The Media in America

A History

Fourth Edition

On the cover:

"The Evening Tribune, 1890"

Watercolor, 16 x 20
By James G. Stovall

The Media in America
A History

Fourth Edition

EDITORS

Wm. David Sloan
University of Alabama

James D. Startt
Valparaiso University

The Media in America
A History
Fourth Edition

Vision Press
3230 Mystic Lake Way
P.O. Box 1106
Northport, AL 35476

Library of Congress Cataloging-in-Publication Data

The Media in America: a history / Wm. David Sloan, James D. Startt, editors
p. cm.
ISBN 1-885219-13-X
1. Mass media--United States--History. I. Sloan, W. David (William David), 1947- II. Startt, James D., 1932

P92.U5M425 1999
302.23'0973--dc20 CIP

Printed in the United States of America

Editors

WM. DAVID SLOAN is the founder of the American Journalism Historians Association and served a five-year term as editor of its research journal, *American Journalism*. He has published seventeen other books, among them *Historical Methods in Mass Communication* and *The Significance of the Media in American History* (both with James D. Startt); *American Journalism History: An Annotated Bibliography; Perspectives on Mass Communication History; The Early American Press, 1690-1783; The Age of Mass Communication; Great Editorials;* and *Masterpieces of Reporting*. He and Prof. Startt also are co-editors of the seven-volume series "History of American Journalism," a work in progress. He has authored more than eighty articles and papers on history and journalistic writing and has been recognized with several research awards for his work in media history. In 1998 he received the AJHA's Kobre Award for lifetime achievements. He is national president (1998-2000) of Kappa Tau Alpha, the mass communication honor society. A professor of journalism at the University of Alabama, he received the Ph.D. in mass communication and United States history from the University of Texas.

JAMES D. STARTT is co-editor of the series "The History of American Journalism" and *The Significance of the Media in American History* and co-author of *Historical Methods in Mass Communication* and has published numerous articles and essays in American and British journalism and diplomatic history. He served as president of the American Journalism Historians Association in 1997-1998 and has served on its Board of Directors and as chair of its research and oral history committees. From 1986 to 1989 he was Associate Editor of *American Journalism*. A senior research professor of history at Valparaiso University, he received his Ph.D. in history from the University of Maryland.

Authors

Chapter 1
COMMUNICATION BEFORE AMERICA

Paul Alfred (Alf) Pratte is a professor of communication at Brigham Young University, where he specializes in media history and in magazine and opinion writing. A former president of the American Journalism Historians Association, he is the author of *Gods Within the Machines: A History of the American Society of Newspaper Editors, 1923-1993*. His articles have appeared in *Journalism Quarterly, Newspaper Research Journal, American Journalism, Media History Digest*, and other scholarly and professional journals. A former newspaper reporter in Utah and Hawaii, he has taught at the University of Hawaii-Kapiolani, Hawaii Pacific College, and Shippensburg (Pa.) University and has been a guest lecturer at Howard University.

Chapter 2
PRINTING IN AMERICA, 1600-1690

Julie Hedgepeth Williams is co-author of *The Early American Press, 1690-1783*, as well as *The Great Reporters: An Anthology of News Writing at Its Best*. She also has authored chapters on colonial journalism, media and religion, and women in the media for several other books. She is a member of the Board of Directors of the American Journalism Historians Association and chair of its Publications Committee. She received her Ph.D. in mass communication history at the University of Alabama and teaches journalism at Samford University.

Chapter 3
THE COLONIAL PRESS, 1690-1765

Donald R. Avery has served as president and secretary-treasurer of the American Journalism Historians Association as well as managing editor of *American Journalism* and as a member of the Editorial Boards of *American Journalism* and *Journalism Monographs.* He has written extensively on the colonial and early party press periods. Chair and professor of communication at Eastern Connecticut State University, he received his Ph.D. in journalism from Southern Illinois University.

Chapter 4
THE REVOLUTIONARY PRESS, 1765-1783

Carol Sue Humphrey is the author of the books *"This Popular Engine": The Role of New England Newspapers During the American Revolution* and *The Press of the Young Republic, 1783-1833.* She also has authored a variety of articles and book chapters on journalism of the Revolutionary era. She received her Ph.D. in history from the University of North Carolina and teaches history at Oklahoma Baptist University.

Chapter 5
THE PARTY PRESS, 1783-1833

Wm. David Sloan has published a number of articles focusing on the political role of the press in America's first party system. His work is largely responsible for today's historical assessment of the press during that period.

Chapter 6
FREEDOM OF THE PRESS, 1690-1804

Margaret A. Blanchard is the author of *Revolutionary Sparks: Freedom of Expression in Modern America* and *Exporting the First Amendment: The Press-Government Crusade of 1945-52* and of numerous articles on the history of freedom of expression in the United States. She served as editor of the *History of the Mass Media in the United States: An Encyclopedia* and is associate editor for history and law for *Journalism & Mass Communication Quarterly.* A former president of the American Journalism Historians Association, she received her Ph.D. in American history from the University of North Carolina, where she is William Rand Kenan Jr. Professor of Journalism and Mass Communication.

Chapter 7
THE PENNY PRESS, 1833-1861

Michael Buchholz, a member of the Editorial Board of *American Journalism,* specializes in the history of the press of the 1830s. He has served as editor of *The Intelligencer,* the newsletter of the American Journalism Historians Association, and as a member of the AJHA's Board of Directors. A professor of journalism at Indiana State University, he received his Ph.D. in sociology from Oklahoma State University.

Chapter 8
THE ANTEBELLUM PRESS, 1820-1861

Bernell Elizabeth Tripp is the author of *The Origins of the Black Press* and has published a variety of articles and book chapters on African-American journalists of the nineteenth century. A journalism professor at the University of Florida, she received her Ph.D. in mass communication history from the University of Alabama.

Chapter 9
THE PRESS AND THE CIVIL WAR, 1861-1865

Kathleen Endres has published a variety of articles on Civil War journalism and on other topics in media history. She is a recognized authority on magazine history and women in journalism. She received her Ph.D. in history from Kent State University and teaches journalism at the University of Akron, Ohio.

Chapter 10
THE FRONTIER PRESS, 1800-1900

William E. Huntzicker has published numerous articles and reviews on the American West and nineteenth-century journalism. He received his Ph.D. in American studies from the University of Minnesota and has taught there and at Bemidji State University, Macalester College in St. Paul, Minn., and the University of Wisconsin-River Falls. He is the author of *The Popular Press, 1833-1865.*

Chapter 11
THE PRESS AND INDUSTRIAL AMERICA, 1865-1883

Ted Curtis Smythe is the co-editor of *Readings in Mass Communication,* which went through thirteen editions, and *Issues in Broadcasting: Readings in Radio, Television, and Cable.* He is the author of a variety of articles on media history. A professor emeritus of communication at California State University at Fullerton, he was Distinguished Scholar in Residence at Sterling (Kansas) College, 1993-1997. He received his Ph.D. in mass communication from the University of Minnesota.

Chapter 12
THE AGE OF NEW JOURNALISM, 1883-1900

George Everett specializes in the history of technological influences on the media and has published a number of articles on the 1880s and 1890s. A professor emeritus of journalism at the University of Tennessee, he received his Ph.D. in mass communication at the University of Iowa and has served on the Editorial Board of *Journalism and Mass Communication Quarterly.* He is former national president of Kappa Tau Alpha, the mass communication honor society.

Chapter 13
AMERICAN MAGAZINES, 1740-1900

Sam G. Riley is editor of the *Dictionary of Literary Biography's* multi-volume series on *American Magazine Journalists.* He authored *Magazines of the American South,* edited *Corporate Magazines of the United States* and *Consumer Magazines of the British Isles,* co-edited *Regional Interest Magazines of the United States,* and compiled *Index to Southern Periodicals* and *Index to City and Regional Magazines of the United States.* He has published three books on newspaper columnists and has written on media history for a variety of scholarly publications. A professor of communication studies at Virginia Tech, he received his Ph.D. in mass communications research from the University of North Carolina.

Chapter 14
THE DEVELOPMENT OF ADVERTISING, 1700-1900

Edd Applegate has written and/or co-edited six texts on advertising, including *The Ad Men and Women* and *Personality and Products: A Historical Perspective on Advertising in America;* two volumes in the *Dictionary of Literary Biography* series; and several chapters in other books. His articles and reviews have appeared in *Journalism and Mass Communication Quarterly, Journalism and Mass Communication Educator,* and *American Journalism.* He has received grants and fellowships from the Freedom Forum Media Studies Center, Gannett Foundation, American Association of Advertising Agencies, American Press Institute, and other organizations. He received his doctorate in mass communications and higher education from Oklahoma State University and teaches advertising at Middle Tennessee State University.

Chapter 15
THE EMERGENCE OF MODERN MEDIA, 1900-1945

Maurine H. Beasley is professor of journalism at the University of Maryland-College Park. She holds a Ph.D. in American civilization from George Washington University. A specialist on the history of women and journalism, she is the author/editor/co-editor/co-author of seven books, including *Taking Their Place: A Documentary History of Women and Journalism.* She has served as national president of both the American Journalism Historians Association and the Association for Education in Journalism and Mass Communication. In 1997 she received the AJHA's Kobre Award for lifetime achievement in media history, one of only five individuals ever to get the award. The AJHA's award for outstanding research in women's history is named in her honor.

Chapter 16
THE MEDIA AND REFORM, 1900-1917

Richard B. Kielbowicz is the author of *News in the Mail: The Press, Post Office and Public Information, 1700-1860s* and of articles on various topics in journalism history. He received his Ph.D. in mass communication from the University of Minnesota and has held a postdoctoral fellowship at the Smithsonian Institution. He is a professor of communication at the University of Washington.

Chapter 17
THE MEDIA AND NATIONAL CRISES, 1917-1945

James D. Startt is the author of *Journalism's Unofficial Ambassador: A Biography of Edward Price Bell, 1869-1943* and of *Journalists for Empire: The Imperial Debate in the Edwardian Stately Press, 1903-1913.* He is an authority on World War I and has published a number of articles on the presidency of Woodrow Wilson.

Chapter 18
RADIO COMES OF AGE, 1900-1945

Donald G. Godfrey is the author/editor of *Historical Dictionary of American Radio, Television in America: Local Station History from Across the Nation,* and *Reruns on File: A Guide to Electronic Media Archives.* He has published numerous articles on broadcast history in a variety of journals. He is a professor of telecommunication at Arizona State University.

William Ray Mofield is the author of *Paducah: FM Capital of the World* and *WPAD: Silver Anniversary,* and of numerous articles on radio history. He has been a CBS Fellow at Columbia University and a Distinguished Professor at Murray State University. He received his Ph.D. in communications from Southern Illinois University.

Chapter 19
THE ENTERTAINMENT MEDIA, 1900-present

Jana L. Hyde has published several book chapters and book reviews on mass media history, primarily in broadcasting. She received her Ph.D. in mass communication, with an emphasis on history, from the University of Alabama. She has taught at both her alma mater and the University of Colorado at Colorado Springs.

Chapter 20
THE AGE OF MASS MAGAZINES, 1900-present

Darwin Payne is the author of *The Man of Only Yesterday* (a biography of *Harper's Magazine* editor Frederick Lewis Allen); *Owen Wister: Chronicler of the West, Gentleman of the East; Big D: Triumphs and Troubles of an American Supercity in the 20th Century;* and other books and articles. He received his Ph.D. in American Civilization from the University of Texas and is a professor of journalism at Southern Methodist University.

Chapter 21
MODERN ADVERTISING, 1900-present

Bruce Roche is an associate professor emeritus of advertising at the University of Alabama who specializes in the history of mass communication and advertising. He received his Ph.D. in journalism from Southern Illinois University.

Chapter 22
PUBLIC RELATIONS, 1900-present

Karen S. Miller specializes in public relations history and has published numerous articles on that and other topics in media history. She received her Ph.D. from the University of Wisconsin-Madison. Her doctoral dissertation on the history of the Hill and Knowlton public relations firm won the AEJMC's Nafziger-White award for best dissertation in 1995. Her book *The Voice of Business* examines the same topic. Prof. Miller teaches at the University of Georgia.

Chapter 23
THE MEDIA IN TRANSITION, 1945-1974

Harry D. Marsh began his newspaper career in 1949 and has since worked on papers in Texas, Mississippi, Alabama, Arkansas, Kansas, Missouri, and New York. He is the co-author of *Excellence in Reporting* and is author of articles on press history, performance, and technology. He received his Ph.D. from the University of Texas and is retired from Kansas State University, where he had served as a professor of mass communication.

Chapter 24
THE CONTEMPORARY MEDIA, 1974-present

Michael D. Murray is author of *The Political Performers* and editor of *Encyclopedia of Television News,* and he has written numerous articles on the history of broadcast news. He is a former president of the American Journalism Historians Association and a recipient of a Goldsmith Research Award from Harvard University. He was elected a fellow of St. Edmund's College, Cambridge University, and has served as a John Adams Fellow at the University of London. He received his Ph.D. from the University of Missouri and teaches in the department of communication at the University of Missouri-St. Louis.

CONTENTS

INTRODUCTION

Why Study Media History?

"What's the value of studying history?"

That's the question that both students and professionals in mass communication often ask.

The answer could be as simple as a suggestion to visit a class in a local city school, where some seventh graders might be asking the same question. Many of them eventually will recognize, however, the importance of history. Why is it, then, that among educated individuals in communication the question of the value of the study of history so often comes up? Is there something unique about mass communication that makes it difficult for people in this field to recognize what civilized people generally have recognized for centuries?

In answer to the question about the value of history, we can give a variety of answers. We can say that the study of media history is important for the same reasons that the study of any kind of history is. History has been a major form of study for more than 2,000 years, ever since Herodotus wrote his *History of the Greek and Persian War*. In explaining his purpose, he used the Greek word for "research" that came to be used as our designation of history. "This," he wrote, "is an account of the researches [*historia*] of Herodotus of Halicarnassus, which he publishes, in the hope of preserving from decay the remembrance of what men have done...." Furthermore, among the various disciplines for the study of mass communication, none has the long tradition that belongs to history. Isaiah Thomas wrote *The History of Printing in America* (1810) a century before schools for education in journalism were established, and ever since the beginning of those schools the study of history has been an integral part of the curriculum.

Media history, as one branch of historical study, offers the range of benefits common to all areas of history. Very broadly and most fundamentally, we can state that the past has intrinsic value in itself and a strong appeal to a large proportion of human beings living today. Historical study provides the opportunity to inform later generations about the nature of humankind and historical truth; it offers an explanation for the complexity of past thinking and behavior; it contributes to the authentic record of human experience. The primary goal of historians, therefore, is to explain the past truthfully. In doing so, they seek to capture the thought and feeling of a time past. Historical study would need no further justification than that. Like humankind's interest in art or its continuing search for knowledge, history has an innate value.

Still, it is possible to state other values of the study of history. One is that it provides information important for identity and background. It helps us to know ourselves both individually and collectively, and it provides knowledge valuable in helping us to understand people and the world around us. Although we may assume that particular events that occurred in the past will never recur in exactly the same way, we also know that an understanding of them will help us to deal with similar events in the future. Whether we are considering wars or social movements or any other major topic, we can be certain that a knowledge of their history and the answers to the questions they raised serve a purpose for anyone who hopes to be an informed and responsible person today.

More generally, we can state that at the academic level the study of history provides an efficacious means of intellectual stimulation and satisfaction. Because historical understanding requires the full range of rigor, critical thinking, mature judgment, analytical ability, and imagination, it is unsurpassed among scholarly disciplines in exercising the mind.

Even though the study of media history is recognized as valuable from these general reasons, the distinctive nature of mass communication as a field of study and professional practice also offers reasons for studying its history. In such a field, imbued as it is with vocationalism, practicality, and present-mindedness, questions about the usefulness of history are bound to arise. In such a field, a knowledge of history provides a broader perspective than one gets from studying simply the tools of the trade. For that reason alone, it bears serious study.

Among the panoply of other values that one might recite specifically related to professional aspects of mass communication, here are examples:

*History helps us to understand the present through knowledge of how the present came to be.

*It provides comparisons that help us to assess and evaluate the present.

*It provides, for the craft-oriented, insight into how professional practices can be done well.

*It sharpens critical thinking about the operation of media today.

Indeed, the value history can bring to the study of mass communication should not be underestimated. Just as one seeks to understand a person or people by knowledge of their background, so it is natural to seek understanding of a contemporary institution by knowledge of its origins, ethical foundations, development, and interaction with the wider culture in which it exists. Both the personal and impersonal influences that affected the course of development of the media, or of a particular mass medium, need to be assessed. The perspective gained from such inquiry may or may not have a direct effect on the work of today or tomorrow, but it can enlarge one's imagination, perspective, and judgment about matters relating to that work. Most important, the study of past achievement, even greatness, and of past failure associated with a human institution is surely a guide to comprehending the present and envisioning the future.

If, however, one is to gain the full value of studying history, it must be studied properly. Let us take a brief look at how good historians go about doing their job—and at how you as a student are affected by how well they do it.

Imagine that you wish to come to the best understanding possible of how, for example, journalists in a former time approached their profession. What would be the best way to gain such an understanding? Here, let's draw an analogy.

Imagine that, rather than wanting to understand the past, you wanted to come to a full knowledge of a place you have never been, a far country. The best way to do that would be to go there and spend as much time as you needed getting to know the country and its people. If you were unable to travel there, the next best thing would be to talk by telephone to the people, read letters from them, watch television programs they might have produced about themselves, read their magazines and newspapers, and examine any other material or records that they have created. Such items are known, in historical terminology, as "primary sources."

If you wanted to understand the past in its truest sense, you would do the same thing. Obviously, you could not physically travel to the past—but you could examine the records that people have left. You could attempt to find all that is possible to know about life at a specific time and place in the past. You could try to become so thoroughly familiar with them that you might have the sense that you had actually lived then and there. If you did that, you would be a historian.

Let's take one more look at the study of history but from a different perspective. Assume that for the next few months the demands of the classes you are taking will absorb all your time and you will not be able to do the work of a career historian—yet in those circumstances you still wish to gain a true understanding of the past and, more specifically, of the media in the past. If you cannot do the work of the historian, the next best thing is having a good historian doing the work and then sharing it with you.

You would expect the historian to perform according to certain fundamental principles. You would want your historian to be free of ideological and other bias. You would expect that he or she have a true appreciation of the people of the past and be interested in them on their own terms. You would not want the historian, for example, evaluating journalists of 1800 according to rules of journalistic conduct that only developed later—rules that may be appropriate for today but that did not exist 200 years ago. (That error frequently shows up among historians and is known as "present-mindedness.") You also would want your historian to be judicious in dealing with material and fair-minded in dealing with people. If you could get a historian who would do all those things and would be rigorous and thorough besides, you probably would have confidence in what he or she told you, for good history must reflect the fundamental fairness of the historian who created it.

That being the case, we can still ask, what processes do historians undertake when producing an account of some part of the past?

In its simplest form, the question can be answered in four words: (1) understanding, (2) sources, (3) extrapolation, and (4) explanation. First, an historian must gain a basic understanding of the subject at hand from what others have said about it, or from materials available about it. In most cases, this learning stage involves a consideration of historiography (the study of historical writing).

Second, all pertinent sources relating to the subject must be located, collected, and evaluated. This phase of the historical process involves gaining an appreciation of and an ability to analyze the various types of sources that are applicable to the inquiry.

Third, meaning must be extrapolated from those sources. Extrapolation might involve probes into contextual matters or an unraveling of details of content. There are, moreover, various tools of analyses (e.g., content analysis, quantitative analysis, psychoanalysis, and comparative analysis) to use when appropriate. Historians might also use a variety of theories to see if, without bending the facts, their own study can be illuminated by them.

Finally, historians must explain the material they have collected and examined. They do this by addressing certain propositions—causation, generalization, interpretation, and the establishing of significance. In this matter, history is an ongoing process. In studying history, it is well to bear in mind the words of the renowned historian Frederick Jackson Turner, who once explained: "Each age writes the history of the past anew with reference to the conditions uppermost in its own time.... History ... is ever *becoming*—never completed." It is a continuing interpretative effort to understand self and society.

The editors of this book hope that is the type of history you will get in the pages that follow. Each chapter author has been selected for expertise on the topic and for talent in doing historical research, and each is an accomplished writer who can present narrative and explanations clearly. You will note that the bulk of the sources that the authors use is made up of records and other materials left by the people who were involved in the episodes. When the authors have used secondary sources—that is, books and articles written by historians—they have been selective, relying only on works written by specialists and authorities on the particular subject under study.

Even so, the student should not assume that any historical narrative or explanation is necessarily and completely accurate. Despite the best intentions, the most rigorous research, and scrupulous editing, there may be other episodes that one might choose for inclusion, some details left out, or different explanations offered. History should be an honest search for answers to important questions. In seeking those answers, you should approach each chapter in this book inquisitively. You will find that the capacity that history has to interact with the reader is another of its many values.

The Media in America
A History

Fourth Edition

1

Communication Before America

Notwithstanding the modern fascination with the here and now of computers, satellites, cyberspace, and the information highway supposedly guiding us into the future, serious students of mass media must look back to their earliest roots. Only then can they truly understand the fields of study linked to journalism, advertising, public relations, the broadcasting trades, and many others. Such study not only provides an idea of the diversity of our technological and philosophical bloodlines rooted in many nations of the world, but it contributes a sense of the primacy of print and writing as the foundation for communication. Thus, by understanding the genesis of mass communication, each of us is able not only to gain a better understanding of the many ancestors and genealogy of our American media, but is able to relate more fully to the family of humankind.

One of the issues that have confronted historians is whether writing developed slowly over long periods of time, or whether it appeared suddenly. This chapter, like much of the study of the history of early communication, takes a mainly evolutionary point of view. A number of scholars, however, point to yawning gaps of evidence and the fact that ancients unanimously called attention to cosmic forces contributing to communication. Rather than evolving over thousands of years and being utilized primarily for the mercenary hurly-burly of business, writing may have sprung full-blown from the minds of ancient men and women in the mid-East, Asia, and the Americas as an instrument divinely inspired.[1]

Often overlooked, for example, in the traditional evolutionary approach to the origins of writing have been the contributions of Native Americans. Writing in 1973, K. H. Basso and Ned Anderson reported on an "authentic, ingenious, original and highly efficient" writing system that the western Apaches used.[2] Apache shaman Silas John claimed that the entire primitive system came to him suddenly in 1904 as a dream from the Great Spirit for the express purpose of recording ritual prayers and ordinances to be disseminated among his tribe. Basso and Anderson emphasize that, although Silas John knew a little about alphabetic writing, his script and underlying principles departed radically from the English alphabet. Like the Cherokee syllabary that Sequoyah invented around 1820, Silas John's writing system represented the creation of a unique cultural form. As such, Basso and Anderson rank it "among the significant intellectual achievements of an American Indian in the 20th century."

According to the Bible, everything began with the "Word." The word, in human terms, enabled people to speak coherently. That ability placed humans above the animals and allowed them to share thoughts and feelings with others. Before the dawn of civilization, however, human utterances were confined by space and time. Speakers could not be sure that their words and thoughts would be faithfully transmitted beyond their environment or after their death. Thoughts could be distorted by the passage of time, and personal achievements would rapidly vanish into the past. Ancient tongues spoken by clans a million years ago have disappeared.

We do know something about our primitive predecessors, thanks to their practice of keeping records. Although these records lack the clarity of written documents, they reveal much about early humans. Archaeologists have unearthed bones with man-made scratchings that may be 400,000 years old. A younger but particularly interesting bone found in France is engraved with parallel lines, arcs, and other symbols. The signs of this ox rib apparently served to keep track of the seasons, rainfall, river flooding, and other natural phenomena. Radioactive carbon-14 methods indicate the rib is 135,000 years old.[3] No matter how elaborate the carvings of early record keepers, their images and symbols fell far short of expressing ideas, feelings, and abstractions. Perhaps the records also lost their meaning when the original artists were not present to explain them.

To share fully in the thinking of others, *homo sapiens* ("thinking human beings" or literally "wise men") needed some means of

[1]This is the claim of such historians as Hugh Nibley and Curtis Wright. See the works by these historians listed in the "Recommended Readings" at the end of this chapter.

[2]K. H. Basso and Ned Anderson, "A Western Apache Writing System: The Symbols of Silas John," *Science* (June 1973): 1013-22.

[3]James Norman, *Ancestral Voices* (New York, 1957), 7.

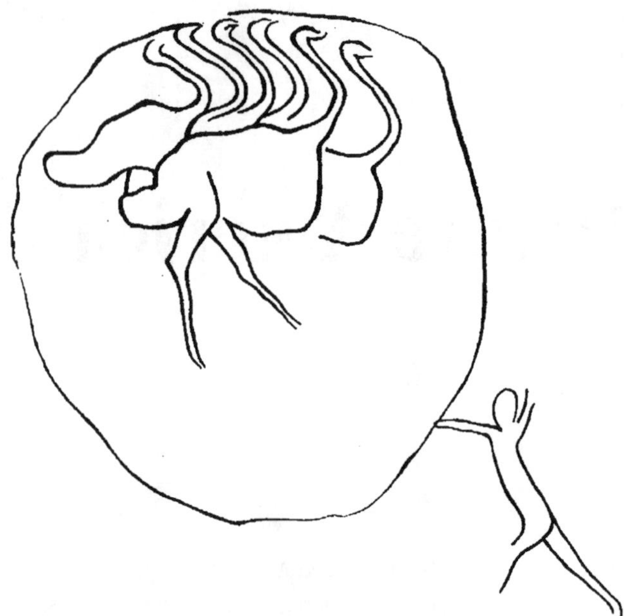

Pictogram
This engraving – technically a *petroglygph*, since it was carved in rock – shows six ostriches in what the hunter probably thought of as his magic circle. The word *pictogram* means "picture sign."

carrying their words across space and time. That means was writing. It is among the most revolutionary inventions in the cultural evolution of humankind.

The Dawn of Writing

Our ancestors had such an appreciation of the importance of writing that many of their myths suggested it had a divine origin. There was a saying among some ancient Indians: "Blessed be he who invented writing."[4] Literary archaeology, a young science, has been concerned with the origins of ancient writing. Literary archaeologists have examined that era when man began composing purposeful messages. They place the origins of writing tens of thousands of years ago when humans learned to convey thoughts and feelings through visible signs. These signs, however, were forms of communication and also, in time, of art rather than forms of writing as one normally defines the term. At first people may have been interested only in marking location, such as piling up stones over a gravesite. Hunters may have stuck small branches or sticks in the ground at angles corresponding to the direction of travel of animal herds.

Early record-keepers used various objects to help them remember. Among these mnemonic (memory-aiding) devices were sticks or bones with carved notches, pebbles in a sack, and knots tied in string. In such a manner, they kept accounts of cattle and agricultural commodities. Mnemonic signs were limited to statistical applications and were probably not used to keep a chronicle of events.[5]

It is likely that the cumbersome nature of these materials provoked the ancients to seek more convenient forms of communicating. Eventually they reduced the size of various constructions like rock piles by simply making representations of them. They took the realities of their world and made pictorial scratchings of them on bones, wood, or stone. In later times, they drew objects on cave walls. Exactly why humans made pictures is the subject of some conjecture, but there seems always to have been an urge to communicate — to leave for others something of oneself. When man began drawing pictures, he demonstrated that he had made considerable progress in his development. Indeed, by making pictures he had reached the first of three successive milestones on the road to writing. The stages were the following:

1. *Pictographic*. A pictogram ("picture sign") was a drawing of a natural object or event. It was often simple, such as a circle with rays emanating from it to suggest the idea of the sun. It could also be complex, such as a drawing of an animal with a spear next to it, to convey the notion of hunting. Pictures carved in rocks are called *petroglyphs*, while those painted on rocks are *petrograms*. While it was possible for a grouping of several pictograms to tell a simple story, the meaning was restricted to the content of the pictures.

2. *Ideographic*. The ideogram provided a more sophisticated technique that remedied a major deficiency in the pictogram. The pictogram by itself was unable to convey ideas or abstract concepts such as love, cold, danger, or happiness. To communicate the intangibles of life, clan members had to convert pictures to ideograms by agreeing among themselves that additional meanings belonged to certain pictures. A primitive society might have agreed, for example, that a drawing of the sun's disk and rays meant heat or warmth, not simply the sun. This stage required more intelligence on the part of the clan and a considerable degree of social organization. The ideogram was a significant advance toward writing because pictures now suggested names of objects or events and thus became symbols.

3. *Phonetic*. This stage saw the linking of the spoken language to the written. Phonetic writing was born when a picture became a single sign that suggested a single sound. The spoken language could now be depicted by combinations of signs. As a result, writing became much easier, and meanings became more precise. This achievement came slowly, and many societies on the road to writing failed to reach this stage. The syllabic writing that developed in the phonetic stage was complicated, and readers were unable to comprehend many of the signs easily. Ultimately, simpler languages appeared that used the alphabet. The latest refinement in the evolution of writing, the alphabet employs a letter sign for each sound instead of a syllable.

[4]Quoted in Ernst Doblhofer, *Voices in Stone* (New York, 1961), 13.

[5]I.J. Gelb, *A Study of Writing* (Chicago, 1963), 4.

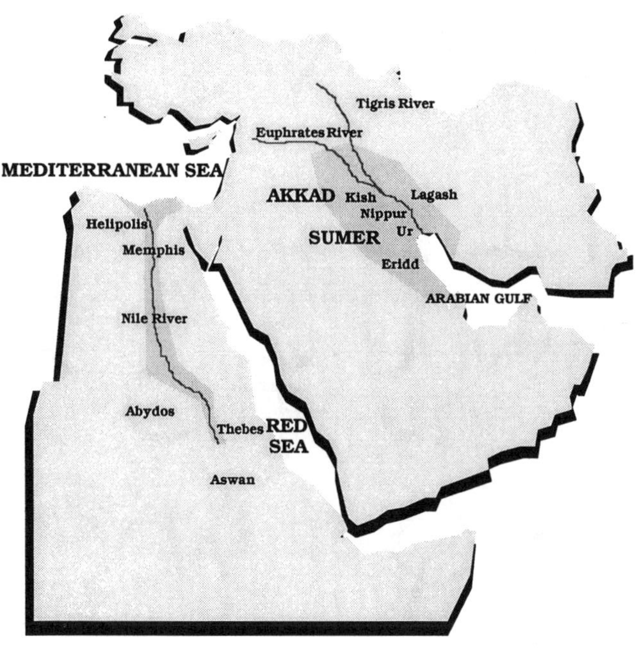

Valley of Civilization
The Tigris-Euphrates river valley in the 25th century B.C. formed one of the earliest centers of civilization and gave humans some of the first forms of writing. It is the site of present-day Saudi Arabia, Iraq, Kuwait, and Iran.

Writing and the First Civilization

Record-keeping and the birth of writing were clearly linked. A few thousand years before the first civilization appeared in the ancient Near East, some peoples began keeping records with a novel system that resembled modern "messages-in-envelopes." This archaic system used *bullae*, or hollow clay balls, which contained tokens representing livestock. The balls were either round or egg-shaped, about the size of a baseball. The small tokens inside were of many shapes, including spheres, discs, cones, cylinders, and triangles. Tokens have been found throughout the Middle East, distributed widely along the Fertile Crescent, that rich area that arches around the top of the Arabian desert from present day Israel to the Persian Gulf and in which the first civilizations appeared.

Historians usually recognize the area of the lower Tigris and Euphrates Rivers as the home of the first civilizations. There, a people known as the Sumerians produced an urban society around 3,000 B.C. Although the exact origins of these people remain a mystery, it is clear that they entered the river valley from neighboring hills. The Neolithic (New Stone Age) Garden Cultures located in the hilly terrain in present-day Iraq and adjacent parts of Turkey, Syria, and Iran may have been their original home. The river valley settlements eventually grew into cities in which life became more complex and more sophisticated in terms of social, political, and economic organization. "Civilization" is the term historians use to describe collective life produced by those conditions. The complexities of city life included the need to keep records of commodities and the need to identify private property. It was in this environment that writing may have first appeared.

Clay tablets unearthed in Egypt in late 1998 contain the earliest writing ever found, but it was the Sumerians who developed the art of writing. These creative, stocky, round-headed, beardless people needed some means of keeping track of their personal property. Their priests required some way to keep accounts of the temple wealth. The priests exacted tribute from the farmers as payment to their gods for use of irrigation water and to ensure divine blessings on future crops.

Records were kept in the early days of Sumer by using marsh reeds to scratch marks on pieces of clay. Later, a more efficient stamp seal was employed. It was an engraved piece of stone or metal, often shaped like a small cone or bell.

A significant advance over the stamp seal was the invention of the cylinder seal. The Sumerians used it to inscribe a continuous record of ownership by rolling an engraved cylinder over a wet clay surface. Historians have noted similarities between the large cylinders of the modern printing press and the rolling printing of the cylinder seal.[6]

It would be difficult to overestimate the importance of the cylinder seal as a step forward for civilization. It promoted cultural diffusion throughout the Near East by transporting abroad pictures of everyday life in Sumer and spreading its literature. One of the earliest and most influential works of literature was the Sumerian *Epic of Gilgamesh*, the legendary ruler of Uruk. The story contains, among other things, an account of a great deluge that killed every living thing except those aboard an ark.

Cylinder printing also contained the first known examples of sensationalism. When the Sumerians were under the domination of the Akkadians and others from about 2340 to 2125 B.C., the themes of cylinder printing exaggerated muscular features of warriors and portrayed an increasing amount of violence.

The Sumerians achieved the last stage in the development of writing — the phonetic — that linked the spoken with the written language. By about 3100 B.C. they had a full writing system in use, the first civilization to accomplish this. But they, like other river valley civilizations, stopped short of achieving an alphabet. The alphabet represents the simplification of syllable writing to single-sound letters. Another alluvial river, the Nile, nourished a civilization that did simplify much of its language to single-sound script. But even the Egyptian civilization failed to reach a completely phonetic writing through an alphabet.

Writing in Ancient Egypt

The origins and early development of Egyptian writing are less certain than of Sumerian writing. Egyptian script does not seem to have been a gradual development through the three stages as in Sumer. There is an element of mystery about the rather startling

[6]Karlen Mooradian, "The Dawn of Printing," *Journalism Monographs* 23 (1972): 9 and 35.

progress the Egyptians made toward a phonetic script very early. At first, in prehistoric times, Egyptians painted pictures on pottery. Their drawings in the pictographic and ideographic stages were skillfully done representations of birds, animals, and deities. Soon after 3000 B.C., however, Egyptian writing abruptly began to use signs phonetically. It became a system of phonetic script written with pictures. Why this happened so suddenly has been a matter of considerable dispute among literary archaeologists.

The early maturity of Egyptian writing probably resulted from Sumerian influence. At the time of greatest cultural diffusion from Mesopotamia, Egypt's writing showed some striking resemblances to Sumerian script. Egypt readily borrowed a number of Sumerian innovations, such as cylinder seal printing, brick architecture, and the potter's wheel. The forms of Egyptian writing were adapted to fit available materials and requirements of Egyptian life. Three kinds of Egyptian writing developed:

1. *Hieroglyphic*. Hieroglyphic, a word with Greek origins, literally means "sacred carved letters." Hieroglyphic writing was used mainly for religious display, for inscriptions on monuments, temple walls, and tombs, and for painted inscriptions on pottery. It has also been found on written documents on papyrus. Hieroglyphic apparently had some secular applications, but it remained largely a sacred, somewhat secret writing used mainly by Egyptian priests. Hieroglyphic characters were a mix of ideograms, phonograms, and other phonetic elements.

2. *Hieratic*. For everyday use in business, letters, medical texts, and literary works, Egyptians employed a cursive script brushed onto papyrus. Although it lacked the pictorial quality of hieroglyphic, it was a rather faithful transcription of hieroglyphic. The main differences were the linkage together of the hieratic characters by the sweep of the brush pen and some minor changes in the signs. Although its name derives from the Greek *hieratikos* ("sacred"), Egyptians used hieratic writing for both secular and religious writing.

3. *Demotic*. The demotic script (from the Greek *demos*, meaning "people") replaced hieratic as the script used in mundane business. Hieratic had, by the seventh century B.C., acquired so many cursive peculiarities and abbreviations that it was difficult to master by any but the priestly class. It then became an almost exclusively sacred script, and demotic came into popular use. Its hieroglyphic beginnings were barely discernible. It combined whole groups of hieroglyphs into a single sign and used a mixture of picture and sound signs.[7]

Although Egyptian writing contained twenty-four single-consonant characters, it was not alphabetic writing. The achievement of a true alphabet eluded the Egyptians for religious and social reasons. Their script depended on scribes who kept hieroglyphics secret, and the social structure of Egypt discouraged a simplification of hieroglyphic so that it could be widely used at all levels of society.[8] The cursive scripts, hieratic and demotic, remained faithful to their hieroglyphic origins and never developed further toward an alphabet.

Phoenician Alphabet
The Western alphabet that is in use today originated with the Phoenicians around 2000 B.C. The twenty-two letters from the alphabet above are from about 1500 B.C. Some letters of our English alphabet of today retain some of the same character designs.

The First Alphabet

The invention of the alphabet was one of the most significant events in human history. A system of signs expressing single sounds of speech, the alphabet had its origins in the ancient Orient. Our own alphabet is a descendant of the Phoenician alphabetic script, following modification of it by the Greeks. The Greek alphabet originated among the Semitic peoples of Palestine and Syria.

There is conjecture as to whether the Phoenicians originated a true alphabet independently or simply adopted the achievement of others and exported it to Greece and elsewhere. The twenty-four monosyllabic symbols in Egyptian hieroglyphics provide evidence of a strong Egyptian influence on the development of the alphabet. There are also strong arguments for a Sumerian picture-script connection. It is virtually certain, however, that the Greeks adopted Phoenician script. The evidence is found chiefly in the nearly identical form of the letters in both alphabets, the order of the letters, and their names. For example, the Semitic *aleph*, *beth*, *gimel* correspond to the Greek *alpha*, *beta*, *gamma*.

Phoenician traders used their alphabet as an important part of a mercantile system that spanned the entire Mediterranean and lasted more than a thousand years. In that manner the Semitic alphabet was exported and borrowed. From their homeland on the Eastern Mediterranean coast, what is now Lebanon and Israel,

[7] Hans Jensen, *Sign, Symbol and Script*, translated from the German by George Unwin (New York, 1969), 71.

[8] David Diringer, *Writing* (New York, 1962), 48-50.

Phoenician merchants sailed to the Greek islands and mainland. Soon they established colonies in Greece, leaving abundant evidence of their presence in alphabetic inscriptions on monuments. The Greek alphabet of classical civilization, built on the letter forms of the Phoenicians, provided the foundation of the Graeco-Roman alphabet. The Graeco-Roman then became the alphabet of Western civilization.

CHINESE WRITING AND PRINTING

Chinese writing ranks alongside other great systems of ancient writing that originated independently. Although writing in ancient Mesopotamia originated more than 5,000 years ago, Chinese writing has the distinction of being the oldest script that is still in use. The script has undergone relatively minor changes in its 4,000-year life. Like other writing systems, Chinese script began from a pure picture form of writing, with phonetic elements added gradually. The oldest evidence of Chinese writing consists of inscriptions on bronze vessels, dating from the Hsia dynasty in 2205 B.C. Bones and tortoise shells were inscribed in the twelfth century B.C. with sacred messages. These "oracle bones" contained divine pronouncements spoken through priests.

Until the third century B.C. the Chinese wrote mostly on bone, stone, wood, metal, and bamboo. In the next three centuries, however, a number of discoveries revolutionized their writing techniques. A bristle brush was developed for applying ink made from pine soot or black earth. It was used with another invention, a writing surface that was cheap, convenient, and quite portable—paper. The superintendent of a weapons factory, Tsai-Lun, created paper in 105 A.D. He cooked a mush made of cut-up plant fibers, bark, hemp, rags, and water, and then poured the cooked pulp onto screens made of bamboo strips. When drained and dried, thin sheets of paper were left. The knowledge of paper-making was exported to Korea and Japan about 600 A.D. and passed to the Arabs in 751. Shortly, paper mills sprang up at several locations in the Middle East, in Baghdad, Damascus, and Egypt. Paper entered Europe through Spain in the eleventh and twelfth centuries. The manufacturing of paper began in Europe in the thirteenth century, and it was associated with the emergence of the Commercial Revolution.

Within a few centuries of their discovery of paper, the Chinese found a way to reproduce writing by carving designs on wooden blocks, inking the designs, and pressing them on paper. This technique marked the birth of the modern process of printing with a press, paper, and ink. Printers carved the necessarily large number of different Chinese characters from wood blocks and began to produce printed books in the middle of the ninth century. Pi-Sheng, a metalworker, invented a press employing movable letters made of metal, clay, and wood in 1045. This achievement was later eclipsed in Europe, where the letter press met with great success because printers did not have to cope with the 40,000 possible characters in the Chinese written language.[9]

Pioneer Printers
The Chinese were pioneers in both writing and printing. They used presses that employed movable type several hundred years before the Gutenberg Bible was printed in Europe.

The ancient Chinese developed a system for gathering news from across the large Chinese land mass. It was used, however, only to provide information for the imperial court and not the masses of people. Beginning in 206 B.C. the imperial court of the Han dynasty set up a postal network to obtain news of events throughout the empire. In the T'ang dynasty (618-907 A.D.), a handwritten official news paper, *ti pao*, was published. It circulated news to government officials that had been gathered through the postal network. During the Sung dynasty (960-1278), the *ti pao* was disseminated among intellectuals, and in the Ming period (1367-1644) an even wider circle of readers received it.

CRETE: PARENT OF WESTERN CIVILIZATION

Writing seems to have sprung up independently in various cultures and civilizations in the centuries immediately following its appearance in southern Mesopotamia about 3100 B.C. The Cretan civilization, centered on the Mediterranean island of Crete, was one of them. Also known as Minoan civilization, it was one of the

[9] Oscar Ogg, *The 26 Letters* (New York, 1961), 188.

parents of the classical civilization of the Greeks and Romans. Crete is particularly interesting because it was the site of one of the great mysteries in the development of printing.

About 2300 B.C. Cretan civilization expanded commercially, culturally, and artistically. These maritime peoples began writing in a pictorial script that was replaced by two kinds of linear script after 1700 B.C., about the time of Crete's peak as a civilization. Their writing, like ours, read from left to right.

A clay disk with strange markings was found in 1908 at the site of what was once the palace at Phaistos in Crete. It was produced from individual pieces of type that had been pressed onto the clay. This earliest known example of movable-type printing, produced between 1700 and 1600 B.C., predates by more than 3,000 years Gutenberg's invention of movable type. Its picture-signs are unlike the rest of Cretan picture-script. The ancient Minoan would have had to rotate the disk to read it. The forty-five different signs used repeatedly on the disk are identical in shape and size. That fact gives rise to the tantalizing speculation that the ancients who imprinted the disk intended to reach a large audience by producing reusable pieces of type.

Classical Civilization

The Greek-speaking peoples of the Mediterranean and the Latin-speaking Romans were the constituent elements of Classical Civilization (950 B.C. to A.D. 550). Greek culture was heavily influenced by its Semitic roots in the Cretan civilization, but Rome simply adopted the same culture from the Greeks about 200 B.C. Generally speaking, classical culture was not the culture of the masses of people. It was the culture of the literate, slave-owning, upper classes who were a small minority of city dwellers. It had no system of general education, and the majority remained illiterate.

The Greeks modified the Phoenician alphabet by changing some unused consonants into much needed vowels. They eventually developed a standard alphabet of twenty-four characters without the *C* and *V* of our alphabet. To accommodate the space and shape of writing surfaces, Greek scribes wrote both left to right and right to left. About the sixth century B.C. they settled on a left to right script.

The Greeks used a variety of writing tools and surfaces, including papyrus imported from Egypt, brush, reed pen, waxed tablet, stylus, and parchment. An improvement over papyrus, parchment came into use after 200 B.C. Both remained as writing surfaces throughout most of the Graeco-Roman period. Around the end of that period, parchment became the basic medium for writing and remained so throughout the early Middle Ages, until paper replaced it in the thirteenth century. Parchment was made by bleaching goat or sheep skin and rubbing the surface smooth. It had many advantages: it was long-lasting, it held ink without smearing, it could be used on both sides, and it could be rolled up or bound into a book.

The Greeks made a remarkable contribution to the technology

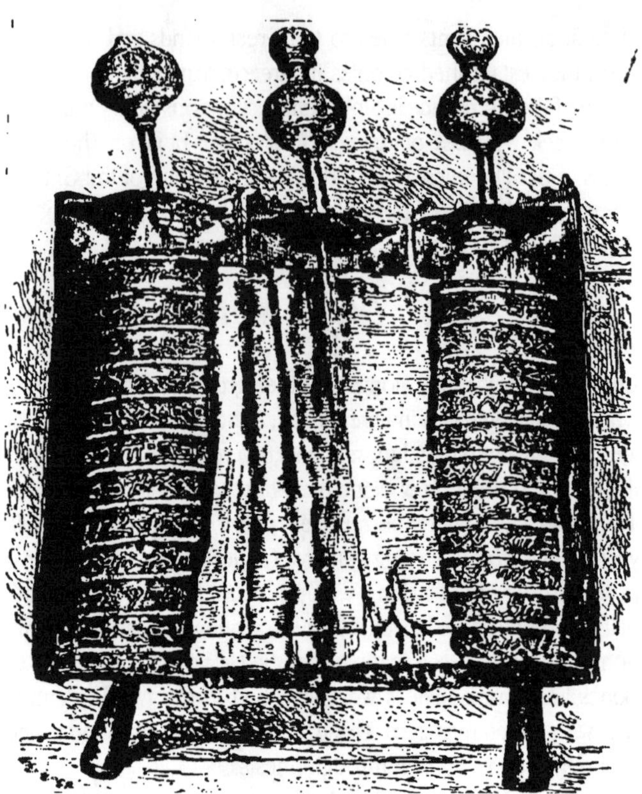

Scrolls
Scrolls, such as this one of the Pentateuch, were one of the earliest means found to keep large manuscripts together. As books grew larger, however, scrolls became inconvenient, and they gave way to codices that resembled today's books.

of communication by developing an optical telegraph for use in warfare. The word "telegraph" means "writing at a distance." Although they lacked electricity, a necessity for modern telegraphy, the Greeks were able to communicate over distances perhaps as early as the fourth century B.C. through the use of signal fires to convey military information.[10]

Ancient Greece provided one of the earliest examples of large-scale censorship. A cleavage in Greek social and political life resulted in the virtual disappearance of certain literary and philosophical works. Between 450 and 350 B.C. the oligarchs, a conservative group that favored the nobility, state authority, and the Spartan approach to life, challenged the adherents of Athenian democracy, who favored commerce and social equality. The Oligarchs eventually triumphed over the democratic forces. Because the Oligarchs were unwilling to pay for making copies of works that did not favor their position, most of the writings of supporters of Athenian democracy have been lost to history. Thus, the works of Plato, Xenophon, and other allies of the nobility have survived while those of the Sophists and Ionian scientists did not.[11]

It seems ironic that the Classical Age of Greece, whose legacy included the works of eminent Greek philosophers, scientists,

[10] Jackson P. Hershbell, "The Ancient Telegraph: War and Literacy," in *Communication Arts in the Ancient World*, Eric Havelock, et al., eds. (New York, 1978), 82-7.

[11] Carroll Quigley, *The Evolution of Civilizations* (New York, 1961), 196-8.

poets, and playwrights, had no system for producing and distributing books. Even in the period of greatest literary accomplishment, relatively few hand-copied books were available. Later, however, during the Hellenistic Age (323 to 30 B.C.), the Greek domination of Egypt led to the emergence of Alexandria as the foremost — and only — center for book production for several centuries before the Augustan age in Rome. Alexandria was the largest city in the ancient world, with as many as a million residents. Its magnificent library held about 750,000 papyrus volumes. The Ptolemaic kings of Egypt developed in Alexandria a systematic approach to book production and marketing. Works considered classics were collected by librarians there and served as sources for copyists employed by publishers. Alexandrian book dealers thus sold the wisdom of the ancient world to the wealthy leisure classes in Rome, Athens, and elsewhere.

Rome and Mass Communication

In the Roman Empire mass communication reached a level of sophistication not previously attained. Greeks and other peoples who had fully developed writing systems produced literature, coinage, trade marks, and other forms of communication intended for a wide audience. But in Rome the task of governing a vast empire and supporting far-flung military and commercial ventures required new applications of existing forms of communication.

The Latin alphabet became the script of the western Roman Empire (and eventually most of Europe and America). It appeared after 600 B.C., having been derived from a local script of the Italian peninsula. At first the alphabet was written entirely in capital letters. Later, cursive forms were employed for everyday use, and gave birth to the small letters of our alphabet. In Rome's later days cursives became so popular that the use of capital letters declined. By the Middle Ages, long after the fall of Rome, Roman capitals became so rare that they might have been lost had they not been chiseled into stone. Fortunately, after movable type was invented, medieval type cutters used the beautiful and graceful Roman letters sculpted on monuments as their inspiration.

There was a high degree of literacy among Rome's upper classes. Many who had the leisure to read were vitally interested in public affairs and had a need for information about government, the markets, and events throughout the empire. Ultimately their thirst for news was quenched by a remarkable chronicle, the *Acta Diurna Populi Romani* (daily acts — or occurrences — of the Roman people). The *Acta Diurna* survived for at least two centuries and was a forerunner of the modern newspaper. The words "journal" and "journalism" derive from *diurna.* The *Acta Diurna* developed from three predecessors:

1. The *Acta Senatus*. The deliberations of the Roman Senate were kept in these official records. Similar in content to our *Congressional Record*, they contained mostly speeches and opinions of senators and were kept in an archives where they could be read by senators. Early forms of the *Acta Senatus* date from 449 B.C.

2. The *album.* This was a white tablet set up outside the home of the Pontifex Maximus at the east end of the Roman Forum. The *album* contained accounts of ceremonies in which the ruling consuls and other officials participated. Updated daily, it also included festivals, eclipses, and dedications. The tablets were taken down at the end of the year and stored. Fortunately for historians, the *alba* were kept for centuries, providing an authentic, official chronicle of Roman history.

3. Newsletters. Scribes were paid to compile a summary of news on a regular basis. Some of Rome's wealthy purchased the service for their news-hungry friends outside Rome. The scribes who collected and copied current information were among history's first professional reporters. The quality of their work was occasionally unsatisfactory, provoking complaints by readers, including Cicero. He employed the learned Coelius to produce a regular, perhaps even daily, newsletter of events in Rome. Coelius hired several literate men as reporters to furnish him with general news of all kinds. Acting as editor, Coelius assembled the news into a collection of articles that he sent to Cicero while the latter was a governor in Asia Minor. Cicero apparently wanted primarily political interpretation in the mix of news and cared little for such trivial matters as gladiatorial contests.

These three traditions culminated in the *Acta Diurna* itself, begun by Julius Caesar in 59 B.C. The *Acta* was an official daily publication at first, covering governmental business such as decrees, proclamations, and senate resolutions. It also contained general information about goings-on in Rome and elsewhere, news of famous persons, executions, fires, and weather. The *Acta* was posted each day in popular places, such as the baths, where illiterates often listened while someone read the news aloud. Many of the wealthy sent literate slaves to make copies of the *Acta* for savoring at a dinner party or for mailing to friends abroad. The *Acta* entertained as well as informed. It departed from its official traditions by the end of the first century A.D. and began reporting court decisions, crime, divorce, marriage, gossip, and bizarre happenings such as the claimed sighting of a phoenix.[12]

Because the *Acta* was written on perishable papyrus, no copies have survived. We know of its existence and some of its contents indirectly. Petronius mocked the *Acta* in the *Satyricon*; and Roman historians such as Tacitus, Suetonius, and Pliny referred to the *Acta* frequently in their works. Fragments claimed to have been found in the late Middle Ages have proven to be spurious.

The Roman emperor Augustus put into operation a worldwide system for the dissemination of information and propaganda. Some historians have called him a genius of government. Reigning from 29 B.C. to A.D. 14, he seemed to understand that an efficient communication apparatus — controlled by him — was essential to the consolidation of his political power. He put the postal system on a regular basis to hasten the delivery of official dispatches to and from governors in the provinces. By this effort he also aided the lively and prosperous book trade in Rome that used the post

[12]C.A. Giffard, "Ancient Rome's Daily Gazette," *Journalism History* 2 (1975-76): 107.

Roman Coin
One of Roman emperor Augustus' successful uses of propaganda was through the printing on coins, with his likeness on one side and information on the other. This coin was created to represent the comet that appeared during his reign, which was claimed to be an epiphany of Julius Caesar, his predecessor.

to send books to locations throughout the expansive empire.

Among Augustus' most innovative contributions to communication was use of the monetary system to disseminate messages. The messages were of great social, political, and economic consequence. They were engraved on coins and thus carried across several continents by Roman armies, government officials, and merchants. The coins were, in addition to the *Acta Diurna*, another kind of "newspaper" that provided current information. The portrait side remained relatively unchanged while officials frequently revised the other side to carry a variety of messages reflecting current events. Augustus used coins to inform the public of his military triumphs, public works, governing policies, important anniversaries, happenings within the imperial family, and other current matters.

His engravers and mint supervisors carefully matched the message to the audience, as evidenced by the geographic selectivity exercised in issuing certain coins. Augustus controlled every element of Roman coinage, providing him with a powerful tool in his efforts to manipulate public opinion. Historians of coins acknowledge that he was among history's most successful propagandists.[13]

Medieval Europe: Copying to Printing

The death of Classical Civilization, a fact even before the end of the Western Roman Empire in 476 A.D., led to cultural disintegration throughout the Mediterranean basin and Europe. For several centuries literacy declined and communications remained inadequate. Among the casualties of the Roman Empire's demise were the well maintained and secure roads and the markets for literature. With the barbarian invasions, these virtually disappeared and the literary activities of Rome effectively ceased. The Christian clergy in Europe possessed what little literacy there was.

The oral tradition in communication, as old as humanity itself, remained strong. Towns employed criers to read aloud handwritten bulletins. Ballad singers, who lived by their wits, collected news as they wandered from one community to another. The balladeer gathered a crowd at the village crossroads and sang or recited his story in doggerel. He ceased singing after completing a part of the ballad, continuing only if paid by the listeners.

The book had already changed physical form by the early Middle Ages. Roman book publishers, between the first and fifth centuries, had begun to abandon the roll and to make books by binding flat leaves into a volume (a codex). Vellum (calf or lamb skin) was the preferred writing surface until the introduction of paper into Europe after 1100. The use of animal skins as pages contributed to the high cost of books and their scarcity. In the nine centuries between the end of Rome and the advent of the printing press, manuscript production was the responsibility of the Christian monasteries and, later, medieval universities. Monks were the only civilizing influence in much of Western Europe. They were skilled farmers, sharing their knowledge of agriculture with the local folk. Some monks became expert in glass making, weaving, wood carving, metal working, and brewing. The monasteries were also centers for nurturing the arts, science, and invention. It was the Irish, once they were Christianized in the fifth century, who founded the monastic movement, copying the books that Germanic invaders were destroying elsewhere.

The prolific period of monastic copying of manuscripts began with the founding of the monastery of Monte Cassino in Italy by St. Benedict in 529. He had an exceptional interest in literature, perhaps as the result of the influence of another monk, Cassiodorus, who later founded his own monastery. The *Rule of St. Benedict*, regulations governing the Benedictine order of monks, specifically instructed the monks to occupy themselves with manual labor and holy reading. The reading requirement was intensified during the Church's holiest season:

> During Lent, let them apply themselves to reading from morning until the end of the third hour, and in these days of Lent, let them receive a book apiece from the library and read it straight through.[14]

Since the rule could not be implemented if books were in short supply, monastic superiors interpreted the rule as requiring the production of books by the monks themselves. The call for daily manual labor, then, meant work for some of the more literate monks as copyists in the *scriptorium*, a large, common workroom overseen by the chief scribe, the *librarius*. In some monasteries it

[13] Frank J. Krompak, "The World News According to Augustus," a paper presented to the annual convention of the American Journalism Historians Association, Tallahassee, Florida, 1984.

[14] *The Rule of St. Benedict*, Chapter 48, quoted in George Haven Putnam, *Books and Their Makers During the Middle Ages* (New York, 1962), 29.

Scriptorium
Before the invention of printing with movable type, individual copies of books had to be done by hand. Monks did most of the work. Under Charlemagne, emperor of the Holy Roman Empire, every abbot, bishop, and count was ordered to employ a copyist and every monastery was required also to maintain a scriptorium, outfitted with desks and writing material. Book copying became a life-long occupation for many people. Flaccus Alcuin, Charlemagne's adviser who oversaw the policy on copyist requirements, wrote that "it is a most meritorious work, more beneficial to the health than working in the fields, which profits only a man's body, while the labor of the copyist profits the soul."

was located near a source of heat, to permit work in cold weather. The monks occasionally worked into the night by the light of oil lamps. Copying was gruelling, tedious work. Many monks preferred the manual labor of the farm to the confinement of the copyist's desk. The Benedictines encouraged literacy and penmanship by having the more practiced monastic scribes teach those with lesser skills. The monopoly on literacy by Christian churchmen was fortunate because they preserved not only the philosophical and religious works of the Classical period, but works of a secular nature as well. One might picture the blushing monk who preserved for the modern world the erotic verses of the Roman poet Ovid from a pagan era.

The monks' achievements as copyists often obscure another important monastic accomplishment in the history of communication in the Middle Ages — their work as chroniclers or reporters. The monks served not only as scribes, but also as historians, teachers, and collectors of information who faithfully kept chronicles of civil, domestic, social, and agricultural life. Most of the accounts of medieval life extant today come from the secular records, called *cartularies,* which monks meticulously collected. *Cartularies* were institutional and personal legal records, and they often contained narratives of events and circumstances needed to explain the subject of the document. They were, therefore, important documents of communication, and they go back at least to the ninth century. Annuals, histories, and biographies were also produced, even in the Early Middle Ages (500-1000 A.D.). Moreover, some of the writers who chronicled history and events in those centuries were among the most important medieval authors. One has to think only of St. Gregory of Tours, who wrote in the sixth century, and of the venerable Bede, the most influential scholar of the seventh and eighth centuries, to appreciate the importance of such figures. Bede wrote history, sermons, textbooks, and much else. More than anyone else in his time, he spread historical, Biblical, and chronological knowledge as well as that about literary criticism. In the process he stimulated interest in history, geography, and science. Consequently, although the literary arts languished in the Early Middle Ages, writing had by no means disappeared.

The prolific publishing of the monasteries in the eleventh century allowed Pope Gregory VII to influence public opinion. He encouraged monks to travel throughout the German Empire to circulate writings that argued on behalf of papal prerogatives and against the schismatic activities of certain German princes. The literary assault by Pope Gregory and the monks displeased Henry IV, the Holy Roman Emperor and the most powerful monarch of that time, yet Henry was unable to prevail in his long series of disputes with the Church.[15] It is ironic that the published work, which so materially aided the Church against her enemies throughout the Middle Ages, later became a powerful weapon against her during the Protestant Reformation.

The clerical monopoly on publishing lasted until the thirteenth century when medieval universities became centers of copying. The first efforts at university copying involved the reproduction of lectures. Book suppliers, called *stationarii*, assembled lecture notes into texts and distributed them to students at such centers of learning as the University of Bologna and the University of Paris. No two hand-copied texts were identical, unfortunately, and the accuracy of the information they contained suffered from multiple copyings. Since the texts were composed from students' notes and copied from their wax tablets, many inaccuracies crept in. Students, then as now, frequently misunderstood their lecturers, causing some rather embarrassing misstatements in the published versions of the lectures. The lack of uniformity in texts plagued medieval universities until the introduction of printing.

[15]Putnam, 81-2.

Johann Gutenberg

Printing's Inventor Remains a Mystery

We know little about the man who probably put together the modern printing system and a method for creating a true masterpiece — the 42 Line Bible. Johann Gutenberg worked in strict secrecy and didn't sign his books — and historians have uncovered no notes by or contemporary narratives about the man or his work. We have only a few fifteenth-century government and legal records about him.

Historians began compiling and analyzing those documents almost 300 years after the fact. Two mid-twentieth century works on Gutenberg, Douglas McMurtrie's *The Gutenberg Documents* and Victor Scholderer's *Johann Gutenberg, The Inventor of Printing*, still rely on those documents reported and analyzed by eighteenth- and nineteenth-century historians.

Historians say Gutenberg was born about 1395 into a patrician family in Mainz, Germany, but was constantly pressed for money throughout his life. In his early thirties he moved to Strasbourg during sharp disputes among Mainz's wealthy classes. He apparently experimented with printing and definitely had some legal and social problems in Strasbourg. He entered into a partnership in 1438 with all parties sworn to secrecy. Testimony from an ensuing legal battle indicates they worked with the tools of printing, but there are no direct statements that they were developing a movable type system.

The historians note that Gutenberg's social problems also brought him to court. One of Strasbourg's gentry ladies sued him for breach of promise of marriage. He apparently won the case and remained unattached for life, but his vehement defense testimony cost him fifteen guilders in defamation damages. The city's tax records showed he had a well stocked wine cellar. He paid tax on 420 gallons of wine in 1439.

The documents show that he had returned to Mainz by 1450 when he entered into a partnership with lawyer Johann Fust, which again landed Gutenberg in court. The lawsuit document shows Fust invested considerable money with Gutenberg for "the work of the books" — the printing of the 42-line Bibles. Fust foreclosed on Gutenberg in 1455 just as the Bibles neared completion, taking his materials, his press, and even his technician, Peter Shoeffer.

The historians propose two possibilities why Fust shut Gutenberg down at this crucial moment. Fust's own creditors may have pressed him to repay money, or he may just have been a sharp businessman. Fust knew that the completion of the Bibles ended his partnership with Gutenberg. Fust would get his initial investment back and his share of the profits on the Bible run, but Gutenberg would then have the printing "secret" to himself with enough capital to subsidize future work. Perhaps Fust saw that foreclosing on Gutenberg gave Fust "the secret" and the printing monopoly. Whatever the reason, Fust and Shoeffer became wealthy and famous through printing while Gutenberg lived out his days printing on borrowed equipment and a small pension by the grace of the local archbishop.

Tom Volek
University of Kansas

The idealized painting above shows Johann Gutenberg inspecting proofs from his press. Although he usually gets credit for "inventing" printing, we know relatively little about him or his work. The bottom engraving, the earliest portrait of Gutenberg, shows him holding a die of twenty-four letters. The portrait, which may have been an imaginary likeness, first appeared in a book in 1584. Blind and impoverished, Gutenberg had died in 1468, after forfeiting ownership of his printing system to a creditor. The creditor, Johann Fust, then grew wealthy printing books and for many years claimed credit as the inventor of printing.

Movable Type

The 5,000-year process begun by the ancient Sumerians culminated in the mid-fifteenth century when a printed sheet was pulled from a printing press in Europe. By 1450, all of the essential ingredients were at hand to permit the mass production of literature: paper already had largely replaced vellum in manuscripts, the codex had long since replaced the roll as the preferred form for books, and experiments in metallographic printing were under way in France, Holland, and Germany. Metallographic printing, a technique begun about 1430, used metal letters as dies that were impressed into clay. A lead printing block or plate was cast from the clay mold. The plate was then inked, and uniform copies could be made. The process, however, produced copies that were frequently illegible. The poor results derived from the irregular manner of impressing each letter die into the clay.

We know little about the contribution of Johann Gutenberg, an inventor whose name is associated with the achievement of printing with movable type. Many of the references to him in history are forgeries, and his name appears nowhere in books claimed to have been printed by him. The evidence that he invented printing with movable type is scanty, consisting mostly of a lawsuit against him that describes the nature of the printing that went on in his Mainz, Germany, establishment. However, it is certain that he — or his contemporaries — pulled together the technology available around 1450 that made printing with movable type a practical reality.

Gutenberg (or others) corrected the problems associated with metallographic printing by employing individual metal letters (instead of a whole printing plate) that could be reused in different combinations. By casting a large number of type pieces and sorting these into type cases, a printer merely had to rearrange pieces of type to create a new text. The pieces of type were set in lines or sticks of roughly equal length to form columns of text. Thin pieces of lead were placed between lines. The columns were locked into a form called a matrix that was then inked. Paper was pressed against the matrix by a device that resembled the grape crusher of the wine maker. In this manner the famous Gutenberg Bible was produced in 1455 or 1456. It had a press run of between 70 and 270 copies. From this modest beginning the size of press runs grew throughout Europe, and a thousand copies became the norm by 1500. As the rate of book production rose, prices fell and book publishing became a profitable and international enterprise.

In the first decades following the invention of movable type, an Englishman, William Caxton, took up residence in Germany, where he learned printing. He printed an English translation of the *Recuyell of the Historyes of Troye* (or *History of Troy*) and shipped it to England. It is considered to be the first book printed in English. Caxton, who may have smuggled type into Britain, returned there in 1476 and set up a print shop in London. He issued a number of noteworthy books, including Malory's *Morte d'Arthur* and Chaucer's *Canterbury Tales*. Caxton is important also because his efforts helped to unify England through a common language.

Printing brought with it an end to the monopoly of church-produced books and made possible the consideration of events and experiences that had previously been ignored. Histories, geographies, biographies, and observations of the physical world replaced the medieval concerns of the spirit. Exposure to new ideas led to a radical transformation in patterns of thought, and many people realized that the pursuit of truth was a communal effort. A rise in literacy in Europe throughout the late Middle Ages assisted that pursuit. Other factors aided reading: the widespread availability of cheaper literature, clear glass windows that allowed the illumination of interior spaces, and the invention of eyeglasses in the seventeenth century.

Printing also accelerated the Protestant revolt against the authority of the Roman Catholic Church. The Reformation's chief protagonist, Martin Luther, used printing to great advantage, as did his Catholic and Protestant opponents. After he nailed his famous "Ninety Five Theses" denouncing the sale of indulgences on the university church door in Wittenberg in 1517, he had the statement printed and sent to various cities in Germany. His *Address to the Christian Nobility of the German Nation* in 1520 had a circulation of more than 4,000.

The skilled use of movable type — combined with the promulgation of the long-stifled messages of reform in religion, politics, and culture — gives credence to the claim that Luther and his evangelical associates became history's first true mass communicators. The part that women played in the spread of the Reformation also must be noted, as many of them took Luther's doctrine of the priesthood of all believers literally and began to proclaim the Word themselves through devotional works, hymns, and religious poetry. Luther himself believed staunchly in the power of the printed word. Speaking of the power that the spread of the Gospel wielded, he declared in 1522 that "the Word [of God] inflicted greater injury on popery than prince or emperor ever did. I did nothing; the Word did everything." Presaging a "marketplace of ideas" concept that would become popular later in England and America, he observed that "when he [the Devil] sees the Word running and contending alone on the battlefield, then he shudders and shakes for fear. The Word is almighty, and takes captive the hearts."

With Christian faith playing a central role in people's lives in the early 1500s, the capacity to print multiple copies of the Bible took on special importance. The cost of reproducing single copies decreased significantly, and reformers could distribute the Scriptures more widely so that access to them was not restricted to the Catholic clergy. With multiple duplication by printing available, reformers began translating the Bible from Hebrew, Greek, and Latin into the common languages of the people. John Wycliffe had translated the New Testament into English by 1382, and Nicholas of Hereford completed the Old Testament translation in 1384. The earliest known printed English version of any part of the Bible

England's First Printer
William Caxton's *History of Troy* is thought to be the first book printed in England. Caxton learned the printing trade in Germany.

was published in 1526 by William Tyndale. The first complete printed version was accomplished by Miles Coverdale in 1535.

The division of Europe into Protestant and Catholic areas in the sixteenth century led to attempts by each faction to control the printed word. Protestants and Catholics employed similar methods of censorship. First, they identified certain works as dangerous. Next, the civil government (in both Protestant and Catholic areas of influence) assisted religious authorities in attempts to prevent printing. Lastly, they attempted to control the commerce in books by searches of bookstores and customs inspections of imported books.[16]

Alarmed by the spreading heresy of Protestantism, the Catholic hierarchy attempted to keep the faithful from reading the Bible and the works of Luther and others who challenged Catholic doctrine. In 1564 the papacy issued the *Index of Prohibited Books*. It listed Protestant and heretical religious works, pornography, books on magic and demonology, and certain political works, such as Machiavelli's *The Prince*, which advised authorities to use any means they wanted, rather than accepted standards of moral behavior, to obtain their ends. Catholics were forbidden to read books on the list under pain of serious sin. The *Index* was updated every fifty years. Even before the issuing of the *Index*, an earlier papal decree forbade Catholics to have books written in Hebrew. The Church was indeed concerned about the possible influence of the printed word.

[16]William Zeisel, ed., *Censorship: 500 Years of Conflict* (New York, 1984), 29-30.

From Letters to Newspapers

Europe's ambitious exploration of the world in the fifteenth and sixteenth centuries led to the creation of prosperous mercantile and banking enterprises. One such banking institution, the German house of Fugger, also became known as Europe's foremost newsgathering service. Firms had a need to keep abreast of business news, political intelligence, and other current events. The Fuggers paid correspondents in distant locations to send newsletters back along commercial routes and even across battle lines when necessary. The news was a mix of firsthand observations and rewrites of published material gathered locally by correspondents.

The seaport of Venice became an early headquarters for news as a result of its concentration of merchants and bankers. We get our word *gazette* from sixteenth century Venice. It derives from the Venetian practice of collecting a *gazeta,* a penny or so, from those who wished to hear newsletters read aloud. The spoken newsletters were later replaced by printed *gazettes*.

Throughout Europe an insatiable appetite for political news developed after the advent of printing. Printed material, however, was too scarce to meet the demand. So Europeans used the most accessible medium — the manuscript newsletter. By the end of the sixteenth century, newsletters had become a common fixture on the continent. Regular production of newsletters in England, however, had to await the Restoration of the Stuart kings in 1660. The British government itself then became the major publisher. The secretaries of state created their own news service with the aid of a network of diplomatic informants. They collected and disseminated news through postmasters and local officials. In this manner a government monopoly of newsletters prevailed in England until unlicensed newsletters flooded the kingdom in the 1680s.[17] Balladeers, whose rhymes carried the news before the age of printing, were replaced by broadsides, another name for printed ballads. The broadside was a single news sheet, printed on one side only, with a woodcut illustration on the top half. Below the fold were two columns of text, each begun with large, decorative initials called swash letters. The printed ballad contained much that is found in the modern newspaper: news, entertainment, and editorials in the form of sermons. Among history's famous broadsides was one in 1493 announcing the results of Columbus' expeditions to the New World. Broadsides were sold by the pile to news hawkers. The hawkers, usually boys but sometimes girls, then disposed of them singly by means of loud salesmanship in the streets.

Another precursor of the newspaper was the news pamphlet, a four-page publication that focused on a single news event. It flourished in Europe and England through the latter part of the six-

[17]Henry L. Snyder, "Newsletters in England, 1689-1715," in *Newsletters to Newspapers: Eighteenth Century Journalism*, Donovan H. Bond and W. Reynolds McLeod, eds. (Morgantown, W.V., 1977), 4.

teenth century. Some pamphlets catered to the public's taste for sensationalism and featured lurid woodcut illustrations designed to entice the prospective purchaser. In 1607 a news pamphlet describing a disastrous flood was printed with the following title:

> A true report of certaine wonderful over-flowings of waters now lately in Summersetshire, Norfolk, and other places in England, destroying many thousands of men, women, and children, overthrowing and bearing downe whole townes and villages, and drowning infinite numbers of sheepe and other cattle.[18]

The pamphlet's dramatic and detailed woodcut showed a cradle with a child in it floating on the water and survivors clinging to trees. Within the narrative of the destruction, the author interspersed pious sayings and scriptural quotations.

The prototype of the modern newspaper was born in Holland in the early seventeenth century. The intellectually tolerant Dutch permitted more diversity of expression than other European nations, allowing the development of news media that resembled modern types. By the first decades of the seventeenth century, Amsterdam had become the preeminent news center of the world. The Dutch began publishing *Corantos,* or currents of news, about 1618. These were likely patterned after German and Belgian commercial newsletters, which the Dutch adapted to include a smattering of local news.

The Dutch — not the British — first published an English-language *Coranto*. A news sheet in English, dated December 2, 1620, appeared without a title in Amsterdam. It described a battle near Prague three weeks earlier that led to the start of the Thirty Years War. Printers imitated *Corantos* throughout Europe. In 1621 Thomas Archer published the first *Coranto* in England but was imprisoned for doing so without the permission of the government.

In the strict sense, neither the newsletter, pamphlet, broadside, nor *Coranto* could be considered a newspaper. Many were published irregularly, and quite a few failed to survive beyond one issue. A number of them lacked the attribute of timeliness, preferring to deal instead with relatively old matters. Some were simply outright copies of imported newsletters and contained nothing of local interest. Not until 1665 did the English have a news sheet that had the characteristics of the modern newspaper.

A semi-weekly newspaper printed on both sides of a single sheet appeared in the university town of Oxford on November 16, 1665. Henry Muddiman was its founder and editor. The Tuesday and Friday paper, the *Oxford Gazette*, was little more than a mouthpiece for the British government. It was published in Oxford only because the plague was ravaging London and much of the government had fled temporarily. In 1666 it became the *London Gazette* when it moved to London and continued publishing government-approved news. The *Gazette*, despite a small circulation and lack of independence, holds the distinction of

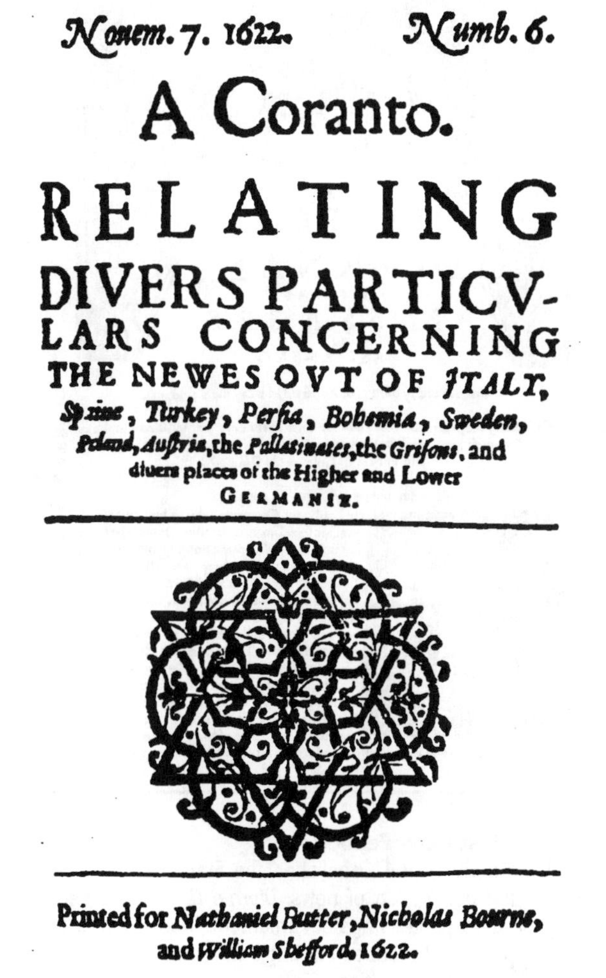

Nouem. 7. 1622. Numb. 6.

A Coranto.

RELATING DIVERS PARTICV-LARS CONCERNING THE NEWES OVT OF ITALY, Spaine, Turkey, Persia, Bohemia, Sweden, Poland, Austria, the Pallatinates, the Grisons, and diuers places of the Higher and Lower GERMANIE.

Printed for Nathaniel Butter, Nicholas Bourne, and William Sheffard. 1622.

Corantos

The corantos ("currents of news") of the 1620s were the forerunners of newspapers. Shown above is a typical weekly coranto with serial numbering and dated issues.

being England's first newspaper in the modern sense.

The honor of founding England's first daily newspaper, the *Daily Courant*, most likely belongs to a woman. The "E. Mallett" associated with the paper probably was Mrs. Elizabeth Mallett. She wrote in the first edition on March 11, 1702: "This Courant [as the title shows] will be Publish'd Daily: being design'd to give all the Material News as soon as every Post arrives: and is confin'd to half the Compass, to save the Public at least half the Impertinences, of ordinary News-Paper."[19] Mrs. Mallett's association with the paper ceased after two weeks, perhaps because the paper seemed headed for extinction. Samuel Buckley took it over and made it a success. The *Courant* was remarkable for its time because it used several techniques practiced by modern journalism: the use of datelines to identify the location and date of news stories, a dedication to objectivity by its avoidance of rumor or gossip, and the clear labeling of opinion and advertising. It lasted thirty-three years.

[18] Mason Jackson, *The Pictorial Press* (London, 1885), 13-4.

[19] Quoted in Calder M. Pickett, *Voices of the Past* (Columbus, Oh., 1977), 12.

A
PERFECT
DIVRNALL
OF THE
PASSAGES
IN
PARLIAMENT.

From Munday the 17. of Aprill till Munday the 24. *Aprill.*

Collected by the ſame hand that formerly drew up the Copy for William Cooke *in Furnevals Inne. And now* Printed *by I. Okes and F. Leach and are to be ſold by* Francis Coles *in the Old Baily.*

Note that here is alſo a true and punctuall relation of the whole proceedings of the ſiedge at Reading for all the laſt weeke unto this preſent.

Munday the 17. *of* Aprill 1643.

THe Lords and Commons taking into conſideration a late Proclamation dated at Oxford the firſt of this inſtant Aprill, for the holding and continuing of the Court of Chanchery and all proceedings herein the Receipt of his Majeſties Exchequer, and of the firſt fruits and tenthes, the Court of the Dutchies of Lancaſter, Court of wards, and Liveries, and Courts of Requeſts, at the City of Oxford for the whole Terme of Eaſter then next enſuing. and for the adjourning the Courts of Kings Bench, Common Pleas, and Exchequer from *Quindena Paſche*, untill the returne of *Quinque Septianas Paſche*, next doe finde that it will much end to the prejudice of the Common-wealth to have the ſaid Courts and Receipts held and continued at Oxford where great part of an Army

England's First News Periodical
After Parliament in 1641 abolished the Star Chamber, which had restricted the publication of news, *Diurnal Occurences* began publishing the daily proceedings of Parliament. In addition to being the first news periodical produced in England, it also was one of the first periodicals to use illustrations. This woodcut of a session of Parliament appeared in several issues.

From Licensing to Liberation

Governmental interference in publishing dates from ancient times when civil or religious authorities controlled information for purposes of maintaining political or religious orthodoxy. In the English-speaking world, official activities affecting printing and publishing originated under the Tudor monarchs. The first of these sovereigns, Henry VII, who reigned from 1485 to 1509, displayed a shrewd awareness of the power of information. He was among history's early managers of the news, taking extraordinary measures to publish news favorable to himself. He authorized the publication of documents of state and carefully controlled the timing of their publication. His publication of a Papal Bull confirming his own title to the throne provided an example. In publishing this document, he made an "end run" around the Church hierarchy and politicians by selecting the time of publication most advantageous to him. In a sense he became his own publisher of news, frequently circulating information regarding state matters.

His successor, Henry VIII, who ruled England from 1509 until his death in 1547, formalized much of the government's interference with the press. After the Church in England was "reformed," the government had considerable authority over it. As a result, the state took over the Church's role as censor. Henry VIII defined heresy, issued censorship rules, and enforced them through the civil authorities. He even issued his own "official" Bible and, along with copies sent to every church in the realm, included instructions that every reader should interpret scripture for himself. Henry VIII inaugurated the system of licensing of the press that lasted until 1695. In his reign the Court of the Star Chamber was created, a court that relentlessly prosecuted printers who challenged the authorities. The Crown justified prior censorship of printing by claiming to eliminate heresy and protect local printers from unauthorized competition. A likelier explanation was Henry VIII's desire to maintain control over the printed word for his own political purposes.

Another Tudor, Queen Elizabeth I, who reigned from 1558 to 1603, controlled the press through the Stationers Company. Printers throughout the realm were placed under its jurisdiction a year before she became queen. In Elizabethan England agents of government censored printed matter, inspected printshops, and kept records on printers' customers, wages of printers, and the number of employees in a printing establishment. The Court of the Star Chamber enforced the laws against unauthorized printing, frequently meting out severe penalties. These included imprisonment, slitting of nostrils, flogging, and even execution in extreme cases.

The Tudor monarchs in sixteenth-century England were effective in their efforts to control the press. In the following century during a time when news became a feature of English public life, control became more difficult. With its two revolutions and prolonged great struggle between the monarchy and parliament over the questions of religion and political authority that so charged the age, the seventeenth century stands as the most turbulent one in modern English history. It was also a confusing time for the press. At the beginning of the century, press restrictions were so severe that only foreign news along with inocuous news could be printed openly. In 1632 the Court of the Star Chamber, at the request of its Spanish ambassador, prohibited the publication of foreign news. Six years later, however, the publication of foreign news was allowed again, but printers had to wait until 1641 for permission to publish domestic intelligence.

In 1640 the famous Puritan-dominated Long Parliament was summoned. It lasted, in some form, until 1660. On July 5, 1641, the parliamentarians abolished the tyrannical Court of the Star Chamber and the Court of the High Commission, the two main chambers of press control. Five months later *Diurnal Occurences in Parliament* appeared (November 29, 1641). The term "Diurnal" in the title was used to describe the contents. It was a record of daily proceedings intended for weekly publication. It was England's first domestic news periodical.

Other periodical publications soon followed. They were known by various names such as mercuries, passages, intelligences, posts, spies, scouts, etc. The abundance of these along with the variety

John Milton and John Locke
The Puritan John Milton (left) wrote *Areopagitica*, that great statement endorsing freedom of discussion, because leaders refused to allow him to circulate a pamphlet on the merits of divorce. *Areopagitica* is one of the most ringing endorsements of free speech ever written, but it is important to note that the core of its argument lay in religious doctrine, not in a political one of free expression. Protestants distinguished themselves from Catholics by claiming broader toleration of dissenting opinion and noted that, for example, it was the Catholic church that had the infamous Index of banned books. Milton was Protestant, as was every member of the British House of Commons, for whom he wrote the *Areopagitica*. Drawing on his understanding of the individual's right to interpret Scripture, the English philosopher John Locke (right) argued that individuals also had the authority to determine the nature of government. That idea served as the basis for the Whig approach to representative government and lay at the heart of the American Declaration of Independence and, indirectly, of American notions on freedom of the press.

of pamphlet publications available in the mid and late seventeenth century made it an exciting time, if a somewhat unheralded one, in journalism history. During those years, notwithstanding some periods of lapse, the government still tried to control the press.

Despite the removal of some constraints on printing, the practice of licensing continued. Poet John Milton composed an eloquent denunciation of licensing in 1644 called *Areopagitica* and addressed it to Parliament. Milton's arguments on behalf of free expression did not, however, extend to Roman Catholics or Royalists. After the Cromwellian revolution installed a Puritan government in England, Milton himself became a censor on behalf of the Puritan regime.

With the restoration of the monarchy in 1660, a period of greater toleration for the press seemed to be close. Indeed, the Licensing Act was allowed to lapse between 1678 and 1682. Nevertheless, the restored Stuart monarch Charles II rejected attempts at toleration after parliament tried to exclude his brother James from the throne. His confrontation with parliament, known as the Exclusion Crisis, took place between 1678 and 1681. Although Charles prevailed in the struggle, he took steps afterwards to protect the public from false and misleading information. For that reason successive governments in late seventeenth-century England wished to control the press. They also hoped to gain political advantage by doing so. Licensing, therefore, returned.

All publications, however, were not licensed. Secret, unlicensed publishing of pamphlets and broadsides was common in the London of the late seventeenth century. A pamphlet written by a daring printer described the activities of those who courted disaster by breaking the law:

> There had long lurked in the garrets of London a class of printers who worked steadily at their calling with precautions resembling those employed by coiners and forgers. Women were on the watch to give the alarm by their screams if an officer appeared near the workshop. The press was immediately pushed into a closet behind the bed; the types were flung into the coal-hole, and covered with cinders; the compositor disappeared through a trapdoor in the roof, and made off over the tiles of the neighboring houses. In these dens were manufactured treasonable works of all classes and sizes, from half-penny broadsides of doggerel verse up to massy quartos filled with Hebrew quotations.[20]

The Licensing Act also promoted corruption. The Stationers Company, which was legally empowered to send government agents to search houses and printers' shops for unlicensed books, sometimes extorted money from publishers who feared prosecution.

While the Licensing Act was in force, the only newspaper in England was the government's own *London Gazette*. It provided readers only with news filtered through the secretary of state's office. A number of periodicals were published; but lacking current news, they were not newspapers in the modern sense. Following the political upheaval known as the Glorious Revolution of 1688-1689, with a newly passed Bill of Rights in force, newspapers began to appear in greater numbers throughout England. Finally, licensing and censorship of the press ceased in 1695. That did not mean, however, that the English government's desire to influence, and to some extent control, the press vanished. It had not, but other means had to be found to implement that desire. In the eighteenth century a number of devices would be used beginning with the Stamp Tax on newspapers and pamphlets that was passed in 1712.

The liberation of expression came slowly. A number of developments combined to assist in the process: the gradual weakening of medieval notions of absolutism of the power of rulers, the rise of the parliamentary system, the emergence of a middle class in Europe, the rise of dissident Protestantism and of science, and an increasing awareness that the search for truth requires free access to knowledge.

Censorship lost legitimacy during the intellectual revolution called the Enlightenment. Begun in Europe about 1680, the En-

[20]Jackson, *The Pictorial Press*, 176-7. He quotes from Thomas B. Macaulay's *History of England*.

lightenment strengthened the notion of individual freedom. Of particular importance to freedom of the press was the work of the Protestant philosopher John Locke. Two of his works, *A Letter Concerning Toleration* (1689) and *Two Treatises on Government* (1690), stimulated the growth of the spirit of toleration in England and established premises of argument that could be used against press restrictions.

His writings condemned absolutism in any form. His ideas on limited government became a foundation for the liberal political tradition that so influenced English politics in ensuing centuries. They also found favor with some thinkers and leaders across the Atlantic. Thomas Jefferson, for instance, shared Locke's hatred of tryanny and distrust of government.

The American notion of press freedom derives, in large part, from the Locke-Jefferson link. Although they lived a century and an ocean apart, Locke's work profoundly influenced Jefferson. Thus British libertarian ideals concerning the press came to be embodied in our founding documents through the pen of Jefferson.

RECOMMENDED READINGS

BOOKS

Bjerken, Mildred Prica. *Medieval Paris: The Town of Books.* Metuchen, N.J., 1973. Explains book production by describing text copying by professional scribes before Gutenberg and publishing by printers afterwards. Essential for understanding the role of the medieval university in publishing.

Bond, Donovan H., and McLeod, W. Reynolds, eds. *Newsletters to Newspapers: Eighteenth Century Journalism.* Morgantown, W.V., 1977. Contains helpful information about newsletters in England in the late seventeenth and early eighteenth centuries.

Brasch, Walter M., and Dana R. Ulloth. *The Press and the State: Sociohistorical and Contemporary Interpretations.* Lanham, Md., 1986. Summarizes 5,000 years of the tension that exists between the press and government, with political philosophy and freedom of the press being major components.

Cahill, Joseph. *How the Irish Saved Civilization.* New York, 1995. The Christianized Irish founded the monastic movement and then preserved and copied books that Germanic invaders were destroyed.

Desmond, Robert W. *The Information Process: World News Reporting to the Twentieth Century.* Ames, Iowa, 1978. Survey history of world news reporting from Acta Diurna in 131 B.C. to the end of the 19th century, along with the social, political, economic, and technological background. Most of the book covers British and American correspondents, agencies, and technology in the last half of the nineteenth century.

Diringer, David. *Writing.* New York, 1962. Concentrates on ancient peoples and places. A complete, global tracing of the origins and development of writing.

Doblhofer, Ernst. *Voices in Stone.* New York, 1984. Lucid explanation of what writing is. Valuable for relating the form of writing to the kind of society that produced it.

Gelb, I.J. *A Study of Writing.* Chicago, 1963. Especially useful for tracing the evolution of the alphabet and writing.

Havelock, Eric A., and Hershbell, Jackson P., eds. *Communication Arts in the Ancient World.* New York, 1978. An excellent and interesting collection of articles on Greek and Roman innovations and practices in writing, poetry, and propaganda. Includes an article on the ancient telegraph of the Greeks.

Hoe & Co., R. *A Short History of the Printing Press and of the Improvements in Printing Machinery from the Time of Gutenburg up to the Present Day.* New York, 1902. History of technological improvements compiled and published by the leading manufacturer of printing presses.

Ingelhart, Louis Edward. *Press Freedoms: A Descriptive Calendar of Concepts, Interpretations, Events, and Court Actions, from 4000 B. C. to the Present.* Westport, Conn., 1987. Encyclopedia of events and quotations about freedom of the press arranged in chronological order.

Jackson, Mason. *The Pictorial Press: Its Origin and Progress.* London, 1885. (Republished in 1968 by Gale Research Co., Detroit). A most valuable classic work on the use of illustrations in early newspapers and broadsides. Contains 150 woodcuts and other engravings from British news publications beginning in the sixteenth century.

Jensen, Hans. *Sign, Symbol and Script.* New York, 1969. This translation from the German attempts to give several sides of scholarly disputes relating to the development of writing. It is lavishly illustrated with line art and photographs.

McKitterick, Rosamund. *The Carolingians and the Written Word.* Cambridge, 1989. Literacy and writing were central to the Carolingian culture in the eighth and ninth centuries.

Morrison, Stanley. *The English Newspaper: Some Account of the Physical Development of Journals Printed in London Between 1622 and the Present Day.* Cambridge, 1932. A well researched and richly illustrated book that historians continue to value.

Nibley, Hugh. *Temple and Cosmos: Beyond This Ignorant Present.* Salt Lake City, 1992. The chapter "Genesis of the Written Word" provides a strong argument for the view that writing originated quickly rather than through a long evolutionary process.

Norman, James. *Ancestral Voices.* New York, 1975. An excellent description of literary archaeology. Provides a wealth of archaeological information about man's earliest efforts to write.

Oswald, John Clyde. *A History of Printing: Its Development Through Five Hundred Years.* New York, 1928. Narrative, encyclopedic account of printing after 1450, with the bulk of attention devoted to Europe.

Putnam, George Haven. *Books and Their Makers during the Middle Ages.* New York, 1962. A reprint of the 1886 edition. Covers the production and distribution of literature from the fall of Rome to the close of the seventeenth century. Detailed descriptions of monks working in scriptoria.

Wright, Curtis. *The Oral Antecedents of Greek Librarianship.* Provo, Utah, 1977. Writing originated in a creative, inspired process rather than through a long evolutionary period.

Zeisel, William. *Censorship: 500 Years of Conflict.* New York, 1984. Published for an exhibition on censorship. A richly illustrated series of essays detailing the struggle against authority.

ARTICLES

Basso, K. H., and Ned Anderson. "A Western Apache Writing System: The Symbols of Silas John." *Science* (June 1973): 1013-22. Provides evidence of the inspired creation of a primitive writing system among American Indians in the early 1900s.

Giffard, C. A. "Ancient Rome's Daily Gazette." *Journalism History* 2 (1975-76): 106-9, 132. One of the best sources of information on Rome's lively daily newspaper, the *Acta Diurna.*

Mooradian, Karlen. "The Dawn of Printing." *Journalism Monographs* 23 (1972). Pulls together archaeological evidence to explain the origins of printing. It concentrates on the stamp seal and cylinder seal of ancient Sumer.

Schmandt-Besserat, Denise. "An Archaic Recording System Prior to Writing." In *5000 Years of Popular Culture*, ed. Fred E. H. Schroeder. Bowling Green, Ohio, 1980. An illustrated article providing evidence that the Sumerians arrived at a system of writing early because their record-keeping was patterned after an already-existing system.

West, Louis C. "Imperial Publicity on Coins of the Roman Emperors." *Classical Journal* 45 (October 1949): 19-26. Details how Roman emperors used the empire's monetary system for propaganda purposes.

2

Printing in America

1600 - 1690

So far as Europeans were concerned, printing appeared in the middle of a long and rich historical timeline. European cultures were well-rooted, steeped in an intellectual history that included a variety of forms of communication such as storytelling, ballad-singing, and the painstaking copying of manuscripts by hand. The printing press interrupted and forever altered the character of European intellectual life, but nevertheless the press came to a Europe which already had an intellectual identity. In its own way, the press had to adapt to serve what already existed. Although well-received, it was a modern convenience that had to weave its way into the thick texture of European life.

But that was Europe. America was a different place altogether. Unlike the nations of the Old World, Anglo-America grew up with the printing press. From the very start of European America, the printed word was on hand to persuade, offer opinion, influence, cajole, entertain, inform, enlighten, chastise, guide, and inspire the mass audience. The printing press did not have to work its way into the history of Anglo-America; instead, Anglo-America worked its way into history by making great use of the press.

That simple fact had a long and indelible effect on the character of the New World and its inhabitants. Without the printed word, European North America would never have begun quite as it did. The printed word coaxed people to the New World, helped guide them there, and gave their presence there a sense of legitimacy and mission. The printed word served as a vital link to Europe in the effort to remake America in the European image. Yet it also helped give Americans an identity different from Europeans by encouraging and spreading concepts that were not the norm in Europe. As transplanted Europeans carved out a new civilization in the wilderness, the printed word helped transform them into Americans.

In the sixteenth and seventeenth centuries, speechmakers and preachers could conceivably reach large audiences, but their words were not readily transportable across time and space to a mass audience. Copyists could write messages in manuscript form, but the human hand can only make so many copies before it must rest. All in all, the cheapest and most convenient way to overcome the constraints of time and human stamina on communication was to use the printed word. The new arrivals in America understood that fact. When they arrived in the New World, they were already accustomed to using the printing press to ease the burdens of communication. They had long enjoyed the printed word for information, enlightenment, and inspiration. They would continue to employ the press to meet those needs, and in so doing they would unconsciously allow the press to help define an America that was different than Europe. Although the first settlers in Anglo-America did not bring a press with them, the Europeans who settled the area had no doubts as to the power and usefulness of the printed word. In fact, many of them had been recruited to America by the printed word.

Printing and Colonization

The earliest American printed literature was not American at all. It came from European presses and had European readers — but nevertheless it was vital to the success and prosperity of the American colonies. During the period of American settlement, promoters and developers flooded Europe with a sea of printed material — pamphlets, books, tracts, flyers, newspaper articles, and anything else they could think of — to reach anyone who might be interested in undertaking or backing American colonization. Through an array of promotional literature, the printing press helped reach a wide variety of readers — wealthy, poor; servant class, merchant class; English, French, Swiss, German; Catholic, Protestant; highly educated, barely educated. Some promoters had a financial stake in the colonization of the region; others had a patriotic interest in seeing their own nation establish colonies. For still others, the issue was survival, pure and simple.

The desperate colonial leader of the French community of Charlesfort fell into the "survival" category. In 1562, Commander Jean Ribault and his band of French Huguenots were struggling to establish a home, safe from religious persecution, in Spanish Flori-

Thomas Hariot

Thomas Hariot was a scientist and explorer in early Virginia who helped issue *A briefe and true report* on the place in 1590. He wrote the text of the book, while his colleague John White drew stunning pictures of American Indians and their towns, as well as of the land's flora and fauna. Hariot wrote in glowing terms of the possibility of converting the Indians to Christianity, a theme that would persist in early American thought. Writers such as Hariot were important in the campaign to persuade Europeans to emigrate to America, but every bit as important were artists such as White, who could depict the strange land in rich detail.

da. The community was failing for want of supplies. Starvation and disease were rampant. In a last-ditch effort to save the distressed colony, Ribault turned to the press. He wrote a book about his adventures in Florida, and in the spring of 1563 he was in England to peddle the work in hopes that it would win financial friends for Charlesfort. The effort was a failure, but the book did have a greater effect. It got Englishmen, who hitherto had been interested only in colonizing Canada, to begin looking at the southern areas around Florida.[1]

Although Ribault failed to raise funds for his colony, his book was one of the first in the mass media of American settlement. The printed word was the lure, the promise, the "official" word about a place so far away that it had been unknown to Europeans a mere seventy years before Charlesfort. Because the mysterious land across the Atlantic could be made thrilling and promising in the pages of books and pamphlets and broadsides, Europeans could begin to discern new opportunities there.

One of the most important promotional writers was the English preacher Richard Hakluyt, who recognized the value of publishing tales that mariners brought back from their voyages. As far as the patriotic Hakluyt was concerned, if England were to build an empire, she had to do it by spreading the gospel of geography. Hakluyt's work featured numerous enthusiastic accounts of far-off lands, such as one from American adventurer Ralph Lane. "[Virginia] is the goodliest and most pleasing Territorie of the world: for the continent is of an huge and unknowen greatnesse...," Lane wrote for Hakluyt. "[I]f Virginia had but horses and kine [cattle] in some reasonable proportion, I dare assure my selfe being inhabited with English, no realme in Christendome were comparable to it." In a piece of boosterism, Lane pointed out that the enjoyable, exotic products of other nations — wines, oils, flax, rosins, pitch, frankincense, currants, and sugar — could be cultivated in Virginia.[2]

Hakluyt was not the only author who peddled the romance of Virginia. In 1590, engraver Theodore de Bry teamed up with artist John White and writer Thomas Hariot to issue a sensationally beautiful, eye-catching tract promoting America. The heavily engraved cover featured the book's title, *A briefe and true report,* framed by a classical doorway, beautifully drawn Indians, and luscious American produce. Inside, engravings that de Bry made from John White's expert drawings depicted the natives of Virginia in stunning detail. Hariot, for his part, discussed the commodities of Virginia and the habits of her people. As publisher of the work, de Bry made sure the book reached a huge European audience; he published it in English, French, German, and Latin.

Despite the glowing nature of reports in books such as Hakluyt's and de Bry's, the first colonists found conditions more like those in Charlesfort than the comfortable beauty depicted in de Bry's engravings. By 1611 it was well known that the natives and the colonists of Virginia's Jamestown were not getting along happily. In the face of negative public sentiment, writers of American promotional literature redoubled their efforts to make the place look attractive and safe. The governor of the fledgling Virginia plantation, Lord De-La-Warre, scrambled to counteract ugly rumors by publishing a glowing report of Virginia's fertility and possibilities.[3] Five years later, adventurer John Smith published a detailed book designed to promote America as a satisfying, safe, prosperous alternative to Europe for people from all walks of life. The work, titled *A Description of New England*, spoke to the common man. Smith wrote:

[1]Alan Smith, ed. *Virginia 1584-1607: The First English Settlement in North America* (Boston, 1957), xvii-xix. Charlesfort was located at present-day Beaufort, South Carolina.

[2]Richard Hakluyt the younger, *The Principal Navigations, Voiages, Traffiques & Discoveries of the English Nation*, vol. I (originally published between 1589 and 1599; reprint, New York, 1927); also, Ralph Lane to Richard Hakluyt, 3 September 1585, in "An extract of Master Ralph Lanes letter" in Hakluyt, vol. VI, 140.

[3]*The Relation of the Right Honourable the Lord De-La-Warre, Lord Governour and Captaine Generall of the Colonie, planted in Virginea* (London, printed by William Hall for William Welbie, 1611), reprinted in Lyon Gardiner Tyler, ed., *Narratives of Early Virginia, 1606-1625* (New York, 1907), 200-14.

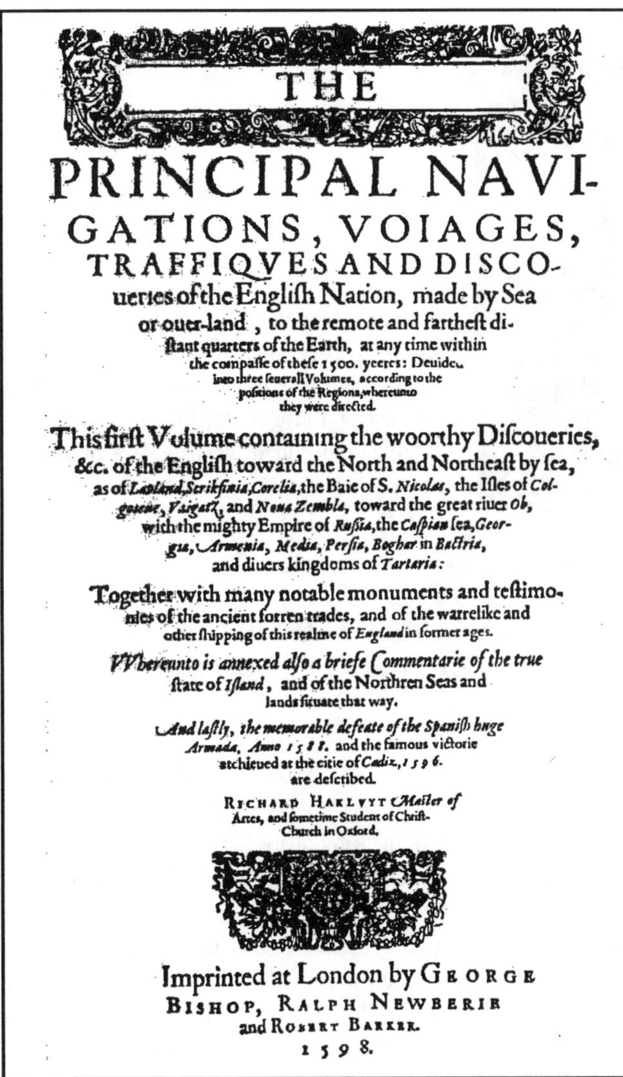

THE

PRINCIPAL NAVI-
GATIONS, VOIAGES,
TRAFFIQVES AND DISCO-
ueries of the English Nation, made by Sea
or ouer-land, to the remote and farthest distant quarters of the Earth, at any time within
the compasse of these 1500. yeeres: Deuided
into three seuerall Volumes, according to the
positions of the Regions, whereunto
they were directed.

This first Volume containing the woorthy Discoueries,
&c. of the English toward the North and Northeast by sea,
as of *Lapland*, *Scrikfinia*, *Corelia*, the Baie of S. *Nicolas*, the Isles of *Col-
goieue*, *Vaigatz*, and *Noua Zembla*, toward the great riuer *Ob*,
with the mighty Empire of *Russia*, the *Caspian* sea, *Georgia*, *Armenia*, *Media*, *Persia*, *Boghar* in *Bactria*,
and diuers kingdoms of *Tartaria*:

Together with many notable monuments and testimonies of the ancient forren trades, and of the warrelike and
other shipping of this realme of *England* in former ages.

Whereunto is annexed also a briefe Commentarie of the true
state of *Island*, and of the Northren Seas and
lands situate that way.

And lastly, the memorable defeate of the Spanish huge
Armada, Anno 1588. and the famous victorie
atchieued at the citie of *Cadiz*, 1596.
are described.

RICHARD HAKLVYT *Master of*
Artes, and sometime Student of Christ-
Church in Oxford.

Imprinted at London by GEORGE
BISHOP, RALPH NEWBERIE
and ROBERT BARKER.
1598.

Promoting Emigration
In promoting British settlement abroad, Richard Hakluyt recognized the value of publishing tales that mariners brought back to England from their voyages. His work, like this 1598 edition of one of his pamphlets, featured enthusiastic accounts of far-off lands.

> And here [in New England] are no hard Landlords to racke us with high rents, or extorted fines to consume us, no tedious pleas in law to consume us with their many years disputations for justice:.... [H]ere every [man] may be master and owner of his own labour and land; or the greatest part in a small time. If hee have nothing but his hands, he may set up his trade: and by industrie quickly grow rich....

Popular Publicity

The technique of printed publicity proved popular. The founders of Maryland created a promotional book that offered a starter's kit for settlement. If a Maryland immigrant were wealthy enough to support an indentured servant, he need only clip and fill in a preprinted blank indenture contract bound into the book. Likewise, the book included a clip-and-use bill of lading form for shipping goods across the Atlantic — and it suggested exactly what a settler needed to include on that bill in the way of food, clothes, bedding, arms, tools, and household goods.[4]

Other works targeted the lower socio-economic classes, painting America as a Promised Land. John Hammond, in a 1656 work titled *Leah and Rachel*, spoke to people who might go to the Maryland/Virginia area as servants. He compared life in Virginia to life in the poor homes of England. He interviewed a destitute and pathetic English fagot seller, whose desperate existence made the hardships of America seem absolutely rosy. Hammond's persuasive intent was obvious: the poor of England were foolish if they didn't opt for work in America.

Promotional materials sought people of many nationalities and religious backgrounds. Even more importantly, people from many of these diverse groups heeded the call to emigrate. That fact produced an interesting population mix in America. A wide variety of people arrived on the continent and created a basis for the pluralistic nature of the American populace. That mixture of people would lay the foundations for democracy. People of lower-class means in Europe could make a decent living and occasionally amass a fortune in America. The sense that a comfortable life was available to anyone who was willing to work hard tended to diminish the chance that America would build its social structure on a strict class society, as much of Europe had. The promotional literature of the colonization era helped develop a population tolerant of such an idea.

American Settlers as Readers

The earliest American settlers were readers. For good reason, it is hard to name an exact literacy rate for the settlers who moved from Europe to America. The new continent was harsh, wild, difficult, and at first no one was able to measure literacy or to set up institutions centered on literacy. Amenities such as schools were secondary to more pressing needs such as clearing land for homes and fields, growing crops for survival, and fending off confrontation with Native Americans. Those difficulties, it would seem, would also stymie intellectual pursuits in the colonies, and no doubt that is partially true. However, a great many American immigrants of all walks of life were literate and were involved in reading.

Time and time again in diaries and letters, newcomer Americans mentioned bringing printed material with them across the ocean. Some brought only the Bible; but others clutched pamphlets, maps, and other printed material. Some brought pamphlets as entertainment for the six- to eight-week voyage across the Atlantic. Many of them religiously packed supplies necessary for starting a new life in America by following guidelines listed in printed tracts. Missionaries came armed with religious texts. Gov-

[4] *A Relation of Maryland; together with a Map of the Countrey* (London, 1635), reprinted in Clayton Colman Hall, ed., *Narratives of Early Maryland* (New York, 1925), 76-7, 99-100.

Harvard College
Harvard College in Cambridge, Massachusetts, was the site of America's first printing press. The Reverend Joseph Glover imported the press in 1638, and printer Stephen Daye had it operating by 1639.

ernors came with books necessary to the smooth operation of their colony.

American immigrants of many social ranks were literate. Literature of the day that dealt with America was not aimed only at so-called "educated" classes. Tracts, pamphlets, and books about the New World were written to entice every level of society, from the servant class to the working class to the merchant class to the extremely rich. They advised readers of the need for individuals as diverse as farmers and haberdashers in America. Authors expected that people from varied occupations and from different socio-economic classes would be both literate and interested in reading the tracts.

Once in America, settlers sent frequent requests to Europe for books, pamphlets, and the latest newspapers. Likewise, it was a time-honored tradition in some families to meet arriving ships to seek the latest printed outpouring of Europe, even though the ships had been weeks in crossing the Atlantic. The Byrd family of Virginia met ships in that manner for generations. A passage from a letter by William Byrd I illustrates how far Americans would go to obtain books from Europe. Byrd had hosted an English traveller at his Virginia plantation in the late 1600s. The two struck a deal: the Englishman would send back much-desired books if the Virginian would first send something uniquely American for the traveller's little boy. Byrd sent off his half of the bargain with this reminder, which proved not only that he had a deep desire to read, but also that children have not changed much since 1686, when the letter was written:

> According to your desire I have herewith sent you an Indian habitt for your boy, the best I could procure amongst our neighbor Indians. There is a flap or belly clout 1 pair of stockings & 1 pair mocosins or Indian shoes allso some shells to put about his necke and a cap of wampum.... These things are put up in an Indian baskett, directed as you desired, and there are bow & arrows tyed to itt.... I therefore intreat you to send mee a treatise or two [on] mineralls & stones the fittest you find for my purpose either of Mr. Boyles or any other English author, allso Salmons Polygraphice the last edition.[5]

The earliest Americans indeed valued the printed word as a form of connection to Europe, as a pastime, and as a carrier of vital information.

God's Word for Indians

One of the potential conflicts in European colonization of America was, of course, the presence of a Native American population that already had towns, crops, and an established culture of its own in the regions targeted for settlement. The natives were a mystery and a great curiosity to Europeans, who had to learn to negotiate and trade with the Indians in order to establish colonies. Sometimes the relationship with the natives was cordial, and in other cases, Indians and Europeans clashed bitterly. As they came into contact with the Native Americans, colonists naturally noticed their cultural habits, which were fascinatingly different from the European way of life. The Indian religion was particularly intriguing. Europeans in general saw it as devil-worship; and that sparked a widespread, passionate fervor to convert the natives to Christianity.

Although the perception of the Indians' spiritual life as a form of demonic worship was misguided, the European settlers' zeal in offering salvation to the Indians was genuine. In pamphlet after pamphlet, the conversion of the "heathen Indians" was put forth as an important goal that would bring an entire race of people to eternal salvation. The desire to convert had some of its roots in Protestants' political need to keep Catholic Spain from bringing the Indians under Spanish rule, and the Spanish had similar aversions to Native Americans becoming a force for Protestantism. Aside from that fact, tracts touting the conversion of natives in America exhibited an honest belief in Christianity as the only way for Indians to find salvation. That evangelistic fervor played into

[5]William Byrd I to John Clayton, 25 May 1686, in Marion Tinling, ed. *The Correspondence of the Three William Byrds of Westover, Virginia, 1684-1776,* vol. I (Charlottesville, Va., 1977), 61-2.

many Europeans' desire to emigrate for their own religious freedom. Truly, America was the land of religious opportunity — Christians of various sects could practice their religion in peace there, and they could at the same time serve God and help the natives by guiding them to true religion.

That idea proved alluring to many settlers. As a pamphlet touting early Carolina explained to readers, the Europeans settling in America might help convert "those poor Indians."[6] That sentiment was typical. A treasury of other tracts sounded the same theme, often in identical words. Convinced by sermon, zeal, and pamphlet, Christian Europeans were ready to show Native Americans how to worship God in order to win spiritual salvation, how to clothe themselves modestly as the Bible required, and how to give up dancing and other heathenish activities.

Therefore, missionaries and ordinary settlers arrived in America with all sorts of religious tracts and books — and, of course, the Bible — to be used in the conversion effort. The printed word was something Native Americans did not have, but they quickly perceived how important it was to the newcomers. A Virginia tribal chief named Wamanto was taken with Englishman John Smith's copy of the Bible. "Hee much wondered at our Bible, but much more to heare it was the Law of our God," Smith recalled in 1624. Smith discussed Genesis with Wamanto, who likened himself to Adam in that he had only one wife at a time. A pleased Smith recorded that the Indian chief seemed ready to learn more about the Bible. To Smith, Indians such as Wamanto proved that the printed word could attract and convert Indians to Christianity.[7]

The Puritans of New England felt a deep commitment to converting the Native American population. As great believers in the printed word and as shrewd employers of the latest technology, they imported their own press in 1638 and set it up for the zealous work of spreading the gospel among themselves and among the unconverted, both in the European and Native American populations. The press, installed at Cambridge, Massachusetts, had other uses, too. The government issued documents to the public via the press, for example, and educational officials used it, but far and away the Puritans used their press most often to produce religious works.

Some of the Puritans' most dramatic evangelistic work featured the energetic John Eliot. He eagerly learned the Indians' language and began the task of converting them to Christianity. Some Indians even formed their own Christian churches and began training for European-style jobs, including printing. Eliot's impressive work, which played a major role in Christianizing American Indians, won much admiration among Englishmen, who read about it in Thomas Shepard's pamphlet, *The Clear Sunshine of the Gospel breaking forth upon the Indians in New England*. That publication and others like it had their intended effect. Amazed after reading about the conversion of Indians, Parliament agreed to incorporate the Company for Propagating the Gospel in New England, an organization dedicated to further evangelizing Indians by producing a Bible for them in their own language. The company underwrote the cost of the Bible, furnishing paper and paying the printers.

John Smith
An adventurer and promoter, John Smith was quite a swashbuckling figure in early America. Famous for his story of being saved from death by the young Pocahontas, Smith's *Generall Historie of Virginia* discussed many other threats to his life as well as his own heroism that helped subdue the Indians, thus opening Virginia to European settlement. He enthusiastically promoted settlement in both Virginia and New England, shrewdly appealing to a wide variety of Europeans either to finance or to undertake American colonization. He assured would-be colonists of the great wealth that America had to offer.

The Bible: First American Book

It was only natural that Eliot be appointed to the painstaking task of translating the Bible into the language of the Algonquin Indian tribe. The work was a historic achievement in American printing. It was the first Bible printed in America, with the New Testament published in 1661 and the Old Testament in 1663. In fact, by many people's reckoning, it was the first actual book printed in Anglo-America, although admittedly many pamphlets of the day were loosely called "books."

Such an amazing American achievement was irrepressibly at-

[6]Edward Bland, Abraham Wood, Sackford Brewster, and Elias Pennant, *The Discovery of new Brittaine, Began August 27, Anno Dom., 1650*, reprinted in Alexander S. Salley, Jr., ed., *Narratives of Early Carolina, 1650-1708* (New York, 1911), 6.

[7]Captain John Smith, *The Generall Historie of Virginia, New England & The Summer Isles* (1624), reprinted in Smith, *Virginia 1584-1607*, 352, 347-8.

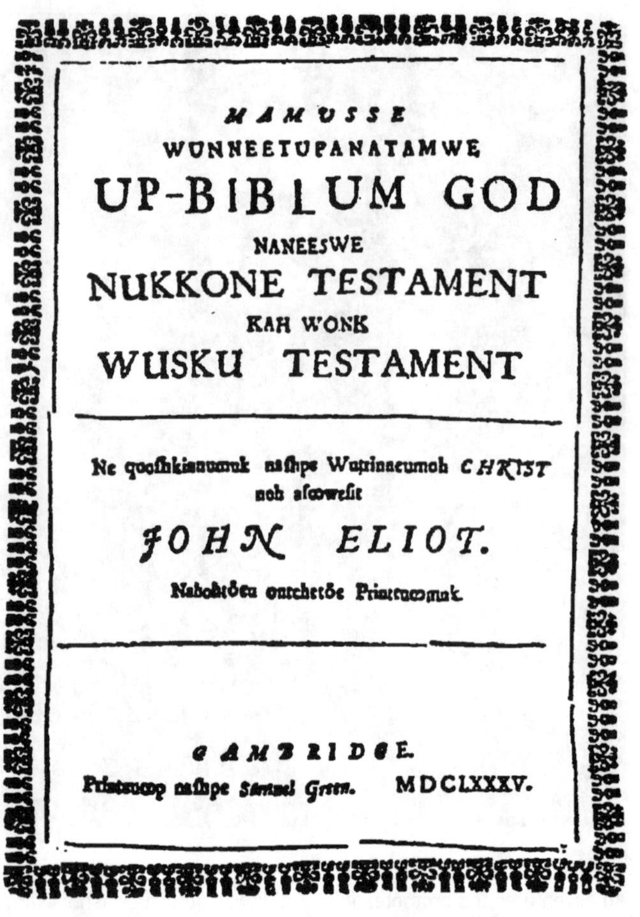

MAMUSSE
WUNNEETUPANATAMWE
UP-BIBLUM GOD
NANEESWE
NUKKONE TESTAMENT
KAH WONK
WUSKU TESTAMENT

Ne quoshkinnumuk nashpe Wuttinneumoh CHRIST
noh asoowesit

JOHN ELIOT.

Nahohtôeu ontchetôe Printeuoomuk.

CAMBRIDGE.
Printeuoop nashpe Samuel Green. MDCLXXXV.

Indian Bible
John Eliot's translation of the Bible into the language of the Algonquins was the first book printed in America. The New Testament appeared in 1661 and the Old Testament in 1663. Together, they were credited with helping to Christianize 24,000 Indians.

tractive. Word spread quickly to Europe of such a wonder, capturing the imagination of religious-minded Europeans all across the continent. Copies found their way to European libraries, and stories of the work remained alive over decades. The Dutch traveller Jasper Danckaerts heard of the Indian Bible in Europe nearly twenty years after its publication, and he was eager to buy the book when he visited America in 1680. He and a friend searched Boston booksellers in vain for a copy and resolved to seek out Reverend Eliot himself a 45-minute ride away in Roxbury, Massachusetts. Persisting until they located the minister, the Dutch travellers discovered that they could not communicate with him. He did not speak Dutch, and they could only speak broken English. The three managed to find a common ground: they were able to converse in Latin. Eliot told them that he had converted a number of Indians to Christianity, but that unconverted Indians despised the Bible and all that it stood for. The words it contained had begun destroying their religion, their worship, their gods. Hating the book, Native Americans had carried away all copies of Eliot's Bible in a recent war. Undaunted, Eliot was in the process of printing a second edition so that distribution and conversion could continue. Not wanting to disappoint religious men who had come so far to see the phenomenon of a Bible written in Algonquin, Eliot gave Danckaerts his own copy of the first edition.[8]

European diseases and gunpowder played a big part in reducing the Native American population, but the role of printed material cannot be overlooked as one factor in subduing Indian culture. Publications pleading with Europeans to convert the Indians not only gave many settlers a mission but also helped plant the idea that the American continent was singled out by God as a place worthy of His best graces, a place that was blessed for the service of God. That notion would grow in years to come, fueled by many factors — but the idea that European settlers could offer Native Americans eternal salvation was a push in that direction.

Preventing False Reports

Jasper Danckaerts was pleased by his copy of the Indian Bible, but he was otherwise frequently displeased with his trip to America. Even the map he was using to find his way around was incorrect! It had been printed and bound into a highly respected atlas, but Danckaerts fumed because it was full of inaccuracies. He made careful corrections and sought out the mapmaker when he returned to Holland. He felt that it was imperative that the man make changes before any more incorrect editions of the atlas fell into other travellers' hands.[9]

Danckaerts was not the only American traveller or settler who was surprised by the inaccuracies in literature about America. A large number of early Americans left behind diaries, letters, and printed matter complaining that tracts about the New World, particularly promotional ones, were exaggerated or even false. Although some readers did, indeed, find America to be similar to the dazzling descriptions of it, it is a safe guess to say that few found the magical America that had been described in promotional tracts. Settlement literature, written somewhat like advertisements of today, had a hyperbolic quality that led many eager readers astray. As an American trader named Christopher Levett said in a 1628 pamphlet seeking to undo the damage done by exaggerated promotional literature:

> And to say something of the Countrey [America]: I will not doe therein as some have done, to my knowledge speak more than is true: I will not tell you that you may smell the corne fields before you see the Land, neither must men thinke that the corne doth grow naturally (or on trees,) nor will the *Deare* come when they are called, or stand still and looke on a man, untill he shute him, not knowing a man from a beast, nor the fish leap into the kettle, nor on the drie Land, neither are they so plentifull, that you may dipp them up in baskets, nor take *Codd* in

[8]Journal entry of 8 July 1680 by Jasper Danckaerts, in Bartlett Burleigh James and J. Franklin Jameson, eds., *Journal of Jasper Danckaerts, 1679-1680* (New York, 1934; translated from the Dutch edition of 1687 by Henry C. Murphy in 1867), 264. The first edition of the Indian Bible was begun in 1660.

[9]Journal entry of 10 October 1680 by Jasper Danckaerts in ibid., 297.

Increase Mather
On a mission to England to negotiate a new governing charter for the colony of Massachusetts, Increase Mather produced a document in 1689 that had the appearance of a newspaper – *The Present State of New-English Affairs.* Mather, however, never intended to publish it again, and thus it did not fit the definition of a periodical. A prolific author, Mather produced 130 books and pamphlets and published numerous sermons.

> netts to make a voyage, which is no truer: then that the fowles will present themselves, to you with spitts through them.[10]

Levett had heard false *good* reports that needed correcting, but most writers who hastened to press over false reports wanted to counteract some negative image. When New England settlers failed in their attempt to raise cattle in North Carolina, they spread the word that the place was unproductive. A group of Carolina-based writers published a pamphlet to answer the rumor. They declared that the land was as good as any they had seen in the entire world, and its timber was superb. The lands in question, they said, would surely accommodate thousands of Englishmen. The pamphlet did not sugar-coat problems with Indians or Spaniards, nor did it gloss over harsh weather conditions of the region, but rather it spelled out the problems in honest detail. The appeal was successful; many people settled in Carolina as a result of reading the pamphlet.[11]

Rumors plagued all of the colonies. As New England leader John Winthrop noted, "...[I]t was so usual to have false news brought from all parts, that we were very doubtful of the most probable reports." He found that confused settlers tended to rely on the printed word to clear up misunderstandings. As governor of Massachusetts, Winthrop found himself involved in a dispute over lands to the west, which France and England both claimed. Frenchmen believed the Englishmen of Massachusetts were planning a hostile raid into French territories. To prove them wrong, Winthrop and the Council of Massachusetts issued a printed order forbidding Massachusetts residents from making any hostile moves towards the French, unless in self-defense. Winthrop and the council considered the printed order to be an important augmentation of mere verbal diplomacy, as well as an effective educational device. It seemed that a printed declaration carried a great deal of weight and authoritative proof of English intentions, and it corrected the falsehoods spreading among the French. It also offered clear direction to Massachusetts settlers who might be contemplating an attack.[12]

Despite communication difficulties, Winthrop did live in the Boston area, which was a communication hub with its busy port and its web of well-travelled roads. Settlers in more remote places fared far worse. From the western part of Massachusetts, for example, John Pynchon constantly sent letters back East in hopes of straightening out the large numbers of rumors that galloped through his community of Springfield. He believed he had a duty to quell false reports. The most trustworthy of all the information that bounced around town, he felt, was that which came from the mass media. At one point a Dutchman appeared in Springfield, claiming that French news publications had told of the defeat of the English fleet by the Dutch. Although Pynchon considered such a defeat to be unthinkable, he was inclined to believe it, as it came from a formal news source. He hurried to get a confirmation. The news was, indeed, true.[13]

Untainted by Falsehood

As Pynchon and so many other colonials agreed, communication with the Mother Country was often distorted by rumor and gossip. At times the printed word seemed to be the most authoritative way to kill those rumors and dissolve that gossip. The desire to keep overseas communication untainted by falsehood led to the publication of a document that had the appearance of a newspaper. Its author, however, never intended to publish it again, and thus it was not a periodical at all. Printed in 1689, the pamphlet was titled *The Present State of New-English Affairs.* It sprang from the pen of Massachusetts leader Increase Mather, who had gone to England to plead for a new Massachusetts charter to replace the

[10]Christopher Levett, *My Discovery of divers Rivers and Harbours* (1628) reprinted in George Parker Winship, ed., *Sailors' Narratives of Voyages along the New England Coast, 1524-1624* (New York, 1968), 282, 286-7.

[11]William Hilton, Anthony Long, and Peter Fabian, *A Relation of a Discovery lately made on the Coast of Florida* (London, printed by J.C. for Simon Miller, 1664), reprinted in Salley, *Narratives of Early Carolina*, 37-61.

[12]Journal entry of 23 May 1644 by John Winthrop in James Kendall Hosmer, ed., *Winthrop's Journal, "History of New England," 1630-1649*, vol. II (New York, 1908), 182-3.

[13]John Pynchon to John Winthrop, Jr., 2 March 1664/65, in Carl Bridenbaugh, ed., *The Pynchon Papers, Vol. I: Letters of John Pynchon, 1654-1700* (Boston, 1982), 53-5. Also, John Pynchon to John Winthrop, Jr., 24 January 1666/67, postscript mistakenly dated 1 January 1666, in ibid., 72. The Dutch had won a naval victory over the English at St. Christopher in the Caribbean on 14 June 1666.

The Present State of the

New-English Affairs.

This is Published to prevent False Reports

An Extract of a Letter from Mr. Mather, To the Governour Dated Sept. 3. 1689 from Deal in Kent.

THe House of Commons Ordered a Bill to be drawn up for the Restoration of Charters to all Corporations. Some Enemies of *New-England* did bestir themselves on that Occasion. But it has pleased God to succeed Endeavours and Sollicitations here so far, as that *N. E.* is particularly mentioned in the Bill.

It has been read twice, and after that referred to a Committee for Emendations. What concerns *N. England* passed without any great opposition. The Bill has been in part read the third Time, and the Charters of *N.-Eng.* then also passed without Objection. Only some Additional Clauses respecting Corporations here, caused Debates; so that the Bill is not as yet Enacted.

In the latter end of *June*, a Vessel from *Mount Hope* arrived here, which brought your Declaration of *April 18.* with an account of the Revolution in *New-England*. The week after I went to *Hampton Court*, and had the favour to wait on His Majesty [illegible] *was well pleased with what was done in* New-England, *and that he would order the Secretary of State to signifie so much, and that His Subjects there should have their Ancient Rights and Priviledges restored to them*.

The King has sent a Gracious Letter (which was delivered to me, and if I reckon not my self, I shall take care that it be sent to you) bearing Date *August 12. Wherein He signifies His Royal Ap*[illegible] of what has been done at *Boston*, [illegible] you that the Government there shall [illegible] so as shall be for the Security and [illegible] of His Subjects in that Colony, and [illegible] time bids you go on to Administer [illegible] manage the Government, according [illegible] you have Petitioned.

[illegible] (now Earl of *Monmouth*) [illegible] that He would be your Friend, [illegible] you from him, *That your* [illegible] *to you by Act of Parliament*. [illegible] of the Kings most Hon[illegible] Council, who have promised to be[illegible] as there shall be occasion for [illegible] I may say, of all the *Leading-men* [illegible]

[illegible] the *Downs* a fortnight, and [illegible] several Nights, but the Wind has [illegible] And we now hear that the Convoyes (on whose Assistance [illegible]) are gone.

[illegible] the *Honourable* [illegible], *Esq;*

[illegible] Colony in N. England.

A Passage extracted from the publick News-Letter, Dated July 6. 1689.

The people of *New-England* having made a thorow Revolution, and secured the publick Criminals. On *Thursday* last, the Reverend and Learned *Mr. Mather*, President of the *Colledge*, and Minister of *Boston*, waited on the King; and in a most Excellent Speech laid before His Majesty, the State of that People; saying, *That they were sober, and Industrious, and fit for Martial Service; and all with their Lives and Interests were at His Majesties Command, to tender the same unto His Majesty: That they desired nothing but His Majesties Acceptance of what they had done, and His Protection; and that if His Majesty pleased to encourage and Commission them, He might easily be Emperour of* America. His Majesty assured him, that He was pleased with what was done for Him, and for themselves in the [illegible] on, and that their Priviledges and [illegible] should be secured unto them.

Extracted from a Letter of Mr Mather, *to his Son, Dated Sept. 3. 1689.*

On *July 4.* The King said unto me, *That He did kindly Accept of what was done in Boston. And that His Subjects in* New-England *should have their Ancient Rights and Priviledges Restored and Confirmed unto them.* Yea, He told me, *That if it were in his power to cause it to be done it should be done*, and bade me rest assured of it.

The *Charter-Bill* is not finished, because some Additional Clauses respecting Corporations here in *England* caused a Debate; and the Parliament is for some weeks Adjourned.

Besides the Letter from the Kings Majesty, whereof we have notice as above; there is now arrived, an Order from His Majesty to the Government, bearing Date, *July 30. 1689.* Requiring, *That Sir* Edmund Androse, Edward Randolph, *and others, that have been Seized by the people of* Boston, *and shall be at the Receipt of these Commands, Detained there, under Confinement, be sent on Board the first Ship, bound to* England, *to answer what may be objected against them.*

Boston, Printed and Sold by *Samuel Green*, 1689.

The Present State of New-English Affairs

Occasionally thought of as the American colonies' first newspaper, Increase Mather's 1689 report, *The Present State of New-English Affairs*, never was intended to be a continuing publication. It did indicate, however, the concern that Mather and other colonists had that there be timely accounts of important events.

one the crown had cancelled. Rumors swirled around his trip — wild rumors, many with no basis in fact. Mather saw the mock newspaper as the surest way to inform the people back home of exactly how their complaints were playing in London. He issued *The Present State of New-English Affairs* with the dramatic announcement: "This is published to prevent false reports."

It is interesting that Mather chose the format of a newspaper to clear up false reports. Even though no newspaper yet existed in America, colonials read European newspapers, which seemed to carry a solemn weight of authority. Readers saw them as purveyors of truth, the definitive word in a world where communication was easily garbled and distorted during the vast numbers of weeks it took for words to travel across the Atlantic. The newspaper was already a trusted form before it finally made its American debut in 1690. Before newspapers ever took hold in English America, the notion of journalism already involved the concept that the newspaper should be true, honest, clear, and trustworthy.

The foundation of the American newspaper industry was built of stones from the colonial era, when highly intelligent people such as Increase Mather recognized that newspapers — even those from faraway England — were the objects of much faith. People believed them and publications like them, no matter how far away they were printed. News told by word of mouth seemed to operate like the game children play by whispering a phrase in each other's ear. The more the message was passed from mouth to ear, the less it resembled the original. Newspapers or pamphlets, however, were printed and therefore were not twisted by repeated telling. They carried a sense of truth. Modern readers of colonial newspapers often complain that the information in them was not timely, especially after six or eight weeks of ocean travel; but that did not really matter so much to colonial Americans. The important thing was, the news in the newspaper or pamphlet had not changed from the original printing. It was the embodiment of truth over rumor.

The idea that the printing press could prevent or cure false reports was a strong one in colonial America and a significant one to people's developing expectations of what journalistic writing was all about. The truthfulness of journalism evolved over time into a permanent fixture in mainstream American journalism. Its ancestry was, at least partially, in the preventing of false reports, a prominent feature of the pre-newspaper press.

Ultimately, it was not surprising in the least that the one and only issue of the first American newspaper, titled *Publick Occurrences, both Forreign and Domestick*, also announced that it was printed to prevent false reports.

THE PRINTING PRESS AND PUBLIC DEBATE

Colonial readers were more easily swayed about the truth of information if its source were the mass media. They also recognized a strong persuasive effect of the mass media. American pro-settlement promotional literature, for example, proved the ability of the press to advertise, lure, coax. Convinced that the printed word was both persuasive and believable, Americans frequently rushed to the printing press when they had disputes among themselves. When an early American citizen passionately felt his cause was the correct one, it was natural for him to try to persuade others that he was right by printing and distributing his ideas for all to read. Frequently parties on the other side of the question would answer in print in a calculated struggle to win public opinion.

The printed word in such cases may or may not have persuaded many readers, but it did frequently spark or perpetuate heavy public discussion. Provocative tracts arguing various points helped build up the democratic notion of a "marketplace of ideas," which would one day be a hallmark of American press phi-

John Winthrop
Puritan John Winthrop had to wrestle with his conscience before deciding to move to America. Although the radical group of Puritans now known as "Pilgrims" had moved to New England in 1620, Winthrop and conservative Puritans believed that they should stay in England to purify the Anglican church. However, as persecution mounted, it seemed that emigrating was the only answer. Winthrop searched the Bible and found justification for fleeing to New England, where he and fellow Puritans could practice their religion in peace. It was he who originated the idea that Puritan New England should be a shining "city on a hill" to enlighten Christians in Europe as to God's true religion. He later became governor of Massachusetts. In that position, he used printing to attempt to counter rumors and false reports as part of his efforts to assure stability in the colony.

losophy. Furthermore, pamphlets, tracts, and books in various wars of words began helping Americans grapple with the concept of what was right, what was correctly a part of the American experience. The literature of debate thus served as seeds of American thought, helping Americans slowly begin to emerge from their European past.

The technique of using print to force American society to confront an issue started early. In 1643 a Mr. Briscoe in Watertown, Massachusetts, challenged the Puritan church rule that everyone pay taxes to fund ministers' salaries. Briscoe himself was not a member of the church and did not wish to be. He audaciously wrote a pamphlet on the taxation question. "This he published underhand, which occasioned much stir in the town," Puritan leader John Winthrop complained. Furthermore, Briscoe went around Massachusetts promoting the book and making reproachful speeches about the tax. Officials brought him before the General Court of Massachusetts, and there he fully admitted both publishing the tract and making the speeches. Cowed by the experience, Briscoe conceded that he had been wrong to challenge the authorities so brazenly. He was fined £10, and one of the publishers of the tract was slapped with a 40-shilling fine.[14] Briscoe may or may not have been successful at winning converts to his point of view on the matter, but he was successful in creating public debate over the issue — his theme that church and state should be separate would come up over and over again as a bone of contention in Massachusetts. The concept of a government independent of church would evolve over time to be a rather unEuropean, very American ideal. By the late 1600s, Puritan congregations were supporting their own churches without help from non-members, and it was the Anglican Church — the state church of England — that believed it was entitled to tax support.

Complaints by individuals such as Briscoe sprang from personal disappointment or small-group discontent. In a bizarre turn of history, however, many of the American colonies experienced unrest of far greater magnitude in the latter half of the seventeenth century. Starting with Bacon's Rebellion in Virginia in 1676 and running through 1690, five colonies underwent violent political upheaval. Angry people in two of them overthrew their colonial governors. Public debate, sparked and augmented by the printed word, fueled the violence in at least three of the colonies. All five of the colonies used written argument to try to convince readers to follow one position or the other.

The colonial revolts took place in Virginia, Albemarle (North Carolina), New York, Massachusetts, and Maryland. The Albemarle and Virginia factions, which were battling over local governmental problems, did not have access to a press in their own colonies. However, revolutionaries in both settlements issued inflammatory writings to stir up the people. Virginia's factions in 1676 debated the insurrection in widely circulated poetry; and a year later, the Albemarle revolutionaries deliberately sent "seditious libells" all over the area "to put all in a flame."[15] Some of the items may have been printed, although probably some were hand-copied.

PRINTING AND THE GLORIOUS REVOLUTION

However, residents of New York, Massachusetts, and Maryland carried on their insurrections through the printed word. The uprisings in those colonies were all linked to rumors and then confirmation of the fact that Protestant William and Mary had been installed as joint rulers of England, ousting Catholic King James in November 1688 in a coup often called the "Glorious Revolution." Printed documents were at the heart of the debate and unrest.

New Yorkers began hearing unconfirmed rumors of James'

[14]Journal entry of 5 March 1643 by John Winthrop in Hosmer, *Winthrop's Journal*, 91.

[15][Unidentified manservant of Nathaniel Bacon], "Bacon's Epitaph, made by his Man," quoted by an anonymous writer in a manuscript entitled "The History of Bacon's and Ingram's Rebellion, 1676"; and "Affidavit of Thomas Miller concerning the Rebellion of Carolina," both in Charles M. Andrews, ed., *Narratives of the Insurrections* (New York, 1915), 75-7, 153.

William and Mary
When William and Mary ascended the British throne following the Glorious Revolution of 1688, their coronation was a cause for celebration in the American colonies. Puritans had supported the overthrow of Catholic King James, and they and his other opponents had used the printing press in their efforts. It was in the aftermath of his overthrow that Increase Mather printed *The Present State of New-English Affairs* and that Massachusetts two years later would get its first newspaper. The British etching above was published in 1689.

overthrow, and immediately people became agitated. The colony's council and representative convention made haste to get a printed copy of the supposed proclamation of the accession of William and Mary. They wrote to Boston for a copy. Hearing that gentlemen from Connecticut were coming to New York with the document, the council sent riders two days out in hopes of meeting them. They missed each other. Eventually the Connecticut riders did arrive in New York and delivered the printed proclamation to the colonial governor, Jacob Leisler. He issued the proclamation without notifying either the council or convention. The council failed to believe Leisler's proclamation until the governing body obtained its own printed version, which eventually arrived dated February 14, 1688/89.[16] In that print, the new monarchs confirmed that office-holders were required to be Protestants. The council turned Catholics out of office but did not explain the action to Leisler. He had no knowledge of why the offices suddenly changed hands without any apparent authorization. So, although a Protestant himself, Leisler accused the new Protestant office-holders of treason.

Inflammatory pamphlets began to appear. One of the most provocative was titled *A Modest and Impartial Narrative*, which was neither modest nor impartial. The writer, Nicholas Bayard, accused Leisler of maliciously attempting to kindle mob violence among the common people. According to Bayard, Leisler worked hand-in-hand with "his assistant vain glory, together with [his] God-Mother Ambition...." The pamphlet accused Leisler of being "a faithful servant to that black prince of the air" who would continue to act for the devil as long as "the many-headed beasts" — the common man — would stand by him. New York was already seething over the factions' handling of events, and writings such as Bayard's did not help cool things off. Leisler was executed a few months later.

New England in Turmoil

Meanwhile, in the united colonies of New England, Governor Sir Edmund Andros had been stirring up hatred for some time. Puritans had been accustomed to governing themselves, as allowed under the original Massachusetts charter, but King James had vacated the charter. He had sent Andros to be the governor of a forced alliance between the various colonies of New England. As an Anglican appointed to rule a largely Puritan population, Andros had always been the subject of public distrust. One of his first actions had been to require the use of a Puritan church for Anglican services, a move that greatly angered Puritan leaders.

They also railed against Andros' heavyhanded leadership, which ran contrary to the freedoms New Englanders had long enjoyed under their own local governments. Puritans singled out restrictions on the printing press as a major blunder by Andros. Increase Mather complained bitterly in a 1688 pamphlet that "the people are at a great loss to ***know what*** is ***Law and what not,***" for Andros had changed the laws without bothering to update the populace with printed copies of the changes.[17] As far as Mather was concerned, printing and distribution of information such as the law were basic necessities.

Massachusetts residents read, repeated, and reprinted Mather's complaints, causing a stern reaction from Andros. He needed to come down hard on rampant anti-governmental expression. Early in 1689, his administration issued an order against seditious publications. It thundered:

> Whereas many papers have beene lately printed and dispersed tending to the disturbance of the peace and subversion of the government of this theire Majesties Colonie....
>
> It is therefore ordered that if any person or persons within this Collony be found guilty of any such like Misdemeanour of printing, publishing or concealing any such like papers or discourses, or not timely discover such things to Authority,...they shall be accounted enemies to their Majesties present Govern-

[16]England and her colonies formally adopted the Gregorian calendar in 1752. Before that, they used the Julian calendar, which (in Christian countries only) featured New Year's Day on March 25. However, some people, including those of Dutch background in New York, accepted the Gregorian calendar, which placed New Year's Day on January 1. Thus, February 14 1688/89 would fall near the end of the Julian year 1688 but near the beginning of the Gregorian year 1689. To avoid confusion, prior to 1752 people were in the habit of writing the two applicable years after all dates between January 1 and March 25.

[17]Increase Mather, *A Narrative of the Miseries of New-England, by Reason of an Arbitrary Government Erected there, Under Sir Edmond Andros* (Boston, printed by Richard Pierce, 1688). This was actually a reprint; the first edition appeared in London, according to *The Andros Tracts,* vol. I (New York, 1868), 5.

Edmund Andros
Among the Puritans' many complaints against Edmund Andros, the Anglican governor of New England from 1686 to 1689, was that he placed heavyhanded restrictions on the printing press. They also charged that he changed the laws without bothering to inform the populace with printed copies of the changes.

ment and be proceeded against as such with uttermost severity.[18]

By November of 1688, Andros was out of a job as King James was forced from the throne, but Andros did not yet know it. Bostonians were hearing rumors of the king's overthrow in December, and more rumors came again in March; but it took the printed word — or the purported printed word — to persuade them that the rumors were true. On April 4, John Winslow arrived from Nevis, West Indies, with a piece of writing that he said he had copied from a print issued by the new King William. It instructed all magistrates who had been turned out by James to return to their jobs. Immediately, someone had the paper printed as a broadside, and it spread through town. The broadside was enough to turn the tide of public sentiment from restlessness to unrest, despite the tenuous nature of Winslow's claims. The fact that the words had somehow, somewhere supposedly been issued as a formal royal print satisfied many readers.

Powerful Bostonians worked quickly to be rid of Andros. On April 18, Puritan leader Cotton Mather, son of Increase, hired the press to print a declaration, which he read from the balcony of the townhouse in a bid to inflame public sentiment. Among other things, he called Andros and his deputies "Horse-leeches...[that] have been sucking of us; and what Laws they made it was as impossible for us to know, as dangerous as for us to break; He would neither suffer them to be printed nor fairly published."[19] Bostonians overthrew Andros later that day, without bloodshed. They finally got a formal, printed proclamation of William and Mary as dual rulers in late May, a month and a half after the coup.

The overthrow of Andros did not end the argument over the legalities of such an action. The debate had just begun, and the sides battled in paper and ink. Nathanael Byfield tried to justify the revolution by printing an account of it in both London and Edinburgh, together with Mather's accusations. John Palmer, an Andros supporter, tried to convince readers of the illegalities and nastiness that went on in Puritan New England by defending Andros in *An Account of the State of New England*, a pamphlet printed in London because, Palmer said, the Puritan majority would not allow such a thing to be printed in Boston. In an attempt to counter Palmer's pamphlet and others like it, a number of men on the colonial governing council wrote a pamphlet decrying Andros as arbitrary and illegally installed. Still other writers gathered and published affidavits by people who had been involved in the coup, supporting the revolutionaries.[20]

The Clash of Catholics and Protestants

As pamphlets fueled public action and debate on the situation in New England, predominantly Catholic Maryland was undergoing upheaval between Catholics and Protestants. Maryland Protestants had gotten word of the change in the English monarchy, and they accordingly felt justified in taking up arms against their Catholic governors. William Nuthead, a printer newly arrived in the town of St. Mary's from Virginia, inaugurated the new Maryland press by printing a controversial tract defending Protestant actions. The writer of the tract, identified only as J.F., complained that Protestant churches had been converted to popery and idolatry. The Catholic governor had tampered with the popular assembly, nullifying some of the laws it had made and sending home some delegates. In fact, J.F. said, the governor had managed to reconfigure the assembly by disbanding it and then calling it anew with far too few representatives. Furthermore, Protestant orphans were given to Catholics to raise, and Catholic leaders looked the other way when Protestants were murdered. Protestants, J.F. concluded, were in constant fear of losing their life and their property.[21]

[18] *Order against seditious publications* (1689), in *Andros Tracts*, vol. III, 107.

[19] Cotton Mather, *Declaration of the Gentlemen, Merchants, and Inhabitants of Boston* (1689), quoted in Nathanael Byfield, *An Account of The Late Revolution in New-England* (London: Printed by Richard Chitwell, 1689), reprinted in Andrews, *Narratives of the Insurrections*, 176-8. The sentence "He would neither suffer them to be printed nor fairly published" was added in Mather's text as a marginal note, marked with an asterisk to be read after the preceding sentence.

[20] Byfield, ibid., 170-82. Also, John Palmer, *An Account of the State of New England* (London, 1690). Also, William Stoughton, Thomas Hinckley, Wait Winthrop, Bartholomew Gedney, and Samuel Shrimpton, *A Narrative of the Procedings of Sir Edmond Androsse and his Complices* (1691), reprinted in Andrews, *Narratives of the Insurrections*, 239-49.

[21] J.F., *The Declaration of Reasons and Motives for the Present Appearing in arms of Their Majesties Protestant Subjects in the Province of Maryland* (St. Mary's, Maryland, printed by William Nuthead, 1689), reprinted in Andrews, *Narratives of the Insurrections*, 305-14.

THE

DECLARATION

OF THE

REASONS and MOTIVES

For the PRESENT

Appearing in Arms

OF

THEIR MAJESTIES

Protestant Subjects

In the PROVINCE of

MARYLAND

Licens'd, *November* 28*th* 1689. J. F.

ALthough the Nature and State of Affairs relating to the Government of this Province, is ſo well and notoriouſly known to all Perſons any way concerned in the ſame, as to the People and Inhabitants here, who are more immediately Intereſted, as might excuſe any *Declaration* or *Apology* for this preſent inevitable *Appearance*: Yet foraſmuch as (by the *Plots, Contrivances, Inſinuations, Remonſtrances*, and *Subſcriptions*, carried on, ſuggeſted, extorted, and obtained by the Lord *Baltemore*, his Depu-

A ties

Maryland Rebellion
Following the change in the English monarchy with the Glorious Revolution, Protestants in Maryland took up arms against their Catholic governors. William Nuthead inaugurated the new Maryland press in 1689 by printing this controversial tract defending their actions. The tract complained that Protestant churches had been converted to popery and idolatry.

It was not a new debate, of course. Protestants and Catholics had clashed in Maryland for many decades. Thirty-four years earlier, Lord Baltimore, the colony's Catholic leader, had tried to counteract public dissatisfaction by issuing a pamphlet titled *The Lord Baltimore's Case*, claiming that he supported both Catholics and Protestants. Protestants responded, charging in print that Baltimore was an enemy to the Anglican Church and that he sought a war with Parliament.

The concept that the press should spark and cultivate public debate was not unique to America, but the fact that European-Americans had some sort of access to the press for their entire history made printed public debate an accepted thing. True, there were restrictions on the press, as was common in Europe, but there was also a wide acceptance that debate about various issues was to be public via the mass media. In fact, if factions on one side or another of an American issue found themselves restricted from printing an argumentative document on a nearby press, they would turn to the press of another colony or even of London. They believed that societal disputes simply needed to be made public. It was important to get the word out so that wrongs might be righted or besmirched reputations might be scrubbed clean.

Episodes of printed debate were pivotal in the formation of American thought about the role of media, about the role of dispute, about the public nature of opposing factions, about the necessity of telling all sides. The American character, conceived in the earliest era of the American mass media, accepted it as natural to see debates printed and distributed for anyone to read.

The Output of the First Presses

Much of the printing work for America took place in Europe, but the importation of a press into America opened the doors of debate, religious instruction, rumor-curing, entertainment, and so on — all the functions of the mass media — on Americans' turf. Theoretically, the press became even more accessible than it had been before.

The first press in Anglo-America arrived in Cambridge, Massachusetts, in 1638. As time passed, other printers moved to the Puritan colony. Before the first American newspaper was published in 1690, what exactly were those Massachusetts presses producing? It's easy to say briefly that they issued broadsides, almanacs, and pamphlets, as well as government documents and occasional books. However, the texture of American thought was evident in those early documents; so the output of the earliest presses, and people's thought about those presses, are worthy of a closer look.

The press was an accoutrement of civilization that seemed to create both great pride and great fear in the American colonies. Showing one type of thought on the presence of an American press, William Berkeley, governor of the Anglican colony of Virginia, was famous for commenting in 1671: "I thank God, *there are no free schools* nor *printing* [in Virginia] and I hope we shall not have these hundred years; for *learning* has brought disobedience, and heresy, and sects into the world, and *printing* has divulged them, and libels against the best government. God keep us from both!" On the other side of the coin, one of the first employees of the Cambridge press was proud that his printshop had a goal of supporting the needs of the government and thus helping a new country to unfold.[22]

The man who imported the first press into Massachusetts, Puritan Reverend Joseph Glover, found plenty of international well-wishers for his American venture. He was able to undertake the expense of importing a press by soliciting the help of Puritan gentlemen in England and in exile in Amsterdam. They, like Glov-

[22]Berkeley made the remark to his superiors in London, who had asked for an accounting of education in Virginia. See David Freeman Hawke, *Everyday Life in Early America* (New York, 1988), 68-9. The other opinion was shown in a letter from Timothy Green to Isaiah Thomas, 8 August 1792, in the Isaiah Thomas Papers, American Antiquarian Society (Worcester, Mass.), Box 2, Folder 2. In the letter, Green was reminiscing about his great-grandfather, Samuel Green, and indicated that Samuel felt that the shop was largely governmental in nature.

America's Primer
Americans of the seventeenth century showed a great interest in the education of the young. The *New England Primer*, printed in Boston in 1690, served as the main textbook for fifty years and was used to teach reading for 100 more.

er, had an interest in seeing a printing press available in the Puritan's model "city on a hill" to spread God's word and the enlightened Puritan thought to the corrupt churches of Europe and their deluded followers.

Although Glover died en route, his press arrived safely in Massachusetts and inaugurated the era of American printing. Others eventually followed Glover's lead; and from 1638 to 1690, American presses churned out documents of varying types, from government decrees to news pamphlets to educational material. The locally produced tracts were not meant strictly for an American audience. Religious writings, especially, found their way back to Europe. Likewise, the Massachusetts press issued 600 copies of the colony's *Book of the General Lauues and Libertyes* with the intention of sending copies to London for distribution to potential settlers. "[T]hey were printed, and now are to be seen of all men, to the end that none may plead ignorance," a Massachusetts settler explained, "and that all who intend to transport themselves hither, may know this is no place of licentious liberty, nor will this people suffer any to trample down this Vineyard of the Lord...."[23] Despite such links with Europe, however, American printed works were most widely distributed in America.

[23][Edward Johnson], *A History of New-England From the English planting in the Yeere 1628. [sic] untill the Yeere 1652* (London, Nathaniel Brooke, 1654), reprinted as J. Franklin Jameson, ed., *Johnson's Wonder-Working Providence, 1628-1651* (New York, 1910), 244.

What type of works were Americans reading from their own presses? Religious publications outnumbered publications of other types, perhaps because the Puritans operated most of the early presses. True, the press came in handy for many other types of documents, but Puritans by definition had a keen interest in spiritual writings. They believed the press had a powerful ability to reach people and influence them and, perhaps more importantly, to be a tool in the search for ultimate truth. They recognized the wide net the mass media could cast, and they used it to better humanity by issuing religious items including sermons, biographies of godly people, book-length works on religious topics, Bibles, catechisms, religious discussions, and answers and challenges to religious heretics or other sects.

Evangelical Writings

It was natural for Puritans to turn to the printed word in their zeal to establish God's kingdom on earth. After all, the Puritans' "errand into the wilderness," as they called their move to America, was justified by nothing less than the word of God as published in the Bible. The Puritans were part of the Protestant movement that shunned the traditional trappings of both the Catholic and Anglican churches, including the priesthood. To devout Puritans, each man or woman had an obligation to read the Scriptures and reason about them for himself. That task was not to be left to a priest or a bishop, as it was in the Catholic and Anglican churches. Thus, the tangible, printed Bible was a personal necessity to Puritans, a treasure that opened the Kingdom of Heaven to each individual reader.

As important as the Bible was to the Puritans, the printed word in other forms also carried deep and important religious significance. The Puritan faith encouraged intellectual understanding of the Bible through interpretation, discussion, and argument — which could all be disseminated through printed matter. To the Puritans, existence on Earth meant a relentless search for truth, and the printed word was an awe-inspiring and powerful tool in that search. A surface reading of the Bible was not enough. It took convincing, wrangling, restating, and debating to understand God's word fully. Thus it was not surprising that church members spent a lot of energy on a great outpouring of printed messages for the purpose of seeking truth, reaching sinners, and keeping the godly on the straight and narrow.

Of course, Puritans relied on sermon and example to reach the straying and to edify the saintly, but they realized that the printed word could bring those very sermons to hundreds who *hadn't* heard the pastor. The printed word could also preserve the character and feats of the saintly in books or pamphlets, which could circulate long and far. Puritans were sure that such writings had the power to convert or to edify, because they knew that many deep and important decisions in their own history had been inspired by the printed word.

John Foxe
John Foxe, who died in 1587, was the author of *The Book of Martyrs*, one of the most widely read books in the American colonies. Even today it is frequently reprinted. With its accounts of hundreds of heroic Christians who had been put to death for their faith, it provided inspiration to the Puritans who settled New England.

Puritan leader William Bradford was one of many church members who had read and been won over by a variety of books about saintly Christians. One of his favorites was John Foxe's famous *Book of Martyrs*, which "recorded how that besides those worthy martires and confessors which were burned in queen Marys days and otherwise tormented, many...fled out of the land to the number of 800." Those Protestant refugees from England set up Puritan congregations around Europe.[24] Like the martyrs in Foxe's book, Bradford and his fellow Puritans were the victims of persecution in England. They identified with the martyrs. Inspired by the *Book of Martyrs* and other such writings, they began fleeing England for Holland, where they could practice their religion as they pleased. When Holland proved less than adequate, they fled further to America.

Bradford's earliest Puritan "pilgrims," as they came to be known, were considered somewhat radical by their Puritan colleagues who remained in England. However, the more conservative sort, including John Winthrop, were finally persuaded to emigrate by the word of God. It was a monumental struggle to decide whether to emigrate, but over and over again, Winthrop turned to the Bible in an effort to convince both himself and others that emigration to New England was the answer to the ever-worsening corruption of the Anglican church.

[24]William T. Davis, ed., *Bradford's History of Plymouth Plantation, 1606-1646* (New York, 1908), 25. The actual title of Foxe's book, although it was commonly called *Book of Martyrs*, was *Acts and Monuments of the Christian Church*.

Since Winthrop was a trusted leader, people looked to him for answers to their fears. Very practical men, for instance, objected to the fact that the area the Puritans intended to settle had no natural fortifications. Winthrop searched the Scriptures and discovered that God intended for His people to learn to trust Him. He argued to the doubters that Paul and his companions in the Bible "were compassed with dangers on every side, and dayley were under the sentence of deathe, that they might learn to trust in the living God." Furthermore, Winthrop pointed out, the book of Deuteronomy confirmed that God had taken the children of Israel into the wilderness, away from "the fleshepottes of Egipt," much like He might be ordering them to leave the fleshpots of a wicked England. That had been a hard lesson for the children of Israel, but Winthrop felt that it had been for the ultimate good of religion.[25] The fact that his answers came from the Bible helped sell the credibility of an American Puritan settlement.

Taking such deep and significant inspiration from the Scriptures and published writings, it was a natural step for Puritans to welcome Joseph Glover's press to their colony in 1638. Printer Stephen Daye had the press up and running in 1638 or 1639.[26] He first printed the governmental *Oath of a Freeman*, which all voting males in the colony were required to take. Secondly he printed an almanac. However, in short order the Cambridge press began turning out pages and pages of religious discussion, more than any other type of document.

A Blessing to Religion

The press was a blessing to religion in the colony. By the 1640s, doctrinal differences were developing among congregations of various New England churches, leading dangerously to false interpretations of God's word. Puritan leaders realized the hazards of such dissent — their colony would no longer function as the model "city on a hill" if it collapsed into disagreement and sects. Calling a synod in 1646, Puritan divines worked out their differences by consulting the New Testament. After agreeing on the direction of the church, they turned to the press to get the word out, to convince erring churches to stay on the right track. True, the rules could and would be preached from the pulpits. But the pastors knew the printed word had authority and clarity beyond mere speaking. They determined that, in print, the rules "might be better scanned and tried of every particular person in the several congregations or churches." Their work, titled *A Platform of Church Discipline,* was published in Cambridge in 1649. Publication meant that all members of the Puritan colony might have the opportunity to read about the true church's strivings for godliness.

[25]John Winthrop, "Objections against this intended Plantation for New E[ngland]: Answered and resolved" (1629), in Stewart Mitchell, ed., *Winthrop Papers*, vol. II, 1623-1630 (Boston, 1931), 114.

[26]The first item from Daye's press was *Oath of a Freeman*. No copies of it have survived. However, several people of the era referred to it in their writings. The dates they gave for the *Oath* were ambiguous, but they suggest that it appeared in either March 1638 or March 1639.

THE OATH OF A FREEMAN.

I ·AB· being (by Gods providence) an Inhabitant, and Freeman, within the iuriſdictiõ of this Common-wealth, doe freely acknowledge my ſelfe to bee ſubject to the governement thereof; and therefore doe heere ſweare, by the great & dreadfull name of the Everliving-God, that I will be true & faithfull to the ſame, & will accordingly yield aſſiſtance & ſupport therunto, with my perſon & eſtate, as in equity I am bound: and will alſo truely indeavour to maintaine and preſerve all the libertyes & privilidges thereof, ſubmitting my ſelfe to the wholeſome lawes, & ordres made & ſtabliſhed by the ſame; and further, that I will not plot, nor practice any evill againſt it, nor conſent to any that ſhall ſoe do, butt will timely diſcover, & reveall the ſame to lawefull authoritee nowe here ſtabliſhed, for the ſpeedie preventing thereof. Moreover, I doe ſolemnly binde my ſelfe, in the ſight of God, that when I ſhalbe called, to give my voyce touching any ſuch matter of this ſtate, (in which freemen are to deale) I will give my vote & ſuffrage as I ſhall judge in myne owne conſcience may beſt conduce & tend to the publick weale of the body, without reſpect of perſonnes, or favour of any man. Soe help mee God in the Lord Ieſus Chriſt.

Oath of a Freeman

Although no original copies of the *Oath of a Freeman* exist, the one shown here is a copy (made at a later date) based on the original text that had survived in hand-written form. The *Oath* was the first item printed in Anglo-America. It appeared in either 1638 or 1639 from the press of Harvard College in Cambridge, Massachusetts, under the operation of Stephen Daye. All "freemen," or voting members of the colony, took the oath. It promised them that they could speak their mind plainly and according to their own conscience, without pressure from the government.

Puritans enjoyed reading printed debates about religious topics. So long as an idea was not so deviant as to be sinful or heretical, it was fair game. Puritan leaders spelled out their feelings about the importance of printed discussion of religious ideas in a tract titled *Propositions Concerning the Subjects of Baptism and Consociation of Churches.* The governing body of Massachusetts had read over the pamphlet, which detailed the controversial findings of a church synod in 1662. The officials announced that they were perfectly willing to let various factions publish their understanding of religious matters. As long as heresy was not allowed, religious debate was an actual obligation. They wrote:

> ...[T]o bear one with another in lesser differences, about matters of a more difficult and controversial nature, and more remote from the Foundation [of church doctrine], and wherein the godly-wise are not like-minded, is a Duty necessary to the peace and welfare of Religion.

Similarly, in 1663 *Another Essay for the Investigation of Truth* called for toleration of printed opinions, even those out of the mainstream. Justifying the publication of views that disagreed violently with certain synodical decisions, the tract's "Apologetical Preface to the Reader" noted calmly that even in the early Christian church, the apostles disagreed with one another. The writer of the preface said:

> Variety of Judgements may stand with Unity of Affections. He that judgeth a Cause before he hath heard both parties speaking, although he should judge rightly, is not a righteous Judge. [Thus] We are willing that the World should see what is here presented.

In fact, the writer announced that it was his moral responsibility to make the dissenters' opinion public so that he would not accidentally withhold the truth from mankind. To the Puritan way of thinking, the press was a tool for learning truth, no matter how much fellow church members disagreed. Contrary to today's popular notions of Puritans, their control on the press was not restrictive. The Puritans allowed — even treasured — the diversified religious discussions available through their press. While they did not tolerate the circulation of "heretical" writings from Anabaptists, Jesuits, and certain other groups, they saw the press as a vital means of uncovering and debating the nature of religious truth.

The only other press in America that had any roots whatsoever by 1690 was operating in Philadelphia. During the four years of its existence, the Philadelphia press had chiefly issued almanacs. However, as the capital of the Quaker colony of Pennsylvania, Philadelphia was the center of Quaker intellectual life. Thus, a number of Philadelphia prints before 1690 were religious in nature, either evangelizing readers into the Quaker religion or carrying on fierce debate with the Puritan press of Massachusetts. The presses of the two religious groups were the bane of each other's existence. No sooner would the Puritan press issue a warning to the flock against Quakerism, than the Quaker press would issue a strong response. Likewise, Puritans often felt they were on the defensive against persuasive Quaker books, especially when brought into Massachusetts by Quaker evangelists. The Quaker sect was far more evangelical in nature than the Puritans preferred — and far more so than it is considered today.

Between the Quakers and the Puritans, the only established presses in America before 1690 largely justified their existence by printing religious material. That fact reflected the importance of religion among the earliest American intellectuals and the devotion of early colonists to evangelism via the printed word. Did the arrival of the secular newspaper mark the beginning of the end of religion as the dominant characteristic of American thought? Americans never entirely gave up religion or swapped it for the

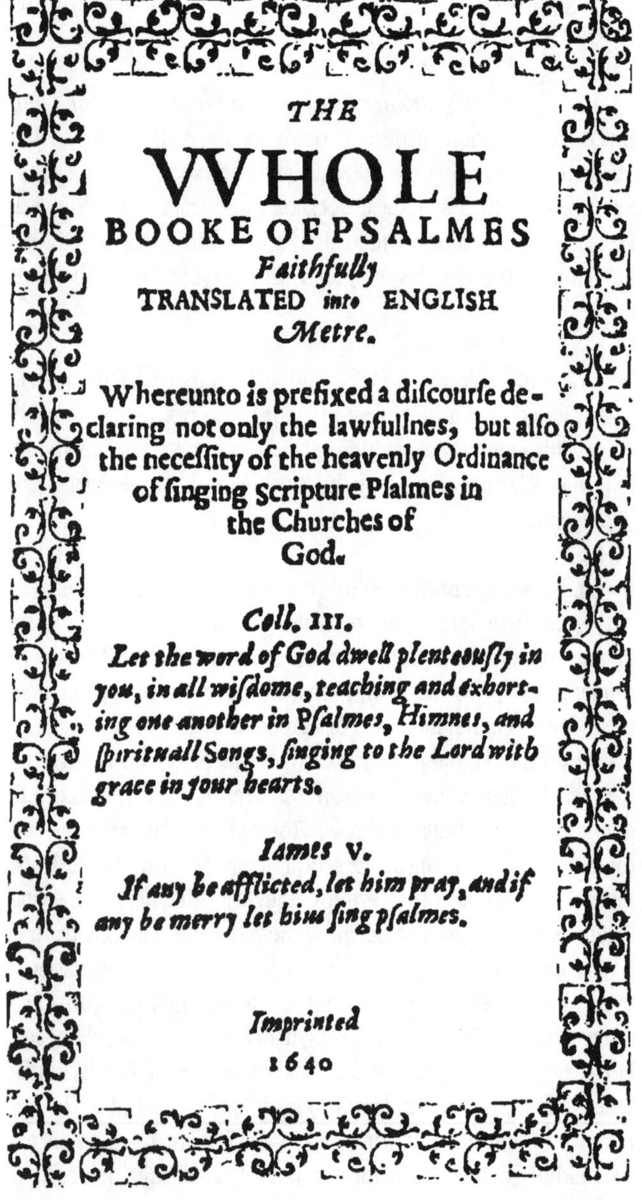

THE

VVHOLE

BOOKE OF PSALMES

Faithfully

TRANSLATED *into* ENGLISH

Metre.

Whereunto is prefixed a diſcourſe declaring not only the lawfullnes, but alſo the neceſſity of the heavenly Ordinance of ſinging Scripture Pſalmes in the Churches of God.

Coll. III.

Let the word of God dwell plenteouſly in you, in all wiſdome, teaching and exhorting one another in Pſalmes, Himnes, and ſpirituall Songs, ſinging to the Lord with grace in your hearts.

James V.

If any be afflicted, let him pray, and if any be merry let him ſing pſalmes.

Imprinted

1640

Religious Printing
To American colonists in the 1600s, the overriding interest was Christianity, and much of the output of the earliest presses consisted of sermons and other religious material. In fact, this publication of the *Book of Psalms*, printed in 1640 by Stephen Daye, has been called by some the first book printed in Anglo-America. However, it resembled a pamphlet more closely than a book, as those terms are defined today.

god of human information, embodied in journalism. However, before the birth of the newspaper in America, citizens thought of the printed word as a primary tool in the search for the universal truth of God. The press could prevent false doctrines as well as false reports. It could turn a floodlight onto the centers of the soul as colonial Americans searched for their spiritual identity and relationship to the Almighty.

The fact that the earliest Americans felt that their very souls should be made bare, that their search for the very meaning of existence should be public, cements the picture of Americans as inhabitants of the "city on a hill," the phrase the Puritans used to describe how their colony should appear to the corrupt churches left behind in Europe. Jesus had promised that the truth would set mankind free, and it was apparent to the earliest Americans that truth came at least in part through the printed word and could be circulated widely via the mass media. In the modern times of the sixteenth and seventeenth centuries, the truth could fly on the printed page to anyone and everyone, and humanity could be set free.

That ambitious goal became a part of the mystique of America. In the centuries to follow, Americans would think of themselves as specially ordained by God to administer a kingdom agreeable to Him on Earth. The concept was not a very far leap from the Puritans' bold assertions in their own search for truth, expressed in their press for the first half-century of printing in America.

Early Americans as Children of the Media

By the time the first American newspaper started and failed all in one issue in 1690, Anglo-America had grown from a few tenuous outposts dotted about the seacoasts to a solid string of towns and colonies populated by people who were no longer struggling to carve out a meager existence. They had homes, jobs, churches, families. And by that time, too, Americans had already begun formulating an intellectual identity that was intimately linked to their use of the mass media. The printed word had driven them to America, encouraged their Europeanization of the place, taught them to quarrel publicly, and allowed them to search for truth openly. It had entertained and educated them, too.

It may seem funny to consider Americans before 1690 as children of the mass media, but indeed they were. Remote as they were, they had nevertheless grown up in the era of the printing press. They had felt its strength, had personally witnessed its persuasive allure. They believed in and read and used the printed word to communicate with their neighbors, whether those neighbors were across town, in another distant colony, or across the ocean in Europe.

As lifetime consumers of the printed word, the European settlers of America unintentionally began creating a nation that featured the mass media as an integral part of its intellectual identity. By the time the seventeenth century began nearing its close, the inhabitants of the New World were prepared for yet-unborn American newspapers to fulfill all the roles of the press that Americans had learned and accepted from childhood. Newspapers would be persuaders, factual truth-tellers, correctors of wrongs, entertainers, and vehicles for public debate and education.

The printed word had played those roles throughout the entire history of Anglo-America, and thus America, in a sense, had grown up and would continue to mature in the public eye, for it would be forever recorded by the printed word and presented to a large

Some Meditations

Concerning our HONOURABLE

Gentlemen and Fellow-Souldiers,

In Pursuit of those

Barbarous NATIVES in the NARRAGANSIT-Country;

and Their Service there.

Committed into Plain Verse for the Benefit of those that Read it. By an Unfeigned Friend.

[1]
THese *Indians strong* have *waited long*
but now intend to see,
If that they can so play the man,
that they themselves may free.

[2]
When I do Muse, I cannot Chuse
but mind Gods hand therein,
How he at first, *Indians* disperst,
that *English* might begin,

[3]
The Ground to Till, the Land to Fill,
with Men and eke with Beasts.
This fifty year, some have been here,
And have Enjoyed Peace.

[4]
The *Indians* then, were as strong men,
as now they seem to be,
And yet *two men* wou'd chace *twice ten*
and make them for to flee.

[5]
They stood in dread and were afraid,
the *English* to offend,
When they did meet 'em in the Street
their word was *What Cheer Friend.*

[6]
It did appear that when they were
in Number many more
Than now they are, both near and far,
abroad, and at our door.

[7]
Then *English* men, there was not Ten,
where Thousands now appear,
And yet alas, it comes to pass,
of them we stand in fear.

[8]
Our Captains stout, they have gone out,
to fight them in the Field:
But in the Wood they were *withstood*,
these Indians will not yield.

[9]
They had a Fight, in Heavens sight,
kept up as in a Pound,
Men strong & tall, were forc'd to fall,
and left upon the Ground.

[10]
Six Score and Ten of Valiant Men,
was wounded in that Fight,
And Fifty more, if not Three Score,
was slain thereby out-right.

[11]
And then at night, they left the Fight,
in Snow up to the knees,
And to their Tent, away they went,
almost ready to freeze.

[12]
And as some say, they lost their way,
and Twenty Miles to go,
Marching all Night, till clear *Day light*,
up to the knees in Snow.

[13]
Some froze to Death, have lost their Breath
with fierceness of the Cold,
Some Froze their Feet, they being wet
'twas sad for to behold.

[14]
It grieves my heart, & makes it smart
I cannot chuse but weep,
To think on those, who on the Snows
are forc'd to take their Sleep,

[15]
In Wilderness, in great Distress,
in Winters fiercest Cold,
'Tis grief to me to hear or see,
'tis sad for to behold.

[16]
Brave Gentlemen, the which have been
brought up most tenderly,
Are now come out, Ranging about,
and on the Ground do ly

[17]
Open your Eyes, and Sympathize,
with those brave Gentlemen,
A heart of Flint, it would Relent,
to think how it hath been.

[18]
All who are wise, will Sympathize,
with this our English Nation,
And sorely grieve, and help relieve
them there in this sad station:

(19)
O Lord, arise, open the Eyes,
of this our English Nation,
And let them see, and also be,
saved with thy Salvation.

(20)
Cast thou a dread, and make afraid
these Indians strong and stout,
And make 'em feel the Sword of Steel,
that so they may give out.

(21)
Lest they do boast of their great Host,
and praise their god the Devil,
From whom indeed, this doth proceed
the Author of all Evil.

(22)
O *New-England*, I understand,
with thee God is offended:
And therefore He doth humble thee,
till thou thy ways hast mended.

(23)
Repent therefore, and do no more;
advance thy self so High,
But humbled be, and thou shalt see
these Indians soon will dy.

(24)
A Swarm of Flies, they may arise,
a Nation to Annoy,
Yea Rats and Mice, or Swarms of Lice
a Nation may destroy.

(25)
Do thou not boast, it is God's Host;
and He before doth go,
To humble thee and make thee see,
that He His Works will show.

(26)
And now I shall my Neighbours all
give one word of Advice,
In Love and Care do you prepare
for War, if you be wise.

(27)
Get Ammunition with Expedition
your Selves for to defend,
And Pray to God that He His Rod
will please for to suspend.

(28)
And who can tell! but that He will,
be Gracious to us here?
I hope that him serve He will preserve
they need it not to fear.

(29)
Though here they dy immediately,
yet they shall go to Rest,
And at that day the Lord will say,
happy art thou, and blest.

(30)
But unto those, that be His Foes,
the Lord to them will say,
Depart from Me, even all ye
that would not Me Obey.

(31)
My Friends I pray, mark what I say;
and to it give good heed,
And to the SON, see that you Run;
and Him Embrace with speed.

(32)
And now my Friend, here I will End,
no more here shall I write,
Or lest I shall some Tears let fall,
and spoil my Writing quite.

December 28, 1675. **W. W.**

Re-printed at *N-London, April 4. 1725*

The Land Settled

By the late 1600s, the colonists who had landed on America's shores three-quarters of a century earlier had effectively settled the new land. For the most part, the Native American population had been subdued, with few conflicts with the Indians becoming serious threats to the settlers. Occasional major disturbances did occur — such as King Philip's War in 1675, the subject of the verse in this broadside — but for the most part the settlements along the Atlantic coast were secure. In the process of creating a new country, the colonists had given particular importance to the printing press, and the printed word had contributed to the character that had become distinctively American.

readership. The character of the American populace was thus deeply linked to the media, and so were such American actions as the subduing of Native Americans, the encouragement of open factional debate, and the acceptance of religious discussion as a basic tenet of American tolerance.

American thought had a basis in the media, for America was never without the presence and influence of a mass medium, not even in the earliest times before Joseph Glover imported a printing press into Massachusetts. There can be no doubt that the American intellectual character, as it evolved into something different from the European intellectual character, was propelled and shaped in some part by the mass media. The qualities of printing — openness, debate, appeal to all types of people, and so on — would color the American intellectual landscape from the very start. There were many, many early influences on the development of America as a distinct place from Europe, but the intellectual notions that showed up in the mass media certainly had an impact on the nature of Americans themselves.

RECOMMENDED READINGS

BOOKS

Barbour, Philip L. *The Three Worlds of Captain John Smith*. Boston, 1964. Examines Smith as an adventurer, colonist, and promoter of America. Gives details on how Smith came to publish his *Generall Historie of Virginia* and how it was received.

Berthold, Arthur Benedict. *American Colonial Printing as Determined by Contemporary Cultural Forces, 1639-1763*, reprint edition. New York, 1970 (originally published in 1934). Colonial America exhibited two styles of thought that molded the press: secular-minded Cavalier thought in Virginia and theocratic Puritan thought in New England.

Brown, Richard D. *Knowledge Is Power: The Diffusion of Information in Early America 1700-1865*. New York, 1989. Early Americans were especially interested in having information about a variety of public affairs, and they used a variety of mass and interpersonal means to circulate it and to obtain it.

Gunn, Giles, ed. *Early American Writing*. New York, 1994. This collection covers early American literature from pre-newspaper, post-newspaper, and Native American traditions. Gunn's introduction discusses the importance of European promotional literature, narratives of exploration, and narratives of colonization as tools for populating the American continent.

Hawke, David Freeman. *Everyday Life in Early America*. New York, 1988. Looks at all facets of early American life, with references scattered throughout to the intellectual life of the era. Among other things, the book addresses the importance of American settlement literature and the significance of printed religious material.

Hulton, Paul. *America 1585: The Complete Drawings of John White*. Chapel Hill, N.C., 1984. A series of introductory chapters offers a biographical sketch of colonial promoter John White and then discusses White's exquisite artistry. The book also examines Theodore de Bry's work as a publisher of White's drawings. The reader is treated to full-color reproductions of White's surviving drawings from 1585 America.

Miller, Perry. *Errand Into the Wilderness*. New York, 1956. Explores not only the intellectual climate that fostered the establishment of Puritan New England, but also the often-overlooked religious literature of Virginia.

Morison, Samuel Eliot. *The Intellectual Life of Colonial New England*. New York, 1956. Discusses colonial printing, bookselling, and libraries. Also devotes detailed sections to various types of intellectual output of the American colonies — sermons, histories, political works, and verse.

Murdock, Kenneth B. *Literature and Theology in Colonial New England*. Cambridge, Mass., 1949. Explores connections between the Puritans' faith and their writings. Puritans published literature "to keep their supporters strong in the faith, to persuade the doubters, and to arouse the unawakened" and also to protect the colony from slander and criticism.

Parks, George Bruner. *Richard Hakluyt and the English Voyages*, 2nd ed. New York, 1961. Excellent biography of colonial promoter Richard Hakluyt. Discusses in detail the work Hakluyt did to publish his famous propagandistic collection of sailors' narratives.

Wright, Louis B. *The Cultural Life of the American Colonies: 1607-1763*. New York, 1957. Discusses books, libraries, literary writings, and the press. The information on press output before 1690 is scanty, but the sections on pre-newspaper reading material are excellent. The work examines why colonists were devoted to reading, and it looks at their enormous outpouring of literature.

Wright, Louis B., *Religion and Empire: The Alliance Between Piety and Commerce in English Expansion, 1553-1629*. New York, 1965. Based on the premise that "the propaganda and influence of the clergy were powerful factors in creating public sentiment for expansion overseas."

Wright, Thomas Goddard. *Literary Culture in New England, 1620-1730.* New York, 1966 (first published in 1920). Illustrates thoroughly the fact that colonial Americans loved to read and amassed well-stocked libraries. Also discusses Puritan writings and offers analysis on the quality of that literature.

Wroth, Lawrence C. *The Colonial Printer,* reprint edition, Charlottesville, Va., 1964 (original edition, New York, 1931). Explores how society shaped printing. Describes the physical needs of the colonial printer, hinting at the intellectual and cultural nature of the colonial era. The press was an outgrowth of colonial life, but it also had some influence on the colonies.

ARTICLES

Dunn, Richard S. "Seventeenth-Century English Historians of America," Chapter IX (pp. 195-225) in James Morton Smith, ed., *Seventeenth Century America: Essays in Colonial History*, New York, 1959. Compares seventeenth-century writings about America from both sides of the Atlantic. These writings "document a most subtle and important phenomenon: the initial development of an American consciousness and a growing sense of distinction between the colonial and his fellow Englishmen at home."

Ford, Edwin H. "Colonial Pamphleteers." *Journalism Quarterly* 13 (1936): 24-36. Examines colonial pamphlets in pre-newspaper America as a form of editorial expression. Such pamphlets set a precedent for the press of times to come by offering intelligent commentary on public affairs. Later newspaper editors would take that notion of editorial-writing and make it their own.

Nord, David Paul. "Teleology and the News: The Religious Roots of American Journalism, 1630-1730." *Journal of American History* 77 (June 1990): 9-38. Puritan writers of news believed that all occurrences took place according to God's plan. The Puritans had a great desire for the entire community to understand God's actions, and thus, it was important that news be published.

Pennington, Loren E. "*Hakluytus Posthumus:* Samuel Purchas and the Promotion of English Overseas Expansion." *The Emporia State Research Studies* 14 (March, 1966, no. 3). Although Richard Hakluyt's successor Samuel Purchas is often decried as a pale star in comparison to the brilliant Hakluyt, he was an important philosopher in the process of American colonization. Through promotions of settlement, he provided an important intellectual/philosophical underpinning for colonization.

Shaaber, Matthias A. "Forerunners of the Newspaper in America." *Journalism Quarterly* 11 (1934): 339-47. It was natural for colonial printers in the pre-newspaper era to publish news in broadsides and pamphlets, for news events were always of high public interest. Broadsides and pamphlets in turn helped establish a news tradition that newspapers would adopt in later years.

3

The Colonial Press

1690 - 1765

The colonial newspaper was not born in isolation but grew out of the milieu in which it was founded. It resulted from a host of interrelated processes: economic, political, religious, cultural, and social. As the newspaper cannot be separated from the environment that nurtured it, neither can colonial life be separated from the larger forces that fueled Western civilization. The roots of the American newspaper are found not in the isolation of the colonies but in the interrelationships of the colonies with each other and with England and Europe.

Economics, Politics, and Religion

The English colonies in North America provided a haven for the religiously persecuted, such as Puritans in New England and Roman Catholics in Maryland. They also provided a refuge from hunger and bankruptcy and a means of acquiring wealth. Regardless of why colonists came, it should be remembered that the vast majority *chose* to come and that from the beginning thought of themselves as a special people. Many believed they were a people with a mission. The English had different views about these people and the colonies they settled. To them the colonies were a major source of wealth, as producers of raw materials for English manufacturers and as buyers of English manufactured goods. Such a relationship was a source of power, for the power of mother countries in the colonial system was based on wealth. Imperial nations needed wealth to function, to run the government, to arm and pay soldiers, to build navies and merchant ships. Acquiring wealth was dependent upon prosperous subjects who could afford to pay taxes.

At the heart of the English scheme was the government's assumption that if expensive manufactured goods were exported to the colonies and less expensive raw materials imported into England, the margin of profit would be great enough to maintain a prosperous population. This favorable trade balance could be established by fostering manufacturing at home, taxing or limiting the import of manufactured goods from abroad, prohibiting the export of raw materials, subsidizing English manufacturing, and limiting competition from the colonies.

Central to this theory of mercantilism, and consequently to the maintenance of national wealth and power, were three ideas that became English policy in the eighteenth century: 1) colonies should produce raw materials that the home country could not; 2) colonies should not harm the home country by competition with it or by trade with her commercial rivals; and 3) colonies should help bear the burden of maintaining the army, navy, and government. Parliament went to great lengths to induce the colonies to produce raw materials that would support English manufacturing. Producers might be exempted from import duties or bounties offered to ensure that desirable materials were imported into England. Government regulations were passed to prevent the colonies from harming home manufacturers. Many colonial industries were proscribed from exporting, sometimes even to other colonies, such items as hats, cloth, and wrought iron. These restrictions were no doubt bothersome to the colonies, but enforcement was so lax as to have little effect on them. The restrictions on commerce were another matter.

The tool used by the English to control commerce was a series of navigation acts. The last, and by far most inclusive, was the Navigation Act of 1660. It required that all imports into England from Asia, Africa, and America be on ships owned and manned by Englishmen. The monopoly extended to goods exported from England. The various acts were particularly burdensome in the North American colonies where a burgeoning shipping industry was trying to grab as much of the shipping business as possible. The commercial policies of the English crown were to bear bad fruit during the eighteenth and early nineteenth centuries. Several causes of the War of 1812 can be traced to them. While English commercial policies had little direct effect on the founding of American newspapers, colonial concern with commerce was a powerful factor in creating the need for newspapers.

With a growing population and merchant class, colonials needed a means of reaching potential customers and of getting intelli-

POLLARD KEARNEY, and JOHN KEARNY,

just imported from London, and to be sold wholesale and retail, by

JOHN ELLIOT,

At his Looking-glass Store, the Sign of the Bell and Looking glass, in Chesnut street, near the State-house, Philadelphia,

A NEAT Assortment of Looking Glasses, in Mahogany and Walnut Frames, carved, gilt and plain, viz. Piers, Sconces, Dressing glasses and Swingers, Hanging glasses, Shaving-glasses, painted and Pocket Glasses, Mahogany and Book Tea chests. He also new Quicksilvers and frames old Glasses, and supplies People with new Glass to their own Frames. Etc.

Just imported in the Ship Friendship, Capt. M'Clelland, from London, and to be sold by

JOHN WHARTON,

In Water-street, near Walnut-street, two Doors below Bayston and Wharton's Store.

A LARGE Assortment of EUROPEAN and EAST-INDIA GOODS. Etc.

To be SOLD by

JOHN JENNINGS,

Very cheap by Retail, at his Shop, the North-East Corner of Front and Arch-streets, and where Mr. John Maydwell lately dwelt,

BLUE and green halfthicks, and flannels, striped lincey, striped cotton ditto, oznabrigs, 3-qr. 7 8ths and yard wide Irish linen, 3-qr. 7 8ths yard wide yard 3-8ths and 6-qr. cotton and linen checks. Irish sheeting, curled [illegible]

[illegible] in Salisbury Township, Northampton County, on the 15th Instant, a bright sorrel Horse, about 14 Hands high, a Star in his Forehead, shod all round, has a short bob Tail, is a natural Pacer, and branded on the off Thigh C H, and is about five Years old. The Owner is desired to prove his Property, pay the Charges, and take him away. LAWRENCE HARTMAN.

CAME to the Plantation of John Rowelan, in the Township of Warwick, Bucks County, the Beginning of April, a bright bay Mare a natural Trotter, about 14 Years old, has neither Brand nor Ear-mark. The Owner is desired to come and prove his Property, pay Charges, and take her away.

Colonial Advertising
One of the primary motives behind the founding of colonial newspapers was to provide a medium for advertising. The most innovative colonial publisher was Benjamin Franklin, who made advertisements more appealing by adding small woodcut illustrations.

gence about not only the comings and goings of shipping but also of the commercial and governmental activity in other colonies and in England. Because of the control that the English crown and English merchants exerted, a colonial shipper of, say, South Carolina indigo might find himself with no market or a depressed market at the exact time he needed to sell his merchandise. Such commercial intelligence might be had by reading English newspapers, but the information was certain to be several months old by the time it was tacked to a tavern wall. Better intelligence was available from ship captains and other travellers, but there was no clearinghouse where an interested party could obtain timely information. Merchants with a shipload of the finest woolens had, as their only means of getting the information to customers, handbills and tavern notices — not a very efficient means of advertising. However, publications issued regularly, as were English newspapers, would provide both merchant and customer with the information needed to bring the two together.

Whether Benjamin Harris intended that America's first newspaper, *Publick Occurrences*, carry advertising is unclear, but that he expected his newspaper to provide commercial intelligence is obvious from his prospectus that the newspaper would "assist [merchants'] businesses and Negotiations."[1] The second newspaper in the colonies, the *Boston News-Letter*, was intended as a commercial vehicle, as editor John Campbell stated in the first number:

> This *News-Letter* is to be continued Weekly; and all persons who have any Houses, Lands, Tenements, Farms, Ships, Vessels, Goods, Wares or Merchandise, etc. to be Sold, or Let; or Servants Run-away, or Goods Stole or Lost; may have the same inserted at a Reasonable Rate, from Twelve Pence to Five Shillings, and not to exceed.[2]

Politics and high matters of state might be the subject of much newspaper content, but it was commerce and advertising that fueled the enterprise.

A growing interdependence among the colonies because of economic and political changes called for an environment that newspapers could help provide. Political needs for cooperation among the colonies grew rapidly toward the end of the colonial period. A recognition that all the American colonies shared common interests in their relationship with England was a strong motivator toward intercolonial cooperation and exchange of information. When the first newspapers were founded in America, government officials apparently did not recognize the value of the press, although the publication of broadsides to counter rumor and falsehood had been common practice for several years. Colonial governments and royal governors, however, quickly began to recognize the value of having a publication friendly to their side as political bickering grew. More than one newspaper printer stayed out of jail because of the conflict and animosity among various government leaders.

Much of what found its way into the colonial printing press was religious in nature. Broadsides, pamphlets, and books carried sermons, doctrinal discussions, religious essays, and proclamations issued from the pulpit. However, early newspapers were primarily concerned with secular events, or "occurrences," as they were more likely to be called. The colonial mind was, to a large extent, a religious mind; and newspapers printed much material that was clearly religious. Promoting religious causes, however, was no more important for most newspaper publishers than informing readers about events. The roots of journalistic practices may be found in that concern for events.[3]

[1] *Publick Occurrences*, 25 September 1690.

[2] *Boston News-Letter*, 24 April 1704.

[3] David Paul Nord, "Teleology and the News: The Religious Roots of American Jour-

Taverns
Colonial taverns were, next to the church, the most important public institution and, before the appearance of newspapers, provided the best means for the spread of news. In some colonies, towns were fined if they did not have a tavern, and the taverns were required to set up outside signs announcing their location.

Besides the increasing population, commercial development, and political changes, the colonies were changing culturally. Particularly in New England there was a growing class of educated citizens interested in the arts, science, and literature. This elite of religious, business, and government leaders provided a ready market for literature in any form. Even the average person who might be more likely to read than write was a steady market for the product of the printers' craft. Though most of seventeenth-century publishing was restricted to religious tracts, pamphlets, and books, by the beginning of the eighteenth century printed matter had become more secular with official documents being printed for colonial governments and pamphlets, broadsides, and other material for more general consumption. A reading class was essential for a successful newspaper enterprise; and by the beginning of the eighteenth century such a class existed, at least in the major cities of Boston, New York, and Philadelphia. Newspapers, of which there were thirty-eight in the colonies by 1775, along with broadsides and a rich pamphlet literature, helped to meet the needs of this reading class. The small literary class found in the colonies was familiar with the writings of Daniel Defoe in *The Review*, Richard Steele in *The Tatler*, and Joseph Addison in *The Spectator*. Not only did colonials eagerly read these English essayists, but colonial writers attempted to copy their style and verve. The concern of many colonial writers with social customs may be traced directly to such English men of letters.

COLONIAL FORMS OF COMMUNICATION

Socially, the colonies were changing. At least in the larger towns social activities grew. Along the coast — where concern was not focused merely on surviving in the wilderness — people began to meet, to talk, and to socialize. While social life in Boston, the birthplace of American newspapers, was dull compared to such towns as Charleston or Williamsburg, even there social activities in the eighteenth century were strikingly colorful in contrast to the previous century. There — as in other major towns — lived the royal governor, a wealthy merchant class, and an educated elite. The taverns of Boston and other towns drew a varied clientele of locals and strangers passing through; and the talk over ale included gossip, political issues, and business matters. While the newspaper might not replace the tavern as a social institution, it could provide snippits of intelligence that could offer grist for a lively evening's discussion. Over time citizens who frequented taverns joined together in discussion clubs and eventually wanted their own newspapers to disseminate their views. The taverns offered a ready market for newspapers.

By the late 1600s all the factors needed to produce a newspaper existed. A growing colonial population, an increasingly wealthy upper-class, a better educated citizenry (brought on to some extent by the desire to read the forerunners of the newspaper), interest in the arts and sciences, and the need to be better informed about government and commerce all help to explain the establishment of newspapers in colonial America. It was a natural development that evolved from a spoken through a written to a primitive printed form. The need for what has been called "surveillance of the environment" may be found in any historical period. It was this need to know that led in Europe and later in the colonies to means of disseminating information. In the colonies the clergy often passed along tidbits of news from their pulpits; the town crier spoke of events and issues in addition to tolling the hour; and citizens in taverns passed along items of interest to others gathered there.

In colonial America it was primarily the pulpit and the tavern that made possible the surveillance of the environment. Before the newspaper's advent the clergy performed many of the functions we now associate with newspapers. Matters of public interest were disseminated from the pulpit. Many sermons dealt with secular issues, politics, and economics, in addition to matters of the soul. Even advertising was not neglected.[4] The clergy were re-

nalism, 1630-1730," *Journal of American History* 77 (June 1990): 9-38.

[4]Such spoken newspapers reached their zenith in Detroit toward the end of the 18th

Town Criers
Before the appearance of newspapers, people relied on church sermons, tavern conversation, and town criers for much of their information about public affairs. This drawing (which first appeared in 1882 in *Harper's Weekly*) shows a town crier reading municipal regulations to a crowd of townspeople.

sponsible also for early near-newspapers, broadsides, and pamphlets. These publications were little different from the first newspapers in the colonies, lacking only regularity of publication. Often broadsides and pamphlets were issued to dispel falsehood and rumor. Not surprisingly, this was often the chief reason given for the founding of early colonial newspapers.

Despite the efforts of the clergy it was the tavern that made possible the widest dissemination of information. At least at the local level the tavern was often the center of government with town meetings, courts, and town officials convening there. Official documents, jury lists, and public notices were all tacked to the tavern's walls along with news items and advertising notices. Because locals as well as travellers frequented the place, the latest news and gossip were apt to be overheard. Tavern owners subscribed to foreign and, later, domestic newspapers and posted them (along with letters and other publications) for customers to read. Patrons not only brought in news but carried away intelligence to be shared with others.

Difficulties of Publishing

Clearly the need existed in colonial America for printed newspapers, which offered a more efficient means of disseminating information. There were also, however, severe constraints upon their establishment.

Printing technology changed little in the two and one-half centuries following Johann Gutenberg's perfection of a method for casting and using movable type. By the early eighteenth century the press Gutenberg used, based on the wine press of the fifteenth century, had not changed at all; and type was still being cast in the same way with the same materials. Paper was still made painstakingly from rags. While inks had not changed, they at least could be made from materials on hand. Combined with the legal constraints of licensing and other forms of press control, the existing technology made establishing a newspaper, or indeed any kind of printing, a costly and difficult undertaking. Circulation problems compounded the difficulty.

century when the Reverend Gabriel Richard provided for a crier to announce news and advertising items outside church each Sunday. The announcements evolved into a written newspaper which was posted near the church door. Richard's efforts were rewarded in 1809 with the founding of Detroit's first printed newspaper.

With the exception of ink, nearly all equipment and materials needed to produce a newspaper had to be imported. Although the first press in colonial America arrived in Cambridge, Massachusetts, in 1638, the colonies had only fifty presses at the beginning of the Revolution. In 1750 Christopher Sower, Jr., began building second-rate copies of English presses, but even then the colonies continued to import presses. Until Sower began casting type in 1772, all type was imported. Despite high costs, equipment was available to the colonial printer. Paper was another matter. Having sufficient paper on hand to produce any kind of publication was a constant irritation to printers. Paper was made from rags, and the scarcity of this raw material made domestic paper manufacture chancy at best. It remained necessary to import foreign paper until late in the colonial period. Paper costs in combination with English hostility to printing in general resulted in more demand for paper than supply.

Printing equipment and materials might be primitive, hard to get, and expensive, but ultimately the success of a newspaper venture depended upon the publisher being able to get his publication to readers. Local distribution of newspapers required only that subscribers pick up their copies at some central location, such as a tavern or the newspaper office, or that servants or apprentices hand-deliver them to subscribers. Beyond the local area, various problems hampered distribution. Not only did printers need to get their publications into a wide circulation area for advertising purposes; they also needed to receive publications from other colonies to provide editorial material. Today the mails are taken for granted. During the colonial period the postal service was nearly nonexistent. Only in 1692 did the English crown grant authority for the creation of an intercolonial mail service. The postal service developed slowly and handled letters only. Newspapers were carried only if the printer were a postmaster or could bribe a post rider. Forty years following the granting of the first royal monopoly for a postal service, the mails still were irreg-

Colonial Printing
Printers in the 1700s used a system in which (left to right, top picture) individual characters of type were kept in separate compartments, then they were arranged into words and lines, and the lines were placed in a page form. In the bottom picture, the workers are inking the pages of type and then printing single impressions on individual sheets of paper.

ular and during winter months might not operate at all. In 1758 fixed postal rates were established for newspapers; and by the Revolution, the value of newspapers to government and the public was recognized, and distribution became easier and faster.

Licensing had ended by the early eighteenth century but not legal constraints on printers. A printing press was a weapon, a source of power, to those who could control it; it could be a source of extreme irritation to those who could not. The royal governors and colonial governments attempted to control printing, first through licensing (which gave authorities the power to prohibit newspapers from being printed) and then through the law of seditious libel. If they were unable to stop the establishment of a printing venture, they could attempt to control what the printer issued. For decades following the demise of licensing in England, colonial governments continued the attempt to prevent publication of selected newspapers, sometimes successfully, sometimes not. A series of events over the years eroded colonial authorities' control of printing. The first colonial newspaper was banned; subsequent attempts were more successful. Although James Franklin was jailed in Boston as was John Peter Zenger in New York, both published in defiance of authority. Other printers saved themselves from incarceration by apologizing, using subterfuges, or getting out of the printing business. Despite the constant threats against their newspapers, printers continued to publish. A slow evolutionary process, freedom of the press had to await the early nineteenth century to become universal in the United States.

It was against this backdrop that the first abortive attempt to publish a regularly scheduled newspaper in colonial America was made. Not surprisingly, it was made in Boston, the largest, wealthiest, and most culturally advanced town in the colonies.

The First Attempt in America

When Benjamin Harris arrived in Boston in 1686, his baggage included not only a knowledge of the newspaper craft but a rebellious spirit. He had begun his publishing career thirteen years earlier in London, and even his early publishing attempts were controversial.[5] An ardent Anabaptist, during his first six years as a printer he became the leading publicist for the Whig political faction and published a number of religious books, several of which attacked Quakers and Catholics. While his early work was no doubt disturbing to the authorities, it was only after the establishment of his London newspaper, *Domestic Intelligences: or News from City and Country*, in 1679, that the authorities began to take notice of his activities. However, it was not the newspaper that led to his undoing. In early 1680 Harris published a pamphlet, *Appeal from the Country to the City*, which was critical of King Charles II. Harris was convicted of seditious libel and sentenced to prison. Following his release, he continued to be a royal irritant and in 1686 published a pamphlet, *English Liberties*, which again led to warrants for his arrest. No doubt having decided that London was no longer comfortable for one of his temperament, he fled with his family to Boston.

There he opened a combination bookstore and coffee house. Despite keen competition he prospered and began to attract the socially inclined, such as the cleric Cotton Mather, to his shop. It was only a matter of time before Harris, an experienced publisher with wide contacts among his clientele, attempted another newspaper. First, he returned to publishing almanacs and other literary works. His greatest success came with his publication of the *New England Primer*, a spelling book that was reprinted for decades.

In the wake of a Puritan rebellion against the British monarchy, on September 25, 1690, Harris used his experience to publish the first newspaper in the colonies. He called it *Publick Occurrences, Both Forreign and Domestick*. It appeared only once; four days later the authorities suppressed it. The paper was a small publication by today's standards. It was four pages, only three of which contained type; the fourth page was left blank, presumably so that

[5]For an account of Harris and his career, see Wm. David Sloan, "Chaos, Polemics, and America's First Newspaper," *Journalism Quarterly* 70 (1993): 108-41.

Numb. 1.

PUBLICK
OCCURRENCES

Both FORREIGN and DOMESTICK.

Boston, Thursday Sept. 25th. 1690.

IT is designed, that the Countrey shall be furnished once a moneth (or if any Glut of Occurrences happen, oftener,) with an Account of such considerable things as have arrived unto our Notice.

In order hereunto, the Publisher will take what pains he can to obtain a Faithful Relation of all such things; and will particularly make himself beholden to such Persons in Boston whom he knows to have been for their own use the diligent Observers of such matters.

That which is herein proposed, is, First, That Memorable Occurrents of Divine Providence may not be neglected or forgotten, as they too often are. Secondly, That people every where may better understand the Circumstances of Publique Affairs, both abroad and at home; which may not only direct their Thoughts at all times, but at some times also to assist their Businesses and Negotiations.

Thirdly, That some thing may be done towards the Curing, or at least the Charming of that Spirit of Lying, which prevails amongst us, wherefore nothing shall be entered, but what we have reason to believe is true, repairing to the best fountains for our Information. And when there appears any material mistake in any thing that is collected, it shall be corrected in the next.

Moreover, the Publisher of these Occurrences is willing to engage, that whereas, there are many False Reports, maliciously made, and spread among us, if any well-minded person will be at the pains to trace any such false Report so far as to find out and Convict the First Raiser of it, he will in this Paper (unless just Advice be given to the contrary) expose the Name of such person, as A malicious Raiser of a false Report. It is suppos'd that none will dislike this Proposal, but such as intend to be guilty of so villanous a Crime.

THE Christianized Indians in some parts of Plimouth, have newly appointed a day of Thanksgiving to God for his Mercy in supplying their extream and pinching Necessities under their late want of Corn, & for His giving them now a prospect of a very Comfortable Harvest. Their Example may be worth Mentioning.

Tis observed by the Husbandmen, that altho' the With-draw of so great a strength from them, as what is in the Forces lately gone for Canada; made them think it impossible for them to get well through the Affairs of their Husbandry at this time of the year, yet the season has been so unusually favourable that they scarce find any want of the many hundreds of hands, that are gone from them; which is looked upon as a Merciful Providence.

While the barbarous Indians were lurking about Chelmsford, there were missing about the beginning of this month a couple of Children belonging to a man of that Town, one of them aged about eleven, the other aged about nine years, both of them supposed to be fallen into the hands of the Indians.

A very Tragical Accident happened at Water-Town, the beginning of this Month, an Old man, that was of somewhat a Silent and Morose Temper, but one that had long Enjoyed the reputation of a Sober and a Pious Man, having newly buried his Wife, The Devil took advantage of the Melancholy which he thereupon fell into, his Wives discretion and industry had long been the support of his Family, and he seemed hurried with an impertinent fear that he should now come to want before he dyed, though he had very careful friends to look after him who kept a strict eye upon him, least he should do himself any harm. But one evening escaping from them into the Cow-house, they there quickly followed him found him hanging by a Rope, which they had used to tye their Calves withal, he was dead with his feet near touching the Ground.

Epidemical Fevers and Agues grow very common, in some parts of the Country, whereof, tho' many dye not, yet they are sorely unfitted for their imployments; but in some parts a more malignant Fever seems to prevail in such sort that it usually goes thro' a Family where it comes, and proves Mortal unto many.

The Small-pox which has been raging in Boston, after a manner very Extraordinary is now very much abated. It is thought that far more have been sick of it then were visited with it, when it raged so much twelve years ago, nevertheless it has not been so Mortal, The number of them that have

Publick Occurrences

Benjamin Harris began publishing *Publick Occurrences*, America's first attempt at a newspaper, to provide information during a period that was marked by much political chaos in Massachusetts. The colony's governing council suppressed it after one issue because Harris had not obtained permission to print it.

subscribers could add their own news as they passed the newspaper on to friends and relatives. The kind of publication Harris intended was obvious from his prospectus. It would be published monthly, he announced, and carry important colonial as well as foreign news. Harris was particularly concerned that unfounded rumors not damage the new Puritan government that had assumed authority in Massachusetts. *Publick Occurrences* contained a variety of news. The stories concerned fire, pestilence, crime, Indians, and French royalty.

Despite Harris' good intentions, the final two items caused authorities to ban the newspaper. They interpreted the Indian story to be a criticism of government and the French story to be in bad taste. The stories recounted atrocities committed by Indian allies of the British against French captives — charging that the government should not be involved with such un-Christian acts — and reported a scandal in which the French king had seduced his daughter-in-law. The governing council banned the publication because it had been issued without a license.

Royal licensing had begun under Henry VIII in 1534 and required printers to obtain the king's permission before establishing a publishing venture. Licensing continued in England until the Whigs allowed it to die in 1695. In fact, one of the last victims of the licensing laws in England was Harris. Licensing continued in the colonies until 1730. The authority for colonial licensing was contained in a provision of the royal governors' instructions:

> [F]orasmuch as great inconvenience may arise by the liberty of printing within our said province, you are to provide by all necessary orders that no person KEEP any press for printing, NOR that any book, pamphlet, or other matter whatsoever be PRINTED without your especial leave and license first obtained.[6]

America's First Continuous Newspapers

Royal authorities had no wish to make their own position more precarious by encouraging colonial publication. It comes as no surprise, therefore, to discover that a license was apt to be issued only to a printer who favored the ruling elite. In fact, this was precisely the kind of newspaper that published fourteen years later and became the first continuously published newspaper in the American colonies. The only newspaper that could succeed would have to get the advance approval of colonial authorities. The ideal newspaper published under these conditions would be an official voice of government.

Historically, one government official did fit the mold of a safe printer: the postmaster. There was precedence for a postmaster-publisher. For decades postmasters in Europe had also served as newspaper publishers. The postmaster occupied an ideal position for obtaining information from newspapers and letters and for mailing copies of his own paper. Being a government-appointed officeholder, he normally also had an inside track for acquiring official information. Neither was it unheard of for a printer-postmaster to gain an edge by denying a competing printer use of the mails. As early as 1700 the Boston postmaster, John Campbell, was sending hand-written newsletters to governors, merchants, and others in the colonies. His newsletters were concerned mostly with commercial news — ship arrivals and departures — but they also contained news items about government activities in Boston. Despite having the assistance of his brother, by 1704 Campbell found the burden of writing the newsletter by hand too great. On April 24, 1704, he turned to the printing press to produce the first regularly published newspaper in North America.

[6]Leonard W. Labaree, ed., ["Licensing of Printing Presses and Printing"], *Royal Instructions to British Colonial Governors 1670-1776*, 2 vols. (New York, 1935) , 2:495.

Numb. 3.

The Boston News-Letter.

Published by Authority.

From Monday May 1. to Monday May 8. 1704.

First Successful Newspaper

The *Boston News-Letter,* for which publisher John Campbell had received approval from the royal governor in advance, was not a very exciting newspaper. It did, however, contain information useful for subscribers, and it set the tone for early American journalism. Most of its content was reprinted from foreign sources, and it included little local news.

The *Boston News-Letter* did not really look like a newspaper. It was a single sheet, 8 x 12$^{3}/4$ inches, printed on both sides. It was dull in comparison to *Publick Occurrences*, for Campbell was postmaster first, journalist second. He lacked Harris' journalistic skill but succeeded where Harris failed because he recognized that his publication must be "safe" to remain in business. Perhaps the most important line of copy in Campbell's newspaper was the notice, "Published by Authority," which appeared in prominent type immediately below the paper's nameplate. The notice indicated that the newspaper had been approved in advance and that the reader should expect only news that supported the royal governor's position. In that regard, Campbell's newspaper maintained an unblemished record of being safe.

The *News-Letter* offered foreign, colonial, and local news. As had *Publick Occurrences*, the first issue of the *News-Letter* contained no advertising, an omission that was corrected in following issues. Advertising in colonial newspapers played an important role. It not only filled subscribers' desire for commercial information; it also was a source of revenue to help meet the expense of producing the publication. Certainly, Boston, with about 10,000 population, could provide an advertising base to help support a newspaper. However, most newspapers during the colonial period were little more than shoestring operations rarely able to support themselves. They included what advertising they could but depended upon other material for the bulk of their content. The *News-Letter* set the pattern: most of the first issue was devoted to news from abroad with the remainder domestic news. This pattern of foreign news dominating newspaper content continued for almost a century.[7] In fact, the early *News-Letter* contained virtually no local news. There is a simple explanation. It was assumed local readers knew about local events, thus giving newspapers no reason to run local news. Having no reporters or correspondents, Campbell met incoming ships to pick up foreign newspapers, pieces of gossip, and the mails. These were his sources of information. He got news from Europe and the other colonies but little from Boston. Campbell began a tradition that lasted well into the next century; he lifted news items from other newspapers. In the beginning all the newspapers were foreign; hence, so was most of the news he printed.

While the *News-Letter* borrowed much of its content, was visually unattractive, and made dull reading, it managed to survive seventy-two years, the first fifteen as a kind of public enterprise. It probably would have continued as a government mouthpiece had Campbell not been removed as postmaster in 1719. Turning over the office of postmaster was one thing, but relinquishing the *News-Letter* was another. Campbell left office but continued to publish the *News-Letter*, now as a private enterprise. The new postmaster, William Brooker, perhaps at the behest of government leaders and perhaps recognizing that there was profit to be made in newspaper publishing, contracted with James Franklin, older brother of Benjamin Franklin, to print a second Boston newspaper.

With the first issue of the *Boston Gazette*, December 21, 1719, competition came to newspapers in the colonies. It was a genuine competition. Brooker attempted to keep the *News-Letter* from using the mails while sending his own *Gazette* through the postal system. While the *Gazette* continued Campbell's practice of being the governor's mouthpiece, competition led to at least one innovation, so-called "Prices Current." This feature was of value to shippers, farmers, and merchants because it gave current prices for commodities and imported goods. Campbell for his part converted the *News-Letter* into a voice of the colonial assembly in

[7]Donald R. Avery, "The Newspaper on the Eve of the War of 1812: Changes in Content Patterns, 1808-1812" (Ph.D. diss., Southern Illinois University, 1982), 213-31.

Cotton Mather and the *Courant*
America's leading religious and intellectual figure in the early 1700s, Cotton Mather provided the target for the operators of the *New-England Courant*. When he proposed inoculating against smallpox, a small group of Anglican opponents started the *Courant* as a forum for attacking him.

contrast to Brooker's *Gazette*, which represented the royal governor's position. Whether the governor considered Brooker's support inadequate is unclear; however, within a year he lost the postmastership, and his successor, Phillip Musgrave, took over the *Gazette*. The change in publisher resulted in the founding of Boston's third newspaper, the *New-England Courant*, and indirectly to the beginning of one of the most notable newspaper careers of the colonial period. Shortly after Musgrave acquired the *Gazette*, he replaced James Franklin with Samuel Green as printer. Out of the newspaper business, Franklin looked around for another printing job.

The New-England Courant

With backing from John Checkley and Dr. William Douglass, Franklin founded a new kind of newspaper, one that, in addition to printing foreign and domestic news, also editorialized. Checkley, Douglass, and other members of Boston's lone Anglican church contributed most of the material that the *Courant* printed.[8] Opponents ridiculed them as the "Hell-Fire Club." Despite claiming that the *Courant* would not attack the Puritan clergy, the paper opened its first issue with a vitriolic attack on the Rev. Cotton Mather for his advocacy of inoculation for smallpox. Most Boston doctors opposed inoculation because they believed it was not scientific, but the primary reason the *Courant* opposed the practice was because Mather favored it. The *Courant*'s open attack on Mather created a sensation, and battle lines were drawn. Mather supporters published in his defense a broadside, *The Little Compton Scourge, or the Anti-Courant*.

Checkley responded in the third issue of the *Courant* with an insulting attack that questioned the morality of Mather's nephew. Checkley's and Franklin's Anglican pastors found the essay so obnoxious that they demanded that Checkley sever his association with the newspaper, and they persuaded Franklin to offer an apology for the article. But the Mather affair was only a beginning. The *Courant* then turned its barbs on Governor Samuel Shute.

Commerce was the lifeblood of New England. It affected the livelihood of farmers, shippers, and merchants. Of particular concern to citizens of Massachusetts was the presence off the New England coast of pirate ships and French privateers. Many believed the colonial government was doing little to rid shipping lanes of the menace. In June 1722 the *Courant* printed an item about a pirate vessel marauding near the coast and reported that the government was outfitting a ship to pursue it "sometime this month, wind and weather permitting." Enraged at the insinuation, Governor Shute induced the General Court to order Franklin to jail for three weeks. While in jail, Franklin apologized for his attack and promised to mend his ways. However, he was no sooner out of jail than he printed a column of satirical verse belittling the General Court for jailing him.

By 1723 the *Courant* was attacking the royal government, along with the clergy, on several fronts. The government officials were certain about one thing: Franklin was simply too bothersome to remain unchecked. The General Court ordered "That James Franklin be strictly forbidden by this Court to print or publish the *New-England Courant* or any pamphlet or paper of the like Nature, Except it be first Supervised, by the Secretary of this Province."[9] When Franklin ignored the order and printed the next issue of the *Courant*, he was held in contempt. He was able to circumvent the order, however, by simply substituting the name of his younger brother for his own as publisher of the *Courant*.

Benjamin Franklin had been apprenticed to his brother James at the age of twelve in 1718. He learned the printing craft from his brother, but writing he apparently learned in secret. His writing style came from the English publication the *Spectator*, of Joseph Addison and Richard Steele, which Franklin admitted to imitating. The first public evidence of Franklin's writing appeared in the *Courant* in 1722 under the pseudonym "Silence Dogood." These letters ran for about six months. They were urbane, witty, and better written than other newspaper articles of the period. James Franklin was unaware of the author's identity in the beginning. Because of the stormy relationship between the two brothers, it is unlikely the elder Franklin would have printed the letters had he

[8] Wm. David Sloan, "The *New-England Courant*: Voice of Anglicanism," *American Journalism* 8 (1991): 108-41.

[9] *New-England Courant*, 14-21 January 1723.

"Silence Dogood"
Benjamin Franklin, then only sixteen years old, contributed the series of letters signed by the widow "Silence Dogood" to the *New-England Courant* – but he kept his authorship secret, for fear that his brother James would stop publishing them if he knew who the author was. Benjamin later wrote about the pleasure he received overhearing the older contributors admiring the letters.

known.[10] When James discovered the authorship, he indeed discontinued the letters, although they were the most popular item in the *Courant*.

Naming Benjamin publisher helped James out of a tight legal tangle, but it also offered the younger Franklin a way out of a disagreeable apprenticeship. In order to name Benjamin proprietor of the *Courant*, James was required to release him from the apprenticeship contract. While James released his brother publicly, he drew up secret arrangements that kept Benjamin apprenticed. Less than a year passed before Benjamin sneaked out of Boston. He had little to fear that James would attempt to force him back to his apprenticeship because to do so would have forced James to admit the subterfuge.

The *Courant* limped on for another three years with James back at the helm, but it was a dull image of its former self. It ceased publication in 1726; and James moved with his family to Rhode Island, where he founded that colony's first newspaper. However, the *Courant* had made its mark. It demonstrated that a newspaper could gain attention with controversy and that local matters could provide a staple for future publications. It also showed that the teeth of government had not yet been dulled.

[10]The brothers appear rarely to have had cordial relations, although, at James' request, Benjamin later accepted James' son as an apprentice in his Philadelphia printing shop.

WOMEN AND OTHER PRINTERS

James Franklin's *Rhode Island Gazette* provided the first opportunity for a woman to be involved in the printing of a newspaper. The *Gazette* was founded in 1732 and ceased publication the following year.[11] Franklin's wife, Ann, was skilled at setting type and performing the other tasks required of a printer. James spent many of the last years of his life suffering from one illness or another; and Ann, like other colonial women, helped her husband in his printing business. Indeed, it is probable that the *Gazette* was a joint enterprise. In a long letter to the readers of the *Gazette* in 1732, James complained of having been ill. Since Ann was clearly able to take over James' printing house when he died in 1735, a reasonable assumption is that she was able to conduct the business, including the newspaper, during his many and protracted illnesses.[12] Some twenty-five years later, Ann, with her son, James Jr., started the *Newport Mercury*. She probably had little to do with the day-to-day operation of the newspaper, being sixty-two years old and in failing health. However, when her son died in 1762, Ann became intimately involved with the *Mercury*. She took in a partner, and the two continued the newspaper until her death the following year.[13]

Four other women are known to have been involved with newspapers in the period before 1765. The least active was probably Anna Zenger, who it is said ran the *New York Weekly Journal* for her husband while he languished in jail charged with seditious libel. During that nine-month period in 1734-1735, she apparently did no writing but merely picked up material from her husband's jail cell and saw that it was set in type and printed.[14] However, Elizabeth Timothy actually served as editor of the *South Carolina Gazette* for seven years following her husband's death in 1738. From the first issue that she published, the newspaper carried the notice that she was editor.[15] Sarah Goddard and her daughter, Mary Katherine, were involved in the publication of the *Providence Gazette and Country Journal*. The newspaper belonged legally to Sarah's son William, but the Goddard women appear to have been the force behind the newspaper from its founding in 1762. After 1765 Mary Katherine managed two other newspapers started by William, the *Pennsylvania Chronicle and Universal Advertiser* and the *Maryland Journal*. Many other women were involved with newspapers after 1765.[16]

The void left by the *Courant* was soon filled by the *New-England Weekly Journal*, founded in 1727 by Samuel Kneeland. He started the *Journal* much in the way Franklin had started the

[11]It is unclear whether James was a poor businessman or, more likely, that Newport was not yet ready for a newspaper. After all, the second attempt, a successful one, was not made for another 30 years. James' widow, Ann, and his son started the second newspaper.

[12]Susan Henry, "Ann Franklin: Rhode Island's Woman Printer," in *Newsletters to Newspapers: Eighteenth Century Journalism*, Donovan H. Bond and W. Reynolds McLeod, eds. (Morgantown, W.V., 1977), 129-43.

[13]Isaiah Thomas, *The History of Printing in America* (Worcester, Mass., 1810; New York, 1970), 325-6.

[14]*New York Weekly Journal*, 18 and 25 November 1734.

[15]*South Carolina Gazette*, 4 January 1739.

[16]Marion Marzolf, *Up From the Footnote* (New York, 1977), 5-6.

Benjamin Franklin, Printer
Even though Franklin later gained greater fame as a diplomat and inventor, he remained a printer at heart. For his own epitaph, he wrote, "The Body of Benjamin Franklin, Printer, (like the cover of an old Book, its contents worn out, and stript of its lettering and gilding) lies here, food for worms! Yet the work itself shall not be lost, for it will, as he believed, appear once more in a new and more beautiful edition, corrected and amended by its Author."

Courant. Kneeland had printed the *Boston Gazette*, but a change of postmaster left him with no newspaper to print. So he started his own. While not a direct descendant of the *Courant*, the *Journal* was influenced by the *Courant*'s discovery of literate journalism. A major difference between the two newspapers was that the *Journal* allied itself with the Puritan majority and not with a small band of controversialists as had the *Courant*. In its early years the *Journal* printed much original material, but by 1730 it was borrowing heavily from the London newspapers. In 1741 the *Journal* brought about the first newspaper merger in America when it combined with the *Boston Gazette* to become the *Gazette and Journal*.

In 1731 a young Boston lawyer, Jeremy Gridley, founded the *Weekly Rehearsal* but published it only a year. Thomas Fleet, previously a writer for Franklin's *Courant*, took over the paper, changed its name to the *Evening-Post*, and eventually transformed it into the best and most widely read paper in Boston. It had many of the virtues of the *Courant* at its best. The *Evening-Post* was well-written and claimed to be impartial (although Fleet's Anglican sympathies were evident). His sons continued the newspaper into the Revolution.

A newspaper that was to become a thorn to the Patriots during the Revolution was the *Boston Post-Boy*, founded in 1734. It was another example of a newspaper having been started because a publisher of the *Gazette* did not survive a change in the postmastership. The *Post-Boy*, following a short discontinuance in the 1750s, survived into the Revolution, espousing the Tory cause.

Philadelphia Newspapers

While somewhat smaller in the early eighteenth century, Philadelphia was in many respects similar to Boston. It was a leading seaport with great commercial activity; it was a center of a growing commercial class; it was literate; by 1740 it had become the largest city in colonial America. All the ingredients necessary for the founding of a newspaper were present when on December 22, 1719, the first issue of the *American Weekly Mercury* was pulled from the press. It was founded by a member of one of colonial America's most illustrious printing families.

The patriarch of that family was William Bradford. He began by printing pamphlets and tracts for Quakers; and because he owned the only press in Philadelphia, he also printed government documents. It was the publication of the latter that led to his censure by Quaker authorities in 1693 and Bradford's departure for New York, where he printed anti-Quaker tracts and thirty-two years later established that city's first newspaper. When Bradford left Philadelphia, he left his printing shop in the hands of an apprentice. The story of Philadelphia newspapers begins with Bradford's son, Andrew.

Andrew Bradford learned the printer's craft in his father's New York shop. In 1712 he returned to Philadelphia to take control of his father's old printing shop. Quaker leadership had mellowed in the intervening years, and Andrew was able to serve both the Friends and the colonial government without the strict oversight his father had endured. In fact he became the official printer and postmaster. These positions placed him in a favorable position to start the Pennsylvania colony's first newspaper. The *American Weekly Mercury* demonstrated a bit more independence than its contemporaries in Boston. It occasionally even criticized the government. However, it did not do so with impunity, for Bradford was arrested for his criticisms of the authorities. He was not prosecuted, however, and the *Mercury* became even more daring. Following Andrew's death in 1742 his widow continued the *Mercury*, but it survived only four years. The newspaper might have continued much longer had it not been for a family dispute.

Some years before his death, Andrew adopted his nephew, William Bradford III, and taught him the printing business. William might have operated the *Mercury* after his uncle's death if not for great animosity between him and his foster mother. On Andrew's death, William founded, as a means of revenge on Mrs. Bradford, a competitor for the *Mercury*, the *Pennsylvania Journal*. If the *Mercury* had been daring, the *Journal* was positively bold. A suc-

Numb. XL.

THE

Pennſylvania GAZETTE.

Containing the freſheſt Advices Foreign and Domeſtick.

From Thurſday, September 25. to Thurſday, October 2. 1729.

THE Pennſylvania Gazette *being now to be carry'd on by other Hands, the Reader may expect ſome Account of the Method we deſign to proceed in.*

There are many who have long deſired to ſee a good News-Paper in Pennſylvania; *and we hope thoſe Gentlemen who are able, will contribute towards the making This ſuch.*

As to the Religious Courtſhip, *Part of which has been retail'd to the Publick in theſe Papers, the Reader may be inform'd, that the whole Book will probably in a little Time be printed and bound up by it ſelf; and thoſe who approve of it, will doubtleſs be better pleas'd to have it entire, than in this broken interrupted Manner.*

Franklin's Newspaper
In his autobiography, Benjamin Franklin claimed that he had planned to start a newspaper but that one of his employees confided his plan to the rival printer Samuel Keimer. After Keimer beat him at founding a paper, Franklin then helped Philadelphia's opposing newspaper to ridicule Keimer and the *Pennsylvania Gazette*. As the *Gazette* foundered, Franklin was able to buy it at a low price from Keimer. He then made it one of the most successful newspapers of the colonial period. By the time he was forty-two years old Franklin had secured enough income through his printing business that he was able to retire to follow other pursuits. This painting is the first portrait of Franklin (inset), made in 1748, the year of his retirement.

cessful newspaper for fifty years under the editorship of William and his son, Thomas, the *Journal* became a powerful and outspoken champion of the Patriots during the Revolution.

BENJAMIN FRANKLIN

The newspaper battles in Philadelphia were not only familial; they also involved other newspapers. Bradford's competition arrived in the form of the best known journalist of the colonial period, Benjamin Franklin. Escaped apprentice and world traveler, Franklin entered Philadelphia inauspiciously but by 1728 was already planning to start a newspaper. When another printer, the eccentric Samuel Keimer, heard of Franklin's plan, he hurried to start his own newspaper. Founded under the clumsy title of *The Universal Instructor in All Arts and Sciences: and Pennsylvania Gazette*, Keimer's paper compared favorably with the *Mercury* and led to Franklin's concern that it might succeed and lock him out of the Philadelphia newspaper business for the forseeable future.

To prevent the *Universal Instructor*'s success, Franklin devised a scheme to destroy the newspaper.[17] He and several friends wrote a number of essays in the tradition of Joseph Addison, who was ever an inspiration to Franklin, for the *Mercury*, satirizing Keimer. The essays attracted considerable attention to the *Mercury* and ensured Keimer's failure. Whether the "Busy-Body" essays were as influential as Franklin believed is unclear; they did allow Franklin, however, to buy the *Gazette* for a pittance.

In 1729 the new owner shortened the newspaper's title to the *Pennsylvania Gazette* and turned the dull news sheet into a solid newspaper. It carried more news and advertising. By 1750 it printed six pages, up to eight pages on occasion, with heavy advertising. Franklin became Bradford's successor as postmaster, which helped Franklin greatly. The *Gazette* and other printing enterprises made him a rich man so that by the age of forty-two he could retire and devote himself to other pursuits. A Franklin protegé from London, David Hall, became sole owner of the *Gazette* in 1766; and Hall's family along with several partners continued the newspaper until 1815.

Franklin did not satisfy himself with only the *Gazette* during his long career. He also published the first foreign-language newspaper in the colonies, the *Philadelphia Zeitung*. Along with Louis Timothee, he founded the German-language newspaper in 1732, but it lasted only a few issues. However, its successors, Christopher Sower's *Germantown Zeitung* and Heinrich Miller's *Wöchentliche Philadephische Staatsbote*, were highly successful newspapers. Another Franklin first had to be shared with his competitor, Andrew Bradford. They produced the first magazines in the colonies within three days of each other. Bradford's *American Magazine* and Franklin's *General Magazine* were both released in January 1741. They were short lived, however, both failing within the year.

NEWSPAPERS IN NEW YORK

The third largest city in the colonies was New York, and it was the third city to have a newspaper. The newspaper was founded by William Bradford. After abandoning Philadelphia when pressure from Quakers became too great, Bradford moved to New York City at the request of the colonial council to continue his printing business. Being a cautious man, he waited three decades to begin his own newspaper, after three newspapers had been founded in

[17] *The Autobiography of Benjamin Franklin* (New York, 1939), 77-8.

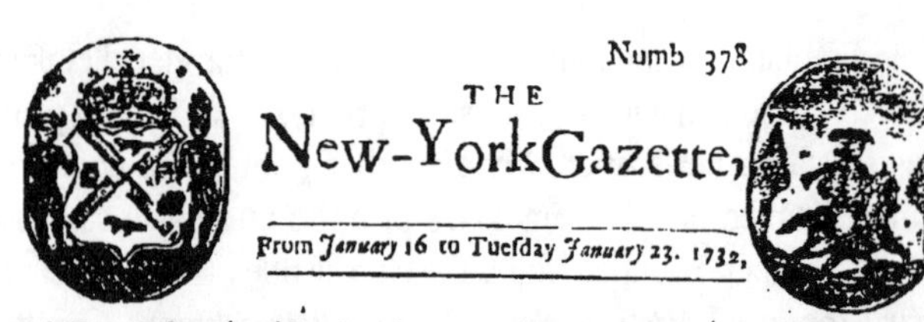

Numb 378

THE New-York Gazette,

From January 16 to Tueſday January 23. 1732,

At the Court at *Kenſington*, the 10th Day of Auguſt, 1731.

P R E S E N T.

The QUEENS moſt Excellent Majeſty, Guardian of the Kingdom of Great-Britain, and his Majeſty's Lieutenant within the ſame.

His Royal Highneſs the Princes of Wales	Duke of Kent
Lord Chancellor	Earl of Scarborough
Lord Preſident	Lord Harvey
Lord Chamberlaine	Lord Delawar
	Mr. Chancellor of the Excheq.

Upon Reading at the Board a Report from the Right Honourable the Lords of the Committee of Council, for Plantation Affairs, Dated the 2d of this Inſtant, in the Words following, *Viz*.

IN Obedience to His Majeſty's Orders in Council of the 10th Day of *April*, 1730. and the 8th Day of *April* 1731. referring to this Committee, the Humble Petition of *Samuel Waldo* of *Boſton*, in His Majeſty's Province of the *Maſſachuſetts-Bay*, Merchant in behalf of himſelf and of *Eliſha Cooke* Eſq; and others, and alſo the humble Petition of Sr. *Biby Lake*, Bart. and others. The Lords of the Committee did ſome time ſince meet and take the ſame into Conſideration; both which Petitions ſet forth *inter al* the Right of the Petitioners to ſeveral Tracts of Land lying between the Rivers *Kennebeck* and *St. Croix*, in that Part of his Majeſty's Province of the *Maſſachuſetts Bay* in *New-England*, lying adjacent to His Majeſty's Province of *Nova Scotia*, which they claimed ſome by Purchaſe from the Indian Sagamores or Sachems allowed of and approved by the General Court for the Government of the *Maſſachuſetts* Province, and others by Grant from the Council eſtabliſhed at *Plymouth*, for the planting, ruling ordering and governing *New-England* in *America*, Ratify'd and confirmed by the ſeveral Charters granted to the Subjects of the ſaid Province, and further ſetting forth; That the Petitioners and their Anceſtors had been, ever ſince the time of ſuch their Purchaſes and Grants, in the Enjoyment and Poſſeſſion of the ſaid Lands, and from time to time laid out very conſiderable Sums of Money in Setling and Improving the ſame, and in Erecting Buildings thereon, and Houſes of Defence, and in defending the ſame from the Indians, and had a Magiſtrate and Courts of Juſtice eſtabliſhed amongſt them, but which Settlements and Improvements were broke up and deſtroyed by the frequent Wars with the Indians, ſaving only as to ſome Block-Houſes of Defence which the Indians were not able to take, whereby the Petitioners, and their Anceſtors, had ſuſtained many and great Loſſes; notwithſtanding which on every Peace with the Indians, they had always endeavoured to effectuate the Settlement of the ſaid Premiſes, and particularly on conclusion of the laſt War with the Indians, which broke out in or about the Years 1722 or 1723, the Petitioners were very vigorouſly puſhing forward the Setling and bringing their Lands into a Capacity of receiving and ſecuring a Number of Inhabitants, and being Intent and Reſolved on continuing and finiſhing their ſaid Settlements, with the utmoſt diſpatch, they had actually laid out ſeveral Townſhips, and provided a Miniſter, and had One Hundred and Twenty Families ready to go and Settle one of the ſaid intended Towns. But further ſetting forth, That to their great ſurprize, diſappointment and loſs, and to the great prejudice of the Province, and His Majeſty's Intereſt there, they had met with an Interruption therein from *David Dunbar* Eſq. Surveyor General of His Majeſty's Woods in *America*, who had forbid the Petitioners going on with their ſaid Settlements, and informed them that he could not permit their going on with the ſame on any other Terms, but their taking Grants from him, in the ſame manner as if they had not already any Title thereto, pretending he had ſome Inſtructions, or a Commiſſion from His Majeſty to make Settlements within the Limits of the Petitioners Lands and in other places in the Eaſtern parts of the ſaid Province of the *Maſſachuſetts-Bay*, and to Erect the ſame into a ſeperate Government from that Province, altho' the ſame is included in the Charter granted to the Subjects of the ſaid Province; and notwithſtanding Mr. *Dunbar* had been waited on, and made fully acquainted with the Petitioners Title to the ſaid Lands and Premiſes, yet he inſiſted he ſhould enter upon and make Settlements therein, unleſs His Majeſty ſhould forbid or reſtrain him there-from.

The Petitioners therefore by their ſaid Petitions pray'd, That His Majeſty would be pleaſed to ſend the neceſſary Orders or Inſtructions to the ſaid *David Dunbar*, not to intermedle with the Tracts of Land to which the Petitioners were ſo Entituled, or moleſt them therein, and that he ſhould not interrupt, obſtruct or diſturb the Petitioners, their Tennants and Agents in carrying on their Settlements on any pretence whatſoever, that ſo the Petitioners might be quieted in the Poſſeſſion thereof, under the Government of His Majeſty's Province of the *Maſſachuſetts-Bay*, and be at liberty to proceed in Setling the Premiſes without Moleſtation.

And the Lords of the Committee thought it proper before they formed any Opinion on the ſaid Petitions, to refer them to the Lords Commiſſioners for Trade and Plantations, with Directions, that they ſhould conſider the ſame, and receive the Opinion of His Majeſty's Attorney and Solicitor General thereon, and afterwards make Report to this Committee, of the whole matter, with what they conceive proper to be done thereupon.

That when the ſaid Lords Commiſſioners for Trade and Plantations received the ſaid Directions, they apprehended it neceſſary for their better Information in the Premiſes, to call the Agent for the ſaid Province before them, and to draw up a State of the Caſe, ſetting forth the nature of the Claim, which the People of the Province had to the Lands in Queſtion, and how little had been done by the Province for the Defence or improvement of the ſaid Country, and alſo Stated the Changes that had happened in this Diſtrict, in point of Dominion by the Conqueſt which the French made over it in 1696, and by the Re-Conqueſt thereof in the Year 1710. by the Engliſh under General *Nicholſon*, and to which Caſe the ſaid Lords Commiſſioners Subjoyned the following Querys, which with the ſaid two Petitions they referred to the Conſideration of His Majeſty's Attorney and Solicitor General, *viz*.

Firſt, Whether the Inhabitants of the *Maſſachuſetts Bay*, if they ever had any Right to the Government of the ſaid Tract of Land, lying between *St. Croix* and *Kennebeck* or *Sagadahock*, have not by their neglect or even refuſal to defend, take care, and improve the ſame, forfeited their ſaid Right to the Government, and what Right they had under the Charter, and now have to the Lands?

Secondly, Whether by the ſaid Tract being conquer'd by the French, and afterwards reconquer'd by General *Nicholſon* in the late Queens Time, and yielded up by *France* to *Great-Britain*, by the Treaty of *Utrecht*, that part of the Charter Relating thereto became vacated? And whether the Government of that Tract and the Lands thereof, are not abſolutely reveſted in the Crown? And whether the Crown hath not thereby a ſufficient Power to appoint Governours, and aſſign Lands to ſuch Families as ſhall be deſirous of ſetling there?

Whereupon His Majeſty's Attorney and Sollicitor General, certifyed to the ſaid Lord's Commiſſioners for Trade and Plantations by their Report of the 11th of *Auguſt*, 1731. That having conſidered the ſaid Caſe and Petitions, and having been attended by Mr. *Paxton* Solicitor for the Affairs of his Majeſty's Treaſury, and by the Reſpective Agents of the Province of the *Maſſachuſetts Bay*, in *New-England*, and of the Petitioners, and having heard Council in behalf of the Crown, and of all the ſaid Parties, at which hearing were laid before them a Copy of the Charter granted by their late Majeſties King *William* and Queen *Mary* to the Inhabitants of the *Maſſachuſetts-Bay*, together with ſeveral affidavits and Copys of divers Conveyances of particular parcels of Land lying within the Tract, in Queſtion, which were certified under the Seal of the ſaid Province, it appeared to them as follows,

That all the ſaid Tract of Lands lying between *Kennebeck* and *St. Croix*, is amongſt other Things, Granted by the Charter to the

New York's First

The *New York Gazette*, a small unattractive sheet, was that colony's first newspaper. After setting up in the printing business, William Bradford, a cautious man, waited three decades before finally starting the newspaper in 1725.

Boston and he had seen his son's success with the *Mercury* in Philadelphia. The *New York Gazette*, first issued November 8, 1725, was a small, unattractive two-page sheet, whose content consisted primarily of stale foreign news. It carried little advertising but managed to survive for nearly two decades.

The importance of New York in the colonial period was not the number of newspapers it produced, or how early, but rather in the freedom of the press issue that was addressed in that colony. In fact, the *Gazette* had no competition for the first eight years of its life. The second newspaper in New York was founded because of political developments. As had occurred in Boston, there arose in New York an opposition group to the royal governor. The group wanted its own newspaper; and on November 5, 1733, the *New York Weekly Journal* was born. A German immigrant, John Peter Zenger, was printer and publisher. He had served his apprenticeship with Bradford and so was a good printer. James Alexander, a lawyer who served virtually as editor-in-chief, stated the newspaper's purpose in a private letter:

> Inclosed is the first of a newspaper designed to be continued Weekly and chiefly to expose him [Governor William Cosby] and those ridiculous flatteries with which Mr. Harison [the Recorder and a member of the Council] loads our other Newspaper which our Governor claims and has the privilege of suffering nothing to be in but what he and Mr. Harison approve of.[18]

The *Journal* did as promised. From the beginning it subjected the governor to scathing attacks. His only defense for the next year appeared in Bradford's *Gazette*. Each defense hastened a new attack.

The controversy between the two factions and the two newspapers revolved around ideological issues. The *Gazette* defended the status quo, the governor, and his council. The *Journal* promoted the opposing faction. The governor decided to crush the *Journal*; and on November 17, 1734, after grand juries twice had failed to indict Zenger, Cosby had him arrested and charged with seditious libel, despite the fact Zenger was merely a printer and had not himself written any of the offensive material. Zenger spent nine months in jail but continued to publish the *Journal* from his cell. Finally brought to trial, he was acquitted by a sympathetic jury. While the verdict did not change colonial law, it did help intensify opposition to British authority.

A number of other newspapers were published in New York during the colonial period. Among them were the *Gazette or Weekly Post Boy*, 1742; *Evening Post*, 1746; *Mercury*, 1752; and *Gazette*, 1759. Of this group one was particularly noteworthy. The *Mercury* was published by Hugh Gaine. During the Revolution he wavered from one side to the other. However, in its early days the *Mercury* was quite neutral, somewhat unusual for the colonial period.

THE SPREAD OF NEWSPAPERS

Newspapers did not appear until later in the other colonies, and New Jersey did not have a newspaper until after 1765. In fact, more than two-thirds of the newspapers printed in the other colonies were founded after 1750. Other newspapers and their founding dates were the *Maryland Gazette*, 1727; *Maryland Gazette*, 1745; *South-Carolina Gazette*, 1732; *South-Carolina Weekly Journal*, 1732; *South-Carolina Gazette and Country Journal*, 1765; *Rhode Island Gazette*, 1732; *Rhode Island Mercury*, 1758 (Newport); *Providence* (R.I.)*Gazette and Country Journal*, 1762; *Virginia Gazette*, 1736; *Connecticut Gazette*, 1755; *New-London* (Conn.) *Summary*, 1758; *New-London Gazette*, 1763; *Connecticut Courant*, 1764; *North Carolina Gazette*, 1751; *Cape-Fear*

18 Quoted in Livingston Rutherford, *John Peter Zenger* (New York, 1941), 28-9.

Gazette and *Wilmington Advertiser* (North Carolina), 1764; *New-Hampshire Gazette*, 1756; *Portsmouth* (N.H.) *Mercury and Weekly Advertiser*, 1765; *Wilmington* (Del.) *Courant*, 1762; and *Georgia Gazette*, 1763.[19]

The advent of newspapers in colonial America was relatively slow. In the early decades of the eighteenth century, the number of American papers was small, and they were slow to spread. However, after about 1750 the effects of increasing populations, wealth, industry, commerce, improved communication, and a more tolerant attitude toward publishers began to be felt. There was an explosion in the number of newspapers after 1750. Twelve newspapers existed in all the colonies in 1750; that number quadrupled in the next twenty-five years. One important impetus for the growth of the American newspaper may have been provided by London.

The famous Stamp Act that Parliament passed in 1765 seemed a reasonable law from England's perspective. The English government was merely looking for a source of revenue and believed that taxing paper was one means of obtaining it. Besides, the English wanted the colonies to help pay for their own defense. The colonists considered the Stamp Act another slight by London. The act's timing was poor because the colonies were suffering through a depression that had followed the French and Indian War (1754-1763). A Stamp Tax on newspapers had existed in Britain since 1712, and similar acts in Massachusetts and New York a decade earlier had met little opposition. The Stamp Act of 1765, however, was vigorously resisted. It may ultimately have been that the colonies were no longer prepared to accept orders from London as meekly as in the past. The Stamp Act hit merchants, lawyers, and printers particularly hard. Surprisingly, however, the number of newspapers increased. While some newspapers ceased publication rather than pay the new tax, a greater number were started as voices in opposition not only to the tax but also to what was seen in the colonies as the cavalier attitude of the English. From this time opposition to English policies grew and newspapers often spearheaded the effort.

RECOMMENDED READINGS

BOOKS

Beasley, Maurine H., and Sheila J. Gibbons. *Taking Their Place: A Documentary History of Women and Journalism*. Lanham, Md., 1994. Reprints of women journalists' work along with an overview of the history of women in journalism.

Brigham, Clarence S. *A History and Bibliography of American Newspapers, 1690-1820*. Worcester, Mass., 1947. An indispensible resource for the colonial journalism historian that provides a compilation of names, dates, locations, and existing copies of virtually all colonial newspapers.

Brown, Richard D. *Knowledge Is Power: The Diffusion of Information in Early America 1700-1865*. New York, 1989. Early Americans were especially interested in having information about a variety of public affairs, and they used a variety of mass and interpersonal means to circulate it and to obtain it.

[19]Many early newspapers carried the same nameplate. Sometimes more than one newspaper used the same name at the same time.

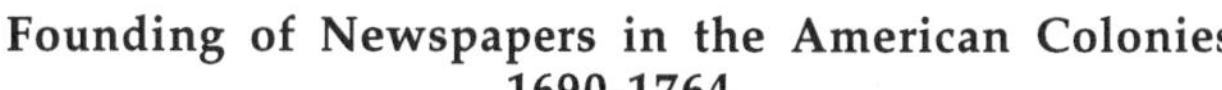

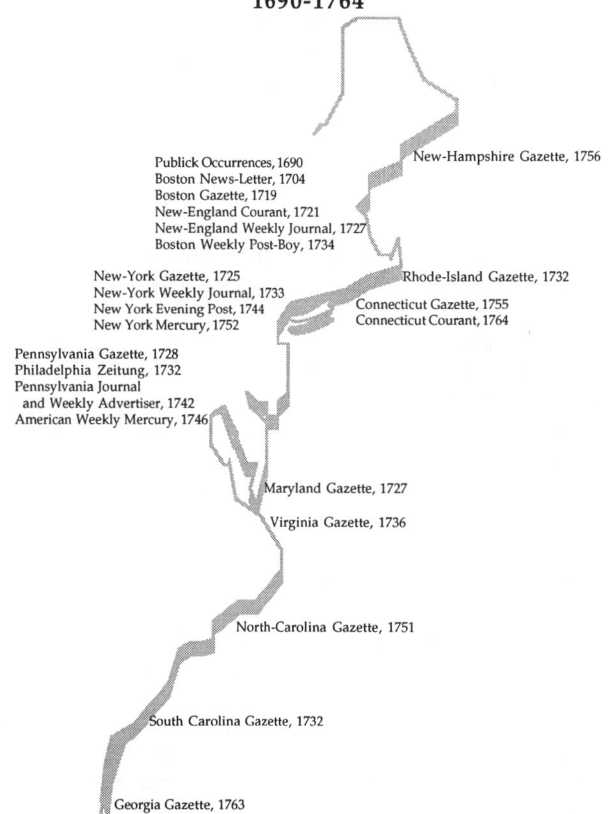

Founding of Newspapers
The founding of newspapers in the colonies was generally based on population growth. The earliest newspapers were located in the larger towns where literacy, a merchant class, and a need by government to present information it considered important provided the impetus.

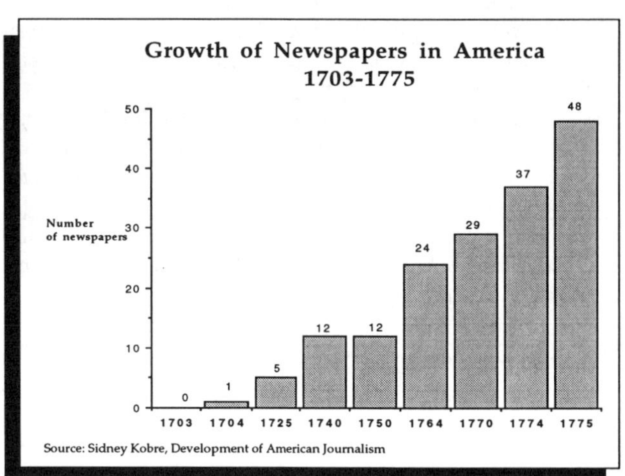

Newspaper Growth
Starting slowly, growth in the number of newspapers in colonial America accelerated after the mid-eighteenth century. As passions increased in the years immediately preceding the American Revolution, newspapers provided a means for Tories and Patriots to present their views.

Clark, Charles E. *The Public Prints*. New York, 1994. Provides details on newspapers and other printed materials, with an emphasis on how newspapers helped to provide a forum for public discussion.

Cook, Elizabeth C. *Literary Influences in Colonial Newspapers, 1704-1750*. New York, 1912. Describes the colonial newspaper as the most important source in the dissemination of non-sectarian literature in the colonies. The colonial newspaper was to a large extent a non-news literary journal.

Copeland, David A. *Colonial American Newspapers: Character and Content*. Newark, Dela.: 1997. The author's explanations in this detailed study are essential to understanding colonial newspapers.

Geitz, Henry. *The German-American Press*. Madison, Wisc., 1992. Book of essays about German-American newspapers, magazines, and books.

Kobre, Sidney. *The Development of the Colonial Newspaper*. Pittsburgh, 1944. An insightful study of the development of the colonial newspaper from a social, economic, and political perspective.

Marzolf, Marion. *Up From the Footnote*. New York, 1977. How women printers and journalists have been treated in the profession. Contains a useful discussion on women in the colonial period.

Richardson, Lyon F. *A History of Early American Magazines, 1741-89*. New York, 1912. Discusses 37 early magazines in terms of colonial thought and culture. Although magazines generally did not survive long, they frequently were important as a focus of opinion and forum for discussion.

Sloan, Wm. David, and Julie Hedgepeth Williams. *The Early American Press, 1690-1783*. Westport, Conn., 1994. This in-depth study, the best general history of the colonial press, looks at newspapers through the end of the Revolution.

Startt, James D., and Wm. David Sloan. *The Significance of the Media in American History*. Northport, Ala., 1994. Sixteen essays profile the various ways media have influenced American life from the colonial period to the present day.

Steele, Ian K. *The English Atlantic 1675-1740*. New York, 1986. An excellent study of the communication relationships between England and her colonies.

Thomas, Isaiah. *History of Printing in America*. 2 vols. Worcester, Mass., 1810. This standard reference for the colonial period includes biographies of printers and a colony-by-colony description of newspapers.

ARTICLES

Aldridge, A. Owen. "Benjamin Franklin and the Pennsylvania Gazette." *Proceedings of the American Philosophical Society* 106 (1962): 77-81. In colonial newspapers, news was the most important content; and essays, opinions, and literary material were only fillers.

Bradley, Patricia. "Forerunner of the 'Dark Ages': Philadelphia's Tradition of a Partisan Press." *American Journalism* 13 (1996): 126-40. Partisanship was strong in newspapers in colonial Pennsylvania, and it laid a foundation for such practices in later journalism.

Copeland, David A. "'A Receipt Against the Plague': Medical Reporting in Colonial America." *American Journalism* 11 (1994): 204-18. American newspapers kept readers informed of epidemics and potential cures.

—. "In All the Papers: Reporting on Religion in Colonial America." *American Journalism* 13 (1996): 390-415. Religion was the focus of early of American life and one of the key subjects appearing in newspapers.

Eberhard, Wallace B. "Press and Post Office in Eighteenth-Century America: Origin of a Public Policy." in Bond and McLeod, *From Newsletters to Newspaper*, 145-54. Except for a supportive postal system, newspapers might have been unable to survive.

Henry, Susan. "Colonial Woman as Prototype: Toward a Model for the Study of Minorities." *Journalism History* 3 (1976): 20-4. Women printers performed a demanding and important service and, as businesswomen, played an important role in the colonial economy.

Hoffman, Ronald. "The Press in Mercantile Maryland: A Question of Utility." *Journalism Quarterly* 46 (1969): 536-44. Argues that newspapers — even though they were helpful, convenient, and useful — were not essential or vital to the prospering of the merchant community or colonial economy.

Kobre, Sidney. "The First American Newspaper: A Product of Environment." *Journalism Quarterly* 17 (1940): 335-45. Examines the economic and social background of the colonial newspaper.

Marzolf, Marion. "The Woman Journalist: Colonial Printer to City Desk." *Journalism History* 1 (1974-75): 100-7 and 146; and 3 (1976-77): 24-7. These two special issues of *Journalism History* are on the history of women in journalism. A general survey history of women in journalism is provided by Marzolf's two-part series.

Mitchell, Catherine C. "Scholarship on Women Working in Journalism." *American Journalism* 7 (1990): 33-8. This bibliography covers the major works concerning women as journalists.

Nelson, William. "Some New Jersey Printers and Printing in the Eighteenth Century." *Proceedings of the American Antiquarian Society* 21, n.s. (1911): 15-56. Describes colonial printers as ideological pioneers who, through the power of their trade and the strength of their ideals, helped create the American nation and the profession of journalism.

Nordin, Kenneth. "The Entertaining Press: Sensationalism in Eighteenth-Century Boston Newspapers." *Communication Research* 6 (1979): 295-320. Argues that sensationalism in American journalism began not with the penny press in the 1830s but with the colonial press.

Oldham, Ellen M. "Early Women Printers in America." *Boston Public Library Quarterly* 10 (1958): 6-26, 78-92, and 141-53. The common characteristic of female printers "was the necessity of supporting themselves, and in most cases their children, upon the death of their husbands." The women had "unusual forcefulness of character."

Sloan, Wm. David. "Chaos, Polemics, and America's First Newspaper." *Journalism Quarterly* 70 (1993): 666-81. Study refutes the assumption that Puritan clergy were behind the suppression of Benjamin Harris' *Publick Occurrences*, arguing instead that it resulted from "a combination of factors working in the political environment."

—. "The *New England Courant*: Voice of Anglicanism." *American Journalism* 8 (1991): 108-41. The purpose of the *Courant*, rather than being to bring about a liberalization of society, as some historians have claimed, was to promote Anglicanism as the official church in Massachusetts.

Spaulding, E. Wilder. "The Connecticut Courant, A Representative Newspaper in the Eighteenth Century." *New England Quarterly* 3 (1930): 443-63. Although colonial newspapers were the "drab, unpretentious by-product of the tiny print shop," they were an integral and important part of American life.

4

The Revolutionary Press

1765 - 1783

The American Revolution may have been the single most important event in the nation's history. During a period of less than two decades of the eighteenth century, Americans developed a political philosophy, declared their sovereignty, fought a war for independence, and transformed a weak intercolonial alliance into an organization of states.

The Revolution gave the colonial press new functions to fulfill. As the thirteen British colonies slowly dissolved their ties with the mother country, newspapers played an increasingly important role in the growing dispute. Both Patriot and Loyalist writers used pamphlets and the weekly papers to attempt to convince their neutral countrymen to support their side. The most successful were the Patriots, so much so that, by the time the Revolution had begun, pro-British newspapers had disappeared from most colonies.

The American Revolution developed out of many circumstances. The ideas behind the separation from Great Britain derived from dissident Protestantism and Enlightenment rationalism, particularly the works of John Locke. Basing their thinking on Biblical tenets, dissident Protestants (that is, those opposed to the official Church of England) argued that all men, since they were created by God, inherited certain rights, including liberty and equality. Political philosophers argued that these "natural rights" should be protected by government. Included among these rights were trial by jury and local participation in government. Heavily influenced by the ideas of the Protestant philosopher Locke, Americans came to believe that governments were created by people to bring order to society. Rulers governed not through divine right but through either usurpation or social contract. The contract did not bestow absolute power on rulers but rather entrusted them only with the power needed to protect people's natural rights. When a ruler broke the contract, reasoned Locke, subjects had a right to replace him.[1]

Englishmen and colonials, who considered themselves Englishmen, believed that the British system of government was the best in the world. Through its balanced system that divided power between King, Lords, and Commons, it gave representation to all sections of society. Maintaining that balance resulted in the preservation of all subjects' rights and interests and thus made tyrannical government impossible. Colonials believed that the British constitution protected their rights as British subjects. They thought that their own colonial governments, which were set up under the authority of the British crown and which were modeled after the British structure, helped extend the rights of Englishmen to all parts of the British empire. When colonials discovered, however, that their "rights" could be abrogated whenever they conflicted with the interests of Britons with ties to the government, they began to question their vision of the British constitutional system. It was at times when colonials felt as if the British government were ignoring their right to representation that colonial protest intensified. The eventual result was rebellion.

Two events served as the catalysts for the beginning of the Revolutionary period in media history. One was the end of the Seven Years' War (known as the French and Indian War in North America). The other, even more important in its effect on the press, was the Stamp Act of 1765. When the Treaty of Paris ended the Seven Years' War in 1763 and drove French troops from North America, colonial soldiers and civilians joined their British compatriots in cheers and toasts. The war had been long and bloody. The victory for the first time guaranteed the safety of the entire eastern seaboard from Upper Canada to Florida and opened up the western frontier for development. But it also shifted attention from troubles with the French and their Indian allies and from the common British-colonial interests to differences between England and the colonies. Even during the war, differences had sharpened, especially disagreements over who should raise and support a militia. With the war ended and the common enemies defeated, other problems that had been submerged surfaced. A number of controversies between the colonies and the home government marked the next decade.

After Britain's years of fighting a global war and suffering the

[1]John Locke, *Two Treatises on Government* (1689).

JOIN, or DIE.

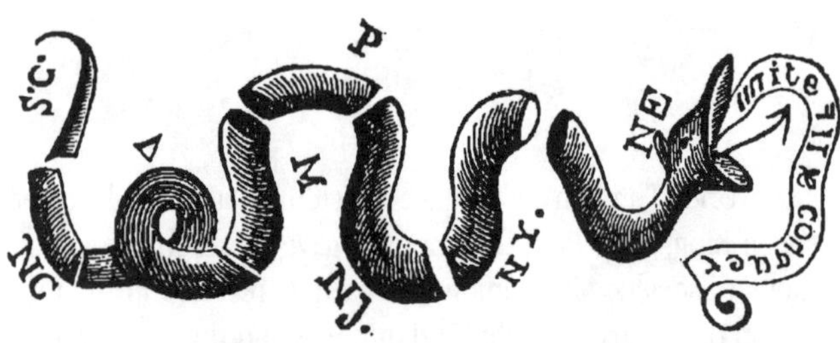

JOIN or DIE

Symbol of a Revolution
Benjamin Franklin created the divided-snake cartoon in 1754 (top drawing) to encourage the colonies to unite in opposition to France's military efforts to extend its power in America. With the end of the French and Indian War in 1763, which removed the danger from the American frontier, British and colonial differences began to intensify. Patriot printers revived the cartoon during the opposition to the Stamp Act in 1765 and the "Intolerable Acts" in 1774. The parts of the snake represented the disjointed colonies. It became the most popular visual symbol during the Revolutionary period. The *Constitutional Courant* used the idea as an engraving in the center of its nameplate (bottom drawing), with the slogan "Unite and Conquer" issuing from the serpent's mouth.

sacrifices required, its treasury demanded immediate replenishment. The war had doubled England's national debt, and military and administrative expenses in America had increased several times. Parliament believed that victory benefited all citizens of the Empire and that all citizens therefore should help pay the costs. Americans, however, looked toward the opportunities that victory offered rather than the responsibilities it required. Theirs was a spirit of increasing self-reliance and a chaffing under restraint. The elimination of the French and Indian threat made the colonials feel far less dependent on the mother country. Coupled with that, 3,000 miles of treacherous ocean kept Britain and America apart, thereby isolating the latter and making a shambles of communication. Sailing ships, the primary mode of communication, took months to make a single Atlantic crossing. The isolation created a pride in what the colonials had created for themselves. While ill-disposed to shoulder the burden for the greatly enlarged British empire, they grew increasingly insistent on their own rights and liberties. They looked with resentment on any attempts by the British government to saddle them with the expenses of war, security, and a mercantile system aimed primarily at benefiting British industry and business. British officials, concerned about economic problems of the home country, seemed ignorant of American attitudes. The only means that Britain's leaders believed existed for solving their problems was to implement new taxes by the quickest means possible.

In America the tax program covered all manner of goods and services. The Sugar Act of 1764 was the first in a series of laws and was followed by the Stamp Act in 1765. British officials thought it only fair that colonials should help pay the costs of security, but Americans argued that they too had incurred debts during the war and that they already were taxed by local governments to help pay the debts. Colonials looking for more independence in their own affairs were eager to use any opportunity to denounce acts of the British government, and the former cooperative attitude of subjects of the crown turned "into distrust, and foreboding," and then eventually into hatred and repudiation.[2] When Britain enacted the Stamp Act, it enhanced the opportunities for these independent-minded colonials.

It was in the conflict over the Stamp Act that newspapers discovered a new role to play. Printers protested the Act for various reasons. Most feared a loss of income; but, more importantly, they believed it was an infringement on colonial rights because no one had the authority to impose taxes but elected representatives. Since Americans did not vote for members of the British Parliament, they reasoned, Parliament could not impose taxes on the colonies. This concept of the power of taxation, which was developed in the newspaper arguments of 1765, became the basic tenet of colonials in all the disagreements with the mother country until independence was declared in 1776.

Literacy, Newspapers, Pamphlets, and Revolutionary Democracy

Interpretations of the American Revolution have varied. Throughout most of the nineteenth century, historians described it as a triumph of the forces of liberty and progress over those of tyranny and reaction. Around the turn of the century an imperial school of interpretation gained popularity. Historians of this persuasion placed the Revolution in a broad setting of colonial empire and tried to rid it of patriotic distortion. At the same time another school of historians appeared to offer yet another interpretation of the Revolution. Known as Progressive historians, they sympathized with the little people, with the farmers and laborers. They believed the Revolution was the result of internal political and social upheavals and of class conflict. It was, in their opinion, as much an internal struggle as it was one against external, or imperial, power. After World War II a number of historians attacked the Progressive interpretation, which had become the most widely

[2]James Parker to Benjamin Franklin, 14 June 1765, *Massachusetts Historical Society Proceedings* 16 (1902), 198.

Family Literacy
Family relationships were particularly important in America on the eve of the Revolution, as illustrated in this portrait, "Family Group" (1773) by Charles Wilson Peale. The Puritans who had settled New England in the 1600s had placed a particular emphasis on spiritual growth and therefore on educating the young. That concern resulted in laws requiring that children be taught reading and other skills. Thus, by the revolutionary era the American populace was highly literate compared with that of other countries.

used one in American history textbooks. The newer interpretation stressed a consensus view that claimed that both radical and conservative colonial leaders shared a commitment to a common body of aims and ideals.

From the first, the press has been an important source for any historian hoping to discover the nature of the Revolution. It has a significant place in both conflict and consensus interpretations. The former, for instance, contends that the true struggle of Revolutionary printers, writers, and other liberal thinkers was to free the common people from the economic and political domination by the elite. According to this "class struggle" concept, a true democratic process in the colonies was non-existent and a small group of eastern "seacoast aristocrats" controlled the country economically and politically. The bulk of the population was herded together under the thumb of the rich. When they could stand the agony no longer, this ragtail, illiterate mob took up weapons and warred against the landlords, who were in league with the British. The Patriot press, through its propaganda, urged colonials forward, keeping the fire of discontent ablaze and succeeding mightily despite the fact that the revolutionaries could not read.

Such an explanation of the Revolution suffers from a shortage of fact. Better evidence suggests that political democracy had taken root in the colonies and that the Patriot press viewed the Revolution not as a struggle between classes but as a fight for political independence from Great Britain. Even though Americans may have disagreed on isolated issues, their differences took place within a broader realm of agreement on underlying principles, including religious freedom, political self-determination, and individual liberty. The Revolution and the press' role in it were primarily democratic rather than economic or social.

The democratic ideas of American colonials, according to the historian Bernard Bailyn, can be traced through the pamphlets published during the Revolutionary period. Pamphlets served as an important forum for the expression of opinion. They revealed that "the American Revolution was above all else an ideological, constitutional political struggle ... and that intellectual developments in the decade before Independence led to a radical idealization and conceptualizaton" of American attitudes. The ideas of some of England's more radical political and social thinkers were transmitted directly to the colonials. American leaders feared that a sinister conspiracy had developed in England to deprive citizens of the British empire of their long-established liberties. It was this fear that lay at the base of the views expressed in the pamphlets and newspapers. The ideas in these publications then became the determinants in the history of the Revolution by leading to a change in colonials' beliefs and attitudes. These ideas challenged traditional authority, according to Bailyn, and argued that "a better world than had ever been known could be built where authority was distrusted and held in constant scrutiny; where the status of men flowed from their achievements and from their personal qualities, not from distinctions ascribed to them at birth; and where the use of power over the lives of men was jealously guarded and severely restricted."[3]

The bulk of the evidence on the public's economic opportunity, the extent of political democracy in the colonies, and the colonial literacy rate reveals that the Revolution was not a class struggle. One of the major differences between living in eighteenth-century Europe as opposed to America was the choice among people about how they would grow as a country. The attitude toward literacy typified the differences. The earliest settlements — Plymouth, Boston, and others — were created by religious groups who wished to make a choice for themselves and their offspring about how to worship God. They could not do so in countries with established churches; they were dissidents, many of whom had suffered in numerous ways as the price of personal religious

[3]Bernard Bailyn, *Pamphlets of the American Revolution, 1750-1776* (Cambridge, Mass., 1965), "Introduction."

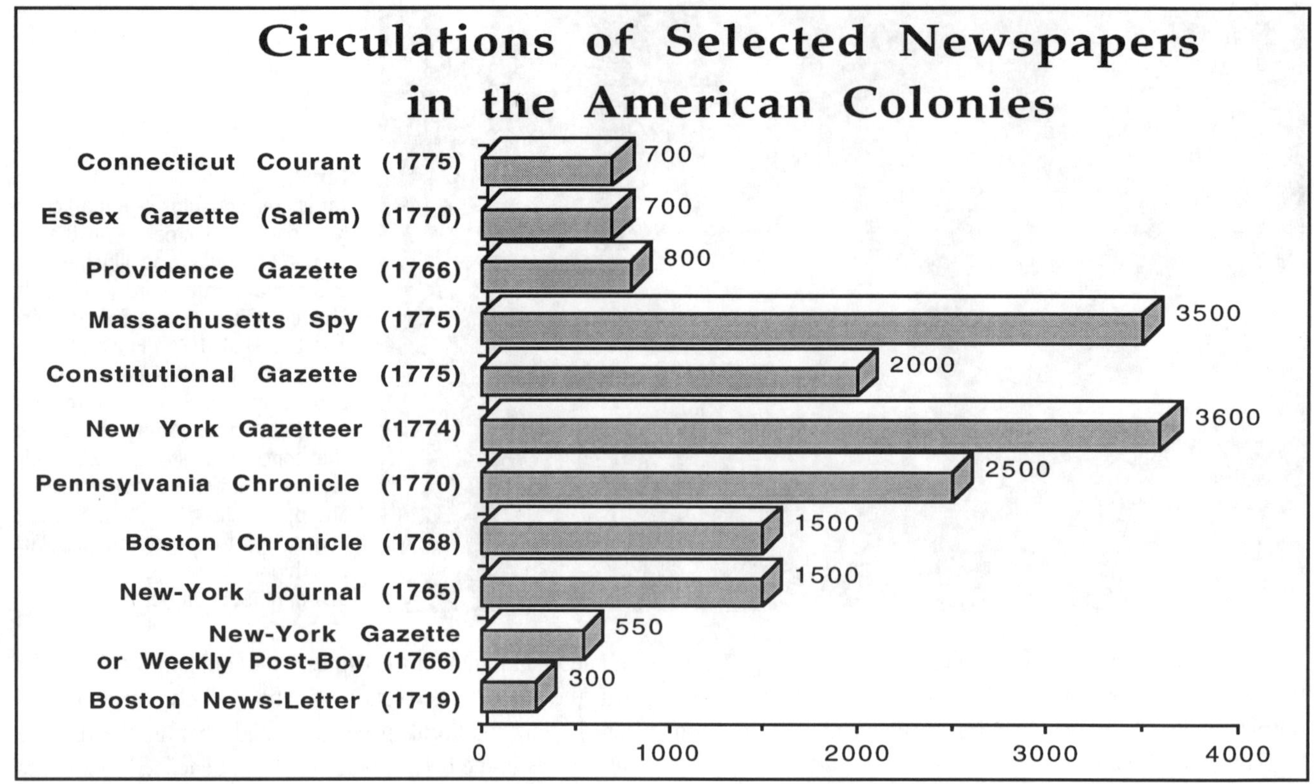

choice. They booked passage to America in the hope of finding freedom in the wilderness. As time passed, more joined them. They tilled the soil, established communities, gave fealty to God, and ultimately became citizens of a truly new social idea. In the process, they instructed their young in Scripture — which required the development of literacy for all. From the earliest days of settlement in America, there was an emphasis on the need for education for the young.

That was particularly true in New England, where colonies founded by religious dissidents, especially the Puritans of Massachusetts, passed compulsory education laws in order to assure that everyone could read the Bible. Parents who did not enforce the rules on education ran the risk of having their children removed from the home and given to others. As the religious requirements abated over time, the practice of requiring schooling for all was maintained as a mark of good citizenship. The emphasis was different in the other colonies, but literacy became increasingly important as the mark of a good citizen. By the time of the Revolution, approximately 85% of the adult men in New England could read, while generally one-half to two-thirds of the adult males in the other colonies were literate.

While such experiences did not produce a mass intellectual elite, they did create opportunities for growth and development of citizens as individuals. Few dreamers envisioned a society in which the majority of its populace could read and write. Still, the educational system that colonials created, supported by public funds, did allow American youth to grow and to participate — through local newspapers, books, and other media forms readily available to them — in public activities at an early age. That outlook did not develop in any other country at that time. Ambrose Serle, a Tory critic of the New York press, wrote in 1776: "One is astonished to see with what avidity they [the colonial newspapers] are sought after, and how implicitly they are believed, by the great Bulk of the People....Government may find it expedient in the sum of things, to employ this popular engine."[4]

The popularity of newspapers provides stark testimony to the interest of a large body of the citizenry in the issues leading to the Revolution. Newspapers circulated widely and were read by the average citizen, not just the aristocrat. Circulation figures reflect a broadly based readership of citizens who were attuned to the events and personalities around them. The Royal Governor of Massachusetts, unnerved over the ranting of the *Boston Gazette*, reported to London: "The misfortune is that seven-eighths of the people read none but this infamous paper."

John Adams testified thus to the reading ability of the American colonials: "The public institutions in New England for the education of youth, supporting colleges at the public expenses, and obliging towns to maintain grammar schools, are not equaled, and never were, in any part of the world."[5] Adams at another point provided further testimony of widespread literacy in America: "A native of America who cannot read and write is as rare an appearance as a Jacobite or a Roman Catholic, that is, as rare as a comet or an earthquake."[6]

Constituting the most literate society in the world at the time,

[4] 26 November 1776, *Journals of Hugh Gaine*, Paul L. Ford, ed. (New York, 1902), I: 57.
[5] Quoted in A.B. Hart, *American History Told by Contemporaries* (New York, 1927), 64.
[6] Quoted in Adrienne Koch and William Peden, eds., *Selected Writings of John and John Quincy Adams* (New York, 1946), 18.

Stamp Act Protests
Perhaps no law in American history evoked such violent opposition as the Stamp Act did. Officials, clergymen, and printers denounced it; and opponents in several towns organized demonstrations against it, hanging effigies of stamp collectors on the community Liberty Tree.

the American colonials used their knowledge to learn about and further their cause in the conflict with Great Britain. Although Americans often disagreed about the details, they generally came to agree that the colonies would be better off if the British monarchy were replaced with a popular form of government.

The Stamp Act of 1765

The clamor over the Stamp Act indicated that relations between the Crown and its colonies likely would worsen. The taxes imposed by the act were, in the colonials' view, excessive. The situation was charged for collision. The Stamp Act, passed March 22, 1765, to become effective November 1, was aimed at raising revenue to help Britain pay its war debts and the costs of protecting American border areas. Unwisely, the British government selected printers, lawyers, and merchants as the targets. Those individuals, along with clergymen, were the best educated and most publicly involved citizens in the colonies. The act required that all legal documents, official papers, books, and newspapers be printed on stamped paper that carried a special tax. It placed an additional tax on each advertisement.

It portended immediate disaster to printers, requiring that taxes be paid at the rate of a halfpenny per halfsheet, a penny for larger page sizes, and two shillings for each advertisement. The income that printers received from subscribers and advertisers was only slightly greater than the taxes. The tax on job printing was just as high, and printing in languages other than English was taxed at double the standard rate. Printers who violated the rules could be fined from forty shillings to ten pounds. If one published anonymously without stamps, he or she would answer in admiralty courts — which had been established originally to try maritime cases — without juries, which seemed a violation of the colonies' traditional rights to try cases of local offenses in local courts before juries of local citizens.

Striking as hard as it did at printers, the tax gave them a special reason to use their newspapers to strongly oppose the Stamp Act. Although at first indecisive, printers shortly began to stiffen their resolve in the face of what they saw as tyranny. David Ramsay, who lived during the Revolution and wrote its history, observed that printers, "when uninfluenced by government, generally arranged themselves on the side of liberty, nor are they less remarkable for attention to the profits of their profession. A stamp duty, which openly invaded the first, and threatened a great diminution of the last, provoked their united zealous opposition."[7] The press war against the Stamp Act began in Boston. Awakened to the dangers building against them, printers there took to their job cases to argue against the act as a frontal assault on the liberty of the people in general and the freedom of the press in particular.

Perhaps no law in American history evoked such violent opposition as the Stamp Act did. Clergymen denounced it from the pulpit. Colonial legislatures and town meetings passed scathing resolutions against it. The Stamp Act Congress in October denounced it as an unconstitutional invasion of the liberties of the colonies. Merchants organized boycotts against British imports. Groups of Sons of Liberty took actions to prevent its enforcement. On May 30, Patrick Henry of Virginia introduced to the House of Burgesses a resolution proclaiming the colonials' right as Englishmen to possess the sole power of taxation. He described anyone who dissented against such a right as an "Enemy to this his Majesty's Colony." It was an astounding pronouncement, especially disturbing to the British authorities because Virginia was the first and most populous colony. Henry's resolution, Massachusetts Governor Francis Bernard feared, "proved an alarm bell to the disaffected."[8]

Meetings called to discuss the Stamp Act sometimes turned into brawls, particularly in Boston and the Middle Colonies; and planned protest rallies and other strategies were devised to nullify the legislation. Trade with Britain dropped precipitously, and colonials refused to pay their British creditors. On June 3, the *New*

[7] David Ramsay, *The History of the American Revolution* (Philadelphia, 1789), I, 61-2.
[8] Letter to Gage, *British Papers Relating to the American Revolution* (Sparks Collection, Harvard College Library, Cambridge, Mass.), I, 43; III, 85.

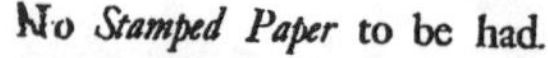
No *Stamped Paper* to be had.

THE PENNSYLVANIA JOURNAL; AND WEEKLY ADVERTISER.

Responses to the Stamp Act
Newspaper printers initially reacted to the Stamp Act of 1765 in a variety of ways. A colonial agent to London when Parliament imposed the Stamp Act, Benjamin Franklin initially tried to get two of his friends appointed as agents to supply the stamps. When he recognized how unpopular the act was, however, he immediately recanted. His printing partner, David Hall, attempted to publish their newspaper, the *Pennsylvania Gazette* (left), safely by noting that publication was continuing without stamps because no stamped paper was available. Their Philadelphia rival, the *Pennsylvania Journal*, took a very different approach. It was among the most defiant. Its front page the day before the law was to take effect was printed in funereal black borders and with a skull of death.

York Post-Boy reported that fewer than a fifth as many ships were working the West Indian routes than before the Stamp Act was enacted. Hard cash was increasingly difficult to find. Business experienced "a most prodigious shock." John Hancock lamented that "times are very bad..., the times will be worse here, in short such is the situation of things here that we do not know who is and who is not safe."[9]

Led by the bolder among them, printers gradually came into full opposition to the law. Eventually, newspapers spoke as if with one voice in opposition to the Stamp Act, as though they had become one "mass medium." They carried detailed accounts of public opposition to the act, noting pointedly the names of tax collectors and stories of their being hanged in effigy. No tax collectors thus dared to distribute the stamped paper, leaving printers on November 1 in a dilemma. The law required that they use nothing but stamped paper, but no such paper was available. The absence of paper did not void the penalties for violation of the law. Printers had to determine what path to take. None intended to pay the tax, but deciding how to proceed was not easy. A few newspapers, mainly in the South, temporarily suspended publication; but others challenged the law one way or another.

Some came out defiantly as usual, appearing without the detestable stamp and proclaiming that the Stamp Act was a direct attack on liberty itself. To protect themselves from authorities, some printers claimed that they continued publishing because of threats from Patriots. John Holt ran an "anonymous" letter in his *New York Gazette or Weekly Post-Boy* threatening his business and his body if he did not publish.[10] Others, unfamiliar with the Stamp Act's fine print, attempted to evade the law by changing their newspapers' names and publishing anonymously. Similarly, some tried to sidestep the letter of the law by removing their serial numbering, thus changing their official status from newspapers to handbills, which were not subject to the act. Even many of those newspapers that suspended temporarily objected vehemently. In late October, the German-language *Philadelphia Staatsbote* outlined its front page in black borders with a skull at the top. On October 31, the day before the act was to take effect, six other papers published with similar make-up, the *Pennsylvania Journal and Weekly Advertiser* assuming the most garish design. It published in the funereal black columns of a tombstone, topped with skull and crossbones, mourning over the death of press liberty.[11] Whatever the course pursued, it is notable that not a single newspaper published on stamped paper.

In March 1766 Parliament, recognizing that the Stamp Act was unenforceable, repealed it. By then, colonial newspapers already had been inspired to oppose British authority. Their continuing opposition helped lead Americans to the Revolution.

Political Passion and Repression

Francis Hopkinson, signer of the Declaration of Independence and member of the Continental Congress, believed the press was vital to Patriot victory in the Revolution, but he argued that newspapers had to play a constructive role in supporting the move for independence. He explained: "[W]hen this privilege is manifestly abused, and the press becomes an engine for sowing the most dangerous dissensions, for spreading false alarms, and undermining the very foundations of government, ought not that government upon the plain principles of self-preservation to silence, by its own authority, such a daring violator of its peace, and tear from its bosom the serpent that would sting it to death?"[12]

Like Hopkinson, Patriots and British officials believed authorities were justified in silencing outrageous speech. Typical of such thinking, a special Patriot commission in Newport, Rhode Island, determined that freedom of the press required "liberal sentiments" but did not allow "wrong sentiments." With a foundation in such thinking, press freedom depended on the issues and circumstances and the degree of clout that Patriots or Tories had. It was permitted for some but not for all.

The Revolutionary period thus created a conflict in terms of modern thinking on freedom of the press. Whereas the modern press is expected to be fair and impartial, a mission, admittedly, it sometimes fails to perform, Patriots and Tories believed that if a

[9]Quoted in *John Hancock: His Book*, A.E. Brown, ed. (Boston, 1898).

[10]*New York Gazette or Weekly Post-Boy*, 7 November 1765.
[11]*Pennsylvania Journal and Weekly Advertiser* (Philadelphia), 31 October 1765.
[12]*Pennsylvania Evening Post* (Philadelphia), 16 November 1776.

Repeal of Stamp Act
When Parliament repealed the Stamp Act in March 1766, colonials eagerly sought details of the news event. They saw repeal as a victory over the unjust taxes of the British government. Colonial newspapers, in leading the opposition to the Stamp Act, gained an important role in the growing opposition to Great Britain.

newspaper were not wholly for their side, it was against them. As a result, as the Patriots gained strength, the greatest danger to freedom of the press came not from British authorities but from Patriot mobs and from threats by groups such as the Sons of Liberty. Relying on extra-legal measures, zealous revolutionaries muffled many voices from New Hampshire to Georgia. The radical Patriots were many and formidable, and they meant business. They trampled on the rights of many people.

One of the few proposals put to the First Continental Congress to strengthen press freedom came from a Tory writing in James Rivington's pro-British *New York Gazetteer*. It read in part: "That whoever, as an instrument of tyranny, or abetter of a mob, shall go about, either by threats, or any other methods to violate the liberty of the press, is an enemy to everything for which a man of sense would think it worth his while to live, or would dare to die."[13]

Such calls for tolerance of dissenting views got a poor reception. Patriots suppressed Royalist papers and condemned Patriot papers when they attempted to be impartial. William Goddard, printer of Baltimore's *Maryland Journal*, quarreled with the local Whig Club, a Patriot organization, over a misunderstood irony in a letter recommending that the colonies accept a British peace offer in 1777. Told to leave town within forty-eight hours, he appealed to the Maryland House of Representatives, the Patriot government. It rebuked the Club. Later, when he printed a letter critical of George Washington, he was mobbed, barely escaped hanging, and was forced to print a recantation. He again appealed for state protection, received it, and printed a repeal of the recantation. In New York, just as the Declaration of Independence was about to be unveiled, Samuel Loudon decided to earn some extra income from the Tory side by printing — not writing — for someone else a rejoinder to Thomas Paine's *Common Sense*. Although Loudon's loyalty to the Patriot cause was undoubted, a mob invaded his home during the night, roughed him up, and destroyed the offending plates. The following day, Loudon received a warning: "Sir, if you print, or suffer to be printed in your press anything against the rights and liberties of America or in favor of our inveterate foes, the King, Ministry, and Parliament of Great Britain, death and destruction, ruin and perdition, shall be your portion. Signed, by order of the Committee of Tarring and Feathering."

[13]Unsigned article by a resident of New Jersey, *Gazetteer*, 2 September 1774.

American Tories

Because of such conditions the British could not use the press effectively. The power of Patriots and the general anti-British sentiment in the colonies made it difficult for Tory newspapers to serve as useful propaganga organs. Life was hazardous for Tory printers. In the pre-war years, they found themselves increasingly intimidated by Patriots, and during the war they had to depend on the British army. They could publish only in those areas the British occupied; they were attacked everywhere else. In the early years of the Revolutionary period, a few printers were staunch Tories, but most who leaned toward the Crown usually tried to be fair, giving both sides. Patriots attacked the latter, however, and finally pushed them fully into the Tory camp. John Mein, one of the notable Tory printers, was typical.

Mein was one of those numerous Europeans who chose to leave their homes and to spend months in the belly of a wooden ship for the opportunity offered in America. A pugnacious Scot, he migrated to Boston, where he opened a bookshop, and soon was on the way to success. Within three years after his arrival, however, he had become the target of radical Patriots. At first, he used the printing firm of Benjamin Edes and John Gill, whose families went back four generations in Boston and who would become two of the most fiery Patriot printers. They frequently published advertisements for Mein in their newspaper, the *Boston Gazette*, thus becoming close business associates. In 1767 Mein launched his own newspaper, the *Boston Chronicle*, intended as a nonpartisan journal.[14] But given the brooding mood of the city since

[14]John Mein, *Proposals for Printing a New Weekly, called The Boston Chronicle* (22 October 1767).

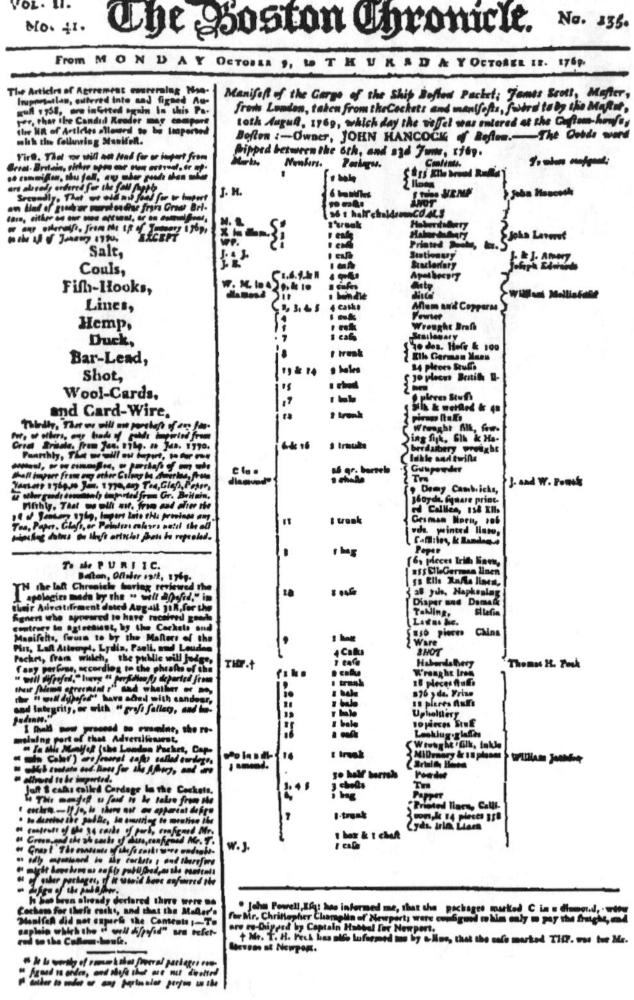

VOL. II. No. 41. **The Boston Chronicle.** No. 135.

From MONDAY OCTOBER 9, to THURSDAY OCTOBER 12. 1769.

The Articles of Agreement concerning Non-Importation, entered into and signed August 1768, are inserted again in this Paper, that the Candid Reader may compare the list of Articles allowed to be imported with the following Manifest.

First, That we will not send for or import from Great-Britain, either upon our own account, or upon commission, this fall, any other goods than what are already ordered for the fall supply.

Secondly, That we will not send for or import any kind of goods or merchandize from Great Britain, either on our own account, or on commission, or any otherwise, from the 1st of January 1769, to the 1st of January 1770. EXCEPT

Salt,
Coals,
Fish-Hooks,
Lines,
Hemp,
Duck,
Bar-Lead,
Shot,
Wool-Cards,
and Card-Wire.

Thirdly, That we will not purchase of any factor, or others, any kinds of goods imported from Great Britain, from Jan. 1769. to Jan. 1770.

Fourthly, That we will not import, on our own account, or on commission, or purchase of any who shall import from any other Colony in America, from January 1769, to Jan. 1770, any Tea, Glass, Paper, or other goods commonly imported from Gr. Britain.

Fifthly, That we will not, from and after the 1st of January 1769, import into this province any Tea, Paper, Glass, or Painters colours until the act imposing duties on those articles shall be repealed.

Manifest of the Cargo of the Ship Boston Packet; James Scott, Master, from London, taken from the Cockets and manifests, sworn to by the Master, 10th August, 1769, which day the vessel was entered at the Custom-house, Boston:—Owner, JOHN HANCOCK *of Boston.—The Goods were shipped between the 6th, and 23d June, 1769.*

To the PUBLIC.
Boston, October 12th, 1769.

IN the last Chronicle having reviewed the apologies made by the "well disposed," in their Advertisement dated August 31st, for the signers who appeared to have received goods contrary to agreement, by the Cockets and Manifests, sworn to by the Masters of the Pitt, Last Attempt, Lydia, Paoli, and London Packet, from which, the public will judge, if any persons, according to the phrase of the "well disposed," have "perfidiously departed from their solemn agreement?" and whether or no, the "well disposed" have acted with candour, and integrity, or with "gross fallacy, and impudence."

I shall now proceed to examine, the remaining part of that Advertisement.

"In this Manifest (the London Packet, Captain Calef) are several casks called cordage, which contain cod-lines for the fishery, and are allowed to be imported."

Just 8 casks called Cordage in the Cockets.

"This manifest is said to be taken from the cockets.—If so, is there not an apparent design to deceive the public, in omitting to mention the contents of the 34 casks of pork, consigned Mr. Green, and the 26 casks of ditto, consigned Mr. T. Gray? The contents of these casks were undoubtedly mentioned in the cockets; and therefore might have been as easily published, as the contents of other packages, if it would have answered the design of the publisher."

It has been already declared there were no Cockets for these casks, and that the Master's Manifest did not express the Contents;—To explain which the "well disposed" are referred to the Custom-house.

"It is worthy of remark that several packages consigned to order, and those that are not directed either to order or any particular person in the

* John Powell, Esq; has informed me, that the packages marked C in a diamond, were for Mr. Christopher Champlin of Newport; were consigned to him only to pay the freight, and are re-shipped by Captain Hubbel for Newport.

† Mr. T. H. Peck has also informed me by a line, that the case marked THP. was for Mr. Stevens at Newport.

John Mein and the *Chronicle*
The publisher of the *Boston Chronicle*, Mein provoked the ire of Patriot committees when he differed with them over policies against importing British goods. In the issue of the *Chronicle* for October 9-16, 1769, he listed names of violators of the non-importation agreements. Facing growing threats in Boston, he eventually fled for England.

the Stamp Act, he immediately got into trouble with Patriot committees over his opposition to the non-importation agreements the Patriots made to resist the Townshend Acts, which Parliament had passed in an effort to raise revenue from the colonies after the repeal of the Stamp Act.

By nature a stubborn man, Mein did not hesitate to criticize the Patriots, and the *Chronicle* grew increasingly pro-British. In 1769 it published a reprint from a London journal that spoke badly of William Pitt, a British statesman who was a favorite of American Whigs. The *Gazette*, which held "impartial" papers in contempt anyway, attacked Mein. The following morning he called on Edes and Gill and demanded that they reveal the identity of the author. When they refused, the Scot invited them outside one at a time. The two held back. Mein then promised "to cane the first one of them I meet..." and departed. On the next afternoon he spied Gill on the street; and "with force of arms, to wit, with a large club," he laid his adversary low with two blows to the head. Then he "beat, wounded, and evil treated" the downed man.[15] Gill won a court judgment of seventy-five pounds. When Mein continued to attack certain Boston "Saints," as he called the radicals, he was hanged in effigy and his home was attacked. When a mob assaulted him on the street, in defending himself he accidentally shot a bystander. To escape prosecution and in fear of his life, he fled to a British ship in Boston harbor and thence to England. The Patriot intimidation of Mein succeeded, noted Tory Peter Oliver, because "the civil power of the country was not sufficient to protect any one who was obnoxious to ye Leaders of the faction,"[16] a statement indicating just how strong the radicals had become. The *Chronicle* ceased publication in 1770.

Of all Tory editors the one with the best imagination and news sense was James "Jemmy" Rivington. The son of a wealthy London publisher, he pursued the family goals of gentility and high style. Something of a rake, he lost in excess of $50,000 playing the horses, one reason he moved to the New World. In Philadelphia he opened a bookstore and then expanded his business to include New York and Boston. Urbane and friendly, he became a popular figure among the upper crust. In 1773 he founded the *New York Gazetteer*. The remainder of the paper's name, *or the Connecticut, Hudson's River, New Jersey, and Quebeck Weekly Advertiser*, indicated something of Rivington's ego and expansive vision. The *Gazetteer* may have been the best printed and most informative newspaper in colonial America. It proved a winner from the outset, with circulation quickly reaching an impressive 3,600 copies, primarily among well-to-do Tories. Included were readers in the West Indies, England, France, and Ireland. But Rivington gained few adherents among Patriots. With his regal bearing and foppish ways, he offered little that they wished to emulate. He thought the Patriot newspapers' claim that they supported truth and justice was ridiculous. As tensions heightened, he vowed that the *Gazetteer*, as it always had done, would continue to offer impartiality equally to the "'sons of freedom' and to those who have differed in sentiments from them." He emphasized the point by running beneath the paper's nameplate the line: "PRINTED at his OPEN and UNINFLUENCED PRESS."

Rivington at first printed both Patriot and Tory contributions. For doing so, the Sons of Liberty hanged him in effigy and destroyed his shop. He then became more openly sympathetic to the British. While most papers had begun to remove royal crests from their nameplates in favor of more "democratic" labels, Rivington made a show of his support for the Crown. Finally the inevitable storm broke. In May of 1775 the paper's office was mobbed, and Rivington barely saved his skin thanks to the action of friends. He then was arrested and forced to sign an oath of allegiance to the colonial cause. Once released from jail, however, he continued to print in favor of the British. In November, "King"

15 *Boston Gazette*, 28 August 1769; 15 and 30 January 1770.

16 Quoted in Douglas Adair and John Shutz, eds., *Peter Oliver's Origin & Progress of the American Rebellion: A Tory View* (San Marino, Calif., 1961), 62.

RIVINGTON'S
NEW-YO[illegible] GAZETTEER;
WEEKLY ADVERTISER.

Jemmy Rivington, Tory
Challenging the radical Patriots' threat that newspapers had to choose sides, the royalist James Rivington claimed to publish an unbiased newspaper. To goad them, he used the slogan "Printed at his Open and Uninfluenced Press" for his *New York Gazetteer.* For his bold opposition to the Patriot cause, Rivington became a target of numerous threats. When a mob hanged him in effigy, he published an engraving of the scene in his own newspaper. He reported that "some of the lower class of inhabitants" of New Jersey had done the deed "merely for [his] acting consistent with his profession as a free printer."

Isaac Sears, a fugitive from justice and a notorious tough, led a Patriot mob, supported by seventy-five members of the Connecticut Light Horse, against Rivington. They demolished his press and carried off the type. Rivington fled to England, where he gained an appointment as the "King's Printer" in New York. Returning to the colonies, he began publishing the *Royal Gazette* (nicknamed "Rivington's Lying Gazette" by Patriots), issuing deliberately warped accounts of battles and Patriot leaders. At the end of the war, he was forced to suspend publication. Although he apologized for his record, he was beaten once and was thrown into debtor's prison for other people's debts. He died in poverty on Independence Day 1802.

Second only to Rivington in New York Tory printing — and as dedicated — was Hugh Gaine, publisher of the *New York Mercury* (later *Gazette and Weekly Mercury*). An Anglican by faith, he was appointed official printer to the English church and identified with it politically. Most of the paper's coverage dealt with political information copied from Boston papers with pro-British leanings. Although Gaine published first with a non-partisan slant, his basic Tory sentiment earned him respectability among Tory readers. With the onset of the war, he moved to Newark, New Jersey, where for a short time he appeared to support the colonials. Within a month, however, he made amends with the British and returned to New York, which the British army recently had captured. Because of his switching of sides, he gained the Patriot nickname "Hugh Gaine, the Turncoat." At the war's end, he was bold enough to petition the New York legislature to permit him to remain and succeeded in escaping official retribution.

The Patriot Press

The Patriot press of the Revolutionary period is best understood as an organ for promoting ideology. Before the war, printers intensified their propaganda efforts against Britain but escaped prosecution because of popular opposition to British authority. Grand juries, made up of colonials, would not indict offending printers; and authorities feared that more high-handed or extralegal measures would invite violent opposition. Despite such complaints as one by Lord Frederick North, First Lord of the Treasury, that no one could "recollect a period when the press groan'd with such a variety of desperate libels,"[17] the government grew increasingly lax in restricting printers. Having set the precedent during the Stamp Act crisis, authorities discovered they had more and more difficulty reining in insolent printers afterwards. They faced the dilemma of wanting to punish offenders while fearing the result if they attempted to do so.

Isaiah Thomas, proprietor of the *Massachusetts Spy*, was one of many printers who flouted authorities because of their quandary. Summoned before the governor's council for essays critical of Governor Thomas Hutchinson, Thomas snubbed the council's messenger and ignored the order to appear.[18] The council then voted to prosecute him for seditious libel, to which Thomas, joined by a chorus of writers in other papers, responded with trenchant attacks on those officials who would regard freedom of the press so lightly and attempt to punish someone for printing the truth. The council persisted in pursuing the case, presenting its charges to a grand jury three months later. The jury refused to indict Thomas. The council believed the jury had been packed but decided to drop the case. "No writer," one essayist in the *Spy* then gibed at Hutchinson, "needs now to stand in fear of you."[19]

Ideologists are most forceful when convinced they are right.

[17] Speech reported in the *Massachusetts Gazette and Boston Post-Boy*, 22 April 1771.
[18] *Massachusetts Spy* (Boston), 14 November 1771.
[19] Ibid., 30 July 1772.

John Dickinson, "Farmer"
In the essays titled "Letters from a Farmer in Pennsylvania," Dickinson, a Philadelphia lawyer, argued effectively against British tax policies in 1767 and 1768. Although he opposed separation from England, once the colonies declared their independence in 1776, he went on active duty as a colonel in the American army.

Patriot printers were no exception. They believed zealously that they advocated justice and that truth was on their side. Those who opposed them supported injustice and were backed only by error and deceit. Such an outlook made necessary a selective use of material in Patriot newspapers, for to publish material opposed to truth did nothing to advance justice and liberty. "My paper," wrote Henry Holt of the *New York Journal*, "is sacred to the cause of truth and justice, and I have preferred the pieces, that in my opinion, are the most necessary to the support of that cause" rather than material that propagated "barefaced attempts to deceive and impose upon the ignorant."[20] To do otherwise, Patriots argued, to print both sides, would give support to those ideas and practices damaging to mankind and liberty. Using such reasoning, printers devoted their newspapers wholeheartedly to colonial freedom and, eventually, separation from Britain. With the coming of the Revolution itself, they did not stint in encouraging the war effort.

Concerted opposition to the British had begun with the Stamp Act. The newspapers' success in helping to get the act repealed emboldened printers to defy British authorities and showed that the press could be used as an effective propaganda tool. The press therefore came to be regarded as a strong arm of the Patriot movement, and several writers and printers gained widespread recognition.

Voices of Revolt

With the calm that had settled in following repeal of the Stamp Act, colonial unrest might not have gotten out of hand if the British treasury's need for revenue had gone away. The problem remained. To solve it, the new Chancellor of the Exchequer, Charles Townshend, devised a plan to place duties on goods imported into the colonies. In a series of "Letters from a Farmer in Pennsylvania to the Inhabitants of the British Colonies," John Dickinson attacked the taxes on the grounds that they were not for regulation of trade but for raising revenue through "external taxes," which Parliament did not have the power to do. The letters were published first in the *Pennsylvania Chronicle* in 1767 and 1768. They were sound in argument, reasonable in tone, and clear and forceful in style. They did not urge independence from the mother country; and indeed Dickinson clearly opposed separation. The letters were, however, important in the move toward independence because of their influence in prompting the merchant and business class to question British policy.

Boston Patriots were the most industrious in the colonies in promoting independence, and to that end they produced a widely circulated "Journal of Occurrences." Published from late 1768 through the first half of the following year, it detailed Boston's suffering under the Townshend Acts and British military rule. Newspapers throughout the colonies picked up items from it, resulting in the publication of Boston Patriots' views throughout the land.

The most aggressive writer was Sam Adams, a leader of the radical Caucus Club in Boston. Members of the Club were committed to independence and, through their writing for the *Boston Gazette* and other activities, exercised a strong leadership in political action in the colonies. It was said that America's course was determined by Massachusetts, that Massachusetts' was determined by Boston, and that Boston's was determined by Adams. It was Adams who, because of his *Gazette* writing and his talent for propaganda, did more than anyone else to promote colonial independence from Britain as a practical, realistic action.

The *Gazette* was the chief radical newspaper in the colonies; and its owners, Benjamin Edes and John Gill, were the most strident newspaper critics of the British prior to the Revolution. Edes, the more belligerent of the pair, was a man for his time. A mover of political causes, he was intelligent, tough, and dedicated. By 1765 he had served as Boston's Town Constable, Town Scavenger, and Clerk of the Market. He was active in the North End Caucus, a political organization that offered opportunities for debating current issues, airing views, and, in time, hatching intrigues against authority. In 1763, John Adams attended a meeting of that

[20] *New York Journal*, 5 January 1775.

For NEW-YORK.

Elizabeth Clark & Nowell,

All sorts of GARDEN SEEDS.

By Elizabeth Greenleaf,

All sorts of GARDEN SEEDS.

Bethiah Oliver,

All sorts of GARDEN SEEDS.

A FARM in Worcester,

TO BE SOLD

On THURSDAY next,

By Benjamin Church,

ON TUESDAY NEXT,

CUSTOM-HOUSE, BOSTON.

John Baker,

A few Bags of the best Cocoa,

Boston Incendiaries

In Boston, the hotbed of the revolutionary movement, Sam Adams (left) kept the fire stoked with his writing and rabble-rousing. Mobs burned British records and pillaged the home of Chief Justice Thomas Hutchinson. Sam's cousin John Adams, future president of the United States, described the situation, "Our Presses have groaned.... The Crown officers have every where trembled." Sam Adams was connected with the chief radical newspaper in the colonies, Edes and Gill's *Boston Gazette*. It was instrumental in stirring up opposition to the British. When British soldiers fired on a Boston mob, Adams, Edes and Gill, and the Sons of Liberty labeled the incident a "massacre." The *Gazette's* account included woodcuts of caskets representing the Bostonians who were killed. At trial, the commander of the soldiers was defended by John Adams and acquitted.

body and attested to its political muscle. Everyone, Adams noted, smoked pipes and drank "Phlip" while selecting "Assessors, Collectors, Wardens, Fire Wards, and representatives" even before they had been selected by the town. Edes also held membership in the "Loyal Nine," that exclusive group of Whigs that would form the nucleus of the Sons of Liberty. Some of its primary functions were to develop strategies to oppose Parliament's authority in the colonies, intimidate Loyalists, and bring moderates into line. Even Sam Adams did not hold membership in that select organization, although he did ally himself with it. Beginning with the Stamp Act crisis, Edes assumed increasing responsibility in the resistance movement.

On the morning of August 14, 1765, residents of Newbury Street stepped from their dwellings to find an effigy of Andrew Oliver, the hated stamp master-designate and secretary of the province, dangling from the Liberty Tree. Alongside hung a huge boot, symbolic of Lord Bute, a power behind the detested tax. Out of the boot peeped a stuffed replica of the devil clutching a copy of the Stamp Act. Oliver's likeness was the creation of Benjamin Edes. The day's activities culminated in the destruction of Oliver's house by the Sons of Liberty, engineered by the Sons' leadership, including Edes. The following week Lieutenant-Governor Thomas Hutchinson's mansion fell to the same fate as the Sons destroyed the place and everything in it. Then they pried all the slates from the roof and cut down every tree on the grounds.

When the Tea Act of 1773 brought the issue of British trade monopoly to a boil, Edes was one of a number of Bostonians who guarded the wharves to prevent the opposition from landing the now-hated herb. Matters deteriorated rapidly until, on the afternoon of December 16, 1773, a group of radicals joined Edes at his home. There they discussed the tea issue, drank considerably from a china punch bowl, and at dark went to the *Gazette* office nearby. Others who had attended another meeting at Old South Church met them, and all donned Indian disguises. They then proceeded to Boston Harbor, where they boarded three ships and dumped 342 chests of tea overboard.

The hapless Boston Tories railed among themselves to salve their frustration. As one of their journalists wrote: "The last Edes and Gill Newspaper is a torrent of envious Calumny, dirtily poured forth from a Sink of Meanness and Defamation." Another complained that "The foul-mouthed Trumpeters of Sedition [Edes and Gill] bellow and rave and drivel like Mad-dogs and clumsy Curdogs, under a dying Man's window...."[21] Even though Edes and Gill had provided the cutting edge for much of the revolutionary movement, they dissolved their partnership in 1775, on the eve of the Revolution. Each attempted a paper on his own, but neither approached the success of the *Gazette*. Both died in poverty after the war.

The best known writer of the Revolution was Thomas Paine, a professional rebel. His pamphlet *Common Sense* (1776) confronted colonials directly with the idea of independence, paving the way, some historians think, for the Declaration of Independence. His first "American Crisis" paper, beginning with the stirring words "These are the times that try men's souls...," was published in the *Pennsylvania Journal* on December 19, 1776, during the colonies' darkest hours of the war. Suffering successive defeats, General George Washington had retreated into New Jersey. Civilians were dejected. Something had to be done. Legend has it that Paine composed the "Crisis" essay on the head of a drum at a fire

[21]Reprinted in *Boston Gazette*, 5 October and 21 December 1767.

Thomas Paine
Paine, the author of the pamphlet *Common Sense*, was one of the most forceful writers of the Revolution. After his death in 1809, Thomas Jefferson said of him: "No writer has exceeded Paine in ease and familiarity of style, in perspicuity of expression, happiness of elucidation, and in simple and unassuming language."

in Washington's army camp, with the cold and ragged soldiers gathered around. After appearing in the *Journal*, the essay was published in pamphlet form. Washington read the essay, was greatly moved, and ordered it read aloud to his assembled troops.

According to tradition, Paine's appeal to patriots, especially its sonorous opening lines, had an immediate and heartening effect on the soldiers. On Christmas night Washington led his troops across the Delaware River through a violent snowstorm, and, early the next morning, they attacked the Hessian mercenaries the British had hired. Washington's surprise attack succeeded. His forces routed the enemy and captured the garrison at Trenton. In the battle, thirty Hessians were killed and about 1,000 were taken prisoner. American casualties were minimal — two officers and two men were wounded. That victory, coupled with another a week later, revived American morale and was one of the major turning points in the war. After the American Revolution ended, Paine went to France to assist in its revolution. He returned to America in 1801 and later died in poverty, ostracized for his attacks on religion.

Whereas Edes and Gill's *Boston Gazette* was the leading radical newspaper before the Revolution, Isaiah Thomas' *Massachusetts Spy* was the most incendiary publication during the Revolution. Prior to the war, Thomas had been outspoken in his support for independence. He revived the "Join or Die" divided-snake device that Benjamin Franklin had created in 1754, and he never softened his attacks on British trampling of colonial rights and liberties. Accounts such as his reporting of the battle of Lexington in 1775 were designed to stir up the anger of colonials. That account began with this call for action:

> Americans! Forever bear in mind the BATTLE OF LEXINGTON! — where British troops, unmolested and unprovoked, wantonly and in a most inhuman manner, fired upon and killed a number of our countrymen, then robbed, ransacked, and burned their houses! nor could the tears of defenseless women, some of whom were in the pains of childbirth, the cries of helpless babes, nor the prayers of age, confined to beds of sickness, appease their thirst for blood! — or divert them from their DESIGN OF MURDER and ROBBERY![22]

After the Revolution, Thomas became manifestly successful as a printer and historian, writing the first history of printing in America and founding the American Antiquarian Society.

More important than any single writer, however, were the Patriots' committees of correspondence. They were created to distribute information and ideas among towns and colonies and to newspapers. Although similar committees had been used on an *ad hoc* basis by clergymen and merchants in the early 1760s, the impetus for the establishment of standing committees devoted to the Patriot cause came in 1772. In the wake of the attempts by Massachusetts' Governor Hutchinson to insulate the courts from colonial influence, Sam Adams issued a call for standing committees to be set up to resist the action. A Boston town meeting in November appointed a standing committee, and Patriots in other towns and colonies soon followed. They eventually established more than eighty committees. Each circulated letters to other committees and provided propaganda to newspapers. In that way, they succeeded through informal organization at their goals of keeping the colonies informed of events, issues, and opinions and stirring up antagonism to British efforts to suppress colonial opponents.

The Press as Morale Booster

During the years of actual fighting, the press played a vital role as it provided information about the war. More than any other institution, it encouraged the people to support the war effort. Thus, newspapers became the primary morale boosters throughout the Revolutionary era. Printers such as Benjamin Edes and Isaiah Thomas used a variety of means to lift public confidence in the drive for independence. Throughout the war, essays and news stories emphasized the tyranny and corruption of the British and

[22] *Massachusetts Spy*, 3 May 1775.

Isaiah Thomas
Thomas produced one of the leading journals favoring the Patriot cause, the *Massachusetts Spy.* After the Revolution, he became the first historian of American journalism.

the glory and justness of the American cause.

Patriot newspapers sought to destroy any remaining colonial ties to Great Britain. Describing George III as the "whining King of Great Britain,"[23] the press urged Americans to discard all loyalty to the mother country. Accusations of cruelty and barbarity by the British and their Tory supporters filled newspapers. In 1781, for example, several printers accused Lord Charles Cornwallis of trying to spread smallpox in the South. This plot, a writer declared, "must render him contemptible in the eyes of every civilized nation, it being a practice inconsistent with the law of nations and as repugnant to humanity."[24]

Even more important for morale than attacks on the British were discussions of American successes and future prospects. Printers filled their pages with discussions of the justness of the American cause and the success of the Continental Army in battle. There was no doubt that the United States would be victorious, for, as one newspaper writer averred, "it is allowed on all hands that the American Army is now equal at least to any in the world for discipline, activity and bravery. There are no soldiers in Europe more exemplary for subordination, regularity of conduct, patience in fatigues and hardships, perseverance in service, and intrepidity in danger."[25] Newspapers worked to increase public resolve by urging all readers to put the war above all other concerns. In 1776, Isaiah Thomas proposed: "Let us not busy ourselves now about our private internal affairs, but with the utmost care and caution, attend to the grand American controversy, and assist her in her earnest struggle in support of her natural rights and freedom."[26] Similar sentiments appeared throughout the war. According to Revolutionary printers, such efforts would produce final victory. Through such discussions, the press sought to help achieve victory by assuring that American morale remained high throughout the armed conflict.

During the war, printers filled their newspapers with stories and essays about the fighting. While obviously seeking to keep readers informed, they also hoped to keep them concerned as well. Newspaper efforts to encourage support and involvement and to boost morale went on for years, for the war proved to be a long one. As it came to a close, Benjamin Franklin praised newspapers for their usefulness, for, he explained, "by the press we can speak to nations.... And we now find, that it is not only right to strike while the iron is hot, but that it may be very practicable to heat it by continually striking."[27] This the patriot newspapers had clearly done, through both defeat and victory, by their nonstop discussion of the war.

The Influence of the Patriot Press

One of the most intriguing questions about the Revolutionary press is what influence it may have had. What role did newspapers, pamphlets, broadsides, and other printed forms have on the initiation and execution of the Revolution? There is no easy answer, for there is no method of determining beyond doubt what the press' influence, if any, was. Today, researchers have enough difficulty determining how persuasive the mass media are, and some argue that the media are only one factor among many that affect people's opinions, with some of the other factors having more importance. If determining causal factors is difficult in contemporary research, it is virtually impossible to do in historical research. No "scientific" measurements such as opinion polls were taken during the Revolutionary period. In the absence of such measures, the historian is left with relying on what contemporaries said about the role of the press. On that issue, contemporaries were in agreement. To a person, they believed that the press exercised a major influence.

Printers, Patriot spokesmen, and government authorities clearly thought the press was important. Otherwise, they would not have placed so much emphasis on it. Washington and other Patriot leaders went to great lengths to aid it, writers and printers used it to express their views to attempt to sway public opinion, and British authorities attempted to suppress it. As early as the mid-

[23]*Boston Gazette*, 19 February 1776.
[24]*Maryland Gazette* (Annapolis), reprinted in *Salem Gazette*, 6 December 1781.
[25]*American Journal* (Providence), 16 December 1779.
[26]*Massachusetts Spy* (Worcester), 28 June 1776.
[27]Benjamin Franklin to Richard Price, 13 June 1782, *Benjamin Franklin: Writings*, ed. J. A. Leo Lemay (New York, 1987), 1049-50.

July 10, 1776. NUMB. 2481.

The PENNSYLVANIA GAZETTE.

Containing the Freshest Advices, Foreign and Domestic.

In CONGRESS, July 4, 1776.
A DECLARATION
By the REPRESENTATIVES of the UNITED STATES of AMERICA, in General Congress assembled.

Independence
Contemporaries and historians have credited the Patriot press with having a large hand in the decision by the colonies to separate from England. When the Continental Congress adopted the Declaration of Independence in 1776, most colonial newspapers, as the *Pennsylvania Gazette* did, printed on page one the document they had helped to initiate.

1760s the view was widespread that newspapers were playing a central role in affecting popular opinion. A writer in the *Maryland Gazette* in 1766, commenting on the newspaper's success in opposing the Stamp Act, expressed that view. "The Press," he declared, "hath never done greater Service since its first Invention."

David Ramsay, a Patriot who participated in Revolutionary activities and then wrote the earliest history of the war, concluded that the press was among the most important ingredients in bringing about the Revolution. He wrote: "The exertions of the army would have been insufficient to effect the revolution, unless the great body of the people had been prepared for it, and also kept in a constant disposition to oppose Great Britain.... In establishing American independence, the pen and the press had a merit equal to that of the sword."[28] The number of such comments by contemporaries could be multiplied indefinitely. They make clear the conclusion of people who lived during the period: the press was indispensable in affecting public sentiment leading to the Revolution.

Most historians have reached the same conclusion. Of the leading studies on printing and the Revolution, only one has challenged it. In *Broadsides and Bayonets: The Propaganda War of the American Revolution* (1961), a study of the years of actual warfare, Carl Berger argued that propagandists' schemes were less meaningful in affecting opinions and beliefs than were events. Words were less important than facts. By 1777 at the latest, Berger argued, most minds were made up, and propaganda efforts could do little to change them. British and American supporters and officials made a number of attempts to convert, persuade, or intimidate people who seemed vulnerable, but most were futile — because hard facts and people's beliefs about what was really occurring held more weight than what propagandists told people to believe. The greatest impact on public opinion, according to Berger, came not from the work of propagandists but from news of the war. As a rule, neither persuasive appeal, nor threats, nor tricks could compare in influence with military success or political and economic facts.

Berger was the exception among historians. Arthur M. Schlesinger, the first historian to provide an extensive documentation of press influence, argued that the most important factor in bringing about the Revolution was public opinion and that in changing public opinion the newspaper was the primary agent. When colonials, Schlesinger said, "began to feel the tightening grip of imperial control after 1763, they naturally resorted to the printing press to disseminate their views and consolidate a favorable public support."[29] Schlesinger's *Prelude to Independence: The Newspaper War on Great Britain, 1764-1776* (1958) studied the role of the press in bringing about what John Adams called the "real American revolution": the "radical change in the principles, opinions, sentiments, and affections of the people" that preceded the Revolution.[30] Unlike most colonials, who saw events from the limited perspective of their own colony, printer-editors often had moved around among several colonies and thus were more continental in their outlook. They therefore held the view that what affected one colony affected all, and they advocated unity among the colonies. The repeal of the Stamp Act was a tremendous victory for the press, Schlesinger argued, and encouraged printers to oppose British authority more intensely. In many events afterward, such as the public uproar against the Tea Act of 1773, it was the newspapers that played a leading role. Eventually, the press' agitation resulted in a declaration of war. While Schlesinger pointed out that a number of factors other than newspapers had helped insti-

[28]Ramsay, *History of the American Revolution*, II, 319.

[29]Arthur M. Schlesinger, "The Colonial Newspapers and the Stamp Act," *New England Quarterly* 8 (1935): 63-83.

[30]Letter to Hezekiah Niles, *The Works of John Adams*, C. F. Adams, ed. (Boston, 1850-56), 282-3.

Cornwallis TAKEN!

BOSTON, (Friday) October 26, 1781.

This Morning an Expreſs arrived from Providence to HIS EXCELLENCY the GOVERNOR, with the following IMPORTANT INTELLIGENCE, viz.—

PROVIDENCE, Oct. 25, 1781. Three o'Clock, P. M.

This Moment an Expreſs arrived at his Honor the Deputy-Governor's, from Col. Chriſtopher Olney, Commandant on Rhode-Iſland, announcing the important Intelligence of the Surrender of Lord CORNWALLIS and his Army; an Account of which was Printed this Morning at Newport, and is as follows, viz.—

NEWPORT, October 25, 1781.

YESTERDAY Afternoon arrived in this Harbour Capt. Lovett, of the Schooner Adventure, from York River, in Cheſapeak Bay, (which he left the 20th inſtant,) and brought us the glorious News of the Surrender of Lord Cornwallis and his Army Priſoners of War to the allied Army, under the Command of our illuſtrious General; and the French Fleet, under the Command of His Excellency the Count de Graſſe.

A Ceſſation of Arms took Place on Thurſday the 18th Inſtant in Conſequence of Propoſals from Lord CORNWALLIS for a Capitulation.—His Lordſhip propoſed a Ceſſation of Twenty-four Hours, but Two only were granted by His Excellency General WASHINGTON. The Articles were compleated the ſame Day, and the next Day the allied Army took Poſſeſſion of York Town.

By this glorious Conqueſt, NINE-THOUSAND of the Enemy, including Seamen, fell into our Hands, with an immenſe Quantity of Warlike Stores, a Forty-Gun Ship, a Frigate, an armed Veſſel, and about One Hundred Sail of Tranſports.

Printed by B. Edes and Sons, in State Street.

Victory!
When Lord Cornwallis, commander of the British army at Yorktown, Virginia, surrendered, news sped through the states. This broadside records the movement of the news north. Cornwallis' troops had laid down their arms at 2 p.m. on Friday, October 19, 1781. Rhode Island got the news on Thursday, October 25, and Boston the following day.

gate the war, he argued that the independence movement could not have succeeded "without an alert and dedicated press." Most historians have agreed with Schlesinger.

Although there is disagreement concerning the impact of the Revolutionary newspapers on public opinion, there is little doubt that they fulfilled an important role during the war. They constituted the primary sources of information about the conflict. Although reports were not always accurate, printers hoped they would boost morale by helping to maintain interest in, and support for, the war effort. By publishing accounts from throughout the colonies, the newspapers helped foster a sense of unity and solidarity of purpose that was essential for a successful revolt.

The War's Effect on the Press

War is not good for the press. Readership may go up and circulation increase because of interest in military events, but war's damages are greater than benefits. Just as that principle has applied to other wars in America's history, it was true of the press during the Revolution. Military operations disrupted publishing, fervor created by the dangers and passions of war restricted freedom of expression, news coverage was made difficult, printing materials were in short supply, and newspaper survival was endangered.

The fortunes of both Patriot and Tory newspapers depended on which army controlled the towns in which they published. Several printers had to flee hurriedly as the opposing army approached. Those who did not move quickly enough had their presses confiscated. Typical was the plight of John Holt of the *New York Journal or General Advertiser*. The British forced him to leave New York City and chased him about Connecticut for several months. Finally he set up a printing shop in Kingston, New York, where he printed a newspaper for less than four months. The British army caught up, burned Kingston, and destroyed part of his materials. He then fled to Poughkeepsie, where he managed to publish a paper with repeated military interruptions until the end of the Revolution. William Bradford, III, Patriot printer of Philadelphia's *Pennsylvania Journal*, had similar experiences. Although he was fifty-seven years old at the onset of the Revolution, he served in the army while continuing to publish the *Journal*. He suspended the paper while fighting with the army in the campaign around Trenton in December 1776-January 1777 and again from September 1777 to June 1778 when the British occupied Philadelphia. When the army left the city, Bradford again resumed publication, but the rigors of his military service left his health and business ruined.

As if military dangers were not enough, Tory printers faced the added threats from Patriot mobs and governing bodies. Although James Johnston of the *Georgia Gazette* was Royalist in sympathy, even after the shots fired at Lexington in 1775 he was able by his impartiality to continue the paper into the following year. At that time, the Georgia Council of Safety forced it to suspend. When the British army occupied Savannah, Johnston resumed publication and was able to continue for three years. At the end of the war, however, Patriots declared him a traitor and forced him to leave Savannah.

Benjamin Towne provides another typical Tory story. At first, he placed his *Pennsylvania Evening Post* on the Patriot side and succeeded in driving his Tory competitor out of Philadelphia through his constant criticism, and he was the first newspaper publisher to print the Declaration of Independence in 1776. When the British took Philadelphia, although several other printers fled, Towne stayed and ingratiated himself to British officers by changing his politics. When the British army evacuated the city, the other Tory printers fled, but again Towne stayed, changed his politics, and was allowed to continue his paper, although he was unable to win back his earlier circulation and was ostracized by Patriots.

For all papers, the war added difficulties to a news gathering system that was not sophisticated, to say the least. Neither newspapers nor British or Patriot leaders provided for anything approaching organized coverage of the Revolution. Newspapers relied for their information on the chance arrival of private letters, official messages, and other newspapers. Each paper printed some local information that others picked up, but even that information was paltry; and reports of major events sometimes consisted of no more than a paragraph. While such a system during peacetime functioned reasonably well for colonial purposes, it was by later standards crude at best, and war added difficulties. News was tardy. The postal service, which barely had developed beyond its infancy, was hampered by the interference of military campaigns, poor financing, and bad roads that stayed in disrepair. English newspapers, which had been a prime source of news before the war, were received irregularly. As a result, news of major events sometimes was delayed a month or more, Americans were ill-supplied with information, and rumors and false news abounded.

One of the Patriot press' biggest problems was shortage of supplies, especially newsprint. As a reaction to the Stamp Act and the Townshend Acts, colonials had agreed not to import certain items from Britain, giving Americans the impetus to begin manufacturing presses and type. Paper mills also multiplied in number; but even though sixty or so existed in the colonies at the time of the Revolution, shortages in the paper supply caused the press much trouble. Paper prices went up sharply, mainly because of the scarcity of rags needed in papermaking. The threat that the shortage might mean a cessation or at least a substantial diminution of newspaper publishing worried Patriot leaders. Newspapers carried pleas for saving rags, and Patriot organizations and town meetings gave prizes to women who showed the greatest patriotism by saving the most rags. Even George Washington took time from his military duties to urge women to save the smallest scraps as a patriotic duty.

Although not telling the whole story, the figures on newspaper mortality reveal something of the effect of the Revolution. At the beginning of the war, thirty-seven newspapers were publishing in the colonies. Seventeen of those died during the war, leaving twenty publishing at its end. Thirty-three new papers were started. Of those, eighteen died and fifteen survived. Thus, at the end of the war, thirty-five newspapers were publishing, two fewer than at the beginning. While a difference of two may seem of little importance, it does not indicate the magnitude of the war's effect. At one time or another, seventy papers were being published during the Revolution; only half survived. Such a high death rate during a period of seven years illustrates the hazards war posed for publishing.

The most important impact of the Revolution on the press, however, lay in the change the War of Independence brought to

THE

GEORGIA GAZETTE.

NUMBER 1. THURSDAY, APRIL 7, 1763.

EUROPEAN INTELLIGENCE.

Moscow, November 15.

THE Empress keeps her apartments, not through illness but precaution. The Count Woronzow has given a grand entertainment to the Earl of Buckinghamshire, to which all the foreign ministers were invited.

Vienna, Dec. 11. We daily expect the news of a general action between the Prince of Holberg and the Prussians in Franconia.

Hamburgh, Dec. 17. The Prussian irruption into Franconia makes a great noise. The princes of the empire once took a resolution to apply for succour to the French King as guarantee of the treaty of Westphalia, but this design was waved on their being informed that the French troops were in consequence of the preliminaries between England and that crown, to evacuate the empire so soon as the ratifications were exchanged, and to return no more during this war.

Hague, Dec. 21. We hear from Madrid, that the King of Spain has granted a pension of ten thousand livres to the widow of Don Velasco, who so bravely defended the Moro Fort at the Havanna; and has given his son a title of nobility in Castile, which he is to bear by the name of the Marquis of the Fort Moro. His Majesty has likewise given directions, that there should be always, for the future, one ship in the royal navy of the name of Velasco.

Paris, Dec. 27. The Duke of Bedford is preparing a grand equipage, in order to his public entry in quality of Embassador Extraordinary from his Britannick Majesty, which is to be made about the middle of February next. This ceremony will give an additional lustre to the festivals then to be celebrated on account of the conclusion of the peace; and, to augment the splendor of this solemnity, an equestrian statue of his present Majesty, already finished, is then to be erected.

LONDON, *December* 24.

Admiralty-Office, December 24.

VICE-Admiral Sir Charles Saunders gives an account, in his letter of the 9th of last month, from Gibraltar, that the day before arrived at that port, his Majesty's ship the Brune, commanded by Capt. Tonyn, with the Oiseau, a French frigate of 26 guns, and about 240 men, which he fell in with and took the 23d of October, about seven leagues N. W. by W. from Carthagena. The Brune had six men killed, and 14 wounded, in the engagement; and there were 49 killed and wounded on board the Oiseau. The Chevalier de Modene, her Captain, lost his right arm: Three of his officers are wounded, and all the rest of them killed. *London Gazette.*

Dec. 27. It is reported that the Earl of Granville will soon resign his place of President of the Council on account of his great age and bad state of health, and that the Lord Chancellor is to resign the seals and succeed him in that important office, which will occasion a general promotion among the gentlemen of the law.

From Ratisbon they send us a rumour that the Ministers of England and Prussia have been ordered by the Grand Signior to quit Constantinople.

Letters by this day's mail advise, that a negotiation between the courts of Vienna and Berlin is in great forwardness.

We have also a report that the Count de Seilern is coming to England with the character of Minister Plenipotentiary from the Empress Queen to renew the good understanding between the two courts.

It is very strongly affirmed that the French have already sent ten men of war to the East-Indies, in order to be beforehand with us, and shew us some true French faith; and that a fleet of ours is already going there.

It is also affirmed that great obstacles to the definitive treaty have arisen, in consequence of some disputes between the French and English East-India companies.

Orders were sent on Thursday night to the War Office, to continue the light troops in full pay till the 23d of next month, not being yet ready to dismiss them.

Yesterday there was a cabinet council at St. James's on affairs relating to the army, at which Lord Ligonier and several officers of the army assisted.

We learn from Spain, that the money and effects of the Count de Superonda, late Viceroy of Peru, which had been landed at Ferrol from the Havanna, had been seized by the government, and the Count himself was expected to be put under arrest: That the money belonging to private persons returned from the Havanna had also been seized, because they had neglected to register it; but it was thought it would be restored.

Advices from Amsterdam pretend, that according to letters received there from Batavia, of the 6th of May, the English have received a considerable check on the coast of Coromandel, by the miscarriage of the attempt against the isle of France, and that, in an action at sea, we have also suffered a very great loss. Other letters from the same place bring accounts, that six of our vessels have been sunk near the isle of France, but it is hoped this will all prove Dutch news.

A gentleman from Portsmouth writes, that the French prisoners there express the utmost dissatisfaction on their being ordered home, and that great numbers of them, who were ordered on board for their return to France, had made their escape.

Last Friday the Buckingham militia was disembodied at Ailesbury, and had given them their regiment cloaths, knapsacks, &c. and each of them 14 days pay to carry them to their respective homes.

The Family Compact privateer of St. Sebastian's, of 10 guns and 100 men, is taken by the Boston frigate, Sir Thomas Adams, and brought into Plymouth.

The Calcutta Indiaman has actually brought home the last Frenchmen that remained on the whole continent of Asia; and Bencoolen, on the island of Sumatra, was retaken about 15 months ago by three of our Indiamen.—Query, *What conquests in the East-Indies has France to restore to England, in order to fulfil the 10th article of the preliminaries?*

By this ship we have also advice, that the forces destined for an expedition against the Manilla islands, were all ready to proceed, and only waited for an account of the declaration of war against Spain, and were in great expectations of success. But we have still a less pleasing account of the intended attack on the French at Mauritius, wisely planned by the late minister, for their utter extirpation from that quarter of the globe. Admiral Cornish, during his cruise and delay, in expectation of the promised succours from Europe, buried upwards of 1000 brave sailors, besides landmen, and returned sickly and distressed.

AMERICA.

Boston, October 18.

WE hear from Biddeford, in the county of York, that at the inferior court lately held there, a cause was tried between Thomas Hammet, of Berwick, in said county, yeoman, plaintiff, and Peter Staple, of Kittery, in the same county, gentleman, defendant, for the defendant's debauching the plaintiff's wife, &c. and after a full hearing of six hours, the jury brought in their verdict for the plaintiff to recover against the defendant 1000l. lawful money, damages and costs.

The Effects of War

The *Georgia Gazette*, founded in 1763 as that southern colony's first newspaper, remained sympathetic to Britain throughout the Revolution. Patriot authorities, however, twice forced it to suspend publication. Most other colonial newspapers also experienced difficulties created by wartime conditions.

America. Freedom had been gained from the mother country, a new political philosophy took firm root, and the foundation was laid on which would be built a wholly new governmental system. While the American press had been instrumental in helping bring about the Revolutionary War, the war thrust the nation and its newspapers into an independence that soon would result in another revolution in politics and government. For a second time, the press would play a critical role in helping shape the American nation.

RECOMMENDED READINGS

BOOKS

Bailyn, Bernard. *The Ideological Origins of the American Revolution*. Cambridge, Mass., 1967. The ideas found in pamphlets indicate that the

American Revolution was primarily an ideological struggle for greater political freedom and equality.

Bailyn, Bernard, and John B. Hench, eds. *The Press and the American Revolution*. Worcester, Mass., 1980. Collection of generally incisive essays by various historians.

Berger, Carl. *Broadsides and Bayonets: The Propaganda War of the American Revolution*. Philadelphia, 1961. Events and real conditions during the war were more persuasive than words, rendering both British and American propaganda ineffective.

Canfield, Cass. *Sam Adams' Revolution 1765-1776*. New York, 1976. "[I]t was primarily Adams who fanned the flame of rebellion and...he did so more effectively than any other major American leader. Without him...American independence could not have been declared in 1776." Adams was a tenacious and uncompromising leader of the independence movement, an agitator, mass organizer, political manipulator, and master propagandist.

Cornebise, Alfred E. *Ranks and Columns: Armed Forces Newspapers in American Wars*. Westport, Conn., 1993. Military journalism from the Revolutionary War through the twentieth century.

Davidson, Philip. *Propaganda in the American Revolution, 1763-1783*. Chapel Hill, N. C., 1941. Without the work of propagandists, independence would not have been declared in 1776.

Foner, Eric. *Tom Paine and Revolutionary America*. New York, 1976. The Revolutionary writer was an important contributor to liberal, democratic philosophy whose main desire was to eliminate inequalities and abuses.

Hixson, Richard F. *Isaac Collins: A Quaker Printer in 18th Century America*. New Brunswick, N.J.: 1968. For the publisher of New Jersey's first newspaper, the *Gazette*, most problems during the Revolution were related to business operations, such as obtaining paper and collecting from subscribers.

Humphrey, Carol Sue. *"This Popular Engine": New England Newspapers during the American Revolution, 1775-1789*. Newark, Del., 1992. During the Revolutionary period, newspapers served as colonials' most important source of information.

Lorenz, Alfred L. *Hugh Gaine: A Colonial Printer-Editor's Odyssey to Loyalism*. Carbondale, Ill., 1972. Gaine, although insisting on fairness when partisanship was expected, was primarily oriented toward business and did whatever was necessary to prosper.

Miller, John C. *Sam Adams: Pioneer in Propaganda*. Boston, 1936. Adams was the total politician, utilizing considerable emotion and a facile mind to convince others that his way should be their way.

Miner, Ward L. *William Goddard, Newspaperman*. Durham, N.C., 1962. Although a pro-Patriot printer, Goddard insisted on freedom to print material from both sides of the conflict and would not withhold news even though Patriot mobs tried to intimidate him.

Morgan, Edmund S., and Helen M. Morgan. *The Stamp Act Crisis: Prologue to Revolution*. Chapel Hill, N. C., 1953. Analyzes colonial resistance to the Stamp Act and the emergence of well-defined constitutional principles.

Schlesinger, Arthur M. *Prelude to Independence: The Newspaper War on Great Britain, 1764-1776*. New York, 1958. Documents newspaper reaction to British authority and the press' role in the growing tide of revolution.

Shipton, Clifford. *Isaiah Thomas: Printer, Patriot, Philanthropist, 1749-1831*. Rochester, N.Y., 1948. Admiring narrative of Thomas' contributions to the field of printing and to other aspects of American life. Thomas was the "father of the modern American printing and publishing business."

Sloan, Wm. David, and Julie Hedgepeth Williams. *The Early American Press, 1690-1783*. Westport, Conn., 1994. This in-depth study provides an insightful account of the role of newspapers before and during the Revolution.

Waldstreicher, David. *In the Midst of Perpetual Fetes: The Making of American Nationalism, 1776-1820*. Chapel Hill, N.C.: 1998. Newspaper reporting of public rituals gave them a "national scope" that helped to reinforce the idea of unity and the concept of "one nation."

Walett, Francis G. *Massachusetts Newspapers and the Revolutionary Crisis, 1763-1776*. Boston, 1974. After 1765, the press became strong in opposition to British authorities. The leading American newspapers were in Boston. The press — through news and propaganda — "played an unusually large part in the movement toward American independence."

ARTICLES

Batchelder, Frank R. "Isaiah Thomas the Patriot." *New England Magazine*, n.s., 25 (November, 1901): 284-305. Thomas, a close friend to many Boston radicals, launched his *Massachusetts Spy* with all the flair and bombast of modern tabloids.

Benjamin, S. G. W. "A Group of Pre-Revolutionary Editors. Beginnings of Journalism in America." *Magazine of American History* 17 (January, 1887): 1-28. The press exercised great power in influencing public attitudes and events to help bring about the Revolution.

Botein, Stephen. "Printers and the American Revolution," in Bailyn and Hench, 11-58. Printers were traditionally neutral and impartial, but their attitudes were often determined by political conditions. In periods of political unrest, they found it profitable to be partisan; in quieter times they could afford to open their presses to diverse opinions. Objectivity and neutrality were principles of the trade.

Calkin, Homer L. "Pamphlets and Public Opinion During the American Revolution." *Pennsylvania Magazine of History and Biography* 64 (1940): 22-42. Study of the influence of pamphlets: "Unquestionably, the pamphlet was considered of prime importance in forming and shaping the minds of the people....[It] must be considered in a study of the American Revolution because of the place it occupied in presenting and forming the ideas and theories of the two sides in the many controversial questions which arose from 1763 to 1783."

Cullen, Maurice R., Jr. "Benjamin Edes: Scourge of Tories." *Journalism Quarterly* 51 (1974): 213-8. Edes was a successful printer who became a leader in the struggle to oppose the Stamp Act.

—. "Middle-Class Democracy and the Press in Colonial America." *Journalism Quarterly* 46 (1969): 531-5. An examination of economic opportunity, the extent of political democracy, and the colonies' literacy rate shows that the Revolution was not a class struggle but a fight for democracy.

Dickerson, O. M. "British Control of American Newspapers on the Eve of the Revolution." *New England Quarterly* 24 (1951): 455-68. Since printing was a business, printers normally ran material that was favorable to authorities who controlled the purse strings.

Frank, Willard C. "Error, Distortion and Bias in the *Virginia Gazette*, 1773-74." *Journalism Quarterly* 49 (1972): 729-39. The Williamsburg printers changed their emphasis from a collection of miscellany to playing the role of conscious editors of powerful journals of opinion. Reports were slanted or distorted and yet were probably believed by radicals, thus playing a large role in urging Virginians to rebel (since the *Gazette* was the only widely-read newspaper available).

Frasca, Ralph. "'The Glorious Publick Virtue so Predominant in Our Rising Country': Benjamin Franklin's Printing Network During the Revolutionary Era." *American Journalism* 13 (1996): 21-37. Even after he finally joined the fight against Great Britain, Franklin urged his printing partners to remain impartial. The pressures of the growing conflict, however, pushed most of them firmly into the Patriot camp.

Harlan, Robert. "David Hall and the Stamp Act." *Papers of the Bibliographical Society of America* 61 (1967): 13-37. Realizing that his newspaper was the most important financial aspect of his printing business, Hall allowed the *Pennsylvania Gazette*'s editorial policies to conform more and more to those of the Patriot faction.

Henry, Susan. "Margaret Draper: Colonial Printer Who Challenged the Patriots." *Journalism History* 1 (1974): 141-4. As publisher of the *Massachusetts Gazette and Boston News-Letter* from 1774 to 1776 following the death of her husband, Draper supported the Tory cause. "Ironically," however, in a period during which women were not fully appreciated, " — and undoubtedly like countless other women in history — her own considerable contribution to a political cause was quickly subsumed beneath her husband's (which, it can be argued, was less substantial)."

Humphrey, Carol Sue. "The Media and Wartime Morale: The Press and the American Revolution," in *The Significance of the Media in American History*, James D. Startt and Wm. David Sloan, eds., Northport, Ala., 1994. The media have always had an impact on public morale during wartime, and the newspapers of the Revolutionary era were no different. The patriot news sheets sought constantly to increase support for the war effort through the materials they published.

—. "'Producers of the Popular Engine': New England's Revolutionary Newspaper Printers." *American Journalism* 4 (1987): 97-117. Describes the typical characteristics of printers.

—. "Selling the American Revolution," in *The Press in Times of Crisis*, Lloyd Chiasson, Jr., ed. Westport, Conn., 1995. A case study of the newspapers of Williamsburg, Va., shows how the press played an important role in setting the public agenda during the Revolution and thus helped convince many Americans to support independence.

Moses, James L. "Journalistic Impartiality on the Eve of Revolution: the *Boston Evening Post*, 1770-1775." *Journalism History* 20 (1994): 125-30. The newspaper's effort to remain impartial resulted in its closing. Just prior to the Revolution, "the printer who attempted to remain partial during the storms of controversy usually found himself in the position of being despised by both sides."

Mott, Frank Luther. "The Newspaper Coverage of Lexington and Concord." *New England Quarterly* 17 (1944): 489-505. Newspaper "coverage was conditioned by the primitive techniques of eighteenth-century news-gathering, by such facilities of communication as existed, and by the stage of development at which the newspaper had arrived." Most newspaper information was not first-hand or timely.

Ours, Robert M. "James Rivington: Another Viewpoint," 219-34 in Donovan H. Bond and McLeod, W. Reynolds, eds. *Newsletters to Newspapers: Eighteenth Century Journalism.* Morgantown, W.V., 1977. Rivington, who was the most hated Tory editor during the Revolution because he was accused of distorting and slanting facts, actually acted as he had promised he would: "impartial and neutral."

Parker, Peter J. "The Philadelphia Printer: A Study of an 18th Century Businessman." *Business History Review* 40 (Spring 1966): 24-46. Printing changed between 1758 and 1800. Before the Revolution, the printer was an artisan and merchant. The Revolution accelerated the growth of his business. By 1800, he thought of his business apart from himself.

Pomerantz, S. I. "The Patriot Newspaper and the American Revolution." In R. B. Morris, ed., *The Era of the American Revolution* (New York, 1939): 305-31. Printers did commendable jobs in news reporting, avoidance of personal abuse, accuracy of information, moderation of tone, open-mindedness toward the conflicting sides, and adherence to other journalistic principles.

Potter, Janice, and Robert M. Calhoon. "The Character and Coherence of the Loyalist Press," in Bailyn and Hench, 229-72. Analysis of the intellectual and ideological content and character of newspaper essays that supported Britain. The most common themes were disaffection, petulance, ingratitude, and disloyalty.

Randolph, J. Ralph. "The End of Impartiality: *South Carolina Gazette*, 1763-75." *Journalism Quarterly* 49 (1972): 702-9, 720. Peter Timothy, printer of the *Gazette*, changed to editorial partiality because of the Anglo-American crisis, although as a general rule he believed in press impartiality.

Skaggs, David C. "Editorial Policies of the *Maryland Gazette,* 1765-1783." *Maryland History Magazine* 59 (1964): 341-9. In Maryland, the *Gazette* was "one of the most significant institutions influencing the change of colonial ideals from dependence to independence, and at the same time leaving such concepts as freedom of religion, speech, and press ingrained in the revolutionary mind."

Smith, Jeffery. "War as Monarchial Folly in the Early American Press." *American Journalism* 10 (1993): 83-97. Colonial journalists linked warfare to royalty, thus undermining monarchs' authority. They argued that republican government would eliminate or at least limit military conflict as a solution to international problems.

Spaulding, E. Wilder. "The *Connecticut Courant*, A Representative Newspaper in the Eighteenth Century." *New England Quarterly* 3 (1930): 443-63. "[A]s a medium for agitation the prosaic little American newspaper had as yet no rival in book or magazine printing. Its only rivals, the broadsides and the pamphlet, it was to overtake and pass by the end of the Revolution, making of itself the most effective mirror of the life and thought of its community. Of such journals none reflected more accurately the ideals, the heart-throbs, and the disappointments of its neighborhood than did the venerable *Courant*."

Thomas, C.M. "The Publication of Newspapers during the American Revolution." *Journalism Quarterly* 9 (1932): 358-73. "The very nature of the printer's business made neutrality in a civil struggle impossible for him. The ordinary inhabitant, even though he favored one side and had no desire to be neutral, could remain in a city and conduct his business regardless of the fortunes of war if he was willing to remain quiet; but the editor of a newspaper could not remain quiet."

Wax, Donald D. "The Image of the Negro in the *Maryland Gazette*, 1745-75." *Journalism Quarterly* 46 (1969): 73-80, 86. A study of Revolutionary newspaper views on race finds that the *Gazette* portrayed the Negro as property and in derogatory terms, thus setting a pattern of race prejudice and discrimination deeply rooted in America's past.

Yodelis, Mary Ann. "Who Paid the Piper? Publishing Economics in Boston, 1763-1775." *Journalism Monographs* 38 (1975). Government printing was not necessary for a successful printing business, and government therefore could exercise little financial coercion.

5

The Party Press

1783 - 1833

As the year 1798 came to an end, Federalist politicians looked to the new year with foreboding. Their party was locked in a battle with their Republican opponents that both sides believed would determine the nature of the new American nation. In the year just closing, the Federalists, in control of the national government, had succeeded in passing the oppressive Sedition Act. Perhaps it would work in silencing the opposition.

Still, the Federalists feared for the future. The Republicans yet might find a way to spread their radical views through their newspapers to the general populace. "Give to any set of men the command of the press," Judge Alexander Addison wrote with worry on New Year's Day of 1799, "and you give them the command of the country, for you give them the command of public opinion, which commands everything."[1] Should Republicans succeed at corrupting public opinion, what could result but despotism? Federalists wondered. "Of such force is public opinion," Addison had written earlier during the furor over passage of the Sedition Act, "that, with it on its side, the worst government will support itself, and, against it, the best government will fall."[2]

Federalists by 1799 had come to realize a fact that had been at the essence of American public life almost since the first colonists had stepped ashore in the early 1600s. Public opinion was the basis for public policy, and the printing press was the means that provided a forum for it. Because of the democratic nature of the American political system, leaders of the early parties recognized the necessity of appealing to public opinion. Only by doing so could they expect their concepts to be the ones that would be adopted and would shape the nation's political ideals. The primary means through which they hoped to mold public opinion was the press.

As parties began to develop following the adoption of the United States Constitution, on April 15, 1789, John Fenno published the first issue of the *Gazette of the United States*, beginning one of the most politically and journalistically vigorous periods in American history. It would see the American political system take shape and the American press play a critical role in determining the direction of that system.

The Federalist-Republican and the Jacksonian periods were passionate political ages marked by intensely bitter partisan opinions. The distinctive characteristic of American newspapers from 1783 to 1833 was political partisanship. That characteristic — combined with the fact that partisan fervor frequently gave vent to abusive personal and political attacks — can give the impression that the party press performed poorly. The nature of the press of the time has to be considered, however, in the context of the role it played in America's social and political environment. The contributions editors made to the political system established them as important figures, both journalistically and politically.

The period of America's partisan press was a critical one for the nation. From the end of the Revolution, America existed as a confederation until 1788. In that year the Constitution was adopted and transformed the loose grouping of states into a unified nation. During the next forty years, Americans set up an elaborate system of national government, organized their first political parties, and laid the base of their foreign policy for years to come. The Federalist-Republican period of 1789-1816 thus represents one of the most important eras in American history, while many historians have viewed Andrew Jackson's presidency (1829-1837) as the culmination of the early fight for American democracy.

The Press and the Confederation

The 1780s marked a new era in American journalism, and many new printers and publishers appeared on the scene. They were optimistic about their young nation's future and the role the press was sure to play. Immediately after the American Revolution ended, however, most of them recognized that the Articles of Confederation were too weak, and they began to support efforts to establish a new form of federal government. Their fears centered on such problems as the difficulty the government had in

[1]*Columbian Centinel*, 1 January 1799.
[2]*Russell's Gazette*, 7 June 1798.

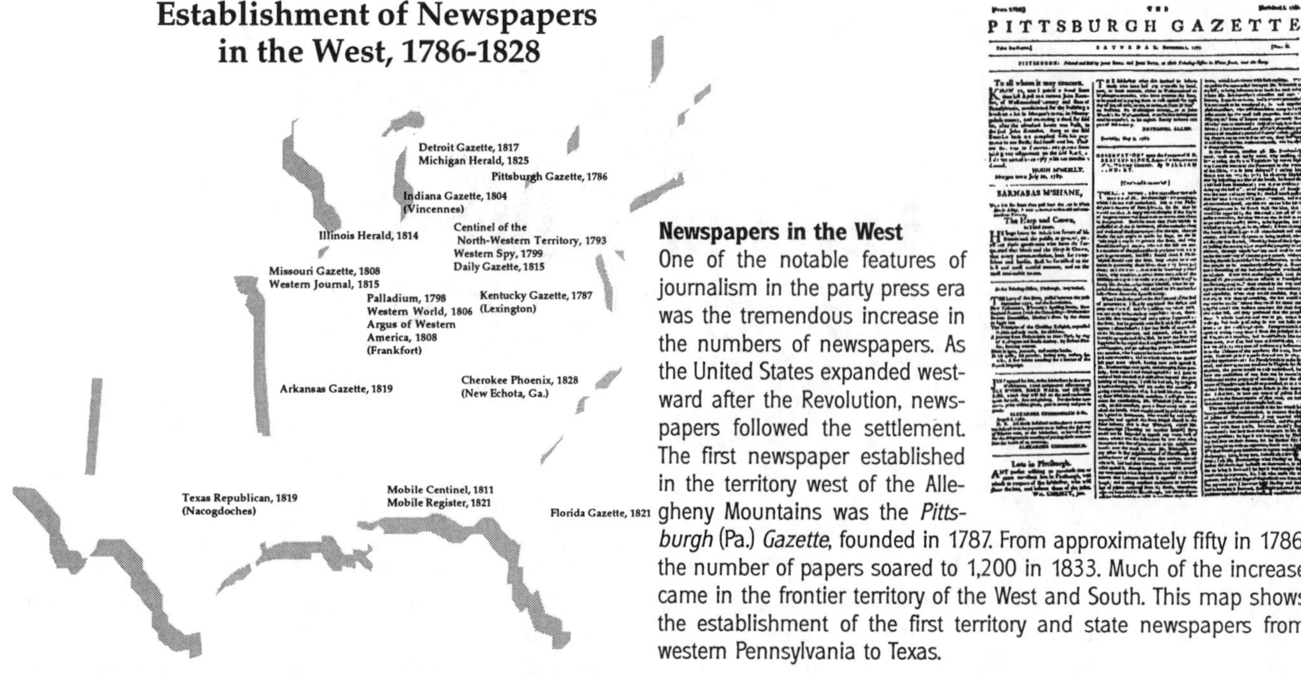

Newspapers in the West
One of the notable features of journalism in the party press era was the tremendous increase in the numbers of newspapers. As the United States expanded westward after the Revolution, newspapers followed the settlement. The first newspaper established in the territory west of the Allegheny Mountains was the *Pittsburgh* (Pa.) *Gazette*, founded in 1787. From approximately fifty in 1786, the number of papers soared to 1,200 in 1833. Much of the increase came in the frontier territory of the West and South. This map shows the establishment of the first territory and state newspapers from western Pennsylvania to Texas.

paying debts incurred during the Revolution, the fact that the individual states were acting in their own selfish interests, and civil unrest as exemplified in "Shays's Rebellion" of rural debtors in Massachusetts and in a mob of disgruntled farmers attacking New Hampshire's state legislature.

Most newspapers supported the call for a Constitutional Convention to work out a more effective national government. When the Convention met for the first time in 1787, its members adopted guidelines for their proceedings that, among other things, closed discussions to the public and the press. Editors agreed that confidentiality was necessary for the convention's frank debate of issues and said little in opposition to the secrecy. Assured of the ability and high character of the men who composed the Convention, they wrote confidently of the expected outcome. The convention was, declared one newspaper, "perhaps the last opportunity which may be presented to us of establishing a permanent system of Continental Government; and, if this opportunity be lost, it is much to be feared that we shall fall into irretrievable confusion."[3]

When the Convention adjourned in September and presented its brief proposed constitution, every newspaper in the country printed a copy, and all immediately opened their columns for a discussion of it. All but twelve newspapers favored its adoption. Editorial support was so strong that opponents claimed their views did not get a fair hearing in the press. Editors responded that they printed all views and that their reason for publishing few articles opposing adoption of the Constitution was that opponents submitted few. Of the hundreds of articles published in favor of adoption, the most widely republished was the series known as "The Federalist Papers." Written jointly by Alexander Hamilton, James Madison, and John Jay, each signing his contributions "Publius," the essays even today are recognized as perhaps the most insightful pieces ever written on America's constitutional form of government. They appeared in the *New York Independent Journal* from October 1787 to April 1788.

By the time the ninth state, the final one needed for adoption, ratified the Constitution in June 1788, the debate had already initiated the appearance of factions in American politics. Supporters of adoption were being called "Federalists." Their opponents, called simply "Anti-Federalists," feared that the new federal government would be too strong, taking power and rights from the states and the people. The animosities between the two factions would quickly intensify as the national government and America's political system began to take shape in the next few years.

The Press and the First Party System

After adoption of the Constitution, Federalists (led by Hamilton) and their opponents (led by Madison and Thomas Jefferson) clashed on several major issues, particularly the federal government's assumption of state debts, the question of whom the United States should support in conflicts between France and Great Britain, and the enactment of the Alien and Sedition Acts in 1798.

The fact that party machinery had not developed to a sophisticated state increased the press' importance. During the first party system, factions at first worked as informal groups rather than as organized political parties, but by 1792 they were exhibiting characteristics of formalized party structure and referring to themselves by the names "Federalists" and "Republicans." Speechmaking and other forms of personal campaigning, however, were

[3]*Freeman's Journal*, 16 May 1787.

"The Federalist"
In the fight for adoption of the Constitution, Virginia and New York, two of the largest states, lagged. In New York, Alexander Hamilton led the battle. Joined by James Madison and John Jay, he and his co-authors produced eight-five "Federalist" essays with the pseudonym "Publius" and published them in the *New York Independent Journal.* Proponents of the Constitution in Virginia and New York found the series especially useful as a handbook for arguments, and both states voted for adoption. After New York ratified in July 1788, New York City held a huge celebration parade, led by the ship *Hamilton.*

not practiced as a part of electioneering. With the 1792 election emphasizing the need for political organization, both parties accelerated their efforts. They tightened party discipline. To promote their cause, Republicans formed numerous "Democratic" societies, with forty or so of these clubs existing by 1794. Debate over the Jay Treaty in 1795 and 1796 helped crystallize parties and accelerated advances in party structure, loyalty, and voting.

In preparation for the 1796 election, Republicans held their first congressional caucuses, and small groups of influential leaders selected the candidates of both parties, the Federalists choosing John Adams and the Republicans, Jefferson. The party ticket had appeared. Jefferson did not campaign, seemingly indifferent to the election; but newspapers waged a vigorous battle.

With Adams' victory, Republicans recognized even more clearly the need of greater efforts at organizing party machinery if they were to win the presidency in 1800. Jefferson, showing a much greater interest in his "campaign" and a determination to win in 1800, early in 1799 wrote out his platform, took every opportunity to express his views in private correspondence, and in other ways generally behaved as a practical politician. Electioneering efforts intensified. Both parties used corresponding committees, circular letters among party adherents, organization committees on the town and county levels, public meetings, party tickets, political addresses, campaign handbills and pamphlets, and newspaper announcements and arguments. Republican efforts, however, were better organized than those of the Federalists; and Jefferson's election may have been as much a result of electioneering methods and disciplined party organization as of his ideology.

The election brought significant progress in party organization and techniques of appealing to public opinion; but generally party machinery was meager, and formal organization had not developed in some states. After 1800, organization improved for Republicans. They used the press, patronage, local committees, legislative caucuses, state nominating conventions, and other mechanisms with more sophistication and intensity.

Although Federalists were less successful in politics, they also attempted to fashion more sophisticated and effective party machinery. Because of the election defeat, many of the older, hardline Federalists deserted politics; but more realistic, and generally younger, Federalists adopted the Republicans' techniques in an attempt to recover from the 1800 debacle and convert their party into one of effective politicians striving for popular support. They were doomed to failure, however, for the ideas of the Federalists were out of line with majority sentiment among the American public. Following Jefferson's election, the Republicans slowly gained the upper hand; and the 1816 presidential election was the last in which the Federalists ran a candidate. About all that was left of the Federalist party by that time were newspapers still carrying on the old fight.

As the party system emerged, both politicians and editors viewed the press as a major instrument in efforts to influence public opinion and gain political dominance. They attempted in a variety of ways to establish and support friendly newspapers and to silence the opposition. As a result, much newspaper content was political, with opinion and argument emphasized rather than news. Editors thrust themselves into the middle of the political struggles. Their purpose was not to be impartial but to fight however they could for their side. The partisan motives of the press were quite clear; the sides in the political conflict well drawn. Since the nature of the political system was based ultimately on the will of the people, appealing to public opinion became crucial. The primary tool was the newspaper. Its intent, unlike that of today's media, was neither to be primarily a news medium nor to be impartial. In the highly partisan political environment, the press took on a political function.

"A Nation of Newspaper Readers"

The press gained its political importance because of the position it occupied as the most important medium for the distribution of news and views. One of the most noticeable features of the period was the growth of newspapers. At the beginning of the period, in 1783, only thirty-five newspapers, all weeklies, served the nation. By 1833, the number had increased to 1,200 and included dailies as well as weeklies.

The early papers published chiefly in the seaports and commercial towns where Federalists were more numerous and most potential advertisers were businessmen with Federalist inclinations. Federalists therefore achieved a decided advantage in numbers of newspapers. In some locales, their papers outnumbered those of the Republicans by margins of five to one. Similarly, the Whig party later was able to maintain superiority in newspaper numbers because more of its members were involved in business than were Democrats.

The primary contributors to newspaper growth were increases in the size of the American population, the appearance of new towns, and the expansion of an ambitious postal system that provided information and inexpensive circulation of newspapers. Much of the increase in the numbers of newspapers occurred with the nation's westward expansion. As population pushed toward the Alleghenies and beyond, newspapers sprang up with the settlements.

How widely read the newspapers were, however, is difficult to determine. The cost of newspapers and the fact that usually they could be purchased not by individual copies but only by yearly subscription limited circulation. The yearly subscription price for a weekly ranged from $1 to $2. For a daily the price was in the $8 range. During a period in which Americans' average weekly income was less than $5, subscription prices tended to keep papers out of the reach of many people. In cities, subscription lists were confined largely to business and mercantile classes. Editors frequently bartered their newspapers, however, for produce and other goods; and small-town newspapers often had substantial circulations in the surrounding areas.

Still, circulation was relatively small. In 1790, America had ninty-one newspapers, only eight of which were dailies, with a combined circulation totaling perhaps 50,000. By 1800 the number had reached 234, including twenty-four dailies, with a combined circulation of approximately 145,000. The total number of copies produced that year has been estimated at a little more than five million, less than one copy per person. By 1808 the number of papers had reached 329, with a combined circulation of around

SATURDAY, April 22, 1784.] GEORGIA. [Vol. III. No. CXXXII.]

THE AUGUSTA CHRONICLE

AND

GAZETTE OF THE STATE.

FREEDOM of the PRESS, and TRIAL by JURY, to remain inviolate forever. *Constitution of Georgia.*

AUGUSTA: Printed by JOHN E. SMITH, Printer to the State; *Essays, Articles of Intelligence, Advertisements, &c. will be gratefully received, and every kind of Printing performed.*

Humorous Relation of the Distress of a Bashful Man.

Seaport Partisans

The earliest partisan newspapers were established mainly in seaports and commercial centers, where business and advertising support were available. Newspapers soon began to proliferate from Maine to the southernmost state of Georgia.

215,000. These low figures, however, do not provide an accurate count of the total number of newspaper readers.

There is, in fact, no way of knowing how many people read a single copy of any paper. A writer to the *New York Journal* in 1795 explained that when the *Journal* arrived in western New York, it was "borrowed from one to the other to the distance perhaps of twenty miles."[4] A single subscription sometimes represented an association of several families, and coffee-houses and taverns subscribed to papers for customers to read. In villages with no newspapers, ministers often read the latest news to their congregations. Such interest led contemporaries to remark that America by 1800 had become "a nation of newspaper readers."[5] The editor Noah Webster declared, "Newspapers are the most eagerly sought

[4] *New York Journal*, 24 February 1795.

[5] *Port Folio Magazine*, quoted in Frank Luther Mott, *History of American Magazines* (Cambridge, Mass., 1938-1968), I: 160. Material on readership of newspapers is gathered from *Monthly Magazine*, I (1799): 13-4; and Philadelphia *Aurora*, 11 September 1799.

after, and the most generally diffused. In no other country on earth, not even in Great-Britain, are newspapers so generally circulated among the body of people, as in America." Because of the circulation that resulted from their cheapness and frequency of publication, he added, newspapers had achieved "an eminent rank in the catalogue of useful publications."[6]

By today's standards, these early newspapers were not impressive. The typical newspaper was a small, four-page tabloid (one sheet printed front and back and folded) with a little political, foreign, and national news, and a few columns of advertising, found among letters and essays by local contributors, political arguments clipped from other papers, and editorials by the editor or a contributor. Grayness pervaded each page. The one-column headlines in use since 1690 remained standard, and newspapers carried even major stories under headlines of small type. Although country papers and those in the West stuck to the fairly small, 12" x 16" page sizes, the metropolitan papers tended to enlarge. As if equating page size with quality, some finally were printing pages three feet wide and five feet deep. By the 1830s the popular, mass-oriented penny papers were jeering at these "blanket" sheets.

The Press as a Political Instrument

The emergence of the newspaper as a spokesman of a political party gave more prestige to the job of editor. Most newspapers continued to function, as they had during the colonial and revolutionary periods, as job-printing operations. Thus most newspaper operators still were printers who also served as writers, typesetters, pressmen, and circulation and advertising managers. Well-developed political argument, however, demanded more intellectual and writing ability from the newspaper operator. Thus emerged the true editor — in the sense of the person who writes opinion and oversees the content operations of the newspaper, in contrast to one who simply prints what others submit — and the standard of ability increased measurably. While many operators of small country papers continued to act more as printers than editors, individuals such as John Fenno of the *Gazette of the United States* and Duff Green of the *United States Telegraph*, Andrew Jackson's spokesman, were primarily editors concerned with editorial and news content.

Close associations between editors and politicians marked the party press period. As political leaders recognized the importance of the press, they worked to encourage newspapers to support their cause. Many new papers started publication. Politicians provided direct support for some of them, while other papers, those founded with the assistance of parties, were able to continue publication because of partisan aid. With the recognition of the newspaper's political significance came a variety of support. Partisan efforts made possible most of the livelihood of some papers. A few editors, enticed by the financial fruits, became little more than sycophants to politicians; but most, despite financial conditions, were sincerely committed to the cause they espoused and continued to publish in support of the party even when they found politicians' support undependable. At a time when advertising and subscriptions brought in little revenue to many newspapers, political support was invaluable. Publishing was not a lucrative business. Advertising often was sparse, and subscription payments were frequently delinquent. Without official favor, many newspapers would have perished. "Subsisting by a country newspaper," the editor of the *Trenton* (N.J.) *True American* wrote in 1802, "is generally little better than starving."[7]

Which party controlled government offices was critical for newspapers. Office-holders from the presidency down to the town council could bestow patronage on editors in the form of printing contracts and political office. Income from printing of congressional and legislative acts and documents and of items such as letterheads required by government officials could be lucrative. During Jefferson's first term, Samuel Harrison Smith of the *National Intelligencer* received nearly $2,000 per year in printing for the State Department alone. On the state and county levels government printing often was highly profitable. The state printer in North Carolina, to cite one case, received approximately $1,200 a year from 1800 to 1810.[8] Other types of political aid included loans and cash contributions, assistance in securing subscriptions and distributing papers, legal assistance, and written contributions in the form of essays, letters, and news items.

Whether a newspaper was published through the support of politicians or the independent efforts of journalists, it was recognized as a party spokesman and as a central part of the political system. Frequently, national, state, or local groups or individuals would provide money for starting a paper by outright contributions of cash or a mortgage or loan for printing equipment. Sometimes a group would hire a printer for a new paper and name one of its own members editor. In either situation, the patrons established the papers in the expectation of getting political support. Such papers came to be regarded as organs of these sponsors. Editors of independently established newspapers brought them into the service of a party and also received support from parties, factions, or individual politicians to assist in continuing publication. Yet while financial support from politicians was imperative for the success of newspapers, the instances of editors basing their political loyalties on monetary considerations were rare. Most supported parties because of their agreement with the parties' political beliefs.

In general, the purpose of editors was to present news and views on political action and secondarily to win adherents to the cause. To accomplish these goals, editors and politicians expected the press to perform a number of functions. These may be categorized as the following: (1) promote political ideals, (2) support

[6]*American Minerva*, 9 December 1793.

[7]*True American*, 26 July 1802.

[8]*Raleigh* (N.C.) *Star*, 29 November 1810. The fullest treatment of the financial relationship between newspapers and the government is provided by Culver G. Smith's *The Press, Politics, and Patronage: The American Government's Use of Newspapers, 1789-1875* (Athens, Ga., 1977).

party principles, (3) defend the party and its politicians, (4) provide a medium for expression of party views, (5) provide "information" — always presented as "truth" from the party viewpoint, (6) influence public opinion, (7) preach the party line to the party faithful, (8) attack opponents, and (9) provide a method of electioneering.

Public opinion played a key role in the American political system. Members of all parties recognized the necessity of appealing to public opinion if their concepts were to shape the nation's political ideals. In their approaches to public opinion, however, the parties exhibited a number of differences. Federalists, with their elitist attitudes, would have eliminated or at least greatly reduced public opinion's role in government if they could have had their way. Republicans, sensing public agreement with their ideas, thought of public opinion as an ally and courted it aggressively. They appealed primarily to people of the middle classes, those who met property-holding qualifications and tax requirements for voting.

Political Importance of the Press

No medium offered such a convenient method for reaching party members and voters as newspapers did. Organizational efforts, mass meetings, and personal correspondence performed to some extent the functions of informing, mobilizing, and persuading party adherents and other voters. The press, however, was able to do these jobs more efficiently and thus became an expeditor of party efforts. Other than pamphlets, newspapers were the only media for general public information. City papers circulated in urban areas containing a significant percentage of the nation's population and frequently had rural subscription lists larger than their city lists. Smaller newspapers throughout the land supplemented their city cousins. Although circulations were relatively small, the importance of newspapers was great because the public possessed limited means of obtaining information. People studied newspapers much more thoroughly — reading every word — than they do today because they had so little reading material available. Many papers with strictly partisan purposes charged artificially low subscription rates to increase their readership; and, because all eligible voters did not exercise the franchise, it is possible that most people who did vote were newspaper readers.

Whatever the readership was, the important factor was that politicians, editors, and general citizens believed the press was critical in the political system. All parties had members who believed in the importance of the press and thought newspapers should be used for partisan purposes. On numerous occasions, Jefferson testified to his belief in the value of newspapers. At the height of the XYZ affair in 1798, fearing that two Republican papers might cease publication, he wrote Madison that failure of the papers would be devastating for Republicanism.[9] Jefferson

Political Passion
The early 1800s marked a period of intense political passion, not only in newspaper columns but in legislative halls. This contemporary cartoon depicts a fight between Matthew Lyon and Roger Griswold. Lyon, a Republican Congressman and editor from Vermont, goaded Griswold with insults until Griswold attacked him with a cane. Lyon responded with fire tongs.

assumed that an informed public would make right decisions and that the press could influence views on political issues. "Our citizens," he wrote in 1799, "may be deceived for awhile, and have been deceived; but as long as the presses can be protected, we may trust to them for light."[10] He had in mind Republican presses, for he believed that Federalist newspapers dealt in "lying and scribbling."[11] As the 1800 election approached, he urged Republicans on a daily basis to write articles for publication — although he did not follow his own advice, rarely contributing to any newspaper. "We are sensible," he wrote Madison, "that this summer is the season for systematic energies and sacrifices. The engine is the press."[12]

Party adherents at all levels attributed to the press a major role in influencing public opinion and, like Jefferson, actively encouraged their parties to make use of newspapers. A Republican stated succinctly and explicitly the accepted view of press importance. "If ink and black paint could overpower the enemy," he said, "we

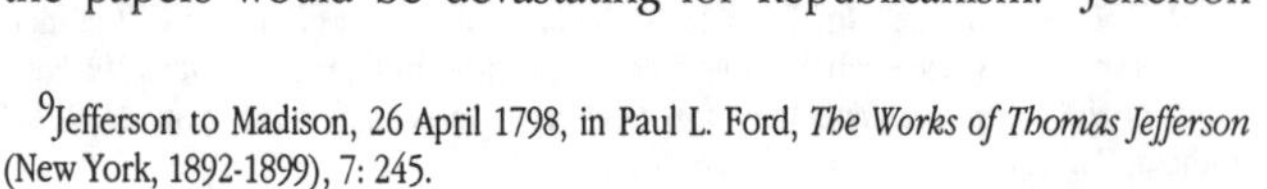

[9] Jefferson to Madison, 26 April 1798, in Paul L. Ford, *The Works of Thomas Jefferson* (New York, 1892-1899), 7: 245.

[10] Jefferson to Archibald Stuart, 14 May 1799, ibid., 378.
[11] Jefferson to John Randolph, 17 September 1792, ibid., 6: 111-2.
[12] Jefferson to Madison, 5 February 1799, ibid., 7: 344.

should have given him an unmerciful beating."[13]

In such a situation, the newspaper editor assumed a major role. Closely involved with politicians and party operations, editors were unusually knowledgeable about political issues and the inner workings of the party. Thus, they occupied ideal positions to serve as party spokesmen and advocates, dispensers of party information, and often political leaders on the local, state, and national levels.

Objectivity Versus Partisanship

Clearly, editors believed the overriding purpose of the press was to serve a partisan cause. Newspapers were intended to be neither non-partisan nor independent of parties. The contrary was true. Editors frowned on impartiality. The Federalist William Cobbett vowed to readers, as if keeping a trust, that he never would be impartial. Upon beginning *Porcupine's Gazette and Daily Advertiser* he proclaimed, "Professions of impartiality I shall make none." He did not intend to be one of those editors "who look on the conflict with perfect indifference, and whose only anxiety is the strongest side." Any editor who "does not exercise his own judgment, either in admitting or rejecting what is sent to him," he claimed, "is a poor passive fool, and not an editor." He would not allow impartiality to make *Porcupine's Gazette* into "an instrument of destruction to the cause I espouse." His "partiality," he declared, was "for the cause of good government, such as we live under."[14]

Because of their disdain for factionalism, Americans expected at least a facade of impartiality during the early part of the period, but by 1800 many editors made no pretense of impartiality. They proclaimed that to be impartial was to do the country an injustice. At a time when partisan feeling was hot, readers sometimes were annoyed that a paper would not take a partisan stand, and they accorded a neutral editor little merit. Samuel Harrison Smith found that readers and editors alike contemptuously referred to his *National Intelligencer* as "Mr. Silky Smith's National Smoothing Plane" because his partisan zeal was not as evident as they thought it should be.[15] Even to consider impartiality, some editors argued, was dereliction of duty. The editor of *The Portfolio* in Philadelphia stated adamantly that "he will not publish an impartial paper." Neutral men, he said, "cry amen to every creed, and venture on all sides, without being trusted by any." He did not intend to be like them. "Of such infamous principles," he declared, "the Editor has the deepest abhorrence, and for the silly scheme of Impartiality, he cherishes the most ineffable contempt."[16] Similarly, the editor of the *Baltimore American and Daily Advertiser* announced that he would declare himself openly in support of "the principles of Republicanism" and in opposition to "toryism and royalty." He would have no part of non-partisanship, he proclaimed, for "it is as incongruous for a publication to be alternately breathing the spirit of Republicanism and Aristocracy as for a clergyman to preach to his audience Christianity in the morning, and Paganism in the evening."[17] The reasoning of these editors is clear. They were publishing during a time of what they believed were important political questions. They would have failed in their devotion to truth and in their duty to serve the best interests of their country had they not stood up for their political convictions. "Objective" news reporting would not have been enough. Advocacy of a cause was imperative.

Newspapers' continual attacks on politicians and government policies were almost always partisan in nature. They did not result from an "adversary" relationship between government and the press as we think of that relationship today. Targets nearly always were members of the opposition party. Republican editors attacked Federalist politicians, and Federalists attacked Republicans; in the second party system, Democrat editors attacked Whigs, and Whigs attacked Democrats. Party and factional loyalties — rather than a belief that the press, per se, should be an adversary of government, per se — accounted for the conflict.

Federalist Editors

Hundreds of editors carried the fight for the parties. One of the first was Benjamin Russell. He and William Warden founded the *Columbian Centinel* in Boston in 1784 as a paper for the mercantile classes. After Warden departed as co-owner, Russell, who revered George Washington, transformed it into a political paper devoutly Federalist, favoring adoption of the Constitution and a strong national government. As the battles between Federalists and Republicans intensified in the 1790s, a choice group of political writers aided the *Centinel*. It also received financial aid through state and federal printing, but Russell regarded serving the nation as important as getting help from the government. In the early days of the Republic, when the national treasury was small, he declined payment for printing the federal laws.

As a strident opponent of Jefferson, Russell threw his support to Aaron Burr when the presidential election became entangled by the electoral system in 1801. After Jefferson was elected, Russell lamented the nation's fallen condition and predicted the demise of the Federalist party. Still, he stridently continued to advocate its principles. Throughout Jefferson's two administrations, Russell virulently denounced him. His opposition to Republicanism continued with the election of Madison, and he fought trenchantly against the war with England in 1812. In 1805 he was elected to the Massachusetts House of Representatives and was re-elected each year until 1821. It was Russell who, with the decline of the Federalist opposition after Monroe's election in 1816, coined the phrase used to describe the few years that followed: "The era of good feeling."

[13]Samuel Mitchell to Tench Coxe, 3 August 1813, quoted in Jacob Ernest Cooke, *Tench Coxe and the Early Republic* (Chapel Hill, N.C., 1978), 211.

[14]*Porcupine's Gazette*, 5 March 1797.

[15]*Richmond Recorder*, 21 May 1803.

[16]Quoted in the *Independent Chronicle*, 7 August 1798.

[17]*Baltimore American and Daily Advertiser*, 16 May 1799.

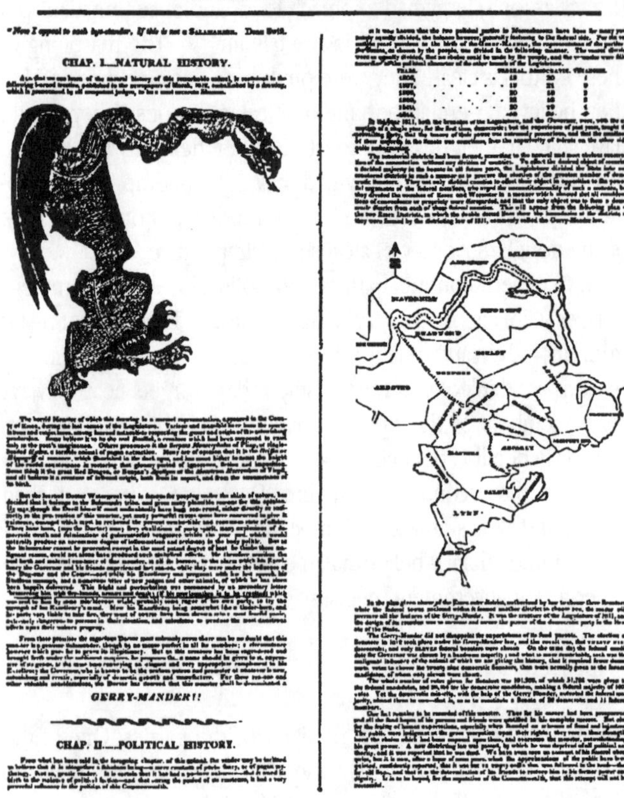

Natural and Political History

OF

THE GERRY-MANDER!

IN TWO CHAPTERS......WITH CUTS.

CHAP. I.—NATURAL HISTORY.

GERRY-MANDER!!

CHAP. II.—POLITICAL HISTORY.

Gerry-Mander

While Elbridge Gerry was serving as governor of Massachusetts, his party in 1812 drew new political districts for Essex County to assure election of fellow Republicans. Benjamin Russell, editor of the Federalist *Columbian Centinel* in Boston, noticed that the shape of one district resembled that of a salamander. He coined the term "Gerry-Mander," and the *Boston Weekly Messenger* ran a cartoon with head, wings, and claws added. In the accompanying map, the districts along the top and down the left side form the Gerry-Mander's outline. Governor Gerry lost the next election, and "gerry-mander" became a part of the American language.

Despite the fact that earlier partisan newspapers had existed, the founding of the *Gazette of the United States* in 1789 marked the real beginning of the party press era. American newspapers before Fenno's had practiced partisan politics, but the *Gazette* was the first founded as an organ of one of the factions comprising America's first party system. It foreshadowed the political and journalistic battles that were to take place for the next generation.

Before the appearance of the *Gazette*, New York City, the new nation's capital, had no strong Federalist newspaper. The faction's leaders believed they needed support other than what they got from the mercantile press that was incidentally Federalist. John Fenno, a 38-year-old Boston schoolteacher, proposed an arrangement by which a pro-Federalist newspaper he hoped to start would be given government printing. Federalist leaders, including Alexander Hamilton, satisfied Fenno on the arrangement, and in three months Fenno began publication. Later, with the transfer of the capital to Philadelphia, he moved the *Gazette* there because of the stipulation in his proposal for establishing the paper that it be "published at the seat of government."[18]

Hamilton and other leading Federalists supported and subsidized the *Gazette of the United States*. They intended it to be the Federalists' mouthpiece in the battle that would determine the nature of the new American government. "To hold up the people's own government, in a favorable point of light," Fenno wrote, "and to impress just ideas of its administration by exhibiting FACTS, comprise the outline of this paper."[19]

From the beginning, Fenno received the support he had requested. Hamilton fed him all the printing of the Treasury Department, he got much of the Senate's printing, and prominent Federalists subsidized him out-of-pocket. It was understood that the *Gazette* would mirror the opinions of its patrons and express the official Federalist positions. Because it was known as the organ of Hamilton, it became the leading paper of the national party leadership, circulating to party leaders and printers in all states. It kept this position throughout the 1790s. Fenno remained as editor until he died of yellow fever in 1798.

His son, John Ward Fenno, then edited the paper for less than two years, after which he became anxious by the loss of political support and sold the *Gazette* to Enos Bronson. Despite the challenge from the newly established *New York Evening Post* — and the weakened position of the *Gazette* — Bronson capably espoused the Federalist cause, and editors throughout the nation continued to rely on the *Gazette* for guidance on political issues. By the final years of the Federalist party, however, leadership had shifted to the *Evening Post*.

With the removal of the *Gazette* to Philadelphia, New York City was left without a strong Federalist organ. A group of ten Federalists — including Hamilton, Rufus King, and John Jay — decided to contribute $150 each to begin a paper and induced Noah Webster to move to the city to edit it. The first issue of the *American Minerva* appeared on December 9, 1793. Webster had established a name for himself for his essays in various papers and his political pamphlets. His columns signed "Curtius" and those by Hamilton signed "Camillus" in the *Minerva* became the most widely reprinted on the Jay Treaty. The paper was an ardent supporter of the administration of Washington and of the national Federalist organization. When Washington left office, Webster's support continued for his successor, John Adams. The new president did not gain the favor, however, of Hamilton.

In 1798 Webster, disillusioned with Hamilton's betrayal of Adams, withdrew from the *Minerva* and placed his nephew, Ebenezer Belden, in charge. The rift between Webster and Hamilton had grown so great by the presidential election of 1800 that Webster wrote a pamphlet charging his former patron with being corrupted by jealousy and ambition. Although it remained Federalist

[18] *Gazette of the United States*, 18 September 1790.

[19] *Gazette of the United States*, 27 April 1791.

Gazette of the United States.

The AMERICAN MINERVA

Patroness of Peace, Commerce, and the Liberal Arts.

Porcupine's Gazette.

Federalist Point Men

In the 1790s the Federalist press was spearheaded by three able journalists. The first party newspaper, the *Gazette of the United States* was founded in the same year as the United States itself, 1789. John Fenno was so devoted to publishing the newspaper that he stayed at his job as a yellow fever epidemic swept Philadelphia in 1793. In a second epidemic in 1798, he again refused to leave the city and contracted the disease. Upon his death, the editorship of the *Gazette* fell to his nineteen-year-old son, John Ward Fenno. As editor of the *American Minerva*, one of the Federalists' leading newspapers in the 1790s, Noah Webster set a comparatively high editorial tone. After leaving journalism, he became famous for compiling the first dictionary of the American language, later editions of which still bear his name. The Federalists' most effective journalist, William Cobbett emphasized the importance of partisanship in newspapers. An editor who did not discriminate in what he published, said Cobbett, was "a poor passive fool." As "Peter Porcupine," he was so effective a writer that he became the target of numerous attacks by Republicans. Reveling in the attention, he wrote his father: "When you used to set me off to work in the morning, dressed in my blue smock-frock and woollen spatter-dashes, ...little did you imagine that I should one day become so great a man as to have my picture stuck in the windows, and have four whole books published about me in the course of one week."

in affection, the *Minerva* developed into a commercial newspaper after Webster left, and its circulation dwindled from about 1,700 to 1,000.

Perhaps the best writer of the period was William Cobbett. Although he lived in America for only six years (1794-1800), he became known as the Federalists' most effective publicist and replaced John Fenno, the official, subsidized party editor, as their leading journalistic advocate. Cobbett began his career as a writer after serving for seven years in the British army, mainly in India. Upon leaving the army, he wrote a pamphlet exposing military corruption. That pamphlet inaugurated a career that would make him one of the most famous figures in British journalism history. At this point, however, unable to substantiate the charges he made, he fled to France. Finding France in the throes of revolution and inhospitable for an English émigré, he departed for Philadelphia in 1794. In the United States, he sided with the Federalists and even began to write with an affinity for the British king and for rule by the aristocratic class in his adopted country. This apparent turnaround in philosophy and his condescension toward democracy may be explained by Cobbett's desire to be a respected "country gentleman" and his belief that the traditional way of life that he preferred was disappearing.

After making a name for himself with two political pamphlets and a periodical titled *The Political Censor*, in 1797 he launched *Porcupine's Gazette* as a daily newspaper, its name taken from Cobbett's pseudonym, "Peter Porcupine." He was the master of invective. Benjamin Russell described his role harshly but probably accurately. Cobbett, Russell said, "was never encouraged and supported by the Federalists as a solid, judicious writer in their cause; but was kept merely to hunt Jacobinic [i.e., Republican] foxes, skunks, and serpents."[20] Cobbett could be hard on anyone, but he especially relished attacking his Republican antagonist Benjamin Bache, editor of the *Aurora* in Philadelphia. He called the *Aurora* "Mother Bache's filthy dishcloth" and described its editor as "the white-livered, black-hearted thing Bache, that public pest and bane of decency." As if that were not enough, he wrote an entire article devoted to Bache, describing him as an "ill-looking devil ... [whose] eyes never get above your knees."[21]

[20] Quoted in Frederic Hudson, *Journalism in the United States, From 1690 to 1872* (New York, 1873), 154.

[21] *Porcupine's Gazette*, 14 November 1797. For a detailed account of party newspapers' use of such language, see Wm. David Sloan, "Scurrility and the Party Press, 1789-1816," *American Journalism* 5 (1988): 97-112.

NEW-YORK EVENING POST.

Federalist Flagship
With support from Alexander Hamilton and other leading Federalists, the *New York Evening Post* was launched with superior offices, supplies, and workmanship. Under the editorship of William Coleman, it quickly took the lead among Federalist newspapers.

Cobbett was closely aligned with Hamilton and in 1799, following Hamilton's lead, broke with Adams in the president's re-election attempt. His denunciation of Adams for sending a peace delegation to France and thereby selling out to the "Jacobinical" Republicans was as strong as the criticism Adams received from Republicans for other actions. Adams privately considered using the Alien Law to get Cobbett deported. Instead, Cobbett lost a libel suit to Republican Benjamin Rush and fled to New York. Faced with having to pay a $5,000 judgment, he returned to England in 1800.

The situation grew bleak for Federalists with the presidential election of that year. Their arch-enemy, Thomas Jefferson, was the victor. To make matters worse for New York Federalists, Republican George Clinton won a landslide victory as governor. He appointed his nephew, DeWitt Clinton, to rid government positions of Federalists. Everyday, he ousted members of the opposition. Not only was Hamilton's political condition declining; he was falling into disgrace. Many Federalists blamed his attacks on Adams for the party's loss of the presidency.

Members of the party in New York, beseiged by the Republican editor James Cheetham, felt they needed a strong organ to present their case. In May of 1801, a group of Hamiltonian Federalists gathered in the home of one of New York's wealthiest merchants, determined to start a newspaper. Needed was $10,000 seed money. Hamilton and his friends secretly circulated a founders' list among trusted Federalists, asking each to contribute at least $100, and they quickly raised the money. Hamilton put $1,000 into the venture. They selected William Coleman, a lawyer and frequent newspaper writer, to edit the paper. The first issue of the *New York Evening Post* appeared on November 16, with 600 subscribers, most from the inner circle of the state's Federalist party. It was affluent from birth. Intended as the flagship paper of the Federalist fleet, it had a printing shop boasting four complete sets of type at a time when most papers did not have one whole set.

Soon, the *Evening Post* was the recognized spokesman of the leading wing of the Federalist party. Its circulation reached 1,100; and its weekly edition, the *New York Herald*, circulated some 1,600 copies around the country. Much of the circulation resulted from the fact that the papers were known to be Hamilton's voice. Immediately upon its appearance, the *Evening Post* challenged the venerable *Gazette of the United States* for leadership of the Federalist press. Less than a year after the paper's founding, the Republican editor James Callender called Coleman the "Field-Marshal of the Federalist editors." As the mouthpiece of the most earnest Federalists, the *Evening Post* virulently opposed Jefferson's administration even though Coleman was considered more dignified and thoughtful than most editors. He continued as editor through the end of the Federalist party, retaining until the end his position as the party's leading journalistic spokesman.

Federalists made various attempts to establish other papers as national and regional organs, but they met limited success. The most determined attempt was that of Boston Federalists on behalf of the *New-England Palladium*. While Hamilton was working out plans for starting the *Evening Post* in New York, Fisher Ames, Timothy Dwight, and other leading New England Federalists envisioned a national paper in Boston of the stature the *Gazette of the United States* had enjoyed under Fenno. They turned to the *Palladium*. To achieve their goals, however, the paper had to be revitalized. In the spring of 1801, Ames wrote fellow Federalists that the new editor, Warren Dutton, would have to be encouraged, the paper's circulation increased, and party adherents engaged in its publication. Of immediate concern were literary contributions, and Ames asked such politician-writers as Rufus King, George Cabot, and Oliver Wolcott Jr. to submit material. The necessary support of leading Federalists, however, did not materialize; and the work of keeping the paper supplied with material fell to a few of the more active party faithful. The *Palladium* still became the leading Federalist organ in Massachusetts for a short time. In 1803, however, despite the bright plans Ames had proposed, its editor resigned, and even Ames abandoned the paper and supported the development of another, the *Boston Repertory*.

The Burr-Hamilton Duel

Political Attack Ends in Death of Federalists' Leading Light

On the morning of July 11, 1804, the Vice President of the United States, Aaron Burr, shot and killed Alexander Hamilton, the first secretary of the U.S. treasury and one of the nation's most influential citizens. The shooting, a duel, occurred after Burr read in a New York newspaper of an attack on his character by Hamilton.

Hamilton, the leading Federalist, and Burr, a Republican, had long been political enemies. After Jefferson and Burr tied in the presidential election of 1800, Hamilton lobbied for Jefferson in the U.S. House of Representatives. Burr became Vice President, but Jefferson distrusted him, and his national career was stymied. In 1804 he sought to become governor of New York by appealing to a group of disaffected Federalists who believed New York and New England should secede from the Union. Hamilton reportedly called Burr "a dangerous man about whom he could detail a still more despicable opinion."

Burr challenged Hamilton to explain or disavow the printed account of his speech. Hamilton's answer failed to satisfy Burr, and so the two men met on a cliff overlooking the Hudson River near Weehawken, New Jersey. It was the same place Hamilton's twenty-year-old son had been killed in a duel three years earlier.

The first eyewitness account of the duel was reported in the *New York Morning Chronicle*, a paper that Burr and other New York Republicans had founded. It reported that both parties took aim and concluded that the conduct of the men involved was perfectly proper, as suited the occasion. In cities such as Philadelphia, Republican papers praised Hamilton as a patriot but were notable for not condemning Burr.

For several weeks, the *New York Evening Post*, a Federalist paper that Hamilton had been instrumental in founding in 1801, ran stories about the duel surrounded by heavy black borders. A dispute arose about whether Hamilton really intended to return Burr's fire, and the seconds almost fought another duel.

Mark Strand
Moorhead State University

One of the most notable of Americans during the early years of the Republic, Alexander Hamilton was continually involved with newspapers. After co-authoring the series of articles known as the "Federalist" papers, he was instrumental in helping to found and support several leading Federalist journals. In 1805, as one of the defense attorneys in the Croswell case, he played a leading role in getting libel law liberalized. He was killed by Aaron Burr in a duel that resulted in part from the trial. In the illustration of the duel at the top, Hamilton is the figure on the right. It is ironic that Hamilton should die for criticizing Burr, a public figure. Hamilton believed the government and its officials should not be immune from criticism, and he urged public figures to take an active role in discussing political affairs through newspapers as he often did. A few months earlier, he represented a young Federalist editor, Harry Croswell, in his appeal of a libel conviction in a New York court. Croswell published *The Wasp* in Hudson, in upstate New York, as a response to *The Bee*, a local Republican paper, but he stung President Jefferson when he accused him of paying a journalist to attack George Washington and John Adams. Hamilton argued that the press should be "free to publish the truth, from good motives and for justifiable ends, though it reflect on government, on magistrates, or individuals." Croswell's appeal ended in a tie vote in the appeals court, but New York later rewrote its libel laws in light of Hamilton's argument.

General Advertiser.

The *Aurora*
Under Benjamin Franklin Bache, Philadelphia's *General Advertiser* (better known as the "Aurora") took the lead among Republican newspapers because of Bache's inside knowledge of politics and hard-hitting writing style. After Bache died of yellow fever in 1798, his assistant, William Duane (inset), married the widow Bache, took over ownership of the *Aurora*, and enlarged its political influence. Duane was forty years old when he married Mrs. Bache. The portrait above was made when he was in his twenties.

Bache, Duane, and the Aurora

Fighting the Federalist newspapers toe-to-toe were a number of prominent Republican papers. Like Federalists, Republican politicians also helped establish newspapers, but no paper during the Federalist-Republican era matched over a long period the leadership that the independently founded *Aurora* in Philadelphia provided. It sustained its leadership without the benefit of inordinate government patronage. Despite the fact that Republicans extended some aid to the paper, its founder, Benjamin Franklin Bache, spent $20,000 of his own to keep it afloat. Started in 1790 when Bache was only twenty-one years old, the paper was consistently strong in opposing the Federalist influence in the national government. Most other Republican editors, who correctly assumed that Bache was on close terms with Jefferson and other national Republican leaders, looked to it for guidance. Grandson of Benjamin Franklin, Bache had spent his early years in France and was kindly disposed to the French cause. When George Washington showed favoritism toward England, Bache turned on him, becoming the first Republican who dared question the president's performance.

Because of Bache's eminence, he became a target of constant Federalist attempts to intimidate and silence him. On one occasion or another, Treasury Secretary Oliver Wolcott threatened to investigate the *Aurora* for treason, Federalist Speaker of the House Jonathan Dayton barred Bache from the House floor, Federalist editors and politicians subjected him to written and verbal attacks, Federalist merchants imposed an advertising boycott on the *Aurora* and barred the paper from their establishments, the government tried Bache for sedition, and individuals and mobs physically attacked him. In the face of such threats, he refused to ease his attacks on Federalist policies. Eventually, as he had expected, a mob assaulted him and his family. On the night of May 7, 1798, during a national crisis over relations between the United States and France, a party of intoxicated Federalist supporters marched on Bache's home. With only the editor, his wife, and their children in the house, the mob banged on the doors and windows and filled the night with insults and catcalls. Soon, however, Bache's friends and neighbors, roused by the commotion, drove off the mob. Two nights later — following a day that President Adams had called to be devoted to prayer and fasting and during which violent denunciations of Republicans had been issued — a mob again marked Bache's home for attack. The editor assembled and armed friends, who prepared for a defense of the home, and the mob that showed up only broke a few windows.

After the failure of the mobs, the United States government proceeded against Bache. Treasury Secretary Wolcott investigated him for treason as a French secret agent after Bache published a secret state paper from the French foreign minister. When the investigation failed, the government then charged him under the Sedition Act for statements he had made in his defense. Before he could be tried, however, yellow fever struck Philadelphia in July of 1798. Residents fled, and by September most newspapers had suspended publication. Like John Fenno, however, Bache remained to carry on his party's fight. On September 6 he contracted the fever and died four days later.

Bache's widow made arrangements to continue the paper; and his assistant, William Duane, took over the editorship. Under Duane, who soon married Mrs. Bache and became sole proprietor of the *Aurora*, the paper continued as the Republicans' leading voice. Because other Republican editors appreciated the prestige Bache had gained for the *Aurora* and admired Duane's own hard-hitting style and exposure of Federalist tactics, they copied much of the material that appeared in the paper, and it became the bible of Republicans in Pennsylvania and other states. Federalists, who called the *Aurora* the "great speaking trumpet of the devil,"[22] so feared Duane that he was arrested for seditious libel of President Adams under the common law, arrested twice under the Sedition Act, and nearly indicted under the Alien Act. Despite attempts to silence him, Duane was undaunted in his loud partisan support of Thomas McKean in his victorious campaign for Pennsylvania governor in 1799 and of Jefferson in his 1800 triumph. Jefferson credited his election in part to Duane's support.

Duane, however, was personally ambitious and eager for government patronage. That led him into bitter factional battles among Republicans for political power in Pennsylvania. He eventually broke with James Madison, and the strife that continued until 1810 finally wore much of the shine from Duane's journalistic stature and political power. Despite his disagreements with the national Republican leadership, his factionalism in state politics, the fact that the national capital moved from Philadelphia to Washington, and the fact that Jefferson shifted much of his support from the *Aurora* in 1801 to the new *National Intelligencer*, the *Aurora* remained the leading national Republican paper. While the *Intelligencer* was a source of news from the capital, the *Aurora*'s editorial comments were reprinted nationwide. "Duane's press," wrote a Madison supporter in 1808, "with all its indecency, is worth for our purposes all others...[because the] circulation of his paper is so universal throughout the United States."[23]

National Gazette

By PHILIP FRENEAU.

Vol. I. MONDAY, October 31, 1791. Numb. 1.

TO THE PUBLIC.

Philip Freneau: Poet, Rascal
Philip Freneau had become a national celebrity with his poetry about the American war for independence. "The Poet of the Revolution," he was called. With, however, his continual attacks on the federal government through the *National Gazette*, President George Washington condemned him as "that rascal Freneau," and the name became better known than his earlier one.

Republican Editors

Despite the prestige of the *Aurora*, Jefferson and his closest political associates twice turned from it to help establish other official organs, the *National Gazette* in 1791 and the *National Intelligencer* in 1800. Madison was the primary force in getting the *National Gazette* started; and Jefferson, an active participant. Madison proposed the idea for the paper to Philip Freneau, a staunch Republican and Madison's roommate at Princeton. He had gained national fame as the "Poet of the Revolution." Jefferson, then Secretary of State, offered him the job of translator of French. The clerkship, however, was of little value, for the money Freneau had to pay to hire assistants exceeded his salary.

Madison and Jefferson expected Freneau to combat Fenno's *Gazette of the United States* and intended his paper from the start to be a national organ. Because of his intellect and writing ability, Freneau conducted the fight with success. Identified as the personal organ of the national Republican leadership, the *National Gazette* quickly became the leader of the nation's Republican press. It circulated to local Republican officials and editors throughout the country and provided the model for partisan thinking and writing. In 1793, however, Jefferson resigned as Secretary of State. With his departure went Freneau's clerkship and the printing patronage the *National Gazette* had been getting from the State Department. The paper, which had boasted a circulation of 1,300, ceased publication two weeks later. After the demise of the *National Gazette*, leadership among the Republican press reverted to the *Aurora*.

It was not until seven years later that another national organ was established under the auspices of the party's leaders. This new paper was Samuel Harrison Smith's *National Intelligencer*. Unlike Freneau's paper, Smith's venture was promoted as much by its editor as by its patrons. Sensing that Jefferson could win the 1800 election, Smith began work during the summer on starting

[22] *United States Oracle*, 22 March 1801.

[23] Thomas Truxton to Madison, 17 March 1808, quoted in Noble Cunningham, *The Jeffersonian Republicans in Power* (Chapel Hill, N.C., 1963), 273.

the paper, and in August he solicited aid from Madison. Assured that help would be forthcoming should Jefferson gain the presidency, Smith began publication even though a major investment of $12,000 to $15,000 would be needed to publish for the first year and extensive patronage was contingent on the election's outcome. Jefferson's victory, however, assured success. In the *Intelligencer's* first year, the Departments of State and the Treasury awarded it the largest share of their printing, and its printing patronage from Congress was substantial. Although Jefferson denied any formal connection with the paper, Smith served as the spokesman of the executive branch of the government and was a close friend of the president.

Throughout Jefferson's two terms, Smith remained a faithful, relatively temperate supporter, with the *Intelligencer* not only serving as the outlet for official views but also providing extensive accounts of national government operations. It continued as a voice of the Republican cause after Jefferson had left the presidency and even after Smith had left the editorship. In 1810 it was sold to Joseph Gales Jr., who had trained for two years under Smith. During the two administrations of Madison, it served as his official organ; but the relationship between the editors and Madison and his Secretary of State, James Monroe, was more distant and formal than the one between Smith and Jefferson. In 1812 William Winston Seaton, Gales' brother-in-law, joined him as co-owner. Gales remained with the paper until his death in 1860; and Seaton, until retirement in 1864.

Among other Republican papers, the most notable were Thomas and Abijah Adams' *Independent Chronicle* in Boston, James Cheetham's *American Citizen* in New York, and Thomas Ritchie's *Richmond Enquirer*. All provided regional press leadership and were involved in party organization. The Adams brothers acquired the *Independent Chronicle* in 1788 and waged a vigorous battle against New England Federalism and Russell's *Columbian Centinel*. In 1799 officials indicted them under both the Sedition Act and Massachusetts libel law. Thomas, the older brother, was too sick to appear at his trial but was found guilty, along with Abijah, who was sentenced to thirty days in jail. The illness and the pending trial forced them to sell the *Chronicle*. Thomas died soon afterward. The *American Citizen* had been established by John Holt in 1766 as the *New York Journal*. In 1800 Cheetham joined the staff as editor and renamed the paper. It was the leading organ of the Clinton faction of the Republican party. The *Enquirer*, founded in 1804, became the organ of Virginia Republicanism and a semi-personal organ of Jefferson.

Regional and Local Papers

While the leading newspapers were found in larger cities, virtually every town in every region of the country had its own partisan papers. In Georgia, Republicans helped establish the *Augusta Chronicle* in 1790. When its editor, John E. Smith, died in 1803, Georgia Senator James Jackson hired Dennis Driscol of Baltimore's *American Patriot* to edit it. Jackson then wrote Gov. John Milledge, "I hope he will be properly supported. I have taken the liberty to promise him yours — as well as much of the public [printing] work, as is consistent with your duty. I shall procure him all the subscribers I can."[24] In Buckstown, Maine, William W. Clapp started the Federalist *Gazette of Maine* in 1805 at the encouragement "of a number of respectable men" in the area. When Anthony H. Holland bought the *Gazette* in 1811, he promised that it would continue to "undeviatingly support the politics of Washington."[25] The Newport Republican Association was organized in 1808 to found the *Rhode Island Republican*. It sold shares for $5 each, with the income administered by a board of directors, which oversaw the operation of the newspaper. In Plattsburgh, New York — after the editor of the existing *American Monitor* married and changed the paper's sentiments from Republican to Federalist in accord with the partisan feelings of his wife — local Republican politicians in 1811 formed a joint stock enterprise to begin the *Plattsburgh Republican*. Even in the West, which was just being settled, parties and factions founded newspapers. The *Reporter* was established in Lexington, Kentucky, in 1806 as the home-state organ of Henry Clay. In Louisiana, where many editors served in the army or militia, James Wilkinson, military governor and an associate of Aaron Burr, effectively controlled the newspapers. Editors were told that "the soldier's back should smart for the printer's insolence."[26]

While parties helped establish numerous newspapers, papers entered party ranks in a number of ways. Editors whose political beliefs were in accord with those of a particular party founded most of them as partisan vehicles. Sometimes editors of a different persuasion bought papers and converted them into partisans of the opposition. William Winston Seaton, as one instance, converted the *North Carolina Journal* from Federalist to Republican when he bought it from William Boylan, who had inherited it from his father. On rare occasions, a new editor would be hired who would bring about a conversion.

Even more infrequently, a party might gain a new paper through its editor's changing his ideology and transferring his paper's allegiance from one party to the other. For an editor to change faith, however, was looked on as political treason, and the party faithful usually attributed unclean motives to journalistic Judases. Besides losing respect, wayward papers usually lost financial support and contributing writers. The effect on the *Castine* (Me.) *Journal and Eastern Advertiser* was typical. When it made a gradual swing to the Republican side in 1801, a policy change contrary to prevailing opinion in the area, it suffered a sizeable loss of advertising and subscriptions, and the editor decided to remove the *Journal* to Hampden.

The most notorious of the turncoats was James Callender, a

[24] 16 March 1803, quoted in Cunningham, *The Jeffersonian Republicans in Power*, 240.

[25] Quoted in Frederick Fassett Jr., *A History of Newspapers in the District of Maine 1785-1820* (Orono, Me., 1932), 168-9.

[26] In William Bass Hatcher, *Edward Livingston: Jeffersonian Republican and Jacksonian Democrat* (University, La., 1940), 132.

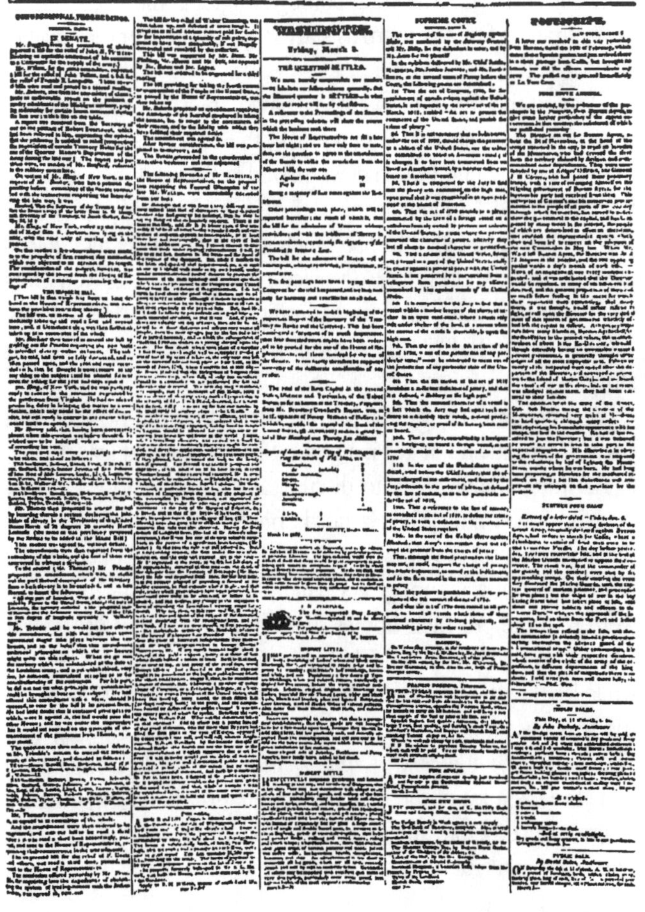

National Intelligencer.

Smith, Gales, and the *Intelligencer*
Under the patronage of the national Republican leadership, the *National Intelligencer* became the official voice of Presidents Jefferson, Madison, and Monroe and something of the official record of government. Partisans who thought Samuel Harrison Smith (bottom left), its founder, was too mild contemptuously referred to the paper as "Mr. Silky Milky Smith's National Smoothing Plane." After serving as Smith's assistant for two years, Joseph Gales Jr. (bottom right) bought the paper in 1810. Under his editorship, it was one of Madison's staunchest supporters during the War of 1812. Gales' brother-in-law, William Winston Seaton, joined him as a partner in 1812 and served as editor until 1864. The partnership of Gales and Seaton provided an official record of debates in the U. S. Congress until that body finally hired its own reporters. Smith died in 1845, Gales in 1860, and Seaton in 1866.

former Republican editor who printed a mass of scandalous material about Jefferson, including the story that Jefferson had fathered children by one of his slaves. While Callender's biography is infamous, however, it did not exemplify political editors. His desertion of Jefferson in 1801 and subsequent attacks were an anomaly and revealed more about Callender's personality than about journalism of the period. The desire for money, for large sales of his works, rather than any desire to aid his party, often motivated his action. He revealed his attitude in a letter to Jefferson in 1799. If only he could sell 1,500 copies of his pamphlets, he wrote, he then would "have some money...and try to find 50 acres of clear land, and a hearty Virginia female, that knew how to fatten pigs and boil hominy, and hold her tongue; and then adieu to the Rascally society of mankind for whom I feel an indifference which increases per diem."[27] Callender also believed that he had suffered great hardship in his fight for Jefferson's election to the presidency and that Jefferson afterwards had neglected him. He professed his anger at "the ingratitude of the Republicans who after getting into power had left him in the ditch."[28]

The Press and the War of 1812

Whether the United States would remain a united nation was soundly tested by the War of 1812. The war, in which the young nation fought against Great Britain, its former master, resulted from several causes. To Americans, the most important were Britain's support of Indian hostilities along the frontier, interference with American trade, and impressment of American sailors into the British navy.

Republicans and Federalists disagreed, however, over whether those were causes strong enough to require war.[29] With the Republican James Madison serving as the nation's president, Republican editors generally favored the war. They urged unity in support of the war effort. "This is not the time for debating the propriety of war," the *National Intelligencer* declared. "WAR IS DECLARED, and every patriot must unite in its support."[30] As the war progressed, they emphasized the successes that the American military achieved and downplayed the defeats.

Federalist editors, on the other hand, believed France was America's real enemy and that war with England was not justified no matter what reason Republicans might give. After Congress declared war, however, they took a variety of approaches. Some stopped all opposition to the war and insisted that their party, along with all other citizens, be loyal to their country. Radical

[27]Callender to Jefferson, September 1799, quoted in Noble Cunningham, *The Jeffersonian Republicans: The Formation of Party Organization, 1789-1801* (Chapel Hill, N.C., 1957), 171.

[28]James Monroe to James Madison, 23 May 1801, James Monroe Papers, New York Public Library, New York, N.Y.

[29]The best treatment of the general subject of the press and the war can be found in Susan Thompson, "The Press and the War of 1812," unpublished paper presented to the annual convention of the American Journalism Historians Association, 27-30 September 1995, Tulsa, Okla.; and Carol Sue Humphrey, "The War of 1812, 1809-1815," chapter 6 in *The Press of the Young Republic, 1783-1833* (Westport, Conn., 1996).

[30]*National Intelligencer*, 7 June 1812.

Federalists, though, continued in their resistance. Typifying their fiery stance, the editor of the *American Daily Advertiser* argued that "THE WAR in which we are engaged is the most hopeless of any ever undertaken by any nation. — It is the fortune of our administration to involve us in a war, in which our success and our defeat would be equally ruinous. If we are defeated, we are overwhelmed with disgrace; if we are victorious, we are victorious over the power which stands between us and the despotism of imperial France."[31]

Maintaining such strident opposition to America's war effort, several of the radical Federalist newspapers became the victims of Republican mobs. The most violent attacks targeted the *Federal Republican* in Baltimore. On June 22, 1812, four days after Congress declared war and following an editorial in the newspaper that lambasted Republican leaders, a mob destroyed the paper's presses and supplies and burned its building. A month later, the paper resumed publication out of a house stocked with ammunition and defended by supporters, including "Light Horse Harry" Lee, the Revolutionary War general. The July 27 issue carried an inflammatory editorial, written by one of its editors, 27-year-old Alexander Hanson, claiming that high-ranking Republicans had instigated the earlier mob attack. That evening, a mob gathered and began its assault by shattering all the windows in the house. The newspaper's defenders fired warning shots to get the mob to disperse, but the noise attracted an even larger number of irate people. The mob then forced its way into the house. The defenders killed one member of the mob and wounded several others. Word spread throughout the city, and the size of the mob continued to increase, swelling to more than 1,500. Finally, law and military officials intervened, just as the mob prepared to fire on the house with a cannon. The officials convinced the newspaper's defenders to surrender and to be jailed until an investigation could be made.

The next night, a mob attacked the jail, killing one of the Federalists and inflicting injuries so severe that several others, including Hanson, were maimed for life or had their lives shortened. The only way they escaped death was by feigning to be dead, but the attackers even then stuck them with penknives and dropped hot wax into their eyes to determine if they were faking. Doctors arrived and convinced the rioters that medical science needed the bodies. They tended to the injured and then secretly removed them to safety out of town.

In covering the war itself, newspapers continued to rely on the techniques of newsgathering that they had used since colonial times. They had no reporters and got their news, instead, from official and private letters. Sometimes written by army generals and eyewitnesses to battles, the letters contained many vivid, objective, and accurate accounts. The major newspapers near the scenes of battles, such as the *National Intelligencer* in Washington and the *New York Evening Post*, also carried first-hand reports. Other papers reprinted the news items for their local readers. Particularly helpful in providing a chronicle of war action were Hezekiah Niles' thorough though Anglophobic *Niles' Weekly Register* and a few war journals started specifically for coverage of the conflict.

Despite the differences among newspapers in their attitudes toward the war, virtually all of them, both Federalists as well as Republicans, celebrated when news arrived in February 1815 that the war had ended. "No intelligence," the *Federal Republican* editorialized, "has occasioned half so much joy."[32] Likewise, all rejoiced at the news of Andrew Jackson's victory at the Battle of New Orleans a few days after the war had officially ended. "ALMOST INCREDIBLE VICTORY!" the *National Intelligencer* headlined its story.[33]

Victory, however, came at just the wrong time for the Federalist party. Near the end of 1814, a group of New England leaders met at Hartford, Connecticut, to discuss, among other topics, secession from the Union. The Hartford Convention concluded by producing only a list of grievances, but the meeting provoked the intense anger of war supporters. Then, just as the conventioneers were returning to their homes, the news of the end of the war arrived. Republican editorials made fun of Hartford delegates, while labeling all their Federalist supporters traitors to their country, an accusation with which most Americans apparently agreed. The *American Watchman and Delaware Republican* exulted that "the enemies of the country [have] shrunk into their native insignificance before the appalling ranks of republican freemen. They have sunk, never more to rise."[34]

Newspapers in the Second Party System

With the demise of the Federalist party, Republicans were left as America's only party. The one-party system was, however, short-lived. Political turmoil marked the "Era of Good Feeling" of 1816-1824 as the membership of the Republican party began splitting into factions. By 1824 party unity and discipline had vanished. By the time of the election of that year, the split had grown bitter. During the election, John Quincy Adams and William Crawford (Republicans), Henry Clay (Whig), and Andrew Jackson (Democrat) all attracted factional newspapers. No candidate gained a majority of votes in the electoral college. Despite the fact, however, that Jackson had received more votes than any of his opponents, Clay threw his support to Adams. After winning election by the disputed vote, Adams appointed Clay Secretary of State.

By the 1828 election, the factions had divided into two parties, the Whigs (made up of conservative Republicans and old-line Federalists) and Jacksonian Democrats (often associated with the "rise of the common man" in American history). As the Republicans had done earlier, Whigs appealed to the middle classes, but Jacksonian Democrats aimed their appeals more at the masses of Americans as changing state laws enlarged the number of voters

[31] *American Daily Advertiser*, 10 February 1813.

[32] *Federal Republican*, 14 February 1815.

[33] *National Intelligencer*, 7 February 1815.

[34] *American Watchman and Delaware Republican*, 21 October 1815

Major Jacksonian-Era Newspapers and Editors

		Regional/State	National
National Republican			
	Official organ		*National Intelligencer* Washington, Joseph Gates, 1810-1864 William Winston Seaton, 1812-1864 *National Journal* Washington, Peter Force, 1823
Whig			
	Official organ	*Evening Journal* Albany, N.Y., Thurlow Weed, 1830-1863	
	Independent	*Republican* Springfield, Mass. Samuel Bowles II, 1824-1844 *Courier and Enquirer* New York James Watson Webb, 1826-1861	
Jacksonian Democrat			
	Official organ	*Argus* Albany, N.Y. Edwin Croswell, 1823 *Enquirer* Richmond, Va. Thomas Ritchie, 1804-1845 *New Hampshire Patriot* Concord, Issac Hill *Argus of Western America* Frankfort, Ky. Amos Kendall, 1824-1829	*United States Telegraph* Duff Green, 1826-1836 *Globe* Washington Francis Blair, 1830-1845

eligible to participate in elections. Although this second party system was more sophisticated than the first, its party machinery still was not elaborate in modern terms. Jackson operated through correspondence committees in the states, congressional leaders, a central committee, and newspaper editors. National organization was not extensive, and people still frowned on candidates who campaigned personally.

The parties, however, strengthened and refined their techniques and structure. On the national level, factions in Congress realigned. They established and patronized numerous newspapers, began campaign funds, attempted national conventions, and constructed party platforms. On the state and local levels, newspapers sprang up, and factions organized committees to coordinate party operations and held conventions to nominate candidates. All parties and factions were aiming at expanding their popular support and tying the electorate more closely to the party. The parties later became electoral machines, nominating candidates for office and organizing efforts to elect them. Active participation increased among the public. One of the key agents in the new system was the newspaper editor, who helped organize and run party operations, mobilize voters, campaign for candidates during a time when personal campaigning was considered improper, and advocate party views.

Jackson's Big Three

Like party spirit, newspaper partisanship also intensified during the second party system. When political dealing took the 1824 election from Jackson, he turned to newspapers as one of the primary components of his political organization. Using them more effectively during the 1828 campaign than had any candidate up to that time, he gained widespread popular support. After a campaign surpassing even the one of 1800 in abusiveness, he got the electoral votes of all states except those of the Northeast.

Most important of the Democratic papers were those personally associated with Jackson, first Amos Kendall's *Argus of Western America* in Frankfort, Kentucky, then Duff Green's *United States Telegraph* in Washington, and finally Francis P. Blair's *Washington Globe*. These newspapers promoted Jackson's presidential candidacy and helped him carry out his programs once he gained office.

Kendall was the most important political force to come out of Kentucky since Henry Clay, the Speaker of the U.S. House of Representatives and one of the towering political figures of the era. An early supporter of Jackson, a fellow Westerner, Kendall was instrumental in organizing Jackson's supporters and his 1828 presidential campaign, tasks at which he worked effectively through

Leaders of a New Party

Among Jacksonian editors, several had a national influence. Three of the most important were (from left to right), Amos Kendall, Duff Green, and Thomas Ritchie. The first two were Andrew Jackson's national spokesmen, while Ritchie was the leading power in the South. Graduating with honors from Dartmouth College in 1811, Kendall quickly climbed the political ladder. In 1814 he moved to Kentucky to serve as tutor to the children of Sen. Henry Clay. In 1815 he was appointed postmaster at Germantown. The following year he became manager of the *Argus of Western America*. After breaking with Clay, he used the paper to support Andrew Jackson. When Jackson won the presidency, Kendall joined his "Kitchen Cabinet," and Jackson appointed him auditor of the U.S. Treasury. An aggressive politician, Green (nicknamed "Rough" by his opponents) served as editor of the *United States Telegraph*. He was instrumental in building the national Democratic party machinery and in getting Andrew Jackson elected U.S. president in 1828. This photograph of Green was made in his later years, but even then his tough personality was evident. For half a century, Ritchie was one of Virginia's leading political figures and a force on the national scene. Having founded the *Richmond Enquirer* in 1804, he made it the voice of Republicanism in Thomas Jefferson's home state. Through the Richmond Junto, the Virginia political machine, he helped forge Andrew Jackson's followers into the national Democratic Party.

personal contacts and editorship of the *Argus*, the spokesman of Kentucky Democrats. It was in the *Argus* that Jackson in 1825 first outlined his views on government and his platform for the 1828 presidential campaign. Kendall originated the slogan "The world is governed too much," a guiding torch of Jacksonian Democracy, and artfully promoted the image of Jackson as the "farmer soldier" and as a thinker with a "lightning mind" in both military and governmental affairs.

Even more integral to Jackson's success, however, was the *United States Telegraph*, established in 1826 in the aftermath of Jackson's 1824 defeat. Vowing they would not allow the presidency to be stolen from Jackson again in 1828, supporters named as its editor Duff Green, an aggressive and energetic politician-editor who savored political fights. Opponents nicknamed him "Rough" Green for his vigorous and hard-hitting writing. He conceived his role as that of developing and promoting party organization. Hard-working and imaginative in his political thinking, he relied on correspondence, travel, individual contacts, and his newspaper to play a central role in building the Democratic party machinery. Directing the Washington Central Committee of twenty-four top Democratic politicians from across the nation, he served as national coordinator of efforts to elect Jackson in 1828 and supervised much of the Democrats' national strategy. Despite the service he gave Jackson, however, Green was more devoted to Vice President John Calhoun; and soon after Jackson's election, when it became evident Green was defecting to Calhoun in preparation for the 1832 election, Jackson and his advisers decided they needed to establish another paper as the presidential organ.

The new paper, founded in 1830, was the *Washington Globe*. Its editor, Francis Blair, had followed Amos Kendall as editor of the *Argus of Western America*. He had served as chairman of the Democratic Central Committee in Kentucky during the 1828 campaign and was an ardent Jackson supporter. Perhaps no editor ever was closer to a president than Blair was to Jackson. He, Kendall (who had gone to Washington with Jackson as a personal adviser), and John C. Rives, the *Globe*'s business manager, were among the most important members of President Jackson's "Kitchen Cabinet," which, though informal, exerted greater influence on executive policy than did the official Cabinet of department secretaries. It was Kendall and Blair who took Jackson's ideas of government, often expressed in rambling fashion, and gave them cogent written form. Blair assumed the national role that Green had brought to the position of editor but increased its importance through his close association with Jackson. Not only did he serve as spokesman for the president's views; he also played a hand in shaping executive policy.

THE JACKSONIAN PRESS NETWORK

While the Democrats could not match the Whigs in numbers of papers, their newspapers increased considerably in the late 1820s and were better organized as part of the party's operation. The initiative for establishing Jacksonian papers came from congressmen; but governors, state legislators, county officials, and local politicians aided the efforts. In most states, the Jacksonians succeeded where the Whigs had failed: they were able to tie their leading newspapers closely to the state party organizations. Whig newspapers to a large extent remained independent, whereas the Democrats integrated their leading papers into the party structure and used them as mouthpieces of state parties.

A network of cooperating newspapers stretching across the nation aided party consensus. The *Albany* (N.Y.) *Argus*, edited by Edwin Croswell, played a central role in the power the Albany Regency exerted in New York politics. The Regency, headed by Martin Van Buren, later United States President, probably was the best organized machine in American politics of its day and provided direction for Democrats in several states. When the Regency threw its support to Jackson in 1828, other state party organizations followed its lead, and it played a critical role in Jackson's election. Croswell, an experienced journalist, was appointed to the post of editor of the *Argus* in 1823 and thereafter rose quickly in the Regency heirarchy, becoming one of the handful of men who directed the organization. Well-educated and tactful, but firmly believing in party politics, he became a leading exponent of Democratic views, and the *Argus* generally was regarded as the most important newspaper in the North.

The influence of the Regency was increased by its association with Democratic machines in other states, the most prominent of which was the Richmond Junto in Virginia. Thomas Ritchie of the *Richmond Enquirer* headed it. In cooperation with Van Buren and John Calhoun, he shared the credit for structuring Jackson's supporters into the national Democratic party. Through his writings in the *Enquirer*, his leadership in Virginia politics, his ties with leading Democratic politicians in other states, and his politically inspired tours around the country, he helped fashion a tight, nationwide party organization. His national influence in party affairs was demonstrated in 1827 when he effectively chose the individual to be named Speaker of the U.S. House of Representatives. The caucus of Democratic congressmen split between Philip Barbour and Andrew Stevenson, both of Virginia. Someone then suggested that the deadlock be broken by asking the head of the Richmond Junto whom he preferred. Ritchie sent word back that he liked Stevenson, who then was selected on the first caucus ballot.

Of considerable importance as other state organs were such papers as the *Charleston Mercury*, *Nashville Republican*, *Baltimore Republican*, and *Philadelphia Palladium*. In New Hampshire, Isaac Hill ran the well-oiled state machine; and the paper he edited, the *New Hampshire Patriot*, served as the state's Democratic spokesman. It was generally acknowledged as New England's leading Democratic paper, and Hill later served as New Hampshire governor and United States Senator. In Massachusetts in the late 1820s the *Boston Statesman*, edited by the scholarly Nathaniel Greene, played a leading role in the Democratic party. It was succeeded by the *Boston Morning Post*, founded and edited by Charles Greene, brother of Nathaniel. Like the *Statesman*, it served as a mouthpiece of the state party and gained prominence throughout New England.

THE WHIG PRESS

Although Jacksonian Democrats used the press more vigorously, Whigs maintained a majority in newspaper numbers. Sensing a critical need for newspaper support, they spent large amounts of money and devoted tireless effort on the establishment and continuation of papers. Aroused by a surge in the number of new Jacksonian newspapers during John Quincy Adams' presidency (1825-1829), Henry Clay declared, "The course adopted by the Opposition, in the dissemination of Newspapers and publications against the administration and supporting presses, leaves to its friends no other alternative than that of following their example, so far at least as to circulate information among the people."[35] Along with the eminent National Republican newspapers in Washington — Gales and Seaton's *National Intelligencer* and Peter Force's *National Journal* — a network of newspapers stretching through all the states and into virtually every town of any sizeable population supported the party.

The preeminent ones were Samuel Bowles' *Springfield* (Mass.) *Republican*, James Watson Webb's *New York Courier and Enquirer*, and Thurlow Weed's *Albany* (N.Y.) *Evening Journal*. Samuel Bowles II founded the *Springfield Republican* in 1824 as an advocate of the National Republican faction in support of John Quincy Adams. It took up the Whig cause in opposition to Jackson. Known for the quality of its editorials, it was considered the best small-town newspaper in America for most of the nineteenth century under the editorship of Bowles, his son, and his grandson.

Thurlow Weed got his start in politics in the fervent but short-lived Anti-Mason movement in western New York in the 1820s. Strongly opposed to Jackson, he moved into Whig politics and soon became the party's leading tactical politician. With the *Evening Journal*, founded in 1830, serving as the national spokesman of Whig views, Weed joined with the politician William Seward and Horace Greeley, who would gain great journalistic fame later with the *New York Tribune*, to control New York politics for a number of years and direct national Whig strategy.

James Watson Webb founded the *Courier and Enquirer* in 1827 primarily as a newspaper aimed at the mercantile class in New York but also as a supporter of Jackson. By 1830 it had gained a sizeable circulation of around 4,500 and therefore was thought

[35]Quoted in Robert V. Remini, *The Election of Andrew Jackson* (Philadelphia, 1963), 128.

James Watson Webb
The *New York Courier and Enquirer*, Webb's newspaper, had the largest circulation of any newspaper in America in 1830. As a result, Webb and the Albany Regency, the pro-Jackson machine in New York State, wielded wide influence. Jealous, however, that the machine made political decisions without consulting him, in 1832 he broke with the Democratic party and became a leading voice for the opposition, which, upon his advice, began calling themselves "Whigs."

of as influential. The pro-Jackson machine, the Albany Regency, that controlled New York State politics, however, neglected to consult Webb on political matters. Jealous at being left out, Webb in the early 1830s intensified his attacks on the machine and eventually became estranged from the Jacksonian party because of differences on a number of major issues, especially the rechartering of the Second Bank of the United States. By 1832 he had become a zealous partisan of his new cause. It was Webb who first suggested that the party assume the name "Whig."

Newspaper Content and Style

Believing the proper role of the press was to support political causes and parties, editors devoted a large amount of space to political discussions. Only a few, however, let politics fill their papers. While some newspapers were nothing other than vehicles for political argument, most editors recognized that readers also wanted news. The news they gave readers was to a large extent foreign or national rather than local. Not only did newspapers in the larger seaboard cities emphasize foreign news, but many small-town papers of the West also devoted a large amount of space to it. European news, comprising the bulk of the foreign information, varied from about one month to six months in age. News from America's political centers was fresher and a little better covered. Local papers reported events, and other major papers picked up their accounts often within a week. Outside the metropolitan areas, national news was somewhat stale. It usually was clipped from other papers or taken from letters written by acquaintances in Washington, Philadelphia, Boston, New York, Baltimore, or another eastern city.

Newspapers largely neglected local news. They often subordinated even important happenings to national and foreign events. Apparently, editors — especially in smaller towns — thought that there was little reason to take up space with news already known to local residents. That did not mean, however, that papers ignored local political events. Most partisan papers covered local politics rather fully. Indeed, politics made up the bulk of local news. In the cities, unlike in the small towns, newspapers frequently published accounts of local non-political happenings. Most of the local non-political news was about such occurrences as deaths and marriages of prominent residents, disasters such as fires and storms, murders and suicides, and local improvements (reported with boasting and pride) such as settlement, water systems, education, and transportation facilities.

Newspapers also included such items as essays (with morality and religion being popular topics, along with social and economic ones), accounts of public lectures, advice on agricultural practices, and letters on local matters. Summaries of current affairs and mercantile or shipping information might fill the remainder of the news columns. Anecdotes and reports of oddities enlivened newspapers; and most editors apparently felt compelled to help improve the cultural appreciation of their readers through poetry, a literary section, excerpts from informative books, and book reviews.

Along with newspapers, several hundred magazines provided political, religious, and literary material. Prominent were the *Farmer's Weekly Museum*, founded by Isaiah Thomas and continued under Joseph Dennie, who also was noted for his political magazine *Port Folio*; the literary and polemical quarterlies *North American Review* and *American Quarterly*; and Hezekiah Niles' news magazine, *Niles' Weekly Register*.

While the writing in some magazines showed real literary style, much in both magazines and newspapers was dry according to later tastes. It was often formal, wordy, flowery, and tedious. At the same time, many editors had broad general educations in the humanities and classics and possessed first-hand knowledge of politics. Thus, such devices as literary allusions dotted their writing, and their political pieces displayed a thorough understanding of issues and arguments.

The most striking characteristics of newspaper writing, however, were personal invective and abusive political attacks. Editors rarely hesitated to call opponents names or accuse them unjustifiably of some evil. Name-calling sometimes approached art, but it often exhibited no quality better than crudeness. Editors referred to opponents as "insane," "incompetent," "cowardly," "worthless," and other epithets. Sometimes, they tried to be a little more imaginative and came up with names such as "prating poppinjay" and "addled cat's paw" and "double-faced weather-cock."

As absurd as some of the name-calling was, accusations were just as bad. Republicans accused George Washington of, among other things, being a blasphemer and John Adams of being subservient to the British. The most repeated and telling charges against Jefferson were that he was an atheist and that he had fathered children by one of his slaves. Although press abusiveness died down somewhat during the presidency of James Monroe (the "Era of Good Feeling"), conditions changed drastically when Andrew Jackson came onto the national scene. Personal deprecation rose again, surpassing even that of the Jeffersonian presidency. Newspapers published such abusive charges during the 1828 election campaign that Jackson and John Quincy Adams refused to speak to one another when Jackson arrived in Washington for his inauguration. Those charges included speculations that Jackson had lived in adultery with his wife before she had received a divorce from her first husband and that Adams had had pre-marital relations with his wife.

Nathaniel Willis
The founder of America's first religious newspaper, the *Boston Recorder* in 1816, Willis also became an important editor in the field of juvenile magazines. In 1827, he founded the *Youth's Companion* in Boston. It had begun as a department of the *Recorder*, and it remained in publication for more than a century, until 1929. In the original proposal for the magazine, Willis wrote, "This is a day of peculiar care for Youth.... Our children are born to higher destinies than their fathers; they will be actors in a far advanced period of the church and the world...." The *Youth's Companion* became one of the most important in the history of juvenile magazines. Willis died in 1870 at the age of ninety.

The Religious Press

A substantial number of newspapers, approximately 100 in 1830, were purely religious publications. Even though their editors considered a religious press necessary for the support of Christianity, most secular newspapers mirrored the Protestant beliefs and mores of the large majority of Americans and published large amounts of material with an obvious religious tone. Many Christian journalists, however, were concerned about how the press had taken on the extreme partisanship of the times; and they believed that American journals needed to be lifted to a higher plane.

The experience of Nathaniel Willis, who started the Christian *Recorder* in Boston in 1816, provided one example. While editing the *Eastern Argus*, a Republican organ in Portland, Maine, Willis found he could not depend on the party's politicians. First, he reluctantly published a libelous article contributed by one of his backers upon the assurance that the writer would bear all responsibility. Then the writer and party members refused to assist Willis in paying the damages a jury assessed. While helping the Republicans turn the Federalists out of office, "I learned," Willis declared, "that politicians are not only ungrateful, but supremely selfish. They used me as the cat's-paw, but took good care to keep all the chestnuts for their own eating."[36]

After experiencing a religious conversion, Willis began to try to tone down the vitriolic writing in the *Argus*. "I am willing to support the Republican cause," he told his backers, "so long as I can with truth and fairness, but I had done with personalities and misrepresentations." His backers criticized the moderation and threatened to start another party organ. Thereupon, in 1808 Willis sold the *Argus* to an editor more committed to Republican partisanship. After moving to Boston and opening a print shop, he produced a variety of religious material and then started the *Recorder* as a means of keeping the public informed of current events and controversies involving religion.

Depending on definitions, the first religious newspaper in the United States may have been the *Herald of Gospel Liberty*, founded by a Baptist minister, Elias Smith, in 1808 in Portsmouth, New Hampshire. Containing mainly the texts of sermons that Smith delivered, however, it resembled a circular more than a newspaper. The first religious publication exhibiting the true characteristics of a newspaper probably was Willis' *Recorder*.

[36]Nathaniel Willis, *Autobiography of a Journalist* (Boston, 1858).

The Origins of Daily Newspapers
In 1783, Benjamin Towne started America's first daily newspaper, the *Pennsylvania Evening Post and Daily Advertiser.* A few weeks later, John Dunlap started a competitor, the *Pennsylvania Packet and Daily Advertiser* (left). The purpose of both was to serve the commercial needs of the city. The competition lasted only briefly, for Towne was forced to suspend publication within the year. The first dailies were begun for financial reasons. Rather than trying to provide the most recent news, publishers started the papers because their weekly editions could not accommodate the abundance of advertising they were receiving. That purpose was reflected in the names of many of the papers, including New York City's first daily, the *Advertiser* (right).

The Pennsylvania Packet, and Daily Advertiser.

NEW-YORK DAILY ADVERTISER.

By the 1830s, numerous religious newspapers, almost exclusively Christian, were publishing throughout the country. Most of their editors had been trained for the ministry rather than for printing or the newspaper business. As a general rule, therefore, they served their editorial functions well, but their lack of an intense profit-motive frequently left them in financial straits. When they did make a profit, most used the money to support other Christian work such as missionary activities or training of young men for the ministry.

The impetus for religious periodicals came from a variety of sources. Many publications were polemical and waged elaborate doctrinal battles with other papers both of the same denomination and of different faiths. The main concern, however, was moral and social issues. The Second Great Awakening in the 1820s sparked a spiritual revival nationwide, and numerous individuals established newspapers to encourage greater efforts. They spent much of their energy promoting the spread of the Gospel, but they also labored at the forefront in such efforts as helping orphans, promoting world peace, eliminating alcoholism, and abolishing slavery. Christians, one newspaper editorialized, should "aim at nothing more or less than the greatest good of our country" by "diffusing the light of the gospel" and engaging in benevolent works.[37]

Developments in Journalistic Practices

Although the purpose and practices of the party press were definitely partisan, today's historian searching for the genesis of purely "journalistic" devices can find a number of them in the party period. One was the daily newspaper. The first was Benjamin Towne's *Pennsylvania Evening Post and Daily Advertiser* in Philadelphia. When Towne converted to daily publication in 1783, he hoped to provide the mercantile class with up-to-date shipping news. A few weeks later, John Dunlap began a second daily, the *Pennsylvania Packet and Daily Advertiser*. It aimed at the same business audience and soon forced Towne to suspend publication.

As interest shifted to political affairs, another innovation occurred: coverage of sessions of Congress. The House of Representatives had opened its doors to the public in 1789, two days after its first session began. Federalists, however, controlled the Senate. They believed they could best conduct the nation's business out of sight of the prying eyes of the public. They barred not only members of the pubic but even members of the House. Into this situation in 1791 stepped the ardent anti-Federalist Philip Freneau. From the first issue of the *National Gazette* he printed proceedings of the House, and in February 1792 he began an editorial crusade for opening the Senate's doors. Finally, responding to public demand, the Senate approved a measure in February 1794 to open its sessions. The leader in coverage of Congress throughout the party press period was the *National Intelligencer*. From 1800 until the Civil War, it served as the authoritative source of information about the national government.

One of the major developments that affected newsgathering was the Post Office Act of 1792. Urged on Congress by James Madison, who believed that government should encourage the extension of knowledge and the exchange of ideas, the act provided that newspapers sending exchange issues to other papers could do so free of charge. Editors used the exchange paper as a chief newsgathering tool. Newspapers were expected to cover impor-

[37] *New York Religious Chronicle*, 13 May 1826.

tant local events and thus furnish other papers with information about those events. The process worked as an informal news service system. The Post Office Act provided a lifeline to many western papers and enhanced the coverage of news by papers all over the country.

Along with changes in newsgathering, changes occurred also in the printing of editorial opinion. Previously, newspapers usually had presented opinions in long essays or even as series of essays, as a long pamphlet would be if divided into sections. Contributors wrote most of them. During the party press period, what is considered the true editorial emerged. Conductors of papers became "editors" and not just printers, and the writing talent of America's newspaper operators improved. In the 1790s these editors began to show a preference for brief comments over long essays. Following the lead of Barzillai Hudson and George Goodwin of the *Hartford* (Conn.) *Courant*, Noah Webster of New York's *American Minerva*, James Cheetham of New York's *American Citizen*, and John Fenno, they began printing opinions in articles separate from the news. Some editors reserved a specific column for their editorials. The column often carried a standing title or signed editorials to signify that the opinion was the editor's. By 1810 the editorial form was widespread; and by the end of the party press period, pamphlet-style opinion virtually had disappeared.

The editorials revealed a variety of qualities that have become commonplace in American journalism. Many were dull and poorly reasoned. Party newspapers, like those of today, sometimes were filled with columns of tedious reading. Little better could be expected when individuals trained as printers rather than writers ran so many papers.

On the other hand, occasional pieces gleamed. Editors of state and national stature were so closely involved with politics that they could comment with knowledge and authority. They were aware of the subtleties of the questions related to the political system, and the editorials of the opposing sides presented thorough and sound debate on the nature of the system. Name-calling and false charges unfortunately stuck out like festering sores, but intermingled with them were many soundly reasoned and well written editorials that both argued the practical political points of immediate importance and provided discussions of essential questions about the American political system.[38]

Partisanship motivated another innovation: the first correspondents assigned to cover the national capital. Until newspapers began using correspondents, they got most of their news from Washington through private letters from acquaintances in the city and from stories in the *National Intelligencer* or other papers such as the *Federalist* located in the capital. The *Federalist*'s accounts, however, were inferior to those of the *National Intelligencer*, and Federalist editors did not like having to rely on the Republican *Intelligencer* for explanations of government proceedings. In 1808, therefore, the *United States Gazette* in New York and then the *Freeman's Journal* in Philadelphia employed individuals of Federalist persuasion to write reports from Washington. Their arrangements ceased prior to the War of 1812, but in the 1820s a number of papers took up the practice of hiring Washington correspondents.[39]

KENNEBEC JOURNAL.

Newspaper Style

Typical of newspapers of the party period, the *Journal* of Kennebec, Maine, emphasized word content rather than graphics. Most of its news was national in nature, taken from newspapers in the nation's major cities and news centers.

Emphasis also changed from foreign to domestic news. Until around 1800 a majority of news content originated in Europe. Americans still considered themselves the offspring of England even after the American Revolution and thought of Europe as the center of important affairs. Furthermore, until the development of a satisfactory system of roads and an efficient postal system in the United States, transportation to and communication with England often were more convenient than among states. With internal improvements, however, communication became easier; and as

[38]The range and quality of editorial writing are documented in Jerry Knudson, "The Jefferson Years: Response by the Press, 1801-1809" (Ph.D. diss., University of Virginia, 1962); and Wm. David Sloan, "The Party Press: The Newspaper Role in National Politics, 1789-1816" (Ph.D. diss., University of Texas, 1981).

[39]Frederick Marbut, "Early Washington Correspondents: Some Neglected Pioneers," *Journalism Quarterly* 25 (1948): 370-5.

Hoe Cylinder Press
In the 1820s R. Hoe & Co. of New York introduced the first cylinder press ever used in the United States. It speeded up printing capabilities to 2,000 four-page papers per hour.

Americans faced more and more serious domestic issues, newspapers' attention naturally turned inward. Even in the late 1700s, when European news still provided most newspaper content, domestic events such as the 1796 and 1800 presidential elections and the furor over the Alien and Sedition Acts of 1798 created periods of intense interest during which domestic news superseded foreign news.

Throughout the party press period, the major newspapers devoted their attention primarily to national affairs. Papers of regional stature, such as the *Independent Chronicle* and the *Columbian Centinel* in Boston, divided their attention about equally between national and state or local political questions; but the papers of national scope, such as the *New York Evening Post* and the *National Intelligencer*, from the beginning devoted most of their space to national politics. In the smaller, local papers, there was a slight trend as the period progressed of expanding interest from local and state affairs to national ones. This change may have been a result of factors such as the development of national party organization or the increasing direct participation readers had in national elections. By 1810 American newspapers' interest had turned irrevocably to domestic rather than foreign news; and the War of 1812, with its military encounters within the boundaries of the American nation, encouraged this trend even more.[40]

Despite improvements in the postal system, the slowness of news plagued editors. Newspapers reported important events in other parts of the country many days and often weeks after they occurred. They got their foreign news, one of the staples of American journalism, from foreign papers brought by ships. Often these ships did not arrive, were late, or did not have the papers expected; and when the news did arrive, it was weeks behind the event. The War of 1812 awakened Americans to the inconvenience of tardiness of news. Slowness made the public impatient, especially when some impending word of a battle was expected, and newspapers experimented with methods to increase the speed of news transmission. Some eastern papers hired private pony express riders to carry reports more quickly than the mails could. At first, the express was used only for special events such as James Monroe's inaugural address to Congress in 1816, but by the 1830s the practice had become common. In the meantime, the national government in 1825 instituted a special "express post" between major cities, tripling postage rates for the service but cutting delivery time in half.

The party-press period also witnessed one development that revolutionized printing: the cylinder press. The previously used flatbed press required that individual sheets of printing paper be pressed against a flat page of metal type by means of a screw mechanism above the bed. The new press replaced the screw mechanism with a rotating cylinder. The bed of type, with a sheet of paper on top of it, moved under the cylinder, which pressed the paper against the type. In 1825 the first newspaper to install the press was the *New York Daily Advertiser*, giving it the capacity to deliver 2,000 four-page papers per hour. In 1832 Richard Hoe invented the double-cylinder press and doubled the capacity to 4,000 copies per hour.

DECLINE OF THE PARTY PRESS

During Jackson's presidency, the press reached its zenith as a partisan voice, and it remained primarily political for years to come. Even with the advent of the popular penny press in the 1830s,

[40]The traditional historical assumption has been that domestic news did not predominate until the War of 1812. Recent scholarship, however, has given evidence that the shift to domestic news occurred earlier. See Donald Avery, "The American Newspaper: Discovering the Home Front," *American Journalism* 1: 2 (1984): 51-66; Sloan, "The Party Press"; and Knudson, "The Jefferson Years."

most papers continued to operate as partisan organs; but the partisan system was dealt a blow in 1846 when Congress passed legislation requiring the federal government to let bids on printing contracts. That requirement took away the most effective tool parties and politicians had for financing newspaper supporters. In 1860, the Government Printing Office was established, removing much of public printing from private newspapers and further separating the operations of parties from the press. Still, the ideological relationship between parties and papers remained strong, and a majority of newspapers continued to identify with and work for partisan political goals. It was not until 1884, many journalists and observers believed, when leading Republican papers bolted James G. Blaine in his campaign for the presidency, that newspapers took on a full degree of partisan independence. Still, newspaper editorial allegiance to parties was vigorous as late as World War II.

Despite the growing autonomy of newspapers from political parties in the late 1800s, the period of the party press had witnessed great vigor, and newspapers had played an important role during some of the most critical years of the American political system. Although the nature of American newspapers would change later, the press perhaps never would be any more vital to the political life of the nation than it had been during the age of the party press.

RECOMMENDED READINGS

BOOKS

Ambler, Charles Henry. *Thomas Ritchie, A Study in Virginia Politics*. Richmond, 1913. Favorable treatment of Ritchie's attempt to run the *Richmond Enquirer* on a high moral plane.

Ames, William E. *A History of the National Intelligencer*. Chapel Hill, N.C., 1972. Argues that the *National Intelligencer* was more interested in news reporting than vituperative political opinion and that the party press played a valuable role in American politics.

Austin, Aleine. *Mathew Lyon: "New Man" of the Democratic Revolution, 1749-1822*. University Park: Pennsylvania State University Press, 1981. Progressive, sympathetic yet critical biography places Lyon in the context of the Enlightenment, viewing him as one of the Americans who embraced both the right of property and the right to pursuit of happiness.

Brown, Charles H. *William Cullen Bryant*. New York, 1971. Definitive general biography of Bryant, focusing on his journalism and literary work. The *Evening Post* was a responsible, respected newspaper, and Bryant was a champion of liberty.

Clark, Mary Elizabeth. *Peter Porcupine in America: The Career of William Cobbett, 1792-1800*. Philadelphia, 1939. The only book-length work on Cobbett's journalistic career in America, providing a favorable treatment of his role in politics. It concludes, however, that although he attempted to help the Federalist cause, his vituperation actually swayed the nation toward Republicanism.

Crouthamel, James L. *James Watson Webb, A Biography*. Middletown, Conn., 1969. Discusses Webb's involvement in New York and national politics, as he worked for political reform.

Elliot, Robert Neal, Jr. *The Raleigh Register, 1799-1863*. Chapel Hill, N.C., 1955. Approaches Joseph Gales as a progressive leader of southern journalism and examines his role in both Jeffersonian and Whig politics.

Fassett, Frederick Gardiner, Jr. *A History of Newspapers in the District of Maine 1785-1820*. Orono, Maine, 1932. Useful state study of the activities of journalists outside the major cities on the eastern seaboard and the conditions under which they operated.

Fäy, Bernard. *The Two Franklins: Fathers of American Democracy*. Boston, 1933. Progressive interpretation of Benjamin Franklin Bache as a leader of democracy among the Jeffersonian Republicans.

Humphrey, Carol Sue. *The Press of the Young Republic, 1783-1833*. Westport, Conn., 1996. The best book on the party press, it provides an excellent overview of the entire period.

Jackson, George. *Uncommon Scold: The Story of Anne Royall*. Boston, 1937. Biography of the "first woman journalist." Special emphasis on the early portions of her life. Deals to a large extent with her personality and character, as well as her writing — comparing her to various landmark individuals.

Kielbowicz, Richard B. *News in the Mail: The Press, Post Office, and Public Information, 1700-1860s*. Westport, Conn., 1989. The postal system played a key role in the distribution of newspapers and the resultant democratization of America.

Leary, Lewis. *That Rascal Freneau*. New Brunswick, N.J., 1941. Attempts to show how Freneau "tried to adapt himself to an essentially uninterested public, and how he failed."

Merriam, George S. *Life and Times of Samuel Bowles*, 2 vols. New York, 1885. A good example of the Romantic school of history, viewing Samuel Bowles II as an important figure in journalism and American society who exercised a wide influence.

Nerone, John. *Violence Against the Press: Policing the Public Sphere in U.S. History*. New York, 1994. Survey of violence against the press over the years, including acts against minority-owned media, the labor press, and mainstream media.

Nevins, Allan. *The Evening Post: A Century of Journalism*. New York, 1922. One of the best histories of an American newspaper. It considers the *Evening Post* under Coleman and William Cullen Bryant as a paper which, although partisan, was interested in accurate news on many subjects and in well-reasoned opinion.

Rosenfeld, Richard N. *American Aurora*. New York, 1997. A detailed history of Bache and Duane's *Aurora*, noting its integral role in the turmoil of the period.

Scudder, Horace E. *Noah Webster*. Boston, 1883. Chronological, descriptive biography (based largely on Webster's diary) set against the background of Federalist-Republican contentions with emphasis on Webster as a literary "man of letters." He "liked to think that he had a hand in pretty much every important measure in the political and literary history of the country." He was for Federalists, "democracy," freedom, and the nation.

Smith, Elbert B. *Francis Preston Blair*. New York, 1980. The editor Blair was a politician. Emphasis on his relations with presidents Jackson, Van Buren, Lincoln, and Johnson as well as with the political dynasty he helped establish and on the politics of which he was a part.

Smith, Jeffrey A. *Franklin and Bache: Envisioning the Enlightened Republic*. New York, 1990. Analyzes the ideas of Benjamin Franklin and grandson Benjamin Bache and their contribution to the optimistic liberal ideology of the Revolution and the new nation.

Stewart, Donald H. *The Opposition Press of the Federalist Period*. Albany, N.Y., 1969. A voluminous study of the content of Federalist and Republican newspapers.

Tagg, James. *Benjamin Franklin Bache and the Philadelphia Aurora*. Philadelphia, 1991. This biography concentrates on Bache's ideological views.

ARTICLES

Avery, Donald R. "The Emerging American Newspaper: Discovering the Home Front." *American Journalism* 1, 2 (1984): 51-66. Content analysis reveals that "American newspapers began giving less attention to matters foreign and more attention to domestic news in the years just prior to the War of 1812.

Far from occurring during the war, as has been suggested by historians, the trend appears to have begun in earnest as early as 1810."

Baldasty, Gerald. "The Press and Politics in the Age of Jackson." *Journalism Monographs* 89 (1984). Argues that newspapers were central to party politics.

Beasley, Maurine. "The Curious Career of Anne Royall." *Journalism History* 3 (1976): 98-102, 136. Anne Royall, a political journalist, "left a 'profile in courage,' the picture of a woman, paranoid or not, who was willing to pursue a man's career and turn into a town freak rather than shrivel up mentally and physically just because convention called upon her to remain quiet."

Benjamin, G. G. W. "Notable Editors between 1776 and 1800. Influence of the Early American Press." *Magazine of American History* 17 (February 1887): 97-127. Views the party press against important and fierce political strife. Biographical sketches of "a few of the more prominent editors who...influenced the destinies of the republic."

Boston, Ray. "The Impact of 'Foreign Liars' on the American Press (1790-1800)." *Journalism Quarterly* 50 (1973): 722-30. Attributes the effectiveness of the Republican press to a group of foreign-born journalists who came to America with common radical political opinions.

Ewing, Gretchen Garst. "Duff Green, Independent Editor of a Party Press." *Journalism Quarterly* 54 (1977): 733-9. Favorable treatment of the man responsible for the great political success of the *United States Telegraph*.

Ford, Worthington C. "Jefferson and the Newspaper, 1785-1830." *Columbia Historical Society Records* 8 (1905): 78-111. Anti-Jefferson and critical of the Republican press which supported him. Jefferson was indecisive and weak in cultivating the press.

Jellison, Charles A. "That Scoundrel Callender." *Virginia Magazine of History and Biography* 67 (1959): 295-306. Study of Callender's political journalism and his relationship with Jefferson. Takes a middle-of-the-road approach, placing less blame on Callender as a completely scurrilous journalist than other historians have done.

Knudson, Jerry W. "Political Journalism in the Age of Jefferson." *Journalism History* 1 (1974): 20-3. Good overview of editors and newspaper methods during Jefferson's presidency, 1801-1809.

Lanman, Charles. "The 'National Intelligencer' and Its Editors." *American Magazine* 6 (October 1860): 470-81. Favorable biography of Joseph Gales (the father) a man of "good sense and probity of purpose," temperateness, and moderation. "[A]midst all the heats of faction, he never fell into violence."

Lee, Robert Edson. "Timothy Dwight and the Boston Palladium." *New England Quarterly* 35 (1962): 229-39. Insightful study of the relationship between Dwight, a religious politician, and the paper he subsidized. Provides a representative illustration of press-party connections.

List, Karen K. "The Role of William Cobbett in Philadelphia's Party Press, 1794-1799." *Journalism Monographs* 82 (1983). Cobbett was a nominal Federalist and was more interested in promoting his native Britain than the Federalist party.

Marbut, Frederick B. "Decline of the Official Press in Washington." *Journalism Quarterly* 33 (1956): 335-41. Attributes the end of the official party paper in Washington to intra-party bickering and competitive Washington reporting.

Martin, Benjamin Ellis. "Transition Period of the American Press — Leading Editors Early in This Century." *Magazine of American History* 17 (April 1887): 273-94. Early critical study of the party press' coarseness and invective.

Murphy, Lawrence W. "John Dunlap's 'Packet' and Its Competitors." *Journalism Quarterly,* 28 (1951): 58-62. This narrative of competition from 1784 to 1796 provides a favorable view of Dunlap, "for he set the pace of early dailies in many cities after 1784 and his ideas were carried over into dailies of other times."

Nord, David Paul. "The Evangelical Origins of Mass Media in America, 1815-1835." *Journalism Monographs* 88 (1984). Religious societies laid the foundation for mass media through mass printing and distribution of evangelical tracts.

Prince, Carl E. "The Federalist Party and the Creation of a Court Press, 1789-1801." *Journalism Quarterly* 53 (1976): 238-41. Examines Federalist officials' appointment of editors and printers in the party's development of a partisan press.

Reitzel, William. "William Cobbett and Philadelphia Journalism: 1794-1800." *Pennsylvania Magazine of History and Biography* 59 (1935): 223-44. The cultural/political atmosphere was favorable for Cobbett's style of partisan journalism. He was oriented toward the past and tradition and thus attacked radical Republicanism.

Sloan, Wm. David. "'Purse and Pen': Party-Press Relationships, 1789-1816." *American Journalism* 6 (1989): 103-27. Editors received a variety of support from parties, but they were motivated primarily by ideology rather than financial considerations.

Smith, William E. "Francis P. Blair, Pen-Executive of Andrew Jackson." *Mississippi Valley Historical Review* 17 (1931): 543-56. Progressive interpretation of Blair as "the greatest partisan journalist and defender of Jacksonian democracy."

Snapp, Elizabeth. "Government Patronage of the Press in St. Louis, Missouri: 1829-1832." *Missouri Historical Review* 24 (1980): 190-216. The *St. Louis Beacon* received patronage from local, state, and national government and played a central role in politics. It "contributed to a more vigorous political debate and enabled a broader segment of the American people to receive a more balanced understanding of the major issues."

Stewart, Robert K. "The Exchange System and the Development of American Politics in the 1820s." *American Journalism* 4 (1987): 30-42. Through the exchange of newspaper subscriptions and the information that newspapers contained, Jacksonian newspapers and party leaders "nurtured a budding party apparatus that enabled the systematic waging of a war of words and ideas from the largest cities to the most remote outposts of the country."

Touba, Mariam. "Tom Paine's Plan for Revolutionizing America: Diplomacy, Politics, and the Evolution of a Newspaper Rumor." *Journalism History* 20 (1994): 116-30. Origins of a 1798 rumor that France planned to invade America reveal diplomats' use of the press.

6

Freedom of the Press

1600 - 1804

Any discussion of the development of freedom of the press in the United States begins with certain inherent difficulties. Today freedom of the press conjures up images of arguments before the United States Supreme Court by newspapers, broadcasting corporations, and other institutions for the right to report the news. The term has become a journalistic talisman invoked to provide protection for an institutional press to cover everything from libel prosecutions to contempt of court citations to invasion of privacy actions.

The term was less precisely understood in early American history; in fact, it did not even exist for many years after the invention of movable type. The revolution in society that the invention of the printing press brought was slow in coming, as was the development of values included in the American concept of freedom of the press. But slowly, early Americans laid the groundwork for the concept of freedom of the press as known today. Even as this foundation emerged, our ancestors discovered many of the concerns about the powers of the press that are expressed today and considered many views about the possible limitations that should be imposed upon such a powerful instrument of communication.

British Roots of Press Freedom

The search for meaning necessarily begins with freedom of the press in Great Britain, for the British emigrants carried their beliefs in religion, in government, and in freedom of speech with them as they established colonies. From these seeds, the ideals and the fears of the new American nation would grow.

Understanding the English heritage of freedom of the press requires abandoning modern definitions and looking instead at practices in context. For instance, when William Caxton set up his press in England in 1476, he did so as a good businessman who had discovered a new way to make money. He had no crusading notions of spreading the truth about government or religion or anything else. A cloth merchant by trade, Caxton even sought royal patronage to increase his chances of selling the books he published. His press printed only books that would be commercially profitable; and, to ensure profitability, he often doctored manuscripts to insert contemporary principles of chivalry and Christian morality as well as English folk heroes into the stories. Through his decision to publish under royal patronage, Caxton gave early printing a close tie to government, a connection that was maintained for many generations. The tie grew as the government hired Caxton's printing press to make multiple copies of documents, a natural extension of the use of the printing press as a mechanical tool for replacing handwritten manuscripts.

This role of the printing press as a mechanical device continued as it came to serve religion, which in sixteenth and seventeenth century England was closely identified with the reigning monarch. When King Henry VIII established the Church of England in 1529, he opened the door for the Reformation that was sweeping the Continent to invade Great Britain. As the teachings of Martin Luther, John Calvin, and other reformers became popular, the printing press became more important in the lives of the English people. The Calvinists, who became the Puritans in England, preached the priesthood of all believers and placed a high value on individual reading of the Bible to understand God's will. Thus, concern for their souls made the printing press important to the Puritans. The person who controlled those presses was immaterial as long as the Puritans had unrestricted access to the Bible.

Only as the Tudor monarchs tried to control the way in which an individual could believe in God and his access to God's word did the printing press become a point of contention. Initial licensing of printing presses in Great Britain stemmed from efforts to restrict access to dissident (meaning non-Church of England) religious materials. This controversy led to increased demands for freedom to speak, initially, on matters of religious beliefs. In turn, the demands for freedom of speech led dissidents to demand access to printing presses to turn out religious documents. Because church and state were so inextricably intertwined, the demands for religious freedom soon expanded into demands for political

Elizabeth I
During the reign of Elizabeth I, England defeated the Spanish Armada and became the most powerful Protestant nation of Europe. Despite her military triumph, she still faced challenges to her authority from Parliament. Its members insisted on considering topics she had banned from discussion, thus opening the door to freer public debate.

freedom.

This battle over the right to believe in God as one wished also affected the struggle for the right of citizens to petition Parliament for redress of grievances. In 1572, for instance, the Puritans issued "An Admonition to Parliament," in which the authors made their traditional arguments against the established church. After they were found and imprisoned, they claimed that their words were protected from royal anger because the document had been written while Parliament was sitting and thus served as a petition to their representatives. Ancient British rights, they argued, protected citizens seeking action. This notion drew a hostile response from the queen's government, but the ability of individuals to petition the government for redress of grievances, even if discussion of those grievances had been barred by the crown, slowly became an important right of British citizens.

While the Puritans were challenging the religious structure of England, Queen Elizabeth was facing additional forays against her royal prerogatives in Parliament. There, for perhaps the first time, representatives began addressing topics that the queen had banned from discussion. Other than religion, the main topics of concern were the queen's marriage and, after it failed to occur, the succession to the throne. Members of Parliament insisted on debating these issues, despite feeling the queen's wrath from time to time. The door now was open for Parliamentary discussion of more issues. Next came protection for members who spoke on forbidden subjects while Parliament sat, individuals who had been subject to arbitrary arrest and imprisonment for broaching such topics in the past. Then came freedom to talk about banned topics in broader English society.[1] A similar pattern of winning the right to speak on diverse topics would occur in the colonies.

When the subject was not religious in nature, printers were not terribly concerned about licensing measures imposed by the crown. In fact, that historically dreaded institution, the Stationers Company, was set up by Queen Mary in 1557 at the request of printers who wanted to limit competition. In return for a royal grant of monopoly, those entrepreneurs promised to aid the crown in suppressing undesirable printing, which they did with vigor. The Stationers Company thus became the first in a list of historic infringements on freedom of the press that journalists down through the ages have cited as tyrannical attempts by government to subvert the press. In time, that list would include the Star Chamber, the prosecution of John Peter Zenger, the odious Stamp Act, and the Alien and Sedition Acts. Each instance would be seen by partisans of the press as an example of government interference with the institution's freedom and usually would be cited at a time when contemporary affairs seemed to threaten a similar intrusion by government to destroy an important civil liberty. Some of the list of horrors came about innocently enough, as in the cases of the Stationers Company and the Stamp Act. Others such as the prosecution of John Peter Zenger and the Alien and Sedition Acts were products of complicated interactions that led to the determination that quieting of dissent was vital to national survival. In the case of the Stationers Company, its founders' main goal was to secure a comfortable living for themselves and their families. The idea that they would be keeping other printers from achieving the same end did not seem to concern them; nor did they worry much about the ethics of the issue. The matter was simply financial.

When the subject was religious, however, the arguments were sharp, and punishments for divergence from the accepted line were severe. The Puritans, who would later settle Massachusetts Bay and bring the first printing press to the American colonies, sought to undermine the established church in Great Britain. One line of attack was against royal prohibitions on the freedom of speech and press. When the Puritans were talking about freedom of the press, however, they were not referring to a newspaper publisher advocating a particular point of view. The term freedom of the press in Puritan England meant freedom for the Puritans to hire a press to produce copies of tracts denouncing the established church. Never, for example, did the Puritans think of extending freedom of the press to Lutherans challenging Calvinist doctrine.

[1]See Harold Hulme, "The Winning of Freedom of Speech by the House of Commons," *American Historical Review* 61 (1956): 825-53.

John Milton
The Puritan John Milton (seated) wrote *Areopagitica*, that great statement endorsing freedom of discussion, because officials refused to allow him to circulate a pamphlet on the merits of divorce. *Areopagitica* is one of the most ringing endorsements of free speech ever written, but it is important to note that the core of its argument lay in religious doctrine, not in a political one of free expression. Protestants distinguished themselves from Catholics by claiming broader toleration of dissenting opinion and noted that, for example, it was the Catholic church that had the infamous Index of banned books. Milton was Protestant, as was every member of the British House of Commons, for whom he wrote the *Areopagitica*. This drawing from 1867 depicts Oliver Cromwell dictating a letter to Milton intended to stop the persecution of religious dissenters.

Although under severe attack, the British system of press control probably would have survived longer had it not been for the avarice of the Stuart kings. Printers who were in the trade as a business, whose ability to make money was based on the possession of royal monopolies to publish certain books, soon found that the Stuarts had sold their patents to others. With their secure source of income gone, some printers looked for other ways to make money and became more willing to put their printing presses at the service of religious malcontents. As the number of such printers grew, so, too, did attempts to regulate what people said about religion and government. The Stuarts, for example, developed the law of seditious libel, designed to protect government from criticism. That law provided for the imprisonment of the printer of the libel until he revealed the writer of the publication. Officials clearly recognized that the person who ran the printing press was usually only a mechanic and not the person who wrote the material. The law covered both authoring and printing false material about the king and other officers of government. This and similar oppressive laws gave the infamous Court of the Star Chamber most of its cases during the reign of Charles I. Because of such laws, England plummeted into a great civil war in the 1640s, which ultimately led to the brief imposition of Puritan rule.

COLONIAL PURITANS AND PRESS FREEDOM

Although the English experience with freedom of speech and press continued, by the 1640s and the start of the civil war, the Great Migration of the English already had occurred. Between 1620 and 1642, close to 80,000 Englishmen (two per cent of the entire population) left Britain. Of those, 58,000 came to North America or to the Caribbean, bringing with them the collective English experience with freedom of speech, press, and religion. To the Puritans who established Massachusetts Bay in 1628, their heritage meant a certain form of religious belief, freedom of speech to support that religious belief, and freedom of the printing press to turn out materials to advance the faith.

Although most of the Puritans who settled in the new world had left England by 1644, colonial concepts of freedom of the press would long be influenced by a pamphlet written in that year by an unhappy fellow Puritan, John Milton. He had wanted to publish an essay he had written on divorce, but officials in the Anglican Church refused to allow its publication. In response, he wrote *Areopagitica*, an argument against censorship, in which he set forth a theory of freedom of the press that found adherents well into the twentieth century: "And though all the winds of doctrine were let loose to play upon the earth, so truth be in the field, we do injuriously by licensing and prohibiting to misdoubt her strength. Let her and falsehood grapple; who ever knew truth put to the worse, in a free and open encounter?"[2] With those words, he established the marketplace of ideas concept, the notion that all ideas ought to be put forward and that truth always would win over falsehood. The doctrine was advanced for his generation, and it was at times cited as an ideal. What Milton himself thought about the ideal is questionable. In one of those quirks of history, when the Puritan Commonwealth was established, Milton became an official censor. Not until the beginning of the nineteenth century did Americans discover that ideas could battle for acceptance without society crumbling.

Taming the new land was the first concern of colonists, but by 1638 the first press was set up at Harvard, where its initial products, quite naturally, promoted the religious beliefs of the colony's founders. The first item off the press was a religious oath that all residents above the age of twenty had to take before becoming citizens, a point that some libertarians today might see as a perversion of the use of the press. This use, however, fit into the role of

[2]The text of *Areopagitica* may be found in numerous sources. One of the most accessible for students of media history is Calder M. Pickett, *Voices of the Past: Key Documents in the History of American Journalism* (Columbus, Ohio, 1977), 8-11.

the press that Englishmen of that generation held. In political commonwealths, such as the one established by the Puritans in Massachusetts Bay, test oaths were commonplace. Using the mechanical device, the press, to publish that oath was only reasonable.

Colonists used the press primarily for reproducing religious materials and publishing important colonial documents. Since the press was carefully supervised at Harvard, no restrictions were placed on its output until 1662. Then, Massachusetts, which already had experienced the heresies of Roger Williams and Anne Hutchinson, saw the arrival of an uncontrolled commercial press as a new challenge to the colony's religious beliefs. To counter the threat, the Massachusetts General Court established a system of licensing similar to the one already operating in England, allowing only the publication of approved documents. The Court was quite frank about the reason for censorship: "For prevention of irregularities & abuse to the authority of this country by the printing press, it is ordered, that henceforth no copie shall be printed but by the allowance first had & obteined under the hands of Capt Daniel Gookin & Mr Jonathan Mitchel, until this Court shall take further order therein."[3]

For their time, Puritans were quite broadminded in their thinking about the publication of differing views, especially on political matters and on theological disputes among themselves. Like dominant groups elsewhere, however, they would not tolerate what they considered heretical religious beliefs. Overall, though, their licensing efforts were sporadic, and their success at limiting what individuals used the press to produce was erratic. But this early experience established a very important principle in the colonies: no printer was ever free to use his press to print exactly what he wished. Some form of control over the output of the press always existed. The basic question throughout these years was who would exert that control.

For many years after the settlement of the colonies, the English were too busy with their own internal problems to be concerned about what was happening on the other side of the Atlantic. With the calming influence that came with William and Mary's ascension to the throne in 1689, the English were ready to turn their attention to all aspects of colonial life, including the way in which the colonists used their presses. In fact, colonial governors increased their concern with what came off those presses even before the first newspaper was published in 1690. Instructions given to governors between 1686 and 1730 included variations of this statement: "Forasmuch as great inconvenience may arise by liberty of printing within our said territory under your government you are to provide by all necessary orders that no person keep any printing-press for printing, nor that any book, pamphlet or other matter whatsoever be printed without your especial leave and license first obtained."[4] Governors' instructions carried such orders, even though Parliament refused to renew the king's right to license the press in 1695.

BY THE

GOVERNOUR & COUNCIL

WHEREAS *ſome have lately preſumed to Print and Diſperſe a Pamphlet Entituled,* Publick Occurrences, both Forreign and Domeſtick: Boſton, Thurſday, *Septemb. 25th.* 1690. *Without the leaſt Privity or Countenance of Authority.*

The Governour and Council having had the peruſal of the ſaid Pamphlet, and finding that therein is contained Reflections of a very high nature: As alſo ſundry doubtful and uncertain Reports, do hereby manifeſt and declare their high Reſentment and Diſallowance of ſaid Pamphlet, and Order that the ſame be Suppreſſed and called in; ſtrictly forbidding any perſon or perſons for the future to Set forth any thing in Print without Licence firſt obtained from thoſe that are or ſhall be appointed by the Government to grant the ſame.

By Order of the Governour & Council.

Iſaac Addington, Secr.

Boſton, September 29*th*. 1690.

Suppression of *Publick Occurrences*
Following the overthrow of the Massachusetts royal governor in 1688, conditions in the colony became chaotic. In an attempt to help bring order, Benjamin Harris published one issue of America's first newspaper, *Publick Occurrences, Both Forreign and Domestick.* The provisional governing council, which included a faction that resented the cleric Cotton Mather's role in the paper, immediately issued an order prohibiting Harris from continuing publication.

In some instances, however, specific language authorizing governors to control the press was not necessary. Some governors were naturally hostile to that mechanical device.[5] Regardless of the attitudes of colonial governors or the feelings of religious leaders, presses continued to arrive in the colonies. So, too, did the problems accompanying their use. But because there were so many colonies and so many officials involved in dealing with the products of the presses, it is impossible to say that the press was treated alike from one end of the Atlantic seaboard to the other. Early in Massachusetts history, religious leaders usually were more important in controlling the press than governors. Presses reached the southern colonies last; and when they finally arrived, the governors and their advisers carefully supervised them. In New York, the governor himself sought an official printer for the colony, and for almost forty years that printer and his press worked calmly and quietly.

Press Freedom and the First Newspapers

Although it is sometimes argued that conflicts over the right to use the press to criticize government or religious leaders did not

[3]*Massachusetts Records*, IV pt. II: 62, quoted in Clyde A. Duniway, *The Development of Freedom of the Press in Massachusetts* (Columbus, Mass., 1906), 41-2.

[4]Quoted in A. C. Goodell, *Proceedings of the Massachusetts Historical Society* (June 1893), 173.

[5]William Berkeley, the Anglican governor of Virginia, for example, remarked in 1671, "I thank God we have no free schools or printing; and I hope that we shall not have them these hundred years. For learning has brought disobediences and heresy and sects into the world; and printing has divulged them and libels against the government. God keep us from both."

begin until the 1730s with John Peter Zenger, several encounters between operators of presses and the authorities occurred before that time. Each clash contributed to the distinctly American heritage of freedom of the press that would develop in later years.

The dispute over the establishment of the first newspaper in the colonies, *Publick Occurrences, Both Forreign and Domestick* in Boston in 1690, provides one such example. An assertive Anabaptist publisher, Benjamin Harris, produced a newspaper intended to provide important information as an antidote to rumors about deteriorating political conditions in Massachusetts, only to have the paper suppressed after one issue. The primary reason for the suppression was that Harris had published without authority, meaning that he had not obtained permission from the governor to print the newspaper. Before granting such permission, the governor or his representative had to approve each item planned for publication, which was prior restraint. No continuous newspaper appeared in the colonies until 1704, when the *Boston News-Letter* was published by authority, meaning its publisher had obtained prior approval of its contents.

Individuals who wanted to publish a newspaper without official permission were not the only printers encountering problems in the colonies. In 1692, Pennsylvania authorities charged printer William Bradford with using his press to print tracts for a separatist faction that mainline Quakers thought heretical. Bradford's first trial ended with a jury deadlocked nine to three in favor of conviction. After waiting almost a year for a second trial, Bradford was released. He quickly left Pennsylvania and headed for New York, where he became the long-sought-after official printer for that colony and set up a profitable business whose only controversial printing was of tracts attacking the Pennsylvania Quakers.

Another early free-press battle, this one in Boston in 1720-1721, centered on who would control the press, which by then had become a pawn in a larger struggle for political and economic control of the colony. The royal governor and his council were on one side, with the commercial classes of Massachusetts on the other. The colonial representative assembly favored the latter group, and the assembly wanted its views on the controversy printed so that colonists would have both sides of the matter to consider. To prevent the assembly from publishing its views, the governor threatened to use the powers to license the press granted him in his royal commission. These instructions had been altered somewhat from their earlier issuance, however, and now required the colonial assembly to participate in the licensing process. The assembly refused. The governor's council, when consulted, pointed out that the king had lost his power to license the press; by extension, so had the royal governor. The Massachusetts assembly thus could have any information published that it wanted. Refusing to concede, the governor asked for a licensing law. Once more the assembly said no. So the governor dissolved the assembly. The *Boston Gazette*, established in 1719, published the governor's dissolution speech; the *Boston News-Letter* printed the full text of the assembly's response. Out of the controversy, then, perhaps for the first time, came the publication of both sides of an important debate.

After the encounter, licensing was dead in Massachusetts, although that reality did not prevent the assembly from trying to exercise the licensing power occasionally. The primary motivation behind such attempts was political, as legislators attempted to solidify their positions in relation to that of the royal governor. Never did anyone think of discontinuing control over the products of the press. The struggle was always over who would control

Kalendarium Pennſilvanienſe,

OR,

America's Meſſinger.

BEING AN

ALMANACK

For the Year of Grace, 1686.

Wherein is contained both the Engliſh & Forreign Account. the Motions of the Planets through the Signs, with the Luminaries, Conjunctions, Aſpects, Eclipſes; the riſing, ſouthing and ſetting of the Moon, with the time when ſhe paſſeth by, or is with the moſt eminent fixed Stars: Sun riſing and ſetting and the time of High-Water at the City of *Philadelphia*, &c.

With Chronologies, and many other Notes, Rules, and Tables, very fitting for every man to know & have: all which is accomodated to the Longitude of the Province of *Pennſilvania*, and Latitude of 40 Degr. north, with a Table of Houſes for the ſame, which may indifferently ſerve *New England, New York, Eaſt & Weſt Jerſey, Maryland*, and moſt parts of *Virginia*.

By *SAMUEL ATKINS*.
Student in the Mathamaticks and Aſtrology.

And the Stars in their Courſes fought againſt Seſera, Judg. 5. 29.

Printed and Sold by *William Bradford*, ſold alſo by the Author and *H. Murrey* in *Philadelphia*, and *Philip Richards* in *New-York*; 1685.

William Bradford and the Quakers
When the Quakers were establishing the colony of Pennsylvania, they engaged William Bradford to do their printing. Most of the work that he produced in his shop – like *Kalendarium Pennsilvaniense*, the first work printed in Pennsylvania, in 1685 – was of Quaker material. Only nominally Quaker himself, however, he readily printed several trenchant and scurrilous attacks that the radical reformer George Keith wrote against Quaker dogma. In September 1692 Quaker officials arrested him and confiscated his printing equipment. At his trial, he argued that the jury should be allowed to determine not only the facts but the law also – that is, not simply that the material had been published but that it was indeed illegal. The jury split in its verdict, with the nine Quaker members voting for conviction and the three non-Quakers against. Both Bradford and Keith later converted to Anglicanism.

that output.

The next major battle over the content of the press also occurred in Massachusetts. In Boston, Anglicans founded the *New-England Courant*, with James Franklin as publisher, as a forum for attacking the Puritan clergy. The government let the attacks pass with no response, but in June 1722 the government jailed Franklin for a month for charging that authorities had not been aggressive enough in suppressing pirates plundering the New England coast. In January 1723, Franklin was in jail again, this time for publishing an essay on hypocrites that had offended members of the colonial assembly. James' difficulties brought forth the earliest support for a press colleague in the colonies when Andrew Bradford, writing in his *American Weekly Mercury* in Philadelphia on February 26, 1723, criticized the Massachusetts authorities for taking away Franklin's means of earning a living without giving him an opportunity to defend himself. Bradford, an Anglican, also criticized the Puritan leaders for their role in the controversy.[6]

Printers encountered problems in Philadelphia as well. William Bradford had been run out of the city in 1693 for using his press to publish allegedly heretical material. In 1722, his son Andrew, publisher of the *American Weekly Mercury* and defender of James Franklin, was in trouble with colonial authorities. Andrew Bradford had published a pamphlet by an anonymous author about the poor credit rating of the colony, which he later reproduced as a news story in his newspaper. The colonial council called Bradford in, demanding to know where he had gotten the article. In a somewhat less than glowing advocacy of freedom of the press, Bradford declared that he did not know where the article had come from and that one of his subordinates must have accepted and printed it without his knowledge or permission, of course. Bradford asked the governor and the council to pardon him for the errant publication. The council accepted his apology and ordered him not to print anything further about colonial affairs without prior approval. Two points made this trial of special interest. First, among the members of the council who imposed prior censorship on Bradford was Andrew Hamilton, who thirteen years later would be John Peter Zenger's chief defense counsel. Second, Bradford, apparently feeling great remorse for his behavior before the council, editorialized on the problems facing fellow editor Franklin a few months later.

During these encounters, colonial printers were trying to determine their place in society. Although they did not speak in terms of freedom of the press, their words would be classified under that general heading today. Benjamin Franklin, in his famous "Apology for Printers," written in 1731, noted that "Printers are educated in the Belief, that when Men differ in Opinion, both Sides ought equally to have the Advantage of being heard by the Publick; and that when Truth and Error have fair Play, the former is always an overmatch for the latter: Hence they cheerfully serve all contending Writers that pay them well, without regarding on which side they are of the Question in Dispute."[7] The notion of letting truth and error compete with one another for acceptance harkened back to John Milton, but in the political climate of the colonies, printing both sides of a story was impossible. Notice, though, that Franklin was talking about opening the columns of his newspaper to "contending Writers." That was a far cry from the concept of modern journalism in which media staff members are the ones who present information, but remember that during the colonial period the printer was still primarily a technician. The contents of the publications usually were provided by others, often those who had paid for publication.

THE ZENGER TRIAL

The most famous encounter between the press and colonial authorities occurred in New York in the early 1730s, and it swirled around just such a printer-technician rather than the writer of the published material. Again the cause of the contest was political power, who wielded it, and who controlled the means to tell their views to the people. The British took over the New York colony, initially established by the Dutch as New Netherland, in 1664 — after the culture, heritage, and power structure of the colony had been well established. Throughout its early years, the English and the Dutch competed repeatedly for supremacy in New York. John Peter Zenger, the printer-technician, was part of one such contest in 1733.

The battle was brought on by the death of an English governor in 1731. The new governor, William Cosby, did not arrive in the colony until fifteen months later. Before his arrival, Rip Van Dam, senior member of the governor's council and a member of a very old and respected Dutch family, served as interim governor. His administration was peaceful, popular, and short. Upon finally arriving in New York, Cosby immediately alienated colonists. He demanded that Van Dam give him the salary that Van Dam had collected as interim governor. Then, when Van Dam refused, Cosby sued. When the chief justice agreed with Van Dam, Cosby replaced him.

Each of Cosby's actions had the practical effect of dividing the colonists into two political groups — a court faction, with Cosby as leader, and an opposition group, which had a large following among the people and within the colonial assembly. The opposition party was a magnet for all who had any grievance against the governor, and it grew rapidly, so rapidly in fact that the governor feared losing control of the colonial assembly through elections in 1734. Cosby managed to keep control, however, with votes won through questionable tactics. When denied their rightful leadership roles in the assembly, the opposition faction turned to England for help, and former Chief Justice Morris went to London to lobby with the king.

With this background of political turmoil, opposition leaders

[6]Anna Janney DeArmond, *Andrew Bradford: Colonial Printer* (New York, 1969), 14-5.

[7]*Pennsylvania Gazette*, 10 June 1731. A similar idea was put forth by Boston newspapermen in the 1740s. See Mary Ann Yodelis, "Boston's First Major Newspaper War: A 'Great Awakening' of Freedom," *Journalism Quarterly* 51 (1974): 207-12.

Political Undercurrents of the Zenger Case
Almost as soon as Governor William Cosby (top left) arrived in New York, he ran into trouble with some of the colony's leading figures. His first dealings with the colonial assembly centered on demands for additional money – a gratuity for his having helped procure the repeal of an obnoxious piece of legislation. In fact, he had not helped in the legislative effort and had been specifically forbidden by the king to accept special gifts from the colonial assembly, but still he succeeded in obtaining £1,000, up from the £750 the assembly had offered initially. Still not satisfied, he demanded half of all the money that Rip Van Dam (top right) had taken in while he was interim governor. The wily Dutchman would have none of that, but he made a counter offer – he would share his income of about £2,000 if Cosby would split his income for the same period of about £6,000. Needless to say, Cosby was not interested in the counter offer, nor was he dissuaded from his goal. He persuaded the supreme court of the colony to sit as a special court of the exchequer, a body empowered to deal with financial matters, to force Van Dam to pay. Chief Justice Lewis Morris (bottom left), however, agreed with Van Dam. Cosby thereupon replaced Morris, another man who commanded much respect within the Dutch community, with a much younger man, James Delancey, a decided royalist and a favorite of the governor. In the meantime, Cosby had used trickery to avoid repaying £1,500 that James Alexander (bottom right) had loaned him. It was Alexander who headed the efforts to found a newspaper, Zenger's *New-York Weekly Journal*, as an organ for opposing Cosby's administration.

began to realize the importance of having a newspaper to circulate their views among the people. They had tried spreading their arguments through pamphlets, but then realized they needed the quickness and regularity of a newspaper. They also needed a way to conceal their identities. Consequently, they quietly set up the *New-York Weekly Journal* as a vehicle to inform the people of Cosby's transgressions and to raise enough protest to force his recall.

Zenger was not the founder of the publication. In fact, the Dutch faction had established the newspaper before naming its printer. Zenger, who had come to the colonies from the Palatine, had learned his trade under William Bradford. After his apprenticeship, he set himself up in business. It was his publication of a pamphlet giving deposed Chief Justice Morris' side of his firing that brought Zenger to the attention of the opposition leaders, now known as Morrisites. On November 5, 1733, relying on the promises of literary and other aid from the Morrisites, Zenger put out the first edition of the *Weekly Journal*. Working with Zenger, the printer, was James Alexander, a young lawyer, who served as chief editor, although he carefully concealed his relationship with the newspaper.

By its seventh edition, in December 1733, the *Weekly Journal* was criticizing the governor for allowing a French warship to enter the New York harbor. Supposedly the ship had entered to obtain supplies, but the newspaper claimed its real purpose was to locate harbor fortifications. Such commentaries were quickly answered by the court party, which used the columns of William Bradford's *New York Gazette* to launch a vicious journalistic war.

Cosby made some early, unsuccessful attempts to silence the *Weekly Journal*. In January 1734, Chief Justice Delancey, the governor's appointee, told the grand jury about alleged seditious libels against the governor found within its pages. The grand jury, however, returned no indictments. A similar attempt during the grand jury's sitting in October 1734 also failed. While the legal system of the colony refused to help the governor silence the newspaper, the *Weekly Journal* added regularly to Cosby's list of reasons for seeking its suppression. In a series of issues of late September and early October 1734, the newspaper criticized the governor for being too selective in choosing members of his council, indirectly implying that only his favorites were eligible for certain jobs. The paper also published an anonymous letter from New Jersey containing a general attack on Cosby and ridiculing the entire

THE

New-York Weekly JOURNAL.

Containing the freſheſt Advices, Foreign, and Domeſtick.

MUNDAY April 8th, 1734.

New-Brunſwick, March 27, 1734.
Mr. *Zenger*;

I Was at a public Houſe ſome Days ſince in Company with ſome Perſons that came from *New-York*: Moſt of them complain'd of the Deadneſs of Trade: ſome of them laid it to the Account of the Repeal of the *Tonnage Aſt*, which they ſaid was done to gratify the Reſentment of ſome in *New-York* in order to diſtreſs Governour *Burnet*; but which has been almoſt the Ruine of that Town, by paying the *Bermudians* about *l.* 12,000 a Year to export thoſe Commodities which might be carried in their own Bottoms, and the Money ariſing by the Freight ſpent in *New-York*. They ſaid, that the *Bermudians* were an induſtrious, frugal People, who bought no one Thing in *New-York*, but lodg'd the whole Freight Money in their own Iſland, by which Means, ſince the Repeal of that Act, there has been taken from *New-York* above *l.* 90,000 and all this to gratify Pique and Reſentment. But this is not all; this Money being carried away, which would otherwiſe have circulated in this Province and City, and have been paid to the Baker, the Brewer, the Smith, the Carpenter, the Ship-Wright, the Boat-Man, the Farmer, the Shop-Keeper, *&c.* has deadned our Trade in all its Branches, and forc'd our induſtrious Poor to ſeek other Habitations; ſo that within theſe three Years there has been above 300 Perſons have left *New-York*; the Houſes ſtand empty, and there is as many Houſes as would make one whole Street with Bills upon their Doors: And this has been as great a Hurt as the Carrying away the Money, and is occaſioned by it, and all degrees of Men feel it, from the Merchant down to the Carman. And (adds he) it is the induſtrious Poor is the Support of any Country, and the diſcouraging the poor Tradesmen is the Means of Ruining any Country. Another replies, It is the exceſſive High Wages you Tradesmen take prevents your being imploy'd: learn to be contented with leſs Wages, we ſhall be able to build, and then no need to employ *Bermudians*. Very fine, replied the firſt, now the Money is gone you bid us take leſs Wages, when you have nothing to give us, and there is nothing to do. Says another, I know no Body gets Eſtates with us but the Lawyers; we are almoſt come to that Paſs, that an Acre of Land can't be conveyed under half an Acre of Parchment. The Fees are not ſetled by our Legiſlature, & every Body takes what they pleaſe; and we find it better to bear the Diſeaſe than to apply for a Remedy that's worſe: I hope (ſaid he) our Aſſembly will take this Matter into Conſideration; eſpecially ſince our late Judge hath prov'd *no Fees are lawful but what are ſettled by them.* I own a ſmall Veſſel, and there is a Fee for a

The Offending *Journal*
The issue of April 8, 1734, was one of two issues of the *New-York Weekly Journal* on which the indictment against the printer Peter Zenger was based. Although he did not write the material, he was arrested on the charge that the *Journal* aroused citizens to question the rule of Governor William Cosby. He spent nine months in jail before being tried. According to legend, he gave his wife, through a hole in his cell door, instructions on how to run the paper.

government of New York.

After an attempt to force the assembly to charge Zenger with libel failed, Cosby resorted to his only sure source of support. He had his council issue its own warrant charging Zenger with raising sedition, inflaming the minds of the people, holding the king's government in contempt, and casting aspersions on the king's officials. Cosby had Zenger arrested in November 1734, and the printer was confined for a week, causing his newspaper to skip an issue. In the next week's paper, Zenger apologized for the missed edition, noting that he was being held in jail without bail and without access to pen and ink. Finally, the legend goes, Zenger resumed editing his paper by giving instructions to his wife through a hole in his cell door. Zenger's bail was set at £400, but he spent nine months in jail even though his Morrisite backers could have raised the money easily. Zenger's hardships created a great deal of public sympathy for him; he was far more valuable to the Morrisites in jail than out.

James Alexander, the actual editor of the *Weekly Journal*, planned to serve as Zenger's chief counsel and to use the trial to challenge the entire system of government established under Cosby's rule. To deprive Zenger of adequate counsel, however, Cosby had Alexander and his partner disbarred shortly before the trial was to begin. Thus, although he had a replacement attorney named by the court, Zenger faced trial without competent representation because the appointee was an ally of the governor. To the Morrisites that was worse than having no lawyer at all. They wanted someone who would vigorously defend Zenger and criticize Cosby's activities at the same time. They chose a friend of Alexander's, Andrew Hamilton of Pennsylvania, one of the most famous lawyers in the colonies.

Charges against Zenger were based on several articles in the *Weekly Journal* accusing the government of jeopardizing the liberties and the property of the people. The controversial pieces also said the governor had tampered with numerous civil liberties including trial by jury and the right to vote. Hamilton's first courtroom move caught most observers off-guard. He admitted that Zenger had printed and published the newspaper issues in question. Under existing law, all the jury could determine was whether the accused had published the offending articles. If Zenger's attorney admitted that his client had published the pieces as charged, then Zenger was guilty of libel. The colonial attorney general, after hearing the plea, insisted that the jury immediately convict Zenger. Hamilton, however, took a different view.

He argued that the prosecution had to prove that the words in the articles themselves were libelous, false, scandalous, and seditious before a conviction was justified. If the words were not, then the jury had to find Zenger not guilty, Hamilton said. Chief Justice Delancey would not permit such an argument; so Hamilton changed his tactics, turned to the jury, and delivered one of the most powerful courtroom addresses of early American history. He appealed to jury members to be their own judges about the truth of Zenger's statements. He denounced unbridled power as exercised by the colonial governor and appealed to the individual juror's love of liberty as the only defense against tyrannical rulers. The basis of Zenger's defense thus became the notion that citizens had the right to criticize their rulers and that citizens as jurors had the authority to determine whether words were false. In fact, Hamilton argued, free speech was essential in the colonies to prevent governors, who were far removed from the restraining hand of their superiors, from abusing their powers:

> Men who injure and oppress the people under their administration provoke them to cry out and complain; and then make that very complaint the foundation for new oppressions and prosecutions. I wish I could say there were no instances of this

Andrew Hamilton and the Zenger Trial
When Governor Cosby ordered Zenger's attorneys disbarred, Hamilton traveled from Philadelphia to take the case. At age fifty-nine, he told the jury that he had been willing, even at his advanced years, to make the long trip for the cause of liberty. Because of that statement, many historians have mistakenly assumed that he was around eighty years of age. The portrait (right) was made when Hamilton was a young man. Known for his strident style of argumentation, Hamilton disregarded common legal practice of the day and admitted that Zenger had published the issues of the paper in question. He then called upon jury members to judge the truth of the material for themselves. "It is not," he declared, "the bare printing and publishing of a paper that will make it a libel: the words themselves must be libelous, that is, false, scandalous, and seditious, else my client is not guilty."

> kind. But to conclude; the question before the Court and you gentlemen of the jury is not the cause of a poor printer, nor of New York alone, which you are now trying: No! It may in its consequence affect every freeman that lives under a British government on the main of America. It is the best cause. It is the cause of liberty; and I make no doubt but your upright conduct this day will not only entitle you to the love and esteem of your fellow citizens; but every man who prefers freedom to a life of slavery will bless and honor you as men who have baffled the attempt of tyranny; and by an impartial and uncorrupt verdict, have laid a noble foundation for securing to ourselves, our posterity, and our neighbors that to which nature and the laws of our country have given us a right, the liberty both of exposing arbitrary power — in these parts of the world, at least — by speaking and writing truth.[8]

The jury returned a "not guilty" verdict, which under the law meant jurors had decided Zenger had not published the material in question.

Although historians argue that the Zenger trial established two important precedents in libel law — the admissibility of evidence about the truth of the alleged libel and the right of a jury to decide whether a publication was defamatory or seditious — more than fifty years passed before these two principles were established in American law. Even if the precepts were not codified immediately, the Zenger trial did make prosecutions under colonial libel laws less certain, showing that a jury could acquit individuals who government officials thought were libelers.

The arguments in the Zenger case were critical to colonial political development, for they established in the popular thinking the individual's right to criticize his government, a right that colonists would employ increasingly as the Revolution approached. Helping this cause along was a pamphlet containing the arguments Hamilton made during the trial that Alexander quickly prepared and circulated throughout the colonies. The transcripts, which were highly dramatic, transcended legal principles. As the *Pennsylvania Gazette* commented in 1738, if the results of the Zenger case were not incorporated into the law, then they were

[8]James Alexander, *A Brief Narrative of the Case and Trial of John Peter Zenger*, Stanley N. Katz, ed. (Cambridge, Mass., 1963), 99.

obviously "better than Law, ... Ought to be Law, and will always be Law wherever Justice prevails."[9] The mass distribution of the Alexander pamphlet discouraged many additional prosecutions, for potential jurors had been made aware of their power in libel prosecutions.

Zenger became a hero in American journalism history. In his own time, he was less important. After Hamilton's rousing victory in court, the Morrisites went out to celebrate, but because of a legal technicality, Zenger spent the night in jail. In early 1736 William Cosby died, and the new governor decided to make friends with the Morrisites. Now part of the power structure, the Morrisites showed themselves just as interested in wielding authority as the Cosby supporters they had condemned a few years earlier. This time, the Morrisites did not forget Zenger; during the final years of his life he was the official public printer of New York and New Jersey—a position given only to those who were on the right side of the people in power.

If a colonial printer did become involved in political controversy, he often surrounded his efforts with essays clipped from English newspapers that proclaimed the importance of press freedom. These essays, produced at the height of partisan journalism in England, were reproduced in the colonies from the 1720s through the Revolutionary period. Colonial editors never seemed to tire of telling their readers about the importance of the basic freedoms of expression.[10] Favorite quotations came from "Cato's Letters," which appeared in English newspapers between 1720 and 1723. Written by John Trenchard and Thomas Gordon, these essays touched on a variety of issues relating to constitutional government, including freedom of expression. In 1720, for instance, Cato told his readers, "Without Freedom of Thought, there can be no such Thing as Wisdom; and no such Thing as publick Liberty, without Freedom of Speech." Such freedom, he wrote, "is the Right of every Man, as far as by it he does not hurt and controul the Right of another; and this is the only Check which it ought suffer, the only Bounds which it ought to know." Citizens, Cato continued, "ought to speak well of their Governors, while their Governors deserve to be well spoken of," but governors who mistreat their subjects should be publicly exposed.[11] This essay on freedom of speech and three others on libel, in which the authors wrote of the right of printers to criticize public officials and measures, formed the heart of the discussion of freedom of expression in the latter part of the colonial period.

The Stamp Act

Despite such high-minded arguments, invocations of freedom of the press often seemed quite self-serving. In New York in the 1740s, another struggle between a royal governor and the provincial assembly led to the insistence that the assembly's point of view on a particular issue be published and to a pious declaration that assembly members were firm in their "Resolution to preserve the Liberty of the Press."[12] What they were firm about was their intention to ensure that the people discover the governor's faults through the newspaper. In Massachusetts, attempts by the royal governor in 1768 to take action against Benjamin Edes and John Gill, printers of the *Boston Gazette* and vitriolic patriots, were met by a smug colonial assembly affirming that "the Liberty of the Press is a great Bulwark of the Liberty of the People: It is therefore the incumbent Duty of those who are constituted the Guardians of the People's Rights to defend and maintain it."[13]

Although much was said about freedom of the press, what that term actually meant remained much in doubt as the colonial period came to a close. Generally when a printer and a government body collided, the printer escaped severe punishment, but the psychological toll on these individuals must have been great. Even trying to determine what could be printed without encountering the wrath of some official was difficult, as Hugh Gaine, printer of the *New York Mercury*, found out in 1753. Gaine's transgression was reproducing without permission the king's instructions to a

Stamps and Press Freedom
When the British government imposed a requirement that newspapers be printed on paper bearing a stamp (above), its main motive was to raise revenue. American editors argued, however, that the Stamp Act was a great assault on freedom of the press.

9 *Pennsylvania Gazette*, 11 May 1738.

10 For a discussion of the importance of these English writers in colonial newspapers, see Gary Huxford, "The English Libertarian Tradition in the Colonial Newspaper," *Journalism Quarterly* 45 (1968): 677-86.

11 John Trenchard and Thomas Gordon, *Cato's Letters*, 6th ed., Leonard W. Levy, ed. (London, 1755; reprint ed., New York, 1971), 1: 96-7 (page citations to reprint edition).

12 Quoted in Clark Rivera, "Ideals, Interests and Civil Liberty: The Colonial Press and Freedom, 1735-76," *Journalism Quarterly* 55 (1973): 52.

13 Quoted in Duniway, *Development of Freedom of the Press in Massachusetts*, 127.

Against Stamps, for Freedom
When the British Parliament passed the Stamp Act in 1765 to raise taxes to help pay debts incurred during the French and Indian War, the aroused public protested with marches and threats. They equated the law with an assault on their freedoms – and they viewed the repeal of the law as a great victory for freedom.

new governor and the governor's speech to the colonial assembly. Gaine was summoned before the assembly and forced to apologize for his efforts to provide news of government to his readers. In the late twentieth century, such information routinely is considered in the public domain and available to journalists to use as they see fit. Seldom do newspapers wish to print the full texts of statements or of laws. In the colonial period, however, publishing any kind of official document — or any debate before the legislature — was dangerous for printers. Information was a closely controlled commodity, perhaps because of the belief that too much knowledge could lead to unrest among the populace. Colonial officials, both the royal governors and the locally elected assemblies, were acting on principles learned from centuries of English experience. Information needed for governance, this heritage maintained, was best left in the hands of those suited to make decisions. The judgment of the general public could not be trusted, and so most citizens were excluded from the process.

As the colonial period ended, those who soon would be patriots clearly understood the value of the newspaper as a medium of communication that was as important as and more timely than the highly favored pamphlet. But the newspaper had to be carefully controlled in order to foment and successfully wage a revolution. The Zenger case had won the colonists some protection for their criticisms of royal government, and the newspaper was the ideal place for those criticisms to appear. Never did the colonists think that the newspaper's printer should be free to take any side of political controversy. In fact, as one historian notes, the freedom to use the press to print all sides or any side of existing controversies depended on the existence of a political stalemate in the colony. Such a condition rarely existed as the Revolution approached. And where one side had the upper hand, the press was carefully controlled. During the Revolution, in those areas where patriot forces were supreme, their leaders eagerly suppressed printers who had the audacity to support the king or who tried to present both sides of the controversy.

Before the Revolution actually broke out, however, the British again challenged press freedom in America, or at least so the patriot leaders thought. The conflict stemmed from the British Parliament's passage of the Stamp Act in 1765. The law, which imposed taxes in the form of revenue stamps on a variety of printed materials including newspapers, almanacs, and pamphlets, was similar to legislation that had been in effect in England for years and was designed to help defer the costs of defending and administering the colonies. To the colonists, it seemed another oppressive law enacted by a government more interested in American money than American well-being. Newspaper publishers, closely tied to the colonial business classes that provided their advertising revenue, joined in denouncing the tyrannical nature of the tax. Among their criticisms was the notion that the act was an attempt to suppress American freedom of the press.

With the act's repeal in 1766, newspapers were in the forefront of those claiming credit for Parliament's action. The episode added to what the press perceived as its power over events; from that feeling of power came an even stronger proprietary interest in a still vaguely defined freedom of the press and a greater willingness to use the term indiscriminately. The phrase had not yet become a slogan, but the time when that would happen was drawing near. As a result of the Stamp Act experience, more printers became active patriots. Some were even key members of the growing Sons of Liberty. These patriot-printers considered their newspapers and their freedom of the press additional weapons to use against a very dangerous foe: the British.

The American Revolution and Freedom of the Press

As the Revolution began, what individuals meant by using the phrase "freedom of the press" is open to question, but they certainly did not mean freedom to print as one pleased. In Boston in 1770, John Mein, publisher of the pro-British *Chronicle*, so of-

The Declaration of Independence
When the signers read the Declaration of Independence on the steps of Independence Hall in Philadelphia, colonials believed that its commitment to "life, liberty and the pursuit of happiness" encompassed press freedom. Newspapers throughout the colonies printed the Declaration, and news of its adoption quickly spread. As the Revolution that followed would show, though, many Patriots felt that "freedom of the press" was to be enjoyed only by those newspapers that supported their revolt against England.

fended patriots that he was attacked in the streets. He fled to England in fear of his life. In 1775 in New York, two patriot leaders, Alexander McDougall and Isaac Sears, led a mob in smashing Tory printer James Rivington's press. Rivington was out of business for eighteen months — the time necessary for him to import new equipment from England. In 1776, the New Hampshire provincial assembly summoned Daniel Fowle before it to chastise him for publishing an article questioning the trend toward independence. Rivington bounced back several times from attempts at intimidation during the war and, indeed, was the leading Tory publisher in the colonies. Fowle, however, was so upset by the assembly's rebuke that he suspended publication.

Samuel Loudon, patriot editor of the *New York Packet* and the *American Advertiser*, who was paid to print a loyalist reply to Thomas Paine's *Common Sense*, also encountered popular disapproval. Besides making the mistake of taking on the job, Loudon erred by advertising the anti-Paine tract in his newspaper. He was rousted from his bed in the middle of the night and forced to lead a patriot mob to the printing plates used to reproduce the pamphlet. He then watched as the mob smashed the type and burned 1,500 copies of the tract plus the original manuscript. The mob considered this a great victory for liberty. The next morning, freedom of the press as known today took a decided trouncing as every printer in New York found on his doorstep an intimidating note: "Sir, if you print, or suffer to be printed in your press anything against the rights and liberties of America, or in favor of our inveterate foes, the King, Ministry, and Parliament of Great Britain, death and destruction, ruin and perdition, shall be your portion. Signed, by order of the Committee of tarring and feathering."[14]

That effectively stopped loyalist publications in the New York area for the moment.

Did the Revolutionary leaders believe in freedom of the press? Yes and no. They certainly believed in their freedom to use the press to advance their own interests but refused to grant equal privileges to their opponents. But since the patriots were so convinced of the rightness of their cause and the evil of their foes, they could convince themselves that they were, indeed, supporting freedom of the press when they limited the abilities of the Tories to reach the public via the press.[15] Patriot leaders also easily could convince themselves that manipulating the contents of their newspapers to bolster support for their cause was perfectly reasonable. This manipulation began when patriot newspapers carried versions of Patrick Henry's Virginia Resolves, which condemned the Stamp Act, that varied substantially from the resolutions enacted in Williamsburg — and when the newspapers failed to tell readers that the Resolves had been passed by a few members of the House of Burgesses and were repealed the following day by the full house. It continued as leading printers, including Benjamin Edes of the *Boston Gazette*, William Goddard of the *Providence Gazette*, and John Holt of the *New York Gazette or Weekly Post Boy*, joined the Sons of Liberty and further manipulated the contents of their papers.

Patriot leaders also clearly understood another cardinal principle regarding the use of the press — that limits to its freedom were set by the wishes of the community. An essay in Samuel Adams' newspaper, the *Boston Gazette*, explained this societal impact on the use of the press in 1767 by saying that "political liberty consists

[14]Quoted in Thomas Jones, *History of New York During the Revolutionary War* (New York, 1879), I: 65.

[15]For a discussion of how the patriots could view their actions as supportive of freedom of the press see Richard Buel, Jr., "Freedom of the Press in Revolutionary America: The Evolution of Libertarianism, 1760-1820," in *The Press and the American Revolution*, Bernard Bailyn and John B. Hench, eds. (Boston, 1981), 59-97.

in a freedom of speech and action, so far as the laws of a community will permit, and not farther."[16] During the Revolution, the patriots had little tolerance for pro-British sentiment, as their actions demonstrated repeatedly. Such an attitude found expression in various calls for restrictions on freedom of information.

The Continental Congress understood the need to place limitations on freedom of expression during the Revolution. Following the pattern of contemporary legislative bodies, its meetings were closed to printers, who probably would not have known how to behave had they been able to attend. Delegates went one step further, however, and adopted a resolution calling for the expulsion of any member who revealed the topics of discussion without permission. Such a person might well know how to use the press to make the problems and disagreements within the Congress public knowledge and thus undermine the effort for independence. Anyone who violated the resolution was to be "deemed an enemy to the liberties of America." The Continental Congress also urged states to pass legislation to prevent people from being "deceived and drawn into erroneous opinion." This, however, was the extent of the Continental Congress' efforts to restrict freedom of expression, for although urged to pass a variety of further limitations, its members steadfastly refused to do so. Part of this reluctance may have been due to the uncertain nature of the Continental Congress' power over the states.

In any event, the states adopted all necessary restrictive measures. By 1778, all states had laws requiring loyalty oaths from all male citizens and legislation to protect military information and to punish individuals who criticized the new government or the war effort.[17] Although George Washington did not ask for any special corrective action, he often expressed concern about the explicit reporting of military matters in patriot newspapers. In a war in which the front lines were so fluid, the chances of the enemy obtaining copies of those publications were good. If that happened, months of planning could be destroyed.

WILLIAM JACKSON,

an IMPORTER; at the

BRAZEN HEAD,

North Side of the TOWN-HOUSE,

and *Oppofite the Town-Pump, in*

Corn-hill, BOSTON.

It is defired that the SONS and DAUGHTERS of *LIBERTY*, would not buy any one thing of him, for in fo doing they will bring Difgrace upon *themfelves*, and their *Pofterity*, for *ever* and *ever*, AMEN.

Sons of Liberty?
While declaring that the move for American independence was aimed at achieving liberty, members of the Patriot group Sons of Liberty threatened people who disagreed with them. Their threats extended to everyone from merchants, the target of the boycott in the flier above, to editors.

The Revolution and Public Opinion

Although concern about the content of news stories was commonplace during the Revolution, the patriots were also aware of the public opinion implications of freedom of the press. If a free press were designed to create a well-informed citizenry, then the people had to be kept apprised of what was going on in Congress and on the battlefield. This belief was best illustrated as a worried George Washington encouraged the creation of camp newspapers for his soldiers to read and as he sent old tenting to be made into paper for civilian newspaper use. For its part, the Continental Congress showed its awareness of the importance of information by creating a postal system that permitted the free exchange of newspapers.

Even more apparent was the patriot awareness of ways to mold public opinion, to create what later leaders would call propaganda designed to enlist allies. Two wartime documents demonstrated the propaganda skills of the patriots. The Declaration of Independence, although not referring to freedom of speech or of the press specificially, appealed to international public opinion by noting that "a decent respect to the opinons of mankind requires that they [the patriots] should declare the causes which impel them to the separation."[18] Despite the fact that the Continental Congress suggested restrictive legislation, its members also wrote the *Address to the Inhabitants of Quebec*, which, in 1774, attempted to convince Canadians to join the thirteen colonies in revolt. The document cited numerous reasons for such a combined effort, listing various rights offered under the new government:

[16]Leonard W. Levy, *Freedom of the Press from Zenger to Jefferson* (Indianapolis, 1966), 95.

[17]*Journals of the Continental Congress, 1774-1789*, 2 January 1776, 4: 18, in Leonard Levy, *Freedom of Speech and Press in Early American History: Legacy of Suppression* (Cambridge, Mass., 1960), 181; and Charles C. Tansil, ed., *Documents Illustrative of the Formation of the Union of the American States* (Washington, 1927), 18.

[18]The Declaration of Independence is reprinted in Bernard Schwartz, *The Bill of Rights: A Documentary History*, 2 vols. (New York, 1971), 1: 252.

The last right we shall mention, regards the freedom of the press. The importance of this consists, besides the advancement of truth, science, morality, and arts in general, in its diffusion of liberal sentiments on the administration of Government, its ready communication of thoughts between subjects, and its consequential promotion of union among them, whereby oppressive officers are shamed or intimidated, into more honourable and just modes of conducting affairs.[19]

The Meaning of Press Freedom: The 1780s

By the early 1780s, printers still were debating just what freedom of the press meant. Once again, they reached back to the familiar strains of *Areopagitica*. Eleazer Oswald wrote in the first issue of his Philadelphia newspaper, "The *Liberty of the Press*, so highly extolled by all Persons, has not been clearly defined by any. Some contend for unbounded Liberty, and that this being equally allowed on all sides, Truth and Justice having fair Play, would necessarily over-power their Opposition, and finally prevail."[20] But did this man, a printer by trade, understand the ramifictions of such a statement? Perhaps Benjamin Franklin, highly astute individual that he was, had some inkling of what he was saying in his "Apology for Printers." But did his successors?

Regardless of their level of understanding, the talismanic value of "freedom of the press" was clearly being claimed by newspaper printers around the country. In 1785 the *Charleston* (S.C.) *Herald* praised the virtues of freedom of the press highly, saying that because of it, "Magistrates cannot oppress the poor; bawds cannot seduce young females; Generals cannot act with cowardice; Guardians cannot betray their trust; Paymasters cannot pocket public money; Stockjobbers cannot impose upon the credulity of the nation for News-papers." Even senators, it contended, could not "betray their trust; convert serious matters into jokes; or transfer mountains into molehills."[21] All of this reliance on a free press occurred in an age in which newspaper content came primarily from local nonjournalists or was clipped from publications from other parts of the country. How could such a watchdog role of the press even be considered under such circumstances? Had the rhetoric outpaced the reality? Or were these printers seeing in their publications something hidden from twentieth-century observers?

Aside from the question of whether they practiced what they preached, printer-editors of the post-Revolutionary period showed some understanding that freedom of the press was most valuable as a protection for comments made about government. As Francis Bailey of the *Freeman's Journal* in Philadelphia wrote in 1791, "Pieces relative to public measures, and evidently wrote with a design to infuse the public good and general interests ... whether they touch on men or measures, things or persons, there ought to be no restriction.... [T]he press should be free and open, leaving the offender to the ordinary course of the law, if his writings have libellous import."[22] One of his Philadelphia competitors, Eleazer Oswald, agreed:

Considerable Latitude must be allowed in the Discussion of Public Affairs, or the Liberty of the Press will be of no Benefit to Society. As the Indulgence of Private Malice and Personal Slander should be checked and resisted by every legal Means, so a constant Examination into the Characters of Ministers and Magistrates should be equally promoted and encouraged.[23]

These arguments would be heard again during debates over the ratification of the Constitution and in calls for a Bill of Rights. Clearly, the press had to be free to discuss governmental issues, regardless of the actual scope of the term freedom of the press. With such general agreement on the need for the press to supervise government, the old notion of seditious libel, a crime that stemmed from the criticism of government, seemed dead.

The Articles of Confederation, the nation's first constitution, provide no clues in the search for the meaning of freedom of the press, for they contained no mention of that particular right. Only when the new states began to draft their constitutions do we begin to see some mention of it. Reflecting the recent colonial experience, the Virginia Declaration of Rights, drafted in 1776, said, "The freedom of the Press is one of the greatest bulwarks of liberty, and can never be restrained but by despotick Governments." The Maryland Declaration of Rights, drafted in the same year, said that "the liberty of the press ought to be inviolably preserved." Pennsylvania wrote the most specific of all the new guarantees: "That the people have a right to freedom of speech, and of writing, and publishing their sentiments: therefore the freedom of the press ought not to be restrained." The Pennsylvania constitution preserved freedom of the press for individual use; no one anticipated the development of an institutional press deserving protection on its own merits. In all, nine of the original thirteen states had constitutions containing free press or free speech clauses prior to or coincidental with the adoption of the Constitution and ratification of the Bill of Rights.[24]

These early state constitutional provisions, however, were all quite vague. In 1789, debate swirled around the interpretation of the Massachusetts guarantee: "The liberty of the press is essential to the security of freedom in a state: it ought not, therefore, to be restrained in this Commonwealth." William Cushing, chief justice of the state, discussed the possible meaning of the language with its author, John Adams. The main thrust of the guarantee, both agreed, was to grant newspapers freedom to comment about the operation of government and about their political leaders. Cushing praised newspapers, believing that without the press the

[19]The address is reprinted in ibid., 223.

[20]*Independent Gazetteer*, 13 April 1782.

[21]*Charleston Herald*, quoted in *South Carolina Gazette and Public Advertiser*, 1 October 1785.

[22]*Freeman's Journal*, 13 June 1781.

[23]*Independent Gazetteer*, 13 April 1782.

[24]Quotes from documents are reprinted in Schwartz, *The Bill of Rights*, 1: 235, 266. See also Margaret A. Blanchard, "Filling in the Void: Speech and Press in the State Courts Prior to *Gitlow*," in *The First Amendment Reconsidered*, Bill F. Chamberlin and Charlene J. Brown, eds. (New York, 1982), 18.

Constitutional Debate on Freedom of the Press

John Adams:
"The liberty of the press is essential to the security of freedom in a state: it ought not, therefore, to be restrained in this Commonwealth." (Massachusetts Constitution)

William Cushing:
"When the press is made the vehicle of falsehood and scandal, let the authors be punished with becoming rigour."

Elbridge Gerry:
"Despotism usually while it is gaining ground, will suffer men to think, say, or write what they please; but when once established, if it is thought necessary ... an imprimatur on the Press ... may silence the complaints ... of an injured and oppressed people."

James Wilson:
"The proposed [U.S. constitution] possesses no influence whatever upon the press ... [A free-press clause was dangerous, for] that very declaration might have been construed to imply that some degree of power was given, since we undertook to define its extent."

American Revolution would not have been possible, let alone successful. "This liberty of publishing truth can never effectually injure a good government, or honest administrators," he wrote, "but it may save a state from the necessity of a revolution, as well as bring one about, when it is necessary." The guarantee entailed the imposition of no previous restraint on publication, Cushing said, but "when the press is made the vehicle of falsehood and scandal, let the authors be punished with becoming rigour." Adams fully agreed with such an interpretation.[25] So another piece of the puzzle begins to fall into place. Freedom of the press initially referred solely to matters concerning government and political leaders. Its guarantees seemed fairly well limited to the absence of prior restraint or prior approval of contents. Punishment was assured for anyone who misused that freedom.

Such understanding extended beyond the borders of Massachusetts; indeed, agreement was widespread throughout the new states. Nevertheless, the new Constitution, proposed in 1787, included no such guarantee. Charles Pinckney, a South Carolina lawyer, suggested that the Constitution include a statement that "the liberty of the Press shall be inviolably preserved." But the delegates to the constitutional convention believed that since the federal government was not empowered to invade such personal liberties, guarantees were unnecessary. They defeated Pinckney's suggestion by a vote of four states for it — Massachusetts, Maryland, Virginia, and South Carolina — to seven against it — New Hampshire, Connecticut, New Jersey, Pennsylvania, Delaware, North Carolina, and Georgia.[26] The New York delegation was evenly divided and did not vote; the Rhode Island delegation was not present.

[25]Quoted in Leonard Levy, *Emergence of a Free Press* (New York, 1985), 198-9.

[26]Federal Convention, 1787, quoted in Schwartz, *The Bill of Right*, 1: 437 and 439.

James Madison on Freedom of the Press

On newspapers and liberty: "Whatever facilitates a general intercourse of sentiments, as good roads, domestic commerce, a free press, and particularly a circulation of newspapers through the entire body of the people...is favorable to liberty."

National Gazette, 1791

On press and religion: "It is to the press mankind are indebted for having dispelled the clouds which long encompassed religion, for disclosing her genuine lustre, and disseminating her salutary doctrines."

Speech in Virginia Assembly, 1799

On newspaper fairness: "Could it be so arranged that every newspaper, when printed on one side should be handed over to the press of an adversary, to be printed on the other, thus presenting to every reader both sides of every question, truth would always have a fair chance. But such a remedy is not ideal."

To N.P. Trist, 1828

Constitutional Debate

The Constitution was sent to the states for ratification without any protection for civil liberties. The lack of such protection stirred great debates in state ratifying conventions and led to powerfully written pamphlets demanding what became the Bill of Rights. Although much of the rhetoric dealt with civil liberties, much of the real concern centered on questions of political and economic power and who would wield it. Such questions were not easy to debate or write about, however, and the lack of a Bill of Rights became the focal point of debates. Unfortunately, though, the debates did not add measurably to an understanding of the meaning of freedom of the press. Often, protests against the lack of protection for freedom of the press combined many guarantees without any differentiation among them, such as this from a pamphlet by Virginian George Mason: "There is no declaration of any kind for preserving the liberty of the press, the trial by jury in civil causes, nor against the danger of standing armies in time of peace." Elbridge Gerry, an Anti-Federalist, or opponent of ratification, from Massachusetts, fearful that the new system at first would seem kindly and beneficent and then would turn oppressive, detailed his feelings with more precision:

> There is no security in the profered system, either for the rights of conscience or the liberty of the Press: Despotism usually while it is gaining ground, will suffer men to think, say, or write what they please; but when once established, if it is thought necessary to subserve the purposes, or arbitrary power, the most unjust restrictions may take place in the first instance, and an imprimatur on the Press in the next, may silence the complaints, and forbid the most decent remonstrances of an injured and oppressed people.[27]

The Federalists, or supporters of the Constitution, felt such criticisms were unmerited. They had no ulterior motives, they said, no plans to subvert the civil liberties of the people. In fact, argued Pennsylvanian James Wilson, "The proposed system possesses no influence whatever upon the press"; he argued that "it would have been merely nugatory, to have introduced a formal declaration upon the subject; nay, that very declaration might have been construed to imply that some degree of power was given, since we undertook to define its extent."[28] Such a concern is heard even today as some purists argue that to take press-related cases into court, asking a judicial body to include a particular right within the list of benefits granted by the First Amendment, gives jurists just as great an opportunity to exclude that right from the panoply of rights granted under the First Amendment as to include it.

The greatest of all Federalist writings on the Constitution was *The Federalist Papers*; and "Federalist No. 84," by New Yorker Alexander Hamilton, reveals someone with a clear understanding of the societal base necessary for the existence of freedom of the press:

[27]Quoted in ibid., 450 and 486.
[28]Ibid., 529.

> What signifies a declaration, that "the liberty of the press shall be inviolably preserved"? What is the liberty of the press? Who can give it any definition which would not leave the utmost latitude for evasion? I hold it to be impracticable; and from this I infer that its security, whatever fine declarations may be inserted in any constitution respecting it, must altogether depend on public opinion, and on the general spirit of the people and of the government.[29]

This statement has held true throughout United States history. When Americans have believed limitations on the right of certain individuals to speak were appropriate — be they abolitionists in the 1830s and 1840s, Southern sympathizers in the North during the Civil War, German-Americans or pacifists during World War I, or Communists in the 1950s — ways have been found to curtail freedom of expression. Such actions later in American history followed the spirit of our patriot forebears who believed destroying Tory presses was congruent with the liberty they were seeking in the Revolution. The importance of public opinion in the preservation of freedom of the press is often one of the most overlooked and underappreciated elements involved in the protection of that right.

The state ratifying conventions featured much rhetoric about freedom of the press but cast little illumination on its meaning. Pennsylvanians probably received the best explanation of freedom of the press when they suggested adding an amendment to the Constitution that would read, "That the people have a right to the freedom of speech, of writing and of publishing their sentiments; therefore, the freedom of the press shall not be restrained by any law of the United States."[30] Responding to questions as to the meaning of the amendment, future United States Supreme Court Justice James Wilson said the amendment certainly would not mean absolute freedom for the press: "The idea of the liberty of the press is not carried so far as this in any country — *what is meant by the liberty of the press is that there should be no antecedent restraint upon it*." He added "that every author is responsible when he attacks the security or welfare of the government, or the safety, character and property of the individual."[31] In this way, Wilson indicated that Americans had accepted the legal precept first expounded by Sir William Blackstone in England in 1769 that "the liberty of the press is indeed essential to the nature of a free state; but this consists in laying no *previous* restraints upon publications, and not in freedom from censure for criminal matter when published."[32]

Although absent from the constitutional debates because of his assignment as ambassador to France, Thomas Jefferson, a strong proponent of freedom of the press, also believed that an amendment prohibiting the federal government from interfering with the press would not restrict a state's ability to enact libel laws. As he wrote to James Madison, "A declaration that the federal government will never restrain the presses from printing anything they please, will not take away the liability of the printers for false facts printed."[33]

Despite the uncertainty of the meaning of freedom of the press, the people wanted a Bill of Rights added, and their approval of the Constitution was based on promises to that effect. The mandate for protecting press freedom was relatively small, however. Twelve states held ratifying conventions between 1787-1788; only Virginia, New York, and North Carolina suggested a press-freedom guarantee.[34] Thus, although the Constitution was ratified and suggestions for a Bill of Rights offered, support for freedom of the press was not overwhelming. The support that existed favored freedom along with responsibility for abuses.

One thing can be said with a fair amount of certainty, however, about the men who wrote the Constitution: they had few compunctions about withholding news of their deliberations from the public. Delegates closed convention sessions to the public and quickly adopted rules to make sure no information was leaked. Guards were posted at the doors, and no official record of debates was kept.[35] To a certain extent, one can understand this shroud of secrecy that fell over Independence Hall that Philadelphia summer. Delegates had convened to revise the Articles of Confederation — not to frame a new government — and the direction that the new government was taking was so dramatically different from that which already existed that the framers decided to wait until the entire document was completed and then to unveil it all at one time. The newspapers tolerated the secrecy. Perhaps they had become accustomed to legislative bodies meeting in secret, for that was the format for most sessions. Or perhaps they simply trusted the men who were serving as delegates to the convention.[36] Whatever the reason, the document that was placed before the American people for ratification came as a complete surprise to most.

THE FIRST AMENDMENT

Shortly after the completion of the ratification process, the first Congress convened, and Madison began moving a Bill of Rights through a body far more interested in other matters. He intended, however, to hold Congress to its promise that a Bill of Rights would be one of its first concerns. In the area of freedom of

[29]Alexander Hamilton, James Madison, and John Jay, *The Federalist Papers*, selected and edited by Roy P. Fairfield, 2nd ed. (Garden City, New York, 1966), 263-4.

[30]Quoted in Schwartz, *The Bill of Right*, 2: 658.

[31]Quoted in Leonard W. Levy, *Emergence of a Free Press* (New York, 1985), 204 (emphasis included).

[32]Quoted in Levy, *Freedom of the Press from Zenger to Jefferson*, 104 (emphasis included).

[33]July 31, 1789, Julian P. Boyd, et. al., eds., *The Papers of Thomas Jefferson* (Princeton, N.J., 1950), 13: 442-3.

[34]For a discussion of the legislative history of the Bill of Rights, see David A. Anderson, "The Origins of the Press Clause," *UCLA Law Review* 130 (1983): 471.

[35]For a study of the role of secrecy in the new nation, see Daniel N. Hoffman, *Government Secrecy and the Founding Fathers: A Study in Constitutional Controls* (Westport, Conn., 1981).

[36]See Carol Sue Humphrey, "'Little Ado About Something': Philadelphia Newspapers and the Constitutional Convention," *American Journalism* 5 (1988): 63-80; and Victor Rosewater, "The Constitutional Convention in the Colonial Press," *Journalism Quarterly* 14 (1937): 364-5.

Thomas Jefferson on Freedom of the Press

On the newly proposed Constitution: "I will now tell you what I do not like. First, the omission of a Bill of Rights providing clearly...for freedom of religion, freedom of the press...."

To James Madison, 1787

On the Alien and Sedition Acts: "I am for...freedom of the press, and against all violations of the Constitution to silence by force and not by reason the complaints or criticisms, just or unjust, of our citizens against the conduct of their agents."

To Elbridge Gerry, 1799

On criticism by Federalist newspapers: "The firmness with which the people have withstood the late abuses of the press, the discernment they have manifested between truth and falsehood, show that they may safely be trusted to hear everything true and false, and to form a correct judgment between them."

To John Tyler of Caroline, 1804

On the power of states to punish newspapers for libel: "While we deny Congress has a right to control freedom of the press, we have ever asserted the right of the States and their exclusive right, to do so."

To Abigail Adams, 1804

On the shortcomings of the press: "It is a melancholy truth, that a suppression of the press could not more completely deprive the nation of its benefits, than is done by its abandoned prostitution to falsehood. Nothing can be believed which is seen in a newspaper. Truth itself becomes suspicious by being put into that polluted vehicle....I really look with commiseration over the body of my fellow citizens, who, reading newspapers, live and die in the belief, that they have known something of what has been passing in the world in their time."

To John Norvell, 1807

speech and press, he suggested two amendments, one of which read, "The people shall not be deprived or abridged of their right to speak, to write, or to publish their sentiments; and the freedom of the press, as one of the great bulwarks of liberty, shall be inviolable." The second proposal read, "No State shall violate the equal rights of conscience, or the freedom of the press, or the trial by jury in criminal cases." Madison argued specifically for adoption of this second amendment, saying, "If there were any reason to restrain the Government of the United States from infringing upon these essential rights, it was equally necessary that they should be secured against the State Governments."[37] Had congressmen adopted this second suggestion, application of the federal guarantees of freedom of the press to the states would have been immediate rather than postponed until United States Supreme Court action in the twentieth century.

Neither version emerged from the Congress. In fact, the language of the First Amendment was revised several times, with the final version being a compromise between advocates in the Senate and the House. Although the House of Representatives held open debates, the Senate, which drafted the final language of the First Amendment, kept its proceedings secret; and its reasons for making changes are unknown. Even the records that are available provide no insight into the meaning of freedom of the press, for that topic was never discussed in debates. The language that emerged, though, is familiar to all:

> Congress shall make no law respecting an establishment of religion, or prohibiting the free exercise thereof; or abridging the freedom of speech, or of the press; or the right of the people peaceably to assemble, and to petition the Government for a redress of grievances.

While Congress was setting up the new federal government, several states, dissatisfied with their initial constitutions, drafted new ones that included clarifications of their ideas about the role of the press in society. In Pennsylvania, a new constitution drafted in 1790 said:

[37]U.S. Congress, House, *Annals of Congress*, 1st Cong., 1st sess., 1: 434, 435, and 755.

> The printing-presses shall be free to every person who undertakes to examine the proceedings of the legislature, or any branch of government, and no law shall ever be made to restrain the right thereof. The free communication of thoughts and opinions is one of the inviolable rights of man; and every citizen may freely speak, write, and print on any subject, being responsible for the abuse of that liberty.

In that clause was found the trend of the future in state constitutions, for many states modeled their versions on it. The printing press, not the newspaper, was to be free for anyone who investigated government. Citizens had the right to share their views on government with each other, but if they abused that right, they could be held responsible in a court of law. The Pennsylvania constitution added, "In prosecutions for the publication of papers investigating the official conduct of officers or men in a public capacity, or where the matter published is proper for public information, the truth thereof may be given in evidence; and in all indictments for libels the jury shall have the right to determine the law and the facts."[38] In this way, Pennsylvania became the first state to write into its fundamental law the principles first debated during the Zenger case fifty-five years earlier.

Freedom of the press during the early days of the nation was clearly associated with the proper functioning of government. Political leaders firmly believed that an informed populace was necessary for the Republic to function satisfactorily; the products of the press made an informed citizenry possible. Some debates focused on whether by listing what press freedom included and excluded, constitutional guarantees might limit that freedom. Concern also appeared about how state and federal protections of press freedom would mesh, although debates and correspondence made it clear that the federal Bill of Rights in no way prevented state governments from acting against abuses of freedom of the press. Most participants agreed that freedom of the press meant freedom from prior restraint; no one wanted to revive the colonial licensing system. Almost everyone agreed that those who used the press should be held responsible for transgressions. Substantial agreement also existed that individual citizens who wanted to use the press to publish their thoughts were the ones protected under state constitutional provisions. Owners and operators of presses were not specifically protected, although the latter obviously merited protection while using their printing presses to disseminate information. Because of the way in which the business of journalism would grow, however, the chief claimants to the right of freedom of the press over the years would become the owners and operators of the presses. Most political leaders of the times also realized how important public opinion was in guaranteeing the press its freedom.

[38] Pennsylvania Constitution of 1790, Art. IX, sec. 7, quoted in Francis Newton Thorpe, comp. and ed., *The Federal and State Constitutions, Colonial Charters, and Other Organic Laws of the States, Territories, and Colonies Now and Heretofore Forming the United States of America*, 17 vols. (Washington, D.C., 1909), 5: 3100.

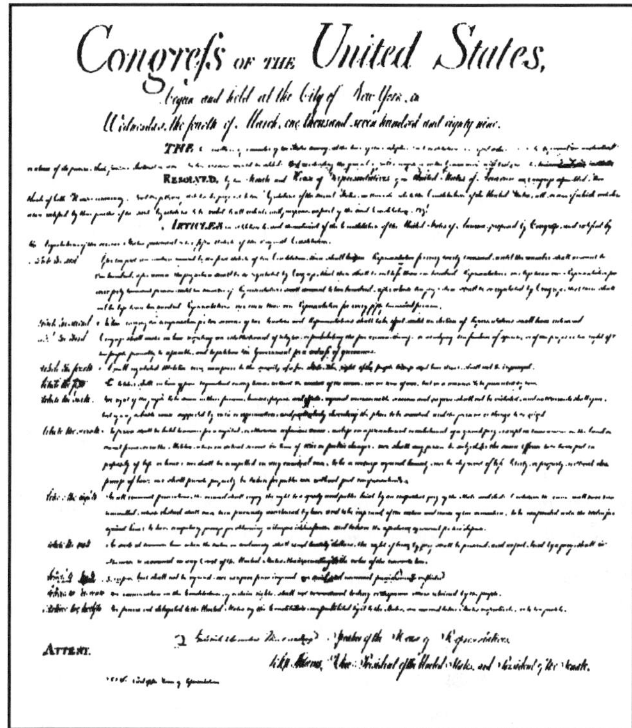

Congress OF THE United States,

begun and held at the City of New-York, on

Wednesday the fourth of March, one thousand seven hundred and eighty nine.

ATTEST.

Bill of Rights

When the Bill of Rights was sent to the states for ratification in 1789, what we know as the First Amendment today was the third in order of priority. The first two proposed amendments dealt with congressional housekeeping affairs. The states rejected the first two proposals, and amendment three became the First Amendment.

The Historical Debate about the Meaning of the Press Clause

The imprecise language used in the debates on civil liberties during these years caused problems for subsequent generations of Americans. In the latter part of the twentieth century, just what the framers meant by freedom of the press — and other Bill of Rights guarantees — became very important. A battle between liberals and conservatives raged over the doctrine of original intent — over whether the document has been interpreted according to the meaning the framers in the late eighteenth century intended. Conservatives argued that the Bill of Rights had been stretched out of shape by liberal judicial interpretations so that it now had eroded fundamental principles touching core religious and family values. To find a way to preserve these values, twentieth-century conservatives sought to uncover the meanings of the amendment when written. Once those original intentions were unearthed, constitutional interpretation could return to the correct foundation rather than being based on the moral and political preferences of judges. Liberals, on the other hand, argued that the Constitution and its Bill of Rights were living documents that used flexible eighteenth-century language as a base for changes as time and circumstance demanded.

Generally unconcerned about abortion and other such issues

that interest some among both modern conservatives and liberals, scholars on the history of freedom of the press have waged their own battle over the meaning of that guarantee.[39] At stake is whether the United States has a libertarian or repressive heritage on this important right and, by implication, what sort of treatment the press merits today as a result of that history. Those supporting the heritage of limited freedom find most of their evidence in legislative and court records and argue that certain restrictions on press freedom were expected during the early days of the nation. Those supporting the libertarian tradition look more at the words of printers about the wide extent of their freedom in those tumultuous times. They also view institutional journalism as a bulwark of American liberty, without which the nation never could have been founded. Those who support the more restrictive view of press freedom argue that only political speech was clearly protected by the Bill of Rights and that even that protection included the expectation that practitioners would exercise their freedom responsibly.

The more liberal version of press freedom has long been advocated by representatives of the institutional press, who see a long and impressive list of journalistic triumphs over attempts to suppress freedom of the press, victories that underscore the vital role of press freedom. Those looking at the repressive treatment of the press are of more recent vintage and find themselves trying to rewrite popular legend. Scholars on both sides of the battle have locked horns for more than thirty years and continue to grapple over the future of this important guarantee. Evidence amassed on both sides is impressive, and often scholars reinterpret their foes' proof to provide support for a different argument.

The problem, of course, focuses on separating rhetoric from reality. Were the laws reality and the printers' comments rhetoric? Or were the printers' comments reality and the laws rhetoric? Or did the truth lie somewhere in between? Obviously there were many federal and state laws on the books that could have restricted press freedom. Just as obviously, printers carried on in the pages of their newspapers as if those laws did not exist. In some cases, laws were enforced; in others, they were not. Today we can only appreciate that a considerable battle was waged over freedom of expression in our nation's early history and that the freedom that exists today was built on that early experience.

Federalists and Republicans

Although many historians consider the development of freedom of the press primarily in terms of laws and constitutions and debates over such documents, a considerable social fabric about freedom of the press was developing as well. Much of the activity centered around George Washington and his concern for the way in which the press operated. During the partisan age of journalism, Washington was a target of Republican editors. He complained liberally in private about the way in which the press treated him, but publicly the president maintained his support of a free press to provide the information citizens needed to operate a republic. Several characteristics of a twentieth-century free press emerged in his administrations (1789-1797) as well, including the freedom to criticize an incumbent president harshly without suffering retribution; the ability to obtain information about governmental activities through a variety of sources, including leaks from authorities; and the ability of a president to manage the press, as Washington himself leaked a copy of his farewell address to a friendly printer in Philadelphia.[40]

George Washington and Press Freedom
The nation's first president detested partisanship and hoped to avoid factionalism in the new government. Republican editors subjected him and his administration to so many bitter attacks, however, that he became exasperated. His reaction, combined with his distrust of the politics of immigrants, particularly of a French conspiracy, led him to support the Alien and Sedition Acts of 1798. He considered the latter not a repression of press freedom but a legitimate means for the government to protect itself from serious danger.

Some journalists also discovered the value of news and attempted to attend legislative sessions, which traditionally had been closed in Europe and in the United States. Thus, there were

[39]The foremost scholar arguing the repressive tradition is Levy, *Emergence of a Free Press*. Among those arguing for a more liberal tradition are Anderson, "The Origins of the Press Clause"; and Jeffery A. Smith, *Printers and Press Freedom: The Ideology of Early American Journalism* (New York, 1988).

[40]James E. Pollard, *The Presidents and the Press* (New York, 1947; reprint, New York, 1973), 1-35.

repeated contests with the Congress about access to its sessions. The House quickly opened its meetings, but sessions of the Senate remained closed for several years.[41]

Finally, the ability of the press to interject itself into foreign affairs became clear. Although problems with the French soon would become of overwhelming importance, the continuing diplomatic crisis during Washington's adminstrations involved the British. During these difficulties and Washington's attempt to secure a treaty to resolve them, an official document was leaked to the press for the first time. A Republican senator gave the text of the Jay Treaty to Benjamin Franklin Bache, who rushed it into print. Although upset by the breach of security, Washington had no recourse against Bache. Congress, which could have been persuaded to launch an investigation, was not in session at the time.[42]

Newspapers during the early days of the Republic were tied closely to political factions, and their publishers and patrons tested the limits of their freedom. The newspaper war between the proponents of the visions of America's future as advocated by Alexander Hamilton and Thomas Jefferson continued unabated as the Adams administration (1797-1801) began. During the Adams years, fears increased about the dangers posed by the French connections of Vice President Jefferson and his supporters. The French Revolution of 1789, which Republicans welcomed, had, by 1793, turned bloody. The primary targets of the revolutionaries were substantial businessmen, the French equivalent to the Federalists. Problems with the French extended into North America, where they were trying to re-establish a presence by getting the Spanish to give them Louisiana and the Floridas, and trying both to win Quebec away from the British and to rebuild their relationship with the Indians beyond the Appalachian Mountains.

President Adams tried to win peace with the French by sending a special mission to France in 1797-1798. The attempt proved futile. The French diplomats with whom the Americans negotiated tried to extort money from the United States. If the Americans did not come up with the required sum, the French threatened to unleash the French party in America, the Republicans, on the Federalists. The underlying threat was a bloody revolution similar to the one in France. The sordid situation was publicized widely as the XYZ Affair, named after the anonymous French envoys; and war fever ran high. Hatred of the Republicans reached a peak, and Federalists tried to make political capital from the affair.

Federalists labeled the Republicans as the country's enemies and determined to destroy their newspapers and to eliminate Republicans as a political force. The newspapers in France had, after all, played an important part in bringing down the monarchy. The newspapers in the colonies had been vital in destroying the relationship with Great Britain. History could repeat itself, and Republican newspapers could help destroy the new Republic and the

Partisan Suspicion
As animosity built up in the 1790s, Federalists feared that Republicans sympathized with the radicalism of the French Revolution. They published this cartoon in response to Thomas Jefferson's statement to a French official that the Federalists favored "despotism." Such suspicions provided one reason behind the Federalists' repressive Sedition Act of 1798.

Federalists. Federalists also wanted to keep individuals whom they viewed as unreliable aliens or immigrant radicals — including a number of Republican editors — from finding a way to express themselves. Thus the Federalists decided their only solution to an unpleasant situation was the suppression first of the Republican newspapers and then of the Republicans themselves.

Such a solution seems unrealistic today; but in the late eighteenth century, American political leaders had not learned that political parties could co-exist without their differences leading to revolution. In fact, the only major transition of power from one political faction to an opposing group to that point in American history had been the Revolution. The first peaceful transition of power from one political faction to another would not come until 1800, and its impact was so far-reaching that historians call it the "Second American Revolution." The years immediately preceding it were ones of great peril for people opposed to the existing government.

Federalists were wrong about the intentions of Republicans. The latter were not attempting to subvert the Constitution. If anything, they wanted to preserve it for the anticipated presidential bid of Jefferson in 1800, which perhaps frightened Federalists more than any dangers from the French. Republican newspapers, although vocal, were in the minority and were definitely weaker

[41]Gerald L. Grotta, "Philip Freneau's Crusade for Open Sessions of the U.S. Senate," *Journalism Quarterly* 48 (1971): 667-71.

[42]Everette E. Dennis, "Stolen Peace Treaties and the Press: Two Case Studies," *Journalism History* 2 (1975): 6-14.

FIFTH CONGRESS OF THE UNITED STATES:

At the Second Session,

Begun and held at the city of *Philadelphia*, in the State of Pennsylvania, on *Monday*, the thirteenth of *November*, one thousand seven hundred and ninety-seven.

An ACT respecting alien enemies.

Alien and Sedition Acts

Federalist officials used the Alien and Sedition Acts as weapons against leading Republican editors. Their goal was to silence any support of revolutionary France that existed in the United States and to ensure that Republican newspapers were unable to back Thomas Jefferson's bid for the presidency in 1800. The French threat failed to materialize, and Jefferson became the third president of the United States.

than their Federalist competitors, which had advantages ranging from use of the mails granted to government-appointed postmasters to incomes from government printing contracts. But the realities of the situation did not stop Federalists from pushing through Congress some of the most oppressive legislation ever enacted in American history.

The Alien and Sedition Acts

In proposing the Alien and Sedition Acts, Federalists contended that they were merely acting to meet a serious foreign threat within the United States. The legislative package actually consisted of four laws: a naturalization law increasing the residency requirement for citizenship from five years to fourteen years, an alien enemies law allowing deportation or imprisonment of aliens during wartime, an alien friends act allowing the president to engage in selective deportation of undesirable aliens, and a sedition act aimed at curtailing criticism of the government. The Sedition Act was all-encompassing:

> That if any person shall write, print, utter or publish, or shall cause or procure to be written, printed, uttered or published, or shall knowingly and willingly assist or aid in writing, printing, uttering or publishing any false, scandalous and malicious writing against the government of the United States, or either house of the Congress of the United States, or the President of the United States, with intent to defame said government, or to bring them, or either of them, into contempt or disrepute; or to excite against them, the hatred of the good people of the United States, or to stir up sedition within the United States, or to excite any unlawful combinations therein, for opposing or resisting any law of the United States, or any act of the President of the United States, done in pursuance of any such law, or of the powers in him vested by the constitution of the United States, or to resist, oppose, or defeat any such law or act, or to aid, encourage, or abet any hostile designs of any foreign nation against the United States, their people or government, then such person, being thereof convicted before any court of the United States having jurisdiction thereof, shall be punished by a fine not exceeding two thousand dollars, and by imprisonment not exceeding two years.[43]

The political motivations of the law were clear. The act protected the sections of the federal government dominated by Federalists and pointedly excluded Vice President Jefferson from its provisions. The law also provided for trial by jury for offenders with truth as a defense and with the jurors allowed to determine both the law and the fact of the matter before them, thus putting into federal legislation the principles of libel law argued in the Zenger case. The provision, however, provided little protection. The journalism of the day liberally mixed news and opinion, and most prosecutions under the law involved opinions. Proving the truthfulness of opinion was impossible.

Reaction to the Alien and Sedition Acts came from partisans of both sides. Federalists almost unanimously lined up in favor of them. Although President Adams later said that he had never recommended the Sedition Act to Congress, he signed it willingly and used its provisions to prosecute political opponents. Alexander Hamilton, who was out of government at the time, found initial proposals too harsh, arguing to his allies that some of the sections might make martyrs out of Republicans prosecuted under its provisions. He approved, however, of the amended act as eventually adopted. George Washington, now in retirement, found within the legislation new hope that the nation would survive the divisiveness brought on by the partisans of France that he so feared.

The only leading Federalist who registered opposition was John Marshall, future chief justice of the Supreme Court and one of the three delegates to France whose involvement in the XYZ Affair sparked the initial calls for anti-sedition legislation. He stated his opposition in a campaign tract issued in an effort to win a Virginia congressional seat. He believed that the legislation was "useless" and would "create unnecessary discontents and jeal-

[43]*Statutes at Large*, 1: 596-7.

Bacon-Face Samuel Chase
Although possessing a keen and respected legal mind, Justice Samuel Chase became notorious for his high-handedness during trials under the Sedition Act. The Republican editor Benjamin Bache wrote that no one could "mistake...the bacon face of old Chase for the face of justice." Chase's violent temperament created personal enemies even of those who shared his ideology.

ousies at a time when our very existence, as a nation, may depend on our union." He pledged to oppose renewal of the legislation should he be elected to Congress.[44]

Congressional debates on the bills brought into sharper focus just how Americans interpreted "freedom of the press." The Federalists saw within the proposals no dangers to freedom of the press. In fact, they argued that the legislation extended freedom because it would purge newspapers of false and malicious comments. As Harrison Gray Otis of Massachusetts pointed out in the House of Representatives, "Every independent Government has a right to preserve and defend itself against injuries and outrages which endanger its existence." Freedom of the press "is nothing more than the liberty of writing, publishing, and speaking one's thoughts, under the condition of being answerable to the injured party, whether it be the Government or an individual, for false, malicious, and seditious expressions, whether spoken or written." The Alien and Sedition Acts, Otis said, would simply punish "licentiousness and sedition" and would not be a prior restraint on the press, which was forbidden.[45] Such an argument for the right of government to preserve itself would not vanish from American history. It was heard again during debates over the adoption of repressive measures during World War I and during the enactment of laws restricting the freedom of Communists in the 1950s.

Another Federalist, Representative James Bayard of Delaware, betrayed the administration's interest in controlling the nature of information circulated. Republicans trusted the people to make the correct decisions; Federalists were more elitist and believed the masses were not able to run a government. The only way a republic based on popular sovereignty could survive, Federalists believed, was by very carefully guiding public opinion, for, as Bayard said:

> This government ... depends for its existence upon the good will of the people. That good will is maintained by their good opinion. But, how is that good opinion to be preserved, if wicked and unprincipled men, men of inordinate and desperate ambition, are allowed to state facts to the people which are not true, which they know at the time to be false, and which are stated with the criminal intention of bringing the Government into disrepute among the people? This was falsely and deceitfully stealing the public opinion; it was a felony of the worst and most dangerous nature.[46]

Republicans viewed the proposals and the abilities of the people quite differently. Albert Gallatin, who would become secretary of the treasury under Jefferson, argued that "the bill was intended to punish solely writings of a political nature" and was aimed at preventing Republicans from putting their views before the American people in an election year. "Laws against writings of this kind had uniformly been one of the most powerful engines used by tyrants to prevent the diffusion of knowledge," he added.[47] John Nicholas, a Republican representative from Virginia, was even more pointed in tying the proposed legislation to the 1800 elections: "The people have no other means of examining their [leaders'] conduct but by means of the press, and an unrestrained investigation through them of the conduct of the Government," he said. "Indeed, the heart and life of a free Government, is a free press." Then he added that to restrict the press would be to destroy the elective principle by taking away the information necessary to election and that there would be no difference between such a deprivation and a total denial of the right of election, but in the degree of usurpation.[48]

The majority of the nation's newspapers, which were Federalist, strongly supported the Alien and Sedition Acts, seeing nothing within their language as a threat to press freedom.

Although Federalists were able to obtain indictments and con-

[44]John Marshall campaign tract, 20 September 1798, in *John Marshall: Major Opinions and Other Writings*, John P. Roche, ed. (Indianapolis, 1967), 32.

[45]U.S. Congress, House, *Annals of Congress*, 5th Cong., 2nd sess., 8: 2146, 2148, and 2149.

[46]Ibid., 3rd sess., 9: 2960.

[47]Ibid., 8: 2162.

[48]Ibid., 8: 2162 and 2144.

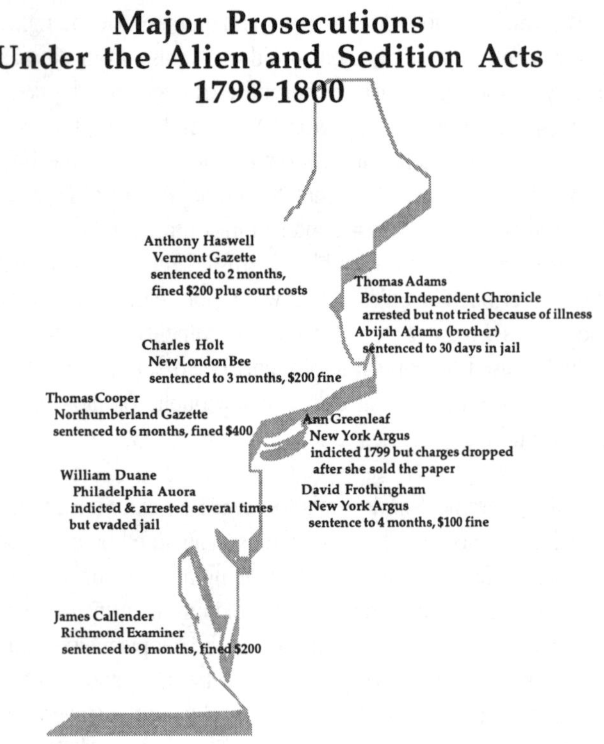

Luther Baldwin's Sedition

Twenty-five Republicans were arrested under the Sedition Act. Most were editors. The unfortunate Luther Baldwin was indicted, however, for remarks he made at a parade honoring President John Adams. The Philadelphia *Aurora* reported that an observer, seeing the cannon fire after Adams had passed, told Baldwin, "There goes the President and they are firing at his a- -." Baldwin, a little inebriated, replied "that he did not care if they fired thro' his a- -: Then [a Federalist] exclaims ... that is seditious." Other papers picked up the story, one of which asked, "Can the most enthusiastic Federalists or Tories suppose that those who are opposed to them would feel any gratification in firing at such a disgusting target as the a- - of John Adams?"

victions of Republican newspaper editors under the Sedition Act, their main target, Jefferson, remained out of reach. He had long had a personal policy against writing for newspapers, a practice that protected him during the two years in which the Alien and Sedition Acts were in effect. So the Federalists settled for actions against leading Republican newspapers in an effort to silence opposition commentary.

The Republican Response

The Republican press carried on as if the laws had never been enacted, and federal courts so zealously enforced the laws that questions arose about whether defendants received fair trials. Judges broadly interpreted the seditious libel formula established in the law to preclude even ordinary political commentary. In all, there were twenty-five arrests, fourteen indictments, eleven trials, and ten convictions under the Sedition Act, eight of which were related to newspaper publications. The legislation and the results of court cases did nothing to discourage Republican newspapers. If anything, editors went to greater degrees of disrespect and criticism of Federalist office holders. Imprisoned Republican editors had the enforced luxury of additional time for writing, and they used it well. As Zenger before them, they became martyrs to a cause and thus built additional support for themselves and their patron, Jefferson.

Republican leaders were not idle either. They considered themselves locked in a struggle for survival and launched a full-scale attack on the Alien and Sedition Acts, taking their cues from Madison and Jefferson, whose Virginia and Kentucky Resolutions provided the philosophical cornerstone for criticism of the laws. Although the Resolutions were primarily an argument for the right of states to nullify federal legislation with which they disagreed—and later would support John C. Calhoun's nullification theory during sectional conflicts leading to the Civil War—they did mention the importance of communication in a free society. Madison noted that the Alien and Sedition Acts were dangerous because they were "levelled against the right of freely examining public characters and measures, and of free communication among the people thereon, which has ever been justly deemed the only effectual guardian of every other right."[49] Jefferson raised the question of the Alien and Sedition Acts violating the First Amendment, which prohibited the federal government from taking action against the press.[50]

Although the constitutionality of the Alien and Sedition laws never was tested, some historians believe that the measures would have been found constitutional by the Supreme Court. During the controversy a number of members of the Court said Congress had the power to enact such legislation.[51] The same decision was reached on the sedition laws enacted during World War I. Foreign dangers long have been seen as endowing Congress with extraordinary powers to act, even to the extent of limiting First Amendment freedoms.

The drafting of the Resolutions did give Madison a chance to think about the meaning of freedom of the press, and from his reflections came a remarkably modern statement about the problems inherent in this complicated right. Everyone, Madison said, agreed that freedom of the press meant freedom from prior restraint. But, he asked, did not laws "inflicting penalties on printed publications ... have a similar effect with a law authorizing a previous restraint on them?" It seemed odd, he said, to allow someone to make a statement and then punish the person for speaking. Madison recognized that abuse of free press was likely at times, but "it is better to leave a few of its noxious branches to their luxuriant growth, than, by pruning them away, to injure the vigour of those yielding the proper fruits." Such a policy was the best one to follow because "to the press alone, chequered as it is with abus-

[49] "Resolutions of 1798," Gaillard Hunt, ed., *The Writings of James Madison*, 19 vols. (New York), 6 (1790-1802), 328-9.

[50] "Resolutions Relative to the Alien and Sedition Laws," Albert Ellery Bergh, ed., *The Writings of Thomas Jefferson*, 20 vols. (Washington, D.C., 1905), 17: 381-2.

[51] Edward G. Hudon, *Freedom of Speech and Press in America* (New York, 1963), 53.

es, the world is indebted for all the triumphs which have been gained by reason and humanity over error and oppression." Counted among those triumphs was the successful revolution from Great Britain, which, Madison said, never would have occurred if a sedition act had been in place. Then, he added a practical political argument. "A number of important elections will take place while the act is in force," he noted, and "will not those in power derive an undue advantage for continuing themselves in it, which, by impairing the right of election, endangers the blessings of the Government founded on it?"[52]

Republicans' fears about the effect of the laws on the election of 1800 were not confirmed; Jefferson became the third president of the United States. The Alien and Sedition Acts expired, and Jefferson pardoned anyone convicted under them and still serving prison terms. The legislation had stirred a public debate on press freedom. Recognition that conflicting voices could exist without the Republic crumbling became an important milestone in the development of freedom of the press; additional advances in the role of the press in America would be built on that precept.

Jefferson, Hamilton, and Freedom of the Press

Concluding a discussion on press liberty with a statement that Jefferson, schooled in the value of a free press, acted differently than his predecessors in dealing with opposition newspapers during his administration (1801-1809) would be ideal. However, he only believed in protecting freedom of the press from federal intervention. As with his contemporaries, Jefferson believed strongly in the restriction of the press on the state level and argued in 1803 for restoring the press' credibility lost during the Federalist era by "a few prosecutions of the most prominent offenders" under state law. Partisanship influenced Jefferson's views on press freedom. Federalist newspapers had so defiled the press, Jefferson argued, that "the people have learnt that nothing in a newspaper is to be believed. This is a dangerous state of things, and the press ought to be restored to its credibility if possible." Just as the Federalists argued that the Alien and Sedition Acts really would not violate the freedom of the press, so, too, did Jefferson think that action against Federalist publications would simply serve to upgrade their quality. He did not want "a general prosecution, for that would look like persecution: but a selected one," thinking such an effort "would have a wholesome effect in restoring the integrity of the presses."[53]

In fact, Jefferson ended the critical early period of development of freedom of the press locked in another conflict with Alexander Hamilton. The cause was a libel suit in 1804 involving a Federalist newspaper, *The Wasp*, published by Harry Croswell in Hudson, New York. Croswell had made the mistake of reprinting some criticism of Jefferson published initially in Hamilton's *New York Evening Post*. Jefferson, upset by the comments, decided that Croswell's republication was an example of the licentiousness of the press that should be punished, and he urged his supporters to bring a libel suit against Croswell. Hamilton defended Croswell on appeal; and, although he lost the case, he delivered a classic statement of freedom of the press:

Harry Croswell
Harry Croswell, editor of the *Wasp* in Hudson, New York, brought down the ire of Republican politicians when he reprinted a charge from another Federalist newspaper that Thomas Jefferson had paid a Republican editor to criticize John Adams. Jefferson agreed with some of his supporters that the government should make an example of Croswell by prosecuting him for seditious libel. Although the trial court found Croswell guilty, the trial led to important changes enlarging press freedom. This portrait was made years later, after he had become a priest in the Anglican Church.

> The liberty of the Press consists, in my idea, in publishing the truth, from good motives and for justifiable ends, though it reflect on government, on magistrates, or individuals. If it not be allowed, it excludes the privilege of canvassing men, and our rulers. This is impossible without the right of looking to men. To say that measures can be discussed, and that there shall be no bearing on those, who are the authors of those measures cannot be done. The very end and reason of discussion would be destroyed....In speaking thus for the Freedom of the Press, I do not say there ought to be an unbridled license; or that the

[52]Report on the Resolutions, Hunt, *The Writings of James Madison,* 6: 386, 389, and 397-8.

[53]Jefferson to Thomas McKean, 19 February 1803, Andrew A. Lipscomb, editor-in-chief, *The Writings of Thomas Jefferson* (Washington, 1904-1905), 9: 449, 451, and 452.

THE

SPEECHES

AT FULL LENGTH

OF

MR. VAN NESS, MR. CAINES,

THE ATTORNEY-GENERAL, Mr. HARRISON,

AND

GENERAL HAMILTON,

IN THE

GREAT CAUSE

OF THE

PEOPLE,

AGAINST

HARRY CROSWELL,

ON AN INDICTMENT FOR A

LIBEL

ON

THOMAS JEFFERSON,

PRESIDENT OF THE UNITED STATES.

New-York;

PRINTED BY G. & R. WAITE, NO. 64, MAIDEN-LANE.

1804.

[Copy right secured.]

Alexander Hamilton and the Croswell Case

When President Thomas Jefferson encouraged a libel prosecution of editor Harry Croswell, the Federalist Alexander Hamilton agreed to serve as one of Croswell's attorneys. The Federalists' intellectual leader, Hamilton enunciated some of America's most insightful ideas on the nature of constitutional government. He also saw clearly the press' role in a democracy and, in the Croswell trial, argued effectively for the right to criticize government. Although the court found Croswell guilty, Hamilton's contention that truth should be accepted as a defense gained wide approval following publication of the arguments in book form. As a result, state governments began adopting the principle.

> characters of men who are good, will naturally tend eternally to support themselves. I do not stand here to say that no shackles are to be laid on this license....I contend for the liberty of publishing truth, with good motives and for justifiable ends, even though it reflect on government, magistrates, or private persons. I contend for it under the restraint of our tribunal. When this is exceeded, let them interpose and punish.[54]

Hamilton lost the case because New York law did not protect the kind of commentary Hamilton was defending. The state legislature, so swayed by Hamilton's argument, though, changed the state's libel law to allow truth to be admitted as evidence and to authorize the jury to determine both the law and the fact of the matter. Thus the home of Zenger finally permitted printers to criticize governmental officials. The ability of those using the press to comment about the functioning of their leaders had been one of the first uses for the press, whether the leaders were spiritual or temporal, royal or colonial, Federalist or Republican. And this freedom to criticize leaders has remained the heart and soul of the American press system regardless of changes over the years.

By 1804, then, the foundation of freedom of the press was well established. It consisted of freedom of individuals to use a press to print their thoughts. Generally, people were given greater freedom when they were discussing public officials; but, in all cases, they were held responsible for the abuse of the press. Federal authorities, the Alien and Sedition Acts notwithstanding, were forbidden to act against the press. State legislatures, however, could enact laws to ensure that those using the press acted responsibly. The principle that freedom of the press meant the absence of prior restraint on publication also was generally accepted.

As the nineteenth century dawned, Americans were beginning to believe that multiple views could be tolerated on the same topic and that those views should be protected through the principle of freedom of the press. This notion, crucial as it is to a true meaning of freedom of the press, did not really become embedded in American thinking until the abolitionist crisis of the 1830s. Despite America's tradition of freedom, tolerance for dissident views was not one of the strongest pillars of its free-press heritage.

[54] *The Law Practice of Alexander Hamilton*, Julius Goebel, Jr., ed., 5 vols. (New York, 1964), 1: 809-10.

RECOMMENDED READINGS

BOOKS

Blagden, Cyprian. *The Stationers Company*. London, 1960. History of the organization responsible for enforcing licensing provisions during early English history.

Brant, Irving. *The Bill of Rights*. Indianapolis, Ind., 1965. Discussion of all parts of the Bill of Rights with emphasis on freedom of speech and freedom of the press.

Chenery, William L. *Freedom of the Press*. New York, 1955 (rev.ed., Westport, Conn., 1977). The tradition in early America was one of freedom of expression, with the people fighting against conservative, repressive government to attain and maintain freedom. Uses history of freedom to argue for freedom in the 1950s. Covers major episodes such as the Zenger trial, Alien and Sedition Acts, Jefferson's writings, etc.

Cheslau, Irving G. *John Peter Zenger and "The New-York Weekly Journal"; A Historical Study*. New York, 1952. The trial, although a milestone in American freedom, did not establish a legal precedent and "did not sweep out the rigors of the common law" of libel.

Duniway, Clyde Augustus. *The Development of Freedom of the Press in Massachusetts*. Cambridge, Mass., 1906. Detailed treatment of the development of the press in this most important part of the American continent through the early nineteenth century.

Eldridge, Larry D. *A Distant Heritage: The Growth of Free Speech in Early America*. New York and London, 1994. Eldridge contests Leonard Levy's theory on repression of free speech, concluding that "colonists experienced a dramatic expansion of their freedom to criticize government and its officials across the seventeenth century."

Gleason, Timothy W. *The Watchdog Concept: The Press and the Courts in Nineteenth-Century America*. Ames, Iowa, 1990. Brief but cogent investigation of freedom of the press and the concept that the press should serve as a guardian against governmental abuses of power.

Hudon, Edward G. *Freedom of Speech and Press in America*. Washington, 1963. This study attempts to establish a historical basis for the libertarian belief in the need for freedom of expression in a complex society. It is a well-documented study of "the British law of speech and press as it existed in England and colonial America prior to the revolution."

Humphrey, Carol Sue. *The Press of the Young Republic, 1783-1833*. Westport, Conn., 1996. Its chapter on the Alien and Sedition Acts is especially good.

Konkle, Burton A. *The Life of Andrew Hamilton, 1676-1741, "The Day-Star of the American Revolution."* Philadelphia, 1941. Chapters 11-14 focus on the Zenger trial. For his service to press freedom, Gouverneur Morris called Hamilton "the day-star of the American Revolution."

Levy, Leonard W. *Emergence of a Free Press*. New York, 1985. Detailed description of the development of press freedom in America. This is a revision of Levy's landmark work, *Freedom of Speech and Press in Early American History: Legacy of Suppression*, published in 1960.

—. *Jefferson and Civil Liberties: The Darker Side*. 1963; reprint, New York, 1973. Chapter on Jefferson's relationship with the press indicates his willingness to curtail its freedom in certain circumstances.

Miller, John C. *Crisis in Freedom: The Alien and Sedition Acts*. Boston, 1951. Brief history of the Alien and Sedition Acts.

Mott, Frank Luther. *Jefferson and the Press*. Baton Rouge, 1943. Very favorable look at Jefferson's record on freedom of the press.

Rutherford, Livingston. *John Peter Zenger, His Press, His Trial, and a Bibliography of Zenger Imprints*. New York, 1904. The standard biography of Zenger, with a bibliography of works on his trial, issues of the *Journal*, and publications by Zenger.

Rutland, Robert A. *The Birth of the Bill of Rights, 1776-1791*. Chapel Hill, N.C., 1955. Detailed tracing of factors leading to the adoption of the Bill of Rights.

Schuyler, Livingston. *The Liberty of the Press in the American Colonies Before the Revolutionary War. With Particular Reference to Conditions in the Royal Colony of New York*. New York, 1905. Good treatment of the relationship between colonial authorities and those using the press.

Siebert, Frederick S. *Freedom of the Press in England, 1476-1776*. Urbana, Ill., 1952. Most widely accepted discussion of free-press heritage of Great Britain.

Sloan, Wm. David, and Julie Hedgepeth Williams. *The Early American Press, 1690-1783*. Westport, Conn., 1994. The treatments of Puritan ideas of press freedom and the chapters on the Zenger trial and the Stamp Act crisis are especially valuable.

Smith, James M. *Freedom's Fetters: The Alien and Sedition Laws and Civil Liberties*. Ithaca, N.Y., 1956. Detailed account of the Alien and Sedition Act controversy.

Smith, Jeffery A. *Printers and Press Freedom: The Ideology of Early American Journalism*. New York, 1988. Examination of the development of the free-press heritage in context of the intellectual and political climate of eighteenth-century America.

ARTICLES

Allis, Frederick S., Jr. "Boston and the Alien and Sedition Laws." *Boston Society, Proceedings* (1951): 25-51. The reaction of Federalists in Massachusetts to the Kentucky and Virginia resolutions against the Sedition Act showed "little sympathy for this Republican nonsense." They favored strict enforcement.

Anderson, David A. "The Origin of the Press Clause." *UCLA Law Review* 30 (1983): 456-541. Discusses the background of the press clause in the Bill of Rights in an attempt to discover its meaning.

Anderson, Frank M. "The Enforcement of the Alien and Sedition Laws." *Annual Report of the American Historical Association* (1912): 113-26. High Federal officials were energetic in enforcing the laws. Republican charges of unfairness were numerous. Juries were packed, judges interpreted the acts favorably in accord with Federalist intent, and the deportment of some judges was questionable.

Baldasty, Gerald J. "Toward an Understanding of the First Amendment: Boston Newspapers, 1782-1791." *Journalism History* 3 (1976): 25-30, 32. Discussion of the way in which newspaper printers defined the right to freedom of the press as the right to criticize public officials as compared with the legal definition existing at the time.

Berns, Walter. "Freedom of the Press and the Alien and Sedition Laws: A Reappraisal," 109-59 in *Supreme Court Review*, 1970. Chicago, 1970. "The men principally responsible for the development of liberal law of free speech and press ... were the Federalists Alexander Hamilton and James Kent who were able to do this because, unlike Jefferson and his colleagues and successors, they were not inhibited by an attachment to the institution of slavery."

Buel, Richard, Jr. "Freedom of the Press in Revolutionary America: The Evolution of Libertarianism, 1760-1820," in Bernard Bailyn and John Hench, eds., *The Press and the American Revolution* (Worcester, Mass., 1980), 59-98. Although there were many obstacles to absolute freedom, early Americans viewed freedom as a good ideology — but they believed that freedom should be used for the public good.

Buranelli, Vincent. "Peter Zenger's Editor." *American Quarterly* 7 (Summer 1955): 174-81. The lawyer James Alexander played a key role in the New York *Weekly Journal* and the Zenger trial. Zenger's fame rightfully "grows with the years." The *Weekly Journal*, directed and edited by Alexander, was "the great spokesman for freedom, attempting to educate its readers into the meaning of the concept, and at the same time giving a practical demonstration of the concept in action."

Carroll, Thomas F. "Freedom of Speech and the Press in the Federalist Period: The Sedition Act." *Michigan Law Review* 18 (1920): 615-51. Federalists believed Congress had the right to prohibit publications that interfered with the government in the exercise of its constitutional duties.

Covert, Cathy. "Passion Is Ye Prevailing Motive: The Feud Behind the Zenger Case." *Journalilsm Quarterly* 50 (1973): 3-10. James Alexander developed his ideas of press freedom because of his feud with Gov. William Cosby. His concepts of press freedom — which became important to the American ideology of press freedom — were developed for their usefulness in political battle.

Fisher, Joshua Francis. "Andrew Hamilton, Esq., of Pennsylvania." *Pennsylvania Magazine of History and Biography* 16 (1892): 1-27. Hamilton was "one of the earliest and boldest asserters of the liberty of Speech and Writing" and was pre-eminent "in the enunciation of the now universally accepted doctrine of the law of libel."

Grotta, Gerald L. "Philip Freneau's Crusade for Open Sessions of the U.S. Senate." *Journalism Quarterly* 48 (1971): 667-71. A review of Freneau's efforts to open the Senate to journalists.

Heming, Thomas J. "A Scandalous, Malicious and Seditious Libel." *American Heritage* 19:1 (December 1967): 22-27, 100-06. Narrative of the Croswell case.

Humphrey, Carol Sue. "'That Bulwark of Our Liberty': Massachusetts Printers and the Issue of a Free Press, 1783-1788." *Journalism History* 14 (1987): 34-8. In the face of attempts by the state government to limit freedom of the press, Massachusetts printers "praised the benefits of a free press and supported the removal of all restrictions."

Huxford, Gary. "The English Libertarian Tradition in the Colonial Newspaper." *Journalism Quarterly* 45 (1968): 677-86. Traces the influence of "Cato" (John Trenchard and Thomas Gordon) and other British Libertarian writers, through the first half of eighteenth century, on American writers.

Leder, Lawrence H. "The Role of Newspapers in Early America: 'In Defense of Their Own Liberty.'" *Huntington Library Quarterly* 30 (November 1966): 1-16. Examination of the attitudes of American editors from 1690 to 1762 toward press freedom. Speculation on press freedom did not appear in the first thirty years and later only as newspapers tried to break a press monopoly.

Montagno, George L. "Federalist Retaliation: The Sedition Trial of Matthew Lyon." *Vermont History* 26 (January 1958): 3-16. Narrative of the trial, conviction, imprisonment, and political martyrdom of Lyon.

Morris, Richard. "The Case for the Palatine Printer: Zenger's Fight for Free Press," 69-95 in *Fair Trial*. New York, 1953. "The Zenger case destroyed once and for all the notion that government officials were entitled to unqualified allegiance and support and that they were untouchables immune from criticism."

Nelson, Harold L. "Seditious Libel in Colonial America." *American Journal of Legal History* 3 (April 1959): 160-72. After the Zenger trial, legislatures or governors' councils, rather than courts, disciplined printers. The colonial assembly became the major force in limiting the press and freedom.

Plasterer, Nicholas N. "The Croswell Case: Paradox of History?" *Journalism Quarterly* 44 (1967): 125-9. The Croswell case was an important trial that "apparently had a direct and important causal relationship with our present libel laws."

Price, Warren C. "Reflections on the Trial of John Peter Zenger." *Journalism Quarterly* 32 (1955): 161-8. The background to the Zenger case was political, not that of press freedom. The situation of Zenger gained public support probably because of the unpopularity of the corrupt Gov. Cosby. The case did not set a legal precedent.

Rivera, Clark. "Ideals, Interests and Civil Liberty: The Colonial Press and Freedom, 1735-76." *Journalism Quarterly* 55 (1978): 48-53, 124. A re-examination of colonial theory and practice regarding freedom of expression.

Robbins, Jan C. "Jefferson and the Press: The Resolution of an Antimony." *Journalism Quarterly* 48 (1971): 421-30, 465. Jefferson's attitudes toward freedom of expression, sometimes thought contradictory by historians, sprang from the same philosophy. He believed self-preservation to be a right of more ultimate importance than freedom of expression,.

Sloan, Wm. David, and Thomas A. Schwartz. "Historians and Freedom of the Press, 1690-1801: Libertarian or Limited?" *American Journalism* 5 (1988): 159-77. Historiographical essay explains the various interpretations historians have applied to early Americans' views on freedom of the press.

Smelser, Marshall. "George Washington and the Alien and Sedition Acts." *American Historical Review* 59 (1954): 332-4. Gives the first president's view on the controversial legislation.

Stevens, John W. "Congressional History of the 1798 Sedition Law." *Journalism Quarterly* 43 (1966): 247-56. Narrative of the congressional debates over the Sedition Act and its provisions. "[T]he debate on the sedition law opened a dialogue on the role of free expression within a democracy (particularly at a time of crisis) which has continued to this day."

Terwillings, W. Bird. "William Goddard, Victory for Freedom of the Press." *Maryland History Magazine* 36 (June 1941): 139-49. In 1777 Goddard withstood the vigilante pressures of a local Whig Club and refused to reveal the name of the author of an article in the *Maryland Journal*. He received the support of the Committee of Grievances of the Maryland House of Delegates to whom he referred the case.

Yodelis, Mary A. "Courts, Counting Houses and Streets: Attempts at Press Control, 1763-1775." *Journalism History* 1 (1974): 11-5. Summary of the "constraints exercised against all the Boston newspapers and publishers: legal, economic, violent, symbolic, and rhetorical." The press "remained relatively free, often in spite of bitter partisanship. In fact, freedom may have developed from such partisanship."

7

The Penny Press

1833 - 1861

A revolution in American journalism occurred in the 1830s when the penny press appeared. Its presence had a great impact both on the press and on society, and some of the most famous figures in American journalism were instrumental in its development. As we shall see, a number of explanations have been advanced to account for the emergence of this new dimension of the press, but at this point it is important to hold some basic ideas in mind. The penny press began as the nation was becoming more industrial and urban. It started in the midst of major advances in transportation and communication. Finally, it is worth noting that with the penny press one can begin to see the growth of many of the qualities associated with the content, production, and distribution of newspapers that have come to characterize the modern metropolitan press.

Birth of an Idea

The idea of publishing a cheap newspaper occurred not to a journalist but to a medical student by the name of Horatio David Sheppard. While attending the Eldridge Street Medical School in New York, he often had passed along Chatham Street, known for its "penny a piece" sales, on his way downtown. He noticed how quickly people bought items for a penny. James Parton, a contemporary writer and biographer who was interested in the beginning of the penny press, once reconstructed Sheppard's thoughts about those penny sales in this manner:

> The difference between a cent, and no money, did not seem to be appreciated by the people. If a person saw something, wanted it, and knew the price to be only a cent, he was almost as certain to buy it as though it were offered him for nothing. Now, thought Sheppard, to make a fortune, one has nothing more to do than to produce a tempting article which can be sold profitably for a cent, place it where everybody can see it, and buy it, without stopping—and lo! the thing is done! If it were only *possible* to produce a small, spicy daily paper for a cent, and get boys to sell it about the streets, *how* it would sell! How many pennies that now go for cakes and peanuts would be spent for news and paragraphs![1]

Unfortunately for Sheppard and his pocketbook, his attempt to put his plan into action failed, even with the help of Horace Greeley and another printer. Greeley would later found an important penny daily, the *New York Tribune*.

But describing the penny press, as these newspapers came to be called, does not explain why they happened at this particular time in history. Thousands of words have been spent on theories, and historians still disagree on how and why the changes came about.

When Benjamin Day brought out the *New York Sun*, the first successful penny daily, on September 3, 1833, there were about 1,200 newspapers publishing in the United States on a regular basis. Most were political, and most were expensive.

The largest of the afternoon newspapers in New York was the *Evening Post*, which had been founded in 1801 as a Federalist publication and funded by Alexander Hamilton and other party leaders. Editing the newspaper at the dawn of the penny press era was William Cullen Bryant, who is better known in American literature as a poet than a newspaper editor. He joined the newspaper in 1826 as the assistant of the first editor, William Coleman. When Coleman died in 1829, Bryant took over, gradually acquiring a half interest in the newspaper and editing it for the next half-century. He was a Jacksonian and eventually turned the newspaper into a Democratic organ. As he grew more concerned with the Democratic Party's support of slavery, he embraced the Free Soil Party and then the Republican Party when it was founded in 1856. He had a strong reputation as an editorial writer but also supported the news side of the operation by hiring correspondents in other American cities and employing Europeans to submit articles from abroad. Although the *Evening Post* failed to keep up with the burgeoning circulations of the newer, cheaper publications, Bryant

[1]James Parton, *The Life of Horace Greeley, Editor of the New York Tribune* (1855; reprint, New York, 1970), 140.

William Cullen Bryant
Even though his newspaper, the *New York Evening Post*, never achieved the huge circulations of Horace Greeley's *Tribune* and his sensational rivals, the *Sun* and the *Herald*, William Cullen Bryant was a towering figure in nineteenth-century journalism. He served as editor of the *Evening Post* for fifty years, from 1829 to 1878. While establishing himself as one of America's pre-eminent editorial writers and spokesmen on political issues, he also enlarged his international reputation as a poet and a literary critic.

built it into a prosperous, prestigious newspaper. He semi-retired in 1870 to translate Homer and continued with the paper until he died in 1878.

Day's new penny newspaper was a sharp contrast to the more expensive papers like Bryant's. "A daily newspaper in those days was a solemn thing," as Parton explained:

> People in moderate circumstances seldom saw, never bought one. The price was ten dollars a year.... It was not a thing for the people; it appertained to the counting-house; it was taken by the wholesale dealer; it was cumbrous, heavy, solemn. The idea of making it an article to be cried about the streets, to be sold for a cent, to be bought by workingmen and boys, to come into competition with cakes and apples, must have seemed to the respectable New Yorkers of 1831, unspeakably absurd. When the respectable New Yorker first saw a penny paper, he gazed at it (I saw him) with a feeling similar to that with which an ill-natured man may be supposed to regard General Tom Thumb, a feeling of mingled curiosity and contempt; he put the ridiculous little thing into his waistcoat pocket to carry home for the amusement of his family; and he wondered what nonsense would be perpetrated next.[2]

Less than twenty years later, according to Horace Greeley, there were about 2,500 newspapers, 250 of them dailies that issued a million copies a day. Greeley told a parliamentary committee in London in 1851 that each county in the United States usually would have at least a weekly newspaper, and counties of 20,000 population, at least in the free states, often would have two. Someone usually started a daily newspaper when a town's population grew to about 15,000.[3] Many of the new dailies differed from the older papers, which not only were more expensive but were distributed by subscription only. The cheaper papers relied more on advertising and boasted of their political independence from parties. Their emphasis was on news, not views.

What created the phenomenon of the cheap press? Most historians assumed that it was part of the natural development of the modern newspaper. Frederic Hudson, a newsman of that era who also had the distinction of writing the first comprehensive history of American journalism after the advent of the penny press, claimed that the newspapers of the 1830s were so dull that a change, a revolution, was needed and that it occurred naturally. Another writer of the period, Augustus Maverick, describing the birth of the *New York Times*, said that readers in the 1850s hungered in the vacuum left by the insufficient and unsatisfactory newspapers of the day and that natural forces were at work to produce the *Times* to satisfy them.[4] Hudson and Maverick were both journalists on penny newspapers who believed that the history of journalism was the story of how newspapers and journalism practices had progressively developed over time to reach the advanced stage existing in their own time. Most journalism historians since then have held the same assumption. They have considered the penny press to be the origin of "true" journalism, that is, journalism independent of political parties, emphasizing news rather than opinion, and appealing to a mass audience.

Others credit technology and suggest that changes in printing, transportation, and communications had to occur before the penny press could develop. In the 1820s, newsprint manufacturers figured out how to make cheap paper from wood pulp instead of rags. Press manufacturers developed steam-operated web presses that were able to use improved ink to print both sides of a continuous roll of paper at the same time and cut it into sheets. With the introduction of the Hoe type-revolving press, newspapers could print their product more cheaply and faster. When the *New York Herald* acquired the new stereotyping process, multiple copies of the same page could be printed at the same time from papier-mâché impressions of one form of type. Advances in the speed of communication came when the postal service set up a

[2]Ibid., 141-2.

[3]Greeley's testimony is reprinted in Parton, ibid., 355-61, and in Frederic Hudson, *Journalism in the United States, from 1690 to 1872* (New York, 1873), 540-2.

[4]Hudson, ibid., 408-9, and Augustus Maverick, *Henry J. Raymond and the New York Press for Thirty Years. Progress of American Journalism from 1840 to 1870* (1870; reprint, New York, 1970), 53.

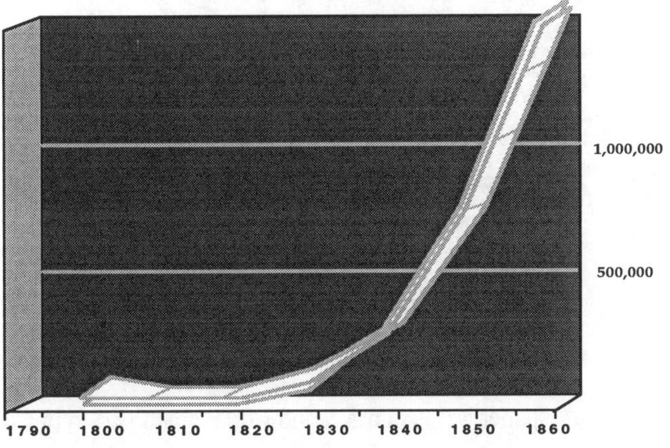

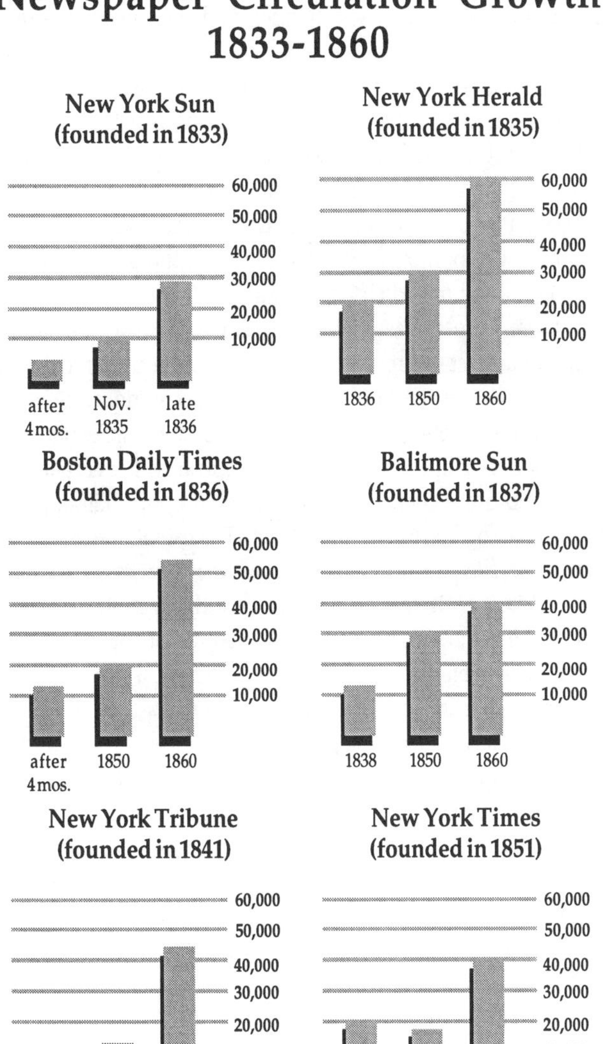

pony express run between Philadelphia and New York in 1835; but railroads, steamships, and the telegraph were much faster. Railroads began to crisscross the nation in the late 1830s and early 1840s. By the end of the 1830s new steamships were capable of crossing the Atlantic in less than three weeks. Such speed spurred the creation of a number of newspapers that summarized recent developments on one side of the Atlantic and printed them in time to catch the steamships as they departed for readers on the other side.[5] The telegraph was introduced in 1841, and in 1851 attempts began to lay cable for telegraphic communication across the Atlantic.

Still other historians claim that the nation's growing literacy spurred the development of the penny press. They contend these papers were forced to stress human interest and local news to attract a new and relatively unsophisticated audience. Between 1833 and 1860, the population increased 233%. The development of public education dropped the illiteracy rate to 9%, calculated on the basis of whites over twenty years of age.

Historians have argued recently, however, against these three theories. The history of the penny press as the development of later or modern journalism can be criticized, according to some historians, because it uses current assumptions to analyze newspapers of the past for which the assumptions were not necessarily true, and because it assumes that progress, defined by current standards, is inevitable.[6] Michael Schudson wrote that most of the mechanical changes could have been developed years before and that the press itself supported some inventors and encouraged technological change. While it contributed to the emergence of the mass press, he wrote, technological change did not cause the cheap newspaper or have much influence on its content. Greater literacy, Schudson argued, may not have created a demand for cheap reading material but may have itself resulted from more material being available to read.

Schudson, a sociologist, attributed the rise of the penny press to the growth of what he called a democratic market society. More members of the middle class were immersing themselves in business and politics than ever before. In business, the movement was expressed in the growth of a capitalistic middle class; in politics, it was known as Jacksonian democracy. The penny press, Schudson argued, was a product of this new spirit of individualism in business enterprise and independence in politics. It expanded the market by opening up advertising and making the newspaper something cheap enough to be consumed at home.[7]

But even revisionist historians like Schudson have been criticized in the continuing debate over the origins and significance of the penny press. John C. Nerone accused most historians, whe-

[5]Richard Schwarzlose discusses these newspapers in "The Foreign Connection: Transatlantic Newspapers in the 1840s," *Journalism History* 10 (1983): 44-9, 67.

[6]For a discussion of the approaches that various historians have taken to the penny press, see James G. Stovall, "The Penny Press, 1833-1861: Product of Great Men or Natural Forces?" in Wm. David Sloan, *Perspectives on Mass Communication History* (Hillsdale, N.J., 1991), 123-38.

[7]Michael Schudson, *Discovering the News: A Social History of American Newspapers* (New York, 1978), 30-50.

The Rotary Press
The Hoe Company built its first Type Revolving Press in 1846 for the *Philadelphia Ledger*. Although the process that it used was fast, the centrifugal force of the rotations sometimes flung the thousands of pieces of type from the pages and scattered them around the pressroom. The 10-cylinder press shown here was introduced in 1855.

ther developmental or revisionist, of perpetrating a "mythology" of the penny press. He wrote that "the gist of the mythology is that a small number of daring innovators, working especially in New York City, revolutionized the content and style of American journalism by creating what was essentially the modern popular commercial newspaper. These penny papers were the first commercial papers, the first popular papers, the first politically independent papers, and the first 'news' papers. They were the ancestors of contemporary U.S. newspapers."[8]

Nerone disagrees with some of these statements and contends that the evidence to support others is lacking. Instead, he argues that changes in American journalism were more evolutionary than revolutionary, brought about by changes in society and culture. Instead of focusing on large newspapers operated by well-known journalists in Eastern cities, Nerone says, historians should shift their focus to the "typical" newspapers in smaller American communities. Historians should recognize, he says, that American newspapers and newspaper readers in the nineteenth century were not all the same, that there were different classes of newspapers, and that the audience was segmented. Yet, Nerone himself has been criticized because of the nature of his research and because of his efforts to make generalizations about the penny press from a study of other types of papers.

Early Failures and the First Success

Like several other aspects of American journalism, the penny press had historical precedents in England. There the radical press, which shared the penny press' sympathy for the common people and a penchant for government reform, was started almost single-handedly by a man whose name was already familiar to American readers — William Cobbett. "Peter Porcupine," the partisan journalist who had returned to England from America in 1800, established the weekly *Political Register* in 1815 to espouse radical principles such as universal suffrage for men and annual elections as part of the movement's natural rights philosophy. At its start, the paper was expensive, and workingmen had to buy it in groups in order to afford it for reading aloud at their local alehouses. But on October 26, 1816, Cobbett announced a new edition that would sell for twopence, and the cheap press movement in England was born. Cobbett published the cheap version in foolscap size — a broadsheet of 13" x 16" that displayed articles in four columns — to get around the Stamp Act. Legislators angry at opposition editors placed a heavy tax on newspapers that were folded, but they had failed to write into the law a tax on unfolded papers. Cobbett's paper was successful and widely imitated.

Another aspect of the penny press, its sensationalism, was foreshadowed by another British development, the Sunday newspaper. One of the first such papers was published in 1779, and by 1812 there were at least eighteen in London. They were controversial for at least two reasons. First, they were considered antireligious because they required the workers who produced them and the citizens who bought them to break the Sabbath. Second, their contents were risqué. Still, they were popular with a certain readership, and other cheap newspapers seized upon their approach and began to flourish in the 1820s. Typical of these was the *Terrific Register: or, Record of Crimes, Judgments, Providences and Calamities*. It regaled its readers with horrendous tales of violence, illustrated with gruesome pictures of murder, mutilation, and cannibalism. Along with these papers, a revived version of the radical press was also popular in the 1830s, including a new entry from Cobbett, the *Twopenny Trash*.

Early attempts at cheap newspapers in the United States failed. Frederic Hudson, who became the managing editor of the *New York Herald*, wrote that James Gordon Bennett, who in 1835 founded the *Herald*, started the cheap press movement by founding the *New York Globe* on October 29, 1832. Actually, the *Globe* was not cheap. A subscription cost $8 a year — cheap compared to the price of the $10 newspapers but still not inexpensive enough for working people to afford. The newspaper failed, Hudson wrote, when the *Globe* tried to show some political independence and politicians moved to cut off its funds and kill it.[9]

[8]John C. Nerone, "The Mythology of the Penny Press," *Critical Studies in Mass Communication* 4 (1987), 376.

[9]Hudson, *Journalism in the United States*, 409-11.

Horace Greeley, who like Bennett played a large role in the development of the penny press, was involved in another false start. It was he and his partner at that time, Francis Story, who printed Dr. Sheppard's ill-fated and short-lived *New York Morning Post*. As we have seen, Dr. Sheppard dreamed of producing a cheap daily paper, and he managed to launch the *Post* on January 1, 1833. Sheppard's naivete, however, coupled with the New Year's holiday and an overnight blizzard, seemed to conspire against the two-penny sheet. He had wanted to sell the paper for a penny, but Greeley did not think any newspaper could make a profit if it sold for less than two. Sheppard agreed to go along with the higher price to get Greeley in on the venture. Greeley, who was in his early twenties at the time, remembered thirty-five years later that Sheppard thought the newspaper would sell because it was cheap and failed to advertise that the new journal was coming out. But New Yorkers did not read much of anything on New Year's Day, he added, and the snow storm blocked the streets. The few papers that were delivered to doorsteps were lost in the snow. Few people wanted to stop in the frosty weather to pay for a copy, and the carriers finally gave up and went home.

The paper struggled for two and a half weeks. The printers had started with $150 between them, and Greeley had persuaded someone to give them some credit. Sheppard, rumor had it, had come to New York with $1,500, but Greeley surmised that most of the money must have disappeared before the *Post* came out. The bills were only $200 a week, but Sheppard was unable to pay them after the first week. When the circulation limped along at two or three hundred a week, he reduced the price to a penny. "The public would not buy it even at that," Greeley wrote, "and we printers, already considerably in debt for materials, were utterly unable to go beyond the second or third week after the publisher had stopped paying."[10] The printers lost between $50 and $60, more than a month's wages.

Young Horace Greeley
Horace Greeley, a printer in his early twenties, was involved in one of the first, but ill-fated, attempts at a cheap newspaper, the *New York Morning Post*. Launched on January 1, 1833, the morning after a blizzard had blanketed New York City, the newspaper never recovered from the disaster. Despite the failure, Greeley later would become one of America's most important journalists.

The New York Sun

But while Greeley was losing money on the *Morning Post*, others were dreaming of making a cheap daily a success. A struggling job-printer named Benjamin Day thought such a newspaper could help his business make ends meet during the cholera epidemic that struck New York in 1832. Day had spoken to Sheppard about his penny daily and held on to the idea even after the *Morning Post* had failed. Two of Day's friends, Arunah S. Abell and William M. Swain, thought it impractical even to think about making a success of a cheap daily.[11] Day, too, at first was pessimistic about the project and put off his plans to publish until August 1833. The first, four-page issue of his paper, the *New York Sun*, came off Day's double-cylinder press on September 3 — a third of it advertisements and another fourth of it a combination of poetry, anecdotes, and a short story. But most of the remainder of the issue was filled with a variety of shipping, police, and general news. The *Sun* started a revolution in the newspaper business.

Day was able to turn ideas that spelled early failure for other men into a profitable success. He put out a newspaper that had a circulation of 34,000 and was worth $38,000 by the time he sold it in 1838. He proved that a general, non-partisan newspaper could be sold on the streets to the masses for a penny, and he showed that new readers could be attracted to a newspaper written in language that was not stuffy or pretentious. While most newspapers dealt with business or politics, the *Sun* published stories about ordinary working people doing ordinary and sometimes embarrassing things. The emphasis was on sensation and human interest.

During the *Sun's* first two years, its editor and main writer was George W. Wisner, who appeared when the newspaper was a day old and offered to cover the police court and set type for $4 a week. His stories about the drunks, vagrants, prostitutes, and abused women who appeared before police magistrates at four in the morning were some of the most popular items in the news-

[10]Greeley discussed his experiences with the *Morning Post* in his autobiography, *Recollections of a Busy Life* (1868; reprint, New York, 1970), 91-3.

[11]Following Day's subsequent success with the *New York Sun*, however, Abell and Swain started their own penny newspapers, the *Philadelphia Public Ledger* and the *Baltimore Sun*.

The Moon Hoax

The *New York Sun* Stuns Readers with Discovery of Lunar Life

In August 1835 the *New York Sun* astounded readers with the news that life had been discovered on the moon. In a six-part series titled "Great Astronomical Discoveries," the penny newspaper revealed that an astronomer in South Africa had found that the lush lunar surface was covered with trees looking like firs and palms and that animals resembling bison and zebras roamed over it. Then, in the last few installments, readers discovered that the moon also was home to "rational beings," creatures who looked and acted very much like humans — except they had batlike wings and could fly.

The moon stories, supposedly discovered by the *Sun* in a Scottish scientific journal, caused a sensation. Other newspapers rushed to copy them, and the *Sun* saw its own circulation soar.

The articles had barely concluded, however, before both the *New York Herald* and the *Journal of Commerce* denounced them as a hoax.

The latter paper, in particular, had reasons for its claim, because the writer of the stories, Richard Adams Locke, had confessed to a colleague at the *Journal* that he had made the whole thing up.

The *Sun*, however, never openly admitted that the articles were a hoax, still claiming in mid-September that their source was a credible scientific journal reporting the activities of a respected astronomer. At the same time, it delighted in the fact that the authenticity of the articles had become a news event in itself. The truthfulness of the articles was not even that important, according to the *Sun*, because even those who doubted the stories' veracity admired the skillful writing and appreciated the amusement they had brought.

As the moon hoax showed, entertainment was as much a part of the function of early penny newspapers as information.

Ulf Jonas Bjork
Indiana University-Indianapolis

THE SUN.

NEW YORK, TUESDAY, SEPTEMBER 3, 1833.

PUBLISHED DAILY,

AN IRISH CAPTAIN.

The first big story of the penny press era appeared in the *New York Sun* in 1835. The owner, Benjamin Day (lower left), had recently hired Richard Adams Locke (middle left) as his reporter. Locke in short time produced what came to be known as the "moon hoax." The series of stories gained such international attention that other publications reported the discovery of life on the moon, and some created illustrations (above) to try to depict the lunar landscape and beings as Locke described them.

paper. By October 24, 1833, Wisner was listed as co-publisher on the *Sun's* masthead.[12] But Wisner and Day quarreled over abolition, and Day bought him out for $5,000 and hired Richard Adams Locke as a replacement.

Some contemporaries were not impressed with the *Sun*. It was the first to publish the full names of minor offenders while other, more squemish newspapers were publishing only their initials or batches of ellipses. Hudson said the best thing the *Sun* ever did was to publish the infamous Moon Hoax, a fictional account of lunar observations that it passed off as truth. Locke was the author of the Moon Hoax, a series of articles that purported to describe what a well-known astronomer saw on the moon through a specially built telescope. The first articles provided great detail on the telescope and how it came to be built. Later articles, in increasingly startling revelations, described the lunar terrain, plants, and wildlife. As interest grew and the public and other newspapers clamored for the story, the *Sun* focused on the moon's most sophisticated inhabitants, a race of winged people who had built temples and other structures on the satellite's surface.[13]

About ten years later, Edgar Allan Poe made a rather feeble claim that a story he had published in his *Southern Literary Messenger* three weeks before the hoax began to appear had been an influence. Poe's story, now known as "The Unparalleled Adventures of One Hans Pfaall," was about the hero's journey to the moon in a balloon and what he saw there. Poe said he did not believe the *Sun*'s stories for a minute and that some of the other newspapers reprinted the *Sun*'s stories side by side with Poe's, thinking that Poe had written them all. But Poe had little success convincing other readers that the *Sun*'s stories were fabrications, primarily because people lacked knowledge of astronomy. After a competing newspaper exposed Locke's deception, he denied having read Poe's story, and Poe said he believed him.[14]

THE NEW YORK HERALD

More controversial than either Day or Locke was James Gordon Bennett, the innovative, competitive founder of the *New York Herald*. He once had approached Greeley about putting out a cheap daily, and Greeley, perhaps still smarting from his experience with the *Morning Post*, suggested that Bennett look elsewhere. Bennett followed the suggestion, believing he had a mission — to use the daily press to reform and revitalize American society. Consequently, he pulled together $500 and published the first issue of the *Herald* on May 6, 1835, in competition with seven six-penny morning papers, four six-penny afternoon papers, and four small, cheap papers. In the first issue, Bennett declared that the *Herald* would be a newspaper for everyone. It would refuse to support the line of any political party, as most of the other newspapers did, and would instead report the facts as briefly and honestly as possible. As Bennett said in the second issue, the *Herald* would try to "give a correct picture of the world — in Wall Street — in the Exchange — in the Police-office — at the Theatre — in the Opera — in short, wherever human nature and real life best display their freaks and vagaries."[15]

Bennett's attempts to carry out his plan shocked New Yorkers of the mid-1830s. His language was frank. He referred to "shirts" instead of linen, "pantaloons" instead of inexpressibles, and "legs" instead of limbs. Once he wrote of the "branches" of public dancers; and to goad his critics he once wrote, "Petticoats — petticoats — petticoats — petticoats — there — you fastidious fools — vent your mawkishness on that!"[16] His detailed coverage of crime and the courts put readers in the middle of the story. He angered some with his critical comments about Wall Street and others with his coverage of politics and organized religion. Typical was this piece:

> Religion — true religion — consists not in eating and drinking — not in high salaries — not in hanging around the apron strings of rich old women — not in presuming to judge the opinions of others beyond what their acts will justify. Neither does true religion — nor real Christianity consist in believing the dogmas of any church — or [dogmatic statements] of any man. The Bible is before me. Have I not a right to read that book — to draw out from it religious opinions — and to create a belief and a church of my own? ... I went to the source of true religion, and drank of the pure stream, uncontaminated by priest or prelate, parson or minister; and as long as we have these sacred volumes in full circulation here below, defiance may alike be set to the bigots of Catholicity or of Protestantism. We care for neither. We are independent of all. Like Luther — like Paul, we go on our own hook.[17]

The reaction of competitors to Bennett was immediate and negative. The *Sun* and the *New York Transcript* immediately withdrew their business from the firm that was printing the *Herald*. After five years of Bennett and the *Herald*, his opponents organized what became known as the Moral War of 1840. The war broke out in May, and in the vanguard of the attack were the Wall Street press, a few of the smaller New York newspapers, and a number of out-of-town Whig newspapers, all led by the *New York Courier and Enquirer*. Its editor and proprietor, Col. James Watson Webb, once had physically attacked Bennett in the street. The newspapers attacked Bennett and the *Herald* in their columns and tried to persuade businesses to withdraw their advertising. Hotel owners were implored to ban the *Herald*, and anyone who even looked at it was called impious and immoral. The *Herald*'s

[12]See James Stanford Bradshaw's "George W. Wisner and the New York *Sun*" and Wm. David Sloan's "George W. Wisner: Michigan Editor and Politician" in *Journalism History* 6 (1979-80): 112+ and 113-6, respectively.

[13]The series appeared in the *Sun*, 21-29 August 1835.

[14]Edgar Allan Poe, "The Literati," a series of articles in *Complete Works of Edgar Allan Poe* (New York, 1902), 7: 312-87, and 9: 1-96. The article on Locke is in 9: 83-96. The articles originally were published in the popular *Lady's Book* magazine in 1846.

[15]*New York Herald*, 7 May 1835.

[16]Quoted in Isaac C. Pray, *Memoirs of James Gordon Bennett and His Times* (1855; reprint, New York, 1970), 266.

[17]Quoted in ibid., 276-7.

THE NEW YORK HERALD.

NEW YORK, THURSDAY MORNING, JULY 15, 1841.

James Gordon Bennett and the *New York Herald*
The editor of the *New York Herald* matched his journalistic energy and imagination with a huge idea of his own importance. "My ambition," he wrote, "is to make the newspaper Press the great organ and pivot of government, society, commerce, finance, religion, and all human civilization. I want to leave behind me no castles, no granite hotels, no monuments of marble, no statues of bronze, no pyramids of brick – simply a name. The name of James Gordon Bennett, as one of the benefactors of the human race, will satisfy every desire and every hope." Despite Bennett's personal eccentricities, he seemed to know intuitively what would interest readers. By emphasizing news and sensationalism, he made the *Herald* one of the most popular and successful newspapers of the nineteenth century.

managing editor, Frederic Hudson, said the war had more to do with Bennett's independence than his "immorality," and that "the issue and success of this independent paper aroused four powerful interests against its editor: the politicians, the clergy, the stock brokers, and the managers of the old newspapers." It was Bennett's "continued boldness and success in 1838 and '9," he claimed, that "brought on the general war of 1840."[18] Hudson contended that the Moral War had little lasting effect on Bennett; but the *Herald* lost circulation, and Bennett tried to curb some of his excesses to gain it back.

One of Bennett's contemporaries commented that the Moral War was actually the third attempt to beat down Bennett and that it grew out of the envy of his competitors. "It was conducted with vindictive pertinacity, by the strongest alliance of spleen, passion, folly, and intellect ever known in the history of Journalism, for such a purpose," wrote Isaac Pray, Bennett's sympathetic biographer. "Never was there arranged a more determined or extensive machinery to destroy the position and prospects of one man, at least by means of the small musketry of words, and the heavier artillery of opinions and denunciation." The newspapers and editors, Pray said, "were chagrined and maddened to see jocose, quizzing, and lampooning paragraphs maintaining favor in the public mind, while their own carefully written, and sometimes brilliant essays, were wholly neglected. Instead of rebuking public taste, however, they undertook to destroy the oracle of it itself."[19]

Pray thought the effort was doomed to fail from the start, because some of those accusing Bennett of immorality "had outraged taste and the feelings of humanity for years upon years," and the public was quick to recognize the hypocrisy. Nor, in Pray's opinion, did the Moral War have much effect on the changes that Bennett introduced at about the same time. "Mr. Bennett was about to exchange his isolated life for the delights of wedlock, and it was his regard for the happiness of others that caused him to modify that style of expression which naturally enough offended cultivated minds," Pray wrote. Bennett, he claimed, had accomplished his purpose. He had made the newspaper a necessity for thousands and had cured society of its inability to tolerate frank expression. Thus, Pray said, Bennett could afford to tone down his language.[20]

At times Bennett seemed to pay little attention to all his opposition and at others responded editorially in kind. On June 3, 1840, he listed the circulation of the "Wall Street Holy Allies" and claimed that his circulation was higher than all of theirs combined. He also listed the "horse power" of the "lies, impudence, ignorance, hatred, jealousy, cash, credit and virtue" of his opponents — the last three were zero — and compared it to the "horse power" of his own "energy, sobriety, moral courage, intellect, wit, poetry, virtue and cash."[21]

Bennett the Innovator

Regardless of the effect Bennett may have had on the prudery of New York society, he deserves credit for a number of innovations in the newspaper business. He put the *Herald* on a pay-as-you-go basis, requiring subscribers to pay for their newspapers in advance and ending the long-standing complaints of editors about their thieving readers. He added money to the newspaper's cash box by creating the "Personals" column and requiring advertisers to change their ads every day. In the past, advertisers ran ads for up to a year at a time without changing copy. Bennett thought the

[18]Hudson, *Journalism in the United States*, 456. Hudson discusses the Moral War on pages 456-61.

[19]Pray, *Memoirs of James Gordon Bennett*, 264.
[20]Ibid., 265-6.
[21]*New York Herald*, 3 June 1840.

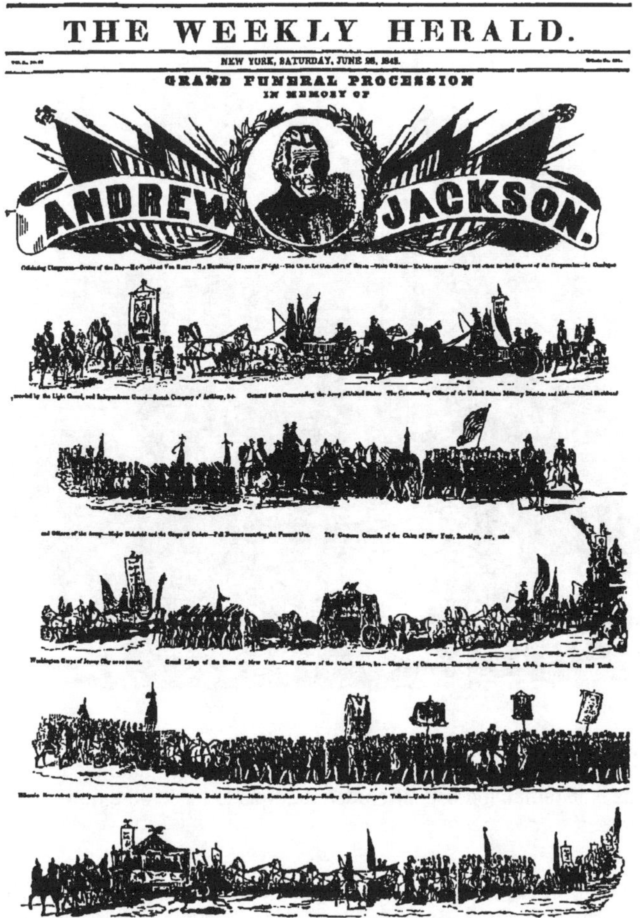

THE WEEKLY HERALD.

NEW YORK, SATURDAY, JUNE 28, 1845.

GRAND FUNERAL PROCESSION IN MEMORY OF

ANDREW JACKSON.

Bennett the Innovator

With the *Herald,* James Gordon Bennett pioneered many newspaper practices that are still with us. One of his most innovative was this, the first full-page news illustration to appear in an American newspaper, published on the occasion of the death of former President Andrew Jackson. The *Herald* printed the illustration on June 25, 1845, followed by publication in the paper's weekly edition the next day.

practice was "silly" and a good way to lose money. He refused to let the same ad appear for more than two weeks, and in 1848 he began to accept only one-day runs.

Bennett's most important contribution, however, was his redefinition of the concept of news. In colonial days, editors and printers had treated news as if it were history. Their newspapers came out only once a week, and some of the printer-editors were excessively slow about getting information into print. Nor were they or their readers much concerned about the tardiness of news. If people had not read or heard about some event, they still would be interested in it regardless of how late the news was. With improvements in technology and the needs of business for more timely information, however, newspapers began to rush news into print. But even in the 1840s, some news reports could be weeks late. Reports of congressional debates often appeared in the Washington press several weeks later, and since other newspapers depended on the Washington press for their reports on Congress, citizens were behind in learning what their elected representatives were doing.

Bennett, on the other hand, wanted the *Herald* to publish the reports promptly and in 1841 hired Robert Sutton to set up a corps of Washington correspondents. Sutton, however, wanted extra income, prompting him to revise and polish reports of debates to suit congressmen. Because the reports were no longer verbatim, they lost much of their value. From that time on, congressmen used the reports as a way of addressing their constituents rather than as a way of debating the questions with each other.[22] Similar to Bennett's innovative Washington reporting were his efforts to strengthen foreign news. When the first steamship crossed the Atlantic in April 1838, cutting the time between Europe and the United States from six weeks to less than three, Bennett booked passage on the return voyage and started setting up a system of European correspondents. While in Europe, he covered Queen Victoria's coronation and put stringers in Berlin, Brussels, Glasgow, London, Paris, and Rome. After returning home, he hired stringers in Canada, Mexico, and the Republic of Texas. One stringer was Thomas Oliver Larkin, the U.S. consul in Monterey, California, which was then a part of Mexico. When war broke out between the United States and Mexico in May 1846, Larkin reported on military activity from the West Coast.

Bennett's *Herald* also pioneered in such areas as sports, business news, and coverage of women. In 1855 Bennett hired Jane Cunningham Croly ("Jennie June") to write about "society." Her byline soon became famous with articles about fashion, beauty, and social gatherings. After leaving the *Herald*, she became a journalism pioneer. She wrote the first syndicated column intended for women. In 1868 when she discovered that the New York Press Club limited its reception honoring Charles Dickens to men, Croly reacted by organizing a club for women. "Sorosis" was one of the earliest women's clubs to endure. In 1889 she founded the Women's Press Club of New York City. Late in life when she was appointed to a chair in journalism and literature at Rutgers Women's College, she became the first woman to teach journalism at the college level.[23]

NEWSPAPER COMPETITION

Augustus Maverick, who was one of Bennett's contemporaries, credited (or blamed) him for introducing the era of newspaper competition: "The ruthless Bennett," he contended, "shocked the staid propriety of his time by introducing the rivalries and the spirit of enterprise which have ever since been distinguishing characteristics of New York newspaper life.... The only cheap papers, in 1840, which pretended, with any show of reason, to publish all the

[22]Ben Perley Poore, *Perley's Reminiscences of Sixty Years in the National Metropolis*, 2 volumes (Philadelphia, 1886), 1: 261-2. Poore's discussion of the situation begins on page 260.

[23]Madelon Golden Schilpp and Sharon M. Murphy, *Great Women of the Press* (Carbondale, 1983), 90-3.

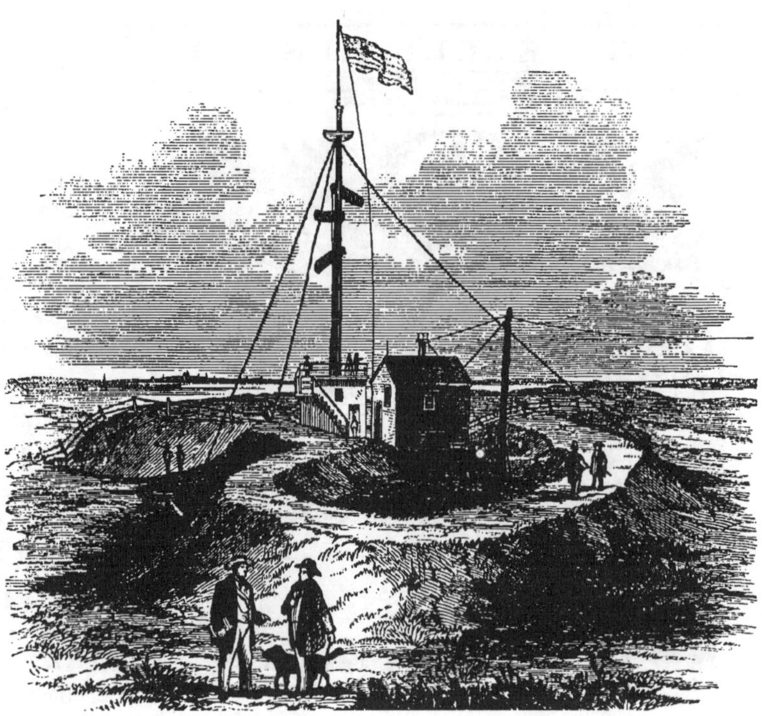

Samuel Morse and Telegraphic News
When Samuel F. B. Morse was granted a patent for his magnetic telegraph in 1844, stations began to spring up throughout the United States. When words could speed from one point to another electrically, there was little remaining use for cruder attempts to hasten the news – the pony express, the railroad, fleets of news boats, and carrier pigeon expresses.

news of the day, were the *Herald*, and Moses Y. Beach's *Sun*; and although the former of these was low and often scurrilous, and the latter silly, they attracted readers among the younger inhabitants of New York, who had begun to tire of the Dutch phlegm."[24]

Until Greeley entered the scene in 1841 with his *New York Tribune*, most of the competition centered around the *Herald* and the *Sun*, which Day had sold to Beach in 1838. These two newspaper rivals spent thousands of dollars in trying to beat the other with the news. They set up pony express systems and hired trains and used carrier pigeons. Once begun, competition became keener. New York newspapers, including even some of the more somber commercial ones, financed a news boat to meet incoming ships from Europe so the news could be in New York newspaper offices before the trans-Atlantic ships could dock. A breakdown in the system forced many of the newspapers to finance their own boats; so New York eventually had a fleet that would race to incoming ships and race back with the news.

Bennett tapped into a "pigeon express" founded by Daniel H. Craig, editor and proprietor of the *Boston Daily Mail*. Craig gathered news from the ships sailing into Boston harbor from Europe and sent reports to Bennett by carrier pigeon. From New York, Bennett sent the reports winging to Swain of the *Philadelphia Public Ledger* and Abell of the *Baltimore Sun*. Each paper in the pigeon chain contributed its own news items, and the operation got European news to American newspapers three days faster than before. Bennett's rival in New York, the *Sun*, formed its own group of pigeon-linked newspapers, and the competition turned deadly after Craig got access to ships arriving in Halifax, Nova Scotia, before they docked in Boston. The pigeons were forced to fly through a barrage of bullets from the rifles of sharpshooters to ensure that the news got into print.

What doomed the pigeon express, however, was not the mostly inaccurate fire of rooftop riflemen, but a development that revolutionized communications. In 1837, Samuel F.B. Morse applied for a patent for his magnetic telegraph, which used electricity to send signals over wires. The patent was granted in 1844, and soon a line connected Washington, D.C., and Baltimore. Operators, who could transcribe twenty-five to thirty words a minute, used code to send messages, including news about the national nominating conventions of the Whig and Democratic parties. Columns headed "Telegraphic News" began appearing in newspapers. When the telegraph line went up between New York and Boston in 1847, the days of the pigeon express were over.

Bennett exploited the telegraph and used it as a weapon in the New York circulation wars. Other newspapers were forced to drop out of the race or join in the potentially ruinous competition. Salvation for many came in the form of the news agency, a cooperative service that the magnetic telegraph made possible and, at the same time, necessary for survival. Only five agencies existed in 1853, but all were operating on the general pattern established by Charles-Louis Havas when he set up Agence Havas in 1832. The organization, which employed Dr. Bernhard Wolff and Paul Julius Reuter before they founded their own agencies in Europe, es-

[24]Maverick, *Henry J. Raymond*, 37-8.

tablished a sub-agency in New York in 1845.

Three years later was born the agency that would become today's Associated Press. The organization grew out of the old Harbor News Association set up by six New York newspapers in 1848 to operate a news boat. In 1850 the newspapers formed the Telegraphic and General News Association of New York to get telegraphic news from Boston, Washington, and other places. The organization went through two name changes before settling on the New York Associated Press in 1858, the name it would keep until it shortened it to the Associated Press in 1893. The NYAP, which had access to its six original members, representatives in other major American cities, and the Reuters news agency, eventually contracted with other regional news agencies in other parts of the United States.[25]

Sometimes the competition to get the news first went to extremes, and reporters played tricks on each other. Maverick recounted, for instance, an occasion when "a messenger for the *Tribune* quietly gathered up the details of some important news, in a distant part of the country, and then ran away with it to New York on an engine which was waiting, under a full head of steam, for the use of the representative of the *Herald*. Of course, the *Tribune* had the news exclusively; and Bennett, very naturally, uttered blasphemies."[26]

Greeley and Bennett were convinced that their innovations in newsgathering and distribution were sound. The former commented in 1851 that apparently the public had gotten used to the competition and to getting news in a timely fashion. "The fact that certain journals have the earliest news soon becomes notorious," he said, "and almost every one wants his newspaper with his breakfast, delivered between the hours of five and half past seven. They take the morning papers to read with their breakfast."[27] Bennett also placed great value on timely news. He was so tough to work against that sixteen newspapers in Boston, New York, Philadelphia, Baltimore, and Washington banded together to try to get the news out before the *Herald*, or so, at least, Bennett told the story. He also declared to his readers that the *Herald* intended to compete against this "Holy Alliance," noting that it was the *Herald* that had introduced such competition into American journalism. "With our fleet of news clippers, manned by the hardiest men in existence, cruising always outside the Hook [Sandy Hook], at distances varying from fifty to two hundred and fifty miles from land, failure in getting news in the speediest way possible may appear out of the question," he stated.[28]

Before the advent of the penny press, newspapers relied on the chance arrival of ships and mail for most of their news. Bennett had had his share of problems with the slowness of the mail. He had been the Washington correspondent for the *New York Enquirer* in 1828 when he was thirty, and like other Washington correspondents he had been forced to put his letters in the mail by midnight to make sure they got off to northern cities early the next morning. New York newspapers were unable to publish the reporters' letters until two days after they were written, and Boston papers usually could not publish them before the fourth day. Had it not been for the *Herald*, Bennett told readers, "the public would be to this day trusting to Uncle Sam's mail-bag for the earliest intelligence, both foreign and domestic."[29]

The competition also led to some of the pressure that made a newspaper job such demanding work. "Only those who have been placed upon the treadmill of a daily newspaper in New York know the severity of the strain it imposes upon the mental and physical powers. There is no cessation," one newsman explained. "A good newspaper never publishes that which is technically denominated 'old news,' — a phrase so significant in journalism as to be invested with untold horrors," he said. "All must be daily fresh, daily complete, daily polished and perfect; else the journal falls into disrepute, is distanced by its rivals, and, becoming 'dull,' dies."[30]

The Influential Greeley

Greeley knew all about hard work, too. Before starting the third major penny newspaper, the *New York Tribune*, he had been a job printer. He had also edited a literary paper and a couple of political papers that supported the Whigs. The first of these was the *New-Yorker*, begun on March 22, 1834, while Greeley was running a job-printing business that he had returned to after the *Morning Post* had failed. The *New-Yorker*, which he founded in partnership with another printer by the name of Jonas Winchester, contained mostly literary material picked up from American and foreign publications, some editorials, and some political news. James Parton, a contemporary biographer of Greeley, claimed that the newspaper was politically neutral; but Thurlow Weed, one of the Whig leaders in New York, was so impressed with the newspaper that he asked Greeley to put out a statewide campaign newspaper for the party in 1838. Campaign newspapers were a common part of politics; and Weed and the Whigs' state committee chairman, thinking that Greeley favored the Whigs' plans for a strong tariff and other Whig policies, offered Greeley $1,000 to edit the publication. Greeley agreed. Although the paper was supposed to be a weekly costing fifty cents a year, most of its circulation was free, and wealthy party members paid its operating expenses.

Greeley was so willing to take on another job partly because he was desperate for money. Although the *New-Yorker*'s original list of twelve subscribers gradually grew to about 9,000, the newspaper never made much money, in part because Greeley sent copies to subscribers on credit, and many never paid. Greeley lost about $100 a week throughout 1837. "It was in vain that I appealed to

[25]See Robert W. Desmond, *The Information Process: World News Reporting to the Twentieth Century* (Iowa City, Iowa, 1978). Chapter 7 covers the pigeon express, Chapter 8 the telegraph, and Chapter 9 the news agencies.

[26]Maverick, *Henry J. Raymond*, 39-40.

[27]House of Commons, report (London, September 16, 1851), quoted in Hudson, *Journalism in the United States*, 542.

[28]*Herald*, 1846, quoted in Pray, *Memoirs of James Gordon Bennett*, 375.

[29]Ibid.

[30]Maverick, *Henry J. Raymond*, 220.

LOG CABIN

NO. 12. PRICE--25 CENTS IN ADVANCE. DAYTON: O

LOG CABIN.

LOG CABIN CANDIDATES.

FOR PRESIDENT
WM. HENRY HARRISON.

FOR VICE PRESIDENT,
JOHN TYLER,
THE INDEPENDENT VIRGINIAN

FOR GOVERNOR OF OHIO,
THOMAS CORWIN,

FOR CONGRESS,
PATRICK G. GOODE.

FRIDAY—SEPTEMBER 18.

Tippecanoe and Tyler, Too
Before founding the hugely successful *New York Tribune*, Horace Greeley edited several Whig newspapers. One of them, the *Log Cabin*, was published during the 1840 campaign to promote William Henry Harrison for president, with John Tyler as his running mate.

delinquents to pay up," he recalled years later. "Many of them migrated; some died; others were so considerate as to order the paper stopped, but very few of these paid; and I struggled on against a steadily rising tide of adversity that might have appalled a stouter heart."[31] Greeley felt morally committed to continue the *New-Yorker* because at least 3,000 subscribers had paid in advance.

Thus Greeley took on the Whigs' campaign paper, the *Jeffersonian*, to help make ends meet, and the newspaper's year of existence was an exhausting one. The *New-Yorker* was published in New York, but the *Jeffersonian* operated out of Albany, 150 miles away. Greeley would no sooner get the *New-Yorker* to press and assign part of the copy for the next edition than he had to rush to catch the boat to Albany. The hard work, however, paid off. The *Jeffersonian* distributed about 15,000 copies a week and may have been one reason the Whigs won a decisive victory in New York while suffering defeat in other states. In New York, the party took the governorship and the lieutenant-governorship, won control of the state assembly, and made gains in the state senate.

Whig leaders then asked Greeley to edit a newspaper for General William Henry Harrison's run for the presidency in 1840. The newspaper was named *The Log Cabin* to foster the legend that Harrison, after returning to Ohio from his military ventures, had lived in a log cabin. It was published between May 1 and November 1, 1840, with a subscription costing $5. The first page had campaign material, and the second had editorials and letters. There were reports of party victories on the third page, and the fourth page had campaign music and miscellaneous articles. One of the early tiffs — there were to be others — between Weed and Greeley centered around the campaign music. Greeley wanted to publish the songs with music, but Weed thought the plates took up too much space.

Greeley was the type of man and hard-working journalist who won the respect of many of his contemporaries. Weed represents a case in point. He was a journalist of considerable repute as well as a power in the Whig party and, after that, in the Republican party. Greeley was "unselfish, conscientious, public spirited, and patriotic ... [and] had no habits or tastes but for work, steady, indomitable work," Weed wrote of Greeley some years later. Regarding their differences, Weed could also recall: "Our sentiments and opinions of public measures and public men harmonized perfectly; our only difference was, that upon the temperance, slavery, and labor questions he was more ardent and hopeful. In this I gave him credit for fresher and less disciplined feelings."[32]

Another astute observer, Benjamin Perley Poore, also was impressed with Greeley, and wrote of him: "He was a man of intense convictions and wielded an incisive, ready pen, which went straight to the point without circumlocution or needless use of words. Although he was a somewhat erratic champion of Fourierism, vegetarianism, temperance, anti-hanging, and abolition, there was a 'method in his madness,' and his heretical views were evidently the honest convictions of his heart. Often egotistical, dogmatic, and personal, no one could question his uprightness and thorough devotion to the noblest principles of progressive civilization. Inspired by that true philanthropy that loves all mankind equally and every one of his neighbors better than himself, he was often victimized by those whose stories he believed and to whom he loaned his hard-earned savings. The breath of slander did not sully his reputation, and he never engaged in lobbying at Washington for money, although friendship several times prompted him to advocate appropriations for questionable jobs — the renewal of patents which were monopolies, and the election of public printers who were notoriously corrupt."[33]

The New York Tribune

When Greeley put out the first issue of the *Tribune* on April 10, 1841, there were about a hundred periodicals and twelve daily newspapers in New York City. Four Whig papers sold for $10 each a year, and two other political newspapers that sold for the same

[31]Greeley, *Recollections*, 95.

[32]Thurlow Weed, *Autobiography of Thurlow Weed*, edited by his daughter, Harriet A. Weed (Boston, 1883), 467.

[33]Poore, *Perley's Reminiscences*, 1: 238-9.

New-York Tribune.

Greeley, the *Tribune*, Morality, and Liberalism
Horace Greeley was not impressed with other sensational penny dailies when he founded the *New York Tribune* in 1841. He attempted to keep his newspaper on a high moral plane while exposing his readers to the latest in liberal philosophy. He attracted to the staff the most talented group of journalists of the era. This early, rare daguerrotype by Matthew Brady shows Greeley (seated, second from right) flanked by his top assistants. They are (standing, left to right) Thomas McElrath, Charles Dana, John F. Cleveland, (seated, left to right) George N. Snow, Bayard Taylor, Greeley, and George Ripley.

price supported the Democratic party. There were three cheap, non-aligned dailies, along with Beach's *Sun* and Bennett's *Herald*. For all practical purposes the latter was Democratic. The absence of a cheap, Whig-oriented daily was one reason Greeley brought out the *Tribune* on that "leaden funereal morning, the most inhospitable of the year." It was the morning of New York's funeral parade and pageant for President Harrison, who had died after serving only a month in office.

But Greeley had ideas other than politics for his newspaper. He did not intend to establish a strictly Whig paper. In fact, as he later recollected, he had as much disdain for "servile partisanship" as he did for "mincing neutrality." What political position, then, did he wish to support? He later answered that he had tried to find the "happy medium" between the extremes of partisanship. The position he wished to defend was that "from which a journalist might openly and heartily advocate the principles and commend the measures of that party to which his convictions allied him, yet frankly dissent from its course on a particular question, and even denounce its candidates if they were shown to be deficient in capacity or (far worse) in integrity." He even argued "that a journal thus loyal to its guiding convictions, yet ready to expose and condemn unworthy conduct or incidental error on the part of men attached to its party, must be far more effective, even party-wise, than though it might always be counted on to applaud or reprobate, bless or curse, as the party's prejudices or immediate interest might seem to prescribe."[34]

[34]Greeley, *Recollections*, 137.

Greeley also hoped to publish a newspaper in which readers could find everything they needed to keep up with important events by reading only that one paper. Noticing Bennett's success with his stable of correspondents, Greeley moved to establish his own. He sent his city editor, Charles A. Dana (who later was to become one of the nation's outstanding journalists), to Europe during the political upheavals of 1848 and 1849 to cover events in Berlin, London, and Paris. Greeley also had four stringers in Europe, two in Canada, and still more in Mexico, Cuba, and Central America. Bayard Taylor, who was famed for his travel writing and poetry, worked as a roving correspondent for Greeley from 1844 to 1854. He covered the 1849 California gold rush and Commodore Matthew Perry's attempts to open up Japan to western trade in 1853. He also wrote extensively from Africa, China, Egypt, India, and the Middle East.

In Rome for the Italian revolution of 1848-1849 was Margaret Fuller, the first woman to work regularly for a newspaper and the first female foreign correspondent. Greeley had been publishing her work since 1844 after being impressed with her influential feminist tract, *Woman in the Nineteenth Century*. Fuller brought to her job as literary critic and general reporter a keenly honed mind that was largely self-educated, a wealth of contacts among the Transcendentalists, and experience as co-editor of *The Dial*, the Transcendentalist publication. In 1846 she left for Europe, following a German Jewish immigrant with whom she had had a secret romantic relationship. Greeley published her articles from London about a number of British literary figures and her later

Margaret Fuller
The first female foreign correspondent, Fuller began writing for Horace Greeley's *New York Tribune* in 1844. Returning to the United States from Europe in 1850, she died, along with her Italian husband and their son, when their ship struck a sand bar near New York Harbor during a storm.

articles from Rome, where she went in 1847 after getting caught up in the cause of Italy, struggling to free itself under the banner of Giuseppe Garibaldi from French and Austrian domination. She became the secret lover of the Marchese Giovanni Angelo d'Ossoli and bore him a son in 1848. She took d'Ossoli's name, although they probably never were married, and continued writing articles about European politics and the Italian revolution. When the revolution collapsed during the French bombardment of Rome in February 1849, the d'Ossolis fled to Florence, where their questionable marital status shocked the English-speaking community and outraged Greeley to the point that he refused to continue printing Fuller's correspondence. Fuller, her husband, and their child perished in 1850 while trying to return to the United States. Their ship struck a sand bar near New York Harbor during a storm and later sank.

While Greeley developed an excellent reputation for covering the news, he offered his readers more. The *Tribune* published lectures, book excerpts, serialized novels, poems, and book reviews. It took such a high moral ground — refusing to publish reports of police courts, sensational murder trials, and the theater — that it became known as the "Great Moral Organ."

The thing that set the *Tribune* apart, however, was its editorial position, which was a reflection of its owner. He neither smoked nor drank and was an ardent prohibitionist. He was against slavery and capital punishment, and he supported labor unions and westward expansion.

Having seen the sufferings of the poor during the terrible winter of 1838, Greeley became a socialist for a number of years. It was, in fact, his interest in socialism of the Brooke Farm variety that produced the first major difference between him and Weed. In 1842, Greeley allowed a group to buy the right to run the articles of Albert Brisbane, a well-known socialist, in one column a day on the front page of the *Tribune*. Weed thought that Brisbane would try to remodel the American social system and replace it with his own brand of socialism. The disagreement, Weed remembered, was friendly, and he noted that Greeley later changed his views on socialism. But the change did not occur before Greeley allowed his managing editor, Charles A. Dana, to publish many articles between 1851 and 1862 under the byline of Karl Marx, the founder of communism. Dana was impressed by Marx, whom he had met in Cologne in 1848, and a few years later employed him to contribute bi-weekly articles on European affairs. Friedrich Engels, Marx's loyal collaborator, wrote many of these articles at first, but by 1853 Marx was writing most of them himself. After the Crimean War ended in 1856, American interest in Europe waned; and, as the boom of the early 1850s faded, the *Tribune* had to economize. Consequently, Dana cut back the number of articles he could accept from Marx. In doing so he tried to find other work for Marx in this country with *The American Encyclopedia* and with various magazines. By 1862 when Marx's work for the *Tribune* ended, he had contributed almost 500 articles to the paper.

There is no question of the newspaper's controversial nature. Parton wrote that "men have been heard to talk of their Bible, their Shakespeare, and their *Tribune*, as the three necessities of their spiritual life." But those who did not like the paper, he added, "dislike it excessively, and are wont to protest that they should deem their houses defiled by its presence."[35] A piece appearing in the *Tribune* in the early 1850s demonstrated its position. The writer explained that "in a world so full as this is of wrong and suffering, of oppression and degradation, there must be radical causes for so many and so vast practical evils." Much of the world's progress, he went on to say, resulted from "the fearless thought and speech of those who dare be in advance of their time — who are sneered at and shunned through their days of struggle and of trial as lunatics, dreamers, impracticables and visionaries — men of crotchets, of vagaries, or of 'isms.'"[36]

Other newspapers did not greet Greeley's *Tribune* with joy. The *Sun* tried to destroy the *Tribune* shortly after it came out for fear that the *Sun* would lose its business to Greeley. It attempted to bribe Greeley's carriers to give up their routes and threatened that they would not be allowed to sell the *Sun* if they also sold the *Tribune*. It also sent newsboys to beat up Greeley's carriers.

[35] Parton, *Life of Horace Greeley*, 383.
[36] Ibid., 384.

Go West Greeley
Horace Greeley's impact on American life was great, but nowhere could it be seen more than in the westward migration of America. He repeated the counsel to move west so frequently that by the 1830s he had been tagged with the nickname "Go West Greeley." "Go west, young man" became a national slogan. He continued to urge westward movement after founding the *New York Tribune*. No editor probably ever played a more decisive role in an issue of such national moment.

Despite the intimidation, Greeley secured 500 potential subscribers from names his political colleagues provided, printed 5,000 copies of the first issue, and almost managed to give away all that he could not sell. During the first three weeks, he acquired 300 new subscribers a day; and by the seventh week, the *Tribune* was printing 11,000 copies, all that its press could handle. The four columns of ads in the first issue ballooned to thirteen in the hundredth issue. Such growth and profits forced Greeley to buy new presses that could print 3,500 copies an hour; and at the end of the first year, the *Tribune* had 12,000 subscribers.

While the *Tribune* did not always live up to Greeley's professed moral standards, it was an influential newspaper. Farmers treated its weekly edition as gospel, and Greeley's Chautauqua circuit lectures always were well attended. In most of the paramount national issues of the mid-nineteenth century — from abolition to internal improvements, from temperance to westward expansion — Greeley played a pre-eminent role.

THE PENNY PRESS AND THE MEXICAN WAR

Many of the penny press' innovations helped it cover its first big war, the Mexican War of 1846-1848. At issue was much of the territory that is now the southwestern part of the United States but that then was part of Mexico. Tension had existed between the United States and Mexico ever since the successful Anglo revolution in Texas in 1835-1836, which ended in the creation of the Republic of Texas. When the U.S. Congress approved annexation of Texas in March 1845, the Mexican government cut diplomatic relations with the United States and both nations posted troops to face each other across the Rio Grande. The United States failed in subsequent attempts to buy Texas and the California and New Mexico territories. After a border clash near Matamoras in April 1846, the United States declared war the following month.

With his network of stringers, Bennett had positioned himself well to cover the war, but he also had an agreement with the *New Orleans Picayune* to supply him with news. The *Picayune*, founded by George W. Kendall and Francis Lumsden in 1837, was one of twelve English-language dailies that published in New Orleans during the war and was the city's first cheap daily. Kendall, who rode with Gen. Zachary Taylor and saw action at Monterey, Buena Vista, and Vera Cruz, set up an express to speed war news to Bennett's *Herald*. Riders, often forced to evade the fire of Mexican soldiers, carried Kendall's dispatches from the interior of Mexico to Vera Cruz or Port Isabel on the Gulf of Mexico. Ships ferried the reports to New Orleans and the *Picayune*, and from there a relay of sixty riders sped the news to the southern tip of the nation's telegraph system at Richmond, Virginia. This "Great Southern Daily Express" cut two days off the ten-day period it took mail to get from New Orleans to New York. Northern readers now waited only two to five weeks to read news of the fighting in Mexico.

Other northern newspapers made similar arrangements. The *New York Sun*, along with the *Charleston Courier* in South Carolina, was associated with the *New Orleans Crescent*; and Philadelphia's *North American* and the *Boston Journal* had an agreement with the *New Orleans Delta*. Both New Orleans newspapers had correspondents in the field. American newspapers generally were unable, however, to post correspondents in Mexican cities. Filling the gap was *La Patria* of New Orleans, which was to become the first Spanish-language daily in the United States. Many American newspapers reprinted reports from *La Patria's* correspondents.[37]

RAYMOND AND THE NEW YORK TIMES

Working for Greeley during the *Tribune*'s first two years was a young reporter who later would establish the only New York penny newspaper still surviving today, the *New York Times*. In 1843, the 23-year-old Henry Raymond thought that he was overworked

[37]See Desmond, Chapter 10; and Tom Reilly, "'The War Press of New Orleans': 1846-1848," *Journalism History* 13 (1986): 86-95.

and underpaid. He had joined Greeley as a staffer on the old *New-Yorker*, and for his first three weeks he was not even paid. "I added up election returns, read the exchanges for news, and discovered a good deal which others had overlooked; made brief notices of new books, read proof, and made myself generally useful," Raymond recalled.[38] When he got a teaching job and was about to leave, Greeley rather offhandedly remarked that he could match the salary the school would pay; so Raymond joined the payroll at $8 a week.

Raymond moved with Greeley when he founded the *Tribune* and became the editor's first assistant. Although his pay remained the same, his duties increased, and he found himself covering public meetings, writing editorials and book reviews, clipping material from other newspapers to print in the *Tribune*, and making up the newspaper. By 1843, he had had all he could stand and went to work for the *New York Courier and Enquirer*. Although Raymond later was to become Greeley's political rival, Greeley charitably assessed Raymond's years on the *Tribune*. In his autobiography, which was published a year before Raymond's untimely death at the age of forty-nine, Greeley wrote of him: "I never found another person, barely of age and just from his studies, who evinced so signal and such versatile ability in journalism as [Raymond] did. Abler and stronger men I may have met; a cleverer, readier, more generally efficient journalist, I never saw."[39]

James Parton also lamented Raymond's departure from the *Tribune*, saying that Raymond could have made the paper into "the great, only, undisputed Metropolitan Journal" sooner than destiny would allow. Greeley was more of a legislator, a person who could suggest how to solve problems, than he was an editor, and it was as an editor that Raymond could have been of help. Parton observed that "Mr. Raymond is not a man of first-rate talent — great talent would be in his way — he is most interesting when he attacks; and of the varieties of composition, polished vituperation is not the most difficult. But he has the right *notion* of editing a daily paper, and when the *Tribune* lost him, it lost more than it had the slightest idea of — as events have since shown."[40] Whether Parton, writing in 1855 after Raymond founded the *Times*, was right about his talent, he was certainly right about Raymond's newspapering ability.

When the *Times* appeared in 1851, the *Herald* and the *Tribune* each had its following, but there was a third group of readers who cared for neither paper. It was to this group of "quiet domestic, fireside, conservative readers," as Hudson called them, that Raymond and the *Times* appealed.[41] Most people of the mid-nineteenth century took a daily newspaper to find out what was going on in the world. "They are averse," Parton noted, "to profligacy and time-serving [a reference to Bennett's *Herald*], and yet are offended at the independent avowal of ideas in advance of their own [a reference to Greeley's *Tribune*]."[42]

Before the appearance of the *Times*, the reader was faced with little choice. As Augustus Maverick, Raymond's contemporary and biographer, once complained, the alternative was "either the sixpenny journals of Wall street, with meagre supplies of news, or the cheaper *Tribune* and *Herald*, with all the intelligence of the day overlaid and almost extinguished by the Socialistic heresies of the one and the abominable nastiness of the other." What choice was that? Maverick claimed that "heads of families feared to take the *Tribune* to their homes, because its teachings were the apotheosis of vice. They could get their tidings of the news of the world through Bennett's *Herald* only at the cost of wading through heaps of rubbish. The predicament was unpleasant."[43]

Although in appearance the *Times* was much like the others — it had four pages of six columns each, with the front page displaying foreign and local news — it would offer a new alternative. Raymond planned to publish a paper comprehensive in content and independent in terms of political preference. His paper would champion "the public good." Sometimes that would lead it to be conservative; sometimes, radical. "We do not believe," he wrote in the paper's prospectus, "that *everything* in society is either exactly right or exactly wrong; what is good we desire to preserve and improve; what is evil, to exterminate and reform."[44] With time, the paper developed a reputation for fair, careful, accurate reporting with an emphasis on foreign affairs. It was a newspaper designed for the masses but without the sensationalism of the *Sun* and the *Herald* or the sometimes scatterbrained ideas of the *Tribune*.

At first, the *Times* faced uncertainty. Raymond spent six months in Europe recuperating from health problems immediately before the first issue of the *Times* appeared, relying on his employees to get the newspaper ready to go. Some of the other newspapers threatened their carriers with loss of routes if they also carried the *Times*, but the *Times* lived long enough to attract some of its rivals' best employees. The circulation climbed to 20,000 in the first ten weeks, partly because Raymond had the paper delivered free for a week to thousands of homes. At the end of his first year, Raymond estimated the newspaper had spent $13,000 on editors, $25,000 on mechanical work, $40,000 on paper, and $50,000 on the press and "general outfit," a total of $128,000 — and all before turning a profit. His own salary was $50 a week, and he was forced to take it because he was having trouble getting some of his back salary from his previous employer. The other investors, however, had to wait until the newspaper became profitable before they could begin to get their money back.

Because of his first-year expenses, Raymond raised the price of the *Times* to two cents an issue, the same price readers were paying for the *Herald* and the *Tribune*. He used the extra income to double the number of pages, but the price increase lost him a third of his circulation, which he had claimed at the end of the first year to be 25,000. The loss was only temporary, though, and by

[38]Quoted in Maverick, *Henry J. Raymond*, 29.
[39]Greeley, *Recollections*, 138-9.
[40]Parton, *Life of Horace Greeley*, 205.
[41]Hudson, *Journalism in the United States*, 621.
[42]Parton, *Life of Horace Greeley*, 382.

[43]Maverick, *Henry J. Raymond*, 53.
[44]*New York Times*, 18 September 1851.

New-York Daily Times.

Henry Raymond and the *New York Times*
In contrast to the approaches of Horace Greeley's *New York Tribune* and James Gordon Bennett's *Herald* – and in a pointed gibe at his rivals – Raymond stated that in starting the *New York Times*, "[w]e do not mean to write as if we were in a passion, – unless that shall really be the case; and we shall make it a point to get into a passion as rarely as possible."

1860 the *Times* was not far behind the *Tribune* in circulation. Both trailed the *Herald* and the *Sun*.

The Political Raymond

Raymond was as much involved in politics as Greeley, although Raymond worked much more successfully with party machinery. In fact, he might have been able to make the *Times* much better had he not spent so much time on politics. At various times he served in the New York legislature, participated in national political conventions, and was elected lieutenant governor of New York. In 1852, he decided to be a journalist and stay out of politics, but the pledge lasted only two years before he jumped back into the political arena. Maverick thought that was "the great misfortune of his life" and wrote: "Had Raymond remained a journalist, untouched by the corrupting influences of party chicanery, and unsullied by evil association, the record of his life would have had no deep shadows."[45]

Nevertheless, some of Raymond's political efforts were of consequence in state and national politics. He played a major role in the Whig party in New York during the early 1850s, and he served as a Whig in the New York assembly from 1849-1851. In 1856 he became a supporter of the recently formed Republican party. Thereafter, he remained active in that party and was one of its key figures. He became President Lincoln's steadiest supporter in New York during the Civil War. By 1864, he was considered one of the nation's Republican leaders. While serving as a congressman from New York from 1865 to 1867, he became the administration's leader in the House of Representatives. He was a supporter of President Andrew Johnson's moderate reconstruction policy after the Civil War; but when that policy failed, his political influence was severely damaged. In 1866 he was expelled from the Republican national committee when it became clear that his opinions differed from those of the majority of that body. Afterwards, until his death in 1869, he devoted most of his efforts to the *Times*.

Even though the character of newspapers had changed by the 1850s, friends still gave some of them political favors. The superintendent of the federal Bank Department, for example, had been a shareholder in the *Times* and gave it the contract to publish the weekly statements of the metropolitan banks. The *Times* was supposed to pass on the proof-slips so other newspapers could publish the information as news, but it invariably was late in getting the proof-slips to the *Tribune*. Greeley wrote a nasty letter to the superintendent in 1853, beginning an acrid exchange of letters between the two in which the banking official denied a conflict of interest. In one of the letters, Greeley charged:

> I have a most insolent and scoundrelly letter from your favorite, Raymond, offering to send me these returns at his own convenience if I will credit them to the *Times* (not to the Bank Department, of which only have I asked them), and talking of his willingness to *grant favors* to those who prove worthy of them, but not to be "*kicked into benevolence*," etc. *All this insolence of this little villain is founded on your injustice*.[46]

Raymond was known as the "little villain" for the rest of his life. The bad feelings between Greeley and Raymond had been growing ever since Raymond left the *Tribune* for the *Courier and Enquirer*. The first public notice of their differences was contained in a debate between the two over socialism, published by both newspapers before Raymond founded the *Times*. The main source of the trouble, however, may have been that both aspired to political office. Raymond achieved it, but Greeley did not (except for filling out an unexpired term in Congress). "These political honors made the *Times* more antagonistic to the *Tribune*," Hudson wrote. "More favors were showered upon Raymond than upon Greeley, and the latter looked upon the fact as one of ingratitude in every way and sense."[47]

In spite of his political work, Raymond made sure that the *Times* was aggressive in covering the news. When a steamer was lost in 1854, for example, *Times* reporters went all over the city

[45] Maverick, *Henry J. Raymond*, 142.

[46] Greeley to D.B. St. John, 16 August 1853.

[47] Hudson, *Journalism in the United States*, 626.

checking out rumors that a survivor had turned up, but they were unable to find him. As the city department editor went home in his horse-car at 3 a.m., he overheard a conversation that indicated that the *Herald* had given the survivor a bottle of wine and was keeping him in the *Herald* offices. The *Herald* paid well for exclusive news. The *Times* man returned to his office and got a pressroom worker to obtain, somehow, a copy of the *Herald*, which was being withheld from street circulation until 9 a.m. Then the *Times* called all its compositors back to work; and the whole story, stolen from the early edition of the *Herald*, was set in an hour. The *Times* was on the streets by 8 a.m., beating the *Herald* on its own story. The city editor got a $5 a week raise, and the sticky-fingered pressman got a $50 bonus.

***New York Times*, 1851**
The building at 113 Nassau Street was not ready when, "on the night of the 17th of September [1851], the first number of *The Times* was made up" amid construction debris, wrote staff member Augustus Maverick. "All was raw and dismal," as staff worked in "open lofts, destitute of windows, gas, speaking tubes, dumb waiters, and general conveniences." He remembered "sitting by the open window at midnight, looking through the dim distance at [Henry] Raymond's first lieutenant, who was diligently writing brevier [editorial copy] at a rickety table at the end of the barren garret; his only light a flaring candle, held upright by three nails in a block of wood; at the city editor and the newsmen and the reporters, all eagerly scratching pens over paper, their countenances half lighted, half shaded, by other fluttering candles; at Raymond, writing rapidly and calmly, as he always wrote, but under similar disadvantages. And all the night the soft summery air blew where it listed, and sometimes blew out the feeble lights, and grim little [printers'] 'devils' came down at intervals from the printing-room, and cried for copy; and ... every man in the company, from the chief to the police reporter, gave his whole mind to the preparation of the initial sheet."

Reflections on the Cheap Press

The innovations of the cheap newspapers in New York were picked up by newspapers in other major American cities, and contemporary observers thought that the revolution in the daily press would bring about a revolution in American society. Bennett boasted that a free press conducted by genius and talent could be the real government of a civilized people. He even believed that his type of journalism had "defended pure religion from the insults and attacks of its professed friends." He claimed, "We can at least declare that the aim of this journal [the *Herald*] has ever been to show that religion stripped of cant, hypocrisy, and sectarianism, is the only foundation on which the prosperity and happiness of nations or individuals can repose."[48]

The early biographers of the leaders of the penny press shared their subjects' enthusiasm. Greeley's biographer, James Parton, thought that the penny press would have more effect on the nation than anything that had happened in the first seventy years of its history. He predicted:

> Its results, in this country, have already been wonderful indeed, and it is destined to play a great part in the history of every civilized nation, and in that of every nation yet to be civilized.... The Cheap Press — its importance cannot be estimated! It puts every mind in direct communication with the greatest minds, which all, in one way or another, speak through its columns. It brings the *Course of Events* to bear on the progress of every individual. It is the great leveller, elevator and democratizer. It makes this huge Commonwealth, else so heterogeneous and disunited, think with one mind, feel with one heart, and talk with one tongue. Dissolve the Union into a hundred petty States, and the Press will still keep us, in heart and soul and habit, One People.[49]

Isaac Pray, Bennett's biographer, thought that the press's increasing ability to disseminate quickly the words of speakers would profoundly affect the nation and its politics. People could be galvanized to get out from under the control of the old-style political parties and their journals. "Thus Journalism and popular eloquence go hand in hand throughout the country," he wrote, "exciting men to thought and action, not in the old beaten track of political dictators, but on the broad ground of justice and the common welfare."[50]

Even a rival of the cheap press could print words in its praise. Less than two months after the appearance of the *Herald* in 1835,

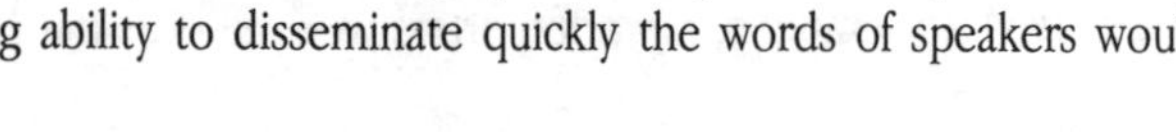
[48]Quoted in Pray, *Memoirs of James Gordon Bennett*, 278.

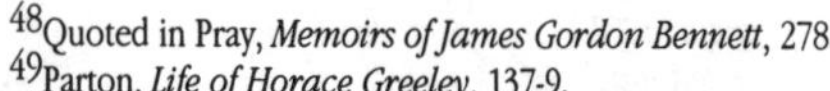
[49]Parton, *Life of Horace Greeley*, 137-9.

[50]Pray, *Memoirs of James Gordon Bennett*, 418.

the editor of New York's *Journal of Commerce* wrote that the penny papers were conducted with as "much talent" as their more expensive rivals. He even reflected that "in point of moral character we think candidly they are superior to their sixpenny contemporaries.... The number of newspaper readers is probably doubled by their influence, and they circulate as pioneers among those classes who have suffered greatly from want of general intelligence." Believing the cheaper papers were "less partisan in politics than the large papers, and more decidedly American, with one or two exceptions...," he concluded by wishing his "penny associates all success, hoping that they will grow wise, good, and great, until they make every sixpenny paper ashamed that tells a lie, or betrays its country for the sake of party, or does any other base thing."[51]

The penny press, of course, did not live up to all these expectations; but it did bring about important, if gradual, changes to the nation's newspapers. New readers were attracted to the changes in writing style and content — the increased emphasis on sensationalism, human interest, and local news. While there was an abundance of examples of newspaper hoaxes and while even the mass circulation dailies still were tied to political parties, the relatively neutral reporting of facts — what would be called "objectivity" later — became increasingly prevalent. Specialization in personnel and newswriting increased as newspapers became larger organizations. Bennett introduced his "money articles," and editorials began to become distinct from news stories. Sportswriting appeared, and there was more on-the-scene reporting from the political battlegrounds in Washington, D.C., and the military battlegrounds of the Mexican War and European revolutions. The printing technology that let the penny press reach its mass audience also let it change the appearance of the product. The newspaper became larger, and there was a greater use of headlines in "decks" (one-column headlines followed by subheads).

Just as important as changes in content were the changes in distribution and financing. The London Plan of circulation on the streets — rather than circulation by subscription only — gave publishers a powerful tool to reach readers who could not be reached by mail. New types of advertising — want ads, personals, and display ads — and the decision to force advertisers to change ad copy every day shifted the financial base of the newspaper from subscriptions to advertising.

The one-person shop was a thing of the past. The newspaper now was often an organization of more than a hundred persons, and its voice spoke to thousands more. It was becoming a ubiquitous institution in American society.

RECOMMENDED READINGS

BOOKS

Bryant II, William Cullen. *Power for Sanity: Selected Editorials of William Cullen Bryant, 1829-1861*. New York, 1994. A chronological collection of the editorials of Bryant, one of the greatest opinion writers of all time.

Carlson, Oliver. *The Man Who Made News*. New York, 1942. Discusses James Gordon Bennett's development of news as an instrument to sell newspapers.

Copeland, Fayette. *Kendall of the Picayune*. Norman, Okla., 1943. Considered the definitive biography of George W. Kendall, who brought the penny press revolution to New Orleans. He was one of the first American war correspondents.

Crouthamel, James L. *Bennett's New York Herald and the Rise of the Popular Press*. Syracuse, N.Y., 1989. Chronicle of Bennett's contributions to journalistic practices.

Hale, William Harlan. *Horace Greeley: Voice of the People*. New York, 1950. Explains Greeley as an advocate of the interests of the common man.

Huntzicker, William E. *The Popular Press, 1833-1865*. Westport, Conn.: 1999. The best survey history of the penny press, along with journalism in general during the period.

Johnson, Curtiss S. *Politics and a Belly-full*. New York, 1962. Provides the only book-length study focusing primarily on William Cullen Bryant's newspaper work.

Johnson, Gerald W., Frank R. Kent, H.L. Mencken, and Hamilton Owens. *The Sunpapers of Baltimore*. New York, 1937. Narrates a history of the *Baltimore Sun*, that city's leading penny newspaper.

Maverick, Augustus. *Henry J. Raymond and the New York Press for Thirty Years. Progress of American Journalism from 1840 to 1870*. Hartford, Conn., 1870. A look at Raymond and the cheap press by a contemporary newsman.

Mitchell, Catherine C., ed. *Margaret Fuller's New York Journalism: A Bibliographical Essay and Key Writings*. Knoxville, Tenn., 1995. Focuses on Fuller's journalistic writings at the time she was in charge of the *New York Tribune's* literary department under Horace Greeley.

O'Brien, Frank M. *The Story of the Sun*. New York, 1918. Narrates the history of the first successful penny newspaper from its founding in 1833 into the twentieth century.

Oslin, George P. *The Story of Telecommunications*. Macon, Ga., 1992. Detailed and anecdotal history of wired communication, from the telegraph to television.

Parton, James. *The Life of Horace Greeley, Editor of the New York Tribune*. New York, 1855. Probably the best biography of Greeley, written by a contemporary and filled with detail.

Pray, Isaac C. *Memoirs of James Gordon Bennett and His Times*. New York, 1855. An important but sometimes inaccurate account by a contemporary journalist of a major figure in nineteenth-century newspapering. Unfortunately, in writing the book the author was determined not to consult Bennett.

Schwarzlose, Richard A. *The Nation's Newsbrokers: Volume One, The Formative Years: From Pretelegraph to 1865*. Evanston, Ill., 1989; and *The Nation's Newsbrokers: Volume Two, The Rush to Institution: From 1820 to 1920*. Evanston, Ill., 1990. History of cooperative newsgathering, emphasizing the interrelationship among newspapers, telegraph companies, and news agencies.

Seitz, Don C. *Horace Greeley: Founder of the New York Tribune*. Indianapolis, 1926. Greeley was influential yet contradictory, earnest and honest, courageous yet lacking deep insight.

Seitz, Don C. *The James Gordon Bennetts; Father and Son; Proprietors of the New York Herald*. Indianapolis, 1928. Narrative biography of the Bennetts, who ran the *Herald* from 1835 to 1918 and formed "the longest newspaper dynasty we Americans have known."

Sloan, Wm. David, Cheryl Watts, and Joanne Sloan. *Great Editorials*, 2nd ed. Northport, Ala., 1997. An anthology of newspaper editorials, with special attention to those of thirteen of the best writers that American journalism has produced. Includes works not only from the penny press era but from colonial times to the present.

Solomon, Martha M. *A Voice of Their Own: The Woman Suffrage Press, 1840-1910*. Tuscaloosa, Ala., 1991. Efforts by women's suffrage publications resulted in heightened awareness of women's issues, which were often ignored by the

[51]*New York Journal of Commerce*, 29 June 1835.

mainstream newspapers.

Stevens, John D. *Sensationalism and the New York Press*. New York, 1991. From the penny-press era to the present, New York City readers have been particularly interested in tabloid journalism.

Stoddard, Henry L. *Horace Greeley: Printer, Editor, Crusader*. New York, 1946. Narrative biography showing Greeley as brilliant, independent, generous, resolute, and industrious, yet changeable, profane, lonely, and unhappy. He supported various serious reforms but also was inclined to fads.

Van Deusen, Glyndon Garlock. *Horace Greeley: Nineteenth Century Crusader*. Philadelphia, 1953. Portrays Greeley as a symbol of his age and the *New York Tribune* as a national institution, mirroring mid-19th century ideas on such issues as nationalism, reform, and party politics.

Weed, Thurlow. *Life of Thurlow Weed*. Edited by Thurlow Weed Barnes and Harriet Weed. 2 vols. Boston, 1883-1884. Interesting details of nineteenth-century journalism by a major journalist and politician of the period.

ARTICLES

Bjork, Ulf Jonas. "The Commercial Roots of Foreign Correspondence: The New York Herald and Foreign News, 1835-1839." *American Journalism* 11 (1994): 102-15. Bennett built up a staff of foreign correspondents to compete with the commercial press.

—. "Sketches of Life and Society: Horace Greeley's Vision for Foreign Correspondence." *American Journalism* 14 (1997): 359-75. Greeley's concept of foreign correspondence was that of travel letters that went beyond matters of politics to describe the "feelings, hardships, hopes and antipathies" of people abroad.

Bradshaw, James Stanford. "George W. Wisner and the New York *Sun*." *Journalism History* 6 (1979-1980): 112, 117-21. A closer look at the man who wrote one of the *Sun*'s most popular features.

Commons, John R. "Horace Greeley and the Working Class Origins of the Republican Party." *Political Science Quarterly* 24 (1909): 468-88. Greeley was an idealistic thinker who put together a constructive program for improving the conditions of the working class and providing land for farmers. His ideas helped form the Republican party, which "was not an anti-slavery party ... [but] a homestead party."

Eberhard, Wallace B. "Mr. Bennett Covers a Murder Trial." *Journalism Quarterly* 47 (1970): 457-63. As a reporter for the *New York Courier and Enquirer*, James Gordon Bennett challenged the contempt power of the court trying a murder case in Salem, Mass. Bennett's work demonstrated his audacity and his "deep dedication" to the profession of journalism.

Endres, Kathleen. "Jane Grey Swisshelm: 19th Century Journalist and Feminist." *Journalism History* 2 (1975-1976): 128-32. A study of what it was like to be a woman and journalist in the times of the penny press.

Hoffert, Sylvia D. "New York City's Penny Press and the Issue of Woman's Rights, 1848-1860." *Journalism Quarterly* 70 (1993): 656-65. The New York penny press gave wide attention to the woman's rights movement in the antebellum period and provided a voice for movement activists who lacked a newspaper of their own.

Nelson, Anna Kasten. "Secret Agents and Security Leaks: President Polk and the Mexican War." *Journalism Quarterly* 52 (1975): 9-14. Demonstrates that presidents had problems with national security and the press even during the penny press period.

Nerone, John C. "The Mythology of the Penny Press." *Critical Studies in Mass Communication* 4 (1987), 376-404. Criticizes the standard portrayal of the penny press and questions its importance. Followed by several critical responses from other scholars.

Nilsson, Nils Gunnar. "The Origin of the Interview." *Journalism Quarterly* 48 (1971): 707-13. In the 1830s, penny press reporters, led by James Gordon Bennett, began using question-and-answer story forms and placing an emphasis on human interest material. "From there the step to the interview was very short."

Pickett, Calder. "Technology and the New York Press in the 19th Century." *Journalism Quarterly* 37 (1960): 398-407. For newspapers in the mid-nineteenth century to survive, they had to adopt the new communication and printing technology.

Reilly, Tom. "Newspaper Suppression During the Mexican War, 1846-1848." *Journalism Quarterly* 54 (1977): 262-70. Demonstrates that military-press conflict is not just a modern-day problem.

Robinson, Elwyn B. "The *Public Ledger:* An Independent Newspaper." *Pennsylvania Magazine of History and Biography* 64 (1940): 43-55. In Philadelphia, the penny newspaper pursued a political course not tied to parties and a "civic-minded editorial policy ... combined ... [with] unusual enterprise in securing news of important events at the earliest possible moment."

Russo, David J. "The Origins of Local News in the U.S. Country Press, 1840s-1870s." *Journalism Monographs* 65 (February 1980). A major study that details news content in smaller newspapers of the penny press era and afterward.

Shaw, Donald Lewis. "At the Crossroads: Change and Continuity in American Press News, 1820-1860." *Journalism History* 8 (1981): 38-50. A study of the content of American newspapers reveals that the influence of the major newspapers was slow to reach the hinterlands.

Smith, Henry Ladd. "The Beauteous Jennie June: Pioneer Woman Journalist." *Journalism Quarterly* 40 (1963): 169-74. As a member of the *New York Herald* staff, Jane Cunningham Croly was a superior journalist and a leader in the feminist movement. She had a number of significant accomplishments and "firsts."

Taylor, Sally. "Marx and Greeley on Slavery and Labor." *Journalism History* 6 (1979-1980): 103-6. An interesting study of Greeley's relationship with the cofounder of communism.

8

The Antebellum Press

1820 - 1861

Sectional controversy leading up to the Civil War can be attributed to many factors. Some historians point to the threat of industrialism and the ultimate conflict between farm and factory. Northerners of the nineteenth century were intrigued by concepts of industry and trade, while Southerners were more concerned with land and farming. Other historians view the conflict as a struggle between cultures: one in the South dominated by a pro-slavery philosophy and another in the North shaped by the increasingly influential forces of reform and democracy. However, one issue, slavery, served as the catalyst and rallying cry for the controversy that eventually would culminate in war between both cultures. The *New York Commercial Advertiser* declared in 1821 that slavery was responsible for "shedding sectional animosity" upon the country.[1] The question of slavery could be argued on several different levels — financial, moral, patriotic, religious. These were all principles for which men and women pledged their lives to support.[2]

The years prior to the Civil War represented a turning point for America's press. Newspapers had become a mass medium, reaching most of society, and editors were forced to choose sides in the intersectional strife over slavery. The slavery issue threatened not only the country, but also the role and development of the American press. Although the first shots of the Civil War were not fired until April 12, 1861, newspapers in the United States had declared a war of words years earlier, with slavery as the core issue. A press dominated by party loyalty was beginning to give way to a group of editors and publishers concerned with the press' broader civic responsibilities.

The Abolitionist Press

Antislavery publications began to appear throughout the country during the early 1800s. Among the earliest antislavery editors were Charles Osborn, Elihu Embree, and William Swain. Osborn established the *Philanthropist* in Mount Pleasant, Ohio, in 1817, followed two years later by Embree's *Manumission Intelligencer* in Jonesboro, Tennessee. In 1820 Embree changed his weekly, probably the first paper devoted exclusively to the abolition of slavery, to a monthly and changed the name to the *Emancipator*. Swain began publication of the *Greensboro* (N.C.) *Patriot* in 1828, publishing his antislavery material despite local opposition.

Perhaps the most influential early abolitionist publication belonged to Benjamin Lundy, a proponent of the antislavery cause since 1815. Lundy is often credited with keeping antislavery sentiments from dissipating as early as the 1820s. Born in New Jersey, the only child of Quaker farmers, Lundy devised a plan for an antislavery organization to be based in Mount Pleasant, Ohio. The organization, named the "Union Humane Society," operated on the principle that its members would use all legal means to end racial prejudice, to attain civil rights for free blacks, and to secure the freedom of those blacks enslaved illegally.[3]

Lundy continued to espouse his ideas about the abolition of slavery through his paper, the *Genius of Universal Emancipation*, established in 1821 in Mount Pleasant. The *Genius* was often referred to as "the little paper with the great name." Lundy's dedication to his cause was evidenced in his methods of operating his paper. He spent much of his time traveling, selling subscriptions for his paper, and lecturing. In some instances, although slight of build, he walked to his destination carrying his office equipment with him in a large pack. When he arrived in a town that had a printing press, he would stop long enough to write, print, and mail an edition of his paper.

In 1822 Lundy decided to move his operation to a place where slavery existed in its more blatant form — Greeneville, Tennessee. He journeyed 800 miles to Tennessee, making one-half of the trip by steamboat and the other half on foot. He hoped that his *Genius* would serve as a replacement for Embree's *Emancipator*. Before his death in 1820, Embree and the *Emancipator* had provoked widespread hostility in its location so close to the enemy, and

[1] Quoted in William B. Hesseltine and David L. Smiley, *The South in American History* (Englewood Cliffs, N.J., 1960), 147.
[2] Harriet Martineau, *The Martyr Age of the United States* (Boston, 1839), 3.

[3] Merton L. Dillon, *Benjamin Lundy and the Struggle for Negro Freedom* (Urbana, Ill., 1966), 18.

GENIUS OF UNIVERSAL EMANCIPATION.

EDITED BY BENJAMIN LUNDY.

"We hold these truths to be self-evident; that all men are created equal, and endowed by their Creator with certain un-alienable rights, that among these are life, liberty, and the pursuit of happiness."—*Declaration Independence U. S.*

No. 10. Fourth Month, 1822. Vol. I.

Genius of Universal Emancipation

The most influential of the early abolitionist papers was Benjamin Lundy's *Genius of Universal Emancipation,* founded in 1821 in Mount Pleasant, Ohio. The only child of Quaker parents, Lundy had been reared with a strong belief in the sanctity of human life. He moved the paper to Greeneville, Tennessee, in 1822 so that he could publish from a place in which slavery was legal. He produced uncompromising material and provoked widespread hostility. He kept alive his "little paper with the great name" by selling subscriptions while he traveled and lectured. When he came to a town with a printing press, he would stop long enough to produce an issue.

Lundy's *Genius* would fare no better. Despite opposition, Lundy produced antislavery material that insulted slaveholders throughout the country. In one particularly scornful article, he proclaimed slaveholders to be "whoremongers" who dared to oppose emancipation on the grounds of their lust and greed, making a "business of raising bastards and selling them for money."[4]

In hopes of getting support, Lundy later moved his operation to Baltimore, Maryland. Failing to gain adequate allies, however, he was forced during the winter of 1828-1829 to discontinue his efforts because of lack of funds. By late 1829 he was able to scrape together enough money to resume publication of the *Genius*, later increasing its publication frequency to weekly. At that point Lundy was joined by a young man who would later establish his own newspaper and become the most militant and best-known abolitionist editor of the period. He was William Lloyd Garrison.

Garrison came to Lundy as an experienced journalist. Taking a route typical of early American journalists, he served as a printer's apprentice and later worked as a journeyman printer. At age twenty he became the youngest editor and publisher in the United States when he took control of the *Free Press* in his hometown of Newburyport, Massachusetts. He later became editor of the *National Philanthropist* in Boston, a temperance newspaper. Prior to joining Lundy, he had founded and edited the *Journal of the Times* in Bennington, Vermont, a paper established to support John Quincy Adams for the presidency in 1828.

At the *Genius* Garrison was to be the editor-in-residence, while Lundy went about the country holding meetings and selling subscriptions. The partnership should have been ideal. The two shared strong beliefs that slavery was wrong and should be abolished. They did not agree, however, on what should happen to slaves once they were freed. Garrison, a master of fiery rhetoric, issued pronouncements of his personal faith and commitment to the cause. Having once supported gradual emancipation, he later advocated immediate emancipation and enfranchisement. Lundy, having passed through this passionate stage a decade earlier, preferred to examine more practical measures that he hoped would free some slaves immediately and more as time passed. Along with gradual emancipation, Lundy also favored plans for colonization in Africa.

Because of this major difference in philosophies, Lundy offered this solution: "Well, thee may put thy initials to thy articles, and I will put my initials to mine, and each will bear his own burden."[5] The two shook hands, and the *Genius* became a paper with two voices. However, Garrison was the abler journalist of the two, and his voice emerged the louder. Later explaining his unorthodox approach to attacking slavery, Garrison wrote:

> I am aware, that many object to the severity of my language; but is there not cause for severity?...[U]rge me not to use moderation in a cause like the present![6]

Garrison's advocacy of immediate emancipation met stiff opposition in Baltimore. Lundy's appeal for gradual emancipation had been tolerated, but Garrison's bold proposal enraged the citizenry. He soon faced libel charges, and the outcome of the case clearly indicated that antislavery sentiments were at a low ebb in the North. Upon learning that a ship belonging to Francis Todd of

[4]*Genius of Universal Emancipation*, June 1823.

[5]Quoted in Oliver Johnson, *W. L. Garrison and His Times* (1880; reprint, Salem, N.H., 1969), 29.

[6]*Liberator*, 1 January 1831.

THE LIBERATOR.

VOL. I.] WILLIAM LLOYD GARRISON AND ISAAC KNAPP, PUBLISHERS. [NO. 1.

BOSTON, MASSACHUSETTS.] OUR COUNTRY IS THE WORLD—OUR COUNTRYMEN ARE MANKIND. [SATURDAY, JANUARY 1, 1831.

William Lloyd Garrison
The editor of the *Liberator* wrote harshly and uncompromisingly about the inhumanity of slavery. His views gained tremendous public attention because his writing possessed a shock effect and a power to arouse violent opposition. Garrison was one of the first to argue that slaves were humans equal to whites and to urge immediate emancipation.

Newburyport, had sailed from Baltimore to New Orleans with a cargo of slaves, Garrison took pen in hand and attacked. He was enraged because the ship's owner was from his hometown. After giving the facts of the story, he editorialized in bold print:

> It is no worse to fit out piratical cruisers, or to engage in the foreign slave trade, than to pursue a similar trade along our own coasts; and the men who have the wickedness to participate therein, for the purpose of heaping up wealth, should be SENTENCED TO SOLITARY CONFINEMENT FOR LIFE; *they are the enemies of their own species — highway robbers and murderers*; and their final doom will be, unless they speedily repent, *to occupy the lowest depths of perdition*.[7]

Garrison did not wait for Todd to read his attack in the *Genius*; he sent him a marked copy. Todd sued for $5,000 for defamation. A grand jury also indicted Garrison for having written and published "a gross and malicious libel." Both Garrison and Lundy were initially charged, but the charges against Lundy were dropped after the judge determined that his absence from the city at the time absolved him of all responsibility for the article. However, although a leading lawyer of Baltimore offered his services free of charge and defended Garrison, after less than fifteen minutes' deliberation the jury returned a verdict of guilty. Garrison was fined $50 and court costs, totaling $100. Unable to pay either, he was jailed for forty-nine days. It is ironic that the only factual error in Garrison's account was that eighty-eight slaves were aboard the ship instead of the eighty-five he reported.

[7]Quoted in Ralph Korngold, *Two Friends of Man* (Boston, 1950), 38.

The Liberator

After completing his jail term, Garrison parted company with Lundy. Lundy contended that financial difficulties had forced an end to the weekly paper, and he was thus returning to the monthly format with less expensive production costs.[8] Using his previous format, Lundy continued his efforts to expose the evils of slavery and praise the merits of colonization. It is uncertain whether Lundy and Garrison separated on a sour note or dissolved their partnership on good terms. Since the issue of colonization had been compromised at the beginning of their relationship, it is likely that the latter was the case. Lundy admired much of Garrison's work, once stating that "nothing but this will reach the adamantine hearts of slavites."[9] Garrison's tribute following Lundy's death in 1839 indicated a great deal of admiration, respect, and gratitude: "Now, if I have in any way, however humble, done anything toward calling attention to slavery, or bringing about the glorious prospect of a complete jubilee in our country at no distant day, I feel that I owe everything in this matter, instrumentally and under God, to Benjamin Lundy."[10]

On January 1, 1831, Garrison founded the *Liberator* in Boston. Free of any obligation to Lundy, he exerted all his efforts to gain immediate emancipation and enfranchisement for freed blacks. In the first issue of the *Liberator* he declared that blacks were as entitled to "life, liberty and the pursuit of happiness" as any white man.[11] He also explained why he had chosen Boston to launch his newspaper. In the North, Garrison claimed, he "found contempt more bitter, opposition more active, detraction more relentless, prejudice more stubborn, and apathy more frozen, than among slaveholders themselves." To show his determination, Garrison wrote: "I *will be* as harsh as truth, and as uncompromising as justice. On this subject, I do not wish to think, to speak, or write, with moderation.... I am in earnest — I will not equivocate — I will not excuse — I will not retreat a single inch — AND I WILL BE

[8]*Genius of Universal Emancipation and Baltimore Courier*, 5 March 1830.
[9]Ibid., December 1830.
[10]Quoted in Korngold, *Two Friends of Man*, 41.
[11]*Liberator* (Boston) 1 January 1831. Also see Johnson, *W. L. Garrison and His Times*, 50-66, and George M. Fredrickson, *William Lloyd Garrison* (Englewood Cliffs, N.J., 1968), 244-5.

The Liberator
In a sense, the founding of the *Liberator* represented the birth of abolitionism. William Lloyd Garrison turned his back on the gradualism and moderation of many of his past antislavery allies. Slavery, he believed, was a sin and had to be abolished. Many of the political radicals, including Senator Charles Sumner and Massachusetts Governor John Andrew, read the *Liberator.*

THE LIBERATOR.

VOL. I.] WILLIAM LLOYD GARRISON AND ISAAC KNAPP, PUBLISHERS. [NO. 33.

BOSTON, MASSACHUSETTS.] OUR COUNTRY IS THE WORLD—OUR COUNTRYMEN ARE MANKIND. [SATURDAY, AUGUST 13, 1831.

HEARD."[12]

Garrison and his *Liberator* raised fear among Southerners and stiff opposition from Northerners. Slave owners feared Garrison's appeals would spark more slave rebellions, while Northerners believed Garrison would destroy any chance of compromise between the two regions.

Several efforts were made to suppress, or at least limit, distribution of the *Liberator*. The year the paper was founded, the Georgia legislature offered $4,000 for the arrest of Garrison. South Carolina offered $1,500 for the arrest of anyone caught distributing the paper. In the North even James Gordon Bennett of the *New York Herald*, who earlier had argued vigorously for freedom of the press, saw nothing wrong with gagging Garrison. In 1833 a mob stormed a building in which Garrison was holding an antislavery meeting but failed to recognize the editor, who prudently had mingled among the crowd. In 1835 a mob in Boston attacked him, and he had to be jailed for protection. On his cell wall, he inscribed the details of his harrowing adventure, concluding that the "respectable and influential" had attempted to destroy him "for preaching the abominable and dangerous doctrine, that 'all men are created equal,' and that all oppression is odious in the sight of God."[13]

Garrison's infamous reputation created a profound effect upon his newspaper's popularity. The *Liberator* was not an instant success, its circulation never surpassing 600. In the long run, however, Garrison did manage to reach those who were apathetic on the issue of slavery and reinforce the views of those who already embraced antislavery sentiments. He even opened his columns to blacks so they might be able to express their views about the subject of slavery. His may have been the first effort by any white editor in America to provide such an opportunity to blacks. His creation of the "Ladies' Department" in the *Liberator* probably offered the first widespread opportunity for black women to voice their opinions in a public forum.

Blacks flocked to join the antislavery movement. For the first three years of the *Liberator*'s operation, the majority of the subscribers and supporters were black. In April 1834 only one-fourth of the subscribers were white.[14] This support was partially due to Garrison's fervent vow to devote his life to atoning for the wrongs inflicted upon blacks. He was also respected for his tendency to seek out free blacks and ex-slaves in the North to ascertain their opinions on how to improve the condition of the race. Garrison's children later wrote that this passion and devotion led many blacks to assume that Garrison was a black man.[15]

It has been said that Garrison was "the most articulate spokesman of militant abolition. For a generation he was one of the most important forces working for the freedom of slaves."[16] Contrary to the impression created by some of the revolutionary articles that appeared in the *Liberator*, however, Garrison was not an advocate of violence. He was a strong believer in "nonresistance" (or "nonviolence" as it would be called today). He claimed his philosophy "was simply to desist from the sin of slavery under moral suasion so that the oppressor and the oppressed could enter with clean hands into a new reconciliation and brotherhood." In 1837 he declared, "Next to the overthrow of slavery, the cause of PEACE will command our attention."[17] However, he did have some difficulty in defending the Nat Turner-led slave rebellion in Virginia in 1831 and John Brown's raid in 1859 without compromising his stand on nonresistance. He managed well. In reference to Turner, he contended that the rebellion was an example of the ultimate violence that slavery would produce. Slavery, therefore, should be abolished immediately. In defense of Brown he wrote:

> A word or two in regard to the characteristics of John Brown. He was of the Old Puritan stock — a Cromwellian who "believed in God," and at the same time "in keeping his powder dry." He believed in "the sword of the Lord and of Gideon," and acted accordingly. Herein I differ widely from him. But, certainly, he was no "infidel" — oh no![18]

As if Garrison's stand on slavery were not enough to irritate the majority of whites in the United States, North and South, he also strongly advocated the rights of women. In conjunction with abolition of slavery, Garrison declared: "As our object is universal

[12] *Liberator*, 1 January 1831.
[13] *Liberator*, 7 November 1835.
[14] Benjamin Quarles, *Black Abolitionists* (New York, 1969), 20.

[15] W.P. Garrison and F.J. Garrison, *William Lloyd Garrison, 1805-1879; The Story of his Life as told by his Children*, Vol. I (New York, 1885-1889), 258.
[16] An assessment of William Lloyd Garrison by John Hope Franklin, *From Slavery to Freedom* (New York, 1948), 241.
[17] *Liberator*, 15 December 1837.
[18] *Liberator*, 16 December 1859.

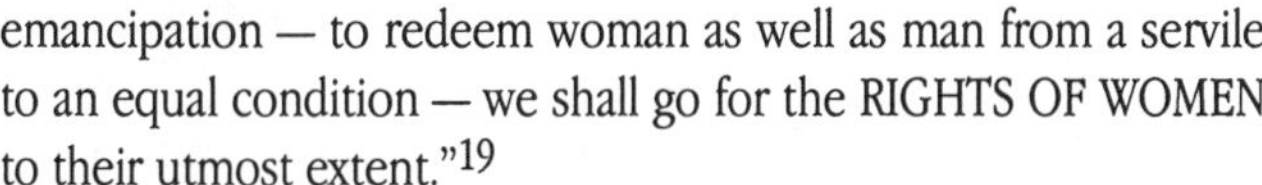

Elijah Lovejoy, Martyr
Facing threats in St. Louis, Elijah Lovejoy moved his print shop across the Mississippi River to Alton, Illinois. Twice, mobs destroyed the office and press. The third time, in 1837, a mob not only demolished his office but killed Lovejoy as well. He became a martyr to the antislavery cause, and today the annual Elijah Lovejoy Award for Courage in Journalism recognizes journalists who do their job in the face of great dangers.

Lewis Tappan
After breaking with William Lloyd Garrison over the latter's aggressive demands for abolition, Tappan founded the *National Era*, which emphasized moderation and gained the largest circulation of any abolition newspaper.

emancipation — to redeem woman as well as man from a servile to an equal condition — we shall go for the RIGHTS OF WOMEN to their utmost extent."[19]

Lovejoy, Birney, and Tappan

Several abolitionist papers would rise and fall by the end of the Civil War; the *Liberator*, however, appeared every week for thirty-five years. Followers of Garrison, "Garrisonians" as they were often referred to, accounted for the establishment of several leading antislavery newspapers. The *National Anti-Slavery Standard* was published in New York from 1840 to 1870. During the 1850s, Garrisonian organizations published the *Pennsylvania Freeman* in Philadelphia and the *Anti-Slavery Bugle* in Ohio. One advocate of the abolitionist movement would become a martyr for the cause.

The issue of slavery had been whipped to such a feverish pitch by the 1830s that attempts were made to restrict freedom of expression on the issue in both the North and the South. In 1835 Elijah Lovejoy, a former Presbyterian minister, established the *St. Louis Observer*. The *Observer* was a reform paper, and Lovejoy angered numerous readers with his anti-Catholic editorials. Denying that he was an abolitionist, Lovejoy, nevertheless, altered the focus of his paper to include attacks on slavery. When he criticized the leniency of a judge in a trial of persons accused of burning a black man alive, the citizens of St. Louis presented Lovejoy with a resolution informing him that freedom of expression as guaranteed in the Bill of Rights did not extend to editors such as he.

Lovejoy moved his press across the river to Alton, Illinois. There he set up the *Alton Observer* and continued his crusade against slavery and the injustices inflicted on the black man. In 1837, he prophesied: "God has not slumbered nor has his Justice been an indifferent spectator of the scene.... In due time they [the souls of dead slaves] will descend in awful curses upon this land, unless averted by the speedy repentance of us all."[20]

As had happened in Missouri, Lovejoy again became the object of public outrage. Twice mobs destroyed his office and threw his printing press into the river. Determined and with financial help from antislavery organizations, Lovejoy set up his third shop in Alton. The mob then took the ultimate step. In 1837 it demolished his office and killed Lovejoy. The antislavery movement had gained a martyr. Abolitionists now possessed persuasive evidence that slave power threatened all of humanity. John Quincy Adams declared that Lovejoy's murder sent "a shock as of an earthquake through the continent." The *Haverhill Gazette* announced that the "late attack upon the freedom of the press at Alton, Illinois, which has at length been consummated in blood and murder, should arouse every press and every voice in the country."[21]

James G. Birney was more fortunate than Lovejoy. As the first editor of the *Philanthropist* in Cincinnati, he was considered a "reasonable" abolitionist. Kentucky-born, he took his slaves to Ohio, emancipated them, and took up the antislavery cause. Although Birney was mild in sentiments, in 1836 a mob destroyed his printing press, and he barely escaped with his life.

As the antislavery movement grew, it became fragmented. For those who preferred a moderate approach, there was Lewis Tappan, who had broken with Garrison and had helped to form the American and Foreign Anti-Slavery Society. In 1847 he founded the *National Era* in Washington, D.C., and named Gamaliel Bailey editor. He started the paper to "help coordinate anti-slavery senti-

[19] *Liberator*, 31 May 1844.

[20] *St. Louis Observer*, 16 April 1835.

[21] Reprinted in *Liberator*, 8 December 1837.

Uncle Tom's Cabin

Harriet Beecher Stowe's *Uncle Tom's Cabin* originally appeared in serialized form in 1852-1853 in the *National Era* and soon was issued as a book. It was the most widely read literature of the time. Within months of publication in book form, its sales reached 300,000. It was the single most important writing in increasing the demand that slavery be abolished. This illustration shows a child, having just been sold by her master, being separated from her mother.

ments and action among governmental officials." Although modest in its demands, the *Era* opposed "discrimination against blacks" and called for "an end to prejudice." In terms of circulation, the *Era* was probably the most successful of all abolitionist papers. It has been estimated that in 1853 its circulation reached 25,000, while most papers of its kind failed to exceed 3,000. One factor that may have contributed to its success was its publication in 1852-1853 of installments of Harriet Beecher Stowe's *Uncle Tom's Cabin*, probably the most widely read literature of the time. It might also have been because of Bailey's moderate abolitionist philosophy, in which he envisioned a more effective strategy that occupied a middle course between compromise and impractical or unpopular tactics. Bailey reasoned that "a majority of the anti-slavery people of the free states without abating their zeal, or compromising their principles, clearly see that mere denunciation may inflame but not convince — may terrify the cowardly, but must arouse the indignation and resistance of men of courage and intelligence."[22] Consequently, according to Bailey's reasoning, Southerners who realized that slavery could not survive might be willing to listen to discussion that did not require the complete dismantling of their established way of life.

Although divided, abolitionist editors had gained some support for their cause by 1861, the year the Civil War began. In the North the apathetic began to ponder the question of slavery and in many cases sided with the movement. Some ministers began to see slavery as sinful but were horrified that the "war of words" was now producing human casualties.

[22]*National Era*, 7 January 1847.

The Black Press

From its founding in 1827 the black press became a strong ally of the abolitionist press. Approximately forty black newspapers were founded in the United States before the Civil War. The first, *Freedom's Journal*, was established in 1827 in New York City. Initially, the Reverend Samuel E. Cornish, a Presbyterian minister born in Delaware, served as editor, while the proprietor was Bowdoin College graduate John B. Russwurm, a half-black Jamaican who was one of the first blacks to graduate from a U.S. college. In addition to taking a strong stand against slavery, the paper launched an attack against plans of the government and some white and black leaders to establish colonies of American blacks in Africa and Cuba. Cornish believed the plan might benefit some blacks — those who reasoned that full citizenship rights would never be achieved inside the borders of the United States — but it offered little promise to the majority. It would, he believed, substantially reduce the black population in America and deny enslaved blacks access to their most important spiritual ally, free blacks. This attack on colonization was made almost four years before William Lloyd Garrison founded the *Liberator* and expressed a similar philosophy.

Cornish and Russwurm were not together long before they disagreed on what policy should be adopted for blacks in the United States. Cornish favored emancipation and enfranchisement, while Russwurm leaned toward colonization, preferably in Liberia. After six months Cornish ended his association with the paper, leaving the operation solely in the hands of Russwurm, who became a staunch supporter of the American Colonization Society. He reversed the paper's position on colonization and continued publication for almost a year, but not without arousing the ire and outrage of much of the paper's black readership. In 1829 he closed shop and left the United States for Liberia to participate in the colonization program.

Following the departure of Russwurm, Cornish returned to the *Journal* with hopes of reviving it and making it a powerful voice against slavery and the colonization movement. In an effort to pump new life into the paper, he changed its name to *Rights of All*. However, in 1830 a lack of financial support forced him to give up his effort. This was not an uncommon dilemma for black-owned newspapers before the war. Financial difficulties would continue to plague the black press throughout the nineteenth century.

After the demise of *Rights of All*, blacks made several efforts to establish a voice of freedom for slaves. The *African Sentinel and Journal of Liberty* appeared in Albany, New York, in 1831. The *National Reformer* was established in Philadelphia in 1833, and the *Spirit of the Times* in New York City in 1836. All were short-lived.

In 1837, however, the *Weekly Advocate* appeared in New York City with Philip A. Bell as proprietor and the veteran Samuel E. Cornish as editor. Due to its longevity, the *Advocate* often is referred to as America's second black publication. It survived for five years, a long life for a black newspaper during this period. Except for a brief period in 1840, the paper was published until 1842. After two months of publication, the name was changed to the *Colored American*. One of Cornish's first duties as sole editor was to explain the name change to the readers. He argued that the new name emphasized that blacks were actually "more exclusively 'American' than our white brethren," and "colored" was considered an inoffensive word that was a more acceptable term for addressing blacks than other well-known labels and could be used to unify the black community.[23] As did its predecessors, the *Colored American* drew most of its support from antislavery advocates and was established to promote "the emancipation of the enslaved and the elevation of the free colored people." In 1841 the *Colored American* justifiably claimed to be "the only paper in the United States, published and edited by a colored man, and expressly for colored people." The editorship and proprietorship changed hands several times. Following the retirement of Cornish in 1839, Dr. James McCune Smith and Bell became co-editors and Charles Bennett Ray proprietor. Despite the division of authority, the paper managed to maintain consistency in its beliefs, efforts, and editorial content. As part of its attacks against colonization, Ray reasoned in an editorial entitled "This Country, Our Only Home":

> Now, probably three-fourths of the present colored people are American born, and therefore American citizens. Suppose we should remove to some other country, and claim a foothold there, could we not be rejected on the ground that we were not of them, because not born among them? Even in Africa, identity of complexion would be nothing, neither would it weigh anything because our ancestry were of that country. The fact of our

FREEDOM'S JOURNAL.

"RIGHTEOUSNESS EXALTETH A NATION"

NEW-YORK, FRIDAY, MARCH 30, 1827 [Vol. I. No. 3.

***Freedom's Journal's* Founders**

Samuel Cornish (left) and John Russwurm (right) started *Freedom's Journal*, the first African-American newspaper, in 1827 out of a desire to improve the conditions of their race. Cornish, a Presbyterian minister, and Russwurm, one of the first black Americans to get a college degree, particularly emphasized the spiritual, moral, and educational improvement of free blacks. They also wanted to promote racial unity and the progress of blacks in the North. In starting the paper, they explained, "We wish to plead our cause. Too long have others spoken for us...for though there are many in society who exercise towards us benevolent feelings; still (with sorrow we confess it) there are others who make it their business to enlarge upon the least trifle which tends to the discredit of any person of colour.... We are aware that there are instances of vice among us, but we avow that it is because no one has taught its subjects to be virtuous..."

[23] *Colored American*, 4 March 1837.

not having been born there would be sufficient ground for any civil power to refuse us citizenship.[24]

Black religious organizations founded and sponsored several newspapers. These religious publications took a strong social stand and added their voices to the abolitionist press in its fight for freedom. One such paper was the *Christian Recorder* founded in 1846, still surviving as the oldest continuously published black newspaper in America. It was not merely by chance that many of the early black editors were ministers — the Revs. Samuel E. Cornish of *Freedom's Journal*, *Rights of All* and *Weekly Advocate*; C.B. Ray of the *Colored American*; and Richard Allen of the *Recorder*, to mention a few. In addition to the fact that an education was more readily accessible to potential clergymen than to the general black population, the Christian concept of love of humanity was a key factor. Furthermore, one authority on the black press has explained, "With the church tied to the largest Negro groups, thus assuring a ready readership, and with the clergymen quite often the most learned individuals in a particular community, it was natural for newspapers to be attached to religious groups and for the ministers to be editors."[25]

Of the black newspapers founded in America before 1856, most, if not all, promoted the antislavery philosophy. However, the circumstances leading to the founding of many of these papers did not involve the question of the existence of slavery, but the fact that blacks were denied access to the established press to voice their opinions on the slavery issue, as well as other concerns, such as education, employment, and moral development. *Freedom's Journal* was founded after black leaders in New York were refused an opportunity to respond to anti-black editorials appearing in several papers owned by Mordecai M. Noah. In 1843 Martin R. Delaney was prompted to establish the *Mystery* in Pittsburgh because the papers in that city refused to publish letters on slavery from blacks.

In 1847 the *New York Sun* urged its readers to vote "NO" on a state constitutional amendment that would have repealed a clause that allowed blacks to vote only if they owned $250 worth of real estate while whites were not required to own any land. Willis Hodges, a black businessman, prepared a rebuttal to the *Sun*'s editorials and submitted it to the paper. The rebuttal was actually a lengthy "letter to the editor"; however, it was not published until after Hodges had paid a $15 fee. The *Sun* modified the article and placed it in the classified advertising section of the paper. When Hodges complained, the editor informed him that, contrary to the paper's slogan "The Sun Shines For All," the real policy was "The Sun shines for all white men, and not for colored men." Hodges was told if he had something to say, to start his own newspaper. He worked as a "whitewasher" and sold fruits and vegetables for a year to earn enough money to unveil to the citizens of New York the first issue of the *Ram's Horn* on January 1, 1847. The paper carried the motto: "We are men, and therefore interested in whatever concerns men."

Frederick Douglass
An escaped slave, Douglass wrote eloquently of the plight of members of his race while exhorting them to self-improvement. "The fact that we are limited and circumscribed," he wrote, "ought rather to incite us to a more vigorous and persevering use of the elevating means within our reach, than to dishearten us. The means of education, though not so free and open to us as to white persons, are nevertheless at our command to such an extent as to make education possible."

Frederick Douglass

The *Ram's Horn* managed to survive for about eighteen months and once listed 2,500 subscribers. Hodges assumed the role of editor, while Thomas Van Rennselaer, an old friend and well-known restaurateur, served as business manager. Among its contributors and supporters appeared the names of John Brown and Frederick Douglass, two major figures in the antislavery movement. Although Douglass was listed as an assistant editor in August 1847, there is no evidence that he contributed to the *Ram's Horn* anything more than the prestige associated with his name.

Douglass was the best-known black man in America during the period. Born in Tuckahoe, Maryland, he was the son of a white father and a black slave mother. Escaping from slavery in 1838, he settled in New Bedford, Massachusetts, and became a popular speaker. From 1845 to 1847 he lectured in Great Britain and Ire-

[24]Quoted in I. Garland Penn, *The Afro-American Press and its Editors* (1891; reprint, New York, 1969), 44-5.

[25]Armistead S. Pride, "The Negro Newspapers: Yesterday, Today, and Tomorrow," *Journalism Quarterly* 28 (1951): 183-4.

land on the evils of slavery. British sympathizers then bought his freedom from the slaveholder who, legally, still owned him. On his return to the United States, he thus was able to travel throughout the North freely proclaiming the message of immediate abolition of slaves.

A few issues before the demise of the *Ram's Horn*, it had carried a prospectus for a new antislavery newspaper to be called the *Northern Star* (shortened to *North Star*) and to be edited by Douglass. The prospectus read in part:

> Frederick Douglass proposes to publish in Rochester, New York, a weekly antislavery paper with the above title. The objective of The North Star will be to attack slavery in all its forms and aspects; advocate universal emancipation; exact the standard of public morality; promote the moral and intellectual improvement of the colored people; and to hasten the day of freedom to our three million enslaved fellow-countrymen.[26]

The *North Star* began publication on November 1, 1847.

Although Douglass had not been known as a journalist, his paper, according to a nineteenth-century historian, was "readily accepted as one of the most formidable enemies to American slavery. Its aims and purposes, as set forth in the prospectus, drew to it good support from those of the whites who favored abolition."[27] Not everyone, though, welcomed Douglass. His house was burned, and several issues of his paper destroyed. The *New York Herald* advocated that he be "exiled to Canada and his presses thrown into the lake."[28]

The founding of the *North Star* also caused a break between Douglass and some of his supporters. Douglass had received strong support from leading abolitionists, including William Lloyd Garrison, once his chief sponsor. However, the two parted ways over a dispute over dissolution of the Union. Some abolitionists advocated dissolving all ties with slaveholding states. Douglass did not believe a break-up of the nation would solve the problem of blacks still held as slaves. Nor did he believe the U.S. Constitution was pro-slavery, although he argued that government officials often misinterpreted it. Moderate though he was, Douglass did not hesitate to attack when an official took a pro-slavery stand, at one time calling President James Buchanan "the pliant tool of pro-slavery propagandists, the subsidiary of Southern despotism and a consummate hypocrite."[29] Garrison and Douglass also held differing opinions on the need for a newspaper devoted solely to the concerns of a black readership. Garrison maintained that the abolitionist press could aptly respond to the needs of blacks without forcing a split in the loyalties of black subscribers who wished to support both types of newspapers. Douglass, by comparison, believed that only someone who had experienced a similar fate could fully understand the plight of blacks in the United States.

Four years after its founding, the *North Star* was merged with the *Liberty Party Paper* in Syracuse, New York, and renamed the *Frederick Douglass' Paper*. The *North Star*'s financial difficulties appear to have been the major reason for this merger, but Douglass remained as editor after the merger. John Thomas, former editor of the *Liberty Party Paper*, became assistant editor. The paper remained essentially the same. It continued its attack on slavery until publication was suspended in 1860.

The Black Press' Dilemma

In 1856 the first black paper to be published on the Pacific Coast appeared in San Francisco and was called the *Mirror of the Times*. John H. Townsend and Mifflin W. Gibbs served as editors. The *Mirror* grew out of a meeting of delegates attending the First Colored Convention of California in Sacramento in 1855. It was decided that a black voice was needed in the state — a black newspaper. However, publication did not begin immediately. As outlined by the delegates, its primary concern was to be with problems encountered by blacks within the state and not, primarily, with the national or international issue of slavery. The delegates outlined their purpose:

> Our sole objective is, to present our grievance to the people at large in our way, and through columns of our own press; show them [whites] the disabilities we labor under; ask them, in respectful terms, to remove them, and we have every reason to believe they will be stricken from the statute-books.[30]

The statement referred to several restrictive laws against blacks in California, especially the Testimony and Witness Law which barred blacks from giving testimony or appearing as witnesses in court cases involving whites. The *Mirror* fought vigorously against these laws; but when efforts failed to have them repealed, Gibbs became discouraged with the lack of change in San Francisco and moved to Victoria, British Columbia, in 1858. Shortly afterward, Townsend returned to New York, and the *Mirror* was discontinued. Until 1862 the Pacific Coast would be without another black publication; however, the black press had spread from coast to coast. For obvious reasons, though, no effort would be made to publish a black newspaper in the South until after the Civil War.

From its founding, the black press had to deal with the dilemma of colonization or enfranchisement. Most papers chose the road to enfranchisement; however, at least one chose to support a colonization scheme. In 1859, Thomas Hamilton founded the *Anglo-African Magazine*. At first it was a strong antislavery publication with the motto, "Man must be free; if not through the law,

[26] *Ram's Horn* (New York), 5 November 1847. Also see Carter R. Bryan, "Negro Journalism Before Emancipation," *Journalism Monographs* 25 (1969): 19.

[27] Penn, *The Afro-American Press and its Editors*, 68.

[28] Quoted in Lionel C. Barrow, Jr., "Historic Role of the Black Press in the Liberation Movement," *National Black Monitor* (November/December 1975): 2.

[29] Quoted in Lionel C. Barrow, Jr., "Role of the Black Press in the Liberation Struggle," *Black Press Handbook*, 1977 (Washington, D.C., 1977): 32-4.

[30] Accounts of these meetings are documented in Philip Montesano, "Some Aspects of the Free Negro Question in San Francisco, 1849-1870" (MA thesis, University of San Francisco, 1967); and J. William Snorgrass, "The Development of the Black Press in the San Francisco Bay Area, 1865-1900," *California History* 60 (1981/82): 306-17.

Anglo-African Magazine.

VOL. I. JANUARY, 1859. NO. 1.

Apology.

(INTRODUCTORY.)

The publisher of this Magazine was 'brought up' among Newspapers, Magazines, &c. The training of his boyhood and the employment of his manhood have been in the arts and mysteries which pertain to the neighborhood of Spruce and Nassau streets in the city of New York. Of course the top of the strata, the upper-crust of the laminæ in his geologic region is—the Publisher. . . . To become a Publisher, was the dream of his youth (not altogether a dream, for, while yet a boy he published, for several months, the People's Press, a not unnoticed weekly paper,) and the aim of his manhood. He understands the business thoroughly, and intends, if the requisite editorial matter can be furnished, to make this Magazine 'one of the institutions of the country.'

He would seem to be the right man in the right place; for the class of whom he is the representative in Printing House Square, sorely need an independent voice in the '*fourth estate.*' Frederick Douglass has said that 'the twelve millions of blacks in the United States and its environs must occupy the notice and the care of the Almighty:' these millions, in order to assert and maintain their rank as men among men, must speak for themselves; no outside tongue, however gifted with eloquence, can tell their story; no outside eye, however penetrating, can see their wants; no outside organization, however benevolently intended, nor however cunningly contrived, can develope the energies and aspirations which make up their mission.

The wealth, the intellect, the Legislation, (State and Federal,) the pulpit, and the science of America, have concentrated on no one point so heartily as in the endeavor to write down the negro as something less than a man: yet at the very moment of the triumph of this effort, there runs through the marrow of those who make it, an unaccountable consciousness, an aching dread, that this *noir faineant*, this great black sluggard, is somehow endowed with forces which are felt rather than seen, and which may in 'some grim revel,'

'Shake the pillars of the commonweal!'

Thomas Hamilton and the Anglo-African

With black readers hungry for material relevant to them, founder Thomas Hamilton filled his *Anglo-African Magazine* with informative essays and articles on issues and events important to the black community. Raised in the newspaper district of New York City, Hamilton became involved with black publications early in his teen years as a carrier for the black newspaper *The Colored American.* He introduced the *Anglo-African Magazine* to New York City in 1859 in hopes of bolstering the intellects of his fellow black men. The first issue contained his statement of purpose. "In addition to the expose of the condition of the blacks," he declared, "this Magazine will have the aim to uphold and encourage the now depressed hopes of thinking black men, in the United States."

then above it." However, in 1860 the paper was sold to James Redpath, who was interested in the Haitian Emigration Movement, a project to encourage blacks in North America to emigrate to Haiti. Under the changed name of the *Weekly Anglo-African* and later the *Pine and Palm*, the paper was used primarily to support the emigration movement. After a year Redpath resigned his position as emigration agent for the organization, and the paper reverted to the Hamilton family with a brother of the deceased founder as editor. Robert Hamilton chose to use the paper's original name of *Anglo-African* and continued publication until 1862.

Regardless of how harsh their tone, most of these papers advocated non-violence, as did the abolitionist press. All had the same appeal: the elevation of blacks in the United States to first-class citizenship.

The Southern Press

Unlike the abolitionist and black papers, southern newspapers were not established, primarily, to fight for a specific cause. The southern press was founded on the same basic business/political principles as leading newspapers in the North. However, the slavery issue forced everyone in the United States to choose sides, and agitation from the abolitionist press forced southern newspapers to take a stand. Considering their economic predicament, southern editors could choose only one road — to support slavery.

Economically, the southern newspapers were at a greater disadvantage than their northern counterparts. According to the 1860 census, the South lagged behind the North in industry, wealth, education, and "free" population. Not only did this mean that southern newspapers had a significantly smaller advertising base, but it also meant fewer subscribers. The South's free population was the real market for political, religious, literary, and miscellaneous periodicals. Fewer readers resulted in far smaller circulation numbers and fewer newspapers in the South than in the North. Despite these drawbacks, the southern antebellum press was strong. There were several profitable triweekly, biweekly, and especially weekly newspapers. These publications showcased the spirit and lifestyle of the southern region, but they still were not ready for open debate on the issue of slavery.

In the early years of the nineteenth century, the South had few restrictions on discussions regarding slavery. A few abolitionist newspapers were even published in southern and border states, including Elihu Embree's *Manumission Intelligencer* and the Northern Carolina Manumission Society's *The Patriot*. However, several occurrences, along with slavery, began to influence the South's tolerance for open discussions. Two incidents that contributed to this intolerance were the Nat Turner Rebellion of 1831, in which fifty-seven whites were killed in Virginia, and the 1830 publication of *Walker's Appeal* by abolitionist David Walker, whose pamphlet was the first militant assault on slavery and racism. In both instances blacks were encouraged to use all means, including violence, to secure their freedom. To further frustrate efforts for open debate, two gag measures surfaced on the national level in the mid-1830s, reflecting southern attitudes toward abolitionist activities. First, Postmaster General Amos Kendall gave southern postmasters the authority to remove incendiary antislavery literature from the mails. Second, Congress passed a law that required antislavery petitions to be tabled without review.

Individual states also began to apply measures to protect themselves from inflammatory antislavery material, including imposing severe restrictions on newspapers and sanctions on individuals who gave any indication of sympathy toward abolition. In 1832 William Gilmore Simms was threatened and forced to sell the *Charleston City Gazette* because of his pro-Union sentiments, and a New York State student working in Tennessee received twenty lashes from the Committee on Vigilance for selling one abolition-

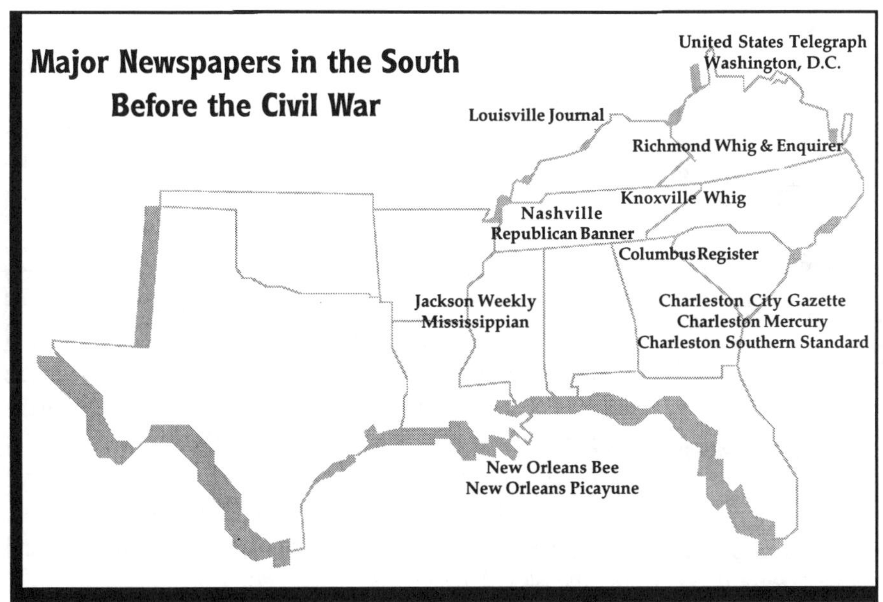

The Fire-Eaters of the South
Because the South did not have an industrialized economy and because it had few cities of substantial population, the region had fewer newspapers than did the North, and they were for the most part of smaller circulation. As the antislavery issue took on growing importance, southern newspapers reacted aggressively. With time, the most prominent editors became the "Fire-Eaters." Among those, the most vocal was Robert Barnwell Rhett. A native of Beaufort, S.C., he changed his name from Smith in 1837, the same year he was elected a congressman in South Carolina. A states'-rights extremist, he used his *Charleston Mercury* as a mouthpiece of secesionist sentiment.

ist work and carrying another. By 1836 most southern states had laws against literature that had a tendency to "incite to insurrection," and anyone who dared to subscribe to an abolitionist paper did so at the risk of being jailed. Some southern states even considered imposing the death penalty on captured abolitionists.

The South was reacting aggressively to antislavery pressure, and it had its own set of supporters in a group of newspaper editors. They were strong in their devotion to the South and its way of life. The *United States Telegraph* in Washington, *Richmond Whig* and *Enquirer*, *Columbia* (S.C.) *Register*, the *Bee* and *Picayune* of New Orleans, *Louisville Journal*, *Nashville Republican Banner*, and *Knoxville Whig* were well-established papers and influential sectional spokesmen on issues concerning the South. They occupied the same role in opinion-making in the South as clergymen and politicians. One group of Southern editors, known as "Fire-Eaters," supported slavery as strongly as Garrison and Douglass opposed it. Among the best known was Robert Barnwell Rhett, owner of the *Charleston Mercury*.

Rhett, who changed his name from Smith in 1837, was a successful lawyer and real estate operator. He acquired valuable property in Charleston, including the *Mercury*, which he made one of the leading newspapers in the South and which made him one of the most powerful men in the region. He and his followers strongly supported slavery and secession of the South from the Union. In the battle over whether slavery was to exist in Kansas, Rhett urged Southerners to support that state's advocates of slavery. He reasoned in the *Mercury*:

> Upon the proposition that safety of the institution of slavery in South Carolina is dependent upon its establishment in Kansas, there can be no rational doubt. He, therefore, who does not contribute largely in money now, proves himself criminally indifferent, if not hostile, to the institution upon which the prosperity of the South and this state depends.[31]

Rhett was no less adamant about secession. In 1837 when it was proposed in Congress that slavery be abolished in the District of Columbia, he exploded and declared that "the Constitution had failed to protect the South in the peaceful enjoyment of its rights and that, therefore, it was expedient that the union be dissolved."[32] He also claimed that the North had made tremendous profits from southern products and called the South "the best colony to the North any people ever possessed."[33]

By the mid-1800s a younger group of editors who endorsed the wisdom of the Fire-eaters emerged to take their place alongside the established leaders. Many came from the ranks of newspaper owners, editors, and writers. In 1846, James DeBow, at age twenty-six, founded *DeBow's Review* and vigorously defended the South and its institution of slavery. In 1854, 30-year-old Ethelbert Barksdale became editor of the pro-slavery *Weekly Mississippian* in Jackson, and 35-year-old Leonidas W. Spratt became widely known throughout the South as editor of Charleston's *Southern Standard*.

[31]Quoted in Hesseltine and Smiley, *The South in American History*, 242.
[32]Ibid., 159.
[33]Ibid., 204.

CHARLESTON

MERCURY

EXTRA:

Passed unanimously at 1.15 o'clock, P. M., December 20th, 1860.

AN ORDINANCE

To dissolve the Union between the State of South Carolina and other States united with her under the compact entitled "The Constitution of the United States of America."

We, the People of the State of South Carolina, in Convention assembled, do declare and ordain, and it is hereby declared and ordained,

That the Ordinance adopted by us in Convention, on the twenty-third day of May, in the year of our Lord one thousand seven hundred and eighty-eight, whereby the Constitution of the United States of America was ratified, and also, all Acts and parts of Acts of the General Assembly of this State, ratifying amendments of the said Constitution, are hereby repealed; and that the union now subsisting between South Carolina and other States, under the name of "The United States of America," is hereby dissolved.

THE

UNION

IS

DISSOLVED!

Secession
Robert Barnwell Rhett produced this special "extra" of the *Charleston Mercury* immediately after South Carolina voted to secede from the Union.

Although all shared a commitment to maintaining the Southern way of life, differences other than age did exist among the Fire-eaters. Rhett and his colleagues had direct contacts with the North and Northerners. The DeBows and Barksdales did not. Those who followed Rhett had some hesitation in trying to defend slavery on moral grounds; the DeBows and Barksdales did not. Many of these young men were, according to one historian, "pro-slavery moralists, aggressively avowing their belief in the rightness of slavery." However, one thing bound both groups of editors together in their philosophy: their careers were based on patterns of sectionalism rather than nation-building.[34]

As the words "secession" and "disunion" became more common in the South, the Fire-eaters began to justify the option of the South going it alone. The *Mercury* declared that the South would not be hurt economically by a separation from the North. In fact, it stated, the region would benefit. It claimed that the South was "in control of her own commerce and destinies" and would "bound forward in a career of prosperity and power, unsurpassed in the history of the world." So strongly did Rhett believe in the future of the South that when South Carolina did secede from the Union in December of 1860, he predicted that "the historians of 2000 A.D. would write glowingly of the Southern Confederacy." He envisioned an empire "extending across the continent to the Pacific, down through Mexico to the other side of the Gulf, and over the Isles of the Sea."[35]

The Jackson *Weekly Mississippian* took a similar approach to secession. It was said of Barksdale and the *Mississippian* that when the paper roared in Mississippi all the little country papers yelped. It was common for the paper to brand any scheme with which it did not agree as "abolitionist" or "traitorous," words that were quick to arouse southern outrage. Thus, the paper pointed a finger at the North as the primary cause of the South's leaving the Union. It declared:

> It does not seem to occur to the aggressors [the North], that if there is any disunion, in consequence of the aggressors, that they are the disunionists. Disunion, which follows a perverted Union, is the work of the pervertors. He who violates the contract is the author of a dissolution of the contract made, in consequence of his violation.[36]

All newspaper editors in the South were not Fire-eaters; nor did they agree on the issue of secession. There were some who supported immediate withdrawal from the Union, while others believed that secession should depend on some future event or grievance and not on past ones. Some editors did not believe any type of change would benefit the country, and they advocated continuation of the Union with few changes in conditions. Some editors were unsure of what road to take. However, following the election of Abraham Lincoln, most southern papers moved toward immediate secession. When the six seceded southern states adopted the provisional constitution for the Confederate States in 1861, Robert Barnwell Rhett's was the first of fifty signatures.

Regardless of their stand, most editors believed that if secession should come, it would take place in a peaceful manner. It is difficult, if not impossible, to determine just how much the papers of Garrison, Douglass, Rhett, DeBow, Barksdale, Spratt, and others had to do with bringing about the Civil War; however, they

[34] Ronald T. Takaki, *Pro-Slavery Crusade* (New York, 1971), 22.
[35] Quoted in Hesseltine and Smiley, *The South in American History*, 606.
[36] *Jackson Weekly Mississipian*, 27 June 1860.

FRANK LESLIE'S ILLUSTRATED NEWSPAPER

NEW YORK, SATURDAY, JUNE 27, 1857.

Dred Scott Decision
The fugitive slave who sued in court for his freedom, Dred Scott became the subject of front-page coverage throughout the North. Despite the Supreme Court's decision against him in 1857, his master granted freedom to him, his wife, and two daughters. This story in *Leslie's Illustrated* appeared right after the Court decision and recounted the story of Scott and his family.

must be credited with fanning the flames of hatred that helped turn a war of words into one of weapons.

THE NORTHERN PRESS

By the mid-1800s the northern press had become a strong voice in the affairs of the North. The *Evening Post*, *Herald*, *Tribune*, and *Times* of New York, the *Springfield* (Mass.) *Republican*, and *Chicago Tribune* all were established leaders. Although these newspapers, with the exception of the *Herald*, supported the antislavery movement, it would be erroneous to put them in the same category as Garrison's *Liberator* or Lundy's *Genius*, which were founded to attack slavery. The established papers were founded primarily as journalistic ventures that happened to support the abolitionist movement, or at least to oppose the spread of slavery.

From a business point-of-view, northern newspapers were far more successful than their southern counterparts, and during the antebellum period they experienced enormous growth. For every paper in the South, there were three northern newspapers. The North had three times the political papers and almost four times the number of religious, literary, and miscellaneous publications. Dailies flourished in the cities, while towns seemed to be ideal locations for weeklies. For example, by 1860 the *New York Herald* had a circulation of 77,000 daily, while the weekly edition of the *New York Tribune* averaged 200,000. In the South, the *Richmond Dispatch*, one of the South's most successful papers, had a daily circulation of only 8,000 and 5,500 for its weekly edition. Rhett's *Charleston Mercury* had only 550 paid subscribers. Many of the differences in the number of publications and subscribers can be attributed to the different economic base in the North. Unlike the southern newspapers, the North's newspapers and magazines benefited from the urban, industrial, and retail strengths of the cities.

The *Evening Post*, the oldest paper in this northern group, had gained a reputation as a fighter for the "common man" and freedom of the press. It aligned itself on the antislavery side of the issue and, under the leadership of William Cullen Bryant, had run the spectrum from Jacksonian Democrat to Free Soil to abolitionist Republican. Bryant argued that abolitionist editors had as much right to freedom of expression as any other editors. The *Evening Post* was also a strong pro-Union paper. When the southern states seceded, the paper branded them "traitors."

Of the four leading New York papers, the *Herald* came closest to promoting the views of the South. It supported the compromising attitude of the Kansas-Nebraska Bill of 1854, which called for Kansas to be a slave state and Nebraska a free state. The South took the bill as a positive gesture toward slavery, and the *Herald* enjoyed wide acceptance in the region. James Gordon Bennett, the *Herald*'s owner, also represented the Democratic party's and the South's view on states' rights, which reasoned that the federal government had no right to interfere with slavery in states that chose the institution. The *Herald* did not, however, support secession from the Union by the southern states.

The *New York Tribune*, under its dominating editor, Horace Greeley, became a strong supporter of the antislavery movement. Greeley, a teetotaler, fought for prohibition, opposed capital punishment, and hated slavery. At one point he favored allowing the southern states to withdraw peacefully if they wished. "Whenever a considerable section of our Union shall deliberately resolve to go out, we shall resist all coercive measures to keep it in," declared the *Tribune*. "We hope never to live in a republic whereof one section is pinned to the residue by bayonets."[37] This attitude changed as war came closer. By 1850 the *Tribune* had become the most influential, and one of the most anti-southern, papers in the country. Of the popular daily newspapers, it had become the leader of those opposed to slavery. It was so hated in the South

[37]Quoted in Donald E. Reynolds, *Editors Make War* (Nashville, Tenn., 1966), 157.

Joseph Medill
Editor of the leading newspaper in the Midwest, the *Chicago Tribune*, Joseph Medill was antislavery and staunchly pro-Union. He considered secessionists to be traitors. In giving directions for the operation of the paper after his death, he declared: "I desire the Tribune as a party organ never to be the supporter of that party [Democratic] which sought to destroy the American union or that exalts the state above the nation."

that a southern news agent, who made the mistake of accepting an order for fifty copies of the *Tribune*, was seized and arraigned by a vigilance committee, determined to be an abolitionist, and sentenced to hang.

The *New York Times* maintained a more neutral stance on slavery. In 1851, in the prospectus of its first issue, the *Times* declared that it did not believe "that everything in society is either exactly right, or exactly wrong; what is good we desire to preserve and improve; what is evil, to exterminate, or reform."[38] That statement set the tone for the paper. However, this stance by editor Henry J. Raymond was probably more political than emotional. In 1854 after the Whig party split over the free-soil issue, Raymond, an aspiring politician, joined the new Republican party. Although unalterably antislavery, the new political organization formulated a program that would attract those who were undecided on the issue of slavery, as well as those opposed to slavery. Raymond and the *Times* had also developed a reputation for "reasonableness" in reporting and, unlike Greeley, used a minimum of invective. Not until war actually began did the *Times* take a strong stand on the slavery issue.

In Springfield, Massachusetts, Samuel Bowles III was proving that a newspaper outside New York could have national influence. After taking over the reigns of the *Springfield Republican*, following the death of his father Samuel Bowles II in 1851, Bowles thrust the weekly paper into the mainstream of political and moral thought. Like Raymond, Bowles was a Whig who later turned to the Republican party. Also, like Raymond's *Times*, the *Republican* was not always a staunch supporter of the antislavery movement. Prior to passage of the Kansas-Nebraska Act, it had approved of the Fugitive Slave Law, and it frequently attacked abolitionists for their views. Bowles did not approve of slavery; but he was strongly pro-Union, and he believed that quarrels between the North and South threatened the Union's existence. Later, after abandoning the Whig party, he denounced the execution of John Brown and became one of the first mainstream editors to endorse the Republican party and Abraham Lincoln.

The newspaper field in the West was led by Joseph Medill's *Chicago Tribune*, a strong pro-Union and antislavery paper. Like Bowles, Medill was a pro-Unionist, and the *Tribune* militantly opposed disunion and considered those who advocated secession as abandoning the true principles on which America was founded. Although it appears most Republican papers had to gradually accept the idea of Abraham Lincoln for president — and some never did — he was the *Tribune*'s choice from the beginning. After Lincoln received the nomination in 1860, a *Tribune* editorial said of him: "He will take to the Presidential chair just the qualities which this country now demands to save it from impending destruction — ability that no man can question, firmness that nothing can overbear, honesty that can never be impeached, and patriotism that never despairs."[39]

By 1861, battle lines between the North and South had been drawn. There was no "one" issue that brought them to arms, but a combination of several that were rolled into the emotional issue of slavery. As with the rest of the country, most newspapers had been forced to take a stand. It can also be observed in hindsight that the war about to begin, which would so influence this nation's history, also would change American journalism.

RECOMMENDED READINGS

BOOKS

Blassingame, John W., Mae G. Henderson, and Jessica M. Dunn, eds. *Antislavery Newspapers and Periodicals*, 5 vols. Boston, 1980-1984. Index to the contents of the publications.

Bullock, Penelope L. *The Afro-American Periodical Press, 1838-1909*. Baton Rouge, 1981. An overview of the development of black magazines and journals and an analysis of their contents.

Cain, William E., ed. *William Lloyd Garrison and the Fight Against Slavery: Selections from the Liberator*. Boston, 1995. A selection of Garrison's editorials from the Liberator, highlighting his political philosophies in relation to such

[38] *New York Times*, 18 September 1851.

[39] *Chicago Tribune*, 23 May 1860.

topics as slavery, women's rights, and the nature of reform.

Daniels, Walter C., ed. *Black Journals of the United States.* Westport, Conn., 1982. Historical profiles of more than 100 black periodicals published in the nineteenth and twentieth centuries in America.

Dann, Martin E., ed. *The Black Press, 1827-1890: The Quest for National Identity.* New York, 1971. A collection of items drawn from black newspapers over a 63-year period and grouped according to prevalent themes, along with an overview and chapter introductions that explain the ideals and purposes of the black editors and writers.

Dickerson, Donna Lee. *The Course of Tolerance: Freedom of the Press in Nineteenth-Century America.* Westport, Conn., 1990. A readable introduction to the subject, with significant material devoted to the dangers posed to press freedom during the antebellum and Civil War periods.

Dillon, Merton L. *Elijah P. Lovejoy, Abolitionist Editor.* Urbana, Ill., 1961. Sympathetic biography of the martyr-editor from Alton, Ill. In advocating emancipation, Lovejoy was motivated by religious zeal.

Dumond, Dwight L., ed. *Southern Editorials on Secession.* New York, 1931. Anthology of 183 editorials selected from seventy-two newspapers, "showing the variety, conflict, and concurrence of opinion in the southern states during and shortly before the crisis of secession."

Fredrickson, George M., ed. *William Lloyd Garrison.* Englewood Cliffs, N.J., 1968. A two-part documentation of how Garrison viewed the world and how his contemporaries viewed him.

Gill, John. *Tide without Turning: Elijah P. Lovejoy and Freedom of the Press.* Boston, 1958. Not only was Lovejoy a martyr to the antislavery cause, but he staunchly advocated the First Amendment guarantee of press freedom.

Harrold, Stanley. *Gamaliel Bailey and Antislavery Union.* Kent, Ohio, 1986. Through the *Philanthropist*, the organ of the Ohio Anti-Slavery Society, and the *National Era* in Washington, D.C., Bailey played a central role in the abolitionist movement.

Hutton, Frankie. *The Early Black Press in America, 1827-1860.* Westport, Conn., 1993. Black editors emphasized social responsibility, morality, and democratic ideals.

Kessler, Lauren. *The Dissident Press.* Beverly Hills, Calif., 1984. Historically black-owned newspapers served as a voice for black Americans because the mainstream press overlooked, distorted, and downplayed their concerns and accomplishments. Several functions of the black press included engendering racial pride, educating its readers, and advocating for change.

Kinshasa, Kwando M. *Emigration vs. Assimilation: The Debate in the African American Press, 1827-1861.* An examination of the soical-political foundation of the black press and the position the various editors maintained on the issue of assimilation of free blacks within the United States or emigration to other countries.

Korngold, Ralph. *Two Friends of Man.* Boston, 1950. A story of William Lloyd Garrison and Wendell Phillips and their relationship with Abraham Lincoln.

Kraditor, Aileen S. *Means and Ends in American Abolitionism: Garrison and His Critics on Strategy and Tactics, 1834-1850.* New York, 1967. Analysis of the ideas of abolitionists argues that Garrison was a realistic, successful abolitionist and social thinker rather than an irrational zealot. "The unrealism was not the abolitionists' for feeling guilty [about slavery] but their neighbors' for not feeling guilty."

Perkins, Howard C., ed. *Northern Editorials on Secession,* 2 vols. New York, 1942. Anthology of editorials during the crisis of 1860-1861, preceded by an introduction describing the general characteristics of the period's newspapers.

Pride, Armistead Scott and Clint C. Wilson II. *A History of the Black Press.* Washington, D.C., 1997. Emphasizes the social and political context surrounding the development of black newspapers from 1827 to the 20th century, stressing the function of the press to serve as a voice for blacks.

Ripley, C. Peter, ed. *The Black Abolitionist Papers.* Chapel Hill, N.C., 1985. A three-volume collection of black newspaper items published in the United States, Canada, and the British Isles from 1830 to 1865, including analyses of people and events connected with the topics addressed in those items.

Sadlier, Rosemary. *Mary Ann Shadd: Publisher, Editor, Teacher, Lawyer, Suffragette.* Toronto, Ontario, 1995. The biography of the first black woman editor in North America and the role she played in the development of racial pride and nineteenth-century equal rights.

Simon, Paul. *Lovejoy, Martyr to Freedom.* St. Louis, 1964. Readable popular biography that presents nothing new about Elijah Lovejoy, the antislavery editor killed by a mob in Alton, Ill., in 1837. He was a model of moral courage. Following a religious conversion, he slowly became an abolitionist.

Streitmatter, Rodger. *Raising Her Voice: African-American Women Journalists Who Changed History.* Lexington, Ky., 1994. Eleven influential black women journalists from the 1830s to the present.

Tripp, Bernell. *Origins of the Black Press: New York 1827-1847.* Northport, Ala., 1992. The early black press emphasized self-expression and improvement for blacks, not just abolition.

White, Laura A. *Robert Barnwell Rhett: Father of Secession.* New York, 1931. The definitive biography of the fire-eating editor of the *Charleston* (S.C.) *Mercury.* He argued for secession as early as 1850 and remained a staunch advocate of slavery and southern extremism throughout the Civil War.

Wolseley, Roland E. *The Black Press, U.S.A.* Ames, Iowa, 2nd ed., 1990. An historical overview of the black press in America from its founding to the present.

ARTICLES

Barrow, Lionel C., Jr. "'Our Own Cause': *Freedom's Journal* and the Beginnings of the Black Press." *Journalism History* 4 (1977): 118-22. The newspaper "gave blacks a voice of their own and an opportunity not only to answer the attacks printed in the white press but to read articles on black accomplishments, marriages, deaths, that the white press of the day ignored."

Bond, Donovan H. "How the Wheeling Intelligencer Became a Republican Organ." *West Virginia History* 11 (April 1950): 160-84. During 1856-1858 the Virginia newspaper advocated "free speech for all" and had a "policy of letting all parties express their views in its columns." These approaches "did not fit well with the practices of its orthodox Southern and Democratic contemporaries." Editor A.W. Campbell then became a leading spokesman for separating from Virginia and forming the new state of West Virginia.

Brewer, William M. "John B. Russwurm." *Journal of Negro History* 13 (1928): 413-22. Biography of the editor of *Freedom's Journal,* America's first black newspaper, and advocate of colonization of former slaves.

Bryan, Carter R. "Negro Journalism in America Before Emancipation." *Journalism Monographs* 25 (1969). A listing of black newspapers published prior to the Civil War and a discussion of their origins, content, and purpose.

Burks, Mary Fair. "The First Black Literary Magazine in American Letters." *CLA Journal* 19 (March 1976): 318-21. The *Anglo-African Magazine* "succeeded in creating a tradition of *belles lettres* among blacks and in establishing a nascent countermovement ... to assimilationist literature, which often was no more than an imitation of a white culture, unknown to millions of blacks."

Cornish, Lori L. "Samuel Cornish: Co-founder of Nation's First Black Newspaper." *Media History Digest* 7, 1 (1987): 25-28. Cornish published *Freedom's Journal* with meager financial support and advocated self-help and education for blacks.

Cullen, Maurice R., Jr. "William Gilmore Simms, Southern Journalist." *Journalism Quarterly* (1961): 298-302, 412. In addition to being "the recognized leader of Southern literary endeavor in the period spanning the American Civil War," the South Carolinian also "was a dedicated journalist who, in several instances, placed his life in jeopardy in order to tell in print what he felt *had* to be told." Although he originally had been pro-Union, with the Civil War he "emerged as a fire-eating editor."

Domke, David. "Journalists, Framing, and Discourse About Race Relations." *Journalism & Mass Communication Monographs 164* (December 1997): 1-55. Examines racial values and attitudes of a group of leading newspaper editors from the nineteenth century, including Whitelaw Reid and Frederick Douglass.

Floan, Howard R. "The New York *Evening Post* and the Ante-bellum South." *American Quarterly* 8 (Fall 1956): 243-53. William Cullen Bryant, *Evening Post* editor, in the 1830s attempted to play down divisive issues. As differences between the North and South worsened, however, he grew stronger in his condemnation of southern attitudes and actions.

Gross, Bella. "Freedom's Journal and the Rights of All." *Journal of Negro History* 17 (July 1932): 241-86. The most complete early scholarly narrative of the two early black newspapers.

Holmes, J. Welfred. "Some Antislavery Editors at Work: Lundy, Bailey, and Douglass." *CLA Journal* 7 (1963): 48-55. "These three men of diverse talents and viewpoints, while editing their papers in a highly individual manner, struck telling blows against slavery."

Johnson, David W. "Freesoilers for God: Kansas Newspaper Editors and the Antislavery Crusade." *Kansas History* 2 (Summer 1979): 74-85. In the 1850s fight for a free Kansas, editorials emphasized slavery as a violation of the Bible and God's principles.

Malone, Henry T. "The Weekly Atlanta Intelligencer as a Secessionist Journal." *Georgia Historical Quarterly* 37 (December 1953): 278-86. With the secessionist crisis of 1860-1861, the *Intelligencer* "became defiantly pro-Southern. For the period between Lincoln's election and the fall of Fort Sumter, the *Intelligencer* offers an interesting and representative picture of Atlanta journalism during critical times."

Martin, Asa Earl. "Pioneer Anti-Slavery Press." *Missouri Valley Historical Review* 3 (March 1916): 509-28. Between 1800 and 1830, journals (published primarily in the border states) "kept alive the anti-slavery sentiment, organized it and formulated definite plans of operation....They were the pioneers of the movement, struggling almost single-handed against the numerous difficulties that threatened to overwhelm them."

Nord, David Paul. "Tocqueville, Garrison and the Perfection of Journalism." *Journalism History* 13 (1986): 56-63. Garrison's *Liberator*, rather than the penny newspapers, embodied Tocqueville's concept of a democratic press.

Nordin, Kenneth D. "In Search of Black Unity: An Interpretation of the Content and Function of 'Freedom's Journal.'" *Journalism History* 4 (1977): 123-8. The first black American newspaper "tried to establish a sense of fraternity among blacks and chart the course people of color should take to improve their positions in American society. It tried also to provide its readers with a sense of culture and to furnish them with the significant news of the day."

Nye, Russel B. "Freedom of the Press and the Antislavery Controversy." *Journalism Quarterly* 22 (1945): 1-11. Southern states abridged freedom with the argument that freedom did not allow the distribution of obnoxious doctrines. Northern legislatures refused to abridge press freedom, and abolitionists quickly recognized the relationship between their cause and constitutional liberty.

O'Kelly, Charlotte G. "Black Newspapers and the Black Protest Movement: Their Historical Relationship, 1827-1945." *Phylon* 43 (1982): 1-14. Content of black newpspapers and the response of the black press to the black protest movement were influenced by interrelationships of changes, events, issues, problems, and ideologies of particular eras. Beginning with the abolitonist movement, O'Kelly reviews the antebellum press through the Booker T. Washington era and post-world war years.

Perry, Patsy Brewington. "The Literary Content of *Frederick Douglass' Paper* through 1860." *CLA Journal* 17 (December 1973): 214-29. Douglass was "an arbiter of cultural and literary taste....[He] provided rich literary fare for his readers — ...he was, in fact, a champion of belles lettres." (214)

Potter, David M. "Horace Greeley and Peaceable Secession." *Journal of Southern History* 7 (1941): 145-59. Greeley's argument that the southern states should be allowed to secede peaceably was impractical and illusory. It "obscured the clarity of the true alternatives — compromise and war." His tone was like that of other prominent Republicans: "generally either blustering or vacillating, and, in either case, unrealistic."

Reed, Barbara Straus. "The Antebellum Jewish Press: Origins, Problems, Functions." *Journalism Monographs* 139 (June 1993). The Jewish press in antebellum America addressed issues facing American Jews and served a religious and cultural purpose for its audience.

Reilly, Tom. "A Spanish-Language Voice of Dissent in Antebellum New Orleans." *Louisiana History* 23 (1983): 325-39. In opposing American intervention in Cuba in 1851 and the Mexican War, *La Union* stood up against prevailing sentiment among the Anglo-American populace of New Orleans.

Rhodes, Jane. "Race, Money, Politics and the Antebellum Black Press." *Journalism History* 20 (1994): 95-106. Account of the *Provincial Freeman*, a Canadian newspaper published in the 1850s for fugitive slaves and abolitionists.

Robinson, Elwyn Burns. "The *Pennsylvanian*: Organ of Democracy." *Pennsylvania Magazine of History and Biography* 62 (1938): 350-60. In antebellum Philadelphia, the *Pennsylvanian* received patronage from Democratic politicians and supported Democratic, southern interests in slavery and secession.

Snorgrass, J. William. "The Black Press in the San Francisco Bay Area 1850-1900." *California History* 60 (Winter 1981-82): 306-17. The newspapers had two objectives: "to provide a platform from which blacks could express their views and combat racial prejudice and discrimination in the United States."

Stewart James B. "The Aims and Impact of Garrisonian Abolitionism, 1840-1860." *Civil War History* 15 (1969): 197-209. The radical "Garrisonian approach to northern politics was not nearly as unsophisticated and unproductive as historians have assumed."

Whitby, Gary L. "Horns of a Dilemma: The *Sun*, Abolition, and the 1833-34 New York Riots." *Journalism Quarterly* 67 (1990): 410-19. The penny *Sun* provided a popular forum for advocating abolition — even though its two co-editors disagreed on the speed at which abolition should proceed.

The Press and the Civil War

1861 - 1865

The Civil War represented the dawning of a new era in war reporting. In part, this was made possible by the economic condition of newspaper and magazine publishing, particularly in the North. The climbing circulations and increasing advertising revenues of newspapers and magazines in major metropolitan areas meant more money could be spent on reporting — and illustrating — the Civil War. Even in the South, where circulation and advertising revenues could not match northern figures, cooperative news enterprises allowed extensive war reporting at affordable prices.

The Civil War also represented the dawning of this new era for reasons quite apart from economics. Technological innovations made this the most immediate war that the general public had ever witnessed. The Civil War was one of the first in which reporters made widespread use of the telegraph. They could wire their newspapers with the most up-to-date information on the battles, and editors could quickly get that news to the reading public via "extras," or added editions of the newspaper. Those "extras" — with the latest information on a battle — were snatched up by readers with insatiable appetites for war news. The premium was on reporting and speed but not necessarily accuracy. The emphasis on speed sometimes caused shoddy reporting, incomplete dispatches, and unethical practices. In the Civil War, the reader's focus was increasingly shifted to the reporter, who had to get the story — and get it first.

Ever in search of a good story, reporters dodged bullets at battlefronts, endured the endless boredom of camp life, and sometimes invoked the ire of generals because of the stories they wrote. They also shared the risks of war. Some died from disease or wounds sustained in the line of duty. Others found that the rigors of war reporting had permanently damaged their health. War reporting was not done, however, just at the front. Reporters were also covering Richmond and Washington, D.C. — ever on the lookout for a good story.

Speed of reporting was not the only aspect of coverage that made the Civil War stand apart from earlier American wars. The Civil War also marked the beginnings of "visual" war reporting. Artists roamed the front, sketching battle scenes, leaders, and camp life. These drawings seemed to appear instantaneously in a new type of publication, the illustrated news weekly. The speed of publication was made possible by technical changes in the engraving process. Readers could follow the war in detailed maps that charted battles and troop movements, though not necessarily accurately. These maps were primarily in the newspapers and news weeklies of the North. These, in turn, posed a new set of national security questions, which were never satisfactorily answered during the war.

Photography was an even newer innovation that provided an additional dimension to war coverage. No other American war had been so extensively photographed. Although the photos could be reproduced in newspapers or magazines only as line drawings, the public flocked to studios or to traveling photographers to see and to buy photos of the war.

The Telegraph and the Civil War

The 1860s found the nation strung with telegraph lines. About 50,000 miles of wire crisscrossed the nation in a network that could assure virtually "instantaneous" transmission of news. No longer would the public have to wait weeks for the latest news on battles. Thanks to the telegraph, the reporter could get his story into the editor's hands within hours of the fighting (and, in some instances, while the battle still raged); and the editor, through the use of the "extra," could get the information quickly to readers. The telegraph used in conjunction with the "extra" meant that newspaper war coverage was fast. It could do nothing, however, to improve accuracy.

Using the telegraph for transmitting news came at a high price. In the North, the telegraphing of battle reports was one of the largest single expenditures a newspaper faced. The *New York Herald* and the *Chicago Times* faced especially high bills because they emphasized the use of the telegraph. The *Herald* paid $1,000, a

"Bull Run" Russell

William Howard Russell of the *London Times* was a celebrated reporter at the beginning of the Civil War. The engraving on the left, which appeared in *Harper's Weekly* in June 1861, showed Russell inspecting a cannon at a Confederate-held fort in Georgia. Russell's image changed, however, shortly after the first Battle of Bull Run in July. Despite the fact that he sympathized with the Union, he was disturbed about the conduct of Union soldiers at Bull Run. In writing about the battle, he called their behavior "scandalous" and "a disgrace." He endured much press criticism for the report, such as the engraving (right) that appeared in the *New York Illustrated News*. Critics gave him the nickname "Bull Run." By the next spring, he had returned to England.

substantial amount in the 1860s, for its telegraphed story of the capture of New Orleans. Nonetheless, such costs were prices editors were happy to pay — especially if they got the story first. As one northern reporter complained, editors were ever pushing the reporters to get and transmit their stories quickly. "To print first, however incorrect and incomplete intelligence," the reporter declared, "was the height of ambitions."[1]

In the South, the pressure to get the story quickly was just as real; but the problem of telegraph expense was relieved somewhat by a cooperative news venture called the Press Association of the Confederate States of America (PA), which negotiated lower telegraph rates for its reporters. After the Civil War began, southern newspapers lost the services of the New York Associated Press. Out of necessity, the Confederate dailies formed a cooperative news venture. Under agreements worked out by the PA, its reporters had access to military and commercial telegraph lines at reduced rates. Newspapers with correspondents in the field found that telegraph expenses were just another cost to be added to the skyrocketing costs of production. Later in the war, southern reporters could not even depend on telegraph transmission as lines rusted on the poles or burned before invading armies.

In the North and the South, the high telegraph rates as well as the uncertainty of transmission led to a certain amount of streamlining of reporter copy. Compared to the reporting of earlier nineteenth-century wars, Civil War stories seem concise and to the point. Compared to twentieth-century dispatches, the stories appear stilted and wordy. The dispatch reporting the surrender of Fort Sumter at the beginning of the war illustrated the writing style of the Civil War period:

> FORT SUMTER HAS SURRENDERED.
> The Confederate flag floats over its walls.
> None of the garrison or Confederate troops are hurt.
> Another correspondent says: —
> *Major Anderson has drawn down the stripes and stars, and displays a white flag, which has been answered from the city, and a boat is on the way to Sumter.*[2]

The telegraph was not the only means of transmission of news. Reporters continued to rely on the mails or special messengers, who rushed the dispatches via train, boat, or horseback to newspaper offices.

The emphasis on speed led, in many cases, to inaccurate, shoddy reporting. It also led to unnecessary national security problems. Reporters transmitted everything they learned; but editors, particularly in the North, seldom deleted the information that could aid the enemy. The concept of press responsibility in wartime had failed to keep up with the lightning speed of the telegraph.

Union Reporters

This emphasis on speed put the spotlight on the reporter. Basking in the light was a group of northern reporters who labeled themselves the "Bohemian Brigade." Although the term originally applied to that one group, it could be — and has been — applied to northern reporters in general. They lived the high-spirited, unsettled lives that the term "Bohemian" implies. Many northern reporters, at one time estimated at 500, often lived on the edge. They were a bit disreputable in the public's mind and reprehensi-

[1]Henry Villard, "Army Correspondence," *Nation*, 27 July 1865, 116.

[2]*New York Herald*, 14 April 1861, 1.

ble to many generals. Nonetheless, they went to the front, suffered diseases, braved danger, and faced death to report the war.

The names and numbers of all the "Bohemian Brigade" will probably never be known. Some floated into war reporting as "occasionals," paid at space rates, and then disappeared. Others were soldiers who contributed letters to newspapers or magazines back home. Perhaps only 200 were full-time, professional reporters, who spent extended periods covering the conflict.

Many were ill prepared in training, temperament, or skill to report this or any other war. Special qualities were needed to cover the conflict. One Union correspondent contended that reporting required the "gifts of omnipresence, omnivision and supernatural capacity of intellectual production." As the war continued, this correspondent found fewer reporters were equal to this task. By midwar, he observed, a new set of men, "an altogether inferior class of persons," had made their way into the ranks of army correspondents:

> Men turned up in the army as correspondents more fit to drive cattle than to write for newspapers. With a dull or slow perception, incapable of logical arrangement of facts, innocent of grammatical English, they were altogether out of place in the positions they tried to fill. Many added to these defects a lowness of habits and vulgarity of manners that rendered them unfit for association with the higher ranks of the army, and confined them in their intercourse to like-minded subalterns. They could not and did not gain the respect, and with it the confidence, of those high in command, with whom to be on good terms was a prime condition of professional success. They got to be looked upon, as a distinguished general expressed it, "as intolerable and unavoidable nuisances."[3]

Surprisingly little is known about all these "nuisance" war reporters. A number of them drifted into the war, covered a campaign or two, and then gave up the trade. Others assumed pseudonyms and thereby eluded identification. What is known about them is pieced together by contemporary accounts or by published biographical data on the best known of the reporters. Most of the northern reporters were young — in their twenties. Most had some journalism experience before the war. Of a group of fifty of the best known reporters, nearly half attended college, when few Americans could afford to do so, and more than half were urban born in a primarily rural country.[4]

The vast majority of the reporters were white males. Few minorities covered the war. One notable exception was Thomas Morris Chester, an African American who returned from Liberia to report for the *Philadelphia Press*. His best known reports emanated from captured Richmond, where he reported — sometimes from slave jails — on freedman reaction to President Lincoln. The few women covering the war reported primarily from Washington, D.C. Of these, the best known was Jane Grey Swisshelm of the *St. Cloud* (Minn.) *Democrat*, who supplemented her journalistic income with a clerkship in the Quartermaster General's office. Nonetheless, she critically reported on the quality of Union hospitals, carrying on a personal, bitter campaign to improve conditions. Mary Livermore also reported on hospital conditions. As an agent of the Northwestern branch of the Sanitary Commission (Chicago), she traveled to hospitals, ministering to soldiers and writing for her husband's paper, the *New Covenant*.

These three were not representative of the typical reporter. New York papers sent the greatest number of reporters to the front. The *Herald* alone dispatched more than sixty. Its tent and wagon became a familiar sight at the front. The *Tribune* and the *Times* never sent as many, yet their reporters would often beat the *Herald* with battle coverage. Other New York papers sent some reporters to cover the war but lacked the reporting presence of the other three dominant New York papers.

New York reporters were not the only ones at the front. Midwestern papers, particularly, came into their own during the Civil War. The *Cincinnati Gazette* may not have had many reporters in the field; but it had one of the best, Whitelaw Reid, who after the war became editor of the *New York Tribune*. The *Gazette's* competition, the *Cincinnati Commercial*, was one of the most popular papers with the men of the western armies. It came to be known as the "soldier's paper." In Chicago, the *Tribune* and the *Times* jockeyed for predominance in battlefield reporting. At one time, the *Tribune* fielded twenty-nine special correspondents. In spite of his pro-southern sentiments, Chicago *Times* editor Wilbur F. Storey emphasized telegraphic speed. He was alleged to have instructed a reporter: "Telegraph fully all news you can get, and when there is no news send rumors."[5]

However, no single newspaper, not even the mighty *New York Herald*, could match the number of correspondents dispatched by the New York Associated Press. Formed in 1848 as a cooperative venture of New York newspapers, the AP found itself at a real advantage during the Civil War since it had just negotiated special rates with both Union telegraph companies in 1860. Before the war, the AP had a network of reporters throughout the country. Their number increased once the hostilities started. AP coverage came, however, at a price. Newspapers outside of New York were forced to pay exorbitant rates for AP coverage and even more for "special reports." Western newspaper publishers, incensed with the high charges and the inconsistent quality of the New York AP reporting, organized their own cooperative in November 1862. It became known as the Western AP.

Wire and newspaper reporters found that their jobs meant long hours, stress, danger, and low pay. The typical pay for the reporter was just $15 to $35 a week, less than a typesetter made, plus expenses.

Despite the low pay, editors expected reporters to get the news first and get it any way they could. A circular to reporters from the

[3] Villard, "Army Correspondence," 115-6.

[4] Louis M. Starr, *Bohemian Brigade: Civil War Newspapermen in Action* (New York, 1954), 61.

[5] *Chicago Daily Journal*, 22 April 1924.

***New York Herald's* Field Headquarters**
The *Herald* sent more than sixty reporters into the field to cover the Civil War. Its tent and wagon became a familiar sight to soldiers at battlefronts. The *Herald's* editor-owner, James Gordon Bennett, believed that news had to be timely if readers were to be interested in it. To get timely news, a newspaper had to place reporters on the scene and employ the fastest means available to gather and transmit their stories.

New York Herald explains the pressure these journalists worked under: "In no instance, and under no circumstances, must you be beaten."[6] To this end, reporters were known to use any device, ethical or not. A reporter was not above bribery, fabricating eyewitness accounts, and hoaxes. More than one train engineer was bribed by a reporter heading for a telegraph office after a battle. *Herald* reporter William Shanks found that his bribe of a locomotive engineer not to let anyone else on the train did him little good. A reporter for a competing newspaper was already aboard. *New York Tribune* reporter Junius Browne missed the Battle of Pea Ridge, Arkansas, but that did not stop him from writing a stirring, albeit fictitious, report. A British newspaper reprinted the story as an example of the finest war reporting.[7]

This is not to say there was no good reporting or ethical reporters. Many journalists risked their lives or their health to cover the war and get their stories back to the newspaper office. *New York Herald* reporter Phineas Homans perished when he fell from the deck of a steamer in South Carolina. Another *Herald* reporter, George Alfred Townsend, nearly died of "Chickahominy Fever" following General McClellan in the Peninsula Campaign of 1862. Some reporters were captured by the opposing armies and imprisoned.[8]

Wherever troops fought, reporters usually followed. Reporter George Smalley followed them to bloody Antietam and tried everything to get his story back to the *New York Tribune*. That included riding through a hail of bullets to cover the battle and then traveling day and night to deliver his story to the *Tribune* offices. That story, considered one of the best of the war, was the first on the battle to hit the streets of New York City, the second morning after the fight.

Henry Villard had a different problem covering the Battle of Fredericksburg: he had to convince the *Tribune* to publish his story. He witnessed the terrible destruction at Fredericksburg, where there were more than 12,000 Union casualties, and rushed to Washington, D.C., to file his story. The government censor refused to clear it. Villard was not about to be stopped. He sent his graphic account of the battle by special messenger to New York — but the powerful *Tribune* delayed and eventually published only a watered down version. President Abraham Lincoln, however, wanted to know the full details of the fight and summoned Villard to the White House for his eyewitness account.[9]

These reports — and the best of Union reporting — conveyed not just the bare facts of the war but also a sense of the battle. In the last days of the war, George Alfred Townsend, by then with the *New York World*, shared some quiet moments with General Philip H. Sheridan's men after the Battle of Five Forks:

> I am sitting by Sheridan's camp-fire, on the spot he has just signalized by the most individual and complete victory of the war. All his veterans are around him, stooping by knots over the bright faggots, to talk together, or stretching upon the leaves of the forest, asleep, with the stains of powder yet upon their faces. There are dark masses of horses blackened into the grey background, and ambulances are creaking to and fro. I hear the

[6] Albert Richardson to Sydney Gay, 11 April 1863, reprinted in Starr, *Bohemian Brigade*, 233.

[7] Franc B. Wilkie, *Pen and Powder* (Boston, 1888), 126-9.

[8] George Alfred Townsend, *Rustics in Rebellion: A Yankee Reporter on the Road to Richmond 1861-1865* (Chapel Hill, 1950), 121-30. Junius Browne, *Four Years in Secessia: Adventures within and Beyond the Union Lines* (Hartford, 1865), 229-368.

[9] George W. Smalley, *Anglo-American Memories* (New York, 1911), 150-2. Henry Villard, *Memoirs of Henry Villard, Journalist and Financier, 1835-1900*, Vol. I, 1835-1862 (New York, reprint, 1969), 388-90.

> sobs and howls of the weary, and note, afar off, among the pines, moving lights of burying parties, which are tumbling the slain into the trenches. A cowed and shivering silence has succeeded the late burst of drums, trumpets, and cannon; the dead are at rest; the captives are quiet; the good cause has won again, and I shall try to tell you how.[10]

The good writing, the tenacious reporting, and the critical analysis of Townsend, Smalley, and Villard never eradicated the new national security problems that reporters and the military had to deal with. Reporters and editors of the North had much difficulty dealing with the concepts of press responsibility as it related to national security. Newspapers throughout the Union carried stories about troop movements, reinforcements, and numerical strength of units. Maps in newspapers, particularly the *Herald*, even pinpointed troop locations at battle sites. Confederate officers soon saw benefits of such coverage. General Robert E. Lee and other officers regularly read northern papers for military intelligence.

Yet, on the positive side (at least as far as military security was concerned), many of these reports were inaccurate. The emphasis on speed meant little time to check for accuracy. During the course of the Civil War, according to newspaper accounts, Richmond surrendered any number of times, General Lee resigned, and Confederate President Jefferson Davis died. Such news must have brought much joy to the reading public in the North, but it had no basis in fact. Sometimes, however, the reporters were not to blame. Union war officials liked to fiddle with the facts, and censors played with casualty figures in reporters' dispatches. At Harper's Ferry in 1862, more than 10,000 Union troops surrendered. A reporter's dispatch contained the correct figure, but censors lowered it to 6,000.[11]

Reporters for the Union
Among the hundreds of reporters who covered the Civil War at the front, a small number stood out for their exceptional work. Among the best from the New York City newspapers were (clockwise from top left) Henry Villard, *New York Herald* and *Tribune*; George Alfred Townsend, *New York Herald* and *World*; Charles Anderson Page, *New York Tribune*; and George Smalley, *New York Tribune*. Although many people believed that reporters led glamorous lives, even the best ones worked with difficult conditions and faced daily dangers. Townsend, for example, nearly died of camp fever while covering the Peninsula Campaign of 1862. Page described the reporter's life as one of "constant danger, without the soldier's glory." Villard described many reporters as "more fit to drive cattle than to write for newspapers."

CONFEDERATE REPORTERS

The Confederate reporters had some things in common with their northern brothers, but it was the differences that became the most obvious as the war wore on. Like their northern counterparts, Confederate reporters were just trying to fully cover a bloody, destructive war. For them, however, the war was much more immediate, fought near their homes and in the cities they knew so well.

The war's proximity meant chronic and serious shortages of almost everything needed in publishing — paper, type, ink. The Confederacy had only negligible paper production facilities and type foundries. Editors could, at least, "make do" with homemade ink. Even shoe blacking did the trick for some newspapers. The paper and type shortage was not as easily solved. By 1862, because of the paper shortage, editors had to reduce the number of pages, dimensions of the sheet, and frequency of publication. By the end of the war, some editors even tried innovative alternatives — printing on writing paper, brown paper, waste paper, even the backside of wallpaper. Type seldom could be replaced. It was merely used and used until it was barely legible.

Manpower shortages, likewise, plagued newspapers. One editor per newspaper was specifically exempt from the draft. In addition, the editor could request an exemption for every employee indispensable to the operation of the publication. The editors, apparently, took their responsibilities seriously and used their exemption requests sparingly. Some 75% of the Confederate printers saw military service. That meant that newspapers were chronically understaffed. As compared to the North, far fewer reporters — only about 100 — covered the war for newspapers and wire services in the South. Included in that number were many soldiers

10"The Battle of Five Forks," *New York World*, 4 April 1865, 1.
11*Boston Daily Journal*, 19 September 1862.

Keeping up with the News of War
This painting, titled "War Spirit at Home" and done by Lilly Martin Spencer in 1866, shows a family of a Union soldier reading a newspaper account of the northern victory at Vicksburg, Mississippi. Along with letters from relatives fighting in the Civil War, civilians got nearly all their information about the progress of the war from newspapers. Through their emphasis on battlefield reports and the use of such means as the telegraph, newspapers were able to provide news soon after it happened.

and officers serving as "volunteer" correspondents. The major dailies of the Confederacy did send reporters to the field. They were joined there by wire service reporters, including the southern AP, which no longer had relations with New York, and, in 1863 and after, the Press Association of the CSA.

Reporters faced serious difficulties communicating with their home offices as telegraph and mail service broke down. Even at the beginning of the war, the Confederacy was not as strongly linked via telegraph as the Union, nor was it as well supplied for repairs. Nonetheless, southern reporters made ample use of existing lines. The readers in the Confederacy, like the readers of the Union, searched futilely for up-to-date news on the war. As the war turned against the Confederacy, particularly in 1864 and after, reporters had to get their stories back via the most primitive communication network. The Confederate telegraph system was rotting on the poles. Wires rusted, making transmission of news uncertain at best. The telegraph system often fell victim to Union forces. The mail service did not offer a real alternative. With the destruction of railroads and roads, the mail service was crude and military transmissions always had priority. That meant battle reports might take days or weeks to reach the newspapers. In one instance, it took almost a month for a report from Richmond to reach Mobile.[12]

Coverage often became a matter of guesswork. Battles expected to be important or generals who were friendly drew the largest number of reporters, while unexpected battles or hostile generals attracted far fewer. That meant battles and sometimes whole campaigns went, at best, underreported. Few reporters were present to cover the opening of the 1862 campaign in the west or the fall of New Orleans. In spite of actions limiting press access at the first battle of Manassas and other campaigns, General Pierre G.T. Beauregard remained popular with newspapers because of his successful military record and his personality. In contrast, General Braxton Bragg would not abide journalists. As Bragg began the invasion of Kentucky in August and September 1862, he gave orders that no one who was not attached to the army — thus excluding reporters — could accompany him. Those who continued faced the prospect of arrest.

Politicians posed a whole different set of problems. The attitude of the Confederate Congress was perhaps best illustrated when it refused to allow the quartermaster's office to sell food to reporters who were covering the army for the Press Association of the CSA.

The PA had a large contingent of reporters in the field. It had been established in 1863 as a cooperative news enterprise of all the southern dailies east of the Mississippi and a number of triweeklies.[13] John S. Thrasher, a newsman from Galveston, Texas, oversaw a staff of about twenty reporters. Working under a specially negotiated agreement with the military, the reporters were under orders from Thrasher to keep their dispatches factual and objective — and ahead of all the special correspondents of the newspapers.

That proved difficult. Southern newspapers had some outstanding reporters. Peter W. Alexander and Felix Gregory deFontaine were among the best. Alexander illustrates how some southern reporters were able to service more than one master. Although the greatest portion of his work appeared in the *Savan-*

[12]*The War of the Rebellion, A Compilation of the Official Records of the Union and Confederate Armies*, Series iv, vol. 2 (Washington: Government Printing Office, 1900), 160-2, 731. J. Cutler Andrews, *The South Reports the Civil War* (Princeton, N.J., 1970), 43, 479-80.

[13]An initial meeting was held in 1862 to set up the PA, but it was poorly attended. The PA was finally formally established March 1, 1863, in Augusta, Georgia.

nah Republican, he also contributed to the *Atlanta Confederacy*, *Mobile Advertiser and Register*, *Richmond Dispatch*, and *Times* of London. A master writer, he was a lawyer at the outbreak of the war but left his practice in Georgia to resume his writing for the *Republican*, where he had served as editor-in-chief during the 1850s. DeFontaine, son of a French nobleman, was born in Boston. After working for several New York papers, he moved to Charleston just before the Civil War. Both reporters came to be known for their finely crafted and fairly accurate dispatches. While Alexander, "PWA" in many of his dispatches, remained in the field for much of the war, deFontaine, "Personne" to readers of the *Charleston Courier*, left much of his battlefield reporting behind in late 1863.

Like their northern counterparts, southern reporters were underpaid, overworked, and physically endangered. Confederate and Union reporters made about the same. The PA paid $25 to $30 a week plus travel and maintenance allowance, but wartime inflation in the South greatly reduced the buying power of these wages. The physical dangers of war coverage were compounded for the southern reporter. At least three Confederate reporters died during the course of the war — and perhaps more since not all southern war correspondents have been identified. Others suffered the diseases that ravaged the Confederate troops.

The work of southern reporters also suffered from many of the same flaws as that of the Union reporters. A number of southern dispatches revealed information that today might be considered national security material. Troop movements and plans of generals were published, a fact not lost on Union officers who read southern dailies for such intelligence.

Confederate generals were not, however, without their methods of control. Some, including Generals Joseph Johnston, Bragg, Beauregard, and Thomas "Stonewall" Jackson, kept reporters out of their camps during certain campaigns. That step, however, did not always stop journalists. One PA reporter eventually tracked down Bragg — after traveling twenty-six miles on foot. Sometimes, generals took extreme actions against reporters. Wallace Screws of the *Montgomery Advertiser* languished in jail ten days after writing a comment on movements of the Army of Mississippi. John Linebaugh of the *Memphis Appeal* was arrested for treason after his anti-Bragg reports and his dispatch that mentioned troop movements. For more than two weeks, he was shuttled from detention center to detention center until finally released. Perhaps the greatest punishment was that he missed covering the battle of Chickamauga.

There was more to the southern journalist's job than just reporting the news. He also had to carry on that job in a matter consistent with keeping up public morale, a role that gained greater importance as the war ground to a close.

In this regard, the women "correspondents" in the Confederacy had a role to play. The use of pseudonyms by women — and especially southern women — makes it difficult, however, to identify the women who wrote for publication. Constance Cary, a Richmond resident, identified herself as the author of the exchange between "Secessia" (a southern sympathizer in Baltimore) and "Refugitta" (a loyal Confederate woman in Richmond) that appeared in a southern newspaper. In this exchange, Cary wrote about the extravagance of the Union women compared to the frugality and patriotism of the women of the Confederacy.[14]

Cary's exchange illustrated how women — and men — correspondents could build up Confederate morale. War dispatches could not always be so uplifting. Just how candid should dispatches be during wartime? Southern reporters did write about the extensive amount of disease in camps, but few reported General John B. Hood's staggering casualties in Georgia in 1864. DeFontaine and others wrote of the terrible destruction at Shiloh. "While I write I am sitting on the floor of one of the corridors, with bodies of the living and the dead ranged on either side, and opposite as far as the eye can reach," deFontaine described the field hospital. "Groans fill the air, surgeons are busy at work by candlelight, a few women are ministering to the wants of the suffering, the atmosphere is fetid with the stench of wounds, and the rain is pouring down upon thousands who yet lie upon the bloody ground of Shiloh."[15] Yet few editors would admit in their newspapers the possibility of defeat. Even the disastrous loss of Atlanta was described by the PA thusly, "Whilst the fall of Atlanta is regretted, the people are not at all discouraged."[16]

In the South as in the North, the war had brought revolutionary changes to the press. News was assuming primary importance. The reporter was gaining stature. Even when communications began to break down within the South, both editors and the public continued to demand speed of transmissions and constant up-to-date information. Readers wanted the freshest information on the war. Too often these demands would go unfilled because of the destruction in the South. Yet, in spite of the breakdown in the telegraph and the mail systems, the contentious generals, the risks of death and disease, reporters did their best to cover the war. They were too often inaccurate and, according to certain generals, unmindful of national security matters — but, given the limits of their time, their training, their experience, and their numbers, the reporters of the South probably did the best that could be expected.

THE ARTISTS

The 1850s witnessed the phenomenal growth of a new type of publication, the illustrated news weekly. By the end of the decade, two weeklies in particular were locked in a battle for dominance, *Frank Leslie's Illustrated Newspaper* and *Harper's Weekly*, both published in New York City. *Leslie's* was the older of the two. Launched in 1855, it became the rock upon which the Leslie family of magazines grew. *Harper's* was launched in 1857 as a literary

[14]Mrs. Burton Harrison (Constance Cary), *Recollections Grave and Gray* (New York, 1911), 124-5.

[15]Personne, "Our Army Correspondence," *Charleston Daily Courier*, 15 April 1862, 1.

[16]PA report reprinted in Andrews, *The South Reports the Civil War*, 462-3.

Illustrated War News

Leslie's and *Harper's Weekly* led in the use of illustrations during the Civil War. The two-page spread above from *Harper's*, with each page measuring about the size of a tabloid newspaper today, was drawn by Winslow Homer and titled "War News Illustrated." It shows the work of artists and reporters in providing the news. The panels (clockwise from the lower left) are captioned "Our Special Artist," "For the Fleet," "News for the Staff," "Wounded," "From Richmond," and "The Newspaper Train."

and newsweekly that soon adopted the illustrated look. The Civil War only heated up the competition that already existed between these two.

Each of these publications — along with the *New York Illustrated News*, another weekly — dispatched artists to the front from the very beginning of the Civil War. *Leslie's* once claimed to have had eighty artists covering the war. It is unclear how many artists *Harper's* or the *Illustrated News* had in the field. Northern soldiers who sometimes doubled as "special artists" complicated estimates. The identifiable artists were young, as a group probably younger than the reporters. Financially, they were no better off. Many were paid by space rates: one amount for a simple illustration, more for a double-page spread, still more for the grandiose four-page illustrations that *Leslie's* sometimes published.

That money never compensated the artist for the life he lived. The artist maintained a nomadic existence — roaming from camp to camp, battle to battle, East to West, and back again. The rigors of the work and the travel took their toll. As one artist wired Leslie, "I am deranged about the stomach, ragged, unkempt and unshorn, and need the co-joined skill and services of the apothecary, the tailor and the barber...." But sheer exhaustion was not the only occupational hazard these artists faced. The same artist found that he was mistaken for an enemy scout as he searched for the best location to sketch. As artist Henri Lovie of *Leslie's* observed, he expected some risks — but not from the Union army. He explained he had "no objection to running reasonable risks from the enemy, but to be killed by mistake would be damnably unpleasant!"[17] Damnably unpleasant from a financial perspective was the risk of losing sketches at a battle. C.E.H. Bonwill of *Leslie's* lost his entire portfolio of the Red River campaign in Louisiana when General Nathaniel Banks' army was beaten back at Sabine Cross Roads in 1864.

Some artists went on to distinguished careers after the war. Political cartoonist Thomas Nast began his style of allegorical cartooning during the Civil War, in addition to his romanticized drawings of battle scenes. Indeed, his version of Santa Claus as a roly poly, bearded figure debuted during the Civil War — visiting Union troops — in *Harper's Weekly*.[18] Winslow Homer, also of *Harper's*, went on to a career in oils and watercolors. During the

[17] *Frank Leslie's Illustrated Newspaper*, Vol. 14, No. 66 (17 May 1862); *Cincinnati Daily Gazette*, 29 June 1861.

[18] *Harper's Weekly*, 20 September 1862; 18 July 1863; 3 September 1864; 12 November 1864; and 3 January 1863.

war, his specialty was camp life. The fame of other artists never reached the post-war stature of Nast or Homer, but their Civil War illustrations stand as lasting reminders of their talent. Their beautiful illustrations in news weeklies and other magazines provided romanticized representations of the war. Alfred Waud of *Harper's*, for example, was a favorite among the reporters in the field and was considered the consummate war artist. George A. Sala of the *London Daily Telegraph* described him as "blue-eyed, fair-bearded, strapping and stalwart, full of loud cheery laughs and comic songs, armed to the teeth, jack-booted, gauntleted, slouch-hatted."[19] There was another Waud in the field. Younger brother William earned his way at *Leslie's*. He made his debut as a war artist sketching Fort Sumter. At *Leslie's*, he was joined by a battery of other talented artists.

These individuals represented only one part of a three-way artistic partnership that produced the magnificent illustrations of the Civil War. The artists in the field, the artists back in New York, and the engravers worked as a team. The pictures that appeared in the illustrated news weeklies and magazines represented the product of that partnership — with all its strengths and weakness.

The artist in the field was the illustrator in a hurry. He drew everything from battles to leaders, from camp life to sieges. The pencil sketches, never meant to be published, were designed as reference points to be embellished in the editorial offices. Many battlefield drawings carried notes to allow other artists and engravers in New York to fill in the details. They transformed the rough drawings into single, double, and even four-page illustrations. These were powerful illustrations, many with meticulous details only hinted at in the original sketch.

The illustrations appeared surprisingly soon after the event pictured. The speed and the detail were possible because of a method Leslie is said to have brought from England. Before the introduction of this method, illustrations were the result of a long, tedious process. Each had to be drawn on a block, then engravers cut away wood from the artist's line, then and only then could the relief block be used for printing. The process could take days, weeks, even months.

Readers during the Civil War did not have to wait that long. With the engraving process brought over from England, the rough battle drawing was transferred to the wood block. The master engraver would then cut the main outlines and indicate the engraving technique to be used. The block was then separated into different pieces to be engraved by a number of craftsmen. When all the parts were completed, they were bolted back together. A master engraver provided the finishing touches, and the illustration was ready to be printed. A process that formerly had sometimes taken weeks had been reduced to hours.

The speed of production had failed, however, to remedy all the problems associated with these illustrations. They suffered from two of the flaws associated with the reporting of the period: inaccuracy and a lack of concern for national security. The inaccu-

[19]Quoted in Starr, *Bohemian Brigade*, 254.

Alfred Waud, Artist
Soldiers considered Alfred Waud of *Harper's* the complete artist. Union army general George Meade sometimes used his talents as an observer. At his request, Waud once scaled a tree to draw enemy lines. "Rebel sharpshooters," he reported, "kept up a fire at me the whole time." Like other artists, he also faced the hardships of the battlefield and frequently was confined to bed because of illness.

racies stemmed from honest mistakes to deliberate misrepresentation. Because artists traveled the front, they ran the risk of missing an important battle or skirmish. Accordingly, a number of "on-the-spot" illustrations were actually created by artists many miles away who had never witnessed the action. Other inaccuracies resulted from obstructed views at the battle site, the enthusiasm of the artist in the field or back in New York, or the ignorance of the artist.

The illustrations sometimes posed national security problems. The problems emanated not from the romantic and highly imaginative battle scenes but from the illustrations of military fortifications, diagrams of troop movements, and maps.[20]

PHOTOGRAPHERS

The Civil War was the first American war extensively captured on film.[21] The daguerreotype had been introduced to America in 1839 by Samuel F. B. Morse, inventor of the telegraph. The Americans and British tinkered with the invention, eventually per-

[20]As examples, see "War Maps and Diagrams," *New York Herald*, 27 July 1861, 1-4; and "The National Battle Ground," *New York Herald*, 12 September 1861, 1.

[21]It was neither the first war nor the first American war photographed. The Crimean War had been extensively photographed for primarily a European audience, and war scenes of the Mexican War had been taken by unidentified daguerreotypists. James D. Horan, *Mathew Brady, Historian with a Camera* (New York, 1955), 40.

The Black Wagons
The so-called "What-is-it wagon" that Mathew Brady's field photographers used during the Civil War was a combination portable darkroom and storage unit. Soldiers dreaded seeing the black, hooded wagon rumble into camp because it too often meant a battle was planned. The images the field photographers captured were the most starkly real of the war, often showing bodies of soldiers just killed.

fecting the "wet-plate" process that was used in the mobile darkrooms at battle sites of the Civil War.

An army of photographers shot the war. The most famous was Mathew Brady, a successful antebellum photographer with studios in New York and Washington, D.C. It was Brady who photographed Bull Run and came up with the idea of putting together a photographic history of the war. For that, however, he needed War Department approval. Secretary of War Edwin M. Stanton approved the idea; but, aside from offering the services of Allan Pinkerton and the Secret Service for protection, he offered no support for Brady's scheme.

Brady would have to underwrite the project, hire the men, and equip the portable darkrooms, the so-called "what-is-it wagons." This was an expensive venture. Brady invested some $100,000 in salaries, equipment, and miscellaneous expenses of his crew of at least twelve photographers. He was banking on a return for his money. He sold his pictures to the general public. Newspapers and magazines purchased some of his pictures but could not reproduce them as photographs for technical reasons. They had to be converted to line drawings before printing, and the conversion process did not always do justice to the photograph.

Brady's photographers followed the troops in black wagons that stored the glass plates used in photography and doubled as darkrooms. They traveled to various theaters of war, waiting for battles or just chronicling camp life. Their photographs captured the horrors of the war. They stood in stark contrast to the romanticized illustrations of the period. The photographs showed bloated corpses on the battlefield and the tormented wounded in the hospitals, the heroes and the nameless, the desolation of the countryside and the destruction of once great cities, the living skeletons of a Confederate prison and the hanging of the assassins of a president. It was as Oliver Wendell Holmes wrote when he saw some Brady war prints: "It is so nearly like visiting the battlefields to look over these views that all the emotions excited by the actual sight of the stained and sordid scene, strewed with rags and wrecks, came back to us, and we buried them in the recesses of our cabinet as we would have buried the mutilated remains of the dead they too vividly represented."[22]

It is difficult to gauge precisely how many of the photos were actually taken by Brady. The Brady name was attached to all photos taken under his sponsorship. That led to tension among certain "Brady" photographers. Several of his best photographers eventually left his employ. Alexander Gardner and Timothy O'Sullivan continued to photograph the war but under their own names. Brady and his photographers were not the only ones in the battlefield. Brady was soon facing competition from talented former employees, professional photographers who had been competitors before the war, and War Department cameramen.

The Confederacy had its own war photographers. George S. Cook of Charleston was the best known. He had been in charge of Brady's New York studio before he struck out on his own. It was his ambrotype of Fort Sumter commander Major Robert Anderson that became so popular in the North early in the war. Andrew B. Lytle of Baton Rouge photographed the war for three years and through several campaigns from a Confederate perspective. He assumed another role — camera spy, perhaps the first in U.S. his-

[22]Quoted in ibid., 33.

The Prayer of Twenty Millions

HORACE GREELEY. "Mr. President, '*do you propose to ignore, disregard, and in effect defy*' these twenty millions here present, whom I command?"

Horace Greeley's opponents lampooned him mercilessly when he wrote an open letter to President Lincoln in 1862 urging him to proclaim southern slaves free. This caricature from *Harper's Weekly* ridiculed Greeley for being so presumptuous to imply that he could speak for the citizens of the North. In his open letter to the President, which Greeley titled "The Prayer of Twenty Millions," he had begun,

"To ABRAHAM LINCOLN, president of the United States:

"DEAR SIR: I do not intrude to tell you — for you must know already — that a great proportion of those who triumphed in your election, and of all who desire unqualified suppression of the Rebellion now desolating our country, are sorely disappointed and deeply pained by the policy you seem to be pursuing with regard to the slaves of the Rebels. I write only to set succinctly and unmistakably before you what we require, what we think we have a right to expect, and of what we complain...."

Greeley and Lincoln Spar over Freeing Southern Slaves

By the beginning of the Civil War, Horace Greeley was clearly America's best known newspaper figure. His weekly edition of the *New York Tribune*, some said, was the country's first national newspaper. His was the leading voice on many of the most important issues of the day.

Consistently an outspoken opponent of slavery, Greeley had supported the candidacy of Abraham Lincoln in 1860 but had grown impatient with him over his seeming reluctance as president to issue an emancipation proclamation.

So on August 20, 1862, with the war not yet going well for the Union, Greeley decided to give Lincoln a personal editorial nudge. He published an open letter to the president headlined "The Prayer of Twenty Millions." Abolitionists cheered him, but critics called him arrogant and intemperate for the assumption that he spoke for everyone in the North.

"What an immense majority of the loyal millions of your countrymen require of you is a frank, declared, unqualified, ungrudging execution of the laws of the land," Greeley wrote. He urged Lincoln to declare slaves who came within Union lines immediately free and to insist that military commanders enforce and obey that law.

Perhaps unwittingly, Greeley provided Lincoln with the very opportunity he needed to explain to the country his exact stand on the issue of slavery.

The president's answer came three days later, not in a private letter to Greeley, but in the pages of the old, respected *National Intelligencer*. It had not supported Lincoln and had been outspoken in favoring a system of slavery for economic reasons. Some suggested Lincoln chose the *Intelligencer* just to needle Greeley.

If Greeley's "Prayer" was his most famous editorial, the response by Lincoln is often touted as one of his most elegant messages. "My paramount object in this struggle is to save the Union, and is not either to save or to destroy slavery," he wrote. In a concluding statement, he explained, "I have here stated my purposes according to my view of official duty; and I intend no modification of my oft-expressed personal wish that all men everywhere could be free."

The *National Intelligencer*, celebrating its good fortune to have been the recipient of the president's letter, took a swipe at the presumption of Greeley for his editorial. Other papers suggested he needed a lesson in etiquette. Greeley published an apology. "Nothing was farther from my thought," he explained, "than to impeach in any manner the sincerity or the intensity of your devotion to the saving of the Union."

When Lincoln made public his preliminary announcement of the Emancipation Proclamation on September 22, just a month after the "Prayer" appeared in the *Tribune*, Greeley's loyal readers were quick to praise the editor, to credit him with hurrying Lincoln along on the freedom issue. In their eyes, he still had plenty of editorial clout left.

Randall L. Murray
California Polytechnic State University

JIM CROW JUMPING ABOUT SO.

"On to Richmond! The Rebel Congress must not be allowed to meet there in July."—(*See N. Y. Tribune, May and June*, 1861.) | "Let us bow to our destiny, and make the best allowable peace." (*See N. Y. Tribune, Jan.*, 1863.)

The Changeable Greeley
Horace Greeley's critics lampooned him for the unpredictability of the positions he took toward executing the Civil War. In this cartoon, the panel on the left refers to the *New York Tribune's* aggressive recommendation that the Union army should attack Richmond at the beginning of the war, resulting in the northern defeat at Bull Run. The panel on the right ridicules Greeley's contrasting contention in 1863 that the Union should let the South secede in peace.

tory — photographing Union troops and armaments and sending his pictures to Confederate headquarters.

Lytle, Cook, and the other southern photographers faced special problems. Lacking an extensive Confederate supply of cameras, equipment or materials, they had to rely on the same northern photographic house that supplied Brady and other Union photographers. Supply was irregular because materials had to be smuggled through Union lines.

For Americans, photography meant that the Civil War — with all its horror, death, and destruction — became the stark reality that no news story or illustration could ever convey. Even today, the photographs stand as powerful reminders of the destruction of war. The Civil War photography pointed to a new direction in wartime reporting. Every future American war would be captured on film. The photographer had won his place in wartime journalism.

Censorship

Censorship is the official control of editorial comment and news content before they appear in a publication. Typically, in the United States, censorship has been done in wartime and, ideally, only to limit the amount of national security material — especially military information — to the enemy. Conventionally, censorship is interpreted as a duty of the military, with accompanying memos, directives, and guidelines issued to the press. In the Civil War, censorship was not as structured, nor was it merely a function of top military leadership. It was also carried on by communities through "mob censorship" or by invading armies.

Before the war, a number of pro-Union editors in the South were intimidated. A.B. Norton of the *Fort Worth* (Tex.) *Chief* was threatened with hanging. He took the hint, sold his paper, and moved on. Mobs destroyed the offices of the *Galveston* (Tex.) *Union*, a name that belied the paper's editorial position.

Once the war commenced, little mob action was required. Most southern editors came to support secession and the war soon after Fort Sumter. The few laggards were kept in line via economic harassment or threats. Economic boycotts drove several Unionist papers in the Confederacy out of business.

Mob intimidation played its role in the North as well. Pro-South editor Wilbur Storey of the *Chicago Times* started to transform his editorial rooms into a mini-armory, with loaded muskets and hand grenades ever available in case readers decided to carry out their threats. He rarely left the office unarmed, the wise thing to do in light of the many threats upon his life. Proper Union sentiment was not even enough to protect newspapers from mobs. During the New York draft riots of 1863, one of the targets of mob attention was the *Tribune*, which had been a leading proponent of the war.[23]

Hostile military armies also effectively censored newspapers and newsmen. When Union troops took Confederate cities, they sometimes also took control of the newspapers, as they did, for example, with the *Picayune* after the capture of New Orleans. Union occupation did not always silence a newspaper's voice. When Memphis fell to the Yankees, the *Appeal* joined the growing numbers of the southern "refugee" press, newspapers that moved rather than yield to Union control. At various times, the *Appeal* was published in Mississippi, Georgia (including Atlanta), and Alabama, trying to stay one step ahead of northern forces.

Obviously, with so many cities falling to Union forces, the

[23]*New York Times*, 28 October 1884, 5. George Smalley, *Anglo-American Memories* (New York, 1911), 161-3.

Giving Aid and Comfort to Rebels
Critics accused some northern newspapers, in their competition to provide war news, of providing military information to the South in the process. This cartoon caricatures the *New York Herald, Tribune,* and *Times.* The caption reads: "*Herald* – Posters of the Sea and Land, we three travel hand in hand. *Tribune* – Of each secret expedition, letting out the sealed commission. *Times* – So that nothing private here may vex the rebel privateer. *All* – Double, double. Nay, we treble aid and comfort to the rebel!"

northern army had more opportunities to exercise censorship than the southern troops. There were times, however, when the Confederate army captured and imprisoned northern newsmen. Typically, captured correspondents were quickly turned over for return to the North. That was not the case in the instances of Junius Browne and Albert D. Richardson of the *New York Tribune*. Greeley's *Tribune*, with its longtime abolitionist/reform editorial stances, represented a particularly odious publication in the Confederacy. For twenty months, Browne and Richardson languished in Confederate prisons, including the notorious Libby at Richmond. Not even the efforts of President Lincoln could secure their release. Finally, the reporters escaped and made their way back home. The Confederacy had, however, accomplished its mission. For almost two years, these two had been prevented from filing any dispatches.

On a day-to-day basis, it was the military that assumed the mantel of censor. The censorship systems of the Union and the Confederacy were designed to keep military information out of the hands of the enemy. Both armies believed that troop movements, armaments, military plans, strengths, and weaknesses were all legitimate topics to exclude from newspapers. Thus, such information was to be deleted from telegraph dispatches back to the home newspaper office. However, as the Confederate and Union military soon discovered, just because censorship provisions might be in place, they were not necessarily effective. The military on both sides found that reporters could — if they were resourceful enough — evade the most structured censorship system. In the North, particularly, reporters soon excelled in the fine art of foiling the army censor.

The northern army censor found that his best weapon of control was the telegraph. The telegraph office represented one central location for monitoring reporter dispatches. From the very beginning, the War Department attempted to capitalize upon that link. The earliest battles of the war were reported under an agreement between General Winfield Scott, then the Supreme Commander of Union forces, and the press. No reports on army movements, mutinies, or anticipated military activity were to be transmitted. Reports of battles in progress were to be cleared by the army censor. Union losses at Bull Run prompted Scott to rethink his policies. He slapped a strict censorship on the telegraph. No word of the defeat went over the wire until long after the battle.

It soon became apparent that some sort of formalized censorship system had to be imposed on reporters. In August 1861, Simon Cameron, then Secretary of War, ordered that no information about army movements, "without the authority and sanction of the major general in command," be telegraphed. Violators could be executed. Unfortunately, censorship authority was put in the hands of the State Department, which exercised its power unevenly. Early the next year, the War Department took over and substantially beefed up monitoring and threats. Newspapers that published "unauthorized" military news, news not cleared by the army censor, were warned that they could lose the use of the telegraph.[24]

Even that threat, however, did little to stem the flow of military information. If a censor refused to transmit — or substantially eliminated information before transmission — the reporter could simply send his dispatch via special messenger or hand deliver it himself. Then editors sometimes published these reports without considering security issues. However, the reporter in the field sometimes paid a heavy price. Thomas W. Knox of the *New York Herald* sent reports back to New York with the estimated size of General William T. Sherman's army just before Vicksburg, a clear breach of established guidelines. Knox was arrested on three counts: giving intelligence to the enemy, directly or indirectly; being a spy; and disobeying orders. If found guilty, Knox could have been executed; Sherman threatened to hang him. Instead,

[24]*The War of the Rebellion*, Series 3, Vol. 1 (Washington: Government Printing Office, 1899), 324, 390, 454-5, 394, 899.

Attack on the *Tribune*
One of the targets of the New York draft riots was the *Tribune* offices. The mob shattered windows, but the presses escaped damage. The police countercharge saved the paper from more extensive harm.

Knox was found guilty of only the last charge and was expelled from the Army of Tennessee and ordered never to return.

Another method of control was suspension. In the North, there was a range of opinion on the war: from the pro-southern (Copperhead) papers to the rabidly pro-Union dailies. It was the Copperhead papers that posed the greatest problems. In a number of instances, Union generals found that the best way to control a Copperhead newspaper was with a chain and a lock on the door. General Ambrose Burnside shut down the *Chicago Times* for two days for its continuing "disloyal and incendiary sentiments."[25] No such suppressions were needed in the South. Soon after the war began, community pressure had effectively silenced pro-Union papers. Thus, suspensions of newspapers by the Confederate military were not required.

Southern reporters, however, had to live with a set of censorship guidelines. The guidelines were enacted almost from the beginning of the Confederate government itself. In May 1861, the Provisional Congress of the Confederate States of America passed a bill giving President Jefferson Davis power to set up censorship of the telegraph. He did so quickly. Thus, from almost the first battle of the war, the Confederacy already had a telegraph censorship system in place. The next month, the government set up official restrictions on the mail. Postmasters could open and censor mail, although they seldom monitored reporter dispatches.

By July, Secretary of War Leroy Walker outlined for the press the specific areas that posed national security problems. Reporters, he wrote in an open letter to all Confederate journalists, should avoid providing information that could hurt the southern cause. That included information on armaments, troop movements, fortifications, or weaknesses. This letter set the pace for the voluntary censorship that marked Confederate reporting through much of the war. Reporters sometimes obtained and transmitted information that did not specifically follow the guidelines. However, editors exercised considerable restraint in publishing such information. For example, reporters for both the *Richmond Dispatch* and *Richmond Enquirer* had transmitted dispatches that included details on General Jubal Early's plan to invade Maryland in 1864, but neither paper published the information. Only two reporters accompanied Early in his thrust north, and neither could communicate with his paper until the general returned to Virginia.

Another way Confederate generals controlled the press was by excluding reporters from their campaigns. Many times southern reporters had to rely on northern newspapers to keep up with the news of what the Confederate troops were doing.

This does not mean that the southern press never published anything that was of aid to the enemy. A good deal appeared that could be of use, and northern officers regularly monitored southern papers. In many instances, however, Union officers were misled by what they read, for the Confederate papers published inflated estimates of enemy casualties and underestimated the number of southern dead and wounded.[26]

The Civil War represented one of the first U.S. wars in which

[25]Ibid., Series 1, Vol. 17, Part 2 (Washington: Government Printing Office, 1887), 889-93; and Vol. 23, Part 2, 381.

[26]See *New York Times*, 28 October 1884, 5.

large-scale censorship had to be imposed. The generals, the politicians, the editors, and the reporters had no real precedents to follow. In general, censorship was ineffective. In spite of the threats, the trials, and the belligerent generals, reporters could and did avoid the army network of censorship. Northern editors seemed less likely to exercise restraint in publishing what today might be considered information that could give aid to the enemy than the Confederate editors. This would not be the last system of wartime censorship. Americans have tinkered with their wartime censorship systems ever since. The Civil War was just one experiment.

AFTERMATH

American journalism was never quite the same after the Civil War. It could not be. The war had brought too many changes.

The reporting, in spite of all its limitations, helped establish standards for immediacy in wartime coverage that continue even today. Reporters used every possible technological innovation to get their stories back to their editors quickly. Certainly, the immediacy of Civil War journalism never equalled the "immediacy" of television coverage of the Persian Gulf War in our time. Yet, by nineteenth-century standards, the Civil War had its own "instantaneous" quality that earlier wars had never captured.

The writing was, likewise, changing. While by twentieth-century standards, it appears stilted and flowery, nonetheless the writing was much improved over the reporting of earlier wars. The Civil War set high standards for powerful news reporting, stories that not only told what happened but captured a sense of the battle, the personality of the generals, and the trauma of the event. Alexander, deFontaine, Chester, Townsend, Villard, Smalley, and many others showed later reporters what war reporting could be. It was not a lesson lost on the generations that followed. The best reporting would detail not only what happened but captured a "sense" of the war.

The Civil War also transformed how the public viewed war. No longer would wartime coverage be a matter of words. Photography, especially, would become an accepted part of wartime journalism. It had won its place on the battlefields of Manassas, Antietam, and Gettysburg.

Finally, as a result of the Civil War, the *expectations* of the reading public had changed. Readers would no longer be satisfied with dispatches printed weeks or even months after a battle. The American public had come to demand immediate war information.

The Civil War posed a new set of national security questions that today's reporters, editors, broadcasters, government officials, and military officers still have not definitively answered. The balance between the people's right to know and the protection of military information has never been successfully struck.

RECOMMENDED READINGS

BOOKS

Andrews, J. Cutler. *The North Reports the Civil War*. Pittsburgh, 1955. This is the most thoroughly documented, authoritative history on Civil War reporting of the several books that have been published. Despite various obstacles, reporters performed well.

Andrews, J. Cutler. *The South Reports the Civil War*. Princeton, N.J., 1970. Well documented narrative of southern reporters in their attempts to cover the battles of the war.

Blackett, R.J.M., ed. *Thomas Morris Chester, Black Civil War Correspondent*. Baton Rouge, 1989. A short narrative biography tells Chester's story. Part II includes 277 pages of his war dispatches chronicling the activities of black troops.

Carlebach, Michael J. *The Origins of Photojournalism in the America*. Washington, D.C., 1992. Photojournalism history from the age of daguerreotypes to the digital era.

Clinton, Catherine, and Ninal Silber, eds. *Divided Houses: Gender and the Civil War*. New York, 1992. Drew Gilpin Faust's essay, "Altars of Sacrifice: Confederate Women and the Narratives of War," points out the importance of women in sustaining Confederate morale.

Cornebise, Alfred Emile. *Ranks and Columns: Armed Forces Newspapers in American Wars*. Westport, Conn., 1993. Both Union and Confederate troops had newspapers. This account notes the troop and hospital papers in the Civil War as well as subsequent wars.

Coulter, Ellis M. *William G. Brownlow: Fighting Parson of the Southern Highlands*. Chapel Hill, N.C., 1937. Well researched and interestingly written biography of the zealous Tennessee editor, preacher, and politician. He lived a fiery life, first as a Methodist attacking Baptists and Presbyterians, then as an ardent abolitionist and anti-secessionist.

Crozier, Emmet. *Yankee Reporters, 1861-1865*. New York, 1956. A look at the activities of northern reporters during the Civil War.

Fahrney, Ralph Ray. *Horace Greeley and the Tribune in the Civil War*. Cedar Rapids, Iowa, 1936. Greeley and the *Tribune* exercised a powerful influence, although the editor was inconsistent, sometimes even enigmatic, in his stands.

Harper, Robert S. *Lincoln and the Press*. New York, 1951. Lincoln was tolerant and patient with the press despite the difficulties and complexities of the Civil War, many of which the press created, with the Copperhead newspapers especially troublesome.

Horan, James D. *Matthew Brady: Historian with a Camera*. New York, 1955. Collection of 500 photographs by Brady, who believed that photographs should serve as an historical record, thus making him a reporter of first rank.

Horner, Harlan H. *Lincoln and Greeley*. Urbana, Ill., 1953. Study of the relationship between two men who played critical roles in America from 1860 to 1865. Lincoln and Greeley had similar backgrounds and attitudes, but Lincoln was more compassionate and Greeley egotistical.

Marszalek, John F. *Sherman's Other War: The General and the Civil War Press*. Memphis, 1981. Despite Sherman's anti-press attitude, he and journalists, with little precedent to follow, developed a relatively open working relationship.

Reynolds, Donald E. *Editors Make War*. Nashville, Tenn., 1966. An examination of the role southern newspapers played in bringing on the Civil War.

Smart, James G., ed. *A Radical View: The "Agate" Dispatches of Whitelaw Reid, 1861-1865*, 2 vols. Memphis, 1978. Collection of the Radical-Republican Civil War correspondent's articles for the *Cincinnati Gazette*.

Starr, Louis M. *Bohemian Brigade: Civil War Newspapermen in Action*. New York, 1954. Entertaining story of how colorful reporters from the North, especially New York City, contributed to the development of journalism through their reporting of the Civil War.

Venet, Wendy Hamand. *Neither Ballots nor Bullets: Women Abolitionists and the Civil War*. Charlottesville, Va., 1991. This important account highlights women abolitionists who continued their work on newspapers and magazines during the Civil War.

Weisberger, Bernard A. *Reporters for the Union*. Boston, 1953. During the Civil War, the status of reporters advanced from that of inferior newspaper staff members to that of prominent public figures and professional journalists.

ARTICLES

Abbott, Richard H. "Civil War Origins of the Southern Republican Press." *Civil War History* 43 (March 1997): 38-58. Union military support in the occupied South encouraged papers supporting the Union cause and the Republican party, serving as the foundation for that party's press in the region.

Beasley, Maurine. "Pens and Petticoats: Early Women Washington Correspondents." *Journalism History* 1 (1974): 112-5, 136. "[W]omen journalists established national reputations....Their careers illustrated that the Civil War social climate permitted women a foothold in the masculine field of Washington reporting in spite of cultural conflicts between their roles as women and as journalists."

Cappon, Lester J. "The Yankee Press in Virginia, 1861-1865." *William and Mary Quarterly* 15 (January 1935): 81-8. Union troops published as many as a dozen newspapers in occupied Virginia territory. "Most of these crudely printed sheets served as a means of relaxation for the soldier...[but to] the civilian they were a source of irritation."

Endres, Kathleen L. "The Women's Press in the Civil War: A Portrait of Patriotism, Propaganda, and Prodding." *Civil War History* 30 (March 1984): 31-53. Most women's publications during the Civil War period can be classified as either "reform" or "mainstream." Although the two types had various differences, editors agreed "that the women's press had a responsibility to build up the spirits of their readers."

Goldsmith, Adolph O. "Reporting the Civil War: Union Army Press Relations." *Journalism Quarterly* 33 (1956): 478-87. "Restrictions on handling of war news...were extremely loose as a general rule, but unnecessarily tight in specific instances. The haphazardness of controls resulted in more damage to the war effort than if there had been no controls at all."

Guback, Thomas H. "General Sherman's War on the Press." *Journalism Quarterly* 36 (1959): 171-6. "Most generals had trouble with the press, but Sherman "was plagued mercilessly by the press during the entire war." He "hated" the press because he felt it treated him unfairly.

Hughes, Thomas Andrew. "The Civil War Press: Promoter of Unity or Neutral Reporter?" *American Journalism* 6 (1989): 181-201. Analyzes the various perspectives historians have used in explaining the press.

Jensen, Oliver. "War Correspondent: 1864. The Sketchbooks of James E. Taylor." *American Heritage* 31 (August/September 1980): 48-64. Taylor, an artist, covered the Civil War for *Frank Leslie's Illustrated Newspaper*, providing the combination of words and pictures that readers craved about the battlefront.

Kielbowicz, Richard B. "The Telegraph, Censorship and Politics at the Outset of the Civil War." *Civil War History* 40 (June 1994): 95-119. The telegraph made censorship necessary and feasible.

Logue, Cal M., Eugene F. Miller, and Christopher J. Schroll. "The Press Under Pressure: How Georgia's Newspapers Responded to Civil War Constraints." *American Journalism* 15 (Winter 1998): 13-34. Georgia newspapers faced three wartime problems — problems maintaining profitability, problems of newsgathering and reporting because of disrupted communication channels, and problems with censorship.

Malone, Henry Thompson. "The Charleston *Daily Courier*: Standard Bearer of the Confederacy." *Journalism Quarterly* 29 (1952): 307-15. The *Courier* remained a consistent and enthusiastic supporter of Jefferson Davis and of the Confederacy throughout the Civil War.

Marten, James. "For the Good, the True and the Beautiful: Northern Children's Magazines and the Civil War." *Civil War History* 41 (March 1995): 57-75. Children's magazines in the North encouraged readers to get involved with the war effort by inspiring them with tales of bravery and patriotism and explaining the history and causes of the war.

Mindich, David T. Z. "Edwin M. Stanton, The Inverted Pyramid, and Information Control." *Journalism Monographs* 140 (August 1993). Among the earliest examples of the "inverted pyramid" structure of news stories were the news releases written by Stanton, Lincoln's Secretary of War.

Nye, Russel B. "Freedom of the Press and the Antislavery Controversy." *Journalism Quarterly* 22 (1945): 1-11. Southern states abridged freedom with the argument that freedom did not allow the distribution of obnoxious doctrines. Northern legislatures refused to abridge press freedom, and abolitionists quickly recognized the relationship between their cause and constitutional liberty.

Randall, James G. "The Newspaper Problem in its Bearing upon Military Secrecy During the Civil War." *American Historical Review* 23 (January 1918): 303-23. Northern newspapers "undoubtedly did the national cause serious injur...[but] actual governmental interference with the freedom of the press was comparatively slight."

Risley, Ford. "Peter W. Alexander: Confederate Chronicler and Conscience." *American Journalism* 15 (Winter 1998): 35-50. Alexander was one of the few southern journalists providing consistent, reliable reporting throughout the war and helped define the professional role of correspondents covering subsequent wars.

Sears, Stephen W. "The First News Blackout." *American Heritage* (June-July 1985): 24-31. The compromises during the Civil War conflict between a free press and the need for military security "may not have provided all the answers, but they had raised all the modern questions."

Skidmore, Joe. "The Copperhead Press and Civil War." *Journalism Quarterly* 16 (1939): 345-55. The Copperhead press in the North was "vigorous and fearless in the face of official suppressions and unofficial mobbings and lootings."

Tenney, Craig. "To Suppress or Not to Suppress: Abraham Lincoln and the Chicago *Times*." *Civil War History* 27 (September 1981): 248-59. Even though Lincoln rescinded Gen. Ambrose E. Burnside's order to suppress the *Times*, he did so out of political motives rather than for concern for First Amendment principles.

Thorp, Robert K. "The Copperhead Days of Dennis Mahony." *Journalism Quarterly* 43 (1966): 680-6, 696. "A Democratic Iowa editor,... Mahony was a persistent critic of Abraham Lincoln and the Union War effort. But his Copperhead stand was in reality a conservative's attempt to hold back change."

Wilson, Quintus C. "The Confederate Press Association: A Pioneer News Agency." *Journalism Quarterly* 26 (1949): 160-6. Narrative of the founding and operation of the CPA. One of the major problems it faced was military censorship.

10

The Frontier Press

1800 - 1900

Frontier editors at their hand-operated presses exerted an influence beyond the dusty towns in which they published. Working within a national tradition that had promoted western expansion and development, the press played a significant role in the settlement of the American West. Colorful editors and their Wild West news stories are among the legends — and provide some of the myths — of the frontier.

After the American Revolution, as white settlers moved west across the North American continent, agricultural development of the land from a wilderness to an agrarian garden was romanticized as basic to the creation of a new nation. In the late eighteenth century, Thomas Jefferson said the nation's moral future depended upon its farmers and the countryside. "Those who labor in the earth are the chosen people of God," he wrote. Farmers and the land would bear many fruits for the new nation while "the mobs of great cities add just so much to the support of pure government, as sores do the strength of the human body." In his first inaugural address in 1801, President Jefferson applied his view to westward expansion, saying the continent had "room enough for our descendants to the hundredth and thousandth generation."[1] He later implemented his vision with the purchase of the Louisiana Territory.

Pioneers craved news of the world they had left behind. They often congregated at the stage depots and railroad stations, not only to see who was arriving and departing, but also to be the first to get a copy of a big-city newspaper. Saloon keepers subscribed to urban newspapers as a means of enticing patrons. Some towns, taking a page from the past, called meetings at which people could pay a small admission to hear the news read. Competing newspapers in small towns worked out novel ways to get their exchanges ahead of the competition, thereby making the local paper appealing to those who didn't get the papers from New York, Denver, Chicago, San Francisco, or Atlanta. In these ways, newspapers served as a link between urban and rural life.

Newspapers promoted expansion. The most basic assumption of frontier promotion in eastern newspapers was that white settlers had a right to the wilderness. British colonists, in particular, considered themselves "civilized" and, therefore, more qualified to manage the land than the "savages" who occupied the continent. Contrasts in dress, religion, and social habits were seen as evidence of white superiority. A more destructive weaponry gave further evidence of more advanced, superior culture. Even natural disasters or plagues that affected the Native Americans often became evidence of God's displeasure with them and support for white control.

Expansionism became an issue for the Federalist press attacking Jefferson. In 1803, William Coleman, editor of the *New York Evening Post*, worried about an increased French presence on the continent. Claiming Jefferson was Napoleon's dupe, he maintained that the "destiny of North America" belonged to the United States, not France. "The country is ours," he wrote; "ours is the right to the rivers and to all the sources of future opulence, power and happiness, which lie scattered at our feet; and we shall be the scorn and derision of the world if we suffer them to be wrested from us by the intrigues of France."[2] While the Federalists were ready to go to war with France over continental control, Jefferson defused the issue by purchasing the Louisiana Territory from France in 1803. Despite his major expansionist move, Jefferson believed the nation would not need the western land for generations; his agrarian society would end at the Mississippi River, leaving the Far West as a large Indian reservation until the vacant land east of the river became settled.

Manifest Destiny

John Louis O'Sullivan, editor of the *United States Magazine and Democratic Review*, gave life to the concept of continental expansion with the phrase "manifest destiny," coined when Texas was annexed in 1845. The "reception of Texas into the Union," he

[1]Thomas Jefferson's *Notes on the State of Virginia* and "Inaugural Address, 1801" are found in a number of places, among them Adrienne Koch and William Peden, eds., *The Life and Selected Writings of Thomas Jefferson* (New York, 1944), 280-1 and 323.

[2]*New York Evening Post*, 28 January 1803.

Manifest Destiny
When John O'Sullivan editorialized in 1845 that America's "manifest destiny" was to spread from the Atlantic to the Pacific, the phrase galvanized Americans' vision of what the country was intended to be. That year, Florida and Texas were granted statehood, and President James K. Polk rode a wave of enthusiastic expansionism aimed at incorporating California and the Oregon territory into the Union. Buoyed by newspaper support for such aims, Polk added more territory to the United States than had any president since Jefferson. O'Sullivan's phrase has remained a driving force for the idea that the United States' natural boundaries should be the two oceans on its east and west coasts.

wrote, defeated all attempts by past rivals Spain, England, and France, who operated "in a spirit of hostile interference against us, for the avowed object of thwarting our policy and hampering our power, limiting our greatness and checking the fulfillment of our manifest destiny to overspread the continent allotted by Providence for the free development of our yearly multiplying millions." California, O'Sullivan predicted, would "fall away" from Mexico next and join the United States. The hand of "Providence" would then join with technology — railroad and telegraph — to unite the nation. The arguments for the railroad were so convincing, O'Sullivan wrote, "that the day cannot be distant which shall witness the conveyance of the representatives from Oregon and California to Washington within less time than a few years ago was devoted to a similar journey by those from Ohio: while the magnetic telegraph will enable the editors of the 'San Francisco Union,' the 'Astoria Evening Post,' or the 'Nootka Morning News' to set up in type the first half of the President's Inaugural, before the echoes of the latter half shall have died away beneath the lofty porch of the Capitol, as spoken from his lips."[3]

The sensational penny papers provided jingoistic editorials advocating annexation of Texas, war with Mexico, and the acquisition of Oregon from Britain in the 1840s. The partisan Democratic press was the most outspoken in favor of expansion. Frontier papers spoke even more vociferously than those in the East. "Nothing would please the people of the entire West half so well as a war with England," proclaimed the *State Register* in frontier Illinois. British leaders had said enough about the Oregon issue, the paper continued, to justify retribution. "We are all for War! War!"[4] Later while the nation was at war with Mexico, the same newspaper advocated acquisition of the entire Mexican nation to turn a war of self-defense into a "war of philanthropy and benevolence" to free an oppressed people.[5] Mexico should indemnify the United States for its war expenses, said the *Cincinnati Enquirer*, or else "we are willing to extend the 'area of freedom' by accepting a portion of her territory most contiguous to our own, and important to our commercial, mercantile and industrial interests."[6]

War broke out in May 1846 — six months after the annexation of Texas — over whether the Rio Grande was the Texas-Mexico border. When the Treaty of Guadalupe Hidalgo ended the war in 1848, the United States got more than a third of Mexico's territory.

By the time of the Mexican War, simple printing presses were common in frontier settlements. Although presses with revolving cylinders allowed urban eastern papers to turn out 2,000 impressions per hour in the 1830s, their $20,000 to $25,000 price tag assured that they would not be used in small frontier towns. Frontier editors used smaller, hand-operated presses. One of the most common presses, the Washington hand press patented by Samuel Rust of New York in 1821, rode on many covered wagons to frontier outposts where editors, setting type one letter at a time, placed their handiwork into an iron form on the flat bed of the press. The printer then rolled ink across the type and laid a dampened sheet of paper over the form. By turning a hand crank, the printer rolled the bed along a track below the platen, which then was lowered to make an inked impression on the paper. The bed was then returned along the track and the sheet of newsprint removed. The printer could make 250 impressions of two pages at a time per hour in this manner. To print the back two pages, the printer removed the type, set the other two pages, and repeated the process on the back of the original sheet. Rust's press won the West primarily because of innovations, including hollow legs, which made the bulky machine somewhat lighter to transport than its cast iron competitors.

Soldiers frequently established newspapers when they were stationed near a town for any length of time. The *Corpus Christi Gazette*, started by an itinerant Texas printer in 1846, was the first of a series of newspapers to spring up around American camps in

[3]*United States Magazine and Democratic Review* 17: 85 (July and August 1845).
[4]*State Register* (Illinois), 9 May 1845.
[5]Ibid., 12 November 1847.
[6]*Cincinnati Enquirer*, 18 August 1847.

The Press of the West
Because its cast-iron legs were hollow, the Washington hand press was lighter to transport by wagon than its competitors were, and it became the printing press favored by frontier editors.

Texas. The United States army established the first English-language newspaper in the Territory of New Mexico, with soldiers serving as printers. Before the invasion by white Americans, three Spanish-language newspapers appeared in Santa Fe during the 1830s and 1840s. The army's *Santa Fe Republican* proclaimed its purpose as the spread of reliable news from the States and information about the army to both the American and Mexican populations.

Spanish-Language Newspapers in the Southwest

The Mexican War added a huge territory to the United States. The Southwest — comprising the future states of Texas, New Mexico, Arizona, Nevada, and California — continued to be inhabited by former Mexican citizens, and Spanish-language newspapers increased in numbers. In a dynamic situation created when two cultures meet, newspapers mirrored intense feelings and changes. The American government and newly arrived Anglo-Americans set out to Americanize the region. New settlers expected that they should wield influence and should prosper from the region's resources. The Mexican-Americans were divided about how they should respond. Some believed that they should adapt to the culture of their new nation, while others argued that they should retain their own heritage. Editors reacted in the same ways. Some editors encouraged assimilation into the dominant Anglo system; others resisted.

By this time, Spanish printing had a long history on the continent. The first press set up in the Americas was Spanish-language, established in 1535 in Mexico City. The first Spanish periodical, *Mercurio Volante*, was founded in 1693, just three years after Boston's *Publick Occurrences*. Although the first Spanish-language newspaper in United States territory — *El Misisipi* in New Orleans — was not started until 1808, the number of newspapers in the Southwest soon began to increase rapidly, the first paper being Texas' *La Gaceta*, published in 1813. The end of the Mexican War gave a strong boost to newspapers, and the Southwest saw more than 130 founded in the next half-century. Local, state, and national governments subsidized many of them.

Like their English counterparts, Spanish-language newspapers boosted their communities, affiliated with political parties, provided news, and advocated the causes and interests of their readers. Although some editors resented the American influence on their communities and culture, a large number of newspapers advocated pro-Anglo-American points of view. Many had been started as Spanish-language sections in bilingual American newspapers, following the lead of the *Santa Fe Republican*, the first New Mexico paper to divide its pages between English and Spanish.

Spanish-speaking Anglo-Americans wrote for the bilingual newspapers intended for Mexican-American readers, and newspapers employed only a small number of workers of Spanish descent, mainly to translate. Well-educated and prosperous Mexican-Americans owned most Spanish-language newspapers. They tended to accept American values and fit more comfortably into the American system than did their more numerous lower-class countrymen.

Still, the newspapers tended to reflect the interests and lifestyles of their Mexican-American readers and to promote cultural unity. They helped maintain a sense of identity and community among readers by reporting community events, supporting efforts to solve the problems their readers faced, and emphasizing the importance of retaining close links with their Mexican-American heritage. Some editors worried about the danger of assimilation of Mexican-Americans into the dominant Anglo-American culture. Others feared that the children and grandchildren of former Mexican citizens were losing the ability to speak Spanish. While these tendencies worried some editors, others believed the best future for Mexican-Americans lay in mastering their new nation's system and adapting to it.

In the cultural debate, the most notable participant was Francisco Ramirez, who in 1855 founded Los Angeles' *El Clamore Publico* (*Public Outcry*) at the age of seventeen. At first moderate in tone, Ramirez changed the tenor of his weekly after Anglo-American mobs lynched several Mexican-Americans. He argued that Anglo-Americans were barbaric and inhumane and that the

American system subjugated and oppressed Mexican-Americans. He concluded that the best course for Mexican-Americans was to emigrate to Mexico. Despite the fact that *El Clamor Publico* received extensive support from government printing, it suffered financial difficulties. Ramirez shut it down in 1859, and no other editor stepped forward to fill the activist role he had played.

Newspapers and Indian-White Conflict

The doctrine of manifest destiny assumed an empty or heathen-infested wilderness awaiting Anglo-American civilization. Public law and national sentiment, said the *New York Morning News* in 1845, called for the immigrants from Europe and their offspring to own the continent. "We are contiguous to a vast portion of the globe, untrodden save by the savage and the beast, and we are conscious of our power to render it tributary to man." Little regard, thus, was given the original inhabitants of the land. "We take from no man," the *Morning News* said; "the reverse rather — we give to man. This national policy, necessity or destiny, we know to be just and beneficent, and we can, therefore, afford to scorn the invective and imputations of rival nations."[7]

In the early nineteenth century, leaders of the Five Civilized Tribes began adopting some of the white man's ways. Sequoya, a Cherokee, recognized the power of written language; in 1809 he began creating symbols for more than 2,000 Cherokee words. He abandoned that system for a simple 86-character language. In 1828 the Cherokee Nation established the *Cherokee Phoenix*, the first Indian newspaper, in New Echota, the Cherokee capital near what is now Calhoun, Georgia. The newspaper was written partly in English and partly in Sequoya's Cherokee. Elias Boudinot, a college-educated Cherokee school teacher, was among its founders. A missionary and clerk of the Cherokee National Council, he hoped the paper would improve both the living conditions and the image of American Indians. The idea of improving a people's image through a newspaper had become a common premise of frontier journalism.

In 1829, however, the Georgia legislature stripped Cherokees of all their legal rights. From that point on, they had no standing in Georgia courts. "Full license to our oppressors, and every avenue of justice closed against us," the *Phoenix* said in an editorial. "Yes, this is the bitter cup prepared for us by a republican and religious government — we shall drink it to the very dregs."[8] A year later the newspaper reported on harassment, arrest, and threats of physical harm to its staff members. When it protested the postmaster's sale of liquor to Indians, he retaliated by cutting off its mail. The *Phoenix* was left without its source of supplies and exchange papers.[9]

The Cherokees fought to maintain a free press, but Boudinot slowly came to agree with a growing minority of Cherokees that their removal from their lands was inevitable. Principal Chief John

Elias Boudinot and the *Cherokee Phoenix*
Born Buck Watie, Elias Boudinot attended a missionary school and adopted the name of a white hero of the American Revolution. In 1828 he founded the *Cherokee Phoenix*, in part to help Christianize fellow Cherokees and, in part, to promote the idea of a separate Cherokee nation. He hoped that this, the first newspaper published by American Indians, would help improve their image and conditions. He faced threats from white neighbors who wanted Cherokee land and tribal leaders who resisted removal from Georgia and Tennessee. In 1839, after his nation was removed to Indian Territory in Oklahoma, members of an opposing faction murdered him.

Ross told him not to publicize dissension within the Cherokee National Council; instead, he was to present a united front of Cherokee resistance against white encroachment. Boudinot, however, joined the "treaty faction" seeking accommodation with whites.

In a published letter of resignation in 1832, he revealed his painful decision that he could not manage the paper without a free discussion of issues so important to his readers. "I should think it my duty to tell them the whole truth," he said. "I cannot tell them that we shall be reinstated in our rights when I have no such hope." Ross appointed his brother-in-law Elijah Hicks editor, but Hicks lacked his predecessor's rhetorical power. Meanwhile, pressure from the outside continued. The paper became erratic in publication, and, in 1834, it was suspended. Hicks' parting editorial asked readers not to give up the fight. "Although our enemies are numerous we are still in the land of the living and the JUDGE of all the earth will impart the means for the salvation of our suffering Nation."[10]

Although most local whites pressed for the Indians' removal, not all agreed. Two Alabama newspapers printed an article la-

[7] *New York Morning News*, 13 October 1845.
[8] *Cherokee Phoenix*, 29 May 1830.
[9] Ibid., 11 July 1831; 19 August 1831.
[10] Ibid., 11 August 1832; 31 May 1834.

menting the theft and destruction of Indian land and property. The article said such was the work of individuals who took "mean advantage of these who were unprotected and defenseless. Such villainy may go unpunished in this world, but the day of retribution will most certainly come."

In 1838, federal troops rounded up Cherokee men, women, and children and forced them to march to Indian Territory, which is now Oklahoma. One of every four died on this "Trail of Tears" to their new home. For signing the treaty, Boudinot and two other leaders of the treaty faction were killed by Cherokees sympathetic to Chief Ross. Tribal leaders granted amnesty to the killers.

Although the Cherokee nation was unable to start another newspaper for nine years, Samuel Worcester, who had been jailed in Georgia for his support of the Indians, helped establish printing in Indian Territory with the *Cherokee Almanac*, which was published more or less annually beginning in 1835. The second American Indian newspaper, the *Shawnee Sun* (*Siwinowe Kesibwi*), began in 1835 under the editorship of Johnston Lykins and with the assistance of the Reverend Jotham Meeker, a missionary who took a printing press with him to the large Baptist mission in Kansas. The press at Shawnee Mission published part of the newspaper in the Shawnee language using the English alphabet. Meeker also translated religious messages and songs and published Indian material in the native language. The newspaper, a monthly or semimonthly, was published until 1839. Resuming publication in 1841, it ran for three more years. The first press in the area that is now Kansas, it was put out of business temporarily by the removal of the Shawnees south into Oklahoma. This was the last in a long line of moves for the Shawnees, with whom the British had first negotiated in the woodlands of Kentucky in 1774.

THE SCIOTO GAZETTE.

Growth and Prosperity
By 1835, when the *Scioto* (Ohio) *Gazette* was founded, settlement was spreading rapidly along the Ohio River. This particular issue of the *Gazette* carried an article entitled "Commerce of the Mississippi Valley" that painted a vivid picture of the region's economic growth.

Newspapers and Frontier Cities

The westward surge of white Americans had roots stretching back into colonial times. Indeed, their determination to move west from the original thirteen colonies became so troublesome to the British Crown that it imposed a Proclamation Line in 1763 prohibiting settlers from crossing the Appalachian Mountains. Although the Indians did more than the British to enforce the line, the colonists blamed the King for their frontier troubles. By freeing the colonists from British control, the American Revolution opened western lands to migration. Settlements followed scientific and military expeditions into the newly opened regions. Newspapers followed settlement and, in turn, encouraged additional settlement. Along with improved roads and postal services, newspapers linked remote towns to the older regions. Towns and their newspapers grew as commerce increased.

Western migration is reflected in the dates the first newspapers appeared in each state along the Ohio River. The first Kentucky newspaper, the *Kentucke Gazette*, was founded by John Bradford in 1787, thirteen months after the *Pittsburgh Gazette*. In 1793, Cincinnati had its first newspaper, *Centinel of the North-Western Territory* edited by William Maxwell.

Most editors had learned the printing trade at newspapers farther east. Elihu Stout, who began as a printer on the *Kentucke Gazette*, founded the *Indiana Gazette* in 1804 at Vincennes. After a year and a half of weekly publication, his printing plant and office were destroyed by fire. Obtaining a new press and supplies from Kentucky, he began the *Western Sun* in 1807. Irishman Joseph Charless, who learned the printing trade in Philadelphia, published the first *Missouri Gazette* at St. Louis in 1808. Subscriptions were payable in flour, corn, beef, or pork. The following year Charless changed the name of the paper to *Louisiana Gazette* in recognition of the entire territory, but he returned to the original title three years later upon the organization of Missouri as a separate territory and the creation of Louisiana as a state. Illinois was detached from Indiana in 1809, and, five years later, the *Illinois Herald* became the first journal in the new territory. It was published at Kaskaskia by Matthew Duncan, who had owned a small Kentucky publication called *Farmer's Friend*. Like many frontier editors, Duncan would become a prominent figure in state politics.

Newspaper editors frequently had an interest in expansion and town development. John Bradford of Lexington, Kentucky, and

THE
CENTINEL of the *North-Western TERRITORY*

Open to all parties—but influenced by none.

SATURDAY, June 14, 1794.

PUBLIC NOTICE

WHEREAS many good Citizens of this Territory, with a design to check the incursions of the hostile Indians, now at war with the people of the United States, have voluntarily entered into, and subscribed their names to certain articles; each name having a sum annexed thereto, and have severally bound themselves their heirs &c. to pay the same, as in the said articles are mentioned.

We the subscribers therefore, being nominated and appointed to superintend the business of collecting and paying the money thus subscribed; hereby give notice, that the following arrangement is made, *for the reward to be given for Indian scalps* taken and produced within the period of the eighteenth of April last past, and the twenty fifth of December next ensuing, and within the boundaries following, to wit, beginning on the Ohio ten miles above the mouth of the little Miami, on a direct line thence northwardly, the same distance from the said Miami, until it shall extend twenty five miles above where *Harmar's trace* first crosses the said Miami, thence due west, crossing the said little Miami, until it shall extend ten miles west of the great Miami, thence southwardly, keeping the distance of ten miles from the said great Miami, to the Ohio, thence up the middle of the said river Ohio, to the beginning; that for every scalp, having the right ear appendant, for the first ten Indians who shall be killed within the time and limits aforesaid, by those who are subscribers, to the said articles, shall, whenever collected, be paid the sum of *one hundred and thirty six dollars*; and for every scalp of the like number of Indians, having the right ear appendant who shall be killed, within the time and limits aforesaid; by those who are not subscribers, the *federal troops* excepted, shall, whenever collected, be paid the sum of *one hundred dollars*; and for every scalp, having the right ear appendant, of the second ten Indians who shall be killed within the time and limits aforesaid, by those who are subscribers to the said articles, shall whenever collected as aforesaid, be paid the sum of *one hundred and seventeen dollars*; and for every scalp having the right ear appendant, of the said second ten Indians who shall be killed within the time and limits aforesaid by those who are not subscribers to the said articles, except before excepted, shall whenever collected, be paid the sum of *ninety five dollars*.

Cincinnati. Levi Woodward, Darius C. Orcutt, James Lyons, Columbia. Wm. [illegible], Ignatius Ross, John Reily. } Committee

Fifty Dollars
Reward.

DESERTED from Fort Washington, [illegible]

FORTY DOLLARS REWARD

DESERTED off their posts at Greenville on the night of the [illegible] of April, 1794, [illegible]

D. STRONG, [illegible]
Fort-Washington, May [illegible], 1794

TEN DOLLARS REWARD.

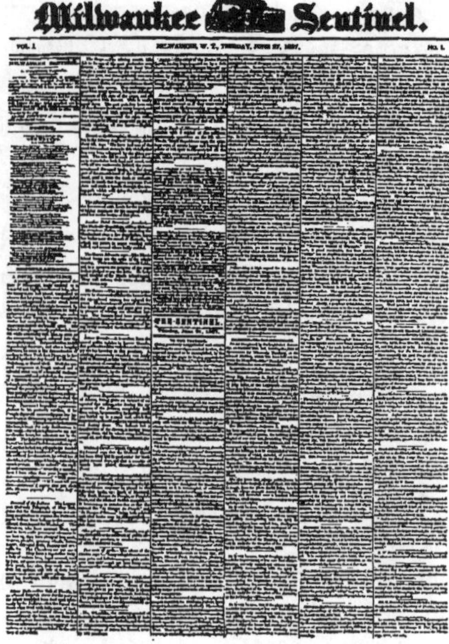

Settling the Frontier
Editors on the American frontier took on two preeminent issues as settlement moved westward. One was the constant conflict with the native inhabitants, and the other the promotion of their towns. Founded in 1793 as the first newspaper in Cincinnati, the *Centinel of the North-Western Territory* typified the approach of early newspapers. It devoted much of its space to the Indian wars in the territory. The lead article in this issue detailed the bounties to be paid to settlers for each Indian they could kill. In 1813 the *Western Intelligencer* of Worthington, Ohio, carried a front-page story about "The Savage Tomahawk," which it described as an "agonizing weapon of murderous destruction." The conflicts between settlers and Indians continued until most of the latter were finally subdued in the late 1800s. In attempting to encourage town growth, newspapers in frontier communities usually pointed with pride to local progress. In the first issue of the *Milwaukee Sentinel* (1837), the editors declared that "the records of past ages may be searched in vain, for evidence of a community with so magical a growth as that witnessed in the new and flourishing Territory of Wisconsin."

Joseph Charless of St. Louis, like many other editors, were members of their towns' governing councils. Most editors, however, were of lower social levels than the merchants who ran the towns. Still, if they had less income, they often had as much prestige. Although separated by background and training from the merchants, editors helped unify the budding frontier cities. The number of newspapers grew faster than the successful towns. The *Missouri Republican* in St. Louis noted in 1829 that newspapers promised to be "thick as blackberries in the spring" on the frontier.[11] Many towns soon had two weeklies; by 1830, Cincinnati had seven weeklies and two dailies. The number of newspapers, of course, indicated growth in the number of towns and cities. Urbanization had begun to infect Jefferson's agrarian utopia.

Because a newspaper's survival depended upon the growth and prosperity of the town in which its subscribers and advertisers lived, editors became town boosters. Not all of the early frontier towns prospered, of course. Many towns and their newspapers died, and many successful ones rode through several boom-and-bust cycles related to unpredictable economic growth. Despite the odds, town-promotion rhetoric revealed incredible optimism — at least in print. Essays and advertisements in neighboring towns and eastern cities extolled the town's potential. Typical was the promotion of Town of America at the junction of the Ohio and Mississippi rivers, whose proprietors said no other point on the continent "has ever presented a fairer prospect of a greater inland commercial city."[12]

This first generation of town boosters spawned another western tradition: the spoof of boosterism. In 1819, the *Augusta* (Ga.) *Chronicle* ran a widely reprinted advertisement from "Andrew Air Castle, Theory M'Vision, and L. Moonlight Jr., & Co.," who were described as proprietors of the City of Skunksburgh. After a folksy description of the town and its location as the middle ground between all major North American cities, the "proprietors" concluded with its potential: "A line of Velocipede stages will be immediately established from Skunksburgh straight through the O-ke-fin-o-cau Swamp, to the southernmost point of the Florida peninsula; and, as soon as a canal shall be cut through the rocky mountains, there will be direct communication with the Columbia river, and thence to the Pacific Ocean. Then opens a theatre of trade bounded only by the Universe!"[13]

Editors depended on exaggeration to attract new settlers and on optimism to assure stability of their towns. They gave hope and encouragement to struggling pioneers. They also sought to alleviate hardship by promoting civic development and reform. As the consciences of their communities, they editorialized about the health hazards of urban living. The *Pittsburgh Gazette* in 1802 attributed the increase in disease to a sudden increase in population

[11]*Missouri Republican* (St. Louis), 17 February 1829.

[12]Quoted in Richard C. Wade, *The Urban Frontier: Pioneer Life in Early Pittsburgh, Cincinnati, Lexington, Louisville, and St. Louis* (Chicago, 1950), 31.

[13]Reprinted in *Cincinnati Liberty Hall*, 1 October 1819.

combined with a stench in the air from "filthy gutters, putrid vegetables and matter, the stench from the foul slaughter houses, the exhalations from ponds of stagnant water."[14] Editors advocated improved sewage disposal and the regulation of privies. They supported such reforms as abolition of debtors' prison, humane treatment of the insane, free education for the children of working people, and the establishment of Bible and missionary societies. Most sought to improve the level of local culture, through the literary quality of their own columns and reviews of local entertainment and cultural events. Newspaper publishers also published books, operated bookstores, encouraged local philosophical and literary societies, and sponsored private circulating libraries. Thus newspapers served as both boosters and reformers.

Advertising columns often reflected frontier social life more accurately than the news columns. Newspapers in backwoods communities frequently carried advertisements for the sale of slaves or indentured servants and for the return of runaways. An early ad in the *Pittsburgh Gazette* was typical: "To be sold. A Negro Wench. She is an excellent cook and can do any kind of work in doors or out of doors. She has been registered in Westmoreland County. Produce will be taken or cattle of any kind."[15] Other ads mentioned a willingness to accept payment in kind, such as firewood, pelts, or farm produce, in exchange for service or merchandise. Editors frequently took such payment for advertisements or subscriptions. An improving economy was reflected in the fabrics advertised by local stores. A boarding and day school for young ladies advertised that it taught how to lace by both bobbin and needle, how to knit and do other crafts, and how to read English.

Newspapers took differing attitudes toward local news. Some editors relied entirely on exchanges and even apologized when the mail failed to bring enough news. In small towns, word of mouth spread news faster than the printed word. But editors still used editorials, essays, and letters for local reports. Other editors believed their very survival depended upon local news to build a sense of community. Editors liked to write about local people, but they continued to report much of their news by reprinting official documents, such as speeches and texts of legislative proceedings. Such reprints often filled the pages, especially in papers with contracts to do government printing. Other news was reprinted from "exchange" papers from farther east. Although such news was weeks or months old, it was new to the frontier. Many long, anonymous essays carried such pseudonyms as "Subscriber," "Farmer," and "Cato." Subjects varied, covering such topics as political reform, education, weather, women, laughter, and gallantry. Backwoods philosophy and poetry added local color, and frontier newspapers often carried fiercely partisan political articles. Later, the telegraph offered timely news, and more towns could publish daily newspapers.

Westward migration nudged American newspapers closer to the modern concept of news. In the late eighteenth century, frontier news traveled faster and was covered more thoroughly in personal letters and by word of mouth than in newspapers. Many early frontier publishers may not have viewed local news coverage as an important function of newspapers. Nevertheless, when the new nation began to create its own cultural identity in the early nineteenth century, editors reflected the change by including more domestic as opposed to foreign news. Most uniquely American news came from the West. Exchange papers, including special-interest publications, supplied easily reprintable material for the West while colorful western stories found their way into the eastern press.

Town promoters often pointed to the growth of newspapers along with churches and schools as an outward sign of culture. Even though citizens bragged about their newspapers, the publications seldom did well financially, even with dramatic growth. The *Liberty Hall*, founded in Cincinnati in 1804 with 150 subscribers, published 2,000 copies weekly by 1813. Pittsburgh's *Mercury* had 1,400 subscribers by the end of its first year. The number of papers per city varied. The original paper might squeak by without opposition. More likely, however, an opposition political party would set up a competing newspaper. The party in power could award local printing contracts to its own newspaper. Other factions and interests also established newspapers. Mining journals appeared in the West; specialized farm publications sprouted across the continent. Ethnic groups, such as the Irish and Germans, established newspapers in some communities, many of which appeared in languages other than English. Freed slaves and abolitionists established newspapers as did many religious denominations. Although New York City became the center of black journalism, some freedmen communities on the frontier published newspapers. A black political convention in Ohio voted to publish a newspaper, *The Voice of the Oppressed*, edited by William H. Day and Charles H. Langston. African Americans published at least four periodicals in New Orleans before the Civil War. By the end of the war, three black newspapers in California provided a strong voice for civil rights.[16]

Ethnic communities founded newspapers to provide news from the old country, help preserve cultural identities, and promote common interests. Foreign-language papers could be found in urban centers as well as isolated ethnic communities. French, Chinese, German, Spanish, Jewish, and Italian groups launched thirty-six newspapers in metropolitan San Francisco during the decade beginning in 1850. Germans started more than a hundred newspapers in California during the following century. Like other western newspapers, many ethnic ones were short-lived. Some thrived, however. Czech immigrants settling on the Great Plains in the 1880s turned publishing into a big business. Edward Rosewater, a Czech Jew in Omaha, founded the first Czech-language newspaper in Nebraska, taking advantage of the Union Pacific Railroad's settlement-promotion advertising. After six years, Jan

[14] *Pittsburgh Gazette*, 23 July 1802.
[15] Ibid., 23 May 1787.

[16] William Loren Katz, *The Black West*, 3d ed. (Seattle, 1987), 44, 128; and Lauren Kessler, *The Dissident Press* (Newbury Park, Calif., 1984), 26-34.

Thomas Hart Benton and Cheap Land
Along with Horace Greeley of the *New York Tribune*, Thomas Hart Benton of Missouri was one of the nation's strongest advocates of westward expansion. A United States senator, he also was co-editor of the *St. Louis Enquirer*. Born in 1782 in North Carolina, he moved to Tennessee after becoming a lawyer and then in 1815 to St. Louis. After election to the senate in 1820, he promoted westward expansion through such policies as lowering the price of land from $1.25 to 25 cents an acre.

Rosicky bought the paper and began a Czech-language chain of fourteen newspapers and specialized journals. Other ethnic newspapers worked to hasten assimilation into American life. Along these lines, missionaries started Chinese-language newspapers to convert immigrants to Christianity. For similar reasons, missionaries printed the earliest Hawaiian newspapers in the native language of the islands.[17]

Politicians occasionally founded newspapers in hope before an election only to close them if the party suffered a bad defeat. While death awaited some partisan newspapers after an election, government printing contracts could go to the victors. Town, county, and state governments designated official printers to handle official business, such as the printing of laws, notices of public auctions, legislative proceedings, and registration of land sales and cattle brands. In an era in which type was set one letter at a time, a contract to publish government proceedings could save time by allowing the editor to set type once for a speech in both the newspaper and a government publication. A speech could fill an entire newspaper page.

With survival on the line at election time, some political debates became desperate fights for survival. Political discussion on the frontier, one historian noted in a monumental understatement, "has never been characterized by an excess of deference to an opponent's opinions, or by over-indulgence as to his personal shortcomings."[18] Political fights in newspaper columns could turn into personal abuse. Yet many editors helped neighbors, even political rivals, when their newsprint ran out or their shops burned down.

Every frontier editor faced the prospect of physical violence. William Gilpin's vitriolic attacks in the *Missouri Argus* increased the threatening mail to his boss, proprietor Andrew Jackson Davis. Despite protests, Davis kept Gilpin as editor. One opponent, holding Davis rather than Gilpin responsible, beat the owner over the head with an iron cane; Davis died after surgery. Gilpin lived on, eventually to become the first governor of the Territory of Colorado in 1861. Another Missouri editor, Joseph Charless, was attacked by a long-time political opponent who carried a pistol and spit in the editor's face. The politician retreated when Charless retaliated with stones. Charless and rival editor Isaac N. Henry, a co-editor with Thomas Hart Benton (a future U.S. senator) of the *St. Louis Enquirer*, engaged in an extended editorial argument and court battle over a street fight between Henry and Charless. Charless' articles about the case led to a $20 fine for contempt of court. Refusing to pay the fine, Charless went to jail. On another occasion, he was shot at as he walked in his garden.

Religious Newspapers

Churches founded many newspapers in the uphill battle of taking civilization, not only to the frontier "savages," but also to the many pioneer whites in need of redemption. Religious newspapers grew rapidly in the Old Northwest through the 1840s and 1850s. By the middle of the nineteenth century, most Christian denominations had at least one journal. Jews were the only major group to found their first paper after 1850. Religious journals contained serious discussions of theology, morality, history, science, and literature. News of local congregations and such special-interest topics as useful items on farm and household management worked their way into religious papers. Generally, the early nineteenth-century religious papers were of better quality in terms of paper, printing, editing, and style than their secular counterparts.

Unlike secular editors, religious editors were not trained as printers. Nearly all were clergymen poorly prepared for managing a newspaper. One moral dilemma they faced was the selection of advertising. While some ruled out the quack patent medicines widely advertised at the time, others permitted the advertise-

[17]See Edward C. Kemble, *A History of California Newspapers, 1846-1848* (Los Gatos, Calif., 1962); T.L. Broadbent, "The German-Language Press in California," *Journal of the West* 10 (1971): 637-61; Emerson Daggett, supervisor, *History of Foreign Journalism in San Francisco* (San Francisco, 1939); and Paul Alfred Pratte, "Ke Alaka'i: The Role of the Honolulu *Star Bulletin* in the Hawaiian Statehood Movement," Ph.D. dissertation, University of Hawaii, 1976.

[18]Reuben Gold Thwaites, "The Ohio Valley Press before the War of 1812-15," *Proceedings of the American Antiquarian Society* 19 (April 1909): 321.

ments in the belief that, since business was not a religious concern, the advertising sections should not be subjected to religious scrutiny. The placement of advertising, however, did separate secular from religious papers. Secular papers often placed advertising on the front page; religious papers seldom did.

Religious editors had much to say about the morality of their countrymen. Protestant editors advised against smoking, drinking, and attending the theatre and horse races. Catholic and Jewish publications generally ignored and occasionally ridiculed such Protestant taboos. The politics of the religious press varied as much as the politics of the religious leaders today. The publications frequently advocated such reforms as improved living conditions and education. Catholic and Protestant papers differed on the war with Mexico; Catholics did not share the euphoria of white Protestant expansion into the Southwest controlled by Indians and Spaniards. Most newspapers shared the nation's assumption of its "manifest destiny" to conquer the North American continent, redeeming the land from a "degenerate and less energetic race," but some worried about the "idol of Manifest Destiny" taking control over the national temper. Some religious newspapers worried about living conditions among the Native Americans, and many of them took the lead in the crusade to end slavery.

The most controversial of the special-interest papers on the frontier were those founded in the crusade against slavery. The frontiers of Tennessee and Kentucky hosted early abolitionist papers. Like the religious papers, abolitionist papers generally were published by sponsors. Four anti-slavery papers established before 1826 were in slave states west of the Allegheny Mountains. Sponsored by religious groups or anti-slavery societies, the papers reprinted laws, arguments, opinions, essays, speeches, statistics, congressional proceedings, colonization efforts, and notices of books and pamphlets on abolition. Editors risked their lives and property in their pursuit of social reform. One abolitionist editor, Elijah Lovejoy, became a martyr when he was killed by a mob in Alton, Illinois, in 1837.

John Stuart Skinner, Farm Publishing Pioneer
Skinner founded the first national farm journal, the *American Farmer*, to provide useful information and to promote effective farming methods.

Agricultural Journalism

A major impetus for special-interest frontier newspapers came from New England and New York State with the creation of agricultural journalism. The nation's pioneer national farm journal was the *American Farmer*, created in 1819 in Baltimore by John Stuart Skinner, who had a farm background and experience as a postmaster. "The great aim, and the chief pride, of the *American Farmer*," Skinner announced in his first issue, "will be, to collect information from every source, on every branch of husbandry, thus to enable the reader to study the various systems which experience has proved to be the best, under given circumstances."[19] Under the flag on page one, a line in all capital letters read: "Rural economy, internal improvements, news, prices current." Skinner's example was followed by *The Cultivator*, founded in 1834 by Jesse Buel, editor of the *Albany Argus* and state printer for New York, and the *Genesee Farmer*, founded in 1831 by Luther Tucker, who published it along with his *Rochester Daily Advertiser*. In 1840 the *Cultivator* and the *Genesee Farmer* merged, and in 1853 the combined paper became the *Country Gentleman*. When the *American Farmer* suspended publication in 1834, at least fifteen publications with the same purpose survived it.

From these beginnings, agricultural journalism spread westward across the continent and encouraged more specialized publications. More than 400 farm papers were begun in the thirty years after 1829; most lasted less than three years. Tucker was among the founders of the *Horticulturist*, one of the first specialized agricultural publications. Newspapers devoted exclusively to dairy farming were founded in Ohio and New York in 1859. Many general farm newspapers began specialized sections, including ladies' departments. The *Rural American* opened a matrimonial bureau as a reader service.

Agricultural papers zealously picked up on the Jeffersonian agrarian ideal. They reprinted speeches, poems, and editorials depicting the "happy plodding farmer" who lived a contented, easy, chaste, and independent life. One such poem was "The Farmer's Song" from *Yankee Farmer* in 1835:

[19] *American Farmer* (Baltimore), 2 April 1819.

AMERICAN AGRICULTURIST,

FOR THE

Farm, Garden, and Household.

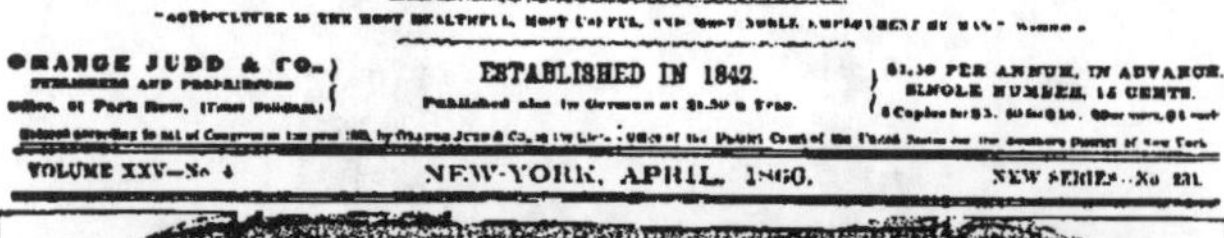

ORANGE JUDD & CO.

ESTABLISHED IN 1842.

VOLUME XXV—No. 4 NEW-YORK, APRIL, 1866. NEW SERIES—No. 231.

HEAD OF BARON OF OXFORD.

Agricultural Journalism
Specialized publications developed in the first half of the nineteenth century to serve frontier farming interests. Like the *American Agriculturist*, founded in 1842, they both provided useful information and extolled the virtues of farm life.

I envy not the mighty king
 Upon the splendid throne —
Nor crave his glittering diadem,
 Nor wish his power mine own,
For though his power and wealth be great,
 And round him thousands bow
In reverence — in my low estate
 More solid peace I know.[20]

Similar was "The Farmer's Life" from *Southern Cultivator* in 1843:

I love the farmer's quiet life —
His peaceful home, devoid of strife,
 With gay contentment bless'd.
I love the virtues of his heart,
Which peace, and joy, and love impart
 Around his tranquil rest.[21]

[20]*Yankee Farmer*, 20 July 1835, 120.
[21]*Southern Cultivator*, 11 October 1843, 168.

Poems and essays extolled the virtues of farm life and praised the pleasures of God's creation. They idealized nature, farming, and the work ethic. Besides soothing a sense of inferiority, such romanticism had a serious purpose: keeping people on the farm. Eastern cities and western gold fields tempted young men to leave the farms, particularly in New England, where the soils were losing productivity. The farm, said the *New Genesee Farmer*, provided stability: "The young of both sexes foolishly give up such a birth-right, for a bare-foot existence in the western wilderness — amid privation, and toil, and sickness — where pork is the greatest luxury, and a log-house raising the most exciting recreation."[22] Cities, meanwhile, were pictured as dens of iniquity, seats of corruption, and places filled with sin and sorrow. "The farm," said the *Indiana Farmer*, "is the natural home of man. Placed in any other condition he naturally degenerates, both physically and morally, and soon acquires an inferior type."[23]

Agricultural journalists took the lead in the "worn-out soil" issue in New England and New York, the state with the most farm newspapers. Frequently published by agricultural societies, the newspapers popularized such notions as fertilizing with manure and using scientific innovations in agriculture. They promoted agricultural fairs at which farmers showed their crops and judged the results of one another's harvests. They promoted tours of farms, essay contests, and agricultural societies. They tested new machinery and promoted such new devices as the steel plow, seed drill, corn planter, cultivator, thresher, mower, and reaper before 1860. Occasionally, they editorialized on such issues as women's rights, temperance, and, gradually, abolition as well as various tilling techniques and breeds of cattle. They encouraged farmers to exchange seeds and conduct experiments. In all of these activities, the pages of the newspaper were opened to the exchange of ideas.

The farm papers and agricultural societies forged a strong interest group to lobby for agricultural education and a federal agriculture department. The harvest of their editorial seeds came in 1862 when President Lincoln signed into law bills creating the Department of Agriculture and agricultural colleges to be financed by grants of land from the public domain in the West. Within weeks, Lincoln also signed the Homestead Act and the authorization for a transcontinental railroad. These agricultural reforms passed Congress only after southern states had withdrawn from the Union. The South had opposed most of them to prevent expansion of northern influence into the territories. The Homestead Act was to create the Jeffersonian utopia with a farmer on every 160 acres across the continent.

"Go West"

The important characteristics of the newspaper editor seen later

[22]*New Genesee Farmer*, January 1847, 17.
[23]*Indiana Farmer*, June 1858, 65.

California News
Artist William Sidney Mount, who sought a popular audience, completed this "California News" painting in 1850. "Paint pictures," he advised, "that will take with the public – never paint for the few, but the many." The many followed the California Gold Rush of 1849, which attracted settlers, speculators, and interest to the West more effectively than any previous promotional campaigns. President Polk stimulated interest by lending credibility to exaggerated reports of the promise of gold. Newspapers promoted gold fields in Nevada and Colorado to attract settlers when the Civil War broke out in the East. Caravans of settlers and adventurers transformed the prairie within a few decades after the California Gold Rush.

in the Wild West originated in the frontier between the Appalachian Mountains and the Mississippi River. Frontier editors east of the Mississippi before the Civil War trained apprentices who moved farther west. Editors learned to live on a shoestring, contend with unreliable mail and transportation, promote their hometowns, batter their political opponents, face violence, and, through exchange papers, cooperate with their counterparts in other cities. These "exchanges" provided a ready source of copy for editors usually too harried to cover their own towns thoroughly. Despite hardships, some editors developed a rugged independence.

Regardless of their locale, frontier editors faced hard times and isolation. First, they had to transport their heavy presses in horse- or oxen-drawn wagons on rough roads over difficult terrain. Once the presses were in place, they depended upon an unreliable transportation system for paper, ink, and replacement type. They relied upon the same transportation system and the occasionally unpredictable postal service to distribute their newspapers.

Subscribers and advertisers also experienced the hard times of isolation. They, in turn, passed hardships on to the newspapers. Editors often lectured advertisers and subscribers on their responsibility to pay bills, although they often carried unpaying clients and accepted goods and services in lieu of money.

Although some editors were well educated, they were primarily printers. Knowledge of the mechanical printing process was a basic job requirement. Editors often had to be resourceful in repairing their own equipment and substituting available materials. Their survival often depended upon the quality of their printing, and newspapers often operated job printing shops to supplement their income or to keep the newspapers going in difficult times. Editors also worked outside the newspapers. Most were printers who did job printing on the side, but many were also teachers, lawyers, or postmasters.

The discovery of gold in California, along with what a historian called "one of the most effective promotional campaigns in history," stimulated a gold rush to the West Coast. "The accounts of the abundance of gold in that territory," President James K. Polk said in December 1848, "are of such an extraordinary character as would scarcely command belief were they not corroborated by the authentic reports of officers in the public service." Skeptics who had refused to believe newspaper accounts took the president's word seriously. Two days after his message, the Philadelphia mint assayed a 230-ounce sample conveyed in a tea caddy, confirming the reports of gold. Newspapers abandoned all caution. "The Eldorado of the old Spaniards is discovered at last," one proclaimed. "We are on the brink of the Age of Gold," reported another. "The coming of the Messiah or the dawn of the Millennium," said another, "would not have excited anything like the interest" that the tea caddy generated.[24] The combination of national idealism and material rewards injected the nation with gold fever. The fever became an epidemic, drawing hordes of Americans westward.

At the same time, economic depravity in the cities forced people to look for dreams in a new land. *New York Tribune* publisher Horace Greeley was among the most visible promoters of western settlement as a "safety valve" to release unemployed urban dwellers from the pressure cooker of the inner city. During the Panic of 1837, Greeley wrote, paupers arrived in New York City at the rate of 1,000 per day. Stop immigration from Europe, he said;

[24]Quotations are from Ray Allen Billington, "Words that Won the West 1830-1850," address before the Public Relations Society of America, 18 November 1963, San Francisco, Calif. Published as a booklet by the Foundation for Public Relations Research, New York.

Uncle Horace Greeley
Horace Greeley, America's leading advocate of westward migration, had followers throughout the country. This illustration, from *Scribner's Monthly* magazine in 1883, accompanied an article by William Dean Howells. Reflecting on his life on a country newspaper, Howells wrote that rural readers opened the weekly edition of Greeley's *New York Tribune* expectantly. "Well," they would say, "let's see what old Horace says this week."

encourage emigration to the frontier. His often-quoted advice "Go West, young man, and grow up with the Country" dates from 1837, four years before he founded the *Tribune*. Every laborer could find opportunity in the limitless frontier. "If he go prepared to throw off his coat, fare rudely, work heartily, sleep soundly, and rise reasonably," Greeley wrote, "he will likely thrive there."[25] Unceasingly, Greeley promoted the Homestead Bill, agricultural societies, land-grant colleges, the transcontinental railroad, and other reform measures to promote western expansion and settlement. When the Homestead Act made 160 acres of the Great American Desert available to each settler, Greeley could hardly contain his excitement. "Young men! Poor men! Widows! resolve to have a home of your own! If you are able to buy and pay for one in the East, very well; if not, make one in the broad and fertile West!"[26] Ironically, Greeley's safety valve failed to account for the fact that poor inner-city immigrants could not afford the trip west. So Greeley continued to lobby for inexpensive transportation and free homesteads. And his weekly edition of the *Tribune* provided encouragement and practical tips for farmers — some of whom were ill-prepared for the hardships of western farming. Nevertheless, the weekly *Tribune* ranked with the Bible as one of the most read publications in the Midwest.

Native Americans in the Press

The period between the Civil War and the end of the nineteenth century saw the most violent of the conflicts on the American frontier and provided the backdrop against which the national western mythology was created. Images in the press often fit preconceived notions and political bias as much as real conditions on the frontier. Editors' views on frontier issues, such as Indian policies and railroad development, became complicated by the popularization of frontier stereotypes of such characters as mountain men, gunfighters, soldiers, and Indians. People such as Buffalo Bill Cody, Wild Bill Hickock, Marthy "Calamity Jane" Cannary, "General" George Armstrong Custer, and Wyatt Earp fulfilled expectations of eastern writers. Journalists saw the familiar Civil War military men — Custer, Phil Sheridan, Winfield Hancock, among others — transferred to the plains wars against the Native Americans.

Most eastern newspapers grew impatient with the cavalry's failure to solve the Indian situation, but only two — the *Chicago Times* and the *New York Herald* — reported regularly on the major campaigns between 1867 and 1881. Covering frontier violence required commitment by the newspaper and the special correspondent. "If he [the journalist] goes out on such business," John F. Finerty of the *Times* wrote, "he must go prepared to ride his forty or fifty miles a day, go sometimes on half rations, sleep on the ground with small covering, roast, sweat, freeze, and make the acquaintance of such vermin or reptiles as may flourish in the vicinity of his couch; and, finally, be ready to fight Sitting Bull or Satan when the trouble begins, for God and the United States hate non-combatants."[27] Correspondent Mark Kellogg, of the *Bismarck Tribune* and *New York Herald*, died with Custer and five companies of the Seventh Cavalry at the Little Big Horn in 1876.

For coverage of the frontier, most eastern newspapers depended upon local papers from which they lifted stories and upon volunteer correspondents, such as local writers, editors, or soldiers. Many of these special correspondents had stronger powers of imagination than observation, and most reporting was biased. Stories of Indian warfare provided the most dramatic examples of distortion. Eastern editors sought sensational stories for a public used to reports from Civil War battlefields; western writers wanted enough alarming news to pressure the federal government to

[25] *New Yorker*, 22 April 1837; Greeley attributed the quotation, "Go West, young man," to Indiana editor John Soule of the *Terre Haute Express*.
[26] *New York Daily Tribune*, 6 June 1862.

[27] John Finerty, *War-Path and Bivouac or The Conquest of the Sioux* (1890; reprint, Norman, Okla., 1962), 80-1.

Gold in the Black Hills
When gold was discovered in 1874 in the Dakotas, mining camps sprang up from the rush of prospectors. Printing establishments and newspapers followed closely afterward. The *Black Hills Champion* began publication in 1877 in Deadwood City.

send more troops. Reports by wire were received in the East before the mails could arrive, and they appeared in print complete with illustrations from wood engravings. The illustrated newspapers, which frequently based their pictures on descriptions from the field, provided some of the most sensational accounts of Indian battles.

Newspapers, including Greeley's *Tribune*, became occasional victims of faked stories. In the spring of 1867, the *Tribune* reported a massacre of eighty people at Fort Buford at the mouth of the Yellowstone on the Upper Missouri River. The story said soldiers held off 2,000 to 3,000 Indians before being overwhelmed. A colonel was said to have shot his wife to save her from a fate worse than death. Four days after this sensational story, the *Tribune* reported that General Sherman could not confirm the story of the massacre. A month later, it reported the story as "a base fabrication." The two major illustrated newspapers, however, reported the "massacre" complete with the colonel's killing of his wife and neglected to mention that the story had been exposed as a fraud.[28]

As the frontier moved west, the natives who had been pushed ahead of settlers were squeezed with no place left to go. For a time, Indian Territory was set aside for them. When Indians were no longer in their backyard, eastern newspapers became more liberal toward them. At the same time, western editors became more violent in their rhetoric. Characteristically throwing subtlety to the wind, the *Arizona Miner* vowed that the territory was worth fighting for and that the government should not protect "the murderous savages who now bar the door to prosperity in Arizona."[29]

Exaggeration and racial hatred colored many stories. The three English-language papers in Arizona Territory in 1871 contributed to the special fear of Apaches and the defeat of the plan for reservations that, in the local view, threatened white opportunity for private ownership of the land. The papers got carried away with their rhetoric. The *Arizonian* suggested a policy toward the Indians "to receive them when they apply for peace, and have them grouped together and slaughtered as though they were as many nests of rattlesnakes." The paper recommended "first class apartments in a Lunatic Asylum" for advocates of reservations.[30] Such overblown rhetoric did not prevent some eastern papers from depending on local weeklies and small dailies as sources for news stories. The widely reprinted *Arizona Citizen* account of the Camp Grant massacre in which Tucson residents attacked an Indian camp, killing eighty-five Indians and capturing twenty-eight, mostly women and children, began: "The suffering and exasperated people have commenced the work of retaliation on the Indians. Their patience has been remarkable."[31] Editors encouraged the massacre if they did not participate in it. They could have reported the plans, widely known in Tucson, of organizers plotting the 55-mile march to attack the village.

Generally, frontier editors regarded Native Americans as inferior beings or even less than human. Many called for extermination. "A dead Indian can always be counted as reliably good," said an Albuquerque newspaper.[32] A Las Vegas, New Mexico, paper said the residents of a nearby town had subscribed $2,000 for the payment of $100 for every Indian killed and brought in. "There is a royalty for wolf scalps and why not for Indian scalps?" the paper asked.[33]

Editors continually fought the eastern image of Indians that, they said, romanticized them. A Santa Fe weekly suggested that the Indians be relocated to New England, where philanthropists could become educated as to the "true character" of these people whose natural inclination was toward hunting, stealing, murdering, and scalping.[34] Mark Twain, a product of the frontier press,

[28]Elmo Scott Watson, "The Indian Wars and the Press, 1866-1867," *Journalism Quarterly* 17 (1940): 301-12.
[29]*Arizona Miner*, 16 April 1870.

[30]*Arizonian*, 28 January 1871.
[31]See William B. Blankenburg, "The Role of the Press in an Indian Massacre, 1871," *Journalism Quarterly* 45 (1968): 61-70.
[32]*Daily Citizen*, 25 June 1890.
[33]*Daily Optic*, 4 February 1881.
[34]*Weekly New Mexican*, 11 November 1879.

The Last Plains Indian War
The Sioux War of 1876 was the last major attempt of the Plains Indians to resist intrusions by the white population onto native lands. This drawing from Richard Dodge's collection "Our Wild Indians," published in 1882, depicts a cavalry raid on a Sioux village. In 1876 General George Custer led a major expedition to force Sioux, Cheyenne, and others to move to reservations. As he prepared to attack a large village on the Little Big Horn River in southeastern Montana, Crazy Horse's force of 6,000 warriors surrounded and wiped out Custer's 600 troops. The battle gained popularity in the press as the "Custer massacre" and "Custer's Last Stand" and intensified demands that the Indians be subdued once and for all. Some newspapers called for the extinction of the entire Sioux nation.

satirized the Indians and philanthropists when he suggested that soap and education would be more successful than a massacre in eliminating the Indians: "Soap and education are not as sudden as a massacre, but they are more deadly in the long run; because a half-massacred Indian may recover, but if you educate him and wash him, it is bound to finish him some time or other. It undermines his constitution; it strikes at the foundation of his being."[35]

Some editors supported Native Americans, but they often did not understand them. To identify with Indian causes, sympathetic whites often expected natives to get a white education in Protestant schools and adopt "civilized" lifestyles. Indians were encouraged to learn English and remain on clearly defined reservations much smaller than their original territories. Newspapers sprouted on reservations, where tribal councils sponsored many of them. In 1844, the Rev. Samuel A. Worcester and printer John F. Wheeler, Boudinot's friends who had gone to jail for working on the *Phoenix*, helped editor William P. Ross, the chief's nephew, start the *Cherokee Advocate* in Indian Territory. In 1876 the Creek Nation started the *Indian Journal*, which continues today as a small weekly.

No single event united the moderate and the extremist, the eastern and the western press, as strongly as the Battle of the Little Big Horn in which Custer led five companies of Seventh Cavalry troopers to their deaths in an attack on a Sioux and Cheyenne village in Montana Territory in 1876. The news startled a nation celebrating its centennial with little thought of Indian wars on the remaining frontier. The sense of frustration felt by nearly all the newspapers was perhaps summed up best by the *New York Herald*, which called for "one grand, consummate campaign" to settle the Indian question. "Let us," the paper editorialized, "treat the Indian either as an enemy or as a friend — either as a savage or a human being. Let us exterminate or capture him." The number of Indians in North America, the *Herald* said, was less than the population of Brooklyn; yet the Indians demanded more space than the German Empire. "If the Indian will not submit to civilization, let us cage him as we would a tiger or wolf."[36]

News accounts referred to Indians as animals, savages, demons, devils, and vampires. "The only proper monument to Custer's memory," proclaimed the *Helena Herald* in Montana, "will be the extinction of the Sioux nation." Characteristic of frontier papers, the Helena newspaper said it was time to abandon the notion that Indians had any right to the soil: "They ought to be compelled to live within their reservations, the same as wild beasts are confined in cages. If they cannot be forced to work and earn their own living, they must be supported as national paupers, we suppose, until they naturally die out."[37] Even the *Indian Journal* agreed that the Sioux must be punished and driven to a reservation, but it reminded those calling for extermination that white cruelties, including the slaying of men, women, and children, had been as severe as any committed by Indians.[38]

Coverage of the Little Big Horn battle demonstrated the strength of the manifest destiny idea to justify westward expansion. Democratic and southern papers were not as nostalgic in their lamentations of Custer, a Union Civil War hero, and many newspapers opened their columns to opposing viewpoints. The Battle of Little Big Horn and the resultant press and congression-

[35]Mark Twain, "The Facts Concerning the Recent Resignation," in Arthur P. Dudden, ed., *The Assault of Laughter: A Treasury of American Political Humor* (South Brunswick, N.J., 1962), 204-5.

[36]*New York Herald*, 9 July 1876.
[37]*Helena Herald*, 13 and 27 July 1876.
[38]*Indian Journal*, 10 August 1876.

Editors and Vigilantes
Many editors supported the vigilante justice of the West. In this 1874 illustration from *Harper's Weekly,* a New York publication, vigilantes guard three horse thieves while waiting for a telegraph pole to be rigged up as a gallows. Some editors believed lynchings were the only effective means of bringing law to the lawless frontier.

al debates rallied public opinion behind the final campaign to subdue the remaining free Indians on the Northern plains.

Cowboys, Law, and Order

Frontier editors shared one basic dilemma. Should they boost their towns and overlook the shortcomings? Or should they report the seamy side and possibly undermine the town by scaring families away? One way or another, each editor had to find a way through this tricky problem. Before becoming concerned about long-term settlements, editors paid little attention to crime. Six lynchings had occurred near an early newspaper office in Albuquerque, but the editor did not consider them newsworthy enough to report. In the end, most editors devised methods of advocating community reform without calling unnecessary attention to problems. Most advocated public education, promoted churches, and called for wholesome recreational facilities. Particularly in the rowdy mining towns, most editors worked for the imposition of law and order as the first step toward bringing civilization to the frontier and making towns inviting for families and other long-term settlers. But some editors were anything but civilized; many supported mobs and extralegal action.

Campaigns for law and order frequently involved anonymous committees of local citizens operating outside the law to rid the community of undesirables. Most editors backed these "vigilantes." "The hempen rope," *New York Herald* reporter Henry M. Stanley wrote from Colorado, "proved to be a necessary auxiliary to justice."[39] Montana's first newspaper, the *Montana Post* of Virginia City, romanticized about the vigilantes who had lynched a corrupt sheriff and his gang of outlaws. The editor, Thomas J. Dimsdale, wrote a series in 1865 on the vigilantes later published as the first book printed in the territory. "Reason and civilization then drove brute force from Montana,"[40] Dimsdale wrote, apparently missing the irony of using extralegal force to bring conformity to the law. This impromptu system of justice purged the society of corruption and proved that outlaws could not dominate respectable citizens.

As they sought to attract families to their towns, editors stressed the need for a legal system. The *Post* reported on and opposed two riots, reckless horseback riding in the streets, public dueling, and the carrying of firearms. The *Miner's Register* in Central City, Colorado, threatened to help enforce the law by printing the names of people who persisted in wild riding through the streets. Editors often balanced calls for law and order with comments about the increasing number of families peaceably making their homes within the town.[41]

Some editors — particularly in towns dependent upon the cattle trade and mining — turned their backs on reformers. Saloons, gambling, prostitution, and a tolerance of violence often helped local business. The relationship between the editor and the saloons became complex. The editor wanted to put a good face on town news, while the saloon, often a source of conflict, attracted business to the town. The major saloons were dependable advertisers. In fact, some critics said frontier newspapers contained too many liquor advertisements. A gift of liquor from the local saloon could purchase a favorable mention in the press. Some editors even solicited such donations in their columns, occasionally mentioning the gifts when the editors reviewed the product. Although temperance advocates frequently wrote letters and occasionally

[39]Henry M. Stanley, *My Early Travels and Adventures in America* (1895; reprint, Lincoln, Neb., 1982), 173.

[40]Thomas J. Dimsdale, *The Vigilantes of Montana* (1866; reprint, Norman, Okla., 1972), 205.

[41]*Central City* (Colo.) *Daily Miners' Register*, 29 September 1866; *St. Paul* (Minn.) *Pioneer*, 14 January 1851.

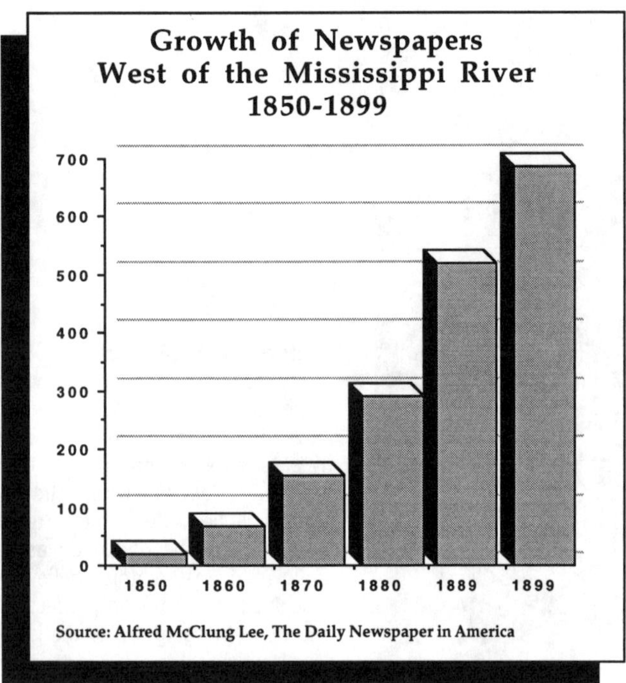

became editors, miners and cowboys generally showed little interest in receiving temperance lectures through the press.

Editors in railhead towns at the end of the Texas-to-Kansas cattle drives ignored the indiscretions of visiting trail hands who spent their wages at local recreational centers. A series of cattle towns built in the 1870s in southern Kansas competed to attract the cattle drives. Town delegations occasionally met the drives on the trail to persuade the drovers to come to their town instead of others. Editors depended upon the cattle trade because their towns did.

Not everyone favored the annual visits by the drovers. Besides bringing bored and lonely cowboys who sometimes made trouble, the cattle drives posed other problems. The large herds trampled farmers' pastures and crops and sometimes brought infectious livestock diseases and parasites to the growing indigenous ranches. Local politicians and their newspapers feuded over quarantine statutes and other laws restricting the movement of cattle. Without herd laws, the farmers, not the cattlemen, were responsible for keeping the cattle out of the fields. Editors and politicians who at first sided with cattle drovers eventually came to look at the future differently as railheads moved west and waves of immigrants settled in the surrounding countryside. Cattle drives had provided quick prosperity, but the long-term future depended upon homesteaders and ranchers.

The battle between the future and the past reached its most dramatic climax in Tombstone, Arizona. Governor John Gosper described the situation as a "rivalry between the civil authorities." The sheriff, a Democrat, was on one side, and Republican Marshal Virgil Earp with two of his brothers, deputies Wyatt and Morgan Earp, on the other side. "I found," Gosper said, "two daily newspapers published in the city taking sides with the deputy marshal and the sheriff, respectively, each paper backing its civil clique and berating the other."[42] The Earps sided unofficially with town leaders in a vigilante group. They were opposed by the cowboys, who had the support of the sheriff despite their record of crimes. The town's Republican leaders considered the cowboys gangsters who threatened progress toward peaceful settlement; the cowboys fought to protect a way of life that did not have room for fences, homesteaders, and railroads. A showdown came mid-afternoon October 26, 1881, in one of the most celebrated street fights in American history near a place called the O.K. Corral. After an exchange of about thirty shots, Tom and Frank McLaury were dead; Billy Clanton, another cowboy, lay mortally wounded; and "Doc" Holliday and Morgan and Virgil Earp were injured.

Characteristically mixing news and editorial comment, the first paragraph of the *Tombstone Epitaph*'s story began by saying the previous day's shooting broke the town's peace long maintained by Marshal Virgil Earp and that "all good citizens" supported the Earps' effort to rid the country of outlaws: "If the present lesson is not sufficient to teach the cow-boy element that they cannot come into the streets of Tombstone, in broad daylight, armed with six-shooters and Henry rifles to hunt down their victims, then the citizens will most assuredly take such steps to preserve the peace as will be forever a bar to further raids."[43] The Earps and the *Epitaph* clearly represented the townspeople. John. P. Clum, the mayor and postmaster, founded the paper, and it was he who appointed Virgil Earp town marshal. Although his tenure lasted only two years, Clum was a reputable *Epitaph* editor who went on to a career in the U.S. postal service and on the lecture circuit. He believed that "every tombstone needs an epitaph" and that the name alone would assure his newspaper a place in history.

Conflict among editors in the same town often had an economic as well as political basis. In Butte, Montana, newspapers played a key role in the fights among the copper barons for control over state politics and what the boosters called "the richest hill on earth." Both sides poured money into a newspaper war, including bribes of editors and outright purchases of opposing papers. The more distant press looked upon the whole affair with revulsion. "They are all liars," said the *Yellowstone Journal* in rural Miles City.[44] The Amalgamated Copper Company finally emerged from the fight with control of politics and of more than half the state's newspaper circulation. By the 1920s, it owned eight of the state's nine largest dailies.

The war of Butte's copper kings symbolized a change in the mining frontier. Gold and silver had created wealth for individual miners; copper required complex processing and large corporate investments. Journalism changed with the mining industry. Newspapers consolidated and, in some places, came under the control of corporate interests that used them as political parties had in the

[42]Gosper to U.S. State Department, 30 September 1881, quoted in *Tombstone Epitaph*, 9 December 1881.

[43]*Miners' Register* (Central City, Colorado), 27 October 1881. The most relevant *Epitaph* stories are in Douglas D. Martin, *Tombstone's Epitaph* (Albuquerque, 1951), 176-203.

[44]*Yellowstone Journal*, 8 February 1900.

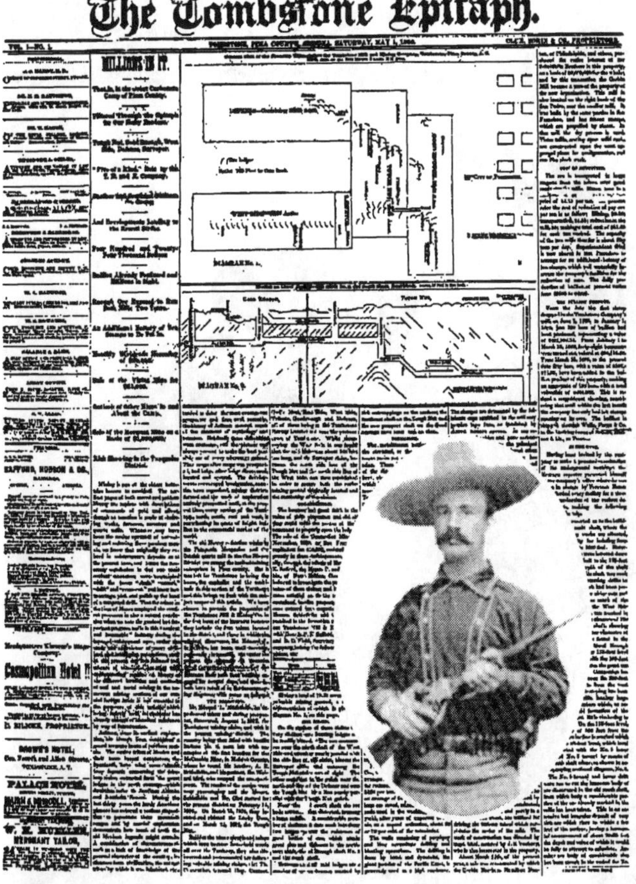

The Tombstone Epitaph.

MILLIONS IN IT.

John Clum and the *Tombstone Epitaph*
Although Tombstone, Arizona, was best known as the site of the gunfight at the O.K. Corral, it was also important because of nearby mining interests. The first issue of its most famous newspaper, the *Epitaph*, demonstrated the high degree of local interest with a story about plans for a new mining operation that filled all but the left-hand column of page one. John Clum (inset), who had resigned as an Indian agent after Washington superiors ignored his protests about treatment of the Apaches, founded the *Epitaph* in 1880. He soon became Tombstone's mayor and postmaster. As an editor, he became an unabashed advocate of Republican U. S. deputy marshal Wyatt Earp against his Democratic rivals who controlled the county government. As mayor, he appointed Earp's brother Virgil as police chief and brother Morgan as a special officer under him. In daily and weekly editions, the Republican *Epitaph* and the Democratic *Nugget* fought over everything from county printing contracts to the proper approach to law and order in violent local feuds. Clum's support of the Earps became the basis for the later versions of the 1881 gunfight at the O.K. Corral. He sold the *Epitaph* to his rivals in 1882.

past.

Such changes in newspapers revealed that journalism had moved into its modern era. In journalism as in other professions, corporate power and professional associations replaced the influence of the cantankerous individual.

The Character of Editors

Although newspapers promoted westward expansion and economic development, historians disagree over the extent of their influence. The disagreement illustrates the classic debate about the mass media and society: Do the media shape society, or vice versa? "Just as the six gun, the windmill and barbed wire were regarded as the principal tools in the conquest of the Great Plains, so the frontier newspaper may be regarded as another important instrument in the civilizing of the West," wrote historian Oliver Knight.[45] Newspapers were catalysts for social change. Yet, as historian William H. Lyon wrote, the pioneer editor put out the same monotonous paper year after year. "Society forced changes upon him; he did not change society," Lyon observed. "He stood among the colorful men striving for recognition and influence in frontier society; but changing conditions of journalism, his own individualistic personality, his itineracy, and his lax business methods deprived him of the stature he sought."[46] Even though editors were an independent lot, Lyon contended, they became too dependent upon patronage and the debts of advertisers and subscribers to exercise much independence.

Yet editors were motivated by a belief that their newspapers raised the community's educational level and maintained a democratic government, and they were committed to freedom of the press. The frontier editor in the Trans-Mississippi West, Knight said, promoted social change through regular and frequent publication, dissemination of timely information, and advocacy of controversy. Through this process, the newspaper helped transform a "chance grouping of individuals" from diverse backgrounds into a community. It promoted schools and other institutions familiar in the metropolis, and it provided a link between the small, isolated town and the outside world. Thomas Heuterman, biographer of printer Legh Freeman, took a cautious look at the editor's influence. "While literary features served an entertainment function," Heuterman noted, "frontier newspapers by their mere existence are said to have raised the educational level of society, civilized the West, and been an agent of literacy. Frontiersmen were avid readers, but whether racist editorials or land promotion schemes achieved such enlightenment is questionable."[47]

Frontier editors defy generalization. They lived in different times and places over a century and across the continent. While involved in land-speculation and town-promotion schemes, Freeman tried to live the stereotypical life of a frontier scout. At times, his wife and family ran the paper while he traveled and sent home columns. This wanderlust was illustrated when he operated his "press on wheels," the *Frontier Index* newspaper that moved from town to town just ahead of the Union Pacific Railroad westward across Nebraska, Colorado, Wyoming, Utah, and Montana. The editor tried to stay ahead of advancing civilization.

Newspaper attacks often got personal. Editors frequently responded to criticism with comments about their opponent's

[45] Oliver Knight, "The Frontier Newspaper as a Catalyst in Social Change," *Pacific Northwest Quarterly* 58: 2 (1967): 74-81.

[46] William H. Lyon, *The Pioneer Editor in Missouri 1808-1860* (Columbia, 1965), 35-7 and 164-5.

[47] Thomas H. Heuterman, *Movable Type: Biography of Legh R. Freeman* (Ames, Iowa, 1979), 50-1 and 143-4.

Women of the West

Virginia Lady Remakes Herself into a Frontier Editor

Some women were as involved in efforts to start frontier newspapers as their husbands and town developers were. Typical of these women was Ada Miller Freeman. Moving from town to town with her husband — proprietor of a newspaper known as the "press on wheels" — she died violently, a way that was not uncommon on the frontier. But even at the time of her death — from a falling shotgun — she was trying to do what she had done throughout her married life: provide stability for a growing family.

She was married in 1869 in Virginia to Legh Freeman, a dashing, tall-tale telling newspaper publisher who for some time had been operating various publishing ventures and writing her letters from the western frontier. Within ten years they had had four children and she had remade herself into a newspaper woman. Legh Freeman worked at a variety of occupations, including frontier scout. While he traveled and sent home pieces about his adventures, Ada and the family ran the paper.

Although the couple was making its home in inhospitable territory, her work received compliments. She herself wrote of her efforts with these words:

"Be it recorded as part of the history of Utah, that a Virginia Born and Bred lady, came into Utah unacquainted with a single soul, and, within a period of six weeks, organized, established, and conducted the Ogden 'Freeman,' took charge of two infant sons, and gave birth to a third, and in that time was never censured because her endeavors to assist her husband did not accord with notions."

During her last of many household moves — this one from Utah to Montana — a shotgun fell from the wagon and discharged a load of birdshot into her hip. According to her son, she died with a great deal of pain.

Her husband remarried another would-be newspaper woman and yet another when the second one died.

Ann Colbert
Indiana University/Purdue University

Like Ada Freemen, women played a prominent role in frontier journalism, although their lives were not often as dramatic as pictured by the *National Police Gazette* in 1882 (above). Women began a number of the early prohibition and suffrage newspapers in the West. Town promotion, frontier fantasies, and real-estate deals occupied the time of Ada Freeman's husband, itinerant newspaperman Legh Freeman (left). They published several papers, but he usually moved by the time railroads and civilization reached the towns he promoted. Another Montana editor noted that all the towns in which Freeman published had died but that his *Frontier Index* always managed to start anew in another place.

drinking habits or sex life. The *Arizona Sentinel* called the editor of the *Arizona Miner* a cuss, a dirty nincompoop, a drunk, and a miserable liar and referred to the newspaper as "his dirty abortion."[48] The *Miner*'s editor responded by claiming that the *Sentinel*'s editor had been everything but independent: "Had you changed your shirts as often as you have changed masters, there would be one sand-bar less in the Colorado river."[49] The most vitriolic language was reserved for corrupt politicians, especially from the opposite party. A Minnesota editor characterized the U.S. marshal for the territory as "utterly destitute of moral principle, manly bearing or even physical courage." Of course, each editor noted that the opponent was not worthy of the attention he was receiving. Despite such examples of vituperation, for the most part newspapers didn't engage in violent rhetoric.

Editors needed the support of their communities, and even though they made personal sacrifices for their papers, they seldom set out as individuals without support. Historians recently have uncovered a rich variety of motives and financial arrangements for newspapers. Besides town boosters and partisan politicians, other groups founded newspapers to support causes like temperance, women's suffrage, abolitionism, churches, and medical groups. Editors often looked for the towns most likely to provide sustained growth for their newspapers. Some cooperated with newspapers in nearby towns for financial assistance.

More than one editor surely stifled his views rather than vent his true feelings about his newspaper's patrons. The primary audience might be the exchange papers in the East where, editors hoped, columns would be reprinted extolling the virtues of the frontier. Minnesota winters, for example, actually looked good in booster columns. "In fact," wrote *Minnesota Pioneer* editor James M. Goodhue, "we have no wind; so that we actually suffer less in the coldest weather than they do in the cutting winds of Illinois, at a much milder temperature."[50] Boomtown newspapers extolled their communities' peaceful future, while on Saturday nights drunken cowboys loped their horses through the streets, yelling and shooting their guns into the air. Editors in homesteader towns dreamed in print of the day when miraculous dry farming techniques would transform barren plains into a blooming garden.

THE EDITOR AS CELEBRITY

But some editors like Jane Grey Swisshelm would not bend from their beliefs; she could not be purchased at any price or intimidated by any threat. Swisshelm was not more accurate in her reporting or less caustic in her comments than her male counterparts. She fought hard for the abolition of slavery and for stronger retribution against the Indians. The first part of her newspaper career was spent in Pennsylvania and Washington, D.C. After the failure of her marriage, she fought for women's legal rights to pre-

[48]*Arizona Sentinel*, 7 November 1874.

[49]*Arizona Miner*, 5 January 1875.

[50]*Pioneer*, 19 December 1849.

Jane Grey Swisshelm and the *Visiter*
Despite her journalistic intemperance, Jane Grey Swisshelm had many accomplishments during her newspaper career. She used her newspaper, the *St. Cloud* (Minn.) *Visiter*, to champion abolition, Republicanism, and women's rights.

vent her husband from taking her property. Leaving behind an unpleasant family situation, she fled in 1858 with her six-year-old daughter to St. Cloud, Minnesota, where she hoped to find some peace.

St. Cloud's newspaper had failed, and a local Democrat with an idle press on his hands asked her to edit a newspaper. To her declaration that she was an abolitionist who could not edit a paper without full control over the columns, he replied that "all Democrats recognized a lady's right to talk any kind of politics she had a mind to." And talk she did. She approached St. Cloud's most influential politician, Sylvanus B. Lowry, seeking his backing for her fledgling newspaper. He agreed to help if she would support the re-election of President James Buchanan. Outraged at the suggestion, she began attacking Lowry, who she said enticed newcomers to become Buchanan Democrats through control of political appointments and removals. The newcomers' "knees double up and their backbones double down like the fibers of a green cabbage blade held over the escape pipe of a steam engine," she wrote.[51] In response, Lowry's lawyer made a speech on the subject of women, whom he categorized as coquettes, flirts, old maids, and advocates of women's rights who write for newspa-

[51]*St. Cloud Visiter*, 4 March 1858.

pers. Swisshelm responded with an insulting description of a woman who vaguely resembled the lawyer's wife.

Within a week, the office of Swisshelm's newspaper, the *Visiter*, was broken into, the press destroyed, and the type scattered in the streets and thrown into the Mississippi River. A note from the committee of vigilance warned her not to repeat her offense. The citizens of St. Cloud, the note said, "have decided that it [the *Visiter*] is fit only for the inmates of brothels, and you seem to have had some experience of the tastes of such persons." Nothing could have more outraged the strictly Protestant Swisshelm.

With financial help from embarrassed moderate St. Cloud residents and support from newspapers across the state and nation, she rebuilt the newspaper. She got so much mileage out of the attack that Lowry pleaded for an agreement from Swisshelm's backers that the *Visiter* would no longer mention the incident. "The men pledged their honor that the *Visiter* should not 'discuss the subject,'" Swisshelm responded. "We pledged our honor that the paper we edit will discuss any subject we have a mind." Changing the paper's name to the *St. Cloud Democrat*, Swisshelm continued to write about Lowry and the mob's attack. During the Civil War, she left Minnesota for an appointment in the War Department, but later her fierce criticism of President Andrew Johnson provoked him into firing her.

Like Swisshelm, other editors became local celebrities. They were important because their patrons believed the press to be necessary to the region, the party, or the cause. They were well known because of the attention they called to themselves with their language and their antics. In Denver, the site of a bitter newspaper feud, New York reporter Henry M. Stanley said the reputation of "these plain-speaking journalists" has "positively frightened me" from visiting them. After a time in the West, however, Stanley began to admire the competition, politics, and eccentricities of the editors and their environment. "I had heard that the editors were savage fellows," he wrote, "ever ready with the pistol and bowie-knife to fight anybody who differed with them; but such stories are pure slanders I think, and the next time I visit Colorado territory I shall try to see more of them."[52]

Editors left their mark on the frontier. The adventurous editor "did not pass away with the frontier," historian Thomas Heuterman wrote; "a legacy of tall tales, boosterism, and even racism seems to make inaccurate the statement that the frontier press bequeathed nothing that the West of the immediately succeeding era wanted to keep."[53]

MARK TWAIN

The most lasting legacy came from a frontier journalist who was a poor reporter and, except in the absence of his boss, not an editor. Fortunately, editor Joe Goodman of the *Territorial Enterprise* in Virginia City, Nevada, enjoyed the articles he received signed "Josh." Publication of the articles mocking a local judge encouraged the anonymous writer, Samuel Clemens, to become a staff writer for the newspaper. Clemens was a former riverboat pilot who was failing as a miner. The *Enterprise* was a rare frontier newspaper in that its staff, which included five full-time printers, was large enough to allow the reporters to be full-time writers, and Goodman was liberal enough to publish good writing regardless of its factual accuracy.

Roughing It
Samuel Clemens dabbled at silver mining in Nevada until Virginia City's *Territorial Enterprise* offered him $25 a week to write full-time. It was at the *Enterprise* that he took on the pen name "Mark Twain." He later wrote about his Nevada experiences in the book *Roughing It*. This illustration of Twain at his desk in the *Enterprise* office appeared in the book.

On assignment to Carson City, where he was supposed to stay one day but enjoyed the festivities so much he stayed a week, Clemens sent back a series of typically exaggerated reports, one of which he signed "Mark Twain." The *nom de plume* was from a river term indicating water two fathoms deep. His account of the Washoe delegation to the legislature, headed "The Grand Bull Drivers' Convention," included a description of one man dancing around in his red night clothes and another similarly attired trying to convince him he was a humbug. "A suspicion crossed my mind that they were partially intoxicated," Twain wrote, "but I could not be sure about it on account of everything appearing to turn

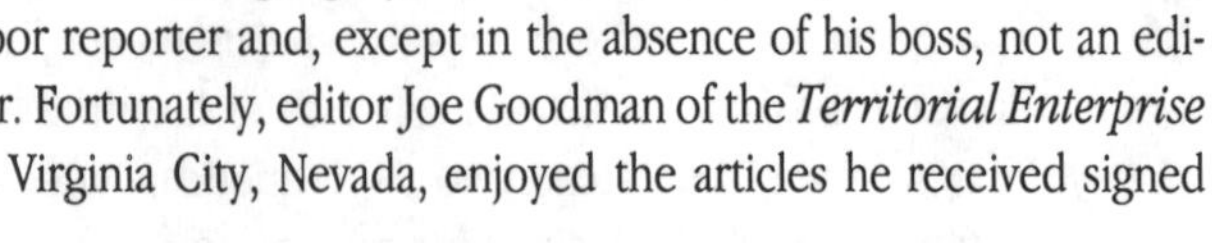

[52]Stanley, *My Early Travels*, 176-7.
[53]Heuterman, *Movable Type*, 145.

around so."[54]

Twain's stories were so widely reprinted in the exchange papers that he told his mother that people knew him wherever he went. "I am proud to say," he added, "I am the most conceited ass in the Territory." Many of his colleagues agreed.[55]

Twain's talent for satire owed a debt to both the wild Nevada boomtown and a tradition of American humor. His cynicism received plenty of reinforcement from the environment, reflected in this "Stock Broker's Prayer" written by Twain or one of his colleagues:

> Our father Mammon who art in the Comstock, bully is thy name; let thy dividends come, and stocks go up, in California as in Washoe. Give this day our daily commissioners, forgive us our swindles, as we hope to get even on those who have swindled us. "Lead" us not into temptation or promising wildcat; deliver us from law-suit; for thine is the main Comstock, the black sulphurets and the wire-silver and from wall-rock to wall-rock, you bet![56]

In Virginia City, Twain got to know several colleagues including William Wright (pen name Dan De Quille). De Quille was well known locally and influenced Twain's professional development. Twain probably also listened to and told tall tales around campfires and at social gatherings. He lifted his expository method from a tradition of American humor. Humorists of the Old Southwest had spun tales for which the setting just as easily could have been Twain's Nevada.

Like most western journalists, Twain owed a debt to his predecessors in the Ohio Valley, where many newspapermen adopted pen names for the purpose of writing satire of life and politics. Charles Farrar Browne, who as city editor of the *Cleveland Plain Dealer* created the character Artemus Ward, was well known before Twain began writing for the *Enterprise*. An avid reader of Ward, Twain borrowed ideas, phrasing, and tangled syntax from the Ohio writer; and when Browne visited Virginia City, Twain made the most of the occasion, spending a good deal of time discussing technique with him. Browne advised Twain on his writing and offered him a letter that helped him to publish a humorous piece in New York in 1864. For his part, Twain never acknowledged his debt to Browne.

A humorist who followed Twain in popularity by writing books, touring the lecture circuit, and writing widely reprinted columns was Edgar Wilson (Bill) Nye, who edited newspapers in Laramie, Wyoming.

One of Nye's suggestions for reform on the frontier was the creation of a School of Journalism. Questioning the idea that it was possible to train someone in journalism — a profession requiring the same information possessed by the Almighty and a willingness to work for less — he outlined a proposed course of study. Two years were necessary for meditation and prayer to compensate for the profanity resulting from years of spelling "God" with a lower case "g," five years to grasp the "mirth-provoking orthography" of English, three years of athletics to build up physical strength, ten years to learn typography and type setting, five years of proofreading and learning to correct proofs by marking "on the margin like a Chinese map of the Gunnison country," at least fifteen years to understand American politics and the civil service and to learn the relative importance of political parties, five years in medicine to learn how "to bind up contusions, apply arnica, court plaster or bandages, plug up bullet holes, and prospect through the human system for buck shot," ten years to study law to understand the difference between "a writ of mandamus and other styles of profanity," ten years of theology, and ten years of practical knowledge in areas ranging from cutting wood to winning the affections of the opposite sex. "At the age of 95," Nye con-

Artemus Ward
Charles Farrar Browne, later taking on the pen name of the humorist "Artemus Ward," established his early following as a writer of brief, fanciful "locals" for the *Cleveland Plain Dealer*. He soon gained a popular following because of his comic ability, and from his local stage he expanded to a national audience and became a writer and speaker of wide fame. This caricature from *Vanity Fair* magazine in 1862 showed him as a popular public speaker.

[54]Quoted in Louis L. Snyder and Richard B. Morris, eds., *Treasury of Great Reporting*, 2nd ed., (New York, 1962), 162.

[55]Forest Hill, Nev., *Placer Weekly Courier*, 17 January 1863; reprinted in ibid., 159-62.

[56]Reprinted in Edgar Marquess Branch, *The Literary Apprenticeship of Mark Twain* (Urbana, 1950), 61.

The Frontier Standardized
By the late 1800s, "frontier" newspapers had become standardized. Rather than being the romantic, adventurous enterprises that some of the earlier newspapers may have been, by the 1890s they had become typical small businesses. After Oklahoma territory was opened for settlement, many printers started newspapers as offshoots of their shops. Their offices, like this one of the *Minco Minstrel*, had poor lighting and heating, with equipment and supplies cluttering their limited work space.

cluded, "the student will have lost that wild, reckless and impulsive style so common among younger and less experienced journalists." At that point, the student's pressing question would be whether to invest in government bonds or real estate in a growing town.

In a satire on sentimentality in writing about children, Nye observed that "statistics show that the ratio of good boys who die, compared to bad ones, is simply appalling." Printing presses attacked the surviving boys: "Most job presses feel gloomy and unhappy until they have eaten the fingers off two or three boys. Then they go on with their work cheerfully and even hilariously."[57] Despite its popularity with nineteenth-century readers, Nye's humor was not as lasting as Twain's.

The Changing Frontier

Mass production contributed to a growing uniformity of small-town newspapers even before the Linotype machine came into use in 1886. Syndication services supplied "ready prints" — pages already printed on one side — to local printers who then printed local news and ads on the back of the pages. The same syndicates also supplied "boiler plate" containing preset stories, illustrations, or pages. These services provided editors with prepared material, leaving a small space for type that was set locally. Ready prints substantially reduced the need for local typesetting, thereby allowing editors to establish newspapers on a short-term basis, such as the length of an election campaign, without investing much time in the print shop. To further simplify typesetting, many legal notices such as those claiming cattle brands or homesteads were required to run for several consecutive weeks. Once a printer had a number of the notices set in type, he was left with only a column or so to fill and could devote the rest of his time, wrote one historian, to commercial printing or "to the comforts of the saloon across the street."[58]

The syndicated services allowed publishers to create small newspaper chains in which several towns could have virtually the same paper with some minor changes. Obviously, the content of newspapers dependent upon syndicated ready print or boilerplate services lacked immediate news value. Sentimental poetry, historical pieces, fiction, and biographies of celebrities were common. The ready prints also carried advertisements, a service that allowed the syndicate houses to supply the pages to the local printer with little expense compared to the cost of printing local news.

The economic structure of frontier papers reflected the changing business climate at the end of the nineteenth century. The earliest printers in the Ohio Valley had learned the printing trade as apprentices in the shops of other printers, probably farther east. Occasionally, they borrowed money from their master to help with the costs of starting a business. Even in colonial times, Benjamin Franklin held an interest in a number of the newspapers he helped young printers establish, but chain ownership was more a mark of the twentieth than the eighteenth century. Financial records of few newspapers are available, but there are indications of inter-newspaper relationships on the frontier. As early as the 1860s about one-fourth of Wisconsin newspapers were operated as parts of chains or other financial arrangements involving more than one newspaper.

As the nineteenth century drew to a close, small-town newspapers began showing the conformity of industrialism evident in their urban counterparts. Like the urban paper, which moved toward stricter standards of news, the weekly newspapers became businesses; many publishers showed little resemblance to the early printers who took pride in their printing craft and their bombastic political essays. Still, some courageous small-town weekly newspaper editors continued to throw caution to the wind in at-

[57]T. A. Larsen, ed., *Bill Nye's Western Humor* (Lincoln, Neb., 1968), 50-3, 63.

[58]John Cameron Sim, *The Grass Roots Press: America's Community Newspapers* (Ames, Iowa, 1969), 42-6.

tacking local corruption or waging a fight over the county printing contract.

RECOMMENDED READINGS

BOOKS

Barnard, Sandy. *I Go With Custer: The Life and Death of Reporter Mark Kellogg*. Bismarck, N. D., 1996. The product of years of painstaking detective work, this book brings together more information about Kellogg than has ever been assembled before. At the same time, it reveals the difficulties of making a living as a journalist in the West.

Beebe, Lucius. *Comstock Commotion: The Story of the Territorial Enterprise*. Stanford, Calif., 1954. The *Territorial Enterprise* of Virginia City, Nev., in the 1860s-1870s was "the pattern and archetype of all western newspapers in pioneer times.... [It had] gunfighting editors, celebrated news beats, authority and power in affairs of state, and its hilarious and uninhibited way of life." The paper was prosperous and boisterous.

Bennion, Sherilyn Cox. *Equal to the Occasion: Women Editors of the Nineteenth-Century West*. Reno, Nev., 1990. Looks at the lives and works of thirty-five female editors of newspapers and other western periodicals.

Cloud, Barbara. *The Business of Newspapers on the Western Frontier*. Reno, Nev., 1992. Business and economic dimensions of small-town frontier newspapers published in the late nineteenth century.

Coward, John M. *The Newspaper Indian: Native American Identity in the Press, 1820-1890*. Champaign, Ill., 1999. Examination of newspaper reporting and how it shaped popular opinion of American Indians in the nineteenth century.

Dary, David. *Red Blood and Black Ink: Journalism in the Old West*. New York: Knopf, 1998. Anecdotal overview of western journalism with rich detail and quotations from colorful editors.

Demaree, Albert Lowther. *The American Agricultural Press 1819-1860*. New York, 1941. The best book on the early history of agricultural journalism.

Dwyer, Richard A., and Richard E. Lingenfelter. *Lying on the Eastern Slope: James Townsend's Comic Journalism on the Mining Frontier*. Miami, Fla., 1984. Editors in the Sierra Nevada, as exemplified by the roving editor "Lying Jim" Townsend, fabricated much of the content in their newspapers, including wild tales, details of mining prosperity, comic episodes, etc., mostly in good humor in the nature of Mark Twain.

Dykstra, Robert R. *The Cattle Towns*. Lincoln, Neb., 1968. Social history of Kansas cattle centers including newspaper boosterism and competition.

Fatout, Paul. *Mark Twain in Virginia City*. Bloomington, Ind., 1964. Follows the famous writer through his formative years as a frontier journalist.

Hage, George S. *Newspapers on the Minnesota Frontier 1849-1860*. St. Paul, Minn., 1967. Valuable, entertaining look at the earliest Minnesota newspapers and the antics of their editors.

Halaas, David Fridtjof. *Boom Town Newspapers: Journalism on the Rocky Mountain Mining Frontier, 1859-1881*. Albuquerque, N.M., 1981. Looks at newspapers in the mining towns in Arizona, New Mexico, Colorado, Wyoming, and Montana.

Hamilton, Milton W. *The Country Printer: New York State, 1785-1830*. New York, 1936. This sympathetic study covers such topics as problems of publishing, apprenticeships, freedom of the press, ethics, how financing, partisanship, shortage of capital, meager public support, the inadequacy of printers' education, newspaper content (including inadequate news), the fierce independence of pioneer printers, circulation, newspaper influence, and finally the encroachment of city papers.

Heuterman, Thomas H. *Movable Type: Biography of Legh R. Freeman*. Ames, Iowa, 1979. Valuable, fascinating look at the colorful editor of the "press on wheels" and his adventures and speculations.

Karolevitz, Robert F. *Newspapering in the Old West: A Pictorial History of Journalism and Printing on the Frontier*. Seattle, 1965. Anecdotal, illustrated treatment of newspapers from 1840 to the latter part of the 1800s. Frontier journalism was rough and tumble; and newspapermen were individualists, not fitting any common characeristics or stereotype.

Knight, Oliver. *Following the Indian Wars*. Norman, Okla., 1960. Looks at correspondents and press coverage of the plains wars from 1866 to 1891.

Lyon, William H. *The Pioneer Editor in Missouri 1808-1860*. Columbia, Mo., 1965. Best look at frontier editors and their place in frontier life and journalism.

Lyon, William H., ed. *Journalism in the West*. Manhattan, Kan., 1980. Reprints special issue of *Journal of the West* on the press and adds three essays.

Martin, Douglas D. *Tombstone's Epitaph: The History of a Frontier Town as Chronicled in Its Newspaper*. Norman, 1958; reprint ed., 1997. Heavy on excerpts from newspaper articles, this book focuses mostly on the politics and feuds involving the Earp brothers and editor John Clum's role in them.

Murphy, James E., and Sharon M. Murphy. *Let My People Know: American Indian Journalism*. Norman, Okla., 1981. A brief overview of American Indian media and treatment of Indians in white newspapers.

Myers, John Myers. *Print in a Wild Land*. Garden City, N.Y., 1967. Sweeping look at western editors, their problems, and adventures.

Norton, Wesley. *Religious Newspapers in the Old Northwest to 1861: A History, Bibliography, and Record of Opinion*. Athens, Ohio, 1977. Frontier religious newspapers and their contributions to reform.

Sibley, Marilyn McAdams. *Lone Stars and State Gazettes: Texas Newspapers before the Civil War*. College Station, Tex., 1983. The main purpose of most newspapers was to support or oppose politicians, political causes, or religious ideas. When financial support ended, most papers ceased publication.

Stratton, Porter A. *The Territorial Press of New Mexico 1834-1860*. Albuquerque, 1969. Readable, comprehensive history of New Mexico's frontier press and its role in major political and social debates.

Wheeler, Keith. *The Chroniclers*. Alexandria, Va., 1976. Colorful picture book in Time-Life Old West series considers writers, editors, photographers, and painters in the Far West.

ARTICLES

Dyer, Carolyn Stewart. "Political Patronage of the Wisconsin Press, 1849-1860: New Perspectives on the Economics of Patronage." *Journalism Monographs* 109 (1989). Patronage was a major source of income for frontier editors, and thus partisans used it to influence them.

Ellison, Rhoda Coleman. "Newspaper Publishing in Frontier Alabama." *Journalism Quarterly* 23 (1946): 289-301. Printers and their environment in the early southeast.

Endres, Fred F. "'We Want Money and Must Have It': Profile of an Ohio Weekly." *Journalism History* 7 (1980): 68-71. Financial problems were severe for the frontier newspaper.

Endres, Kathleen. "Jane Grey Swisshelm: 19th Century Journalist and Feminist." *Journalism History* 2 (1975): 128-32. A reporter for the *New York Tribune* in the 1850s, Swisshelm advocated equal treatment of women. She took strong stands on several public issues.

Fisher, Paul. "A Forgotten Gentry of the Fourth Estate." *Journalism Quarterly* 33 (1956): 167-74. Tramp printers provided a mobile working force for country newspapers. The printer "was a colorful figure and the subject of many a backshop yarn. But he also played a vital role in the expansion of newspapers after the Civil War, until modern efficiency spelled his doom."

Gower, Calvin W. "Kansas 'Border Town' Newspapers and the Pike's Peak Gold Rush." *Journalism Quarterly* 44 (1967): 281-8. Historians have unjustly criticized newspapers for inciting gold fever by publishing exaggerated, reckless, and false claims.

Gutierrez, Felix. "Spanish-Language Media in America: Background, Resources, History." *Journalism History: Spanish Language Media Issue* 4: 2 (1977): 34-41 and 65-7. Gutierrez's article is most useful as a general history. This special issue of *Journalism History* also includes seven articles on the history of the

Spanish-language media in the United States.

Hall, Mark W. "1831-49: The Pioneer Period for Newspapers in California." *Journalism Quarterly* 49 (1972): 648-55. California's first two newspapers, produced very crudely during the American army's occupation during the Mexican War, were similar to eastern papers of the colonial period. They were begun as a means of a printer's supplementing his meager income and carried little local news, relying primarily on news clipped from other papers. Most were vitriolic.

Hirsh, Jeffrey L. "Tocqueville and the Frontier Press." *Journalism Quarterly* 51 (1974): 116-9. Between 1835 and 1840s, in the papers of Ann Arbor, Mich., "[p]olitical struggles, violent and seemingly tasteless personal attacks, and promotion of schemes they considered beneficial to the people, were all promiment."

Housman, Robert L. "The End of Frontier Journalism in Montana." *Journalism Quarterly* 12 (1935): 133-45. Frontier journalism was a mirror of the political, social, and economic frontier. Editors brought with them the "tradition of personal journalism characteristic of the general newspaper work of the period."

Jones, Douglas C. "Teresa Dean: Lady Correspondent Among the Sioux Indians." *Journalism Quarterly* 49 (1972): 656-62. While writing about Indians for Chicago newspapers, before she had met any, Dean deplored "the state of Sioux existence, brought on, she indicated, primarily through a native laziness and indolence." After getting to know the Sioux, however, she blamed the American government's Indian affairs policies for the problems.

Journalism History, Special Frontier Issue, edited by Thomas H. Heuterman and Jerilyn S. McIntyre, 7 (Summer 1980). Essays on economics, census data, women and their relationship to frontier newspapers, and letters and handwritten newspapers.

Jordan, Philip D. "The Portrait of a Pioneer Printer." *Journal of the Illinois State Historical Society* 23 (April 1930): 175-82. James G. Edwards, a printer in Illinois in the 1830s, was a "typical frontier newspaperman who set his type by hand, pulled the galley proofs, ran off the edition, delivered it, and then attempted to collect from his subscribers.... [I]n these chores he was no different from other printers who were hoping to build up a publishing business on the frontier."

Katz, William A. "The Western Printer and His Publications, 1850-90." *Journalism Quarterly* 44 (1967): 708-14. Publications in Washington territory indicate "a level of banality matched only by lack of individuality." Most were printed as official government records and laws and minutes of meetings. Printers relied on government work for most of their income.

Kindig, Everett W. "'I am in purgatory now': Journalist Hooper Warren Survives the Illinois Frontier." *Illinois Historical Journal* 79 (Autumn 1986): 185-96. Narrative of the trials and tribulations of an editor who began one of Illinois' earliest newspapers.

Lent, John A. "The Press on Wheels: A History of *The Frontier Index*." *Journal of the West* 10 (1971): 662-99. "[I]t was newspapers such as the *Index* and newspapermen such as [brothers Legh and Fred Freeman, publishers of the *Index*] who had a big hand in promoting, developing, and, in the *Index's* unique situation, laying out Western cities and towns. They truly opened up the West as much as did the buffalo hunter, Indian fighter or railroader."

Lorenz, Larry. "Harrison Reed: An Editor's Trials on the Wisconsin Frontier," *Journalism Quarterly* 53 (1976): 417-22, 462. Frontier editors, as exemplified by Reed, succeeded or failed depending on their ability to deal with financial, social, and, above all, political pressures.

—. "'Out of Sorts and Out of Cash': Problems of Publishing in Wisconsin Territory, 1833-1848." *Journalism History* 3 (1976): 34-9, 63. Editors managed to establish newspapers on the Wisconsin frontier despite a host of problems, including primitive mail service, difficulties with obtaining needed supplies, and subscribers and advertisers who would not pay their bills.

Luebke, Barbara F. "Elias Boudinot, Indian Editor: Editorial Columns from the Cherokee Phoenix." *Journalism History* 6 (1979): 48-51. Boudinot edited the first American Indian newspaper, the *Cherokee Phoenix*, for four-and-one-half years. It became increasingly politicized.

Martin, Asa Earl. "Pioneer Anti-Slavery Press." *Mississippi Valley Historical Review* 2 (March 1916): 509-28. Shows the origins of early abolitionist newspapers in the frontiers of slave and border states.

McIntyre, Jerilyn. "Communication on a Western Frontier — Some Questions About Context." *Journalism History* 3 (1976): 53-5, 63. In the 1850s in California and Oregon, the conditions of the frontier exercised a major influence on the methods of communication.

Nelson, Jack A. "The Comic Frontier." *Media History Digest* 6, 1 (1986): 46-9. "Those enduring the isolation [of the western frontier] often had little enough to laugh about, and most editors ... saw it as part of their function to offer a laugh now and then."

Nichols, Roger L. "Printers' Ink and Red Skins: Western Newspapermen and the Indians." *Kansas Quarterly* 3 (Fall 1971): 82-8. In recommending how to deal with Indians, journalists "viewed aborigines through glasses tinted by attitudes of racial or cultural superiority."

Quebral, Nora C. "Wilmer Atkinson and the Early Farm Journal." *Journalism Quarterly* 47 (1970): 65-70, 80. The *Farm Journal*, an agriculture magazine, succeeded because it "met the current need of a specific class of readers for a low-priced source of information tailored to their frame of interest."

Raitz, Karl B., and Stanley D. Brunn. "Geographic Patterns in the Historical Development of Farm Publications." *Journalism History* 6 (1979): 14-5, 31-2. "The earliest journals printed little more than general information on plant and animal husbandry, but as agricultural science developed and specialized farming regions evolved, the farm magazine gradually became less descriptive and more analytic and demonstrative of scientific farming techniques."

Reed, V. Delbert. "A Last Hurrah for the Frontier Press." *American Journalism* 6 (1989): 65-84. Newspapers in Wallace, Idaho, in the 1890s exhibited the diverse characteristics of frontier journalism.

Riley, Sam G. "The Cherokee Phoenix: The Short, Unhappy Life of the First American Indian Newspaper." *Journalism Quarterly* 53 (1976): 666-71. Describes the six-year life of the paper and stresses the effect that acts of the Georgia legislature had on its demise.

Robbins, William G. "Some Perspectives on Law and Order in Frontier Newspapers." *Journal of the West* 17 (January 1978): 53-61. Like other Oregonians between 1850 and 1890, editors advocated law and order "in the name of community building and economic progress."

Sloan, Wm. David. "The Frontier Press, 1800-1900: Personal Journalism or Paltry Business?" 104-22, in *Perspectives on Mass Communication History* (Hillsdale, N.J., 1991). Analyzes the approaches that historians have taken.

Thwaites, Reuben Gold. "The Ohio Valley Press before the War of 1812-15." *Proceedings of the American Antiquarian Society* 19 (April 1909): 309-68. A history of the first newspapers in each territory of the region.

Watson, Elmo S. "The Indian Wars and the Press, 1866-1867." *Journalism Quarterly* 17 (1940): 301-10. "Depending mainly upon volunteer correspondents more gifted in imaginative writing than in accurate reporting, [eastern newspapers] spread before their readers the kind of highly-colored accounts of Indian raids and 'massacres' that the most sensational yellow journals of a later period might have envied."

Williams, Nudie. "The Black Press in Oklahoma: The Formative Years, 1889-1907." *Chronicles of Oklahoma* 61 (1983): 308-19. "[W]hile ... black newspapers defended blacks almost to the point of losing objectivity, most were true newspapers in every respect...."

Wrone, David R. "John Sterling Harper, Founder of 160 Papers." *Journalism Quarterly* 45 (1968): 538-41. "'The Father of Western Journalism' ... [who] founded more newspapers than any other man ... followed a pattern.... He would found a newspaper in a promising community, it would fail or he would sell out at a good offer, and he then would...start anew."

11

The Press and Industrial America

1865 - 1883

The Civil War was a watershed in American journalism, although the participants did not recognize it as such until a decade or so had passed. The world had changed. The country was politically united. People began to speak of the United States in the singular rather than the plural: "The United States *is*" rather than "The United States *are*" as they had done before the war. Historian Shelby Foote said the war "made us an 'is.'"[1] The Civil War had been fought over that issue. So the shift in public consciousness was not surprising.

On the other hand, the country still was riven with sectionalism. The South was prostrate from the war, which had been fought largely in the South and had bled the region of men and capital. Major cities in the Carolinas, Georgia, and Virginia were in ruins. The South's economy, relying on cotton and tobacco and having only a small industrial base, was a shambles. The slaves, freed by the war, were adjusting to the new realities, to paid jobs, ownership of stores and businesses, and political activism. Southern resistance to black enfranchisement exacerbated the situation, giving northern Radical Republicans reason to institute military reconstruction in the South in 1867.

A Changing Nation

The West was changing as well. What then was called *The West* extended as far as the Missouri River but centered in Illinois, Indiana, Michigan, and Ohio, states that were on their way to great wealth through agriculture, natural resources such as coal, iron and wood, and manufacturing based on those same abundant resources.

Immigration into the United States had slowed during the Civil War, except for young men who came to fight; now that flow began afresh. In addition to foreign immigration, Americans emigrated from the East into the exploding cities of what would become the Middle West. Political power followed their settlement. Political power, particularly given the disenfranchisement of the South under Radical Republicans, was related to population, wealth, and communications. The House of Representatives had 237 members before Lincoln's inauguration; in his first administration, the 37th Congress had only 178 members as a result of southern secession. The South had only spasmodic representation in the years after the war until the 43rd Congress in 1873-1875 — during Grant's second administration — when the House had grown to 300 members, a result of southern reenfranchisement, black enfranchisement, and new states and territories in the West.

In the Far West, the enormous territory west of the Missouri River, cities and towns sprang into life, like desert flowers in the spring. Like those flowers, many lasted no longer than the first heat of summer; but most were quite sturdy, and the settlement of the West occurred rapidly. Indian Territory began to disappear, and new territories were created out of existing territories. Colorado, in what had once been the distant West, gained statehood in 1876, the centennial of the nation. The frontier had not yet closed officially, but signs of its closing were everywhere to be seen. Most of the remaining free Indian tribes were relocated to reservations. The long white-topped wagon trains, which had wound their way across the rugged plains, deserts, and mountains like a dirty white ribbon, began to be replaced with ribbons of iron that invariably altered the character as well as the face of the land. With the completion of the transcontinental railroad in 1869, passenger trains carried settlers west, especially to San Francisco and points along the way. Freight trains carried the region's bounty east: wheat from Minnesota and Kansas, fruit from California, and beef on the hoof from Texas and Oklahoma (shipped via rail from Kansas). By the 1880s, processed meats would be shipped east in refrigerated railway cars from the slaughterhouses of Chicago.

The changing landscape of the country was but a reflection of fundamental changes taking place in the issues that concerned Americans. Slavery was dead. The debate on the issue had convulsed political parties for decades and had spawned multiple newspapers to keep the issue fresh in the minds of the people.

[1]Interview with Shelby Foote in Geoffrey C. Ward, *The Civil War, An Illustrated History* (New York, 1990), 273.

A PHILOSOPHER IN ECSTASY.

Horace Greeley, Candidate
When Democrats nominated Horace Greeley, editor of the *New York Tribune*, as their presidential candidate in 1872, opponents immediately began to ridicule his eccentricity. Comparatively gentle was this Currier & Ives engraving lampooning his glee at getting the nomination.

That issue disappeared, supplanted by women's rights and political parity for freed blacks in the South. Reconstruction dominated Congressional politics for a decade. It was a mixture of revenge, concern for blacks, and greed. Education received increasing attention, in both the North and the South. Change was slow in coming, however, and changes wrought by education would have an impact on the press long after the period we are examining. For instance, the literacy rate of all whites ten years and older was 88.5% in 1870, but only 20.1% for blacks. A decade later the figure had not changed dramatically. Native whites had a literacy rate of 92.3%; foreign born, of 88%. Blacks had reached 30%.[2] The residual effects of slavery, and its prohibition against teaching blacks to read, would continue for several generations. The issue of hard money versus soft currency galvanized parties, as did immigration, tariff, and national sovereignty. The citizen's world was turned upside down — and everything affecting society affected the American press.

Editors and publishers were as confused about the issues, the direction in which the country should go, as were politicians, businessmen, laborers, and farmers. Newspapers became increasingly outmoded and wallowed chaotically in the social, economic, and political changes. Journalists not only did not know in what direction to head, but newspaper owners were inadequate for the boiling environment. Some continued in the old ways and eventually sank, swamped by popular sentiment and political change. Others adapted by emphasizing vigorous newsgathering and increased advertising, thereby keeping themselves afloat for years. Still others recognized that these social and economic times were different. To survive and prosper, they experimented to see what methods would work. Prospering took seers and risk takers and a lot of good luck, but the successful newspapers trimmed their political sails, strengthened their financial base through advertising, and changed their news to ride through the swirling, changing times.

A New Generation of New York Editors

The northern states and their commercial centers dominated economic and political life after the Civil War, and no city was more important than New York. Its newspapers reflected its own mercantile power as well as the political power of the state. Newspapers known for their thoroughness in news coverage during the war now retained their prominence, although most still were closely allied with political parties and politicians.

The seeds of independence from party and politician had been planted during the war as the exciting news attracted readers to metropolitan dailies. But for seeds to grow and produce they need water and fertilizer and protection from weeds. Advertising would enable the newspapers to grow and produce; the careful weeding of the news would attract readers for advertisers. The growth would not occur overnight, but the newspapers that grew independent of party would become the healthiest ones.

The old guard editors in New York City, as elsewhere around the urban centers of America, began to slip from the scene through death and retirement. Henry J. Raymond of the *New York Times* died in 1869; James Gordon Bennett of the *Herald* died in June 1872; Horace Greeley of the *Tribune* died later that year following a grueling and acrimonious run for the United States presidency. They were giants of the personal journalism that had marked American newspapers.

An astute observer, who knew all three men personally, summarized their different editorial philosophies with a telling anecdote about Greeley. Radical Republicans did not trust President Andrew Johnson, who had become Lincoln's vice-president as a War Democrat. Johnson attempted to follow most of Lincoln's reconstruction policies. Dissatisfied, Radical Republicans muttered

[2] *Historical Statistics of the United States, Colonial Times to 1970*, Part 1. Bureau of the Census (Washington, D.C., September 1975), Table H, 664-8.

A New Generation of Editors
With the passing from the scene of such notables as Horace Greeley, James Gordon Bennett, Henry Raymond, and William Cullen Bryant, many observers thought the "golden age of journalism" had passed. The post-Civil War decades, however, saw the emergence of a new generation of outstanding editors. Among them were such figures as Charles Dana of the *New York Sun*, Murat Halstead of the *Cincinnati Commercial*, Joseph Medill of the *Chicago Daily Tribune*, James Gordon Bennett Jr. of the *New York Herald*, and Henry Watterson of the *Louisville Courier-Journal*.

about "impeachment." Greeley objected, suggesting that Johnson would hang himself if given enough rope. One day, when Greeley was on a lecture tour, Johnson removed Secretary of War Edwin Stanton from office. Republican politicians immediately attacked the action — since Stanton had been leaking Johnson's plans to them — and a *Tribune* writer editorialized, "Impeachment is Peace." Although Greeley opposed impeachment, he kept the *Tribune* on the course the editorial laid out because he felt the newspaper should be consistent, and he would not have it publicly vacillate on the issue. If the same thing had happened to Bennett, the contemporary said, he would have fired the staff and written an editorial espousing *his* view; Raymond would not have fired anyone, but the paper would have ended up reflecting *his* views. Despite his personal opinion, Greeley revered the *Tribune* and was willing to subordinate his views to the greater good of the paper.[3]

Soon after the old giants of New York journalism — Raymond, Greeley, Bennett, and William Cullen Bryant — passed from the scene, a whole new generation of editors was ready to step into the void. The most prominent were E. L. Godkin at the *Nation* and later the *Evening Post*, Charles Dana at the *Sun*, and James Gordon Bennett, Jr., at the *Herald*.

While politics and industrialization influenced these new editors, tradition also had a major impact. The penny press, which had wrought a revolution in its own time, had contributed practices that were widely adopted by metropolitan editors. New editors took those practices and refined them. To some extent, the metropolitan press after the war was a sophisticated version of the penny press. While it made use of the inventions of technology and industry, it still emphasized entertainment and news with mass appeal. Even though news took up the majority of space,

[3]John Russell Young, "Men Who Reigned: Bennett, Greeley, Raymond, Prentice, Forney," *Lippincott's* (February 1893): 187-91.

many editors continued to express strong opinions and to give their papers a distinctive personality. As some newspapers were taking on certain characteristics of big business, the leading ones still were those that readers identified with particular editors.

The pre-eminent model of that personal style was Charles Dana, editor of the *New York Sun*. He bought the *Sun* in 1868 and gained prominence by his writing style and his concept of news. Under stiff competition from James Gordon Bennett's *Herald*, the *Sun* had lost the circulation lead in the 1850s. It languished at a circulation of 43,000 until Dana bought it. In 1876 it reached 131,000, a remarkable circulation increase in just eight years. The popularity resulted from Dana's commitment to sparkling writing and interesting news, a goal he stated in the very first issue: "[The *Sun*] will study condensation, clearness, point, and will endeavor to present its daily photograph of the whole world's doings in the most luminous and lively manner."[4] He looked for bright young writers, many of them college graduates, and provided them with adequate salaries, training, assurance of tenure, and freedom to write as they chose — as long as the writing was interesting. The *Sun*'s writing style was especially evident on the editorial page, the part of the paper into which Dana put most of his effort and the work of his most talented staff members. That page became famous for its "casual essays" on everyday life. Perhaps the most famous editorial ever to appear in a newspaper was the *Sun*'s "Is There a Santa Claus?" in which Francis Church gave the answer, "Yes, Virginia, there is...."[5] Although not written until shortly after Dana's death, it typified his approach in its style and subject matter.

In its treatment of news, the *Sun*, like its chief competitor, the *Herald*, emphasized murder, scandal, and gossip. Dana, however, particularly stressed stories of human interest about events with little significance but considerable emotional impact and stories of the unusual. The classic summary of that approach was the definition of news given by Dana's city editor, John Bogart. "When a dog bites a man," he told a young reporter, "that is not news, because it happens so often. But when a man bites a dog, that is news."[6] When criticized for the *Sun*'s sensationalism, Dana responded in a manner that well illustrated his theory of news coverage: "The first thing which an editor must look for," he said, "is news..., and by news I mean everything that occurs, everything which is of human interest.... I have always felt that whatever divine Providence permitted to occur I was not too proud to report."[7]

Despite his writing genius, Dana did not accomplish all that he might have. Increasingly cynical, he was flippant, almost perverse, in his editorial opinion, and as a result never achieved much editorial influence. In the 1880 presidential campaign, for example, the *Sun* endorsed Democrat Winfield Scott Hancock as "a good man, weighing 250 pounds."[8] Dana's favorite editorial technique was the derisive, clever epithet, such as his continual reference to President Rutherford B. Hayes as "his fraudulency Mr. Hayes," an approach that made for interesting, colorful reading but that made it difficult for readers to know when Dana was serious or jesting. In spite of such fatuousness, Dana was considered by contemporaries to be the leading editor of the post-war period, and the *Sun* generally was referred to as "the newspaperman's newspaper."

Dana's closest competitor as the period's outstanding journalist was E.L. Godkin, editor of both the *Nation* (1865-1899) and the *New York Evening Post* (1881-1899). He was the opposite of Dana: deadly serious about his editorial views. After William Cullen Bryant retired from the *Evening Post* in 1870 to translate Homer, his son-in-law, Parke Godwin, served as editor until 1878, when he sold the paper to Henry Villard. In 1881 Villard made Godkin a co-editor and in 1883 the sole editor. Neither the *Nation* nor the *Evening Post* could compete with the *Sun* for news coverage or popularity; nor did Godkin wish them to. He was not interested in the news departments of his papers and concentrated instead on the editorial pages. Because of his intellect and forceful writing style, he was the foremost leader of public opinion in his day. The philosopher William James wrote of him: "To my generation, his was certainly the towering influence in all thought concerning public affairs, and indirectly his influence has assuredly been more pervasive than that of any other writer of the generation, for he influenced other writers who never quoted him, and determined the whole current of discussion."[9] During his editorship of the *Nation* and the *Evening Post*, Godkin never had more than 35,000 subscribers, but they included leaders of public opinion such as clergymen, lawyers, and college professors, who helped disseminate his views to large audiences.

From an upper-middle-class background, Godkin had little sympathy for the masses in America's growing cities. Yet he was the nation's most effective advocate of many reforms. He preferred to look beneath the surface of issues to find underlying principles, thus bringing an insight that few people could match and offering penetrating analyses of public questions in a clear, forceful writing style. While his writing could be light and witty, it also could be sharp and cutting. The story was told of an old woman in upstate New York who was asked if she was afraid living alone in the country. No, she replied, for every evening the carrier threw her copy of the *Evening Post* onto her porch, and "it just lay there and growled all night."

The other major figure in New York journalism was James Gordon Bennett, Jr., heir to his father's newspaper, the *New York Herald*, as well as to his father's taste for sensational news. In 1872 he inherited a fortune valued at more than $2 million and a newspaper with an international reputation. Spoiled from childhood by his doting parents, he was raised on wealth; during his fifty-year

[4] *New York Sun*, 27 January 1868.
[5] *New York Sun*, 21 September 1897.
[6] Quoted in Frank M. O'Brien, *The Story of "The Sun"* (New York, 1918), 241.
[7] Quoted in ibid.

[8] *New York Sun*, 19 October 1880.
[9] Quoted in Kenneth Stewart and John Tebbel, *Makers of Modern Journalism* (New York, 1952), 79.

Giants of Personal Journalism: Dana, Godkin, and Bennett
In the post-Civil War era, three newspaper owner-editors maintained the American tradition of great individuals in journalism. Charles Dana, E. L. Godkin, and James Gordon Bennett Jr. made lasting marks on the field. Upon hearing of Dana's purchase of the *New York Sun* in 1868, the paper's founder, Benjamin Day, declared that the new editor-in-chief would "make a newspaper of it." With the help of the profession's brightest writers, Dana made an international name for himself, his staff, and his newspaper. He proclaimed that a newspaper's duty is to give readers good writing. "The invariable law of the newspaper," he declared, "is to be interesting." As editor of the opinion journal *The Nation*, Godkin was America's leading thinker on the public issues of the last quarter of the nineteenth century. For many of the problems of society he blamed "newspapers and other cheap periodicals ...[which] have diffused through the community a kind of smattering of all sorts of knowledge, a taste for reading and for 'art' – that is, a desire to see and own pictures – which...pass with a large body of slenderly equipped persons as 'culture.'" The son of the *New York Herald's* founder, James Gordon Bennett Jr. brought to the newspaper a similar instinct for news and sensationalism that his father had possessed. Despite his lavish expenditures on himself from the *Herald's* income, the paper was able to remain a circulation leader throughout the last part of the 1800s.

ownership of the *Herald*, he withdrew an estimated $30 million for his personal fancies. In 1877 his engagement to a New York City socialite was broken off after the inebriated Bennett urinated in the fireplace at a social gathering. After his fiancee's brother horsewhipped him, the embarrassed Bennett fled to France. From there, he served as absentee owner and editorial director of the *Herald* for the remainder of his life.

Despite his egotism and other faults, Bennett recognized that it was news that had made the *Herald* successful. During the 1870s it remained the nation's leading paper in the amount, speed, and thoroughness of its news coverage. Like his father, Bennett sensed what people wanted. Two of the most famous episodes in American news resulted from the *Herald*'s initiative. The paper financed Henry Stanley's successful search for the physician and missionary David Livingstone; and it perpetrated the "wild animal hoax," which terrified New York City residents with reports of animals escaped from the zoo roaming the streets.[10] The paper always had emphasized human interest and sensational subjects. Its approach was exemplified by the observation of one of its editors that "a dogfight in New York is more newsworthy than a revolution in China." The *Herald* maintained its circulation until the 1880s, when Joseph Pulitzer arrived in New York City. Still, in 1890, it and Bennett's two other newspapers, the *New York Telegram* and the *Paris Herald*, the paper's international edition, were making a combined annual profit of $1 million. The *Herald*, however, gradually was sinking. Bennett died in 1918, and the *Herald* merged with the *Tribune* in 1924.

Some of the new editors after the Civil War, such as Dana and Godkin, continued to imprint a highly personal character on their papers and to consider editorial opinion the most important function of the press. Others, however, followed the path laid down by the senior Bennett in the 1830s; their newspapers began to put more effort into producing news than presenting views. A number of circumstances encouraged this shift in the role of newspapers. For one thing, the modern daily newspaper was rapidly becoming a huge, heavily capitalized industrial plant. No longer would an editor-owner, with a modest political subsidy and a printing business on the side, be able to finance a mass daily in which to press his party's opinions. The need for abundant capital would split the functions of ownership and management, so that editors from the 1870s on would serve increasingly as hired help.

An Independent Press

The metropolitan press was first to undergo a metamorphosis from political partisanship to political independence, but there were rough times as the great newspapers in New York, Boston, and Philadelphia worked out their reason for being. The changing social, economic, and political structures of the country required changes, but change required effort and involved risk. Not everyone saw clearly the signs around them. A few who did pushed and

[10]The hoax story appeared on the front page of the *Herald*, 9 November 1874.

Stanley and Livingstone

Epic Adventure Concludes with History's Most Famous Greeting

The *New York Herald's* publisher gave correspondent Henry Morton Stanley a two-word assignment in October 1869: "Find Livingstone." The veteran reporter barely survived the search.

British missionary and medical doctor David Livingstone had disappeared four years earlier in East Africa's equatorial jungles. Known for his good works and books about the largely unexplored African continent, Livingstone was a Victorian Era celebrity. But rumors now circulated among the enclaves of Europeans on the African coast that cannibals had killed him. Finding Livingstone, dead or alive, would help the *Herald* maintain the preeminence earned by its Civil War coverage, reasoned publisher James Gordon Bennett, Jr.

He ordered the *Herald's* star reporter to work his way to Africa. Late in 1869, Stanley covered the Suez Canal opening and spent 1870 filing stories from the Middle East and North Africa. Starting from the island of Zanzibar early in 1871, he sailed to the southeast African coast and began his trek toward Livingstone's last known camp more than 600 miles inland on Lake Tanganyika. During his 236-day journey, he contracted malaria and lost forty pounds. He also participated in a war between Arab traders and Africans that delayed his expedition for months.

But two years and twenty-four days after receiving his assignment, Stanley finally reached the object of his search and asked the question that would link him forever with one of the great scoops of journalism: "Doctor Livingstone, I presume?"

Stanley spent four months with the doctor before returning to Zanzibar. Livingstone died a year after they parted, and Stanley served as one of his pallbearers during a Westminster Abbey funeral. He returned to Africa to take up Livingstone's exploration work.

He conducted other African expeditions, but his relationship with Bennett soured. The publisher often noted that Stanley might have found Livingstone, but Bennett paid for the trip.

Randall Scott Sumpter
Texas A&M University

To increase circulation and advertising, newspapers began to rely on "big news" and "stunts." The most successful in the 1870s was Bennett's *New York Herald.* The biggest stunt was reporter Henry Morton Stanley's search for the "missing" missionary doctor David Livingstone in southern Africa. Stanley's final story in his account ended with the famous words, "Dr. Livingstone, I presume?"

cajoled their reluctant comrades.

One of those reformers was David Croly, managing editor of the *New York World*. During his tenure a contemporary claimed the *World* could have been a model for city newspapers because its news dealt with the important issues of the day and included something of interest to the genteel as well as the proletariat. Croly argued for impartial news, "given regardless of parties or persons, and without the slightest tinge of personal or partisan bias." He believed the public's views had changed, which "compelled the leading papers to refrain from printing distorted news, so that now the reports of meetings and the statements of political opponents are, in the main, correctly stated." Nevertheless, three years after the war, only the *New York Herald* practiced what Croly preached. To his mind, it was the outstanding paper in the country. It would hold that position until someone else equaled "it in enterprise and independence, and surpass[ed] it in earnestness, ability, dignity, and moral purpose."[11]

Political independence meant editors were free to criticize their own parties' political leadership and policies when those leaders and policies were incorrect or corrupt. Some made a distinction, however, between parties and politicians. Whitelaw Reid's *New York Tribune* outlined the distinction in 1876 in response to a critical letter from a reader. Using a metaphor in which the Republican Party was a ship, the editor wrote: "We have scraped the barnacles from the bottom of the hull, but we have not sought to blow up, or burn, or scuttle the ship. In 1874, when a piratical gang [unscrupulous supporters of President Grant] gained possession of the decks and drove the regular ship's company into the hold, we joined the enemy's boats and attacked, not the ship, but those who had seized control of her and cast her adrift.... The pennant of Grantism has been torn down and the Old Republican colors are today flying at the masthead."[12] Even political newspapers could criticize the Party when pirates had gained control of the ship. Independence did not mean "neutrality." Nearly everybody agreed on that.

Despite the growing party independence, daily newspapers did not adopt a standardized, non-partisan approach. The urban centers of the country contained a considerable mix of newspapers that defied neat classification. In Chicago, for instance, the two leading newspapers were the *Times* of Wilbur F. Storey and the *Tribune*, after 1874 under Joseph Medill's editorial control. Both editors actively covered city news, generally avoided shaping news to conform to politics, and took editorial positions independent of their respective parties, but they nevertheless expressed strong views on opposite sides of political questions. There were many well known papers such as these in the urban centers.

Some independent editors had even recanted of their heresy. Murat Halstead, editor and proprietor of the *Cincinnati Commercial*, late in his career recounted his personal odyssey:

Whitelaw Reid
Taking over the *New York Tribune* from Horace Greeley, Whitelaw Reid eschewed Greeley's advocacy of popular causes and turned the paper into a voice for the "respectable" class. He argued that newspapers should be independent of politicians but not of parties.

> One who gave a good many years to independent journalism — preached it, and strove to practice it — held that the position of the journalist was outside and above parties — that the greater the men of the party the greater the necessity for hostile watchfulness, and for holding them in restraint by healthful severities; that the more certain the party was good, the clearer the duty to inform it of its faults — one with such an experience may speak of this theory [of independence] with freedom. The difficulty is that professional and dominating independence inclines to the habit of fault-finding, and leaves the fault-finder hanging rather to the fringes, or wandering on the edges of affairs, than taking them by the handle or the helm and guiding the course of events. It is the better way to go with parties, to be devoted to them, on the inside of them, to make the best of them, stick to them, maintaining their discipline, asserting the principles that they represent.... If the party will go unteachably, irreclaimably wrong, get out of it and try another.[13]

Despite Halstead's forceful views on partisanship, most independents felt otherwise, and they offered many reasons in justification of their views: politicians were not to be trusted, for they reneged on promises of postmaster positions or government printing

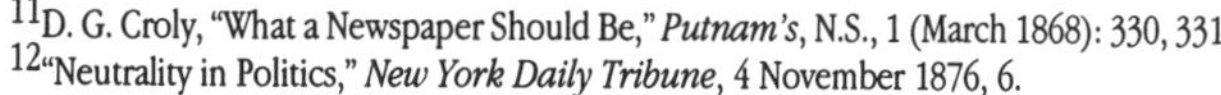

[11] D. G. Croly, "What a Newspaper Should Be," *Putnam's*, N.S., 1 (March 1868): 330, 331.
[12] "Neutrality in Politics," *New York Daily Tribune*, 4 November 1876, 6.

[13] "Maxims of the Press," *New York Tribune*, 24 January 1889, 7.

when they got into office; readers no longer were interested in so much political coverage and comment; and more readers were attracted to the independent press, which was an inducement to advertisers.[14]

In 1881 a southern writer offered a stronger view: Partisan editors were fools. A newspaper that is "An 'organ' [for a political party] makes only such music as its master may order;...the editor supplies the place of the monkey in picking up the coppers." The only safety for an editor was to be "right and independent."[15] This expression came late in our period, for the southern press was slow to embrace the idea of political independence. In the convention minutes of Mississippi publishers from 1866 to 1884, it was mentioned only twice. It was not a popular topic in the South.[16]

The widespread criticism of political or class influence on the news[17] indicated, however, that editors and publishers were adopting different news values, for few people in the pre-Civil War era had expected the press to be independent. Several reasons accounted for the change in editorial values. One was the new generation of journalists coming on the scene. Their views of politics and government, as well as of journalism's role in portraying them, had been shaped in the crucible of the Civil War. They could never be the same as the generation whose "righteousness" had brought about the war. This rejection played an important role in shaping news values for the next several decades.

Equally important were three concurrent changes occurring in journalism, changes that fostered the independence movement: Editors increasingly questioned the value of editorials as compared to news in shaping public opinion and attracting readers; stock ownership became the mode for financing newspapers; and advertising became increasingly important as a means of support and profit.

As for the first change, astute observers, including many in journalism itself, recognized that news shaped public opinion more than editorials. A hundred years later journalism scholars would call this "agenda setting." Several arguments were advanced in the 1870s and '80s to support this view. Many readers took the paper for the news rather than opinion and tended to neglect the editorial page.[18] One experienced writer claimed, "Editorials are read and forgotten. Facts remain and are remembered. It is the news column, not the editorial page, which forms public opinion. In the long run, men do their own thinking [based] on the facts which are stored in their memory...."[19] The influence of the editorial had long since waned, according to these critics. It was the events — and the reporting of them — that shaped opinion.[20]

Other writers thought the editorial still had an impact on public opinion, but only when editors recognized public concerns. In their view, it was the public that influenced the press, and successful editors molded and shaped that ill-formed opinion, but not if they fought it. Cincinnati's Murat Halstead, basing his conclusion on long experience, wrote, "The press does not form, it reflects public opinion. It does not make, it partakes of the charac-

Murat Halstead
Reflecting journalism's move toward political independence, Murat Halstead of the *Cincinnati Commercial* had taken that approach during much of his career. In later years, however, he recanted. "Dominating independence," he declared, "inclines to the habit of fault-finding," leaving journalists on the fringe of the political system.

[14]Eugene H. Munday, "Sunday Dispatch," *The Proof-Sheet* 4 (November 1870): 42, noted that the owners of the *Philadelphia Sunday Mercury* became disenchanted because the Democratic party leadership did not reciprocate the support from the paper; so the publishers charged cash for all political ads and made themselves independent of the party's managers. The views of readers were discussed by H. P. Hall, "Independent Journalism" (speech given in Minneapolis, 3 February 1874), appendix to *Eighth Annual Session of the Minnesota Editorial Association*; reprinted in *Proceedings of the Minnesota Editors and Publishers Association, 1871-1874* (St. Paul, 1874); and Howard Owen, "Advertising Rates and Agencies" (speech, 1874), *Transactions of the Maine Editor and Publishers Association, From 1870 to 1874, Inclusive* (Wiscasset, Me., 1874), 25. Owen was publisher of the *Kennebec Journal* of Augusta, Maine.

[15]Hugh Wilson's speech reported in *Seventh Annual Meeting of the South Carolina State Press Association* (Greenville, S.C., May 4, 1881), 23, 24.

[16]*Proceedings of the Mississippi Press Association from May 1866 to May 1884* (Jackson, Miss., 1885). Only George W. Harper, "The Country Press," June 1879, 147, and R. Walpole, president of the Mississippi Press Association in 1882 and publisher of the *Yazoo City Herald*, 205, mentioned the idea. It should be noted that the southern press was in large measure a country press, and the country press generally was slower to espouse "independence" than its big-city contemporaries.

[17]M. J. Savage, "A Profane View of the Sanctum," *North American Review* 141 (August 1885): 49; "Wendell Phillips on the Press," New York *Tribune*, 5 December 1879): 2; George William Curtis, *Ars Recte Vivandi* (New York, 1898), 99; Anonymous, "The Newspaper," *Printers' Circular* 13:3 (May 1878): 55, reprinted from the *San Francisco Argonaut*, and Anonymous, "The Adulteration of News," *The Nation*, 12 August 1880, 107.

[18]Editorial, "News Versus Editorials," *Printers' Circular* 10:10 (December 1875): 266.

[19]An Old Journalist, "Power-Centres," *Lippincott's* 27 (February 1881): 179.

[20]David Croly claimed that public opinion is "created or moulded by public events,...the fluctuations of commerce,...changes in population, the rise, progress, and decay of religious and industrial organizations,...the conflict of races." Croly, "What a Newspaper Should Be," 333.

ter of the people."[21] Couple these concepts with the view that newspapers should present news the "public most desires to read,"[22] as Charles Dana argued, and one can see why the press had to adopt different news values.

The reasons for starting newspapers also changed. That newspapers were established to make money had always been true — but publishers and editors talked so much about politics and the public opinion role of the press that people forgot its money-making purpose. Contemporary commentators did not forget. Time and again they remarked about this aspect of journalism and noted that it had come to dominate journalism. Charles Dudley Warner, an editor who with Mark Twain in 1873 wrote *The Gilded Age* — a name that stuck to the period — said of the press: "The newspaper is a private enterprise. Its object is to make money for its owner. Whatever motive may be given out for starting a newspaper, expectation of profit by it is the *real one*, whether the newspaper is religious, political, scientific, or literary."[23] (Italics added.)

To attain this crass objective — to make money — publishers and editors increasingly sold stock to raise capital. Selling stock ultimately would cause editors to lose financial control of their papers, but not during our era. Where the editor did not maintain control, the manager might use his authority over the budget to maximize profits. Dividends became more important than politics. When Horace White gained editorial control of the *Chicago Tribune* following the war, he redirected the paper's policies toward liberal rather than radical Republicanism. The change may have cost the paper circulation, but since expenses were kept low and advertising made the paper profitable, no stockholder criticized White's redirection of the editorial page. When the paper lost money following the Panic of 1873, however, the business manager and chief stockholder asked Joseph Medill to become editor.[24]

The means by which profit could be earned also changed. Advertising support became more important than political and government subsidies for the metropolitan newspapers and even surpassed circulation income. By 1879 nearly 54% of all newspaper income was derived from advertising. These figures included daily newspapers with weekly editions.[25] Metropolitan dailies probably had a much higher percentage of income from advertising. The daily edition of the *New York World*, for instance, earned 47% of its income from advertising in 1866, the first full year of peace. The next year that figure reached 50%. Only once in the next nine years did it drop below 50%, and that was because 1868 was a year filled with important news, including the impeachment of President Andrew Johnson and the election campaign of Gen. Ulysses S. Grant on a Radical Republican platform.[26] That year newsstand sales of the *World* jumped 43%, while advertising increased less than 1%. In 1873 the paper earned *61%* of its income from advertising. The *World* was weak compared with such New York newspapers as the *Herald* and *Tribune*, leading one to think that the strong papers earned a higher percentage of income from advertising than the census figures reveal. The Panic of 1873 was devastating to the *World*. Advertising dropped in 1874 and did not recover to pre-1873 levels until after Joseph Pulitzer bought the paper in 1883.[27]

Horace White
As a correspondent for the *Chicago Press and Tribune* before the Civil War, White formed a close, friendly relationship with Abraham Lincoln, a fellow opponent of slavery and leader in the new Republican party. During Reconstruction, he was prominent as the reform-minded, liberal Republican editor of the *Tribune*.

The importance of advertising support was not lost on other editors and publishers. To sell more advertising, publishers responded to the new realities of the marketplace. They justified their conversion by arguing that advertising freed editor and publisher alike from political partisanship.

[21] "Maxims of the Press," *New York Tribune*, 24 January 1889.

[22] Quoted in Frederic Hudson, *Journalism in the United States, From 1690 to 1872* (New York, 1873), 680. Hudson reprints the article "The Newspaper Press" from the *New York Tribune* of 1850. Dana expressed this view *before* the Civil Wax.

[23] Charles Dudley Warner, *The American Newspaper* (Boston, 1881), 5. Originally read before the Social Science Association, Saratoga Springs, N.Y., 8 September 1881.

[24] Lloyd Wendt, *Chicago Tribune. The Rise of a Great American Newspaper* (Chicago, 1979), 243-7.

[25] S. N. D. North, "The Newspaper Press of the United States," *International Review* 12 (1882): 200. An analysis of the census figures shows that 49.17% of newspaper income was from advertising, but North used a figure of 53.79% in the *International Review* article. The reason for the discrepancy is unclear. Weeklies by themselves got only 38.95% from advertising. S. N. D. North, *History and Present Condition of the Newspaper and Periodical Press of the United States, With a Catallogue of the Publications of the Census Year.* (Washington, D.C., 1884), Table IV, 179. This was a special report of the Census.

[26] *New York World* account book, Manton Marble Papers, Vol. 42, Folio #9346, Library of Congress. The accounts run from 1863 to 1875.

[27] Calculations from a memo in *New York World* Papers, Box 1882-1885 Nov. The memo is in the January 1883 folder and summarizes advertising income for 1878-1882. It does not provide circulation income.

Changing Strategies in Advertising

Just as journalism was responding to changes in society, so too were advertisers and agents. America's increased manufacturing capacity, a result of the Civil War, produced a situation of surplus capacity in some goods. The difficulty lay in distributing and selling those goods since wholesalers or "jobbers," as they were called, determined what goods would be produced and distributed. Manufacturers submitted bids to supply wholesalers with the finished product. Since products did not have brand names, wholesalers were interested in them only as generic goods, and the lowest bid got the order.

A few manufacturers, however, did not pursue this practice. The patent medicine industry already had shown manufacturers there was a way for them to gain control of their products, if they were willing to take a risk. Patent medicines had brand names, thus allowing producers to advertise them directly to the ultimate buyer, the consumer. The consumer, in turn, spurred by advertising and the "efficacy" of the medicine, asked the retailer for the medicine by name. If the retailer could not substitute another nostrum, he then ordered that product from his supplier, usually a wholesaler or the manufacturer himself. Patent medicines were ideal for marketing because they were distinctive and cheap to produce and had a large profit margin, thus enabling producers to advertise extensively to build a market.

In the post-Civil War era other manufacturers began to think of their products as distinctive, too, and to affix a brand name that they then could advertise. Thus the growth of brand names, coupled with new products coming on the market in the next several decades, provided the rationale for extensive advertising in the newspapers and on fence posts and the sides of barns.

Another distinctive change was occurring simultaneously in retailing. One-product stores, such as men's clothing, or women's clothing, hardware, or silverware, were too small to advertise extensively in the metropolitan newspapers. Most of them served a small area rather than the entire city. That situation changed, however, with the advent of the department store, in which numerous specialty stores became departments within a large store. A. T. Stewart in New York City opened what was to be the first department store in the United States in 1853. Macy's started in New York a decade later, as did Wanamaker in Philadelphia. All were fixed-price stores — that is, customers could not dicker and clerks could not reduce the price. The department stores emphasized extensive advertising in newspapers. Wanamaker hired an advertising writer to prepare his.

This revolution in retailing affected the newspaper in ways in addition to advertising. It stimulated the development of evening editions, which were targeted to women in the home, and spurred the spread of the Sunday newspaper, which carried news directly to the home to reach women and children.

In addition to these manufacturing and distribution changes, a change was occurring within the advertising industry itself. Especially important was the development of the advertising agency.[28] Under the influence of such people as Volney B. Palmer, George P. Rowell, and Francis Wayland Ayer, agencies instituted practices that benefited both advertisers and newspapers alike.

Rowland Macy
Macy went broke four times, but he was one of the handful of entrepreneurs who revolutionized retailing with the department store. One of the most important advances that the stores made was to advertise extensively in newspapers.

The development of brand products, the growth of department stores, and the development of advertising agency services stimulated the growth of advertising. Despite the Panic of 1873, which depressed the economy for five years, total advertising grew from $40 million in 1867 to $175 million in 1880. Publishers eagerly tapped into this burgeoning market.[29]

Advertising flowed increasingly into the coffers of newspapers, freeing editors from financial pressures to serve political parties and politicians. The freedom, however, was not absolute, nor was it without its own cost. Publishers and editors soon found that advertisers were little better than politicians when it came to demands. At editorial convention after editorial convention, in the East, South, and West, editors condemned advertising agents because of their constant demands for discounts and preferred placement of ads, the use of reading notices,[30] and refusal to pay

[28]See chapter 12 for an account of the history of advertising agencies.

[29]These are total advertising figures from various government sources. Newspaper and periodical advertising was always less than this. In 1867 it was about $10 million, and in 1880 nearly $40 million.

[30]Reading notices were of two kinds, but both were written by the advertiser and appeared in the news columns disguised as news stories: 1) Reading notices were published "free" as a bonus to advertisers who had purchased "display" ads, or 2) space for

bills if the advertiser failed.[31] These demands were irritating, but they dealt with business issues. More important was the impact the increased advertising had on the news product.

Advertising's Influence on the Press

Editors expressed concern about advertisers who acted as if their dollars gave them the right to influence editorial positions of the newspaper, or news itself, especially if the news was about their store, product, or family. Yet, the *indirect* and *unintended* influences of advertising on the business offices and news values were more important. These latter influences were seldom noted publicly during this era. Only in retrospect can we determine their importance.

Believing they had a legitimate right to the editorial or news columns of papers that carried their advertising, many advertisers threatened boycotts of newspapers because of editorial positions on candidates, critical news coverage, or increases in advertising rates. Every element of the paper ultimately was influenced. Most boycotts were undertaken by local rather than national advertisers; and few, it is fair to say, were a response to political positions. After all, until newspapers truly became independent of party, advertisers expected them to take political stances. Few general advertisers felt so strongly about a paper's politics that they would club together with competitors to boycott a paper. Still, if they got excited enough, they could and would apply pressure. During the nationwide strike of railroads in 1877, for instance, local merchants, most of them advertisers of the *Chicago Daily News*, claimed the paper was "inflaming" public opinion against the railroads. They asked the paper to stop publishing the news. Melville E. Stone, editor, and Victor Lawson, publisher, refused their request.[32]

Advertiser pressure on editors and publishers would increase in the years ahead, spurred in part by national efforts of patent medicine manufacturers. Such overt pressure would become an oft-told tale in journalism, and it would influence the content of American newspapers. Because it is the most obvious kind of pressure, it has been criticized through the years. In the total scheme of journalism, however, such pressure has been minimal.

Other changes, however, did have a great influence on the Industrial Press. Earlier business managers had accepted advertising as it came to them. The growth in advertising, however, caused business managers to hire advertising managers. Along with the traditional job of preparing ads for display in the newspapers, they were expected to solicit advertising as well. Soon, they hired more men — women were not employed in the job — to try to sell advertising space to retailers, manufacturers, and advertising agents. As newspapers courted more advertising, they made themselves vulnerable to advertiser demands.[33]

Product Brand Names
In the post-Civil War era, some manufacturers began to think of their products as distinctive and to use brand names that they could advertise. Two of the earliest brand-name logos were Smith Brothers cough drops and Levi Strauss pants.

Most of these demands were legitimate. Wanting to know what they were getting for their money, advertisers asked business managers to provide circulation figures. When that finally occurred, advertisers then pressed for *accurate* circulation figures as well as *meaningful* circulation figures. For decades, publishers and their business managers had refused to provide circulation figures. Since they were not actively seeking advertising, they could be cavalier. Solicitors, though, found that selling space required circulation figures; so they importuned their managers to publicize circulation figures to advertisers.[34] Publishers and managers responded by publicizing circulation. Unfortunately, they exaggerated their figures in order to beat competing papers in the

reading notices was purchased along with the display ads and alternated publication dates. Patent medicine proprietors were particularly prone to reader ads, frequently using their entire space in such copy. In every case, the reader notice was set in the same type as the news columns and appeared in those columns.

[31] Several agents did pay their bills, even if the advertiser failed. Both Rowell and Ayer were noted for this practice.

[32] Charles H. Dennis, *Victor Lawson. His Time and His Work* (Chicago, 1935), 41-4.

[33] See Ted Curtis Smythe, "The Advertisers' War to Verify Newspaper Circulation," *Journalism History* 3 (1986): 167-80, which summarizes the development of advertising departments in newspapers and offers conclusions about their influence on management and advertising practices.

[34] Don C. Seitz, *Training for the Newspaper Trade* (Philadelphia, 1916), 98-9.

chase for advertising. Inflated figures were a widespread problem. Francis Wayland Ayer spoke of it in 1876, after claiming that advertisers had as much right to know the correct circulation as a merchant buying a barrel of flour had the right to know the correct weight of its contents. Ayer divided publishers into four classes:

1. Those who willingly state their circulation and do it correctly, affording facilities for proof of their statements if desired.
2. Those who decline to give figures, on the ground that if they give them at all they will do so honestly, but as their neighbors are given to falsifying, such a statement would be unjust to themselves.
3. Those who are always willing to give the desired information, but invariably add very largely to the actual figures, and when requested to furnish proof have no recourse but to decline.
4. Those who falsely report their circulation, and for proof try to palm off spurious affidavits or some similar device.[35]

Still, many publishers did offer accurate circulation figures and fixed advertising rates that could not be whittled down by crafty advertising agents. Perhaps it is not surprising that these new publishers, coming on the scene in the 1870s, were the leaders in the new journalism that began to dominate the press in the 1880s. The leaders were in the West, but New York, Boston, and Philadelphia each had honest publishers willing to stand on their circulation and rates.

Another influence of advertising was in shaping the content of the newspaper. Newspapers relied upon "big news" to sell the paper. "Big news" was defined as news that attracted readers of all classes — political campaigns, disasters, crime, and so forth. Really "BIG news" attracted even larger numbers of readers. It included such items as hotly contested presidential elections, marathon walking matches, and bicycling events.[36] Major news events, however, did not occur regularly; so circulation would fluctuate dramatically. On some days there was little news of significance or interest, resulting in significant declines in circulation. These fluctuations could occur because many metropolitan dailies relied upon street sales rather than subscriptions. From the advertiser's standpoint, such fluctuations amounted to poor business.[37] An advertisement placed in a newspaper on the day of a major news event earned far more readership than was paid for; but some days — and one never knew when they would occur — a dearth of news earned less readership. The editor and publisher sought ways of eliminating these "dips" by raising circulation to a straight line, punctuated only by the "bumps" resulting from major news events. Subscriptions would have accomplished the goal, but major newspapers never relied entirely on subscriptions.

Instead, they reduced the dips by increasing "small news," news attractive only to a small audience, but for which that audience would return day after day. This kind of news required departmentalization — putting news into columns devoted to sports, society, labor, business, law, and other areas.[38] The list expanded as editors found readers attracted to the news and advertisers attracted to those publications that carried departmentalized news. Specialized news quickly expanded from a column to several columns and then, as papers increased in size, to a full page.

Advertising was a motive force for developing this form of news. "[A]s a rule," one successful publisher said, "a newspaper can secure more satisfactory growth out of specialties than by the extravagant exploitation of general news. In a competitive field a newspaper either succeeds or fails according to its features and individuality."[39]

New Publishers and Editors

Not every publisher and editor understood these changes or wanted to participate in them. The old ways were comfortable and familiar. The new ways required hard work and great risk. During the period after the Civil War, several publishers and editors stood out for their leadership in the new, independent journalism based upon legitimate business practices that attracted advertising for support and profit.

Those publishers were largely in the West and in two major eastern cities, Boston and Philadelphia. New York had no one who grasped the new way of journalism, not even James Gordon Bennett, Jr., and Charles A. Dana. They had led the way in New York City, but now even they were to lag behind the kind of journalism personified by the newcomers. Perhaps they were of the wrong generation.

The new publishers and editors understood the role not only of the news and editorial side of the paper but also the business side. One of the members of this breed was 27-year-old Charles H. Taylor. He was hired as editor of the year-old *Boston Globe* in 1873, a few months after the first department store opened in Boston and one month before the great panic of 1873. Knowing nothing about managing a newspaper, he threw himself into resurrecting a badly run paper, what one wag called a "weekly paper published every day."[40] A Republican paper, it was losing $60,000 annually and would continue to lose money until Taylor gained

[35]"Newspaper Circulation," *N. W. Ayer & Son's Advertisers Guide* 1 (September 1876): 51.

[36]"News and Newspaper Circulation," *New York Sun*, 21 May 1882, 4. Until 1882 the largest circulation the *Sun* had ever attained followed the presidential election of 1876 between Tilden and Hayes. Sales reached 222,390. Presidential election reports normally increased circulation 73 per cent, indicating that some political news was of interest to some people.

[37]Circulation income also fluctuated, making it important to level out the dips in order to keep circulation income at a steady level and to reduce the number of copies returned to the publisher by newsstand dealers.

[38]Helen MacGill Hughes, "The Social Interpretation of News," *The Annals of the American Academy* 219 (January 1942): 13. This issue was entitled "The Press in the Contemporary Scene," edited by Malcolm M. Willey and Ralph D. Casey. Hughes called such items news for "big publics" and "small publics."

[39]Jason Rogers, *Newspaper Building. Applications of Efficiency to Editing, to Mechanical Production, to Circulation and Advertising* (New York, 1918), 252.

[40]Quoted in James Morgan, *Charles H. Taylor. Builder of the Boston Globe* (N.P. [Boston], 1923), 49. Morgan is the source for most of this sketch.

CHICAGO DAILY NEWS.

VOL. I. NO. 1 CHICAGO, THURSDAY, DECEMBER 23, 1875. PRICE, ONE CENT

2 O'Clock EDITION

The Cameron Case

A Disgusting Story Told in Judge Moore's Court This Morning.

STARTLING CONFESSION.

Success in the Midwest
With the *Chicago Daily News*, whose first issue was published December 23, 1875, Victor Lawson and Melville Stone built a highly successful newspaper based on fairness in reporting and on political and commercial independence.

control in 1878 and had total freedom to revamp it. He had started a Sunday paper in 1877, which became a huge success, and twice cut the price of the daily, finally arriving at two cents in 1878. He started an evening edition that same year. Although he changed the political support of the paper to the Democrats, he gave fair and accurate treatment to Republican views. He added news for women, forcing men to take the paper home where it was more valuable to the advertiser, especially the department store. He added sports, reporting important sporting events on the front page — which appalled old-time journalists but attracted new readers. Within a year the paper broke even. The second year, it made a profit and Taylor became one of the notable leaders of the new journalism.

Another leader was Victor F. Lawson. He bought controlling interest in the penny evening *Chicago Daily News* in July 1876, several months after his high school friend Melville E. Stone had established the paper and four months before his twenty-sixth birthday. With Stone continuing as editor, Lawson's business and journalistic skills turned the paper around, making it financially successful. Together they carved out of Chicago's highly competitive environment a new kind of journalism based on fairness in reporting, and political and commercial independence in the editorial columns.

From the first, Lawson demanded accuracy in circulation figures, based upon actual sales instead of print runs, and asked low — but fixed — prices for advertising based on circulation. He began publicizing average weekly circulation when, within a year of the paper's founding, it climbed above 10,000. Lawson would not lie about circulation, but when December figures did not appear in the paper — and November's average remained — one knew the circulation had fallen. In 1878 Lawson bought the assets of the bankrupt *Post and Mail* for its evening Associated Press franchise. In 1881 he began the six-day *Morning News*, later renamed the *Record*, a reversal of the usual practice in which morning papers started evening editions. Also unlike most new journalism publishers, Lawson would not start a Sunday newspaper, despite its certainty of money making, because of his religious beliefs.

Melville E. Stone, meanwhile, was exploring local news and exploiting it for readership. During the Hayes-Tilden presidential campaign of 1876, the *Chicago Daily News* supported neither party editorially and did not comment on the candidates, yet it provided full coverage of campaign events and the contested results. Although sympathetic toward labor, both Stone and Lawson believed in an evenhanded approach to the news, thus providing a new kind of journalism in Chicago.[41]

In St. Louis, a rapidly growing city just behind Chicago in the West, two men led the way toward the new journalism. The first was Joseph B. McCullagh, who, at the age of thirty-one, became editor of the *Morning Globe* in 1872. With wide experience as a war correspondent and editor in Cincinnati and Chicago, he brought a fresh journalistic style to St. Louis. He demanded that the news be accurate and free of political taint, and he vigorously sought news in all corners of the city. In 1874 he bought a morning Associated Press franchise, which forced the competitive *Democrat* to agree to a consolidation, creating the *Globe-Democrat*, a paper that would dominate St. Louis journalism for years. McCullagh started special columns of religious news and daily railroad reports, for the city was finally becoming a railway hub.

A competitor, Joseph Pulitzer, soon joined the newspaper wars. The 31-year-old Pulitzer successfully bid for the bankrupt *Evening Dispatch* in 1878. His prize was the paper's evening Associated Press franchise, because the paper's assets were nearly worthless. John Dillon of the *Evening Post* quickly met with Pulitzer. The *Post* was one of two evening papers recently to start in St. Louis. A merger of the *Post* and *Dispatch* resulted from the meeting. Both Pulitzer and Dillon already had established their political independence although neither was politically neutral.

[41]David Paul Nord claims the *Evening News* differed from other newspaper leaders in Chicago by being truly urban, "an activist portrayer and promoter of the public community." His article, "The Public Community: The Urbanization of Journalism in Chicago," is conveniently reprinted in Jean Folkerts, editor, *Media Voices. A Historical Perspective* (New York, 1992).

St. Louis Post and Dispatch

VOL. I.

ST. LOUIS, THURSDAY EVENING, DECEMBER 12, 1878.

AFTER LOOKING AROUND

The "Golden Eagle!"

DAN'L C. YOUNG & CO.

ARTISTIC POTTERY

Miller & Stephenson's

Christmas is Coming

OUR SHAW PATENT

Easy and Reclining Chair

APPROPRIATE PRESENT

FOR A

HOLIDAY GIFT!

BURRELL, COMSTOCK & CO.

SIEGEL & BOBB,

HOLIDAY GOODS.

SIEGEL & BOBB,

SCRUGGS

VANDERVOORT

& BARNEY

Large Daily Additions

Holiday

Presents.

FINE LACES

421,423&425

NORTH FOURTH ST.

2d EDITION!

5 O'CLOCK

St. Louis Post-Dispatch
Even though Joseph Pulitzer is best known for his news and circulation successes, page one of the first issue of the *St. Louis Post-Dispatch* under his ownership clearly demonstrates the emphasis he placed on advertisements, which filled four of the page's seven columns.

Pulitzer was the driving force in the newsgathering and business side of the paper. It was not in his nature to share control, and within a year he bought out Dillon, gaining sole ownership of the paper.

Pulitzer developed a vigorous newsgathering and exploitative journalism, adopted the "known circulation" policy, and followed a vigorous solicitation policy for advertising by building "Wants" through free insertions until the "object of the wants" had been attained. This promotional campaign lasted through the summer and fall of 1879. The morning *Globe-Democrat* carried far more columns than the *Post-Dispatch*, but Pulitzer built a steady source of income and readership, especially notable for an evening paper in St. Louis.[42]

The next year Pulitzer brought in John Cockerill as managing editor. Cockerill installed a more vigorous news style, one more sensational and active even than Pulitzer's. The 35-year-old Cockerill had wide experience in western journalism, but when he killed a local attorney in 1882 readers turned from the paper. Although he was acquitted in a grand jury hearing, the *Post-Dispatch's* circulation dropped drastically, and Cockerill resigned early in 1883. He soon joined Pulitzer as managing editor of the *New York World*, which Pulitzer had just bought.

WEST COAST JOURNALISM

Pacific Coast journalism, like the region itself, was relatively undeveloped during this period. Yet the journalism practiced in two cities drew attention from around the country. The cities were San Francisco, where Michel H. and Charles de Young had founded the *San Francisco Chronicle*, and Portland, where Harvey W. Scott was editor and part-owner of the *Oregonian*.

The de Young brothers founded the weekly *Dramatic Chronicle* on a borrowed $20. Three and a half years later, September 1, 1868, after they had had a very successful run covering the stage, they converted their publication into the *San Francisco Chronicle*, publishing it morning and evening in addition to a weekly. Soon the paper, through aggressive reporting and editorial leadership, became the dominant paper in Northern California. It won the fight for a new state constitution, despite an array of well-heeled opponents, and boosted its circulation dramatically.

Michel de Young claimed the paper was not sensational, but he spoke those words after William Randolph Hearst, the guru of garish journalism, had entered and left San Francisco. De Young may have been comparing the *Chronicle* with the sensationalism of Hearst's *Examiner*. The *Chronicle* was at least very aggressive. De Young said the brothers modeled their paper on James Gordon Bennett's *New York Herald*.[43]

Scott became an editor for the *Portland Oregonian* in April 1865 after graduating from Pacific University. He was known for his fluency in English, thoughtful analysis of events, and lack of invective. He gave direction to the development of Portland and Oregon over forty years, and political leaders and newspaper publishers throughout the rest of the country carefully followed his editorial comments.

Yet he was not without his foibles and biases. During Reconstruction he spoke for leniency to the South. He abhorred slavery and state sovereignty, yet "he was never reconciled to Negro suffrage," one historian claimed. During the free-silver passions of the 1890s, he was a nearly lone voice in the Pacific Northwest for a gold standard, and his advocacy was considered the reason Oregon was the only state along the Pacific Coast to vote for the gold standard and against presidential candidate William Jennings Bryan.[44]

[42] This sketch is based on Julian Rammelkamp, *Pulitzer's Post-Dispatch 1878-1883* (Princeton, N.J., 1967). Memoranda in the Pulitzer Papers suggest that Pulitzer believed want ads stimulated circulation. They also provided *steady* income.

[43] Addison Archer, *American Journalism. From the Practical Side* (New York, 1897), 319-22. Archer published an extensive interview with de Young.

[44] George S. Turnbull, *History of Oregon Newspapers* (Portland, Ore., 1936), 118-21.

Publishers in many other cities — Philadelphia, Detroit, Cleveland, Cincinnati, and Kansas City — were designing newspapers adapted to 1880s and '90s America. Their journalism varied, but they shared several characteristics. Independent of political parties, they emphasized news and conducted vigorous newsgathering. Their newspapers were low priced, designed to reach the largest audience. Most of their newspapers also were of the new generation of evening journals. No less important, they relied upon advertising to support the news, practiced business openness by providing accurate circulation based on the sale of papers, and adhered to their advertising rate cards. These papers generally campaigned against corruption in government, both local and national. There was a lot of campaigning to do.

The Tweed Ring and Urban Corruption

The Tweed Ring in New York City marked one of the low points in American journalism, although historians have seldom emphasized the press' role in allowing the gang of Tammany Hall politicians to steal millions and millions of dollars from the taxpayers. An exception was the *New York Times*, which risked all in attacking the Ring.

Upon Henry Raymond's death in 1869, George Jones became editor of the *Times*. He previously had handled the paper's business affairs. He decided to attack the Tweed Ring's rapacious ways. He launched the campaign in September 1870, with Louis J. Jennings, an Englishman, writing the editorials, and John Foord, a recently immigrated Scot, the news stories. When documents detailing the Ring's financial malfeasance were given to the *Times*, the Ring's fate was sealed. Democratic Tammany Hall no longer could accuse the Republican *Times* of acting only out of partisanship.[45]

Along with the *Times*, *Harper's Weekly* also helped bring down the Tweed Ring. Thomas Nast, the political cartoonist on the illustrated magazine, pilloried the ringleader, the rotund William Marcy Tweed, and his gang week after week. Tweed retaliated by removing Harper's Brothers school books from the public schools. Although the company suffered a severe financial loss, it did not back down. Nast drew a cartoon showing Tweed ripping Harper's books from the hands of school children.

Among the other New York newspapers, however, only the *Herald* supported the campaign against the ring. Where were the others? Why did not the vigorous New York press attack the wholesale thievery practiced by Tweed and his gang? The answer lay in the counting house — the business office of the press. The ring bought off the newspapers through lucrative advertising contracts with the city, which Tweed's cohorts administered. When an investigation was made after the gang's fall, the comptroller found

"Let Us Prey"
The *New York Times'* efforts to topple the Tweed Ring were joined by the cartoonist Thomas Nast of *Harper's Weekly*. One of his contributions was this cartoon, which painted Boss Tweed and his cohorts as vultures preying on the city.

eighty-nine papers had received patronage. Twenty-seven died when the patronage spigot was turned off. All "...with possibly three exceptions, were solely dependent upon this kind of advertising for support."[46] The magnitude of the thievery can be found in the comptroller's report. Joseph Howard, who owned the *New York Star*, received $218,477 from 1867-1871, and he claimed an additional $23,233. The *Daily News* received $431,623 during the same period. Tweed's *Transcript* received $783,498! A critic of New York's papers wrote:

> In those halcyon days of roguery people used to glance in their morning paper over a mayor's message of six or eight columns, innocently supposing it part of the news of the day, while bookkeepers were at the same moment charging it to the city as an advertisement at a dollar a line. Petty evening papers received a thousand dollars a month; and after the newspapers had been

[45]Meyer Berger, *The Story of the New York Times* (New York, 1951), 35-53, gives a well written account of the *Times'* role in bringing the Tweed Ring to justice. He is too kind on the other publishers, although he acknowledges they knew—or should have known — of the graft at City Hall. An insightful discussion that raises many questions about the *Times'* performance can be found in Thomas C. Leonard, *The Power of the Press. The Birth of American Political Reporting* (New York, 1986), chapter 4.

[46]In *Clippings About Journalism*, Vol. 2, Library of Congress. The clipping, from an unknown newspaper, is of an article reprinted from *Harper's Weekly*.

The New *Chicago Tribune* Building
Through Joseph Medill's emphasis on departmentalization and specialized news, the *Chicago Tribune* rapidly gained circulation and grew in size, requiring the construction of a much larger building to house its operations in the 1880s. Based on the design of the building that had been destroyed in the Great Chicago Fire, the new building added an extra floor, increasing its space by 25 per cent.

> bought and silenced at this rate for five years, and the Ring had no longer control of the treasury, the unsettled "claims" of the various counting-rooms amounted to more than two millions of dollars. The writers for the press got little of this. *They* were put off with a ridiculous gratuity of two hundred dollars a year, voted by the aldermen to the reporters who omitted twice a week to tell the public what the aldermen had done.[47]

One printer set city reports in type, ran off thousands and thousands of copies, and sold them in bulk to publishers to be run in their own papers. Those publishers charged the city as though they had set the reports themselves.[48] The wholesale bleeding of the city's finances was possible only because the press, including the quality newspapers, was bought off.

Corruption was widespread in other cities and in the national government. Most papers were only tangentially involved in reporting it. They might respond if the corrupters were of a different political party, but most newspapers were not yet willing to take on any person and any political party.[49] A survey of 130 cities in 1877 found that their collective debt, at $644.4 million, was nearly three times larger than it had been a decade earlier. That figure probably was on the low side since it relied upon self reports from city comptrollers. New York City's comptroller, for instance, claimed debt at $91.4 million while a city report to the State Senate revealed debt at $149.3 million, 63% higher. The enormous funds needed for rapidly growing cities were simply too tempting for many "public servants" to overlook. Newspapers, in a few cases, reported the skullduggery, but the press generally was not alert to the corruption.

Differentiating the News

The journalism that developed in the post-war period required vigorous, enterprising young men and women in the newsrooms actively pursuing the news. When the *Chicago Daily News* was established in 1875, the existing Chicago papers sold for five cents a copy and were, a *Daily News* editor claimed, "eight vast pages of long, closely printed columns." Ads crowded the front pages. "Space was devoted to the printing of railroad time tables, in return for which much transportation was obtainable on request. The news was "actual or so called, all of it diluted to a painful degree,...reprinted matter swept up from everywhere."[50] The "big news" was that which all newspapers tended to get, and at about the same time.

If a major story occurred, the newsgathering agencies — the New York Associated Press, the Western Associated Press, or the numerous regional agencies — covered it, and no newspaper receiving the service had an advantage over competitors receiving the same service. The key phrase is "receiving the same service," for the news agencies allowed those newspapers that first subscribed to the service to monopolize the news. Newspapers were bought for no reason other than to gain access to their Associated Press franchise, as happened in St. Louis with the *Globe-Democrat* and the *Post-Dispatch* and in Chicago with the *Daily News.*

News brokering became very competitive. The Western Associated Press had begun as a subsidiary to the New York Associated Press, despite the strength of the western newspapers. A contract in 1867 provided for news from the NYAP to be shared with the WAP, but also restricted the WAP from supplying other state or regional news agencies that might start up in the future. News was to be distributed exclusively over Western Union lines. Despite the contract, the WAP set up subsidiary agencies in the West, a move vigorously contested by the NYAP. Control, nevertheless, largely remained in the hands of the NYAP for a multitude of reasons, not the least of which was the agreement the two groups

47James Parton, "Falsehood in the Daily Press," *Harper's New Monthly Magazine* 49 (July 1874): 274.

48*Clippings About Journalism*, Vol. 2, in the Library of Congress, contains numerous newspaper clippings that dealt with the Ring's handling of newspaper advertising. See especially "A Great Leak Stopped," "The 'Subsidized Press,'" and "Subsidies to the New York Press."

49An exception was the Whiskey Ring fraud in which liquor taxes were diverted from the U.S. Treasury during Grant's administration. It was uncovered by a *St. Louis Globe-Democrat* reporter. Grant was Republican, as was the paper.

50Charles H. Dennis, "Lawson and Stone Hailed as Pioneers," *Editor & Publisher* (21 July 1934; Golden Jubilee Number): Sec. 2, 52.

Charles H. Taylor
Few editors grasped the emerging mode of journalism in the 1870s as did Charles H. Taylor of the *Boston Globe*. He emphasized independent journalism, new types of news content, and sound business practices to attract advertising. Losing $60,000 when Taylor took control, the *Globe* began making a profit in his second year at the helm.

had made in 1867. By 1882, however, the WAP had grown so powerful it was able to persuade the NYAP to merge into one association with two divisions. Control still remained in New York — not a completely satisfactory arrangement for western newspapers — but at least it was diffused. In any case, this powerful new entity was able to provide large quantities of news to its subscribers and to cut off overlapping services into the same states.

This growth and conflict resulted in distribution of national and international news cheaply and quickly to a significant portion of America's dailies. In 1880, one-third of all dailies took the Associated Press news report.[51] A weak competitive news service provided many of the non-AP papers with most of the major national news. As a result, competitive dailies contained the same "big news" stories, although some always were at a competitive disadvantage.

For those who did share this news "budget," how then could an editor gain a news advantage over competitors? The answer was through local and specialized news and special columns. This kind of reporting required larger staffs. Chicago journalism generally may have been stodgy before the arrival of the *Daily News*, but certainly not all papers were. An exception was the *Tribune*. In 1874, when Joseph Medill again took over editorial control of the paper, he promoted departmentalization of specialized news: foreign, city, financial and commercial, books, religion, sports, women, and others. These changes had a positive effect on circulation. Charles Taylor did much the same thing on the *Boston Globe*, but added serials and short stories, a column on housekeeping, and humor. This specialized news — "small news" — was treated differently from "big news" in that it tended to be more accurate and timely.[52]

To gather this news required reporters, lots of them. Editors cast around for "knights of the pen" only to find there were not enough experienced men or women to meet their needs. The old route through the backshop as an apprentice did not provide enough people. Editors hired willy-nilly, hoping to find jewels by throwing young men and women unprepared into the workplace.[53]

Working conditions varied from city to city. New York, which had a surfeit of applicants, developed a system not widely used outside the city until the 1880s. Reporters would be "hired" as space men. This meant they would sit and wait for the city editor to assign them to a story. If they were given a lead to pursue and they found publishable stories, they were paid by the number of column inches their stories filled in print. Those inches were totaled at the end of the week; and, depending upon the paper, the reporters were paid from $6 a column to $8. If reporters were not able to get a story, they were paid up to fifty cents an hour for the time they spent gathering the information (provided they had not taken too long on the story). If they were not assigned a story, they sat all day long and received nothing. It was a vicious system, but the aggressive newsgatherers with the willingness to stick it out eventually would win a place on the paper. Many talented reporters with experience in less competitive markets faded into other jobs.[54]

One of the effects of the space system was to cause reporters to pad their stories. The problem was obvious even in 1871. "Men do not drink wine," one critic complained, "but 'indulge in a little stimulating fluid.'" Many writers buried the news under a pile of verbiage. One story began: "As the gray beams of morn began to pencil the eastern sky with the advancing light of day...." The writer finally got around to telling the reader a neighbor's hen-house had been robbed at dawn.[55] Editors fought such flowery and exag-

[51]Richard A. Schwarzlose, *The Nation's Newsbrokers. The Rush to Institution from 1865 to 1920.* Vol. 2. (Evanston, Ill., 1990), Table I, 248.

[52]Editorial, "Journalism and Jealousy," *New York Tribune*, 1 December 1879, 4. When the *Tribune* was accused of publishing financial information for personal reasons, the editor defended the paper's early news beat. He criticized those editors who resorted to innuendo to disparage competition just because they were beaten.

[53]When Charles A. Dana took over the *New York Sun* he quickly increased its circulation. George P. Rowell, a close observer of the paper, attributed the increase in part to the paper's improved news coverage, made possible because Dana picked good reporters, not relatives of proprietors. George P. Rowell, *Men Who Advertise* (New York, 1870), 124.

[54]North, *History and Present Condition*, 83. For a fuller discussion of working conditions and their effect upon the news, see Ted Curtis Smythe, "The Reporter, 1880-1900: Working Conditions and Their Influence on the News," *Journalism History* 7 (1980): 1-10.

[55]Jaimes Parting, "Grasping After Sublimity," *Advertiser's Gazette* 5 (October 1871): 79. It was probably a pseudonym. The article appeared first in the *Utica* (N. Y.) *Daily Observer*.

Congressional Reporters
A handful of women reporters covered Washington in the 1870s. Few of them, however, covered Congress. Although they were eligible to apply for admission to the Reporters' Galleries in the Capitol building, they chose instead to report from the Ladies' Gallery. This 1874 illustration of congressional reporters showed only two women, and both were spectators.

gerated writing, but reporters were desperate for column inches.

Even though reporters were not paid well, the large numbers of men and women needed to cover city news ate up the editorial budget. In an effort to make his reporters more efficient, Charles Taylor of the *Boston Globe* put his *regular* reporters on salary, but he found they would not produce enough copy. When they were put on space, however, some produced so much copy they earned $240 a month, a princely sum for a reporter. Taylor solved the dilemma by putting reporters on a regular, but small salary, with a quota for the amount of news required and a bonus based on one-third of all space over the salary.[56]

Such conditions led George William Curtis of *Harper's Monthly* to assert that journalism was not a profession because there was no course of study required, no examination to test what one knew, and no certification by degree. "It is a pursuit rather than a profession," he concluded.[57]

Reporters were one cog in an industrialized press — one requiring more capital to start, more investment in machinery and talent, and larger staffs and expenses. Because of the financial considerations, the larger papers, like their industrial counterparts, needed to economize. It was as important for the solicitor to get the ad into the newspaper as for the reporter to get the news in, and both had to meet deadlines. The key was to operate efficiently in gathering and writing news and in selling space and writing advertisements. As a means of efficiency, both advertising manager and editor sought to systematize office routine.

The people who rose to the top of these new industrial organizations usually had come up through other newspapers, but not always as reporters. By 1875 it no longer was true, if it ever had been, that metropolitan editors arose from the rural areas, coming out of the small towns to make a career and name for themselves. A few prominent editors had indeed come from rural communities, but by 1875 the top editors of the largest newspapers were like other industrial executives: 64% of the editors versus 67% of the industrialists had fathers with business, professional, or public official backgrounds. Thirty-seven per cent of the editors had started work at age fifteen or younger, reflecting the long apprenticeship many underwent in the backshop of the newspaper. But they did not stop there. Forty per cent had college degrees, while only two per cent of the American population had graduated from high school. These editors did not reflect American society. Perhaps of equal importance, nearly 63% held a controlling interest in their papers; another 14% held part ownership. The editor was a member of the elite in education, background, and, often, because of ownership, in income.[58]

African Americans in Journalism

Black Americans who wanted to work on newspapers following the Civil War had but three options: they could write for a black newspaper, which was issued weekly; work in the backshop of a white-owned paper as a compositor or printer; or start their own newspaper. No African American worked as a journalist on a metropolitan daily until 1887, when T. Thomas Fortune began writing for the *New York Sun*.

Fortune was born a slave but early became interested in newspapers, working on black-owned weeklies in both the South and the North after the war. He got further journalistic experience by buying the *Globe* in New York (1879-1884) with a colleague. They kept it going by working as compositors on another paper.[59]

[56]*Minutes of the Ninth American Newspaper Publishers Association Convention* (1895), 54-5. Taylor was recounting an earlier period.

[57]George William Curtis, *Ars Recte Vivendi* (New York, 1898), 120. This essay appeared originally in *Harper's Monthly* (October 1882).

[58]Jack R. Hart, "Horatio Alger in the Newsroom: Social Origins of American Editors," *Journalism Quarterly* 53 (1976): 14-20. Hart's study compares both 1875 and 1900 editorial profiles with surveys of industrialists during roughly the same periods. He dispels the myth of most metropolitan editors starting from humble backgrounds.

[59]Clint C. Wilson II, *Black Journalists in Paradox*. Contributions in Afro-American and

Certainly the most famous black journalist during the post-Civil War era was Frederick Douglass. He had made a name for himself during the antebellum period as both a public speaker and newspaper editor. Having discontinued his *Frederick Douglass' Paper* during the war because of financial difficulties, he did not again contribute regularly to a newspaper until 1870, when the *New Era* was formed to help former slaves adapt to their new status. The paper fell on hard times; so Douglass bought a half-interest, became editor, and then renamed the paper *The New National Era*.

It continued to struggle until he closed it in 1875 and left journalism for good. The abolitionist fervor of some white supporters in the antebellum period dissipated after the war. Financial support faded as quickly as the fervor cooled, and advertising and subscription income was inadequate to keep the paper going. Douglass continued to make speeches; and he fought vigorously for passage of the Fourteenth Amendment to the U.S. Constitution, which guaranteed equal protection of the laws for everyone under United States jurisdiction. He was named Marshal of the District of Columbia, giving him status as well as power to employ blacks.[60]

Both Fortune and Douglass serve to illustrate the state of African-American journalism in the first two decades following the Civil War. It was precarious and generally unrewarding. In the census of 1880, there were an estimated thirty-one black newspapers, all weekly, but they died almost as rapidly as they were started.

Women in Journalism

Reporting and editing were largely male domains after the Civil War. The few female reporters generally covered meetings, weddings, and social events. There were few exceptions. The 1870 census listed only thirty-five women as journalists, 0.6% of the total number. By 1880 that figure had climbed to 288, but it still represented only 2% out of 12,308 journalists.[61]

A notable exception to those who covered women's topics was the handful of women who covered Washington, D.C., but even they were confined largely to background or social topics. They seldom covered hard news. Mary Clemmer Ames filed a "Women's Letter From Washington" for the *New York Independent* beginning in 1866 and continued it for twenty years. Yet, though eligible to apply for the Reporters' Galleries in the Capitol building, she never did so, instead reporting on Congress from the Ladies' Gallery.

Emily Briggs, under the pen name "Olivia," during the Civil War began writing on Washington government and society for the *Philadelphia Press*. She continued to write five or six letters a week after the war. Senate Historian Donald Ritchie called Briggs "one of the first women correspondents to use the telegraph for 'spot news,' a sudden flash of important and late-breaking information. Yet, since telegraphing 'cost a fortune,' she generally corresponded by letter, writing long and detailed accounts of the people and events she observed from the reporters' galleries or at an evening social gathering." Her most important talent, Ritchie noted, "lay in her colorful descriptions, her keen eye for social and fashion trends, and her witty style of writing."[62]

In the late 1870s, twenty women were accredited to the House and Senate press galleries. The Standing Committee of Correspondents, however, issued a new rule that required that members represent daily newspapers *and* use the telegraph to file copy. The rule was aimed at keeping lobbyists and other non-journalists out of the galleries; but, since most women worked for weeklies and the few who represented dailies wrote stories that were sent by mail, no woman qualified for the galleries in 1880.

Increases in Dailies and Circulation, 1850-1880

	Dailies	*Circulation*
1850	254	758,454
1860	387	1,478,435
1870	574	2,601,547
1880	971	3,566,395

Source: North, *Newspaper and Periodical Press*, 187.

Technology and the Press

Other changes were altering the character of the American newspaper. The number of newspapers increased dramatically, and circulation increased even faster than the population.[63] One factor in the circulation growth was a number of technical advances enabling publishers to reduce newspaper prices, print news closer to its time of occurrence, and increase rapid distribution to the suburbs or even to other states.

Newsprint costs were substantial and fluctuated over time. The high costs were particularly troublesome for those newspapers that tried to maintain cheap prices in order to reach a popular audience. A change in the paper making process, however, offered a solution. In Germany during the 1840s, wood pulp was used to make newsprint. That process moved to the United States in the 1860s, and the first American newspaper to convert was the *New Yorker Staats-Zeitung*. This conversion began January 1, 1868, although the paper did not switch entirely to wood pulp until 1870. For a decade or two, rag content was mixed with wood pulp to produce newsprint. As a result, the price of newsprint at first stabilized and then began a steady decline. It quickly fell from $344 a ton in 1866 to $246 in 1870. Yet, the New York Public Library found that only five of fifteen newspapers in its files converted to

African Studies, No. 145 (New York, 1991), 38-41.

[60]Robert Conniff, "Frederick Douglass Always Knew He Was Meant to be Free," *Smithsonian* (February 1995), 36-8.

[61]Maurine H. Beasley and Kathryn T. Theus, *The New Majority* (New York, 1988), 7.

[62]Donald A. Ritchie, *Press Gallery* (Cambridge, Mass., 1991), 150. Ritchie devoted an entire chapter to women correspondents, most of it covering the period of this chapter.

[63]North, "Newspaper Press," 202.

Improving Press Speeds
The web-perfecting press enabled newspapers to print thousands of copies quickly. "Perfecting" designated the process of printing on both sides of a sheet of paper at the same time. The "web" referred to the continuous roll of paper that ran through the press. The top illustration shows the Taylor company's perfecting press from 1856. Robert Hoe's "web printing machine" (bottom) attracted crowds of spectators at its exhibit in 1876. It could deliver 30,000 copies of an eight-page paper in the brief time of one hour.

wood entirely in the 1870s. Nevertheless, after the price dropped further to $138 in 1880, six more converted. The price continued to decline dramatically, so that by 1890, after manufacturers introduced chemicals to process the wood pulp, the 1880 price had been cut in half. It would be cut in half again by 1900.[64] Newspapers that stayed with rag paper or some mixture of rag and pulp faced a cost disadvantage.

Technical improvements in production also reduced costs while increasing speeds. All news and advertising copy was set by hand rather than by machine. The type was then fixed on rotary power presses, inked, and pressed against sheets of newsprint. For a newspaper to increase production by adding presses meant that duplicate pages had to be set, requiring a duplicate set of compositors and thus doubling labor costs.

A solution offered itself, however, in the stereotyping process that had been developed in the 1850s. In stereotyping, molds were made by pounding papier-mâché into the flat pages of type. Metal plates then were cast from the molds. At first this process slowed production, taking forty-three minutes to cast two plates in 1856, but a publisher could add as many presses as needed to speed production, since several plates could be made from the same matrix. Costs dropped because a second set of type did not need to be bought and a second set of compositors did not need to be hired. The process provided an additional bonus by saving wear on type, which no longer had to be used to print thousands of copies day after day.

In 1861 stereotyping was adapted to the large printing presses used by urban newspapers when the R. Hoe company designed a rotary press that used a curved matrix. Faster processes of making molds also were tried. By 1880 it had become possible to produce

[64]Anonymous, "When Did Newspapers Begin to Use Wood Pulp Stock?" *New York Public Library Bulletin* 33 (October 1929): 745; David C. Smith, "Wood Pulp and Newspapers, 1867-1900," *Business History Review* 38 (Autumn 1964): 335, 337; H. A. Innis, "Technology and Public Opinion in the United States," *The Canadian Journal of Economics and Political Science* 17 (February 1951): 13.

Reporting by Phone
Drawing on principles he had learned as an instructor for the deaf, Alexander Graham Bell invented the telephone in 1876. After the first telephone exchange opened in 1878, journalists were slow to make use of the device. By the 1880s, however, reporters in large cities were beginning to work as two-member teams. The "leg man" gathered the information and then phoned it to the "rewrite man" in the newspaper office.

two plates in nine and a half minutes, with the second and succeeding plates ready in two minutes.

Coupled with these technical changes was the development of the web-perfecting press. The perfecting technique had been developed before the Civil War. William M. Bullock of Philadelphia in 1863 refined it into web-perfecting, and the process was improved by Robert Hoe of New York City in 1871. The press fed paper automatically from a continuous roll instead of sheets hand fed by pressmen. The paper ran between two forms (stereotype plates) on two presses, allowing both sides to be printed simultaneously. As the paper left the forms it was slit with a knife, making two separate sheets, which then were folded and cut apart automatically. A Hoe double web-perfecting press installed in the *Missouri Republican* in 1880 could deliver 30,000 finished eight-page papers an hour.

With such technological advances, deadlines were moved closer to the time of printing.[65] Newspaper production had become systematic, like factory work.[66]

Distribution varied from city to city, with independent news agents handling most distribution in New York City and Chicago, but in Philadelphia newspapers tended toward subscriptions and handled distribution themselves. Technology also entered the distribution field, as papers could be sent only short distances if they were to be fresh upon arrival. Boston newspapers were limited to twenty miles on Sunday because the railroad operated no farther. The *Springfield* (Mass.) *Republican* had to run its own train in order to deliver papers to Birmingham, Vermont, the longest distance of any paper in the Northeast.

New York and Philadelphia were able to distribute newspapers as far as Chicago when the Pennsylvania Railroad began operating a fast mail train in 1875. This service was arranged with the U.S. Postal Department, which also allowed the train to carry a few first-class passengers. The train, running seven days a week, originated in New York City loaded with morning newspapers and delivered them in Philadelphia the same morning. It then took on Philadelphia newspapers and reached Pittsburgh with them at 6 p.m. and Chicago the next morning.[67]

These developments supplemented earlier technological changes. The telegraph had already demonstrated its utility in reducing the time lag between an occurrence of an event and a report in the press. From almost the beginning of telegraphy, the press had used it extensively, not only for information from distant sources but for news transmission from reporters in the suburbs, until the spread of the telephone in the cities.

The first telephone exchange opened in New Haven, Connecticut, in 1878. The telephone would not have much impact on newsgathering, however, for several years, largely because the telegraph was so well established in journalism.

The underwater cable connecting North America with England and Europe had been laid before the Civil War, but it failed. After the Civil War, another cable was laid. The cable company then picked up and repaired the earlier cable, thus providing the United States with two links with Europe. The cable reduced by days the time for transmitting news from Europe, yet because of the high costs only a few newspapers, in addition to the news agencies, would make consistent use of the cable. Nevertheless, the technology was in place for those newspaper entrepreneurs who would use it for competitive advantages in the future.

The South — A Distinctive Difference

Like the eleven states that had seceded from the Union, the press of the South also was devastated by the Civil War. It took several decades to recover. Abraham Lincoln's program of reconciliation with the South was put into effect by President Andrew Johnson. This first Reconstruction Act failed. Whether Lincoln himself could have succeeded against the entrenched power of Congress is debatable. In southern states, white governments had denied polit-

[65]"Stereotyping the Sun," *New York Sun* 8 January 1883, 3; North, "Newspapers and Periodicals," 103.

[66]Eugene H. Munday, "The Public Ledger (and Daily Transcript)," *The Proof-Sheet* 4 (July 1870): 1-2.

[67]"A Lightening Fast Mail and Newspaper Train," *Proof-Sheet* 10 (October 1875): 209.

Connecting Continents
The first transatlantic cable was completed in 1866. This engraving from the *Illustrated London News* of that year shows its landing in Newfoundland. The cable made the transmission of news from Europe to the United States almost instantaneous, but its high cost limited its use to only a handful of newspapers.

ical equality to qualified blacks, and Confederate leaders had been returned to influential political positions. The Radical Republicans gained control of Congress and, reacting to political developments in the South, set new criteria for readmitting former Confederate states to the Union. All but Virginia of the eleven Confederate states fell under Radical Republican rule. All black males were enfranchised, and many whites were disenfranchised.

The southern press generally opposed Republican rule. Editors articulated the opposition to Republican leaders and programs, sometimes flamboyantly and intemperately. They had particular reasons for opposing Republican newspapers. The Republican administrations subsidized party newspapers through state and federal payments for printing and advertising. During the three-year administration of the "Carpetbag" governor of Georgia, party newspapers received $98,000 for printing his proclamations. During the five years just prior to the war, Georgia had spent only $5,000 for the same purposes. Most Republican papers had little standing in their communities, but some prospered handsomely.

The newspapers in several states still had not recovered to prewar circulation levels by 1880. This was particularly true in Louisiana, Virginia, and South Carolina. Both Louisiana and Virginia increased the number of dailies from 1860 to 1880. Louisiana went from eight to thirteen, and Virginia from fifteen to twenty, even with the loss of West Virginia as a result of the war. Daily circulation, on the other hand, declined, with Virginia dropping by 27%. Adding the minuscule daily circulation of West Virginia would have had little impact on the percentage. South Carolina was hit harder, although the decline began earlier. In 1850 the state had seven daily newspapers which dropped to two in 1860, but recovered to four in 1880. The circulation of those four papers was 50% *less* than the seven dailies of 1850.[68] Although papers in the other secessionist states had increased and circulation had held steady or marginally improved, the press still remained weak in comparison to the North.

It seems strange, then, that perhaps the most representative figure in the South who would persuade his northern colleagues that a New South was arising was from South Carolina. He was Francis Warrington Dawson of the *Charleston News and Courier*, a newspaper resulting from the merger of the *Courier* with Dawson's *News* in 1873. He was a leader of the editors who would become identified with the New South, who stressed crop rotation, industrialization (especially by bringing the mills to the South where the cotton was located), and small farms. Independent on some social and racial issues, he still was partisan and intensely involved politically. Equally important, he owned his newspaper, which allowed him to make it his instrument for civil reform in South Carolina and the nation. His political interests were in tune with changes occurring on the national scene, and he was a member of the Democratic National Committee. He was on the executive committee of the Society of Political Education, a northern group promoting free trade and civil service reform. These contacts, and his views regarding the South, gave him a voice in the North even as he remained a political power in South Carolina.[69]

Better known than Dawson as a leader of the New South movement was Henry Grady, who in 1880 bought a quarter interest in the *Atlanta Constitution* and became its managing editor. His oration in New York City titled "The New South" brought him nationwide fame as the leading spokesman of the movement. Like other advocates of that cause, he emphasized diversified agriculture and increased manufacturing, but he also had a vision of his home city of Atlanta becoming the political center of his new South. The practical result was that he made his most intense efforts promoting Atlanta rather than the entire region.[70]

[68]Calculated from North, "Newspapers and Periodicals," Table XI, 187.

[69]E. Culpepper Clark, "Francis Warrington Dawson: The New South Revisited," *American Journalism* 3 (1986): 5-23.

[70]Harold E. Davis, "Henry Grady, Master of the Atlanta Ring—1880-1886," *Georgia Historical Quarterly* 69 (1985): 1-38; and Davis, "'A Brave and Beautiful City': Henry Grady and the New South," *American Journalism* 5 (1988): 131-44.

Southern Leaders

The leading advocate of a "New South" was Henry Grady (left) of the *Atlanta Constitution.* He used the newspaper as a pulpit from which he promoted industrial development, with Atlanta as the center of growth. As editor of the *Courier-Journal* in Louisville, Kentucky, for half a century, Henry Watterson (right) was a leading voice of a progressive South after the Civil War. He focused most of his efforts on the editorial page and became one of the most skilled opinion writers that American journalism has produced.

The most insistent voice of the New South was "Marse Henry" Watterson. As editor of the *Louisville Courier-Journal*, he was the most widely quoted southern editor in the North for fifty years. Active as an editor during the war years — always retreating but barely staying ahead of the advancing Union army several times — he settled down in Nashville, Tennessee, as part-owner and editor of the *Banner.* There he undertook a campaign for reconciliation, what he called "The New Departure," promoting investment by northern capitalists in the North and diversified farming in the South. He moved to Louisville, Kentucky, in early 1868 to become editor of the *Journal*. By the end of the year he had persuaded the publisher of the *Courier* to merge the two papers. The *Courier-Journal* resulted from the merger, and Watterson became editor and one-third owner. This gave him a base to promote his views to both the South and the North. He became active in Democratic politics at the national level beginning with the 1872 campaign. His paper succeeded, but largely on its editorial views rather than its news. That fact may well indicate the difference between southern journalism and that developing in the expanding urban centers of the North. Watterson did not agree that news shaped public opinion more than editorials, and at various times the *Courier-Journal* had more editorial page writers than reporters.[71]

Many publishers in the North and West may well have agreed with Watterson, but theirs was the journalism of the past. The social, economic, and technological changes resulting from the Civil War had set in motion a different society, one that would require different media from pre-Civil War newspapers. The editors and publishers of the emerging journalism emphasized vigorous, impartial news policies based on independent journalism. This new newspaper design, powered with advertising and circulation, could support a massive superstructure capable of succeeding in the new urban environment. The press would be refined and shaped during the next several decades, but the form was designed in the post-Civil War era.

[71]Joseph Frazier Wall, *Henry Watterson. Reconstructed Rebel* (New York, 1956). Walter N. Haldeman was majority owner and manager of the paper.

RECOMMENDED READINGS

BOOKS

Armstrong, William M. *E. L. Godkin: A Biography*. Albany, N. Y., 1978. A study of the founder of the *Nation* and one of the most politically active editors of his era.

Caudill, Edward. *Darwinism and the Press: The Evolution of an Idea*. Hillsdale, N. J., 1989. Newspaper and magazine treatment of Darwinism demonstrated the media's inherent difficulty in covering ideas.

Clark, E. Culpepper. *Francis Warrington Dawson and the Politics of Restoration: South Carolina, 1874-1889*. Tuscaloosa, Ala., 1980. Political biography of the *Charleston News and Courier* editor focuses on his state, regional, and national influence.

Clayton, Charles G. *Little Mack: Joseph B. McCullagh of the St. Louis Globe-Democrat*. Carbondale, Ill., 1969. McCullagh successfully combined the news emphasis of Bennett with the editorial ability of Greeley. He emphasized ethics and good writing.

Davis, Harold E. *Henry Grady's New South: Atlanta, a Brave and Beautiful City*. Tuscaloosa, Ala., 1990. Grady's efforts for a "New South" had as their primary goal the political and economic condition of Atlanta rather than of the South as a whole.

Dicken-Garcia, Hazel. *Journalistic Standards in Nineteenth-Century America*. Madison, Wis., 1989. Analyzes what critics and journalists understood journalistic standards to be. In the latter part of the century, as newspapers became more complicated and less understood by the public, criticism increased.

Hershkowitz, Leo. *Tweed's New York*. New York, 1977. Describes in detail the newspaper crusades against Tammany Hall that led to the campaign against the Tweed Ring.

Lancaster, Paul. *Gentleman of the Press: The Life and Times of an Early Reporter, Julian Ralph of the Sun*. Syracuse, N. Y., 1991. This biography of one of the leading reporters for the *New York Sun* provides insight into the nature of reporting on America's urban newspapers after the Civil War.

Marcosson, Isaac. *Marse Henry: A Biography of Henry Watterson*. New York, 1951. Detailed chronological biography of the Louisville editor and noted editorial writer. Watterson was a colorful "personal" editor.

Nevins, Allen. *The Evening Post, a Century of Journalism*. New York, 1922. A gracefully written newspaper history that devotes much attention to the wider social and historical context of the 1860s and '70s.

O'Connor, Richard. *The Scandalous Mr. Bennett*. New York: Doubleday, 1962. Popularized, colorful biography of James Gordon Bennett, Jr., owner of the *New York Herald*.

Ogden, Rollo, ed. *Life and Letters of Edwin Lawrence Godkin*, 2 vols. New York, 1907. Godkin loved justice and honesty and wrote with acumen and forceful expression. He was intelligent and scholarly, but also could be overly proud of his British background and culture.

Paine, Albert Bigelow. *Thomas Nast, His Period and His Pictures*. New York, 1904. Nast was the "father of American caricature." He believed his primary goal should be the moral and political advancement of America.

Rosewater, Victor. *History of Cooperative News-Gathering in the United States*. New York, 1930. Standard work on the history of the Associated Press and other newsgathering organizations.

Steele, Janet E. *The Sun Shines For All: Journalism and Ideology in the Life of Charles A. Dana*. Syracuse, N.Y., 1993. Intellectual history of the editor of the *New York Sun* from 1868 until the 1890s.

Stone, Candace. *Dana and the Sun*. New York, 1938. This readable biography emphasizes Dana's editorial comment and his role in public affairs.

Summers, Mark Wahlgren. *The Press Gang: Newspapers and Politics, 1865-1878*. Chapel Hill, N.C., 1994. Describes the interconnection of politicians and newspapers after the Civil War.

Thompson, Julius Eric. *The Black Press in Mississippi: 1865-1985*. Gainesville, Fla., 1993. Black newspapers in Mississippi were hampered by financial problems and repression from whites.

Thompson, Robert L. *Wiring a Continent: The History of the Telegraph Industry in the United States, 1832-1866*. Princeton, N. J., 1947. Best account of the rise of the Western Union monopoly.

Wingate, Charles F., ed. *Views and Interviews on Journalism*. 1875; reprint, New York, 1970. Fascinating collection of interviews with the most famous editors and publishers of the post-war era.

ARTICLES

Caudill, Edward. "E.L. Godkin and His (Special and Influential) View of 19th Century Journalism." *Journalism Quarterly* 69 (1992): 1039-49. Godkin held a multi-dimensional attitude toward journalism, which he saw as a haven for both reformers and money-grubbers.

Dickerson, Donna L. "From Suspension to Subvention: The Southern Press During Reconstruction, 1863-1870." *American Journalism* (1991): 230-45. Outlines the methods of control over editors and newspapers after the Civil War.

Fedler, Fred. "Mrs. O'Leary's Cow and Other Newspaper Tales About the Chicago Fire of 1871." *American Journalism* 3 (1986): 24-38. Demonstrates how fanciful, erroneous reports were picked up and reprinted by other newspapers.

Goble, Corban. "Mark Twain's Nemesis: The Paige Compositor." *Printing History* 18:2 (1999): 2-16. Readable account of Twain's disastrous financial investment in James Paige's efforts to perfect a typesetting machine.

Hart, Jack R. "Horatio Alger in the Newsroom: Social Origins of American Editors." *Journalism Quarterly* 53 (1976): 14-20. Editors of the largest newspapers during 1875-1900 were comparable in origin to executives in other major industries; they were from the business class, forming a socio-economic elite.

Hyde, Jana. "The Industrial Press, 1865-1883: Professional Journalism or Pawn of Urbanism?" 186-98 in Wm. David Sloan, *Perspectives on Mass Communication History* (Hillsdale, N. J., 1991). Analyzes the approaches that historians have taken to explaining the press of the period.

Knights, Peter R. "'Competition' in the U.S. Daily Newspaper Industry, 1865-68." *Journalism Quarterly* 45 (1968): 473-80. The trend toward independence was well under way in the years after the war.

—. "The Press Association War of 1866-1867." *Journalism Monographs* 16 (1967). Detailed history of squabbles between the Associated Press and the Western Associated Press, and the role of Western Union.

Kolchin, Peter. "The Business Press and Re-construction, 1865-1868." *Journal of Southern History* (1967): 183-96. The business press generally favored moderate measures rather than the Radical Republican platform during Reconstruction.

Nord, David Paul. "The Business Values of American Newspapers: The 19th Century Watershed in Chicago." *Journalism Quarterly* 61 (1984): 265-73. Chicago newspapers shared a commitment to the "public interest" despite the differences in their nominal allegiances to various ideologies.

Spencer, David R. "Bringing Down Giants: Thomas Nast, John Wilson Bengough and the Maturing of Political Cartooning." *American Journalism* 15:3 (1998): 61-88. Nast and Bengough helped to expose corrupt political figures.

Thorn, William J. "Hudson's History of Journalism Criticized by His Contemporaries." *Journalism Quarterly* 57 (1980): 96-106. Based on an analysis of newspaper reviews of Frederic Hudson's 1873 history of journalism, Thorn concludes that journalists considered the newspaper's role in promoting democracy more important than its function of providing news.

Whisnant, David E. "Selling the Gospel News, or: The Strange Career of Jimmy Brown the Newsboy." *Journal of Social History* 5 (1972): 269-309. Describes the process by which the newsboy became a figure in American mythology and social life.

12

The Age of New Journalism

1883 - 1900

In 1883 the young St. Louis publisher Joseph Pulitzer went to New York to take over the *World,* rightly convinced that the greatest opportunity for a hardworking and talented journalist was to be found in America's fast-growing metropolis. He updated and improved the formula of Day and Bennett for reaching the masses and soon was hailed as the creator of a "new journalism" in America. He quickly built the largest circulation and the tallest building in New York and spawned considerable optimism about the future of journalism.

By 1900, however, the new journalism had been renamed "yellow journalism," and disillusioned young reporters like Will Irwin and H. L. Mencken observed perfidious practices that they would describe in blunt words a generation later. Irwin said of yellow journalism's vices: "Its falsity was chief and its rowdy denial of the right of privacy in news-getting only second."[1] Mencken recalled, "The public position of a journalist was above that of a street-walker but below that of a police captain.... [Papers] were ignorant, partisan and puerile, and most of the men who owned them were for sale."[2]

What happened during the last years of the nineteenth century to cause such a turnabout? So many publishers became rich, the time was literally the Golden Age of newspaper journalism. What went wrong, then, between 1883 and 1900? The answers to such questions lie deep in the newspaper industry of the period.

One of the simplest indicators of newspaper growth in America over the past century may be found on a library shelf with a complete set of the *American Newspaper Annual* (now called the *Gale Directory of Publications*) published each year since 1880. Volume I is no larger than a good-sized novel, but later gold-stamped hardbound directories grow fatter and fatter, three inches thick by the late 1880s and so fat by the 1890s that the binding strained to contain the 2,000 or so pages required to list the nation's periodicals. The books begin to thin down around the time of World War I, and by the 1990s (before radio and TV were added) were back to the two-inch thickness of the first volume.

The largest increases in the number of dailies came during the decades of the 1880s and 1890s. (See Figure 1.) The number of weeklies was increasing at a similar pace, going up by about 4,000 in the 1880s (including semi-weeklies and tri-weeklies, too) and about 3,500 in the 1890s to total 16,000-plus in 1899. Both dailies and weeklies slowed their growth after 1900, and each peaked about 1914.

Because the nation had fewer people then, total daily and weekly circulations were lower than today. The number of daily papers in the 1890s was about the same as the number of dailies in the United States in modern times (about 1,500 in 1999). But today's dailies are spread over three times as large a population.

What made the American market so ripe for selling newspapers in the 1890s was the urbanization of the U.S. population. In 1860, only about a fifth of Americans lived in urban places (population of 8,000 or more), but the flood of immigrants swelled the cities so that a third of the population was urban by the 1890s. Daily circulation totals came to about half the total urban population — one paid daily newspaper circulated for every two people in American cities. That was more than one copy per household, a higher saturation than one finds today in an age when so many city-dwellers have turned to television as their sole news source.

A number of other factors also encouraged circulation growth. The percentage of children attending public schools rose from 57% to 72% between 1870 and 1900, and illiteracy was cut in half. Newspaper prices generally declined from the end of the Civil War to 1900, and daily papers selling for a penny became common again. People became less provincial as transportation and communication improved; and from the Civil War on, it became normal and appropriate for citizens to want to know what was going on beyond neighborhood and community. In short, the United States was building a sizeable urban middle class, and it was only natural that newspapers would grow along with such a potential market. The newspaper industry soon became one of the country's largest manufacturing industries.

[1] Will Irwin, "Yellow Journalism," in *Highlights in the History of the American Press,* Edwin H. Ford and Edwin Emery, eds. (Minneapolis, 1954), 281.

[2] Fenwick Anderson, ed., *Quotations from Chairman Mencken* (Urbana, Ill., 1974), 16.

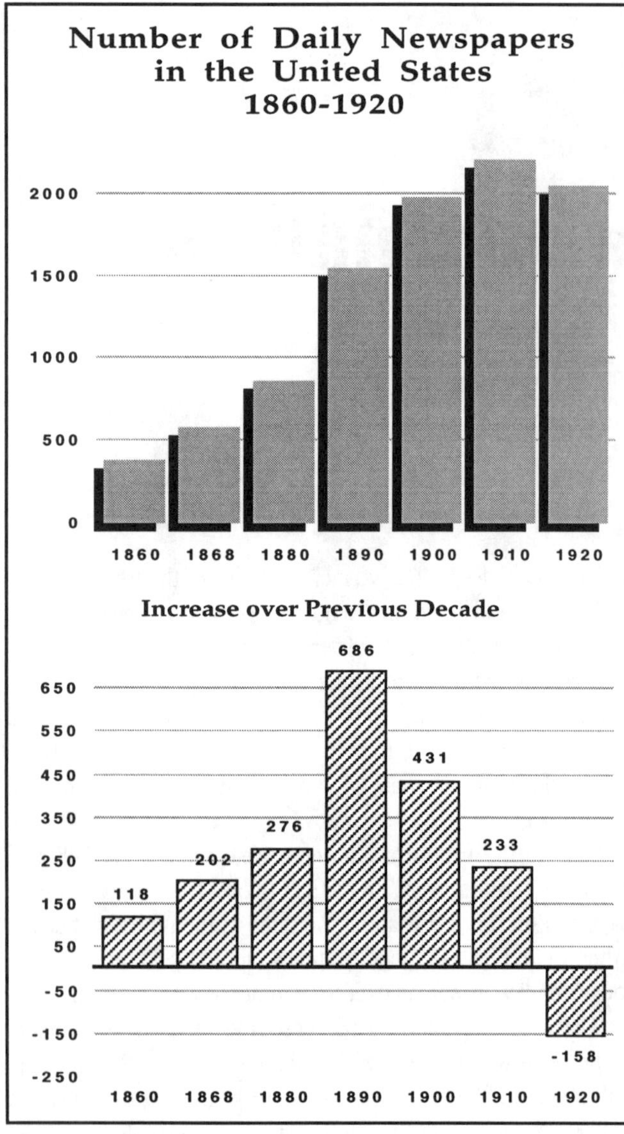

FIGURE 1

In colonial America, newspapers had been the dominant medium. The printing of books required more capital and equipment than most colonial printers could furnish; so they turned to newspapers more than did their European counterparts. Thus it was for reasons both historical and demographic that America became a nation of newspaper readers. It was believed that newspapers in America in the 1880s exercised a greater influence than in any other country. Inevitably, some people even worried that newspapers were too strong. Archbishop Corrigan of New York once made this typical comment about the abundance of newspaper readers: "Here everyone reads; everyone, even the poorest, is rich enough to buy the daily papers; here more than elsewhere, in our characteristic hurry to save time and labor, we are willing to allow others to do our thinking and to serve us not only with the daily history of the world, but with lines of thought and suggestions of conduct ready for use."[3] A more recent critic of the newspaper's place in society at this time reflected: "In the post-Civil War period the newspaper had too little outside intellectual competition for its own good.... The late Nineteenth Century American commoner was notoriously a consumer of newspapers and of little or nothing else.... Such opinions...as got a wide acceptance were those propagated through the newspapers."[4]

The market was in place and the newspaper tradition was established. But for publishers to exploit these conditions, they needed the tools to deliver enough papers to meet the demand.

Explosion in Communication Technologies

Printing technology was advancing toward a peak. After 1900, inventors would turn to other communication and transportation technologies, and little would happen to printing until computers and electronic typesetters emerged late in the twentieth century. But in the years 1883-1900 there was action on several fronts.

Newspaper presses were reaching speeds undreamed of by the framers of the First Amendment. The *St. Louis Republic*, begun in 1806 on a wooden handpress of the type that was standard in colonial times, in 1890 was installing a Hoe press that would produce 72,000 copies (printed on both sides) and needed ten pressmen to operate it.

The last four presses that the Republic had used all printed on both sides of a continuous roll (web) and probably used stereotype plates. By the 1890s the Hoe factory was turning out huge presses superior to any others in the world for newspaper work, and for the next sixty years there would be no basic changes in the design. Many newspapers today are using presses that print about 72,000 copies per hour — roughly the same speed at which copies were produced a century earlier.

By the 1890s additional improvements had been made to permit the use of spot color, a development that gave the era its name. Pulitzer's *World* had introduced comics, and the color man in the pressroom came up with the idea of running colors in the comics, beginning by using yellow ink for the ridiculous-looking wide skirt worn by a single-toothed child in Richard Outcault's "Hogan's Alley." This comic-strip character was quickly dubbed "The Yellow Kid." The strip was changed to that name; and when Outcault was hired away by William Randolph Hearst, Pulitzer continued the strip with another artist. Thus, both Hearst and Pulitzer had strips named "The Yellow Kid" running at the same time. The Pulitzer/Hearst methods soon came to be called yellow journalism.

Folding machines had been around for a while, but none could keep up with the speed of the rotary presses. The unfortunate juveniles who picked up metropolitan dailies for street sales had to struggle with cumbersome stacks of huge unfolded sheets thrown over their shoulders. In the days of the penny press, the *Sun* and *Herald* emerged as sheets about 15 x 20 inches, to be

[3]Quoted in James Edward Rogers, *The American Newspaper* (Chicago, 1909), 101.

[4]Eric W. Allen, "Economic Changes and Editorial Influence," *Journalism Quarterly* 8 (1931): 342-59.

The Linotype
Ottmar Mergenthaler, the inventor of the Linotype machine, gave an early demonstration to Whitelaw Reid, editor of the *New York Tribune*. It was Reid who originated the name "Linotype." The machine dominated newspaper typesetting for almost a century.

folded once. After that, the size of newspapers had grown through enlargement of the pages. The standard number of pages remained at four. Some of the "blanket sheet" papers opened out to prodigious widths. The *Free Press* at Burlington, Vermont, was given to newsboys in sheets fifty-two inches across.

In 1883 Hoe and Co. introduced triangular forming bars that could fold papers as they came off the press. The fast-moving web of paper was passed over a V-shaped plate with curved edges. The edges of the web turned downward, and the middle of the web passed over the point of the V forming a continuous crease or fold the full length of the web. It only remained for a revolving blade to chop the folded papers off the end of the web, and a conveyor belt could carry forth completed four-page newspapers just as fast as the press could print them. Larger papers could be produced just as fast, by running two or more webs over the plate so that multiple sheets would be folded inside one another.

Typesetting machines were badly needed, and it appeared for awhile that printing press technology was going to pull away and leave behind the technology of typesetting. The newest presses of the *Republic* had made it possible for one pressman to produce 400 times as many sheets in 1890 as in 1806, but there had been no increase in typesetting speed. Typesetters still were setting all the type laboriously by hand, one letter at a time. In 1890 the *Chicago Herald* boasted of a new "Hall of Compositors," an area of 7,000 square feet containing work-spaces for 150 men to set type. Each man had his own cabinet of type, and "large wicker baskets and brown rubber spittoons are plentifully provided throughout the floor, and every compositor is provided with an oak stool by the management."[5] No matter how luxurious these working conditions may seem, the fact remains that each man was setting type the same labor-intensive way it had been done since Gutenberg.

The breakthrough originally was made by an immigrant German watchmaker, Ottmar Mergenthaler, whose Linotype machine went on sale in 1890. Mergenthaler had been working on the machine since 1876, but he (and some Washington legal stenographers) had been concentrating on a device for courtroom or congressional notetaking. He was about to give up when Whitelaw Reid of the *New York Tribune* got a group of publishers to back the development of a linecasting machine. Reid was considered an enemy of the printer's unions, and he doubtless wanted the machine to make his paper less vulnerable to strikes. The machine was introduced at the *Tribune* in 1886 and, after some modifications, was put on the market. The larger newspapers snapped it up, and 90% of the big dailies had Linotypes by 1897. One machine could do the work of five human typesetters. The machines made it possible to use more non-advertising material in papers.

Photoengraving was introduced during the 1880s, and the use of pictures began to increase rapidly. During the 1880s and most of the 1890s the process could use only line drawings, but in the late 1890s Stephen H. Horgan sufficiently perfected a halftone process that permitted photographs to be reproduced on newspaper presses. Illustrated newspapers had been around since before the Civil War, but they had relied on the tedious handwork of skilled woodcarvers or electrotypers, and only the high-circulation papers could afford them. By the 1880s, line drawings were being photographed onto the surface of zinc plates for acid etching. This mechanical process not only made illustration cheaper; it shortened deadline time so that last night's fire could be portrayed pictorially in the morning paper. Horgan's process gave printing the halftone screen — the same basic method used to print photographs today. But when critics of yellow journalism decried the use of too many pictures, they were referring primarily to the line drawings of the 1880s and early 1890s, rather than the halftones that began to appear in large daily newspapers only at the end of the period.

Papermaking also advanced rapidly after 1860, and it usually is not given proper recognition by historians searching for the causes of the nineteenth-century newspaper boom. When Pulitzer published a 200-page issue of the *World* in 1893, his achievement created a great excitement in the newspaper world, but the papermakers deserved much of the credit for that feat. True, newspapers had grown considerably since the days of the four-page standard size, but paper prices were dropping. (See Figure 2.)

Paper was cheapest in 1897-1901, and prices have climbed ever since, averaging about 40¢ per pound today. Publishers less talented than Pulitzer could publish 200-page issues if paper could

[5]"A Few Words About the Chicago Herald," *Inland Printer* 9 (January 1892): 329-44.

First Halftone
The *New York* Graphic, founded in 1873 to make fullest possible use of photography, experimented with several processes before its photo-mechanical manager, Stephen Horgan, produced this halftone in 1880. He copied the original photograph – a picture of New York's Shanty Town – through a fine screen, producing an engraving that could give the illusion of continuous tones of gray even thought it was printed with black ink. The same principle is employed in printing of pictures today.

be bought at 2¢ a pound.

Other printing technologies were important advances when introduced. Some of these have become obscured by time: the standardization of the point system (in 1886) used to measure type; the use of electricity to drive printing presses; mechanical tension controls to replace the erratic hand-braking of webs of paper; and modular designs for stacking or lining up press units much as they are still arranged in pressrooms today.

Newsgathering technologies were particularly important, although the economies they produced were sometimes harder to measure. James Gordon Bennett may have introduced the beat system in days long past; but it would not reach perfection until reporters could cover the city on bicycles, streetcars, or telephones, could write their stories on typewriters with the aid of electric lights, and could benefit from reduced telegraphy and cable toll charges (lowered by Western Union's loss of monopoly status) and from the widespread use of railroad passes.

Invention and innovation were the watchwords, and the newspaper industry was ready to employ any new machine or device that promised to speed production or save money. Consider, for example, the use of pneumatic transmission. When city transportation proved too slow for Chicago's energetic journalists, a cooperative called City News Bureau of Chicago built a tube system in 1892 to serve the thirteen newspapers in the city. Cannisters were propelled through three-inch brass tubes by steam jets delivering a pressure of 125 pounds per square inch. The fifteen-mile underground system served the Board of Trade and other non-newspaper customers as well. It was not exactly perfect; the steam kept the tube so damp that dispatches sometimes arrived as wet as if they had been submerged. The tubes had to be dug up, removed, and put into tunnels, so that stuck cannisters could be freed more easily. Vacuum pumps had to be purchased to replace the steam pumps. But it was a new technology, and the drive to speed up publication of news was so strong that journalists were ready to try just about anything.

One other experiment bears mention. In 1899 young Guglielmo Marconi loaded his equipment onto a steamer and set out to cover the Kingstown Regatta, sending wireless messages ashore for the *Dublin Express* in Ireland. The news of the race made it to the streets before any of the ships had returned to port, and the feat earned Marconi an invitation to cross the Atlantic and provide similar coverage of the America's Cup race for the *New York Herald*. He did so, successfully, in October 1899 — the first commercial use of wireless to transmit news in America.

The traditional technologies of printing, papermaking, and typesetting all had achieved rapid advance by the 1890s. The inventors — and the market that demanded their inventions — had provided the tools to make possible a great change. How would these tools be used? Would the cheaper, larger newspapers with their new capabilities for illustration and color strive to use these tools to produce a better-informed, more thoughtful citizenry? Or would the publishers concentrate on making themselves rich?

Before judging the publishers, it is advisable to take a brief look at the cultural and intellectual environment. It was a complex time in American history.

The Social Context for the Great Newspaper Boom

The national political environment in America after 1861 was generally dominated by the Republicans. Grover Cleveland was the only Democrat elected between James Buchanan (elected 1856) and Woodrow Wilson (1912). Sandwiched around Cleveland were ten Republican presidents. They did not always have Republican Congresses to support them, but government policy leaned toward business. Laws provided high protective tariffs, but little regulation of business. Some early bipartisan efforts were made to curb trusts such as Standard Oil and Amalgamated Sugar, but communications trusts were largely ignored. The notorious financial manipulator Jay Gould was able to dominate the telegraph business with Western Union, and there was some public outcry. But the eventual solution — if it were one — lay in new competition from the express companies and in a trans-Atlantic cable war between Gould and millionaire William Randolph Hearst. The

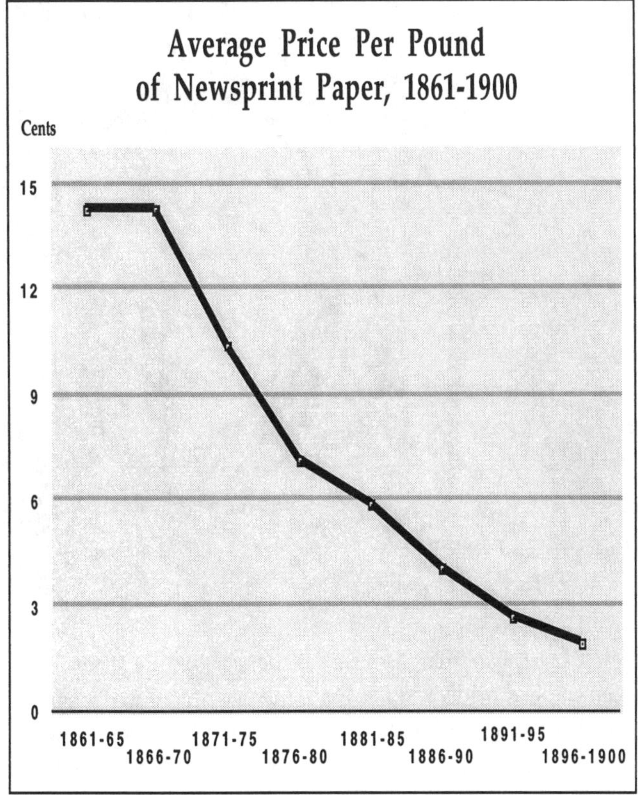

FIGURE 2

Spread of Technology
Printing technology spread from urban newspapers to small-town ones. In the 1880s, the *Daily Evening Press* and the *Orange County Press* in Middletown, N.Y., were publicizing the fact that their press was steam-driven.

market simply expanded faster than could the monopoly, and new competition eased the situation.

Publishers avoided antitrust stories, and sometimes they colluded. The Associated Press, itself a near monopoly, made such tight deals with Western Union that by 1880, 91% of the press messages — $3 million worth that year — were carried over Western Union. Newspaper trade journals were spotted with news of a paper trust, an ink trust, a type trust — but, unlike oil and sugar, the prices of printing materials kept going down.

Getting competitors together, organizing the market, getting rich by charging all the traffic would bear — this seemed to be the American way. Business was king, and in business the word of the day was "Organize."

With business carrying the nation into a period of great expansion, the increased wealth, particularly in the growing middle class, led to the establishment of a broad popular culture. P. T. Barnum had recognized it back in 1852, when he helped start the first news picture weekly in America. In the 1880s newspapers published columns upon columns of material that had nothing to do with straight information: doggerel poetry; sugar-sweet romance stories; idealized woodcuts of blushing, innocent maidens; ethnic jokes used as filler material; sports; and cartoons. An aristocratic class, which once had dominated media content with its patronizing decisions about what was fit for the public to know, had lost its influence. Popular culture had arrived.

Occurring simultaneously was a newfound faith in science and in pragmatism. Charles Darwin was at peak influence, and his disciple Herbert Spencer had coined the expression "the survival of the fittest." Various opportunists argued that there was a sort of "social Darwinism," under which the afflicted and the poverty-stricken were victims of a natural evolution process. The lower class was simply being weeded out by natural selection. Of course, Karl Marx (who, like Darwin, died during the 1880s) would have explained that capitalism concentrates wealth in the hands of a few owners and leads to exploitation of the workers. But the Darwinian explanation was more "scientific"; and science, at that time closely associated with engineering, was responsible for all the wonderful technology that was perceived as advancing civilization in America.

Under the influence of Spencer and of educator/philosopher John Dewey, the social sciences flourished in America. Men of inquiry began to think of society as a huge laboratory, in which behavior, if studied scientifically, could be analyzed, explained, and predicted, just as reliably as predicting that mixing hydrogen and oxygen will produce water. Influenced by such ideas, journalists began to think of themselves as scientific observers, and the notion of news objectivity was conceived. Newsmen began to believe that what they wrote was some kind of scientific truth, rather than viewpoint: "I don't make the news — I just report it."

The Kansas City Evening Star.

The Old and the New
Mrs. Frank Leslie and William Rockhill Nelson typified the stark differences between the old and new approaches to journalism in the 1880s. The mawkish Mrs. Leslie, Miriam Follin Leslie, changed her own legal name to "Frank Leslie" after her husband's death and became publisher and editor of the Leslie publications. To gain control of the business, she had to fight nineteen lawsuits brought by a variety of challengers, including Leslie's son from an earlier marriage. She established a solid foundation for the publishing company and then leased it to a syndicate. In 1900, her partners forced her into retirement. With the *Kansas City Star*, Nelson eschewed the garish sensationalism of Hearst and Pulitzer. By emphasizing solid news, civic improvement, and a strong business base, he built a potent and profitable newspaper in the Midwest.

Counter-Trends in American Society

The intellectual environments here described can be seen as dual — the prevailing view, and the alternative view. There was the Darwinian view, but there was the Marxist view. There was the "scientific" journalist, but there was also the writer of personal views and of doggerel. There were the pro-business Republicans, but there were some pro-regulation Democrats, too. American society was growing schizophrenic.

These counter-trends were exemplified vividly by two pairs of individuals in the field of journalism. Each was an important figure in mass communications in this period that Mark Twain once called "the Gilded Age," but in each pair one person represented a lifestyle or viewpoint that was on the way out, and the other represented the future.

Mrs. Frank Leslie and William Rockhill Nelson were apt examples of the old and the new in 1880s journalism. Mrs. Leslie, whose third husband, Frank Leslie, founded the first successful illustrated news weekly in America, *Frank Leslie's Illustrated Newspaper*, had her own name legally changed to Frank Leslie when he died in 1880. Leslie had started about thirty weekly and monthly publications, most of them with "Frank Leslie's" as part of the title; his widow presumably wanted the name to facilitate her continuing control.

Both Leslies kept a high profile, trumpeting their transcontinental railroad trip and their pavilion in the 1876 Centennial Exposition. Mrs. Leslie, who had written prolifically for their various magazines on fashions, travel, manners, and literature, seemed to "report" on obscure places and customs not because they were important, but because she was so important herself that the public should read anything she wrote. It was inevitable that when she took the helm so assertively, she was dubbed the "empress of journalism," a nickname that followed her until 1905, when the Frank Leslie Publishing House was merged out of existence. (By then she had made a trip to France to acquire a more legitimate title, becoming the Baroness de Bazus.) She was a good business manager, and it is no discredit to her acumen that she sold the illustrated newspaper in 1889, recognizing that photoengraving would soon make the woodcut-illustrated pictorials obsolete. When a publication seemed to decline, she sold it or killed it; Victorian writing style may have been full of romance, but sentiment did not interfere in her business. She kept a firm hand on the tiller; and in her nickname, the emphasis should be placed on "empress" — not "journalism." She was not so much a journalist as a public figure, and a notorious one at that.

Mrs. Leslie became engaged to an ersatz marquis, was wooed by a Russian prince, frequented the literary soirees presided over by Oscar Wilde's mother in London, and in 1891 married Oscar Wilde's brother William. The Leslie stable of publications included a gossip journal or two, and there were competitors. When she asked Marshall Wilder to serve as best man at her fourth wedding, one catty rival editor remarked, "The bridegroom was Wilde, the best man was Wilder, but the bride was wildest."[6] Mrs. Leslie was a skilled manager and marketer of popular culture, but as a journalist she was little more than a caricature, a fading blossom from the flowering of a past generation.

Nelson, on the other hand, was the editor of the future. With a background in law and business, he arrived in Kansas City in 1880 when the fast-growing town was in its adolescence, ripe for the guidance of a solid newspaper. Nelson started his *Kansas City Star* at 2¢ a copy, 10¢ a week, when competitors were selling for 5¢ a copy. The paper grew with the city, reaching 10,000 circulation in 1883, 25,000 in 1886, 31,000 in 1889. Moving to Kansas City with only one year of journalistic experience at the *Fort Wayne Sentinel* (as co-owner), Nelson seldom wrote, but always supervised.

[6] Madeleine B. Stern, *Purple Passage, The Life of Mrs. Frank Leslie* (Norman, Okla., 1953), 156.

He was a tough businessman, paying his employees only as much as he had to, but he campaigned relentlessly for the betterment of Kansas City and showed no fear of any politician. He was not above expediency and was known to make payoffs to city commissioners to get ordinances passed that he thought would be good for the city.

Fat and stubby, Nelson walked with a waddle and often with a bodyguard at his side. He never spoke in public. He apparently had no desire to become a figure of national importance, but he fully intended to be a guiding force in his city, and he succeeded. His weapons did not include charm, charisma, or enchanting pen; instead he used a cunning business sense. He concentrated on building a sound base of local retail advertising, and his paper was comparatively immune to the vagaries of national advertisers such as patent medicine producers and booksellers, who were much more likely to pull their ads during hard economic times. He recognized the potential of a city's trade area, and in 1890 he marketed a weekly edition of his paper at the unheard-of price of 25¢ a year, capturing Kansas farmers by the thousands and widening the *Star*'s geographic reach, to the immense discomfort of publishers in Lawrence, Leavenworth, and Topeka.

Nelson, who died in 1915, left behind a monumental newspaper establishment, a journalistic legacy that would be carried on by such pupils as William Allen White, and a city replete with a wide range of civic improvements the *Star* had fought for with effective persistence. Mrs. Leslie left a reputation, a legacy of outmoded Victorian notions, and a business record admittedly remarkable for a woman in the nineteenth century.

Richard Harding Davis and Ambrose Bierce offer as strong a contrast in reporter/writers as Leslie and Nelson do in editor/publishers. Davis was indisputably handsome, with the perfectly sculpted kind of features that later would bring fame to actors such as Leonardo DiCaprio and Brad Pitt. He was a doer, a romantic who managed to live the life of high adventure many Americans dreamed of but never came close to experiencing.

A popular nickname for Davis was "Gibson Boy," because his flawless looks seemed ideally paired with the Gibson Girls so popular in 1890s illustrations. He appeared for his first reporting job dressed as an English dandy and soon was fired for sitting down to type still wearing his yellow kid gloves. But he did not repeat the mistake, and on a later assignment in Texas he did not hesitate to leap onto a horse to join in pursuit of a Mexican bandit, riding across thirty miles of scorching, dusty prairie.

Davis went to New York and the *Evening Sun*, where he served one of the country's most talented editors, Arthur Brisbane; but he found a daily newspaper's routine confining and accepted an editorship at *Harper's Weekly*. Gradually his career evolved toward freelance writing, and he did news work for both magazines and newspapers, including Hearst's *New York Journal* during the Cuban insurrections. He also wrote considerable fiction, much of it autobiographical, drawing from a wide variety of experience. He covered the coronation of Czar Nicholas II, traveled in Central and South America, and reported on Queen Victoria's Diamond Jubilee and numerous other events abroad. An impressive and talented figure, he was welcomed into many places correspondents dream of entering — the courts of royalty, or the dens of bandits and adventurers. Davis was perhaps the first true swashbuckling hero figure in American popular culture. His ties to nineteenth-century romanticism are clearly seen in one of his best-known short stories, "Gallegher," published in 1891. The story describes the rise to fame and success of a pressroom helper who scoops the experienced reporters and exposes corruption and vice. Many decades later the story was done for television by Walt Disney Studios, and it is likely that many of today's reporters — along with most other American children during the 1960s and 1970s — got their first glimpse of the idealistic life of the cub reporter by watching Gallegher on "The Wonderful World of Disney." Whether such glamorizing of the journalistic trade is a disservice to innocent children is open to question, but Davis' classic stereotype of the adventuresome reporter serves as a prime example of unrealistic idealism fashioned in America's Age of Innocence.

Ambrose Bierce provides the antithesis. Like Davis, he was both journalist and writer of fiction stories, many dealing with war. But the similarity beyond that point is hard to find. Consider, for example, their view of the Spanish-American war. Describing the 1898 Battle of San Juan Hill in a dispatch that brought new fame to Theodore Roosevelt, Davis wrote: "I speak of Roosevelt first because... Roosevelt, mounted high on horseback, and charging the rifle pits at a gallop and quite alone made you feel that you would like to cheer. He wore on his sombrero a blue polkadot handkerchief... which, as he advanced, floated straight behind his head, like a guidon...." Davis explained his own feelings about this episode in a private letter he wrote at the time: "I got excited and took a carbine and charged the sugar house [on San Juan Hill]. If the men had been regulars, I would have sat in the rear as [Stephen] Crane did but I knew every one of them, had played football and all that sort of thing, so I thought as an American I ought to help."[7]

To Davis, war could be great fun. Aboard Admiral Sampson's flagship during a naval battle off Cuba's coast that same year, he wrote: "The other night, we were heading off a steamer and firing six-pounders across her bows, the band was playing the 'star' song from 'Meistersinger.'...Wagner and War struck me as the most fin de siecle idea of war that I had ever heard of."[8]

Bierce, on the other hand, thought war — specifically the Spanish-American War in 1898 — could be caricatured as a gross kind of play. As a columnist writing in San Francisco, he remained away from the conflict unlike Davis, who was present on the battle line, but Bierce knew war from experience. He had seen four years of hell in 1861-1865, and his short story on that war, "An Occurrence at Owl Creek Bridge," captured much of the terror and despair of America's tragic conflict. He may have been 3,000 miles away from

[7]Richard Harding Davis, *Notes of a War Correspondent* (New York, 1910), 95-7. The Davis letter is quoted in John Hohenberg, *Foreign Correspondence* (New York, 1964), 135.
[8]Quoted in Larzer Ziff, *The American 1890s* (New York, 1966), 179.

A Study in Contrasts
Richard Harding Davis (left) and Ambrose Bierce (right) worked in journalism as if they were from two different ages. One of the best writers that American journalism has ever produced, Davis was a reporter for such newspapers as Charles Dana's *New York Sun* and William Randolph Hearst's *New York Journal*. He gained immense popularity not only for his writing but for his athletic good looks. A cynic, Bierce provided an early model for later journalists. He is best known, however, for the infamous quatrain that read, "The bullet that pierced Goebel's breast/ Cannot be found in all the West./ Good reason: it is speeding here/To lay McKinley in his bier." William Goebel was the assassinated governor of Kentucky. When President William McKinley was assassinated, critics recalled the quatrain and condemned both Bierce and his boss, William Randolph Hearst.

the battlefield in 1898, but he was sure he knew what was going on in Cuba. He called war

> ...a game; it is played, as football is played, because men love it — love to play it, love to see others play it, love to read about it and talk about it and look at pictures of it. Like many other games, it is played for stakes, but nobody really cares very much for what profit may come of success — all think they care most for that, but what really engages their interest and enthusiasm is the blood-letting — just as in pugilism and bull-fighting. Cloud the matter as we may with the cant of patriotism, humanity, promotion of commerce, or what you will, it is essentially and in the last analysis a sport.[9]

Bierce wrote many a column attacking the war in general and Davis's coverage of it in particular. Their differences extended to a full range of subjects — and not just their positions on various topics, but in the style of their approaches. Davis would set each small slice of society on the optimist's pedestal, viewing it with hope and enthusiasm. Bierce, on the other hand, was a cynic and, as a journalist, the master of the critical attack on those things he found unworthy of society. His appraisal could be scathing, but it was usually sound and realistic reasoning.

Like Samuel Clemens and Stephen Crane, Bierce was an intellectual with literary skill who viewed journalism as a labor sometimes necessary to keep the writer in groceries and in front of his audience. His forty years of journalism were devoted mostly to the writing of commentary, and his most productive years were spent writing for — of all people — William Randolph Hearst. Anti-war, anti-patriotism, anti-sensation — in fact, anti- just about anything — Bierce seemed the opposite of Hearst, and many wondered why (and how) Hearst kept him on. One of Hearst's editors later offered this explanation: "If I ever wondered why Mr. Hearst hired and tolerated Bierce that wonder was dispelled years later when I received a communication from W. R. instructing me to hire the late Harold Ickes as a columnist. It read: 'Ickes is a bitter bastard but hire him. The public loves abuse.' Mr. Hearst perhaps wrote the identical line in suggesting the hiring of Bierce."[10]

Hearst lured Bierce out of the literary circles in 1887 when he took over his first newspaper, the *San Francisco Examiner*. Bierce stayed with Hearst until 1906. After that he devoted himself to editing his *Collected Works* until he retired from writing in 1913. Eventually he wandered off into the Mexican desert and was never heard from again. It may have been just as well; to a man with Bierce's fanatic hatred of war, the slaughter of World War I would have been unbearable. Bierce was brilliant, if unlovable. But certainly he the skeptic, more than Davis the romantic, was the journalist of the future.

In these two pairs of contrasts — Leslie/Nelson, and Davis/Bierce — can be seen the old journalism giving way to the new: the condescending, high-profile, personal style of Mrs. Leslie replaced by the behind-the-scenes businessman's approach of city-builder Nelson; the romantic swashbuckler Davis yielding to the cynical but logical realist Bierce. The romance was going out of newspaper journalism.

[9]Ambrose Bierce, *Skepticism and Dissent—Selected Journalism from 1898-1901* (Ann Arbor, Mich., 1980), 148.

[10]Quoted in Lawrence I. Berkove, "Introduction," in ibid., xix.

The "New Journalism" Phenomenon

But if Mrs. Leslie and Davis were the Victorians and Nelson and Bierce were men of the future, that still doesn't explain why historians have named the 1880s and 1890s the "Age of New Journalism." There did appear to be a transitional period, before excess sensationalism led to a marked sobering of the press after 1900, when journalism was remarkably lively, innovative, brash, self-conscious, impetuous, and — well — sensational. The icon of this age was Joseph Pulitzer, and when in 1934 the newspaper trade journal *Editor and Publisher* celebrated its first fifty years with a poll asking editors to name the greatest American journalist, Pulitzer got the most votes, more than two decades after his death. His life and work are chronicled in the next section, but first an examination of this "New Journalism" is needed to get a better feel for what he symbolizes.

At the core of the New Journalism was an increased emphasis on news. The traditional urban journalism of the nineteenth century was that of thoughtful, patrician editors clipping articles from exchanges and writing editorial essays. The new method was to scour the city for the latest events of interest and to write them up in a brazen style appropriate to the leather-lunged boys who sold newspaper excitement on busy street corners.

Gossip, titillation, shouting newsboys, scoops, the 24-hour news cycle — these are the legacies of James Gordon Bennett, and many of the roots of this 1880s New Journalism are certainly to be found in Bennett's *New York Herald*. But the New Journalism drew on other innovations not usually found in Bennett's bag of tricks, such as big-letter headlines, action pictures, and popular crusades.

The *New York Times* and *Chicago Times* experimented with these bold new headlines in the late 1860s and 1870s. The New York paper showed the brazen insensitivity of the new style when it proclaimed in 42-point bold capitals, "EXIT GREELEY," after the Democratic nominee had just been crushed, both politically and emotionally, by his wife's death and his defeat in the 1872 presidential election. In the 1870s the Chicago paper won the prize for callousness with headlines like "Jerked to Jesus," over the story of a Bible-quoting prisoner hanged at a public execution; "Brooklyn Bake," on the story of 350 patrons trapped by a fire in a Brooklyn theater; and "Hell's Halo," over the story of a massacre during an Indian uprising. By the 1880s, smaller papers were getting into the act, and an Arkansas paper headlined a story about the lynching of some black people with "Chocolate Drops." Alliteration, puns, doggerel, and even acrostics appeared in newspaper heads, often depicting tragedy or disaster in ways tasteless or crass, but nevertheless engaging.

The use of action pictures invaded the mainstream press from the illustrated news weeklies (*Harper's* and *Leslie's*) that had reached full flower during the Civil War. Their success spawned a more frivolous pictorial something like the tabloids that accost shoppers in supermarket lines today. In the 1880s the *National*

1880s Tabloids
The *National Police Gazette*, by emphasizing illustrations and sensational stories, led the pack of tabloid newspapers in the late 1800s. Its circulation exceeded 100,000, allowing it to promote itself as "the leading illustrated sporting journal in America." It was printed on pink paper.

Police Gazette led the pack, printed on pink paper with an action picture covering most of page one. Its circulation exceeded 100,000. It did not pretend to be a general news medium, but the effectiveness of its illustrations was not lost on innovative publishers of mainstream newspapers, who incorporated action pictures into the new journalism mix.

The journalistic crusade also had been around for decades before it became a symbol of the New Journalism. One of the earliest had been the 1858 "swill milk" campaign, in which Frank Leslie filled his *Illustrated Newspaper* week after week with drawings of diseased and dying cows propped up so they could provide tainted milk to New York's babies. The *New York Times* had published lengthy series on Boss Tweed and on insurance company misdeeds, and *Harper's Weekly* was known for its long battle with Tammany Hall. But Pulitzer was the most successful at captivating public attention with crusades. The most effective ones usually were associated with humanitarian causes that were difficult to fault, but their broad popular appeal seemed somehow to threaten the establishment. The marketplace of ideas was changing. The small, select reading audience that had been engaged in serious discussion of the issues and of classical culture was now replaced by a larger public indulging in shallow trivia and intrigue.

Joseph Pulitzer

As measured by the magnitude of their lasting contributions to journalism, the giants of this period were Joseph Pulitzer and Adolph Ochs. These two men also are a study in contrasts — the noisy crusader and the quiet chronicler, the dashing and the prosaic, the man of the nineteenth century and the man of the twentieth.

Joseph Pulitzer, when he went to New York City in 1883, had been practicing his new kind of bright, lively journalism at the *St. Louis Post-Dispatch* since 1878. A gangling Hungarian immigrant, he had had to force his way into the American middle class with energy and cleverness; he was not going to win his way by first impressions. Coming to America in 1864 to join the Union Army, he began an association with Carl Schurz, then commander of a cavalry regiment and later editor of a German-language newspaper in St. Louis. Schurz hired Pulitzer as a reporter in 1868, despite a total lack of experience. Pulitzer showed a surprising aptitude for politics and was elected to the Missouri legislature when he was but twenty-two. A liberal within the Republican Party, he soon grew impatient (a lifelong trait) and left both legislature and party at the end of his term.

He scraped together enough money to combine two struggling English-language newspapers into the *Post-Dispatch* and announced, "The Post and Dispatch will serve no party but the people...will oppose all frauds and shams wherever and whatever they are; will advocate principles and ideas rather than prejudices and partisanship."[11] In days when one did not ask how many morning and evening papers a city had, but rather how many Republican and how many Democratic papers, it was a rather unusual plan. Especially so in St. Louis, where the strong *Republic* (noted earlier in this chapter for its press speeds) and the morning *Globe-Democrat* were like Goliaths towering over the new David.

Seizing and holding the initiative, Pulitzer began a series of crusades against corruption and complacency, establishing himself not just as a printer of news but as a non-partisan social critic. He published a list of owners of houses of prostitution, interviewed a prominent local heiress who had eloped, and charged a singer with drunkenness on the night of her performance. It was not the kind of news St. Louis' staid burghers could ignore; the news had taken on new life.

Within two years the upstart *Post-Dispatch* had city sales as large as the *Republic*, and the next year it absorbed the failing *St. Louis Star*. Profits were running $40,000 to $85,000 per year. But

Joseph Pulitzer
When Pulitzer bought the *New York World* in 1883, it was losing $40,000 a year. Within four months, he doubled its circulation to 40,000. In 1892, when he established the *Evening World*, the two papers' combined circulation of 374,000 surpassed that of any other two newspapers in the United States.

Pulitzer was working at such a relentless pace he was encountering increasing health problems; and when he headed east in 1883, it was for rest and recuperation. On his way to Europe he learned the *New York World* was for sale, and he bought it, assuming new responsibilities that would make him a famous, powerful, wealthy man, but broken in health.

The *World* had been losing money, and it was hardly noted for prestige. Pulitzer bought it (at the asking price of $346,000) from Jay Gould, the unscrupulous stock manipulator who had used it to promote his financial dealings. Before that the president of the Pennsylvania Railroad had owned and used it as a public relations tool. But it had a franchise with the Associated Press and afforded Pulitzer entry into the biggest newspaper market in America. Never mind that New York already had twenty-six English-language dailies (eleven of them business papers);[12] it did not have one quite like the *St. Louis Post-Dispatch*. A neurotic dynamo named Joseph Pulitzer was now ready to try his successful formula in the nation's chief metropolis.

[11] *St. Louis Post-Dispatch*, 12 December 1878.

[12] *American Newspaper Catalogue* (Cincinnati, 1885).

The announcement of the *World*'s new editorial and news policies was similar to Pulitzer's opening lines in St. Louis five years earlier. He was going to provide more news, brighter news, news for everybody. Demonstration was not long in coming. The Brooklyn Bridge was just about to be opened, and Pulitzer surprised readers with an unusual three-column illustration on page one. To Pulitzer, "bright" meant well illustrated, among other things, and the use of pictures was widely understood to be one of the standard characteristics of sensationalism.

Pulitzer wanted to create a newspaper for the underdog, and underdogs were plentiful in immigrant-filled New York. He scrupulously avoided news or features that seemed to put down the foreign-born and would not permit ethnic dialect writing even though it was one of the most popular forms of cheap literature. In 1887 he hired Elizabeth Cochrane ("Nellie Bly") to feign insanity and investigate conditions at the infamous Blackwell Island asylum. She found poor sanitation, unhealthy food, and abuse of patients. Her stories resulted in an official investigation and improvements. While she later would gain greater fame for her stunt to travel around the world in fewer than eighty days to break the record set by Jules Verne's fictional character Phileas Fogg, her exposure of Blackwell typified Pulitzer's crusading. He took stands popular with the poor: a federal income tax, inheritance taxes, civil reform, and relentless prosecution of corruption among the privileged. It was a remarkable turnabout for the *World*, which just two years earlier had been used by Gould to drive the stock of the Manhattan Transit Co. (New York's streetcar utility) so low that he could gain cheap control of another monopoly.

If Pulitzer planned to attack corruption, he was especially obsessed with that most readable of subjects, prostitution. His critics differ as to whether the elimination of vice and corruption was his primary goal, or the extra newspaper sales drawn by titillating headlines. More to the point, Pulitzer recognized his market and what it wanted to read; and if it made him rich, it did so by rewarding a talent basic to the free-enterprise system.

Continuing the extended crusades of the type he had originated in St. Louis, Pulitzer reached a zenith with his campaign to raise $200,000 for a base for the Statue of Liberty, a gift from the people of France. Bringing in nickels, dimes, and pennies from countless poor immigrants, he succeeded not only in building circulation, but also in giving the masses a sense of ownership of an important civic monument.

It took Pulitzer just two years to gain the highest circulation in New York City with 207,000 subscribers, passing the one-cent *Evening News*.[13] He set the trade journals to buzzing in admiration, not for his innovation so much as for the remarkable success he was having in building profits. The *World*, reminiscent of James Gordon Bennett Sr.'s *Herald* two generations earlier, became the trendsetter, the paper others imitated. In 1884, for example, the *World* put in its own photoengraving plant, the first newspaper in the city to do so; within ten years every major daily in the country

TO CYCLERS!!

NEW YORK JOURNAL

WHEELWOMEN!!

BRYAN GREETED IN M'KINLEY'S STATE.

Democratic Candidate Given an Enthusiastic Welcome.

VERMONT NAMES A GOVERNOR TO-DAY.

WALL STREET WISHES A NEW GUARDIAN OF THE TREASURY.

New York Journal
William Randolph Hearst hoped to appeal to the masses by using strong graphics in the design of the *New York Journal* and by supporting the populism of Democrat William Jennings Bryan. The column on the left of this cartoon by Homer Davenport recounts Bryan's recent successes in the 1896 presidential campaign.

had one.[14]

Pulitzer himself became less and less aware of his reputation. By the late 1880s he was the victim of near-blindness and a nervous disorder that prevented him from working at the World Building. He ran the paper by dispatch, and messengers were kept busy carrying memos back and forth, reading each day's paper to the editor-in-chief, trying to calm the crackling atmosphere around their increasingly irritable employer. Had he been more aware of his admirers and imitators, he might have been forewarned that one of them, an upstart young editor in California, was about to increase his irritation many times over.

WILLIAM RANDOLPH HEARST

The arrival of William Randolph Hearst in New York in 1895 marked the end of Pulitzer's golden years when the *World* ran far ahead of the pack. The *World*'s success was not lost on the ambitious young Hearst, who earlier had begun imitating *World* tactics at the *San Francisco Examiner*. He went to New York, as a matter of fact, to see whether he could out-Pulitzer Mr. Pulitzer.

[13] *American Newspaper Annual* (Philadelphia, 1886).

[14] *The Fourth Estate* 1 (5 April 1894): 8.

Nellie Bly

Stunt Reporter Was the Central Character in Her Own Stories

Nellie Bly (1865-1922) achieved fame as a newspaper reporter at a time when fewer than 5% of full-time journalists were women. She was able to do that through a combination of daring, self-promotion, and a talent for recognizing what the highly competitive newspapers of the late 1800s wanted.

Born Elizabeth Cochrane, she entered newspaper work at the *Pittsburgh Dispatch* in 1885 armed with a high school education, an attitude, and the need to support herself. Within two years she secured a job at the sensational *New York World* by getting herself committed to a lunatic asylum and then reporting her story in lurid detail. Her most renowned stunt was her 1889 trip around the world in seventy-two days — in a quest to beat the fictional Phileas Fogg's eighty-day feat — but she also wrote about social issues, including labor strikes, the living conditions of workers, gambling, and prostitution.

She married in 1895 and temporarily left newspaper work, but by 1913 she was widowed and in debt. She used her newspaper connections to win a position at the *New York Evening Journal*, where she was soon publishing first-page bylines and her own column. She worked as a war correspondent in Austria from 1914-1918 and following World War I returned to the United States to cover the plight of orphans.

Readers and sources alike found Bly a warm and sympathetic champion of those about whom she wrote. In addition to this characteristic, part of her success was due to her highly personal and somewhat breathless style of writing and her direct appeal to readers' emotions. But above all, no matter what story she was covering, she always made herself a central character in the drama.

She never let her readers forget for a moment that this was Nellie Bly who was telling them this story.

Elizabeth V. Burt
University of Hartford

Nellie Bly's attempt to go around the world in a shorter time than had the fictional Phileas Fogg in Jules Verne's *Around the World in Eighty Days* made her internationally known. She carried with her only what she was able to pack in her handbag, and her checkered coat became famous. The *New York World* published the cartoon at the bottom on the day of her return, showing her with other famous travelers from history. Along with her news stories in the *World*, she published her account in a popular book (below).

Hearst had been expelled from Harvard a decade earlier, much more interested in the newspaper business than in college. Such an interest was not unique, but Willie Hearst wanted to start at the top. His father, rich from his western silver mines, had acquired the *San Francisco Examiner* and was using it, at a loss, to further his political interests. Kicked out of Harvard, young Hearst pressed his father again for permission to run the paper. When George Hearst refused, Willie moved to New York and got a job on the much-talked-about *World*. He went to the *World* because it reportedly had raised its circulation from 15,000 to 250,000 in three years, and he wanted to do likewise with the *Examiner* someday. He wanted to be the Pulitzer of the West.

When George Hearst was appointed to the Senate in 1886, then elected for a full term in 1887, he gave his son control of the *Examiner*. W. R. took over in March 1887, when he was not yet twenty-four. He called his paper "The Monarch of the Dailies" and claimed for it "the most elaborate local news, the freshest social news, the latest and most original sensations" — all in large type.[15] He used more pictures, conducted Pulitzer-style crusades, spent his father's money lavishly, and built circulation. By 1890 the *Examiner* was in the black, and W. R. was sending agents east to see what was available in New York. The *New York Times* was in poor condition, but the price was unreasonable. The *Journal* was failing, but it was owned by Joseph Pulitzer's brother Albert. However, another owner obtained the *Journal*, and by 1895 he in turn was ready to sell. Hearst sent his agent with authority to pay a bundle, but he got the paper for a mere $180,000 — far less than Pulitzer had paid for the *World* ten years earlier. It was fortunate that Hearst saved on the purchase price; he would soon be spending extravagantly on salaries.

What followed was one of the most interesting and tackiest episodes in American journalism. Having received a family fortune of $7.5 million from his widowed mother in 1895, Hearst had the financial means to create competition on his own terms. He conceived a daring plan for quick success. He would hire away Pulitzer's best staff people, not only bolstering his own paper but dealing a body blow to his chief competitor as well. After hiring the entire staff of the *Sunday World*, including R. F. Outcault, the artist who had been drawing the popular comic strip "The Yellow Kid," Hearst continued to raid the *World* staff. On more than one occasion the contest took on the character of a high-stakes poker game with Pulitzer and Hearst each trying to outbid the other. Reporters soon found themselves in a seller's market, each awaiting the legendary card in the mailbox reading, "Mr. Hearst would be pleased to have you call." In 1897 one of Pulitzer's top editors, Arthur Brisbane, went over, and the *World* was beginning to hurt for talent.

The hiring of Brisbane proved especially fortunate for Hearst. The young editor had served as reporter and foreign correspondent for Dana's *Sun* but joined the *World* in 1890, where he fit in especially well with Pulitzer's new journalism. When Hearst, in an early raid, lured Sunday editor Morrill Goddard away from the *World*, Brisbane took his place, and the two engaged in a vigorous and colorful battle for Sunday readers. It may have been too colorful. Pulitzer had what Brisbane later recalled as "an attack of responsibility" and began to tighten the reins on the talented young writer-editor, moving him over to the *Evening World*.

Arthur Brisbane
In many respects the man responsible for the mass popularity of Pulitzer's and Hearst's sensational newspapers, Arthur Brisbane at the same time was one of the most popular editorial writers of all time. Upon his death in 1936, a fellow journalist pronounced, "The death removes one of the most gifted and contradictory personalities in American journalism."

Before long, Brisbane found himself in Hearst's posh apartment, talking terms. He said he didn't want Pulitzer to think he would quit because of money; so he asked that his base salary be no more than the $200 he got at the *World* — but he suggested a novel incentive. He asked Hearst to add a dollar a week to his salary for every 1,000 he added to the *Evening Journal's* circulation. Hearst gladly agreed. Brisbane had built the *Evening World* circulation to 325,000, and now he was essentially starting over at the *Evening Journal* with 40,000.

Brisbane loaded his new paper with banner headlines, huge pictures, and his piquant commentary. In less than two months he had almost pulled even in circulation and earned a $9,000 commission. When circulation later jumped again during the Spanish-American War, the contract was renegotiated; but even with the

[15]*San Francisco Examiner*, 12 March 1887.

William Randolph Hearst
Hearst, ever seeking popularity, aspired to be United States President. After being elected to the U.S. House of Representatives in 1902, where he served poorly, he lost the Democratic bid for president in 1904, lost his bid to be New York City mayor in 1905, lost a race for New York governor in 1906, lost another bid for New York City mayor in 1909, and lost a race for lieutenant governor in 1910. With that – and after having spent $2 million in his campaigns – he decided to quit running.

new arrangement, Brisbane eventually earned $260,000 a year plus benefits. For decades he was the highest paid journalist in America. For several years he also had the largest personal following of any writer in the world.

As Pulitzer lost key employees, he was losing profits, too. Hearst had started his evening paper at one cent a copy, and Pulitzer felt forced to retaliate by cutting the *World*'s price from 2¢ to 1¢. The *World*'s vaunted profit margin was dissipating.

For the rest of the 1890s, the two newspaper tycoons attacked each other — with bigger type, more sensational features, raids on talent, price-cutting, and exclusives — as new journalism rapidly turned to yellow journalism.

YELLOW JOURNALISM

Yellow journalism was an extension and a caricature of the New Journalism phenomenon. Put simply, it was New Journalism overstated and deprived of its soul. It is appropriate that this brief, unkindly labeled era got its name from a cartoon character, because illustration was a key component of yellow journalism. So also were big headlines, known tellingly as "scare heads," and exaggerated news display.

Nowadays, most people with some idea of yellow journalism have formed their impressions with the help of Orson Welles, whose 1941 film *Citizen Kane* was based on the life of William Randolph Hearst. Consider this dialogue, in which Kane (Hearst) explains his new approach to the old-time editor of the paper he has just bought:

> Kane (pointing to the rival paper): The "Chronicle" has a two-column headline, Mr. Carter. Why haven't we?
>
> Carter: The news wasn't big enough.
>
> Kane: If the headline is big enough, it *makes* the news big enough.

This script was written by Herman Mankiewicz, an experienced New York newspaperman before he went to Hollywood in the 1920s. Does it depict 1890s journalism fairly? Unfortunately, the element of truth is substantial enough to make the dialogue credible, even though the script is overdrawn in the standard Hollywood style.

A fairer point of view, though biased in the other direction, was offered by Hearst's own business manager, T.T. Williams, interviewed for an 1897 book. He made a persuasive argument:

> Sensationalism is largely a matter of type — of head lines, display, illustrations. The most eminently respectable newspapers in this country at times print matter that the so-called sensational newspaper would never dare to print — but the so-called respectable newspaper escapes uncriticized because it does not look sensational.[16]

This was an aspect of yellow journalism where Hearst undeniably led the way: the display of news. Newspapers like the *Boston Globe* and *San Francisco Chronicle*, and even smaller papers like the *Knoxville Journal*, began to run headlines in which the type size was measured in inches rather than points. This new style of news display spread across the country in a wave of imitation something like later newspaper fashions — the 1920s papers trying to emulate the highly successful *New York Daily News*, or today's papers trying to look like *USA Today*.

But other aspects of yellow journalism were harder to condone: hoaxes, fake interviews, a variety of inaccuracies, and a reportorial passion for personality and human interest. Inevitably, some of the nation's opinion leaders began to make this kind of journalism a public issue, laying the groundwork for a tradition of press criticism that would blossom in generations to come. The most likely 1890s forum was the issue-oriented magazines (like *Cosmopolitan* or *Century*) that opinion leaders read. Some proposed newspaper reform, calling for endowed newspapers or for more religious publishers. Others advised turning away from

[16]Charles Austin Bates, ed., *American Journalism* (New York, 1897), 314.

$50,000 REWARD.—WHO DESTROYED THE MAINE?—$50,000 REWARD.

EDITION FOR GREATER NEW YORK.

NEW YORK JOURNAL AND ADVERTISER

DESTRUCTION OF THE WAR SHIP MAINE WAS THE WORK OF AN ENEMY.

$50,000!

$50,000 REWARD! For the Detection of the Perpetrator of the Maine Outrage!

Assistant Secretary Roosevelt Convinced the Explosion of the War Ship Was Not an Accident.

The Journal Offers $50,000 Reward for the Conviction of the Criminals Who Sent 258 American Sailors to Their Death. Naval Officers Unanimous That the Ship Was Destroyed on Purpose.

$50,000!

$50,000 REWARD! For the Detection of the Perpetrator of the Maine Outrage!

NAVAL OFFICERS THINK THE MAINE WAS DESTROYED BY A SPANISH MINE.

Hidden Mine or a Sunken Torpedo Believed to Have Been the Weapon Used Against the American Man-of-War—Officers and Men Tell Thrilling Stories of Being Blown Into the Air Amid a Mass of Shattered Steel and Exploding Shells—Survivors Brought to Key West Scout the Idea of Accident—Spanish Officials Protest Too Much—Our Cabinet Orders a Searching Inquiry—Journal Sends Divers to Havana to Report Upon the Condition of the Wreck. Was the Vessel Anchored Over a Mine?

BY CAPTAIN E. L. ZALINSKI, U.S.A.

Assistant Secretary of the Navy Theodore Roosevelt says he is convinced that the destruction of the Maine in Havana Harbor was not an accident.

The suspicion that the Maine was deliberately blown up grows stronger every hour. Not a single fact to the contrary has been produced.

863,956 WORLDS CIRCULATED YESTERDAY

The World.

863,956 WORLDS CIRCULATED YESTERDAY

MAINE EXPLOSION CAUSED BY BOMB OR TORPEDO?

Capt. Sigsbee and Consul-General Lee Are in Doubt—The World Has Sent a Special Tug, With Submarine Divers, to Havana to Find Out—Lee Asks for an Immediate Court of Inquiry—260 Men Dead.

IN A SUPPRESSED DESPATCH TO THE STATE DEPARTMENT, THE CAPTAIN SAYS THE ACCIDENT WAS MADE POSSIBLE BY AN ENEMY.

Dr. E. C. Pendleton, Just Arrived from Havana, Says He Overheard Talk There of a Plot to Blow Up the Ship—Capt. Zalinski, the Dynamite Expert, and Other Experts Report to The World that the Wreck Was Not Accidental—Washington Officials Ready for Vigorous Action if Spanish Responsibility Can Be Shown—Divers to Be Sent Down to Make Careful Examinations.

The Battleship *Maine*

The *New York Journal's* and *World's* reporting of the sinking of the American warship *Maine* in Havana harbor in February 1898 helped lead the nation's sentiment to war with Spain.

newspapers to magazines and books, until the fad passed. Most longed for a more serious approach to newspapering, and they soon recognized what they were looking for in the person of an 1896 New York arrival, Adolph Ochs. A new type of criticism began to be heard also from the emerging science of social psychology. The concept of social responsibility was proposed, and academicians began to report some empirical research in scholarly journals.

However, it may have been that catharsis was needed most of all, and this soon came about in the form of a swashbuckling journalist's dream war just a few dozen miles from our shores. It was an accident of history that the Spanish-American disagreement came just at the height of the Pulitzer-Hearst competition and of a national craving for sensation. The two publishers, however, did more than their share of promoting it. As a result, that little war received aggressive news coverage unlike anything else in human experience.

The Spanish-American War

The year 1898 was pivotal in both the Pulitzer-Hearst contest and in American news reporting history. On February 15, the AP correspondent in Havana cabled bulletins reporting that the battleship *Maine* had been blown up and hundreds of sailors killed in the harbor. Hearst was at home that night and received the news by phone from the *Journal*'s office. "Good Heavens!" he exclaimed. "What have you done with the story.... Have you put anything else on the front page?" "Only the other big news," his editor replied. "There is not any other big news," said Hearst. "Please spread the story all over the page. This means war."

It was the news Hearst had been waiting for. He already had a corps of writers and artists in Cuba covering the insurrection against Spanish rule, and on occasion had trouble convincing them there was a war to be reported. His artist, Frederic Remington, the famous illustrator of the American West, felt that the publisher was wasting his money, and cabled, "Everything is quiet. There is no trouble here. There will be no war." Hearst responded with the most famous wire in newspaper history: "Please remain. You furnish the pictures and I'll furnish the war."[17] When the *Maine* was blown up, and when inept Spanish diplomats failed to neutralize the incident, Hearst and Pulitzer (in concert with imperialist politicians like Theodore Roosevelt) were able to urge Congress into a formal declaration of war on Spain by April.

The first exclusive of the new war fell to Pulitzer, through a stroke of luck. He had a stringer with Commodore Dewey at Manila when the Spanish fleet was destroyed on May 1, and he was able to get the news first when the American fleet put in at Hong Kong, where a cable to Europe was available. But from then on it was Hearst's show. He spent about $3,000 a day on war coverage alone, totaling about $500,000 for the year. Pulitzer spent a bit

[17]Quoted in James Creelman, *On the Great Highway* (Boston, 1901), 177-8. Some historians doubt the accuracy of this oft-told story.

NEW YORK JOURNAL

RICHARD HARDING DAVIS AND FREDERIC REMINGTON IN CUBA FOR THE JOURNAL.

The *Journal's* Stars
Hearst's *New York Journal* gave star billing to two of its staff members covering the Spanish-American War from Cuba. The artist Frederic Remington (left) illustrated the war, and Richard Harding Davis reported on it.

less; and the *Herald*, the *Sun*, and the Associated Press are estimated to have spent about $250,000 each. The AP had five dispatch boats in the area, and when a Spanish squadron was destroyed off Santiago, the AP man sped to Jamaica and put the entire story on the cable at the urgent rate; cable charges alone totaled $8,000 for that one story. But the Hearst yacht, the *Sylvia*, cut the most impressive figure, and the publisher must have felt most gratified when he was able to pick twenty-nine Spanish prisoners out of the water after the sinking of the Spanish fleet.

The Spanish-American War brought Hearst's style of journalism and his flagship paper, the *New York Journal*, to their peak. On its best day the *Journal* printed 1,068,000 copies. Brisbane later said 200,000 more could have been sold. Pulitzer had less luck with his correspondents, and for once he was not able to match his rival's enterprise and resourcefulness.

The contributions of Pulitzer and Hearst have been compared relentlessly by historians, and Pulitzer usually gets a lion's share of the credit. He was the innovator, the energetic pioneer who developed the new sensational journalism for whatever it was worth. His crusades certainly did some tangible good, and he brought a great many New Yorkers into the newspaper audience who apparently had read nothing before the *World* stirred them from their lethargy, boredom, or semi-literacy.

Pulitzer's chief contributions came in those first twelve years before his nemesis arrived. The subsequent spending contest, coupled with Pulitzer's health problems, blindness, and forced absence from the newspaper office, prevented his regaining the industry's leadership once the public tired of sensation and things settled down after the turn of the century. Ironically the St. Louis paper, which he neglected after 1883, continued to grow and to become a great American newspaper. But the *World*, to which he gave so much of his energy, his health, and his fortune, entered a period of slow but terminal decline.

Hearst was imitator more than innovator, but his contributions were hardly insignificant. He did bring higher salaries, bylines, and other recognition to an under-rewarded profession; and he never hesitated to employ, or even experiment with, the latest in printing technology, if it would sell more papers. Clearly, he was no villain. What may appear to modern generations as war-mongering was fairly common behavior in the western world in the 1890s. In fact, the United States was a come-lately in the great imperialist movement of the nineteenth century. If the Hearst/ Pulitzer efforts seemed a bit intense, the two publishers did have some reason to make up for lost time.

ADOLPH OCHS

Perhaps the greatest contribution to journalism in the 1890s was made by an unimposing latecomer who sent no dramatic telegrams and launched no blaring crusades. But he did turn the moribund *New York Times* into the premier newspaper of the twentieth century.

Adolph Ochs started delivering newspapers in Knoxville, Tennessee, when he was nine years old. At fourteen he became a printer's devil at the local *Chronicle*, and by the time he was seventeen he decided he had learned all there was to learn in Knoxville. He headed west toward gold country. He got as far as Louisville, where he worked briefly setting type for the *Courier-Journal*, and then returned home to help with the family income. He was the oldest of six children; and his father, a scholarly lay rabbi, was a poor businessman. Adolph and a partner went to Chattanooga to start the *Dispatch* in 1877, but the paper expired within months. At nineteen, he did not have enough money to return the 120 miles to Knoxville.

Showing a dogged persistence that he would often call upon, he published a city directory in Chattanooga and paid off the newspaper's debts. He won the community's confidence; and when he bought the near-bankrupt *Chattanooga Times* in 1878, a local banker co-signed a note for the $250 down payment. Not yet twenty-one, the youth had to have his father travel from Knoxville to make the transaction legal. The post-reconstruction years were lean in the war-torn town, and Ochs was hard-pressed to build circulation; the paper had 250 subscribers when he bought it. But Ochs had declared: "We shall give the people a chance to support

Ochs and the *Times*
Reacting against the sensationalism of the *New York World* and *Journal*, Adolph Ochs emphasized news and objectivity over opinion. The *New York Times*, which was losing $1,000 a day when Ochs took over its management in 1896, began turning a profit within a year. With Ochs' emphasis on operating on sound business practices, the *Times* became the model for newspapers.

that which they have been asking for — a newspaper primarily devoted to the material, education and moral growth of our progressive city and its surrounding territory."[18]

The community accepted the proposal sufficiently to bring him enough profit in four years to gain sole ownership and move his family from Knoxville. His brothers helped on the paper, and the Ochs family has operated it ever since.

While he was still in his twenties, Ochs became intrigued with Chattanooga's growing role as a southern mountain resort city, and he speculated in real estate. By the 1890s he still had a profitable newspaper, but he had a lot of nearly worthless land and staggering debts. In 1896 he went to New York in search of fortune. His Chattanooga circulation had risen to near 5,000, but he had a New York-sized debt. He saw his solution in the venerable *New York Times* and managed to finance its purchase for $75,000 in an auction in a New York courtroom. He announced his intention to continue the tradition of past editors Henry Raymond and George Jones, and added:

> It will be my earnest aim that The New York *Times* give the news, all the news, in concise and attractive form, in language that is parliamentary in good society, and give it as it can be learned through any other reliable medium; to give the news impartially, without fear or favor, regardless of any party, sect or interest involved; to make the columns of The New York *Times* a forum for the consideration of all questions of public importance, and to that end to invite intelligent discussion from all shades of opinion.[19]

Before the year was out he had shortened that statement considerably, to "All the news that's fit to print." In either the long or the short version it was not remarkable, except in that it resisted the temptation to join the sensational trend so dominant since Hearst had entered New York journalism the year before. Ochs was determined to keep the *Times* a decent newspaper.

Using business experience that had elevated him to the presidency of the Southern Newspaper Publishers Association and established him as one of the South's leading publishers, Ochs set about cutting costs and building revenue. After two years of improvement, things looked dark in 1898. Pulitzer and Hearst were locked in a costly combat that affected the other New York papers. Rather than lower his standards, Ochs lowered his price. At a time when the *World* and *Journal* were selling lavishly illustrated, sensational papers at 2¢ each, Ochs cut his price to a penny. It turned out to be a shrewd business move. By 1900 circulation was up to 82,000 — a ninefold increase — and his Chattanooga debts were paid. He had, moreover, maintained the New York newspaper's quality.

Ochs' good business sense was quickly recognized. He received several offers of $2 million or more for his majority stock in the paper in 1900. One of the industry's trade journals, *The Newspapermaker*, sought to explain the *Times*' remarkable success over the four-year period when Pulitzer and Hearst had been getting all the attention. It said:

> The success of The New York *Times* has astonished and pleased those publishers who feared the "yellow peril".... The answer is found in "All the news that's fit to print." It has modestly attempted to reflect, not to make public opinion. It has aimed to be a complete daily newspaper, edited for the self-respecting man, his wife, son and daughter. It does not print pictures, neither does it indulge in freak typography. It has avoided sensationalism and fakes of every description. It has not attempted to do stunts in the name of public service. It has cultivated impartiality and independence. It does not print any advertisement in the ordinary news type of the paper, and it prints "readers" [ads that look like news stories] in agate type only, with "Adv." after them.[20]

[18]Ruth Sulzberger Holmberg, "Adolph S. Ochs — A Granddaughter's Perspective," address to Chattanooga Rotary Club, 1976.

[19]*New York Times*, 19 August 1896.

[20]*The Newspapermaker*, 21 February 1901.

New Leaders
In the 1880s, the old newspaper leaders of New York City – such as the *New York Tribune* that Horace Greeley had founded in 1841 (whose building is pictured in the left foreground in this 1888 drawing) – were beginning to fade in competition with Pulitzer's *World* and Hearst's *Journal.* Those two newspapers themselves, however, would in later years succumb to a new competitor, Adolph Ochs at the rejuvenated *New York Times.* Even though it occupied impressive offices (center building, above) at the time that he took over its management, it had fallen on difficult times. Ochs, however, established new policies for its approaches to both news and business, and it eventually would become the model for other newspapers.

This statement overdrew the case a bit, for certainly the *Times* would soon be printing pictures, too; but its implication was clear — many readers and journalists were tired of sensation, and they welcomed a more mature brand of journalism.

OTHER NEWSPAPER LEADERS

While Pulitzer, Hearst, and Ochs were setting trends in New York, other important newspapermen were making their marks elsewhere in the country. Unlike the three men who left important newspapers in St. Louis, San Francisco, and Chattanooga because only New York offered sufficient challenge, these others were content with establishing newspaper traditions in lesser cities. No longer did a newspaper editor have to look to New York to make it to the top. The West — everything beyond Pittsburgh — was assuming new importance.

The Scripps family had been involved in western papers since the 1850s; and the first Scripps-founded paper was an important one, the *Detroit News*, started in 1873. Other papers were established in Cleveland, St. Louis, and Cincinnati; and soon Edward W. Scripps emerged as the energetic driving force of the family. By the mid-1890s, with five papers already Scripps-owned, he and his business manager formed the Scripps-McRae League. Other chains had existed technically — newspapers in two cities with the same person owning both papers, as with Pulitzer — but Scripps was the first to give his energies to the group, rather than to a single paper. He was generally successful, prompting one enthusiastic historian to call him the Benjamin Franklin of his day.[21] Such comparisons exaggerate the importance of the Scripps papers, usually penny afternoon dailies in mid-sized cities. But Scripps was indeed the father of the modern media chain, and it is probably fitting that the Scripps name lives on in modern newspaper and broadcasting companies, and most recently in Scripps Howard Cable TV, one of our larger cable television operators.

Other western and southern publishers, unlike Pulitzer, Hearst, Ochs, and Scripps, built both financial strength and journalistic tradition in one location. The best known among them were Joseph Medill at the *Chicago Tribune*, Henry Watterson at the *Louisville Courier-Journal* and the *Times*, Henry Grady at the *Atlanta Constitution*, Charles Taylor at the *Boston Globe*, and Kansas City's William Rockhill Nelson. Each had established his leadership in the pre-1883 period, but continued to strengthen his paper in the 1880s and 1890s (except Grady, who died in 1889).

On the other hand, some journals with established reputations declined during the 1880s and 1890s. Among the New York editors crowded from the limelight by Pulitzer, Hearst, and Ochs were the *Tribune*'s Whitelaw Reid, devoted now to politics and diplomacy; the *Sun*'s Charles Dana, who stubbornly resisted new methods and machines; James Gordon Bennett Jr., erratic absentee publisher whose *Herald* went into a long, gradual decline; and the *Post*'s E. L. Godkin, whose devotion to a sharp, witty editorial page came at the expense of newsgathering effort.

Two other newspapermen of the period deserved no particular notice at the time, but they later laid the foundations of media empires. In the 1890s Harry Chandler was working for his father-in-law, Harrison Otis, on the *Los Angeles Times*; and Frank Gannett, just out of college, began a career with a paper he would later own, the *Syracuse Herald*. Unlike the Scripps chain, Times-Mirror and Gannett were not founded in the 1890s; but their roots are there.

[21]J.M. Lee, *History of American Journalism*, rev. ed. (Garden City, New York, 1923), 417.

E. W. Scripps, Chain Magnate
In operating his newspaper chain, Scripps believed in singleness of control, independence from banks and advertisers, and publishing papers for the underdog. He involved his sons in the business by starting them at the top; but even though he ran his newspapers from his central office, he treated his managers well by sharing profits with them. He was particularly interested in local political reform, but he also gave a great deal of attention to the business soundness of his papers and their profitability.

Structure of the Newspaper Industry

After whom would these founders of future chains pattern their causes? Would they emulate the high-profile leadership of Pulitzer and Hearst, with close personal supervision of editorials, crusades, and news policy? Or would they look to Scripps, who later boasted that he owned newspapers in some cities he had never visited; or Nelson, who apparently did not write for his own newspaper; or Ochs, the quiet publisher and policymaker who tried to divert the limelight from himself to his paper and its solid reputation?

The last two decades of the nineteenth century saw the last major efforts at personal journalism. Inspirational leadership gave way to more sophisticated behind-the-scenes management. The newspaper industry, like many other old-time manufacturing businesses in America, was maturing. The publishers and business managers were taking over.

Emphasis on organization increased. The trend permeated much of American business. Some competitors merged and formed monopolies (i.e., exclusive control of a particular market) or oligopolies (i.e., control of a market by a few sellers) and tried to raise prices. More often, businesses with common interests simply formed trade associations. One of today's most powerful media associations is the American Newspaper Publishers' Association, which recently reorganized and changed its name to the Newspaper Association of America. Its first national meeting, in 1887, began by dealing with the problem of unethical and unscrupulous advertising agents. Within a decade advertising agents had established their own group, the American Advertising Agents Association, partly to deal with unscrupulous publishers. A primary need for the new ANPA came from what the publishers felt was the ineffectiveness of the previous National Editorial Association and the older state press associations. With their new, more modern structure, newspapers needed a new group aimed at meeting publishers' needs. Publishers and editors now had separate organizations; the functional distinction was clear. An editor's role was to fill half the paper with news and commentary. The position of advertising manager became common, with responsibilities for the other half of newspaper content. The publisher's job was to oversee both and to be sure the newspaper made money.

Increasingly, the money came from advertising. American newspapers and periodicals had received 56% of their revenue from circulation and 44% from advertising in 1879. By 1889 the split was approximately 50-50, and by 1899 it was 45.5% from circulation and 54.5% from advertising. Department store advertising was beginning to replace patent medicine ads, and a new breed of professional advertising men was evident. Whereas advertising agents of the 1880s were primarily brokers, shopping for the newspaper that would give the lowest rate, the ad men and women of the 1890s were often professional artists and copy writers providing creative services for their clients. They also began to look at demographics, beginning with the discovery that large numbers of women were reading newspapers and shopping accordingly.

In short, America's newspapers were becoming an integral part of the country's new national marketing system. The old-time newspaper, driven by a dynamic editorial personality, was beginning its evolution into the market-driven mass medium of the twentieth century. Inevitably, the roles of publisher, ad manager, and circulation manager took on increasing importance.

The Provincial Press

At the same time that mainstream daily papers were establishing themselves as important ad media, there was a rising tide of small local newspapers, marginally profitable and often quite unprofessional. Estimates of the total number of newspapers and periodicals in America at any given time in the 1890s usually run around 15,000 or 16,000, but a significant portion of them are of little journalistic importance. A few were papers subsidized by special interests such as prohibitionists, free-silver advocates, or populists. A

LATE NEWS.

THE SATURDAY BLADE.

LUETGERT.

Over One Million Five Hundred Thousand Readers a Week.

PRICE 5 CENTS.

GIRL IS MISSING.

Hundreds of Men on Trail of Abductor.

Stranger Captured Narrowly Escapes Being Lynched.

LUETGERT'S DEATH

IS YELLOW FEVER.

30 Cases, 10 Deaths at Hampton, Va.

Inmates of Soldiers' Home the Victims—4,000 Men Exposed.

WHAT MRS. M'KEE SAW IN WOODS NEAR BLOOMINGTON, IND.

"Shut Up! You'll Cry Worse Than That Before You Are Through With Me," Yelled the Strange Man, With an Oath.

PALMER HOUSE RIOT.

Opposing Forces Meet in the Hotel Foyer.

SEA MONSTER SEEN.

Story Confirmed by 300 Ocean Voyagers.

LABOR IS IN DEMAND.

Great Scarcity of Men in the Northwest.

BACK FROM ICY NORTH.

The Spread of New Journalism
With the circulation successes of Pulitzer and Hearst in New York City, their techniques spread to cities around the country. The *Saturday Blade* of Chicago was one newspaper on which the influence of New Journalism was apparent.

larger number were propped up by a unique system of syndicates that enabled untrained workmen in rural villages to establish "newspapers" on the thinnest of shoestrings.

The system worked this way. A syndicate (sometimes called a co-op or a newspaper union) would start up in a state's centrally located city, such as Des Moines or Nashville or Denver. Its purpose was to provide pre-printed sheets of newsprint to small-town editors, who then would add a bit of local news and sell the entire paper to their fellow townsmen. These sheets were called readyprint and could be furnished with two or three pre-printed pages. A local printer could fill half of the unprinted front page with a house ad (mostly white space) and the paper's nameplate, and all that remained was to fill a few columns with local gossip. All he needed was a few dollars worth of type and an old hand-press of colonial vintage; and he could print a hundred or so copies, sell a few dozen subscriptions, and eke out a living.

The syndicates filled the other three pages with jokes, stories, travel features, and other non-local material, plus a generous portion of advertising. The ad sales covered the syndicate's expenses, and the pre-printed pages could be given to the local printer free. The general public often thought little of such papers, and sometimes with good reason — as when Minnesota farmers read in their paper instructions on safely boarding a cable-car, and southern Californians read advice on teaching cows to drink from frozen ponds. Readyprint papers commanded about as much esteem as some of the poorly produced free-circulation papers (sometimes called "shoppers") of today.

Less objectionable standardized content was columnar plate material that some syndicates distributed. They shipped stereotype plates of news and features by train daily or weekly, and local editors could make day-to-day decisions on how much of it to substitute for locally produced type. The material, called boilerplate, could include some breaking news — reports from the state legislature, for example — and in some ways the plate houses resembled wire services. However, they could furnish plate material, as they advertised, with "politics to suit," and they slanted the news Republican or Democratic to accord with a printer's views.

In the 1890s more than half the country's weeklies were using readyprint, and a leading plate house said it was supplying its material to 8,000 journals. The plate matter sold for $1.20 to $2 a page, and the readyprint was furnished free. It did not cost much to get into the newspaper business, and doubtless many people entered it who had no business being there. Although these cheap papers may have helped marginal communities get established, they inflicted much senseless material on the general public, and the image of the newspaper industry was probably damaged as much by boilerplate and readyprint in small towns as it was by sensational yellow journalism in large cities.

A minority of small papers stood out from the canned sheets. Doing all one's own typesetting and printing was a mark of quality. A few country editors refused to print canned features and editorials and insisted on writing their own. In 1896 a young editor in Emporia, Kansas, wrote his resounding "What's the Matter with Kansas?" editorial[22] and saw it quoted and reprinted all across the country. He was William Allen White, and he was no readyprint man. His fame grew rapidly, and one day he would exemplify the solid small-town newspaperman, a grassroots voice representing America's weekly press long after most of the boilerplate and readyprint had disappeared.

ALTERNATIVE NEWSPAPERS

Despite the fact that thousands of newspapers were operating in the mainstream of American journalism, many demographic groups were living at the margins of society where they were insufficiently served.

In this period of heavy immigration, foreign-language newspapers filled important functions in readying the newly arrived for assimilation and citizenship. The German-language papers were the most numerous, with the 1880 census showing 641 newspapers with an aggregate circulation of about 2.5 million. Eighty of them were dailies.

[22] *Emporia Gazette*, 15 August 1896.

Immigrants and the Press
In a period of heavy immigration, foreign-language newspapers helped prepare the newly arrived for assimilation and citizenship. This cartoon from *Leslie's Weekly* in 1888 illustrated the attitudes between old Americans and the newcomers. Many immigrants preferred to retain their native language rather than learn English, and numerous foreign-language newspapers were started to appeal to them. About 1,000 such periodicals, most of them German, were publishing by the 1890s.

Native Americans, especially in Indian Territory (now part of Oklahoma), needed their own papers to help preserve their culture and provide forums for discussion of the many difficult issues they faced. The Cherokee Nation led the way, using the alphabet that Sequoya had invented, and by 1891 had its own newspaper, the *Daily News*.

Other groups lived in mainstream communities but, though not confined by geography or ethnic origin, felt consigned to the philosophical margins of society. Anarchists founded their own press, with several newspapers representative of different views. *Liberty* (1881-1908) was edited by *Boston Globe* writer Benjamin Tucker, who advocated freedom and laissez-faire capitalism, not unlike the position of America's revived Libertarian Party press today. But Tucker's energy was also needed to combat the more militant anarchist following of Johann Most and his German-language *Freiheit* ("freedom"). Along with the anarchist newspapers *Truth* and *Alarm*, the *Freiheit* ran articles on how to make bombs and nitro-glycerin. One masthead read, "*Truth* is five cents a copy and dynamite forty cents a pound." These inflammatory papers probably abetted the public overreaction to the violence at the Haymarket Riot (1886) and the Homestead Strike (1892).

Many other newspapers advocated diverse interests. Numerous papers served the labor movement. One of them, the *Standard* (1887-1891), gained national attention as the voice of its editor, political economist Henry George of single-tax fame. Another hundred or so papers, scattered around the country, were devoted to the causes of temperance and prohibition. Populist papers numbered around 1,000 at their peak in the early 1890s.

Without doubt, however, the group in greatest need for a voice was African Americans. Six-and-a-half-million strong, they saw their recently won freedom taken away bit by bit under the sharecropper system and forced labor laws in the South, followed by new Jim Crow laws that the U.S. Supreme Court affirmed in 1896 in *Plessy v. Ferguson*. Despite the hardship of targeting a newspaper to such an economically bereft market, many Black editors emerged to serve a news-starved people.

In the four decades following the Civil War, 1,200 Black newspapers were started, mostly in the South. John P. Mitchell established the *Richmond Planet* as the largest-circulation weekly in Virginia with 13,000 subscribers. T. Thomas Fortune reached his peak influence at the *New York Age*, which he edited from 1889 until 1907. He was African Americans' leading voice in the denunciation of lynching, disenfranchisement, and Jim Crow laws. Ida B. Wells-Barnett emerged as the leading Black woman editor, using the Memphis *Free Speech* to vigorously condemn the lynchings that were frequent in the heart of the South. Threatened with violence, she moved to New York City to write for Fortune's *Age* and then to Chicago, where she earned fame as an effective organizer and lecturer, both here and abroad.

The armed forces, numbering only about 40,000 in the mid-1800s, were served by the *Army & Navy Journal* from 1863 on, but the Spanish-American War brought new needs. For the first time, significant numbers of American troops were stationed overseas, and military papers sprang up in Cuba and the Philippines.

The dominant medium, the newspaper, demonstrated its ability to serve a wide variety of social needs. But the time had come for newspapers to share the stage.

Competition from Other Media

Historians of media economics have found much evidence to support what has been called the Principle of Relative Constancy. The principle holds that a fairly constant proportion of personal income will be spent on media, and if a new mass medium enters the picture, its share of media revenue comes at the expense of re-

Dime Novels

Cheap Fiction Brings Western Adventure into America's Parlors

Termed the "first profitable mass literature in the United States," the dime novel from 1860 to about 1920 played much the same role television does today. The favored form of entertainment read by nearly everyone, including adolescents and the working class, the inexpensive books sold millions of copies, often in long-running series.

Like television, dime novels both reflected and helped shape society. Also, like television, they were blamed for crime and other societal ills. Clergy and other critics proclaimed dime novels immoral, an ironic charge since publishers went out of their way to edit sex and rough language from their manuscripts.

Because the nation was enamored by the frontier after the Civil War, and because the frontier offered unlimited opportunity for tales of derring-do, it was natural for the Western adventure story to be the first, most successful dime novel genre, supplemented later by detective and self-improvement books. Historical figures like Buffalo Bill, Calamity Jane, and Kit Carson took on heroic proportions and mixed with fictional characters created by Edward Ellis, Ned Buntline, Edward Wheeler, Prentiss Ingraham, and other writers.

Dime novelists were competent, though perhaps second-rank, authors who were unceremoniously dubbed hacks because of their commercialism. They cranked out prodigious amounts of copy using pen and ink and, later, typewriters. Ingraham produced more than 600 novels, once, it is claimed, writing a 35,000-word book in twenty-four hours. Authors generally received $75 to $300 per manuscript. The most important publisher was the House of Beadle and Adams in New York, which originated dime novels by publishing Ann Stephens' *Malaeska: the Indian Wife of the White Hunter* in 1860. Beadle and Adams alone published more than 7,500 novels.

Dime novels succumbed in the 1920s to changing times, postal regulations, pulp fiction magazines, and movies.

Glenn Himebaugh
Middle Tennessee State University

Beadle & Co. inaugurated dime novels in 1860 with *Malaeska; the Indian Wife of the White Hunter* under the slogan "Books for the Millions!" Because of the book's popularity, Beadle reissued the novel with the illustrated cover above. It promoted its line of dime novels as "the choicest works of the most popular authors." Among the most popular of the dime novelists was Ned Buntline (left), who played to the hilt the public image of a western adventurer.

duced shares for existing media.[23] Data to support this proposition (also called the Scripps Hypothesis) are derived mainly from the twentieth century, because records on consumer spending before 1900 are almost non-existent. But it is clear that in the 1880s and 1890s other media began to challenge newspapers' dominance. The ensuing gradual newspaper decline can be explained by the new competition just as logically as by public reaction to sensationalism, or readyprint, or fad, or fashion.

Books, of course, had been around longer than newspapers. However, mass production and cheap transportation began to deliver unprecedented numbers of books to the marketplace. Not only did public school attendance increase, but also sales of school books went up even faster as pupils bought their own readers and spellers. The popular McGuffey textbooks were selling more than two million copies a year in the late 1880s. In popular literature, the increase in sales was even more dramatic. The most widely published author was Horatio Alger, whose first novel appeared in 1867 and who wrote about 100 more before he died in 1899. Sales of Alger books are estimated at about 250,000,000. It was the era of the dime novel, and hundreds of writers (few of whom took their craft as seriously as Alger, a former minister) ground out hackneyed plots and well-worn characterizations to meet the demand for cheap literature. A third market appeared as paperback collections, or "libraries," came into vogue. The growing middle class wanted an inexpensive introduction to serious literature; and the classics and best-sellers were increasingly sold in groups.[24] By 1887, twenty-six libraries were on the market, including the full range from cheap romance to the classics. A forerunner of the book club, Funk and Wagnalls had a subscription list of 16,000 who had signed up at $4 a year to receive a book every two weeks. Serious readers could fill a bookshelf with the same few dollars they might otherwise spend for the canned contents of a readyprint newspaper. No doubt many of them did.

Magazines were expanding their markets. Magazine prices were cut in the 1890s so that monthlies like *Munsey's* and *McClure's* could be put within the purchasing power of almost everyone. When Frank Munsey cut his price from 20¢ to 10¢ a copy and quintupled circulation from 40,000 to 200,000 (1893 to 1895), he brought a new kind of competition to newspapers.

The motion picture, an entirely new form of mass medium, began to reach large numbers of people by the end of the 1890s. Thomas Edison had patented his Kinetoscope in 1891, and by the mid-'90s short films were being shown in vaudeville theatres. Meanwhile, Edwin Porter, who would later (1903) make his mark with *The Great Train Robbery*, was touring fairs and small towns with his own movies before he joined the Edison company in 1899. Various kinds of peep shows were marketed through penny arcades, but Edison's equipment showed the greatest potential, and his vigorous fight to control the patents through the courts indicated his recognition that the new medium had great promise. Biograph and Vitagraph produced films also; and by 1900 they, along with Edison, were maneuvering industriously to control the burgeoning market. Oscar Hammerstein produced a film showing William McKinley in the 1896 presidential campaign, and the semiliterate laborer who saw it in a penny arcade suddenly felt he knew more about the Republican nominee than he could learn in hours spent looking at woodcuts and working his way laboriously through wordy newspaper descriptions.

The phonograph provided still another mass medium available to the general public. Its inventor Edison had been pushing it for more than a decade as a means of point-to-point communication — not a mass medium — but in the early 1890s he began to market it as an entertainment medium. When Emile Berliner introduced the disc to replace Edison's cylinder, mass production became practical. Berliner called it the Gramophone, and by 1896 the disc was being called a phonograph "record." In 1897 Edison designed a machine for the mass market, priced at about $20. The most common use of the phonograph, though, was in arcades where machines would play a record for a nickel.

Other mass communication technologies began to appear in the outer edges of the arena; and although they provided no serious competition for newspaper sales, they gave sign of rivalry to come. One medium already on the market was the stereograph, a device with a separate lens for each eye to look at dual photographs, giving a 3-D effect. These stereopticon slides were printed in fairly large numbers, using the new halftone process, and found their way into many thousands of middle-class living rooms.

Meanwhile Marconi was conducting his wireless experiments; and Paul Nipkow's scanning disc, ancestor of television, had been patented in Germany. In 1898 the Danish engineer Valdemar Poulsen patented a radical new device that he called a "telegraphone." He theorized that if sound could be converted to magnetic impulses in some electrically charged carrier, such as a wire, then the impulses could be converted back to sound, and after use the magnetic field could be erased and the carrier used to record over and over again. It was demonstrated successfully at the 1900 Paris Exposition, where it created quite a sensation, although witnesses could hardly know that it would take most of a century before the principle could be successfully applied and disseminated into the average middle-class home. Almost 100 years later, Poulsen's invention — magnetic recording — finally reached its full development in the 1990s.

Why Did the Golden Age Turn Yellow?

The 1880s and 1890s provided a fertile period for the introduction and development of new mass communication technology. Clearly, the days of newspaper hegemony were numbered. In 1883 things looked bright for the press, but by 1900 critics were applying all kinds of unflattering labels. What had changed during those

[23]See Maxwell E. McCombs, "Mass Media in the Marketplace," in *Journalism Monographs*, No. 24 (1972); and Benjamin M. Compaine, *Who Owns the Media?* (White Plains, N.Y., 1979).

[24]Novel collections in the 1880s and 1890s were sold much as record libraries ("all the great melodies from the classics in one pair of CDs for just $19.95") have been sold on late-night television in recent times.

seventeen years?

The framers of the U.S. Constitution had lit a very long fuse 100 years earlier, and the explosion finally took place. When the First Amendment prohibited Congress from abridging press freedom, regulation fell by default to the marketplace. The newspapers that survived would be the ones that sold their ads and subscriptions at the greatest profit. The principle of *cultural democracy* had been established: every citizen had the right to vote (with his money) for that portion of the culture he wished to consume. As with food and drink, that cultural material the buyer chose to consume was not always the most beneficial.

In the nation's early years, newspapers went mostly to the better educated citizens, to the more discriminating members of the population. As newspapers were democratized, reaching full circulation into all levels of the citizenry, choices of what to read were not always made wisely. By the 1880s all adult males had become part of both the voting and the consuming public, and newspapers hardly could afford to ignore any of them.

A key to the changing character of newspapers was a shift in sources of income. Papers became primarily dependent on advertising revenue, rather than on circulation. As the nation's manufacturing and marketing systems became more highly developed, the newspaper's role gained importance. Advertisers wanted their messages delivered to large numbers, and they wanted to deal with the newspaper in businesslike fashion. In the earlier days, when the subscriber often bought a paper because of the person (editor) or political interest it represented, circulation was foremost. In 1900 when an advertiser bought an ad, he was interested in audience, not editor, and he would just as soon work with the newspaper people responsible for advertising and distribution.

Furthermore, subscribers, who still counted for 45% of newspaper revenue, by 1900 had alternative media from which to choose. If newspapers grew wearisome with their incessant sensations and crusades, there were new forms of media to which the audience could turn. There would appear more new media, and still more, and more, as the new century wore on. The public reaction to excessive sensationalism was probably a factor in the newspapers' descent from the pinnacle of media dominance and influence. But any lowering of the level of journalistic quality should be attributed to the demands of the new marketplace, more than to sensational excesses of a Pulitzer or a Hearst.

From Golden to Yellow Journalism
As Pulitzer and Hearst tried to outdo one another in sensational techniques, some publications and many members of the public reacted negatively. This cartoon – which appeared in 1897, even before the height of the newspaper hysteria surrounding Spain – caricatured Pulitzer and Hearst as being swept away by their own excesses.

The Lessons of New Journalism

History, of course, never repeats itself. It is foolish, therefore, to make predictions based on the past. Yet we can examine the past for clues to help us understand the present, and some of the generalizations that can be applied to the 1883-1900 period may add insight into some present trends. A few seem to suggest themselves:

1. The market is not necessarily geared to quality journalism. This condition is hardly new, and recent studies have offered supportive evidence. A newspaper's profits correlate to how well it meets market needs and usually do not correlate to journalistic excellence. If the market is there, a poor newspaper can serve it. If it is not, even a good newspaper can fail.

2. The personality factor fades as a medium matures. As the medium reaches full stature, it relies more on sophisticated management techniques and less on intuition and high profile. To the consumer, the medium seems more impersonal. Network broadcasting, with occasional exceptions, is not run by popular figures with whom the viewer identifies; and as cable television matures, perhaps we cannot expect to see any more Ted Turners in that field, either.

3. Tradition can be self-defeating. Late-nineteenth-century journalists like Dana, Bennett Jr., Reid, Davis, and Mrs. Leslie tended to live romantically in the past, and their influence declined. Newspaper people of today, if they expend too much effort trying to maintain the traditions of Bennett Sr., Greeley, or even Ochs, may get left behind.

4. Self-promotion can become tiresome. When Pulitzer and Hearst went to New York, each had to climb a pedestal and proclaim his presence. But after several years, the public, like a weary grandparent, grew tired of the no-longer-cute child who kept saying, "Look at me, look at me!" Television marketers and news consultants who urge incessant promos may be approaching the same threshold Pulitzer and Hearst crossed at the end of the Yellow Journalism era.

5. A mature medium does not have to be inflexible. Large, vigorous newspapers showed that they could adapt to, and embrace, new technologies such as wireless, telephones, and high-speed trains (as used in boilerplate distribution). There is no reason to believe that modern newspapers cannot make efficient use of electronic information retrieval, fibre optics, digital imaging, the Internet, or technologies still unnamed. As the medium with the longest history and the most experience in delivering news to the American public, newspapers just might prove to be the best, not the least, able to implement and exploit the new technologies destined to deliver information to the twenty-first century.

RECOMMENDED READINGS

BOOKS

Baldasty, Gerald J. *The Commercialization of News in the Nineteenth Century*. Madison, Wis., 1992. During the 1800s, newspapers were transformed from a political to a commercial base, with the change becoming virtually complete in the last two decades.

Brown, Charles H. *The Correspondents' War*. New York, 1967. Approaches the Spanish-American War as a convenient war for reporters to cover and describes reporters as a self-important bunch.

Carlson, Oliver. *Brisbane: A Candid Biography*. New York, 1937. Arthur Brisbane, Hearst's top editor, preferred the esteem of businessmen and material success to social and journalistic ideals.

Churchill, Allen. *Park Row*. New York, 1958. Entertaining, popular history of the colorful era of personal journalism from the 1880s to the 1930s.

Dreiser, Theodore. *Newspaper Days*, T.D. Nostwich, editor. Philadelphia, 1991. Reprinted and expanded version of the American novelist's recollections, first published in 1922, of his newspaper reporting days in the 1890s.

Fowler, Gene. *Timber Line*. New York, 1933. Highly entertaining, readable account of Bonfils, Tammen, and the *Denver Post*.

Frasca, Ralph. *The Rise and Fall of the Saturday Globe*. Cranbury, N.J., 1992. Account of the first national weekly newspaper, published from 1881 to 1924.

Johns, George S. *Joseph Pulitzer: His Early Life in St. Louis and His Founding and Conduct of the Post-Dispatch up to 1883*. St. Louis, 1932. At the *Post-Dispatch*, Pulitzer developed a new form of journalism, combining the news techniques of Bennett with the enlightened editorial approach of Greeley.

Johnson, Gerald. *An Honorable Titan*. New York, 1946. Credits Adolph Ochs' belief in traditional American values for his success with the *New York Times*.

Johnson, Icie F. *William Rockhill Nelson and the Kansas City Star*. Kansas City, Mo., 1935. As owner-editor of the *Star*, Nelson devoted himself and his paper to the improvement of Kansas City, and he was the premier reason for the town's progress from a small pioneer town to a metropolis.

Juergens, George. *Joseph Pulitzer and the New York World*. Princeton, N.J., 1966. Views the *World* as the originator of the modern newspaper and its approach to illustrations, appearance, sports, women's news, concern for the underprivileged, and other features.

Kilmer, Paulette D. *The Fear of Sinking: The American Success Story in the Gilded Age*. Knoxville, Tenn., 1996. Some new ideas on the Horatio Alger "myth" help to relate this popular cultural theme to the media of the time.

King, Homer W. *Pulitzer's Prize Editor: A Biography of John A. Cockerill, 1845-1896*. Durham, N.C., 1965. Cockerill, as the managing editor of the *New York World*, was the true originator of "New Journalism."

Kobre, Sidney. *The Yellow Press and Gilded Age Journalism*. Tallahassee, 1964. During the Gilded Age, American journalism changed from one of personal journalism to an industry marked by mechanization, urbanization, centralization, and standardization.

Kroeger, Brooke. *Nellie Bly: Daredevil, Reporter, Feminist*. New York, 1994. Account of a daredevil woman reporter who worked in turn-of-the-century New York.

Lubow, Arthur. *The Reporter Who Would Be King: A Biography of Richard Harding Davis*. New York, 1992. Biography of the dashing reporter and editor who became widely known in the 1890s for his reporting and fiction.

Marks, George. *The Black Press Views American Imperialism (1898-1900)*. New York, 1933. The American black press identified with colored people around the world and protested American imperialistic exploitation of them.

Marzolf, Marion Tuttle. *Civilizing Voices: American Press Criticism, 1880-1950*. New York, 1991. As "new journalism" changed the nature of American newspapers, critics raised "the issues of moral purpose and democratic idealism to counter the strong forces of commercialization and impersonality."

Milton, Joyce. *The Yellow Kids: Foreign Correspondents in the Heyday of Yellow Journalism*. New York, 1989. The highly competitive reporters for Pulitzer's *World* and Hearst's *Journal* were both dashing and devious.

Morris, Roy Jr. *Ambrose Bierce: Alone in Bad Company*. New York, 1995. Bierce's acidic view of the late nineteenth century is explained by events in his life, particularly his Civil War experiences, and the literary quality of his writings is given just due.

Oriard, Michael. *Reading Football: How the Popular Press Created an American Spectacle*. Chapel Hill, N.C., 1993. The press popularized modern football in its crucial formative years from 1880 to 1912.

Stern, Madeleine B. *Purple Passage, The Life of Mrs. Frank Leslie*. Norman, Okla., 1953. Mrs. Leslie was one of the most colorful journalists of all time.

Swanberg, W. A. *Citizen Hearst*. New York, 1961. Critical biography of Hearst, a newspaper owner and politician driven by a desire to have things his way.

Taft, Robert. *Photography and the American Scene, A Social History, 1839-1889*. New York, 1938. Photojournalism brought a new dimension of journalistic impact on American society.

Thompson, Mildred I. *Ida B. Wells-Barnett: An Exploratory Study of an American Black Woman, 1893-1930*. Carlson, 1990. Examines journalist Wells-Barnett as a writer and reformer within the social context for her work.

Wilkerson, Marcus. *Public Opinion and the Spanish-American War: A Study of War Propaganda*. Baton Rouge, La., 1932. A serious study examining the influence of the press on the Spanish-American War.

ARTICLES

Auxier, G.W. "Middle Western Newspapers and the Spanish-American War, 1895-1898." *Mississippi Valley Historical Review* 26 (1940): 523-34. Analysis questions historians' claim that yellow journalism precipitated the war. Middlewestern newspapers did not all adopt the jingoistic journalism of Pulitzer and Hearst.

Bekken, Jon. " 'The Most Vindictive and Most Vengeful Power': Labor Confronts the Chicago Newspaper Trust." *Journalism History* 18 (Spring-Summer

1992): 11-7. The Daily Newspaper Association of Chicago, founded in 1884, included most of the major English-language daily newspapers, which collaborated on editorial policy and labor matters.

Berg, Meredith, and David Berg. "The Rhetoric of War Preparation: The New York Press in 1898." *Journalism Quarterly* 45 (1968): 653-60. Although it is impossible to determine the exact influence that the New York press had in preparing the public for the Spanish-American War (or bringing about the war), there was "a powerful linkage between the press and the people."

Bradley, Patricia. "Joseph Pulitzer as an American Hegelian." *American Journalism* 10:3-4 (1993): 70-82. The titan's intellectual associations explain how his idealist New Journalism could coexist with sensational journalism.

Buchstein, Frederick D. "The Anarchist Press in American Journalism." *Journalism History* 1 (1974): 43-5. Anti-statists reasoned and argued, but the more radical pro-violence groups got most of the attention in the 1880s and 1890s.

Colbert, Ann. "Philanthropy in the Newsroom: Women's Editions of Newspapers, 1894-1896." *Journalism History* 22 (1996): 91-9. The 1890s phenomenon — turning over editions of newspapers to be run by women for a day — showed not only what opportunities and limitations women faced but also the responsiveness of newspapers to their communities' needs.

Connery, Thomas. "Julian Ralph: Forgotten Master of Descriptive Detail." *American Journalism* 2 (1985): 165-73. The *New York Journal* reporter, although not as well known as some other reporters of the time, was an accomplished writer.

Domke, David. "The Black Press in the 'Nadir' of African Americans." *Journalism History* 20 (1994): 131-8. Black newspapers' coverage of Supreme Court decisions in the 1880s and 1890s that upheld discrimination against blacks.

Gleason, Timothy W. "The Libel Climate of the Late Nineteenth Century: A Survey of Libel Litigation, 1884-1899." *Journalism Quarterly* 70 (Winter 1993): 893-906. Compares libel suits filed by public officials and public figures in the late nineteenth century and compares them to the libel climate of the present day.

Henry, Susan. "Reporting 'Deeply and At First Hand': Helen Campbell in the 19th-Century Slums." *Journalism History* 11 (1984): 18-25. Depth reporting on urban problems was a feature of New Journalism, and in this case it illustrated the problems that women reporters encountered.

Howard-Pitney, David. "Calvin Chase's *Washington Bee* and Black Middle-Class Ideology, 1882-1900." *Journalism Quarterly* 63 (1986): 89-97. The *Bee's* black editor "was neither exclusively accommodationist nor protest-oriented, but a pragmatic blend of the two."

Hyde, Jana. "New Journalism, 1883-1900: Social Reform or Professional Progress?" 199-212 in Wm. David Sloan, *Perspectives on Mass Communication History* (Hillsdale, N.J., 1991). Analyzes the approaches that historians have taken to explaining the press of the period.

Lorenz, Larry. "The Whitechapel Club: Defining Chicago's Journalists in the 19th Century." *American Journalism* 15:1 (1998): 83-102. In this bohemian club, journalists helped to define professional values. They also created an image of the hard-drinking, wise-cracking, cynical reporter that lasted well into the twentieth century.

Mander, Mary S. "Pen and Sword: Problems of Reporting the Spanish-American War." *Journalism History* 9 (1982): 2-9, 28. Motivated by a sense of personal responsibility, correspondents performed well despite many difficulties.

Murray, Randall L. "Edwin Lawrence Godkin: Unbending Editor in Times of Change." *Journalism History* 1 (1974): 77-81, 89. The thinking man's editor, Godkin provided a voice of authority, though he never reached the mass reader.

Nord, David Paul. "Working-Class Readers: Family, Community, and Reading in Late Nineteenth-Century America." *Communication Research* 13 (1986): 156-81. Balances the overattention to New York newspapers with detailed analysis of Americans' other reading habits in the Gilded Age.

Olasky, Marvin. "Late 19th-Century Texas Sensationalism: Hypocrisy or Biblical Morality?" *Journalism History* 12 (1985): 96-100. While criticizing New York-style yellow journalism, many Texas newspapers during 1880-1900 were publishing the same type of material. Texas editors, however, were trying to use the sensationalism to point out what they considered to be biblical morals.

Perry, Clay. "John P. Mitchell, Virginia's Journalist of Reform." *Journalism History* 4 (1978): 142-7. Fired as a teacher by a prejudiced school board, Mitchell established the *Richmond Planet* as the largest-circulation weekly in Virginia and had the second largest Black-owned publishing house in America.

Ponder, Stephen E. "Conservation, Community Economics, and Newspapering: The Seattle Press and the Forest Reserves Controversy of 1897." *American Journalism* 3 (1986): 50-60. The *Seattle Post-Intelligencer's* changing stands on creation of a new national forest indicated that daily newspapers in the late nineteenth century were "subject to ... complex influences on local editorial policy...."

Simpson, Roger. "Seattle Newsboys: How Hustler Democracy Lost to the Power of Property." *Journalism History* 18 (1992): 18-25. Story of the establishment of the Seattle Newsboys Union in 1892, its effort to protect newsboys, and its subsequent decline.

Smythe, Ted Curtis. "The Reporter, 1880-1900. Working Conditions and Their Influence on News." *Journalism History* 7 (1980) 1-10. Economic conditions such as low salaries resulted in poor reporting and sensationalism.

Steele, Janet E. "The 19th Century *World* Versus the *Sun*: Promoting Consumption (Rather than the Working Man)," *Journalism Quarterly* 67 (1990): 592-600. Pulitzer's success against Dana signalled "the erosion of traditional American values such as hard work, thrift and self-sacrifice, and the emergence of a value system that increasingly celebrated consumption, leisure, and self-indulgence."

Stevens, Summer E., and Owen V. Johnson. "From Black Politics to Black Community: Harry C. Smith and the Cleveland *Gazette*." *Journalism Quarterly* 67 (1990): 1090-102. Smith used the *Gazette* "to serve as a forum for political debate and to promote the development of a black identity and community."

Watson, Elmo Scott. "A History of Newspaper Syndicates in the United States, 1865-1935." Supplement to *Publisher's Auxiliary*, 16 November 1935. This mini-history explains the rise of boilerplate and readyprint, and the beginnings of the feature syndicates that began to proliferate before 1900.

Winfield, Betty Houchin, and Janice Hume. "The American Hero and the Evolution of the Human Interest Story." *American Journalism* 15 (1998): 79-99. The rise of the human interest story gave readers heroes they could relate to just as Horatio Alger did in fiction. Today's fascination with celebrities in television news can be traced to this fascination.

13

American Magazines

1740 - 1900

American magazines grew from tentative eighteenth-century beginnings as a "cottage industry" serving a small, elite audience, to the brink of becoming a national industry by the end of the nineteenth century. Editors and publishers developed their product in reaction to wars, social changes, and economic developments that transformed the American nation itself from a child to an adolescent.

The American magazine had its roots in the periodical tradition of the British Isles — a tradition that had begun with a learned journal in 1665[1] and that had progressed through a variety of other forms. Other seventeenth-century periodicals mixed news and low humor to amuse the not-so-learned and usually identified themselves by the title "Mercurius": *Mercurius Fumigosus*, for example. More dignified periodicals of the late 1690s such as the *Athenian Mercury* entertained by answering readers' questions. The earliest English periodical to give readers a taste of fiction and verse was *The Gentleman's Journal* (1692); and Daniel Defoe's *Weekly Review* (1704) included some essays, thus presaging the essay papers that would soon follow.

Influencing the style of popular writing for many decades to come was Irish-born Richard Steele's *Tatler* of 1709, a thrice-weekly essay paper that was closed after a year and replaced with the *Spectator*, edited daily by Steele and his even more talented partner, Joseph Addison. In these two periodicals and their legion of imitators, writers commented in a witty, urbane, entertaining way on the vices, virtues, and conventions of the day.

The earliest English periodical to call itself by the name "magazine" was *The Gentleman's Magazine* of 1731, which left the reporting of the day's news, or "tydings," to the newspapers and instead emphasized elegant writing, amusement, and instruction via miscellaneous content that included the literary, political, biographical, and critical. The designation "magazine" caught on rapidly among competitors.

[1]In March 1665 Henry Oldenburg founded the *Acta Philosophica Societates Anglia*, later re-titled the *Philosophical Transactions of the Royal Society*, a learned periodical of scientific bent that was modeled after Paris' *Journal des Savans*, founded slightly earlier in January 1665.

By 1740 the American colonies' great innovator, Benjamin Franklin, had resolved that the time was ripe for an indigenous monthly magazine modeled roughly after the British miscellanies then being read by a fairly select Colonial audience. The busy Franklin engaged John Webbe, who earlier had contributed to Franklin's newspaper, the *Pennsylvania Gazette*, to handle the project as editor. In an apparent bid for better pay, Webbe revealed the plan to Franklin's rival printer, Andrew Bradford, who gave Webbe a sweeter deal and succeeded in bringing out his *American Magazine* just three days before the February 1741 appearance of Franklin's *General Magazine and Historical Chronicle*. Both magazines were indifferently received. Bradford's lasted for only three monthly issues, Franklin's for six.

More American magazines soon appeared. In 1743 two were introduced in Boston. The first printed a mere three issues; but the second, lawyer Jeremiah Gridley's *American Magazine and Historical Chronicle*, managed to publish for three years. New York City was home to the next American magazine, a four-page political essay paper of Whig leanings and reformist outlook. Similarly political was *The American Magazine and Monthly Chronicle*, founded in 1757 and continued for a year in Philadelphia by another of the Bradfords, William III. It was a pro-British, anti-French periodical published in the midst of the French and Indian War (1754-1763) and also entertained with *Tatler*- and *Spectator*-inspired essays of manners, most notably the "Timothy Timbertoe" series.

Yet another interesting though short-lived colonial title was Isaiah Thomas' *Royal American Magazine*, which was founded in Boston prior to the Battle of Lexington and appeared in 1774 and '75. Despite the word "Royal" in its title, it was sympathetic to the Patriot cause and is noteworthy not only for its solid articles on serious topics and its Paul Revere cartoon engravings, but for its entertaining copy and for having introduced song lyrics and scores to the American magazine market.

A final American magazine founded prior to the Revolution was Philadelphia's *Pennsylvania Magazine* (1775-1776), edited by

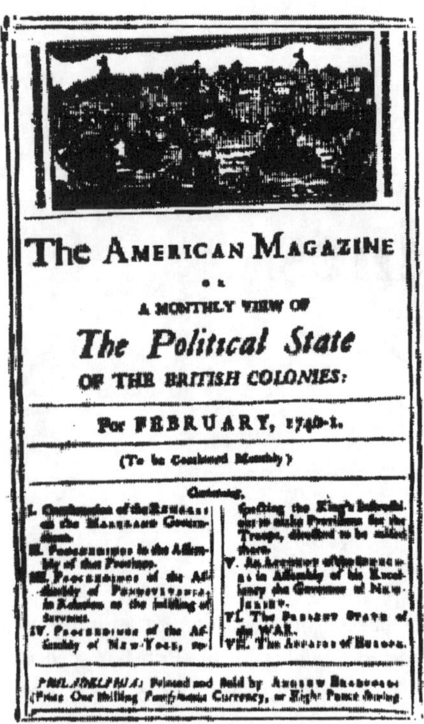

The AMERICAN MAGAZINE

OR

A MONTHLY VIEW OF

The Political State

OF THE BRITISH COLONIES:

For FEBRUARY, 1740-1.

(To be Continued Monthly)

Containing,

I. [illegible]

II. [illegible]

III. [illegible]

IV. [illegible]

V. [illegible]

VI. The PRESENT STATE of the WAR.

VII. The AFFAIRS of EUROPE.

PHILADELPHIA: Printed and Sold by ANDREW BRADFORD. (Price One Shilling *Pennsylvania* Currency, or Eight Pence Sterling

United States Magazine,

A

REPOSITORY

OF

Hiſtory, Politics, and Literature.

For MARCH, 1779.

PARTICULARS.

Political Diary, 98
Notes to Correſpondents, 100
Notes to the Public, ibid.
An Oration on the Advantages of American Independence, ſpoken at Charleſtown, on the fourth of July 1778. Concluded, 101
The cave of Vanheſt, continued. Containing ſome particulars relative to the battle of Monmouth. 106
The Anſwer of Continental Currency to the Repreſentation and Remonſtrance of Hard Money; alſo addreſſed to the People of America, 110
On Keeping of Secrets, 121
Viſion of the Paradiſe of Female Patriotiſm. By Clariſſa, a Lady of this City. 122
Account of the Iſland of St. James; in a Letter to Mr. A. A. 124
Account of New Publications.— Obſervations on the American Revolution. Publiſhed according to a Reſolution of Congreſs. By their Committee, 125
Some ſucceſsful Experiments for deſtroying the Fly in Wheat, and for preventing its Depredation in that Grain, 129
Experiments on the Effects of Elder in preſerving growing Plants from Inſects and Flies. Alſo a Hint for preſerving freſh Fiſh or Meat from being Fly-blown in Summer, 130
Query to the Public, by a Correſpondent from the State of Delaware, 132
A New Queſtion, ibid.
Poetical Eſſays,
The Cornwalliad, an Heroi-comic Poem, Canto I. 133
On the Attempt of the Ingenious Mr. F--le, to take the Likeneſs of Miſs ---- a Young Lady of this City. 134
To Janus on New-Year's Day, 135
Foreign Affairs,
Origin of the Debate between the King of Pruſſia and the Emperor of Germany. Tranſlated from the Journal Hiſtorique & Politique, publiſhed at Geneva, 136
Domeſtic Affairs,
Operations of the American and Britiſh Armies in Georgia—Auguſta evacuated by the Britiſh—Succeſs of Gen. Moultrie, 137
Account of an Incurſion of the Enemy to Horſeneck, State of New-York, 140
Account of the Attempt of the Enemy to ſurprize the Poſt at Elizabethtown, New-Jerſey, 141
Various Intelligence, 143
Captures at Sea,—by the Britiſh—by the French—by the States, 144

PHILADELPHIA:

Printed and Sold by FRANCIS BAILEY, in Market-Street.

THE

COLUMBIAN MAGAZINE:

OR

Monthly Miſcellany.

For SEPTEMBER, 1786.

Sketch of the Life of the Late NATHANIEL GREENE, Major General of the Forces of the United States of America:

Embelliſhed with his Portrait, elegantly Engraved.

THIS gallant officer, whoſe death is ſo generally and ſo juſtly regretted, was born in the town of Warwick, Kent county, Rhode-Iſland, in or about the year 1741, and was the ſecond ſon of a reſpectable citizen of the ſame name, (deſcended from ſome of the firſt ſettlers in the colony) who was extenſively concerned in lucrative iron-works, the property of which, at his death, prior to the war) he left to his children.

The ſubject of this ſketch was endowed with an uncommon degree of judgment and penetration, which, with a benevolent manner and affable behaviour, acquired him a number of valuable friends, by whoſe intereſt and influence, he was, at an early period of life, choſen a member of the aſſembly of the then colony of Rhode-iſland. This truſt, in which he gave the higheſt ſatisfaction to his conſtituents, he continued to poſſeſs until, and at, the period, when the folly and madneſs of England ſevered a world from her empire.

After the ſkirmiſhes at Lexington and Concord, when a ſpirit of reſiſtance ſpread, like wild-fire, over the continent. Rhode-iſland was not deficient in her contributions for the general defence. She raiſed three regiments of militia, the command whereof was given to Mr. Greene, who was nominated brigadier-general. The liberty, ſafety, and proſperity of his country being expoſed to imminent danger, the pacific principles of quakeriſm, in which he had been educated, proved inſufficient to combat the ardent ſpirit of liberty with which his boſom glowed.

He led the troops under his command to Cambridge, and was preſent at the evacuation of Boſton, by a force which had in England been vauntingly ſtated treble the number that would be requiſite

America's Magazine Pioneers

Magazines have enjoyed a long, rich history in America. Several early ones stood out in their attempts to bring a new form of periodical material to the reading public. Andrew Bradford, publisher of the *American Mercury* newspaper in Philadelphia, announced his intentions of offering America its first magazine in October of 1740. The announcement sparked a controversy between Bradford and Benjamin Franklin, who also planned to begin a magazine. The argument played out in the pages of the *Mercury* and Franklin's newspaper, the *Pennsylvania Gazette*, for longer than either magazine actually lasted. Once Bradford's *American Magazine, or a Monthly View of the Political State of the British Colonies*, actually appeared in February 1741, it lasted only three months. Bradford abandoned the venture without explanation. Coinciding with the American colonies' revolution against Great Britain, the *United States Magazine* began publishing in Philadelphia in 1778 despite the chaotic social and political conditions that threatened to douse its fire from the start. Its publisher, lawyer and writer Hugh Henry Breckenridge, attempted to use the Revolution as a selling point, filling the pages with essays and literature of a patriotic nature. When the magazine folded after a year, he blamed its failure on the disinterest of the colonists in the welfare of America. In the years immediately following the Revolution, five Philadelphians joined together in a publishing venture in the 1780s. Their combination of talents spelled immediate success. Writer Mathew Carey, engraver John Trenchard, printer Charles Cist, bookseller William Spotswood, and T. Seddon introduced *The Columbian Magazine* in the wake of the American Revolution. The partnership began to disintegrate after three months of publication, when Carey defected to publish his own magazine. However, the *Columbian* endured in its original form for four years, after which it published primarily as a history of the Revolution.

Robert Aitken, who on the recommendation of Ben Franklin hired Thomas Paine, later to become better known for his contributions as a propagandist pamphleteer in both the American and French revolutions.

The only magazine to be introduced during the war years was Newark's *United States Magazine* (1779), edited by H.H. Breckenridge.

OBSTACLES AND SUCCESSES

In the mid to late 1700s a great many Americans were still too busy seeing to their basic needs to devote much time to reading. Even if time were not a problem, most were unable to afford the cost of a magazine subscription.[2] On the supply end of the picture, relatively few colonial writers were adept at providing good magazine copy, and many early magazines were filled largely with "selected" material taken, usually without either payment or permission, from books, newspapers, and other magazines, frequently those of English origin.

Early editors and publishers also faced challenging distribution problems — few and poor roads, uncertain mails, and unfavorable postal rates. The postal act of 1792 gave magazine publishers no break at all from the ordinary letter rate; and though the act of 1794 allowed them a lower rate, postmasters were given the right to refuse the mails to magazines if carriers could not conveniently handle the extra load. With a small population spread thinly over an enormous geographic area, getting magazines to distant subscribers was difficult; collecting from those subscribers was often even more challenging. Also, presses, type, paper, and ink had

[2]See David Paul Nord, "A Republican Literature: A Study of Magazine Reading and Readers in Late Eighteenth-Century New York," *American Quarterly* 40 (March 1988): 42-64. In this study of *The New York Magazine* of 1790, the writer concludes that magazine reading in that period might have been "more broadly democratic than has usually been supposed."

to be imported at no small cost at a time when magazines contained very scant advertising.

Even so, a desire for cultural independence from England, oddly coupled with the hope of emulating the success of the leading English periodicals, led a number of Americans to found new magazines between the end of the Revolution and the start of the new century. Noteworthy examples were Noah Webster's *American Magazine* (1787) of New York, the graphically impressive *Columbian Magazine* (1786-1792), and its co-founder Mathew Carey's next venture, the *American Museum* (1787-1792) of Philadelphia. Also published in Philadelphia was Joseph Dennie's *Port Folio* of 1799, a Federalist organ and the first U.S. magazine to achieve substantial national circulation. Virginia's first magazine, the *National Magazine* (1799-1800) of Richmond, was in the opposite political camp: Anti-Federalist. The favorite target of its outspoken editor, James Lyon, was Alexander Hamilton, whom Lyon called "the most dangerous man in the Union."[3]

Clearly the foremost magazine publishing centers in eighteenth-century America were Philadelphia, Boston, and New York. Unless one includes the *North Carolina Magazine, or Useful Intelligencer* (1764-1765), which was part magazine, part newspaper, the earliest magazine south of Philadelphia was the *Free Universal Magazine* (1793) of Baltimore, a city that thereafter made impressive strides in publishing and produced five more titles before the new century. The only other southern city to gain any real importance in 1700s magazine publishing was Charleston, South Carolina, where three titles were published before 1800. That city's first magazine appeared in 1796. To the west, the first important magazine city was Lexington, Kentucky, although no titles appeared there until 1801.

Vol. I. [57] No. 8

The NORTH-CAROLINA

MAGAZINE;

OR,

UNIVERSAL INTELLIGENCER.

From FRIDAY July 20, to FRIDAY July 27, 1764.

O ſacred Hunger of pernicious Gold,
What Bands of Faith can impious Lucre hold!

IT is to me aſtoniſhing, *ſays that immortal Prince, that Chriſtian Heathen*, Marcus Antonius, that Man, (allowing Mercy to be the moſt amiable Attribute of the Gods, and having daily Inſtances of their Forbearance, notwithſtanding the repeated Affronts offer'd) can have the Heart to injure his Fellow Creature, or even to return Wrongs; for if the Gods were ſo ſevere in their Puniſhment, and meaſur'd with the ſame Meaſure Mortals do, one only Offence would be ſufficient to deprive us of Life. Who, *continues he*, can be cruel, either through Wantonneſs, Revenge, or filthy Lucre, deſerves not the Appellation of *Man*; for *Man* the Gods (as is evident by his Make) deſign'd an inoffenſive ſociable Creature: He is not furniſhed with one natural Inſtrument for Cruelty, but with many for Mercy and Compaſſion: He has two Eyes to behold and commiſerate the Indigent and Helpleſs: He has two Feet to carry him to the Temples, to praiſe the Gods; and to thoſe who want his Aſſiſtance, to imitate their Goodneſs, he has two Hands to diſtribute on either Side: He has a Tongue to plead for the Widow, Orphan, and helpleſs Priſoner; he has a Heart to love the Gods, Underſtanding to [illegible] Evil, and Diſcretion to chuſe what's Good. He has not the Horns of a Bull, the Hoof of a Horſe, the Claws of a Tyger, the Teeth of a Lyon, or the Venom of a Serpent; for as the Gods are merciful, ſo have they deſign'd us mild and compaſſionate, and Nature has given us no Means or Inſtruments for Revenge and Miſchief.

Thus far that good Emperor, in a Letter to his Friend *Antigonus*. But where the Love of Money has taken Poſſeſſion of the Heart, there is no Beaſt ſo cruel as Man: They ſeek their Prey to ſatiſfy their Hunger, which may be appeas'd; but the Avaricious can never be ſatisfy'd, and none eſcapes him with whom he is able to cope. Covetouſneſs baniſhes not only every Virtue, but even Humanity itſelf; and changing Nature, the Groans of the Oppreſſed become Muſick, and the Miſeries of Mankind a grateful and delighting Spectacle. What Miſeries has not this Vice brought upon whole Nations? How many have been made deſolate by Avarice? There is ſcarce a Crime which does not take Riſe from the *Auri ſacra fames*. This makes the Miniſter betray his Truſt, and ſell the Proſperity of his Country: Inſtigated by this inſatiable Thirſt of Riches, Men not only proſtitute their Wives and Daughters, but give up their Liberties, and joyfully exchange their native Rights for gilded Fetters. There is nothing the Avaricious will ſtop at: Murder, Treaſon, Sacrilege, are puny Crimes, and Gold renders them imperceptible, appeaſes or prevents the Stings and Remorſe of Conſcience, argues and convinces. Avarice corrupts the Judge, ſides with the Powerful, and treads the Poor under Foot. Where a Man once is enſlaved by the Love of Money, he never aſks what's juſt, but what's lucrative; nor what's reaſonable, but what makes for his Intereſt. Did the Life of a Son or Father ſtand in the Way of ſuch a Man's Gain, he would think it no Crime to remove him. But what

First Southern Magazine

Although the *North-Carolina Magazine* had some of the characteristics of a newspaper, it sometimes is considered the first magazine published south of Philadelphia. Founded in 1764, it lasted only one year. The first true southern magazine was the *Free Universal Magazine* of Baltimore, founded in 1793.

MAGAZINES GAIN GROUND

In the early decades of the 1800s, editors began to find original copy easier to obtain. Original stories and other contributions were frequently identified as such under their headlines, yet most items were run without credit to the author or were signed only with initials, a pen name, or a line such as "by the author of...." This preference for anonymity in early American periodicals can be attributed in part to the Puritan belief that art and literature should be their own reward; partly to the notion that writing for the public was not an altogether respectable occupation for the genteel; partly to the selfish, if often necessary assertion by the editors/publishers that if their writers remained unknown to the reading public, they would not be able to command much compensation for their writing. Also, magazine proprietors sometimes declared that by running unsigned copy, the work of new, unknown writers would be on a more nearly even footing with that of more famous contributors. In case after case, however, giving bylines actually would have been an embarrassment to the editor, who frequently had to write most of an issue's original copy himself.

Although most early American magazines can be described as "miscellanies," they usually had a generous measure of political content, entirely natural in such politically charged times. Later, especially after the War of 1812, "literary miscellanies," magazines whose editors wished to popularize native American literature, emerged. Also in the decade from 1810 to 1820 appeared what writer Neal Edgar has termed "special miscellanies,"[4] magazines that directed their still rather general content at identifiable groups — members of specific organizations, women interested in fashion, persons who still had a keen interest in our nation's English heritage, and the like.

The magazines were largely elitist — published by and for the American "aristocracy" and a small but growing middle class. Subscribers could be more accurately viewed as supporters than cus-

[3]See Sam G. Riley, *Magazines of the American South* (Westport, Conn., 1986), 136. This quotation appeared in the *National Magazine's* first issue (p. 91).

[4]Neal L. Edgar, *A History and Bibliography of American Magazines, 1810-1820* (Metuchen, N.J., 1975), 20.

tomers, and writers were usually educated business and professional people or clergy who wrote for pleasure, not for profit. A feeling of *noblesse oblige* pervaded much of the magazine copy. The writers' polished, genteel prose and verse, replete with classical allusions, often reflected on the civic virtue of the higher orders of society.

On the whole, magazine copy of the late 1700s and early 1800s was far less frivolous and much less commercial than its present-day equivalent, usually employing the essay style popularized in England by Addison and Steele. It was not until the 1840s, the era of Jacksonian democracy, that the hold of elitism began to relax substantially. Fiction occupied little space in these magazines, although today's magazine reader would likely be surprised at the plentiful amount of poetry, both reprinted and original. By today's standards, some of the most memorable magazine verse was satirical; some of the worst, sentimental.

In the early part of the new century, magazines increased in number, emphasized fiction content, and, except for the verse they carried, paid increased attention to Americanizing their content. In 1800 only a dozen American magazines were being published, yet in the two decades that followed, the total increased to well over 100. During this period of growth, fiction increased in popularity, and homegrown verse took a back seat to the work of British poets, especially Sir Walter Scott and Lord Byron. On balance, though, the first two decades of the nineteenth century exhibited a strong nationalistic expression.

Increasing the quantity and quality of the nation's literary output was hampered by the overriding importance of commerce and politics to most educated citizens and by the almost complete absence of full-time, professional writers. In various cities small literary societies lent their support to the efforts of the magazines. Prominent among them were Boston's Anthology Club, New York's Friendly Club, Baltimore's Delphian Club, and Philadelphia's Tuesday Club. Despite these efforts, the larger share of the prose remained ponderous and the verse less than memorable. Articles continued to be run unsigned, but a few periodicals began to pay their contributors. In this period of highly personalized publishing, when the same person sometimes held the titles of editor and publisher and profits were insignificant, editors often worked without compensation.

An interesting assortment of individuals were involved in magazine work in the early years of the new century. Novelist Charles Brockden Brown, for example, attempted to further American letters through his editorial work with four short-lived literary magazines. The flowery writer Stephen Carpenter edited an ambitious "journal of record" for both political history and literature in Charleston. Washington Irving of "Rip Van Winkle" and "Ichabod Crane" fame co-edited a satirical New York periodical titled *Salmagundi* (after a kind of hash) and then became editor of the *Analectic Magazine* (1813-1820) in Philadelphia, a year of which convinced him that the life of a magazine editor was not for him.

In the early 1800s magazines were largely limited to local circulation, if not always to local outlook. As a consequence, circulations remained small. Boston's population growth and importance as a magazine center fell behind the pace set by Philadelphia and New York. Philadelphia had begun the 1800s as the nation's leader so far as magazines were concerned, but New York's impressive growth in population and commerce gradually helped it overtake its rival city.

AMERICAN TURF REGISTER

AND

SPORTING MAGAZINE.

VOL. I.] SEPTEMBER, 1829. [NO. 1.

INTRODUCTION.

"There are intervals when the studious and the grave must suspend their inquiries, and descend from the regions of science; and to excel in those innocent amusements which require our activity, is often one of the best preservatives of health, and no inconsiderable guard against immoral relaxation."
Rev. W. B. Daniel.

THE want of a repository in this country, like the English Sporting Magazine, to serve as an authentic record of the performances and pedigrees of the *bred* horse, will be admitted by all, whether breeders, owners, or amateurs of that admirable animal. The longer we remain without such a register, the more difficult will it be to trace the pedigrees of existing stock, and the more precarious will its value become. Is it not, in fact, within the knowledge of many readers, that animals known to have descended from ancestry of the highest and purest blood, have been confounded with the vulgar mass of their species, by the loss of an old newspaper or memorandum book, that contained their pedigrees? Sensible for years past of the danger which in this way threatens property of so much value, and persuaded that it is not yet too late to collect and save many precious materials that would soon be otherwise lost, the subscriber hopes to supply the long looked for *desideratum*, by the establishment of "THE AMERICAN TURF REGISTER." But though an account of the performances on the American turf, and the pedigrees of thorough bred horses, will constitute the *basis* of the work, it is designed, also, as a Magazine of information on veterinary subjects generally; and of various rural sports, as RACING, TROTTING MATCHES, SHOOTING, HUNTING, FISHING, &c. together with original sketches of the *natural history and habits of American game of all kinds*; and hence the title, *The American Turf Register and Sporting Magazine.* It will of course be the aim of the Editor to give to his journal an original *American* cast, conveying at once, to readers of all ages, amusement and instruction, in regard to our own country, its animals, birds, fishes, &c. In the absence of domestic materials, the magazines received from abroad will supply an ample stock of appropriate matter.

Of the Rev. Dr. Parr, a man profoundly learned, and, what might be expected to follow, an exemplary minister, and a liberal christian,

Sports Pioneer
Among the many magazines published in Baltimore in the early 1800s was the ground-breaking sports periodical *American Turf Register*. It was founded in 1829 and published for fifteen years. Its purpose was to provide amusement as a diversion from "studious and...grave" inquiries.

Baltimore remained a lively magazine center in the early 1800s, with such long-lasting titles as Hezekiah Niles' prototype news magazine *Niles' Weekly Register* (1811-1849) plus postmaster John S. Skinner's early agricultural magazine *The American Farmer* (1819-1897) and his ground-breaking sports periodical *The American Turf Register and Sporting Magazine* (1829-1844). To the

Magazines for Women

Women's Magazine Founder (left)
Sara Josepha Hale started the first successful American women's magazine in 1828. Published in Boston, it was the *Ladies' Magazine* and lasted until 1836. Although it was short-lived, hundreds of later publishers took up the idea of aiming periodicals at a female audience.

Amelia Bloomer (right)
The editor and publisher of America's first woman's suffrage magazine, the *Lily*, Amelia Bloomer scandalized popular opinion when, in 1853, she appeared in trousers to deliver a speech criticizing the requirement that women cover their legs. Her fashion design took on the name "bloomers."

south and west, Charleston, Lexington, and Cincinnati were important.

Renewed Growth and Development

The 1830s, '40s, and '50s brought unprecedented magazine growth. By the eminent historian Frank Luther Mott's reckoning, the total number of magazines being published in 1860 was 600.[5] Of the general monthlies, *Graham's Magazine* (1840-1858) of Philadelphia and Lewis Gaylord Clark's *Knickerbocker Magazine* (1833-1865) of New York City stood out.

Sara Josepha Hale's *Ladies' Magazine* (1828-1836) of Boston was the first successful American women's magazine, but it was the next such periodical she edited, Louis A. Godey's *Godey's Lady's Book* of Philadelphia, that really epitomized the genre. Running a combination of prose and verse by the best writers, alongside more average fare, and hand-colored fashion plates, by 1850 *Godey's* reached the largest circulation attained by any American magazine to that time — roughly 40,000. Imitators were many, but probably the best was *Peterson's Magazine* (1842-1898), also of Philadelphia, edited by the prolific sentimentalist Ann Sophia Stephens, best remembered as the author of the first Beadle Dime Novel (a profitable series of low-priced popular novels heavy on adventure, sentimentality, and moralism).

Unlike today's magazines, which so often are geared to practical concerns, most of the periodicals of the 1820s-1850s mainly provided popular literature — reading for the sake of reading. The *Saturday Evening Post* (1821-1969) is an example of the many literary weeklies that became popular. Similar in content, but distinct in appearance were *Brother Jonathan* (1839-1845) and *New World* (1840-1845), both of New York, which used enormous page sizes to provide readers heavy doses of popular fiction, including whole novels.

Taking their cue from earlier English periodicals, a few U.S. publishers contributed to the cause of popular education. More serious or scholarly readers could opt for another magazine genre copied from British predecessors: the sober, often ponderous quarterly review. Among the most noteworthy were the Harvard-connected *North American Review* (1815-1914) and, in the South, Hugh Swinton Legare's *Southern Review* (1828-1832) and Daniel Whitaker's *Southern Quarterly Review* (1842-1857), both of Charleston. In addition, another extremely serious periodical, the *Dial* (1840-1844), allowed New England's Margaret Fuller and Ralph Waldo Emerson to show literary America a different kind of quarterly: a journal that combined opinion and *belles-lettres* and that became the forum for American transcendentalism.

Other serious-minded Americans were moved more by social than by literary motives. As the debate over the slavery question intensified, numerous periodicals were founded as forums for addressing this crucial issue. The most important was the *Genius of Universal Emancipation*, founded by the Quaker Benjamin Lundy, who underwent extreme difficulties to continue publishing and speaking out against what he decried as the nation's greatest evil. The nation's earliest woman suffrage periodical (and also an advocate of temperance) was the *Lily* (1849-1856), edited and published by Amelia Bloomer, for whom the then scandalous garment known as "bloomers" was named. Bloomers were pantaloons, or women's "trowsers," which the *Lily's* editor wore and defended as more sensible than the ordinary women's fashions of the day.

Magazines at Mid-Century

Mid-century found America's cities jockeying to secure, maintain, or improve their positions as influential magazine centers. By 1850 New York's population was vastly larger than that of any other U.S. city, and its lead in periodical publishing was greater than ever. Its outstanding new entry in 1850 was *Harper's New Monthly* (1850-

[5]Frank Luther Mott, *A History of American Magazines, 1741-1850* (Cambridge, Mass., 1930), 321.

HARPER'S

NEW MONTHLY MAGAZINE.

No. I—JUNE, 1850.—Vol. I.

A WORD AT THE START.

HARPER'S

NEW MONTHLY MAGAZINE.

No. LXII.—JULY, 1855.—Vol. XI.

JOHN PAUL JONES.

WHEN the quarrel between Great Britain and its American subjects resulted in actual war, and blood flowed at Lexington and Concord in the spring of 1775, the "rebels," as the haughty ministers called the resisting colonists, had not a single armed vessel afloat to defend their exposed coast of several hundred miles in extent. Then, as now, the British navy was the right arm of English puissance; and every seaport town of the feeble colonists might have been cannonaded by a hundred guns at the same time. Although a

Nineteenth-Century Leader
Founded in 1850 by Fletcher Harper, *Harper's New Monthly* became the leading American magazine of the nineteenth century. By publishing the writings of some of the nation's outstanding literary figures, it not only influenced popular reading but helped make New York City the center of magazine publishing in the United States. Within a short time after its founding, it had taken on a stronger graphic appearance (illustrated by the issue from 1855 on the right) than it had when it had begun publication only five years earlier.

current).[6] The magazine was well illustrated and fat in number of pages per issue. Thanks to the combined efforts of such major Massachusetts literary figures as Henry Wadsworth Longfellow, James Russell Lowell, Ralph Waldo Emerson, Henry David Thoreau, Nathaniel Hawthorne, and Oliver Wendell Holmes, Boston's influence in periodical literature had outstripped that of Philadelphia. To the south, Baltimore continued to be important. Farther south, Charleston's William Gilmore Simms was the dominant figure, editing several literary magazines. The most acclaimed single magazine in all the pre-Civil War South, though, was Richmond's *Southern Literary Messenger* (1834-1864). Providing the region a widely noticed cultural forum of its own, the *Messenger* was edited for about a year by the brilliant but troubled Edgar Allan Poe. The South and North each had its own dominant magazine of general commerce: *DeBow's Review* (1846-1880) in New Orleans and *Hunt's Merchant's Magazine* (1830-1870) in New York. In the South, which had no really large cities, magazines were overwhelmingly regional in appeal. In the Midwest, Cincinnati, Louisville, St. Louis, and Columbus, Ohio, gained in importance as publishing sites. The Pacific Coast was founding a few new magazines of its own, mainly in San Francisco.

With added attention being given New World literary efforts, this mid-century period was marked by intensified rivalry between American and English writers. Much space was occupied in U.S. magazines by replies to the charges leveled at American cultural life by European authors Charles Dickens, Harriet Martineau, Frances Trollope, and Frederick Marryat. All the same, this animosity did not prevent the continuing practice of pirating British writers. In return, British periodicals did their share of stealing the work of the best American writers.

One reason for American magazines' use of pirated material was economic; another was that quality American fiction was still sparse. Despite the fine work of Poe, Washington Irving, and Hawthorne, the short story was not yet a well defined literary genre in the United States, and much short fiction by Americans, especially in the women's magazines, was cloyingly sentimental and moralistic. That situation, though, was to improve, due in part to the increasing professionalism of magazine publishing. The 1840s marked the emergence of a few individuals designated "magazinists," men and women who made their living by writing for, and sometimes editing, magazines. Nathaniel Parker Willis was perhaps the first, followed by Poe, Park Benjamin, Simms, Lydia Sigourney, Ann Stephens, and others. By 1850 the popular magazines, especially women's magazines and the literary weeklies, had begun giving bylines, and a few leaders had started to pay at least their better-known contributors.

By 1850 a far greater variety of periodical reading was available to the public. The magazine business had not yet become "the magazine industry," but with the advent of better and more regular payment to writers, a new class of magazine specialists was able to emerge, promoting stronger editorial standards and encouraging the development of American authorship.

The next half-century was one of tremendous upheaval in American life: first the Civil War, then enormous changes as the nation urbanized and industrialized. The country's magazines duly reflected all these developments.

As the nation moved toward war, the number of political periodicals grew, roughly doubling during the 1850s. The vast majority of magazines were still either regional or local in circulation. Only a handful of general and women's magazines and a few journals of law, medicine, and religion had national circulations of any size. Even most magazines having "U.S," "American," or "National"

[6] "New" was dropped in 1900 and "Monthly" in 1939 when the title was altered to *Harper's Magazine*. Since 1976, the title has been simply *Harper's*.

Edgar Allan Poe
One of the most important American fiction writers of the nineteenth century, Edgar Allan Poe helped to popularize American short stories through his magazine writing in the 1840s and 1850s. This portrait of him appeared on the cover of the March 1853 issue of *The National Magazine.*

in their titles were unable to gain much circulation outside their own locales, and when war came, this localism intensified. By 1860 about one-third of all magazine circulation was accounted for by the titles published in New York City. After New York came Philadelphia, Baltimore, and Boston. The most important of the new magazines, *Harper's New Monthly* and the dignified *Atlantic Monthly*, positively influenced the standard of popular reading.

Of considerable importance were the large-format, abundantly illustrated weeklies, led by *Gleason's Pictorial Drawing-Room Companion* (1851-1859); *Frank Leslie's Illustrated Newspaper* (1855-1891), which actually was more of a magazine than a newspaper; and *Harper's Weekly* (1857-1916). They offered a combination of large wood engravings, light literature, and news. They also provided another instance of U.S. magazines directly following the lead of their counterparts in Great Britain, where engravers, many of whom had their start at the *Illustrated London News*, had recognized the commercial potential of lavish pictorial content and had founded their own illustrated magazines. These British publications pioneered the use of steam-driven multiple-cylinder stereotype printing in the mass-production of large, low-cost pictures. A number of illustrated British magazines became enormously popular. By 1855, when English-born Frank Leslie launched his first U.S. title, they had reached circulations over 200,000, and then eventually became the first magazines to gain circulations of 1,000,000 or more.[7] Leslie's real name was Henry Carter. He initially used "Frank Leslie" to hide his identity because his father disapproved of his interest in drawing. He retained the name, however, after becoming the wealthy publisher of a whole stable of magazines that bore the Leslie name. Curiously, following his death, his widow, Miriam, had her own name legally changed — to Frank Leslie.

Mass culture took a giant step in the 1840s and '50s, inasmuch as the illustrated weeklies were the first magazines to reach a truly mass audience. The visual images they presented so affordably — of great leaders, faraway places, art works, exotic animal life, noteworthy architecture, and so on — appealed to all segments of society and did not demand formal education to be enjoyed. They became a readily accessible window on the world, especially for those whose horizons had previously been much closer.

Other content was changing. A popular weekly in the 1850s was *Saturday Press* (1858-1866), the magazine in which humorists Mark Twain and Josh Billings first reached a large, widespread audience. The staid quarterly reviews had lost some of their former importance. Some had broadened their traditional content and had taken on the look of the more dignified general monthlies; and, correspondingly, some general magazines had begun to run book reviews.

A variety of magazines on special topics proliferated. The largest single genre in number of titles was the religious periodical — quarterlies, monthlies, and weeklies published all over the nation by a wide array of faiths. After religious titles, the most active category was the agricultural periodical, a prominent example of which was *Country Gentleman* (1853-1955). As the Midwest and West became more developed agriculturally, the number of their farm periodicals increased accordingly. Although their great growth period had not yet begun, specialized business periodicals proliferated.

MAGAZINES AND THE CIVIL WAR

In the prewar years women's magazines for the most part kept clear of political controversy. Most northern religious periodicals spoke out against slavery, while their opposite numbers, and many other more general magazines in the South, sought to rationalize their region's "peculiar institution." One of the leading antislavery magazines was William Lloyd Garrison's *Liberator* (1831-1865). A terrific outpouring of magazine comment on both sides of the conflict followed publication of the era's best-selling book, *Uncle Tom's Cabin* (1852), which already had appeared serially in the Washington, D.C., magazine, *National Era*. Also exciting much comment was John Brown's Harpers Ferry raid in 1859. In addition to abolition, temperance was a leading cause, supported

[7]See Patricia J. Anderson, "A Revolution in Popular Art: Pictorial Magazines and the Making of a Mass Culture in England, 1832-1860," *Journal of Newspaper and Periodical History* 6 (1990): 16-25.

THE CHILD AT HOME.

VOL. V. NOVEMBER, 1864. NO. 11.

PUBLISHED BY THE AMERICAN TRACT SOCIETY, BOSTON.

Illustrating the Civil War

Magazine illustration continued to increase lavishly even during the Civil War. Much magazine content, however, naturally focused on the war. *The Child at Home*, a specialty magazine produced by the American Tract Society, a Christian missions organization, illustrated both trends. The lead story in this 1864 issue was titled "'Thanksgiving' in the Hospital," with the accompanying illustration showing a woman and girl visiting the wounded.

by various issue-specific periodicals.

Before the Civil War most magazine writing was still being done by "ladies and gentlemen" as a leisure pursuit rather than in expectation of payment, but some of the larger or better magazines were paying a few dollars a page. Advertising did not yet provide much of a magazine's income, and sales were mostly by subscription. The typical monthly of the 1850s sold for three dollars yearly, most weeklies for two dollars.

Whereas intensified demand for war news kept newspaper subscriptions from declining during the war, magazines — especially those few that previously had enjoyed substantial national circulation, such as *Harper's* and *Godey's* — suffered major losses. In the North the financial panic of 1857, followed by the war, which cut off southern subscriptions, caused a decline in the overall number of magazines. In the South shortages of paper, ink, and printing equipment that had formerly been brought in from the North; high postal rates; a labor shortage; and finally, the arrival of hostile troops caused most southern magazines either to discontinue publication until war's end or to fold permanently. On the other hand a surprising number of new magazines were founded in the South during the conflict.

In the North the illustrated weeklies provided good war coverage, giving the region's newspapers stiff competition. In addition, several northern military periodicals were published. A handful of periodicals took a dim view of the North's role in the war.

England had long served as the model for many American magazines. At mid-century American readers were still bound to the "Mother Country" by the enormous popularity of English writers, especially Charles Dickens for fiction, Thomas Carlyle for nonfiction, and William Wordsworth and Alfred Lord Tennyson for verse. Also heavily represented in American magazines were William Makepeace Thackeray, Henry Fielding, Jane Austen, and Elizabeth Barrett Browning. Among French writers, George Sand, Alexandre Dumas, Honore de Balzac, and Victor Hugo were popular, as to a lesser extent were the Germans Johann Wolfgang von Goethe, Heinrich Heine, and Jean Paul Richter. By the 1870s, however, some American magazines were finding readers on the English side of the Atlantic. *Scribner's*, *Century*, and *Harper's Monthly* were selling well in Britain, their popularity due in large part to their voluminous illustration.

Magazine content continued to change. Novels were popular and were run serially in magazines. Some encouraged domestic novelists, while others continued to take advantage of the absence of international copyright agreements and predominantly used English material without permission or payment. The short story still had not come into its own. Much short magazine fiction and most verse were sugary and sentimental. History and biography were more in demand, probably due to the politically charged times, and travel articles appeared everywhere. Humor writing was a staple by mid-century. Especially popular were the dialect humorists Artemus Ward (whose real name was Charles Browne), Petroleum Vesuvius Nasby (David Locke), Bill Arp, and Finley Peter Dunne (Mr. Dooley). An example of the period's humor periodicals was the Artemus Ward-edited *Vanity Fair* (1859-1863). Another, *Southern Punch,* (1863-1865), surprisingly, commenced publication in Richmond, Virginia, after Lee's defeat at Gettysburg and quickly attained a sizable circulation. Prize fighting and horse racing were the sports that got the most magazine attention, although sports and games were not yet as popular as they would later become in America. Even so, many specialized periodicals were published. Spiritualism was an 1850s craze that resulted in magazines of its own. Secret societies such as the Freemasons and Odd Fellows were also popular and had their own periodicals.

Illustration at mid-century was done by both wood and metal engraving. The pictorial weeklies led the way with wood, while older magazines stayed mainly with steel and copper.

Petroleum V. Nasby
Humorists writing in dialect were especially popular during the Civil War era. Among the most successful was David Ross Locke, who wrote under the pen name "Petroleum Vesuvius Nasby." Locke began the satirical Nasby character in 1860 for the *Toledo* (Ohio) *Blade* and used him to criticize slavery, southerners, secessionists, and Democrats.

Post-War Growth

The years following the Civil War were a period of dramatic growth in magazine publishing. Mott counted 700 periodicals in 1865, and in dramatic contrast, 3,300 by 1885.[8] Even in the Reconstruction South magazine activity was considerable. Magazines began going after subscribers more aggressively, boosting circulation by using premiums such as books and pictures to reward new or renewed subscriptions. Ebenezer Butterick's *Dilenator, A Monthly Magazine Illustrating European and American Fashion*, for example, used dress patterns as premiums and boosted circulation to an impressive 200,000 by 1888.

There were other changes as well. During the lean economic years 1873 to 1878, advertising became more important. *Scribner's Monthly* (1870-1881) and *Galaxy* (1866-1878) took the lead in attracting advertisers by touting their large circulations.

Also changing was the style of writing. It lightened and became less didactic. Most articles were run signed instead of anonymous, as the prudish manners of the prewar years began to fade. Even so, many of the most popular "magazinists" of that era, such as Eugene Benson, Junius Browne, Frederick Perkins, Titas Coan, and David Wasson, have been all but forgotten. The quality of literary magazines ranged from the high-toned, non-illustrated *Atlantic* to many of more humble quality.

Regional interests continued to play a role in the magazine field. In the South the most active magazine cities of the 1870s were Atlanta, Baltimore, Louisville, Richmond, and New Orleans. New Orleans was also remarkable for the number of French-language periodicals — roughly forty — published there during the 1800s. Atlanta's *Sunny South* (1875-1907) and Louisville's *Home and Farm* (1876-1918) were the leaders in a region where a circulation of 100,000 was considered an enormous success. Reconstruction was a common topic in northern magazines, and such southern writers as George Cable, George Egbert Craddock, and Thomas Nelson Page found ready markets in the North for their work. At the end of the 1870s a great westward population shift occurred; and Chicago, St. Louis, Cincinnati, Milwaukee, and Topeka became more active in magazine publishing.

The many religious newspapers that had become popular in the 1820s began withdrawing from the coverage of secular news in the 1870s, probably due to the growth of big-city dailies better equipped to handle hard news. Overall, however, the total number of religious periodicals doubled between the Civil War's end and 1885.

Magazines for women increased in number. Most of the major magazines came out against woman suffrage, despite the fact that far more women than men were subscribers. Consequently, smaller journals sprang up all over the country to speak for women's rights: not just the legendary *Revolution* (1868-1879) that Susan B. Anthony and Elizabeth Cady Stanton conducted in New York, but many others in a variety of locations. The most outspoken of them all was *Woodhull and Claflin's Weekly* (1870-1876). Not all women joined the movement, however, as was evidenced by the antisuffrage *True Woman* (1870-1873). At the same time, fashion magazines became more popular than ever. *Harper's Bazar* (1867-current) took the lead. Two especially successful home magazines were *Woman's Home Journal* (1878-1909) and Cyrus Curtis' *Ladies' Home Journal* (1883-current), with which editor Edward W. Bok introduced to the women's market the concept of service journalism, and which was the first American magazine to reach 1,000,000 subscribers (in 1903). Circulation growth in general was given a major boost by the Second Class Postage Act of 1879, which allowed magazines a more favorable postal rate.

The growth of specialized or "class" periodicals was enormous in the decades following the Civil War. Many new journals appeared in all the sciences; and as the nation industrialized, innumerable engineering, manufacturing, and mechanical periodicals

[8]Frank Luther Mott, *A History of American Magazines* (Cambridge, Mass., 1938),3: 5.

Mary Booth

Harper's Bazar Editor Succeeds Through Intuition and Taste

Give the reader what she wants. That was the philosophy of *Harper's Bazar's* founding editor, Mary L. Booth.

"An editor's first qualifications are sagacity to discover what the public wants, and knowledge how to supply the demand," she explained.

And Booth, a luminary among nineteenth-century magazine editors, had both.

Her magazine was a sort of *Harper's Weekly* for women. Owned by Harper & Brothers, *Harper's Bazar* debuted with Booth at the helm on November 2, 1867. From an upstart fashion magazine, she built a journal known more for its literary leanings than its fashion prowess. Thomas Nast and other leading artists and novelists such as William Dean Howells found a forum in *Harper's Bazar.*

Booth herself scoffed at critics who dismissed her magazine as a fashion folio. "It seems to me," she asserted, "that a journal which numbers among its constant contributors the best writers of light literature, both of Europe and America, which treats, in the course of each volume, of almost every subject that would be likely to interest the family circle, and which contains some of the finest art illustrations published in any newspaper in the country, can hardly be ranked by any one as a mere journal of fashion."

Booth used her magazine forum to encourage women to achieve beyond their domestic sphere. By her very presence at the head of a respected, high-circulation magazine, she became a celebrity and role model for other women of her era.

She believed women like herself were "eminently" qualified for journalistic work because "[t]heir acute and subtle intuition, and habits of keen observation, readiness of thought, and refined taste, fit them to succeed both as contributors and editors."

Booth herself had lots of that intuition. She led the highly successful, mass circulation, national weekly from its first issue until her death in 1889.

Agnes Hooper Gottlieb
Seton Hall University

HARPER'S BAZAR
A Repository of Fashion, Pleasure, and Instruction

NEW YORK, SATURDAY, OCTOBER 3, 1868

In the popular trend toward fashion magazines in the post-war period, *Harper's Bazar*, founded in 1867 and still publishing, took the lead. For more than twenty years, Mary Booth served as its editor.

were established. Literature in a real sense was being elbowed aside by science and a consuming interest in commerce and industrial progress. Professional journals, especially in medicine, also enjoyed considerable growth, and education journals published by teachers' organizations or by state government agencies were plentiful. "Booster magazines" began to appear and with newspapers extolled the virtues of their regions to attract economic development. Also, the number of agricultural journals roughly tripled between 1870 and 1885. To further the farmers' interests, thousands of local granges were formed in the late 1860s and early 1870s, and many of them published their own periodicals.

Interest in sports broadened, and each sport had its own magazines. Hunting, fishing, boating, and bicycling were served by periodicals. The earliest bicycling periodical was published in New York City in 1869, but cycling suffered a decline in popularity until the solid rubber tire was introduced in the early 1870s. Then *American Bicycling Journal* (1877-1879) and several similar periodicals capitalized on the revived craze. Of the spectator sports, horse racing remained preeminent and was represented by several specialized periodicals. Second in popularity was baseball, the first periodical for which was *Ball Player's Chronicle* (1867) of New York.

More than any other nation, America published magazines for young readers. About half were Sunday school or other denomination-affiliated periodicals, although they did not match the overall circulation of the secular juveniles. An older juvenile magazine was *Merry's Museum* (1841-1872), edited for a time by Louisa May Alcott, author of *Little Women*. New titles sprang up. The best of them all was the lavishly illustrated *St. Nicholas* (1873-1943), ably edited by Mary Mapes Dodge, author of *Hans Brinker, or the Silver Skates*. Contributors to *St. Nicholas* included Mark Twain, Rudyard Kipling, and Theodore Roosevelt.

A new process of electrotyping made wood a practical medium for long pressruns, and wood engraving began to replace steel and copper in the late 1850s and early '60s. Especially known for their wood-engraved illustrations were *Appleton's Journal* (1869-1881) of New York, *Scribner's Monthly*, *St. Nicholas*, and the pictorially splendid, large-format *Harper's Weekly*. A steam-powered lithographic press developed in France reached the United States in the 1860s, and illustration in American magazines increased so greatly that some critics began to worry that pictorial content had encroached too far on space that might otherwise have been occupied by written copy.

A variety of genres of writing increased in popularity. Fiction was in a strong position during the latter part of the nineteenth century. The importance of the serial novel continued to increase, thanks in large part to the popularity of foreign novelists. The 1870s and '80s were a time of growing importance for the short story, although most short fiction continued to be blighted by what *Harper's New Monthly* editor Henry Mills Alden characterized as the precious, the mock-heroic, and the morbid. Similarly

No. 17.—With Supplement] SATURDAY, JULY 24, 1869. [Price Ten Cents.

ON THE ROAD TO LAKE GEORGE. By Winslow Homer

Growth of Illustration
With the steam-powered lithographic press available beginning in the 1860s, magazine illustrations increased so greatly that some critics began to worry that pictures were encroaching on the space available for text. One of the most visual magazines was *Appleton's Journal*.

dreadful was much of the poetry, although Walt Whitman, Sidney Lanier, and Lowell provided quality verse for various magazines. After fiction, travel writing was next in popularity with magazine readers, who reportedly wanted fewer pretty descriptions, less sentiment, more historical treatment, and more attention to mores in their travel copy. Travel writing had to become more practical because more Americans had begun to travel abroad. Supplying the South's need for historical accounts of former glories and the Lost Cause were several magazines designed specifically for that purpose, such as North Carolina's *Our Living and Our Dead* (1873-1876).

Among humor magazines, the preeminent one was *Puck* (1877-1918), edited for many years by the gifted parodist H.C. Bunner. In the 1880s came two other outstanding ones, *Judge* (1881-1939) and *Life* (1883-1936), with its splendid drawings by Charles Dana Gibson, creator of the "Gibson man" and "Gibson girl." *Texas Siftings* (1881-1897) began in Austin and later was also published in New York, providing a sort of humor bridge between East and West; and Opie Read's *Arkansas Traveler* (1882-1916) was in Little Rock before it offended too many locals and had to "travel" to Chicago.

Once again politics began to be discussed in more of the general magazines. The old prewar partisanship was breaking down, and most of the magazines that ran political material were not tied to a particular party. A thoughtful new journal of opinion was E.L. Godkin's *Nation* (1865-current). It developed an avid nationwide following among the educated and professional classes. Labor unions organized and became politically active after the Civil War, and by 1885 around 400 labor periodicals were being published, most of them local in scope.

As the cities grew, so did their social problems — awful living conditions for the poor, prostitution, violent crime, corrupt government — but Victorian public reticence was still too strong for most magazines and newspapers to risk offending their readers with frank attention to these problems. In the celebrated fight against New York City's Tweed Ring, the only magazine to commit itself fully was *Harper's Weekly*. Still, the progress of science and technology, plus the democratization of politics, made more intense by great waves of immigration, eventually served to weaken the hold of traditional values on the American mind, causing a great deal of interest in changing manners and mores. Many travel articles of this era, for instance, were in reality comparative glimpses at how other peoples lived.

Toward Century's End

In the late 1880s and the 1890s some of the larger national magazines reduced their prices and thus set the stage for the era of low-priced, giant-circulation monthlies and weeklies of the early 1900s. The prices of the most popular magazines generally were in the range of 20¢ to 35¢, but *Munsey's* (1889-1929), *Peterson's*, and *Godey's* went to 10¢ in the 1890s. *Collier's* began as *Once a Week* in 1888, gaining a large circulation at 7¢ a copy. The *Ladies' Home Journal* likewise built an enormous circulation in the 1890s at 5¢ a copy, and the low-priced *McClure's* (1893-1933) reached a circulation upward of 350,000 by 1900 by emphasizing biographies and stories of success. These price cuts were made possible in part by cheaper paper, lower printing costs, and halftone photoengraving, which by the early 1890s was on its way to replacing the far more costly wood and metal engraving processes.

The popular magazines of the 1890s were not sensational in content, but they were heavily illustrated compared to earlier decades. Subject matter had gained in variety, and articles on the problems of the day had become more common. Fiction was de-emphasized in favor of history, politics, and economics. Even the *Atlantic Monthly* became less literary and followed the trend.

Magazine growth in the 1880s and '90s was furthered by still other influences. Mail rates for magazines were reduced in 1885, and in 1897 rural free delivery was inaugurated. Magazine adver-

THE LADIES' HOME JOURNAL AND PRACTICAL HOUSEKEEPER.

FIVE CENTS PER COPY — PHILADELPHIA, FEBRUARY, 1884. — FIFTY CENTS PER YEAR.

Jeremiah Jones's Housekeeping.

Circulation Leader
Founded in 1883, *Ladies' Home Journal* became an enormous success by providing useful information to homemakers at a low price. Selling for 5¢, it achieved one of the nation's largest circulations in the 1890s, and in the early 1900s it became the first American magazine to reach a circulation of 1,000,000. Founded by Cyrus Curtis, it provided the cornerstone for the Curtis Publishing Company, one of the most successful magazine publishers of the twentieth century, and remains today one of the nation's leading periodicals.

tising headed up sharply the last decade of the century, and full-page ads became fairly common. Single-copy sales increased, as well.

By 1890 magazines were able to recruit editing and writing talent from a substantial pool of persons who had worked for other magazines. Prior to that time most staffing had come from newspapers or from contributors who had little or no full-time experience with any kind of magazine. It became common for writers to prepare copy first for magazine publication, and then collect it and try to have it published in book form. Even the very best writers were happy to use magazine publication as a means of pre-promoting their books.

Illustrated weeklies were losing ground by the 1890s, although the finest of them, *Harper's Weekly*, still enjoyed a solid position, as did *Frank Leslie's Illustrated Weekly* (renamed *Leslie's Weekly* in 1895).

Local and regional magazines became much more popular in the 1890s. One type of local periodical was the city weekly, which offered a mix of politics, commentary on the entertainment scene, humor, society chit-chat, and light literary fare. Most large cities had at least one such periodical. Humorous, but hardly a society-oriented periodical, was *Rolling Stone* (1894-1895) in Austin, Texas, owned and edited by William Sydney Porter, later to find lasting fame as O. Henry, America's premier short-story writer. Regional magazines were published in most parts of the country, from Florida to the Rocky Mountains to the Pacific Northwest. Students of magazine history should resist the temptation to think of city and regional magazines as inventions of the 1960s and 1970s, a more recent major growth period for this genre.

Sports got heavy attention from the magazine industry in the 1890s, both from general and specialized periodicals. Two of the period's most resilient titles were *Sports Afield* (1887-current) and *Field and Stream* (1896-current).

In the more literary magazines of the 1890s the short story finally had become an important staple, and by the later years of the decade writers were supplying what came to be called the "short short story." The major literary debate was over the merits of realistic as opposed to romantic fiction. *Harper's* and *Dial* spoke for realism, but most magazines that aimed at a mass circulation and had to please popular taste retained their faith in romanticism. By the end of the decade poetry was receiving far less space in magazines than it had previously.

During the 1880s and '90s general magazines developed a more practical bent, decreasing their emphasis on literature, history, and travel in favor of politics, the economy, and social problems. Thus the content of magazines and newspapers became more similar. Much attention was directed at monopolies and trusts, imperialism, protective tariffs, and socialism as the nation's magazines tried to deal with the ramifications of the country's growing wealth and influence. Speaking out on issues important to black women in America was *Woman's Era* (1894-1898), published in Boston and edited by Josephine St. Pierre Ruffin. By this time, in fact, quite a number of magazines by and for African Americans were in publication, although they still suffered the difficulties in attracting good contributors and willing advertisers that had troubled mainstream publishers in the early 1800s. Religious or other organizations supported many of them, and the first black magazine in the South did not appear until 1890.

Poised on the brink of a new century, the American magazine had changed a great deal. It was already in the process of becoming a part of a large industry led by national magazines of enormous circulation, and overall it informed, as opposed to entertained, more than it had done in the mid 1800s. A far greater range of practical specialized periodicals had come into being, and even the general content magazines were placing more emphasis on providing their readers with useful factual matter. Historian Agnes Repplier once described nineteenth-century magazines as characterized by propriety-bound patronization — editors seeming to say to their readers: "We will help you. We will uplift and improve you."[9] By century's end the tone was less gentle and polite, more frankly journalistic. Less literary in purpose than before, the American magazine was nevertheless stronger and soon would be ready to enter a period in which magazines shined in investigative reporting.

RECOMMENDED READINGS

BOOKS

Alden, Henry Mills. *Magazine Writing and the New Literature*. New York, 1908. Examines the relationship of periodicals to general literature and the changed nature of periodical writing in the late 1800s.

Ballou, Ellen B. *The Building of the House*. Boston, 1970. A history of the influential *Atlantic Monthly*.

Chielens, Edward E., ed. *American Literary Magazines: The Eighteenth and Nineteenth Centuries*. New York, 1986. Includes a general essay covering the years 1774-1900 and sketches of ninety-two titles.

Edgar, Neal L. *A History and Bibliography of American Magazines, 1810-1820*. Metuchen, NJ, 1975. A well written commentary on the general magazine history of this period, followed by thumbnail descriptions of 223 individual periodicals.

Endres, Kathleen, and Terese Lueck, eds. *Women's Periodicals in the United States*. Westport, Conn., 1995. A useful reference source on an important sector of the magazine business.

Entrikin, Isabelle Webb. *Sarah Josepha Hale and Godey's Lady's Book*. Lancaster, Pa., 1946. As editor of *Ladies' Magazine* and *Godey's Lady's Book*, Hale made many contributions to magazine editing and American literature. She was especially concerned about improving social and cultural conditions.

Exman, Eugene. *The House of Harper: One Hundred and Fifty Years of Publishing*. New York, 1967. A useful history of this important publishing house.

Fackler, Mark P., and Charles H. Lippy, eds. *Popular Religious Magazines of the United States*. Westport, Conn., 1995. Profiles 100 of the more important magazines in this genre, past and present.

Hoover, Merle M. *Park Benjamin: Poet and Editor*. New York, 1948. As editor of the *New England* magazine and of the weekly *New World* (1839-1845), Benjamin influenced American literature.

John, Arthur. *The Best Years of the Century: Richard Watson Gilder, Scribner's Monthly, and Century Magazine, 1870-1909*. Urbana, Ill., 1981. A detailed history of the important American magazine that was founded as *Scribner's Monthly* and in 1881 became *The Century Illustrated Monthly Magazine*.

Lomazon, Steven. *American Periodicals: A Collector's Manual and Reference Guide*. West Orange, N.J., 1996. A handsome, well-illustrated book by a major collector.

Luxon, Norval Neil. *Niles' Weekly Register: News Magazine of the Nineteenth Century*. Baton Rouge, 1947. Until 1832, the *Register* took strong editorial positions in favor of a protective tariff, aid to western development, Clay's American System, etc.

Lynn, Kenneth S. *William Dean Howells: An American Life*. New York, 1971. Literary biography of the magazine editor and novelist whose earliest career was briefly in newspapers.

McClure, S.S. *My Autobiography*. New York, 1914. An inside look at the birth of American mass magazines.

Meyer, S.E. *America's Great Illustrators*. New York, 1978. A useful perspective for readers who are usually more word- than picture-oriented.

Mott, Frank Luther. *A History of American Magazines*. Cambridge, 1930, 1938,

[9] Agnes Repplier, "American Magazines," *Yale Review* 16 (1926-27): 261-74.

1957. Volume I of this encyclopedic five-volume work covers 1741-1850; Vol. II, 1850-1865; Vol. III, 1865-1885; and Vol. IV, 1885-1905.

Price, Kenneth M., and Susan Belasco Smith, eds. *Periodical Literature in Nineteenth-Century America*. Charlottesville, Va., 1995. Excellent essays on a variety of magazine topics.

Richardson, Lyon F. *A History of Early American Magazines, 1741-89*. New York, 1931. Some of the thirty-seven magazines, although they lasted for only short periods, were important as forums for the expression of opinion and for discussion.

Riley, Sam G. *Magazines of the American South*. Westport, Conn., 1986. Descriptive sketches of eighty-nine southern magazines.

–, ed. *American Magazine Journalists*. Vols. 73 (1741-1850) and 79 (1850-1900) of *Dictionary of Literary Biography*. Detroit, 1988, 1989. Provides detailed biographical essays on most of the important magazine editors/publishers for each period.

Schneirov, Matthew. *The Dream of a New Social Order: Popular Magazines in America, 1893-1914*. New York, 1994. Useful for a look at magazines at the turn of the century.

Smyth, Albert H. *The Philadelphia Magazines and Their Contributors, 1741-1850*. Philadelphia, 1892. Good detail on developments in this important magazine city.

Tebbel, John, and Mary Ellen Zuckerman. *The Magazine in America, 1740-1990*. New York, 1991. A general history of American periodical publishing.

Wells, Daniel A., comp. *The Literary Index to American Magazines, 1850-1900*. Westport, Conn., 1996. An excellent source for the literary content of magazines.

Zuckerman, Mary Ellen. *A History of Popular Women's Magazines in the United States, 1792-1995*. Westport, Conn., 1998. Women's magazines played an important role in the lives of readers, while culture and economics were especially important in the lives of the magazines themselves.

ARTICLES

Cardwell, Guy A. "The Influence of Addison on Charleston Periodicals, 1795-1860." *Studies in Philology* 35 (July 1938): 456-70. Demonstrates how important Addison's style was in providing a pattern for American magazine writing well into the 1800s.

Burks, Mary Fair. "The First Black Literary Magazine in American Letters." *CLA Journal* 19 (March 1976): 318-21. The *Anglo-African Magazine*, founded in 1859 in New York, "succeeded in creating a tradition of *belles lettres* among blacks."

Dennis, Everette E., and Christopher Allen. "*Puck*, the Comic Weekly." *Journalism History* 6 (1979): 2-7, 13. *Puck* (1877-1918) was the "first and most important" comic magazine in the late nineteenth century. This study examines the reasons for its success.

Endres, Fred J. "The Pre-Muckraking Days of McClure's Magazine, 1893-1901." *Journalism Quarterly* 55 (1978): 154-7. What this popular, important magazine was like before its better-remembered muckraking period.

Garcia, Hazel. "Of Punctilios Among the Fair Sex: Colonial American Magazines, 1741-1776." *Journalism History* 3 (1976): 48-52, 63. Men wrote most of the magazine material about women and dealt with love and marriage, but that written by women showed them asserting themselves.

Kitch, Carolyn. "Changing Theoretical Perspectives on Women's Media Images: The Emergence of Patterns in a New Area of Historical Scholarship." *Journalism & Mass Communication Quarterly* 74 (Autumn 1997): 477-89. Surveys the historical research on images of women as portrayed in magazines and other media.

Linneman, William R. "Southern Punch: A Draught of Confederate Wit." *Southern Folklore Quarterly* 26 (June 1962): 131-6. A look at a humor magazine that was founded at a most unlikely time.

Sheppard, Carol. "The Blighted Life of the Writer, Circa 1840." *American Heritage* (August-September 1986): 102-5. Rough rejections and rotten pay, but the writers continued to write anyway.

Stearns, Bertha Monica. "Early New England Magazines for Ladies." *New England Quarterly* 2 (July 1929): 420-57. An examination of the first women's magazines in this region, with special emphasis on the contributions of Sarah Josepha Hale. Related works by Stearns include "Southern Magazines for Ladies." *South Atlantic Quarterly* 31 (January 1932): 70-87; and "Early Philadelphia Magazines for Ladies." *Pennsylvania Magazine of History and Biography* 64 (October 1940): 479-91.

Taketani, Etsuko. "The *North American Review*, 1815-1835: The Invention of the American Past." *American Periodicals* 5 (1995): 111-27. The periodical played an important role in the creation of the new country's national identity.

14

The Development of Advertising

1700 - 1900

When volcanic ash was removed from Pompeii, which was destroyed by an eruption of Mt. Vesuvius in 79 A.D., the names of three prostitutes were found on a wall outside a bar. Another sign carried the name of a candidate for political office. These signs were typical of the advertisements of early merchants and promoters. They were used to direct prospective customers to a shop or to identify it. Like the barber's red, white, and blue pole of modern times, the signs often were symbolic.

Along with signs, early advertising also took the form of criers and trademarks. Signboards were carried in some ancient cities, and criers told the public about merchants' wares. As products moved beyond local consumption and were marketed in nearby towns, trademarks were used to assure the purchaser of a particular level of quality. Advertising remained in a primitive state for most of human history — until the development of movable type during the Renaissance made possible the newspaper, the first mass medium.

Early American Advertising

Although criers and hawkers were popular in England, they were not in the American colonies. The earliest commercial advertising in America appeared in pamphlet and signboard forms. Pamphlets, which were popular, explained in-depth what was available. Signboards, on the other hand, usually contained only symbols and addresses. Various symbols were used, for example, for tobacco shops — from the black boy and the Indian to the Smoking Dutchman. Addresses consisted of brief copy. Signs for taverns were the most visible. Although these signs were popular among businesses throughout the colonies, the most colorful appeared in large towns, such as Philadelphia and Baltimore.

Newspaper advertisements appeared less than a century after the founding of the first settlement in New England at Plymouth, but the printing press had been in the colonies for sixty-six years before it was used to print an advertisement in a newspaper. Boston had several presses, while Philadelphia and New York had at least one each. These presses printed the *Bible*, the *Freeman's Oath*, tracts, almanacs, and other books. The colonies' first newspaper, Boston's *Publick Occurrences, Both Forreign and Domestick*, carried no advertising in its sole issue in 1690.

The earliest newspaper ads, which were published in the *Boston News-Letter* in 1704, resembled today's classified or want ads. When John Campbell, the postmaster in Boston, began the *News-Letter*, space was at a premium in the two-page newspaper, and he limited advertising to a maximum space of twenty lines. The cost per line was about 1 1/2 cents. The ads consisted of several lines of small type with no display elements. Runaway servants, slaves for sale, and some merchandise for sale were the most commonly advertised items.

The third *News-Letter*, dated May 1-8, 1704, contained the first paid advertisements. Although there were three advertisements, together they occupied only four inches of space in one column. The only typography that separated them from the news was the word "advertisements." Two advertised rewards for the capture of thieves. The third advertised real estate. This, the first real estate advertisement to appear in an American newspaper, read:

> At Oysterbay, on *Long Island* in the Province of *N. York*, There is a very good Fulling-Mill, to be Let or Sold, as also a Plantation, having on it a large new Brick house, and another good house by it for a Kitchen & work house, with a Barn, Stable &c. a young Orchard, and 20 acres clear Land. The Mill is to be Let with or without the Plantation: Enquire of Mr. *William Bradford* Printer in *N. York*, and know further.[1]

As Campbell's *News-Letter* continued, other kinds of advertising appeared. Advertisements for slaves appeared frequently. Advertising remained meager, however. Even after three years, five inches devoted to advertising was rare. Some issues were devoid of any advertising whatsoever.

Colonial advertising received its greatest boost when Benjamin

[1]*Boston News-Letter*, 1-8 May 1704.

Sloop Samuel, James White, for S. Carolina.

Cleared.

Ship Dolphin, J. A. Denormandie, to St. Christophers.
Snow Phenix, Henry M'Murrain, to Dublin.
Snow Britannia, Thomas Harron, to Jamaica.
Scooner Speedwell, William Weldon, to Antigua.
Sloop Frederica, John Goodwin, to Georgia.
—— Winyaw. Richard Painter, to Winyaw.
Ship Southampton, Henry Magger, Cadiz.
—— Lancashire Gally, Angel Corbin, } to Antigua.
—— Ranger, John Hamilton,
Sloop Diamond, Nathaniel Wyatt, to Rhode-Island.
Ship Ruby Gally, Joseph Arthur, to St. Christophers.
Sloop Sarah, Ebenezer Hawes, to Boston.

THIS is to give Notice, That HAIR-CLOTH and HAIR-LINES of all Sorts, still continues to be made by the Widow Rakestraw, at the upper End of Front-street, Philadelphia, where all Persons may be supplied with the same as usual.

*** Note, There are two large Rooms with Fire places in them, to be let by the said Widow Rakestraw.

RUN away about the 6th of November past from Mathew Clarkson, a Servant Man named Johannes Paluck, born in Switzerland, about Twenty Years of age, of a middle Stature, hath two Thumbs to the right Hand, and keeps it bound over with a Rag, came over from Holland, in the Brigt. Prince Frederick, Joseph Willson, Master, to New-York, about the middle of September last: Had on, a new Felt Hat, a double worsted ... Cap, a double breasted Pea-Jacket with flat brass buttons, two ... Shirts, new leather breeches ... Whoever apprehends the said Servant & delivers him to the Goal of Philadelphia, any Goal in New-Jersey or at New-York, giving Notice to Mr. Arent Hassert of Philadelphia, Gerardus De Peyster at New-Brunswick, or Mathew Clarkson in New-York shall receive Three Pounds reward and reasonable Charges.

Lately Imported from London & Bristol,
To be SOLD by Thomas Williams,

AT his Store on Fishbourn's Wharff, Kersys and Broad Cloths of all Prices, a good Choice of Rugs, Blankets, Oznabrigs, ... and fine Broad Cloth in Suits with Trimming ... plain narrow Cloth, Bed Ticks ... Money or at the usual Credit.

LEnt, or left somewhere abroad, about three or four Months ago, a very large Kersey GREAT-COAT, burnt almost through in one or two Places, with the Edge of the Taylor's Goose, in making it. Whoever brings it to the Printer hereof, shall be thankfully rewarded.

JOHN GOODWIN,

SHOP-KEEPER, who formerly liv'd in Chesnut-Street, is Removed into Front-Street, next Door ... at the Sign of the SUGAR-LOAF; where his Country Friends and others may be supplied with sundry Sorts of European and other Goods, on reasonable Prices.

And all Persons in Debt to the said John Goodwin, are desired to make speedy Payment.

CHOICE Lisbon SALT to be sold cheap by Thomas Griffitts in Philadelphia.

THIS is to give Notice, that John Wilkinson, BRUSHMAKER, in Second-Street opposite the Post-Office, Philadelphia, desires all Planters, ... Pedlars and others, to save and gather all the Hog's Bristles they can, and bring or send them to him, who will give from Six Pence or Eight Pence to Ten Pence a Pound, according as they are in Goodness, combed or uncombed, it being no more Trouble, when People are scalding their Hogs, than to take all the Bristles that grow on the Back, and throw them from the rest of the Dirt, and afterwards either comb 'em or lay 'em by in the rough. Note, That he buys from the largest Quantities to the smallest, he using large Quantities every Week.

At the same Place People may be furnished with all Sorts of BRUSHES; as Sweeping-Brushes, Scouring-Brushes, Limners Brushes, Hatters Brushes, Whitewashers Brushes, Clothes-Brushes, Hat-Brushes, and all other sorts of hard and soft Brushes, by wholesale or Retail, at reasonable Rates. He has brought over a good Quantity of English, Irish and Russia Bristles, and furnishes Shoemakers with all sorts fit for their Use.

To all Storekeepers, Shallop Men and Pedlars in all Parts, to desire all they trade with, to bring in their Bristles to them, that they may gather large Quantities, and send them to me, or to Thomas Shreeve of Burlington, or to Thomas Hutton or William Atley Merchants in Trenton, who will give the Price above mentioned.

John Wilkinson.

Philad. Nov. 17. 1736.

A LIKELY Servant Man's Time to be disposed of, having three Years and a half to serve, Enquire of the Printer hereof.

For LONDON directly,

THE Ship Charming Nancy, John Stedman, Master, will certainly sail in five Weeks, Wind and Weather permitting.

For Freight or Passage agree with the said Master at Fishbourn's Store in Water-Street.

N. B. He will carry Goods at a very reasonable Freight, and has several sorts of European Goods to sell Cheap for ready Money. Philadelphia, Decem. 16. 1736.

VEry good SACK sold by Joseph Wharton, at 8s. per Gallon.

CHOICE double-refin'd Loaf Sugar at 17d per Pound, by the half Dozen Loaves, single-refin'd Sugar at ... per Pound by ditto, Powder Sugar, Muscovado Sugar suitable for Shops or Family Use, Sugar Candy, Molasses and Bohea Tea, sold at very reasonable Rates by Peter Delage, at the House of John Dillwin, at the upper End of Second Street.

Just published,

POOR RICHARD's ALMANACKS for the Year 1737, containing besides what is usual, a particular Description of the Herb which the Indians use to cure the Bite of that venomous Reptile a RATTLE-SNAKE, an exact Print of the Leaf of the Plant, an Account of the Places it grows in, and the Manner of using it, &c. made publick for the general Good. With Variety of other Matters useful, serious and comical. Printed and Sold by B. Franklin.

ARENT HASSERT, intending to go for London and Holland in the first or second Month next, desires all Persons that are Indebted to him, to pay their respective Dues. To be sold by the said Arent Hassert, at his House in ... Court, sundry sorts of Bolting-cloths, as fine, middling, and coarse; also Madder, and sundry other Goods very reasonable, for ready Money.

To be SOLD,

A Very likely breeding Negroe Woman, and a Boy about two Years old. The Woman is fit for any Business either in Town or Country. Enquire of William Bus..., near ... Coffee-House in Front Street.

VERY good LAMPBLACK made and Sold by the Printer hereof.

PHILADELPHIA: Printed by B. FRANKLIN, at the New Printing-Office near the Market. Price 10 s. a Year.

Where Advertisements are taken in, and BOOK-BINDING is done reasonably, in the best Manner.

Benjamin Franklin's *Gazette*

After purchasing the *Pennsylvania Gazette* in 1729, Benjamin Franklin turned his creative mind to advertising, and the newspaper soon was crowded with ads. It was one of early America's most prosperous newspapers.

Franklin, while still in his early twenties, purchased the *Pennsylvania Gazette* in 1729. He turned his inventive and creative mind to upgrading the newspaper's finances, and it soon grew crowded with advertisements. He brought his genius as a writer to bear on the advertising as well as the editorial content. He was the first advertising copywriter worthy of the name in American history. In fact, his contributions to American advertising are so important that the American Advertising Federation selected him as one of the first members of its Hall of Fame.

Franklin increased the number of pages in the newspaper from two to four so he could handle more advertisements and news stories. He separated each advertisement with white space. He used at least a 14-point heading for each advertisement. Later, he incorporated small stock cuts or illustrations. Realizing that illustrations could enhance an advertisement, he used half-column and column cuts made especially for certain advertisers. A cut of a clock face, for example, was used to identify a watchmaker's advertisement. Readers could recognize what was being sold merely by glancing at the illustration. Retailers who had stayed away from advertising in newspapers realized they could increase sales by advertising in Franklin's newspaper. As a result, he had to enlarge his newspaper again. Instead of two short columns, he put in three deep columns, which made the newspaper about the size of a modern tabloid. He advertised numerous products and services, including glasses, wine, cheese, chocolate, mathematical instruments, codfish, tea, coffee, and stoves. No other colonial printer did more for advertising.

Although John Peter Zenger is best known for the fact that his trial in 1735 enlarged freedom of the press, he also helped advance advertising. His *New York Weekly Journal* normally contained eight to ten advertisements, while the other papers usually contained two or three. Zenger used column rules to separate advertisements, and he did not restrict advertising to a particular amount of space. One advertisement was more than a half-page deep. Like Franklin, Zenger realized the importance of illustrations and used various cuts to improve the appearance of advertisements. He charged three shillings (36¢) for the first insertion and one shilling for each insertion thereafter. He realized that advertisers would advertise more often if they received a discount.

Another innovator in advertising was James Parker, who founded the *New York Weekly Post-Boy* in 1742. Advertisements in the *Post-Boy* occupied as much as six columns, or half of the paper. Advertisements were for real estate, slaves, runaway apprentices, books, wines, medicines, and lotteries. Their captions were capitalized in 10-point and sometimes 14- or 18-point type. By 1760, type sizes and typefaces varied within most advertisements, with captions at least eighteen points. Display advertisements sometimes filled entire columns. The newspaper became so successful with advertisers that advertisements filled three of the four pages. The October 30, 1760, issue's entire front page was covered with advertisements, the first time that had occurred in a colonial newspaper.

As the American Revolution approached, however, events began to affect advertising deleteriously. The British Parliament taxed ads with the Stamp Act of 1765, which the colonists aggressively opposed. In 1765, primarily because of a shortage of paper in the colonies caused by the Stamp Act, Benjamin Franklin cut display advertising from the *Pennsylvania Gazette*. Instead of large type and illustrations, he filled advertising columns with small type and thumbnail art.

When the Revolution started, George Washington used posters, an advertising medium, to recruit soldiers. Conditions worsened in the colonies during the war, and many newspapers died. One newspaper, though, the *Pennsylvania Packet and the General Advertiser*, founded in 1771 by John Dunlap, illustrated how advertising could help sell newspapers. It is obvious that Dunlap learned from Franklin. He realized the importance of how an advertisement looked. As a result, the *Packet's* advertisements

DUNLAP's ... Packet ... THE ADVERTISER.

DECEMBER 20th, 1773.

TO-MORROW, AT ONE O'CLOCK, AT JOHN HART's VENDUE-STORE, At the corner of SOUTH and FRONT-STREETS, Will begin the SALE of a large and neat assortment of MERCHANDIZE, Amongst which are, BROADCLOTHS, Naps, Kerseys, Half-thicks, Plains, Coatings, &c.

O BE LET, On GROUND-RENT forever, ... WILLIAM COATS.

O BE SOLD, ... JOHN IMLAY, ISAAC WIKOFF, and CURTIS CLAY.

NOTICE is hereby given, ... MICHAEL FISHER, SAMUEL HARRISON, Esquires.

GRACE PARKER, From LONDON, WILL open a School on Monday the 20th instant (December) ... GRACE PARKER.

ZEBULON RUDULPH, Has removed his store ...

WEST-INDIA, Philadelphia and New England rum; sugar, molasses, tea, coffee ...

For NEWRY, The SHIP JUPITER, SAMUEL BROWN, Master; A GOOD stout ship, with excellent accommodations for passengers, will sail in ten days, ... BARCLAY and MITCHELL.

STOLEN OR STRAYED, From a pasture near the Play-house, A LARGE dark brindled COW, with a white belly and legs, ... FIFTEEN SHILLINGS reward ... FIVE POUNDS ... ROBERT MORRIS.

THREE POUNDS REWARD. RANAWAY from the subscriber, ... JOHN MORGAN, ...

Advertising Design

During the American Revolution, John Dunlap's *Pennsylvania Packet* succeeded in part because Dunlap recognized the importance of how an advertisement looked. He frequently used woodcut illustrations to enliven ads.

were easier to read and attracted reader interest. The newspaper featured commercial news, too, rather than political stories. Commercial news attracted merchants. Thus Dunlap was able to attract those who needed to advertise. He revived the illustration and created special cuts for certain advertisers. Within two years, the newspaper was so successful that Dunlap had to enlarge its size and increase its columns. Advertising accounted for two-thirds of the paper's content. In 1784, the newspaper, which had started as a weekly, became the second daily to be published in America. The reason was not because of readers' hunger for news. Rather, Dunlap received so much advertising that he found it necessary to increase the frequency of publication.

Another daily appeared a year later. Published in New York by Francis Childs, the *New York Daily Advertiser* contributed to advertising by running captions in type as big as 36-point. Usually one word, the captions were bold to capture attention.

By the early 1800s, the number of newspapers published in the United States had grown to more than 300. Despite the fact that advertising volume was increasing, few newspapers depended on advertising revenue. Most were operated for political purposes and were supported by private contributions or subscriptions. Most publishers were satisfied with their advertising. Few worried about how advertisements appeared. Thus advertising remained constant in appearance for many years. In most cases, no more than one cut illustrated each advertisement. The copy was dull and usually small in size.

Yet, advertising remained popular among businesses. The reason was simple: cities were growing. Consequently, proprietors realized that prospective customers were increasing in number every day; thus they had to be informed. Otherwise, advertising, if it had depended on the creativity of publishers, may have failed.

Advertising in the Penny Press

When Benjamin Day began the *New York Sun* in 1833, he not only revolutionized journalism but newspaper advertising as well. By the second year, the *Sun* was selling 20,000 copies, more than twice the number of any other newspaper in the United States. The large circulation made it a popular medium for advertisers.

Advertising in the *Sun* cost $30 a year for a "square" of ten lines a day. This equalled one cent a line. Day wrote most of the copy, which, in most cases, consisted of ten lines or less. The advertisements were similar to those in other newspapers, except for their size. Day realized the importance of the want ad, which had been used by advertisers in London. He solicited these small advertisements from businesses and readers and placed them under the heading "Wants." Each, two or three lines in length, cost 50¢. Day also published advertisements for theaters and museums as well as marriage and death notices.

As the number of advertisements increased, Day had to increase the *Sun's* page dimensions. By 1836 the size was 12 x 19. Advertising accounted for thirteen columns a day. In 1839, two years after Day sold the *Sun* to Moses Beach for $40,000, advertisements accounted for seventeen columns in the 24-column newspaper.

Penny journalism grew as the result of the *Sun's* success. In New York alone, thirty-five penny papers were started between 1834 and 1839. Not all survived. In 1835, James Gordon Bennett founded the *New York Herald*, which, like the *Sun*, presented news of every type. Eventually, the *Herald* surpassed the *Sun* in circulation, and Bennett was more creative than his rivals in dealing with advertisers. Most newspapers followed standard practices in regard to advertising. Like the *Sun* and the *New York Daily Advertiser*, the *Herald* catered to merchants and manufacturers by the kind of news stories printed. Advertising rates applied to a "square" of space — from $30 a year to 50¢ a day. These rates changed, however, as physical changes occurred in typography and size. Advertisements were separated by lines but contained no boldface headings. Bennett preferred lightface.

Most advertisements carried little, if any, illustrations. A few papers in Boston and Philadelphia were exceptions to the rule. Most advertisements were similar to want ads. They contained small first-line headlines, small amounts of copy, and thumbnail cuts of houses, hats, ships, and other illustrations that identified a certain kind of business.

In 1836, Bennett's *Herald* published a two-column advertisement for the American Museum that contained a two-column illustration. For several years after that, the *Herald* and other New York newspapers published two-column advertisements, some with illustrations. In the late 1840s, advertisers who placed small advertisements every day complained so much about the few advertisers who placed large display advertisements occasionally that the *Herald* finally banned all display. Consequently, the *Herald's* advertising columns looked the same, and advertising — at least, in the *Herald* and other New York newspapers — seemed to regress.

The Industrial Revolution that reshaped the United States in the nineteenth century produced dramatic changes in advertising. Newspaper advertisements frequently were intended as much for personal as for business purposes. Before the 1830s, the United States had few industries. Agriculture provided unprocessed food, and a slow craft system and foreign sources supplied the clothing, furniture, and other hard goods necessary to society. Power came from animals and water. The Industrial Revolution brought steam power and machines that could be connected to it to produce more goods — merchandise in search of a market. Advertising helped supply the market. With the spread of railroads and other forms of transportation and new manufacturing plants, newspaper advertising became important to these industries as well as to new small businesses. These forms of transportation also helped newspapers increase their circulations, thus encouraging a growth in advertising volume.

In addition, there was an influx of immigrants from Europe. Those who could read English read newspapers and magazines to learn about their new home and to obtain employment. While most immigrants moved into cities and became a part of urban society, others migrated west. Territorial expansion was rapid, and advertisers realized new markets.

In the 1850s, Robert Bonner, who had worked as a compositor on the *Hartford* (Conn.) *Courant*, purchased the *Merchants' Ledger*, a business sheet, and changed the name to the *New York Ledger*. He at first accepted no advertising. However, he made advertising history by publishing stories that appealed to women, which resulted in women becoming more interested in reading stories in newspapers and in advertisements directed to women. Bonner serviced advertising in another way, too, when he advertised his publication in other newspapers. He broke the barriers against display and soon made publishers of penny papers realize they had made a mistake, monetarily speaking, by restricting the format that advertisers were allowed to use. He experimented with copy and typography, which caused other publishers to do the same. His *New York Ledger*, which sold for 4¢, soon had a circulation of 400,000.

Bonner's advertisements in other newspapers were similar to those by auctioneers in London, who split their messages into separate announcements and ran ads of equal length down a column. Each ad began with the same two lines in capital letters. Like

THE NEW

WHOLE NO. 8180. MORNING

Robert Bonner

In the 1850s, Robert Bonner (inset) established a number of firsts in advertising. One of his accomplishments was to begin publishing stories in the *New York Ledger* that appealed to women, thereby creating a market for advertising of products of particular interest to them. When James Gordon Bennett banned display advertising from the *New York Herald*, Bonner got around the prohibition by printing small lines and repeating them endlessly, sometimes filling an entire page with the same message. These two columns in 1859 urged readers to buy Bonner's own *New York Ledger*. The reason for Bennett's ban was that he did not want small advertisers' messages to be lost among large ones.

the auctioneers in London, Bonner wrote his advertisement in the want-ad style, repeated it ninety-three times, and filled a column in the *New York Herald* in this manner:

> ORION, THE GOLD BEATER is the title of Cobb's sensation story in the *New York Ledger*.
> ORION, THE GOLD BEATER is the title of Cobb's sensation story in the *New York Ledger*.
> ORION, THE GOLD BEATER is the title of Cobb's sensation story in the *New York Ledger*.

It was difficult for any reader of the *Herald* to miss Bonner's advertisement.

Bonner soon went to two columns with reiteration, then to a full page. Some of his advertisements included the following line printed more than 600 times: "Don't go home to-night without the *New York Ledger*." He was the first advertiser to spend $27,000 a week. Only the patent medicine advertisers spent as much in a single year. Bonner's methods had an immediate effect on advertising. Although large bold display advertisements were not published by most newspapers until the late 1800s, most newspapers experimented with type faces and sizes.

In New York, after the Civil War, two large department stores — Macy's and Lord & Taylor — broke away from agate and column rules and moved to two-column advertisements. Lord & Taylor's ads contained announcements of specific products or groups of products. Its logo was usually the largest type — 30-point. The size was increased to 36-point in the 1870s. Lord & Taylor also broke up copy so that three or four ads could be printed one under the other in one column. Thus its logo was seen by the reader more than once. Other advertisers, such as John Wanamaker in Philadelphia, copied this style.

Not every merchant, however, wanted to advertise, as Daniel Frohman, a young advertising solicitor, realized. In 1869, in a brochure titled *Hints to Advertisers*, he discussed the average merchant's attitude toward advertising:

> The man who doesn't believe in advertising is constantly doing what he deprecates. He hangs costs outside of the door, or puts dry goods in his window — that's advertising. He sends out drummers through the country, or puts his name on his wagon — that's advertising. He labels the articles of his manufacture — that's advertising. If he has lost his cow, he puts a written notice at the post office, or tells his sister-in-law about it — that's advertising. He has his name put up in gilt letters over his door — what is that but advertising?... A man can't do business without advertising; and the question is whether to call to his aid the engine of the world — the printing press ... or to go back to the days when newspapers, telegraphs and railroads were unknown.[2]

[2]Quoted in Frank Presbrey, *The History and Devlopment of Advertising* (Garden City, N.Y., 1929), 255-6.

Frohman also noted that newspaper reporters as well as novelists were writing advertising copy and that there were two schools of writing. One school produced flowery language; the second produced advertising copy that was interspersed with news copy. Patent medicine advertisers employed the second form, particularly when they advertised in rural newspapers. Some advertisers also used jingles and teaser copy to arouse readers' curiosity.

Magazine Advertising

The first ad to appear in an American magazine was a reading notice about a ferry. Dated May 10, 1741, it ran under the heading "Advertisement" in Benjamin Franklin's *General Magazine*.

Magazines, however, lived only briefly in the 1700s. Many merchants refused to place advertisements in them. No merchant wished to advertise in a magazine that had financial problems, and without advertising most magazines had financial problems. Would-be advertisers wondered: Would the printer be paid? Would the merchant's advertisement appear? Or would the magazine die as a result of too few readers or too few advertisers?

In the 1800s, in order to attract advertisers, magazine publishers allowed advertisements to appear on the covers. Special sections of four to eight pages catering to advertisers were common. These sections allowed numerous businesses to advertise products and services in copy-filled blocks. Display was seldom used.

Many magazine publishers refused to carry advertising because they believed doing so was demeaning and lowered their magazines' value. The only advertising appearing on the pages of *Harper's Weekly* was for the company's forthcoming books. In the mid-1800s, however, several of the most popular magazines began running advertising for the first time. The *Atlantic Monthly* had fourteen pages of advertising in its December 1865 issue. The *American Whig Review*, in an attempt to stay afloat, carried advertising in its last year of publication.

Women's periodicals such as *Godey's Lady's Book*, *Peterson's*, and *Ladies' Wreath* carried advertising of numerous products and services — from musical instruments, sewing machines, and silverware to schools. These advertisements contained copy and some illustrations. *Frank Leslie's Illustrated Newspaper*, a weekly periodical, published a full-page advertisement of Mason & Hamlin musical instruments on October 20, 1860. The advertisement contained eleven illustrations, which was unusual. Most advertisements contained one or two.

Many magazines depended on patent medicine advertising. Typical was this ad in the August 2, 1862, issue of *Vanity Fair*:

> To Soldiers, Sailors, and the Public
> THE PREVAILING DIFFICULTY
> a general lassitude seizes the frame,
> which often resembles the torpor preceding death....
> Now whether this be in
> THE NORTH OR THE SOUTH

Frank Leslie's Illustrated Ads
Magazine advertising in the mid-1800s began to carry illustrations of products. In the October 20, 1860, issue of *Frank Leslie's Illustrated Newspaper* appeared this full-page ad for Mason & Hamlin musical instruments.

> the remedy is the same.
> Take at once six or eight of Brandreth's Pills....[3]

As a result of such advertising, journalists criticized the industry. One of them, Frank Leslie, wrote:

> The art of advertising is one of the arts most studied by our literary vendors of fancy soaps, philanthropic corn doctors, humanitarian pill-makers, and all the industrious professions which have an intense feeling for one's pockets. Every trick that can be resorted to for the purpose of inducing one to read an advertisement is practiced, and, it must be confessed, very often with complete success....[4]

Such tricks were used primarily because newspapers refused to accept display ads. Magazines, however, preferred full-, half-, or quarter-page display ads from large advertisers. Profits, after all, were greater from these than from the small copy-filled ads.

After the Civil War advertising in magazines became popular. Circulations increased as more Americans learned to read. *Scribner's*, which enjoyed a large circulation, was one of the first magazines to attract numerous advertisers. The December 1880 issue contained forty-nine pages of advertising. *Galaxy* was the first high-class magazine to run a variety of miscellaneous ads in color. From 1868 to 1870, it used colored inserts — one of the main reasons it had at least twenty-four pages of advertising a month.

Magazine advertising increased until 1873. In that year, businesses saw profits decrease because of a depressed economy and, consequently, for the next several years withheld advertisements. Magazine publishers tempted advertisers with various offers. Many of their offers, however, went unnoticed; and their magazines died.

Advertisements contained brief but bold captions, bold logos, copy in various sizes and typefaces, and one or more illustrations, depending on the sizes of the ads.

Advertising rates in the late 1800s reflected circulations. In 1865, the *Saturday Evening Post*, which had a circulation of 20,000, charged 30¢ an agate line. In 1885, it charged 25¢ an agate line; yet it had a circulation of 40,000. The explanation for the apparent paradox is that as circulations increased, the cost of advertising decreased. This was the case for such periodicals as the *Spirit of the Times*, *Harper's Monthly*, *Century Magazine*, *Ladies' Home Journal*, and *Godey's Lady's Book*.

By the beginning of the 1890s, new industries had been founded and old industries had grown. Businesses realized that magazines were reaching more consumers, especially in December, and consequently placed more advertising. Advertising rates in some magazines were expensive. *Harper's* charged $250 for a full-page advertisement, while the *Ladies' Home Journal* charged more than $2,000. As the century ended, magazines accounted for about one-fourth of the dollars businesses spent on advertising. One reason for this growth was national advertising by manufacturers such as W.L. Douglas, Lydia Pinkham, and Royal Baking Powder. Among the firms with large advertising expenditures were ones such as Warner's Celebrated Coraline Corsets, Plymouth Rock $3 Pants, and Cluett Shirts and Collars. Agencies for many of these firms used pictures in advertisements to illustrate the benefits of the product.

Other big advertisers included manufacturers of pianos and other instruments, housewares, appliances, bicycles, cameras, breakfast foods, phonographs, soaps, safety razors, and medicine, to name a few. Some companies became famous as a result of their advertising. Consumers remembered Pears' after reading its slogan: "Good morning, have you used Pears' Soap?" Procter & Gamble's Ivory Soap was remembered, too, because it was "99 44/100 per cent pure."

Although many magazines advertised practically anything and

[3]*Vanity Fair*, 2 August 1862.
[4]*Frank Leslie's Illustrated Newspaper*, 3 October 1857.

"He Stole from My Bodice a Rose"
Magazine circulations increased so substantially in the latter decades of the 1800s that publications such as *Godey's Lady's Book* became important vehicles for advertising. Many ads, such as this one for a patent medicine, combined interesting text with appealing illustrations intended to grab readers' attention.

everything during the late 1800s, some publishers protected their readers by not running fraudulent advertisements. Fake remedies were especially troublesome. However, even the most reputable magazines ignored other complaints, including those about the use of pictures of women to sell corsets and underwear, which was considered taboo.

How P.T. Barnum Changed Advertising

Phineas Taylor Barnum learned to advertise early in life. Before he was twenty he created advertisements for lottery tickets. They consisted of handbills, circulars, gold signs, and colored posters. When he was twenty-one, he edited and published *The Herald of Freedom* at Danbury, Connecticut, and claimed that a church deacon had "been guilty of taking usury of an orphan boy." Barnum was jailed for the libel — and, in true promotional style, he used the occasion to his advantage. When released, he rode in a parade, preceded by a brass band and forty horsemen and followed by carriages filled with friends and supporters. Of course, the press gave much attention to the event.

Three years later he and his wife moved to New York, where he learned about Joice Heth, an African American who, supposedly, had been the slave of George Washington's father. She was, she said, 161 years of age. Barnum purchased her for $1,000. Through handbills, posters, and newspaper advertisements, the public learned that she was the first to clothe young George. Within the first week of her appearance Barnum earned a profit. After New York, Barnum took Heth to other cities.

To sell Heth's appearances he placed informative advertisements in newspapers and mailed anonymous letters to editors denouncing her credibility. Income increased until her death a few months later. Barnum claimed that he learned only after her death that she had been about eighty years old. He, like the public, had been deceived.

In 1841 — after several years of earning a meager living and supporting a family of four through such jobs as writing advertisements for the Bowery Amphitheater for $4 a week — Barnum acquired Sudder's American Museum. Filled with natural and unnatural curiosities, the museum brought Barnum fame and fortune. He entertained the public with educated dogs, industrious fleas, jugglers, ventriloquists, giants, dwarfs, mechanical figures, and American Indians. More importantly, he knew how to advertise the museum. He placed newspaper ads to announce acts. Sometimes the ads had qualities of incantations, as illustrated by the following one:

VISION OF THE HOURIS
VISION OF THE HOURIS
VISION OF THE HOURIS
A Tableau of 850 Men
Women and Children
CLAD IN SUITS OF SILVER ARMOUR
CLAD IN SUITS OF SILVER ARMOUR
CLAD IN SUITS OF SILVER ARMOUR[5]

Other advertisements appeared in other forms. A brass band, which could be heard for several blocks, played on the balcony of the museum. Barnum placed gas lights, which had the effect of modern electronic spectaculars, on top of the museum, where they illuminated lower Broadway. He had large paintings of rare animals made in panels and placed on the outside of the museum. Banners announcing a rare find were strung across streets. Barnum also used handbills, as well as the reliable news-column, which he had perfected. "I thoroughly understood the art of advertising," he later wrote, "not merely by means of printers' ink, which I have always used freely, and to which I confess myself so much indebted for my success, but by turning every possible cir-

[5]In E.S. Turner, *The Shocking History of Advertising* (New York, 1953), 130.

Barnum's Jumbo
One of P.T. Barnum's great promotional gimmicks was an elephant he claimed to be the largest in the world and which he named "Jumbo." This cartoon by Thomas Nast, titled "Mutual Admiration," has Barnum telling Jumbo, "You are a HUMBUG after my own heart. You have even beat me in advertising."

cumstance to my account. It was my monomania to make the Museum the town wonder and town talk. I often seized upon an opportunity by instinct, even before I had a very definite conception as to how it should be used, and it seemed, somehow, to mature itself and serve my purpose."[6]

When ordinary forms of advertising failed, Barnum improvised. For instance, he instructed a man to place bricks on the corners of several streets and then to carry at least one brick to each corner and exchange it for the other. The man was not to comment to anyone. On the hour, he was to go to the museum and present a ticket, then enter. Within the first hour, approximately 500 bystanders stood and watched, trying to solve the mystery. When the man went to the museum, the crowd followed and purchased tickets, hoping to learn the answer inside. Barnum's walking advertisement attracted so many people that after a few days the police asked Barnum to withdraw the man from the street. Newspapers played up the event for several weeks.

Another example of improvisation was his invention of "Dr. Griffin" and his preserved mermaid. ("Dr. Griffin" was actually Levi Lyman, an associate of Barnum's.) To promote the mermaid to the public, Barnum placed stories in numerous newspapers. They said Dr. Griffin had purchased the mermaid in China for the Lyceum of Natural History in London but would be exhibiting it at Concert Hall for one week. A week later Barnum announced that he had secured the rare specimen for the American Museum. When the museum displayed the mermaid, the exhibition was a huge success.

Barnum also put on baby shows, baby contests, and beauty contests to arouse the public's curiosity. He was probably the first in the United States to use these shows and contests to attract attention. He was responsible for implementing the first successful advertising campaigns primarily because he realized that they increased sales.

"Tom Thumb"

Charles Stratton, a midget, was born in Connecticut. When he was five, his parents signed an agreement with Barnum that allowed Barnum to exploit the child. Of course, the parents could accompany their son and would get paid.

In order to sell "Tom Thumb," Barnum had him tour the United States. He advertised "Tom Thumb's" age as eleven instead of five and his place of birth as England instead of Connecticut. He had Tom introduced to prominent families, which was mentioned in ads. He printed biographies as well as lithographs and distributed them wherever Tom toured. Newspaper editors published stories about him, which sparked additional interest. When he appeared at the American Museum, most of the public had read about him and desired to see him. Barnum introduced him as "General Tom Thumb freshly arrived from England," and the crowds laughed. In the thirteen months he was at the American Museum, almost 100,000 persons paid to see him.

Barnum applied reverse psychology in his advertising. Before the General appeared anywhere, Barnum had an announcement posted. He directed the public not to get excited but to keep quiet. He perfected those techniques during a tour of Europe that lasted three years. In England and on the Continent, Barnum and the General entertained royalty, including Queen Victoria. Dressed like Napoleon, Tom made an unforgettable impression on the noble class. He and Barnum were invited to palaces, estates, and chateaus. Of course, news stories featured these exploits primarily because readers desired to learn about society's elite. In Paris the General was so popular that a cafe was named "Tom Ponce." Artists begged him to sit for them. Composers wrote songs about him. Shop windows had statuettes of him. After Paris, he and Barnum toured southern France, Spain, Belgium, and other countries. General Tom Thumb was greeted with the same enthusiasm wherever he toured. During the three years in Europe, approximately 5,000,000 people paid to see him. The tour's profits were more than $1,000,000; Tom's share was half. He and Barnum remained friends for life.

Jenny Lind

Jenny Lind, the "Swedish Nightingale," was the most famous performer in Europe in the 1800s. Barnum offered her $1,000 per

[6]P.T. Barnum, *Barnum's Own Story: The Autobiography of P.T. Barnum* (New York, 1961), 102.

Barnum's Stars

During his day, Tom Thumb was the most popular star in the world. England's Queen Victoria invited him and P. T. Barnum to visit her palace, and she took him by the hand and showed him around her art gallery. He told her, in his high treble voice, that the gallery was "first rate," one of his favorite expressions. He sang and danced for members of the royal court for an hour, at the end of which Victoria invited him to return at a time when the Prince of Wales might meet him. Jenny Lind, already a famous European soprano singer called the "Swedish Nightingale," was contracted by Barnum in 1850 to tour the United States. He – like most Americans – had never heard her sing, but he believed he could promote her well enough to take a chance. The tour saw concert halls packed at every engagement.

concert, plus expenses, for touring America. She accepted with stipulations. Barnum had to assure her that he would pay for her conductor, composer, and pianist, as well as a sixty-member orchestra. He also had to deposit in a London bank $187,500 before she left Europe.

When Barnum realized that most Americans had never heard of Jenny Lind, he used press releases to publicize her. He then distributed an authorized biographical pamphlet and photograph that informed readers of her inimitable talent.

Before Lind left for the United States, she gave, at Barnum's request, two concerts in Liverpool. Both sold out. A London critic wrote a review praising her performances. Barnum was able to get the review published in newspapers throughout America before she arrived.

When Lind's ship docked in New York harbor on Sunday, September 1, 1850, Barnum, accompanied by a reporter from the *New York Tribune*, and about 40,000 persons greeted it. The crowd followed her and her entourage as they traveled in Barnum's carriage to the Irving House Hotel.

Barnum then promoted the Great Jenny Lind Opening Concert Ticket Auction. He persuaded his friend John Genin to be the first person in America to purchase a ticket to hear Lind sing. Barnum then visited Dr. Brandreth, who was known for his patent medicines, and persuaded him to buy the first ticket at auction. Barnum assured him that it would be an excellent opportunity to advertise his medicines. Several thousand attended the auction to bid against one another, including Genin's bookkeeper and Dr. Brandreth's cashier. The publicity was so encouraging that Barnum repeated the auction in several cities.

The tour covered fifteen cities in the United States and Havana, Cuba. Reviews of Lind's performances were filled with superlatives; some critics claimed she was the greatest singer they had heard. Barnum was ecstatic. Lind gave ninety-five concerts.

In June 1851, however, she informed Barnum she was ending the tour. She tried to go it alone but was not successful. Organizing the advertising was too much for her. In May 1852, she performed her last American concert where she had performed her first, except this time the Castle Garden was half empty.

The campaign for Jenny Lind was characteristic of Barnum's brilliance. Because of his imagination and energy, Barnum influenced these advertising techniques: (1) keeping one's name or business before the public; (2) using unique or original devices to produce conversation as well as attention; (3) taking advantage of every opportunity to bring about editorial comment or news; and, of course, (4) providing more real value than one's competition. Like advertisers today, Barnum advertised primarily to generate interest and consequently income.

The Birth of the Advertising Agency

The advertising agency in America developed in the 1800s, in a time of quacks and promotional geniuses like P.T. Barnum. Before the country's first major multi-service agency, N.W. Ayer & Son, was founded in Philadelphia in 1868, ad agencies had passed through four stages.[7] The earliest agencies represented newspaper publishers, serving mostly as wholesalers of newspaper space. Orlando Bourne was acting as an agent as early as 1828. The pioneers, however, were Volney B. Palmer, who by 1846 had offices in Boston, New York, Baltimore, and Philadelphia, and John L. Hooper, who worked in New York. Whereas most agencies worked for one or a few newspapers, Palmer and Hooper represented several. In addition, they promoted advertising as an integral part of marketing and produced as well as delivered ads to publishers. Palmer was particularly active in those techniques.

[7]For a detailed discussion of these stages, see Ralph M. Hower, *The History of an Advertising Agency* (Cambridge, Mass., 1949), 13-9.

Promoting Modern Conveniences
By the mid-1800s, advertising was seen as an integral part of the process of marketing products, and modern conveniences became increasingly popular. Magazine advertising, like this ad for a new washing machine with two cylinders, emphasized explanatory text and frequently included illustrations.

The second stage in the development of agencies occurred in the 1850s when agents became independent. Space-jobbing, as this stage was called, became popular as agents realized they could earn more by selling space to advertisers. When advertisers purchased space, the agents would buy it for them in newspapers. This stage caused many agents to question their role. After all, they did not work for publishers, and they did not work for advertisers. Yet, they referred to themselves as agents.

The third stage developed out of the second when George P. Rowell purchased large amounts of space in newspapers and then resold it in small amounts to advertisers. This stage, which has been called space-wholesaling, began in 1865.

The fourth stage was based on Rowell's idea and appeared in the late 1860s. Marked by the advertising concession agency, this stage occurred when Carlton & Smith (later the J. Walter Thompson Company) purchased most — if not all — of the advertising space in certain publications for a specified period of time. Consequently, the agency — not the publisher — was responsible for securing advertisers for the entire publication. This practice actually closed the gap between agent and publisher, but the agent worked as an independent middleman nonetheless.

Volney B. Palmer

Volney Palmer, who had worked in real estate, started advertising his business in 1842 in *M'Elroy's Philadelphia Directory*. One of his early ads read:

> V.B. Palmer's
> REAL ESTATE AND COAL OFFICE
> No. 104 South Third Street (a few doors below the Exchange) Philadelphia
> Agency for the Purchase and Sale of Houses and Lots, Farms, Farming, Timber and Coal Lands, Bonds and Mortgages, Ground Rents, Anthracite Coal, &c. ADVERTISEMENTS and Subscriptions received from some of the best and most widely circulated newspapers in Pennsylvania and New Jersey, and in many of the principal cities and towns throughout the United States, for which he has the agency, affording an excellent opportunity for Merchants, Mechanics, Professional Men, Hotel and Boarding House Keepers, Railroad, Insurance and Transportation Companies, and the enterprising portion of the community generally, to publish extensively abroad their respective pursuits — to learn the terms of subscription and advertising, and accomplish their object here without the trouble of perplexing and fruitless inquiries, the expense and labor of letter writing; the risk of making enclosures of money &c, &c.[8]

Palmer remained in real estate for the next several years, even though his advertising interests were fruitful. In 1849 he used "Advertising Agency" in an advertisement for the first time. Advertisers would have Palmer place their ads in selected newspapers. After assuring that an ad had been printed, he then billed the advertiser and paid the publisher. He claimed to be the sole representative of 1,300 newspapers, thus allowing merchants to be selective about where they advertised. He also created speculative presentations for prospective advertisers.

Of course, advertisers had to pay the total cost for Palmer's services, not just the space rates for each newspaper selected. Palmer received a 25% commission from the publisher upon payment. The 25% commission rate remained standard among agents into the 1860s. Increasing competition among agents, however, allowed advertisers, who frequently ran three or more campaigns a year, to seek the lowest bid on each campaign. Some agents responded by haranguing publishers for lower and lower rates and cheating on the number of times an ad was published or on the number of newspapers in which it was run. The commission sys-

[8] *M'Elroy's Philadelphia Directory* (1842), 1.

tem is still used today, except agencies normally receive 15%, not 25%.

Palmer provided a number of other services. According to his *Almanac* of 1850,

> • he is Agent for the best papers of every section of the whole country.
> • he is empowered by the proprietors to make contracts and give receipts.
> • his long experience and practical knowledge qualify him to give valuable information.
> • the same prices only are charged to advertisers as are exacted by his principals, the publishers.
> • a selection can be made suitably adapted to the various pursuits of advertisers.
> • a complete system of advertising can be adapted upon either a large or small scale.
> • the papers are on file at the Agency, where advertisers can examine them, see the terms, and obtain all requisite information to enable them to advertise judiciously, effectively and safely.[9]

The list of services made it clear that Palmer's agency did more for advertisers than most other agencies.

Both publishers and advertisers were delighted to use his agency. He promoted his services by using endorsements from publishers. By the mid-1850s, with numerous clients considering him a godsend, his agency grew. He opened offices in four major cities. He maintained the office in Philadelphia and hired others to manage the other three. He visited the other offices at various times throughout each year.

In the late 1850s, John E. Joy, W.W. Sharpe, and J.E. Coe became partners. When Palmer retired, in either 1862 or 1863, Joy and Coe operated the Philadelphia and the New York offices. Sharpe eventually purchased the latter office. S.R. Niles controlled the Boston office.

Palmer died in 1864 at the age of sixty-five. Perhaps no other agent did more for advertising than Palmer. Not only did he help advertisers; but he also helped newspaper publishers. Indeed, he sold the idea of advertising to advertisers and consequently made hundreds of proprietors realize how important a role advertising played in a capitalistic society.

George P. Rowell

George P. Rowell and his partner Horace Dodd founded an advertising agency in Boston in 1865. Like Palmer, they made up a list of newspapers for advertisers to consider. Unlike Palmer, they persuaded some publishers to give them an additional discount based on continued patronage. They received an additional 3% if they paid in cash within thirty days. They did not have to pay more than 25% of the card (that is, the advertised) rate for most of the newspapers they handled. Rowell was responsible for the cash discount in addition to the commission.

George P. Rowell
Although Rowell is best remembered as founder of the first trade journal of advertising, *Printer's Ink*, he also brought legitimacy, stability, and other needed improvements to the advertising agency system. After starting his own agency in 1865, he established the practice of guaranteeing newspapers payments for ads himself (rather than waiting until his own clients paid him). He also began the practice of buying space annually rather than on an ad hoc basis. In 1869 he produced *Rowell's American Newspaper Directory*, the first complete list of newspapers throughout the country and their circulation figures.

He was also responsible for buying space in bulk and selling it to advertisers. He used the system first with newspapers in New England, and then he instituted it in other regions when the George P. Rowell & Co. agency opened its headquarters in New York in 1867. His early success was based on his novel "select list" of newspapers, most of them weeklies, in which he would guarantee the publisher a column of advertising each issue for an entire year. To get this guarantee, publishers gave Rowell such discounts on the regular rates that he could sell a one-inch advertise-

[9]V.B. Palmer's *Business-Men's Almanac* (New York, 1850).

ment four times in 100 papers for $100 and still clear 25% to 40% or more. Rowell was not the first to offer select lists, but he was the first to require that advertisers take the entire list. The select list required that he take a risk — he had to fill those yawning columns of space with ads or suffer financial loss, but the profits made the risk worthwhile.[10]

Rowell tried to assure that circulation figures claimed by publishers were accurate. As he candidly pointed out in an agency flier,

> In fixing the value of advertising space in any particular journal, the first question to be considered is the number of copies issued; next the character or quality of the circulation. A well-printed paper is worth more than one badly printed; an influential journal carries more weight than one without reputation. So also a paper which habitually charges high prices for its advertising thereby makes its columns exclusive, and will have fewer, and as a rule, a better class of advertisements, and is worth something more on that account. The value of all these considerations is recognized, but exactly *how* much each one is to be considered becomes a question of judgment.[11]

Rowell realized that if his agency could supply advertisers with accurate information about newspapers and their readers, then advertisers would know how much to pay for the space they purchased. As Rowell pointed out, that was one purpose of his agency.

In 1869, as a service to all who were interested in advertising, his agency published the first issue of *Rowell's American Newspaper Directory*, which listed circulations of more than 5,000 publications in the United States and more than 300 in Canada. Although Rowell had tried to eliminate the so-called private list — a list containing inflated circulation figures created by the publisher — other agents criticized him for making available at a nominal cost more information than they offered. Publishers criticized him for printing conservative circulation figures. They accepted advertising from his agency nonetheless. As a result of his publication, publishers eventually changed their circulation claims to reflect accurate figures.

Rowell was responsible for the *American Newspaper Reporter*, a house organ published for the purpose of informing advertisers and publishers about advertising and how to do it. In the November 20, 1871, issue, he wrote about "The Principles of Advertising":

> Honesty is by all odds the very strongest point which can be crowded into an advertisement. Come right down with the facts, boldly, firmly, unflinchingly. Say directly what it is, what it has done, what it will do.... Do not claim too much, but what you do claim must be claimed without the smallest shadow of weakness.... Say flatly "the best," or say nothing. Do not refer to rivals. Ignore every person, place or thing except yourself, your address and your article.... Be serious and dignified, but active and lively. Leave wit, however good it may be, entirely aside.[12]

Rowell realized that advertising copy, which suffered from too many words and overstatement, needed improving. He also realized that every advertisement — even small ones — had to attract attention. Rowell's house organ became *Printers' Ink* in 1888. By then it had become famous as an instrument in improving advertising. Rowell retired in 1905.

N.W. Ayer & Son

Francis Wayland Ayer, who was born in 1848, was influenced by the changes occurring in agencies and by his father, Nathan Wheeler Ayer. A graduate of Brown University, N.W. Ayer named his son after Dr. Francis Wayland, one of Brown's presidents. N.W. Ayer, a devout Baptist, practiced law for several years in Massachusetts, taught in Massachusetts and New York, then purchased a seminary in Philadelphia in 1867. He was not successful financially, earning only a modest living until he suffered from ill health.

Francis Wayland Ayer learned from his parents, particularly his father, the basic principles that helped him throughout his life. He knew what responsibility, integrity, and honesty meant. His value system was never questioned. When he was fourteen, he taught in a country school in New York State. A year later he was offered a position in a village school. For the next several years one promotion followed another. He desired to go to college, however, and in 1867 he attended the University of Rochester. Within a year he had spent his savings. His father, who was barely earning an income, was unable to help. F.W. Ayer left the university in search of a job. The publisher of the *National Baptist*, a weekly religious newspaper, hired him to solicit advertisements. Ayer earned $1,200 in commissions in less than a year. His employer offered him $2,000 a year to stay with the firm. Ayer refused the opportunity, certain he could earn more on his own. He persuaded his father to work with him, and on April 1, 1869, he opened his agency, N.W. Ayer & Son. The agency bore the name of his father for several reasons. He not only admired his father, but he also preferred using the combined name of father and son. It sounded more impressive than one name alone, he thought, and his father already had agreed to join him.

The Ayer agency began with eleven religious newspapers. Like other agents of his day, Ayer solicited advertisements from merchants and then placed them in the publications listed with his agency. He also purchased the total advertising space in certain publications and then resold it in parcels to advertisers. Thus he acted as a manager of advertising departments of some publica-

[10]George P. Rowell, *Forty Years an Advertising Agent, 1865-1905* (New York, 1906). Rowell had some flexibility. He guaranteed to send a group of ads every month and always provide at least one-quarter of a column and never more than two columns without the publisher's consent. See "The List System," *American Newspaper Reporter* 7 (3 March 1873): 173-92. This is an advertisement for the list system, including sample contracts and advertisements. The *Reporter* was Rowell's house organ.

[11]Quoted in Presbrey, *The History and Development of Advertising*, 269.

[12]*American Newspaper Reporter*, 30 November 1871.

Francis W. Ayer
In 1869, at the age of twenty, Ayer began his advertising agency with about $250 from his father. Believing that combining his name with his father's would add a sense of stability to the agency, he thus came up with the name "N. W. Ayer & Son." His father, a devout Baptist and owner of a seminary, had taught him responsibility, integrity, and honesty. Applying these principles to the advertising business, Francis Ayer had made his agency the largest in the nation by the late 1880s.

tions. He also placed advertisements in publications that were not on his list. With those, he estimated how much the space would cost and then quoted a price to advertisers that was slightly higher than his estimated cost. He earned income the best way he knew: by selling and bargaining. There was little time for experimenting, especially during the agency's formative years. By the end of its first year, the agency represented several newspapers in addition to the original eleven. Growth continued, and in 1870 Ayer had to move to a larger office and hire his first employee, George O. Wallace, who was responsible for the bookkeeping.

Within two years, the agency had to move again. It was handling more than 300 publications located in twenty-seven of the thirty-seven states that made up the nation. In addition, it placed advertisements for clients in other publications through other agents.

In 1873, N.W. Ayer died. Since his mother did not have the experience or the interest to be a partner, Francis purchased his father's share of the business. He reasoned that his mother's absentee ownership would not be beneficial to the clients. The same year, as a result of growth, he asked Wallace to become a partner, and Wallace accepted the one-fourth interest in the firm.

Throughout the 1870s, the Ayer agency grew. In 1875, Ayer created a printing department so the agency could produce most of the advertisements in-house. Thus, by the following year, his agency could place advertisements in any newspaper published in the United States or Canada. This gave the agency an advantage over other agencies since most agencies hired independent printers to produce their advertisements.

In 1877, Ayer purchased Coe, Wetherill & Co., another agency in Philadelphia. Coe, Wetherill & Co. had succeeded Joy, Coe & Co., which had acquired Palmer's agency. Ayer's agency, like Rowell's, also published its own directory, *Ayer & Son's Manual for Advertisers*, to promote its list of publications and later *The Advertiser's Guide*, a quarterly magazine filled with informative features and promotional pieces on advertising.

Ayer followed the lead of other agencies and placed advertisements for patent medicine. Some of these included "Compound Oxygen," "Kennedy's Ivory Tooth Cement," "Rock & Rye," and "Dr. Case's Liver Remedy and Blood Purifier." Of course, Ayer represented other firms, too, including John Wanamaker, Montgomery Ward, Whitman's Chocolates, Blackwell's Durham smoking tobacco, and Singer sewing machines. He also represented manufacturers of farm machinery as well as educational institutions such as Harvard College.

It was during this time that Ayer analyzed Rowell's methods of handling publishers and clients and realized that Rowell had put himself in the middle. That is, he was being paid by the publisher, yet he was representing the advertiser. How could Rowell serve both? Ayer wondered. He decided to represent the advertiser. Unlike Rowell, he would inform an advertiser as to how much space cost. Furthermore, he would inform an advertiser what the agency received for its services. Instead of being merely a space-seller like other agencies, Ayer's agency would become a space-buyer and therefore be paid by the client. Ayer believed this plan was fair to the client and actually superior to Rowell's plan.

Ayer persuaded a longtime client to allow Ayer's agency to handle all of his advertising for an entire year. They agreed upon a 10% commission (a figure Ayer soon regretted and changed to 15% with other advertisers) with Ayer to charge the advertiser only what he himself was charged by publishers. This gave the advertiser the benefit of all discounts Ayer arranged. Ayer also chose the best newspapers in which to place the ad. Under the bid system, in contrast, each agent strived to use the cheapest papers rather than the best ones. If Ayer felt a publisher's space rates were too high, he had the right to change newspapers during the campaign. This prerogative kept the list "open," thus giving the practice the name "The Open Contract." This new way of doing business forced the agent to work for the advertiser. If the advertiser succeeded, he rewarded the agent by renewing the contract.

The Ayer open-contract-plus-commission plan was initiated in

1875. Through trial and error, Ayer learned how to earn a profit from his commission system. That was not as difficult as persuading advertisers to look at advertising from a different perspective. Indeed, the advertiser had to trust Ayer and vice versa. Ayer would buy space at the lowest possible cost for the advertiser. The advertiser would have access to Ayer's lists of rates. Thus the advertiser could determine the cost of advertising space in a specific publication and consequently the commission to the agency.

This system allowed Ayer to buy advertising space wisely as well as consider the advertiser's needs, which are hallmarks of modern agencies. The system, although sound, was not adopted by every agency, but it forced every agency to recognize that advertisers had interests that needed servicing and, to a certain extent, protecting.

In 1879, the Ayer agency started another service when it conducted a market survey of the nation to entice the Nichols-Shepard Company, which manufactured threshing machines, to advertise. The survey examined the production of grains by counties and states. The agency also included an in-depth advertising plan in its proposal to Nichols-Shepard. The resulting campaign was the first based on a market survey. The company hired Ayer as a result of the survey, and Ayer realized that this particular service could be performed for other advertisers.

In 1880, the agency focused on writing advertising copy in addition to printing advertisements. It explained to prospective clients:

> The Composition, Illustration and Display of Newspaper Advertisements has so long been a study with us that we have become admittedly expert in preparing the best possible effects.
>
> Having at command the services of an Artist, a Wood Engraver, and a number of Printers who have been for years engaged almost exclusively in this work under our direction, we possess entirely unequaled facilities for serving those who desire to entrust their business to our care.[13]

During the same year, the agency issued the *American Newspaper Annual*, which listed every newspaper and magazine published in the United States and Canada. This annual later became the *N.W. Ayer & Son's Directory of Newspapers and Periodicals*, which is still published as the *Gale Directory of Publications and Broadcast Media*. Revenue came from advertising that newspaper publishers placed in the annual.

In the late 1880s Ayer began to refuse advertising that would discredit the agency or would disappoint the advertiser. In 1887 he presented his agency's philosophy in a circular:

> *We do not wish* any advertising which cannot reasonably be expected *to pay the advertiser*.
>
> *We do not wish* any advertiser to deal with us unless it is to *his interest to do so*.
>
> *We always say just what we believe*, even though we have to advise a man not to spend any money in newspaper advertising.
>
> *We aim to give* as conscientious consideration to little as to larger matters. Small orders entrusted to us receive just as careful attention as the largest ones get.
>
> *We thoroughly believe in newspaper advertising*, and that there is more value in it than most people think. We therefore contend that the subject deserves an intelligent and unprejudiced consideration, to which should be applied as good business sense as any other matter of business commands.
>
> *We are not anxious* for any order with which there does not come the reasonable expectation, *first*, that the advertising will pay our customer; and *again*, that we can so handle the business as to convince him that his interests will be best served by entrusting to us all his future advertising orders.[14]

Most of the advertising the agency handled in the 1880s came from small businesses such as retail stores and from schools and colleges. With time, however, it added many large accounts, such as Hires' root beer, J.I. Case threshing machines, and Procter & Gamble soaps. In 1891, it added the N.K. Fairbanks soap company and Mellin's Baby Food. From 1894 to 1898, some clients were affected by the recession and consequently reduced their advertising budgets. When these businesses expanded in the late 1890s, so did Ayer. It started to handle advertising for Standard Oil and several of its subsidiaries. In 1899 it handled the major campaign that introduced the "Uneeda Biscuit," the first such product to be mass marketed in individual airtight packages. The campaign, which was for the National Biscuit Company and was the largest up to that time, included newspaper, magazine, and outdoor advertisements. The campaign was an overwhelming success. Consumers asked for the product by name.

Ayer realized that advertising specific brands was just as important as advertising new products. He made sure that businesses were aware of this principle as well. When in 1900 he conducted a massive campaign for the agency, he advertised in trade journals and other periodicals, informing businesses that his agency put this principle to practice.

The business that Ayer received from respectable clients made up for the loss he incurred when he stopped handling accounts for questionable products. In 1896 his agency dropped beer advertising. Three years later it halted whiskey advertising, and in the early 1900s it stopped patent medicine advertising.

By 1900 Ayer saw his agency, which was based on his character and innovative ideas, grow into the largest in the nation, with more than 160 employees.

13 Folder advertisement for N.W. Ayer & Son (April 1880).

14 "Our Creed." Folder advertisement for N.W. Ayer & Son (1887).

GUITAR-BANJO-MANDOLIN-VIOLIN

Self-Taught, without Notes, by Figure Music. Send stamp for Big Illustrated Catalogue of Self-Instructors and Instruments. We ship the first Instrument in each locality at a big discount, simply to advertise our goods and establish a trade. Address E. C. HOWE, 429 Bay State Building, CHICAGO.

When Writing Mention Chicago Sat. Blade.

WETO GRAPH

The Great Secret Writing System

FOR LOVERS AND OTHERS.

Every lover and everyone who writes letters should have a Weto Graph. It is a system of secret sign writing for correspondence, etc. If you have a Weto Graph you can preserve recipes, secret memorandum, addresses, or information you do not want anyone to find out. You can write to your friends on a postal and no one can find out what you have written. Lots of fun to have a Weto Graph. Don't miss it. Send 10 cents and we will send the Weto Graph by mail, with full instructions. Address,

PENN PUBLISHING CO., PARNASSUS, PA.

When Writing Mention Chicago Sat. Blade.

AGENTS WANTED

$8 TO $10 PER DAY at Fairs with FUTURESCOPE. Jonas N. Bell & Co., 586 W. Lake St., Chicago

When Writing Mention Chicago Sat. Blade.

GIRLS earn a handsome ring or camera selling our toothpowder. We trust you. N. IMPORTING CO., Box 204, Detroit, Mich

When Writing Mention Chicago Sat. Blade.

SEND $1.00 and I will send receipt whereby you make $12 to $28 on $1 invested. C. G. WHITE, 660 9th St., Oakland, California

When Writing Mention Chicago Sat. Blade.

SALESMEN to sell Perfumes, Toilet Soaps, etc., to dealers. $100 monthly and expenses; experience unnecessary. Plumer Perfumery Co., St. Louis, Mo

When Writing Mention Chicago Sat. Blade.

$75 Month and Expenses; no experience needed; position permanent; self-seller. Pease Mfg. Co., Stat'n O, Cincinnati, O.

When Writing Mention Chicago Sat. Blade.

DETECTIVE. Shrewd, reliable man wanted in each locality. Act under orders; no experience necessary; write

---

Newspaper Advertising, 1899

As the recession of the 1890s ended, advertising increased, and newspapers again experienced the prosperity that came with it. Typical advertising columns, as exemplified by this 1899 one from the *Chicago Blade*, retained some of the characteristics that earlier newspapers had exhibited, but a stronger emphasis on graphics was evident.

Patent Medicine Advertising

Before 1900, several kinds of questionable advertising appeared in newspapers and magazines. The two worst offenders were patent medicine advertising and abortion advertising.

Colonial Americans depended on homemade remedies to cure illnesses. Usually, the formulas were passed from one generation to another. Colonists who lived in towns could visit physicians who would charge them for their herbal remedies. However, many colonists could not afford physicians. As an alternative they could purchase patent medicines which, in most cases, caused drunkenness and nothing else.

Patent medicine advertising appeared in newspapers during the 1700s and 1800s partly because it paid the bills. Many newspapers would have died after a few issues had it not been for such advertising.

A number of advances in medicine were made during the colonial period. The most dramatic was the use of inoculation against smallpox. After the Rev. Cotton Mather had advocated the practice, Boston newspapers initiated a heated debate in the 1720s. Despite the vituperative attacks in the *New-England Courant*, inoculation eventually gained general acceptance. In newspaper advertisements, however, makers of patent medicines continued to make exhorbitant claims. Their products could cure, they said, not only minor ailments such as common colds but also noxious ones, including smallpox. Most of the advertisements were straightforward. By 1736, creativity had replaced the straightforward style in copy. The following advertisement for Dr. Bateman's Pectoral Drops was typical. It appeared in the *Pennsylvania Gazette* on July 1, 1736:

> Dr. Bateman's PECTORAL DROPS, which are given with such great Success in all Fluxes, Spitting of Blood, Consumptions, Small Pox, Measles, Colds, Coughs, and Pains in the Limbs or Joints; they cure Agues, and the most violent Fever in the World, if taken in Time, and give present Ease in the most racking Torment of the Gout; the same in all sorts of Pains (be they ever so violent) they give Ease in a few Minutes after taken; they ease After-Pains, prevent Miscarriages, and are wonderful in the Stone and Gravel in the Kidneys, Bladder and Ureters; bringing away Slime, Gravel, and oftentimes Stones of a great bigness, and are the best of Medicines for all Stoppages or Pains in the Stomach, Shortness of Breath, and Straitness of the Breast, re-enkindling the almost extinguish'd natural Heat in diseas'd Bodies, by which Means they restore the languishing to perfect Health: Their manner of working is by moderate Sweat and Urine. For Children's Distempers, no Medicine yet discover'd can compare with it: For it cures the Gripes in their Stomach and Bowels, by expelling Wind upwards and downwards. It causes weak and forward Children to take their natural Rest. It is taken with great Success in the Rickets, and, in a Word, it hath restored Hundreds of poor Infants to their strength and liveli-

HOW A LIFE
WAS SAVED.

THE LIFE OF
Chas. S. Prentice
SAVED
BY THE USE OF
WARNER'S
SAFE
KIDNEY and LIVER
CURE.

The following letter proves that BRIGHT'S DISEASE, in its worst form, IS CURABLE:

TOLEDO, O., Sept. 25, 1879.

Messrs. H. H. WARNER & Co., Rochester, N. Y.—Gentlemen: Having escaped death from Bright's disease by the use of your Remedy, I feel it a duty not only to acknowledge my gratitude to you personally, but also to bring my case before the public, and have those who are suffering similarly to judge whether a medicine not prepared by the "regulars" will cure this frightful malady or not.

In the summer of 1872 I was first taken ill with symptoms which, I was informed, were those of

Patent Medicine Advertising, Late 1800s

ness, that have been reduced to meer Skeletons.

Sold by *Miles Strickland* in *Market-Street, Philadelphia*, price 3 s. a Bottle, with Directions.

This remedy, according to the advertising, cured more than thirty illnesses, diseases, or abnormalities. Only three shillings (36¢) a bottle, the product sold well throughout the century. Other imported patent medicines were also advertised throughout the colonies; and most, like Dr. Bateman's Pectoral Drops, offered the consumer relief from practically any illness or disease.

As newspapers increased in size and in number of pages, they carried more medicine advertising. Some advertisers pointed out that their concoctions were sanctioned by royalty. In the February 19, 1770, issue of the *Boston Chronicle*, the London Book-Store of Boston advertised the "Essence of Pepper-Mint, by his Majesty's Royal Letters Patent."[15] The product sold for one shilling four pence. In return, the consumer received "speedy relief" from colic, gout, and other illnesses.

During and after the Revolutionary War, advertisements for imported medicines were curtailed, yet Americans realized that the need for medicines was great. Consequently, they started producing medicines domestically. Lists of medicines sold at apothecaries were advertised weekly in newspapers. Physicians also served as dentists, veterinarians, druggists, and barbers, and often advertised their services and cure-all potions.

In the 1800s, patent medicine advertising occupied most of the space in numerous newspapers. Products such as Dr. Ryan's Incomparable Worm-Destroying Suger-Plums, Turlington's Balsam of Life, Godfrey's Cordial, Steer's Genuine Opodeldor, Stoughton's Bitters or Elixir, Antipertussis, Lockyer's Pills, James' Fever Powder, Dalbey's Carminative, and Anderson's Pills, just to name a few, were advertised from New England to Florida. Their sellers seemed to imply that certain names and labels could ward off illnesses even if the product could not.

Mineral waters, such as Dr. Willard's Mineral Water, Ballston or Congress Mineral Water, and Godwin's Celebrated German Water, were advertised like patent medicines: the copy was filled with outrageous claims. In a mineral water advertisement that appeared in the June 15, 1803, issue of the *New York Herald*, Dr. Willard claimed that the water from his mineral spring in Connecticut could cure such maladies as "Erisipelas, Salt Rheum, Leprous Affections, and indeed almost every cutaneous complaint," including cancer, gout, paralytic disorders, and other diseases.[16]

In the 1830s and 1840s, some patent medicines romanticized the American Indian through illustration, name, and advertising copy. Advertisements for Dr. Freeman's Indian Specific pointed out that the product was made from herbs that Indians used to cure consumption. Wright's Indian Vegetable Pills, which sold exceptionally well in the 1840s, were advertised as "THE ORIGINAL

[15] *Boston Chronicle*, 19 February 1770.
[16] *New York Herald*, 15 June 1803.

Lydia Pinkham

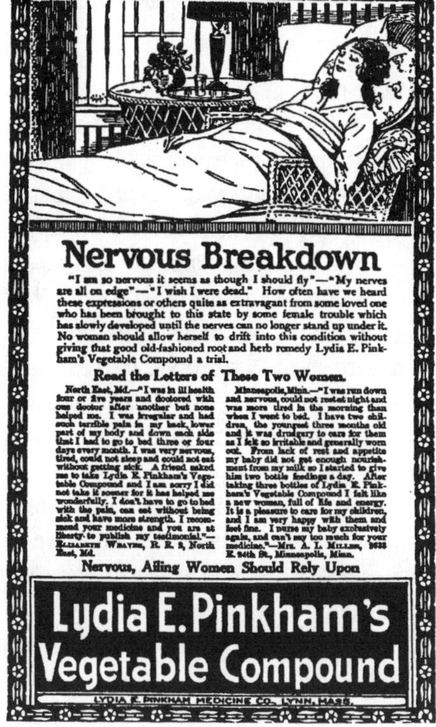

On this page are some of the ads for Lydia Pinkham's Vegetable Compound — although the banner spanning the Brooklyn Bridge (top) was only one dreamed of. The portrait of Mrs. Pinkham showing her in robust condition (bottom left), above the slogan "Yours for Health," was used even after her death.

Vegetable Compound Brings Fortune and Fame to Its Brewer

America's first successful businesswoman and perhaps first millionairess, Lydia E. Pinkham was one of the most widely known women of the nineteenth century. A devotee of natural foods, a worker for temperance, abolition, and woman's rights, she was, like many women, disenchanted with orthodox medicine that prescribed dangerous cathartic drugs and bleeding for most female ailments.

She concocted root and herb-based home remedies laced with a 20% alcohol preservative and at first gave away gallons to friends and neighbors. The dire financial straits inflicted on the nation by the Panic of 1873, however, forced her to begin selling her brew as "Lydia Pinkham's Vegetable Compound."

Sales soared after Dan Pinkham placed a $60 ad in the *Boston Herald*. The Pinkhams built a factory in Lynn, Massachusetts. They trumpeted the Compound's effectiveness for male as well as female ailments from kidney disease to uterine prolapse, and they got rich off the patent medicine.

Key elements in the ad campaign were the trademark countenance of the handsome 55-year-old grandmother, her advice service, and testimonial letters. Her *Guide for Women* was reprinted over the years in millions of copies. Originally a four-page folder describing in plain language women's physiology and its many potential disorders, by 1901 the booklet had sixty-two pages and was printed in five languages, with her image and her motto on the cover: "Yours for Health, Lydia E. Pinkham."

She died in 1883, but her Compound lived on, with users unaware of her death. In 1902 a muckraker tried exposing her in the *Ladies' Home Journal* by juxtaposing current letters, signed with her name, with a photograph of her tombstone. After a brief setback, the Compound doubled its sales within ten years and reached its all-time high in 1929. The company sold out to Cooper labs in 1968, sixty-two years after passage of the Pure Food and Drug Act.

Maureen J. Nemecek
Oklahoma State University

Advertising Posters
Advertising that took the form of posters had been used since the colonial period. In the late 1800s, following in the footsteps of city growth, posters became a popular medium for advertisers to use. Pasted to building walls along city streets, they attracted the attention of the thousands who passed by each day. This drawing is from an issue of *Frank Leslie's Illustrated Newspaper* of 1882.

AND ONLY GENUINE INDIAN MEDICINE."[17]

Makers of patent medicines soon realized that it was more profitable to manufacture and advertise several remedies for a variety of illnesses than to produce one remedy and advertise it as a cure-all. Dr. Bardwell had Aromatic Lozenges of Steel, Re-Animating Solar Tincture or Pabulum of Life, Genuine Ague and Fever Drops, and Annodyne Essence — all for different illnesses.

Some companies manufactured gadgets that were to be worn as a cure. Supposedly using electricity, these devices were said to restore the nervous system as well as cure all kinds of disease. Of course, the gadgets could cure nothing. Yet, like advertisements for patent medicines, the advertisements for these contraptions were filled with testimonies, superlatives, and claims of being "genuine," "original," or "nature's own."

By the end of the 1800s, the nation's households were filled with patent medicines and devices. They did not die until the early 1900s, when newspapers began receiving an adequate amount of advertising from other manufacturers and businesses. By then, muckraking journalists had begun discrediting the patent medicine industry and consequently encouraged lawmakers to enact legislation that would eliminate or at least restrict the cure-alls. As a result of the efforts of advertising professionals and the muckrakers, the Associated Advertising Clubs of America embarked on a "Truth-in-Advertising" crusade in 1911, which led to the establishment of today's better business bureaus. The federal government also joined the effort to clean up advertising. In 1914, Congress established the Federal Trade Commission (FTC), which exercises a measure of control over all advertising. Court decisions and later congressional additions gradually have enhanced the power of the FTC.

[17]Quoted in Cedric Larson, "Patent-Medicine Advertising and the Early American Press," *Journalism Quarterly* 19 (December 1937): 338.

Abortion Advertising

In the early 1800s, advertising for abortifacients and abortion appeared, although the word "abortion" was not used. Most of the advertisements for "female monthly regulating pills," for example, contained such words as "suppression," "irregularity," or "stoppage" in reference to menses.

Advertisements for "Madame Restell" (Anna Lohman), the most notorious of the abortionists, which appeared in newspapers in New York City, were carefully worded to guard against prosecution. Abortion was illegal. Thus, she was committed to secrecy for her clients, as the following advertisement indicated:

> MADAME RESTELL, FEMALE PHYSICIAN, residence 148 Greenwich Street, where she can be consulted with the strictest confidence on complaints incident to the female frame.[18]

In another advertisement, she hinted that pregnancy, if not desired, should not be tolerated. "Irregularity and suppression," the advertisement claimed, caused "violent and convulsive headaches, derangement of the stomach, gnawing in the side, burning in the chest, disturbed and feverish sleep, frightful dream, languor, debility, weakness, a most distressing lethargy." The ad claimed that certain women who become pregnant also suffered from depression and, as a result, contemplated suicide. The reader was reassured: "These dreadful and alarming symptoms and all others arising from female irregularity or suppression are removed in a few days by Mme. Restell."[19]

Madame Restell advertised her products and services differently from 1839 to 1846 in the *New York Herald* and the *New York Sun*. Some newspapers, such as Horace Greeley's *New York Tribune*, refused to run her ads. Nonetheless, her business prospered. She opened offices in Boston and Philadelphia and sold

[18]*New York Herald*, 15 July 1841.

NATIONAL POLICE GAZETTE.

NEW-YORK, SATURDAY, MARCH 13, 1847. FOUR CENTS A NUMBER.

"Madame Restell"
Anna Lohman became notorious for performing abortions under the name "Madame Restell." She built her trade through advertising that thinly veiled her practice, and police finally arrested her.

abortifacients through seven franchises in three cities.

Another advertiser, Catherine Costello, copied Madame Restell. Identifying herself as a "female physician," she advertised pills, her services, and a place to recover. In the early 1840s she and Madame Restell engaged in an advertising war. They called one another's pills counterfeit, and the two battled for three years. Both were criticized in print. The *National Police Gazette* publicized the trial of Costello's husband, Charles Mason, who sold the corpse of one of his wife's patients. This series ended Costello's career, as prospective patients grew concerned. The magazine then attacked Madame Restell. In 1847 she was arrested for conducting an abortion and was found guilty. She served a one-year sentence, but upon her release she resumed advertising her services. In 1878, she was arrested a second time and committed suicide the evening before her trial was to begin.

By this time, some newspapers refused abortion ads. Eventually, most — if not all — did so, much to the delight of the public, who for years had cried for political pressure or police action to close or prosecute abortionists.

There were other efforts as well to clean up advertising. People associated with the business began taking note of the negative impact on legitimate advertising produced by false and misleading advertisements. They talked of collective action against such advertising and the advertisers who ran it. The result was the earliest advertising clubs, the first of which may have been one founded in Denver in 1891. Regional advertising organizations with similar interests followed.

RECOMMENDED READINGS

BOOKS

Advertising: Today, Yesterday, Tomorrow — Printer's Ink. New York, 1963. Contains articles on the most influential shakers in advertising as well as the growth of advertising in the various media.

Applegate, Edd. *Personalities and Products: A Historical Perspective on Advertising in America*. Westport, Conn., 1998. Examines advertising in colonial America as well as certain advertisers from the 1800s and 1900s.

Brigham, Clarence S. *Journals and Journeymen: A Contribution to the History of Early American Newspapers*. Philadelphia, 1950. Contains a section on advertising in the early 1700s.

Goodrum, Charles, and Helen Dalrymple. *Advertising in America: The First 200 Years*. New York, 1900. Discusses the major changes in American advertising since its beginning. Illustrated with numerous advertisements.

Harris, Neil. *Humbug: The Art of P. T. Barnum* (Chicago, 1973). Not just an ordinary huckster, Barnum used advertising and publicity techniques and capitalized on Jacksonian democracy and cultural trends to become the most famous showman of his time.

How It Was In Advertising: 1776-1976. Chicago, 1976. This study, which is compiled by the editors of *Advertising Age*, highlights some of the most important advertisers and agencies.

Hower, Ralph M. *The History of an Advertising Agency: N.W. Ayer & Sons at Work 1869-1939*. Cambridge, Mass., 1939. Institutional, business history of a company, whose founder, Francis Wayand Ayer, typified the nineteenth-century success story: beginning with no money, he worked hard and used good judgment to build an enterprise.

Mott, Frank Luther. *A History of American Magazines, Vol. I, 1741-1850*. New York, 1930. Contains information about advertising in magazines. Additional information appears in the following volumes.

Presbrey, Frank. *The History and Development of Advertising*. Garden City, N.Y., 1929. An in-depth history of advertising filled with illustrations.

Rowell, George. *Forty Years as an Advertising Agent*. New York, 1906. George Rowell's autobiography.

Sutphen, Dick. *The Mad Old Ads*. New York, 1966. Looks at advertising in the latter half of the nineteenth century.

Turner, E.S. *The Shocking History of Advertising!* New York, 1953. A critical history.

Wood, James Playsted. *The Story of Advertising*. New York, 1958. A brief history of advertising in America.

Young, James Harvey. *The Toadstool Millionaires*. Princeton, 1961. The history of the "patent medicine era."

ARTICLES

Atherton, Lewis E. "The Pioneer Merchant in Mid-America." *University of Missouri Studies* 14 (April 1939): 121-5. Discusses retail advertising as it appeared in publications in the early 1800s.

Endres, Kathleen L. "Strictly Confidential: Birth Control Advertising in a 19th-Century City." *Journalism Quarterly* 63 (1986): 748-51. Birth-control advertisers used carefully worded classifieds in Cleveland newspapers. However, advertising fell victim to state anti-abortion legislation and the anti-obscenity campaign in the 1870s.

Holland, Donald R. "Volney B. Palmer (1799-1864): The Nation's First Advertising Agency Man." *Journalism Monographs* (1976). A brief biography of the pioneer advertising agent.

Larson, Cedric. "Patent Medicine Advertising and the Early American Press." *Journalism Quarterly* 14 (1937): 333-41. Examines the "evolution" of patent medicine advertising from 1720 "until the press had come of age toward the middle part of the nineteenth century." Widespread advertising campaigns made patent medicine a highly complex industry. Colonists had simple faith in the claims of advertisers.

Lawson, Linda. "Advertisements Masquerading as News in Turn-of-the-Century American Periodicals." *American Journalism* 10 (1988): 81-96. Reading notices permeated publications in the second half of the nineteenth century. These notices were advertisements that appeared in news and editorial columns.

Olasky, Marvin. "Advertising Abortion During the 1830s and 1840s: Madame Restell Builds a Business." *Journalism History* 13 (1986): 49-55. Some advertising in the penny press, as Restell's ads demonstrated, was motivated by the desire for profit, not by morals. Even though abortion was against the law and the ads made it clear what service they were offering, the *New York Sun* and *New York Herald* did not control the advertising. It is possible that the advertising influenced them not to criticize abortion editorially.

Schafer, Judith Kelleher. "New Orleans Slavery in 1850 as Seen in Advertisements." *Journal of Southern History* 47 (February 1981): 33-55. An analysis of advertisements in nine New Orleans newspapers indicates "a booming slave trade in which the equivalent of one in five of the bondsmen in New Orleans were sold annually."

Shaw, Steven J. "Colonial Newspaper Advertising: A Step Toward Freedom of the Press." *Business History Review* 33 (Autumn 1959): 409-20. Advertising revenues helped free newspaper publishers from political subsidies and/or political parties.

Smythe, Ted Curtis. "The Advertisers' War to Verify Newspaper Circulation, 1870-1914." *American Journalism* 3 (1986): 167-80. Beginning in the 1870s, advertisers and advertising agencies "worked together to force publishers to provide circulation figures, then to provide *accurate* and *meaningful* circulation figures....[They] also sought equitable advertising rates." Their efforts culminated in the founding of the Audit Bureau of Circulations in 1914.

15

The Emergence of Modern Media

1900 - 1945

Major changes in the media in the United States occurred in the years between 1900 and 1945. They began with the printing press dominating channels of information. They ended with print being challenged by the electronic media. They started with an emphasis on written words as the primary means of imparting knowledge. When they were over, visual images and words spoken over the airwaves had become major contenders for public attention.

Unknown in 1900, the term "mass media" entered the language in the 1920s, denoting a new world of communication to the masses transmitted, or mediated, through technological means. When commercial television burst on the scene after World War II, the population was prepared to welcome it. But print still held its own. Newspapers had learned to incorporate visual elements and remained powerful forces for interpreting the world.

The first decades of the twentieth century saw tremendous change in the United States amid tumultuous social upheaval. The nation confronted the shock of World War I, the frenzy of the Roaring '20s, the poverty of the Great Depression, and the horror of World War II. It grappled with the problems of increased industrialization counterbalanced by labor organization and governmental efforts to ensure benefits for the majority of citizens. Increasingly, mass media became the institution that glued together most of society. They created a consumer culture based on mass marketing. Popular forms of news and entertainment drew a mass audience for national advertisers.

Newspapers, which depended on advertising for more than half their revenue, laid claim to a unique status in the nation's economic and political power structure. As an industry, they professed a philosophy of journalism that rested on a concept of public good. It included support for democratic institutions based on freedom of the press as guaranteed by the First Amendment, a claim of adherence to the ideals of truth and objectivity as primary journalistic values, and service to the public as its champion and watchdog on government.

Translation of this ideology into the news product varied. Newspapers differed in terms of appearance, content, political loyalties and control, ties to advertisers, editorial opinions, appeals to reader, and class, racial, and ethnic orientation. Although the number of foreign-language newspapers declined after World War I, the African-American press gained circulation and fought for civil rights.

Some publishers attracted millions of readers by employing formulas that stressed pictures and simply-written stories. Improved photographic and reproduction equipment produced new kinds of newspapers and magazines that emphasized images over words. Tabloid newspapers (a term applied to those half the size of regular newspapers) sprang up in cities after World War I. Relying on photography, they targeted an audience of relatively low reading skills.

Using automated transmission equipment, the Associated Press and other wire services created uniform news products that went to small towns as well as big cities and served to standardize the formats of news articles. Teletype machines (that combined the telegraph and typewriter to print out news stories), teletypesetting equipment, and phototransmission devices as well as national radio networks that were set up by 1926 sent news across the country with breathtaking speed.

As the mass media searched for subjects to catch the attention of their vast, variegated audience, the new fields of advertising and public relations moved into professional image-making. The "celebrity" was born, personified by entertainers and even Prohibition-era gangsters — individuals heralded not because of performing heroic deeds but simply because of being well-known. Celebrities and professional models endorsed products and became part of the national media scene, appealing, in particular, to women, who were identified as key consumers.

Formal study of mass communications as a discipline began. It was initially pegged to efforts to learn more about propaganda, defined as one-sided or distorted communication to influence action, which had been used as a psychological weapon in World War I. New methods in social science research led to the use of

Old Newspapers and New Challenges
In 1900, newspapers were the unchallenged means for providing information. Founded in 1801, the *New York Evening Post* of the 1920s typified the old-style newspapers that provided a variety of news and thorough coverage. The newspaper industry, however, had grown so large that it was slow to meet new conditions; and many of the old newspapers such as the *Post* faltered against the competition. To revive it, later owners redesigned it as the sensational tabloid *New York Post*.

polls and surveys to measure public opinion. Both government and private industry set up public relations arms, often called information offices, in attempts to build goodwill with the public.

The growth of the film industry added another dimension to the field of mass communications. Silent motion pictures, which were followed by talking pictures in the 1920s, dimmed the line between news and entertainment. Newsreels, which purported to show actual news events but depended heavily on reenactments, became staples of theaters. Movies helped prepare the public for the advent of television after World War II ended in 1945.

As the twentieth century dawned, however, it was hard to conceive of any medium other than newspapers dominating the news scene. This chapter tells how newspapers reacted to the changes that swirled around them and redefined their place in mass communications.

The Newspaper as King

In the early years of the twentieth century, the number of newspapers stood at a record high. In 1910, there were 2,200 English-language daily newspapers of general circulation and about 14,000 weekly newspapers. Cities commonly had numerous competing newspapers, with afternoon papers purchased by workers on their way home. In New York City alone, considered the epitome of metropolitan journalism during most of the twentieth century, there were twenty-nine daily newspapers in 1899.

Daily newspaper circulation far outstripped increases in population. Representing about a three-fold increase, the population of the United States grew from 23.2 million in 1850 to 75.9 million by 1900. But the circulation of newspapers increased by twenty-fold, from about 758,000 in 1850 to 151.1 million by 1900.

By the turn of the century, big-city newspaper owners had discovered the something-for-everyone formula of news, sports, entertainment and advertising that still characterizes the daily press. With the advent of cheap newsprint in the nineteenth century, Anthony Smith, a scholar of technology, has noted, "it became apparent that great fortunes could be made by turning the medium into a universal one, rather than restricting it to ... special groups."[1] In the last few years of the nineteenth century, most newspapers changed from organs of editors' personal opinions to impersonal vehicles for the luring of mass audiences so advertisers could gain entry into large numbers of households.

To facilitate the gathering and transmission of news, newspapers in the early 1900s utilized a wide variety of inventions that symbolized the nation's technological progress. These included electric lighting (which facilitated the operation of newspaper plants around the clock), colored ink, high-speed presses, Linotypes (keyboard-operated machines for setting hot metal type one line at a time), mechanical folders, the halftone process for printing photographs, the wireless telegraph, long-distance telephone, and radiophone service. Metropolitan newspapers with different sections for men and women put out as many as nine or ten editions per day, feeding readers' appetites for the latest happenings. Children yelled out the headlines on crowded streets, selling papers for a penny or two. Newspapers rushed into print with "extras," unscheduled editions that offered the latest news developments.

Yet competition from an array of new media soon would cause retrenchment and consolidation in the newspaper business. More and more newspapers would come under the control of chain ownership. Media barons would transform local, family-owned newspapers into complex, interlocking corporate structures at the same time the industry shrank. By 1946, the number of daily newspapers would decline to 1,763.[2]

[1] Anthony Smith, *Goodbye Gutenberg: The Newspaper Revolution of the 1980s* (New York, 1980), 13-4.

[2] This drop has continued as population growth has outpaced newspaper circulation. By 1993 the number of daily newspapers had gone down to 1,556 and the number of weeklies to 7,437. In 1994 only 33 cities had two or more newspapers under separate ownership compared to 562 cities with competing dailies in 1900. By 1994 a total of 473 afternoon newspapers had folded since 1946, direct casualties of television and changing life styles.

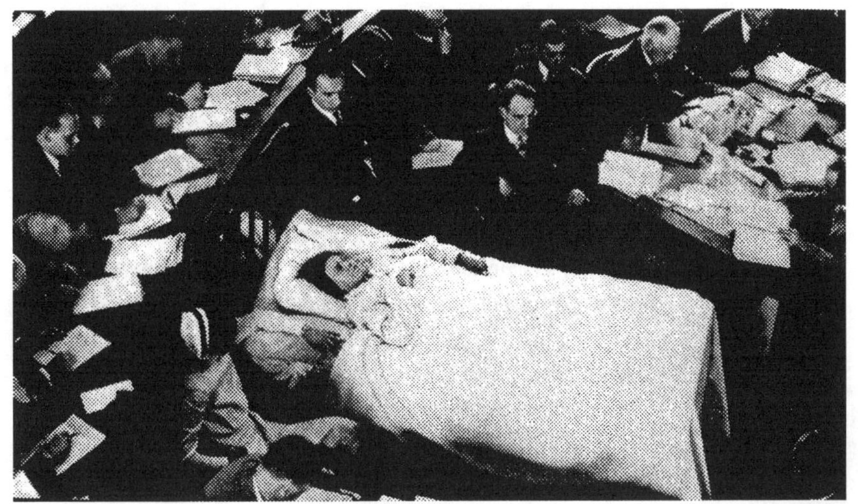

Pig Woman Testifies
Of the varied murder trials the tabloids played up, hardly any was more sensational than that of Mrs. Frances Hall for the murder of her husband and his mistress, Mrs. James Mills. The key witness was Jane Easton, whom the newspapers dubbed the "pig woman" for the stock she raised. Stricken with cancer, she had to be carried into court on a bed. Reporters ringed the courtroom and filed stories for newspapers around the nation.

THE NEWSPAPER AS TABLOID

In the 1920s the success of the tabloids helped divide newspapers into two broad categories. The first, often associated with Adolph Ochs, who bought majority ownership of the *New York Times* in 1896, presented information in a staid, middle-of-the road fashion that became the standard for journalism considered of high quality. Newspapers that followed this course prided themselves on recording official events, used a factual format in the news columns, and frequently developed close ties with the governing elite, who became sources of information.

The second, highlighted by the tabloids, updated the late nineteenth-century innovation of "yellow journalism" promoted by Joseph Pulitzer and archrival William Randolph Hearst. The tabloids enlivened the earlier sensationalism of blaring headlines, garish comic strips, and tear-jerking feature stories with bold new elements: eye-catching, sometimes faked, photography and a condensed, colorful style of news writing. Reporters, previously the romantic figures of newsgathering, now shared top billing with photographers, since advances in photography led newspapers to depend more heavily on pictures.

The two contrasting models were keyed to class divisions within the reading audience. According to Michael Schudson, a sociologist, the emphasis on story-telling and unusual events in the sensation-oriented newspapers reflected the life experience of somewhat unsettled individuals who were newly literate and newly urban. The more respectable newspapers, on the other hand, aimed at a middle and upper-class audience and spoke in rational, reasonable tones to individuals who lived a more orderly existence.[3]

Originated in England, the tabloid newspaper was brought to the United States by Joseph Medill Patterson, grandson of Joseph Medill, founder of the *Chicago Tribune*. Patterson launched the *New York Daily News* in 1919, billing it as an "illustrated" newspaper. It was subsidized by the *Tribune*, which was run by the autocratic Col. Robert R. McCormick, Patterson's cousin.

The tabloid captured buyers with an emotional mix of sex and crime news pushed by coupons and promotional schemes. Its size made it convenient to read on crowded subways and buses. Apparently finding an audience that had not read other newspapers, the *Daily News* hit the million mark in circulation in 1925. Within a decade of its founding, it had imitators in New York and other major cities — Washington, Baltimore, Los Angeles, San Francisco, Buffalo, Philadelphia, Miami, and Chicago.

Tabloids personified the "jazz journalism" of the Roaring '20s when alcoholic beverages were outlawed under Prohibition. Photographers carrying bulky cameras roamed the streets, looking for scenes that recorded the frenzies of an era known for excitement over bootleggers, speakeasies, love nests, movie stars, bathing beauties, and the foibles of the rich and famous. In a reversal of the traditional newspaper reliance on words, pictures splashed across the entire front page became the story. Brief captions, sneered at as "picture-writing" by the intellectuals, served to explain the illustrations. Relating to readers who increasingly sought entertainment from newer media — motion pictures and radio — the tabloids furnished terse, melodramatic accounts of crimes and scandal and sometimes resorted to falsification.

Perhaps the most famous example of the tabloid photographer's work ran in the *Daily News* in 1928. Taken by Tom Howard, who sneaked into Sing Sing prison with a concealed camera strapped to his left leg, it showed Ruth Snyder, a convicted murderer, literally frying to death in the electric chair. Along with her lover, a corset salesman, Snyder had been sentenced to be electrocuted for the murder of her husband following a much-publicized trial. The huge headline above the picture screamed "DEAD!" Although a "storm of protest was aroused," as one writer of the day put it, "the *News* could afford disapproval of an action which sold an estimated 500,000 extra copies of the paper."[4]

With the advent of the Depression, the excesses of "jazz" journalism died out. The nation turned its attention to serious eco-

[3]Michael Schudson, *Discovering the News: A Social History of American Newspapers* (New York, 1978), 119.

[4]Simon M. Bessie, *Jazz Journalism: The Story of the Tabloid Newspapers* (New York, 1938), 117.

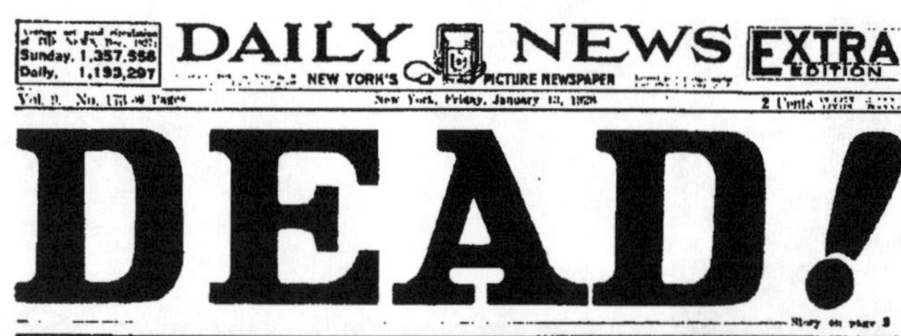
DAILY NEWS EXTRA

NEW YORK'S PICTURE NEWSPAPER

DEAD!

Tabloid Journalism
Like other tabloid newspapers of the 1920s, the *New York Daily News* brought new approaches to design and illustration. The *Daily News'* boldest play was this page-one photograph of the execution of the convicted murderer Ruth Snyder.

nomic problems, overturning Prohibition and looking to the federal government for new programs to aid citizens. Some tabloid newspapers left the scene, but the *Daily News* continued to enthrall a working-class audience with its snappy combination of pictures and words.

Efforts failed to aim a New York tabloid at more affluent readers. In 1940 Ralph Ingersoll, formerly publisher of *Time* magazine, and associates started *PM* (for Picture Magazine) to reach an audience that supported liberal causes. This tabloid accepted no paid advertisements, but, recognizing the news value of advertising, gave readers synopses of ads in other papers. With an editorial policy that stressed social justice and consumer rights, it became a journal of interpretation. Unable to attract a sufficient audience, it died after eight years in spite of a heavy infusion of funds from Marshall Field III, the wealthy grandson of a Chicago department store owner.

Although lamenting the excesses of the tabloids, which critics called gutter journalism, contemporary observers praised the metropolitan newspaper as a manifestation of progress. Willard Bleyer, an early journalism educator, blamed sensationalism on the audience. It resulted from immigration, Bleyer said, since it "flourished in larger cities where the number of half-assimilated foreigners was the greatest."[5] He believed newspapers, in spite of their imperfections, functioned as vehicles of democracy and viewed them as products of technological evolution.

Others saw newspapers more negatively, accusing the press of cowardly caving in to advertising pressures. In a scathing attack in 1919, Upton Sinclair, the muckraking novelist, compared journalists to patrons of prostitutes. In a tongue-lashing to reporters, he wrote, "[it is] you who take the fair body of truth and sell it in the market-place, who betray the virgin hopes of mankind into the loathsome brothel of Big Business."[6]

THE NEWSPAPER AND CONSOLIDATION

For all of their collective popularity, individual daily newspapers confronted a saturated marketplace. A case in point was Pulitzer's *New York World*, the largest newspaper in the United States in 1897, with combined morning and evening circulations of one million copies. In 1931, twenty years after Pulitzer's death, his family, faced with huge operating losses, sold the newspaper, which had abandoned its sensationalism to become a liberal voice, and it disappeared, consolidated with Roy Howard's *Telegraph*. The end came after the *World* found itself squeezed between two types of competitors: the "establishment" press, symbolized by the *New York Times* and the newly created *Herald Tribune*, itself the merged descendant of James Gordon Bennett's *New York Herald* and Horace Greeley's *Tribune*, on the one hand; and the *Daily News* and its imitators, on the other. By 1940 New York was down to eight daily newspapers, equally divided between morning and afternoon publications.

Mergers became common in the World War I era and thereafter, as newspapers succumbed to many of the same financial pressures that created giant corporations in other industries. Whether the manufactured product was steel, shoes, or whiskey, businesses sought to consolidate in the name of increased efficiency and greater market shares. Efforts to restrain competition resulted in trusts and monopolies that were exposed by muckraking journalists and made illegal under the Federal Trade Commission Act of 1914 and earlier legislation.

Consolidations made economic sense in the newspaper field. It was cheaper for advertisers to buy space in one paper with wide circulation than in two with overlapping circulations. Also, combinations of morning and afternoon newspapers allowed for efficient, round-the-clock utilization of plant facilities. To critics, however, mergers led to further standardization of the newspaper and a decrease in opportunities to express conflicting viewpoints.

Chain ownership — or "group" ownership, as the newspaper industry prefers to call it today — played an important role in consolidations. While only one-tenth of all newspapers at the turn of

[5] Willard G. Bleyer, *Main Currents in the History of American Journalism* (Boston, 1927), 390.

[6] Upton Sinclair, *The Brass Check* (Pasadena, Calif., 1919), 436.

the century were group owned (meaning that one individual or company owned newspapers in two or more cities), by 1945 the proportion had increased to two-fifths. (Today it stands at four-fifths.[7])

Among those most active in this phenomena were Hearst and E. W. Scripps, a self-proclaimed "damned old crank," who championed the cause of labor. Hearst, the prototype for "Citizen Kane" in the Orson Welles movie of that name, assembled a complex media empire of newspapers, magazines, feature syndicates, wire services, and motion picture interests. His newspaper chain, which backed nationalistic policies and engaged in hunts for Communists, reached its peak in 1935 with twenty-six dailies. Two years later his empire had collapsed, in part because of the Depression, but also because of his personal extravagance, symbolized by the exotic art treasures and lavish entertainment that characterized life at his palatial California estate, San Simeon.

By loaning money to bright young men who ran his enterprises, Scripps established tightly edited, low-cost afternoon newspapers aimed at working people in smaller cities. Although he lived in style on a 2,100-acre ranch, Miramar, near San Diego, he recognized the political importance of labor. He insisted that his newspapers editorialize in favor of the poor against the rich. Over the years, his holdings grew to include the Scripps-McRae and Scripps-Howard newspaper chains, United Press, feature syndicates, and other companies. After mergers and restructuring, by 1940 nineteen newspapers survived out of a total of fifty-two once associated with Scripps.

It was Frank Munsey, a businessman dubbed the Grand High Executioner of newspapers, who occupied a special and unrevered place in the annals of consolidation. His efforts to build a chain by purchasing newspapers in New York, Washington, Boston, Baltimore, and Philadelphia ended with the death of most of the publications. His unfeeling attitude toward newspapers as civic entities brought a stinging attack from William Allen White of Emporia, Kansas, the best-known small town editor of his day. In the *Emporia Gazette* White wrote a widely reprinted obituary of Munsey. It declared, "Frank Munsey contributed to the journalism of his day the great talent of a meatpacker, the morals of a money-changer and the manners of an undertaker. He and his kind have about succeeded in transforming a once-noble profession into an eight percent security. May he rest in trust."[8]

Although the newspaper industry underwent the same tendency toward oligopoly (control of the market by a few sellers) as other industries, individual newspapers were viewed as local, not national, enterprises. They were rarely candidates for anti-trust action by the federal government in its efforts to break up monopolies. Wire services were a different matter. The Associated Press, a cooperative owned by member newspapers, kept out new members until 1945 when the U.S. Supreme Court ruled that it was illegally restraining trade.[9]

Frank Munsey
Munsey was notorious for merging and killing newspapers. He believed that they should use the same economic principles that other businesses used. Multiple competitors, he believed, did not make for efficiency; and he set out to reduce the number of newspapers in New York City. He began by buying the *Sun* in 1915, and then in 1920 he bought the *Herald* and combined the two papers. All told, he merged five New York newspapers into a single publication.

The decision favored the *Chicago Sun*, a liberal newspaper established by Marshall Field, the department store magnate who also backed *PM*, in opposition to McCormick's *Tribune*. The *Tribune* had blocked the *Sun*'s attempt to have access to AP service. Before the court ruling, newspapers with AP memberships could — and did — refuse to let competing publications gain membership. This meant that publishers either had been forced to buy weak newspapers with existing AP memberships or subscribe to competing, but less complete, private wire services like United Press.

Important though they were, wire services did not replace local news staffs. With printing presses rolling out thousands of copies several times a day, the news became a hot commodity endlessly pursued by zealous reporters and photographers. Newspaper offices, dirty, noisy, and cluttered, acquired a romantic image in a culture that pictured reporters and photographers as daring bohemians with front-row seats for human dramas. In reality, journalism represented an insecure, underpaid, male-oriented occupation. Women who managed to break through barriers of discrimination had to display spectacular talents and ingenuity.

[7]Erwin K. Thomas and Brown H. Carpenter, *Handbook on Mass Media in the United States: The Industry and Its Audiences* (Westport, Conn., 1994), 94.

[8]*Emporia Gazette*, 23 December 1925.

[9]*Associated Press v. United States*, 326 U.S. I (1945).

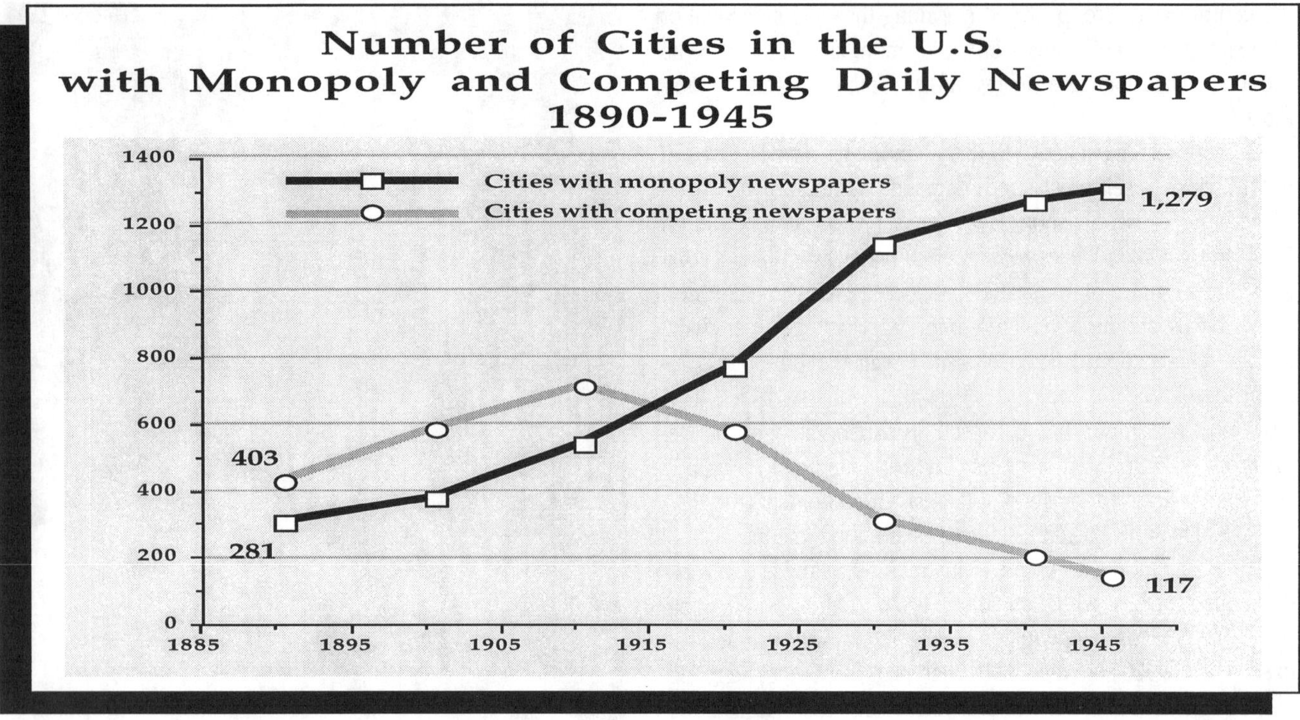

THE NEWSPAPER AS MALE PRESERVE

In the first history of women journalists written in 1936, Ishbel Ross, a veteran of New York journalism, described scores of women who followed in the footsteps of "Nellie Bly" (Elizabeth Cochrane). "Bly's" race around the world for Pulitzer's *World* in 1889 had made her famous as a "stunt girl," but by the early 1920s Cochrane was eking out a living writing a column on abused and missing children for Hearst's *Journal*. Her fame had long since gone; yet just as Pulitzer had once capitalized on her adventurous spirit to attract readers, editors continued to exploit women journalists.

With the advent of the tabloids, "stunt girls" came back into vogue. Since the tabloids "had to astonish, bemuse, dazzle or horrify the reader," Ross wrote, "editors did handsprings to startle the town.... A group of clever girls adopted the new technique with success."[10] In pursuit of material that would shock and excite, tabloid women reporters purloined photographs, tracked down gangsters, and charmed murderers into giving them exclusive interviews.

A few women, like Lorena Hickok of the Associated Press, gained recognition as reporters and attained what Ross called the coveted designation of "front page girl." These women displayed almost superhuman effort to convince male editors they could perform as well as, or better than, their male counterparts on all assignments. An example was Hickok's attempt to produce a scoop while covering the 1932 kidnapping of the infant son of aviator Charles A. Lindbergh. This was a story so big it pushed the Depression off the front page as readers followed every detail of the crime, the discovery of the baby's body, and the subsequent trial, conviction, and execution of the convicted murderer, Bruno Hauptmann.

A top political writer, Hickok was determined to go to the kidnapping scene in Hopewell, New Jersey. After a fruitless search for clues to find the baby herself, she crawled on her hands and knees up a snow-covered mountain at 2 a.m., peering in the windows of Lindbergh's isolated home to check out a vague rumor that the infant might have been returned. All she received for her exertion was flu due to exposure. Her editors were annoyed — not at her ethics but at her failure to produce a story.

Relatively few women journalists could ever hope for front page bylines. In most cases the women's and society pages provided their only viable opportunities for newspaper careers. The product of the late nineteenth century, the women's pages aimed at drawing a large audience for department store advertising. Their success constituted one important factor in the expansion of daily newspaper readership, which doubled in the period from 1892 to 1914.

Despite their role in the newspaper organization, the women's pages were barely tolerated by male journalists. Segregated from the main city room in areas given such names as the "hen coop," women's page staff members received even poorer pay than their male counterparts. Often male editors limited the women's pages to a trite formula of fashion, beauty hints, and domestic chitchat. Nevertheless, coverage of women's organizations and community interests served to make these sections into a limited means for women to communicate among themselves. To some degree women's pages showcased women of achievement, although most of the women pictured there were portrayed as wives of prominent men.

[10] Ishbel Ross, *Ladies of the Press* (New York, 1936), 262.

Lindbergh Kidnapping

The Media Cover 'the Greatest Story Since the Resurrection'

In 1927, 25-year-old Charles Lindbergh accomplished the first nonstop solo flight across the Atlantic Ocean and became one of the most admired people in the world. His fame brought him great fortune and also great misfortune.

On March 1, 1932, his 19-month-old son, Charles Jr., was kidnapped from the Lindbergh home in New Jersey. A ransom note was found on the nursery window sill, and a ladder was left against the outside wall of the house.

Although the Lindberghs paid a ransom and were given the baby's pajamas as evidence that he was alive, the child was not returned. Authorities found his body in woods near the house two months later.

The abduction of "The Little Eagle," as the media affectionately dubbed the baby, captivated public attention, and newspapers and newsreels avidly reported every detail of the crime and its aftermath. News photographers even managed to photograph the baby's body in the morgue.

For two and a half years, investigators struggled to solve the Lindbergh case. Finally, in September 1934, some of the marked ransom bills began showing up, and police traced them to an illegal German immigrant, Bruno Richard Hauptmann. Police found some of the marked money in his garage, and experts later said his handwriting matched that on the ransom note. More than 700 reporters and photographers descended on Flemington, New Jersey, in January 1935 for the final chapter of what many called "the crime of the century" — the trial of Hauptmann. Author H.L. Mencken called the trial "the greatest story since the Resurrection." Emotions were so high that several journalists openly expressed their opinion that Hauptmann was guilty.

After Hauptmann was convicted and sentenced to death, the Lindbergh family moved to England to escape publicity.

Jane S. McConnell
University of Oklahoma

Section 1 "All the News That's Fit to Print."

The New York Times.

THE WEATHER

NEW YORK, SUNDAY, MAY 22, 1927.

LINDBERGH DOES IT! TO PARIS IN 33½ HOURS; FLIES 1,000 MILES THROUGH SNOW AND SLEET; CHEERING FRENCH CARRY HIM OFF FIELD

COULD HAVE GONE 500 MILES FARTHER

Gasoline for at Least That Much More—Flew at Times From 10 Feet to 10,000 Feet Above Water

ATE ONLY ONE AND A HALF OF HIS FIVE SANDWICHES

Fell Asleep at Times but Quickly Awoke—Glimpses of His Adventure in Brief Interview at the Embassy.

LINDBERGH'S OWN STORY TOMORROW.

MAP OF LINDBERGH'S TRANSATLANTIC ROUTE, SHOWING THE SPEED OF HIS TRIP.

LEVINE ABANDONS BELLANCA FLIGHT

LINDBERGH TRIUMPH THRILLS COOLIDGE

CROWD ROARS THUNDEROUS WELCOME

Breaks Through Lines of Soldiers and Police and Surging to Plane Lifts Weary Flier from His Cockpit

AVIATORS SAVE HIM FROM FRENZIED MOB OF 100,000

Paris Boulevards Ring With Celebration After Day and Night Watch—American Flag Is Called For and Wildly Acclaimed.

All the News All the Time

Los Angeles Times

In Two Parts — 32 Pages

TIMES OFFICES

WEDNESDAY MORNING, MARCH 2, 1932. DAILY, FIVE CENTS

LINDBERGH SON SEIZED BY KIDNAPERS

JAPAN DRIVES FOES BACK ALONG SHANGHAI FRONT

Fall of Tachang Reported as Air Raid Smashes Nanking Rail; New Army Pushes South

TOKIO READY TO PARLEY

China Insists on Truce First

"Criminal Procedure!"

ABDUCTORS CARRY BABY FROM CRIB OUT NURSERY WINDOW

Note Found at Scene by Maid Who Discovered Crime Three Hours After Putting Boy to Bed; Three States Take up Search

NEW YORK, March 2. (Wednesday)- Charles Augustus Lindbergh, Jr., 20-months-old son of Colonel and Mrs. Charles A. Lindbergh was kidnaped sometime between 7:30 and 10 o'clock last night from his crib in the nursery on the second floor of his parents' home at Hopewell, N. J., near Princeton. His disappearance was discovered at 10 p.m. by Miss Betty Dow, his nurse.

KIDNAP BILL VOTE NEAR

Death Provided as Penalty

The Columbus Enquirer-Sun

VOL. CIV Columbus, Georgia, Friday Morning, May 13, 1932

LINDBERGH BABY FOUND MURDERED

GRAND JURY ACTION IS EXPECTED SOON IN LINDBERGH CASE

Compromise Relief Plan Tentatively Accepted Thursday

FEDERAL JUDGE TO ACCOMPANY INVESTIGATORS

Son of Lindberghs Is Dead

CHARLES A. LINDBERGH, JR.

DEATH CAUSED BY FRACTURE OF THE SKULL

BODY IS IDENTIFIED

HOW NEWS BEAT WAS FLASHED IS EXPLAINED

Negro Details Story Of Stumbling On Body

LINDBERGH HIGHSPOTS

These front pages from New York City, Los Angeles, and Columbus, Georgia, illustrate how Charles Lindbergh's Atlantic flight and the kidnapping of his child filled the news media.

The Old Guard
James Gordon Bennett Jr., whose father had entered the newspaper business in the early 1800s, epitomized the traditions that were giving way in the early 1900s. Bennett's *New York Herald* was faltering, and numbers of women were beginning to enter what had once been a virtual male domain.

One woman journalist who built an extraordinary career appealed to millions of readers, chiefly women. Elizabeth M. Gilmer, who wrote as "Dorothy Dix" from 1895 until 1949, achieved fame, first as a "sob sister," who wrote highly emotional feature stories for Hearst newspapers, and then as a syndicated advice columnist, whose counsel on personal relationships was avidly sought by her devoted followers. In an era when newspapers featured narrative and told stories more than today, "sob sisters" emoted in lurid human interest accounts that built circulation. As a reporter Gilmer specialized in covering trials of women charged with murder and befriended the accused, picturing them as victimized by males. Conventional in her views on women's behavior, in her advice columns she urged women to seek inner happiness as a way of overcoming their misfortunes.

A noteworthy woman, Mary Baker Eddy, founder of the Christian Science Church, established a daily newspaper, the *Christian Science Monitor*, in 1908, not as a religious organ, but as a protest against sensationalism in news coverage. The newspaper featured high-quality foreign and cultural news and downplayed news of crimes and tragedies. In the World War I era it had a circulation of 120,000 and was distributed more widely over the United States than any other daily newspaper.

Coverage of the campaign for women's right to vote, which ended with the adoption of the Nineteenth Amendment to the U.S. Constitution in 1920, enhanced the visibility of women's issues and women reporters. It brought together women who worked on newspapers and women who sought publicity for the suffrage cause. In Washington, D.C., for example, women journalists and women publicists (an early term used for public relations practitioners) joined forces in 1919 to form their own organization. They established the Women's National Press Club that served as an outlet for the professional development of women, who were denied admission to the male-only National Press Club until 1971. Similarly, the New York Newspaper Women's Club, still in existence today, was founded in 1922 after women reporters who had covered the suffrage campaign together found they missed the camaraderie of frequent gatherings.

Other women edited and published suffragist newspapers. Alice Stone Blackwell, the daughter of Lucy Stone and Henry Blackwell, both of whom were dedicated to the cause of woman's rights, edited the *Women's Journal*, the leading woman's-rights newspaper, for thirty-five years after her graduation from Boston University in 1881. Rheta Childe Dorr, a journalist who exposed injustices against working women and was a World War I war correspondent, became the first editor of the *Suffragist*, the publication of the militant wing of the suffrage movement, in 1914.

Another veteran of the movement, Clara Bewick Colby, started her newspaper, *The Woman's Tribune*, in Nebraska in 1883. Four years later, she shifted it to Washington, D.C., where she published it until 1904. That year she moved the newspaper to Portland, Oregon, where it continued until 1909, although the emphasis remained on national, not local, suffrage news.

In spite of the presence of a limited number of capable women on daily newspapers in the early twentieth-century, editors assumed that most women were unfit to be general assignment reporters and did not belong in city rooms. One reporting textbook in the 1930s stated bluntly, "The general tempo — with the deadline-fighting element always present — is such to bar many women because of nervous temperament."[11]

The rakish, smoke-filled atmosphere within big city newspaper offices was dramatized by Ben Hecht and Charles MacArthur, former reporters, in their 1928 play, *The Front Page*. The drama, which revolved around a love-hate relationship between two males — a cynical reporter and a manipulative city editor — presented a fantasized notion of journalism as a disreputable, but enthralling, occupation for men only. It was made into a movie that has been remade three times and become an icon of newspaper lore. In the modern version the reporter is a woman, a theatrical touch that highlights the eventual acceptance of women on newspaper staffs. Women, however, remained marginal figures in the newspaper world until passage of civil rights legislation in 1964

[11] Philip W. Porter and Norval N. Luxon, *The Reporter and the News* (New York, 1935), 8.

Dorothy Dix
Under the pen name "Dorothy Dix," Elizabeth Meriwether Gilmer for more than half a century worked as a reporter, a "sob sister," and syndicated advice columnist. She was one of the most popular newspaper writers of the twentieth century, advising women that the means to happiness in the face of difficulties was contentment.

that outlawed discrimination in employment on grounds of sex as well as race.

In small towns and rural areas the journalistic pace was far slower than the frenzied race to meet deadlines that marked the newsrooms of metropolitan dailies. Still, the work was just as hard and the hours just as long, if not longer, than in the big cities for even less monetary reward. Country weeklies, which remained an important element in journalism during the first decades of the twentieth century, required skill and devotion from their owners who sometimes were the only staff members. With 51% of the population of the United States still classified as rural before World War I, small newspapers played vital roles in their respective communities, serving as boosters and bulletin boards as well as political voices.

The preeminent exemplar of a weekly journalist was William Allen White of the *Emporia* (Kan.) *Gazette*. He purchased the languishing newspaper in 1895 and moved back to the small town where he had been born in 1868. Then he quickly gained national fame with a single editorial in 1896. He wrote it in answer to a group of Populist farmers who cornered him on a street on a Saturday morning when they had come into town to do their weekly shopping. They challenged him to defend his conservative opinions, demanding that he explain his argument that the Populist political movement was harming Kansas. Befuddled and angered, he could not give them a coherent answer. He rushed back to his office and, employing bold sarcasm, wrote out his answer, an editorial titled "What's the Matter with Kansas?"[12] He and his wife then left on their summer vacation. Unbeknown to White, Republican newspapers around the country reprinted the editorial, and he returned to his office two weeks later to find himself famous. In later years, his political views moderated, while his writing style improved. He won the 1923 Pulitzer Prize for an editorial dealing with press freedom, but his most enduring editorial was a masterpiece on the death of his seventeen-year-old daughter in 1921. Among all editorials ever published in American newspapers, it comes closest to being a genuine classic of literature.[13]

Country weeklies often were family businesses, involving husbands, wives, and children, with some women as adept as males in setting type and performing backshop mechanical chores. To cite one example, in Oklahoma Territory Elva Ferguson founded the *Watonga Republican* in 1892 with her husband, Thompson, who became territorial governor. Also a powerful figure in politics, she carried on the newspaper following her husband's death in 1921 until she sold it in 1930.

The Newspaper and Professionalization

Before World War I, journalism, in line with other technically oriented occupations like accounting, business, public management, and engineering, moved toward attaining professional status. Universities established journalism schools, enabling graduates to move into the field without long apprenticeships as "cub" reporters. Countering the perception of newspaper work as an unconventional, if not shady, occupation, both formal training programs and newly organized professional associations called on journalists to act as responsible public advocates.

The first school of journalism, which emphasized practical experience on its own newspaper, opened in 1908 at the University of Missouri. From the beginning, the idea of university preparation met hostility from some editors and publishers who ridiculed academic instruction, foreshadowing a debate that goes on today over the worth of journalism degrees. Summing up criticism of the need for university education, the *Moberly* (Mo.) *Democrat* sniffed at the Missouri school: "So long as men can embark in the newspaper business without education, character, brains or money, there is very little inducement to take higher courses in journalism."[14]

Frequently located in the Middle West, where public universities had a tradition of assisting farmers and businesses, the early journalism schools were backed by state press associations. Their

[12] *Emporia Gazette*, 15 August 1896.

[13] "Mary White," *Emporia Gazette*, 17 May 1921. For this and other editorials, see Wm. David Sloan, Cheryl S. Wray, and C. Joanne Sloan, *Great Editorials*, 2nd ed. (Northport, Ala., 1997).

[14] Quoted in Robert F. Karolevitz, *From Quill to Computer: The Story of America's Community Newspapers* (National Newspaper Foundation, 1985), 117.

members wanted to elevate the status of newspapers as well as have a supply of trained employees. As contrasted with the Missouri model, some journalism schools followed the pattern set up at the University of Wisconsin, which stressed social science research along with skills training.

Journalism schools were part of a broader movement to professionalize the editorial side of newspaper work by establishing standards of conduct. Organized in 1922, the American Society of Newspaper Editors (ASNE) one year later adopted its "Canons of Journalism," an ethical code with high-minded phraseology that contrasted sharply with prevalent tabloid practices. "Journalism... demands of its practitioners the widest range of intelligence, of knowledge, and of experience, as well as natural and trained powers of observation and reasoning," the code said. "To its opportunities as a chronicler are indissolubly linked its obligations as teacher and interpreter."[15]

The code's weakness was illustrated the following year. An attempt was made to censure and possibly expel Frederick G. Bonfils, co-publisher of the flamboyant *Denver Post*, which printed giant headlines in red ink and was run from an office with red-painted walls known as the "Bucket of Blood." At issue was an accusation that Bonfils had accepted a payoff to withhold news of the Teapot Dome oil scandals. ASNE members disagreed on the interpretation of the code, and Bonfils was allowed to resign.

One institutionalization of the concept of journalism as a public trust was the Pulitzer Prizes, long considered journalism's most coveted professional awards.First given in 1917, the prizes were endowed with funds left by Joseph Pulitzer to Columbia University, where he helped establish a school of journalism that started in 1912.

In setting up the prizes that recognized work in literature, drama, and music as well as journalism, Pulitzer described a vision of newspapers as progressive social forces untainted by selfish, commercial considerations. He specified three different types of annual prizes in journalism: One for "the most disinterested and meritorious public service rendered by any American newspaper during the preceding year"; the second for the best editorial, "the test of excellence being clearness of style, moral purpose, sound reasoning, and power to influence public opinion in the right direction"; the third for reporting based on "strict accuracy, terseness, the accomplishment of some public good commanding public attention and respect."[16]

Over the years the prizes have been expanded to include additional categories — such as foreign correspondence, photography, and criticism.

In 1937 Anne O'Hare McCormick of the *New York Times* became the first woman journalist to be honored, receiving a Pulitzer Prize for foreign correspondence. She was one of the first journalists to interview the leaders of the totalitarian regimes in Europe that led to World War II. She began sending columns to the *Times* from Europe while accompanying her husband on business trips abroad. In spite of the high quality of her work, she referred to herself as a "stepchild" in the *Times*' family and was not allowed to become the first woman on the newspaper's editorial board until 1936, after the death of publisher Adolph Ochs. Like other publishers of his day, Ochs did not think women belonged in newspaper offices.

Dorothy Thompson
The first American woman to head a European news bureau, Dorothy Thompson covered Germany from 1924 until expelled in 1934. She was one of the first foreign correspondents to recognize the dangerous nature of Nazism.

McCormick was not the only woman to achieve distinction as a foreign correspondent. Dorothy Thompson became the first American woman to head a European news bureau when she was made chief of the Berlin office of the *Philadelphia Public Ledger* and the *New York Evening Post* in 1924. She decided to pursue foreign correspondence to escape being limited to writing about women's groups in the United States. In 1936 she signed a contract with the *New York Herald-Tribune* for a syndicated column of European political analysis that reached an audience of 8 million at its peak. Another influential woman foreign correspondent during the 1930s was Sigrid Schultz of the *Chicago Tribune*.

THE NEWSPAPER AND OBJECTIVITY

The concept of "the public" as a force that could be influenced to

[15]Quoted in John L. Hulteng, *The Messenger's Motives: Ethical Problems of the News Media* (Englewood Cliffs, N.J., 1976), 18-20.

[16]Quoted in John Hohenberg, *The Pulitzer Prizes: A History of the Awards in Books, Drama, Music, and Journalism Based on the Private Files Over Six Decades* (New York, 1974), 20.

The Metropolitan Daily
In the first half of the twentieth century, newspapers continued on the growth spiral that had begun in the 1830s. Along with circulation increases, they expanded their staffs in all departments of their operations. Simply taking care of sending copies to subscribers and newsstands required a major operation, as illustrated in this drawing from the early 1900s. On average, major dailies employed approximately sixty workers in their mail rooms.

the good by responsible journalism fit well with the pragmatic views of an American society that had an optimistic faith in democracy. To some philosophers the reportorial search for facts became a search for truth that could be laid out before a reasoning audience. As J. Herbert Altschull, a journalism historian, put it, according to this belief system that continues to motivate investigative reporting, it is necessary for the journalist not only "to help educate the citizen, [and] to supply him with information, but it is equally necessary for the journalist to serve as the citizen's eyes and ears in scrutinizing the powerful."[17]

Not all theorists saw the gathering of factual information as likely to provide enlightenment. The increasing complexity of a society torn apart by modern war spread disillusionment with the idea of purported facts speaking for themselves. To some it seemed almost impossible to obtain true facts in a world where citizens were subjected to downright lies by devious sources.

In 1920, Walter Lippmann, an intellectual who became the last editor of the *New York World*, reacted to the propaganda that had characterized World War I: "But where all news comes at secondhand, where all the testimony is uncertain, men cease to respond to truths, and respond simply to opinions. The environment in which they act is not the realities themselves, but the pseudo-environment of reports, rumors and guesses."[18] To deal with this situation, Lippmann called for the professionalization of journalism and urged that reporters be trained to be as objective as possible. Lippmann later achieved fame for his syndicated column of political commentary that alternated with Dorothy Thompson's column in the *New York Herald-Tribune*.

The ideal of objectivity led journalists to subscribe to techniques of reporting that now are standard. These included attributing information to official sources, trying to balance coverage by giving both sides of issues, and attempting to offer some context, or background, for news events. The objective reporter no longer presented facts in isolation but strived to paint a broader picture.

Many reporters themselves realized that objectivity might be an unattainable quest, particularly since some editors and publishers wanted news slanted to suit their own preferences. In a study of Washington correspondents in the 1930s, a researcher found forty-two reporters who agreed that "it is almost impossible to be objective." But another twenty-four disagreed with the statement.[19]

Lippmann was a leading thinker in the new area of public opinion. In his influential book *Public Opinion*, first published in 1922, he outlined the concept of the "public" as an emotional, rather than a logical, entity. He contended that each individual thinks in terms of stereotypical pictures carried in the mind rather than in realistic terms. He wrote that the press is too weak an institution "to supply spontaneously the truth which democrats hoped was inborn. And when we expect it to supply such a body of truth we employ a misleading standard of judgment...an appetite for uninteresting truths which is not discovered by any honest analysis of our own tastes."[20] To Lippmann news was a limited commodity and the public's ability to absorb facts and act on them for its own good a questionable concept.

The Newspaper and Public Relations

The idea of the public as a somewhat inert mass subject to persuasion lay behind the emerging profession of public relations. Notable for its mid-nineteenth century roots in the ballyhoo of press agents who promoted circuses and theatrical events, the field of publicity broadened into public relations as politicians and

[17] J. Herbert Altschull, *From Milton to McLuhan: The Ideas Behind American Journalism* (New York, 1990), 263.

[18] Walter Lippmann, "The Basic Problem of Democracy: What Modern Liberty Means," *Atlantic Monthly* 124 (November 1919): 624.

[19] Leo C. Rosten, *The Washington Correspondents* (New York, 1937), 351.

[20] Walter Lippmann, *Public Opinion* (New York, 1922), 273.

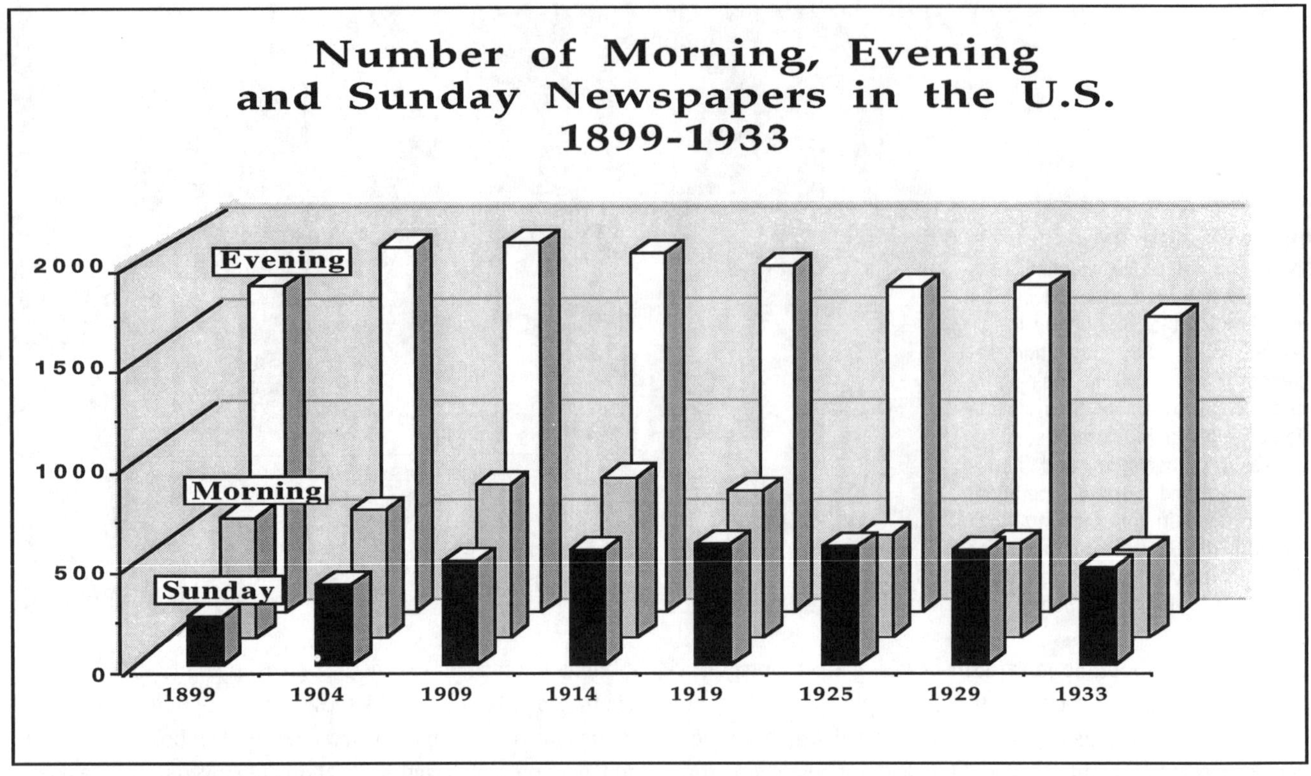

representatives of big business employed publicists to present them to the public in a favorable light. John D. Rockefeller Jr., criticized for strike-breaking and other "robber baron" activities, hired Ivy Lee, one of the first public relations practitioners, to improve his personal image in 1914.

Other public relations pioneers included Edward L. Bernays and his wife, Doris E. Fleischman. Bernays, the nephew of Sigmund Freud, approached public relations from an intellectual, rather than a business management, viewpoint. Writing the initial theory in the field, he expressed an elitist belief that the public could be manipulated positively for its own good.

Some journalists saw public relations as a threat to their professional autonomy. PR practitioners, many of whom were former reporters, sought to furnish stories to newspapers on behalf of their clients. Although journalists made use of this material, questions arose as to what degree the practice of accepting public relations "handouts" compromised the ideal of objectivity. Journalists maintained they were advocates of the public interest and therefore purer than PR practitioners who represented specific clients. Persons in public relations, on the other hand, resented being seen as inferior to journalists.

In both academic and commercial realms, a new science of mass communications research emerged. George H. Gallup, a journalism teacher at Iowa State University, originated scientific public opinion polling as a result of measuring reader interest in newspaper content. Starting in the 1930s, advertisers and political candidates used his polling to assess public reaction to their campaigns. Newspapers covered his findings as news, informing readers which candidates were leading in the polls. Another pioneer researcher, Harold Lasswell, a political scientist, developed a technique called content analysis to study communication messages. He classified their components into different categories for statistical measurement. As the leading member of a Rockefeller Foundation seminar on communication in 1939-40, Lasswell originated a five-question model for communication study that dominated the field for many years: "Who says what to whom in what channel with what effect?"

The ideas of Lasswell and others influenced the U.S. government, as well as the news media, during World War II when social scientists were involved in efforts to enhance support for the war effort. Convinced that the war represented a battle for the minds of individual citizens as well as for physical territory, Lasswell headed a project in Washington to analyze media content for propaganda from both allies and enemies and to advise government officials on the best way for the United States to carry out its own propaganda/information program. His staff worked with various agencies concerned with mobilization, including the U.S. Office of War Information, which employed journalists and public relations professionals to prepare and coordinate news releases pertaining to the war. Motivated by patriotism, newspapers supported the war overwhelmingly and made use of this material.

The Newspaper as Minority Voice

Among specialized publications the ethnic press played an important role in preparing immigrants to support the U. S. government and to play an active role as citizens in their new environment. Its number peaked in 1914 when about 1,300 journals, including 140 dailies, were being published in thirty-six languages. About 40% were printed in German, a percentage that declined rapidly after the United States fought Germany during World War I.

Characterized by high mortality, the ethnic press waxed and waned in response to succeeding waves of immigration. From 1884 to 1920, some 3,444 newspapers were begun, while 3,186 ceased publication, although some merged into stronger publications. By 1948 only 973 foreign-language newspapers remained.

The ethnic press was the subject of one of the most influential academic writings on the newspaper. Robert E. Park, a former reporter in Minneapolis and an important figure in the "Chicago School" of sociology, which pioneered in applied social research at the University of Chicago, published *The Immigrant Press and Its Control* in 1922. It was written in response to concerns about whether the foreign-language press was loyal to the United States during World War I.

Along with the philosopher John Dewey, also a key intellectual at the University of Chicago, Park saw the newspaper as a unifying element in American society. He considered it a means of restoring personal communication between individuals lost in the anonymity of big city life. In his book he concluded that most publications in foreign languages helped immigrants adjust to the United States and did not emphasize loyalty to their original homelands.

In the case of the Spanish-language press of the Southwest, one authority estimated that 248 newspapers were begun between 1900 and 1958.[21] These publications served an audience of Chicanos (American citizens of Mexican background) that increased markedly from 1910 to 1920 in response to economic dislocation created by the Mexican Revolution. Editors took diverse positions toward the revolution and the question of whether the United States should intervene, but the press helped maintain a sense of cultural identity among the Chicanos and encouraged sympathy for the Mexican people.

Large numbers of African-American newspapers were started in the late nineteenth and early twentieth centuries. The total begun between 1865 and 1950 was some 2,700. Of those, only 175 remained in existence at the middle of the twentieth century. The average life span was nine years. Many of the papers faced difficulty in establishing an advertising base and died, while others received political subsidies that did not last beyond a particular political campaign. These subsidies came from Republican interests, since until the Depression African Americans remained loyal to the party of Lincoln, who was credited with releasing them from slavery during the Civil War.

The newspapers articulated the aspirations of an oppressed portion of the population. Although local publications often were in no economic position to challenge the white power structure, weekly papers with multiple editions and national circulations highlighted racial inequities. Their influence can be judged, in part, from the campaigns waged against them. According to a contemporary observer, in Somerville, Tennessee, in 1919, an order was issued that no "colored newspapers" could be circulated in the town and that the "darkey" population had to read a local white paper edited by a Confederate veteran.[22]

SPECIAL

Extra The Chicago Defender Extra

SUNDAY, NOVEMBER 14, 1915

Booker T. Washington

DEAD!

1:23 Sunday Morning at Tuskegee

Full Particulars in Saturday's Paper

The *Chicago Defender*
Founded by Robert S. Abbott in 1905, the *Chicago Defender* built its huge success by using a formula emphasizing sensational news geared to racial issues. Abbott's news sense was demonstrated with its special issue upon the death of Booker T. Washington in 1915. The most popular African American of his time, Washington emphasized moderation in race relations. By the time of this issue, the *Defender's* circulation had reached 230,000.

National newspapers, particularly the *Chicago Defender*, played a major role in promoting the "Great Migration." This was a movement of African-American agricultural workers from the South to the North in the World War I era and thereafter to seek better opportunities. Other leading newspapers included the Baltimore-based *Afro-American*, the *Pittsburgh Courier*, whose editor, Robert Lee Vann, championed social justice under law, and the *Norfolk Journal and Guide*.

Founded by Robert S. Abbott in 1905, the *Defender* developed an attention-getting formula for sensationalized news geared to racial issues. By 1915 its circulation had reached 230,000. Its call to African Americans in the South to leave the cotton fields and head North so threatened the existing order that in some areas it was banned from regular channels of distribution. Instead, African

[21]Cited in Felix Gutierrez, "Spanish-Language Media in America: Background, Resources, History," *Journalism History* 4 (Summer 1977): 34.

[22]Frederick G. Detweiler, *The Negro Press in the United States* (Chicago, 1922), 1.

Americans who were railroad porters handed it out surreptitiously. Other African-American newspapers adopted the *Defender* formula as they attempted to meet the needs of an audience largely cut off from the mainstream press.

As black and white communities became increasingly separate worlds in the first decades of the twentieth century, African-American newspapers served as a platform for action to secure civil rights. At the end of the nineteenth century, T. Thomas Fortune, the editor of the *New York Age*, stood out as a champion of opposition to disenfranchisement, unequal school funding, and other injustices. His influence, however, waned after he became closely allied with Booker T. Washington, who advocated that African Americans seek vocational training and accommodate themselves to segregation, at least in the South. Washington was instrumental in obtaining subsidies for some African-American newspapers.

To counter the ideas of Washington, in 1901 William Monroe Trotter, an African American who was a Phi Beta Kappa graduate of Harvard University, founded the *Boston Guardian* that continued in existence until his death in 1934. He was an initial backer of W.E.B. DuBois, who emerged as the most articulate and important of the anti-Washington forces. The holder of a doctorate from Harvard University, DuBois, a professor who was one of the most significant figures in African-American history, acted as director of publications for the National Association of Colored People and founded its official journal, the *Crisis*, in 1910.

Since white newspapers in general refused to hire minorities and covered racial news mainly as reports on crimes, the African-American press provided a crucial journalistic service for its readers. Most cities with sizeable African-American populations sustained black newspapers that protested against discrimination as well as offered social and cultural news missing from white publications.

The activism of the black press led the *Kansas City Call* in 1939 to back efforts by Lucile Bluford, its managing editor, to gain admission to the University of Missouri's school of journalism. Although she had an undergraduate degree in journalism from the University of Kansas, Missouri turned down her application to its master's program on grounds of her race. Unlike Kansas, the state of Missouri was legally segregated. Bluford brought suit in state court, but her plea was rejected, highlighting the lack of educational opportunities for African Americans to study journalism. (In 1989 Bluford, then editor and publisher of the *Call*, received an honorary doctorate in humanities degree from the University of Missouri in recognition of her outstanding political writing.)

DAYTON CRIES FOR LIGHT AS SCIENCE PLEA RINGS

THE PREACHER

When William Jennings Bryan yesterday trumpeted his challenge to science in the Dayton courtroom his mein was far from that of Sunday when he occupied the pulpit in a Dayton church. Photo shows the shirt-sleeved Commoner in the pulpit at the beginning of his sermon.

Scopes Defender Drives Out Effect of Bryan's Wrathful Tirade and "Sells" Modernism to Tennesseeans

WAVES OF APPLAUSE DRAWN BY ADDRESS

Stern Fundamentalists Join in Ringing Ovation for Man Who Would Open New Book of Revelations

Dayton, Tenn., July 16—"Shall the parents have a right to say that no teacher paid by their money shall rob their children of faith in God and send them back to their homes, skeptical, infidels, agnostics, or atheists?"

Thus William Jennings Bryan set forth the case for the prosecution in the Scopes trial today.

"Close no doors of knowledge from them. Let science and theology both be loved, but let them not be confused."

Thus Dudley Field Malone put the case for enlightenment.

BY PHILIP KINSLEY

(Special to The Times-Picayune)

Dayton, Tenn., July 16—Dayton began to read a new Book of Revelations today.

If God spoke, at this climax of the Scopes trial, on this day of days in Tennessee, it was in a strange tongue, in favor of science, rather than through the lips of William Jennings Bryan.

The Monkey Trial

When the Tennessee teacher John T. Scopes challenged the state law prohibiting the teaching of the theory of evolution, his 1925 trial became a national media event. More than 100 journalists descended on the small town of Dayton. Most portrayed the local residents as yokels and religious zealots. Much of their reporting reflected the prejudice of the journalists, treating Scopes' lawyer, Clarence Darrow, heroically and the state's attorney, William Jennings Bryan, as a man of small intellect. The *New Orleans Times Picayune* contrived the "photograph" accompanying the story above by superimposing the shot of Bryan on a scene of a church.

The Newspaper and Radio

The devastating Great Depression, which hit the United States with the collapse of the stock market in 1929, brought additional changes to newspapers. Even during the economic boom of the 1920s, the newspaper ran into unexpected competition from a new medium: radio. First thought a mere toy, radio soon received recognition as a potent instrument of mass communication. With the advent of widespread commercial broadcasting in the 1920s, the public discovered that it could obtain news and entertainment with far greater immediacy and impact via the airwaves than on the printed page.

The period between World War I and World War II was an era of memorable voices and strong personalities able to project well behind a microphone — President Franklin D. Roosevelt, who led the news agenda from his inauguration in 1933 until his death in 1945; Adolf Hitler, who screamed his totalitarian message to fanatic Nazi followers; and Benito Mussolini, who rallied his Fascist following in Italy. Listeners were enthralled as they gathered around their radios to hear world leaders speak, to find out election results, and to receive actual coverage of events such as the Scopes "monkey" trial in Tennessee in 1925 over the teaching of evolution in the public schools.

Publishers found it hard to adjust to the new reality of broadcasting. When the Depression hit in 1929, radio continued to flourish, but newspapers did not. Radio easily attracted the mass audience that once had been the newspaper's sole province. A total of 584 daily newspapers stopped publication from 1931 to 1945, although this number was offset somewhat by 386 that began publication.

Newspaper advertising plummeted, forcing newspapers to cut salaries and production costs. In 1929 newspapers received 54% of all national advertising in mass media, magazines 42%, and radio only 4%; but by 1939 the percentage had fallen to 38% for newspapers and 35% for magazines but had risen to 27% for radio. While newspapers continued to lead in local advertising, here too radio threatened them. Newspapers received 45.2% of all advertising expenditures in 1935, but ten years later their share had fallen to 32%. Radio's share had increased from 6.5% to 14.6%.

Newspapers reacted by attempting to cut off radio access to news. In the early days of radio, stations often were owned by newspapers, which expanded into broadcasting as a way of enhancing local prestige. When it became apparent that radio was endangering newspaper profitability, however, publishers attempted to reestablish their monopoly over news transmission. In 1933 the American Newspaper Publishers Association brought pressure on the Associated Press and private wire services not to furnish news to radio stations except for brief bulletins that would encourage newspaper readership.

The publishers' effort proved futile. Radio networks struck back initially by setting up their own news operations. This costly undertaking ended in 1934 when the leading press associations agreed to set up a Press-Radio Bureau to furnish two brief news broadcasts daily to the networks. Nevertheless, news agencies not bound by the bureau agreement soon sprang up and supplied reports directly to broadcasters. By 1935 the bureau experiment had ended; radio had emerged as the victor in the press-radio war. Not until 1940, however, did the Associated Press start a service aimed at radio clients. By then newspapers were running radio columns and giving readers news of their favorite programs and personalities. Among them were network radio commentators with their personal views of the news.

When World War II broke out in Europe in 1939, radio brought the sounds of actual warfare into Americans' living rooms. News of the Japanese bombing of Pearl Harbor on December 7, 1941, precipitating the entry of the United States into the war, reached Americans via their radios hours before they read about it in their newspapers. Newspapers realized that they could not compete with radio for timeliness, but they could, and did, offer far more details and background reports.

Total newspaper circulation increased, although it failed to keep pace with population growth. Radio news limited the need for newspaper extras; nevertheless, they continued to be published during the war. Motion pictures as well as radio and new types of magazines drew down the potential newspaper audience. From a high of 1.36 copies per day per household in 1910, newspaper circulation fell to 1.18 by 1940. This figure, still quite impressive, showed an industry that remained profitable.

The Newspaper and Newsreels

Newsreels, ten-minute productions that showed news events before feature films in theaters, drew attentive audiences from 1911 until their demise in 1967. They provided a dramatic mixture of actual news pictures, staged reenactment, sports, war coverage, and human interest material. In part because early equipment was hard to transport, newsreel companies had a history of faking prize fights and other events. Parades were popular features since cumbersome cameras, which had to be fixed in place, could record news subjects as they marched passed by.

One enterprising newsreel company signed a contract in 1914 with Pancho Villa, a Mexican revolutionary, for exclusive coverage of his battles during the Mexican Revolution. The company paid Villa $25,000 and 50% of the royalties from the newsreel. In exchange, he delayed raids until cameramen arrived and scheduled them during daylight hours. Whether the footage that resulted was authentic or faked is unclear, but audiences flocked to see it.

As camera equipment became more portable, newsreels showed footage of spectacular news events. Among them: Charles Lindbergh's takeoff for his historic solo flight across the Atlantic from New York to Paris in 1927, the explosion of the German zeppelin "Hindenburg" in 1937, and scenes of World War II, many of which were supplied by the U.S. military. Leading movie companies and publishers, including Hearst and Henry Luce of the *Time-Life* media empire, entered the newsreel business.

In 1935 Luce started *The March of Time*, a twenty-minute series that lasted sixteen years. These programs, seen by some 25 million moviegoers monthly in more than 9,000 theaters, used a documentary format — one based on real people and events — to explore social issues, although they employed dramatizations that merged fact and fiction. *The March of Time* emphasized interpretation and touched on political issues. This made it different from conventional newsreels that sought to avoid controversy. The series ran not only in newsreel form but on the radio and later in television.

Credible or not, newsreels were received as quasi-journalistic sources of news by millions, even though they emphasized showbusiness values. Starting in 1929, movie theaters that screened newsreels exclusively were opened in New York and other cities. The *All-American News*, a newsreel for African Americans, was shown regularly in most of the nation's 450 black motion picture theaters in the World War II period. Newsreels lasted until the widespread use of television caused their death.

The Newspaper and New Magazines

New types of magazines that presented news as well as views also challenged the newspaper. In 1923 Luce and a Yale classmate, Briton Hadden, started *Time*, the first weekly newsmagazine. Responding to the pressures of urban life, *Time* promised to save time for the "busy man" by organizing the news into separate cat-

Los Angeles Times

VOL. LVI — FRIDAY MORNING, MAY 7, 1937. — DAILY, FIVE CENTS

ZEPPELIN BLAST KILLS THIRTY-FIVE

Giant Dirigible Blazing Wreck

BLASTS SEND GIANT BALLS OF FLAME SPURTING FROM AIRSHIP

C.I.O. Joins Film Strike

JURY QUIZZES MRS. SHELBY IN TAYLOR DEATH MYSTERY

Survivor Tells Leap to Safety

TENTATIVE LIST OF MISSING AND KNOWN CRASH SURVIVORS

AGE-PENSION MEASURE VOTED

LIST OF KNOWN SURVIVORS

The *Hindenburg*
Of the many world news events of the 1930s, few were bigger than the crash of the German zeppelin *Hindenburg* on her maiden voyage to the United States in 1937. Radio and newspaper reporters, along with newspaper and newsreel photographers, were all on hand to record her arrival in Lakehurst, New Jersey. The corps of journalists quickly spread the news to readers, listeners, and viewers across the nation.

egories — national, foreign, business, education, art, and other areas. Not pretending to be objective, it offered opinions intermingled with facts in a somewhat flippant style.

Luce, who took charge after Hadden died, recognized the public's unquenchable appetite for the visual. In 1936 he inaugurated *Life*, a sophisticated weekly picture magazine designed to appeal to a nation increasingly interested in buying cameras for home use. In an era predating color film, *Life* featured striking photographic essays in black and white. Readers soon demanded five to six million copies a week, far more than could be produced. Crowds almost came to blows in the street to get fresh copies. Clearly, the public wanted a photographic report on the world, just as it wanted a photographic record of personal life. Other picture magazines, particularly *Look*, began publication in clear imitation of *Life*.

Photographers, not reporters, starred at *Life* and its imitators. Among them was Margaret Bourke-White, whose spectacular pictures brought her international fame. Chosen to shoot the first cover for *Life*, Bourke-White, a pioneer in industrial photography, pictured a dam in Montana built as part of a Depression work relief project — a symbol of the nation's belief in technology to solve problems.

Although not able to provide slick paper reproduction of photographs, newspapers adjusted to their new competitors. They made more attempts to departmentalize their contents, with front-page news summaries becoming regular features during the 1930s. They used more bylines and allowed reporters more latitude to express themselves, even though most news continued to be written impersonally in line with the ideal of objectivity.

The Newspaper and the Federal Government

Franklin D. Roosevelt was elected President of the United States four times — in the Depression years of 1932 and 1936 and in the World War II years of 1940 and 1944 — in spite of overwhelming opposition from a majority of the nation's newspaper publishers. As a group, the publishers, who tended to be conservative Republicans, like other business people, feared the social and economic consequences of Roosevelt's Democratic New Deal. Roosevelt himself spoke out against "press lords" like Hearst (after Hearst, an initial backer, broke with the administration in 1935) and Robert McCormick, contending that 85% of the nation's newspapers editorially were against the New Deal.

While Roosevelt exaggerated the extent of the enmity, it was formidable. According to surveys, about 40% of the nation's dailies supported his first election in 1932 and 36% backed his re-election in 1936, while only 22% endorsed his election to an unprecedented third term in 1940 and to a fourth term in 1944. The fact that he won overwhelmingly served as proof that newspaper endorsements meant relatively little in presidential elections. Nonetheless, newspapers were potent influences in the entire political process.

Roosevelt showed himself to be a master at political communication in spite of hostility from publishers. Aided by his press secretary, Stephen T. Early, he cultivated the Washington press corps more than his predecessors had done. Inspiring confidence with his melodious voice, he also took his case for economic recovery directly to the American people in a series of twenty-eight radio "fireside chats." These presented his programs in terms that the public could understand.

Roosevelt took steps personally to make front page news that was favorable to his administration. During his presidency he held a total of 998 press conferences, an average of eighty-three per year, a figure far higher than that of his successors. Displaying his warm and magnetic personality, he provided an endless source of stories for reporters. In return, they valued his friendship and admired his leadership. His popularity with the White House press corps, many members of which he knew by name, was illustrated in his relations with still and newsreel photographers. Although Roosevelt, as a result of infantile paralysis, was unable to walk without assistance, photographers acceded to a "gentleman's

UNIONIST BOMBS WRECK THE TIMES; MANY SERIOUSLY INJURED

A PLAIN STATEMENT

All Business for THE TIMES Will be Transacted at Their Branch Office 531 SOUTH SPRING ST.

Heywood Broun and Organized Labor
The leader of the American Newspaper Guild, Broun was a hero of liberals in the 1920s and 1930s. His columns about what he considered to be injustice often were bitter, but acquaintances said that he was friendly and kind, and many held him in deep affection. In the efforts to unionize newspapers, organizers were hampered by isolated instances of violence. A member of a union (unconnected with the Newspaper Guild) in the American Federation of Labor confessed to having thrown the bomb that killed twenty employees at the non-union *Los Angeles Times* in 1910. AFL membership declined nationwide for the next several years.

agreement" not to snap pictures of him in a wheelchair.

Newspaper publishers took particular exception to New Deal legislation that had an impact on their own businesses. Roosevelt's National Recovery Act of 1933, which set up codes of fair practices for industries, was outlawed by the U.S. Supreme Court in 1935, but it promoted the organization of labor and led to the founding of the American Newspaper Guild. The guild was the first union of newspaper personnel not involved in mechanical operations like printing, which long had been unionized and paid better than editorial work.

Led by Heywood Broun, a syndicated columnist, the guild fought for contracts that raised pay and provided for job security, sick leave, and other benefits. Based on a standard forty-hour work week, the contracts helped improve the atmosphere of newspaper city rooms, described by novelists as refuges for aged alcoholics worn out by years of long hours and low pay. Higher pay led to the employment of better-educated individuals.

Faced with resistance from Hearst and other publishers, guild units went on strike against some twenty newspapers in the 1930s. The right of reporters and other personnel to join the guild was upheld by the U.S. Supreme Court in 1937 when it ruled against the Associated Press for discharging an employee engaged in union activity. The AP argued that the formation of unions in editorial offices was contrary to the constitutional guarantee of freedom of the press. In its ruling, the high court made a distinction between newspapers as a business, subject to general laws governing all businesses, and newspapers as an instrument of free expression operating under the First Amendment.

Six years earlier the Supreme Court had ruled by a 5-4 decision that a Minnesota statute, known as the "Gag Law," which outlawed malicious and scandalous publications by court injunction, violated the freedom of the press clause. The case, *Near v. Minnesota*, involved a newspaper of questionable reputation, the *Saturday Press*, that had attacked public officials. The majority of the justices held that a court injunction represented prior restraint on publication and was illegal under the U. S. Constitution, no matter how unsavory the newspaper might be.

As the Roosevelt administration put through a complicated legislative agenda to deal with the Depression and World War II, newspapers, influenced in part by the popularity of news magazine analysis and radio commentators, turned to interpretative reporting to explain involved economic, political, and social questions. Interpretative reporting offered an approach to news, often provided by syndicates, that stressed interconnections between facts and permitted specialists in areas such as science, economics, and labor to share their expertise with readers. It bore relatively little relationship to the slap-dash race for scoops that remained part of journalistic lore.

Background material for interpretative reports came from government public information offices, which Roosevelt saw as important facets of New Deal activities. To argue the case for relief programs, the administration tried to document the extent of Depression-era poverty. In part this was because newspapers did not cover the Depression in great detail, hoping for a return of consumer confidence to boost economic conditions. Roosevelt's Farm Security Administration sent out teams of photographers, including Dorothea Lange, Walker Evans, and other well-known professionals, who captured on film the plight of rural Americans affected by drought and dust storms. The same agency also commissioned notable documentary films.

Some Washington correspondents became syndicated political columnists called "pundits," who pontificated on national and international issues. Representing opposite extremes were the somber Lippmann, known as the dean of the pundits, and Drew Pearson, who gave a behind-the-scenes view of Washington political shenanigans. Syndicates also sold comic strips, features, and gossip columns. One of the most popular columnists was Walter Winchell, a Broadway "insider" who offered intimate gossip about show business personalities for both newspapers and radio.

One syndicated columnist occupied a class by herself. It was

The New York Times.

ROOSEVELT WINNER IN LANDSLIDE! DEMOCRATS CONTROL WET CONGRESS; LEHMAN GOVERNOR, O'BRIEN MAYOR

SWEEP IS NATIONAL

Democrats Carry 40 States; Electoral Votes 448.

Bingham, Watson, Moses and Smoot Are Defeated.

The Electoral Vote

Wets in Control in Both Houses, But Short of Two-Thirds in Senate

The Roosevelts
Upon Franklin Roosevelt's election as President in 1932, both he and his wife, Eleanor, became accomplished at working with the media. He initiated regular meetings with journalists and appealed effectively to the public through his radio "fireside chats." Mrs. Roosevelt wrote a syndicated newspaper column, "My Day," held press conferences, and made frequent radio broadcasts. She became one of the best known radio personalities in the country during and after the twelve years she was in the White House, from 1933 to 1945.

the First Lady, Eleanor Roosevelt, whose column, "My Day," ran from 1936 until her death in 1962. It gave an informal, diary-like account of the people she met and the places she went. Like her husband, Eleanor Roosevelt held press conferences, scheduling some 348 during her twelve years in the White House. She also gave sponsored radio broadcasts.

The First Lady limited her press conferences to women reporters only, attempting to help them hold jobs during the Depression by giving them news that, as she expressed it, "the women reporters might write up better than the men."[23] In initiating the press conferences just after her husband's inauguration in 1933, she received guidance from Lorena Hickok, an intimate friend. Hickok left the Associated Press to become an undercover reporter for the Roosevelt administration, touring the country to write confidential reports on relief efforts. In 1934 she accompanied the First Lady and a small group of women reporters on a fact-finding mission to Puerto Rico and the Virgin Islands.

At the time of Franklin Roosevelt's death in 1945, shortly after the start of his fourth term, newspapers retained their status as mass vehicles of news and entertainment. Yet the Roosevelt years had seen enormous changes in the mass media — changes that Franklin and Eleanor Roosevelt had recognized and in which they personally had participated. Newspapers still provided a quantity of news and advertising oriented to local communities and not available from other sources.

But the public had been primed for change. Fascinated with radio, motion pictures, and still photography, it stood ready for the advent of network television, which had been delayed by World War II. Newspapers had yet to meet their most formidable challenger.

[23]Eleanor Roosevelt, *This I Remember* (New York, 1949), 102.

RECOMMENDED READINGS

BOOKS

Abramson, Phyllis Leslie. *Sob Sister Journalism*. Westport, Conn., 1990. Examines the evolution of the newspaper "sob sister" in relation to the celebrated Thaw murder trial of 1907.

Beasley, Maurine H. *Eleanor Roosevelt and the Media: A Public Quest for Self-Fulfillment*. Urbana, Ill., 1987. Shows how Eleanor Roosevelt became the most notable woman in American public life by skillful use of the media.

Berman, Ronald. *Advertising and Social Change*. Beverly Hills, Calif., 1981. Offers a discussion of how social forces and changes in the marketplace have shaped media economics.

Blanchard, Margaret A. *Revolutionary Sparks: Freedom of Expression in Modern America*. New York, 1992. A comprehensive history of freedom of speech and press from the 1870s to the Reagan presidency.

Britt, George. *Forty Years, Forty Millions: The Career of Frank A. Munsey*. New York, 1935. Munsey made journalism into a business with a primary concern for money.

Cochran, Negley. *E.W. Scripps*. New York, 1933. Details the history of the Scripps-Howard chain, treating Scripps as a great public servant.

Cohen, Jeremy. *Congress Shall Make No Law: Oliver Wendell Holmes, The First Amendment, and Judicial Decision Making*. Ames, Iowa, 1989. The noted Supreme Court justice was more concerned with jurisprudence than with free expression.

Covert, Catherine L., and John D. Stevens, eds. *Mass Media Between the Wars: Perceptions of Cultural Tension, 1918-1941*. Syracuse, N.Y., 1984. Offers essays that examine the growth of mass communications and their impact on American society.

Czitrom, Daniel J. *Media and the American Mind: From Morse to McLuhan*. Chapel Hill, N.C., 1982. Presents an intellectual history of modern communication rooted in social context.

Emery, Edwin. *History of the American Newspaper Publishers Association*. Minneapolis, 1950. Explains the newspaper industry from the publishers' viewpoint, including its position on governmental and labor issues.

Ewen, Stewart. *Captains of Consciousness: Advertising and the Social Roots of the Consumer Culture*. New York, 1976. Explains how capitalists used advertising to expand consumption and control the marketplace after 1900.

Goldberg, Vicki. *Margaret Bourke-White: A Biography*. Reading, Mass., 1987. Relates Bourke-White's career to the evolution of photojournalism.

Good, Howard. *Acquainted with the Night: The Image of Journalists in American Fiction, 1890-1930*. Metuchen, N. J., 1986. A synopsis of fictional treatment of reporters in relation to social changes.

Griffith, Sally Foreman. *The Autobiography of William Allen White*. 2nd ed., Revised and Abridged. Lawrence, Kansas, 1990. Makes the *Autobiography*, published in 1946, more accessible to the modern reader.

—. *Home Town News: William Allen White and the Emporia Gazette*. New York, 1989. This biography of the prominent Kansas editor especially emphasizes his political dimension.

Hohenberg, John. *The Pulitzer Prize Story*. New York, 1959. Tells the history of the Pulitzer Prizes and reprints examples of prize-winning work.

Keever, Beverly Ann Deepe, Carolyn Martindale, and Mary Ann Weston. *U.S. News Coverage of Racial Minorities: A Sourcebook, 1934-1996*. Westport, Conn., 1997. Draws together scholarly work assessing news coverage of Americans of African, Native, Asian, Hispanic, and Pacific Islander origin in the mainstream U.S. media.

Knight, Oliver, ed. *I Protest: Selected Disquisitions of E. W. Scripps*. Madison, Wis., 1966. Contains a biographical introduction and key documents from Scripps' papers that present his thinking on journalism, politics, and related subjects.

Kobre, Sidney. *Modern American Journalism*. Tallahassee, 1959. Details the growth of newspapers by region in the first half of the century.

Marzolf, Marion T. *Up From the Footnote: A History of Woman Journalists*. New York, Hastings House, 1977. Tells the story of efforts by women to be accepted as professional equals with men in the field of journalism.

Meyer, Karl E., ed. *Pundits, Poets, and Wits: An Omnibus of American Newspaper Columns*. New York, 1990. An anthology of newspaper columns from colonial times to the present.

Pfaff, Daniel W. *Joseph Pulitzer II and the Post-Dispatch*. University Park, Pa., 1991. Biography of the elder Pulitzer's middle son reveals how the liberal *St. Louis Post-Dispatch* handled major critical issues from World War I through the 1950s.

Rogers, Everett M. *A History of Communication Study: A Biographical Approach*. New York, 1994. Relates the personal histories of leading communications scholars to the establishment of communication study as a formal discipline.

Seldes, George. *Lords of the Press*. New York, 1938. Offers a liberal argument that big newspapers were controlled in most instances by wealthy money-makers who were conservative and failed to ensure fair news treatment for labor and for social and economic reforms.

Sloan, Wm. David, and Cheryl S. Wray. *Masterpieces of Reporting*. Northport, Ala., 1998. An anthology of outstanding examples of news writing, many covering the first half of the twentieth century.

Sloan, Wm. David, Julie Hedgepeth, Patricia Place and Kevin Stoker. *The Great Reporters: An Anthology of News Writing at Its Best*. Northport, Ala., 1992. Includes biographies of and famous news stories by well-known reporters from World War I through the 1940s.

Smith, Wilda M., and Eleanor A. Bogart. *The Wars of Peggy Hull: The Life and Times of a War Correspondent*. El Paso, Tex., 1991. Life of a pioneer woman foreign correspondent in the early twentieth century.

Snyder, Louis L., and Richard B. Morris, eds. *A Treasury of Great Reporting*, 2nd ed. New York, 1962. Of the many anthologies of news reporting, this is one of the best. Including articles from the Zenger trial in 1735to the early 1960s, it is particularly strong on articles from the 1920s to 1940s.

Stevens, John D. *Sensationalism and the New York Press*. New York, 1991. From the penny-press era to the present, New York City readers have been particularly interested in tabloid journalism.

Stott, William. *Documentary Expression and Thirties America*. New York, 1973. Explains how conditions were documented in spite of opposition from interests that preferred not to make a record of the Depression.

Swanson, Walter S.J. *The Thin Gold Watch, A Personal History of the Newspaper Copleys*. New York, 1964. Paints a favorable picture of Ira Copley as one of the first 20th-century businessmen to recognize that the newspaper was a business that could make a profit.

Trimble, Vance H. *The Astonishing Mr. Scripps: The Turbulent Life of American's Penny Press Lord*. Ames, Iowa, 1992. Comprehensive biography of the penny press baron of the late nineteenth and early twentieth centuries.

Villard, Oswald Garrison. *The Disappearing Daily: Chapters in American Newspaper Evolution*. New York, 1944. Offers a liberal criticism that too many newspapers had given up crusading in the interests of the public, growing concerned instead with "crass materialism."

Williamson, Samuel T. *Imprint of a Publisher: The Story of Frank Gannett and His Newspapers*. New York, 1948. Tells the success story of a poor boy who went from rags to riches through buying and merging newspapers.

Winfield, Betty Houchin. *FDR and the News Media*. Urbana, Ill., 1990. Relates the steps taken by Franklin D. Roosevelt to manage the news during critical periods in American history.

ARTICLES

Asher, Brad. "The Professional Vision: Conflicts Over Journalism Education, 1900-1950." *American Journalism* 11 (1994): 304-20. Journalism schools were part of a trend toward professionalization, but newspapers did not embrace the concept.

Beasley, Maurine H. "Lorena A. Hickok: Journalism Influence on Eleanor Roosevelt." *Journalism Quarterly* 57 (1980): 281-6. Describes the role of Hickok in covering Mrs. Roosevelt for the Associated Press and advising her on press relations.

Bekken, Jon. "The Chicago Newspaper Scene: An Ecological Perspective." *Journalism & Mass Communication Quarterly* 74 (1997): 490-500. Examines the media environment in Chicago from 1880 to 1930 in terms of the variety of specialized and foreign-language newspapers that coexisted with the English-language dailies.

Bennion, Sherilyn Cox. "Reform Agitation in the American Periodical Press, 1920-29." *Journalism Quarterly* 48 (1971): 692-9, 713. Discusses the reluctance of the mass magazines of the 1920s to bring up subjects related to social reforms because their readers were not interested in such topics.

Brazil, John R. "Murder Trials, Murder and Twenties America." *American Quarterly* 33, 2 (1981): 163-84. Pictures tabloids competing for public attention with cheap literature and movies.

Carlebach, Michael L. *American Photojournalism Comes of Age*. Washington, D.C., 1997. Traces the development of photojournalism as a profession from 1880 through the 1930s, focusing on the news photographer as a witness to history.

Christians, Clifford G. "Fifty Years of Scholarship in Media Ethics." *Journal of Communication* 27 (Autumn 1977): 19-29. Explains the way that definitions of ethics changed from the 1920s to the 1930s.

Del Castillo, Richard Griswold. "The Mexican Revolution and the Spanish-Language Press in the Borderlands," *Journalism History* 4 (Summer 1977): 42-7. Mexican-American editors helped promote an emerging sense of nationalism in Mexico.

Egan, Kathryn S. "A Constructivist's View of an Earthquake: Edith Irvine Photographs San Francisco 1906." *Journalism History* 20 (1994): 66-73. Account of the independent woman who took surreptitious photographs of a devastated San Francisco after the 1906 earthquake.

Harrison, Stanley L. "'The Wayward Press' Revisited: The Contributions of Robert Benchley." *Journalism History* 19 (1993): 19-25. From 1927 to 1939, Benchley wrote the "Wayward Press" column in the *New Yorker* and used it to uphold high newspaper standards.

Johnson, Thomas J., and Wayne Wanta, with John T. Bird and Cindy Lee. "Exploring FDR's Relationship with the Press." *Political Communication* 12 (1995): 157-72. Uses Roosevelt's efforts to examine the process of agenda setting.

Kaul, Arthur J., and Joseph P. McKerns. "The Dialectic Ecology of the Newspaper." *Critical Studies in Mass Communication* 2 (1985): 217-33. Traces the ecological cycle of how the newspaper industry became an oligopoly.

Marzolf, Marion. "The Woman Journalist: Colonial Printer to City Desk, Part II." *Journalism History* 2 (1975): 24-7, 32. Tells how women fought for the right to be treated as professionals in journalism in spite of discrimination.

Mirando, Joe. "Lessons on Ethics in News Reporting Textbooks, 1867-1997." *Journal of Mass Media Ethics* 13 (1998): 26-39. Textbooks on reporting and news writing devoted little attention to matters of ethics and often overlooked important moral and intellectual questions.

Olasky, Marvin N. "When World Views Collide: Journalists and the Great Monkey Trial." *American Journalism* 4 (1987): 133-46. Reporters covering the Scopes trial in 1925 considered themselves open-minded, but they were opposed to fundamental Christianity and thus interpreted the trial and its participants to fit their prejudices, giving biased and inaccurate accounts.

Ponder, Stephen. "That Delightful Relationship: Presidents and White House Correspondents in the 1920s." *American Journalism* 14 (1997): 164-81. Management of the press by executive officials became institutionalized during the decade.

Rogers, Everett M., and Steven H. Chaffee. "Communication and Journalism from 'Daddy' Bleyer to Wilbur Schramm: A Palimpsest." *Journalism Monographs* 148 (December 1994). The origins of journalism and communication as a separate branch of study at American universities.

Schiller, Dan. "An Historical Approach to Objectivity and Professionalism in American News Reporting." *Journal of Communication* 29 (Autumn 1979): 46-57. By the turn of the century, objectivity was increasingly threatened, becoming "professionalized" and incorporated into ethical codes in hopes of preserving it.

Sloan, Wm. David. "Historians and the American Press, 1900-1945: Working Profession or Big Business?" *American Journalism* 3 (1986): 154-66. Historiographical essay examines how historians have explained the press of the period.

Smith, Carol, and Carolyn Stewart Dyer. "Taking Stock, Placing Orders: A Historiographical Essay on the Business History of the Newspaper." *Journalism Monographs* 132 (1992). Examines the treatment by historians of newspaper economics and business practices.

Stevens, John D. "The Black Press Looks at 1920's Journalism." *Journalism History* 7 (1980): 109-13. The black press "had always been a 'fighting press,' and while it did not abandon that opinion-leader role, it turned more and more to news as its staple" in the 1920s. Black newspapers became "viable businesses."

Strother, T. Ella. "The Black Image in the Chicago 'Defender,' 1905-1975." *Journalism History* 4 (Winter 1977-78): 137-41, 156. Concludes the *Defender* presented a positive black image throughout the newspaper although it headlined anti-social behavior to sell newspapers.

Suggs, Henry Lewis. "Black Strategy and Ideology in the Segregation Era: P.B. Young and the *Norfolk Journal and Guide*, 1910-1954." *Virginia Magazine of History and Biography* 91 (1983): 161-90. A founder of the NAACP, Young nevertheless was cautious and favored black accomodationism.

Sullins, William S., and Paul Parsons. "Roscoe Dunjee: Crusading Editor of Oklahoma's 'Black Dispatch,' 1915-1955." *Journalism Quarterly* 69 (1992): 204-13. The weekly newspaper editor was a crusading civil rights activist who urged peaceful change.

Teel, Leonard Ray. "W. A. Scott and the *Atlanta World*. *American Journalism* 6 (1989): 158-78. Presents the *World*, the first African-American daily newspaper in the United States, as the result of the owner's business sense.

Weigle, Clifford F. "The Young Scripps Editor: Keystone of E.W.'s 'System.'" *Journalism Quarterly* 41 (1964): 360-6. Scripps got promising young men to start new papers by directing them to a city, advancing them capital, and then leaving them alone and allowing them to buy a share of the paper. Many were so inspired by these principles that they worked tirelessly on starvation budgets.

16

The Media and Reform

1900 - 1917

The mass media have long been a valuable resource for reformers working on behalf of social and political change. The same is just as true, too, of those interested in forestalling reform. They exerted a great deal of influence, both direct and indirect, over the means of mass communication. This paradoxical relationship between the press and reform can be seen in the Progressive era of American history, roughly the period from the inauguration of Theodore Roosevelt as president in 1901 until the United States entered World War I in 1917. "The fundamental critical achievement of American Progressivism was the business of exposure," historian Richard Hofstadter has written, "and journalism was the chief occupational source of its creative writers. It is hardly an exaggeration to say that the Progressive mind was characteristically a journalistic mind, and that its characteristic contribution was that of the socially responsible reporter-reformer."[1]

One brand of journalism these reporter-reformers practiced earned the title "muckraking." Expressing his displeasure with the 1906 magazine series "Treason of the Senate," President Roosevelt compared the over-zealous reporters to the man with the muckrake in John Bunyan's *Pilgrim's Progress*. In off-the-record remarks before a club of Washington, D.C., journalists, Roosevelt said the man could "look no way but downward, with muckrake in his hands; ...was offered a celestial crown for his muckrake, but... would neither look up nor regard the crown he was offered, but continued to rake to himself the filth of the floor."[2] Roosevelt's label stuck. Indeed, some journalists wore it as a badge of honor.

Muckrakers, although the most visible reform journalists, were hardly alone in their efforts. Socialist and labor groups sponsored newspapers that explored the deleterious effects of the new economic order, the feminist press criticized unjust social arrangements, and some civic improvement associations found newspapers ready allies for their municipal reforms. Still, muckraking marked a new departure in reform journalism. For the most part, muckraking exposés appeared in national consumer magazines. Hence, they were aimed at the middle class and could tackle a wide range of topics. Typically, muckraking journalists and magazines claimed independence from interest groups, although many worked loosely with insurgent Republicans and reform-minded Democrats. The better muckraking articles marshaled details unearthed in thorough investigations. Significantly, the exposés derived their power from well-selected facts, not the forceful polemics characteristic of earlier journalistic essays. For a relatively short period at the beginning of the century, then, reform journalism in mainstream magazines flourished as never before or since.

The concerted journalistic effort during the Progressive era was a by-product of developments in the mass media, particularly the magazine industry. The ultimate question, perhaps, is whether the press succeeded in promoting worthwhile reforms.

The Progressive Movement

Although Roosevelt's ascension to the presidency often is cited as marking the beginning of the Progressive era, another event of symbolic importance had occurred several months earlier. In April 1901, United States Steel became the first American firm incorporated with more than $1 billion in capital stock. The event had been preceded by several decades of growth of giant industries. The power associated with such economic concentration was, in the eyes of the Progressives, wielded without concern for the public good. Government regulation of the industrial behemoths was virtually unknown, although Populists in the West and South had been fighting the railroads, banks, and grain companies for decades. The Progressive movement picked up elements of the Populist agenda, but tended to concentrate more on problems connected with urban America.

The specific goals varied among the individuals and groups that assembled under the banner of Progressivism, but a few reforms

[1] Richard Hofstadter, *The Age of Reform: From Bryan to F.D.R.* (New York, Vintage Edition, 1955), 186.

[2] Quoted in Harvey Swados, ed., *Years of Conscience: The Muckrakers* (New York, 1962), 10.

were shared by most. Curbing the excesses of big business, principally through government regulation, was high on the agenda. Progressives worried about business corrupting the political process. Thus, they sought to reduce the political influence of special interests by making government more responsive to the electorate. Ameliorating social problems associated with industrial, urban America occupied the attention of many. Of interest to fewer Progressives but still noteworthy were concerns about racial discrimination in both the North and South.

Despite the generally liberal nature of the Progressive movement, it did embody conservative elements, at least in the eyes of some historians. The reform wrought by the Progressives enhanced the competitive edge of big business, it has been argued; federal regulations tended to eliminate competition in some industries and gave remaining firms greater control of markets. Other historians accurately point out that all but a few Progressives, far from being wide-eyed radicals, subscribed to basic American values — responsible corporate capitalism, individualism, representative democracy, and social order. Their acceptance of the basic structure of the American political and economic system limited the extent and nature of change that they envisioned. Rarely did they advocate sweeping structural changes in the system.[3]

Forerunners of Muckraking

Reformers had used the press as an instrument of change long before the advent of the Progressive movement. Abolitionists launched an antislavery pamphlet campaign in the 1830s that provoked a violent backlash. Later in the century, women suffragists, temperance groups, and other reform movements sponsored publications to promote their causes and to communicate with like-minded citizens throughout the country. But these efforts to communicate messages of reform suffered one major handicap — for the most part they were read by the already-converted and failed to reach large, mass audiences.

An important precursor of muckraking was the reform press of agrarian activists in the 1880s and 1890s. Populists and the Farmers' Alliance waged much of their battle against railroads, banks, and food processors on the pages of their newspapers. Many promoted alternative economic structures such as agricultural cooperatives. In 1891, the editors formed the National Reform Press Association, which eventually attracted more than 1,000 members. Although most of these papers were small weeklies, at least one claimed a circulation approaching 100,000.

At the same time, urban citizens' groups were forging loose alliances with sympathetic city newspapers. These reformers understood the new environment of large cities with their mass-circulation newspapers. The press was the best means to communicate with disparate groups in urban areas that now were too large and socially complex for personal contacts to suffice. In a sense, mass communication took the place, at least in part, of communication through city-wide political machines. For example, the *Chicago Daily News* and *Chicago Tribune* helped put problems of transportation, utilities, and pollution on the political agenda. But elsewhere (St. Louis, for instance) most of the press was indifferent or opposed to reform.[4]

Much of what the reporter-reformers did in the early twentieth century built on venerable traditions in American journalism. Occasionally reporters had entered prisons, asylums, and similar institutions to describe conditions. Such excursions seemed to be motivated as much by a desire to titillate readers with sensational details as to expose inhumane conditions. The sins of big corporations had been chronicled, too, long before the Progressive movement. Charles F. Adams, Jr., had exposed some of the machinations of the Erie Railroad and associated financiers as early as 1868. W.T. Stead cleverly titled his 1894 study of Chicago's seamy underbelly *If Christ Came to Chicago*. And in the same year Henry Demarest Lloyd published *Wealth Against Commonwealth*, a weighty book that anticipated much of the later muckraking. Police courts and tenement life had regularly furnished stories since the 1830s. Although this kind of reportage was not part of concerted campaigns to reform urban life, the better writers captured the plight of the disadvantaged in big, impersonal cities. There were also precedents for editorial leadership on behalf of city improvement. Joseph Pulitzer campaigned in his *New York World* to abate the sufferings of the poor, while in Kansas City William Rockhill Nelson and his *Star* promoted plans to beautify the city.

The nineteenth-century reform tradition culminated in the work of Jacob Riis, one of the first important photojournalists and a reporter who influenced muckrakers of the Progressive era. Born in Denmark in 1849, Riis immigrated to the United States in 1870 and held a number of odd jobs before becoming a reporter for New York area newspapers. He covered the police for the *New York Tribune* and thus saw firsthand the consequences of life in the city's poorer neighborhoods. Even though many of his stories dealt with people who had run afoul of the law, he tried to affirm the humanity of his subjects and assure his middle-class readers that the newly arrived immigrants wanted the same kind of life they enjoyed. He then expanded his purview to include the city's health department. He began accompanying inspectors as they made nightly rounds of overcrowded flop houses, but his newspaper stories, Riis felt, made no impression. It then occurred to him to take photographs at night using dangerous flash techniques. In his autobiography, *The Making of an American*, Riis described how he and the inspectors would enter a room crowded with sleepers, ignite the flash powder to take the picture, and trigger a panic. Twice his flash set fire to houses and once to him-

[3]See Gabriel Kolko, *The Triumph of Conservatism* (New York, 1963), 1-9, for the argument that the Progressive movement had more conservative consequences than most historians imagined. Hofstadter, *The Age of Reform*, 196, notes that the Progressives were hardly revolutionaries. For a incisive analysis of historians' discussions of muckraking, see Wm. David Sloan, "The Muckrakers, 1901-1917: Defenders of Conservatism or Liberal Reformers?" in *Perspectives on Mass Communication History* (Hillsdale, N.J., 1991), 271-82.

[4]David P. Nord, *Newspapers and New Politics: Midwestern Municipal Reform, 1890-1900* (Ann Arbor, Mich., 1981).

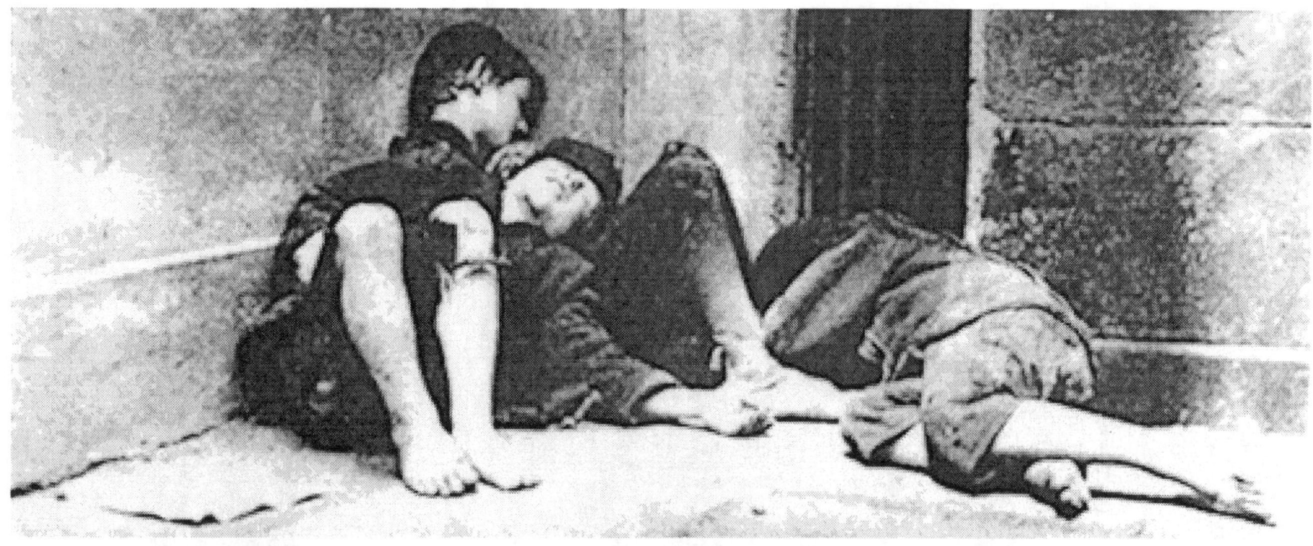

Jacob Riis, Photojournalist Reformer
In the 1880s and 1890s, reporter Jacob Riis began photographing the squalid conditions in which many poor New Yorkers lived. The subjects of this photograph were three "Street Arabs," homeless boys living in the Mulberry Bend district. Riis' work led to the renovation of the district, one of the worst in New York City. His reform efforts also foreshadowed the work of the muckrakers in the twentieth century.

self. Many of his photographs were collected in the book *How the Other Half Lives* (1890), and his work led to the renovation of one of the worst areas, Mulberry Bend. Like many of the reporter-reformers who followed, Riis combined his observational powers with literary techniques. He even wrote short stories that were little more than thinly disguised versions of his newspaper reports.

In fact, the move toward realism in literature left its mark on muckraking. Literary realism in the United States started with the works of Mark Twain, Stephen Crane, and William Dean Howells. Its most extreme adherents were such writers as Jack London and Theodore Dreiser. All these men had worked on newspapers; and, in varying degrees, their outlook on life had been shaped by what they had seen as reporters. Dreiser is a good example. Having spent his boyhood mostly in small Indiana towns and in the middle-sized city of Terre Haute, he first experienced the world as a newspaperman in Chicago. He covered both the inner-city poor and industrialists, two extremes of American society. The contrasts troubled him and influenced the tone of his novels. Characters in such works as *Sister Carrie* (1900) were buffeted by social and economic forces over which they had no control. Frank Norris' *The Octupus* (1901) made a fictional indictment of predatory railroads akin to later factual stories. Many muckrakers, aspiring novelists themselves, were influenced by this major current in American literature.

MUCKRAKING MOVES TO MAGAZINES

Muckraking was a distinctly twentieth-century phenomenon in at least one respect: it was closely associated with the rise of nationally circulated, inexpensive magazines that reached millions of readers. As a medium, national magazines were ideally suited to the purposes of the muckrakers. They permitted a more developed and coherent presentation of complex facts than was possible in daily newspapers. Much muckraking endeavored to show broad patterns that transcended any one city or state; national magazines were the logical vehicle. Other stories dealt with national institutions — Congress and big business were two favorites — and needed to be placed before a national audience. Extensive research often was needed to document charges, and daily newspapers lacked the resources to allow reporters to undertake such digging. Finally, local scandals could be broken by national publications, whereas community interests might pressure newspapers to remain silent.

Muckraking can be viewed at least in part as a by-product of structural changes in the magazine industry. Until the late nineteenth century, most magazines were very expensive or specialized. A few religious magazines attained huge circulations but were limited in scope. The more eclectic magazines, on the other hand, set subscription rates so high that they restricted readership. Changes began in the late 1800s. Underlying the emergence of general-audience magazines — the first true national media of mass communication in the United States — were basic changes in the nation's economy.

Manufacturing was becoming the economy's driving engine, and the hallmark of manufacturing was the cheap production of goods for mass consumption. Accompanying this change was the growth of a national distribution network, based largely on railroads. The retail sector of the economy shifted, too, from exclusively local, independently owned outlets to national chains and department stores. Together, these developments brought about the mass marketing of goods, which depended on advertising for the large volume of sales needed to sustain huge capital investments. Beginning chiefly in the 1890s, advertisers sought national markets, and inexpensive general-circulation magazines provided

Ida Tarbell Exposes Standard Oil
Ida Tarbell made her reputation with magazine biographies of Napoleon and Abraham Lincoln. Her exposé on the Standard Oil Company began as a biography of its head, John D. Rockefeller. It was so popular that it initiated the flood of muckraking articles that filled American magazines over the next decade. *McClure's* printed the first of the series' eighteen parts in November 1902, helping *McClure's* assume the leadership role in exposure journalism.

McClure's Magazine

VOL. XX *NOVEMBER, 1902* NO. 1

THE HISTORY OF THE STANDARD OIL COMPANY

BY IDA M. TARBELL

Author of "The Life of Lincoln"

CHAPTER I—THE BIRTH OF AN INDUSTRY

ONE of the busiest corners of the globe at the opening of the year 1872 was a strip of Northwestern Pennsylvania, not over fifty miles long, known the world over as the Oil Regions. Twelve years before, this strip of land had been but little better than a wilderness its only inhabitants the lumbermen, who every season cut great swaths of primeval pine and hemlock from its hills, and in the spring floated them down the Allegheny River to Pittsburg. The great tides of Western emigration had shunned the spot for years as too rugged and unfriendly for settlement, and yet in twelve years this region avoided by men had been transformed into a bustling trade center, where towns elbowed each other for place, into which the three great trunk railroads had built branches, and every foot of whose soil was fought for by capitalists. It was the discovery and development of a new raw product, petroleum, which had made this change from wilderness to market-place. This product in twelve years had not only peopled a waste place of the earth, it had revolutionized the world's methods of illumination and added millions upon millions of dollars to the wealth of the United States.

GEORGE H. BISSELL

The man to whom more than any other is due the credit of what is called the "discovery" of oil; for it was he who first took steps to find its value and to organize a company to produce it. It was he, too, who suggested the means of getting oil which proved practical. After the oil company which he organized obtained oil in the Drake well, he aided in establishing the needed industries and institutions in the new country.

Petroleum as a curiosity was no new thing. For more than two hundred years it had been described in the journals of Western explorers. For decades it had been dipped up from the surface of springs, soaked up by blankets from running streams, found in quantities when salt wells were bored, bottled and sold as a cure-all—"Seneca Oil" or "Rock Oil," it was called. One man had even distilled it in a crude way, and sold it as an illuminant. Scientists had described it, and travelers from the West often carried bottles to their scientific friends in the East. It was such a bottleful, brought as a gift

7

the best vehicle. Ironically, this economic transformation produced both the social problems that the muckrakers critiqued as well as the means the reporter-reformers used to investigate them. In a further irony, muckrakers' exposés often appeared alongside advertisements for products created by the very system they were attacking.

While economic changes provided the stimulus for large-circulation magazines, technological improvements made their publication feasible. In the 1880s and '90s, magazines began adopting the rotary presses that had revolutionized newspaper publishing. Switching from flatbed to rotary presses increased the potential output of some magazines tenfold. Also important to attracting larger audiences was the artwork that magazines could offer readers. The old methods of reproducing drawings, especially in color, were time-consuming and expensive. Sketches had to be engraved by hand. To add color, *Godey's Lady's Book* hired 150 women to tint illustrations. But by 1893, rotary presses could handle multicolor reproductions. The introduction of more sophisticated and expensive technology provided another impetus for publishers to seek massive audiences. Huge capital investments were needed to equip printing plants, and their fixed costs could best be recouped through large circulations.

In addition to improved technology, delivery systems — both public and private — extended the market of periodicals. The U.S. Congress, through the Post Office Act of 1879, bestowed the fullest mailing privilege on magazines — the low rates long enjoyed by newspapers. The American News Company virtually monopolized the distribution of non-local newspapers and magazines carried outside the mails. It served the thousands of newsstands that increasingly carried magazines as the century drew to a close.

McClure's and Ida Tarbell

On this foundation of printing technology, economic supports, and delivery systems, a few enterprising publishers began issuing magazines, usually priced at ten cents, for larger audiences that could never afford the more typical 25¢ or 30¢ subscriptions. Some of the new publishers, such as Frank A. Munsey, simply applied principles of mass production and distribution to magazines in order to make a profit. Others, though partly impelled by the profit motive, also hoped to reach an untapped class of readers with interesting fare. S.S. McClure was one, and through the magazine bearing his name he provided a forum for many muckraking journalists.

A native of Ireland who had emigrated to Indiana as a boy, McClure ran a newspaper feature syndicate with his partner John S. Phillips for eight years. In 1893 they launched *McClure's Magazine* as an outlet for feature material they already owned. They initially invested $7,300. From the first number, the magazine made liberal use of illustrations and sold for fifteen cents a copy. Unfortunately, the magazine appeared just as a general financial decline started. Circulation hovered between 30,000 and 40,000, and *McClure's* stayed alive only through the loans of friends, contributors, and advertisers.

The magazine found its formula for success with the publication of "Napoleon," a well-illustrated feature by Ida M. Tarbell, who became one of the most important muckrakers. This biography boosted the circulation of *McClure's* and was followed by a series on the "Early Life of Lincoln" in 1895. With circulation rising, *McClure's* lowered its price to ten cents, joining the two other major illustrated ten-cent monthlies, *Munsey's* and *Cosmopolitan*. *Munsey's* sold more copies; but because of *McClure's* better content, it attracted more advertising. By 1896, it claimed to carry more pages of advertising than any other magazine in history.

McClure's most noteworthy contribution began in 1902, when it carried the first major magazine pieces identified as muckraking journalism. The January 1903 issue recognized that something unusual was happening:

> We did not plan it so; it is a coincidence that this number contains three arraignments of American character such as should make every one of us stop and think. "The Shame of Minneapolis," the current chapter of the history of Standard Oil by Miss Tarbell, Mr. Ray Stannard Baker's "The Right to Work" — they might all have been called "The American Contempt of Law." Capitalists, Workingmen, Politicians, Citizens — all breaking the law or letting it be broken. Who is there left to uphold it?...There is no one left — none but all of us.[5]

The three articles in the issue outlined concerns that were central to the Progressive reformers, and the closing injunction — that all citizens should become involved — was the movement's rallying cry.

Ida Tarbell was the first to begin working on muckraking articles for *McClure's*, though hers were not the first to be published. Building on her earlier successes, the sketches of Napoleon and Lincoln, she persuaded her editors to let her undertake another biography of sorts — a serialized history of the Standard Oil Company headed by John D. Rockefeller. Her series capitalized on two interests of American readers: the infatuation with the rags-to-riches stories of millionaires and the growing unease over the increasing power of trusts and combinations in big business. Tarbell's father had been an independent oil producer who suffered from the business practices of Standard Oil.

A painstaking researcher, Tarbell spent more than four years gathering information and writing her stories on Standard Oil. Fortunately, the magazine allowed her the time and the resources — nearly $50,000 — to pursue the story. She worked like a historian, poring over the evidence, mostly public documents available to anyone with the patience to sift through them. Old law suits and the reports of congressional investigations furnished many of the details. She made only sparing use of information from confidential sources, unlike investigative reporters today. In an eighteen-part series, she detailed the illegal or at least underhanded practices that Standard Oil used to drive competitors out of business. Shedding light on some of the ignoble journalism of the day, she found that Standard Oil's public relations agency had contracted with at least 110 Ohio newspapers to run editorials and "news" favorable to the company.[6]

What did her history-exposé accomplish? It prompted government investigations of Standard Oil, leading to the 1911 U.S. Supreme Court ruling that dissolved the giant corporation into smaller companies. When government investigators retraced the ground that Tarbell had covered, they verified most of her important allegations against the company. Rockefeller responded to Tarbell's and others' characterizations of him by employing public relations counsels to restore his repuation. Tarbell's labors yielded rewards for her employer, too. *McClure's* circulation climbed, a result, at least in part, of "The History of Standard Oil."

Lincoln Steffens and "The Shame of the Cities"

While Ida Tarbell was readying her work for publication, a colleague at *McClure's*, Lincoln Steffens, published "Tweed Days in St. Louis" in October 1902. This first installment in what became "The Shame of the Cities" series was hardly distinguished, especially in comparison to Tarbell's work. But some accounts credit it with being the "first muckraking article."[7] Whether it was is open to debate, and arguments over historical "firsts" are usually unproductive. Without a doubt, the series was one of the most important contributions to muckraking journalism, and in many ways Steffens epitomized the reporter-reformer of the Progressive era. Because he left a detailed and engaging *Autobiography* (1931) — one of the best written by any American — it is possible to trace his method of investigation and reflections on his own work.

Born in 1866 in San Francisco, Steffens enjoyed the amenities of an upper-middle-class life. He majored in history at the University of California-Berkeley (after failing the admissions test on his first try) and then began graduate studies in Germany. In 1892, following three years of study and travel in Europe, he went to New York, where, using his father's connections, he landed a reporting job on the *Evening Post*. He encountered some of the leading Wall Street figures of the day and began honing his interviewing skills. He also covered the police beat and became acquainted with New York's reformers, including Theodore Roosevelt. Although working on the *Evening Post* exposed him to a world he never had experienced, he chafed under the heavy-handed editing of Edwin Lawrence Godkin.

Steffens left the *Post* in 1897 to become editor of the *New York Commercial Advertiser*, a position he hoped would permit him greater latitude. He assembled a group of talented writers, not reporters, as he fondly recalled, and freed them to capture the life of the city in their graceful prose. Many of them went on to distinguished literary careers. During Steffens' tenure on the *Commercial Advertiser*, a friend he had met while studying in Germany left him an inheritance that, through careful investment, Steffens used as the basis for the financial security and editorial independence he enjoyed the rest of his life.

He left the *Commercial Advertiser* in 1901 to devote himself to writing fiction, his first love. His wife already had published a novel, but that attainment eluded him; so he joined *McClure's Magazine* as managing editor. Restless with life in the office, Steffens traveled in pursuit of stories. He noticed that newspapers sometimes focused on corruption in their communities; but, with

[5]Quoted in C.C. Regier, *The Era of the Muckrakers* (Chapel Hill, N.C., 1932), 55.
[6]Ida M. Tarbell, *All In The Day's Work: An Autobiography* (New York, 1939), 202-53.

[7]Ibid., 59.

Lincoln Steffens and Cities' Shame Corruption in the governments of some of America's cities in the early 1900s surpassed that of New York City's earlier Tammany Hall. Following Lincoln Steffens' exposé of Minneapolis in *McClure's Magazine* in 1903, the mayor resigned, and many officials were prosecuted. Steffens' goal in his exposés was to reform modern urban life on the ideals of Christianity. "I have been contending all my life," he wrote at the end of his autobiography, "and always with God."

McClure's Magazine

VOL. XX *JANUARY, 1903* NO. 3

THE SHAME OF MINNEAPOLIS

The Rescue and Redemption of a City that was Sold Out

BY LINCOLN STEFFENS

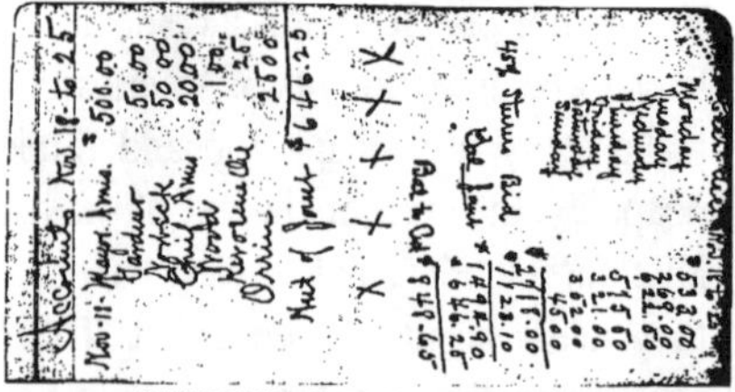

FAC-SIMILE OF THE FIRST PAGE OF "THE BIG MITT LEDGER"

An account kept by a swindler of the dealings of his "Joint" with City Officials, showing first payments made to Mayor Ames, his brother, the Chief of Police and Detectives. This book figured in trials and newspaper reports of the exposure, but was "lost"; and its whereabouts was the mystery of the proceedings. This is the first glimpse that any one, except "Cheerful Charlie" Howard, who kept it, and members of the grand jury, has had of the book

WHENEVER anything extraordinary is done in American municipal politics, whether for good or for evil, you can trace it almost invariably to one man. The people do not do it. Neither do the "gangs," "combines," or political parties. These are but instruments by which bosses (not leaders; we Americans are not led, but driven) rule the people, and commonly sell them out. But there are at least two forms of the autocracy which has supplanted the democracy here as it has everywhere it has been tried. One is that of the organized majority by which, as in Tammany Hall in New York and the Republican machine in Philadelphia, the boss has normal control of more than half the voters. The other is that of the adroitly managed minority. The "good people" are herded into parties and stupefied with convictions and a name, Republican or Democrat; while the "bad people" are so organized or interested by the boss that he can wield their votes to enforce terms with party managers and decide elections. St. Louis is a conspicuous example of this form. Minneapolis is another. Colonel Ed. Butler is the unscrupulous opportunist who handled the non-partisan minority which turned St. Louis into a "boodle town." In Minneapolis "Doc" Ames was the man.

a glut of other news, accounts in the papers often failed to make an impression with the readers. He reasoned that similar stories developed comprehensively in a monthly magazine might prove to be a more powerful stimulus for change. His chance to test the idea came while he was in St. Louis, where a courageous district attorney was trying to prosecute corrupt city officials. Steffens commissioned a local writer, Claude Wetmore, to prepare an article for *McClure's*. Wetmore, however, feared local pressures if he published all the facts he uncovered; so Steffens added his name to the byline to diffuse responsibility. Wetmore's trepidation probably explains why reporters sometimes shied away from exposing corruption in local papers where outside pressure could more readily be exerted on them.

Steffens' second installment, "The Shame of Minneapolis," appeared in the January 1903 *McClure's*, an issue that attracted so much attention that it sold out. "The Shame of Minneapolis" was also the first muckraking article that Steffens researched himself, exercising the interviewing skills he had cultivated as a newspaper reporter. He went to Minneapolis when the broad outlines of corruption were already well known. He talked to reporters for the local papers who often knew much more than they put in print. Typically, Steffens would also draw out the grafters themselves, sometimes playing the role of a knowledgeable police reporter, other times ingenuously marveling at the criminals' accomplishments. Whatever guise he adopted, he refrained from treating his subjects in a condescending manner, and he never passed judgment or moralized in their presence. In short, he developed a rapport with his subjects.[8]

The corruption uncovered in 1902 revolved around Minneapolis Mayor Albert Alonzo Ames. He had served three terms as mayor in the 1880s, both as a Republican and as a Democrat. He was, by some accounts, the most popular man in the city. After winning the election again in 1900, Ames and his cohorts set about creating a system of graft eclipsing that of his previous administrations. On inaugural day, he appointed his brother chief of police and dismissed 107 of the 225 policemen. As mayor-elect, Ames had been screening replacements, personally interviewing all the finalists. With hand-picked officers in all key police department posts, he and his lieutenants devised various schemes to gather graft. Criminals were invited to Minneapolis to work under the auspices of the police. Saloons, brothels, and gambling houses flourished by paying for police protection. The police even guarded burglars as they worked, and they dissuaded victims of rigged gambling games from filing complaints.

Two Minneapolis newspapers, the *Journal* and the *Times*, had opposed Ames' election. The *Tribune*, a recipient of city printing contracts, was a quasi-official organ of the administration. As crime mounted, the *Journal* and *Times* intimated that the police were involved, but such stories appeared too infrequently for the average reader to sense the extent of the graft. An aggressive grand jury eventually uncovered the corruption. Empaneled in April 1902, the grand jury decided to work with the assistant prosecutor to tackle the Ames gang. The chief prosecutor was afraid, and prominent citizens urged the jurors to drop the investigation. As the grand jury heard testimony, stories began appearing in the *Journal* and *Times* linking the mayor to police graft. The pro-administration *Tribune* rallied to Ames' defense until a ledger was produced that showed his share of the take. Even the *Tribune* then had to concede that "there is a state of affairs in the municipal government of Minneapolis that discounts anything Tammany Hall ever dreamed of."[9]

[8] This discussion of "The Shame of Minneapolis" is based on Richard B. Kielbowicz, "The Limits of the Press as an Agent of Reform: Minneapolis, 1900-1905," *Journalism Quarterly* 59 (1982): 21-7 and 170.

[9] *Minneapolis Tribune*, 1 June 1902.

The Ames administration crumbled. Detectives and police captains were convicted or fled the city, and the mayor resigned. The president of the city council assumed duties as mayor and began enforcing ordinances against prostitution and gambling. But the tangible results of the grand jury's digging and the newspaper's coverage were rather limited. Existing laws were better enforced, but ineffectual statutes were not rewritten. Despite massive publicity linking Ames to the graft — some of which he admitted in court — four juries failed to convict him, probably because of his popularity. Vested interests that profited from the Ames regime, including church-going landlords who collected rent from brothels, resisted reforms. The possibility of alternative government structures — for example, a city manager form — was never raised in the columns of the city's papers. Driving the guilty from office, a comparatively modest change, was the principal improvement.

Steffens did not unearth the story. His contribution was to synthesize the uneven newspaper coverage, add details from interviews with several of the principal figures, and elevate the story to a national arena. Publication of the story in *McClure's* came at a critical moment. Interest in the scandal had waned in Minneapolis by late 1902, and Ames quietly left town after resigning as mayor. The Minneapolis papers lost interest. But publication of "The Shame of Minneapolis" in a national magazine spurred the local press and the authorities to seek Ames' return for prosecution.

Steffens went on to muckrake other cities — St. Louis again, then Pittsburgh, Philadelphia, Chicago, and New York. He dismissed claims that he was a scientist, but his method combined the techniques of journalism with those of social science. He examined the structure of city politics, looking for patterns as well as unique features, and thus was able to generalize about the state of city governance. The shame of the cities, he concluded, was the shamelessness of citizens. In most cities he visited, he found that "corruption was not merely political; it was financial, commercial, social...."[10] Respectable business owners colluded with politicians to secure privileges from government. Such corruption was hardly a secret in most places; indeed, leading citizens often were involved.

Finally dissatisfied with the superficial reforms of the Progressive movement, Steffens turned to more radical solutions. Intrigued by the Russian communists' claims of social and economic justice, he traveled to the Soviet Union in 1917 and 1919 to observe their progress firsthand. He was impressed with long-range Soviet planning and the translation of theories into practice. When asked of his reaction, Steffens' well-rehearsed answer was "I have seen the future, and it works." Such a candid endorsement of Soviet communism earned him many enemies during the American "red scare" after the First World War. Toward the end of his life, he spoke less enthusiastically of the Soviet system.

[10]Lincoln Steffens, *The Shame of the Cities* (New York, 1904), 14.

America Under the Muckrake

About 2,000 muckraking articles appeared in the first decade and a half of the twentieth century, but some stand out. One of the most sensational efforts was "The Treason of the Senate." Sitting in the Senate press gallery one day, Charles Edward Russell noticed that many of the men on the floor below were little more than "butlers for industrialists and financiers." Russell proposed a series of articles on the subject for *Cosmopolitan,* just purchased by William Randolph Hearst. Another project sidetracked Russell, however, and Hearst assigned the story to David Graham Phillips, a noted political journalist and novelist. A historian did much of the research for the series, though Phillips wrote the stories. The series opened with a salvo: "The treason of the Senate! Treason is a strong word, but not too strong, rather too weak, to characterize the situation in which the Senate is the eager, resourceful, indefatigable agent of interests as hostile to the American people as any invading army could be...."[11] Phillips named senators who consistently voted on behalf of certain interests. Heavily promoted by Hearst, the series triggered quite a reaction, including Roosevelt's famous "The Man With the Muck-rake" speech. Historians have credited Phillips' stories with unseating some of the senators.[12]

Even churches came under the muckrake. Among the most biting investigations was Charles Edward Russell's "The Tenements of Trinity Church," published by *Everybody's* in 1908. The story turned on a bitter irony: Trinity Church raised money for its charities from rents it collected on some of the worst tenements in New York. According to Russell, the tenements were firetraps, lacked sanitary facilities, and bred diseases, particularly tuberculosis. Trinity fought back by criticizing Russell and *Everybody's* for their sensationalism, and much of the public seemed to agree. A few years later, Trinity quietly tore down about four blocks of its most miserable buildings. Russell went on to expose the abuses of the convict labor system in Georgia.

Even more restrained magazines such as *Ladies' Home Journal* entered the fray, at least on some topics. The *Journal* spearheaded the war against patent medicines, which, at the turn of the century, had sales of about $100 million a year. Magazines had a self-interest in the sales, for patent-medicine producers were among the biggest advertisers. Some of the big sellers were Lydia Pinkham's Vegetable Compound, Dr. Williams' Vegetable Jaundice Bitters, and Colden's Liquid Beef Tonic. Ads claimed that these nostrums cured everything from cancer to catarrh, piles to eczema. These formulas were more than ineffective; they were dangerous. Most contained alcohol, and some used narcotics. In 1892, long before most other publications exhibited any interest in reform, *Ladies' Home Journal* announced that it would no longer accept

[11]David Graham Phillips, "The Treason of the Senate," *Cosmopolitan* 40 (March 1906), 488.

[12]Two anthologies of the best muckraking journalism are Swados, *Years of Conscience: The Muckrakers,* and Arthur Weinberg and Lila Weinberg, eds., *The Muckrakers* (New York, 1961). The articles discussed in this section can be found in these collections.

Teddy and the Muckrakers

President Roosevelt Wants Journalists To 'Let in Light and Air,' Not 'Sewer Gas'

Theodore Roosevelt was mad. An article in *Cosmopolitan Magazine*, under the title "The Treason of the Senate," had attacked Senator Chauncey Depew. Roosevelt liked "poor old Depew." A man of reform, the president nevertheless sensed that the exposé of one of the Senate's most venerable members — even though he was receiving $20,000 annually from an insurance company — went too far and could disrupt social order. He vented his rage in a dinner address at the Gridiron Club, an association of old-timer journalists, by comparing the crusading journalists in 1906 to "the man with the muckrake." He took the metaphor from John Bunyan's *Pilgrim's Progress*.

Ray Stannard Baker, a "muckraker," reminded the president that the president himself had contributed to the "letting in of light and air" by exposing "rascals." Roosevelt replied: "I want to 'let in light and air,' but I do not want to let in sewer gas."

Despite muckrakers' arguments, Roosevelt's talk to the Gridiron Club had been well received, and he decided to go further with his idea. On April 14, 1906, on the occasion of the laying of the cornerstone of the United States House of Representatives office building, he made the muckrakers the main topic. With teeth gleaming beneath his dark, bristling mustache, the stocky and energetic president thundered: "The man who never does anything else, who never thinks or speaks or writes save of his feats with the muckrake, speedily becomes, not a help to society, not an incitement to good, but one of the most potent forces of evil."

Lincoln Steffens, Roosevelt's close friend, told him, "Well, Mr. President, you have put an end to all these journalistic investigations that have made you." Roosevelt replied that he had no such design and that he hadn't intended to include Steffens in his criticism.

To Roosevelt's embarrassment, the applause for his speech came from newspapers he branded as "organs of the criminal rich." And the reporter-reformers took pride in the term Roosevelt had coined, which has lived ever since in the language of American politics.

Jiafei Yin
Central Michigan University

Cosmopolitan Magazine

Vol. XL MARCH, 1906 No. 5

DEPEW'S JOVIALITY AND POPULARITY, ACCORDING TO MR. PHILLIPS, HAVE COST THE AMERICAN PEOPLE AT LEAST ONE MILLION DOLLARS

The Treason of the Senate

BY DAVID GRAHAM PHILLIPS

Treason against the United States shall consist only in levying war against them, or in *adhering to their enemies, giving them aid and comfort.*
—THE CONSTITUTION OF THE UNITED STATES, Article III, Section 3.

ONE morning, during this session of the Congress, the Senate blundered into a discussion of two of its minor disreputables, Burton and Mitchell, who had been caught with their fingers sliding about in the change pocket of the people. The discussion on these change-pocket thieves was a fine exhibition of "senatorial dignity and courtesy," which means, nowadays, regard for the honor and dignity of the American people smugly sacrificed to the Senate's craftily convenient worship of the Mumbo-Jumbo mask and mantle of its own high respectability. In closing the

After David Graham Phillips' series "The Treason of the Senate" began appearing in *Cosmopolitan Magazine* and exposing that body's corruption, one reader wrote to the magazine: "Glory Hallelujah! You have found a David who is able and willing to attack this Goliath of a Senate." One of the targets was Senator Chauncey Depew. This photograph of him (top right) ran in the magazine above the caption "Here is the archetypal face of the sleek, self-satisfied American opportunist in politics and plunder." President Theodore Roosevelt (bottom right) thought the article had gone too far and gave his famous "muck-rake" speech in response. Phillips (seen here in the bottom left photograph, which accompanied his article in the magazine) was aloof and goal-oriented. One friend said that he had a "secretiveness, especially about his own affairs, purposes, and hopes.... He intended to get all he could out of newspaper work ... as a training in the study of men and social conditions.... [H]e would then make a big name for himself as a writer of books." In 1911 he was shot and killed by a manic depressive who thought one of Phillips' novels was about the man's family.

ads for these spurious remedies. The *Journal*'s editor, Edward Bok, stepped up the campaign in 1904, encouraging boycotts of periodicals that still carried ads.

Muckraking journalism was not confined to magazines, as Upton Sinclair proved. His book *The Jungle* possibly touched more Americans than any other exposé of the period. Sinclair was born into a poor family, though some of his relatives enjoyed an upper-class lifestyle. Living and attending college in New York City, he witnessed the effects of urbanization and industrialization on those around him. His early novels were undistinguished, but about 1902 he was exposed to the writings of a Grinnell College professor who argued that socialism was the natural culmination of Christianity. Nearly all Sinclair's subsequent works bore the marks of his socialist ideology. In 1904 he began writing a series of articles on an unsuccessful strike in the Chicago meat-packing industry for the *Appeal to Reason*, a Kansas-based socialist magazine. He decided to expand these into a novel about wage slavery.[13]

Although he planned to write a work of fiction, Sinclair researched the topic much as a journalist would today. In Chicago he interviewed laborers, social workers, lawyers, doctors, saloon-keepers, and others. He visited the homes of workers and toured the meat-packing plants both as an official visitor and, disguised, as a worker. The result was *The Jungle*. Shocked by the book's descriptive realism, five publishing houses rejected the manuscript. Doubleday, Page & Co. then expressed interest and commissioned a report by a Chicago journalist to verify Sinclair's allegations. The journalist, it turned out, was a publicity agent for the stockyards; and he advised against publication. But Sinclair persisted and was able to persuade the publisher to send its own investigator, whose report substantiated Sinclair's claims. Doubleday published *The Jungle* in 1906.

Sinclair wrote to dramatize the plight of exploited laborers. His unstated goal was to generate support for the socialist movement, but his descriptions of the packinghouse conditions were so vivid that they overshadowed the problems of the workers. "I aimed at the public's heart and by accident I hit it in the stomach," he said of the reaction to his book.[14] The novel focused on the life of Jurgis Rudkus, a Lithuanian peasant lured to Chicago by the promises of high wages in the packinghouses. Rudkus slowly succumbed to the inhumane conditions of the packing plant. He was injured, members of his family contracted horrible diseases, and the women turned to prostitution. Rudkus almost gave up all hope until he heard the promises of socialism. Although the characters were fictional, the situations and conditions were real. Sinclair reported that diseased carcasses were sold as prime meat, that rats and rat feces were ground up with the meats, and that inspectors routinely accepted bribes. But his most stunning scene underscored the callous disregard for human life: workers fell into open vats "and when they were fished out, there was never enough of them left to be worth exhibiting. Sometimes they would be overlooked for days, till all but the bones of them had gone out to the world as Anderson's Pure Leaf Lard!"

Virtually all aspects of American society fell under the muckrake sometime between 1902 and 1912. The range of inquiry is suggested by the following articles, some of the most distinguished writings of the period. Unchecked businesses were scrutinized in much the same way that Tarbell had studied Standard Oil: Charles Edward Russell told "The True Story of the Great Vanderbilt Fortune" (*Hampton's*, 1909); and Louis D. Brandeis, in "The Great Life Insurance Wrong," explained how the interests of the insured were ignored (*The Independent*, 1906). Racial problems received serious attention in print for the first time since the Civil War: Ray Stannard Baker wrote of "The Clash of the Races in a Southern City" (*American Magazine,* 1907), while William English Walling noted the terrible irony of white mobs killing blacks in Springfield, Illinois, Abraham Lincoln's home ("The Race War in the North," *The Independent,* 1908). The special problems of working women and children were ably detailed by Rheta Childe Dorr in her book *What Eight Million Women Want* (1910) and in Robert Hunter's "The Children Who Toil" (*World's Work,* 1905). Confidence in the quality of justice was shattered by such articles as C. P. Connolly's "Big Business and the Bench" (*Everybody's,* 1912).[15]

Muckraking the Press

One important American institution, the press, escaped incisive examination until muckraking's declining years. One historian has speculated that interest in the press was piqued when the muckraking magazines were being purchased and forced out of business by some of the very companies they had criticized.[16]

Before muckraking's heyday, criticism of the press was mainly episodic or internal and hence limited in its effect. News coverage, for instance, of major events such as the Spanish-American War provoked cries of sensationalism and jingoism but then ebbed as the story receded from front pages. When journalists talked among themselves at conferences or on the pages of trade journals, they also raised some ethical concerns. This self-examination, however, typically focused on a limited range of business concerns — exaggerated circulation claims, advertisements disguised as news stories, and the like.

It remained for Will Irwin to undertake a systematic study of the press. He examined it in a fifteen-part series on "The American Newspaper" for *Collier's* that began in January 1911. Little had been written on the press; so Irwin obtained most of his information in remarkably candid interviews with reporters and editors. Before the first word was set in type, Irwin was offered a bribe and William Randolph Hearst threatened to sue for libel, a threat he carried out — although his $500,000 suit was dropped before

[13] The best biography of Sinclair is Leon Harris, *Upton Sinclair: American Rebel* (New York, 1975).

[14] Upton Sinclair, "What Life Means to Me," *Cosmopolitan* (October 1906), 594.

[15] See the anthologies by Swados, *Years of Conscience,* and Weinberg and Weinberg, *The Muckrakers*, for these articles.

[16] Regier, *The Era of the Muckrakers*, 165.

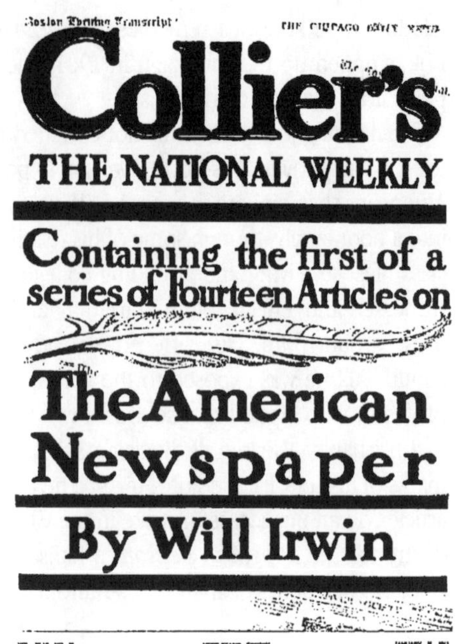
Collier's
THE NATIONAL WEEKLY
Containing the first of a series of Fourteen Articles on
The American Newspaper
By Will Irwin

Scrutinizing the Press
Although journalists are quick to examine other institutions, they rarely have brought the same energy to scrutinizing themselves or the institution of the press. The first systematic attempt to critique journalism was that by Will Irwin, a veteran reporter, in the 1911 series "The American Newspaper" in *Collier's* magazine. It remains a model work even today.

reaching court. Irwin was not intimidated. He showed that the Hearst newspapers ran news stories and editorials favorable to those who purchased advertising. A $1,000 theater advertisement, for instance, bought an editorial lauding a play. In such cities as Pittsburgh and Cincinnati, Irwin revealed, the papers excluded news about citizens' reform efforts, a problem that Lincoln Steffens had encountered before.[17]

One news organization, the Associated Press, was the object of several critics. In the most extreme view, the AP was a monopoly that suppressed news unfavorable to capitalistic institutions. Irwin, writing in *Harper's Weekly* on March 28, 1914, had a more moderate view. He did express concern that a few of the older, more conservative newspapers exerted disproportionate influence in conducting the affairs of the AP, a cooperative. AP bylaws made it virtually impossible for a new, perhaps more liberal publisher to receive a franchise in a community with an established, usually conservative member. Irwin discounted the claim that the AP conspired with banks, utilities, industries, and others to keep unfavorable news off the wires. He did believe, however, that the association (and many newspapers) tended to hire reporters and editors who were generally conservative in outlook. The most vitriolic attack on the AP and the American press, Upton Sinclair's *The Brass Check* (1920), came after the muckraking movement had waned. Much of the evidence for his attack, however, was drawn from the period, when the practices of big business made it particularly susceptible to criticism.

Muckraking generally, and the exposés of corrupt press practices in particular, prompted some institutional self-reflection. While Irwin, Sinclair, and others pointed to the press' shortcomings, the general thrust of the muckrakers underscored journalism's power to affect public opinion and people's lives — for better or for worse. Cultivating journalistic professionalism was one way to channel this power and prevent its abuse. Universities launched the first formal degree programs in journalism, students organized Sigma Delta Chi (now known as the Society of Professional Journalists), and some state press associations began adopting codes of ethics — all as muckraking peaked. Also, in keeping with Progressives' faith that experts could remedy social problems, more idealistic measures were proposed to improve the press. The most notable, though unsuccessful, were the licensing of journalists to improve the quality of reporters, accuracy bureaus to judge the truthfulness of news accounts, and even adless or endowed publications that could report without having to favor commercial interests.[18]

The Decline of Muckraking

The heyday of muckraking journalism was relatively brief. It peaked about 1906 and started its decline within two years. The movement enjoyed a brief resurgence at the time of the 1912 presidential campaign when Roosevelt ran as the Progressive party candidate, but it ebbed until it all but disappeared at the outbreak of the First World War. Several reasons have been advanced to explain muckraking's demise: vested interests killed the reform-minded magazines; the public grew tired of a continuous stream of exposés; the best reporter-reformers moved on to other endeavors; muckraking journalists lost their base of support as the Progressive impulse in the nation declined; and, in the most optimistic view, the jounalistic investigations had prompted reforms and thereby diminished the need for further muckraking. Some combination of these reasons probably best explains the decline of muckraking.

[17]See Will Irwin, *The Making of a Reporter* (New York, 1942), 164-9.

[18]For a fuller discussion of such efforts, see Marion T. Marzolf, *Civilizing Voices: American Press Criticism, 1880-1950* (New York, 1991), 34-75.

Writers for Social Justice
Scores of writers practiced muckraking at the beginning of the twentieth century, but the works of a handful of them stood out – and they were motivated by a sense of the need to restore justice to America's social system. Among the most important were (left to right) Frank Norris, Upton Sinclair, and Ray Stannard Baker. Norris' powerful indictment of slum life in San Francisco became the novel *McTeague* in 1899. It was to have been followed by a trilogy of novels excoriating the transportation trusts and corrupt exchanges trading in wheat. Norris died, however, a year after the first of the trilogy, *The Octopus*, was published in 1901, exposing unethical practices among railroads. He was only thirty-one when he died. The author of the best-selling muckraking novel about the meat-packing industry, *The Jungle*, Sinclair saw himself as a critic of a "materially prosperous but spiritually starving" generation. Baker, best known for his work "Railroads on Trial" and his investigation of southern race relations, was a Wisconsin-born Presbyterian who decried "a lack of moral vision" in American public life. The effort to achieve "social justice," he was convinced, required a journalism of "righteous indignation."

Most interesting is the claim that some of the companies that had suffered at the hands of the muckrakers drove the offending magazines out of business. There is evidence for this allegation, but it has to be weighed carefully with the knowledge that its source was often the frustrated muckrakers themselves. *Hampton's Magazine* may have suffered such a fate. The owner, Benjamin Hampton, had boosted circulation to 440,000 in 1910 when his was possibly the most aggressive muckraking magazine left in the field. As part of a series on the great railroads, Charles Edward Russell did a story on the New York, New Haven and Hartford line. The story charged that the company secretly had been able to monopolize just about all public transportation in New England, steamship as well as railroad traffic. Before the story was printed, Hampton later wrote, an agent of the railroad visited him and threatened reprisals unless the articles were pulled. Hampton refused, and the December 1910 issue carried "The Surrender of New England."

Hampton claimed that spies planted in his office by the railroad stole a list of the magazine's stockholders and then bombarded them with notes undermining confidence in the publisher's ability to run the publication. When Hampton sought a loan to tide the magazine over a slow summer, bankers refused to provide funds despite the firm's substantial collateral. Hampton was forced to sell. The new owners, he claimed, drained the magazine's assets and were guilty of criminal mismanagement, but he was unable to prove his case in court. Other accounts place more of the blame on Hampton's poor management. For whatever reason, the magazine folded in 1912.[19]

Similar pressures were claimed to have been brought to bear on other muckraking magazines. Shortly after *Success* assailed the powerful speaker of the U.S. House of Representatives, Joseph Cannon, advertising dwindled, paper suppliers started demanding cash, and banks refused loans. The magazine, which had been worth about $400,000, was sold for $2,250. At about the same time, *Twentieth Century* was sold when its muckraking editor failed to secure credit. Another journal that ran occasional muckraking pieces, *Human Life*, changed ownership in 1911 while running a serialized novel that dealt with New York City's chief of police. The new owners suspended the series. Even the pathbreaking *McClure's* ended up as the property of West Virginia Pulp and Paper Co. S.S. McClure blamed his own mismanagement, but Upton Sinclair and others seized on the sale as another example of a muckraking magazine that succumbed to special interests.

Some muckrakers believed that their distribution channels were threatened, too. They accused the American News Company, which distributed magazines to newsstands, of choking *The*

[19]Regier, *The Era of the Muckrakers*, 175-6, and Louis Filler, *The Muckrakers: Crusaders for American Liberalism*, rev. ed. (Chicago, 1968), 366-8, tend to accept Hampton's claims that the railroad killed the magazine. A contrasting opinion can be found in Frank Luther Mott, *A History of American Magazines*, 5 vols. (Cambridge, Mass., 1930-1968), 5:150-1. Mott seems to believe that Hampton's careless business practices were responsible. The best treatment of this topic is Michael D. Marcaccio, "Did a Business Conspiracy End Muckraking? A Reexamination," *The Historian* 47 (1984): 58-71.

Arena. And when President William Howard Taft and his postmaster general proposed raising magazine postage rates in 1909, some muckraking journals interpreted it as an assault on them.

Even if big business had killed some of the muckraking magazines, it is doubtful that such interests, no matter how powerful, were ultimately responsible for the death of the muckraking movement. Part of the explanation lies in the nature of the magazine business itself. Once a few magazines such as *McClure's* demonstrated the popular appeal of muckraking, imitators entered the field. *Success*, for example, originally had thrived by featuring stories about successful people. Converting to a muckraking formula — with stories critical of successful businesses — the magazine may have alienated its original readership. At some point, there were just too many muckraking magazines vying for a limited audience. Since these publications depended on mass circulations, splintering the readership might have been a fatal mistake. In addition, not all publishers combined imaginative editorial leadership with the business acumen needed to survive.

Muckraking journalism, moreover, suffered from its own excesses and an evaporating political base. Roosevelt's 1906 speech lashing the muckrakers had signaled growing doubts about the motives and goals of the reporter-reformers. When muckraking journals began attacking such institutions as the church, some readers felt they had gone too far. By the close of the decade, critics were complaining that many so-called muckrakers were little more than shrill and careless imitators of Steffens, Tarbell, and Russell.

Support eroded further when Roosevelt fragmented the Progressive movement with his third-party bid for the presidency in 1912; some supporters gravitated to Roosevelt's Progressive party while others backed Democrat Woodrow Wilson. The Progressive party's agenda shifted from an emphasis on domestic reforms to a preoccupation with preparing for the impending war. Once America entered the war in 1917, a frenzy of idealism and patriotism preempted debates about social reforms.

Muckraking journalism did not disappear with the advent of World War I; it entered a different phase. In its heyday, muckraking articles were appearing in major magazines with a combined circulation of about three million. By the outbreak of war, most muckraking articles had disappeared from mass-circulation magazines, but stories were reappearing in different forums. Opinion magazines such as *The New Republic* filled part of the void, though they reached a much smaller audience. Books became the most important outlet for the muckraking that once had appeared in popular magazines. Upton Sinclair and others sustained the muckraking tradition by publishing their exposés between hard covers, and some of them sold rather well.

The radical press, especially socialist and feminist publications, proved particularly durable. They had preceded muckraking, thrived with less public attention during its heyday, and survived after the major popular magazines had lost interest in reform journalism. In 1912, about 1,000 socialists held public offices in the United States, and their candidacies were often boosted by allied publications. The International Workers of the World, a socialist group, had at least seventy newspapers. The *Daily Milwaukee Leader* claimed a circulation of 31,000. *The Masses*, edited by Max Eastman, published radical views on politics, sex, and art from 1911 until policies of the Post Office Department drove it out of business in 1917.

Margaret Sanger, Reproductive Rebel
Feminist publications had begun in the nineteenth century and were especially active in the early twentieth. One of the most notable was *The Woman Rebel*, edited by Margaret Sanger. She used it as a platform for asserting women's reproductive rights. Police arrested her, but her supporters remained faithful. This photograph was made after her arraignment in January 1917.

A healthy mix of periodicals that dealt with issues of interest to women coexisted with the muckraking magazines. Some lobbied almost exclusively for the right of women to vote. Others had a much broader reform agenda and worked to improve the social and economic lot of women. Margaret Sanger used her publication, *The Woman Rebel*, to press for women's reproductive rights despite harassment by federal authorities. These and similar organs of dissident groups formed an important reservoir of reform journalism in the United States.

In terms of circulation, however, mainstream women's magazines eclipsed the feminist press. At the outset of the Progressive era, the *Ladies' Home Journal* reached a circulation of one million, the first magazine in the world to pass that milepost. The *Journal* and kindred magazines succeeded by appealing to traditional interests and developing a formula that defined women's roles largely in terms of consumption. Yet, that idea was not necessarily antithetical to the feminist publications, for the popular magazines conveyed a sense that consumption could partly liberate women from drudgery. Some of the mainstream magazines embraced Progressive reforms such as limits on patent medicines. And even when they resisted reforms, their female readers might disagree. For instance, Edward W. Bok, who replaced Louise Curtis as editor of the *Journal*, opposed women's suffrage although a poll of readers revealed that they supported it.[20]

Many mainstream newspapers also advocated various reforms. The conservative *New York Evening Post*, for example, through the work of its women's page editor, Rheta Childe Dorr, helped lead efforts to improve the lot of working women. She focused attention on hard conditions, long hours, and low pay, arguing that women should receive treatment in the workplace equal to that given men. While the mainstream press occasionally featured muckraking reporting, the publications of radical groups were continually practicing reform or revolutionary journalism.

Reform's Decline and Accomplishments
A number of factors led to the end of muckraking. Many of the causes that the reformers had advocated, such as woman's right to vote, were accomplished; and they entered the mainstream of American thinking and found their way into a variety of publications. This cover of a 1920 issue of *Leslie's Illustrated Weekly Newspaper* demonstrated both reasons, illustrating the effect of the Nineteenth Amendment, approved in August of that year.

The Accomplishments of Muckraking

Histories of the Progressive period offer somewhat divergent and imprecise assessments of the impact of the press on reform. Carl N. Degler sees the muckrakers' most enduring contribution as throwing "a flood of light upon the social results of the factory and the city." Investigations by the press altered middle-class attitudes by introducing "principles of political realism," according to Vernon L. Parrington. Other historians — C.C. Regier, Louis Filler, and Fred Cook, for example — assert that the press had a more profound and tangible impact. They argue that the muckrakers' works aroused public opinion and compelled substantial legislative reforms. Richard Hofstadter takes the more cautious view that legislative reforms short of "structural alterations in the American social and economic system" resulted from journalistic investigations. The muckraking journalists themselves expressed opinions that covered a similar gamut.[21]

Muckrakers have been credited, at least in part, with producing an impressive array of legislative reforms. Passage of the Pure Food and Drug Act followed publication of *The Jungle* and, some said, marked the culmination of the long war against patent medicines. A few states adopted an eight-hour work day for women, and more passed child-labor laws. More than half the states had workers' compensation laws by the end of the muckraking period. Prison reforms were enacted, too. Journalistic efforts also helped make government more responsive to the people. A constitutional amendment providing for the popular election of U.S. senators was the most notable accomplishment along these lines. Reforms at the state level included the adoption of the referendum, recall, and initiative. Exposés preceded and perhaps propelled the legal actions that broke up Standard Oil and the huge tobacco companies. Charles Edward Russell's study of the Southern Pacific Railroad helped break its stranglehold on California politics, and the Trinity Church cleared some of its tenements after he focused attention on its hypocrisy.[22]

To be sure, these reforms were realized. But what was the role of the press? In many of the reforms, a close look reveals that the press functioned chiefly as an auxiliary to larger forces. Grand claims, for example, have been made for the effects of Sinclair's *The Jungle*. That the Pure Food and Drug Act was passed after the publication of the book is undeniable. Often overlooked, however, are the other influences that contributed to this important leg-

[20]For an elaboration of this idea, see Helen Damon-Moore, *Magazines for the Millions: Gender and Commerce in the Ladies' Home Journal and the Saturday Evening Post, 1880-1910* (Albany, N.Y., 1994).

[21]Carl N. Degler, *Out of Our Past* (New York, 1955), 364; Vernon L. Parrington, *Main Currents in American Thought: Beginnings of Critical Realism in America* (New York, 1930), 407; Filler, *The Muckrakers*, 379-94; Regier, *The Era of the Muckrakers*, 197 and 210; Fred Cook, *The Muckrakers* (Garden City, N.Y., 1972); Hofstadter, *The Age of Reform*, 197.

[22]Filler, *The Muckrakers*, Regier, *The Era of the Muckrakers*, make the grandest claims for the effects of muckraking. For a thorough assessment of *The Jungle*'s impact on pure food laws, see James W. Davidson and Mark H. Lytle, *After the Fact: The Art of Historical Detection* (New York, 1982), 232-62.

Legislative Reforms Resulting From Journalistic Muckraking

Hepburn Act (1906)
Authorized the Interstate Commerce Commission to tighten regulations on railroads after *McClure's* published Ray Stannard Baker's "Railroads on Trial."

Meat Inspection Act (1906)
Passed after Upton Sinclair's book *The Jungle* exposed meat-packing practices in Chicago. The book was first serialized in several newspapers.

Pure Food and Drug Act (1907)
Passed after Samuel Hopkins Adams' exposé of the patent medicine industry, "The Great American Fraud," appeared in *Collier's.*

Mann Act (1909)
Prohibited the transportation of females across state lines for immoral purposes after Burton J. Hendrick's article "Daughters of the Poor" appeared in *McClure's.*

islation. Earlier exposures had alerted the public to the problem of adulterated meats. In fact, some of the moguls of the meat-packing industry already had been indicted. President Roosevelt, sensitive to the issue ever since his troops had eaten tainted meat in Cuba during the Spanish-American War, introduced legislation. Publication of *The Jungle* kept public pressure on Congress but was hardly a sufficient stimulus for change.

Typical, too, was the experience of Steffens as he investigated "The Shame of the Cities." He never uncovered municipal corruption himself; he wrote about others' discoveries in an engaging fashion for a national magazine. In just about all cases, a local reform group or an agency of government had initiated the investigations. As Will Irwin explained, the press generally waited until an incident or problem came "before court or commission, thus becoming news in the conventional sense."[23] Besides government agencies, reform groups often raised the issues that muckraking journalists explored.

The ultimate barrier blocking some reforms was the public itself. The press could and did direct the public's attention to problems, a power that communication researchers today label the agenda-setting influence. Doubtless the public's awareness of social problems associated with modern, industrial America was increased by the muckraking articles. Attitudes, however, were not so easily altered by journalistic exposés. Although historians lack sophisticated methods to detect shifts in past public opinion, evidence suggests that in some matters muckraking journalism indeed touched public attitudes. This power was probably most important on issues that could be dramatized graphically and affected readers directly. But where readers' interest in an issue was remote, and where the audience was predisposed to disagree with the findings of an exposé, muckraking probably was less effective in changing attitudes.

Reforms more tangible than shifts in public opinion — removing corrupt officials from office, enforcing existing laws, and rewriting statutes — followed some muckraking efforts, but journalists usually contributed ammunition to a campaign initiated by other reformers. The most fundamental reforms — structural changes in the political, economic, and social system — were the hardest to realize. The most noteworthy changes occurred in the political system, with a number of reforms that increased the direct participation of people in government. All but a few of the muckrakers were more interested in fine-tuning the system than overthrowing it. Thus, they rarely advocated radical changes, which irritated some in the socialist movement.

Some of the most astute students of the press' new-found power to influence public opinion and legislation were the era's American presidents, notably Theodore Roosevelt. Whereas previous presidents had courted publishers and editorial writers, Roosevelt discovered the power of news and reporters. He cultivated reporters and, mindful of newspapers' publishing routines and constraints, managed news about his administration to good effect. At first he engineered publicity to secure congressional passage of such reform measures as the Hepburn Act, which strengthened

[23]Will Irwin, *The American Newspaper* (1911; reprint, Ames, Iowa, 1969), 35.

federal control of railroad rates. Later, however, he applied the same news-management techniques for overtly partisan ends. He deftly orchestrated publicity, for example, to undercut the presidential bid of Charles Evans Hughes and to deflect criticism of his own role in acquiring the Panama Canal.[24]

For journalism, the enduring legacy of the muckraking period was not so much that the press worked on behalf of reform. More important, it taught reporters the power — and limitations — of facts. A bit naively, some journalists embarked on their muckraking careers believing that reforms flowed naturally from stories laying a problem before a rational public. Facts, indeed, had power, but by themselves they accomplished little. Interestingly, the growing realization that facts were weapons contributed to the rise of modern public relations. It was more than coincidental that the first American public relations firm had as clients some companies that were subjects of the muckrakers' exposés.[25] The muckrakers also discovered the value of gathering and reporting facts in a systematic manner. In a sense, they anticipated the social science techniques reporters use today. Journalists can look to this period with pride, but that pride should be tempered with the knowledge that certain elements of the press played a less than noble role during the Progressive era.

RECOMMENDED READINGS

BOOKS

Applegate, Edd. *Journalistic Advocates and Muckrakers: Three Centuries of Crusading Writers*. Jefferson, N.C., 1997. The 101 biographies shed light on crusading and muckraking journalism.

Baker, Ray Stannard. *American Chronicle: The Autobiography of Ray Stannard Baker*. New York, 1945. Baker traces his years with the *McClure's* group and after.

Chalmers, David M. *The Social and Political Ideas of the Muckrakers*. New York, 1964. A good, quick overview of the ideology underlying the works of leading muckrakers.

Chamberlain, John. *Farewell to Reform*. New York, 1932. Chamberlain, a Marxist, was critical of Progressivism because of its superficial approach to solving deep-seated problems, when radical solutions were needed. Muckrakers accomplished many reforms, but they were powerless to solve the underlying problems of the system.

Cook, Fred J. *The Muckrakers*. Garden City, N.Y., 1972. Provides a readable overview of the leading writers.

Crunden, Robert M. *Ministers of Reform: The Progressive Achievement in American Civilization, 1889-1920*. New York, 1982. The author sees muckrakers as key players in building public support for Progressive reform.

Filler, Louis. *The Muckrakers: Crusaders for American Liberalism*. Chicago: Gateway edition, 1968. Filler has spent much of his scholarly career studying muckraking and Progressivism; this is the best of the traditional approaches.

Harrison, John M., and Harry H. Stein, eds. *Muckraking: Past, Present and Future*. University Park, Pa., 1973. A collection of essays on specialized themes.

Hofstadter, Richard. *The Age of Reform: From Bryan to F.D.R.* New York, 1955. Provides the context for the period and pays considerable attention to journalism.

Hudson, Robert V. *The Writing Game: A Biography of Will Irwin*. Ames, Iowa, 1982. Irwin, a noted critic of the press, was a versatile writer with a deep concern for public issues.

Kaplan, Justin. *Lincoln Steffens: A Biography*. New York, 1974. The best biography of the leading muckraker.

Kochersberger, Robert C., ed. *More Than a Muckraker: Ida Tarbell's Lifetime in Journalism*. Knoxville: University of Tennessee Press, 1996. Collection of Tarbell's writing demonstrates that she contributed greatly to the origins of modern journalism.

Lawson, Linda. *Truth in Publishing: Federal Regulation of the Press's Business Practices*. Carbondale, Ill., 1993. Federal regulation of newspapers' business practices in the Progressive era culminated in the Newspaper Publicity Act of 1912, which used second-class mailing privileges as the basis for some government regulation of the press.

Lyon, Peter. *Success Story: The Life and Times of S.S. McClure*. New York, 1963. An insider's look at the McClure's group and their influence on the age of reform.

McClure, S.S. *My Autobiography*. New York, 1914. An inside look at the birth of American mass magazines and muckraking.

Miraldi, Robert. *Muckraking and Objectivity: Journalism's Colliding Traditions*. Westport, Conn., 1990. Chronicles the move away from the activist approach of the muckrakers to an objective, neutral stance of later journalists.

Regier, C. C. *The Era of the Muckrakers*. Chapel Hill, N.C., 1932. The muckrakers exposed many social, economic, and political evils. This study examines the conditions which stimulated muckraking, the rise of popular-priced magazines which provided a medium, the subjects of exposure, the results, and the reasons for the decline of muckraking. Muckraking was "the inevitable result of decades of indifference to the illegalities and immoralities attendant upon the industrial development of America."

Steffens, Lincoln. *Autobiography*. New York, 1931. Perhaps the most engaging autobiography of an American journalist, this work is full of useful information, too.

Steinberg, Salme H. *Reformer in the Marketplace: Edward W. Bok and the Ladies' Home Journal*. Baton Rouge, 1979. Even fairly traditional magazines engaged in some muckraking.

Swados, Harvey. *Years of Conscience: The Muckrakers*. Cleveland, 1962. One of the better anthologies of muckraking journalism.

Tarbell, Ida. *All in a Day's Work*. New York, 1939. The life and work of one of the earliest and best of the muckrakers.

Tomkins, Mary E. *Ida M. Tarbell*. New York, 1974. Tarbell was primarily a defender of traditional, Puritan New England values. She was concerned for morals, democracy, justice, and individual independence, and thus in her Standard-Oil exposé attacked Rockefeller because of his lack of concern for morality and his ruthless methods, similar to those that had been used to drive her father and middle-class oil producers out of business.

Ware, Louise. *Jacob A. Riis. Police Reporter, Reformer, Useful Citizen*. New York, 1938. In his career as a police reporter on the *New York Evening Sun*, Riis helped reform housing conditions because he believed that such conditions as those found in the slums were the true cause of people's troubles and wrongdoing.

Weinberg, Arthur, and Lila Weinberg, eds. *The Muckrakers*. New York, 1961. This anthology features useful background and many interviews with the muckrakers.

Wilson, Harold. *McClure's Magazine and the Muckrakers*. Princeton, 1970. A good account of the leading muckraking magazine.

—. *Progressivism and Muckraking*. New York, 1976. A critical bibliography of muckraking throughout American history.

[24]For the fullest treatment of this subject, see George Juergens, *News from the White House: The Presidential-Press Relationship in the Progressive Era* (Chicago, 1981).

[25]See Scott M. Cutlip, "The Nation's First Public Relations Firm," *Journalism Quarterly* 43 (1966): 269-80.

ARTICLES

Cassedy, James H. "Muckraking and Medicine, Samuel Hopkins Adams." *American Quarterly* 16 (1964): 85-99. Adams progressed from a muckraker exposing problems in medicine to a medical writer. In 1920s he left medical writing because medicine had advanced and more knowledgeable writers were available. As a muckraker, he was not an expert on medicine. However, he did serve an important function by educating the public and helping bring about reform.

Chalmers, David. "The Muckrakers and the Growth of Corporate Power." *American Journal of Economics and Sociology* 18 (1959): 295-311. Provides good details on the muckrakers' opposition to big business.

Clark, John G. "Reform Currents in Polite Monthly Magazines, 1880-1900." *Mid-America* 47 (1965): 3-23. Argues that the muckraking magazines did not represent a radical departure.

Cobb-Reiley, Linda. "Not an Empty Box With Beautiful Words On It: The First Amendment in Progressive Era Scholarship." *Journalism Quarterly* (1992): 37-47. The Progressive era produced influential interpretations of the constitutional guarantees of free speech and press.

Evensen, Bruce. "The Evangelical Origins of Muckraking." *American Journalism* 6 (1989): 5-29. The muckrakers' primary motivation was religious.

Grenier, Judson A. "Muckraking and Muckrakers: An Historical Definition." *Journalism Quarterly* 37 (1960): 552-8. Tries to define muckraking and what it meant to different individuals.

Hays, Samuel P. "The Politics of Reform in Municipal Government in the Progressive Era," *Pacific Northwest Quarterly* 55 (1964): 157-69. A case study probing the role of muckrakers in achieving municipal reform.

Marcaccio, Michael D. "Did a Business Conspiracy End Muckraking? A Reexamination," *The Historian* 47 (1984): 58-71. A sensible analysis of the reasons for the decline of muckraking.

Marmarelli, Ron. "William Hard as Progressive Journalist." *American Journalism* 3 (1986): 142-53. Hard was the typical muckraker: "a champion of order and efficiency, and of social justice and social control."

McCormick, Richard L. "The Discovery That Business Corrupts: A Reappraisal of the Origins of Progressivism," *American Historical Review* 86 (1981): 247-74. McCormick argues that Progressive era reform stalled out because the muckrakers prematurely encouraged control over the trusts that did not go far enough.

Reynolds, Robert D. "The 1906 Campaign to Sway Muckraking Periodicals." *Journalism Quarterly* 56 (1979): 513-20, 589. Some magazines were more interested in economic survival than journalistic integrity.

Schultz, Stanley K. "The Morality of Politics: The Muckrakers' Vision of Democracy," *Journal of American History* 52 (1965): 527-47. Schultz probes the view of democracy that led to muckraker agitation for a re-moralized America.

Semonche, John. "The American Magazine of 1906-1915: Principle vs. Profit." *Journalism Quarterly* 40 (1963): 36-44. Discusses the tension between idealism and the need for a realistic business sense at one of the leading muckraking magazines.

Shultz, Stanley Key. "The Morality of Politics: The Muckrakers' Vision of Democracy." *Journal of American History* 52 (1965): 527-47. Analyzes the political objectives of the muckrakers.

Sloan, Wm. David. "The Muckrakers, 1901-1917: Defenders of Conservatism or Liberal Reformers?" 271-82 in *Perspectives on Mass Communication History* (Hillsdale, N.J., 1991). Analyzes the approaches that historians have taken to explaining the muckraking period.

Stein, Harry H. "Lincoln Steffens: Interviewer." *Journalism Quarterly* 46 (1969): 735-6. Describes the techniques that made Steffens so successful in eliciting incriminating information.

Thelen, David P. "Social Tensions and the Origins of Progressivism," *Journal of American History* 56 (1970): 323-41. An excellent summary of the social context within which muckrakers agitated for the creation of a civil society.

Uselding, Paul, ed. "In Dispraise of Muckrakers: United States Occupational Mortality, 1890-1910," 334-71 in *Research in Economic History I.* Greenwich, Conn., 1976. This is a pro-business interpretation of muckraking. Muckrakers served "admirably as the press agents of reform." However, in their attacks on industry for its danger to mortality, they exaggerated or misread the statistics.

17

The Media and National Crises

1917 - 1945

Between 1917 and 1945, the United States faced some of the greatest tests in its history. These were pivotal years of crisis and challenge, including two world wars of unparalleled scope and destructiveness as well as the most severe economic crisis in the nation's history. Having reached their twentieth-century position as major institutions, the media were in a state of constant interaction with the great events and issues of the time. Their role in the life of the nation was crucial. Their involvement in the crises that shaped the period began on the eve of this country's entrance into World War I.

The Quest for American Support

American entrance into the war has been a topic of ongoing dispute among historians. The most prominent interpretations center on the following propositions: (1) that a German-dominated Europe would imperil American security, (2) that American economic ties to the Allies were so important that intervention to preserve them was necessary, (3) that President Woodrow Wilson and his advisors risked serious encounter with Germany in order to defend law, morality, national prestige, and Americans' traditional beliefs in neutral rights as they understood them, (4) and that Germany's resorting to submarine warfare against neutral ships in European war zones represented an intolerable infringement on American rights. Accompanying these major themes, a number of diplomatic exchanges and declarations usually are cited as well as some specific events, such as the sinking of the *Lusitania* on May 7, 1915, which resulted in the loss of 1,198 lives, including those of 128 Americans. Finally, the theme of the pro-Allied stance of American public opinion runs throughout interpretations of U.S. intervention in the war.

The last point is of particular significance for the media. Once the war began, favorable American opinion was well worth having, and both Britain and Germany courted it. The British, however, proved better at winning it. They sent an avalanche of material to numerous people and public agencies in this country who were in a position to influence American opinion.[1] Consequently, the press was one of their prime targets, as it was for the Germans, but the British were more successful at influencing it for several reasons. First, after cutting the German transatlantic cables as one of their initial actions in the war, they had better communication facilities at their disposal. Furthermore, since the 1890s, an Anglo-American rapprochement had been developing that now produced a friendly spirit for the British to exploit. Then, too, the democratic war aims that the British advanced resonated better with Americans than did the content of German publicity.

When German propagandists tried to create sympathy for German *kultur*, they not only failed to touch American sensitivities but even gave the British an additional subject to exploit. Moreover, German actions such as the invasion of Belgium, use of submarine warfare, and sinking of the *Lusitania* in 1915 discredited their cause in this country. The same can be said about German sabotage activities and of revelations about several of their agents working here.[2] They damaged Germany's own cause as they enhanced that of the British and increased anti-German feeling among Americans.

World War I

When President Wilson asked Congress to declare war on Germany on April 2, 1917, he had the majority of public and press opinion behind him. The American people had been jarred out of their neutrality, at the end of January, by Germany's announcement that it would launch unrestricted submarine warfare against neutral ships entering European war zones. Then on March 1, news of the Zimmerman Note flashed across the country. The

[1]"British Propaganda During The Great War 1914-1918," *Ministry of Information Records*, INF 4/4A, #4140, Public Record Office, London, 13.

[2]See H. C. Peterson, *Propaganda for War: The Campaign Against American Neutrality, 1914-1917* (Norman, Okla., 1939), 134-58. The best known of these misfortunes involved Dr. Heinrich Albert, a German espionage agent, who let his portfolio containing information about German sabotage activities out of his sight for a few minutes on a New York streetcar. An American secret-service agent seized the portfolio, and the government published the incriminating contents in August 1915.

Propaganda Loses to Action
Despite their efforts to influence American opinion through propaganda, German actions eventually swayed Americans to favor joining the war in Europe against Germany. The Germans' sinking of the British liner *Lusitania* in May 1915 provided a major turning point in American and press sentiment. Although the *Los Angeles Times'* news treatment of the event (left) was straightforward, many newspapers published editorials attacking Germany for its submarine warfare. When American agents intercepted the note that German Foreign Minister Arthur Zimmerman had sent to Mexico, newspapers across the United States published the story (right). Offering Mexico the American Southwest if it would join the Central powers, the note galvanized American opposition to Germany.

The Los Angeles Times

OVER A THOUSAND LIVES PROBABLY LOST WHEN THE GERMANS SANK THE LUSITANIA.

SUSPEND JUDGMENT, SAYS PRESIDENT WILSON.

FIVE TO SIX HUNDRED SURVIVORS LANDED ALONG THE IRISH COAST.

LUSITANIA SURVIVORS LANDED AT QUEENSTOWN.

BRETHERTONS OF LOS ANGELES AMONG THE PASSENGERS SAVED.

THE NEW YORK HERALD.

JAPAN AND MEXICO ASKED BY PRUSSIANS TO JOIN THEM AND MAKE WAR ON AMERICA; DARING PLOT LONG KNOWN TO MR. WILSON

ARMED NEUTRALITY MEASURE IN MOST DRASTIC FORM IS CERTAIN TO BE PASSED AT THIS SESSION

INVASION OF UNITED STATES BY MEXICO A PART OF GERMAN SCHEME TO CONQUER WORLD

ARMING OF AMERICAN VESSELS MEANS FIGHT AND CERTAIN WAR

KINSMAN OF AMERICAN WOMEN LOST WITH THE LACONIA MAKES APPEAL

note stated that if Germany and the United States went to war, Mexico should be invited to ally with Germany. In return, Mexico would receive New Mexico, Arizona, and Texas, pending the victory of the Central Powers. The German Minister in Mexico also was to ask President Carranza to invite Japan, one of the Allies, to join the compact. Intercepted in transit to the German embassy in Mexico, the message was released and published. It was one of the great news breaks of this century, and it electrified the American people and press. On March 18 German submarines sank three American merchant ships without warning, and many lives were lost. President Wilson saw no alternative but to ask Congress to recognize that a state of war existed as a result of Germany's actions. Although some Americans opposed entrance into the war, most accepted it. Most newspapers, notwithstanding various degrees of enthusiasm, endorsed it overwhelmingly.

During the three years of American neutrality, there were more correspondents from this country covering the war than from any other nation except Britain. As neutrals they were in a position to report the war from either side. This they did, and the American public received a more comprehensive picture of the war than did the people of any other nation. American correspondents, however, were not free agents. Authorities in the warring nations controlled their movement and censored their work. This was as true for special war correspondents, even for Richard Harding Davis, the best-known correspondent in the world, as it was for regular foreign correspondents whom papers such as the *New York Times* and *Chicago Daily News* had stationed in the various European capitals. In the opening weeks of the war a handful of correspondents by their own ingenuity reached the front lines, but after that only a few were allowed there. The privileged normally went in groups conducted by authorities. Nevertheless, correspondents' reports were numerous. They were often based on official communiqués. War news, consequently, filled many pages of the American press and, particularly during the early stages of the war, included reports of atrocities committed by the belligerent forces. Many of the atrocity stories were unfounded — either the results of exaggerated reports or of propaganda.

With the entrance of the United States into the war, a new group of correspondents went to France to cover the American Expeditionary Forces (AEF). Gen. John J. Pershing, who commanded the American troops, appointed Frederick Palmer, an American correspondent and previously the only one accredited to the British Expeditionary Force, Chief Press Officer of the AEF with the rank of major. He had to organize his own department and formulate censorship regulations that had to conform in general to those of the Allies. According to the correspondents, Palmer distributed too little information and exercised too much censorship. By the end of 1917, he welcomed the chance to remove himself in order to visit the United States on a mission for Gen. Pershing. By early 1918, his successor, Gerald Morgan, had liberalized restrictions on movement and censorship as conditions allowed. The military censor, however, remained the ultimate guardian of news from the front.

Was the day of the war correspondent gone, as some disillusioned correspondents claimed? That was hardly the case. American correspondents were active across and beyond Europe. Floyd Gibbons of the *Chicago Tribune* and Irvin S. Cobb of the *Saturday Evening Post* were among the most widely read and flamboyant. Some — such as Heywood Broun, Westbrook Pegler, and George Seldes — would become well known in later years as polemical journalists. A few worked their way into Asia to report on the Eastern front of the Russian Civil War, the fate of the Czechoslovakian Legion fighting its way across Siberia, and on other repercussions of the war in that part of the world. Women correspondents were also active. The Newspaper Enterprise Association's Peggy Hall, the first woman correspondent to receive accreditation from the War Department, not only reported news from Europe but also went to Siberia with the American expedition to Vladivostok at the end of the war. The best-known woman correspondent was Rheta Childe Dorr. She managed to accompany the Russian women's Battalion of Death to the front. The *New York Mail* carried her dispatches on the front page, and she later reproduced them in an engaging book, *Inside the Russian Revolution*.

Yet, in a sense, the time of the dashing reporter sending dispatches from the front had been passing for some years — at least from the beginning of the century. In modern war, to inform the public is also to inform the enemy. Consequently, with the evolution of war came the need to restrict the freedom of operations of the press. Correspondents, editors, and readers had to adjust to that condition as did newsreel cameramen, who by this time roamed near and far to film events.

Since first appearing in this country in 1911, newsreels had grown rapidly as a popular news medium. But once the war began, all the belligerents restricted civilian cameramen both at the front and at home. After the United States entered the war, the U.S. Army Signal Corps produced most of the newsreel footage that American audiences saw. The film was carefully edited to serve military and national war goals.

War conditions also influenced how the press at home treated the war. The Committee on Public Information (CPI) coordinated the media and the war effort. Established by executive order on April 14, 1917, just eight days after the declaration of war, the CPI included the secretaries of state, war, and navy. George Creel, a newspaper editor, writer, and devotee of President Wilson, headed the organization. It was divided into a Foreign Section that dealt with propaganda for use abroad and a Domestic Section that dealt with mobilizing opinion on the home front. Many intellectuals and journalists, including a number of ex-muckrakers, served the Committee.

Among its myriad of activities, the CPI made a particular effort to inform and influence the press.[3] It published the first daily government newspaper in the country's history. Called the *Official Bulletin*, it reached a peak circulation of 118,000. The CPI also published a *War News Digest* to send to country newspapers upon request. Small rural papers by the hundreds used it. The CPI sent various releases to the press and through its Division of Syndicated Features produced articles for use in Sunday newspapers. The CPI also published a weekly series of news films, the Official War Review. It appeared regularly in half of the country's movie theaters. To publicize it, the CPI published a bi-weekly *Official Film News*. The Committee's Foreign Language Newspaper Division sought to influence the several hundred non-English newspapers published in the United States. Beyond all of these home-front activities the CPI created a sprawling propaganda operation

THE SATURDAY EVENING POST

WHEN THE SEA-ASP STINGS

By IRVIN S. COBB

War Correspondence
American war correspondents provided much on-the-scene reportage of World War I. One of the leading correspondents was Irvin S. Cobb of the *Saturday Evening Post.* This story in March 1918 recounted a submarine attack on a ship crossing the Atlantic.

that stretched across Europe, Asia, and Latin America.[4]

From the beginning, both the Committee and Creel himself received a great deal of criticism. After the war, Creel reflected that many people believed he and the CPI suppressed free speech and a free press. He contended, however, that he had opposed censorship as such except for cable censorship and had argued for "expression, not suppression" as the real need.[5] In 1917 he opposed a proposed censorship law and asked the press to accept a voluntary arrangement in which editors would act as their own censors. To this end, the CPI issued guidelines in May 1917 that delineated the types of information that should be kept secret.

There was, however, some official censorship. Modern wars tend to infringe on civil liberties, including freedom of speech and freedom of the press. Three federal acts during World War I gave the government ranging power of control: the Espionage Act (1917), the Trading-with-the-Enemy Act (1917), and the Sedition Act (1918). Furthermore, by an executive order in April 1917, President Wilson gave the government control of telegraph and

[3]For the activities of the CPI see George Creel (Chairman), *Complete Report of the Chairman of the Committee on Public Information* (Washington, D.C., 1920); James R. Mock and Cedric Larson, *Words That Won The War: The Story of the Committee on Public Information* (Princeton, N. J., 1939); Stephen Vaughn, *Holding Fast the Inner Lines: Democracy, Nationalism and the Committee on Public Information* (Chapel Hill, N. C., 1980). For his own lively defense of the CPI see George Creel, *Rebel At Large: Recollections of Fifty Crowded Years* (New York, 1947).

[4]For examples of the CPI's activity abroad, see James D. Startt, "American Propaganda in Britain During World War I," *Prologue: Quarterly of the National Archives* 28 (1996): 17-33; Startt, "American Film Propaganda in Revolutionary Russia," ibid., 30 (1998): 167-79; and Gregg Wolper, "Wilsonian Public Diplomacy: The Committee on Public Information in Spain," *Diplomatic History* 17 (1993): 17-34.

[5]Creel, *Rebel At Large*, 157.

THE SATURDAY EVENING POST

GERMAN POISON

The Propaganda That Imperils Patriotism and Preparedness

By Isaac F. Marcosson

German Propaganda

The German government and several German-language newspapers in the United States carried on an intense campaign to keep America from entering World War I and continued the efforts once America was involved. This article from the *Saturday Evening Post* in 1918 warned about the German methods and the dangers.

cable lines leaving the country; and by another executive order in October, he created a Censorship Board to coordinate all official activities of that type. Creel represented the CPI on the Censorship Board, and he did attempt to bar some "dangerous" material and to stop certain periodicals from leaving the country. Consequently, while it is technically true that the CPI had no power of censorship, as Creel claimed, it is also true that as the chairman of the CPI he engaged in censorship activities. It is clear, too, that the government created machinery to control the press and to outlaw criticism of the war effort.

PRESS SUPPORT OF THE WAR

Throughout the war the mainstream of the American press supported the war effort and cooperated with the CPI. To be sure, the Hearst papers and some others, such as the *Washington Post*, sometimes were at odds with the government. As a rule, the press printed all the news the government allowed and spared no expense in gathering it. Even if some of the news was slanted, the war was an absorbing and commanding event that deserved and received ongoing publicity. Nor should it be forgotten that President Wilson was an inspiring leader who placed American participation in the war in an idealistic mold. His methods, in turn, engendered even more public and press support. The statement of war aims contained in his famous "Fourteen Points" address was a superb articulation of the objectives Americans hoped would be achieved. Little wonder it won such widespread public and press acclaim. Support for the nation at war, however, sometimes led to overzealous, even crude and disgraceful, action.

The tempo of war created a demand for loyalty and conformity. American opinion quickly gravitated around the need to mobilize thought as part of the war effort. Strong currents of nativism and anti-radicalism ran amid the swelling tide of support for the war. If the public came to accept the war in terms of right and wrong, as a struggle of democracy against autocracy, it should be remembered that, in some respects, the press prepared the way for such thinking. In the first decade of the century, the exposé and "advocacy journalism" of the muckrakers made a deep impression on American thought. Some of the same traits that had characterized muckraking appeared in exaggerated form in war propaganda. American opinion grew intolerant of criticism and impatient with suspected or imagined cases of disloyalty. Responsibility for this attitude rested, in part, with government officials and with the CPI. It also rested on the shoulders of journalists who allowed the war spirit to impair their sense of discretion.

Once America entered the war, a wave of superpatriotism spread across the country. Only two months after the United States' entry, *The Literary Digest* invited readers to clip and send to that journal any editorial that seemed "seditious or treasonable." Under the Espionage Act, people committing disloyal activities could be fined or imprisoned. The act also empowered the postmaster general to exclude from the mails newspapers and periodicals containing treasonable or seditious material. The Sedition Act of 1918 was even more drastic in curtailing freedom of expression and of the press. During the war the Post Office Department threatened to deny mailing privileges to more than seventy-five newspapers and periodicals. Some of them actually were barred from the mails. Even the prestigious liberal journal, *The Nation*, was denied use of the mails at one point. In that case, however, President Wilson intervened to have the ban lifted after four days.

Other publications were not so fortunate. Radical, Socialist, and German-language papers were hardest hit. The well-known radical periodical *The Masses*, as well as several Socialist papers such as the *New York Evening Call* and the *Milwaukee Leader*, lost mailing privileges. English-language papers serving communities with concentrations of German population were held suspect. German-language newspapers, especially ones of radical or Socialist inclination, suffered from a number of pressures. Many other newspapers attacked them, sometimes in subdued language and sometimes with all caution thrown aside. The *Topeka Capital*, for example, demanded the suppression of all German-language newspapers. On October 6, 1917, President Wilson signed into law a measure requiring German-language newspapers to supply Eng-

George Creel and the CPI
Headed by newspaper editor George Creel (left), the Committee on Public Information was appointed by President Woodrow Wilson to prepare propaganda for use abroad and to help mobilize public opinion at home. Although receiving some criticism, it provided informative and usually accurate material to newspapers across the country. It produced much material aimed at aiding the war effort. One of its first concerns was preventing loose talk from providing useful information to German secret agents. This poster of Uncle Sam (right) presented the message effectively with one word: "Shhhh!"

lish translations of all articles relating to the American government and to the war. Translation was a costly operation that a number of newspapers could not afford. Many simply ceased publication.

Various forms of pressure impaired those remaining in business. In some cases, advertisers refused to place ads in these papers, while in other instances government officials broke into the offices of some radical and Socialist publications in search of subversive material and arrested a few editors. One historian writes that "in other instances, trainmen threw off bundles of German-language newspapers at wrong stations; Boy Scouts burned stolen bundles; and teachers discouraged their pupils from delivering 'disloyal' newspapers."[6] Consequently, many German-language papers closed down despite the fact that the vast majority had shifted their position soon after the United States entered the war and patriotically supported the country.

Most black newspapers also supported the nation's war aims.[7] Some militant black journalists, however, wondered if the problems of their race were receiving the attention they deserved. Between the 1880s and the opening of World War I, hundreds of black newspapers had been founded. Many failed to survive for long; but at least 173, and perhaps as many as 288, existed in 1914. Among them were some that became venerable publications such as the *Baltimore Afro-American*, the *Indianapolis Recorder*, and the *Pittsburgh Courier*. Some of the leading black journalists, such as Robert S. Abbott, the editor and publisher of the *Chicago Defender*, and William M. Trotter, the editor of the *Boston Guardian*, were militant, angry with the conciliatory philosophy of Booker T. Washington. So was W.E.B. DuBois, the editor of *The Crisis*, the monthly journal of the National Association for the Advancement of Colored People.

Wilson's relations with black leaders became strained during his first administration because of the segregation and discrimination practiced in government departments and agencies. America's entry into the war made matters worse. Racial intolerance and violence grew, and although about 200,000 black Americans served in France, only 42,000 were combat troops — and they had to fight to gain a place on the front lines. A tide of black protest arose. Black editors questioned Wilsonian idealism. "Poland? The President loves it," complained DuBois in a typical instance. "His interest in everything that concerns it is very deep....But twelve million American Negroes? Silence! Distance from Washington certainly lends enchantment to Democracy."[8] A. Philip Randolph's socialist magazine *The Messenger* announced that rather than make the world safe for democracy it "would rather make Georgia safe for the Negro."[9]

Given the force of the black press protest, it was uncertain how far its critique of the government would go. In June 1918, however, Creel organized a meeting of thirty-one leading black editors in Washington. The editors adopted and published a petition strongly urging black Americans to "make every sacrifice to win the war."[10] Then, in July 1918, DuBois, whose popularity among blacks was second only to that of Booker T. Washington, wrote a much-heralded editorial titled "Close Ranks" characterizing the war against German power as "the crisis of the world." He urged

[6]Frederick C. Luebke, *Bonds of Loyalty: German-Americans and World War I* (De Kalb, Illinois, 1974), 243.

[7]See Lester Jones, "The Editorial Policy of Negro Newspapers of 1917-1918 as Compared with That of 1941-1942," *Journal of Negro History* 29 (January 1944): 24-31.

[8]*The Crisis*, March 1918, 216.

[9]Quoted in Robert H. Brisbane, *The Black Vanguard: Origins of the Negro Social Revolution 1900-1960* (Valley Forge, 1970), 58.

[10]*Afro-American* (Baltimore), 5 July 1918, 1.

W.E.B. DuBois
The founder and editor of *The Crisis*, the monthly journal of the National Association for the Advancement of Colored People, W.E.B. DuBois provided militant leadership for African Americans on issues of racial equality during World War I. He argued that President Wilson was more concerned about conditions in Europe than about the plight of black Americans.

black Americans, as the war entered its final four months, not to hesitate. "Let us," he said, "while the war lasts, forget our special grievances and close our ranks shoulder to shoulder with our white fellow citizens.... We make no ordinary sacrifice, but we make it gladly...with our eyes lifted to the hills."[11]

The war stimulated black hopes for better treatment at home. As it went on, faith in democracy increased across the Western world, and black Americans shared in the expectation of its greater implementation. Rarely had our government placed such emphasis on democracy, and never had it publicized American idealism to the extent that it did in the final years of the war.

When a democracy enters a major war, the masses must be mobilized, not only in terms of manpower and resources but also in terms of thought and opinion. During World War I, the liberal Woodrow Wilson and the liberal George Creel ended up with what one historian calls "perhaps the most gigantic propaganda campaign in all American history."[12] The press played an instrumental role. Wilson led the United States to war with the bulk of American press opinion behind him, and during the war much of the nation's press believed in his peace program and the hope for a better world order that it appeared to promise. World War I was a conflict of unprecedented proportion, a total war. For good or ill, it affected all institutions in the participating countries and beyond. The press was no exception.

[11]*The Crisis*, July 1918, 110.

[12]Selig Adler, *The Isolationist Impulse: Its Twentieth Century Reaction* (New York, 1961), 37.

THE UNSETTLED AFTERMATH OF WAR

Following the signing of the Armistice on November 11, 1918, the press and the nation engaged in a year-long debate over the negotiation and ratification of a peace settlement. Wilson himself shattered precedent and ventured abroad to head the American delegation at the Paris Peace Conference, and the stormy ratification debate that followed invariably centers on him.

In the fight for treaty ratification during the summer and fall of 1919, Wilson needed all the support he could muster. Arrayed against him were many elements in the American press. The papers owned by two "press lords" — as their liberal critics called them — Frank A. Munsey and William Randolph Hearst, denounced the settlement. Some of the leading liberal journals such as *The Nation* and *The New Republic* also opposed the treaty, believing that Wilson had compromised away liberal principles at the conference table. The Irish-American and the German-American press attacked the treaty. Across the country many newspapers, particularly in the Northeast and Midwest, opposed the treaty on a number of grounds. Many partisan newspapers were virulent in their attacks on Wilson and the treaty. Nevertheless, public opinion as reflected by the press was for the treaty (including the League of Nations) but urged compromise on some of its major provisions. Wilson's failure to act upon that fact contributed to the treaty's defeat.[13]

The debate over the treaty occurred against the backdrop of widespread domestic disturbances: a wave of strikes across the land, some of the worst race riots in American history, and the nation's first Red Scare. Newspaper response to the crises was far from constructive. The press resorted to sensational reports and scare headlines, thus increasing public alarm. It showed an inclination to support the anti-radical persuasion then sweeping the country.[14]

Yet, some liberal journalists maintained their principles. *The Nation* and *The New Republic* chastised the press at large for the role it played in abetting public disorder and violence. Perhaps the *New York World's* Frank Cobb was correct when he reflected at the end of 1919 that the nation's newspapers "were not prepared for the waves of discontent and unrest that spread over the coun-

[13]For press opinion regarding the ratification of the treaty, see Wolfgang J. Helbich, "American Liberals in the League of Nations Controversy," *Public Opinion Quarterly* 31 (1967): 568-96; James L. Lancaster, "The Protestant Churches and the Fight for Ratification of the Versailles Treaty," *Public Opinion Quarterly* 31 (1967): 597-619; Luebke, 322; Kenneth R. Maxwell, "Irish-Americans and the Fight for Treaty Ratification," *Public Opinion Quarterly* 31 (1967): 620-41; and James D. Startt, "American Editorial Opinion of Woodrow Wilson and the Main Problems of Peacemaking in 1919" (Ph.D. diss., University of Maryland, 1965).

[14]Robert K. Murray, *Red Scare: A Study in National Hysteria, 1919* (Minneapolis, 1955), 178. Also, numerous examples of anti-radicalism and anti-labor press opinion can be found in the many *Literary Digest* articles published on the subject in 1919.

LATE The Citizen NIGHT

TRUCE TERMS PUT HUN ARMIES BEHIND RHINE

TERMS OF THE ARMISTICE IN BRIEF

Peace to Bring Liberty for World

CANCEL DRAFT CALLS NOW OUTSTANDING

How Yanks at Front Took The News

Greatest Celebration Is Staged Here

WAR IS OVER!

SAY HINDY NOT WITH "BILL"

CAPTURE MORE AUSTRIANS

CHURCHES CELEBRATE TONIGH

War's Aftermath
Americans and their Allies were jubilant over Germany's surrender to end World War I. The exhilaration that the *Citizen* of Columbus, Ohio, displayed typified the reaction. Allied leaders' failure, however, to work out enduring settlement terms sowed the seeds of greater international problems to confront Europe beginning in the 1930s.

try. They were not prepared for the social ferment that followed the war. They were not prepared for the industrial upheavals that came."[15]

There was, however, a limit beyond which the press in general refused to go. In time, a number of newspapers feared that mob rule was becoming a national menace as a result of the race riots and lynchings. They demanded that the "supremacy of law" be reasserted over "jungle rule" and that some permanent remedy to the fundamental causes of the trouble be found. Early in 1920 the New York State Legislature denied five elected Socialist members their seats in the assembly. That action may have marked the beginning of the end of the public hysteria, for it received the condemnation of many of the nation's newspapers. The conservative *Chicago Tribune* commented that it was "an unusual piece of small-bore politics."

The Great Depression

Seldom in history can one find two more crowded decades than those that fell between the two world wars. Movements grew across the world that would challenge an international order that had been evolving for centuries. In the West, the period began with widespread cultural disenchantment, the result of the experience of World War I and of long-growing strains and doubts regarding modern life. Communism, fascism, and nazism all developed and spread during these years. Midway through the period there occurred one of the most agonizing episodes known in American life, the Great Depression. The 1920s and 1930s were also important years in the life of the American press. More than ever it became an integral part of the nation's life, playing an essential role in the country's great domestic and international challenges.

The greatest challenge to domestic stability was the Great Depression. It was, in fact, the severest domestic test the country had faced since the Civil War. The economic collapse of the early 1930s is hard to imagine today. A few statistics might provide a rough picture of the economic collapse. By 1932, the country's industrial production was down by half, its foreign trade had declined 70%, and unemployment soared to about twelve million. The national income in 1932 was $49 billion (down from $81 billion in 1920), and per capita income declined from $681 in 1929 to $495 in 1932. Salaries decreased by about 40%; manufacturing wages by about 60%. Banks closed by the thousands.

The Depression lingered on in some form until 1940, but the worst of it hit in 1931 and 1932. It was preceded by a number of economic tremors such as the languishing state of American agriculture, wild investment in the stock market starting in 1927, the unnerving stock market crash of 1929, the failure of banks, the disruption of world trade and the world monetary system, and a decline of investment. Once it struck, it occasioned widespread human anguish and frustration.

Did the press help the nation to foresee this unprecedented tragedy? It is impossible to dismiss George Seldes' indictment of the press regarding the country's economic collapse. In 1937 this veteran journalist and liberal critic of the press charged: "It is held by many people that the failure of our newspapers to inform us honestly and accurately about the economic situation from 1927 to 1929, and the wish-fulfillment policy from 1929 on, constituted its [the press'] greatest failure in modern times."[16]

There may be grounds to support that accusation. To begin with, one might question if the tendency in the press of the 1920s to stress sensational "big stories" and give the trivial equal coverage with the significant served the public well. Did the popularity of tabloid journalism, with its stress on brevity and simplicity, somehow impair the mental condition of the average American? Did the press' emphasis on prosperity as well as its fawning and flattering of Wall Street barons create a false sense of confidence among newspaper readers? Did journalists have either the inclination or the ability to take a longer and deeper view of major eco-

[15]Frank I. Cobb, "The Press and Public Opinion," *The New Republic*, 31 December 1919, 147.

[16]George Seldes, *Freedom of the Press* (Garden City, N.Y., 1937). See also Margaret A. Blanchard, "Press Criticism and National Reform Movements: The Progressive Era and the New Deal," *Journalism History* 5 (1978): 36.

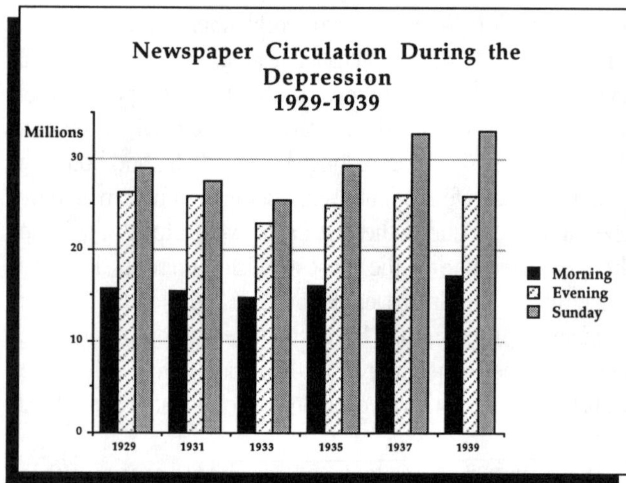

nomic issues? Such questions, of course, defy easy answers, but they do suggest that the press throughout the 1920s spent too much of its time and energy on a dramatic, sensational, and episodic type of journalism and too little on the comprehensive and orderly presentation of news. There was, to be sure, journalism of the latter type. Yet there is reason to question whether the American press strained to inform the public about the social and economic factors that conditioned its life. Such serious journalism, perhaps, would not have sold newspapers.

As an agent for stimulating public debate and participating in the shaping of a public agenda, the press floundered at the beginning of the Depression. One study of front-page news stories of newspapers with major circulations indicates that there was no significant increase in stories about economic matters before the crash of 1929 or during the early years of the Depression. An increase only occurred in 1931. Economic stories reached their peak of 26% in 1935. Moreover, the number of stories that linked economic matters to political action was much less than of those that merely described economic events and conditions. The author of the study concluded by underscoring "how little economic coverage the early years of America's greatest depression received and how reluctant the press was to politicize economic issues and bring new, unorthodox solutions into the political arena."[17]

A number of writers, in fact, have criticized the press for its treatment of the Depression. Some have charged that strong antilabor prejudices prevailed in the press. Some liberal critics accuse the press of bowing to the interests of the government and of the business community. President Herbert Hoover advised caution and asked the press not to overreact to the crisis and make matters worse.[18] One recent writer reflects: "Newspapers probably did not need the nudge. Most appeared ready to maintain discreet silence until the Depression blew over."[19]

[17]Richard L. Rubin, *Press, Party, and Presidency* (New York, 1981), 124.

[18]"The President's News Conference of November 29, 1929," *The Public Papers of the Presidents of the United States: Herbert Hoover* (Washington, 1974), 292-3.

[19]James Boylan, "Publicity for the Great Depression: Newspaper Default and Literary Reportage" in *Mass Media Between the Wars: Perceptions of Cultural Tension, 1918-1941*, eds. Catherine L. Covert and John D. Stevens (Syracuse, 1984), 161.

Was the press more interested in saving the nation's business than in reporting what had happened to the public? There appears to be substance in these charges, as one of the astute observers of journalism at that time commented. In 1932, William Allen White, the Republican editor of the *Emporia* (Kan.) *Gazette*, wrote to Kent Cooper of the Associated Press: "It is so easy for a reporter, copy-reader, the city editor, and the staff of our prosperous papers to take the Country Club attitude, the boss's slant, toward those who for one reason or another are whacking the established order."[20]

There are, however, several mitigating factors to consider. First of all, it is easier to recognize the Great Depression in retrospect than it was to perceive it in its early years. The stock market crash of 1929 had not directly affected the majority of Americans. Most people had not invested in the market. No one knew in 1930 that the Great Depression had begun. There was, moreover, a natural tendency to believe that recovery would come. As the Depression deepened and spread, there may have been a natural impulse among journalists not to be alarmists and to attempt to act as a restraint on public emotions. Without excusing the press response, particularly to the initial phase of the Depression, it might be admitted that the disaster was a soul-searching and baffling experience. It confused many Americans and, no doubt, many journalists, too.

At least two additional points should be mentioned. First, even during the initial stage of the Depression, quality periodicals such as *The Nation*, *The New Republic*, *Harper's*, *Scribner's*, and *The Atlantic* performed well in treating the economic collapse. Second, after 1932 the coverage by the newspaper press increased sharply. Along with mainstream newspapers, a number of social-issue, advocacy periodicals attacked the problems. The *Catholic Worker* provided a leading voice. Founded in 1933 by Dorothy Day and Peter Maurin, the monthly tabloid focused especially on labor issues — unemployment, unions, strikes, low wages, exploitation of black workers — and gained an impressive circulation of 110,000 within two years.

The Press and the New Deal

It is no exaggeration to say that, with the election of Franklin D. Roosevelt in 1932, the country and the press entered one of their most exciting times. His recovery program, the New Deal, became a center of public debate for the remainder of the decade. Against the backdrop of totalitarianism abroad, the New Deal offered hope and action for the American people. Roosevelt's buoyant leadership and experiments with economic policy inspired the majority of Americans with feelings of a democratic resurgence. To others, he appeared as a charlatan, even a dictator. Critics viewed his New Deal as a program for an unwanted revolution. As part of the vortex of the public debate surrounding Roosevelt and

[20]William Allen White to Kent Cooper, 29 August 1932, in Walter Johnson, ed., *Selected Letters of William Allen White 1899-1943* (New York, 1947), 326.

NEW YORK Herald Tribune LATE CITY EDITION

Roosevelt Wins, May Exceed '32 Landslide; Leads in N.Y., Pennsylvania, Ohio, Illinois; Lehman Re-elected; New Charter Adopted

FDR and the Press

Even the considerable press opposition to Franklin Roosevelt and his New Deal could not overcome his immense popularity. In his campaign for reelection in 1936, he challenged his critics directly and won the biggest electoral victory since 1820. Liberals claimed that newspaper owners were more interested in their own profits than in the welfare of the nation as a whole.

the New Deal, the press displayed a vigor regarding public affairs that it had not demonstrated for years.

That vigor was many-sided. For years the news media had been expanding their role in the political culture of the nation, and by the time of Roosevelt's presidency they reached into American life in an unprecedented manner. Before World War I news film had gained considerable prominence in this country, and during the war it played a significant role in covering the conflict. The years 1911 to 1927 might be called the "Age of the Silent Newsreel," but with the addition of sound the newsreel entered a golden age that lasted until the 1950s. There may have been some truth in Oscar Levant's remark that a newsreel was "a series of catastrophes, ended by a fashion show," but the American people welcomed newsreels. By the 1930s they had become an accepted and widely popular news medium.

Roosevelt's buoyant personality and confident approach to the nation in distress made him a natural subject for the newsreel camera. When Americans by the millions went to the "movies" during the New Deal years, they saw the president and watched and listened as he popularized his administration's programs and achievements. Aside from their attraction to news showing dramatic, sensational, and even tragic events, newsreel editors appreciated the positive news that Roosevelt was able to supply. Considering that newsreels were shown along with feature films in practically every theater, they afforded FDR an ideal communications opportunity, and he was able to take advantage of it.

The radio was another new medium with a huge political potential. Since its first scheduled broadcast in the United States in 1920, its popularity had grown enormously. Roosevelt and his administration recognized its publicity value and, from his first days in office, sought to maximize it as a political instrument. His Fireside Chats, beginning the month he took office, became legendary as a means of connecting him and the people in an intimate way. In these and his longer broadcasts, Roosevelt, working with a team of speech writers and mobilizing his superb rhetorical skills, was able to reach a vast audience. The networks also extended public speaking privileges to Mrs. Roosevelt and to members of the president's cabinet. Beyond that, the networks produced numerous informational programs, and while claiming to be politically neutral, they carried "administration information" as a public service. By 1941 radio had become the most significant source of public information, and Roosevelt was masterful in using it.

Meanwhile the print media were busy extending political journalism. New periodicals, many designed for specialized audiences, appeared. Some were immensely popular. News magazines such as *Time*, founded in 1923, and *Newsweek*, founded in 1933, enjoyed large circulations. No media development vitalized American political life more than the advent of public affairs syndicated columnists. Hundreds of newspapers subscribed to popular columns such as Walter Lippmann's "Today and Tomorrow," begun in 1929; and Raymond Clapper's "Watching the World Go By," begun in 1936.

A great deal has been written about Roosevelt and the press. At his first press conference, he exhilarated the correspondents. After the disappointing relations the Washington press corps had experienced with his predecessors, it is no wonder that journalists were impressed by Roosevelt's jaunty personality and his efforts from the start to establish rapport with them. He told the reporters that they would no longer have to submit written questions in advance and that he would attempt to handle questions in a spontaneous manner. There would be, of course, ground rules regarding which of his comments could be published and which would be intended as "background information" and as confidential "off the record" remarks. The old rule of "no direct quotes without authorization" would be retained.

The first press conference typified many of his early meetings with the correspondents, and it has become something of a legend among journalists. It ended with the reporters spontaneously applauding the President. As the years went on, however, some correspondents began to complain about his using his wit to evade questions and, particularly after 1935, about his limiting of news by labeling certain remarks as "off the record." It is clear, however, that Roosevelt had the correspondents' support during the crucial early years of the New Deal.

The President found it more difficult to accept certain members of the press. Some mass-circulation columnists such as Frank Kent, Westbrook Pegler, David Lawrence, Mark Sullivan, and Walter Lippmann opposed Roosevelt and the New Deal. Others such as Walter Winchell, Drew Pearson, and Robert S. Allen generally supported him. Roosevelt, however, had little respect for most columnists and could even be contemptuous of them. He was antagonistic also toward publishers as a group although he enjoyed friendly relations with a number of individual publishers and editors. On behalf of the American Newspaper Publishers Association, William Allen White told the President at one point: "Most of us have agreed with most things that you have tried to do. If some of us have disagreed with a few of the things, it was in sorrow, not in anger, and it hurt us much more than it did you."[21]

Such a conciliatory gesture, however, does not alter the well-publicized hostility that Roosevelt had for the press in general. He repeatedly said that 85% of the nation's press opposed him. That was an erroneous appraisal of the strength of his press opposition, and a recent investigation shows that he had reason to know it was exaggerated.[22] The idea of a largely hostile press, however, no doubt added a degree of public sympathy to the President's support.

Although it did not reach the degree he claimed, Roosevelt and his New Deal did attract a great deal of press hostility. Conservative papers thought his program too liberal while liberal journals thought it too conservative and weak on principles. The general pattern of press treatment of the New Deal was strong support at first followed in ensuing years by a more critical tone. Sometimes, as the criticism mounted, it became bitter, but at other times it was temperate. Even the President's most extreme opponents in the newspaper press — William Randolph Hearst and the *Chicago Tribune's* Colonel Robert McCormick — supported the New Deal at first. McCormick broke with Roosevelt rather quickly, as a result of the spending policies of the New Deal and his conviction that the New Deal was a threat to press freedom. Hearst's departure was slower. By 1935, however, he decided he could not endure what he thought were socialistic, even communistic, tendencies in the New Deal.

Roosevelt's administration was not defenseless. It could give as well as receive penetrating barbs. The President, consummate politician that he was, could be harsh in his treatment of individual journalists and papers. So could other New Dealers. The head of the National Recovery Administration, Hugh Johnson, not the most temperate of men, lashed out at an article in the *Washington Post* in this manner: "With little less than libel, a trifle more than backstairs gossip, this writer in whose veins there must flow something more than a trace of redent [sic] blood, exalts some who are weak and throws mud at some who are strong, for no other apparent reason than to provide salable copy." Then he called the *Post* a "dying newspaper."[23] The most famous critique of the press by a New Dealer was that of Harold Ickes, Roosevelt's Secretary of the Interior, who, in his *America's House of Lords*, made a trenchant attack on the press as a business. Such criticism provides an indication of the stormy involvement the press had in the public debate after 1932.

Harold Ickes and Editorial Cartoons
Among President Roosevelt's New Dealers, his Secretary of the Interior, Harold Ickes, was the most pugnacious in dealing with opposition newspapers. As a result, he became the subject of frequent editorial cartoons. This one shows him fighting all types of enemies, including the press, fascism, academics, and the Ku Klux Klan. Having punched out those four, the cartoon caption has him asking, "Anybody else?"

There was another factor of consequence in Roosevelt's relations with the press: his expertise at organizing publicity. The New Deal's publicity organization was one of major dimension.[24] Many of the newly created government agencies had their own publicity bureaus. Stephen Early, Roosevelt's press secretary, was in charge of publicity for the President. Modeling his work on George Creel's CPI organization of World War I days, Early created an effective and centralized information distribution center.

The press benefited from that organization and its mountain of news releases, but it also discovered that it faced a new vigorous

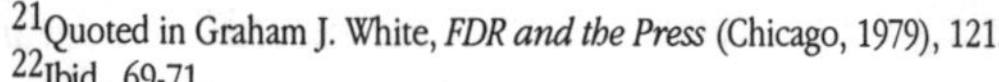
[21]Quoted in Graham J. White, *FDR and the Press* (Chicago, 1979), 121.
[22]Ibid., 69-71.

[23]Quoted in an untitled address by Eugene Meyer, 5 March 1935, Box 85, Eugene Meyer Papers, Manuscript Division, Library of Congress, Washington, D.C., p. 5.
[24]Betty Houchin Winfield, "The New Deal Publicity Operation: Foundation for the Modern Presidency," *Journalism Quarterly* 61 (1984): 40-8.

competitor in its efforts to mold and direct public opinion. Lorena Hickok, one of the first female reporters for the Associated Press, gave up her job in 1933 to gather information for the Federal Emergency Relief Organization. As a chief investigator for the FERA, she traveled the nation on fact-finding tours to observe relief programs and reported directly to the FERA's chief, Harry Hopkins, and to Eleanor Roosevelt, whose friend and confidante she was. Some of her reports formed the basis for newspaper articles, while others resulted directly in government efforts to solve problems.

The Press and Modern Revolutions

Even more than in domestic affairs, the media helped shape public thought about foreign affairs. At the beginning of the interwar years, two modern revolutionary movements established themselves in two major Western countries — Russia and Italy. Now that the United States had become a world power, it was imperative that the public be informed about these movements, since from the start they challenged the international order. The press, however, was far from accurate and exhaustive in its handling of these revolutions.

In Russia's case the revolution occurred in 1917 in the midst of the World War. At that time the Bolsheviks seized power, but it took them several more years and a civil war to establish themselves. During those years the general picture Americans had of Russia in revolution was marred by distortion. For the most part, the problem was due to the radicalism of the revolutionaries and to the extremely restrictive and difficult conditions that they placed on foreign correspondents there. In part, it resulted from the inability of some of the correspondents to understand the Bolsheviks, about whom they knew little, and the dynamics of their revolution. "One of the main reasons for the gross misinformation that these reports [of Russian news] spread," writes one radical critic of the Western press and the Russian Revolution, "was a growing apprehension as to the nature of Bolshevism, which encouraged wishful thinking about its early demise. As details of Lenin's new social order filtered through the West, the first signs appeared of the strong anti-Bolshevik sentiment that was soon to become fanatical."[25]

The misunderstanding also came as a product of ideological differences between American newspapers and Marxist revolutionaries. In 1920, Walter Lippmann and Charles Merz studied Russian news as it appeared in the *New York Times* between 1917 and 1920. They discovered that the *Times* had misled its readers about Russia in revolution, an event destined to change world history. The paper's poor reporting and its reckless imposition of editorial bias in news columns, they claimed, had misinformed the public about events in Russia. They questioned if the professional standards of journalism were high enough to serve the public dur-

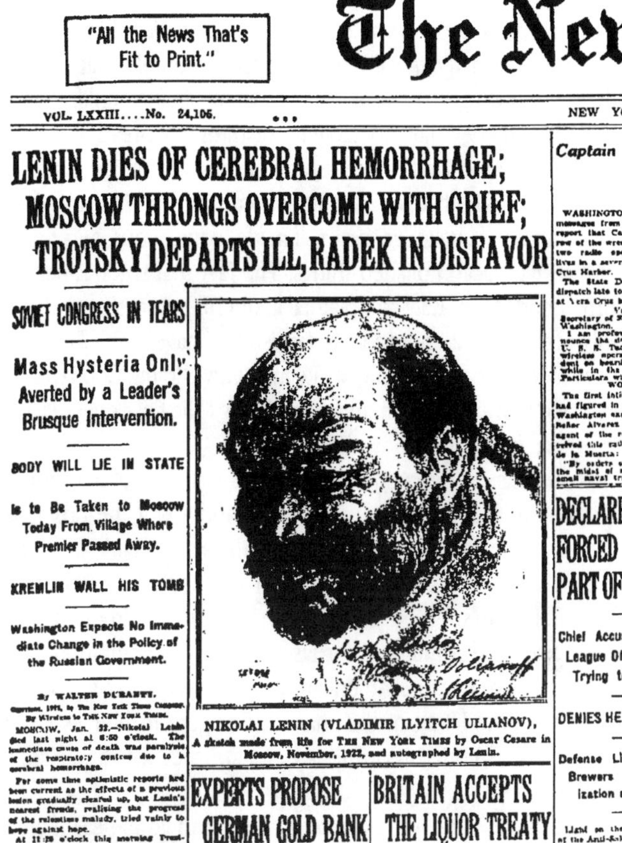

"All the News That's Fit to Print."

The New

VOL. LXXIII....No. 24,106. NEW Y

LENIN DIES OF CEREBRAL HEMORRHAGE; MOSCOW THRONGS OVERCOME WITH GRIEF; TROTSKY DEPARTS ILL, RADEK IN DISFAVOR

SOVIET CONGRESS IN TEARS

Mass Hysteria Only Averted by a Leader's Brusque Intervention.

BODY WILL LIE IN STATE

Is to Be Taken to Moscow Today From Village Where Premier Passed Away.

KREMLIN WALL HIS TOMB

Washington Expects No Immediate Change in the Policy of the Russian Government.

By WALTER DURANTY.

MOSCOW, Jan. 22.—Nikolai Lenin died last night at 6:50 o'clock. The immediate cause of death was paralysis of the respiratory centres due to a cerebral hemorrhage.

For some time optimistic reports had been current as the effects of a previous lesion gradually cleared up, but Lenin's nearest friends, realizing the progress of the relentless malady, tried vainly to hope against hope.

At 11:30 o'clock this morning President Kalinin briefly opened the session of the All-Russian Soviet Congress and requested every one to stand. He had not slept all night and tears were streaming down his haggard face. A

NIKOLAI LENIN (VLADIMIR ILYITCH ULIANOV),
A sketch made from life for THE NEW YORK TIMES by Oscar Cesare in Moscow, November, 1922, and autographed by Lenin.

EXPERTS PROPOSE GERMAN GOLD BANK

R Would Be Absolutely Inde-

BRITAIN ACCEPTS THE LIQUOR TREATY

Document Is Approved by All of

Captain

DECLARE FORCED PART OF

Chief Accus League Of Trying t

DENIES HE

Defense Li Brewers ization

Lenin's Death and a New U.S.S.R.
By the time Nikolai Lenin died in 1924, the American press had developed news bureaus around the world. Newspapers had followed Lenin's seizure of power during World War I when Germany had helped him return to Russia to topple its liberal provisional government. Upon his death, the western press focused on the struggle for power among his followers and was particularly interested in the direction that the Soviet Union would take in international affairs.

ing such a severe test as the Russian Revolution posed.[26]

Years later, the veteran foreign correspondent Raymond Swing recalled that he had been in Russia in 1921 to report on the famine that had reached critical proportions. While there, without instructions to do so, he gathered material for a series of articles on Russia under Bolshevik rule. He sent them to the *New York Herald*, the paper for which he was working. They were not used. Later, he said he learned that the only news the *Herald*'s editor "was going to print about Russia was that Lenin and Trotsky had gone into the backyard and cut their throats."[27]

Between 1922, when he came to power, and 1933, Italy's Benito Mussolini held the center of attention in terms of world leaders covered in the American press. Mussolini was anything but

[25]Phillip Knightley, *The First Casualty: From the Crimea to Vietnam: The War Correspondent as Hero, Propagandist, and Mythmaker* (New York, 1975), 149.

[26]Walter Lippmann and Charles Merz, "A Test of the News," *The New Republic*, 4 August 1920, 1-41.

[27]"American Newspapers and Foreign News," an address by Raymond Gram Swing, 31 May 1938, Box 1, Raymond Gram Swing Papers, Manuscript Division, Library of Congress, Washington, D.C., p. 8.

passive in creating a positive image for himself. American journalists of all persuasions traveled to Italy to interview him, and he welcomed them. *Il Duce* impressed most of them. The fact that he showed more restraint as a national leader before linking arms with Hitler in 1936 fails to account for the widespread, favorable treatment he received in the American press. He enjoyed an image as a man who had saved Italy, as someone who had answered the communist challenge, as a self-made, courageous, and practical man who accomplished things. The fact that some American correspondents in Italy complained about his censorship and control of the press did not seem to tarnish his image in the American press. Will Rogers called him a "Regular Guy"; Irving Cobb said he was "one of the most human human beings" he ever saw; Ida Tarbell called him a "despot with a dimple."

There was, to be certain, some press criticism of and apprehension about Mussolini's use of force and about the brutal aspects of his regime. Nevertheless, until the start of Hitler's regime in 1933 and the Italian-Ethiopian War of 1935-1936, Mussolini's popular image survived in the American press. Although journalists had little admiration for fascism, many did admire Mussolini. It appears that the American press allowed its own and the public's natural liking of the charismatic figure to blur its vision and deflect its criticism of the fascist state over which Mussolini presided.

"Stalin's Apologist"
A reporter for the *New York Times*, Walter Duranty gained prominence covering World War I and became one of the most respected foreign correspondents of his time. Sympathetic to the Russian Revolution and the Marxist regime that it placed in power, however, after the war he misrepresented Soviet conditions to readers by ignoring serious economic and social problems and by downplaying Joseph Stalin's ruthlessness. With time, his bias became apparent, and critics gave him the nickname "Stalin's Apologist," a title later used by his biographer.

Nevertheless, the American press deserves a good deal of credit for the effort it made to cover the world in the 1920s. Europe, of course, was a center of news, and a number of old internationally minded papers expanded their services there. Some newcomers such as the *Baltimore Sun* also entered the field. In Asia, Japan became the center of operation for a small group of correspondents serving the major news agencies, and some of the major American dailies such as the *Chicago Daily News*, the *Chicago Tribune*, the *Christian Science Monitor*, the *New York Herald Tribune*, and the *New York Times*. Conditions were more difficult in China, but a few American correspondents survived handicaps of distance and poor communications to report on the new republic of Dr. Sun Yat-sen and, after him, Chiang Kai-shek. Reuters, the British news agency, covered India extensively after the World War; and in 1930 the Associated Press opened its own bureau in Calcutta. Moreover, a handful of special correspondents visited Asia from time to time for American publications.

Although Americans in the 1920s were drawing back from world affairs, an impressive group of foreign correspondents gave them better knowledge of the world than they had in 1914. The media's coverage of world affairs improved even more in the 1930s. A number of prestigious foreign correspondents won Pulitzer Prizes for their work. They included Leland Stowe of the *New York Herald-Tribune*; H.R. Knickerbocker of the *Philadelphia Public Ledger* and *New York Evening Post*; Anne O'Hare McCormick, Frederick T. Birchall, and Walter Duranty of the *New York Times*; Edgar Ansel Mowrer of the *Chicago Daily News*; Wilfred C. Barber of the *Chicago Tribune*; and Louis P. Lochner of the Associated Press.

The events in the 1930s forced the American public to become more involved in debating international affairs. As the controversies of that intensely political decade ensued, the media occupied a powerful position in shaping and supporting the various positions of argument. Japan's invasion of Manchuria in 1931, the advent of Adolf Hitler in 1933 and Nazi Germany's subsequent persecutions at home and expansion abroad, the Italian invasion of Ethiopia in 1935, and, with these events, the collapse of collective security, all combined to create a dangerous international atmosphere. Meanwhile, the Soviet Union, racked by famine, by Stalin's Five Year Plans of collectivization, and by the purges beginning in 1934, shifted its position and assumed a more cooperative stance vis-a-vis the West.

There was more response to Stalin's diplomatic moves of the mid 1930s. In 1934 the Soviet Union joined the League of Nations and a year later signed mutual assistance pacts with France and Czechoslovakia. These moves met strong and varied press reaction. Liberal journals of opinion, long sympathetic to the Russian people and the Soviet experiment, applauded them. Conservative journals generally still perceived ideological expansion as the prime goal of Soviet policy. Opinion was divided among the nation's major newspapers. Of the country's thirty-five leading papers, twenty-two viewed the moves as motivated by Soviet security needs rather than by the dictates of communist expansion.

The Press and International Aggression

Events elsewhere between 1931 and 1936 also attracted widespread attention in the press. Hitler's coming to power in 1933 and the Nazi reconstruction of Germany that followed caused a great deal of uneasiness throughout the American press. The Italian invasion of Ethiopia in 1935 shattered Mussolini's previously favorable image in the press. Italy became an aggressor nation. When Japan invaded Manchuria in 1931, the American press was at first divided. Among other things, that invasion was a violation of the Nine Power Pact that both the United States and Japan signed in 1922. To some papers, as well as to some diplomats, it still seemed possible at that point to construct a case for Japan. As the crisis continued, however, American press opinion gravitated around hostility to Japan coupled with the hope that a settlement could be reached without hostilities between the United States and Japan. The idea was widespread that the United States had no interest in the Far East that justified a confrontation with Japan. Some papers did support sanctions against Japan, but the press in general felt relieved when they were not employed. Before long, however, events did threaten to draw the United States into intervention, even war, as aggression continued in Europe and Asia.

In the late 1930s this country faced one of the greatest crises in its history. Germany's reoccupation of the Rhineland in 1936, its incorporation of Austria in 1938, and its subsequent destruction of Czechoslovakia jarred American opinion. Meanwhile, in 1937 the Sino-Japanese War began. When the Second World War started in Europe, with Hitler's invasion of Poland on September 1, 1939, the United States was pushed to the brink of decision. After the fall of France in the spring of 1940, whether or not the United States should supply Britain became an acute question. If Germany won, what would be the nature of the Nazi menace to the Western World, and to the Western Hemisphere in particular? Seldom has popular clamor over American policy been as severe as it was in the years between 1936 and 1941. It is difficult to quarrel with the judgment that "never before in their history had Americans been so well informed about events abroad and never before had they followed them so closely."[28]

"Isolationism" is a word perhaps used too loosely. Some isolationists in the 1930s, for instance, were internationally minded. They simply did not wish to have the country again enter war. Some preferred the label "neutralist." Many were isolationists of a traditional type who thought of the interests and character of the United States as separate from those of European countries and

PIECE PEACE?

Isolationism
In the 1930s American and press sentiment opposed involvement in European affairs. When Adolf Hitler demanded that Czechoslovakia cede part of its territory to Germany during the "Munich Crisis," American newspapers, like this cartoon from the *Boston Post*, generally criticized Hitler without urging that the United States take any action to stop him.

who viewed the Atlantic Ocean as a sufficient barrier to guarantee that difference. Regardless, a great surge in isolationist sentiment occurred in the late 1930s. Isolationism was, after all, one of the oldest traditions in American history. After World War I and the frustrations of peacemaking of 1919, American opinion turned away from the international idealism that had characterized its brief departure from the isolationist impulse, and became disillusioned about participating in the international controversies of Europe and Asia. Rejecting the League of Nations, the American people felt secure in their geographical position, buffered on east and west by oceans separating them from foreign turmoil.

As the events of the 1930s unfolded in Europe and Asia, an abhorrence of war grew in America. Coupled with this was the idea that with its depression-shattered economy, the country needed to direct its energies toward curing domestic problems. Moreover, as fear of involvement in another war emerged, revisionist writing about World War I reached its hightide. The revisionists argued that the United States should have stayed out of the First World War and, indeed, that the British had manipulated our intervention in that conflict to serve their own self interests.

[28]William L. Langer and S. Everett Gleason, *The Challenge to Isolation 1937-1940* (New York, 1952), 11.

America First
American opposition to involvement in the problems of the rest of the world took a number of media forms in the 1930s. One was music, with the song "America First" proclaiming that Americans should place the welfare of their own country ahead of international troubles caused by the other countries themselves.

Broad and deep were the currents of isolationist sentiment. The press vitalized all shades of opinion. Its pronouncements ranged from crude expressions of chauvinistic and ill-informed nationalism in some editorials to fair-minded critiques found in papers like the *Kansas City Star*. Liberal journals such as *The Nation* and *The New Republic* favored isolationism as did old progressive organs. Conservative papers endorsed it. Newspapers opposed to Roosevelt's New Deal policies tended to be isolationist. So did many that agreed with those policies. Hearst's papers campaigned hard for the isolationist cause, and in so doing, like the *Chicago Tribune*, tried to mobilize anticommunist and Anglophobic sympathies. In the hands of a Hearst, the cause could be sensationalized. On the other hand, in 1938 the journalist Elmer Davis, an internationalist, commented: "Twenty years ago we went on a crusade which would have made sense if we had got what we wanted; but we failed to find the Holy Grail, and the experience ought to have cured us of our inclination to go grailing."[29] Isolationism was truly heterogeneous; and the majority of Americans, for one reason or another, believed in it.

The isolationists' persuasion, however, was not complete. When Roosevelt suggested in a 1937 speech that aggressor powers be "quarantined," his idea received strong press support. Among the major papers supporting him were the *New York Times*, *Washington Post*, *Washington Evening Star*, *Cleveland Plain Dealer*, *Chicago Daily News*, *Portland Morning Oregonian*, and *New Orleans Times-Picayune*.

Nevertheless, Roosevelt retreated from putting his words into action. American opinion on isolation was not as settled as it might seem. The liberal journals *The Nation* and *The New Republic* were shocked by the Allied capitulation at Munich in 1938, by the Nazi-Soviet Pact of the following year, and by the Nazi blitzkrieg of Denmark, Norway, and the Lowlands in the spring of 1940. Slowly these stalwarts of liberal opinion relinquished their resistance to intervention. Even the *Saturday Evening Post*, the voice of middle-class America and an outspoken isolationist magazine, became interventionist in 1941.

Organizations formed to advocate both sides of the controversy. One was the Committee to Defend America by Aiding the Allies, a group that had William Allen White as one of its organizers and leaders. He was one of the most respected figures in the country, and he explained his purpose in a radio interview:

> Two views are honestly held up by intelligent people. One group contends that by isolating ourselves we can let the Allies fall and Hitler rise and then retire behind our own barriers.... The other group believes that isolation is impossible. The Nazis have overrun Czechoslovakia by force, Poland by force, Norway by force, Denmark by force, Holland by force, and are now by force overrunning France and will conquer England by force if they can. We are next.... It makes no difference whether it is a war with guns or an economic war, or a social upheaval which will menace our way of life.[30]

That idea was gaining in the public mind.

Why the weakening of the isolationist impulse? Perhaps isolationism floundered as a result of the mass media's publicizing the war in Europe after 1939. After the war began, the British government engaged in no propaganda activities in the United States as it had in 1914. It simply gave out "information on demand." But a strong, latent pro-English sentiment existed in this country, and it surfaced as news of the Battle of Britain filled the American press. "This...is London," Edward R. Murrow's dramatic opening of each of his broadcasts from the British capital while the Germans were bombing it, conveyed the reality of the Blitz to millions of Americans and created sympathy for the beleaguered British. Murrow put together a team of correspondents for CBS, and together they became the first broadcast "news stars" to achieve that status not as commentators but as on-the-air reporters.[31] Meanwhile, popu-

[29]Quoted in Allan M. Winkler, *The Politics of Propaganda: The Office of War Information 1942-1945* (New Haven, 1978), 33.

[30]"Radio Interview with W. A. White," n.d., William Allen White Papers, Series D, Box 13, Manuscript Division, Library of Congress, Washington, D.C., pp. 1-2.

[31]The team Murrow assembled included Mary Marvin Breckinridge, Cecil Brown, Winston Burdett, Charles Collingwood, William Downs, Thomas Grandin, Richard C. Hottelet, Larry Le Sueur, Eric Sevareid, William L. Shirer, and Howard K. Smith.

lar radio commentators such as H. V. Kaltenborn and Raymond Swing favored intervention. No doubt these things impressed American opinion. The Germans, moreover, had operated an active propaganda organization in the United States since 1933. It tried to foster isolationism and even worked to attempt to defeat Roosevelt for re-election in 1940. In the end such activity probably damaged the isolationist cause, for most of the Americans who had little desire to intervene had even less respect for nazism. They were recognizing the dangers the Axis powers posed.

Gradually events exposed the fallacies of the isolationist position. But that persuasion remained alive in some quarters of the American press. It could erupt and strike violently at the various measures taken by Roosevelt in 1940 and 1941 to aid the countries fighting Germany. The hard-core anti-Roosevelt isolationist newspapers refused to budge from their contention that he was leading the country into war. Just three days before Pearl Harbor, in fact, the *Chicago Tribune*, in an effort to discredit the administration, splashed a story across its front page announcing that Roosevelt had war plans. A strategic plan drawn up by the War Department to be used in case the United States should declare war on Germany had been leaked to the *Tribune*, and the paper made full use of it. That such a document existed was not surprising, but its publication during times so critical for the world shows the degree to which the isolationist press would go in making its case. In the end, dramatic events abroad overtook the isolationist cause and revealed the falsity of its premises. The attack on Pearl Harbor removed most of the remaining doubt.

Honolulu Star-Bulletin 1st EXTRA

WAR!

(Associated Press by Transpacific Telephone) SAN FRANCISCO, Dec. 7.—President Roosevelt announced this morning that Japanese planes had attacked Manila and Pearl Harbor.

OAHU BOMBED BY JAPANESE PLANES

SIX KNOWN DEAD, 21 INJURED, AT EMERGENCY HOSPITAL

Attack Made On Island's Defense Areas

Hundreds See City Bombed

Names of Dead and Injured

Schools Closed

Editorial

Pearl Harbor

When Japanese planes bombed the American naval base at Pearl Harbor on December 7, 1941, the act immediately brought the United States into World War II as a combatant. The report reproduced above was from the same day in the *Star-Bulletin* of Honolulu, the site of the bombing.

The Second World War

With the Japanese attack on Pearl Harbor on December 7, 1941, the debate ended over the position the United States should take regarding the war. It is difficult today to recapture the shock and indignation felt by the American people as they heard over their radios that afternoon that Japan had attacked the American "Gibraltar of the Pacific." The fact that, with some exception, the bulk of the press' attention had been directed toward Europe magnified the shock. On December 8, Congress responded by declaring a state of war existed between the United States and Japan. Three days later, Germany and Italy honored their Tripartite Pact with Japan and declared war on the United States. The United States reciprocated with a declaration of war against the Axis powers on the same day.

America had entered a war of unprecedented magnitude and faced one of the most severe crises in its history. It confronted a staggering combined menace, for by late 1941 Hitler had overrun Europe. His armies were poised to strike at the Middle East. Where they would move after that no one could say — perhaps eastward to join forces with Japan, which was already in China and had begun to overrun Southeast Asia.

Unlike during World War I, the United States had been attacked, and Americans were saying that this was "our war." The Pearl Harbor disaster united the country. "We must from now on think not only in terms of total war, but also in terms of a world-wide area of conflict," editorialized *The New Republic*. On the other end of the political spectrum, William Randolph Hearst wrote in his newspaper column: "Well, fellow Americans, we are in the war and we have got to win it."[32]

The war, however, was not to be won entirely on distant shores. Most Americans applauded the war aims, but questions were raised in some corners. Before Pearl Harbor, the *Pittsburgh Courier* and the *Chicago Defender*, black papers, questioned the nature of the war then underway. Was it a white man's war for the preservation of the status quo? For black Americans to receive the human freedoms that all Americans believed were theirs, the status quo would have to be changed. After Pearl Harbor the NAACP's *Crisis*, edited since 1934 by Roy Wilkins, who had gained a reputation as a forceful advocate of civil rights, announced, "Now is the time *not* to be silent." The *Pittsburgh Courier* agreed and advanced the "Double V" slogan for "victory over our enemies at home and victory over our enemies on the battlefields

[32]"Our War," *The New Republic*, 15 December 1941, 812; and W. A. Swanberg, *Citizen Hearst* (New York, 1961), 499.

abroad."[33] Discrimination in the armed services and in war industries as well as the racial segregation and exclusivism practiced across the country seemed intolerable to many black editors. In retrospect, their exertions helped to establish the groundwork for the civil rights movement of the 1950s and 1960s, but at the time the issue of discrimination was a matter of serious concern for the Roosevelt administration, which moved only hesitantly toward redressing black grievances.

Black citizens appear to have supported both the militancy of their press and the nation's war effort. When the armed forces moved toward greater racial equality in 1944 and sent more black units into combat, black correspondents were permitted to accompany them and reported on their accomplishments. "No previous venture in public relations," surmises the historian John Morton Blum, "had the impact on blacks of the reports of the war correspondents of Afro-American newspapers."[34] As important as the correspondents' work was to the black community, it also can be seen as a part of the larger and unprecedented news coverage of the war.

Radio also was able to make a unique contribution to the coverage. At a time when listening to the news had become a national habit, the American public could hear about the war on its fifty-six million radio sets. Overseas broadcasts by Edward R. Murrow, William Shirer, and others placed American listeners in direct touch with the war in Europe. Meanwhile, the war brought radio commentators and their listeners into the most intimate relationship they have ever experienced. Walter Winchell's rapid fire opening, "Good evening, Mr. and Mrs. North America and all the ships at sea. Let's go to press," echoed in millions of homes. There was a reassuring quality in Lowell Thomas' melodious sign off, "So long until tomorrow." Entire families gathered around their radios in the evening to hear commentators report the day's war news. The commentators, with their individual rhetorical styles, were national figures and a vital part of the nation at war.

Americans also were able to watch news of the war. In some respects the newsreel reached its peak during the war as it responded to the public's great demand for war news. As in World War I, the work of both civilian and military cameramen again underwent censorship because of the conditions imposed by a war of great magnitude. Yet the newsreels gave the public an unparalleled graphic picture of the many sides of modern war with films ranging from portrayals of national strength and unity to scenes of actual battle and to film reports of appalling discoveries the Allies made upon entering the Nazi death camps at Buchenwald and Dachau.

The full extent of the news coverage of the war can only be appreciated by considering the efforts of the 1,646 print correspondents who, although they could not be everywhere, traveled across the world into all the war zones. They made it possible for newspapers and magazines to blanket their pages with reports of this truly global war. In their ranks were journalists such as Leland Stowe of the *Chicago Daily News*, William Laurence of the *New York Times*, and Ernie Pyle, the most beloved of all the correspondents and a reporter who found meaning in the unheroic dimension of war, and the photojournalist Margaret Bourke-White, who covered the conflict for *Life* magazine. The men and women of the press corps contributed to the many-sided vision of war that the press gave the American public. Whatever else might be said about the media at war, the individual contribution that these and many other correspondents made to war reporting should be kept in mind.

News of the war and its cost in human suffering went beyond reports from the various fronts. The ugliest aspect of the war dealt with the Nazi persecution of the Jews and the implementation of Hitler's "final solution" for them. The tragic fate of the six million European Jews who paid with their lives for Nazi racial ideology and its consequences is, of course, well known today. The media did publish news of the persecution beginning in the 1930s and during the war made known the horrors of the extermination to the limits that information was available. Although it was impossible to comprehend the full meaning of "extermination" and despite the fact that suspicion of exaggeration existed (based partly on memories of erroneous World War I atrocity stories), the Allied nations, by joint declaration on December 17, 1942, confirmed that the Nazis had killed two million Jews. Such news made the front pages, but did not hold them for long. Impossible as it was to rescue most European Jews from the grasp of Nazi savagery, something might be done for the refugees who were trying to flee. Some newspapers raised their voice to demand that action be taken and helped to bring about the Anglo-American Bermuda Conference of 1943 to deal with refugees. That conference merely confirmed the idea of rescue through victory.

Many disturbing questions surround the media and public reaction to the Jewish tragedy. Why did such news fail to make a greater impact on the public than it did? Why did the American press fail to launch a major campaign for a modification of immigration policy that would have provided some relief for refugees? Answers to these questions lie in understanding the currents of American culture, the tendency of the press to reflect popular sentiments, and an understanding of the bitter dilemma that the necessities of war forced upon the public and policy makers.

The Government and Information

As was the case in World War I, an elaborate system of government censorship and publicity existed during World War II. Censorship began even before the United States entered the war, subjecting correspondents to the various regulations of the belligerent nations. As conditions grew more perilous for the United States, the government asked the press to apply its own "voluntary censorship." In some cases the press heeded that appeal; in others, it did not. In Hawaii, the press regularly reported the movements of the

[33] Quoted in John Morton Blum, *V Was for Victory: Politics and American Culture during World War II* (New York, 1976), 208.
[34] Ibid., 209.

War Propaganda

Axis Powers Fight the Enemy with Racism and Black Ink

The war of words and images became one of the most important struggles of World War II. Axis nations used the news and entertainment media — and even the arts — to build national unity among their own people, to try to bolster or gain support from other nations, and to try to discourage their enemies.

Germany's effort, led by Josef Goebbels, was the most comprehensive. He believed propaganda should be omnipresent. Long before the war began, the press, films, radio, literature, theater, and art promoted Hitler, the Nazi Party, and such ideas as "one people, one nation, one leader," and "the Jews are our misfortune."

Unlike the Nazis, the Fascists did not attempt to make party views a new national religion. Propaganda aimed at Italians focused on God, national pride, and family values. Later, however, Italians were fed increasingly racist depictions of the enemy, similar to much German and Japanese propaganda. Like the Nazis, the Fascists believed in early indoctrination. Even comic strips in youth newspapers promoted Fascist military values.

The Japanese embraced what they termed "thought war" later than did most Western nations, but they also had a propaganda system firmly in place by the mid-1930s. Interestingly, many of the themes and much of the style came from German propaganda, with the two nations even co-producing two films.

Propagandists used "leaflet bombings" and radio to try to demoralize enemy soldiers. Radio stations, which could be used to broadcast propaganda, became key prizes for advancing armies. A common theme was the suspicion of what lonely wives and girlfriends of "naive" soldiers might be doing at home. Americans Iva Toguri and Mildred Gillars — termed "Tokyo Rose" and "Axis Sally" — both later went to prison for their wartime radio work in Japan and Germany. Toguri, apparently a victim of post-war hysteria, later was pardoned.

James B. McPherson
Peace College

The Nazi party in Germany had used propaganda beginning in the 1920s to advance its ideas, including German racial superiority. Its most vicious campaign was against the Jewish population of Europe. The most infamous example of the campaign was *The Eternal Jew*, a film and exhibit that presented Jews as subhuman. Despite such material, journalists of the Allied nations found it difficult to believe later that the Nazis were carrying out the systematic extermination of Jews, as they were indeed doing. Nazi propaganda like the cartoon at right provided clear evidence to many black Americans that, even though problems existed in the United States, German ideas of racial superiority made it imperative that they support the war effort against the Axis. In the cartoon, one black G.I. declares, "We are fighting for culture, Jimmy." The other replies, "Yes, but what is culture?"

"Silence"
The Office of War Information, headed by veteran journalist Elmer Davis, was responsible for propaganda abroad and information distributed domestically. One of its continuing campaigns, of which the poster reproduced above was a part, was to warn Americans not to talk carelessly about details that enemy agents might pick up and that thus could endanger the war effort.

American fleet despite the request by Secretary of Navy Frank Knox that such information be withheld from publication. Immediately after the attack on Pearl Harbor, the army and navy imposed military censorship.

To deal with the home front, President Roosevelt created the Office of Censorship on December 18, 1941. He appointed as its head Byron Price, formerly executive news editor of the Associated Press. Price established a Code of Wartime Practices for newspapers and radio stations and urged a system of "voluntary censorship." His office's policies were far less restrictive than the direct military censorship. The press cooperated, but there were a few exceptions.

The best known case was that of the *Chicago Tribune's* front page story of June 7, 1942, reporting the American naval victory at Midway. The headline read "Navy had Word of Jap Plan to Strike at Sea," and authorities believed this statement gave the enemy direct access to vital information implying that the navy had broken the Japanese code. In fact, that had been one of the reasons for the American success. Consequently, the government charged the *Tribune* with violating the Espionage Act as well as the Censorship Code.[35]

During World War I, George Creel's CPI controlled both censorship and publicity. President Roosevelt separated the functions and moved hesitantly toward the creation of a publicity organization. Bitter memories of Creel's committee still could be recalled; revisionist writers in the 1930s had denounced the propaganda activities of the First World War; and many thought of propaganda in reprehensible terms because of the shadings it acquired in Nazi hands in the 1930s. Always sensitive to public opinion, Roosevelt avoided creating an organization with the latitude the CPI enjoyed. But the need to mobilize opinion and to coordinate the release of information remained. Consequently, on June 13, 1942, he created the Office of War Information (OWI) to consolidate the activities of several publicity agencies then in existence and under criticism. To head the OWI, Roosevelt chose Elmer Davis, a veteran reporter and radio commentator.

The OWI had a number of responsibilities. It was in charge of propaganda abroad (except for Latin America); and it supervised the government's war information programs in radio, motion pictures, and other mass media. It also was responsible for public information and in this capacity served as a liaison between the press and the government. In terms of scope of activity, the OWI differed from the CPI. There were also differences in operations. A few years after the war, Davis explained that Creel had no problem in coordinating information "because there was nobody to coordinate."[36] In 1917, Creel simply placed his own men in the various departments of government to handle publicity, but in 1942 each of the departments of government had its own public information office. Consequently, Davis worked out a system in which he consulted daily with representatives of the Departments of War and Navy to discuss what war news should be made public. That news then was issued by communiqué from those departments where the press associations and large papers normally stationed their military experts.

The system worked only to a limited degree. Davis wanted the American people to be informed about the war, but the key Departments of Navy and War claimed they controlled what material in their possession would be made public. While disputes over the release of information could be referred to the White House, Roosevelt tended to be deferential to military demands. Davis scored some victories but, in general, had to accept less than what he sought. "He got," as one historian has observed, "only what the others were willing to give."[37]

Press criticism emerged about the Roosevelt administration's control of information. There were, in fact, several sources of dissatisfaction. One was the feeling that the Army and Navy pre-

[35]The illegality of willful publication in wartime of information about national defense useful to the enemy was implicit in the Espionage Act of 1917. Still in effect, that Act had been amended in 1940 to increase penalties for peacetime violation. The government believed that the *Tribune* also had violated the Voluntary Censorship Code.

[36]"Role of Information in World War II," an address by Elmer H. Davis, 16 November 1951, Box 4, Elmer H. Davis Papers, Manuscript Division, Library of Congress, Washington, D.C., pp. 9 and 21.

[37]Winkler, *The Politics of Propaganda*, 51.

NIGHT EDITION

The Sun

LATE NEWS SCHOOLS—PICTURES

BRITISH PLUNGE DEEP BEHIND FOE

New York Boys in Normandy Battle

MONTGOMERY'S MEN 23 MILES INLAND

EXTRA!

9 A.M. FINAL

Los Angeles Times

9 A.M. FINAL

V-E DAY!

War Is Just Half Over!

What God Hath Wrought

Nazis Surrender Unconditionally to Allied Powers

BULLETINS ON SURRENDER

Stores Will Be Open Today

The Big News
The events of World War II resulted in some of the biggest news coverage in history, as illustrated by these two front pages from the last year of the war in Europe. With almost 2,000 American news personnel covering the war around the globe, readers were kept well informed of events as they happened daily. One of the biggest stories was the Allied invasion of Europe, D-Day, on June 6, 1944. In the days following the invasion, newspapers provided detailed accounts of the advance of the armies into France. The story reproduced here (left) is from the June 14 issue of the *New York Sun*. With the front page of this special edition (right), the *Los Angeles Times* of May 7, 1945, captured the overwhelming excitement over the defeat of Germany. Many newspapers throughout the country published the news in similar page designs.

vented the OWI from fulfilling its purpose regarding the release of information. This led some papers, mainly conservative journals, to charge that muddling and bickering ran rampant in Washington. Another source of dissatisfaction was the President himself. Once the war began, he placed restrictions on the press' coverage of his movements. Furthermore, correspondents found his press conferences less and less useful and felt that they were unfairly treated at the various wartime conferences Roosevelt held with other heads of state. So, old antagonisms continued and grew between the President and the press.

The Media's World War II Performance

The role of the media went beyond reporting the war. That public opinion is a prime factor in total war is beyond question, as is the belief that the media help to shape that opinion. During the Second World War, the media helped to create a number of the popular persuasions of the day. Consider, for example, the public and press response to bombing. In the 1930s, American opinion had been shocked by the act of bombing civilian populations in Spain and China. Once World War II began, and particularly after the United States entered the conflict, that attitude changed. Little criticism of "area," "saturation," or "obliteration" bombing appeared in the American press. The distinction between proper and reprehensible acts of war diminished. While Axis bombings of Warsaw, London, or Coventry might be denounced, there was only scant questioning of later Allied bombings of Berlin, Dresden, and Tokyo. The wide endorsement the dropping of the atomic bombs on the Japanese cities of Hiroshima and Nagasaki received in the American press was simply the final demonstration of how popular opposition to bombing had been neutralized in this country and the press. That response also demonstrated how the totality of this great armed conflict had led to acceptance of a double standard regarding proper and improper acts of war. The media, as well as the government, helped to shape that standard. Of course, when assessing the performance of the American press, it is instructive to keep in mind the utter subservience of the Axis press to its national war aims.

The media also were instrumental in shaping American attitudes toward other nations during the war. The American people, for instance, despised the Nazi leaders but displayed little hatred of the German people. Animosity toward the Japanese people, on the other hand, ran much deeper. In the public mind, the Japanese became a treacherous, fanatical, and warlike people. The media confirmed such stereotypes. In the case of the Soviet Union, they worked to replace public suspicions with an image of a worthy ally. The press contributed, in large measure, to the sympathetic, even admiring, image of Chiang Kai-shek and China that was so widespread in the public mind at least until 1943. By that time, criticism of Chiang's corruption and inefficiency began to emerge in the press as a result of revelations published by Vincent Sheean, Hanson Baldwin, and a few other journalists and writers.

While the majority of Americans supported the war, they voiced many complaints and had a number of differences of opinion on important issues. Nothing better illustrated the dissension in the press than the mixed opinion that surfaced regarding the role the United States should play in world affairs after the war. By 1943 there was a widespread sentiment among Americans favoring collective security and participation in a new international organization. It would appear that the isolationist persuasion that was so strong in the 1930s had died or was dying, but too much evidence to the contrary can be found in the press to allow an unqualified acceptance of that conclusion. The nationalistic temper of the Hearst press, for instance, could not tolerate the "idle dreams" of the internationalists and demanded that the United States be strong enough to stand alone. Toward the end of the war, on January 10, 1945, Senator Arthur Vandenberg, an old Republican isolationist who from 1906 to 1928 had edited the *Grand*

The Knoxville News-Sentinel

EXTRA EDITION

KNOXVILLE, TENNESSEE, MONDAY EVENING, AUGUST 6, 1945

Oak Ridge Has Over 425 Buildings

ATOMIC SUPER-BOMB, MADE AT OAK RIDGE, STRIKES JAPAN

Story of Secret Officially Told

Even Plant Chiefs Didn't Know What Work Others Did

Two Views of Giant Oak Ridge Production Plant

First Test in Desert Waste Was Blast Beyond Description

First Atomic Target Was Big Supply Port

End of the War — Dawn of a New Age
The dropping of the atomic bomb on Hiroshima and Nagasaki forced Japan to surrender. Newspapers recognized the bomb as a new, tremendous weapon of war — but few realized that they were seeing the dawn of a new nuclear age.

Rapids (Mich.) *Herald*, reversed his position and announced his conversion to internationalism. To that the *Chicago Tribune* yelled "Benedict Arnold."

In the history of the American press in World War II, there was much that was impressive. There were also some things that invite criticism. As a social institution the press kept much of its liveliness and retained a semblance of its critical voice. In reporting the largest war known to history, it performed a Herculean task with much credit.

In some other respects, its record was far from impressive, as in the case of Japanese-Americans living on the West Coast. In the days following the Pearl Harbor attack, there was a sharp outcry against their presence in that area because of a fear that some might aid Japan's military efforts. For this and other reasons thousands of Japanese-Americans were shipped to internment camps known as "relocation centers."

Some papers were restrained on the issue, but others were not. The latter, which included the powerful California Hearst papers, supported the campaign that led to the removal of the Japanese-Americans. Even the nationally syndicated columnist Westbrook Pegler joined in the emotion of the moment. "The Japanese in California," he wrote, "should be under armed guard and to hell with habeas corpus until the danger is over."[38] Ironically, his column bore the standing title "Fair Enough." Criticism of the press during the war, however, cannot be limited to specific instances.

Critics then and later have suggested that coverage of the war was less than accurate. There is reason to believe the validity of such criticism, and one is left with many questions about the press' handling of war news. How much of it was only an illusion of reality? Why did so many American heroic stereotypes appear in war reports? In describing those heroes, why were there so many allusions to sports? Indeed, the historian John Morton Blum has speculated that "a culture that had made heroes of its athletes could hardly avoid making athletes of its heroes."[39] Why did the press present the war so much in terms of the country's dominant culture? Little about the contributions made by black Americans or Japanese-Americans surfaced in the mainstream of the press. Why did headline writers too often distort the news? That tendency reached an exaggerated point following the raid at Dieppe, France, in 1942 by a Canadian force and a few American Rangers when the *New York Post* headlined: "Yanks invade Europe." Such practices demonstrate the impact that times of momentous national and international crises had on the news media.

RECOMMENDED READINGS

BOOKS

Bassow, Whitman. *The Moscow Correspondents: Reporting on Russia from the Revolution to Glasnost*. New York, 1988. Foreign correspondents' unfamiliarity with Russia, its language, and culture — combined with Soviet restrictions — led to distorted reporting.

Best, Gary Dean. *The Critical Press and the New Deal: The Press versus Presidential Power, 1933-1938*. Westport, Conn., 1993. Describes press opposition to New Deal policies as providing a check against expanding government power.

Carlisle, Rodney P. *Hearst and the New Deal: The Progressive as Reactionary*. New York, 1979. Examines Hearst's position on foreign and domestic policies during the Roosevelt era and his developing anti-liberalism.

Cloud, Stanley, and Lynne Olson. *The Murrow Boys: Pioneers on the Frontline of Broadcast Journalism*. New York, 1996. A vivid and personalized account of the wartime development of broadcast reporting.

Cornebise, Alfred E. *The Stars and Stripes: Doughboy Journalism in World War I*. Westport, Conn., 1981. The military newspaper covered the war from the common soldier's perspective, rather than that of the brass; it was a true newspaper rather than a public relations organ, subject to little interference from military authorities.

Covert, Catherine L., and John D. Stevens, eds. *Mass Media Between the Wars: Perceptions of Cultural Tension, 1918-1941*. Syracuse, N.Y., 1984. Collection of fourteen essays by various authors dealing primarily with the relationship between the media and American culture.

Culbert, David Holbrook. *News for Everyman: Radio and Foreign Affairs in Thirties America*. Westport, Conn., 1976. Commentators' broadcasts, although differing widely in their political beliefs, changed public opinion on American involvement in World War II from isolationist to interventionist, thus greatly influencing the foreign affairs process.

[38]Quoted in Blum, *V Was For Victory* 155.
[39]Ibid., 58.

Desmond, Robert W. *Crisis and Conflict: World News Reporting Between Two Wars 1920-1940*. Iowa City, 1982. An indispensable reference for international journalism and world crisis.

Doenecke, Justus D. *When the Wicked Rise: American Opinion-Makers and the Manchurian Crisis of 1931-1933*. Cranbury, N.J., 1984. A study of American opinion-makers and the Manchurian crisis using the press as an articulator of opinion.

Fielding, Raymond. *The American Newsreel 1911-1967*. Norman, Okla., 1972. Engaging history and the standard work on the topic.

Finkle, Lee. *Forum for Protest: The Black Press During World War II*. Cranbury, N.J., 1975. Black editors were more conservative than their readers. While they favored elimination of discrimination, they believed a world crisis was no time to demand a complete change in racial practices.

Hohenberg, John. *Foreign Correspondence: The Great Reporters and Their Times*. New York, 1967. The standard work on the topic.

Hosley, David H. *As Good as Any: Foreign Correspondence on American Radio, 1930-1940*. Westport, Conn., 1984. American correspondents performed well in covering the events leading to and including the early years of World War II despite the fact that they were working under technical constraints.

Juergens, George. *News from the White House: The Presidential Relationship in the Progressive Era*. Chicago, 1981. The best account of Woodrow Wilson and the press. The flow of power from Congress to the White House during the Progressive era created both the modern Presidency and the modern Washington press corps. Presidents and reporters needed each other, but also at times antagonized each other.

Koppes, Clayton R., and Gregory D. Black. *Hollywood Goes to War: How Politics, Profits, and Propaganda Shaped World War II Movies*. Berkeley, Calif., 1990. The movie industry and the federal government used films to further the Allied effort.

Kurth, Peter. *American Cassandra: The Life of Dorothy Thompson*. Boston, 1990. Chronicle of the career of the syndicated columnist and international correspondent during the turbulent decades of the 1920s and 1930s.

Liebovich, Louis W. *Bylines in Despair: Herbert Hoover, The Great Depression, and the U.S. News Media*. Westport, Conn., 1994. Hoover was innovative in his dealing with the media but nonetheless had a rocky relationship with reporters.

Mock, James R. *Censorship, 1917*. Princeton, N.J., 1941. Although there were occasional excesses, World War I censorship generally was done acceptably. The danger was the threat to American democratic government resulting from carrying over into peacetime the repressive measures used during the war.

Reporting World War II, 2 vols. New York: 1995. An anthology of American reportage during the war covering the years from 1938 to 1946 and based on a variety of print journalism sources and radio transcripts.

Shulman, Holly Cowan. *The Voice of America: Propaganda and Democracy, 1941-1945*. Madison, Wisc., 1990. The fullest account of the role the Voice of America played in advancing American views in World War II.

Short, K.R.M., ed. *Film and Radio Propaganda in World War II*. Knoxville, Tenn., 1983. Governments used movies and radio on a massive scale. Essays by various authors examine the use of propaganda by the Allies, Germany, Italy, and Japan.

Soley, Lawrence C. *Radio Warfare: OSS and CIA Subversive Propaganda*. Praeger, 1989. Political, military, and communication strategies shaped the use of radio during World War II.

Steele, Richard W. *Propaganda in an Open Society: The Roosevelt Administration and the Media, 1933-1941*. Westport, Conn., 1985. A sophisticated treatment of presidential-press relations that includes broadcast, film, and the print media.

Taylor, S.J. *Stalin's Apologist, Walter Duranty: The New York Times' Man in Moscow*. New York, 1990. Reporter Duranty, although respected in the journalism profession, downplayed Soviet problems and Stalin's ruthlessness in doing away with his opponents.

Vaughn, Stephen. *Holding Fast the Inner Lines: Democracy, Nationalism and the Committee on Public Information*. Chapel Hill, N.C., 1980. An excellent, well-balanced study of the CPI as a nationalizing agent in a democratic society.

Wade, Betsy. *Forward Positions: The War Correspondence of Homer Bigart*. Fayetteville, Ark., 1992. A collection of correspondence from the famous reporter for the *New York Times* and *New York Herald-Tribune*.

Wagner, Lilya. *Women War Correspondents of World War II*. Westport, Conn., 1989. This collection of biographies brings attention to journalists who often have been overlooked.

Winfield, Betty Houchin. *FDR and the News Media*. New York, 1994. Franklin Roosevelt gradually became more secretive with the press during his presidency.

Winkler, Allan M. *The Politics of Propaganda: The Office of War Information 1942-1945*. New Haven, Conn., 1978. The best study of the OWI, portraying it as an organization reflecting American policy and American values.

ARTICLES

Bishop, Robert L., and LeMar S. MacKay. "Mysterious Silence, Lyrical Scream: Government Information in World War II." *Journalism Monographs* 19 (1971). This study outlines the "main problems encountered in setting up U.S. information agencies for World War II."

Boorstin, Daniel. "Selling The President To The People: The Direct Democracy of Public Relations." *Commentary* 20 (1955): 421-7. An analysis of Franklin D. Roosevelt's public relations tactics including the style he used with Washington correspondents.

Bowles, Dorothy. "Newspaper Support for Free Expression in Times of Alarm, 1920 and 1940." *Journalism Quarterly* 54 (1977): 271-9. "A content analysis of editorials in sixteen large-city newspapers reveals a pattern of support for free expression."

Costrell, Edwin. "Newspapers' Attitudes Toward War in Maine 1914-17." *Journalism Quarterly* 16 (1939): 334-44. American attitudes toward participation in World War I as reflected by six Maine newspapers refute the notion that U.S. leaders got America into war contrary to popular desire.

Diggins, John P. "Mussolini and America: Hero-Worship, Charisma, and the 'Vulgar Talent.'" *The Historian* 28 (1966): 559-85. An excellent examination of Mussolini's image in the American press from 1922 to 1935.

Ellis, Mark. "America's Black Press, 1914-18." *History Today* 41 (1991): 18-27. Good overview of how black newspapers reacted to World War I and the steps the government took to influence them.

Frank, Larry J. "The United States Navy v. the Chicago Tribune." *The Historian* 42 (1980): 284-303. Account of the grand jury investigation of the *Chicago Tribune* for its publication of an article on the Battle of Midway that appeared to be in violation of the World War II Voluntary Censorship Code and of the Espionage Act.

Kornweibel, Theodore, Jr. "'The Most Dangerous of All Negro Journals': Federal Efforts to Suppress the Chicago Defender During World War I." *American Journalism* 11 (1994): 154-68. The government targeted the *Defender* for its legitimate criticisms of lynching and other injustices against blacks.

Larson, Cedric. "Censorship of Army News During the World War, 1917-1918." *Journalism Quarterly* 17 (1940): 313-23. The censorship operations of the Military Intelligence Section were necessary for control of information during wartime.

Maddux, Thomas R. "American News Media and Soviet Diplomacy, 1934-41." *Journalism Quarterly* 58 (1981): 29-37. An examination of newspaper opinion regarding the diplomatic objectives of Stalin's foreign policy during the period of Nazi expansion in Europe.

—. "Red Fascism, Brown Bolshevism: The American Image of Totalitarianism in the 1930s." *The Historian* 40 (1977): 85-103. An examination of the discussion of Stalinism and Nazism in the American press during the 1930s that makes an important contribution to the historical debate about how American opinion perceived similarities and differences in those two forces.

Mander, Mary S. "American Correspondents During World War II: Common Sense as a View of the World." *American Journalism* 1,1 (1983): 17-30. "The hallmark of the imagination and manners of the journalist reporting World War II...was *common sense*.... Gone were the days of the flamboyant romantic of the nineteenth century; in his place stood the down-to-earth, realistic reporter of modern times."

"The Media and World War II," special issue of *American Journalism* 12:3 (1995). Along with the articles, especially useful are five historiographical essays: Maurine Beasley, "Women and Journalism in World War II: Discrimination and Progress," 321-33; Louise Benjamin, "World War II American Radio Is More Than Murrow," 334-41; Margaret A. Blanchard, "Freedom of the Press in World War II," 342-58; Patrick S. Washburn, "The Black Press: Homefront Clout Hits a Peak in World War II," 359-66; and Betty Houchin Winfield and Janice Hume, "Shhh, Do Tell! World War II and Press-Government Scholarship," 359-66.

Moffett, Albert E. "Hometown Radio in 1942: The Role of Local Stations During the First Year of Total War." *American Journalism* 3 (1986): 87-98. Local radio stations "preached national unity, sought and got unrestrained community participation, and showered listeners with unabashed patriotism — all helping to create a national consensus on the World War II home front."

Ponder, Stephen. "Presidential Publicity and Executive Power: Woodrow Wilson and the Centralizing of Governmental Information." *American Journalism* 11 (1994): 257-69. Wilson tried to centralize the release of government information in the White House to better manage the news.

Pratte, Alf. "The Honolulu *Star-Bulletin* and the 'Day of Infamy.'" *American Journalism* 5 (1988): 5-13. The work of the *Star-Bulletin* on the day the Japanese bombed Pearl Harbor "provides one of the more dramatic illustrations in American history of the press' performance in a major, fast-breaking crisis."

Ross, Felecia Jones. "The Cleveland *Call and Post* and the New Deal: A Change in African-American Thought." *Journalism History* 19 (1993): 87-92. The African-American newspaper rejected New Deal reforms in favor of economic self-help as espoused by the Republican opposition.

Sloan, Wm. David. "The Media in Trying Times: Propagandists, Patriots, or Professionals?" 283-99, in *Perspectives on Mass Communication History*. Hillsdale, N.J., 1991. Analyzes the approaches that historians have taken to explaining the press during this period.

Somers, Paul P., Jr. "'Right in the Führer's Face': American Editorial Cartoons of the World War II Period." *American Journalism* 13 (1996): 333-53. Cartoonists completely supported the war effort.

Stevens, John D. "From the Back of the Foxhole: Black Correspondents in World War II." *Journalism Monographs* 27 (1973). The twenty-seven black reporters who covered World War II did an admirable job despite the problems they faced because of their race.

Theoharis, Athan. "The FBI, the Roosevelt Administration, and the 'Subversive' Press." *Journalism History* 19 (1993): 3-10. At the behest of the Roosevelt Administration, the FBI investigated isolationist reporters and newspapers.

Washburn, Patrick S. "The *Pittsburgh Courier's* Double V Campaign in 1942." *American Journalism* 3 (1986): 73-86. The *Courier*, a black newspaper, adopted an editorial policy aimed at gaining civil rights advances for black Americans by supporting American victory in World War II.

18

Radio Comes of Age

1900 - 1945

The history of broadcasting is a story of electronic information services — journalism and entertainment. It is the story of a revolutionary technology — from wire to wireless and back to wire. It is the story of the role of technology in the evolution of the information age, prophetically described by Senator Clarence C. Dill as the "whispering gallery of the skies."[1]

Radio had its roots in the late 1800s with the development of electronic telegraphy. The telegraph was the first rapid information medium. It enhanced the ability of the printing press by overcoming the obstacle of time. Whereas printing was hampered by the requirement that it be carried physically from place to place, the telegraph allowed information to be transmitted instantaneously by wire.

Pioneers of Electronic Technology

Michael Faraday and Samuel F. B. Morse were the names associated with the development of telegraphy. Faraday's discovery of electromagnetic induction led to Morse's development of the telegraph and experimentation in distance communication. Morse acquired the patent and sent the first official message May 24, 1844. Dictated by Annie Ellsworth to Morse, the message asked, "What hath God wrought?"

Following the invention of telegraphy several people made individual contributions that combined to produce wireless telegraph transmission. Two Americans who did early work were William Henry Ward of Auburn, New York, and a dentist of Washington, D.C., Mahlon Loomis. Both received patents for an aerial conduction telegraph. Ward began his work before the Civil War, with a long series of experiments. The telegraphic tower he patented in 1872, he said, would permit the crossing of oceans without cable. Loomis, too, began his work before the Civil War. He conducted trial runs in the Blue Ridge and Catoctin Mountain ranges of Virginia and Maryland and secured some support in Congress. When the panic of 1873 struck, however, funds for experimentation dried up.

The early era in radio history was a complex period of experimentation, litigation, and financial turmoil for the many inventors who had vision but who often missed out on the rewards of success. James Clerk Maxwell (1831-1879), a Scottish physicist, theorized about electromagnetic energy in 1873. His theories ignited the interest of a German physicist, Heinrich Hertz (1857-1894), who was able to demonstrate the projection of the magnetic field into the air. The name "Hertz" (Hz) has been carried forward today as a credit to his contribution to broadcast technology.[2]

A recluse named Nathan B. Stubblefield has been credited by many as the "inventor of radio." Beginning about 1890 he broadcast speech and music around Murray, Kentucky. He did not use the Hertzian, electromagnetic wave radio we know today but an induction system. It worked without wires and covered five or six miles. He first demonstrated his wireless telephone publicly in 1892, but it was sixteen years before he patented the system. One of the great mysteries for historians is why he waited so long.

To bring his invention to the attention of the public, he staged a giant, open demonstration on January 1, 1902. Guglielmo Marconi had just demonstrated telegraphy across the Atlantic, and Stubblefield compared his own achievement to that of Marconi:

> I have solved the problem of telephoning without wires through the earth just as Signor Marconi has of sending signals through space. But, I can also telephone without wires through space as well as through the earth, because my medium is everywhere.[3]

After a report of the demonstration appeared in the *St. Louis Post-Dispatch*, it created a great deal of national interest, and Stubblefield became widely known among experimenters and scientists.[4]

[1]C.C. Dill, "Traffic Cop For The Air," *American Review of Reviews* 75 (February 1927): 191.

[2]Electromagnetic radiation is known as "Hertzian waves," and a "hertz" is a unit of frequency equal to one cycle per second.

[3]*St. Louis Post-Dispatch*, 10 January 1902.

[4]Waldon Fawcett, "The Latest Advance in Wireless Telephony," *Scientific American*, 24 May 1902, 363.

ork Times.

THE WEATHER.

FIRST WIRELESS PRESS MESSAGE ACROSS THE ATLANTIC

MARCONI CONGRATULATES THE NEW YORK TIMES

FROM THE PRIME MINISTER OF FRANCE.

WIRELESS JOINS TWO WORLDS

MISS VANDERBILT

H. P. WHITNEY ARRESTED?

DEUTSCHLAND STOCK

Guglielmo Marconi
Among the individuals who were conducting experiments with radio in the early 1900s, Guglielmo Marconi received the most attention. His most publicized experiment was the simultaneous transmission and reception of a transatlantic signal in 1901. He soon began transmitting for official agencies, and in 1907 his company began sending transatlantic wireless messages for the public. The *New York Times* published an account of the first such transmission as its lead story on page one on October 18, 1907.

A short time later, Stubblefield became the first person to conduct a marine broadcast. It occurred at a public demonstration in Washington, D.C., on March 20, 1902, from the deck of the steamship *Bartholdi* off the Virgina bank of the Potomac River where he sent wireless messages to receivers on the shore.[5]

Two years later, Stubblefield told a reporter for the *Washington Post*, "Eventually [radio] will be used for the general transmission of news of every description."[6] Most others at the time seem to have thought about wireless as point-to-point communication and not as broadcasting. Stubblefield's statement predated by more than a decade the oft-quoted 1915 memorandum of David Sarnoff, later to be president of RCA, who urged his firm to manufacture a "radio music box" for home use that might also pick up the news. After perfecting his device, Stubblefield was granted a patent in 1908.

Despite Stubblefield's early discoveries, Guglielmo Marconi (1874-1937) was the best known experimenter. He was, however, more than an inventor; he was an entrepreneur. He foresaw the commercial value of his inventions and patented each experimental development. As his work progressed rapidly, he established the British Marconi Corporation, the Canadian Marconi Corporation, and the American Marconi Corporation.

In 1901, Marconi conducted his most publicized experiment. He succeeded in sending a wireless signal from Cornwall, England, to St. Johns, Newfoundland, Canada. Soon after, he began establishing coastal radio stations meant to replace the aging transatlantic telegraph cables. The purposes of the stations were to provide ship-to-shore communication and issue warnings of storms and dangerous ice flows — and to make profits.

While Marconi was sending wireless Morse code signals, Reginald A. Fessenden succeeded in adding voice communication to a transmission. The broadcast occurred Christmas Eve, 1906. It featured Fessenden's talents beyond his scientific telecommunications experimentation. He narrated the opening, read from the Bible, played a phonograph of Handel's *Largo*, performed a violin solo, and sang before finally wishing his audience, comprised of men at sea, a Merry Christmas. He conducted a similar broadcast on New Year's Eve.[7] Although Fessenden's first broadcasts were advertised for a general audience, the audience was made up only of the radio operators aboard ships in the harbor. Radio, up to this stage of its development, was a laboratory toy that was becoming increasingly important as a means of point-to-point informational maritime and ship-to-shore communication. It was a wireless telephone of sorts.

Lee De Forest is regarded as the "father of radio," a title he gave himself, for developing the Audion tube in 1906. This vacuum tube was a keystone to industrial development. Today's chip technology traces its history to this invention: the chip was preceded by the transistor, a series of vacuum tubes, and the Audion tube. In his most famous experiments, De Forest transmitted speech via radio in laboratory tests conducted in New York and Europe. His most publicized test was one from the Eiffel Tower, with reception reported as far away as 500 miles. Like many of his predecessors, De Forest was an inventor and not an entrepreneur. He formed his own company, but lawsuits with Fessenden and his own financial problems plagued his career. Eventually, he sold his interests to the American Telephone and Telegraph Company (AT&T)

At the beginning of the twentieth century, major corporate players began taking an interest in radio's development. The General Electric Company developed the alternator to assist Fessenden in his voice experiments. AT&T, which had acquired De Forest's Audion tube, and the Marconi companies were growing rapidly.

[5] *Washington Times*, 21 March 1902.
[6] *Washington Post*, 10 August 1904.

[7] For a description of the experiment see Reginald A. Fessenden to S.M. Kinterner (vice-president of Westinghouse, Electric & Mfg. Co.), 29 January 1932, Clark Manuscript Collection, Smithsonian Institution, Division of Electricity and Nuclear Energy.

The Titanic Disaster and the 1912 Radio Act

The event that catapulted radio technology into national prominence was the sinking of the *S.S. Titanic* in April 1912 after it collided with an iceberg. The ship *Carpathia* was also at sea, about fifty-eight miles from the *Titanic*. When its wireless operator received the *Titanic's* emergency transmission, the *Carpathia* began steaming to the scene of the disaster. By the time it reached the site, however, the *Titanic* already had sunk. With no rescue ship at hand, 1,513 passengers lost their lives. The disaster created national headlines, at the same time focusing attention on a new technology. The press coverage did more to increase public awareness of wireless communication than any historic experiment had done. The disaster brought attention to the role that radio could play in ship safety on the high seas and to the need for laws governing emergency transmissions.

The Radio Act of 1912 was a direct result of the *Titanic* disaster. America's isolationist tendencies previously had kept it from joining the first world radio conferences to control broadcasting at Berlin in 1903 and London in 1906. But Congress did pass the Wireless Ship Act of 1910 requiring ocean vessels to have both licensed equipment and operators. That act, the precursor of the Radio Act, was simple legislation — less than a page long — acknowledging the potential of radio as a ship-to-shore and ship-to-ship communications tool. The Radio Act of 1912 placed the Secretary of Commerce in charge of licensing radio stations and assigning operational wave lengths. It gave priority to distress signals and established the SOS standards. It also mandated the use of "special call letters" and gave priority to shipping over commercial experimentation.

"All the News That's Fit to Print."

The New York Times.

TITANIC SINKS FOUR HOURS AFTER HITTING ICEBERG; 866 RESCUED BY CARPATHIA, PROBABLY 1250 PERISH; ISMAY SAFE, MRS. ASTOR MAYBE, NOTED NAMES MISSING

Col. Astor and Bride, Isidor Straus and Wife, and Maj. Butt Aboard.

"RULE OF SEA" FOLLOWED

Biggest Liner Plunges to the Bottom at 2:20 A.M.

RESCUERS THERE TOO LATE

The Lost Titanic Being Towed Out of Belfast Harbor.

PARTIAL LIST OF THE SAVED.

CAPT. E. J. SMITH.

The *Titanic* Disaster
When the liner *Titanic* struck an iceberg and sank on April 15, 1912, the disaster alerted the public to the possible uses of wireless transmission in emergencies. Much of the story in the *New York Times'* right-hand column about the disaster dealt with the role that wireless played.

The 1912 act had a maritime focus, but with more regulatory discretion than its 1910 predecessor. The new law was the first comprehensive governmental action dealing with radio, and it lasted fifteen years. However, while it recognized the maritime possibilities of the developing technology, it did not envision the regulatory standards necessary for the events and technology that would occur as soon as radio made the transformation from a maritime device to a medium of general public importance.

World War I and the Patent Pools

Radio did not develop by unanimous consent but through an evolutionary process that reflected the social, political, and technological environment of the time and that witnessed a variety of social, corporate, and individual conflicts. The issues included monopoly, censorship, news and educational programming, advertiser support, and regulation. The resolution of each conflict contributed to the structure of the broadcasting system.

As World War I approached, radio's usefulness shifted from general maritime shipping to defense and the Navy. When the United States entered the war on April 6, 1917, the government ordered all wireless stations closed and on April 7 placed them under the administrative control of the Navy. The government then combined the patent resources of the heretofore competitive experimenters toward a common wartime goal. The individual and corporate rivalries that had previously existed were forced into cooperation. Patents were brought together to facilitate the war effort. The practical result was that previously competitive patent ideas were pooled, thus laying the groundwork for the rapid commercial development that followed the war. The patent pools quickly moved electronic telecommunications from a period of experimentation and maritime communication into an era of commercial broadcasting in the 1920s.

At the conclusion of World War I, the pool was dissolved, and the patents were returned to their owners. The date July 11, 1919, when the Navy returned the patents to private enterprise, marked the beginning of renewed competition and growth on a new corporate scale. First, at the urging of the Navy and U.S. government, Marconi's patents were sold to General Electric. The government did not want a foreign power operating a monopoly — American Marconi — in the United States. General Electric formed a new company, Radio Corporation of America (RCA), to control Marconi's patents and assets. Second, the release of the patent pool meant that the growing corporations had access to almost 2,000 patents. In heated competition, they battled for exclusive and competitive rights to the integral parts of the radio system. The results of the competition left AT&T in control of the manufacture and sale of transmitters, while General Electric and Westinghouse manufactured receiving sets and RCA operated as a sales agent collecting royalties for the use of its patents in manufacturing. The patent pools and the intense rivalries marked the beginning of an age of corporate monopoly in broadcasting within an extremely competitive atmosphere and with a government that would grow suspect of the radio monopoly.[8]

Radio's Growing Popularity

While some called radio a fad, its popularity soon reached into all the nation. The number of stations was only about thirty in 1921, but the total had soared to 600 by 1923. At first, all the sets were handmade at home; but Westinghouse began marketing its model number one in 1920 with the building of radio station KDKA, and the total number of receiving sets in 1923 climbed to 600,000.

With the growth in radio's popularity, major corporations became a part of the radio landscape, and each pioneered practices to give it a competitive edge. KDKA, Pittsburgh, the Westinghouse station, earned its place in history with a broadcast on November 2, election night, 1920. It obtained voting results through an agreement with the *Pittsburgh Post* newspaper and then reported them in what KDKA claimed was "the world's first scheduled broadcast." KDKA was eager to know if anyone was listening and asked, "Will anyone hearing this broadcast please communicate with us, as we are anxious to know how far the broadcast is reaching and how it is being received?"[9]

The broadcast was, indeed, the first scheduled one in the United States, but other stations throughout the world earlier had conducted similar experiments. CFCF, Montreal, Canada, a station owned by Marconi, had broadcast a scheduled experimental program a few months earlier. CFCF's program, which aired May 20, 1920, was aimed at Canadian radio hobbyists and the mariners whose ships were anchored in the St. Lawrence River. Eager, like KDKA, to know if it had an audience, CFCF advertised the broadcast and even prearranged for an audience of Canadian dignitaries.[10]

Such experimentation helped to refine programming and to publicize a growing new telecommunications service. Popular enthusiasm for radio grew rapidly during the 1920s as did the number of radio stations. The traveling Chautauquas around the country offered dazzling displays of radio, importing distant signals for

[8]See John Michael Kittross, "Patent Pools," in *Historical Directory of American Radio*, Donald G. Godfrey and Frederic A. Leigh, eds. (Westport, Conn., 1998), 297-8.

[9]For a description of KDKA, see Westinghouse Radio Stations, Inc., Histories of KDKA, Shortwaves, WBZ, KYW, Frequency Modulation, and KEX. Unpublished manuscript (n.d.) "History of KDKA," 10, in Lawrence W. Lichty and Malachi C. Topping, *American Broadcasting: A Source Book on the History of Radio and Television* (New York, 1975), 102-10.

[10]Donald G. Godfrey, "Canadian Marconi: CFCF, The Forgotten First," *Canadian Journal of Communication* 8:4 (1982): 56-69.

Radio's Popularity
As the popularity of radio surged in the early 1920s, a number of companies worked feverishly to capture the market for receiving sets. General Electric, RCA, De Forest, AT&T, and others developed new equipment and innovations and advertised them extensively. In 1923 Magnavox was selling items to boost the sound from "feeble" receivers. The Latin name "Magnavox" means "great voice."

an audience who had never before witnessed such a marvel. Along with the station program experiments and the Chautauqua publicity, significant advances were made in technology, and industry-wide operational patterns began to develop. WEAF's engineers contributed to the development of the control board, an important tool in programming that is still used today.

With increased popularity, the industry grew. In 1925, the Department of Commerce issued more than 1,400 station authorizations.[11] In 1930 the number of receiving sets stood at 14,000,000. Some were in automobiles; and while the classic custom cars such as Packard and Pierce Arrow had them earlier, the assembly-line 1930 Model A Ford could be had with radio. The 1940 census showed 44,000,000 radios around America. In 1945, there were radio sets in 33,000,000 homes, with many having more than one.

Radio and Advertising

Radio station WEAF in New York City set a precedent when it started to sell advertising. Licensed to operate a "toll" station in 1922, it made commercial airtime available to businesses. On August 28, it broadcast its first income-producing program: a ten-minute message from the Queensboro Corporation to sell apartments in suburban Jackson Heights. The sponsor paid $50.

The WEAF experiment created profound and, at times, heated debate. Some people considered advertising outrageous. Secretary Herbert Hoover felt that "the quickest way to kill broadcasting would be to use it for direct advertising."[12] Congressman Emanuel Celler of New York denounced the "pabulum and disguised advertising...." He felt that too many stations would be given over to deceptive marketing practices. Criticizing radio station advertising from the floor of the House of Representatives, Celler satirized the approach: "This is station KOKO broadcasting lectures from the sanitarium on Pink Pills for Pale People."[13]

Despite the opposition, radio advertising seemed a viable means of financing the new industry. The concept that advertisers could operate a station, or talk about their products on a station, was attractive for many manufacturers and station operators. Programs such as the American Tobacco Company's *Lucky Strike* soon went on the air. During the 1920s no station was well financed by advertising revenue, but advertising provided an allure to investors. Thus, the first WEAF "toll" broadcast gave the fledgling broadcast industry an impetus — a dollars and cents reason to improve. For the listening public, advertising provided a popular system of financing radio, for hardly anyone wanted a tax on receiving sets.

At first no government knew how to finance a broadcast system. The British opted for a system that gave exclusive control to a government corporation funded by a license fee on receiving sets. The BBC developed programs based upon the idea of elevating the taste of the general public. Many other countries owned the systems outright, but the British attempted to insulate broadcasting from political interference through an independent corporation.

In the United States similar arguments arose, but a privately owned commercial system was chosen. In the beginning it was felt if one wanted to advertise he would have to build his own station. Thus Westinghouse built KDKA and other stations to help sell its radio receivers on the sensible theory that one could not sell a radio set if there were nothing to listen to. Rudy's Department store built a station in Paducah, Kentucky; and the American Telephone & Telegraph Company built WEAF in New York. The Bell System, which owned telephone lines needed for radio transmissions, believed it was the only firm that legally could sell time over its lines for advertising. When an intense legal contest arose over Bell's monopolistic theory, Bell decided to duck the fight and sold its radio interests to RCA for $1 million. Others quickly followed the lead of WEAF in broadcasting advertising, and the present commercial system was soon established for American radio.

Soon advertising agencies were buying air time on individual stations and the networks just as they did from newspapers and magazines. Stations began to hire time salesmen. The station representative firm then was organized, selling time to agencies and advertisers for a group of stations. The rise of networks saw advertising grow by leaps and bounds.

The prices for network advertising were high, but the broadcasts seemed to be worth the cost. By 1930 the average family kept its radio on 3.9 hours per day. The 1940 figures showed that 86% of all families listened more than five hours per day — something like a total of 122,000,000 hours every day in all homes across the nation. The Hooper Ratings (of Claude C. Hooper) were giving advertisers the figures on all the major programs. By World War II, with the resultant newsprint and other shortages, radio was one of the few places advertisers could turn to promote their wares and services.

Pioneers of Network Broadcasting

With the increasing popularity of radio, the industry began to look for ways to manage the growth. One of the innovations was the network system. WEAF — which had broadcast the first commercial — also was first to provide network broadcasting. AT&T, which owned WEAF, already had telephone lines reaching all over the country. Linking chains of stations together for purposes of programming became a logical extension of that technological opportunity. It would give AT&T the competitive edge. AT&T's first network experiment, in 1923, linked two stations together, WEAF in New York and WNAC in Boston.[14] In October 1924, a network broadcast featuring a speech by President Calvin Coolidge was sent to twenty-two stations coast-to-coast.

[11]*Broadcasting Yearbook, 1939* (Washington), 11.

[12]Herbert Hoover, *Third National Radio Conference, Proceedings and Recommendations for Radio Regulation, October 6-10, 1924* (Washington, D.C., 1924), 4.

[13]*Congressional Record, 1926*, 67:5:5488.

[14]*Report on Chain Broadcasting*, Federal Communications Commission, Order 37, Docket 5060 (May, 1941): 5-20.

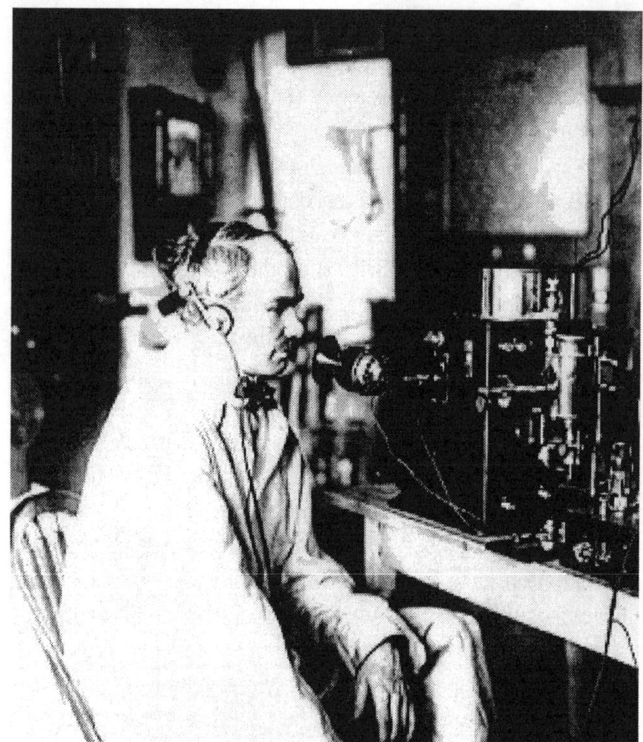

"Father of Radio"
Lee De Forest has been given the title of the "father of radio" for his development of the Audion tube. It was a key to industrial advances, and De Forest sold his original ownership of technology to the American Telephone and Telegraph Company.

By the end of the following year, AT&T had a permanent network linking twenty-six stations. A pattern had been established, in which early experimental stations evolved into "key stations" owned and operated (0&0) by a network corporation. The network was organized around the key stations and strong affiliate contracts.

At the same time that AT&T was making its debut into toll and network broadcasting, its chief competitor, RCA, began network experimentation with stations WJZ and WGY. The former was the RCA-owned station in New York City, and WGY, the General Electric station in Schenectady, New York. Since AT&T claimed the exclusive right to sell broadcast time and thus prevented competitors from using its telephone lines, RCA contracted the lines of Western Union. Thus, its network did not grow as rapidly.

By 1926, however, RCA had created a separate unit to conduct its broadcast and network operations — the National Broadcasting Company (NBC). Shortly thereafter, AT&T's involvement in broadcasting came to an abrupt halt, and it sold its radio interests to RCA. The combination of its own existing operation, plus the newly acquired WEAF-AT&T operation, placed RCA in the dominant position. Nineteen permanent stations were on the RCA network in 1926, and in 1928 RCA established its first permanent national network. The former WEAF-AT&T operation became known as the NBC Red Network, and RCA's WJZ-based network was known as the NBC Blue. Since the Red network had the pick of programming and most of the advertising revenue, it assumed the lead position.

The pioneer who developed NBC was David Sarnoff. Kenneth Bilby, Sarnoff's biographer, wrote that Sarnoff, more than any other industry leader of the time, not only had a vision but "the implacable determination to fulfill it." His vision of a "radio music box" transformed the industry and the listening public. His leadership created one of the largest networks in broadcast history, and he became one of the giants of industrial history.

The inaugural broadcast by NBC, the first network, was aired from 8 p.m. until midnight (Eastern time) on November 15, 1926, from the grand ballroom of the Waldorf-Astoria. Dr. Walter Damrosch conducted the New York Symphony Orchestra. The broadcast featured a comedy team, two singers, an oratorio group, actor-comedian Will Rogers, both a grand and a light opera company, a brass band, and four dance bands. The cost was $50,000, a high price at the time, and yet the prices for network programming continued to rise as they have ever since. When Dodge introduced its new Victory Six automobile with the *Dodge Victory Hour* in 1928, it had to pay NBC $67,000 for time and talent, including Will Rogers, Paul Whiteman, and Al Jolson, among several others.

CBS had it roots in the activities of George A. Coates. He was a promoter who had taken up radio's cause in its battle with the American Society of Composers, Authors and Publishers (ASCAP) over music rights. During the mid-1920s, ASCAP — which saw radio as a new profit opportunity for its artists — demanded higher royalty fees for music played on the air. The struggling new radio industry argued that the rates were too high and unfair. Coates and the National Association of Broadcasters (NAB), which was organized to help the broadcasters win their battle with ASCAP, worked with Arthur Judson, the business manager of the Philadelphia Orchestra. They formed the United Independent Broadcasters, Inc. (UIB). Their plan was to provide network programming for affiliated stations, purchase time from them, and sell advertising on the programming. UIB programming debuted in 1927, but UIB's financing was weak. It was not long before it needed additional backing.

UIB and Columbia Phonograph Corporation joined forces in 1927. Columbia's motivation was to sell records. It was afraid that RCA, which was talking about a merger with the Victor Talking Machine Company, would dominate the record industry. So Columbia merged with UIB and established a sixteen-station lineup. The agreement gave UIB a temporary financial boost and a name change — the Columbia Phonograph Broadcasting System (CPBS-UIB). Advertisers, however, still did not flock to CPBS-UIB. In contrast, RCA was growing rapidly. When it appeared that the RCA/Victor merger would not occur, Columbia Phonograph decided to sell its interest in the CPBS-UIB network.

William S. Paley, the young vice-president of the Congress Cigar Company of Philadelphia, then purchased UIB. Shortly thereafter, the network began showing a profit. Paley retained the

"Unlimited Importance to Humanity"
In the mid-1920s, with radio's popularity increasing rapidly, companies expanded by developing networks of stations and manufacturing equipment. This ad for a new vacuum tube from General Electric, one of the early station owners, noted the popularity and value of radio by listing historic achievements ranging from Marconi's transatlantic transmission to the role radio had played in the *Titanic* disaster and World War I.

name Columbia and purchased as its first key station WABC, New York (now WCBS). A decade later, the Columbia Broadcast System (CBS) purchased the American Record Corporation, which included the Columbia Phonograph label.

There were a number of attempts at other radio network operations, including the Quality Network, the Amalgamated Broadcasting System, and numerous regional networks. However, following NBC and CBS the most significant network was the Mutual Broadcasting System. Mutual was different from both NBC and CBS. Begun in 1934, it was not developed from a key station but as a cooperative among WXYZ Detroit, WLW Cincinnati, WGN Chicago, and WOR New York. In fact, it had no studios or central ownership. Its popularity was built around one strong program, the *Lone Ranger*. It then added such features as *The Green Hornet* and Gabriel Heatter as a leading newsman, and it always aired the World Series. As Mutual grew, it promoted itself as "the largest network in the world." The claim was true: it did have a larger number of affiliate stations. However, they were mostly smaller and rural operations. Mutual was never able to attract the powerful stations that were already firmly tied to NBC and CBS.

A federal government rule forcing divestiture upon individuals and companies that owned more than one station or network in the same service made NBC sell its Blue Network in 1943 to Edward J. Noble, whose millions had come from selling Lifesavers, "The Candy Mint With the Hole." He renamed the organization the American Broadcasting Company.

By 1945 network revenues were up to about $130 million, with one client alone, Procter & Gamble, spending $11 million for advertising time. The 900 stations employed about 25,000 full-time workers at an average weekly wage of $60.52.

The Regulatory Debates, 1922-1934

As more and more stations took the airwaves, they began to interfere with each other, ruining the use of the resource for both broadcaster and listener. People both inside and outside the industry quickly recognized the need for government oversight and regulation to bring order and usefulness to broadcasting. The Radio Act of 1927 established the fundamental principles of broadcast regulation and, as revised in the form of the Communication Act of 1934, continues today as the legal foundation of the broadcast industry.

The legislative history of the 1927 Radio Act began within the Hoover Radio Conferences. Secretary of Commerce Herbert Hoover was in charge of regulating radio. He had the responsibilities placed upon his office by the 1912 Radio Act. As the industry began to grow during the early 1920s, it became apparent that new legislation would soon be needed. In order to draft a legislative proposal, Hoover organized a series of conferences in 1922, 1923, 1924, and 1925.[15] They included representatives of industry

[15] Edward F. Sarno, Jr., "The National Radio Conferences," *Journal of Broadcasting* 13 (1969): 189-202.

and government, and they grew in number and intensity as the radio issue grew in popularity.

Each year, different bills were formulated and, under the direction of Wallace H. White, a Maine Republican, submitted to a disinterested Congress. Few on Capitol Hill understood the legislation, and radio was simply not yet an issue for most congressmen. White, however, persevered. As a member and later chair of the Merchant Marine and Fisheries Committee, he played a key role in generating and drafting several legislative proposals, including one of the first radio bills in 1923. After it failed, White, an outspoken advocate of the public's right in broadcasting, continued to hammer away at drafting legislation from several subsequent proposals until 1927.

The legal catalyst that led to the law finally adopted was a breakdown of the Radio Act of 1912. It had placed the Secretary of Commerce in charge of assigning wavelengths and issuing licenses. However, as radio grew from a maritime instrument into one of general public interest, the law proved inadequate. The legislative crisis came to a head when, in 1926, the Zenith Radio Corporation challenged the powers of the Secretary and the courts ruled in favor of Zenith. The ruling created chaos, as it left the Secretary with no discretionary regulatory power. He was in a position of merely granting licenses upon request. Since he had no regulatory control, stations could change power and use "other wavelengths at will," declared Attorney General William J. Donovan. He told Hoover that "if the present situation requires control, I can only suggest that it be sought in new legislation, carefully adapted to meet the needs of the present and the future."[16]

The crisis finally caught the attention of Congress, but its members were arguing.[17] Senator Cole Blease (D-S.C.) wanted censorship provisions to prevent the discussion of evolution on radio. Senator William E. Borah (R-Idaho) wanted stronger monopoly restraints against what he saw as the growing power of the RCA monopoly.[18]

At that point, Clarence C. Dill played a key role in drafting legislation and getting it passed in the Senate. Compared to White, Dill was a latecomer to radio legislation, but his influence was important. He modified White's proposals by adding a commission to replace White's recommendation that the Secretary of Commerce have control over broadcasting. He then fought forcefully for passage of the amended bill. It was not until February 1927, however, that "Congress woke up," Secretary Hoover said, "and finally passed the law which we recommended and which establishes the public ownership and regulation of the wavelength channels."[19]

A clause in the law that states that broadcasting must operate

Number of Households with Radios in the United States 1925-1985

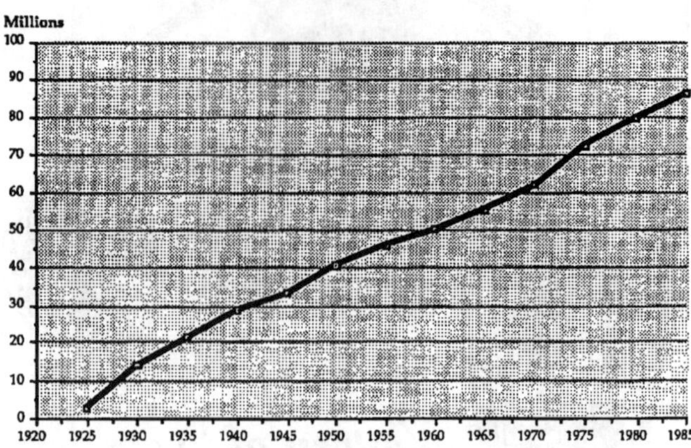

Per Cent of Penetration of Radios in U. S. Households

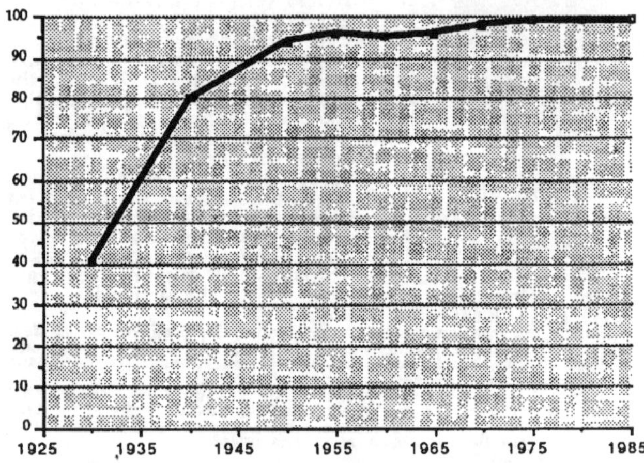

As the number of radios increased in the 1920s, calls for regulation grew louder.

in the "public interest, convenience and necessity" remains the governing principle of electronic media regulation. It has been interpreted within the following seven basic hypotheses:[20]

(1) The radio waves belong to the people.

(2) Broadcasting is a unique service.

(3) Service must be equally distributed.

(4) Not everyone is eligible to use a channel.

(5) Broadcasting is a form of expression protected by the First Amendment.

(6) The government has discretionary regulatory powers.

(7) Government's powers are not absolute.

The 1927 Radio Act established the "commission" as the regulatory agency over broadcasting. Among the first things the new Federal Radio Commission did was to revoke all radio licenses. The revocation forced the stations to reapply and gave the Commission time to consider the administrative law that would govern broadcasting. This body of law became an elaborate set of "Rules and Regulations" and a code of "Standards of Good Engineering Practices," which have been expanded, contracted, and amended

[16]Quoted in Marvin R. Bensman, "The Zenith-WJAZ Case and the Chaos of 1926-27," *Journal of Broadcasting* 14 (1970): 423-40.

[17]Donald G. Godfrey, "The 1927 Radio Act: People and Politics," *Journalism History* 4 (1977): 74-8.

[18]*Congressional Record, 1926*, 67:11:12615. See also Donald G. Godfrey and Val E. Limburg, "The Rogue Elephant of Radio Legislation: Senator William E. Borah," *Journalism Quarterly* 67 (1990): 214-24.

[19]Herbert Hoover, "The Reminiscences of Herbert Clark Hoover," Oral History Project, Columbia University Oral Research Office, 142.

[20]Sydney W. Head, *Broadcasting in America*, 2nd ed. (New York, 1972), 160-1.

in many different forms. These rules and regulations remain in a state of continual evolution, but they embody a strong directive force behind the electronic media development.

There was considerable debate about radio in the hectic years of change after 1927. The networks were still growing, the educational nonprofit broadcasters were being shunted aside by commercial interests, and new technology and regulatory standards were still developing. As conditions changed, it became clear that the Radio Act could not adequately cover them, and new legislation was proposed. When President Franklin Roosevelt asked for an expansion of the Federal Communications Commission in 1934, however, he felt the old Radio Act could scarcely be improved.

The resulting Communications Act of 1934 may have seemed to have changed little in the regulations. It brought forward the same fundamental hypotheses from the Radio Act, and some have said that it was one of the least significant pieces of Roosevelt legislation. However, it was not a carbon copy of the Radio Act.

The new law enlarged the commission from five to seven members and changed its name from the Federal Radio Commission to the Federal Communications Commission. It included a larger role for the commission, extending its control over wire and wireless communication — television, telephone, telegraph, undersea cables, and all radiated and "wired communications" — both interstate and foreign.

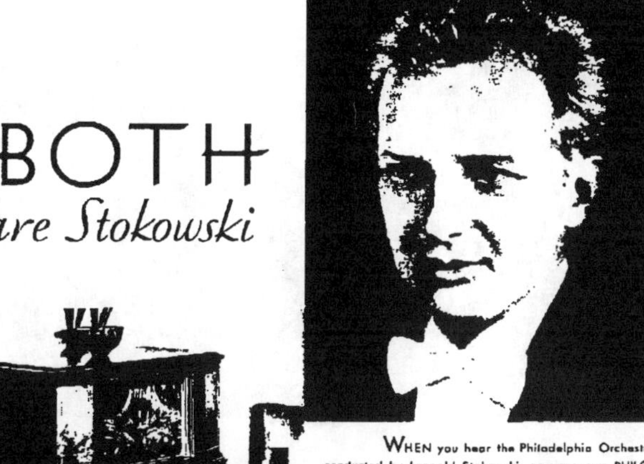

Music Brought "to You in Person"
Music, ranging from country to classical, has been a staple of commercial radio since its beginning. In 1932, Philco advertised its receivers as having the capacity to make listeners feel as if they were in a concert hall with Leopold Stokowski conducting the orchestra.

Music: Classical to Country

At first, networks and local stations offered only irregular programming. When radio was new, programming did not have to be good or interesting. Just the fact that one heard something — anything — was a wonder to hold attention for hours on end. Regular scheduling evolved with the stations' technological ability and with audience demand.

Programming was mostly music, most of which was classical.[21] As early as 1910 Enrico Caruso was heard over Lee De Forest's station in New York. Frank Conrad of Westinghouse with his 8XK — later to be KDKA — began to play phonograph records over the airways in 1919 for the entertainment of his fellow amateurs.

Most music, however, consisted of live performances. Musicians were more than willing to perform on radio in hopes of increasing their own popularity. At first, they were afraid of radio as a competitor of their recordings. Later they realized that they could receive fees for broadcasting and promote the sales of their records at the same time.

The networks had their own orchestras and designed programs for studio performance. The studios were large and draped with curtains, and performers dressed in formal attire for a show's performance even though they would not be seen. All broadcasts were live and were scheduled during the evening.

The audience for this new medium was a receptive one; and as the audience grew, so did the demand for more information and entertainment. Stations responded by increasing their offerings. In Detroit, WWJ of the *News*, another claimant to be America's oldest radio station, picked up a full dance orchestra in September 1920. One of the most popular violinists in America was Fritz Kreisler. He performed over KDKA Pittsburgh in January of 1922. Judith Carey Waller, first station manager of WMAQ in Chicago, presented as its first program a performance by opera star Sophie Braslau the following month. The telephone company station WEAF in New York (now WNBC) pulled a *coup* on January 1, 1925, when it presented a concert by noted Irish tenor John McCormick and Metropolitan Opera star Lucrezia Bori. That same year WEAF sold a regular Sunday series featuring stars of the opera and the concert stage. When NBC began operations in 1926, concert mu-

[21] In February 1925, music accounted for 71.5% of the programming time. Other programming proportions were as follows 0.1% drama; 11.5% information-oriented—education, market reports, politics, news, and sports; 6.8% children's and women's entertainment; and 10.1% religion, health, and miscellaneous. See John W. Spaulding, "1928: Radio Becomes A Mass Advertising Medium," *Journal of Broadcasting* 8 (1963-64): 31-44.

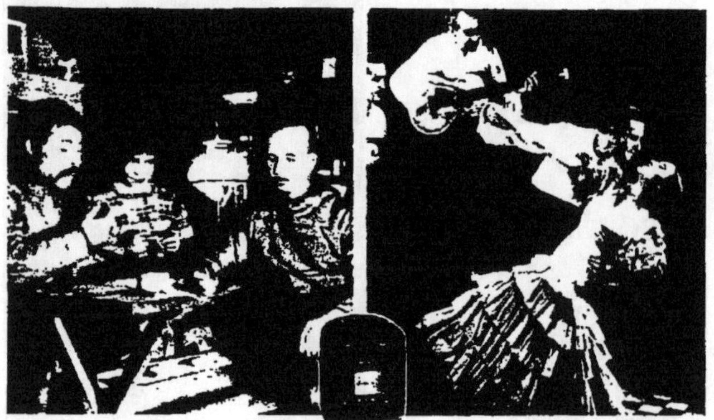

Programs from Around the World

Like other manufacturers, General Electric tried to sell radio receivers by emphasizing the programming available to listeners. This 1934 ad mentioned several varieties of music, news, celebrity gossip, messages from police and ham operators, and network programs.

sic was often on the schedule.[22] In 1927, when CBS began competing with NBC, it ran an original opera by Deems Taylor, *The King's Henchman*. The poet Edna St. Vincent Millay helped on the lyrics. In 1930 CBS began airing the Sunday afternoon concerts of the New York Philharmonic Symphony Orchestra.

Radio began to make talent famous, too. On WDAF in Kansas City, a group called the Nighthawks starring Leo Fitzpatrick as the "Merry Old Chief" kept Americans up half the night. There was also the Coon-Sanders band from the Plantation Grill of the Muehlebach Hotel. The band would play fifteen minutes and rest ten. Desperate to fill the breaks with something on these remote broadcasts, announcers read telegrams and told jokes that proved almost as popular as the music.[23]

Radio tried to please the taste of every type of listener. Country music was one of the early favorites, with the first of the big national barn dances arriving on WLS Saturday night, April 19, 1924. Sears executives (the call letters stood for World's Largest Store) exploded when they heard "Turkey in the Straw" on the air, but 400 telephone calls and a bushel of mail showed that their customers loved it. George D. Hay, "the Solemn Old Judge," was the announcer. The biggest star of the early years was Bradley Kincaid of Kentucky. He moved to WLW in 1931 and stayed there through its day as a half-million watt station. He drew more than 20,000 people to one performance. Hay moved on to WSM in Nashville in 1925 to begin an even more popular barn dance called the *Grand Ole Opry*. John Lair began the *Renfro Valley Barn Dance* in Kentucky over WHAS Louisville a little later. All these became so popular they made the national networks for at least a half hour per week. Chicago and Nashville fed theirs to NBC while Louisville's was programmed through CBS.

Popular music provided many hours of programming in the early years. In CBS's battle to catch the older NBC, William Paley began running dance bands every night. Three pick-ups were used each evening beginning at 11:30 p.m. (Eastern time). New York and Chicago hotels were the favorites for such bands as Paul Whiteman's. In later years, there were Glenn Miller, Tommy and Jimmy Dorsey, and Kay Kaiser. Many other sites made the list, too, including the Roosevelt Hotel in New Orleans fed by WWL and the Peabody in Memphis fed by Hoyt Wooten's WREC. Local stations, of course, did the same, broadcasting local orchestra performances from nightclubs and hotels.

Drama and Comedy by Radio

It took radio some time to realize that the world's greatest stage is the human mind. As the early radio historian E. P. J. Shurick said, "In imagination colors are more brilliant, the pageantry more spectacular, and the action more robust."[24]

General Electric at WGY led the way in drama. It aired the stage play "The Wolf " by Eugene Walter in 1922. WGY was so encouraged with the broadcast's popularity that it began a regular weekly feature and broadcast more than 200 Broadway favorites. Some became motion pictures. Far from hurting attendance, they whetted the appetite of the audience.

In 1923, KDKA Pittsburgh broadcast "Friend Mary" from the Broadway stage as its first dramatic production. WJZ New York, the old Westinghouse station that became the key of NBC's Blue Network (now WABC-770), did Shakespeare's *Romeo and Juliet* from the Henry Miller Theater in the same year. A month later it broadcast *As You Like It* from the 44th Street Theatre. The trend continued, and one of the top rated shows by the end of World War II was the *Lux Radio Theatre* in which noted movie director Cecil B. De Mille put on radio play versions of his own and other famous movies.

The adventure serial drama that was broadcast five days a week

[22]Analysis of NBC "Fiftieth Anniversary of NBC Radio," by Ray Mofield, aired on NBC network November 1976; copies in Library of Congress and various other libraries.

[23]William Paley, from the CBS Taped Radio Show "Fiftieth Anniversary of CBS Radio," aired September 1977; copies in Library of Congress, Washington, D.C., and various other libraries.

[24]Text of Queensboro Corporation spot on Hawthorne Courts in Ray Mofield tape collection (Murray State University; Murray, Kentucky) from Rick Sklar, ABC, New York.

Network Programming

National radio networks in the 1940s were as competitive as the television networks are today. In 1946 ABC used this ad to promote its most popular programs and performers – singer Bing Crosby, "Theatre Guild on the Air," the gossip reporter Walter Winchell, the Metropolitan Opera, and "Cavalcade of Sports."

in the early evening began just a bit later. It was patterned after the continued story approach used in magazines or the *Perils of Pauline* type of movie. The first of these was *Sam 'n' Henry* on WGN. It moved in 1928 to NBC's WMAQ-670 as *Amos 'n' Andy*. It may have been the most popular show of all time. In some areas even theaters stopped their movies while Freeman Fisher Gosden and Charles J. Correll worked their magic as Amos Jones and Andy Brown, along with the Kingfish and other characters. From Peoria, Illinois, Marion and Jim Jordan went to Chicago's WENR to start a once-a-week smash hit called *Fibber McGee and Molly*. It led the ratings for a number of years; and Johnson's Wax, its sponsor, led the sales parade.

These programs gave rise to another kind of daily drama that would attack the problems of the housewife at home. WGN aired the first of these, *Painted Dreams*, in 1930. Soon there were more; and as large audiences were delivered at low cost, the giant soap firms of Procter & Gamble, Colgate-Palmolive-Peet, and Lever Brothers bought up these dramas. They became known as "soap operas." *Ma Perkins* ran for thirty-three years on CBS. There were also *Road of Life*, *Big Sister*, *The Second Mrs. Burton*, and *Our Gal Sunday*.

The power of radio drama was demonstrated in World War II by Kate Smith's successful sale of millions of dollars in War Bonds on her radio programs. It may be, however, that the single most potent story was Orson Welles' Halloween program on CBS in 1938. The October 30 airing of the *Mercury Theatre* is well remembered today, a prime example of the power of broadcasting. The dramatization of H. G. Wells' *War of the Worlds* terrified listeners in the New York-New Jersey area where the story was set. Using the CBS news roundup device of calling in live reports — featuring "news bulletins" that sounded like real announcers reporting news of an invasion from Mars — Welles created such realism that the audience panicked. Many listeners called their local police and left their homes thinking a real attack was taking place. The resulting FCC investigation brought CBS and the other networks to the realization that they would have to be more cautious when playing with radio's dynamite.

Sports Coverage

The 1920s have been called the Golden Era of Sports. Those were the days of Jim Thorpe, Red Grange, Babe Ruth, Jack Dempsey, and the reporting giants such as Grantland Rice who wrote about them. Some feeble efforts were made to air sports in radio's amateur days such as the 1912 University of Minnesota experiment to use a spark gap transmitter to relay telegraph signals of a football game. A university station, WTAW, in College Station, Texas, did the first football broadcast: the Texas A&M Aggie game with the University of Texas on Thanksgiving Day, 1920. But as was often the case, the pioneer among commercial stations was KDKA Pittsburgh. The first play-by-play of a baseball game originated at Pittsburgh's Forbes Field in 1921 as the Pirates took on the Philadelphia Phillies. Almost a year earlier WWJ in Detroit had run the World Series scores as they came in to the *Detroit News* office. Later in 1921 KDKA did its first football play-by-play, and the first ever by a commercial broadcaster, as West Virginia played the University of Pittsburgh Panthers. Another first effort by KDKA was its broadcast of the first Davis Cup tennis matches in 1921.

Boxing was big in the 1920s. The first blow-by-blow description was on KDKA in 1921 in the Johnny Ray versus Johnny Dundee match. The listening audience broke all previous records when later that year KDKA took its remote mike ringside in Hoboken, New Jersey, via a feed from WJY. The attraction was Jack Dempsey against Georges Carpentier.

The first play-by-play World Series came also in 1921. It was an all-New York Series. With a direct line from Pittsburgh, Grantland Rice did the play for KDKA. The Giants of John McGraw took the series that year over the Yankees and repeated the feat in 1922. WJZ took over the World Series play-by-play for 1923. There was a new announcer, Graham McNamee, but the faces on the field were once again the Giants and Yankees, and this time the Bronx Bombers prevailed. When the Yanks came back for the 1926 World Series, McNamee was still around for WJZ, which came up

War of the Worlds

Orson Welles did not foresee the panic he would cause with his Halloween night broadcast of H. G. Wells' novel *The War of the Worlds* in 1938. It caused more panic than any other fictional program has ever done. The top picture shows Welles (arms raised) and the members of his Mercury Theater group rehearsing the production. With the fame he gained from the program, he got a chance to direct and star in his first movie, *Citizen Kane* (right). It is generally considered the greatest movie ever made.

Here's how the *Philadelphia Inquirer* reported on Welles' "War of the Worlds" the day after the broadcast.

Mars Invasion Terrorizes Listeners

Terror struck at the hearts of hundreds of thousands of persons in the length and breadth of the United States last night as crisp words of what they believed to be a news broadcast leaped from their radio sets—telling of catastrophe from the skies visited on this country.

Out of the heavens, they learned, objects at first believed to be meteors crashed down near Trenton, killing many.

Then out of the "meteors" came monsters, spreading destruction with torch and poison gas.

It was all just a radio dramatization, but the result, in all actuality, was nationwide hysteria.

In Philadelphia, women and children ran from their homes screaming. In Newark, N.J., ambulances rushed to one neighborhood to protect residents against a gas attack. In the deep South men and women knelt in groups in the streets and prayed for deliverance.

In reality there was no danger. The broadcast was merely a Halloween program in which Orson Welles, actor-director of the Mercury Theatre on the Air, related, as though he were one of the few human survivors of the catastrophe, an adaptation of H.G. Wells' "The War of the Worlds."

In that piece of fiction men from Mars, in meteor-like space ships, come to make conquest of Earth. The circumstances of the story were unbelievable enough, but the manner of its presentation was apparently convincing to hundreds of thousands of persons....

The realism of the broadcast, especially for those who had tuned in after it had started, brought effects which none—not the directors of the Federal Radio Theatre Project, which sponsored it, nor the Columbia Broadcasting Co., which carried it over a coast-to-coast chain of 151 stations... — could foresee....

Martian Attack Strikes Terror in the Hearts of Earthlings

There are still people who remember the panic that began shortly after 8 p.m. eastern time on October 30, 1938. Hundreds evacuated their homes. Frightened citizens jammed east coast roads and telephone lines trying to warn friends and relatives. Hundreds contacted police, hospitals, newspapers, and radio stations asking how to protect themselves from an unidentified poisonous gas. Some went to church to pray. Some were treated for shock and hysteria. Families huddled on street corners waiting for what they thought would surely be the end of the world.

During Orson Welles' Halloween national broadcast of "War of the Worlds," dance music was interspersed with realistic sounding news bulletins. The adaptation of H. G. Wells' novel created frightening realism and convinced millions of listeners from San Francisco to Boston and from Canada to New Orleans that there had been a Martian invasion and widespread death and destruction.

Listeners believed what they heard because they trusted radio's ability to deliver important information. News bulletins often interrupted programs to report unsettling European developments. Many listeners of Welles' program missed or ignored announcements at the beginning, end, and during the broadcast that emphasized its fictional nature.

Some were indignant when they learned about this Halloween hoax. One New Yorker called it "the most asinine stunt I ever heard of." Another denounced it as a disgrace and an outrage.

In the wake of the controversial broadcast, CBS decided not to use simulated news broadcast techniques "when the circumstances of the broadcast could cause immediate alarm to numbers of listeners." Expressing profound regret and bewilderment that his dramatic efforts caused such consternation, Welles apologized, "I don't think we will choose anything like this again."

This single broadcast remains a prime example of the power of broadcasting to dramatically influence attitudes and beliefs.

Peter E. Mayeux
University of Nebraska-Lincoln

with another first: a nation-wide network broadcast.

Other sports also made it to the airwaves. For Memorial Day 1924, WGN Chicago took its microphones to Indianapolis Speedway for the 500-mile classic and saw the average speed pass ninety-nine miles per hour. That fall, WGN seemed to be everywhere, doing football from every campus of the Big Ten Conference and also Nebraska, Pennsylvania, and Southern California. When 1925 rolled around, WGN headed for Louisville on the first Saturday in May to air the first and most famous of the Triple Crown thoroughbred races, the Kentucky Derby. That "handy guy named Sande" was aboard Flying Ebony in the Run for the Roses. Earl Sande was one of the few jockeys to win the Derby three times. WMAQ Chicago aired every home baseball game of the Chicago Cubs from Wrigley Field in 1924. The networks organized sports divisions in 1927. Ted Husing called everything for CBS including the Kentucky Derby and tennis, though by the 1940s Clem McCarthy did the big horse races, and Red Barber got the nod in baseball. The first live basketball game appears to have been on KGEZ in Kalispell, Montana, at a local high school in 1927. Other sports were added rapidly, and this period of sports broadcasting culminated with the first international coverage of the Olympic games from Berlin in 1936.

Public Service

From the beginning of commercial broadcasting, public service has been a significant part of its work. The earliest radio stations broadcast crime news and police descriptions of suspected criminals. They helped build community and youth centers. Over the years they have aired public service commercials for a variety of organizations such as the National Safety Council, the U.S. Treasury, the Red Cross, and the Girl Scouts, as well as local fire and police departments. Broadcasters do this on both a planned and unplanned basis, and this kind of information can be particularly effective and helpful during natural disasters.

Relief for disasters often was spontaneous as radio presented the need and listeners responded. The most destructive tornado in American history hit Murphysboro, Illinois, in 1925. As WLS Chicago presented the news, a telephone caller asked the question, "Will you accept $5 for the relief of storm sufferers?" George Hay began to plead with the audience to donate. After an all-night run, the station had collected $11,000. Within a week, donations reached $50,000.

Since radio's advent, listeners have depended upon it for the latest weather forecasts. Such has been true everywhere, but especially in farming regions and in the hurricane belt around the Gulf of Mexico. One example was the great hurricane that struck Miami in 1935. The area depended upon WIOD, which went to a half-hourly storm information schedule. Another major hurricane hit New England in 1938, and once more WTIC Hartford gave its microphones to civil defense and governmental authorities. Floods, too, have given radio stations an opportunity for public service. One of the most devastating of all time hit the Ohio Valley in January and February 1937. From Pittsburgh to Cairo, Illinois, WHAS Louisville fed a network of stations that spread information throughout the valley and saved countless lives and brought relief to millions. The stations included WFBM Indianapolis, WEAP Lexington, and two 50,000-watt giants, WSM in Nashville and WCKY in Covington-Cincinnati. Later, much of the information was fed to CBS and NBC, the Canadian Broadcasting Corporation, and even the BBC. The WHAS service continued without interruption from 6 a.m. Sunday, January 24, until 2:30 a.m. Monday, February 1, when the water had begun to recede. Similar activities on a smaller scale were carried on from Paducah's pioneer WPAD. When chased from its transmitter site, the station continued from the home of owner Pierce Lackey. That station gained fame during the Depression years by giving three hours' broadcast time daily during the two weeks before Christmas for Paducah Police Chief William E. Bryant to ask for money to help the city's poor.

Radio has led the way in fighting disease also. One of the first campaigns to gain attention was the March of Dimes organized in the 1930s under the aegis of President Franklin Roosevelt to fight infantile paralysis. Radio provided extensive assistance, and funds thus collected paid for the discovery of both the Salk and Sabin vaccines that have virtually eliminated the disease.

All these historic events were unusual in size and scope, but radio has also brought listeners many smaller items that add to the quality of life. Time and weather are two examples. The first Naval Observatory Time signals were aired in 1922 by WJZ New York, which also started daily weather forecasts on the same day. The year 1922 was a prolific one for WJZ. It also saw the introduction of health talks by a physician, financial news from Wall Street, and a weekly children's story hour. The practice of hiring a meteorologist, almost universal among today's television stations, was begun by Boston's WEEI in 1925 with E. B. Rideout. The practice of providing regular series for minorities was begun in 1944. Titled "New World A-Coming," the series was broadcast on WMCA New York.

The Radio in Politics

Those who wrote the Radio Act of 1927 and the Communications Act of 1934 were wise enough to make provision for political broadcasting. Today broadcasters must make some time available to legally qualified candidates for public office, must treat all for the same office alike, must charge rates comparable to those offered to business, and must give the "lowest unit charge" within forty-five days of a primary or sixty days before a general or special election. Modern commercial political broadcasting began with the 1920 coverage of the Harding-Cox presidential election. The 1924 election saw the candidates campaign by radio and included the first coverage of a national convention, although that was not the first campaign of any kind covered by radio. KDKA got that credit, broadcasting the messages of William A. McGee, Republican candidate for mayor of Pittsburgh. Warren G. Harding was the first U.S. president to address the nation by radio. In 1923 he spoke in St. Louis over KSD on America's participation in the World Court. The broadcast was fed to only one other station, WEAF New York, but was heard over most of the eastern United States since every other station in the nation signed off for the period, allowing WEAF's signal to be received.

The 1924 conventions proved to be quite a sensation for a number of reasons. For one, they marked the first time a presidential convention was broadcast. Since no national network then existed, a special network of sixteen stations in twelve cities was set up to cover the Republican convention from Cleveland. Reception was good, and listeners could hear Vice President Coolidge win the nomination. Graham McNamee put in three days of practice but may not have been prepared for the Democrats, who began their convention nearly two weeks later from New York's Madison Square Garden. The badly divided Democrats went on for sixteen days before settling on darkhorse John W. Davis. During the campaign, the candidates gave several radio speeches. By 1924 there were nearly three million receivers in the country, up from only 400,000 in 1920. Twenty stations broadcast Coolidge's inaugural address.

By 1932 the conventions of the two major parties had become giant media events aimed at the nation more than the people in the arena. Franklin Roosevelt, elected in 1932, was a master at using radio. In his famous "Fireside Chats," he explained to vast audiences the nature of the bank moratorium, farm relief, and the many alphabet agencies developed by his New Deal to solve the problems of the Depression. By 1945 local radio was covering the campaigns of virtually every governor, mayor, and county judge.

The Radio in Rural Life

In 1921 Pittsburgh's KDKA aired the first daily program of farm market reports and in 1923 hired the first full-time farm director. He was Frank E. Mullen, born in Kansas, reared in South Dakota, and recently graduated with a degree in agriculture from Iowa State College at Ames.

For rural America, radio proved to be a unifying force. It reached the farm as nothing had done before. Market news was the life of the farm economic picture. Some stations in the early days were started for the sole purpose of disseminating grain and livestock prices. WDZ in Tuscola, Illinois, was built by grain dealer James Bush in 1921 so he could report prices to elevator operators and not have to make telephone calls.

In the fall of 1928 *Prairie Farmer* magazine bought WLS from Sears. Louisville native Burridge D. Butler, the new owner, pledged to make WLS a voice of agriculture. He announced to listeners:

> I am fired with the deep responsibility which rests upon me as I sit here and think of you millions of farm families sitting about

Front Seats in the theatre of the world

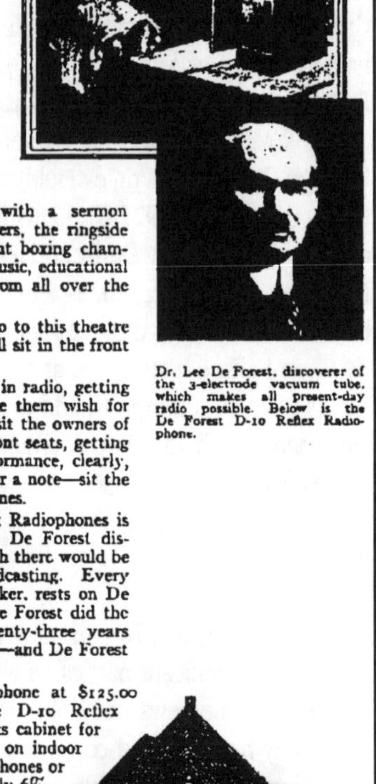

Dr. Lee De Forest, discoverer of the 3-electrode vacuum tube, which makes all present-day radio possible. Below is the De Forest D-10 Reflex Radiophone.

A FASCINATING place, the theatre of the world! Its program for one short week includes addresses by the President of the United States, four great concerts by the New York Philharmonic Orchestra, a Sunday morning full musical church service with a sermon by one of the nation's greatest preachers, the ringside report, blow by blow, of a heavyweight boxing championship, and a bewildering array of music, educational talks, and last-minute news reports from all over the country.

Something over ten million people go to this theatre by radio every week—but they don't all sit in the front seats!

Up in the gallery sit the newcomers in radio, getting enough with their simple sets to make them wish for more. Nearer yet to the great stage sit the owners of more powerful receivers—and in the front seats, getting every word of the great national performance, clearly, distinctly, without the blur of a word or a note—sit the satisfied owners of De Forest Radiophones.

The proved supremacy of De Forest Radiophones is a natural thing. Remember that Dr. De Forest discovered the vacuum tube, without which there would be no present-day radio receiving or broadcasting. Every tube set made, no matter by what maker, rests on De Forest's discovery. Remember that De Forest did the first broadcasting in the world. Twenty-three years ago De Forest was the pioneer in radio—and De Forest is the pioneer in radio today.

The three-tube D-7-A Reflex Radiophone at $125.00 has external batteries; the four-tube D-10 Reflex Radiophone at $150.00 has a drawer of its cabinet for dry cells. Both operate long distances on indoor loop, with wet or dry cells, with headphones or loud speaker. (Prices plus approximately 6% for territories west of the Rockies.)

After you get through experimenting you will come to De Forest, so you might as well get the facts now.

FREE RADIO CATALOGS

for the asking, with prices and full details of De Forest sets, tubes, and parts. Drop us a postcard:

De Forest Radio Tel. & Tel. Co.
DEPT. L3, JERSEY CITY, N. J.

If located west of Pennsylvania address

De Forest Radio Tel. & Tel. Co.
Western Sales Division
Dept. L3, 5680—12th St., Detroit, Mich.

Spectators on the World

With its invention, radio brought events from around the world into listeners' homes. This 1923 ad for the De Forest company's Reflex Radiophone tried to allure buyers with the excitement and entertainment it made possible – a presidential speech, orchestral concerts, church services, a heavyweight boxing match, and news reports from around the world. The genius of Lee De Forest, the "pioneer in radio," provided another selling point for buyers interested in true quality.

your living rooms, listening to this inaugural program. Every day you will be there listening and every night. To give you help in your business by sending you over the air prompt and accurate markets, to help in your production by giving you the best and latest in farm practices, to brighten the home with appropriate musical and educational programs for the mornings and afternoons, to be with you in the evening with restful, inspirational and educational music and talks — to do this every day of the year — and all of the years to come wherein I am given the privilege of serving — to do this I pledge to you my utmost endeavor.[25]

Butler was as good as his word and ran a farm station until it was sold to ABC. The station brought speakers to farm day programs, worked for June Dairy Month with the National Dairy Council, started Peach Week in cooperation with the Illinois Fruit Growers Exchange, and promoted many other efforts.

NBC's *National Farm and Home Hour* on the Blue Network from Chicago brought farmers the information and entertainment they desired until well after World War II. Gardening for farm or city was the topic of CBS's *The Garden Gate*, Saturday mornings with Sam Caldwell, "the Old Dirt Dobber." Some stations built model farms and held demonstrations of the latest methods of farming. One was WLW in Cincinnati. From its 137-acre farm near Mason, Ohio, the farm director began daily remote broadcasts in 1941.

The farm director became a famous person within his coverage area, and many of the big farm stations broadcast on 50,000-watt clear channels. Following in the footsteps of Frank E. Mullen came other pioneers such as George C. Biggar, the first farm director at WLS. While Everett Mitchell was not a farm director, one could scarcely mention farm programming without listing him, announcer for the *National Farm and Home Hour* for most of the years 1928-1960 on NBC. His opening, "It's a beautiful day in Chicago," will forever be remembered by those who lived during the period. One of the best loved programs in the South was WSB's *The Dixie Farm & Home Hour* with Bynum Prance as farm director. In the big midwest farm state of Iowa, there were many farm directors, and most came earlier than the one at WHO Des Moines. But when the station put Herb Plambeck on the air in 1936, he quickly became the most noted because of WHO's 50,000-watt clear channel.

EDUCATION ON THE AIRWAVES

Radio has performed an educational function for every part of the population. Radio's universal tutoring has softened regional dialects, and eventually they may disappear. Commercial stations have reduced the amount of their education programming since World War II with the success of the drive to set aside reserved educational channels in both FM and television and with the passage of the Education Broadcasting Act of 1965.[26]

Though there were no reserved frequencies for education on the AM band, there were, from the first, licensees who voluntarily refrained from using their channels for commercial purposes. Probably the earliest was WHA at the University of Wisconsin, which began in 1919 while it still had the experimental call of 9XM. The following year, the University of Minnesota offered foreign language classes over 9XI. Other efforts of the same type occurred in Iowa and at the University of Illinois, where all three of the WILL stations (AM-FM and TV) were educational. Some colleges built profit-making stations that have virtually supported the schools, thus making them educational in another sense. Among them is WWL, Loyola University of the South, dating from 1922.

At least two of the national radio networks programmed lessons to be used in the classrooms of the country. The *Music Appreciation Hour* with Dr. Walter Damrosch played for years on the NBC network as a supplement to classroom instruction. It began in 1928. Two years later CBS began an even more ambitious project, covering all topics and disciplines usually taught in the American secondary schools. The *American School of the Air* was to be used as a substantial aid to classroom instruction. The network prepared elaborate instructional manuals, and the local CBS affiliates gave them to the schools within their coverage area. Beginning in 1941 WBKN, Youngstown, Ohio, ran *The Student Congress of the Air*, which taught parliamentary procedure and debating ability. WLS in Chicago began national school band contests in 1928, and educational groups have continued them. In 1931 the *University of Chicago Round Table*, intended to stimulate thinking on questions of national importance, began airing on WMAQ. Two years later the Chicago station began feeding the show to the NBC network.

RELIGION AND RADIO

In religious broadcasting, KDKA in Pittsburgh once again was the pioneer. The decision to broadcast Sunday church services was made early in KDKA's first broadcast year. In 1921 it put on the air the full service of the Calvary Episcopal Church in Pittsburgh. Much planning had gone into the project. A special amplifier was built, and microphones were set up to pick up the entire service from the ringing of the chimes in the belfry at the beginning to the organ postlude at the end. Other microphones were installed to broadcast the choir, the congregational singing, certain responses by the congregation, and the sermon. Reaction by the broadcast's audience was enormous, and the program continued. Other stations around the nation inaugurated similar programs.

The networks have provided a pulpit for speakers from almost all religious persuasions on such programs as *The Church of the Air*. Beginning July 15, 1929, KSL in Salt Lake City fed the Mormon

[25]Quoted in James F. Evans, *Prairie Farmer and WLS: The Burridge D. Butler Years* (Urbana, Ill., 1969), 177.

[26]S. E. Frost, Jr., *Education's Own Stations: The History of Broadcast Licenses Issued to Educational Institutions* (Chicago, 1937); and *Broadcasting Yearbook* (Washington, 1984).

The March of Time
Roy Larsen originated the "newscast" in 1928 with weekly ten-minute radio summaries of items taken from *Time* magazine. This 1932 ad announced that after a one-year hiatus from broadcasting, "The March of Time" would resume with "newsacting" vignettes of dramatic events performed by professional actors.

Tabernacle Choir's program *Music and the Spoken Word* to the CBS Network. Today, the program promotes itself as the longest-running radio fare in the United States. Beginning in 1938, KOA Denver has fed the Easter Sunrise Service from the *Garden of the Gods* to the NBC Network. From the early days there were also stations that devoted themselves largely to religious programming, one of which was WMBI in Chicago. This station was operated then, as it still is, by the Moody Bible Institute and began broadcasting in 1926. A month later, it introduced what is believed to be the first children's Bible program, *The Know Your Bible Club*. A standard observation has been that radio provided twentieth-century preachers a larger daily audience for the "Good News" than the Apostle Paul spoke to during his entire ministry.

Early radio stations and networks generally carried religious programming on a "sustaining" basis — that is, at no cost and without commercials. Conditions for religious broadcasting, however, were not always accommodating. Evangelist Aimee Semple McPherson, for example, challenged Herbert Hoover's authority to regulate the frequency of her station. She reasoned that she had the right to fit into God's wavelength and ordered Hoover to leave her station alone. Unfavorable regulation affecting religious broadcasting was not always overt, but owners of religious stations generally did not receive the best spectrum space. In 1940 the National Religious Broadcasters association was organized to lobby Washington for more favorable treatment.

Television has decreased the emphasis on religious radio, but the format remains popular even today. The only radio formats listing more stations than "religious" are country and adult contemporary.

Radio News and Special Events

In today's world of moon shots and space probes, radio listeners and television viewers are all familiar with the special events crews who allow Americans to be present at every major newsmaking happening.

Early radio was the father of on-the-scene news programming. One of the leaders was WGN Chicago. As the home of Clarence Darrow and the birthplace of William Jennings Bryan, Illinois had a special interest in the so-called Tennessee Monkey Trial. Thus, in 1925 at a cost of $1,000 per day for long-distance loops, WGN broadcast the entire trial of J.T. Scopes, who had taught evolution in his high school biology class in Dayton, Tennessee. That same year WHAS in Louisville touched American hearts with Skeet Miller's broadcasts from Horse Cave, Kentucky, where Floyd Collins was trapped in Crystal Cave. The jockey-sized reporter even took a microphone underground for a macabre interview with the dying Collins. Broadcasting of funeral services for presidents began in 1923 when WRC Washingon transmitted the memorial for Warren G. Harding, who died in office. Less than a year later a three-station network aired the funeral of former president Woodrow Wilson, fed by WEAF.

Other special-event shows from outside the studios were often stunts, but the public soon became aware that there were places radio had difficulty going. In 1924 WID Philadelphia broadcast from the bottom of the sea. In 1922 the wedding of Bertha Ann McMunn and George A. Carver was broadcast from Motor Square Garden by KDKA; in 1923 the Al Barnes Circus was broadcast by WFAA in Dallas; that same year KSD St. Louis broadcast from a dirigible in flight; on Easter Sunday, 1924, the Easter Egg Treasure Hunt was staged and broadcast by WCAU Philadelphia. Other such events included Big Ben from London striking midnight over WJZ New York and WRC Washington in 1925; the Liberty Bell from Philadelphia over WCAU on July 4, 1926; the first 24-hour station, KGFJ Los Angeles in 1928; and King Edward VIII's abdication of the British throne for "the woman I love," American divorcee Wallis Warfield Simpson (which was the world-wide broadcast reaching the largest audience of all time) in 1936.

Often the programs were live, but even those recorded for the purpose of later broadcast were soon on the air ahead of the print media reaching the streets. Moreover, radio attracted listeners by

The Fireside Chats
Elected in 1932, President Franklin Roosevelt gave the first of his many "fireside chats" just eight days after his inauguration. Delivered in a friendly, informal manner, the radio addresses did much to show average citizens in the midst of the Great Depression that Roosevelt was interested in them and their problems. Each address began with the salutation "My friends" and was aimed at building confidence in the capacity of the country to solve the grave problems confronting it.

giving them the sense of having been at the event in person. A few papers saw the wave of the future and realized their readers would continue to use both print and broadcast. The *Pittsburgh Post* began to do what almost every paper does today — print the schedules of broadcast stations. It broke new ground in 1921 with the KDKA schedule. It was well into the era of television, however, before all newspapers were printing program schedules.

One unusual piece of news programming grew out of the mind of Roy Larsen, originally circulation manager and then general manager of *Time* magazine. It finally became known as *The March of Time* and eventually moved to the motion picture theaters of the nation. In 1924 Larsen first broadcast a fifteen-minute quiz show called *Pop Question*. It lasted one year. Larsen waited until 1928 to try again with a series of ten-minute news summaries from *Time* magazine featuring what he called a "hair-raising" story. The program was aired on thirty-three major stations in the United States. The programming technique was given the name "newscasting" by Larsen, the first to use the term. Later it incorporated "newsacting" vignettes with professionals dramatizing events for which the program had no recordings of voices. The program was expanded to fifteen minutes and given to any station that would air it along with its built-in promotions for *Time*. More than 100 stations carried it with some regularity.

But Larsen was still unhappy. Lowell Thomas for *Literary Digest* was on NBC. Larsen wanted to top Thomas; and Henry Luce, *Time*'s publisher, promised the money. From the Broadway production of Earl Carroll's *Vanities*, Larsen took Harold Arlen's song "The March of Time" as not only the program title but also the logo music. Ted Husing became the "Voice of Time" followed by Harry Von Zell and, later, Westbrook Van Voorhis. CBS broadcast the first show on March 6, 1931. Agnes Moorehead, Art Carney, Arlene Francis, and Orson Welles were among the noted actors on the program. The show became such a hit that it was expanded to thirty minutes and ran, off and on, until 1945 with such commercial sponsors as Servell Electrolux, Remington Rand, and Wrigley's gum. In 1935 it also began in the theaters and ran until 1951.

THE GREAT DEPRESSION AND THE IMPACT OF RADIO

When the stock market crashed in October 1929, the Roaring '20s ended. The Great Depression that followed was of global proportions and set an emotional tone that was in complete contrast to the optimism of the 1920s. The Depression demanded a New Deal, the name that President Franklin Roosevelt gave to his domestic program.

Even during the sparse conditions of the Depression, radio grew in mass popularity. It had, as a result, a profound effect on the lives of Americans. Historians often equate this period with radio's "golden age." One of the reasons radio was so popular was precisely because of the social context provided by the Depression. People were careful with what money they had, and now instead of going out for entertainment they sat before the large console of a radio receiver. During the Depression, programming matured; and network patterns, advertising practices, and news operations changed.

In the politically charged climate of the Depression, radio was not only the most popular source of entertainment, but also an important platform for the discussion of ideological issues. Some politicians developed political styles well attuned to the new medium. President Franklin Roosevelt epitomized those who successfully made the transformation.

In the 1930s, radio programming matured and grew in popularity. Of the total programming, 64.1% was music (with 23.5% dance music and 4.5% phonographs); 13.3% women's, children's, and feature entertainment; 12.1% informational, education, news, and politics; and 6.5% drama. Programs such as *Suspense*, *Amos 'n' Andy*, *The Shadow*, *Little Orphan Annie*, *One Man's Family*, *March of Time*, and *The Lone Ranger* propelled radio's popularity. In 1938, the number of network quarter-hours of programming in a typical week were of the following types: vaudeville and comedy, 36; general and talk variety, 30; music variety, 52; concert music, 48; light dramas, 17; thrillers, 23; and news, 23.

RADIO NEWS

The development of radio news was one of the important outcomes of the Depression and the oncoming World War II. During the 1930s, and particularly as the war approached, radio news and news gathering practices took on many characteristics that continue today. *Fortune* magazine noted that "The nation's favorite recreation was listening to radio...[and] newscasts ranked third among favorite radio programs." An article in *Scribner's* magazine underscored the impact of the dramatic character of Edward R. Murrow and the importance of radio news. It noted the advantages that Murrow's radio programs had over "the greatest American newspaper."[27] According to William S. Paley of CBS, "Radio news grew up with World War II."[28]

News programming as we know it today did not exist during the 1920s and early '30s. It resembled programming that today would be a parallel to public affairs or special-event coverage. Radio carried speeches, the fireside chats of President Roosevelt, political debates, religious sermons, and celebrations of all sorts. "News staffs" were comprised of a few people at the networks and even fewer, if any, at the local stations.

The network news staffs were there to support commentators and included engineers and producers who arranged for the broadcast of public events. Lowell Thomas had become the first commentator at CBS in 1930. Before the decade was over, CBS had hired the first news director, Paul White. He put together a team of reporters to get the news at the scene of happenings and a commentator back at the studio to tell what it meant. The dean of these was Hans von Kaltenborn, an editor of the *Brooklyn Eagle* who began broadcasting in 1922, joined CBS in 1930, and later completed his career at NBC. Other popular commentators included Boake Carter, Dorothy Thompson, Elmer Davis, Fulton Lewis, Edward R. Murrow, Father Charles Coughlin, and Walter Winchell.

The numbers of commentators rose steadily during radio's golden years (from about 1929 to about 1948). In 1931 there were six network commentators; by 1947 there were more than 600 — if local and national commentators are counted. The best known among them, such as Thomas and Kaltenborn, whose voices and views entered countless American homes regularly, became national personalities. They were, indeed, one of the most color-

My adventure with the invisible

by* Lowell Thomas, *World Traveler—Radio Commentator

MACHINES chattered around me, a bewildering complexity of mechanism endowed with superhuman faculties of precision. They had cost millions of dollars—years of thought and research. As I stood on the fifth floor of the Gillette factory in Boston I reflected: "Imagine this prodigious assembling of technological perfection, just to make a blade."

My guide corrected me, saying: "That isn't what we are turning out here. We are all collaborating here to produce a perfect edge. And that, actually and positively, is a thing that you *cannot see*."

I was to learn he was right. My guide took me upstairs and introduced me to a technician who presided over an amazing instrument. The pet gadget of the blond young modern Merlin from M. I. T. is a "sharpness comparer." Within its mysterious interior an adaptation of the weird usefulness of the photo-electric eye detects to an uncanny degree of accuracy whether that precious edge comes up to Gillette standards of sharpness.

There I realized that what my guide had told me was true. The perfect edge is perfectly invisible. It can be measured only with light-waves!

In my wanderings around the globe this is just about the most astounding spectacle I have observed in modern industry. I mean all this mighty, elaborately mechanized organization engaged in producing the unseeable.

Electric furnaces in which coils of steel are hardened and tempered, furnaces that look like long, miniature tunnels. Inside they are 1500 degrees hot, outside they are so cool you can rest your hands upon them. Diamonds from the fields of Kimberley or Brazil that play their part in the testing machines. Microscopes with a 3000-power magnifying capacity. Cathode ray oscillographs that far outstrip man's poor faculties of perception or accuracy.

And all for what? To turn out something too fine for the human eye to perceive—to produce a shaving edge of incomparable keenness. The doctors of physics, the draughtsmen in the designing room, the toolmakers in the machine shop are constantly experimenting, to produce an even sharper, smoother-shaving edge—and it's difficult for me to imagine that today's Gillette blade could be improved upon. I know—I've tried them all—in all parts of the world.

So in view of what I've seen and experienced, I can't imagine how any shaver could select a blade other than Gillette.

Here are the facts about razor blades. Why let anyone deprive you of shaving comfort by selling you a substitute! Ask for Gillette Blades and be sure to get them.

GILLETTE SAFETY RAZOR COMPANY, BOSTON, MASS.

Celebrity Commentators

In the 1930s, radio commentators became some of the most popular figures in America. Faithful listeners thought of them as family friends. In this 1936 ad, the Gillette Safety Razor Company relied on the popularity of Lowell Thomas, radio's first commentator, to convince men to buy its product by telling of his tour of a razor blade factory.

27 Robert J. Landry, "Edward R. Murrow," *Scribner's* 104 (December 1938): 7-11.

28 William S. Paley, Forward to *History in Sound*, by Milo Ryan (Seattle, 1963), 5.

ful groups of journalists in media history. They enlivened, enlarged, and personalized the public debate of the 1930s and 1940s as they made radio a major force in the political perceptions of millions of listeners.

"This Is London"
With the German Luftwaffe bombing Great Britain in 1940, American journalist Edward R. Murrow provided eyewitness accounts, making famous his nightly introduction, "This is London." Britain's Philips radio company prompted countrymen to buy receivers to get the immediate news of World War II, including "informed, uncensored" comment from American newsmen such as Murrow.

The newspaper industry recognized the potential impact of radio news in the early 1930s. Radio held the advantage over the print media of being able to distribute news instantly to its audience. Threatened by radio's potential, newspapers tried to limit the growth of radio news, contriving rules that forbade the Associated Press to sell news to radio stations. The corporate competition between newspaper and network owners soon led to the "Press-Radio War." Although called a war, it was really a short-lived conflict created by business rivalry. In 1933, the rivalry heated to such a degree that newspapers began to pressure the news information services (Associated Press and United Press International) into withdrawing their services from radio stations. A few newspapers even refused to publish radio program schedules.

At a meeting called to resolve the conflict, broadcasters and newspaper owners reached a compromise (known as the "Biltmore Agreement" after the New York City hotel in which the meeting was held). Newspapers would publish the radio schedules, CBS and NBC would eliminate their news services, stations would limit the amount of news they broadcast, and a Press Radio Bureau would be established to provide stations with news information. The arrangement seemingly limited radio news. However, since the emphasis at the networks was on "commentary" rather than "news," the commentary staffs continued to grow slowly, and producers continued arranging speeches, sporting events, and, according to Murrow, "the Vatican Choir at Easter time."[29] Radio correspondent William L. Shirer, in his *Twentieth Century Journey: The Nightmare Years, 1930-1940*, said he and Murrow were in Europe busy "putting kids' choirs on the air for...Columbia's American School of the Air."

For awhile, the Press Radio Bureau supplied two five-minute news summaries per day, but they could not be broadcast before 9:30 a.m. or after 9:00 p.m. In December 1938, the Biltmore Agreement fell apart, and the Press Radio Bureau ceased to serve the networks. Even after accepting the agreement, however, both NBC and CBS had continued to develop their commentary and public affairs program schedules, even to the point of issuing guidelines for the growing staffs who, according to broadcaster Paul W. White, were to "elucidate and illuminate the news of common knowledge and to point out the facts on both sides."[30] This approach provided the structure that eventually led to today's radio newsroom. The networks were ready to make the transition from commentary to news.

The commentators became news reporters and personalities presenting commentary and eyewitness accounts. Beginning with the Czechoslovakian crisis and the Austrian *Anschluss* of 1938 culminating in the Munich meeting between Hitler and Britain's Neville Chamberlain, networks began a rapid expansion of facilities and personnel. As World War II spread in Europe, the commentators' names became household words, and the network commentary staffs grew into webs of news-gathering bureaus that covered the globe.[31] Following the lead of CBS, all four national radio networks were systematically gathering news for broadcast by the beginning of World War II.

With a new shortwave transmitter, CBS developed the "world news roundup," with correspondents reporting live from the scene of action. Edward R. Murrow was sent to London. From

[29]Edward R. Murrow, "We Take You Back," CBS Radio News Documentary, March 13, 1958. CBS-KIRO Milo Ryan Phonoarchives, National Archives, Washington, D.C., Tape 4065.

[30]Paul W. White, "Covering A War for Radio," *Annals of the American Academy of Political and Social Science* (January 1941): 83. See also Paul W. White, *News On The Air* (New York, 1947), 199.

[31]Donald G. Godfrey, "CBS World News Roundup: Setting the Stage for the Next Half Century," *American Journalism* 7 (1991): 164-72.

there he began to put together a team later known as the "Murrow Boys" to get the news from all of Europe. They included, among others, William L. Shirer in Berlin, who later wrote the well-known standard account of Hitler's Germany, *The Rise and Fall of the Third Reich*. It was radio during World War II that delivered news immediately to Americans at home. Murrow became noted for his "This is London" sign-on with the sound of exploding bombs as background. Speaking in honor of Murrow and his works covering the German bombing of Great Britain, historian and poet laureate Archibald MacLeish reflected the feelings of Murrow's contemporaries. Of Murrow, he said, "[Y]ou have accomplished one of the great miracles of the world.... You have burned the city of London in our homes and we felt the flames that burned it."[32]

By the end of the war, the Hooper Ratings showed half the people in the nation received most of their news from radio. When the Japanese surrender was signed in September 1945 aboard the battleship *Missouri*, the world's people heard it all on radio. They had been there. The event even gave rise to a popular news feature on CBS called "You Are There," re-creating the signing of the Magna Carta, the Battle of Gettysburg, and other historic events.

A number of local stations had made news a part of their standard budget. WPAD Paducah was one of many with one local reporter. WJNT in Jamestown, New York, employed three. WMAZ in Macon, Georgia, hired five full-time, and WHO Des Moines was spending more than $100,000 a year on news. Its news staff totaled twelve persons — not enough to raise eyebrows today but a pioneer effort in the 1940s.

Edwin H. Armstrong
The inventor of FM radio, Edwin Armstrong began to be depressed from his legal battles over ownership of his invention. In 1954, despondent over his inability to reconcile with his estranged wife, he committed suicide by jumping from his thirteenth-floor apartment.

FM Radio's Pioneer: Edwin H. Armstrong

In the late 1920s there were two technical innovations still ahead that would revolutionize the new medium. The developments were frequency modulated (FM) radio and "visual radio" (television). The two inventors responsible for these developments were Edwin Howard Armstrong and Philo Taylor Farnsworth. They were the last of their kind — the individual inventor working independently from corporations.

Armstrong was the father of FM broadcasting. His biographer, Lawrence Lessing, called him "a young man of the twenties." With the "sensitivity of his romantic generation," he "shared the great creativity of the era and [had] more than a touch of its madness."[33] Early in Armstrong's career, he and Lee De Forest, who had been working on similar experiments, wound up in a bitter patent suit. Armstrong's primary work revolved around the elimination of the "static" that interfered with the transmission of the AM (amplitude modulation) radio signal. He conducted his experimentation during the late 1920s and early 1930s. Since he was well-to-do, he funded most of his own work and walked among affluent friends and associates. He was a close friend of David Sarnoff, whose children called Armstrong "the coffee man" because he was always dropping by the Sarnoff home to discuss his experiments over a cup of morning coffee.

The public demonstrations of Armstrong's FM radio were impressive. There was no static in his signal. His most noted public broadcast came in 1935 as a part of a research presentation to an engineering conference in New York. The demonstration was to illustrate and climax his report. As it turned out, it produced moments of surprise even for Armstrong. He had arranged the exhibition with the technical assistance of his friend Randy Runyon. At the point in the report at which the broadcast was to have occurred, a colleague stepped to the podium and whispered to Armstrong, "Keep talking; Runyon has just burned out [the] generator." Armstrong continued reading from his paper until he received the "all clear" signal from Runyon. Then, a glass of water was poured before the microphone — and it really sounded like water being poured — paper was crumpled and torn, Sousa marches were played, and local talent performed from Runyon's living room. The music sounded more alive and crisp than music that had ever been broadcast over radio. Armstrong appeared to have the answer to radio static, the problem on which the audience of engineers had been struggling for years.

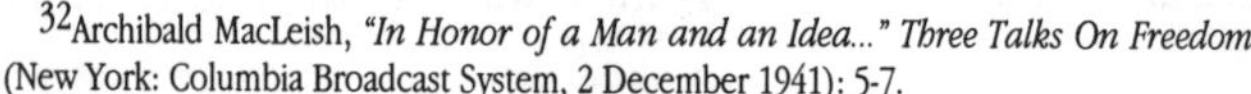

[32]Archibald MacLeish, *"In Honor of a Man and an Idea..." Three Talks On Freedom* (New York: Columbia Broadcast System, 2 December 1941): 5-7.

[33]Lawrence Lessing, *Man of High Fidelity: Edwin Howard Armstrong* (New York, 1969), 169-70.

Armstrong was dedicated to his system. To him, his new FM signal was more than an answer to the static problem of AM. It was a system that would replace AM. Still, some saw it as merely an innovation that would improve the existing signals. Sarnoff and RCA, which were beginning to experiment with television, viewed FM as an opportunity within the development of broadcast television. However, it soon became apparent that those with a financial investment in AM were not willing to consider anything new, and another confrontation began.

The conflict prompted legal delays in the allocation of frequency space for FM. Armstrong's personal relationship with Sarnoff became strained and finally broke. Armstrong, however, never gave up. He spent most of his family's fortune defending his FM system as a revolutionary technology that would make AM obsolete. According to Kenneth Bilby, Sarnoff's biographer, the embittered Armstrong "lacked the Sarnoff stomach for a prolonged battle" with the large growing corporate broadcast industry.[34] FM would be delayed three decades before it would achieve the inventor's vision.

Philo Farnsworth and Visual Radio

The story of the technological development of television has striking parallels to that of FM. Television too had a dominant and independently spirited inventor who was pitted against a major corporation. This time, the inventor was Philo Farnsworth, who battled with the giant RCA and David Sarnoff.

"Visual radio," as television was first called, had two primary pioneers, Farnsworth and Vladimir K. Zworykin. The latter was a Russian immigrant to the United States who worked for Westinghouse as a member of its research staff. Westinghouse's primary interest, however, was radio; so at first Zworykin worked on his own until his television experiments attracted the attention of Sarnoff. He asked Zworykin what it would cost to develop television, Zworykin put the price tag at $100,000. Sarnoff thought it a good investment and hired Zworykin to undertake the job of pioneering television for RCA. Zworykin's estimate would grow significantly over the years as RCA took the lead in the development of television into the 1940s.

The young Farnsworth was the leading competitive and independent inventor of television.[35] He was raised on family farms in Utah and Idaho, but from his youth he took a much greater interest in science than farming. Even his job on the farm was taking care of the family's source of electricity, the Delco generator. While still fifteen years old and attending high school in Rigby, Idaho, he sketched on the classroom blackboard his theory for the development of television. His high school teacher, Justin Tolman, recalled that drawing years later and served as an important witness in the patent suits between Farnsworth and RCA, which had been completely caught off guard by Farnsworth's work.

Philo Farnsworth
Unlike most other inventors, Philo Farnsworth was successful in his legal battles with RCA and David Sarnoff over ownership of his television patents. However, others tried to claim that they – rather than Farnsworth – were the real inventors of television. After his death, his widow, who described how as a teenager Farnsworth had conceived of the technological principle behind television while working in the field on his family farm, continued the fight for her husband to be rightfully recognized.

Like Armstrong before him, Farnsworth the independent inventor ended up in court battling the corporate giant. Elma Farnsworth (Philo's wife, who worked with him in the laboratory) described the confrontation as a "David and Goliath" fight. Farnsworth finally won the court battle, and RCA was forced to come to an agreement with him for use of his patents.

While he won in court, Farnsworth, like Armstrong, did not have the "Sarnoff stomach" for a prolonged war. His health proved a detriment, and after a series of frustrating setbacks and personal tragedies he tired of his television research and its resulting conflict. His work moved from television to nuclear fusion.

While best known for his work in television, Farnsworth also was a leader in radio science and manufacturing. The radio work in his laboratories, though, was primarily in short-wave and audio experimentation to accompany his work in television. In 1938 his company, the Farnsworth Television and Radio Corporation, pur-

[34]Kenneth Bilby, *The General: David Sarnoff and the Rise of the Communications Industry* (New York, 1986).

[35]For details on Farnsworth's career, see Erik Barnouw, *Tube of Plenty: The Evolution of American Television* (New York, 1975); Stephen F. Hofer, "Philo Farnsworth: Television's Pioneer," *Journal of Broadcasting* 23 (1979): 153; T. Ropp, "Philo Farnsworth: Forgotten Father of Television," *Media History Digest* 5:2 (1985): 42-58; and Elma "Pem" Farnsworth, *Distant Vision* (Salt Lake City, 1989).

chased the famous Capehart Company, known for the superior quality of its radio receivers and for its phonographs and jukeboxes. In 1945 Farnsworth purchased WGL-AM, thus becoming a broadcaster as well as an inventor.

Radio Comes of Age

Has radio come of age? Since its inception, radio and electronic media technology has been in a state of continual evolution. In the late 1800s, wireless telegraphy replaced wire. By the 1920s, maritime-oriented wireless was replaced by commercial AM radio. In the 1950s, radio was stunted in its growth by television. Today the quality of FM has created an audience shift away from the AM signal. The evolution continues: color replaced black and white television; the chip has replaced the tube. At first, broadcasting replaced the telegraphic and coaxial cable, but cable now has re-evolved in a new distribution form and eroded the power of the traditional networks. The Internet is the newest form for providing radio services. Using real-time audio from stations and other providers, it extends the service of the broadcaster and expands the opportunities for traditional broadcasting. Today, the audience has greater program selection opportunities, satellite has replaced cable delivery, microwave and satellite have combined to decentralize network news — shifting emphasis to the local stations. The marketplace has made people rethink regulation, and technology is still developing. Who knows what technology will do to the future of the electronic medium?

As with technology, the ideological issues of history bare a striking resemblance to the issues of today. Conflicts over monopoly, network control, news and educational programming, censorship and free speech, the law, and spectrum space are still with us. The platforms surrounding these issues are almost the same. Only the players and the size of the stakes have changed.

RECOMMENDED READINGS

BOOKS

Abramson, Albert. *Zworykin: Pioneer of Television*. Chicago, 1995. This biography reconstructs the inventor's life from his early years in Russia, through his career with RCA, and to his death in 1982.

Archer, Gleason L. *History of Radio to 1926*. New York, 1938. A detailed but ideological history of early radio written mostly from the files of RCA and NBC. Emphasis is on economics and organization.

Baker, John C. *Farm Broadcasting: The First Sixty Years*. Ames, Iowa, 1981. The definitive work; all you ever wanted to know about farm broadcasters.

Barnouw, Erik. *A Tower in Babel: A History of Broadcasting in the United States to 1933*. New York, 1966. The first of a three-volume work. The volumes comprise a detailed history of the electronic media. Volume II, *The Golden Web*, covers 1933 to 1953.

Chase, Francis, Jr. *Sound and Fury*. New York, 1942. This is an "informal history" of the growth of radio in the U.S., told in terms of people and anecdotes: Marconi, DeForest, Sarnoff, early history, the chaos of the early 1920s, the development of networks, FTC, technology, entertainers, etc. This is not a book intended for the serious historian.

Collins, Philip. *Radio: The Golden Age*. New York, 1988. A cultural look at this fascinating period.

Donahue, Hugh Carter. *The Battle To Control Broadcast News: Who Owns the First Amendment?* New York, 1989. Survey history of broadcast regulation since the 1920s, with an emphasis on the concepts of equal time and fairness.

Douglas, Alan. *Radio Manufactures of the 1920s*, vols. 1-3. New York, 1991. This illustrated work provides an excellent reference on manufacturing and corportions.

Douglas, George H. *The Early Days of Radio Broadcasting*. New York, 1987. Technical details not found in every other book of this type.

Edelman, Murray. *The Licensing of Radio Services in the United States, 1927 to 1947*. Urbana, Ill, 1950. Analysis of the policies and actions of the regulatory agencies in licensing radio services 1927-1947.

Everson, George. *The Story of Television: The Life of Philo T. Farnsworth*. New York, 1949. A biography written by the man who worked with and financed Farnsworth's earliest experiments.

Fang, Irving. *Those Radio Commentators*. Ames, Iowa, 1977. Examines fifteen commentators and the influence they had on America from 1929 to 1948.

Fielding, Raymond. *The March of Time, 1935-1951*. New York, 1978. The radio beginnings of the news documentary as well as an important movie newsreel.

Godfrey, Donald G. *Reruns on File: A Guide to Media Archives*. Hillsdale, N.J., 1992. Lists media archives state by state.

Godfrey, Donald G., and Frederic A. Leigh. *Historical Dictionary of American Radio*. Westport, Conn., 1998. Provides an alphabetical listing of topics and terms, with entries covering almost every subject related to radio.

Hilliard, Robert L., and Michael C. Keith. *The Broadcast Century: A Biography of American Broadcasting*. Boston, 1992. Overview of American broadcasting history.

Hilmes, Michele. *Radio Voices: American Broadcasting, 1922-1954*. Minneapolis, 1997. A social/cultural history during its golden era with special emphasis on race, ethnicity, and gender.

Inglis, Andrew. *Behind the Tube: A History of Broadcasting Technology and Business*. Boston, 1990. Survey begins with the origins of the electronic theory and works its way to current developments.

Koch, Howard. *The Panic Broadcast: Portrait of an Event*. Boston, 1970. Story of the Halloween broadcast in 1938 by boy wonder Orson Welles which terrified America and sparked an FCC investigation.

Lewis, Tom. *Empire of the Air: The Men Who Made Radio*. New York, 1991. Chronicle of the inventors of radio and their clashes with the corporations that came to control it.

Lichty, Lawrence W., and Malachi C. Topping. *American Broadcasting: A Source Book on the History of Radio and Television*. New York, 1975. Broadcasting's pre-history to the 1970s, bringing most of the documents, facts, and figures together in one place.

Lyons, Eugene. *David Sarnoff: A Biography*. New York, 1966. Sarnoff played a leading role in the major developments in wireless communications and broadcasting.

MacDonald, J. Fred. *Don't Touch That Dial: Radio Programming in American Life From 1920 to 1960*. Chicago, 1979. Radio in the "Golden Age" reflected a "commerical democracy and the character of the people who made it work."

Maltin, Leonard. *The Great American Broadcast: A Celebration of America's Golden Age*. New York, 1997. Based on oral history interviews, this book is a lively account of radio until the mid-1950s.

McChesney, Robert W. *Telecommunications, Mass Media, and Democracy, 1928-1935*. New York, 1993. Commercial radio's development was heavily influenced by commercial interests that outlobbied reformist opponents.

McMahon, Robert Sears. *Federal Regulation of the Radio and Television Broadcast Industry in the United States, 1927-1959*. New York, 1979. The FCC failed to become an effective guardian of the public's interest, as it was charged to do, in its first twenty-five years.

Paper, Lewis J. *Empire: William S. Paley and the Making of CBS*. New York, 1987. While Paley has told his own story, Paper captures some insights that reveal

Paley's flaws as well as his greatmess.

Ray, William B. *FCC: The Ups and Downs of Radio-TV Regulation*. Ames, Iowa, 1990. Since the FCC was established by the Communications Act of 1934, it has been flawed by political favoritism.

Robinson, Thomas Porter. *Radio Networks and the Federal Government*. New York, 1943. History of the legal relationship of the government and broadcasting with particular emphasis on network broadcasting.

Rosen, Philip. *The Modern Stentors:. Radio Broadcasting and the Federal Government, 1920-1934*. Westport, Conn., 1980. Legislative history of the developing years of broadcasting, especially the formulation of radio regulation and the growth of radio as a business.

Schubert, Paul. *The Electric Word: The Rise of Radio*. New York, 1928. Survey of American governmental and technical developments and the importance of economic factors before 1928.

Smith, Ralph Lewis. *A Study of Professional Criticism of Broadcasting in the United States 1920-1955*. New York, 1979. A study of the ideas and perspectives of selected broadcasting critics, including the background and nature of criticism, program genres, advertising, and the effects of criticisms.

Sterling, Christopher, and John Kittross. *Stay Tuned: A Concise History of American Broadcasting*, 2nd ed. Belmont, Calif., 1990. Narrative history emphasizes the basic events and developments since 1920.

Thomas, Lowell. *Good Evening, Everybody*. New York, 1976. Light, entertaining autobiography detailing Thomas' adventures covering news around the world.

Udelson, Joseph. *The Great Television Race: A History of the American Television Industry, 1925-1941*. Tuscaloosa, Ala., 1982. This study focuses on the history of television technology: survey of research, experiments, and telecasting prior to 1941, when commercial television was authorized.

Will, Thomas E. *Telecommunications Structure and Management in the Executive Branch of Government, 1900-1970*. Boulder, Colo, 1978. The U.S. government played an important role in the formulation of broadcast regulation.

ARTICLES

Baudino, Joseph E., and John M. Kittross. "Broadcasting Oldest Stations: An Examination of Four Claimants." *Journal of Broadcasting* 21 (1977): 61-83. Which station is the oldest in the United States? Awards the crown of first commercial license in continuous operation to KDKA.

Benjamin, Louise. "In Search of the Sarnoff 'Radio Music Box' Memo." *Journal of Broadcasting and Electronic Media* 37 (1993): 325-35. Concise account of the story of David Sarnoff and the development of radio.

—. "Working It Out Together: Radio Policy from Hoover to the Radio Act of 1927." *Journal of Broadcasting and Electronic Media* 42 (1998): 221-36. Traces the development of radio policy and lawmaking from their inception through the Radio Act of 1927.

Bensman, Marvin. "The Zenith WJAZ Case and the Chaos of 1926-7." *Journal of Broadcasting* (1970): 423-37. Historical developments surrounding the period of chaos.

Bohn, Thomas W. "Broadcasting National Election Returns: 1916-1948." *Journal of Broadcasting* 12 (1968): 267-86. The full story from Charles Evans Hughes' surprise to the similar defeat of Tom Dewey.

Chester, Giraud. "The Press Radio War: 1933-1935." *Public Opinion Quarterly* (1949): 252-64. Description of the fight that developed when radio began to compete with newspapers.

Clark, David G. "H.V. Kaltenborn and His Sponsors: Controversial Broadcasting and the Sponsor's Role." *Journal of Broadcasting* 12 (1968): 309-21. Kaltenborn's experiences indicate that commitment to principle by the sponsor appears to be the determining factor in whether a company will sponsor a controversial program in the face of critics and opponents and the resulting economic pressure.

Cranston, Pat. "Political Convention Broadcasts: Their History and Influence." *Journalism Quarterly* 37 (1960): 186-94. The electronic media have helped shape the way in which convention sessions are conducted and have influenced the behavior of delegates.

Garvey, Daniel E. "Secretary Hoover and the Quest for Broadcast Regulation." *Journalism History* 3 (1976): 66-70, 85. Herbert Hoover, as U.S. Secretary of Commerce, 1921-1928, "was a staunch and unceasing advocate of strong federal regulation of broadcasting." (66).

Hammargren, Russell J. "The Origin of Press-Radio Conflict." *Journalism Quarterly* 13 (1936): 91-93. The war between press and radio began "with the formation of chain broadcasting, competition for the national advertising dollar, and sharp focusing of national attention upon the Dodge advertising program of 1928 and the national election of the same year."

Howard, Herbert H. "Broadcast Station Group Ownership: A 20th Century Phenomenon." *Journalism History* 2 (1975): 68-71, 83. Multi-station ownership began in the 1920s, shortly after radio moved from amateur status to commercial.

Jones, Alfred. "The Making of an Interventionist on the Air: Elmer Davis and CBS News, 1939-1941." *Pacific Historical Review* (1973): 74-93. Unique look at Davis and the utilization of broadcast news as primary source materials.

Lewis, Tom. "'A Godlike Presence': The Impact of Radio on the 1920s and 1930s." *OAH Magazine of History* (Spring 1992): 26-33. Discusses the meaning radio had to American culture, religion, and politics during its first years.

Lott, George E., Jr. "The Press-Radio War of the 1930s." *Journal of Broadcasting* 14 (1970): 275-86. Recounts the bitter days when newspapers tried to keep news off the air.

McChesney, Robert. "The Battle for the U.S. Airwaves, 1928-1935." *Journal of Communication* 40 (1990): 29-57. An analysis of the opposition to the network system, with special attention to the social, economic, and political environment.

—. "Media and Democracy: The Emergence of Commercial Broadcasting in the United States, 1927-1935." *OAH Magazine of History* (Spring 1992): 34-40. Political and economic forces shaped broadcasting in its early years.

Michael, Rudolph D. "History and Criticism of Press-Radio Relationships." *Journalism Quarterly* 15 (1938): 178-184, 220. Narrative history of newspaper attitudes toward radio from 1922 to 1938, including competition, use of news, AP regulations, newspaper ownership of stations, etc.

Orbison, Charley. "'Fighting Bob' Shuler: Early Radio Crusader." *Journal of Broadcasting* 21 (1977): 459-72. In the 1920s, California minister Bob Shuler "considered it his responsibility to expose sin and corruption in the wicked city of Los Angeles." He used his broadcasts to do so, and the FCC revoked his radio license.

Pusateri, C. Joseph. "FDR, Huey Long and the Politics of Radio." *Journal of Broadcasting* 21 (1977): 85-95. Politics played an important role in the case of the Federal Radio Commission's 1934 decision allocating a highly desirable channel to one of two competing Louisiana radio stations, thus showing that the FRC was susceptible to political pressure.

Rose, Ernest D. "How the U.S. Heard About Pearl Harbor." *Journal of Broadcasting* 5 (1961): 285-98. Americans heard on radio that they were at war. Although imperfect, the reports helped shape the nation's attitude and world events.

Smith, F. Leslie. "Education for Broadcasting: 1929-1963." *Journal of Broadcasting* 8 (1964): 383-98. The growth of education has coincided with the growth of broadcasting as a profession.

Smith, R. Franklin. "'Oldest Station in the Nation'?." *Journal of Broadcasting* 4 (1959-1960): 40-55. This study proposes criteria by which to judge claims that particular radio stations are the oldest or were the first, attempting to formulate a workable definition of the term "broadcasting station." WHA, which sometimes has been cited as the first, was not the first.

Smith, Robert. "The Origins of Radio Network News Commentary." *Journal of Broadcasting* 9 (1965): 113-22. News commentary began in the 1930s, not during World War II as most historians have argued, from social and political developments of the 1930s.

Spaulding, John W. "1928: Radio Becomes a Mass Advertising Medium." *Journal of Broadcasting* 8 (1963-1964): 31-44. In the late 1920s broadcast facilities, audiences, programs, and station owner attitudes were right for the national advertiser to enter radio sponsorship in a serious way. Radio took advantage of the conditions in 1928 and developed into an advertising-supported medium.

Tenney, Craig. "The 1943 Debate on Opinionated Broadcast News." *Journalism History* 7 (1980): 11-15. The evolution of broadcast news philosophy began with the CBS news rule that stories carry no personal opinions or editorial comment.

Weeks, Lewis E. "The Radio Election of 1924." *Journal of Broadcasting* 8 (1964): 233-43. Radio "grew up" during the 1924 campaign. The campaign introduced new techniques in political campaigning and served as a proving ground for nationwide broadcasting.

Wesolowski, James Walter. "Before Canon 35: WGN Broadcasts the Monkey Trial." *Journalism History* 2 (1975): 76-79, 86. Radio coverage had an impact on the Scopes trial. Since this was the first time radio had covered a trial, participants and officials had no precedents by which to determine their practices.

Wik, Reynold. "The Radio in Rural America During the 1920s." *Agricultural History* 55 (October 1981): 339-50. "The radio was of profound importance for [rural] American people because it opened their ears to the sounds of the world and provided a medium which became an instrument for social change."

Williams, Robert. "The Politics of American Broadcasting: Public Purposes and Private Interests." *Journal of American Studies* 10 (1976): 329-40. Since regulation began in the 1920s, broadcasters have been "pretty much free to pursue their private interests without fear of government controls."

19

The Entertainment Media

1900 - Present

The mass media provide more than just essential news and information. As early as the mid-1700s, newspaper publishers recognized that entertainment was an important selling point. By the mid-1880s, Sunday editions were including feature stories, columns, and comic drawings.

The entertainment media have now expanded from print to sophisticated electronic forms. With the introduction of each new medium came dire predictions that a preceding medium would be sacrificed: the phonograph would hurt live performances; the radio was supposed to kill the phonograph and the newspaper; television was damaging radio and comic books; VCRs would close the movie theaters; cable transmission would kill the broadcasters. In reality, shrewd entrepreneurs in each threatened field adapted to the changes (though some more reluctantly than others) and succeeded in preserving their medium. That process is continuing today. We have more entertainment choices than ever, and the traditional media have found new ways to attract customers.

Americans have embraced the entertainment media, especially the electronic media, with extraordinary passion. In 1998, the average American spent around $593 on the entertainment media.[1] New entertainment media appear steadily, and keeping up with trends has become a full-time job. But are these new media really new? Or are they just updated versions of old media? This chapter discusses entertainment media in a chronological progression from print to electronic media. Although comic books appeared later than the phonograph, movies, or broadcasting, their origins are older than any electronic entertainment medium.

Comic Books

Comic books, like most media, grew and changed over time, combining old and new ideas until the comic book we recognize finally emerged in the 1920s. Cartoons appeared sporadically in American newspapers as early as the 1750s. In the late 1860s, newspapers began publishing cartoons regularly. The first comic strip, however, did not appear until 1896. It was not a true strip, but instead was a single panel full of action. Richard F. Outcault's "The Yellow Kid" depicted the adventures of a youth from the tenements of New York dressed in yellow clothes. It was first published in Joseph Pulitzer's *New York Sunday World*. When a competing paper, William Randolph Hearst's *New York Sunday Journal*, hired Outcault away, George B. Luks drew the panel for the *World*, and New York City enjoyed two Sunday versions of "The Yellow Kid." The cartoon was the inspiration for the term "yellow press," which critics applied to the sensational newspapers of the day.

Seeking to capitalize on the popularity of cartoons and comic strips, publishers released a number of books featuring collections of comics. The modern comic book format did not appear, however, until the late 1920s; and even then, most of the booklets were just reprints of comic strips. Finally, in 1935, a comic book with original material appeared on the newsstands. Titled *New Fun Comics*, it was published by Major Malcolm Wheeler-Nicholson and sold for a dime.

Nicholson may have been a creative talent, but he was not a good businessman. His business mistakes allowed pulp fiction publisher Harry Donenfeld to take over his operation. Donenfeld eventually established DC Comics, one of the most successful comic book companies. In June 1938, with World War II threatening to involve the United States, DC's Superman made his first appearance, to a rather lackluster response. The Superman story was one of several action-packed tales in a new comic book titled *Action Comics*, but the superhero's picture was not even on the cover. The first three issues sold moderately well, but the fourth issue unexpectedly sold out. When Donenfeld learned that Superman was the draw, he had the superhero plastered on the cover of the following issues. Sales of *Action Comics* soon reached 900,000 copies a month. Superman was such a success that DC gave him his own book in 1939, although Superman stories continued in *Action Comics*. By 1940, sales reached 1,250,000 copies

[1]U.S. Bureau of the Census, *Statistical Abstract of the U.S.: 1997*, 117th ed. (Washington, D.C.: U.S. Government Printing Office, 1997), 565.

The Yellow Kid
Created in the 1890s for Joseph Pulitzer's *New York World*, Richard Outcault's "The Yellow Kid" holds the distinction of being the first newspaper comic strip. To critics, the toothless, virtually witless boy seemed to epitomize New York's sensational press, and they began referring to its techniques as "yellow journalism."

a month.

With Superman's success, other now-familiar superheroes followed: Batman in 1939, Captain Marvel in 1940, Captain America in 1941, and Spiderman and the Incredible Hulk in 1962. The superheroes seemed to reflect the mood of the day, and comic book plots often mirrored the concerns of readers. This was most apparent during World War II, when superheroes defended the American way of life by dispatching spies, Nazi troops, and saboteurs. Even before the United States entered the war, patriotic comic book artists joined the fray. Many stories featured superheroes attired in red, white, and blue, and addressed the fears of spies, invasions, and sabotage. The Sub-Mariner and the Wizard attacked German sailors; Yank and Doodle, "America's Fighting Twins," beat up Nazi villains; and Captain America, the superpatriot, battled spies. In 1941 alone, three female patriotic characters debuted: Miss America, Miss Victory, and Pat Patriot. One series, *Military Comics*, devoted its pages entirely to adventure tales of the Army and Navy.

After the war, with enemies not as well defined, superheroes lost much of their appeal. They either disappeared or had to look for new jobs. Batman fought organized crime, and Superman rescued innocent victims of crime and natural disasters. The Korean War encouraged more combat comic books in the early 1950s. The national hysteria surrounding communism provided fodder for characters like Yellow Claw, a Communist Chinese villain. In an unusual twist, however, the hero of the series was also Chinese. Comic book publishers turned to other subjects to boost sales.

Changing Comic Book Characters

Not all superheroes were male, though female characters rarely appeared in the original comic books of the 1930s. A few exceptions — Sandra of the Secret Service, Dale Daring, and Sheena, Queen of the Jungle — appeared in the late 1930s. As early as 1942, Wonder Woman showed she could be just as much the hero as Superman or Batman. When Marvel Comics introduced female comic book characters in 1943, it discovered almost by accident that teenage girls could be comic book fans. Soon, characters designed to appeal to girls populated the newsstand shelves: Miss America, a female version of Captain America; Patsy Walker, a teenager whose antics and adventures eventually led her to assume the mantle of Miss America; Millie the Model; Nellie the Nurse; the Blonde Phantom, a masked crime fighter with movie-star glamour; and Mary Marvel, Captain Marvel's little sister.

Glamour girls, looking every bit the pinup, became popular comic book subjects in the 1940s. These dimwitted, sexy girls did not fight crime but did presage another trend in comics: romance. The late 1940s and early '50s were rife with comics such as *Secret Romances*, *Young Love*, and *Sweethearts* — subjects sparked by pulp magazines like *True Confessions*. By the end of 1949, romance comics outsold every other genre.

Other popular comic book lines emerged around 1950. Horror comics became especially popular. With titles like *Adventures into the Unknown*, *Eerie*, and *Tales from the Crypt*, the stories echoed the trend toward science fiction and horror at the movies. The glut of cowboy programs on television fueled a similar interest in comic books with western themes.

Alongside the western and horror stories and the crime-fighting superheroes, silly and humorous comic books filled the newsstand shelves. Familiar faces like Mickey Mouse, Donald Duck, and Woody Woodpecker shared shelf space with lesser-knowns such as Rufus Lion and Ziggy Pig. Most of the animal humor portrayed slapstick comedy, but *Mad*'s satire and Archie and Jughead's teen humor offered slightly more sophisticated fare.

The 1950s, however, saw growing criticism of comic book content, especially crime and horror. Literary critics, psychologists, and the mass media combined forces to condemn comic books, claiming they contributed to juvenile delinquency. To the alarm of children everywhere, teachers, civic, and religious leaders encouraged the burning of comic books. One photograph taken at the time showed a smug adult tending the fire, while obviously dismayed boys looked on. The misgivings of parents and civic leaders led, in 1954, to the establishment of the Comics Code Authority, which awarded its stamp of approval to comic books that cut out the crime, horror, sex, and gore. A combination of factors, including competition from television and a miniature golf craze,

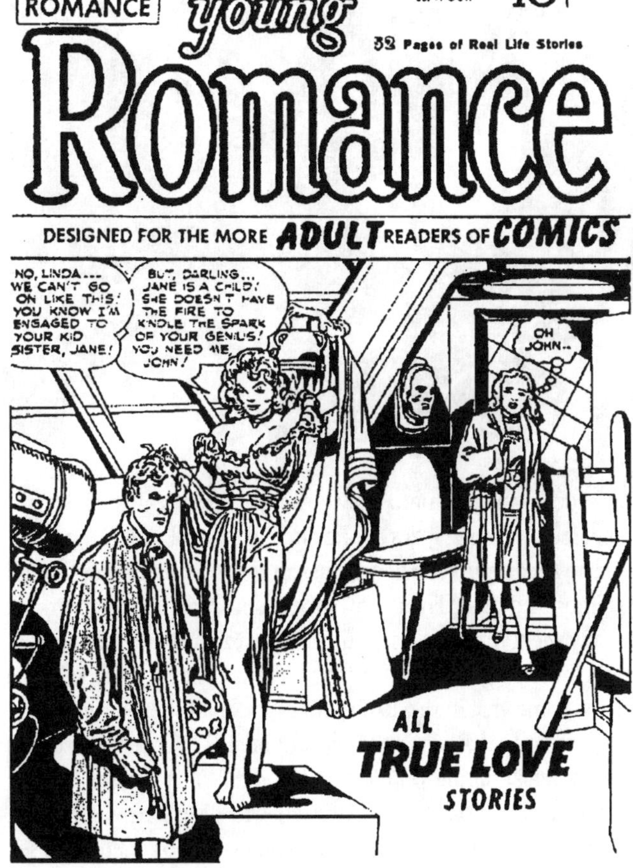

Romance for Young Girls
Shortly after World War II, *Young Romance* introduced the romance genre to comic book publishing. Its main audience was teenage girls, who became comic book readers by the millions. By 1949, romance comics outsold every other genre.

led to a significant decline in comic book sales between 1952 and 1956, prompting some to observe that the Golden Age of comics was over.

Criticized in the 1960s for emphasis on whites and males, Marvel Comics tried to reflect more egalitarian views by including women and minority characters. The superhero Black Panther, who emerged as a character in a story in 1966, eventually claimed his own series in 1973. *Luke Cage, Hero for Hire* was the first series to be named after a black character. Cage, who debuted in 1972, eventually became Power Man and lasted until 1986. *Master of Kung Fu*, in 1974, introduced an Asian hero. A 1972 series featuring a Native American hero, *Red Wolf*, survived for only nine issues.

Few female characters lasted long. When the women's movement intensified in the 1970s, Marvel tried several female characters. Most of them failed, but Spider-Woman and She-Hulk, both spin-offs of male superheroes, became relatively successful. In spite of the success of a few strong female characters, however, most of the women in comic books have been helpless, scantily dressed, and in bondage. Comic book covers have often used voluptuous, practically naked women to attract male buyers. The tactic is similar to that used by beer and automobile ads on television.

Since the beginning of comic books, so-called "underground comics" have tackled subjects that mainstream comics would only skirt around. No subject was taboo for the authors. Highly charged political satire, explicit sex and violence, depictions of bodily functions, and drug use characterized underground comics. Despite several pornography suits in the 1970s, underground comics flourished. They did not account for a large part of comic book sales, but they did stretch the limit of what the "straight" comics considered acceptable.

A Thriving Industry

In recent years, comic book publishers have enjoyed huge success with outside ventures. Batman movies have been tremendously lucrative; the first one grossed well over $250 million. Superman, Dick Tracy, the Rocketeer, and the Crow have all inspired movies. Television networks have benefited from series featuring Superman, Batman, Wonder Woman, Spiderman, and the Incredible Hulk. Action figures and other toys have earned many more millions of dollars. Batman's merchandising alone has sold more than $650 million.

Although other entertainment media have captured the attention and money of youthful consumers, the comic book industry continues to thrive, raking in around $900 million a year. A little over half of that figure comes from comic book sales; the rest, from related merchandising. Clever marketing schemes help push comic book sales figures higher. In 1992, DC Comics killed off Superman, and retailers sold over 3,500,000 copies of the issue. Vintage comic books have a market of their own, as prices of old comic books soar above $100,000. Many new comics supplement television shows, movies, and video games. Some comic books are making it onto computer on-line services.[2] Although the comic book itself is rather low-tech, the comic book industry has found a way to endure competition with more sophisticated media.

The Recording Industry

When Thomas Edison invented the phonograph in 1877, he had no idea how important his little machine would be to music. He believed it would be most useful to business people, who could record letters on the wax cylinders. The device could protect private information from nosy stenographers.[3] In fact, the generic term for the phonograph, "talking machine," reflects its early use. Edison did not focus on the phonograph's musical potential until the early 1890s.

[2]Gayle Sato Stodder, "Comic Book Publishing," *Entrepreneur*, January 1994, 306; Anna Robaton, "Music Chains Add Comics to Mix; Similar Demographics Entice Retailers," *Billboard*, 15 September 1994, 68; "Today's Superheroes are Surfing the Info Highway" *Business Week*, 5 September 1994, 86.

[3]Thomas A. Edison, "The Phonograph and Its Future," *North American Review* (May-June, 1878): 531-2.

Music Recording, 1900
In the early days of music recording, the artists were required to sing into horns attached to the recording device. For quiet passages, they had to lean closer to the horn. Sometimes, singers forgot to change their distance, and their voice was inaudible on the record.

Emile Berliner, in 1887, made some changes and improvements to Edison's phonograph. The result was the Gramophone, which played flat discs instead of the cylinders that Edison used. Berliner also developed a method for duplicating records in 1893. Until then, every record sold was a first-generation recording taken directly from the performance. To make multiple copies of the same musical number, engineers surrounded the performers with several recording phonographs, started them at the same time and recorded the performance on all machines simultaneously. After the song ended, the engineers replaced the freshly recorded discs or cylinders with uncut ones, and the performance was repeated, ad nauseam, until they made enough copies to fill the order.

By 1900, record manufacturers had developed a relatively sophisticated method of recording, especially for the Gramophone disc. Technicians placed a highly polished zinc disc, coated with a thin layer of fat, on a turntable. A sound made through the horn of the recording device vibrated a diaphragm, which in turn vibrated a stylus. The stylus traced a spiral groove through the layer of fat as the turntable revolved, leaving a thin, spiral line of exposed zinc. When the artist and the engineer were satisfied with the results of a take, technicians immersed the disc in acid for about ten minutes. The acid ate at the exposed zinc, leaving a narrow groove that, when played back, reproduced the original sound fairly accurately. A typical record could hold about two minutes of music.

Up until the time musical recordings became available to the public, most popular music gained exposure through sheet music. Since most middle and upper-class homes had pianos, the market for sheet music was large. Publishers devised many creative ways to bring songs to the attention of the public in order to sell sheet music. Song pluggers, employed by publishing houses, helped popularize the songs. Some pluggers played songs from flatbed trucks in downtown areas; others played songs on department store pianos; still more convinced popular vaudeville players to use their songs on-stage. Perhaps the most inventive method of plugging involved prepared pictorial representations of the songs on slides projected onto movie theater screens. The slides also contained the song lyrics so the audience could sing along.

The sheet music business was cut down in its prime, though, by improved recordings. Why should someone go to the trouble to buy sheet music and spend hours learning it when all one had to do was play the song on the Victrola? Sheet music sales declined somewhat in the 1910s, but music publishers did not mind since record sales were soaring. Around 1922, when radio broadcasters began airing popular music, publishing houses howled. Although the broadcasters were able to give a new song phenomenal exposure, the life of that song was shortened from several months or years to only a few weeks. Since broadcasters played popular new songs several times a day, the public tired of them quickly, often before they bought the sheet music or recording. Music publishers, as a result, made less money on each new song and needed a constant supply of fresh tunes.

Early musical recordings consisted mainly of vocal selections and brass bands. Instrumental solos were also common. The first musical recording was a cornet solo of "Yankee Doodle" performed in 1878 in a demonstration of the phonograph in New York City.[4] Recording companies chose their selections with care, to de-emphasize the limitations of the phonograph's recording capabilities. The voice, with its limited frequency range, and the flashy brass band with its ensemble sound were practical choices. Brass bands were so popular, in fact, that they accounted for one-third of the selections offered in the Gramophone Company's catalogues before 1914.

Popular music made up most of the choices in the record catalogues partly because the subtle nuances of most classical compositions would be lost in the crude method used for recording. Compared to today's high-tech studios, early acoustic recording methods were primitive. Some recording studios were merely sheds or rented hotel rooms, containing a piano or small orchestra crammed together on a high platform. The recording phono-

[4]Fred W. Gaisberg, *The Music Goes Round* (New York: MacMillan, 1942), 83; Robert Dearling and Cecilia Dearling, *The Guinness Book of Recorded Sound*, with Brian Rust (Middlesex, England: Guinness Books, 1984), 21, 30.

graph also sat high and had a small horn into which the artists sang or played. In order to be heard, a singer stood and sang into the horn. For quieter passages, the singer had to lean toward the horn so the machine could pick up the words. When the artist increased volume, he or she would have to pull away so the sound would not be distorted. Madame Oberon, a Wagnerian soprano, had to stand ten feet away from the recording horn because her high notes knocked the recording needle off the master disc. Often, the artist would forget to move back and forth. Since it was the engineer's responsibility to ensure the recording was made, he frequently had to pull and push the performer back and forth to get the best results. This frequently created an antipathy between artist and engineer.[5]

Another reason popular tunes made up the bulk of the catalogs was that, for many years, prominent opera stars refused to make recordings. The quality of the recordings had to improve before they would deign to make them. Operatic singers jealously guarded their reputations, believing the phonograph could not display their voices to best advantage. Also, opera singers were accustomed to luxury and adoration from fans. The recording sessions could be long and arduous. The unfamiliar surroundings of the recording studio were distracting; singing into a horn was, to say the least, unfulfilling.

As the mechanics of recording improved sound quality, singers became less reluctant. The most important figure in improving the mechanics was Eldridge Johnson, a New Jersey craftsman and model-maker. He designed a spring motor to replace Berliner's hand-wound apparatus and was granted a contract to produce 200 such motors. He made other improvements to the machine: a mechanism to ensure constant turntable speed, an enhanced sound box, and an improved record using shellac instead of hard rubber. He continually improved Berliner's machine, ultimately salvaged Berliner's Gramophone Company, and reorganized it into the Victor Talking Machine Company. Then, in 1902, operating under the names Victor Talking Machines and Victor Records, he recorded the great tenor Enrico Caruso in Milan, Italy. Soon, other opera stars followed Caruso into the recording business — thus giving birth to popular recorded music.

Caruso's success sparked a new interest in classical music for many people previously unexposed to it. Instead of paying high ticket prices to see an orchestra or opera performance, people could buy an inexpensive record and listen to a piece over and over again.

Enrico Caruso, Superstar
In 1902, Victor Records recorded the great tenor Enrico Caruso in Milan, Italy. Because of his immense popularity as a classic opera performer, he suddenly made recorded music seem respectable to other opera stars. Soon, many of them followed him into the recording business — thus giving birth to popular recorded music. Caruso's recordings sparked a new interest in classical music and made it available to members of the public who could not afford opera tickets.

The Fad Turns Mainstream

At first, the American public looked on the phonograph as a nov-

[5]Gaisberg, *The Music Goes Round*, 38, 40; "How it Feels to Sing for the Phonograph," *Literary Digest*, 10 May 1924, 28-9; Joe Higgins, interview by Columbia University Oral History Office, November 1959, transcript, Columbia University Oral History Collection, New York City, 1935; Arthur Judson, interview, in John Harvith and Susan Edwards Harvith, eds. *Edison, Musicians, and the Phonograph: A Century in Retrospect*, Contributions to the Study of Music and Dance Series, number 11 (Westport, Conn.: Greenwood Press, 1987), 89.

elty or fad. When other inventors made improvements in the performance and sound of the machine, however, the public took notice and phonograph sales jumped. By 1922, over six million families owned phonographs. Record sales jumped, too. Record companies made 2.7 million cylinders and discs in 1899. That number rose to over 27 million in 1914 and to nearly 107 million by 1919. Consumers bought an average of thirty-five records for every phonograph.[6]

When radio broadcasting became wildly popular in the early 1920s, many record companies blamed the new media for a decline in sales. That is partly true, but radio eventually helped popularize records. Many phonograph manufacturers merged with radio manufacturers to create combination units that contained both a radio and a phonograph. The union seems natural today, but during the 1920s and '30s, the two industries were bitter enemies.

Ironically, radio technology contributed to a significant improvement in phonograph technology: electrical recording and playback. The Victor Talking Machine Company introduced the first electrical phonograph in 1925. Using microphones, vacuum tubes, and loudspeakers—all radio technologies—the electrical impulses translated into a "much warmer and more natural" sound, replacing the old morning glory-shaped sound horn on the phonograph.[7]

Artistically, the 1930s and '40s were tremendous years for the recording industry. The Big Band sounds of Glenn Miller and Benny Goodman livened the air with dance music. The crooning style of singing ushered in an era of such stars as Bing Crosby and Rudy Vallee. In 1932, the first disc jockey program hit the airwaves in Los Angeles. Radio stations had been using records for programming since the experimental days, but records were used mostly as filler and were considered inferior to live programming. Los Angeles station KFWB is widely considered to be the first station to program a disc jockey show. Al Jarvis' *Make Believe Ballroom* succeeded, in part, because of the way he highlighted the records. Using his listeners' imaginations, Jarvis created the illusion of a ballroom full of dancers. In this fictitious ballroom, the greatest bands and singers of the day played especially for the listening audience. Jarvis introduced the musicians, pretending to talk to them in between numbers, much like an emcee.[8] The innovative program made an impression on Martin Block, a young announcer who, in 1935, copied the idea for independent station WNEW in New York City. Block later became the highest paid disc jockey in the country, earning as much as $750,000 per year in the late 1940s. By 1955, radio stations across the country played more than 300,000 records a day.[9]

The recording industry did not entirely ignore black performers and listeners, although until the 1950s, record companies promoted "race music" separately from music directed toward whites. "Race music" was a generic term for almost any black-oriented popular music until the terms "blues" and "rhythm and blues" came into vogue in the 1950s to distinguish it from jazz. Many radio stations would not play race music even after it became popular, because the lyrics often were sexually suggestive. White artists recorded cleaned-up versions of popular race records, and often the cover versions outsold the originals. Motown music, a descendant of rhythm and blues, finally brought black artists into the mainstream in the mid- to late-1950s. The Miracles, the Supremes, and the Marvelettes, among others, combined influences from blues, gospel, pop, and jazz to create a recognizable sound that appealed to a wide audience, both black and white. By the mid-1960s, Motown Records was selling more 45 r.p.m. records than any other record company.

With records so popular on the radio, popularity charts began

"The King of Swing"
Along with such "big band" leaders as Glenn Miller, Tommy Dorsey, and Artie Shaw, Benny Goodman pioneered a new music style of "swing." In contrast to the leisurely orchestral dance music so prominent in the early 1930s, swing was a lively music based on New Orleans jazz and attracted a young following. Among the big band musicians, Goodman, pictured above when he was about twenty years old sporting his trademark white pocket handkerchief, is credited with starting the swing craze.

[6] "Phonograph Sales Show Big Growth," *New York Times*, 22 January 1922, sec. II, 13; "Phonograph Rivals Motor Car's Vogue," *New York Times*, 12 March 1922, sec. II, 10.

[7] Milton Gabler, interview by Columbia University Oral History Office, November 1959, transcript, Columbia University Oral History Collection, New York City, p. 1879.

[8] "Radio Showmanship," *Variety*, 14 August 1935, 46.

[9] Paul Ackerman, "300,000 Spins a Day Throw Music Industry Into Whirl," *Billboard*, 12 November 1955, 1.

appearing in the industry trade publications. Prior to 1958, record companies reported their own sales figures. Those claims may or may not have been correct — at any rate, they were unaudited. In 1958, the Recording Industry Association of America (RIAA) began auditing and certifying record sales. At that time, an album needed $1 million in manufacturer's sales to be considered "gold." Since 1975, though, albums must sell half a million copies worth at least $1 million. Singles (records having only one song on each side) need to sell a million copies. The first certified gold record (a single) was awarded on March 14, 1958, to Perry Como for "Catch a Falling Star." The RIAA's program for platinum certification for albums began in 1976. Requirements for platinum albums and singles doubled the requirements for gold albums and singles. The first platinum record was awarded to the Eagles on February 24, 1976, for the album *Their Greatest Hits*. The biggest-selling single of all time is Elton John's memorial to Princess Diana of Great Britain, a remake of his "Candle in the Wind" (originally written as a tribute to the movie star Marilyn Monroe). The perenniel favorite "White Christmas," written by Irving Berlin and sung by Bing Crosby, has sold more 30,000,000 copies in North America alone. In its versions by other singers, it has sold more than 170,000,000. Michael Jackson's *Thriller* is the most successful album ever, selling over 47,000,000 copies worldwide.[10]

Bing Crosby
In the 1930s and 1940s, America's most popular recording star was Bing Crosby. The advertisement above was for his weekly radio show. His song "White Christmas," from the 1942 movie *Holiday Inn*, has sold more copies – 170 million – than any other record in history.

Recording Technology

The introduction of stereo recording and playback in the mid-1950s helped fuel another era of prosperity for the record industry. Prior to stereo, all recordings were monaural, which meant that the sound was recorded on only one channel and sounded like one was listening with only one ear. Stereo recording, on the other hand, uses two channels and is the equivalent of listening with two ears. In a stereo recording of an orchestra, for instance, the violins sitting on the left side of the stage will sound as if they are playing out of the left speaker.

Magnetic tape, brought to the United States after World War II, made multitrack recordings possible. Today, multitrack recording is the standard. Multitrack recording allows an artist to record one instrument or voice at a time on separate tracks. All of the tracks are combined, or mixed down, into two tracks for stereo effect. Multitrack recording is ideal for classical music since the recording engineer can record solos on separate tracks from the whole orchestra and emphasize those solos in the mix-down. Multitrack recording makes it possible for musicians to play more than one instrument on the same song. A six-piece band may actually use only one performer. Todd Rundgren, Paul McCartney, Stevie Wonder, and Prince, to name just a few, have all done this routinely.

The compact disc, introduced to consumers in 1983, was the next important development in recording technology. The CD is significant because it reproduces sound digitally. The disc itself contains strings of microscopic pits that represent the music. A tiny, low-intensity laser beam reads the patterns of pits and translates the data into music. A phonograph needle can wear out the grooves on a record, but a laser does not wear down the data on a CD. Another attractive feature is the fact that the discs are harder to damage than traditional vinyl records or cassette tapes. Originally priced at over $1,000, the first CD players were targeted primarily at audiophiles — those consumers who put a premium on exceptional playback and spent thousands of dollars on stereo systems. Early compact discs were primarily of classical recordings and cost around $25 each. In the late 1980s, CD and CD player prices fell, while the selection of music increased, allowing the average consumer to afford the technology. Today, the CD has displaced the vinyl record and the cassette tape as the medium of choice. Satisfactory players can be bought for under $100 and CDs for as little as $3. The average price of a CD is about $12. In 1996, manufacturers shipped nearly 779 million compact discs.[11]

New digital recording media continued to emerge in recent years but did not grow much in popularity. The Digital Audio Tape (DAT), introduced in the late 1980s, looked like a small cassette tape but recorded and played back the music digitally. Perhaps one reason for its limited success was that the players cost $700 or more. In addition, prerecorded tapes cost $15 and up and were hard to find. Sony introduced its MiniDisc (MD) in 1993. The MD

[10]Irwin Stambler, *Encyclopedia of Pop, Rock & Soul*, rev. ed. (New York: St. Martin's Press, 1989), 769, 831; *Guinness Book of World Records, 1995* (Enfield, Great Britain: Guiness Publishing, Ltd., 1994), 154; "Guinness Touts Elton as World's Hottest," http://www.mtv.com/mtv/news/gallery/j/johne971021.html, accessed 13 January 1999.

[11]U.S. Bureau of the Census, *Statistical Abstract of the U.S.: 1997*, 569.

Elvis Presley

Poor Mississippi Boy Becomes Media's Biggest Superstar

One of the defining elements of the 1950s was the emergence of rock 'n' roll and Elvis Presley, who became known as the King of rock 'n' roll and, later, simply as the King.

From humble beginnings as the son of a Mississippi sharecropper, Elvis became a superstar through his music, movies, and television appearances. He signed with Sun Records in Memphis, Tennessee, in 1954 and a year later contracted with RCA Victor to record some of his biggest hits, "Heartbreak Hotel," "Don't Be Cruel," "Blue Suede Shoes," and "(You Ain't Nothin' But a) Hound Dog."

In 1958, at the height of his initial popularity, he was inducted into the Army and showed that even he, like all young American men, was subject to the demands of the Cold War.

Elvis starred in more than thirty movies, among them *Love Me Tender*, *King Creole*, and *Blue Hawaii*. Most of the movies were merely vehicles to showcase his singing, and it was his musical appeal that kept him among the world's favorite performers.

After a period of relative lackluster success in the early 1960s, Elvis launched a comeback through a series of highly popular concerts and television specials in 1968. His "Aloha from Hawaii" television special in 1973 was broadcast via satellite to half a billion people in forty countries.

On August 16, 1977, Elvis Presley died of an apparent heart attack, complicated by an increasing dependence upon prescription drugs and an indulgent lifestyle. He was buried at Graceland, his stately southern mansion in Memphis, and thousands of fans visit there every year to pay their respects. His legacy lives on as his music, movies, and the industry he left behind bring in millions of dollars from those who still regard him as the King.

Tamara Baldwin
Southeast Missouri State University

Fans of Elvis Presley can argue persuasively that he is the biggest entertainment star ever. After making his first million-selling record, "Heartbreak Hotel," in January 1956, he recorded more than sixty other songs that sold a million or more copies and had twenty that made it to number one on the national music charts. In two consecutive years — 1956 and 1957 — he had the top records of the year: "Don't Be Cruel/Hound Dog" and "All Shook Up." Altogether, his records sold more than 350 million copies. He starred in more than thirty movies, and his soundtrack album to *Blue Hawaii* in 1961 remained at number one for twenty weeks. A later rock star, Bruce Springsteen, said of him, "There have been a lot of tough guys. There have been pretenders. There have been contenders. But there is only one King." The three photographs here show him at different stages in his career: upon his return to performing following service in the U.S. Army (top, with entertainers Joey Bishop, Frank Sinatra, Nancy Sinatra, and Sammy Davis Jr.), early in his career (middle), and later (bottom) when he made a singing comeback with a glitzier approach.

looked much like a small computer diskette but was really a recordable optical digital disc. The MiniDisc suffered from the same problems as the DAT: an MD player/recorder cost at least $500, and the hard-to-find prerecorded discs themselves usually cost between $15 and $40. Another digital recording method, called "tapeless" recording, stores digitally recorded sound in a computer, allowing recording engineers to access easily any part of the recording for corrections and editing. This method of recording is especially useful for movie soundtracks but, at this point, has no practical value for the home consumer.

Criticism of Popular Music

The music industry has been subjected to continuous criticism. In the 1920s, social critics censured popular music recordings, believing they lowered the tastes of the common person. Later, popular music, especially rock 'n' roll, garnered criticism from those afraid that it would atrophy the brain, cause delinquency, or incite crime. Rock 'n' roll music and its descendants have come under especially harsh criticism for language and music video content.

In the 1980s, the Parents' Music Resource Center (PMRC) influenced the recording industry to label albums that contained explicit lyrics. There was no legal reason a minor could not purchase an album, but the PMRC wanted parents to know which albums were "anti-social." That way parents could make decisions about the music their children bought.

Labeling records became common in the late 1980s, but the criticism did not stop. Rap artist Ice-T's song "Cop Killer" created such an uproar that his company pulled the album off the shelves and re-released it without the offending song. Gangsta rap came under fire for the violent content of lyrics. Some crimes have been loosely linked to the music of gangsta rappers. The criticism of pop music is akin to the criticism comic books experienced in the 1940s and '50s. Not all of the music came under attack, just that with violent or sexual content.

While the process of recording music has not changed significantly since the late 1960s, the recording industry has. In the late 1980s and early 1990s, the industry made a move toward consolidation of the larger companies. In contrast, some smaller independent record labels suddenly experienced tremendous success when their artists became stars. DGC, which released the multiplatinum album *Nevermind* by the group Nirvana, grew exponentially as the group and its album climbed the charts. Another small label, Epitaph, also had significant growth when one of its artists, Offspring, released an album that quickly became popular. The success of Offspring's album, *Smash*, is even more remarkable when one realizes that Epitaph, unlike many small labels, did not have a contract with a major record company to distribute the albums to record stores.

A newer and less restricted method of distribution gained in popularity in the 1990s. Some groups, such as Aerosmith, R.E.M., and the Rolling Stones, began offering samples of their new releases over computer on-line services such as America Online and CompuServe. Subscribers to the services could download samples of music to their home computers. This method of distribution allowed artists to bypass the record companies and go straight to the public with their music. The band Cinderella even auditioned new drummers through the on-line service. Applicants downloaded a thirty-second music track, added their own drum track to it, and then uploaded it back to the group.[12]

The recording industry learned early on that it must adapt to new competition. Today, new technologies allow for experimentation with sounds, recording media, and distribution. Some of the larger companies are merging and creating entertainment monoliths. At the same time, the system is fragmenting, allowing unknown bands and labels to get their music to their audiences. But the industry is keeping up with the changes, apparently, and competing successfully for consumer dollars. Annual sales grew from $200 million in the early 1950s to over $12.5 billion in 1997.

The Film Industry

Although Thomas Edison usually gets the credit for inventing the movie camera, his work was based on experiments by others. Eadweard Muybridge started the process around 1874 with his sequential photographs of a running horse. To catch the horse in motion, he ran several wires across a racetrack to still cameras. As the horse ran past each camera, it tripped the wires, causing the camera to take a still picture. The result was a series of still pictures, which Muybridge then placed on a disc that was rotated in front of a projector to give the image of the running horse. Muybridge's results inspired Edison to experiment with motion photography.

In 1891, Edison received the patents for the Kinetograph, or movie camera, and the Kinetoscope, a machine that allowed the viewer to look through a peep-hole at the moving film. Since the Kinetograph weighed about a ton and could not be moved easily, Edison's films were made in a studio that moved to catch the sunlight. The subjects were shot in full sun against a black backdrop. The earliest films, of animals and humans performing tricks, received an enthusiastic response from the public. But Edison moved on to other projects. As with Edison's phonograph, the motion picture was left to others to develop its commercial potential.

A pair of French brothers, Auguste and Louis Lumiere, developed a portable camera and projector combined in one unit. They presented their first films to audiences in the basement of a Paris cafe in 1895. These films were not staged like Edison's Kinetoscope films. The Lumieres simply set up a camera and filmed events taking place in front of them. *Workers Leaving the Lumiere Factory*, *Boat Leaving the Harbor*, and *Fish Market at Marseilles* were typical examples of their slice-of-life films. The subject matter may not have been especially interesting, but audiences en-

[12]James Daly, "Totally Wired," *Rolling Stone*, 1 December 1994, 40.

The Nickelodeon
The earliest movie theaters were "nickelodeons," where audiences paid a nickel to see a short silent film on a small screen with a pianist providing musical accompaniment. When not showing films, the nickelodeons offered live stage performances.

joyed the novelty of seeing events recorded and shown at a later time.

Screenings of films moved from cafe basements to vaudeville theaters, opera houses, and music halls. Proprietors showed the short films in addition to the regular stage program as filler or a curiosity. Soon, these venues were devoting one or two evenings a week exclusively to films. Other entrepreneurs presented films in "black tops" — tents that had the top dyed black to block out daylight. Around the turn of the century the first movie theaters were established. These were usually screened-off sections at the back of an arcade, but as films proved popular with the public, movie houses devoted entirely to showing films sprang up around the country. Most shows cost only a nickel. The term nickelodeon came from combining "nickel" and "odeon," the French word for theater. Although "nickelodeon" later referred to coin-operated musical instruments or phonographs, it originally meant simply "Five-cent Theater." Nickelodeons were often regular buildings with a fancy facade added to attract attention. Around 1912, the nickelodeon era began to die out as theater owners began building movie palaces — large, ornate buildings built specifically for showing movies. These buildings often cost hundreds of thousands of dollars to build. Their primary purpose was to show movies, but most had traditional stages, orchestra pits, fly lofts, and dressing rooms for live stage performances so the theater owners could offer a variety of entertainment.

Early films had no sound. Producers designed them so that the action on the screen told most of the story. If the action got a little complicated, plot cards edited into the film advanced the story line. A pianist or organist usually accompanied films with a musical score that fit the mood of the action on the screen.

Silent films were more sophisticated than most people realize. In fact, most basic film techniques were developed during the silent era: editing, close-ups, multiple exposures, slow- and fast-motion shots, and moving cameras. Improvements on these building blocks have continued as technology has improved. Filmmakers produced silent films in all genres, including drama, science fiction, documentary, comedy, western, and action.

It was during the silent era that movie stars originated. Mary Pickford, Charlie Chaplin, and Douglas Fairbanks all began their careers in the legitimate theater but gravitated toward Hollywood. Many actors could not make the transition from stage to screen, but those who did found more fame and fortune in Hollywood than was ever possible in the theater.

The United States government made good use of that star power during World War I to help sell Liberty Loans to the American public. Pickford, Chaplin, and Fairbanks all helped the war effort by making personal appearances and filming short "trailers," or short films shown along with feature films, exhorting moviegoers to participate in the Liberty Loans program.

Woodrow Wilson, seeking a public relations outlet for war messages, set up the Committee on Public Information (CPI) to take charge of disseminating war films produced by the Signal Corps. George Creel, chairman of the committee, was a sort of press agent for the war effort. As such, he had to invent a method of reaching movie-going audiences with official government war messages. Prior to the CPI's founding, war films produced by the Signal Corps had been distributed rather haphazardly by the Red Cross through its fundraising meetings. Creel realized that, in order to make an impact, government films had to be distributed like commercial motion pictures: through movie theaters. He established the Division of Films in order to do just that. Unfortunately, the film industry was exceedingly fragmented, and it was impossible to get complete dissemination of the films through established channels of distribution. The government had the same distribution problems any commercial film producer had getting the final product to the public. As a result, the Division of Films produced only four war films, but each did achieve fairly wide circulation.

The war in Europe had a favorable effect for American filmmakers. Prior to the war, London was the center of the world film

Movie Milestones
Along with director D.W. Griffith's *Birth of a Nation*, two early motion pictures stand out as landmarks. Produced by Edison's kinetoscope process, *The Great Train Robbery*, made in 1903, was the first film to put together a series of scenes in one coherent narrative. Edison produced this ad to sell the film to exhibitors. *The Jazz Singer*, which was made in 1927, was the first full-length film with synchronized sound. Contrasted with the silent movies, it was a "talkie." Many producers considered sound a passing fad, but by 1929 silents had virtually disappeared.

trade. The war changed that dramatically as American producers capitalized on Europe's misfortune. Hollywood has been the world film leader ever since.

The Talkies Arrive

The introduction of sound to motion pictures was a tortuous process. Edison synchronized phonographs with films as early as 1894, but his attempts were not commercially successful. Other experimenters followed, including radio pioneer Lee De Forest. It was not until 1924 that Western Electric, the same company that invented electrical recording, developed the Vitaphone, a system similar to Edison's. The Vitaphone allowed a musical score to be recorded and synchronized with the film. In 1926, Warner Brothers released the first sound picture, *Don Juan*, starring John Barrymore and Mary Astor. *Don Juan* received a favorable response from the $10-a-seat premiere audience. Nevertheless, most major studios were wary of sound pictures. The earliest Vitaphone pictures did not synchronize voices with the films, but in 1927 *The Jazz Singer*, starring Al Jolson, did just that. Box office records tumbled as enthusiastic crowds filled theaters to see the newest wonder of the world. *The Jazz Singer* ushered in a new era of filmmaking, requiring new studios, new theater equipment, and new acting techniques. Not all actors made the transition from silents to talkies. Some did not have the voices to fit their images; others simply could not act.

Despite the thrill of the talkies, the Great Depression affected the movie industry harshly. Competition from radio, which entertained for free, kept audiences home from the theaters. By 1932, movie attendance had dropped by 30% from the beginning of the Depression in 1929. Many small studios were unable to survive, but others emerged relatively unscathed. While we may think of the movies made in the 1930s as great classic films, many of them were produced inexpensively on assembly-line schedules. There were exceptions, of course. Busby Berkley's intricately choreographed extravaganzas, such as *Gold Diggers of 1935* and *Varsity Show*, used scores of dancers and hundreds of costumes and cost around $10,000 for each minute on the screen. By the end of the 1930s, most studios were regaining strength and preparing to support the U.S. war effort.

When World War II threatened to involve the United States, the movie industry, along with most other industries, swung into wartime production. Much like the comic book industry, Hollywood demonstrated its patriotism by distributing anti-Nazi propaganda with zeal. The U.S. government, through the Office of War Information (OWI), assisted filmmakers in producing war films. Chief of Staff Gen. George C. Marshall recruited celebrated director Frank Capra to produce *Why We Fight*, a series of seven films to indoctrinate recruits. The government encouraged Hollywood to use its resources to keep up morale, instill a sense of duty, and combat Axis propaganda. Many movie stars enlisted in the service or volunteered to entertain troops, setting an example for their fans to follow. Even with shortages of materials needed to make movies, including raw film, the studios churned out almost as many new features during the war as they had during peacetime.

World War II benefited the movie industry in two main ways. First, wartime jobs put an end to the Depression. Many people who had been out of work were now employed and had money to spend. Theaters sold between 85 and 100 million tickets per week. The second thing the war did for Hollywood was to put a temporary stop to television development. America needed all of its resources for the war effort, which meant that unnecessary research and manufacturing slowed to a halt. The Federal Communications Commission stopped issuing licenses for experimental television stations (although existing stations could still broadcast) and television manufacturers converted their plants to war production.

Movie Palaces
As film-going became a hugely popular American pastime in the 1930s, theater owners built larger and more opulent facilities. The Trans-Lux theater in Manhattan offered not only movies but a full schedule of newsreels and other fare.

Competition for Movies

The movie industry suffered, though, when the war ended. Television stations multiplied quickly, and consumers snatched up the primitive television sets at a rate of 200,000 per month in 1948. Movies also felt the effects of the return to one-income families as servicemen returned home to their old jobs and women returned to duty as housewives. New entertainment fads, like miniature golf and bowling, took time and money away from the movies. By 1956, weekly movie attendance had fallen to fewer than 47,000,000 people.

While Hollywood was down economically, it also suffered a blow to its reputation. After the war, U.S.-Soviet relations deteriorated, and anti-Communist passions and fears rose, leading Congress to convene several hearings investigating the Communist influence on the movie industry. The hearings led to blacklists, jail sentences, and suicides for some members of the Hollywood community. Those on the blacklist could not find employment in Hollywood under their own names for a long time, if ever again. Studio executives fired employees who would not cooperate in the hearings, feeling they had to do something to calm public fears that the studios were infested with Communists. Some uncooperative witnesses were charged with contempt of Congress and sentenced to jail. Hollywood's reputation has never fully recovered from the damage done by this "Red Scare."

Ever since a scantily-dressed (for 1895) woman undulated across a Kinetoscope lens, the content of some films has raised public ire. *Dolorita in the Passion Dance* was banned in Atlantic City in 1895, but her legacy continues. The film industry was unable (or unwilling) to abide by a voluntary production code until the mid-1930s, when the Catholic Church's Legion of Decency began its campaigns against objectionable movies. Producers, hesitant to antagonize the meager audiences of the Depression era, began following a strict production code.

If the code were not enough to curb objectionable material in films, filmmakers were often in awe of local and state censorship boards, which held enough influence to ban certain movies. The First Amendment did not apply to movies until 1952, when the U.S. Supreme Court decision in *Burstyn v Wilson* revoked the power of a municipality to license movies for local showing. Several Supreme Court decisions favoring Hollywood, as well as an increasing disregard for the Legion of Decency, mitigated the Legion's influence in the 1950s. The movie industry reached a sort of compromise with its critics by implementing a rating system in 1968. The original system had four categories, but over time, it was expanded and refined. Today, "G" movies are for audiences of all ages; a "PG" rating alerts parents to potentially mature situations; "PG-13" means no one under thirteen will be admitted without a parent; "R" movies are restricted to viewers over age seventeen, unless accompanied by a parent; and "NC-17" movies will not allow anyone under seventeen to enter. Although American society has grown more permissive, blood and nudity still provoke criticism.

Although often overlooked, women have played an important role in the movie industry. We are all familiar with the seductive screen enchantress, the shy ingenue, and the strong-willed rebel who gives in to her man in the end. Hackneyed screen roles such as these made up the typical view of women in film. In reality, however, women were a power behind the camera in the medium's earliest years. As a matter of fact, some historians argue that the first director of narrative films was a woman. In 1896, Alice Guy (later Alice Guy Blache), a secretary for a photographer and early filmmaker, wrote a short play called *La Fee Aux Choux* (The Cabbage Fairy) and filmed it. She soon was making films full-time.

Alice Guy
Perhaps the first director of narrative films was Alice Guy. Working as a secretary for a filmmaker in 1896, she wrote and filmed her first production. Over her career, she produced nearly 300 films.

In her lifetime, she produced nearly 300 films in every genre, including the 1912 science fiction film *In the Year 2000*.

Blache had plenty of company: more women had decision-making power before 1920 than at any other point in film history. We tend to remember the actresses whose faces are so familiar. Often ignored is the fact that many of these famous actresses owned their own production companies and directed some of their own films. Outside of acting awards, nearly 100 women have won Academy Awards for their work behind the camera.

Film histories have also given little attention to minority contributions. Most minority roles have been stereotyped: Blacks as maids, Hispanics and Native Americans as the bad guys in westerns, Asians as enemies in war films. Over the years, some notable minorities have made names for themselves. Paul Robeson, a talented singer and actor on stage and in film, played a variety of roles, including the stereotypical black male. He was recognized as a brilliant actor, but his accomplishments were overshadowed by his political stance against lynching and in favor of friendship with Russia following World War II. No longer able to earn a living in America, he eventually emigrated to England. After several years, he returned to America in poor health and lived the rest of his life in seclusion.

Puerto Rican-born Rita Moreno won an Oscar for her role as the feisty Anita in *West Side Story*. She fought most of her life to overcome type-casting as "the Spanish spitfire." She had to move to Broadway to be cast for her talent and not her ethnic heritage. In the 1990s, though, she was producing films and making decisions about what would appear on screen.

Technological Competition

In 1975, the motion picture environment began to change, forcing production companies to adjust to a powerful new technology. That year, Sony introduced its $1,300 Betamax videocassette recorder. It did not take long for people to realize that the VCR was an ideal companion to movie theaters. Only three years after the VCR hit the market, the video rental industry was born. Business was slow at first, but as VCRs became cheaper and the number of homes owning VCRs rapidly increased, video stores seemed to spring up on every corner. When movie production companies realized how profitable the video rental business had become, they tried to collect a portion of the rental fees. But the courts ruled that, under the First-Sale Doctrine, the purchaser is buying the right to resell a tape or to rent it out. When a studio sells a cassette, it loses the right to any further profits. The purchaser does not, however, gain the right to copy the videocassette. The copyright owner holds that right. Studios make more money from videocassette sales than from theater showings. The videocassette is usually released even before pay-cable channels get the movie. Some movies never even make it to the theater — they go straight to video.

VCRs had a tremendous impact on movie entertainment. By 1995, 77,000,000 American households had VCRs, compared to only 1,000,000 in 1980. Americans spent more money per person on home video than on going to the theater to see movies. In 1995, they spent about 16.3% of their entertainment budgets on home video. They spent only 5% on movies in theaters.[13] In 1995, Disney's *The Lion King* video set a record by selling 26,000,000 copies during its first two weeks on sale.

Even with so much money going to home video, the movie industry continued to thrive, in part, because big stars, special effects, and expensive ads attracted viewers. In 1997, box office revenues set a new record. Theaters sold 1.4 billion tickets for revenues of $6.24 billion. And record box office smashes continued to fill the coffers of studios. *Titanic*, released in 1997, made more money at the box office than any other film in history, grossing more than $600 million in North America and $1.8 billion worldwide.[14]

[13] U.S. Bureau of the Census, *Statistical Abstract of the U.S.: 1997*, 565-6.

[14] "Worldwide Box Office Grosses," http://www.boxofficeguru.com, accessed 13 January 1999; Emory Thomas, "Will Titanic Sink Video Records?" http://dailynews.yahoo.com/headlines, accessed 29 August 1998.

First Radio Broadcast
KDKA, Pittsburgh, earned its place in history with a broadcast on November 2, election night, 1920. It obtained voting results through an agreement with the *Pittsburgh Post* newspaper and then reported them in what KDKA claimed was "the world's first scheduled broadcast." KDKA was eager to know if anyone was listening and asked, "Will anyone hearing this broadcast please communicate with us, as we are anxious to know how far the broadcast is reaching and how it is being received."

The Radio Industry

When a young Italian named Guglielmo Marconi developed wireless telegraphy in 1895, he was far from creating radio broadcasting as we know it. His intention was to improve on the traditional wired telegraph. The "wireless," as it was known, was simply a method for sending Morse code through the air. It proved to be a useful technology for ships and trains that could not use stationary telegraph lines.

The fact that Marconi invented radio telegraphy from materials available to anyone spurred a widespread amateur interest in tinkering with wireless technology. Men and boys built their own transmitting and receiving sets and spent evenings tapping out Morse code or straining to hear messages from faraway stations. Maritime wireless communication before and during World War I demonstrated the usefulness of the technology, and experimentation among amateurs expanded to experimentation among such larger institutions as the military, AT&T, Westinghouse, and General Electric.

Experiments in sending voices and music over the air began as early as 1903. Listeners expecting to hear Morse code were often astounded to hear voices. Reginald Fessenden startled wireless operators on ships in the Atlantic with a 1906 Christmas Eve broadcast of music and a reading from the biblical book of Luke. Around 1909, Charles D. Herrold set up an experimental station in San Jose, California, and he and his wife, Sybil, began broadcasting programs every Wednesday night. Most nights he played phonograph records, but sometimes a singer would perform. When their first child was born, his wife held the baby up to the microphone so listeners could hear it crying.

Although many experimental stations were broadcasting before 1920, KDKA of Pittsburgh usually takes the honors of being the first to broadcast regular programming. KDKA began its history by airing the returns for the 1920 presidential election between Warren G. Harding and James M. Cox. KDKA's importance lies in the fact that it was established not as an experimental station, but one with a commercial purpose: to stimulate sales of radio receivers in the Pittsburgh area. The Westinghouse Corporation, which owned the station, manufactured receiving sets.

Most early station owners viewed radio broadcasting as an indirect way to sell merchandise — and "toll broadcasting," or paid advertising, did not exist until 1922. The earliest stations did not air commercial ads, but their owners considered the stations selling tools. Some had an immediate benefit from owning stations: a station owned by a department store provided customers with a reason to buy a radio set; likewise, a station owned by a radio equipment manufacturer gave people a need to buy vacuum tubes and other parts. Some station owners had no other relationship with the radio industry. Automobile dealers and newspapers, for instance, reasoned that having their names mentioned on a regular basis during their stations' broadcasting provided a kind of advertising. Colleges and universities also obtained licenses for stations to provide educational programs and fodder for research for their engineering and budding broadcasting departments.

Millions of Radio Listeners

Americans' fascination with radio grew with such incredible speed that, in 1922, the Bureau of Standards estimated the radio audience at nearly 1,000,000 people. By September of 1924, that audience had grown to around 5,000,000. A broadcasting industry publication estimated the 1926 audience to be nearly 20,000,000 strong, and 26,000,000 the following year. By the 1930 census, over 12,000,000 American families, or 40%, had radios in their homes. Three years later, that number rose to 16,800,000 families. With an average family size of about four people, that meant radio had an audience of nearly 61,000,000 people after less than thirteen years of existence. Radio sets appeared in even the poorest homes. In 1933, 36% of families with annual incomes under $1,000 owned radio sets.[15]

[15]"Radio Air Police," *New York Times*, 2 April 1922, sec. VII, 2; "Varied News and Comment on Radio," *New York Times*, 21 September 1924, sec. VIII, 14; "Radio Audience

The earliest radio programs consisted mostly of phonograph records, player piano rolls, lectures on various subjects, and a musician or two. AT&T's New York radio station WBAY (later WEAF) included phonograph records in its first day of programming on July 25, 1922. The programmer alternated records with songs played on a piano. Mixing records and piano music worked very well for these pioneers—until the next day, that is, when the Victrola was out of order. From 7:30 to 8:00 in the evening, programmers alternated records and player piano rolls. From 8:00 to 10:30, however, programming was all live.[16]

Because early radio sets had earphones for the operator, most of the audience was made up of the men and boys who were experimenting with the technology. In the early 1920s, the listeners were not so much interested in the contents of the programs as they were in tuning in distant stations. Any programming would do for that purpose. But after the novelty in wore off, programming became more important. In the mid-1920s, loudspeakers were developed and added to radio sets, negating the need for earphones. Programs then became available to the entire family. Listeners did not want programs of phonograph records and piano rolls. Many listeners could play their own phonographs for that matter. They wanted more sophisticated programming — live programming.

Live programming was the mainstay of radio in the 1940s. Broadcasting phonograph records was considered inferior to broadcasting live performers. Local performers filled the airwaves with music from pianos, organs, guitars, and all types of ensembles. Most stations, however, did not have enough local talent to fill the broadcasting day; so many joined a network to take advantage of quality live programming.

Radio Listening, 1920
With improvements in technology, radio's popularity increased tremendously in the 1920s. Whereas the earliest receivers had used leaky batteries for power and headsets for listening, this RCA Radiola from 1926 operated on house electrical current and included a loudspeaker.

RADIO NETWORKS

RCA established the first national network in 1926, the National Broadcasting Company (NBC). Stations across the country, linked by telephone lines, could now deliver the same programming from New York. NBC was actually made up of two separate networks: the Red and the Blue. The two had separate affiliates and separate programming. In 1927, CBS debuted as the Columbia Phonograph Broadcasting System, with programming similar to NBC. The Mutual Broadcasting System, never able to compete successfully with NBC and CBS, began broadcasting in 1934. In 1943, NBC sold one of its two networks to the Lifesavers candy tycoon, Edward Noble, who renamed it the American Broadcasting Company (ABC).

The networks, all headquartered in New York City, had access to the big-name talent — talent the smaller local stations could not afford. A network affiliate, however, could provide listeners with quality live entertainment. Famous musicians, comedians, and actors reached audiences across the country with programs like *Amos 'n Andy*, *Buck Rogers in the Year 2433*, and *Easy Aces*.

Families gathered around the radio and visualized the action of the programs in their minds. Network orchestras, often with famous conductors, provided live performances of classical works for millions of listeners. Although phonograph records had spread interest in orchestral and opera compositions, they could not touch the sheer numbers radio broadcasting reached with classical music. The free entertainment on the radio often took the place of going to movie theaters or buying new phonograph records.

Radio programs were divided into two main categories: sponsored and sustaining. An advertiser paid to sponsor a particular program, and the station promoted the advertiser's name with the show. Pepsodent sponsored *Amos 'n Andy*, Kellogg's sponsored *Buck Rogers*, and Lavoris sponsored *Easy Aces*. Texaco's sponsorship of the Metropolitan Opera's performances is the longest-running on radio. Since 1930, the oil company has participated in bringing classical works such as *Tosca*, *La Traviata*, and *The Bartered Bride* to millions of opera fans. Sustaining programs, on the other hand, had no advertising. They filled in gaps between sponsored shows. Although networks aired sustaining programs, they

Totals 20,000,000," *New York Times*, 3 January 1926, sec. VIII, 13; "Nation-wide Survey Reveals 6,500,000 Sets in Use," *New York Times*, 9 January 1927, sec. VIII, 11; U.S. Department of Commerce, Bureau of the Census, *15th Census of the United States: 1930, Population, Volume VI, Families* (Washington, D.C.: Government Printing Office, 1933), 33; U.S. Department of Commerce, Bureau of the Census, *Vertical Study of Radio Ownership* (New York: Columbia Broadcasting System, 1933), 16, 50-1.

[16]WBAY, Master Programs and Final Program Records for 25 July 1922, 26 July 1922, and 3 August 1922, unpaged, item 1290, NBC Collection, Broadcasting and Recorded Sound Division, Library of Congress, Washington, D.C.

Live, with Sound
When NBC debuted in 1926 as the first national radio network, programming was done live. The ensemble of eleven actors pictured here not only read their lines but also provided sound effects.

were much more common on local stations during non-network hours or on independent (unaffiliated) stations.

Recorded Programming

Despite the emphasis on live entertainment, broadcasters continued to use recorded programming. In the 1930s, though, it became more sophisticated. Programs similar to network programs were recorded on 16-inch discs, called electrical transcriptions (ETs). The ETs were high-quality recordings that usually needed special phonographs on which to play them. Researchers reported that most people could not tell the difference between a live program and an electrical transcription. Some broadcasters implied that the recorded programs were live, prompting accusations of fraud; so the Federal Radio Commission required all recorded material to be announced as such. Some stations used regular phonograph records unapologetically, building such programs around them as disc jockey Al Jarvis' *Make Believe Ballroom*.

Broadcasters learned early on to program for audiences that would be listening at certain times of the day. In the mornings, when most women were home, soap operas and other programs geared toward women filled the airwaves. In the afternoons, children home from school could hear programs like *Little Orphan Annie* and *Skippy*. At night, the programs drew audiences of all ages, when practically everyone was likely to be home. Some stations even experimented with a story time in the late evenings, when children were going to bed.

Radio's Golden Age continued through World War II until television became popular. Television had been introduced in 1939 but did not get far before the country turned its research and manufacturing efforts to the war. Its growth was effectively halted until 1945. After the war, however, a prosperous country was ready for television. Consumers were buying sets at the rate of 200,000 per month in 1948. Applications for television licenses poured in on the FCC, overwhelming the agency and prompting a freeze on application grants from 1948 to 1952. Although New York City and Los Angeles each had seven television stations, most cities had only one. Some major regional cities did not have any stations at all. Some historians have implied that radio's Golden Age ended the minute the war ended and television began ascending. Because of the freeze on licenses for television stations, and because many cities were without television service, however, the radio networks continued to operate, although their primary interests and effort swung toward television. Major radio artists defected to television, and radio lost much of its Golden Age talent.

The freeze on TV applications may have saved radio from complete destruction by giving radio executives time to see what was coming. Many predicted that within a few years, radio would no longer exist. But radio, like film and comic books, adapted to its changing environment. One change was a greater use of recorded programming. Technical improvements in sound recording had muted many arguments against recorded programming, and broadcasters learned to use recordings to attract listeners.

The Disc Jockey

Perhaps the biggest boost to recorded programming was the disc jockey. DJ programs were easy and inexpensive to produce. Many record companies sent records to a DJ for free. Other records were fairly inexpensive to buy. Instead of paying for unionized musicians, actors, scriptwriters, and large studios, broadcasters began paying DJs to spin free records. Sponsoring a disc jockey program cost much less than sponsoring a live music program or a dramatic program. Broadcasters gained an unexpected bonus when DJs and disc jockey programs proved to be popular. Martin Block, of New York's WNEW, was the most popular disc jockey of the 1940s. *The New Yorker* magazine reported that Block's broadcast spiel about an icebox sent over one hundred people out in a blizzard to buy one; and after only a month on the air with Block, a doughnut bakery's sales increased by 432,000 doughnuts per week.[17] With results like that, broadcasters, advertisers, and listeners were happy.

The disc jockey proved to be the savior for radio stations when network program fare diminished and audiences moved to televi-

[17] "Profiles: Socko!" *New Yorker*, 29 July 1944, 27.

sion. DJ programs gained in popularity in cities all over the country, becoming the predominant form of programming in the 1950s. Some disc jockeys and record companies, however, abused the power of the DJ. Companies often paid influential DJs to promote their records, hoping to boost sales. Drugs, trips, prostitutes, and other favors were also common. In 1959, "payola" scandals shook the industry, revealing fraud that had been going on for years. One song promoter said that payola had been around since the late 1930s.[18] It is nearly impossible to estimate the impact payola had on the popularity of certain songs. Many songs that climbed to the top of the charts might have made it without any help from the bribes. On the other hand, some hits may have had only marginal success without the exposure payola ensured. The scandal prompted regulations making payola illegal, although it is widely believed to abound today.

Another factor that helped radio survive after television was the introduction of FM in 1941. Previously, all stations had been on the AM band; and, wondrous as radio was, irritating static and unearthly howls often detracted from the programming. FM, however, utilized a different method for transmission; and although its range was shorter than AM's, it was virtually static-free. World War II did not hamper FM as much as it did the other media. In fact, FM got a chance to prove itself. Although its commercial development was arrested, the military used its technology for tanks, jeeps, and other vehicles. After the war, however, FM struggled for acceptance. RCA attempted to kill FM in favor of television. One FCC decision moved FM's frequency allocation to higher frequencies, making the earliest FM receivers obsolete. Another FCC decision allowed simulcasting of FM programming on AM stations, effectively eliminating the need for listeners to buy a new FM radio since they could listen on their existing AM radios. It was not until the 1960s that FM began to recover from its numerous setbacks. By programming disc jockey shows much like AM radio did, FM attracted listeners with its superior fidelity. Classical music lovers benefited greatly from FM since the transmissions could more accurately reproduce subtle changes in tone and dynamics. Today, 61% of U.S. radio stations are FM.[19]

Alan Freed
One of the disk jockeys who helped to popularize rock 'n' roll in the 1950s was Alan Freed. Along with his radio program, he hosted live concerts with many of the performers of the era. In 1960, however, he suspended his work during the federal investigations of the payola scandals.

Minorities and Women in the Radio Industry

Minorities played important roles in radio, especially during the post-War struggle between radio and television. Other than celebrities like Jimmie Lunceford, Nat King Cole, and Dolores Williams, minorities did not find employment easily in broadcasting. Not until after World War II did blacks begin to make any headway. Of the 3,000 disc jockeys on the air in 1947, only sixteen were black. In the 1950s, black musicians could get their records played on the air, but usually they were played by white DJs. Rhythm and blues (R&B) music traditionally had a black audience, but when white disc jockeys in southern California began playing R&B records on their shows, their white listeners began buying the discs. One disc jockey who also owned an R&B record shop in Hollywood saw his clientele go from almost 100% black to about 40% white. The record distributors in the area credited the increase in non-black buyers of black music to exposure of R&B records on several DJ shows. In the 1990s, although disc jockeys and talk-show hosts were still primarily white, fewer than 3% of radio stations and formats were geared toward black audiences. In large cities, one could find radio stations that programmed blocks of ethnic music, such as Asian, Greek, and Arabic, or whose formats were entirely geared toward a specific ethnic group.[20]

Women have had more success than minorities in the radio industry. In 1909, Charles Herrold's wife, Sybil, experimented with broadcasting alongside her husband. Broadcasters realized early on that their daytime listeners were mostly women working around the house, and they geared programming to that audience. Female radio personalities provided gardening, cooking, and child raising tips; many music programs featured female musicians; soap operas involved the emotions of women listeners; and female characters populated prime time network programs.

[18] Juggy Gayles, quoted in Holly George-Warren, "Leader of the Old School," *Rolling Stone*, 24 March 1994, 14.

[19] "By the Numbers," *Broadcasting & Cable*, 17 August 1998, 78.

[20] Lex Gillespie, "Early-day Black DJs Were Rare," *Colorado Springs Gazette Telegraph*, 25 February 1995, E1; "White Fans Hyping R&B Platter Sales," *Billboard*, 31 May 1952, 20; *Broadcasting & Cable Yearbook, 1998* (New Providence, N.J.: R.R. Bowker, 1998), D-631-2.

Female DJs appeared almost as early as male DJs, and in some cities, were very popular. More often than not, though, their programs were relegated to late-night or the wee hours of the morning. Women also worked in the broadcast stations, not always in positions of management, but some reached the upper echelons and held such positions as National Advertising Sales Manager or Assistant Programming Director. Women did not begin to populate station management until the 1970s, and although their ranks continue to swell, they are still in the minority. The FCC, in the past, has considered women a minority and included them in their minority preference program, helping more women to purchase and program their own radio stations.

Most radio stations in recent years followed a music format, although talk formats have seen a surge of popularity in the last few years. The primary formats were Country, Album Oriented Rock (AOR), News/Talk, Middle Of the Road (MOR), Urban Contemporary, Adult Contemporary, Beautiful Music (Easy Listening), Religious, and Classical. Country was the most common format.

Some popular radio formats were divided into subformats. For instance, within the AOR format, two new formats that grew quickly. Modern Rock (alternative rock) and AAA (Album Adult Alternative) were played on about 150 stations across the country. The Modern Rock format featured many artists found in MTV's *Buzz Bin*, such as R.E.M., Smashing Pumpkins, Green Day, Offspring, and Nirvana. AAA's playlists were more diverse, including such bands as Bonnie Raitt, Steely Dan, Counting Crows, and the Waterboys.[21]

Radio made significant strides in competing with other media by focusing on its sound quality in the late 1980s and early 1990s. For years, some cable systems have offered subscription audio services to their customers. In early 1995, however, the FCC allocated frequency space for digital satellite transmission of audio signals directly to consumer receivers. Terrestrial broadcasters, however, had their own plan for transmitting digital signals. Digital radio will be a reality around the turn of the century, but whether listeners get it from a satellite subscription or free from local radio stations remains to be seen.

Of all the entertainment media, radio has undergone the most radical change in order to survive. Having lost its primary audience, radio made a remarkable comeback and continues to profit each year.

The Television Industry

Television often seems to have sprung suddenly onto the scene as soon as World War II ended. It is true that television's popularity grew quickly, but that could not have happened without a long history of research behind it. As early as 1919, researchers were experimenting with television. Vladimir Zworykin, a Russian immigrant, demonstrated his television prototype to his employers at Westinghouse in 1923. AT&T, also researching television, gave

[21]Eric Boehlert, "Rock Radio Make-Over," *Rolling Stone*, 9 February 1995, 24.

FAR-OFF SPEAKERS SEEN AS WELL AS HEARD HERE IN A TEST OF TELEVISION

LIKE A PHOTO COME TO LIFE

Hoover's Face Plainly Imaged as He Speaks in Washington.

THE FIRST TIME IN HISTORY

Pictures Are Flashed by Wire and Radio Synchronizing With Speaker's Voice.

COMMERCIAL USE IN DOUBT

But A. T. & T. Head Sees a New Step in Conquest of Nature After Years of Research.

Voorhis Hopes When He Is 100 To Visit Smith in White House

"Like a Photo Come to Life"

Bell Laboratories of AT&T demonstrated a system for transmitting images in 1927. President Herbert Hoover made a speech in Washington, D.C., that was sent the 200 miles to an audience in New York City. The system transmitted pictures by wire at the rate of eighteen images per second. In reporting on the demonstration, the *New York Times'* front-page story declared that television had "annihilated" the distance between the speaker and the audience. "It was," the reporter said, "as if a photograph had suddenly come to life and begun to talk, smile, nod its head and look this way and that." Despite television's promise, development was put on hold until after World War II, thus allowing radio time to adjust to its new competitor.

public demonstrations of the new technology in 1927. Ernst F.W. Alexanderson, head of General Electric's television experiments, began testing from an experimental station in Schenectady, New York, in 1928.

In 1939 television was ready for the world — appropriately, at the World's Fair in New York. RCA head David Sarnoff had no doubts about the importance of television to Americans. "It is with a feeling of humbleness," he said prophetically at the dedication of the RCA exhibit, "that I come to this moment of announcing the birth in this country of a new art so important . . . that it is bound to affect all society."[22] President Franklin D. Roosevelt helped Sarnoff unveil the television before the public on April 30. Sets avail-

[22]David Sarnoff, address at New York World's Fair, Flushing Meadows, April 20, 1939. Reprinted in *Looking Ahead: The Papers of David Sarnoff* (New York: McGraw-Hill, 1968), 100.

able to consumers cost between $199 and $600. By 1940, twenty-three television stations across the country were broadcasting.

World War II halted progress in TV's expansion and technical improvements. As with other industries, all efforts were turned toward the war. But when the war ended, the TV boom was on. In 1946, manufacturers produced 6,000 television sets. In an incredible feat of peacetime manufacturing conversion, 1947 saw a jump in TV set manufactures to 179,000 and in 1948 to 975,000. Despite an FCC freeze on new television station licenses in 1948, manufacturers made 3,000,000 sets in 1949. By 1960, 87% of American homes had at least one television set. In 1993, 98.3% of U.S. households owned TV sets.

The Origins of Cable Television

Although the FCC's license freeze in 1948 locked many communities out of television service, some communities got around that problem by erecting community antennas (CATV), the ancestor of cable television. A powerful antenna erected on a tower or hill near the town picked up signals from the nearest television stations. For a one-time fee, residents' television sets were hooked up to the antenna. Subscribers paid a monthly fee for the service. Broadcasters initially welcomed the CATV systems because CATV extended their service areas, allowing them to charge more for ads. By 1952, when the FCC lifted the television application freeze, seventy CATV systems served 14,000 subscribers. Beginning in the 1960s, microwave transmission allowed some CATV systems to receive more distant stations. Now, superstations, such as WOR in New York and WGN in Chicago, are common on cable systems across the country.

Television, 1939
In 1939, RCA exhibited its first commercial television set at the World's Fair in New York. The screen on this model, an RCA Victor, measured 5 1/2 by 7 1/2 inches.

Until 1975, cable television's main purpose was delivering more and better reception of existing broadcast stations. That year, however, subscription movie service Home Box Office (HBO) began broadcasting via satellite to cable systems around the United States. Local cable systems installed $100,000 satellite receiving dishes, three meters in diameter, that picked up signals beamed down from satellites orbiting 22,300 miles above the equator. The cable system then distributed the satellite's signal into subscribers' homes.

What seemed like a revolution in 1975 is commonplace today. Most cable networks are delivered to local cable systems by satellite. Other cable channels may be delivered by microwave signals, a ground-based transmission system. Today there are more than 11,000 cable systems in the United States. Cable is available to about 96% of American homes, 66.1% of which subscribe to it.[23]

With the introduction of non-broadcast programming, cable television became a competitor with traditional broadcasters. To make room for the ever-growing cable networks, some systems dropped local broadcasters. Tensions between the two groups have grown over the last twenty years, prompting the passage of the Cable Communication Act of 1993. Part of that law required cable companies to compensate local broadcasters for the right to carry their signals. Most broadcasters did not receive a cash payment from the cable companies, but received trade-offs in advertising and promotions. As part of the negotiations, some broadcasters even established their own local cable channels.

Competition for Cable

Alternative systems for program delivery are available today, or are in development. Wireless cable, which sounds like a contradiction in terms, allows subscribers to receive many of the same cable channels offered by a traditional cable company. The signal is delivered to the subscriber's home by microwave transmission and is received by a special antenna placed on the roof of the house. Wireless is frequently offered in areas that already have a wired cable system.

C-band satellite service has been available to consumers since 1975, when HBO began its satellite broadcasting. A three-foot Television Receive Only (TVRO) dish can pick up signals sent from many satellites orbiting the earth. Most satellite signals are scrambled, requiring consumers to subscribe to a particular channel, or

23 "By the Numbers," *Broadcasting & Cable*, 17 August 1998, 78.

a package of channels, to get an unscrambled signal. Direct Broadcast Service (DBS) allows subscribers to receive many more channels than wireless cable. The Ku-band signal is received on a satellite dish about the size of a large pizza. Most subscribers to satellite service live in rural areas where cable companies have not run cable, although recently more residents of urban and suburban areas have bought DBS systems.

In the mid-1980s, broadcasters began to look toward the next big development for the television industry: High Definition Television (HDTV). HDTV systems provide dramatically better picture quality on a rectangular screen shaped like a movie screen. Japan introduced its analog (non-digital) HDTV system in the mid-1980s. In the early 1990s, American broadcasters began testing digital delivery of HDTV signals. Implementation of the system was planned for a number of years beginning in 1999.

Television, like movies, comic books, and music, has come under its share of criticism for program content. The sex and violence on television have been blamed for all sorts of social ills from teenage pregnancy to violent crime to illegal drug use. Studies reveal, however, little proof that television is the root of the problems.

Early TV programming took most of its inspiration from radio. In many instances, radio stars simply adapted their radio shows to television's visual demands. Classical music programs beamed orchestral and operatic performances live to millions of people, much as radio networks had done previously. Many Americans now round out July 4th celebrations with stirring performances of the National Symphony or the Boston Pops on television. With television, though, opera fans could see the elaborate sets and costumes and the action on stage. By the 1970s, many TV shows relied primarily on visual aspects to attract viewers. Action programs like *Starsky and Hutch* and comedies like *Laugh-In* relied on visual excitement and visual gags for their success. In the 1980s, with the introduction of the cable channel Music Television (MTV), the audio components of programs regained some importance. *Miami Vice* and *Moonlighting*, for instance, relied heavily on music to establish the mood of certain scenes and to affect viewers' emotions. MTV also influenced the filming and editing of television programs and commercials. Frame composition, rapid cuts between shots, computer graphics and animation, and unorthodox camera angles once found only in music videos are now common in commercials and prime-time fare.

Minorities experienced the same barriers in television as in other entertainment media. Most had stereotypical, subservient roles until 1968, when Diahann Carroll starred in her own show, *Julia*. Julia, the main character, was a nurse but lived like a movie star. Although Carroll's role was an unrealistic portrayal of black life in the '60s, later programs such as *Good Times, The Jeffersons*, and *Cosby* tried to depict black families as more true-to-life. Other minorities have had the same sort of treatment, but have had less exposure. Racial minorities also are underrepresented in television commercials, making up only around 5% of characters, although they are portrayed negatively less frequently than white characters are.[24]

Diahann Carroll
Diahann Carroll, star in her own show, *Julia*, starting in 1968, broke television's color barrier. The show, though, was designed to be palatable to largely white television audiences. Julia, the main character, was a nurse to a physician played by Lloyd Nolan. The two are shown here in the first publicity photograph for the show.

Women's roles in television have paralleled those of radio. Female-oriented programs and soap operas usually featured female personalities. Women in station management have had a harder time than in radio, but more are successful in reaching decision-making positions every year. No woman delivered any network's evening news until 1967, and no woman has ever been the sole anchor of a weeknight network news program, although women have anchored weekend newscasts. Television roles for women are less numerous than roles for males. Female roles continue to portray working women in less powerful jobs, although the number of working female characters has increased over the last twenty years. Despite the progress in women's roles, stereotyping still exists. Women in MTV commercials, for instance, appear less often than men, are usually very beautiful, with fit bodies and skimpy clothing.[25]

[24]Nancy Signorielli, Douglas McLeod, and Elaine Healy, "Gender Stereotypes in MTV Commercials: The Beat Goes On," *Journal of Broadcasting and Electronic Media* (Winter 1994), 91-101.

[25]David Vest, "Prime Time Pilots: A Content Analysis of Changes in Gender Representation," *Journal of Broadcasting and Electronic Media* (Spring 1992), 25-43; David Atkin, "The Evolution of Television Series Addressing Single Women, 1966-1990," *Journal of Broadcasting and Electronic Media* (Fall 1991), 517-23; Signorielli, et al., ibid.

VIDEO GAMES

Americans have used their televisions for more than passive viewing. Video games have been enormously successful. Children and adults have spent countless hours pressing buttons and moving joysticks. Invented in 1966, the first video game consisted simply of two spots that chased each other around the television screen. Nevertheless, the technology had become sophisticated enough to market by 1972.

Odyssey, made by Magnavox, offered consumers twelve different games including Table Tennis, Haunted House, Ski, and Football, all for about $100. An additional set of shooting games was available for another $39.95. To play the games, the user inserted the correct circuit card into the game console and attached a plastic overlay to the television screen to provide the correct background: a green table and net for Table Tennis, a dilapidated house for Haunted House, a map of ski courses for Ski, and a green field with yard lines for Football. The game could not keep score, but Odyssey did provide a cardboard scorecard with the set.

Pong was the first successful video game. It began as an arcade game and then moved into the home in 1975. Pong was an electronic version of table tennis. It needed no plastic overlays to produce the effect of the paddles and net, and it kept score automatically. With the development of microprocessors, video games became much more complex. The video games of today use cartridges and CD-ROMs to store the game information. Hand-held video games are popular, and almost as sophisticated.

As the popularity of video games grew, so did societal concerns over the effects the games had on children. Describing the games as "electronic drugs," some people believed they were addictive. Since most of the games involved destroying an enemy, many adults worried that children were learning antisocial behaviors. School officials took steps to prevent students from skipping school to spend time in the arcades. Recently, games have been criticized for their stereotyped depiction of women and minorities, but through all the criticism, the games have survived and prospered.

All of the entertainment media had to adapt to a changing and competitive media environment. Remarkably, all of the media continued to thrive, but only if they evolved into more sophisticated forms than those in which they originated. Each medium competed with an increasingly crowded arena for a share of consumers' entertainment budgets. Some media enjoyed increasing popularity, while others struggled to keep up with changes.

RECOMMENDED READINGS

BOOKS

Ackler, Ally, *Reel Women: Pioneers of the Cinema, 1896 to the Present*. New York, 1995. Places women in their rightful place in film history: in decision-making positions. Includes short biographies of women producers, directors, and writers.

Andrew, J. Dudley, *The Major Film Theories: An Introduction*. London, 1976. Traces film history and development through a study of major theories.

Andrews, Bart, and Ahrgus Juilliard, *Holy Mackerel!: The Amos 'n' Andy Story*. New York, 1986. Explores the racial stereotypes presented on radio, television, and film, and attempts to explain why this type of program was so popular.

Bowers, Q. David, *Nickelodeon Theatres and Their Music*. Vestal, New York, 1986. Describes the evolution of music in early movie theaters. Includes hundreds of photographs from the author's collection.

Daniels, Les, *Marvel: Five Fabulous Decades of the World's Greatest Comics*. New York, 1991. A behind-the-scenes look at one of the most successful comic book companies in America.

Denisoff, R. Serge, *Solid Gold: The Popular Record Industry*. New Brunswick, N. J., 1975. Traces development of the American record industry, with particular emphasis on the rock and roll era.

Estren, Mark James, *A History of Underground Comics*. Berkeley, Calif., 1974. Illustrated history of non-traditional comic books.

Fornatale, Peter, and Joshua E. Mills, *Radio in the Television Age*. Woodstock, N. Y., 1980. Describes the evolution of radio from its Golden Age before World War II to the formula-format stage it assumed after television arrived.

Gelatt, Ronald, *The Fabulous Phonograph, 1877-1977*. 2d rev. ed. New York, 1977. An account of the phonograph's history from Edison's first tinkerings through technical and musical developments in the 1970s.

Goulart, Ron, *Over 50 Years of American Comic Books*. Lincolnwood, Ill., 1991. Chronological and topical study of the evolution of comic books; includes beautifully reproduced examples of comic book art.

Hilmes, Michele. *Hollywood and Broadcasting: From Radio to Cable*. Urbana, Il., 1990. The relationship of film and broadcasting from the days of network radio to the present.

Lardner, James, *Fast Forward: Hollywood, the Japanese, and the Onslaught of the VCR*. New York, 1987. Examines the effects of the VCR on the American film industry.

Long, Louis S. *The Development of the Television Network Oligopoly*. New York, 1979. Traces the development of the broadcasting networks and the power amassed by a small number of companies.

Jones, Gerard, and Will Jacobs. *The Comic Book Heroes*. Rocklin, Calif., 1997. Recounts the last forty years of comic book history.

Ramsaye, Terry, *A Million and One Nights: A History of the Motion Picture*. New York, 1926. Arguably the first film history. Irreverent, slightly disorganized, but entertaining nonetheless.

Sanjek, Russell, *From Print to Plastic: Publishing and Promoting America's Popular Music, 1900-1980*. Brooklyn, N. Y., 1983. Critical study of the business practices of the recording industry throughout its history.

Smulyan, Susan, *Selling Radio: the Commercialization of American Broadcasting, 1920-1934*. Washington, D.C., 1994. The development of broadcast advertising and how that shaped the content of programming.

Stanley, Robert H. *The Celluloid Empire: A History of the American Movie Industry*. New York, 1978. Hollywood's birth and growth, with particular emphasis on the studios involved.

Toll, Robert C. *The Entertainment Machine: American Show Business in the Twentieth Century*. New York, 1982. Discusses the effects technology has had on entertainment in America.

Wertheim, Arthur Frank, *Radio Comedy*. New York, 1979. Examines the influences on early radio comedies.

Wilder, Alec, *American Popular Song: The Great Innovators, 1900-1950*. New York, 1972. Black music, especially ragtime, influenced American popular music in the twentieth century.

ARTICLES

Austin, Mary. "Petrillo's War." *Journal of Popular Culture* 12 (Summer 1978): 11-8. Examines the factors leading to a successful ban on recording instituted by the American Federation of Musicians.

Benjamin, Louise M. "In Search of the Sarnoff 'Radio Music Box' Memo." *Journal of Broadcasting and Electronic Media* 37 (1993): 325-35. Examines the validity of the memo in establishing David Sarnoff's reputation as a visionary of broadcasting.

Holmes, Marian Smith. "Who Could Resist the Kind of Music They Made at Hitsville?" *Smithsonian*, October 1994, 82-95. A brief explanation of the reasons for success at Motown Records.

Hugunin, Marc. "ASCAP, BMI and the Democratization of American Popular Music." *Popular Music and Society* 7 (1979): 8-17. Describes the formation and competition in the music licensing business.

MacDonald, J. Fred. "Black Perimeters — Paul Robeson, Nat King Cole and the Role of Blacks in American TV." *Journal of Popular Film and Television* 7 (1979): 246-64. Describes the state of Black employment during television's early years.

MacDonald, J. Fred. "Government Propaganda in Commercial Radio: The Case of Treasury Star Parade, 1942-1943." *Journal of Popular Culture* 12 (1979): 285-304. Argues that government-sponsored programming helped convince Americans to support the United States' participation in World War II.

Schultz, Quintin J. "Evangelical Radio and the Rise of the Electronic Church, 1921-1948." *Journal of Broadcasting and Electronic Media* 32 (1986): 289-306. Traces the early history of religious broadcasting and the barriers it encountered from the FCC and the networks.

Wertheim, Arthur Frank. "'The Bad Boy of Radio': Henry Morgan and Censorship." *Journal of Popular Culture* 12 (Summer 1978): 11-18. Entertaining study of renegade broadcaster and his off-beat humor.

20

The Age of Mass Magazines

1900 - Present

As the twentieth century dawned, it was evident that those mass magazines that previously had dominated the American scene were faltering. The high-minded approach that had brought them huge circulations — "leisurely in habit, literary in tone, retrospective rather than timely, and friendly to the interests of the upper classes"[1] — belonged to an era that was ending. The new popular magazines were reflecting instead the hectic pace of a mechanized and urban nation, emphasizing timely information rather than literary fare, and appealing to the tastes of the masses, not the upper classes.

The genteel tradition of literature, represented by and nurtured carefully through magazines such as *Century*, *Harper's Monthly*, *Scribner's*, and *Atlantic Monthly*, had given way to newer, more popular publications. New political forces emanating from the masses — instead of being dictated by the upper classes — were gaining momentum; once-observable class distinctions based on dress, speech, and manners were disappearing; nationwide industries and the mass-marketing of products were promising a revolution in advertising; and new technologies had removed formidable economic barriers that previously limited entry into magazine publishing.

The Appearance of Mass Magazines

The end of the genteel era began in 1893 when an onslaught of inexpensive, lively magazines attracted a huge audience of previously untapped readers. *McClure's*, *Munsey's*, and *Cosmopolitan* were the first to challenge successfully the traditional leaders. The most influential of these was *McClure's*, named for its owner-founder, Samuel S. McClure, who began issuing his magazine in 1893 at 15¢ a copy, less than half the price of the leading magazines. By 1900 the circulation of this lively, readable publication with articles pertinent to everyday life had reached 365,000. *Munsey's*, which had been founded in 1889, lowered its newsstand price to 10¢ in 1893 and, with a content that was less distinguished than that of *McClure's*, achieved a circulation of 70,000 by 1900. John Brisben Walker's *Cosmopolitan*, in existence since 1886, reduced its price from 25¢ a copy to 15¢ in 1893.

In 1896, C.C. Buell, assistant editor of the greatest of the older magazines, *The Century*, counted thirty-five cheap new magazines at a newsstand. He told his editor, Richard Watson Gilder, that in the next few years two or three additional ones a week would be appearing. "I believe," he naively predicted to Gilder, "that the very multiplicity of them is going to reawaken the people to a sense of the value of the serious, 'high-priced' magazines."[2] Buell was wrong. Just three years later *The Century's* associate editor, Robert Underwood Johnson, desperately proposed new measures to counter the "emergency" and "possible debacle" that appeared imminent for the once-powerful magazine.[3] He suggested specific ways to reduce costs and proposed that some bold new editorial project be initiated to restore lagging staff morale.

At *Harper's Monthly* the situation seemed even more critical: the New York magazine and its parent firm, Harper & Bros., had slid into bankruptcy. The great financier J. Pierpont Morgan, holder of the note that Harper & Bros. had been unable to pay, turned over the company to — of all people — the newcomer S.S. McClure, thinking he could provide the magic needed to restore its vigor. In Boston the *Atlantic Monthly* had started losing money in 1894, a trend that continued into the twentieth century.[4]

What had brought about this dramatic decline for established magazines and the emergence of new ones? One of the primary reasons was technological: the established magazines had seemed impregnable for decades because wood engravings, essential to their popularity, were so costly that they discouraged new competitors. The development of photoengraving changed the situa-

[1]Frank Luther Mott, *A History of American Magazines, 1885-1905* (Cambridge, Mass., 1957), 2.

[2]C.C. Buell to Richard Watson Gilder, 25 March 1896, Box 2, Richard Watson Gilder Papers, New York Public Library, New York, N.Y.

[3]Robert Underwood Johnson to Richard Watson Gilder, 30 August 1899, Richard Watson Gilder Letters, Century Collection, New York Public Library, New York, N.Y.

[4]Eugene Exman, *The House of Harper: One Hundred and Fifty Years of Publishing* (New York, 1967), 180-1; Ellen B. Ballou, *The Building of the House* (Boston, 1970), 452 and 463.

204 THE LIFE OF THE MASTER.

whose face is the mirror of Heaven. The wise men open their coffers, and lay their treasures at the feet of the Child, the shepherds do homage with adoring faces, while some gentle animals in the background represent the lower creation at this shrine of holiness. Here indeed is a narrow space, but it is full of Heaven; here is lowliness, but no indignity; here is weakness, but also reverence.

With the after-look the disciples of Jesus may prefer to see the inner glory of His Nativity rather than its outer circumstances; but no one would desire that these should have been different. He was to show unto His time and all ages that the greatest force in life is not position nor wealth, but character, and that character is independent of all circumstances, so that goodness, cradled and reared in poverty, without advantages and without favor, persecuted and slain, is yet the most beautiful and triumphant power on earth. Before this infant, so inhospitably received of the world, lay the cruelty of Herod, and the narrow lot of Nazareth, and the homeless mission of Galilee, and the contempt of the great, and the shame of the Cross. But that would be only the appearance of things, not the heart. Around Him also would gather the loyalty of faithful disciples, and the love of women, and the praises of little children, and the gratitude of the poor, and the reverence of holy souls, and the awe of the wicked, and the sympathy of the saints in Paradise, and the service of the mighty angels of God. On Him also would rest, the true aureole for His head, the Spirit of God and the love of His Heavenly Father.

With the supreme good taste of Holy Scripture it is simply written, that the Child increased in stature and in wisdom, and in favor with God and man. It is enough that Jesus lived His first thirty years at home in Nazareth, since home gathers into it the five factors which influence nature when it is plastic and give it a permanent shape. The first is that word which is of one blood with home, since none can think of home without at the same time saying mother. In the Bible, which is the standard record of human life, the mother has prepared the servants of God from Moses to Samuel, from David to the Baptist, but among all women and mothers surely the most blessed is Mary. Christians may not all unite in paying almost divine honors to the Virgin, or in believing that she is a mediator with her Son, but surely in every reverent mind she must have a solitary

Street scene at Bethlehem.

McClure's, 1900

At the start of the twentieth century, *McClure's* was one of America's most popular magazines. Using well-illustrated biographies, it had a circulation of 350,000. Its lead feature in the January 1900 issue was a story on the life of Christ.

tion: large illustrations could be made at little cost.[5] Other important factors were at work, especially advertisers' search for a national audience. Advertisers would flock to the magazine that could deliver a huge circulation. Magazines could attract huge circulations with cheap prices and popular content, and increased advertising revenues would more than cover the losses incurred by pricing a magazine at less than cost.

The new magazines also reflected a change in editorial philosophy. Nineteenth-century editors typically had sat back and selected the best of whatever manuscripts happened to arrive in the office. *The Century*, without aggressively soliciting manuscripts, received 5,000 in 1882 and about 10,000 a year by 1890.[6] Practically the only solicitation of manuscripts occurred when editors arranged with leading authors to publish their novels.[7]

By 1900 *McClure's*, with a circulation of 350,000, had become the leading magazine in the nation. Its articles explored the wonders as well as the problems of contemporary society. It boasted a staff of excellent writers, the quality of which probably has not been equalled to this day. The staff included, among others, Lincoln Steffens, Ida Tarbell, Ray Stannard Baker, and Viola Roseboro. They wrote about politics, railroads, business, or anything that the editors conceived might appeal to large numbers of readers. Especially popular were profiles of individuals. The long essays that had been the backbone of the nineteenth-century magazine were gone. "The wise editors won't have them any more, because the people won't read them and won't even take magazines that get the reputation of harboring them," observed the writer David Graham Phillips in 1903. Why? Because the "present generation," he offered, was impatient with anything that was not important to the concerns of "here and now."[8] McClure decided that readers wanted "success" stories, and from 1895 to 1901 nearly 65% of the magazine's non-fiction content was "success oriented."[9] On the eve of the great muckraking era that was to be introduced in 1903 by *McClure's* and that magazine's famous staff, Phillips declared that the "real secret" of the revolution was not the reduction in magazine prices but the addition of more meaningful content. The new magazine was written "for the people," and it was a reflection of the "atmosphere of our time."[10]

Two of the four great quality magazines of the nineteenth century succumbed to slow, painful deaths because they failed to adjust. *Century* and *Scribner's* disappeared entirely; *Harper's* and *Atlantic Monthly* survived — barely — with a small, dedicated audience. They were to develop in the twentieth century a reputation for quality journalism rather than for fiction, and no longer would they be dominant publications.

Ironically, those magazines that so abruptly signaled the new age would not continue as the leading magazines of the next era. Their life spans were meteoric — brilliant but short. Among the things they accomplished was to break the dominating hold of the eastern literary establishment. No longer would the few editors of marked similarities and tastes be the arbiters of magazine journalism — and indeed of American culture as well. McClure and Munsey were brash Midwesterners; Walker of *Cosmopolitan* an automobile manufacturer; Walter Hines Page a Southerner. They were "go-getters," involved in things more tangible than literary products. They employed, as the journalist Phillips said, an "almost uncanny energy, a kind of hop-skip-and-jump imagination and mode of action."[11]

One of these new editors, Page, foreshadowed in his publishing career what would be one of the dominant successes of the twentieth century: the news magazine. A North Carolinian, he brought to both the *Forum* and *Atlantic Monthly* a new approach

[5] S.S. McClure, *My Autobiography* (New York, 1914), 207.

[6] Arthur John, *The Best Years of the Century*, 1879-1909 (Urbana, Ill., 1981), 146.

[7] Some notable exceptions should be mentioned, particularly *The Century's* great series on the Civil War and the Old South, both of which brought much acclaim.

[8] David Graham Phillips, "Great Magazines and their Editors," *Success*, May 1903.

[9] Fred J. Endres, "The Pre-Muckraking Days of *McClure's Magazine*, 1893-1901," *Journalism Quarterly* 55 (Spring 1978): 154.

[10] Phillips, "Great Magazines and Their Editors."

[11] Ibid.

THE WORLD'S WORK

VOLUME I NOVEMBER 1900 NUMBER 1

The March of Events

THE concrete results of American character and enterprise during the uninterrupted period since the civil war now appear in such variety and volume as to indicate the rich meaning of life under democratic conditions; for they denote a shifting of the working centre of the world.

The United States is become the richest of all countries. We sell fuel as well as food to Europe, and the rapid increase of our manufactures for export was never matched. We have developed the skilled workman whose earnings are larger and whose product is cheaper than any of his competitor's, because he is a better master of himself and of the machinery that he uses. Our commercial supremacy is inevitable, and European governments are already our debtors for cash as well as for manhood suffrage.

We have constructed industrial and commercial machinery, too, of a scope and of a precision of action that were hitherto unknown. All wise plans for the future must rest on the changes wrought by modern machinery, the organization of industry, and the freedom of the individual; for the perfection of method and of mechanism has done more than to spread well-being among the masses and to enrich and dignify labor: it has changed social ideals and intellectual points of view. It is, in fact, changing the character of men. As soon as material prosperity is won they care less for it; what they enjoy is the work of winning it. The higher organization of industry has for half a century engaged the kind of minds that once founded colonies, built cathedrals, led armies, and practised statecraft; and, to an increasing number, work has become less and less a means of bread-winning and more and more a form of noble exercise. The artist always took joy in his work: it is the glory of our time that the man of affairs can find a similar pleasure in his achievements.

It is with the activities of the newly organized world, its problems and even its romance, that this magazine will earnestly concern itself, trying to convey the cheerful spirit of men who do things.

AT THE CENTURY'S END

AND "THE WORLD'S WORK" begins its career at a fortunate time; for whatever may be thought of the nineteenth century when it can be seen in the perspective of universal history, to men who have caught the spirit of its closing years, it seems the best time to live that has so far come. It is unlike all former periods in this, that it has seen the simultaneous extension of democracy and the rise of science. These have put life on a new plane, and made a new adjustment of man to man and of man to the universe.

An incalculable advantage that we have over men of any other century is the widening of individual opportunity. It has been the century of the abolition of slavery throughout

3

A New Magazine Formula
Eschewing the artwork and fiction that were the staples of most popular magazines, Walter Hines Page's *World's Work* emphasized serious material on timely topics. It presaged the formula that later would make *Time* magazine successful.

in editing: he determined himself what their content would be rather than merely printing what his contributors happened to offer. His emphasis always was on the present and the future, not the past. Literary criticism he regarded as mere "talkee-talkee," and he downplayed it to a secondary role.[12] In 1900 , thinking that he must be owner and publisher if he were truly to establish the ideal contemporary magazine, Page founded the monthly *World's Work*. Its purpose was to describe the nation's progress in the primary aspects of life: education, agriculture, industry, social life, and politics. The concept was novel. The *Chicago Evening Post* observed, "To have literary style injected into articles on American exports, cotton and cotton goods, life and fire insurance, country banks, wholesale and retail dry goods, will be cheerful and inspiring."[13]

The magazine's first issue had a press run of 35,000 copies. In 1909 its circulation peaked at about 125,000. This success was achieved in a manner that contrasted with the formula of *McClure's*, *Munsey's*, and the newly prospering *Saturday Evening Post*, for *World's Work* contained no fiction, not much artwork, a serious tone, and a price of 25¢ per copy. It anticipated what would become one of the outstanding success stories in the years ahead: *Time* magazine. Each issue opened with a section titled "The March of Events" which dealt with a timely subject such as politics, business, or agriculture. Next came between twelve and twenty articles on other topics. By eliminating all fiction, Page boldly rejected the most popular magazine feature of the time. Yet another distinctive feature of the magazine was its exclusive use of photographs for illustrations, eschewing wood engravings. These photographs were spread throughout the pages of the magazine. Page established in *World's Work* a *news* magazine, and to this endeavor he dedicated himself until 1913 when President Woodrow Wilson appointed him ambassador to Britain.[14]

CURTIS' PUBLISHING SUCCESS

While interesting because of its trailblazing format and the formula it provided for *Time* and *Newsweek*, *World's Work* did not otherwise leave its mark on the industry. What was to become the most enduring publishing success of the first half of the twentieth century was a weekly magazine that appealed particularly to the nation's growing middle class, the *Saturday Evening Post*.

Its success initially was tied to that of the *Ladies' Home Journal*, developed by Cyrus H.K. Curtis after his wife laughed at his efforts in covering women's news for a publication called *The Tribune and the Farmer*. She took over the job herself and did so well that in 1879 Curtis, thirty years old, created a separate women's magazine, the *Ladies' Home Journal*. When circulation reached 500,000 in 1889, he turned the publication over to Edward Bok. Two years later he formed the Curtis Publishing Company. By the late nineteenth century *Ladies' Home Journal* had achieved the greatest circulation of any magazine, 900,000. In 1904 it reached the magical figure of 1,000,000 readers, and by 1912 its circulation was approaching two million. Bok boldly carried readers to new areas of interest, including crusades for sex education, which included the use of the word "syphilis" for the first time in any American popular magazine.

The early enthusiastic reception of *Ladies' Home Journal* led Curtis to believe that a similar feat could be achieved with a men's magazine. Thus in 1897 he paid $1,000 for a struggling, unillustrated sixteen-page weekly that was being edited on a part-time basis by a Philadelphia reporter for $10 a week. Its circulation of 1,800 had been dwindling rapidly. The energetic temporary editor Curtis hired from the *Boston Post*, George Horace Lorimer, managed to stay on the job until 1937, creating one of the nation's greatest publishing successes. The original idea for Lorimer's *Saturday Evening Post* and one that provided its motivating force for many years was to romanticize the accomplishments of American business in a way that was neither intellectual nor sensational. The contents of the *Post* of 1895 were decribed as "action stories, ro-

[12]Burton J. Hendrick, *The Life and Letters of Walter H. Page*, I (Garden City, N.Y., 1922), 48-63 passim; Ballou, *The Building of the House* , 454-5.

[13]*Chicago Evening Post*, 29 September 1900, clipping in Walter Hines Page Papers, Houghton Library, Harvard University, Cambridge, Mass.

[14]John Milton Cooper, Jr., *Walter Hines Page: The Southerner as American, 1855-1918* (Chapel Hill, 1977), 162-205 passim.

Cyrus H.K. Curtis
Inspired by his wife's success with a publication titled *The Tribune and the Farmer*, in 1879 Cyrus Curtis started the *Ladies' Home Journal*. In 1905 its circulation reached 1,000,000. Using *LHJ* as a base, Curtis built one of America's leading publishing empires. With the success of *LHJ*, Curtis then bought a struggling weekly publication and remade it into the *Saturday Evening Post*. It claimed to trace its lineage to Benjamin Franklin, but in its modern form it originated in the late 1800s. Originally conceived as a magazine that praised success, it appealed to the growing middle class and emphasized traditional virtues. Its inspirational approach made it the most successful magazine of the first half of the twentieth century.

THE SATURDAY EVENING POST
Founded AD 1728 by Benj. Franklin

MERTON OF THE MOVIES

By Harry Leon Wilson

mances, stories of business; the life stories of successful men of action; articles on economic and political subjects so dramatized that they were at once informing and entertaining; comment on current events; and a modicum of the serious and sentimental poetry countenanced by the businessmen of the period."[15] It was a publication that appealed to what was becoming the dominant force in American society — the middle class. It eschewed radicalism and the bizarre; it championed middle-class virtues. It printed inspirational biographies, factual reports, and fiction.

The competition in the weekly field was formidable. *Harper's Illustrated Weekly*, *Frank Leslie's Illustrated Newspaper*, and *Collier's* were dominant. Lorimer was undaunted by the old leaders and the additional competition of the popular new monthlies, and he solicited fiction from the nation's best authors. In the first four years of the rejuvenated *Post's* existence, the magazine published such noted writers as Stephen Crane, Bret Harte, Richard Harding Davis, Emerson Hough, Owen Wister, and William Allen White. Lorimer also persuaded the nation's outstanding public figures to write about contemporary events — men such as Senator Albert J. Beveridge and Speakers of the House Thomas B. Reed and Champ Clark. He promised that the *Post* would become the largest weekly magazine in the world. It reached a circulation of 1,000,000 in 1908 and surpassed *Ladies' Home Journal*. By 1937, when Lorimer retired, circulation was 3,000,000. In 1968 its circulation would reach 6,800,000.

Advertising revenue climbed as well, reaching $360,000 annually by 1902 and $28 million in 1922. Indeed, it has been said with much justification that the advertising industry and *Saturday Evening Post* and *Ladies' Home Journal* grew and prospered together. One of the chief reasons for the *Post's* advertising growth was the automobile industry's adoption of the *Post* as its favorite advertising medium. By 1914 more than forty manufacturers of automobiles and automotive accessories were advertising in it. Tobacco and liquor advertising were notably missing from the *Post*; they were not accepted until 1930 and 1960, respectively.

Ladies' Home Journal's success was by no means diminished by that of the *Post*. In a 1908 edition, which marked the publication's twenty-fifth anniversary, Edward Bok boasted that his was the first magazine of large circulation to sell at 10¢ an issue, the first to introduce the idea of monthly cover changes, the first to refuse to accept questionable advertising, and the first to create personal columns between editor and reader. Another innovation was yet to occur; the magazine would be the first to introduce color printing in its pages.

Curtis Publishing Company's domination of the magazine industry, led by these two giants, seemed complete during the first third of the century. During the peak years between 1918 and 1929, 48¢ of every advertising dollar spent in American magazines went to either the *Post*, the *Journal*, or a third Curtis publication, *Country Gentleman*. The *Post's* high mark occurred in 1929 when a single issue contained 272 pages and weighed almost two pounds. Lorimer, in a 1927 editorial, commented that the *Post's* readers were the "most intelligent and progressive audience in America — the backbone of the community's buying power." They were, he averred, the kind of people "who support the nation's industries rather than its nightclubs."[16] Among the most notable and popular features of the magazine were the regular covers by artist Norman Rockwell depicting middle-class life.

The *Post's* success emanated from the American heartland, and that success was to continue through the greater part of the twentieth century. When, however, the nation became more urbanized and more sophisticated in its tastes, and when the magazine industry seemed to shift in focus in the 1960s, the *Post* formula would fail to accommodate the new conditions.

Of an entirely different nature was *The New Republic*, a magazine of current affairs founded by Herbert Croly in 1913 as an outgrowth of the Progressive era. Its early staff included a brilliant young journalist named Walter Lippmann, whose recent and

[15]See Walter D. Fuller, *The Life and Times of Cyrus H.K. Curtis* (New York, 1948), 17.

[16]Quoted in Joseph C. Goulden, *The Curtis Caper* (New York, 1965), 32.

thoughtful book, *A Preface to Politics*, called for regulation of monopolies and an expanded role for the federal government. *The New Republic* would maintain a high level of political, cultural, and literary commentary through the present time. Its circulation remained modest, as did that of similar publications such as *The Nation* and *The Progressive*, but its influence was formidable.

While these publications were imbued with the liberals' optimistic view of the possibilities of perfection for the human race, a magazine that emerged in the 1920s with commentary on current affairs took a far more skeptical viewpoint. This publication, the *American Mercury*, was the product of the iconoclastic H.L. Mencken of Baltimore. First appearing in 1924, the *American Mercury* gleefully identified and poked holes in the rosy optimism of the 1920s. Nothing in American life seemed to escape Mencken's caustic attention. The magazine, clad in a bright green cover, attracted widespread popularity, especially among the nation's college youth. As the boom of the 1920s faded into the stark Depression days of the 1930s, however, the magazine's attraction dimmed and Mencken's cynical views lost popularity.

The New
REPUBLIC
A Journal of Opinion

VOLUME I — New York Saturday 7th November 1914 — NUMBER 1

THE New Republic is frankly an experiment. It is an attempt to find national audience for a journal of interpretation and opinion. Many people believe that such a journal is out of place in America; that if a periodical is to be popular, it must first of all be entertaining, or that if it is to be serious, it must be detached and select. Yet when the plan of The New Republic was being discussed it received spontaneous welcome from people in all parts of the country. They differed in theories and programmes; but they agreed that if The New Republic could bring sufficient enlightenment to the problems of the nation and sufficient sympathy to its complexities, it would serve all those who feel the challenge of our time. On the conviction that this is possible The New Republic is founded. Its success inevitably depends on public support, but if we are unable to achieve that success under the conditions essential to sound and disinterested thinking, we shall discontinue our experiment and make way for better men. Meanwhile, we set out with faith.

APART from the narrow margin whereby the Democrats retained control of the House of Representatives, the salient feature of the election is the apparently reactionary revulsion of popular opinion. Progressivism of all kinds has fared badly. The Progressive Party has been reduced to an insignificant remnant. The unprogressive members of the older parties are much more conspicuous on the face of the returns than are their progressive brethren. If we may judge by the fate of the proposed woman's suffrage amendments, progressive legislation has fared as ill as progressive candidates. The revulsion appears to be complete. No explanation can explain it away, but how is it to be explained?

In all probability it is more than anything else an exhibition of fatigue. Popular interest has been strained by a political agitation which has lasted too long and has made a too continuous demand upon its attention. It is tired of Congresses which do not adjourn, of questions which are always being discussed and never, being settled, of supposed settlements which fail to produce the promised results, and of a ferment which yields such a small net return of good white bread. The voter whose interest is flagging reverts to his habits. He had been accustomed to vote as a member of one party when business was good, and sometimes to change over to the other party when business was bad. Business has been undeniably bad. His attention was not diverted from the business depression by the impulse of new and attractive political objects. On the contrary, progressive politics and economics had ceased to be either new or attractive. So the good voter cast his ballot as one or the other kind of a partisan, and the bi-partisan system has regained some of its old vitality. Neither should the substantial contribution which President Wilson has made to this result be overlooked. His scrupulous loyalty to his own party, and his determination to govern by means of a partisan machine and the use of partisan discipline, has resulted in the recrudescence of merely partisan Republicanism, and the increased political importance to the individual voter of a close connection with one of the two dominant parties.

THE severest blow which non-partisan progressivism received at the elections came from the apparently successful Senatorial candidacies of Sherman in Illinois, Gallinger in New Hampshire, and Penrose in Pennsylvania. These three gentlemen are all of them machine politicians with unsavory records, who represent everything most obnoxious to an American progressive. They were to a considerable extent opposed by the progressive elements in their own parties. Yet they were all nominated and elected by popular vote, and no adherent of popular government can question their title to their offices. The meaning of the lesson is unmistakable. Direct primaries and the direct popular election of Senators will not contribute much to the triumph of genuine political and social democracy so long as partisan allegiance remains the dominant fact in the voter's mind. Bi-partisanship will con-

The New Republic
Going against the approaches that made entertaining and inspiring magazines such as the *Saturday Evening Post* hugely popular, Herbert Croly's *The New Republic* emphasized serious, liberal discussion of political issues and current affairs. It had a comparatively small circulation, but its readership consisted of members of influential groups such as college professors.

NEW SUCCESSES IN MAGAZINE PUBLICATION

Three magazines founded in the 1920s seemed to match perfectly the faster pace of the Roaring Twenties. They continued to find favor with the reading public into the 1990s. *Time*, *Reader's Digest*, and *New Yorker* were not at all alike; yet, each found a ready audience. While the *New Yorker's* audience was small and literate, those of *Time* and *Reader's Digest* came from middle America. *Reader's Digest* became for a time the magazine with the greatest circulation in the world. *Time*, the brainchild of two Yale graduates, spawned the nation's most prominent and visible publishing empire. These three magazines survived beyond an age that was noted by the demise of the mass circulation, general interest publication as represented by *Saturday Evening Post* and *Life*.

They were founded during a decade that was unusually important in American life. Radio became in the 1920s a central factor in the daily life of almost every American. Literature blossomed in the post-war years. So, too, did the magazine industry flourish with the advent of these new magazines.

The founding of *Reader's Digest* and its success represented a publishing miracle, giving hope to all aspiring publishers who have an idea but no money. DeWitt Wallace, a Minnesota-born college dropout, discovered the principle upon which the magazine would be based when he was working in St. Paul as a writer of sales promotion letters for a textbook publishing firm. In his reading he noticed an abundance of excellent pamphlets from the Department of Agriculture and state agricultural stations. It occurred to him that the best of these should be digested and reprinted in a single booklet. This he did in 1916, and he sold 100,000 copies of the 120-page booklet, *Getting the Most Out of Farming*, to banks for distribution to their customers. The same thing could be done, perhaps with equal success, he reasoned, by digesting the best magazine articles into a single publication. These thoughts were interrupted by World War I. Serving in the U.S. Army in Europe, Wallace suffered shrapnel wounds, and as he recovered in the hospital the idea forcefully recurred to him as he thumbed through magazine after magazine. As he lay in bed he began to practice tightening up articles, editing out words, phrases, sentences, and whole paragraphs without damaging the articles, often even enhancing them. Returning to St. Paul, he prepared a sample copy of a new publication he called "The Readers Digest." Publisher after publisher refused to sponsor his proposal, and Wallace finally accepted a position in the publicity department of Westinghouse Electric Co. in Pittsburgh.

When a brief recession hit the nation, Westinghouse found Wallace expendable and fired him. Wallace decided he must take his fate into his own hands. He began promoting his magazine project by mail, moved to New York City, rented a storeroom under a Greenwich Village speakeasy as headquarters, borrowed

The Reader's Digest

"An article a day" from leading magazines —each article of enduring value and interest, in condensed, permanent booklet form.

Vol. 5 OCTOBER 1926 Serial No. 54

Gleams of Mark Twain Humor

Anecdotes Reflecting the Whimsical Quality of the Humorist

Excerpts from The Mentor

EVEN as a child Mark Twain gave glimpses of the first outcroppings of the original genius that would one day amaze and entertain the nations. At bedtime he would sit up in bed and tell astonishing tales of the day's adventures, tales that caused his listeners to wonder why the lightning was restrained so long. Friends of his mother asked her if she believed anything the child said.

"Oh, yes," she replied, "I know his average. I discount him 90 per cent. The rest is pure gold. Sammy is a well of truth, but you can't bring it all up in one bucket."

One Sunday morning, during his early married life in Buffalo, Mark Twain noticed smoke pouring from the upper window of the house across the street. The owner and his wife, comparatively newcomers, were seated upon the veranda, unaware of impending danger. Clemens stepped briskly across the street and bowing with leisurely politeness, said: "My name is Clemens; we ought to have called on you before, and I beg your pardon for intruding now in this informal way, but your house is on fire."

The Clemens home at Hartford was next door to that of Harriet Beecher Stowe, and Mark Twain and the author of Uncle Tom's Cabin were the best of neighbors. Mrs. Stowe was leaving for Florida one morning, and Clemens ran over early to say good-by. On his return Mrs. Clemens regarded him disapprovingly: "Why Youth," she said, "you haven't on any collar and tie."

He said nothing, but went up to his room, did up these items in a neat package, and sent it to Mrs. Stowe by a servant, with a line: "Herewith receive a call from the rest of me."

Mark Twain was often subjected to the importunities of young and aspiring authors who sought his advice and, in some cases, asked him to read their manuscripts. One of these had accompanied his request with an inquiry as to the right diet for an author, asking Mark Twain if it was true, as Professor Agassiz had said, that fish was good brain food. Mark Twain replied as follows "Yes, Agassiz does recommend authors to eat fish, because the phosphorous in it makes brain. So far you are correct. But I cannot help

The Reader's Digest 821

Reader's Digest
From its founding in 1922, *Reader's Digest* has used the same formula that has kept it successful until the present. Its editors found interesting stories in other publications and condensed them into brief articles for easy reading.

$5,000 from family and friends, and — on the eve of this risky project — married his longtime sweetheart, Lila, who would become a partner in the venture. When the couple returned from their honeymoon, they found in their mailbox enough subscriptions to pay the printing bill for the first issue of *Reader's Digest*, dated February 1922. It contained "thirty-one articles of enduring value and interest, in condensed and compact form." In the Wallaces' early days as publishers, so short of funds were they that they copied the articles by hand from publications in the New York Public Library.

The formula that Wallace envisioned for the fast-paced life that followed World War I was inherently correct for a nation that, according to the 1920 census, for the first time was predominately urban. The reading public was ready for brevity, and a magazine that condensed the best from other magazines had distinct appeal. Before 1922 ended, *Reader's Digest* could boast of a circulation of 7,000 — not spectacular but certainly satisfactory — and the Wallaces found better facilities in Pleasantville, New York. Actually, the headquarters was no more than a pony shed and garage located on an estate, but here they remained for three years, living above the garage and working in the former pony stalls. In 1925, with circulation reaching 20,000, the Wallaces bought land adjoining their pony stall office, built a home on it, and moved the magazine office into the new ground-floor study.

There was nothing meteoric about the growth of *Reader's Digest*; it was slow but certain. Still, by 1929 circulation had reached 109,000. Wallace introduced the publication on the nation's newsstands rather than relying strictly on subscriptions. He also began signing contracts with certain magazines to ensure his exclusive right to reprint articles.

Despite its reprint policy, *Reader's Digest* developed an editorial formula of its own. In the early years the Wallaces sought to get into every issue something from a long list of categories: science, medicine, education, government, the art of living, international relations, biography, movies, sports, travel, humor, essays, labor, business, nature, and agriculture. In 1933 *Reader's Digest* began to produce its own articles as well. Gradually there emerged a penchant for articles that emphasized the successes of people who worked hard and earned rewards as a result. During the 1940s the magazine began to assume a conservative political stance, lamenting excessive government regulation and championing free enterprise.

The magazine's continuing prosperity was evidenced in 1938 by construction of a four-story building on an eighty-acre site in Pleasantville. In the same year a British edition was published in London. Two years later South American editions were introduced in Spanish and Portuguese. Soon, *Reader's Digest* became the most widely read magazine in South America. Not until the 1950s did the magazine open its pages to advertisers, and in 1950 the firm began a lucrative side-adventure: Reader's Digest Condensed Books. By 1990 *Reader's Digest* enjoyed a world-wide circulation of more than 28 million and a circulation within the United States of more than 16 million. Until the newcomer *TV Guide* surpassed it in the early 1970s, it had been the circulation leader for many years. As usual, such success bred imitation. *Pageant*, *Coronet*, *Fleet's Review*, and *Quick* were among those to challenge, but none achieved lasting success.

Time Magazine

It was this twentieth-century idea of brevity that prompted two idealistic graduates of Yale University, Henry Luce and Briton Hadden, to found *Time* magazine. Their venture started modestly enough but went on to become the most prominent publishing company in the nation, Time Inc., under whose aegis would appear *Fortune*, *Life*, *Sports Illustrated*, *People*, *Money*, a book series, and for a number of years a radio news show and movie newsreel.

Of the two founders, it was Luce with whom the company is identified in the modern public's mind, for Hadden died in 1929, six years after the magazine was founded. The child of Presby-

FIFTEEN CENTS

TIME

The Weekly News-Magazine

VOL. 1, NO. 1 MARCH 3, 1923

***Time*, Master of Brevity**

Observing that the United States had the most highly developed daily newspapers in the world, Henry Luce and Briton Hadden believed Americans still were poorly informed. The reason: busy working people did not have time to read detailed newspaper stories. Their solution was to start *Time* magazine, a weekly summary of current affairs

terian missionaries in China, Luce was reared in that country. Young Luce developed intensely patriotic notions. Upon coming to the United States to attend the exclusive Hotchkiss School in Connecticut, he met and formed a friendly rivalry with the editor of the school newspaper, Hadden. The two went on to Yale; and although World War I interrupted their undergraduate careers, both graduated in 1920. Luce was named "most brilliant," and Hadden "most likely to succeed." After brief careers as reporters, they rejoined one another as newsmen on the *Baltimore News*, where in their off hours they prepared a prospectus for a new magazine they had envisioned since their days at Yale.

They observed that although daily journalism was more highly developed in the United States than in any other nation of the world, its citizens were for the most part poorly informed. Why? "Because no publication has adapted itself to the time which busy men are able to spend on simply keeping informed," they argued. Their working title, "Facts," soon was changed to *Time*. It would be a publication created on a "new principle of complete organization" with materials appearing in a brief, organized manner under fixed department headings: foreign news, sports, and so forth.

Resigning from their positions in Baltimore, the pair moved to New York City to raise the $100,000 they believed would be necessary to begin their publication. They reasoned naively that ten rich Yale men should be willing to contribute $10,000 each toward their goal. After raising $86,000 from seventy-two investors, they had exhausted their list of potential investors and decided to move ahead. In a promotional campaign they offered three free issues before an individual had to decide whether to subscribe for a year at $15. Some 25,000 people accepted the offer.

On March 3, 1923, the first issue of *Time, the Weekly News-Magazine*, appeared. It was divided into twenty-two departments; and since there were no reporters on the staff to generate copy, the news in the magazine was lifted almost entirely from the *New York Times*. Both Hadden and Luce had preferred to be editor, but the publication needed a business manager as well; so the two flipped a coin. Hadden won. The agreement was that they would alternate positions each year, but three years passed before Luce could untangle himself from business affairs to permit him to take his turn as editor.

It was under Hadden's editorship that the peculiar style of writing known as "Time style" evolved. "Backward ran sentences until reeled the mind," wrote Wolcott Gibbs in the famous parody of *Time* that appear in the *New Yorker*.[17] The magazine developed other stylistic mannerisms: "cinemactor" for movie star, "socialite" for one involved in high society, "great and good friend" for mistress, and such sentences as, "As it must to all men, death came last week to...." People in *Time* never said anything; they snapped, gruffed, croaked, chuckled, gushed, or sneered. Neither did they walk; they strode, stalked, bounced, leaped, or shot ahead.

The magazine departed from the standard of journalistic objectivity. There was no editorial page because editorial opinions were inserted in the articles. *Time* did express, however, an interest in achieving a standard of fairness in its coverage.

As the magazine prospered, Hadden and Luce grew apart. Hadden was flamboyant; Luce, serious. In his will, Hadden sought to exclude Luce from gaining his share of the company, but Luce managed to do so anyway; and in the many decades that followed after Hadden's death, Time Inc. and Henry Luce were nearly inseparable in the public mind.

Luce's success with *Time* led the magazine into other ventures. *Fortune*, a monthly designed to give business a publication, was started in 1930 at an inauspicious time — the beginning of the Great Depression — and sold for the startlingly high price of $1 an issue. The magazine did more than survive the hard times; it prospered. Other ventures followed, including a radio news show and the movie newsreel, "The March of Time."

LIFE MAGAZINE

Introduced in 1935, "The March of Time" indicated Luce's growing interest in pictorial journalism, and in early 1936 he an-

[17]Quoted in James Thurber, *The Years with Ross* (Boston, 1957), 217.

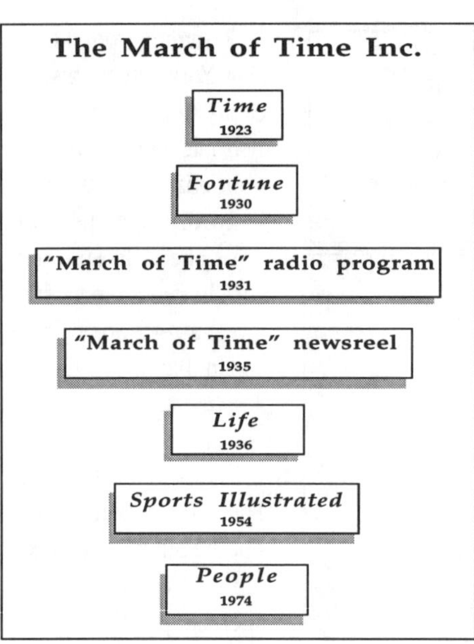

Picture of Success
Time Inc. created a group of magazines whose success was virtually unmatched. For years, its most popular periodical was *Life*, the pioneer among picture magazines. Filled with photographs and photo stories, *Life* was an instant success when Time Inc. introduced it in 1936. Over the years it published some of the best photojournalism ever produced and included work by the most notable American photographers.

nounced his intention to begin a new pictorial magazine. After months of planning and serious in-fighting among the staff, the first issue of the weekly picture magazine, *Life*, appeared on Thursday, November 19, 1936, bearing on its cover the image of Fort Peck Dam in Montana in a black-and-white photograph taken by Margaret Bourke-White.

The magazine was an instant success: the entire press run of 466,000 sold out. The same thing happened in the following few weeks, and the magazine's circulation surpassed 500,000. Just how extensive could the market be? Time Inc. executives got an idea from sales in Worcester, Massachusetts. On the first day of publication 475 copies of the magazine sold out in a few hours. With the December 4 issue the decision was made to flood the city's newsstands with 2,000 copies. These were purchased just as quickly as the 475 copies. In the weeks that followed, shipments were raised to 3,000 then 4,000 and then 9,000. After the latter figure was reached, a Worcester distributor telegraphed: "Send 12,000 next week." The result was yet another sell-out. It was concluded that the potential national demand for the magazine was between five and six million copies a week. The projection proved to be accurate.

Life's impact on Time Inc. was substantial. In 1939 the magazine's annual revenues were just under $30 million; its before-tax profit was nearly $4 million. In 1941 the figures had climbed to $45 million in revenue with before-tax profits of $8.1 million. The average net paid circulation had reached 3,290,480, second to the *Saturday Evening Post*'s 3,386,950. *Life* also was second to the *Saturday Evening Post* in dollar volume of advertising. Its revenues surpassed those of its older brother, *Time*, and its circulation was about four times as great.

Life photographers achieved national fame. They included Margaret Bourke-White, Alfred Eisenstaedt, W. Eugene Smith, Robert Capa, Carl Mydans, David Douglas Duncan, and Gordon Parks. Their candid photographs were made possible through *Life's* adoption of the 35mm camera, so much more portable and discreet than the old 4 x 5 press camera.

Time Inc. began to acquire an international flavor as *Time*, *Life*, and *Fortune* attracted subscribers and developed newsstand sales all over the world. Before World War II a weekly excerpt from *Time* was translated into Spanish and distributed to a number of Latin American newspapers. It was followed by a special edition of *Time* printed on lightweight paper and delivered by air to South America.

Time Inc. was not the only publishing company in the mid-1930s to see promise in a magazine based on photojournalism. At the same time *Life* was being envisioned, John and Gardner Cowles, the brothers who published the *Des Moines Register and Tribune,* were planning their own picture magazine, *Look*. There were no secrets about the separate ambitions, for the Cowles brothers were friends and stockholders of Time Inc. They accordingly shared with Luce dummy copy of their magazine, and even offered Time Inc. a 20% interest in the venture. Time Inc., after careful consideration, accepted the offer, purchasing 45,000 shares of the planned publication. It was acknowledged that *Look* might well succeed where *Life* failed because of *Look's* far more modest scale of operations. After both *Life* and *Look* were in operation, the Cowleses requested that Time Inc. resell its shares in the company. The transaction was made in 1937, and Time Inc. earned a nifty profit of $675,000.

The New Yorker

A third magazine founded in the 1920s, the *New Yorker*, made little attempt to attract a mass circulation. Appealing to a highly literate audience, it endured with hardly any changes in its physical appearance while mass magazines were dying during a struggle for circulation and advertising in the 1960s.

The *New Yorker* was founded in 1925 by Harold Ross, a Colorado native, World War I veteran, and ex-newspaperman. Ross, as did the editors of *Time* and *Reader's Digest*, settled in New York City after the war to establish his publication. Estimating start-up costs at $50,000, he obtained half the amount from Raoul Fleischman, an investor who also provided an office for the publication. Picking a name was no easy chore: "Manhattan," "New York Weekly," "New York Life," "Truth," and "Our Town" were among those considered. One day when the literary crowd that frequented the Algonquin Hotel in mid-town Manhattan pondered the matter, John Toohey suggested "The New Yorker." The name seemed a natural, and Ross rewarded Toohey with stock in the company.

The board of editors that Ross chose included those literary lights with the "Round Table" at the Algonquin: Marc Connelly, Edna Ferber, George S. Kaufman, Dorothy Parker, and Alexander Woollcott. They were supposed to give advice and their own literary output, but the acerbic Ross thought of them as window dressing. "The only dishonest thing I ever did," he said later of his distinguished board.[18]

The first issue of the *New Yorker* appeared on February 21, 1925. No familiar names could be found among the contributors; Ross had used pseudonyms because he wanted the magazine to project its own special personality. The writers protested, and a compromise was reached for future issues: the authors' names would appear at the *end* of articles. Ross, who was to edit the *New Yorker* and to set its unique tone for the rest of his life, intended for it to reflect metropolitan life and to keep up with the affairs of the day in a gay and satirical vein not aimed at "the little old lady in Dubuque." This he did through sophisticated fiction and humor, in-depth profiles of prominent personalities, a gossipy and literate "Talk of the Town" column, lengthy "letters" from around the world, and wry cartoons.

The magazine was slow to take hold; and its readership, never approaching the numbers of *Time* or *Reader's Digest* or *Saturday Evening Post*, reflected an audience that was upperclass, highly educated, literate, and sophisticated. The *New Yorker* developed such writers as E.B. White and James Thurber, and it changed forever the nature of magazine humor.

The *New Yorker*
Once every year since its inception, the *New Yorker* has run the cover shown above. "Eustace Tilly," the fictitious character depicted, seemed to symbolize the sophisticated, literate tone that Harold Ross had envisioned for the magazine when he started it in 1925.

COMPETITION AT THE TOP

There seemed to be plenty of room following World War II for all these magazines. Curtis Publishing Company alone printed more than 25 million copies of its magazines each month. Its annual consumption of ink — more than 10 million pounds — was said to be enough to paint an area of 500 square miles. Despite *Life's* remarkable reception and a circulation of 5.2 million, which was just ahead of the *Saturday Evening Post's*, advertisers continued to view the *Post* as the more reliable vehicle, and the *Post* regularly contained more advertising.

Life's advertising rates, however, were higher than those of the *Post* because of its larger circulation, and the company initiated a campaign to persuade advertisers that their money was better spent in *Life*. Red labels and posters began to appear in shop windows and retail counters proclaiming, "As advertised in Life." Efforts simultaneously were made to boost the circulation to 6,000,000 while the price per issue was increased to 15¢. The increase suggested in a subtle way that *Life* was worth 5¢ more than the *Post*, which sold for a dime.

The *Post* was prepared for the challenge. The era of World War II and afterwards has been called the *Post's* "Silver Age." Editor Ben Hibbs, a Kansan, addressed the conservative American heartland in the magazine's pages. The editors of the other Curtis publications, *Jack and Jill*, *Ladies' Home Journal*, and *Country Gentleman*, also had been born and bred in the Middle West, and their publications reflected that. Hibbs engineered a series of biographical and autobiographical articles on such American heroes as Dwight Eisenhower, Casey Stengel, and Douglas MacArthur. In

[18]Quoted in Jane Grant, *Ross, The New Yorker and Me* (New York, 1968), 210.

a series of "I Call On" articles in the 1950s, senior editor Pete Martin engaged in chatty, intimate interviews with such celebrities as Bing Crosby, Clark Gable, Grace Kelly, and Marilyn Monroe. When entertainer Arthur Godfrey's story appeared in the magazine with his portrait on the cover, the magazine sold 2,000,000 copies on the newsstands alone.

As James Playsted Wood wrote, "There is only one comfortable place for a mass magazine to be — first." Advertising salesmen for the *Post* were unaccustomed to the secondary role in which they found themselves as *Life* pushed ahead in circulation, and an energetic marketing campaign answered *Life's* challenge. According to the *Post's* promotions, people loved and trusted the magazine; more *Post* readers owned their homes; more *Post* readers held executive positions and so on.[19]

The year 1953 saw the *Post's* circulation go above 5,500,000 and advertising sales reach almost $81 million. But 1954 saw a puzzling development: a loss in advertising revenue of almost $2 million. Why? Not for a lack of faithful readers, for there were nearly 6,000,000 of them, but because advertisers were beginning to lose faith in the *Post* and its middle-America predelictions. Madison Avenue was East Coast; advertising account executives tended to prefer *Life* as an advertising vehicle. *Life* was jazzier. It had less type and more pictures. More people saw a single issue of *Life* than saw *Post*. In fact, *Life* produced figures indicating that its readers were better educated and more affluent than the *Post's* and that they tended to be community leaders. Circulation was not declining, for it passed the 6,000,000 mark in 1959. Still, net earnings of $2.8 million that year for Curtis Publishing Company were down from the previous year by about $3.5 million.

In 1942 an entrepreneur named John H. Johnson, noting the success of magazines with broad appeal, decided that a market existed for a national publication directed toward African-American readers. He raised a little money by mortgaging his mother's furniture and used it to start *Negro Digest*, pattered after *Reader's Digest*. Three years later he founded *Ebony*, a publication for African-American readers that was reminiscent of *Life*, although its goal was to emphasize the positive aspects of Negro life. Johnson went on to become the nation's most prominent black publisher, with additional magazines such as *Jet* and *Ebony Jr.* Still other black-oriented publications were emerging in the late 1980s and early 1990s.[20]

PROGRESS REPORT 1964

YEAR OF DECISION

All segments of nation faced crucial decisions — and selected forward steps

Ebony

In 1943 John H. Johnson took the graphic approaches used by *Life* magazine and adapted them to *Ebony*, a publication for African Americans. Celebrating their achievements, *Ebony* helped Johnson become America's leading black magazine publisher.

Magazines in the Age of Television

Besides the growing competition within the mass magazine field, ominous new competition for the advertising dollar had risen from another source: television. It reached audiences in gigantic numbers beyond the range of any magazine. If mass magazines thought they could attract millions of readers by appealing to mass taste, they were hopelessly outmatched by television's ability to do the same. Advertisers readily responded. Between 1952 and 1956, television advertising revenue tripled from $454,000 to $1.2 million. Television had little effect on the public's appetite for general magazines, but its effect on advertisers was devastating. Indeed, while magazine circulation continued to grow in the 1950s, the Golden Age of Television was capturing the imagination of millions more Americans who retired each evening after dinner to their comfortable chairs before the television set.

That problems lay ahead for all mass magazines was clearly suggested in December 1956 with the sudden demise of *Collier's*, a publication that had been in existence for sixty-eight years as a general-interest fortnightly. The magazine's publisher, Crowell Publishing Co., announced at the same time that *Woman's Home Companion*, with an 83-year history, also was suspended. The two magazines, boasting of combined circulations of 8.3 million, had lost $7.5 million between them for the year, threatening the very existence of the parent company.

Look, eager to catch up with *Life* and *Saturday Evening Post* in the circulation war, snatched up *Collier's* subscribers, bringing its list to 4.2 million. Determined to stay in the race, *Look* began pro-

19 James Playsted Wood, *The Curtis Magazines* (New York, 1971), 194.
20 Roland E. Wolseley, *The Black Press, U.S.A.*, 2nd ed. (Ames, Iowa, 1990), 86-9.

moting itself as the magazine that "likes people...what they do, what they feel, what they want, what they think." As a *Look* memorandum to an advertising agency elaborated, "*Life* — in spite of all efforts at informality — remains the lofty pundit, superior, condescending, jesting, ponderous with moral instruction for the lesser masses. Standing shoulder to shoulder with man, *Look* asks questions. *Life* is impersonal; *Look* is personal. *Life* likes theories, causes, paradoxes, heroes and vast movements in time and space; *Look* likes people." Such an approach, Henry Luce felt, was "a sure-fire American line," and he observed that it likely had been inspired by his own personal reputation for being aloof, cold, and inhuman. So long as *Life* demonstrated a capacity for humanness, though, it would be fine, he believed.[21]

Along with television and intensified competition, rising costs for production and distribution were threatening mass magazines. By 1969, despite the 40¢ cover price for *Life*, special subscription rates brought the average price per issue down to 12¢. Yet the cost to edit, print, and distribute was 41¢ per issue. The difference of 29¢ had to be made up by advertisers. At the beginning of 1970, advertising revenues for *Life* were just 27¢ per copy, meaning that each copy sold brought the company a 2¢ loss. Thus, at a time when circulations for magazines such as *Life*, *Look*, and *Post* were higher than ever in their history, at a time when the magazines' acceptance by the public was enthusiastic, these magazines were approaching economic disaster and the end to a long era in publishing. Advertisers who wished to address a mass audience had a better vehicle: television. They were becoming more and more reluctant to pay the high advertising rates that mass magazines were compelled to ask in order to sustain themselves.

The *Post*, in desperation, initiated a series of changes, some of which were revolutionary and none of which worked. It took on as an editorial philosophy "sophisticated muckraking," a stance that offended old readers and won few new ones. It decided to reduce circulation by an arbitrary formula so that it could claim to deliver to its advertisers an elite audience representing the more affluent counties in the nation. To achieve this end, it eliminated 3.8 million of its 6.8 million subscribers. Among the victims, because of accounting errors, were the *Post's* former editor, Ben Hibbs; Arkansas Governor Winthrop Rockefeller; and the magazine's own president, Martin Ackerman. As 1969 arrived, the *Post* found itself losing some $400,000 a month, an untenable situation. Later that year the inevitable occurred: the magazine folded. Several years later it re-emerged as a quarterly under new ownership, and while the product was designed to resemble the *Post* of pre-World War II days, it was a drastically different publication.

Meanwhile, *Life* and *Look* were struggling with the same economic forces. *Look* was next to fail, and *Life* saw its gross advertising revenue drop from $170 million in 1966 to $91 million in 1971. Costs continued to rise, including the price paid for printing paper and a new U.S. Postal Service rate that sought an end to the long-time indirect subsidies for magazine mailing costs.

[21]Quoted in Robert T. Elson, *Time Inc.: The Intimate History of a Publishing Enterprise, 1923-1941* (New York, 1968), 426-7.

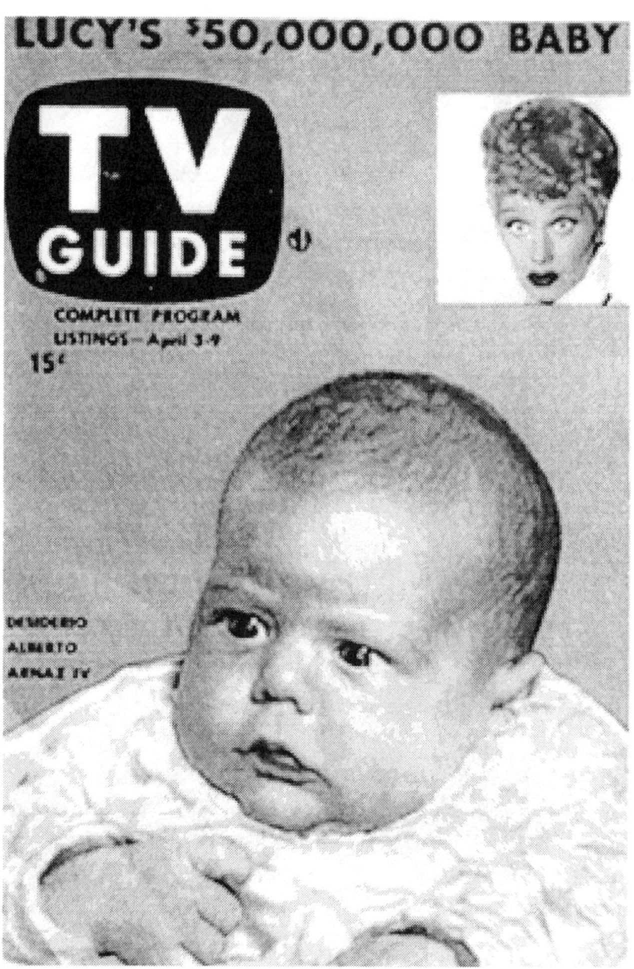

Made by Television
The success of *TV Guide*, which consistently has the highest revenue of any magazine, has coincided with the rise of television in American life. The cover of its inaugural issue in 1953 carried a picture of Lucille Ball and her newborn son.

Life's last regular issue was published December 29, 1972. As was true for the *Saturday Evening Post*, however, *Life* did not disappear forever, for Time Inc. issued occasional special issues at a price of $1.50 to $2 each; and in 1978 it re-introduced *Life* as a regular monthly "specialized" magazine.

A New Magazine Age

As *Post*, *Look*, and *Life* struggled with the new economic forces, other magazines were emerging that seemed to recognize and take advantage of a new age in publishing. These were the specialized magazines, aimed at readers with specialized interests that could not be satisfied in a general publication. Neither could they be satisfied by television and its quest for mass audiences.

Of course, there always had been specialized magazines, but they had existed in the shadow of the mass magazines. Now emerged special-interest magazines that achieved mass-circulation status. The categories were many, ranging from men's magazines such as *Esquire* and *Playboy*; sports magazines such as

Sports Illustrated
Aimed at America's sports enthusiasts, *Sports Illustrated* lost $6 million in its first year. It was ten years before the magazine became a financial success, but it eventually became one of Time Inc.'s most profitable publications.

Sports Illustrated and *Outdoor Life*; business magazines such as *Business Week* and *Forbes*; women's magazines as varied as *Redbook*, *Ms*, and *Mademoiselle*; music publications such as the highly successful *Rolling Stone*; travel magazines such as *Travel and Leisure*; and popular science magazines as varied as the venerable *Scientific American* and *Popular Science*.

Sports Illustrated, founded by Time Inc. in 1954, capitalized on the nation's continuing interest in sports that had been evident in sport magazines dating to the first half of the nineteenth century. *Sports Illustrated* achieved resounding success from its first issue. Yet, despite its acceptance by some 350,000 charter subscribers and excellent newsstand sales, it brought Time Inc. losses of $6 million in 1954. Not until ten years had passed did the magazine achieve its first profitable year. By 1972, however, it not only enjoyed a circulation of 2.2 million but stood second only to *Time* as a profit-maker for the corporation.

Two years later, in 1974, Time Inc. launched yet another weekly publication, *People Weekly*, a magazine that highlighted personal aspects of interesting and important people. *People's* brief, conversational articles, usually about celebrities, accompanied by candid photographs, found a ready audience. After just five years of publication it reached a circulation of 2.3 million, and by the time of its 10th anniversary it had become Time Inc.'s most profitable publication.

A few years earlier, as *Saturday Evening Post* and *Life* had been battling for supremacy during the great circulation wars of the 1950s, another publication devoted to analysis and commentary of current events that was to make a significant contribution to political thought made a quiet debut. This was the *National Review*, appearing for the first time in November 1955 and offering its readers a decidedly conservative outlook with wit and sparkle. From the beginning, the *National Review* was identified with its founding editor, William F. Buckley Jr., who gained the appellation of the "patron saint of conservatism." The *National Review* provided an ideological home for the nation's leading intellectual and political conservatives, nearly all of whom wrote on occasion for the magazine. On its pages were developed the conservative ideology for the nation that reached a pinnacle when Ronald Reagan was elected president in 1980. The magazine, in typical lighthearted fashion, proclaimed that that for the first time it had become "an establishment organ" and that it no longer could indulge in levity. "Connoisseurs of human will have to get their yuks elsewhere," it declared. "We have a nation to run."[22]

By 1970 the "hot magazines" were those such as *TV Guide*, *Playboy*, *Car Craft*, *Southern Living*, *New York*, *Cosmopolitan*, and plenty of other smaller publications that appealed to readers with such diverse interests as skeet shooting, yachting, knitting, photography, drag racing, and gourmet dining. Some 750 magazines for the general consumer were being issued, up 10% from 1965. *TV Guide* sought to escape the economic dilemma that sank *Life* and *Post* by offering regional editions, and in 1970 it had eighty-one different editions. *Time*, *Newsweek*, and other magazines with hefty circulations also offered regional editions that inevitably had identical editorial content but that permitted advertisers to buy space only for a particular geographical area. In 1963 *Time* was the first magazine to offer a "demographic" edition: a special edition that went only to college students. This was followed by special editions for doctors and educators.[23]

This trend toward "targeting" special audiences continued to grow. By 1990 the number of magazines issuing special geographic or demographic editions had passed 200.[24] As the decade of the 1980s yielded to the '90s, a targeted publication, *Modern Maturity*, a slick bi-monthly magazine issued by the American Association of Retired People (AARP), surprisingly stood alongside two other magazines, *Reader's Digest* and *TV Guide*, as having the highest circulations in the nation. *Modern Maturity*, with a distribution of nearly 20 million copies, reflected changing demographics in which an increasing proportion of the nation's population

[22] Quoted in Alan Nourie and Barbara Nourie, eds., *American Mass-Market Magazines* (New York, 1990), 18.

[23] "The Hot Magazines Aim at Special Targets," *Business Week*, 2 May 1970, 64-74.

[24] John Tebbel and Mary Ellen Zuckerman, *The Magazine in America* (New York, 1991), 263-4.

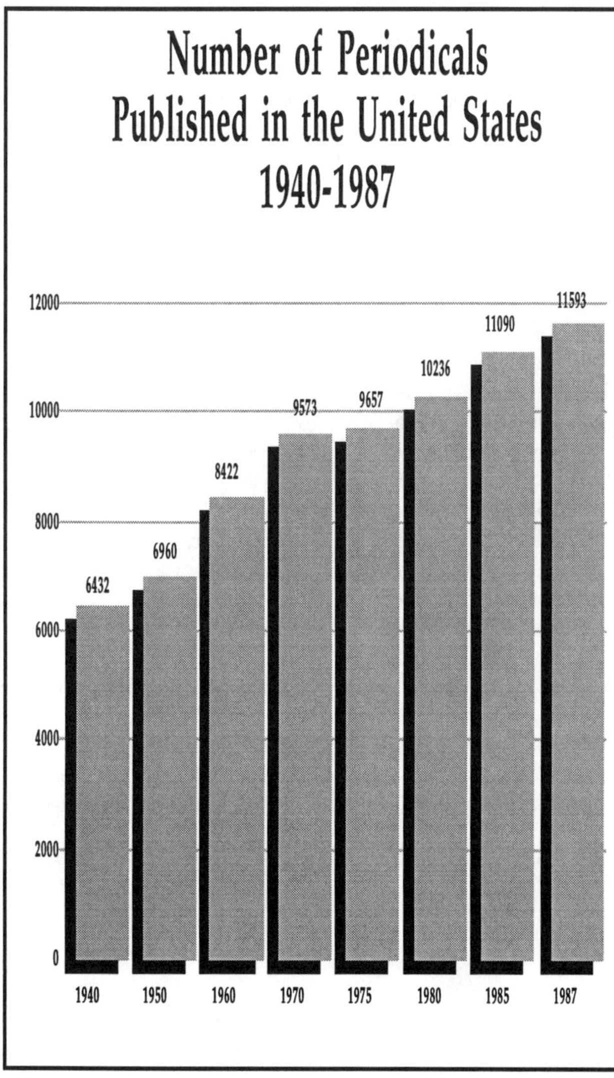

was more than fifty years of age. As AARP grew, so did the magazine's circulation, for all members of the organization received a subscription as a benefit. *TV Guide* was selling approximately 17 million copies a week. The familiar *Reader's Digest*, once the circulation leader, continued to be popular with a monthly circulation of more than 16 million.

Despite a downturn in the nation's economy that brought declining advertising revenues to the industry in the late 1980s and early 1990s, optimism was undaunted. Between 1985 and 1989 a total of 1,238 new magazines were started. As always, the founding of a new publication was a risky venture. Yet, in 1991 some 35% of those new magazines still were in existence, and this was a higher survival rate than that of the first half of the 1980s.

With the beginning of the twenty-first century, then, one thing seems certain: the magazine will continue to be a fascinating, essential part of the increasingly complex communication industry.

RECOMMENDED READINGS

For related books and articles, some of which include the twentieth century, see the list of "Recommended Readings" for Chapter 13 "American Magazines 1740-1900."

BOOKS

Abrahamson, David. *Magazine-Made America: The Cultural Transformation of the Postwar Periodicals.* Cresskill, N.J.: Hampton Press, 1996. General-interest magazines both reflected and reinforced social values.

Ballou, Ellen B. *The Building of the House.* Boston, 1970. A thorough history of the *Atlantic Monthly* covering not only the editorial aspects of the company but also its business side.

Baughman, James L. *Henry R. Luce and the Rise of the American News Media.* Twayne's Twentieth-Century American Biography Series. Boston, 1987. Stresses Luce as a journalist rather than a publisher and analyzes his journalistic style.

Elson, Robert T. *Time Inc.: The Intimate History of a Publishing Enterprise, 1923-1941.* New York, 1968; and vol. 2, *The World of Time Inc.: The Intimate History of a Publishing Enterprise, 1941-1960.* New York, 1973. These two books provide not only an intimate history of Time Inc. and its leading figures, but also insight into the magazine publishing industry as well.

Goulden, Joseph C. *The Curtis Caper.* New York, 1965. An examination into the demise of the *Saturday Evening Post* after so many years of success.

Heidenry, John. *Theirs Was the Kingdom: Lila and DeWitt Wallace and the Story of the Reader's Digest.* New York, 1993. A critical examination of the magazine and its founders and editors.

Kornweibel, Theodore, Jr. *No Crystal Stair: Black Life and the Messenger, 1917-1928.* Westport, Conn., 1975. The *Messenger* was founded as a socialist organ; but once it became clear that the Socialist Party offered no promise for blacks, its publisher moved the magazine to a pro-business position and toward the center of American mainstream politics.

Kunkel, Thomas. *Genius in Disguise: Harold Ross of The New Yorker.* New York, 1995. A significant biography of the founder of *The New Yorker.*

Lyon, Peter. *Success Story: The Life and Times of S. S. McClure.* New York, 1963. McClure "revolutionized American journalism," editing "the best general magazine ever published anywhere." His exposure of political corruption, monopoly trusts, unscrupulous meat packers, etc., had a tremendous influence on legislation. He channeled creative writing into a more meaningful field.

Mott, Frank Luther. *A History of American Magazines, Sketches of 21 Magazines, 1905-1930.* Cambridge, Mass., 1968. Invaluable as a resource for information about the magazines covered; the culmination of Mott's classic five-volume study of American magazines.

Nourie, Alan, and Barbara Nourie, eds. *American Mass-Market Magazines.* New York, 1990. An essential reference for the student of magazines. Contains brief histories with bibliographies of 106 of the most significant mass magazines of the late nineteenth and the twentieth centuries.

Payne, Darwin. *The Man of Only Yesterday: Frederick Lewis Allen.* New York, 1975. Provides an interesting look at editorial workings of *Harper's, Atlantic Monthly*, and *The Century.*

Peterson, Theodore. *Magazines in the Twentieth Century.* Urbana, Ill., 1964. Continues where Mott left off concerning modern magazines.

Sheed, Wilfrid. *Clare Booth Luce.* New York, 1982. Popularized biography of the magazine journalist (managing editor of *Vanity Fair* and originator of the concept for *Life*) who also wrote short stories, satire, and plays. She was a member of Congress, and in the 1950s she was U.S. ambassador to Italy.

Swanberg, W. A. *Luce and His Empire.* New York, 1972. Readable and thorough account of the co-founder of *Time.*

Tebbel, John W., *George Horace Lorimer and The Saturday Evening Post.* Garden City, N.Y., 1948. An uncritical narrative of Lorimer and the *Post* covering the years before the *Post* headed toward its demise.

Thurber, James. *The Years With Ross.* Boston, 1957. An immensely satisfying study of the demanding founder and editor of the *New Yorker*, as well as an intimate portrait of the magazine.

Wainwright, Loudon. *The Great American Magazine: An Inside History of Life.*

New York, 1986. A fascinating anecdotal portrayal of *Life* from one who was there during its heydey.

Wood, James Playsted. *Lasting Interest: The Story of the Reader's Digest.* Garden City, N.Y., 1958. A friendly profile of the magazine and its rise from its origin as an idea.

ARTICLES

Anderson, Fenwick. "Inadequate to Prevent the Present: *The American Mercury* at 50." *Journalism Quarterly* 51 (1974): 297-302, 382. Founded by H.L. Mencken and George Jean Nathan in 1924 to ridicule the attitudes and values of the middle class, the magazine was sold a number of times to publishers who tried to make it succeed financially. By the 1950s it had become conservative.

Bennion, Sherilyn Cox. "Reform Agitation in the American Periodical Press, 1920-29." *Journalism Quarterly* 48 (1971): 692-9, 713. The mass magazines of the 1920s did not talk about reform because their readers did not want to hear about reform. Changes in society had occurred since before World War I, and magazines simply reflected the interests of the public; they were reflectors rather than molders of opinion.

Bullock, Penelope L. "Profile of a Periodical: The 'Voice of the Negro.'" *Atlanta Historical Bulletin* 21 (Spring 1977): 95-114. The establishment of the *Voice of the Negro* in 1904 "marked the substantive beginnings of the commercially published magazine in Atlanta." It reflected black life and provided a black interpretation of events, but it ceased publication after only two years.

Fowler, Gilbert L., Jr., and Edward J. Smith. "The Status of Magazine Group Ownership." *Journalism Quarterly* 56 (1979): 572-6. A well-documented study showing how magazine groups own a large number of the nation's magazines.

Hirsch, Paul M. "An Analysis of *Ebony*: The Magazine and Its Readers." *Journalism Quarterly* 45 (1968): 261-70, 292. Explains the magazine's appeal to a broad group of black readers.

Hoopes, Roy. "Birth of a Great Magazine." *American History Illustrated* 20, 5 (1986): 34-41. *Life* pioneered a new form of journalism and became "one of the great American magazines of the twentieth century."

"The Hot Magazines Aim at Special Targets." *Business Week*, 2 May 1970, 64-74. An in-depth look into the rise of special-interest magazines.

Hynes, Terry. "Magazine Portrayal of Women, 1911-1930." *Journalism Monographs* 72 (1981). Popular magazines did not portray liberated women as typical.

Johnson, Charles S. "The Rise of the Negro Magazine." *Journal of Negro History* 13 (January 1928): 7-21. Since the early 1800s the problems facing black magazines have been "in essence the same.... Increasing literacy, economic improvement, and the shifting facets of such general social questions as temperance, religion and morals, have determined largely the changes."

Julian, Bea. "Mass Magazines, 1900-Present: Serious Journalism or Mass Entertainment?" 259-70, in Wm. David Sloan, *Perspectives on Mass Communication History* (Hillsdale, N.J., 1991). Analyzes the approaches that historians have taken to explaining magazines during this period.

Mott, Frank Luther. "The Magazine Called 'Success.'" *Journalism Quarterly* 34 (1957): 46-50. "The signficance of the magazine *Success* [1897-1911] lies mainly in its embodiment of the cult of success that was so prominent an element of the national spirit at the beginning of the twentieth century, but it was also important as a popular general magazine and as a participant in the last phase of the muckraking movement."

Root, Christine V., and Robert Root. "Magazines in the United States: Dying or Thriving?" *Journalism Quarterly* 41 (1964): 15-22. Describes the transition of magazines between 1938 and 1963 into specialized publications.

Stinson, Robert. "McClure's Road to *McClure's*: How Revolutionary Were 1890s Magazines?" *Journalism Quarterly* 47 (1970): 256-62. A narrative of the background of the founding of *McClure's* in 1893. S.S. McClure took what he considered to be a popular formula for magazines and aimed it at a mass audience through low price.

21

Modern Advertising

1900 - Present

Advertising experienced dramatic change during the twentieth century, and the change expressed itself in virtually every dimension of the business. The advertising industry actively participated in the often chaotic and frenetic events of the century. An integral part of the American business system, advertising was buffeted by forces both inside and outside the industry. It survived internal strife as its practitioners sought the most effective means of appealing to consumers. Detractors used the very methods and messages the industry created to question its value to society.

As the end of the century approaches, advertisers spend 200 times each year what they spent in 1900. The number of messages they place in media has expanded by a similar magnitude. Media that did not exist 100 years ago have exerted a profound influence on advertising. Advertising's role in the marketing of products and services has undergone modification. The advertising agency, one of the most influential institutions in the industry, has radically reconstructed its services to clients.

Much of this change grew out of the nature of American society and the transformations that occurred in it — growth of and changes in population, development of new technologies, and the general affluence accompanying the last half of the century. Changing though it was, advertising participated actively in a dynamic period that may well be called the communications century. Early on, it helped bring an awareness of the fruits of industry into the home. It told the consumer about automobiles, personal products, packaged goods, food, tobacco, candy, alcohol, and television and other appliances. It introduced the nation to figures who became national celebrities: Bob Hope, Jack Benny, Amos and Andy, and even Speedy Alka-Seltzer. As society became more service oriented, advertising was pressed into the cause. In time, it was harnessed to political machinery as never before to help elect candidates to office.

What is modern advertising? It is a process producing persuasive messages that their sponsors pay media to carry. The process is complex. It began simply enough a century and a half ago, but as society grew more complex, people in the advertising industry matched that complexity with activities designed to identify and reach specific groups of people. Some of the twentieth-century history of advertising relates to the development of the advertising process. That history is itself complex. One reason is that advertising is not monolithic. The most visible segment of the industry produces advertisements seen nationwide on television and in magazines. The bulk of this work is done by large advertising agencies in the major business centers of the United States. Most advertising, however, appears locally and comes from small local and regional agencies or from advertisers. In addition, the media themselves produce many of the advertising messages they carry. Moreover, advertising employs all the news media to carry advertisements, thus further dividing the industry along message delivery lines. Some ads promote the sale of products and services. Some deal with political issues and candidates. Others seek to rent apartments or to find lost pets.

Partly because of its diversity, advertising did not respond effectively to several issues that troubled the industry through the twentieth century. Most were incorporated in one fundamental question: what was its job? Was advertising a messenger? Did it exist to sell? Was it a service for consumers?

This basic inquiry led quickly to issues that defined three dimensions of advertising: economic, communicative, and societal. The advertising industry dealt throughout the twentieth century with these dimensions, and they will appear repeatedly as we move through our story.

Economic. What was the role of advertising in marketing? Did it sell? Did it rigidify demand? If so, it was, as economists tended to claim, monopolistic. Or did it produce demand that resulted in economies of scale? If it did, then it had a competitive effect. The economic issue was of greatest interest to economists and marketing people.

Another element of the economic dimension was the financial support that advertising provided mass media. Print media typically derived up to about two-thirds of their revenue from adver-

Magazine Advertising, 1900

Magazine advertising at the beginning of the twentieth century typically included an illustration and display type, with the remaining space filled with informative copy. About one-half of all ads included a mail-in form.

tisers, broadcast media even more. Because advertisers provided the principal support for the American media system, did they deserve influence in the editorial process?

Communicative. Although advertising messages changed over the years, the basic question about the message remained the same: should advertisements be hard-sell or soft-sell? Both views had their articulate and energetic advocates, and they often clashed. Before the present century, little disagreement existed. Most advertisements were informational in nature: for the most part they called attention to the availability of a product, perhaps providing some reasons for purchasing it. During the early years of the twentieth century the concept of advertising as salesman emerged, producing messages that sounded much like sales pitches, in contrast to the earlier informational advertisements. During the teens and 1920s, soft-sell approaches appeared, especially image building. The issue of whether an advertisement should deliver its message within a hard-sell or soft-sell context is most often addressed by people in the advertising business, rather than by outside critics.

Societal. This dimension of advertising involved legal and ethical issues. Did advertising make people buy things they did not want and could not afford? Did it serve or manipulate people? Did advertising frame society's values, or did it reflect independently established conventions? Sociologists were the people principally interested in these questions.

Albert Lasker and the Beginnings of Modern Advertising

The roots of modern advertising are normally associated with the early twentieth century in the United States. The nation was a brawling youngster flooded with immigrants. Manufacturing and other activities attracted large numbers of people to mostly eastern cities. Literacy and educational levels were climbing. Newspapers with sensational content in large cities gained unprecedented circulations. Magazines also experienced extraordinary growth in readership. Both media offered opportunities for manufacturers to reach large markets.

A typical magazine advertisement was one for Baker's Chocolate showing factory scenes in the corners of the ad. A large picture of a maid carrying what appeared to be hot chocolate was situated in the middle of the ad. Large headline type provided the name of the advertiser, Walter Baker & Co., and one of its products, Breakfast Cocoa, above and below the maid. The remaining space was occupied by copy, which said, in part, of the company's chocolate: "The pure product of selected cocoa beans, to which nothing is added, and from which nothing is taken away. Celebrated for more than a century as a delicious, nutritious and flesh-forming beverage. Best plain chocolate in the market for cooking purposes."[1]

About half of the magazine advertisements during the first decade of the century sought a response by mail from consumers, and about a fifth of all ads were for food and drink products. During the decade following, food accounted for slightly less than a third of all ads.

From the standpoint of the message, advertising lacked a sense of direction. It was largely passive. Albert Lasker, a partner in one of the nation's largest advertising agencies, found himself puzzling over the role of advertising and the effects of that on the advertisement itself.

In the first few years of the twentieth century, Lasker rose rapidly to the top of Lord & Thomas, one of three major agencies in the nation, although its billings in 1898 were less than a million dollars. Others were N.W. Ayer & Son and J. Walter Thompson, although the latter was in decline. Lasker was in his early twenties. He was to become one of the dominant and most influential figures in American advertising, playing a major role in its development.

[1]Reprinted in Susan Strasser, *Satisfaction Guaranteed: The Making of the American Mass Market* (New York, 1989), 114.

Albert Lasker
One of the dominant figures in advertising's history, Albert Lasker was instrumental in determining the approaches that ads should take. He asked one question about the effectiveness of an ad: "Will it move the goods profitably?" Arguably a genius with an insatiable curiosity, he never stopped asking questions. His most notable one was the famous, essential inquiry, "What is advertising?" John E. Kennedy gave him the even more famous answer: "Salesmanship in print."

Lasker was born in 1880 and grew up in Galveston, Texas, where his father, Morris, was a prosperous businessman and a towering figure in young Albert's life. By the time he was twelve years old, Albert had established a weekly newspaper that he published for a year. He possessed perseverance. In high school, he involved himself in a busy array of activities, at the same time writing for the local daily newspaper and working for his father. High energy characterized him as a young man and throughout life, and this quality proved both fruitful to him and a burden that led to several breakdowns.

He was also resourceful. While writing for the Galveston daily newspaper as a teenager, he wrangled an interview with a visiting celebrity by posing as a Western Union messenger boy. No other local reporter talked to the visitor. As a young man of eighteen ready to embark on his career, Lasker seemed determined to become a newspaperman, but his father's stern resolve forced him to reconsider. Morris Lasker thought that journalists drank too much, and he extracted from his son a promise that he would take another job for a brief period. The elder Lasker prevailed upon Lord & Thomas to repay a favor and hire his son as an office boy.

In 1898, Albert made the two-day train trip from Galveston to Chicago. He planned to be away only a few months but stayed with Lord & Thomas until, as sole owner, he closed it on December 31, 1942. His starting salary was $10 a week, and his duties involved the usual grubby responsibilities assigned to office boys. He might have made good on his plans to leave Chicago shortly after arrival, but a large gambling debt incurred during his first weeks on the job forced him to borrow from one of the agency's owners and thus remain long enough to repay the loan.

In order to increase his salary and reimburse the lender more quickly, Lasker began focusing his talents on his job. His performance led rapidly to responsibilities as a full-time salesman at a salary ten times that at which he began and then quickly to twenty times his starting salary. The retirement of one of the founders of the firm in 1903 afforded him an opportunity to purchase a partnership, and the death of the other founder made him, in time, the sole owner.

When he became a partner, Lasker's salary rose to $52,000 a year. During his forty-four years with Lord & Thomas, he earned about $45 million.

"SALESMANSHIP IN PRINT"

Lasker as partner became responsible for writing ads at the agency, and he became increasingly troubled by the question, "What is advertising?" He sought the advice of the best men in the business, but none satisfied him. One day a copywriter from another city came to Lord & Thomas and offered to answer the question.

Advertising is salesmanship in print, John E. Kennedy told Lasker and proceeded to give him lessons about making this definition work. Readers of ads must be given reasons why they should purchase the product. Thus, the advertisement must sound much like the presentation a salesman makes to a prospect. It must answer questions a customer may have. Therefore, it must contain long copy that is positive and persuasive.

This concept, sometimes called the "reason why" approach, would guide Lasker throughout his professional career. He argued heatedly against advertisements that strayed away from this hard-sell approach, and this copy philosophy accounted for most of the approximately $750 million in billings that Lord & Thomas placed during its seventy years of life.

Kennedy had learned the idea of advertising as salesman earlier in his career from others who had developed it. Lasker polished the concept and brought attention to it. He trained copywriters — his own and those of other agencies — in this approach. Lord & Thomas printed and distributed thousands of copies of a booklet that touted the idea.

Salesmanship in Print
Albert Lasker and John E. Kennedy believed advertisements must act much like the presentation that a salesperson for a product would make in person. They therefore advocated long copy that was positive and persuasive, as in this automobile ad.

Kennedy, who had drifted from job to job before his meeting with Lasker, joined Lord & Thomas as a copywriter. He worked slowly and ponderously and remained with the agency only about two years. His replacement was Claude C. Hopkins, who shared Kennedy's copy philosophy, but whose work habits were vastly different. Hopkins toiled long hours every day, including weekends. He wrote prolifically and rapidly.

Hopkins' views of advertising were embodied in *Scientific Advertising*, a 1923 volume that supported its title: "The time has come when advertising has in some hands reached the status of a science. It is based on fixed principles and is reasonably exact." And elsewhere in the book: "Advertising is multiplied salesmanship. It may appeal to thousands while the salesman talks to one."[2]

Hopkins proved to be well ahead of his time by employing a technique in his ad copy of emphasizing something unusual and memorable about a product. In one ad, written before he joined Lord & Thomas, he stressed the purity of Schlitz beer because the brewery steam-cleaned its bottles. All breweries, of course, did this, but Hopkins preempted the idea for Schlitz and offered it as an argument for drinking Schlitz. In another ad, written at Lord & Thomas, Hopkins said that Quaker's puffed wheat and rice were "shot from guns." This technique of emphasizing something noteworthy about the product has been popularized in more recent years by Rosser Reeves, president and chairman at the Ted Bates agency, who developed it as a "unique selling proposition," or USP. Hopkins also popularized the use of coupons in advertisements that people could use to obtain a free sample of a product.

[2]Claude C. Hopkins, *My Life in Advertising & Scientific Advertising* (Lincolnwood, Ill., 1986), 213 and 221. Two books are contained in this edition. *Scientific Advertising* was originally published in 1923, and *My Life in Advertising* in 1927.

Stanley Resor and Psychology in Advertising

As Lasker, Kennedy, and Hopkins were mining the hard-sell copy lode, competing agencies were developing other approaches. During the latter part of the nineteenth century, a literary quality had found its way into copy, replacing much of the straightforward listing style most commonly used in American advertising for most of its first two centuries. The literary approach, in turn, was rejected by some people in the field. Arguing that art did not sell, they opened the way for the "salesmanship-in-print" philosophy espoused by Kennedy and promoted vigorously by Lasker. Now came others who found great power in advertising copy that suggested rather than insisted and operated at the consumer's subconscious rather than at the conscious level. Walter Dill Scott's seminal book, *The Psychology of Advertising* (1908), supported this new view of copy.

Among the leaders of this psychological approach were the J. Walter Thompson agency and its dynamic leader, Stanley Resor. Founded under a different name toward the end of the Civil War, JWT handled mostly religious advertising until James Walter Thompson purchased it for $1,300 in 1878 and moved forcefully into the burgeoning field of magazine advertising. Thirty years later, Thompson had tired and had lost touch, and the agency had suffered. In 1908, Resor joined the agency as manager of the Cincinnati office. Four years later he was in New York as vice-president and general manager of JWT. In 1916, a group under Resor bought J. Walter Thompson for $500,000, and Resor became president. The agency was billing about $3 million a year.

Resor's vision of an advertising agency greatly broadened its role. Instead of only buying space and providing copy for advertisements, Resor saw the agency as an integral part of an advertiser's selling program. Moreover, he employed research and the social sciences, especially psychology, to help advertisers in their sales efforts.

Resor was not a copywriter and therefore relied on Helen Lansdowne to develop the advertisements themselves. With one interruption, the two had been together since Resor's days as manager of the Cincinnati office of JWT. In 1917, they married and continued to run the company. While Lansdowne did not totally reject the reason-why approach to copy, her messages tended toward the emotional. For Woodbury's Soap she developed a sen-

The Slogan That Sold Soap
Employing Stanley Resor and Helen Lansdowne's device of appealing to the emotions and the subconscious, Palmolive soap experienced substantial increases in sales in the 1920s using the caption "Keep That Schoolgirl Complexion."

sual advertisement with the theme line, "For the skin you love to touch."

Another example of the type of advertisement that was challenging the popular reason-why approach was developed in 1915 for Cadillac. Titled "The Penalty of Leadership," it promoted pride in the status of Cadillac. The name of the automobile appeared only once in the ad, and the message never mentioned that the product being advertised was an automobile. In a distinguished-looking layout employing a conservative type face and considerable white space, the advertisement delivered this central message:

> The leader is assailed because he is a leader, and the effort to equal him is merely added proof of that leadership. Failing to equal or to excel, the follower seeks to depreciate and to destroy — but only confirms once more the superiority of that which he strives to supplant.[3]

TRUTH-IN-ADVERTISING AND OTHER REFORMS

While the debate about how to write copy continued within advertising circles during the early years of the twentieth century, an external storm of sorts was nearing a climax. It had been developing for many years.

A steady river of advertising messages during the nineteenth century promoting patent medicines and all manner of quackery had created a basic doubt about the honesty and trustworthiness of advertising. Concerned about the future of their livelihood, people in the advertising business began considering options of dealing with false and misleading advertising. By the 1890s they were beginning to organize local advertising clubs: Denver in 1892, Chicago in 1894, New York City in 1896, Seattle in 1902, and Cincinnati and Spokane in 1903. A truth-in-advertising movement appeared within the business to enforce local standards on advertisers.

The problem, however, extended beyond municipal borders. No one city could solve it. Regional advertising organizations were developed, in part to face the issue of false and misleading advertising. In 1904, the West Coast Advertising Men's Association was established, and two years later the Associated Advertising Clubs of America emerged from a meeting in St. Louis.

While undertaking other projects — the west coast group, for example, helped to tell the world that San Francisco after its 1906 earthquake was now an excellent place to live — members of the advertising organizations continued to press their commitment to truth in advertising. A vigilance committee of the San Francisco ad club told members in 1915 that it intended to take "definite action [against] those using illegitimate methods of advertising.... [The committee] is completely organized, it has been assured of the co-operation of Judges, the District Attorney and the Police Department, and its own members are capable and ready to act as special prosecutors in any case undertaken...."[4]

Members of the renamed Pacific Coast Advertising Men's Association pushed legislation in western states that would regulate advertising. In the East, the Associated Advertising Clubs of America organized a national vigilance committee at its 1911 convention, launching a national truth-in-advertising movement and, in the process, the predecessor of the better business bureaus. Moreover, numerous advertising clubs formed local vigilance committees.

In 1911, *Printer's Ink* magazine, an advertising trade publication, offered its model statute for control of false and deceptive advertising. The proposed legislation said that "Any person, firm, corporation, or association who, with intent to sell or in any way dispose of merchandise, securities, service, or anything..., makes, publishes, disseminates, circulates, or places before the public, in this state, in a newspaper or other publication...or in any other way, an advertisement...which...contains any assertion, represen-

[3]Reprinted in "The Centennial of the J. Walter Thompson Company: Commemorating 100 Years of American Advertising," *Advertising Age* (Dec. 7, 1964): 112.

[4]Quoted in Bruce Roche, "AAF ROOTS: A History of the American Advertising Federation," *(E)xchange* (February 1983): 3.

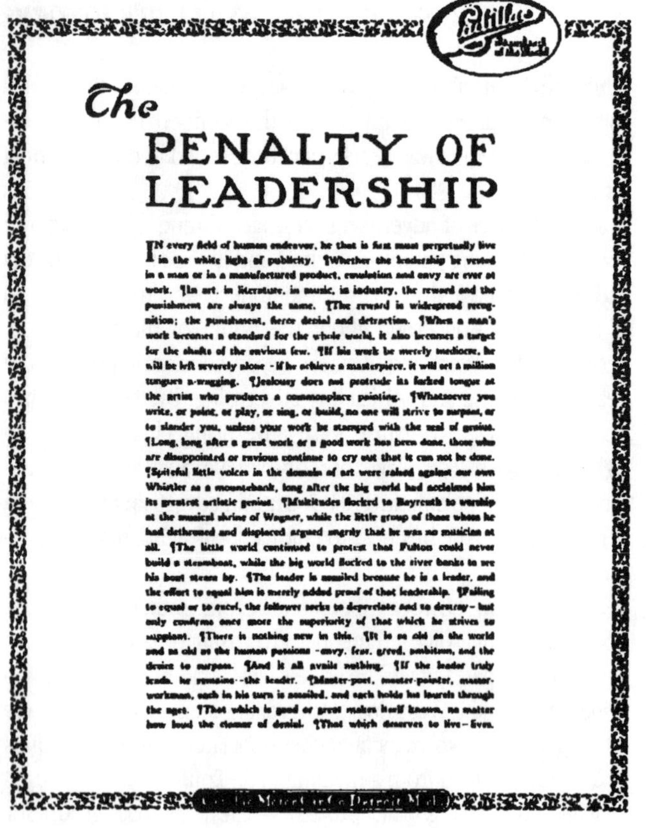

Cadillac Pride

Developed in 1915, "The Penalty of Leadership" advertisement was designed to promote pride in ownership of the Cadillac automobile. The conservative design of the ad was intended to reflect the status of Cadillac.

tation or statement of fact which is untrue, deceptive, or misleading, shall be guilty of a misdemeanor."[5] Most states have adopted the statute in some form.

At the same time that the advertising industry was working its own programs to control abuses, outside parties began pressing their case against the industry. Progressive reformers, with the muckrakers in the lead, wanted to cleanse society. Big business and advertising attracted their attention — patent medicine advertising in particular. The Progressives achieved most of their objectives. In addition to other reforms, they played a role in the passage of legislation that created the Federal Trade Commission (1914), which gradually assumed significant control over advertising. Earlier, they had helped pass the Pure Food and Drug Act (1906), although it held minor implications for advertising. In addition, a 1912 law required that all editorial material for which newspapers and magazines were paid be labeled as advertising.

Also helping to improve advertising was the formation of the American Association of Advertising Agencies in 1917 during a meeting of 150 agency presidents. Of the 1,400 agencies in existence, only N. W. Ayer & Son of the larger agencies did not affiliate. The largest agency in number of clients, Ayer had 391, followed by Lord & Thomas with 139 and J. Walter Thompson with 119.

[5]Quoted in H.J. Kenner, *The Fight for Truth in Advertising* (New York, 1936), 27-8.

Advertising During War and Good Times

As the Progressives and forces within the advertising industry were achieving some victories, the attention of the nation was drawn increasingly to Europe, where a war of unprecedented magnitude raged. After resisting involvement for three years, the United States finally entered World War I in 1917. Albert Lasker's response to that conflict was indicative of how the war engaged advertising. Although a Republican, Lasker served briefly in the administration of President Woodrow Wilson, a Democrat. The secretary of agriculture, for whom he worked as an assistant, used Lasker's familiarity with the marketing of foods to assist with programs designed to encourage the home canning of food.

Lasker symbolized the public-spirited response to the war effort by many in advertising and by the industry itself. Shortly after the Committee on Public Information was established in April 1917 by executive order of President Wilson, its chairman, journalist George Creel, was contacted by representatives of the advertising industry, who offered their assistance in the work of the agency.[6] Wilson authorized the formation of an advertising division within the CPI. By this act, Creel said later, "every advertising man in the United States was enrolled in America's second line, and from the very moment of their enrollment, we could feel the quickening of effort, the intensification of endeavor."[7]

The advertising division harnessed the efforts of media, advertisers, agencies, advertising clubs, and other components of the industry to the execution of numerous campaigns. For example, it developed a communication plan by which 13,000,000 American men between the ages of eighteen and forty-five were told that they must register for possible military service. Creel estimated after the war that the value of the advertising division's work approximated $5,000,000, including contributions of space by media and the time and talent donated by advertising professionals. Creel's figure also included advertising space purchased by private business and given to the government for its use.

While some businesses directly supported the war effort, others chose to reduce or eliminate advertising because they lacked raw materials to produce goods or because their entire output was going to the government. Still others continued regular advertising schedules. In these messages, they sometimes promoted products as usual, but they also used them to tell the public of the advertisers' contributions to the military effort, to promote worthy war-related projects — such as the sale of Liberty Bonds to help finance the war — and to remind people that a company's products would be available again after the cessation of fighting.

[6]Fleming Newbold, chairman of the Bureau of Advertising of the American Newspaper Publishers Association, to George Creel, Nov. 23, 1917; Creel to Newbold, Dec. 1, 1917; Alan C. Reiley, president of the Association of National Advertisers, to Creel, Nov. 21, 1917; and Creel to Reiley, Dec. 1, 1917. This correspondence is in the CPI Records, F.G. 63/CPI 1-A1, box 6, folder 149, National Archives, Washington, D.C.

[7]George Creel, *How We Advertised America* (New York, 1920), 158.

Advertising in World War I
Advertising professionals voluntarily lent their expertise to assist American military efforts in World War I, including the draft registration system. This ad (left) was one of the most famous of its products, featuring the image of Uncle Sam that James Montgomery Flagg created. Many businesses related their products during World War I to the war itself and to the lives of American servicemen. This ad for Ivory Soap (right) was aimed at mothers of servicemen and suggested that they buy the soap and send it to sons, who would be delighted by the gift.

When the war ended in 1918, the nation entered a decade of great, if uneven, prosperity. Although the agricultural sector lagged behind, a general affluence permeated the society. The return of consumer goods and the ability to purchase them produced good times for business and for advertising.

Advertising was maturing by the 1920s. Forty per cent of all ads in print media were full page, and about three out of four ads focused on product benefits. Personal care products replaced food as the largest category being advertised. Sexiness was the dominant theme in magazine advertisements, appearing in one out of four ads.

The appearance of another advertising medium, radio, added to the business mixture of the 1920s. Radio was the first totally new advertising medium since newspapers. The first commercial station went on the air in 1920, and the number of profit-making stations mushroomed. Initially, the use of advertisements on radio encountered resistance. Newspapers saw a threat to their income, and many leaders within radio itself did not favor commercial messages. In spite of this opposition, some stations began offering time to advertisers.

Early radio advertising time was purchased in longer blocks than today's 30- or 60-second announcements. In 1922, New York City radio station WEAF sold several advertisements for $50 to $100 each. The messages were woven into essays on apartments being offered for sale by the advertiser. By the end of the 1920s, advertising messages were no longer enclosed in essays but rather were direct statements designed to encourage listeners to buy the sponsor's product. The amount of money spent on radio advertising grew rapidly. From nothing in 1920, advertisers invested $4 million in network advertising alone in 1927 and $10.5 million in 1928.

After his initial misgivings about radio — keyed no doubt to his belief in long copy, which people could not understand easily by ear — Albert Lasker began to realize the advertising potential of the new medium. During 1927 and 1928, Lord & Thomas alone spent for its clients almost as much money with the National Broadcasting Company as all other advertisers combined. The agency put *Amos 'n' Andy* on network radio for Pepsodent toothpaste, and the show became a sensation. Sales of the toothpaste increased dramatically.

Much of the programming on radio was developed for advertisers. One of the earliest "soap operas" (called by that name because the first programs were sponsored by soap manufacturers), *The Story of Mary Marlin*, went on the air for Kleenex. Another, *Just Plain Bill*, was done for Kolynos toothpaste. Comedians such as Bob Hope and Jack Benny, Bing Crosby and other singers, and radio drama were used to reach audiences — audiences whose members were impressed by and responsive to the new medium. The system worked well for advertisers and also for radio. In a capitalist economy during a decade oriented to business, the emergence of advertising as radio's financial base seems logical.

At the same time that radio was growing as an advertising medium, the reason-why approach to copy was in decline. Several reasons contributed to the loss of popularity by the salesmanship-in-print concept. One, of course, was that print was no longer the only advertising medium. Another related to Albert Lasker's temporary absence from the advertising scene. Still another grew from the affluence of the 1920s.

As World War I was nearing an end, former President Theodore Roosevelt enticed Lasker into serving as the communications chief of the Republican National Committee. The party was out of power and looking forward to both the 1918 congressional elections and the 1920 presidential election by searching for campaign funds. Lasker's job was to handle the promotional aspects of the drive. He devoted three years to that and other political efforts, all within the Republican party, and another two years to a governmental post as chairman of the United States Shipping Board.

In 1923, after a five-year absence, Lasker returned to Lord & Thomas. He was not pleased with what he found. The other two of the big three agencies — N. W. Ayer & Son and J. Walter Thompson — had pulled even with or slightly ahead of Lord & Thomas in billings; and, just as bad, Lord & Thomas had begun to

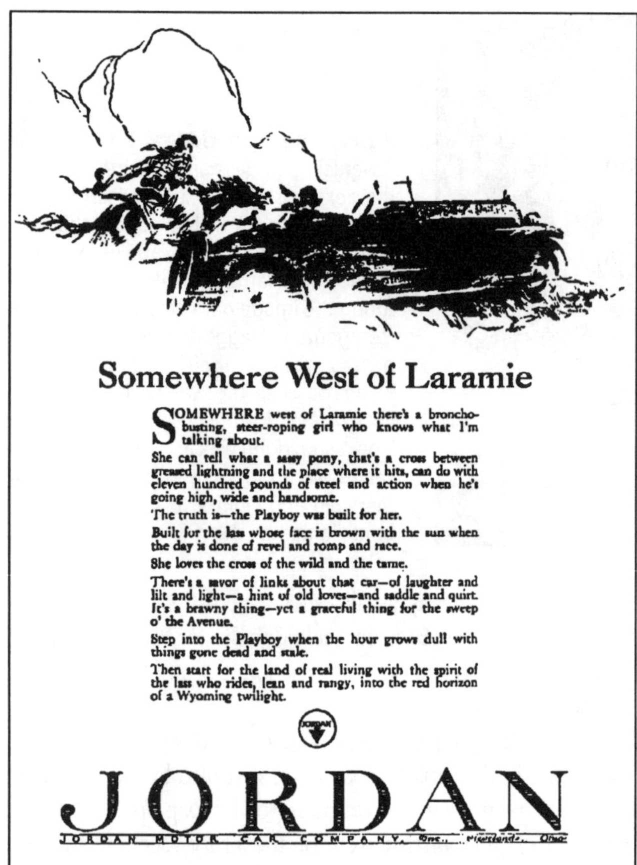

"Somewhere West of Laramie"
This ad for Jordan automobiles is one of the best examples of the image-building approach to advertising. Rather than listing the tangible, mechanical qualities of the cars, it presented an image of the lifestyle that one could obtain through ownership of them.

stray from the gospel of reason-why copy. Lasker applied his energy with renewed dedication to correct these deficiencies.

Lasker was now fighting more, though, than a philosophical war. The times had turned against him. Consumers had more options from which to purchase, including many luxuries. Moreover, the affluence of the 1920s had begun changing the way people viewed the world and the way they responded to persuasive messages. Intangibles became as important as the physical characteristics of a product. Advertisers carried the psychological appeals in a Woodbury's Soap message ("for the skin you love to touch") and the "pride" element in Cadillac leadership yet another step. They began talking about what the consumer became by using a product.

This change provided the introduction of the image-building copy appeal, which sought to establish an atmosphere about a product. No advertisement caught the spirit of this new appeal more than one developed by a former copywriter at Lord & Thomas who had gone into the automobile business. Ned Jordan fashioned a message that created a tight relationship between the spirit of the times and his automobile. In the advertisement, published in 1923 in the *Saturday Evening Post*, and beneath a stylized drawing of a roadster and horse being driven at punishing speed by a young woman and cowboy, respectively, appeared this copy:

> Somewhere west of Laramie there's a bronco-busting, steer-roping girl who knows what I'm talking about.
>
> She can tell what a sassy pony, that's a cross between greased lightning and the place where it hits, can do with eleven hundred pounds of steel and action when he's going high, wide and handsome.
>
> The truth is — the Playboy was built for her.
>
> Built for the lass whose face is brown with the sun when the day is done of revel and romp and race.
>
> She loves the cross of the wild and the tame.
>
> There's a savor of links about that car — of laughter and lilt and light — a hint of old loves — and saddle and quirt. It's a brawny thing — yet a graceful thing for the sweep o' the Avenue.
>
> Step into the Playboy when the hour grows dull with things gone dead and stale.
>
> Then start for the land of real living with the spirit of the lass who rides, lean and rangy, into the red horizon of a Wyoming twilight.[8]

The words painted a sensuous canvas in the mind. They told not of pistons and rings or even of styling or leadership, but of an ambiance. The advertisement implied that the purchaser would buy not just an automobile but a lifestyle. Traditional reason-why copy, on the other hand, sounded like this excerpt from another automobile advertisement:

> In the construction of Dodge Brothers Motor Car, every consideration has been given to the owner's safety. This is particularly evident in the brakes, which, with their 14-inch drums and 2 1/4 inch lining, are appreciably larger than the average. The extra surface thus provided develops friction when the brake bands contract over the drums — and it is this friction which stops the car....[9]

Social psychologist Roger Brown provided, in the 1960s, a rationale for the power of image-building advertisements. "When people," he explained, "are living well above the subsistence level — when food, drink, transportation, and shelter are all adequate — they begin to be interested in buying expressive symbols. A desirable symbol is any product that will suggest that its owner is the kind of person he wants to be — rich, virile, devil-may-care, thoughtful, youthful, cultivated, or what-you-will."[10] Some advertising professionals in the 1920s seem to have learned that lesson more than thirty years before Brown wrote it.

[8] *Saturday Evening Post*, 23 June 1923, 129.

[9] Reprinted in Frank Rowsome, Jr., *They Laughed When I Sat Down* (New York, 1959), 122.

[10] Roger Brown, *Social Psychology* (New York, 1965), 567.

Helps you men look your best

How a certain ingredient in Williams' actually benefits the skin

MEN used to think that all a shaving soap could do was to give a good heavy lather. But the makers of Williams' were not content with a shaving soap that merely did that. They knew the troubles men have with sensitive skins. They knew they could help those men—all men—by giving them a soap which is beneficial to the skin also.

What one ingredient does

There is in Williams' a certain ingredient which is distinctly helpful to the skin, leaving it supple, soft and pliant after every shave. You can feel the smoothness of this ingredient by simply rubbing a bit of Williams' Shaving Cream between your fingers.

Williams' lather containing this ingredient is heavier, thicker, more profuse than you are accustomed to. It acts as a cushion for the edge of your blade, keeping the skin resilient and making the whole shave a delightful one.

Soothing after-effect

After the shave, this same ingredient has a pronounced soothing effect on the skin. You are pleasantly aware of this effect because of the feeling of utter comfort and relief that comes at the end of every Williams' shave. Use Williams' regularly and see how helpful to your face it is.

Trial Tube Free

On request, we will send you a "Get Acquainted" tube which contains enough Williams' Shaving Cream to let you test it fully. Mail coupon below.

For men who prefer the Stick, Williams' Holder Top Stick gives you the genuine Williams' in stick form.

Advertising Prosperity
Reflecting the prosperity of the 1920s, advertising appealed to consumers' desires for social status. Many ads, such as this one for a men's shaving cream, were set in posh locations and included characters of obvious social standing. Ads even for everyday products such as hosiery and canned foods often included maids and butlers or incorporated exotic locales. Although not all Americans lived in such conditions, the ads appealed to their interest in having a high material standard of living.

Prosperity and social status dominated the themes in advertisements of the 1920s in *Ladies' Home Journal*. Automobiles were placed in settings such as the golf course and at resorts. Maids were shown in advertisements for common products such as soaps and polishing wax. Ads for products such as underarm deodorant, coffee, and linoleum suggested that the advertised item would add to the social prestige of its purchaser.[11]

Historian Roland Marchand reflected on this theme in his book *Advertising the American Dream: Making Way for Modernity* (1985), adding that 1920s advertising introduced people into a modern consumer culture. He argued that the images created by the advertisements were more associated with the ideal society as envisioned by the agency copywriters than with reality. His contention conflicts with the general notion among historians that advertisements reflect the values and conventions of their time.

There were other dimensions to advertising in the 1920s. The first Burma-Shave roadside signs offering brief commercial homilies were posted in 1925:

HE HAD THE RING /
HE HAD THE FLAT /
BUT SHE FELT HIS CHIN /
AND THAT WAS THAT /
BURMA-SHAVE

The last year for the signs was 1963.

During the twenties, advertising helped market an army of new products that grew out of technological advances; and the general affluence of the nation permitted a great many people to purchase them: automobiles, radio sets, and refrigerators among other electrical appliances. In addition to conveniences, the items also became status symbols.

At the same time, advertisements began offering solutions to hygienic problems such as bad breath, body odor, and athlete's foot. Some people found abhorrent this intrusion into individual privacy and public discussion of these private matters.

The negative approach that advertisements took to these personal problems also found its way into the volatile cigarette competition that characterized the 1920s. Three major tobacco companies — American, Liggett & Myers, and Reynolds — were fighting for control of the cigarette market. American Tobacco's George Washington Hill and Albert Lasker developed a campaign to encourage women to "Reach for a Lucky instead of a sweet," a reference to Lucky Strike cigarettes. This approach solved two concerns of the decade, women smoking and obesity. The two men saw that if they could overcome society's taboo against women smoking, they potentially could double cigarette sales. To do that, they raised the specter of fatness produced by eating too many candies and other sweet products.

[11]Tammie Byrd-Howard, "Advertising in the *Ladies' Home Journal* from 1923-1945," unpublished masters thesis (University of Alabama, 1991).

Advertising During Hard Times

The wide-open '20s, good times, and affluence ended with the closing months of 1929. An abrupt drop in the stock market spread into a deep economic depression that lasted for more than ten years. Business, the darling of the 1920s, suffered severe losses during the 1930s. Banks closed — more than 2,000 in 1931 — and bankruptcy was common. Industrial stocks fell in 1933 to a fifth of their 1929 value. Agriculture had not shared the prosperity of the 1920s with the rest of the nation, and it experienced even more hardship during the Great Depression. Personal suffering was high. About a quarter of the work force could not find jobs. For those who did work, salaries fell. Welfare assistance was severely limited, compared to the needs of the destitute. Soup kitchens, with their free meals, attracted long lines.

Advertising suffered the same fate as the rest of the economy. Nationally, advertising expenditures had risen from $1.9 billion in 1919 to $2.9 billion a decade later. In 1933, however, at the deepest point of the Depression, advertisers spent only about half of their 1929 expenditures. For most of the 1930s, spending remained at less than $2 billion per year.

Critics attacked business in their search for a culprit, and advertising — one of the most visible components of business — did not escape. Earlier detractors, such as the muckrakers, had directed their fire largely at the content of advertisements. Now the critics turned on the institution itself, raising the issue whether advertising was necessary in a supposedly rational society. As a result, researchers probed into consumer motivation and discovered that purchasing decisions often possessed emotional rather than rational bases.

Society's indictment of the business community produced a web of regulation woven into the fabric of law by the U.S. Congress during the 1930s. Advertising, again, did not escape. The power of the Federal Trade Commission to regulate advertising was greatly strengthened. The Federal Communication Commission was established in 1934 with some indirect authority over advertising. The Treasury Department received power over advertising and other practices of the liquor, wine, and beer industries. Other federal laws were passed tightening controls over advertising.

Society's displeasure with business and advertising also was expressed through an active consumer movement, which led to the formation of the Consumers Union in 1936 as a nonprofit organization. It sought to provide consumers information on products and services by distributing information through a monthly publication, *Consumer Reports*, which carried no advertising. Consumers Union quickly acquired 37,000 members and still exists today, testing and reporting on products and on questionable advertising and marketing practices.

An earlier organization, Consumer Research, was founded in 1927. After the Depression began, it doubled its membership. CR's 1933 book *1,000,000 Guinea Pigs*, which reported on misleading advertising in the drug and cosmetics industry, was a best seller.

Depression Advertising

The hard economic times of the Great Depression of the 1930s saw advertising shift away from the emphasis on prosperity that had characterized the 1920s. In its place appeared the theme of thrift. Gone were the exotic and elegant locales, and replacing them were commonplace situations, such as the modest kitchen in this ad, which was presented as affordable rather than elegant.

Advertisers adapted to the realities of the Depression. Their ads reflected the severe conditions. Fear appeals and testimonials gained widespread use. An increased use of comic strip advertisements demonstrated that advertisers were working harder to deliver their messages to consumers. The use of black-and-white photography increased dramatically. Layouts became bolder and plainer. Hard-sell appeals were employed more often.

In the *Ladies' Home Journal*, themes of economy and thrift, not surprisingly, became more common. Basic products such as household cleaners and toothpaste were more prone to use these themes. Woodbury's Soap changed from its 1920s approach that socially prominent women use its product to one emphasizing that Woodbury's lower price did not mean lower quality. Acknowledging the difficult economic times, one soup company that had advertised its product as part of a complete meal during the 1920s now offered its soup as a meal by itself.

Although advertisers were not moved by altruistic motives, they assisted the national morale during the Great Depression by sponsoring entertaining radio programs that let people forget the misery they saw about themselves daily. These included daytime soap operas such as *Ma Perkins* and *Our Gal Sunday* sponsored by advertisers that used hard-sell commercials. Night-time radio ads were likely to be somewhat more sophisticated. Evening sponsored programs tended to be those by comedians, who attracted large audiences. To a nation burdened with fear, these entertainments offered a measure of stability.

Advertising and World War II

At the end of the 1930s, economic conditions — though not appreciably better than at the beginning of the Depression — had at least stabilized. The nation appeared to face a prolonged future of economic downturn. Events abroad, however, would radically change that prospect. Throughout the decade the nation, wrestling with economic woes, had fearfully watched small wars and preparation for larger conflict occurring in Europe, Africa, and Asia. Then, as the United States was trying to avoid involvement, like a rushing storm, war broke over the nation in December 1941. Business, which so lately had been reviled, was called to deliver the hardware necessary for the country's war effort. The nation went back to work, solving its economic problems. Employment rose, and people again had money to spend. But on what? The entire output of some industries went to the military. Civilian goods were in short supply, many rationed.

Learning from earlier marketers who stopped advertising under similar conditions and subsequently went out of business, many American advertisers during World War II continued to tell the public about their products, advising people that the merchandise would be available again after the war. Governmental policy, which discouraged excess profits, also helped promote this practice. There was some advertising, of course, for products that were available.

Large national advertisers commonly tied into the war effort in some way by encouraging the purchase of war bonds or by promoting a patriotic effort, often related to the company's business. Pabst Brewing Co., for example, toasted the enemy's navy. "Bottoms up," it said in an advertisement, with intended double meaning. A hat company cautioned against spreading rumors with an ad that said, "Keep it under your STETSON."

The formal contribution of the advertising industry to the war effort came through the War Advertising Council. Volunteers from advertising agencies, media, and business joined to produce and distribute advertising campaigns supporting many aspects of the national effort to win the war. Similar to advertising people with the Creel Committee during World War I, except that they functioned outside of government, the advertising volunteers in the 1940s did campaigns for, among others, the Red Cross and war bonds, recruited women through ads for a variety of civilian and military jobs, and encouraged people to grow some of their own food by planting Victory Gardens. The War Advertising Council

War Advertising Council
As it had done in the First World War, the advertising industry during World War II lent its aid to the American military effort. The War Advertising Council led the work. Many of the ads it produced, such as this one, were part of the national effort to raise money for the war through the sale of war bonds to the public.

also served as a means by which the radio industry could handle the inordinate number of requests it received from governmental agencies and other organizations to promote a huge variety of worthwhile projects associated with the war effort.

Altogether, the council produced 150 campaigns during the war. Representatives of advertising agencies and the advertisers designed the campaigns, and media contributed hundreds of millions of dollars in space and time to carry the messages. In terms of the dollar value of in-kind contributions to its efforts, the council was infinitely more successful than its World War I counterpart, so successful in fact that its work was converted to peacetime. The organization dropped "War" from its title and became simply the Advertising Council.

In its fifty years of peacetime service, the council has planned and executed numerous public service campaigns. Best known of its efforts probably is the one for the prevention of forest fires, which features Smokey the Bear. Other campaigns were developed for Keep America Beautiful ("Every Litter Bit Hurts"), the USO, the United Community Funds, and Better Schools. The

World War II Advertising
With many soldiers away during World War II, advertisers frequently used war themes and aimed their messages at women on the homefront. This ad for Listerine as an antiseptic and mouthwash included a serviceman in uniform and encouraged women to keep up their morale and health.

council estimated that about $4 billion in media time and space and in agency commissions had been contributed during its first twenty-five years.

Magazine advertising content during the 1940s showed continued emotional elements, with patriotism, courage, and sacrifice replacing fear. Advertisements were art heavy. As might be expected, war themes became popular. In the *Ladies' Home Journal*, these themes found expression within a woman's context. Readers were urged to remain beautiful for the men in uniform. Other advertisements told women how they could assist with the war effort at home by preparing healthy meals and not wasting food.

The first full year of American involvement in the war was also the year that Albert Lasker decided to retire from advertising. By his own admission, he was tired. The fact may have been that advertising no longer represented a challenge to him. He was a Renaissance man, and his intellect demanded more than advertising could deliver in the 1940s and the seventh decade of his life. Moreover, the structure of American business was changing, with advertising responsibilities moving down the corporate ladder. The change required him to work with the marketing department at corporations rather than top-level management. He did not like the change because he considered the people at the highest echelon of a business his professional equals. One notable exception was the Lucky Strike account at American Tobacco Co., where Lord & Thomas continued to work with the mercurial George Washington Hill, president of the corporation.

So Albert Lasker decided in the waning months of 1942 that he would close Lord & Thomas. He turned to the managers of the agency's three major offices — Los Angeles, Chicago, and New York — and offered to sell them the agency, which he insisted be renamed. They accepted, and the new agency came into existence on January 1, 1943. It was called Foote, Cone & Belding.

Television and Good Times II

Experimental television broadcasting in the United States goes as far back as the 1920s. The first commercial may have been telecast as early as 1940. It appeared that television was on its way to development, but World War II interrupted.

When the end of the war in 1945 brought to a close a four-year shortage of consumer goods, the maturing of television was several years away, but the availability of long-awaited products such as automobiles and appliances came quickly. At first, manufacturers could not meet consumer demand, and waiting lists were common. Advertising was not needed. As supply began to match demand shortly after the war ended, however, advertisements became necessary again in the competition for consumer business.

Radio, outdoor, and print media did most of the work during the last half of the 1940s, since television remained undeveloped. In 1950, advertisers spent $10 million on small screen commercial messages. Today television, although second to newspapers in total advertising expenditures, attracts about $30 billion annually.

The 1950s saw the solution of technical problems, the development of color television, and an explosion in the number of local television stations. The new medium had caught up with the good times of the post-war era, and it grew and prospered along with the economy.

Paradoxically, the rise of this gargantuan mass medium occurred at a time when other mass media were facing decline. As television prospered, radio networks virtually disappeared, and the medium splintered into thousands of local units and, as specialized programming for specific markets appeared, into yet smaller units. Traditional mass magazines began disappearing: *Life*, *Look*, and *Saturday Evening Post*, for example. In their place appeared an army of smaller publications designed for audience members with specialized interests. These new media would produce significant changes in message content. Readers of specialized magazines might, for example, be less prone to respond to image and more likely to read lengthy copy. But this problem lay largely in the future, and the interest of advertising professionals

Percentage of Advertising Expenditures on Various Media 1970-1986

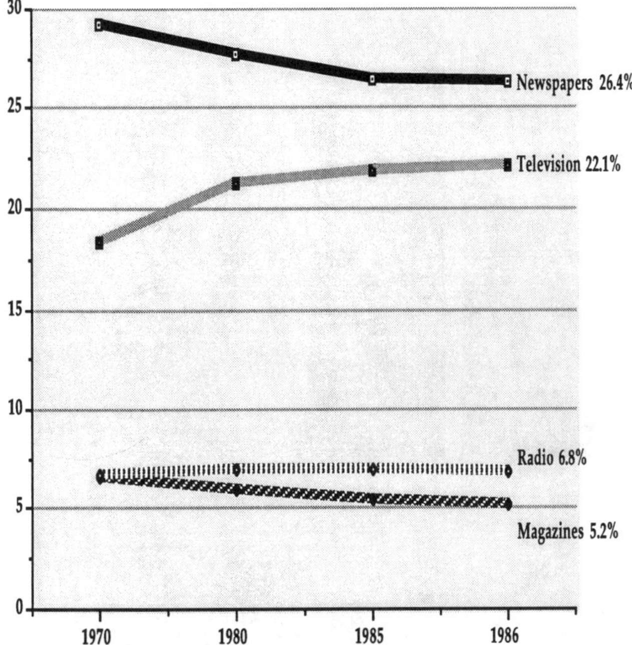

in the 1950s and 1960s focused strongly on television.

Arthur Godfrey emerged as television's first advertising star, although Art Linkletter also became highly visible. Both entertainers had developed popular television programs. Cartoons were a popular format for commercials in the early years of the medium and, of course, continue to be. Speedy Alka-Seltzer began a long run on television in 1952. Ten years later, Volkswagen and its agency — Doyle Dane Bernbach — started its not-always-so-gentle ribbing of American automobiles with a commercial likening its van to a box. That was about the time that Pepsi-Cola began its battle with Coca-Cola. Coke responded to Pepsi's campaign with the slogan "Things go better with Coke."

Most shows during the first twenty years of television were owned by the sponsor, following the radio tradition. By the early 1970s, however, the high cost of sponsorship and other problems associated with ownership — notably involving quiz shows — prompted advertisers to begin relying almost totally on 30- and 60-second spots.

Through print as well as broadcast media, the advocates of hard-sell and soft-sell continued their warfare, both with some success, during the 1950s. Those favoring the primacy of a highly creative message clearly won the battle in the 1960s. Led by Doyle Dane Bernbach, they created messages that got attention — the Marlboro Man, the Jolly Green Giant, the automobile as lemon, and the man with the black eye patch in the Hathaway shirt. A downturn in the economy during the 1970s returned hard-sell copy to the fore, again to be replaced in the affluent '80s by more creative messages. Thus the conflict over copy philosophy continued without letup or permanent victory.

In print advertisements during the 1950s, the overwhelming emphasis was on the benefits of products. During the 1960s, there was heavy use of photographs and a continuing growth in the size of the advertisement. The 1970s were marked by an increase in couponing and in direct marketing. This trend has gathered strength in the years since.

The issue of advertising's role in society entered another dimension during the 1950s as political advertising and television were linked. Early on, critics charged that television emphasized style over content, citing the Eisenhower commercials during the 1952 presidential campaign. One of the most controversial television political commercials, broadcast by the Democratic Party during the 1964 presidential campaign, showed a little girl picking the petals from a flower while a voice intoned a countdown. Then came an atomic explosion and a message implying that the Republican candidate, Barry Goldwater, might lead the nation into a nuclear holocaust. During the 1968 presidential election, advertising — especially through television — stood accused by at least one critic of having "sold" Richard Nixon to the electorate.[12] In recent years, negative political commercials and print advertisements have become increasingly common and have attracted criticism.

Controversy has accompanied television almost since the first commercial. People have called television advertisements manipulative, annoying, boring, in poor taste, misleading, false, too loud, and too hard-sell. No doubt, examples can be found that fit each of these complaints. Likewise, laudable commercials have been run. One of the best was a commercial that Coca-Cola has used during the Christmas season showing young men and women of many races singing together on a mountain top.

The charge that television commercials are manipulative — the same argument that has been leveled at all advertising — has been the most difficult to refute. Television commercials use sound, pictures, motion, immediacy, and emotion to carry the commercial message, and they *are* designed to be persuasive. Critics of television advertising for children have been especially outspoken on this issue and have won concessions from advertisers, especially during Saturday-morning programming. An index of congressional thinking on responsible advertising came in 1970, when Congress barred tobacco advertising from television and radio.

Most visible of the critics of advertising charging manipulation were Vance Packard and Wilson Bryan Key. Their arguments were similar. In his 1957 book, *The Hidden Persuaders*, Packard claimed that advertisers used symbols in their messages to touch consumers' subconscious and stimulate the real reasons behind purchases. Key found all manner of sexual symbolism in advertisements, which he explored in *Subliminal Seduction*, first published in 1973. He said that advertisers embedded these symbols in their messages, and the symbols tapped into the powerful sex

[12]Joe McGinniss, *The Selling of the President 1968* (New York, 1969).

Subliminal Advertising

'Hidden Persuaders' Help Sell Popcorn and Soda Pop

Beginning with early publishers adding woodblock illustrations to attract attention and create a favorable environment for their advertising messages, marketers have searched for more and more subtle ways to influence buyer behavior. Straightforward selling gave way to a gradual blending with other, less direct techniques, employing humor, positive associations, and other devices.

Then, as the practice of advertising began to mature approaching the middle of the twentieth century, innovative practitioners sought ways to utilize tools of the young science of psychology. The ultimate in advertising subtlety was to be subliminal advertising, a technique designed to present a message that could influence buying behavior at an unconscious level. That goal was accomplished, at least in theory, by presenting stimuli that were either so fast, so faint, or so small that a person received them below his threshold of conscious awareness and processed them with his subconscious mind.

The first publicized use of subliminal advertising was in 1956, when a movie theater in Fort Lee, New Jersey, flashed the words "popcorn" and "drink Coca-Cola" on the screen so quickly during the showing of a film that audience members were unaware it was happening. Concession sales of both popcorn and Coke, reports said, were overwhelming.

Public concern at the thought of being secretly manipulated by this type of advertising was fueled in large part by Vance Packard, who in 1957 in his popular book *The Hidden Persuaders* warned that consumers were becoming the unknowing victims of marketing "tricks" like subliminal advertising.

The federal government, as well as broadcast and movie industry groups, were quick to respond, pledging that no such psychological manipulation would be allowed. Today the controversy continues, with print ads most often accused of hiding messages within their artwork.

James A. Hammock
Florida Atlantic University

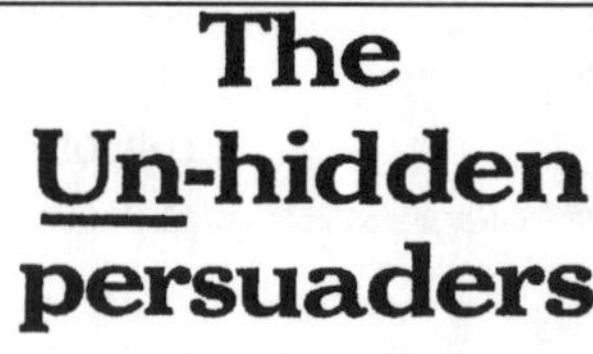

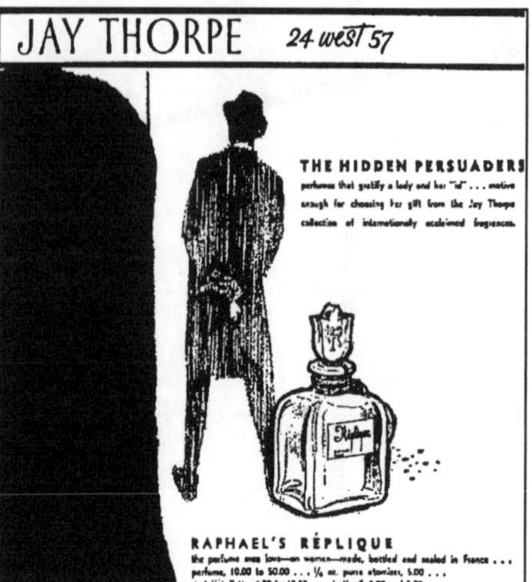

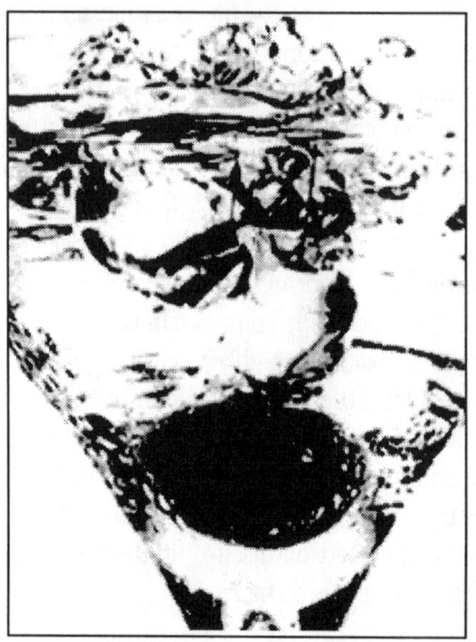

Advertisers responded in different ways to Vance Packard's claims of subliminal messages hidden in ads. One leading agency ran a house ad (top left) debunking the claim and declaring that effective advertising appealed directly to people's real needs. Other advertisers used the concept of sexual subliminal appeal to market their products, as the Jay Thorpe company did (top right) by calling its perfume "the hidden persuaders." Seagram's distillery used the idea of subliminal persuasion humorously in its ad (middle). The picture of the two glasses ran under the caption "Refreshing Seagram's Gin Has Hidden Pleasure. Welcome into the Fold." The ad then instructed the reader to fold the picture so that the two glasses overlapped. The resulting image (bottom) revealed a man and a woman, in a style reminiscent of the 1800s, in a swing.

drive to obtain a response to the messages. Serious research has had difficulty finding support for Key's argument.

In response to some concerns of society, in 1971 the American Advertising Federation, the American Association of Advertising Agencies, the Association of National Advertisers, and the Council of Better Business Bureaus joined in forming the National Advertising Review Board. The NARB has proven effective at its task of policing national advertising and has spawned a number of local review boards.

As the federal government relaxed regulatory controls of advertising after 1980, state attorneys general moved more aggressively against national advertisers, with mixed results. In contrast, the courts have found in recent years that commercial speech — including advertising — enjoys limited First Amendment protection, although decisions have tended to hold advertisers to higher standards than are applied to non-commercial speech.

Of the many women and men who have worked in advertising since World War II, three deserve brief attention: David Ogilvy, Mary Wells, and William Bernbach. Perhaps the most visible advertising person in the United States in recent years was Ogilvy, a principal in Ogilvy & Mather advertising agency and the author of a popular book titled *Confessions of an Advertising Man.*[13] The volume spelled out his advertising philosophy. Ogilvy also obtained considerable attention as one of the more creative people in a business noted for its creativity. A native of England, he came to the United States to study advertising, which fascinated him. He acknowledged the influence in his professional career of both the hard-sell and soft-sell philosophies. In 1951 he developed the idea for the man with the black eye patch wearing a Hathaway shirt in settings that identified him as a person of class. In recent years, Ogilvy — retired and living at his chateau in France — has served as an elder statesman of the advertising industry.

Mary Wells was the first of her gender to rise to the status of principal at a major advertising agency. It was she who painted Braniff jets outlandish colors in the late 1970s. As a young copywriter, she worked at Doyle Dane Bernbach when it was the hottest creative agency in the business.

At DDB, Wells worked for William Bernbach, who perhaps more than any other person in advertising nurtured and symbolized the creative hurricane of the 1960s. Under Bernbach, the agency created some of the most memorable advertising campaigns of that era, indeed, of the entire twentieth century. Bernbach maintained that the power of advertising messages lay in their difference from the ordinary. Disdainful of scientific research, he felt that individuals possessed by inspiration could best establish that difference. He joined with others in establishing Doyle Dane Bernbach in 1949.

The other partners took care of new accounts, management, and financial matters. Bernbach became the creative soul of the shop. He hired people capable of imaginative work, encouraged them, offered ideas, critiqued their work in a positive way, and let

Advertising Bugs
The Doyle Dane Bernbach agency created a new wave in advertising with television and print ads for the Volkswagen Beetle in 1960. Its witty approach was picked up by other advertisers, such as the Avis automobile-rental company, whose slogan became "We Try Harder," referring to its market position behind the Hertz company.

them create. The most memorable work of the agency was done to introduce and sell to American consumers a humble little automobile called the Volkswagen (German for "people's car"). While domestic automobiles were being advertised with an emphasis on size, power, and prestige, the VW campaign advised people to "Think small."

TRENDS IN ADVERTISING

Several recent trends in advertising merit attention. The most historical of the trends traces a linear progression since the early days of American advertising. It is the growth in the number of advertisements and a corresponding growth in the problem of obtaining attention for any one advertisement. A trend that began shortly after World War II is the globalization of American advertising. Large advertising agencies in the United States have offices throughout the world, giving this nation a commercial influence worldwide. Another trend, which has calmed in recent years, is the increase in the size of advertising agencies through merger.

[13]David Ogilvy, *Confessions of an Advertising Man* (New York, 1963).

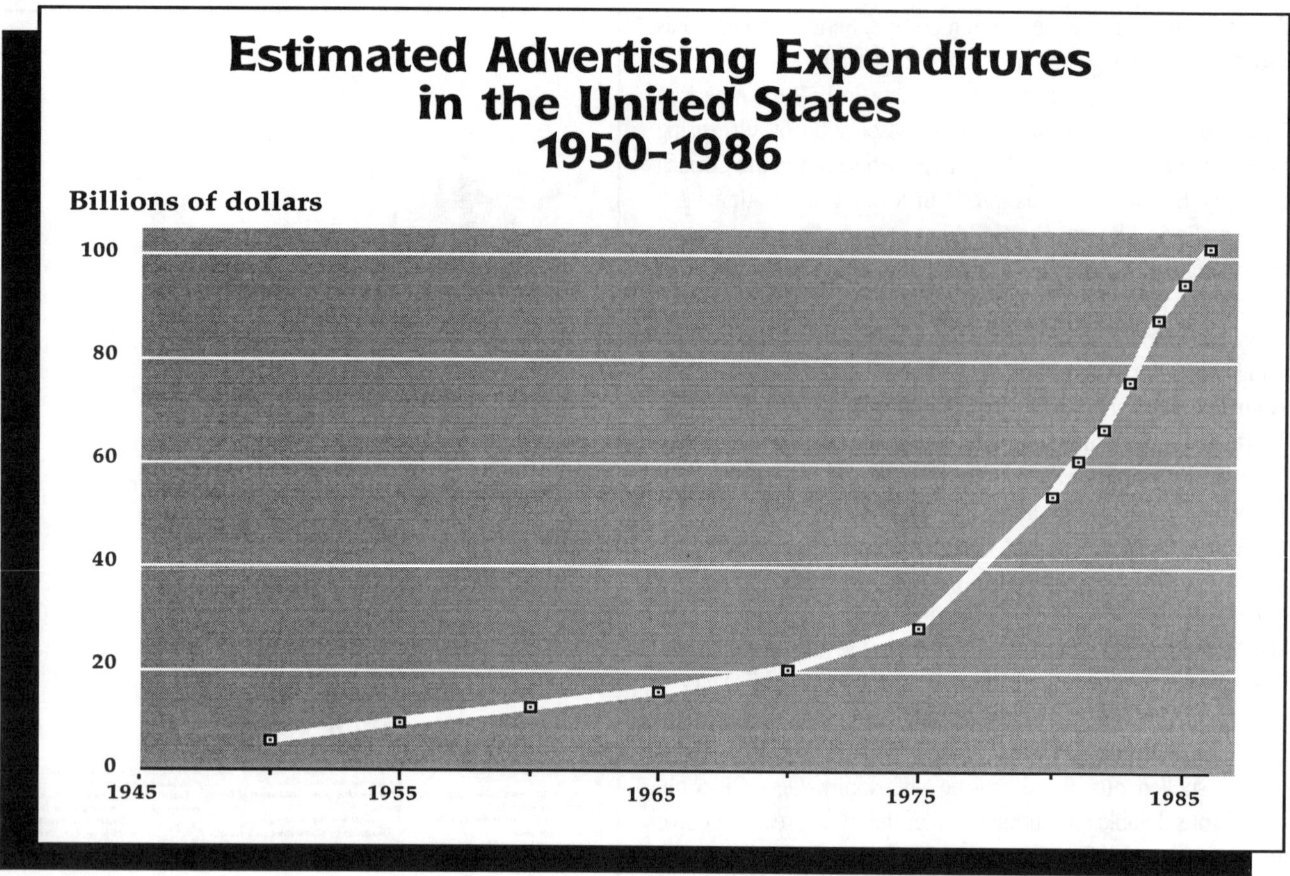

The question that observers of the advertising scene have raised is whether good creative work can be done in large agencies.

A trend and concern of society during the last decades of the century dealt with the role of minority groups and women. An advertising industry controlled by white males for six decades had portrayed African Americans and women in stereotypical roles most of those years: blacks as servants or likable mammies and women as housewives who couldn't solve simple household problems without advice from a male figure speaking for the advertiser. Moreover, the industry itself employed few blacks, and women — with a few exceptions — were limited to secretarial and clerical responsibilities.

Gradually this situation has changed, Mary Wells and William Sharp representing the change most strikingly. Sharp served as advertising manager of Coca-Cola and also held the highest office in the American Advertising Federation, one of the industry's major professional groups.

Perhaps the most profound trend affecting advertising today is the narrowing of target markets — profound because it raises significant questions about the future of advertising. Until twenty-five years ago, almost all advertisements were addressed to large, heterogeneous markets reachable through traditional mass media. In time, targets narrowed to loosely bound groups and mini-groups suitable for specialized publications and cable television — for example, college students — who are reachable most efficiently through several magazines designed for students and through college newspapers. Today, messages often are designed for target markets that are quite homogeneous and extremely narrow. These markets lend themselves best to direct marketing techniques, introducing — as a side issue — some concerns about the privacy of individuals.

Advertising, traditionally a loner on the communications scene, has found itself blended increasingly with direct marketing, sales promotion, and public relations as part of what is being called "integrated marketing communications," which is attracting more of the budget that typically had been dedicated to traditional mass media advertising. The splintering of markets into increasingly smaller and smaller components — triggered initially by the transformation of media into vehicles to reach specialized markets and more recently enhanced by computers and the Internet — has arrived at a point where individuals are reachable. What does this do to an industry such as advertising that has focused primarily on mass markets? Does it predict the decline of advertising as we have known it? What are the implications of this change for mass media and for consumers of those media?

Advertising has matured during the twentieth century. It has changed, and that change continues. The new approaches appear to be taking us away from what we have known in the past as advertising. The future of commercial messages by whatever name seems as tantalizing in prospect as the history of advertising in retrospect.

RECOMMENDED READINGS

BOOKS

Atwan, Robert, Donald McQuade, and John W. Wright. *Edsels, Luckies, and Frigidaires: Advertising the American Way*. New York, 1979. A collection of print ads covering the twentieth century premised on the thesis that advertisements reflect society.

Barnouw, Eric. *The Sponsor: Notes on a Modern Potentate*. Oxford, 1978. The rise and role of sponsors of broadcast programs.

Cleary, David Powers. *Great American Brands: The Successful Formulas That Made Them Famous*. New York, 1981. Discusses the history of more than thirty companies and the products they manufactured.

Cone, Fairfax M. *With All Its Faults*. Boston, 1969. "A candid account of forty years in advertising" by one of the successors to Albert Lasker.

Creel, George. *How We Advertised America*. New York, 1920. Work of the Committee on Public Information, often called the Creel Committee, during World War I.

Diamond, Edwin, and Stephen Bates. *The Spot: The Rise of Political Advertising on Television*. Cambridge, 1984. A study of political advertising from 1952 to 1980, including discussion of styles and effects.

Ewen, Stuart. *Captains of Consciousness: Advertising and the Social Roots of the Consumer Culture*. New York, 1977. Assigns to advertising an ideological role in establishing modern consumer habits.

Foster, G. Allen. *Advertising: Ancient Market Place to Television*. New York: Criterion Books, 1967. A good general survey.

Fox, Stephen. *The Mirror Makers*. New York, 1984. A history of twentieth-century advertising with emphasis on the most influential people in the business.

Gunther, John. *Taken at the Flood*. New York, 1961. Albert Lasker's story by a journalist who also was a friend of the advertising agent.

Hopkins, Claude C. *My Life in Advertising* and *Scientific Advertising*. Chicago, 1986. Two books of personal recollections by one of the great reason-why copywriters.

Johnson, Patricia. *Real Fantasies: Edward Steichen's Advertising Photography*. Berkeley, Calif., 1997. Presents the commercial photography of Steichen as a case study in the development of consumer culture based on images of romance and desirable lifestyle in the 1920s and 1930s.

Jones, Howard A. *50 Years Behind the Scenes in Advertising*. Philadelphia, 1975. Written by an advertising man, this book's focus is on Albert Lasker and Will Grant.

Kenner, H. J. *The Fight for Truth in Advertising*. New York, 1936. Written by the general manager of the Better Business Bureau of New York City.

Kern-Foxworth, Marilyn. *Aunt Jemima, Uncle Ben, and Rastus: Blacks in Advertising, Yesterday, Today, and Tomorrow*. Westport. Conn., 1994. Includes many examples and often disturbing truths.

Lasker, Albert. *The Lasker Story: As He Told It*. Lincolnwood, Ill., 1987. Text of a six-hour lecture in 1925 by Lasker to his staff about his life and principles.

Lears, Jackson. *Fables of Abundance: A Cultural History of Advertising in America*. New York, 1994. Sometimes the book's emphasis is more on culture than on advertising, but it is useful for its study of the cultural setting of advertising.

Marchand, Roland. *Advertising the American Dream: Making Way for Modernity 1920-1940*. Berkeley, Calif., 1985. Argues that advertising distorts reality, employing evidence from two contrasting decades.

Marin, Allan, ed. *50 Years of Advertising as Seen Through the Eyes of Advertising Age 1930-1980*. Chicago, 1980. A collection of ads and articles organized by decade. A nice overview of the decades.

McGinniss, Joe. *The Selling of the President 1968*. New York, 1969. An indictment of political advertising on television.

Ogilvy, David. *Confessions of an Advertising Man*. New York, 1963. The advertising philosophy of one of the most creative men on the contemporary advertising scene.

Pope, Daniel. *The Making of Modern Advertising*. New York, 1983. Development of national advertising since the late nineteenth century, from a business perspective.

Rowsome, Frank Jr. *They Laughed When I Sat Down*. New York, 1959. An informal history of advertising through World War II, especially valuable for its reproductions of early advertisements.

Schudson, Michael. *Advertising, The Uneasy Persuasion: Its Dubious Impact on American Society*. New York, 1986. Advertising lacks the importance assigned to it by critics and advocates.

Seldin, Joseph. *The Golden Fleece: Selling the Good Life to Americans*. New York, 1963. American advertising since World War II.

Sivulka, Juliann. *Soap, Sex, and Cigarettes: A Cultural History of American Advertising*. Belmont, Calif., 1998. One of several recent books exhibiting historians' concerns for the relationship of advertising to culture.

Smulyan, Susan. *Selling Radio: The Commercialization of American Broadcasting, 1920-1934*. Washington, D.C., 1994. How advertising gradually came to be accepted as the appropriate method of supporting radio.

Watkins, Julian L. *The 100 Greatest Advertisements: Who Wrote Them and What They Did*. New York, 1949. Includes background information about each advertisement.

ARTICLES

Advertising Age. "The Centennial of the J. Walter Thompson Company: Commemorating 100 Years of American Advertising" (Dec. 7, 1964), Sec. 2. Special section is keyed but not limited to JWT; includes history, biography, and media.

Avery, Donald R. "Advertising, 1900-Present: Capitalist Tool or Economic Necessity?" Chap. 17 in Wm. David Sloan, *Perspectives on Mass Communication History* (Hillsdale, N.J., 1991). Analyzes the approaches that historians have taken to explaining advertising.

Bowers, Thomas A. "The Bankhead Bill: How a Threatened Press Subsidy Was Defeated." *Journalism Quarterly* 53 (1976): 21-7. The proposed legislation would have subsidized some newspapers during World War I through the purchase of War Bond advertising.

Griese, Noel L. "Rosser Reeves and the 1952 Eisenhower Spot TV Blitz." *Journal of Advertising* 4 (1975): 34-8. Concludes that television commercials were not a factor in the Eisenhower victory.

Hammargren, Russell J. "The Origin of Press-Radio Conflict." *Journalism Quarterly* 13 (1936): 91-3. The war between press and radio began "with the formation of chain broadcasting [and] competition for the national advertising dollar....Only the national advertiser, under our system of private enterprise, really had the power to finance broadcasting."

Kreshel, Peggy J. "The 'Culture' of J. Walter Thompson, 1915-1925." *Public Relations Review* 16:3 (Fall 1990): 80-9. Examines the efforts of Stanley B. Resor to interject "science" into advertising and his desire to elevate the pervasive perception of advertising from a trade to a profession.

Maddox, Lynda M., and Eric J. Zanot. "The Image of the Advertising Practitioner as Presented in the Mass Media, 1900-1972." *American Journalism* 2 (1985): 117-29. As the emphasis on consumerism increased, the image of advertising professionals as presented in books, popular magazines, and professional journals declined. The professional was often depicted in stereotypical terms as a huckster.

McClure, Leslie. "An Analysis of Advertising Volume in World War I." *Journalism Quarterly* 19 (1942): 262-7. World War I influenced the volume of newspaper and magazine advertising, but it did not halt the trend toward more use of advertising by American business.

Miracle, Gordon E. "A Historical Analysis to Explain the Evolution of Advertising Agency Services." *Journal of Advertising* 6 (1977): 24-8 and 10. Traces the evolution of advertising agency services and identifies major factors explaining the evolution.

Mullen, James J. "Newspaper Advertising in the Johnson-Goldwater Campaign." *Journalism Quarterly* 45 (1968): 219-25. Includes data on number, size, and cost of advertisements; appeals used; and campaign expenditures by dates. Suggests that both parties sought to "peak" just before the election.

Nichols, John E. "Publishers and Drug Advertising: 1933-38." *Journalism Quarterly* 49 (1972): 144-7. "[W]hen publishers were faced with a major loss in advertising revenue that would come if Congress approved a bill strengthening the Pure Food and Drug Act of 1906, they fought the bill with inaccurate and distorted reporting, lobbying and testimony before Congress."

Norris, Vincent P. "Advertising History — According to the Textbooks." *Journal of Advertising* 9 (1980): 3-11. Argues that advertising textbooks provide a badly distorted history of advertising.

Pollay, Richard W. "The Subsidizing Sizzle: A Descriptive History of Print Advertising, 1900-1980." *Journal of Marketing* 49 (1985): 24-37. Analyzes the content of magazine advertisements for the first eight decades of the twentieth century.

Pope, Daniel. "Advertising as a Consumer Issue: An Historical View." *Journal of Social Issues* 47:1 (1991): 41-56. Discusses the Federal Trade Commission and consumer movements since the early twentieth century.

Reynolds, Robert D., Jr. "The 1906 Campaign to Sway Muckraking Periodicals." *Journalism Quarterly* 56 (1979): 513-20 and 589. Describes placement of "editorial" advertisements in an attempt to blunt muckraking attacks.

Sullivan, Paul W. "G. D. Crain Jr. and the Founding of *Advertising Age*." *Journalism History* 1 (1974): 94-5. Favorable biography covering 1930 to World War II. Crain, a consumer advocate, referred to *Advertising Age* as "a real newspaper" based on hard news, investigative reporting, and informative columns.

Taylor, James D. "Elliott White Springs — Maverick Ad Leader." *Journal of Advertising* 11 (1982): 40-6. Reviews the twelve-year campaign of controversial advertisements developed by the president of Springs Mills.

22

Public Relations

1900 - Present

In December 1842, master showman Phineas T. Barnum signed a contract with the parents of Charles S. Stratton. For seven dollars a week, plus travel and board expenses, Stratton was indentured to Barnum, and his parents, Sherwood and Cynthia, were bound to the contract for two years. In return, Barnum made young Charles one of the most famous people of his generation — a child most people knew as General Tom Thumb.

Tom Thumb was a midget, who at five years old stood just over two feet tall and weighed fifteen pounds. Barnum bought ponies and tiny carriages for the boy, dressed him in miniature costumes, added a few years to his age, and taught him to dance and sing. The "General" appeared at Barnum's American Museum in New York City, toured the United States, and even traveled to England, bringing in hundreds of dollars a day in box office receipts. Barnum raised his allowance to $25 a week.

Although many such promoters existed, P.T. Barnum was in a class by himself. He used advertising and publicity techniques to draw tremendous crowds to see Tom Thumb and many other attractions, such as the American Museum, his circus, or the singer Jenny Lind. To promote Tom Thumb, for example, in addition to paying for advertising, Barnum commissioned biographies, circulated lithograph pictures of the boy, and stirred interest among newspaper editors, who wrote stories that in turn stirred the interest of many readers. The showman consequently became a very rich man.

Barnum had an unusual flair for publicity, but his efforts to influence public opinion were not unique. While he sold tickets to exhibits, abolitionists advocated the end of slavery, the religious sought conversion, and corporations experimented with imaginative product promotions. People have long conducted organized campaigns to persuade the public to buy, vote, think, or act a certain way.

But nineteenth-century industrialization brought a major change: for the first time, "public relations" became not just an activity but a full-time occupation. Industrialization brought about a host of social and economic changes, creating pressures that led business, government, and other leaders to try new strategies to deal with the changing environment. Among other things, organizations added public relations practitioners to their staffs or hired outside counsel. The field grew from a handful of practitioners at the turn of the century until, in 1990, over 160,000 Americans described themselves to the U.S. Department of Labor as "public relations specialists."

Public relations counselors often say that their role is to present clients' views on an issue before the bar of public opinion or in the marketplace of ideas. They assert that every individual or organization has a right to speak before the public, whether to sell circus tickets or peddle a political candidate. However, the history of public relations reveals that, while it can and often does make positive contributions, PR has not necessarily been a democratic force in American history. As ideas about how best to persuade people changed, practitioners sometimes but not always used their knowledge for the public good.

The Rise of Big Business

Throughout the nineteenth century the United States lagged behind Great Britain in industrial production, but the tremendous boom of railroad building after the Civil War signaled a major change. The railroads spurred steel and machine manufacturing, adding to the already rapid growth in textiles and other industries. The 1900 census showed for the first time that more Americans were employed in industry than in agriculture.

The railroads changed American commerce. They were the nation's first big businesses, and, to make their work more efficient, they developed managerial hierarchies to administer the day-to-day operations of thousands of employees working in widely dispersed locations. They also made it possible for other companies, and farmers, to transport their goods quickly, over long distances, and at relatively inexpensive rates. Instead of small, family-owned businesses that relied on individual artisans, the new corporate

Making Human Junk
Although industrialization provided products that people enjoyed, it also brought with it such problems as child labor, unsafe working conditions, and long hours. Some social activists, such as the photographer Lewis Hine, attacked the problems through campaigns to create public awareness and action. One of his main efforts was against child labor, of which this photograph of a young girl in a cotton factory was a part. He claimed that industry was treating children as "human junk." In the face of such public criticism, many companies began their own public relations efforts to put their practices in a good light.

bureaucracies paid wages to workers who used increasing amounts of machinery to manufacture goods.

Industrialization changed much more than simply the organization of work. With it came a loss in the close connection between owners or managers and their employees and customers; no longer could they call one another by name. Although it gave many people products that they enjoyed, industrialization also brought with it child labor, low-quality products, unsafe working conditions, and working-class slums in cities where corporations located their factories.

During the Progressive era of the early 1900s, social reformers, journalists, and politicians all responded to the negative byproducts of industrialization, often urging political action to curb industry's excesses. A group of muckraking journalists exposed both political evils of the new big cities and abuses by the corporations. Reformers tried to change everything from labor laws to the electoral process, and people began to demand that the federal government regulate industry. While links between the public and the private sectors had always existed, in general Americans believed business should function independently. Business bigness changed this assumption, however, as companies and industries held increasing power over the consumers who grew to depend on them.

The story of the railroads provides a good example. Although railroads drastically improved the nation's transportation system, they also angered many citizens. Railroads had monopolies in some areas, and companies often made agreements among themselves to fix prices. They could charge almost any amount, for people had few viable transportation alternatives. In 1887 Congress created the Interstate Commerce Commission, charging it to regulate the railroad industry. One of its first rules required all railroads to publish their rates and to abide by the published prices.

Railroads were not the only problems, and Congress dealt with other companies, too. "Trusts," giant corporations that controlled entire industries, formed in the oil, sugar, steel, and tobacco industries, among others. In response Congress passed the Sherman Antitrust Act in 1890, making it possible for the courts to break up, or "bust," the trusts.

In other words, pressures from reformers, journalists, and the government combined, creating an environment that seemed increasingly anti-business. In response business leaders developed new managerial strategies in a whole range of areas. Much like mass production created the necessity that fostered innovation in advertising, big business created new sets of problems that managers chose to solve by adding public relations to their arsenals. To mollify public opinion, focus journalists on the more positive aspects of industrialization, and decrease political threats to corporate independence, managers turned to public relations. Not surprisingly, railroads — the first big businesses — were among the first corporations to experiment with press agentry and public relations. The first agency, the Publicity Bureau, formed in Boston in 1900. A belief that public opinion should rule and the availability of urban newspapers and national circulation magazines that could reach large audiences created a climate in which PR appeared to be a good solution to many business problems.

Ivy Lee and the Origins of PR

Ivy Lee's career demonstrates how public relations could be used to respond to employee, media, and public opposition. Lee, often called the "father of public relations," was the son of a Georgia minister and was educated at Emory and Princeton universities. He joined in partnership with George F. Parker to form the first public relations counseling agency, although that term had not yet been coined, in 1904. They issued a "Declaration of Principles" outlining Parker & Lee's policies for the press, because many re-

Ivy Lee, Father of Public Relations
Ivy Lee originated modern public relations in the early 1900s with a philosophy that emphasized openness in dealing with the press. He did not always adhere to his philosophy, but his efforts created a new profession from what had been mere press agentry.

porters and editors objected to corporate demands for "free advertising," as some journalists called publicity. "In brief, our plan is, frankly and openly, on behalf of business concerns and public institutions," they wrote, "to supply to the press and public of the United States prompt and accurate information concerning subjects which it is of value and interest to the public to know about." They also vowed not to hide their sponsorship of work and explained that they would not pay for placement of their stories, as many press agents did.[1] The partnership split in 1913, when Parker went to work for the Episcopal Church, but one of Lee's greatest challenges occurred when he accepted a new account, the Colorado Fuel and Iron Company.

Colorado Fuel and Iron's principal stockholder, John D. Rockefeller, Jr., retained Lee because mine workers had gone on strike in September 1913. The company paid the state militia to subdue the strikers, who were living in tents because they and their families had been thrown out of company housing. Rockefeller's problems peaked when twenty people, women and children included, died in a battle with the mine's armed guards. The guards shot at the mineworkers and inadvertently caused a fire when someone fleeing from the gunfire knocked over a stove in the tent city. Rockefeller hired Lee at $1,000 a month to help to resolve the public opinion crisis that resulted from the deaths. Lee later said that he had insisted on a policy of "absolute frankness," although he did not announce to the press that Rockefeller had hired him for some six months. He issued bulletins "containing the facts of the situation" to prominent individuals and to newspapers — forerunners of today's news release — which were later found to contain inaccuracies.[2] Lee had violated some of his own guidelines for public relations, and muckraker Upton Sinclair thought Lee's behavior was so atrocious that he gave him the nickname "Poison Ivy," which followed Lee for the rest of his life. Still, Lee may have accomplished some good. He recommended that the company create procedures to address workers' grievances.

Corporations such as Colorado Fuel and Iron were by no means the only organizations seeking counsel from public relations practitioners. Many groups came to believe that in the new industrial society, public relations could help to solve problems by reaching large numbers of people with messages, whether requests for funds or votes or simply information about an organization. In fact, two of Ivy Lee's fellow pioneers in counseling, both of whom also founded agencies in the early years of the twentieth century, worked initially on non-corporate accounts. Hamilton Wright promoted the U.S.-occupied Philippines from his San Francisco office, opened in 1908. In New York City the Trinity Church, under attack in the press because it owned a number of ramshackle tenement buildings, retained Pendleton Dudley, who had opened an agency in 1909. Additionally, Edward Bernays, who in 1921 created the term "counsel on public relations," started his career as a publicist for theater, ballet, and opera stars in 1913.

GOVERNMENT, EDUCATION, AND PR

Partly because of the changes brought about by industrialization, the federal government and the electoral process changed, and bureaucracy grew in the public sector just as it did in the private. Progressive reform in many cases led to the creation of new regulatory bodies like the Food and Drug Administration, therefore increasing the number of people working for the federal government. Big government, like big business, soon desired a better public information apparatus. Gifford Pinchot, who headed the U.S. Forest Service, created the first officially designated "press bureau" in the Executive Branch in 1905. He promoted one of President Theodore Roosevelt's pet projects — a campaign for government conservation of natural resources. A Congressional report from 1912 suggests that press bureaus (under a variety of names) existed in the Bureaus of Biology, Census, Education, Public Roads, and Soils, in addition to the Post Office, the State Department, and other agencies.

Politicians, especially presidents, similarly began to designate

[1] Sherman Morse, "An Awakening on Wall Street," *American Magazine* 62 (September 1906), 460.

[2] Henry F. Pringle, "His Master's Voice," *American Mercury* 9 (October 1926), 150.

Gifford Pinchot
Appointed head of the U.S. Forest Service, Gifford Pinchot created the federal government's first "press bureau" in 1905. He used it to promote the conservation of the nation's natural resources, developing today's system of national forests.

individuals to handle public relations-related activities. Some historians believe that the first public relations counselor was Amos Kendall, who during the 1820s and 1830s had served in essence as a press secretary and campaign manager for President Andrew Jackson. Presidential publicity did not become common, however, until the turn of the century. In the 1890s one of President William McKinley's secretaries conducted a nightly press briefing. Theodore Roosevelt worked still more closely with the press, even allowing reporters to interview him during his morning shave. He made presidential messages available to correspondents ahead of time so that they could telegraph their stories to their newspapers. Articles about his speeches appeared on the street almost as he spoke. Although he and many of the presidents who followed did not allow direct attribution of his statements in the press, his practices had created the foundation for a more open discussion of public issues.

Members of Congress were a little slower to begin experimenting with public relations. Representative Frank O'Hair, a Democrat from Illinois, hired Associated Press reporter Lambert St. Clair to be his press secretary in 1912. Six years later California Senator Hiram Johnson hired a San Francisco reporter, Franc Havenner, to handle his publicity and correspondence. The Progressive campaign for the Seventeenth Amendment, the direct election of senators, ratified in 1913, made senators more accountable to public opinion and may have contributed to interest in public relations in the Senate.

Another area of growth for public relations was higher education. After the Civil War, greater competition for enrollment and the growth of the mass media gave rise to a need for recruitment and for better communication within the expanding universities. Much like a hierarchy grew in big business, university administrations began to expand. Unlike the corporate model, however, universities did not rely on outside counsel but turned quickly to "in-house" public relations. The University of Michigan's office opened in 1897, and by 1937 there would be more than 200 such offices in American higher education.

Despite the rapid proliferation of public relations specialists in every area of American life, counseling remained a field closed to many people. Like the clients who retained them, counselors were as a rule white men. Women were excluded in part because industrialization contributed to a major shift in perceptions about the appropriate role of women in the workplace. When the U.S. economy was based on agriculture, both men and women of all races worked to keep their families going. But feminist scholars have shown that during the nineteenth century, changes in the organization of work led many, especially among the white middle class, to believe that men should work and that women, particularly married women, should work only inside the home. Women and people of color were sometimes able to overcome prejudice and secure jobs in advertising by arguing that they were best able to create ads that appealed to other women and people of color. But because public relations practitioners had to work closely with company presidents, journalists, and politicians, who were almost always white men, that argument rarely won jobs for women or minorities. There were exceptions. In 1920, for instance, Pendleton Dudley hired a woman to work with female audiences. The field of paid counseling remained, however, the domain of white men for many years.

Press Agentry, Publicity, and PR

During the first decades of the twentieth century, public relations activities were usually limited to press agentry. A press agent's only goal was to secure favorable mentions of his employer in the nation's newspapers and magazines. For instance, churches promoted special attractions such as giving a Bible to the father and son who looked most alike at one church's Sunday service. This competition could be publicized twice: newspapers might announce the contest ahead of time, and then mention it again when the winners had been selected. Many press agents were former — or current — reporters who understood what newspapers wanted, and they used their knowledge to obtain good coverage.

Public relations counseling was different from simple press agentry in that counselors, in addition to seeking positive press

Teddy Roosevelt Meets the Press
Theodore Roosevelt was one of the earliest American presidents to court the press. He allowed reporters to interview him during his morning shave, and he provided the texts of his messages to them before he gave speeches. This photograph of him talking with reporters was made shortly after President William McKinley, his predecessor, was assassinated.

coverage, also expected their clients to modify their behavior to match public expectations. "Publicity is a one-way street," one PR pioneer later explained; "public relations, a two-way street."[3] In the case of churches, ministers made their sermons more topical (related to current events, for example, by including references to popular books and plays) in an attempt to attract more attention in the press and among newspaper readers who might then choose to attend. In other words, some churches became more responsive to what members or potential members found interesting or important, rather than simply publicizing their usual activities.

Ivy Lee insisted that all public relations counseling, which he simply called publicity, must take on this dual role of informing the public and of advising the client about how to align activities with public interests. "The great publicity man," Lee said, "is the man who advises his client as to what policy he shall pursue, which, if pursued, would create favorable publicity," and, once the policy is set, publicizes it.[4]

During the early years of the twentieth century, most people seemed to assume that publicity techniques were effective. Many believed in the power of the press. The muckrakers, for example, thought that to solve major social issues, they needed only to expose a problem — graphically and with supporting evidence — to the public, who would then take action. Ivy Lee believed people were influenced by a combination of fact and feeling. The people, he said, "are not moved by mind, they are moved by sentiment."[5] Skillfully prepared publicity or news stories, people believed, could influence public opinion and spur public action.

During this formative period, public relations counselors first began to develop the picture of themselves as advocates for their clients before the bar of public opinion. Lee and other practitioners argued that public opinion was the final arbiter. "I believe in telling your story to the public," Lee said. "If you go direct [sic] to the people and get the people to agree with you, you can be sure that ultimately legislatures, commissions, and everybody else must surely give way in your favor."[6] This notion corresponds precisely with the American ideal of free speech. As Justice Oliver Wendell Holmes described the marketplace of ideas, many Americans hold that "the best test of truth is the power of the thought to get itself accepted in the competition of the market...."[7] Public relations practitioners presented their clients' views to the public, believing that individuals would decide for themselves what to believe.

Ray Stannard Baker pointed out a major flaw in the "bar of public opinion" explanation of the role of public relations. Baker, a muckraker, criticized railroad publicity campaigns, asking, "[A]gainst such an organization as [the railroads], supplied with unlimited money, representing a private interest which wishes to defeat the public will, to break the law, to enjoy the fruits of unrestrained power, what chance to be heard have those who believe the present conditions are wrong?"[8] Not all people benefited from public relations representation, and those who *could* organize and pay for public relations expertise apparently had an advantage over others.

Thus, societal changes brought about by the new industrial age gave rise to the counselor, a new development in public relations. Counselors devoted their careers to promoting the interests of a number of clients, and, in their best moments, worked to assure that public interest was served as well as client interest. A new era in opinion management had begun.

The Creel Committee

World War I was in many ways a crucial moment in the history of public relations, not because of innovations in technique or practice, but because of the lessons American propagandists took

[3]Edward R. Bernays, *Public Relations* (Norman, Okla., 1952), 5.
[4]Ivy Lee, *Publicity: Some of the Things It Is and Is Not* (New York, 1925), 41.
[5]Ibid., 47.
[6]Ibid., 60.
[7]*Abrams v. U.S.* (1919), 250 U. S. 616.
[8]Ray Stannard Baker, "Railroads on Trial; How Railroads Make Public Opinion," *McClure's Magazine* 26 (March 1906), 538.

Public Relations and the Great War

To promote the American effort during World War I, the federal Committee on Public Information produced an abundance of material for activities ranging from industrial productivity to public morale. Its campaign to raise revenues to help finance the war, of which this poster (left) was a part, was one of its most successful, raising more than $13 billion. The "Creel Committee" employed a group of speakers known as "Four Minute Men" to spread the war message. They made prepared presentations to various gatherings, such as movie audiences, on "subjects of national importance." The illustration of the right is the front page of one of the program's bulletins.

away from their experiences. The government had, of course, waged campaigns for opinion before, especially in times of war. But the unprecedented scale of operations and the apparent success of campaigns led many Americans, including public relations specialists, to believe that the seemingly irrational public could be easily swayed.

President Woodrow Wilson created the Committee on Public Information (CPI) in April 1917 to censor war information and to coordinate communications from the federal government about American war efforts. The creation of the CPI was not earth-shattering in significance; it was merely an extension of Wilson's ongoing efforts to centralize the flow of information from the executive branch through the White House. Wilson selected George Creel, a muckraking journalist, to chair the committee. Creel believed he could win public support simply by laying out the facts of the situation, and he disseminated information about Wilson's strategy for the United States to "make the world safe for democracy."

Although the committee was called "Public Information," its work was actually propaganda rather than public information or public relations. The Creel Committee did not practice two-way communication as Ivy Lee described. In no instance did it seek to influence government policy; instead, it only sought to inform and persuade people to subscribe to the Wilson administration's view of American participation in the war.

With a multi-million dollar budget, the CPI staff recruited actors, advertisers, artists, educators, journalists, poets, and photographers to spread through every available medium messages explaining U.S. goals and achievements. The Creel Committee wrote short speeches for 75,000 volunteer "four-minute men," who repeated the lectures at movie theaters and other public gatherings across the nation. Special branches of the CPI created brochures, posters, radio programs, films, and handouts for journalists — in English and other languages — in the United States. Others prepared materials for international audiences, both ally and enemy. They planned loyalty demonstrations and other special events to rally public support.

Several factors influenced CPI success. First, because of its budget, the Creel Committee was able to saturate the media with a flood of official information — one clipping bureau located 15,000 CPI-related newspaper stories in eighteen months. Segmentation was a second important element. The committee subdivided the general public into groups, like women or immigrant groups, and targeted each group through different media, such as magazines or the foreign-language press. Finally, the CPI based its work largely on "facts" rather than shrill emotional appeals. The News Division, Creel explained, presented "facts without the slightest trace of color or bias, either in the selection of the news or in the manner in which it was presented."[9] This did not mean that its work failed to stir emotions, only that it was not so obviously propagandistic that people dismissed it.

One of the most significant effects of the Creel Committee was that many of its staff concluded that the public *could* be influenced by media messages. Although the CPI presented what it saw as "the facts," public emotions flared in unexpected ways. For instance, the committee did not as a rule try to stir sentiment against Americans of German descent, but it did sometimes go overboard. A popular poster, called "Spies and Lies," asked citizens to report suspicious activities to the Justice Department. In the wartime atmosphere it is not surprising that some citizens began to harass German-Americans, questioning their loyalty. This extreme response convinced many people that the public was easily influenced — that publicity could herd the crowd. CPI executive Carl Byoir said that the lesson he learned from his World War I experience was that "publicity was a great dynamic force; that if you had the truth, if you had a cause that was right, and could get the facts of that truth or cause over to 130 million people, nobody could hurt you."[10] Creel was so impressed with his committee's

[9]George Creel, *How We Advertised America* (New York, 1920), 72-3.

[10]Carl Byoir, Speech before National Advertising Executive Association, New York City, 7 June 1943.

work that he subtitled his book about the CPI "The First Telling of the Amazing Story of the Committee on Public Information that Carried the Gospel of Americanism to Every Corner of the Globe." Many Americans believed that propaganda had been an important element in the struggle. Although subsequent research on mass communication would dispute propaganda's power, some citizens said that words won the war.

Counseling in the 1920s

Taking these lessons and modeling themselves perhaps after their colleagues in advertising, World War I publicists and their associates made significant strides toward institutionalizing the public relations agency during the 1920s. As the communication center of the United States, New York City became the most favored location for PR firms, which consisted of a principal or partnership, plus other executives and clerical workers. A number of young men who would later found influential agencies got important experience during the war. Edward Bernays worked in CPI's Latin American section, and John Price Jones promoted the purchase of Liberty Loans, which eventually provided more than $13 billion to finance U.S. participation in the war. Arthur Page, William Baldwin, and Carl Byoir all worked at the CPI, with Byoir serving as Associate Chairman, and all later established their own New York agencies. Among the many other agencies founded after the war were two of lasting significance: Carlton Ketchum formed an agency in Pittsburgh in 1919, and in Cleveland in 1927 John W. Hill opened a shop that would later become Hill and Knowlton, the largest agency in the world.

Arthur Wilson Page
At American Telephone and Telegraph in the 1920s, Arthur Page developed the "two-way street" approach to public relations. Along with promoting his company to the public, he attempted to keep AT&T alert to the public's concerns.

Public relations continued its crucial role in employee relations, especially in stopping the organization of labor unions, during the 1920s. John Price Jones found his agency's first client in a group of coal operators who wanted to thwart the growth of the United Mine Workers in West Virginia in 1919. Jones' duties were limited; he mainly provided information on supporters of the UMW campaign. Ivy Lee had a much greater role in trying to suppress the nearly 400,000 striking West Virginians. He entered the fray in 1921 after the "Battle of Blair Mountain," a bloody labor skirmish in Logan County, where as many as seventy men were killed. Lee's strategy included publication of *The Miner's Lamp*, a weekly bulletin much like the one published in Ludlow during the Colorado coal strike, and *Coal Facts*, lengthier background memoranda that provided details about positions the mine operators took. The owners, a group that included the Rockefellers, did halt the workers' attempts to unionize.

Arthur Page's public relations practices at American Telephone and Telegraph (AT&T) stand in sharp contrast to the reactive union-busting maneuvers of Lee and Jones. As AT&T's vice president of public relations, Page practiced the "two-way street" model of public relations: not only did he work to build public acceptance of the company, but he also kept management aware of public opinion. Page sought details on customers' desires about every aspect of service, down to the placement of memo pads in public telephone booths. Most importantly, the company listened and responded to consumers' wishes. Managers wanted to build a good relationship with consumers partly, of course, because they wanted to turn a profit. But they also worried that some people might want to make the company a public utility rather than a private company. AT&T assumed that if consumers were satisfied with their service, they would be content with the status quo. The company therefore tried to keep consumers happy by proactively seeking audience input into company policy.

Between these two extreme proactive and reactive uses of corporate public relations lay the most common use: product publicity. Many companies simply wanted to use public relations techniques to sell more products. Instead of paying for advertising, companies chose to publicize their products in more innovative, and less expensive, ways. Edward Bernays, together with his wife and partner, Doris Fleischman, became especially astute at using the special event to draw attention to their clients' products. Because of a promotion for Ivory, millions of children learned to carve soap — Ivory soap — sculptures in school contests. The Bernays agency attracted attention in the editorial columns rather than in the advertising portions of newspapers by giving awards, announcing the results of scientific surveys, throwing parties, offering symposiums, and holding banquets for such accounts as United Fruit, American Motors, and General Motors. They made news happen.

Government officials also continued to use public relations to advance their goals. The U.S. Secretary of Commerce, Herbert Hoover, conducted several campaigns during the 1920s, including one to improve housing. The Commerce Department's Building and Housing Division, formed in 1921 and chaired by Harvard professor John M. Gries, was the driving force behind the program, although other government offices such as the Departments of Labor, the Interior, and Agriculture also participated. Gries recruited national associations such as the Chamber of Commerce to help reduce housing shortages caused by the suspension of home building during World War I. Hoover joined with the editor of a women's magazine to form a volunteer organization, "Better Homes in America," which was funded by private sources but cooperated fully with the Department of Commerce's campaign. In fact, all "Better Homes" publicity was cleared through Hoover's office. The organization recruited volunteers and sent field agents to visit women's clubs and educational leaders to encourage them to help publicize and end the housing shortage. Hundreds of thousands of homes were built during the 1920s, perhaps in part because of Hoover's program. With that experience in public relations, Hoover, when he became President, created the White House Press Secretary's office in 1929.

Edward Bernays
One of the most important figures in public relations history, Edward Bernays was the first to use the word "counsel," rather than "press agent" for the PR practitioner. He was also instrumental in applying psychology to public relations practice and emphasizing PR as a socially useful practice. In his later years, however, he admitted that it could be "abused and used for anti-social purposes."

As during the Progressive era, after World War I many social reform organizations used public relations tactics to campaign for their causes. The passage of two Constitutional amendments verified their success. After many decades of campaigning, in 1919 advocates of temperance finally achieved Prohibition (the Eighteenth Amendment) and in 1920 suffragists obtained women's right to vote (the Nineteenth Amendment). Although not everyone appreciated these changes, they did show that citizens could form organizations and successfully crusade for changes in government and society.

Public relations could also be applied to less democratic causes. In Atlanta, the Southern Publicity Association, a small agency run by partners Elizabeth Tyler and Edward Young Clarke, helped to revive the Ku Klux Klan, which had been founded after the Civil War but was disbanded by an act of Congress, the Act to Enforce the Fourteenth Amendment, in 1871. In 1915, William Simmons, whose father had been a member of the original Klan, reformulated the Knights of the Ku Klux Klan as a "bottle club," with an elaborate ritual and rules. (Georgia was a "dry" state, and private bottle clubs were the only places where liquor could be served legally.) With the advent of Prohibition, Simmons' club was going bankrupt. So he brought in Tyler and Clarke to reinvigorate the organization. Using the fundraising techniques they had developed for World War I clients like the Salvation Army and the Red Cross, Tyler and Clarke created a national plan for organizing Klans all over the United States. In addition to spreading anti-Catholic, anti-Jewish, and anti-black messages, these Klans actively sought to keep black citizens from voting by marching in parades, burning crosses, and even attacking black sections of some towns.

Public Relations and Psychology

Despite such abuses, public relations flourished during the 1920s, in great part because of a growing fascination with the human mind. Books such as Walter Lippmann's *Public Opinion* and Gustave Le Bon's *The Crowd: A Study of the Public Mind* captivated the public. Viennese psychoanalyst Sigmund Freud, whose work was avidly promoted in the United States by his nephew, Edward Bernays, had tremendous influence. Freud's work suggested that people were driven by irrational desires, which tied directly into Bernays' opinions about the success of the Creel Committee in World War I. Not only did Bernays arrange for translation and sale of Freud's book, *Introductory Lectures in Psychoanalysis*, in the Unites States, but he also began to apply psychology to public relations work.

One example of Bernays' use of psychology in public relations occurred during a cigarette promotion during the 1920s. Bernays' client, American Tobacco, believed that women liked to smoke, but that they chose not to do so in public because of social taboos. Bernays consulted a psychologist, who suggested that women might identify cigarette smoking with the battle for sexual equality. Bernays then had his secretary telegraph thirty New York debutantes with the message, "In the interests of equality of the sexes and to fight another sex taboo I and other young women will light another torch of freedom by smoking cigarettes while strolling on Fifth Avenue Easter Sunday."[11] Ten women smoking cigarettes marched in the "Easter Parade," and their story became big news. Although American Tobacco's premiere cigarettes, Lucky Strikes, were never mentioned, Bernays had managed to make the papers with an angle carefully calculated to appeal to the target audience.

Psychology gave public relations access to a scientific literature that had the potential to make PR a profession rather than an art. Public relations had never been considered an honorable occupation; many people associated it with "Poison Ivy" Lee's inaccurate press handouts at Ludlow or the manipulative activities of Barnum or the railroad press agents. Bernays fought for acceptance of public relations by distinguishing what he did from mere publicity. He taught the first class specifically on public relations (at New York University in 1923) and wrote books about its role in society (beginning with the first book published on public relations, *Crystallizing Public Opinion*, also in 1923). He insisted that a counselor's work "is comparable to that of any special counsel in the highly organized society of today, the lawyer, the engineer, the accountant."[12]

Bernays was also among the first to define his role specifically as "a special pleader before the court of public opinion." He said that counselors owed high ethical standards to the client, the public, the news media, and themselves.[13] To live up to these standards, counselors had to refuse to represent clients who were "unsocial or otherwise harmful," and they had to make certain their clients' policies conformed to public interest.[14] Despite such ideals, this strategy left it to the individual counselor to determine what the public interest was.

Making Smokers of Women
Under the guidance of public relations counsel Edward Bernays, American Tobacco encouraged women in the 1920s to smoke cigarettes in public by equating smoking with social equality and with glamour. The campaign began with debutantes smoking while walking in New York City's 1923 Easter Parade. National advertising related smoking to feminine beauty.

The Great Depression And the Rise of "Big Government"

The Great Depression brought wholesale changes to the American economy and consequently the federal government, resulting in expansion of the role and occupation of public relations. The Depression left industry at a loss — no economic problem of its magnitude and duration had taken place in the industrial age. The economic crisis gave the government license to take over more and more of the decisions traditionally made by management. Business leaders worried about the future of the free enterprise system. Would Americans turn to radical solutions, like the Russian people had during the Revolution of 1917? Not surprisingly, public relations activities increased in both the public and the private sectors as government and industry leaders reacted to the Depression.

President Franklin D. Roosevelt and Congress responded to the Depression with, among other things, new laws that controlled prices and made it easier for labor unions to form. To explain and to sell new laws and regulations to the American people, the Roosevelt administration greatly expanded PR in the government agencies, although no one called it "public relations." Government PR employees worked under such titles as "specialist in information," "director of publicity," "special correspondent," "copy writer," and "editor." At least three separate agencies were responsible for public information, in addition to the information

[11] Edward L. Bernays, *Biography of an Idea: Memoirs of Public Relations Counsel Edward L. Bernays* (New York, 1965), 387.

[12] "Counsel on Public Relations—A Definition," advertisement in *Editor & Publisher*, 29 January 1927.

[13] Ibid.

[14] Edward L. Bernays, *Crystallizing Public Opinion* (New York, 1923), 87.

FDR Masters PR
Perhaps no American president was more effective in working with the press than was Franklin Roosevelt. During the Great Depression, his administration set up numerous government public relations offices. FDR himself enjoyed the company of supportive reporters and held small press conferences in his White House office.

officers in nearly every other agency. Roosevelt also spoke directly to the people through his radio "fireside chats." Some critics denounced the Roosevelt administration for its extensive public relations apparatus. "Reams and reams of statements are issued daily by the 'information' chiefs of the various government departments," one critic wrote in 1935. Despite the fact that he could find little hard evidence of a change in the economy, the author said, "hardly a day passes when some department does not issue a statement to the effect that business is 'picking up.'"[15]

Both government intervention and organized labor were anathema to conservative business executives, who believed that only management and owners should make business decisions. Arguing that Roosevelt's solutions to the problem were little different from socialism, they turned to public relations to sell "the American way": free enterprise. Their campaigns explained that the people had benefited greatly from private industry and that therefore a separation between government and industry should be maintained. The National Association of Manufacturers (NAM), a conglomeration of many smaller groups like the Chamber of Commerce, conducted a campaign that utilized every medium, ranging from motion pictures and film strips, print and outdoor advertising, and direct mail to a speakers' bureau and a radio program. One commentator in 1935 described an audience of manufacturers as "mad — mad at Washington — and keyed, emotionally, to snort defiance at the Administration...."[16] Business executives, including PR practitioners, denounced the government, especially Roosevelt, and labor unions whenever the opportunity arose.

During the Depression, public relations counseling also moved into political campaign management. The first agency dedicated to political PR was founded by a husband-and-wife team, Clem Whitaker and Leone Baxter, in California in 1933. Campaigns, Inc.'s first major battle sought the 1934 reelection of California Governor Frank Merriam. His opponent was Upton Sinclair, a socialist best known for his exposé of the meat-packing industry, *The Jungle*. Whitaker and Baxter did not think Merriam had been a good governor; so, rather than seeking reelection on his record, they maligned Sinclair's reputation. For example, they developed a series of cartoons that ran in dozens of California newspapers that condemned the "blot of Sinclairism." Each cartoon showed a traditional American scene with a giant blob of ink dashed over it, accompanied by a denigrating quote from Sinclair's writings, including dialogue spoken by his fictional characters. One cartoon showed a picture of a Madonna and child accompanied by a quote that called religion "a mighty fortress of graft." Merriam, who had not been particularly popular, won the election.

Other Depression-era campaigns were more constructive. Carl Byoir, formerly George Creel's top CPI lieutenant, together with one of his oil industry clients, Henry L. Doherty, helped to build the National Foundation for Infantile Paralysis. Byoir, whose agency promoted the interests of Chrysler, B.F. Goodrich, and other corporate giants, organized a series of local "birthday balls" held on President Roosevelt's birthday (because FDR was one of the disease's most famous victims, having contracted polio at the age of thirty-nine). Despite the challenge posed by the Depression economy, Byoir raised more than $1 million for polio research in 1934 alone, spending money out of his own pocket to start the program. The program benefited both Byoir's client, who was associated with a good cause, and polio research.

The Depression had a mixed effect on public relations as an industry. New York counsel William Henry Baldwin III found that business at his agency fell about 10% during the economic downturn. Cleveland executive John W. Hill, however, gained so much business that he decided to take on a partner, Donald Knowlton, and open a New York branch office. Trade associations became prime accounts because the National Industrial Recovery Act required companies to work together to write codes to regulate

[15]George Michael, *Handout* (New York, 1935), 11.
[16]Arthur H. Little, "Industry Writes Its Story," *Printers' Ink* 173 (December 19, 1935), 10.

their own industries, giving them an important role in Roosevelt's plan to respond to the Depression.

Three important refinements in the practice of public relations counseling took place during the Depression. First, some counselors began to participate in the formation of a client's policies, so they could advise management about how an organization's plans might affect or be affected by its relationships with key audiences. Two highly respected counselors, Earl Newsom, of Earl Newsom and Associates, and John W. Hill, of Hill and Knowlton, insisted that they work closely with the top management of their client organizations. Although Ivy Lee had long recommended this arrangement, it had not been a regular policy for client-agency relationships for Lee or anyone else. Hill attended virtually every board meeting of the American Iron and Steel Institute for about forty years. Newsom developed close associations with such executives as Frank Stanton, president of the CBS television network, and Henry Ford II. Hill felt so strongly about policy-making that in 1938 he invited a select group of elite counselors (a group nicknamed "The Wisemen") to dinner, and they agreed to participate in monthly dinners and discussions about issues related to counseling.

This period also saw the beginnings of an important trend, the establishment of public relations departments within organizations. United States Steel created its own PR department in 1936, for example, and Standard Oil of New Jersey (later renamed Enco and then Exxon) followed suit in 1942. For the most part, however, outside consulting continued to dominate.

A third development involved codification of the process of creating a public relations program. Edward Bernays developed a set of "four steps essential to formulate a program" of public relations in 1935. In an article titled "Molding Public Opinion," Bernays wrote that the PR counselor must formulate objectives "in the public interest," analyze public attitudes, study that analysis and make the program or policy "part and parcel of the thinking and action of the leaders in the industry," and use the media to carry the policy.[17] Although many objected to the notion that Bernays could "mold" public opinion, these steps are still important in public relations counseling.

Despite such changes, practitioners continued to suggest that the role of public relations was to represent clients' opinions before the bar of public opinion. "For fair judgment," counselor John Price Jones wrote in 1939, "conflicting ideas must be brought into the open for free discussion.... Eventually public opinion will be so crystallized that through action of a majority of the people, new and higher standards will be established in legislation, in public morals and economic methods." Jones also noted that not every idea got a fair hearing. To assure a workable marketplace of ideas, he said, "[t]he nature and meaning of conflicting ideas must be presented adequately, at the bar of public opinion."[18]

[17]Edward L. Bernays, "Molding Public Opinion," *Annals of the American Academy of Political and Social Science* 179 (May 1935): 85-7

[18]John Price Jones and David McLaren Church, *At the Bar of Public Opinion: A Brief for Public Relations* (New York, 1939), 5-6.

Women at War
With many men serving in the military during World War II, women had to take up factory production jobs. Both the government and private industry produced many campaigns to encourage the effort. The government's most famous campaign was "Rosie the Riveter," while companies such as ADEL emphasized the expectation that the factory work women were doing would make it possible for them to quit their war jobs one day and return to caring for their homes and staying with their children.

World War II: "Big Government" Gets Bigger

As in World War I, federal public relations activities during World War II concentrated in the executive branch, but the experiences of its participants were markedly different from those on the Creel Committee. In 1942 the Office of War Information (OWI) replaced the three government information agencies previously created by Roosevelt. The President's team disagreed on the role the OWI should take. Some wanted a centralized office, like the Creel Committee, that would provide not only information but morale-building activities; but Stephen Early, a former journalist and the President's closest communications adviser, opposed a new CPI. Thus, although the new agency was huge, with more than 9,000 employees worldwide, news formed the backbone of the OWI's programs at home and abroad. Respected radio commentator Elmer Davis headed the new agency.

OWI executives believed that years of European propaganda efforts had deafened people to emotional appeals and that honest news stories therefore would be more effective. They relied on

Supporting the War at Home

During World War II, the federal government employed a variety of media to promote the Allied effort among the American citizenry. Movies and films were important, but traditional methods such as posters continued to be used also. The posters pictured here illustrate some of the areas at which the promotional efforts were aimed. The poster on the left encouraged Americans to invest in war bonds by poking fun at Adolf Hitler, Hermann Göring (German military commander), and Joseph Goebbels (propaganda minister). With the need for military personnel, numerous efforts were made to recruit into the armed forces, as illustrated by the middle poster. Both civilians and servicemen also were alerted to the need for vigilance in security and discouraged from discussing topics that might seem innocent but could be of use to the enemy (poster on right).

radio news, especially in Europe, in addition to newspaper and magazine stories and leaflets to reach their audiences. "Before OWI, reporters might obtain from different agencies, on the same day, three or four different versions to the same story — each of them partial, and at least to that extent inaccurate," Elmer Davis reported to the President. "We sometimes made them wait a day, but what we gave them was coherent and correct."[19] The agency spent more than $130 million in its overseas, domestic, and administrative branches to keep people informed.

Although the OWI is usually remembered for its earnest news presentation, it also disseminated propaganda through films, magazines, and other entertainment media. It controlled movie content both by censoring and by offering advice on what should appear. For example, executives wanted the Hollywood studios to prepare citizens for the deaths of American soldiers; so movies like *Tender Comrade* showed scenes of a mother telling her baby that his father "went out and died so you could have a better break when you grow up." The OWI's Magazine Bureau similarly encouraged publishers to include war messages in their periodicals. One of its more famous campaigns, the Womanpower project, provided pictures and reports about women, symbolized by "Rosie the Riveter," who entered the labor force to take the places of men who had gone to war. The campaign also suggested plots for fictional stories about such women.

Unlike the Creel Committee, the OWI did not spawn a large number of new practitioners or agencies. In fact, two of the most important postwar counselors, Farley Manning of Manning, Selvage & Lee and Harold Burson of Burson-Marsteller, worked for the military — which mobilized as many as 100,000 public information officers during the war — not the OWI. Nor did PR practitioners leave their wartime positions with the belief that opinion management was simple or easy.

Unlike the First World War, World War II experiences with propaganda indicated to practitioners that the effects of mass-mediated messages were limited. Theories about persuasion changed during World War II, in large part because of an influential communication experiment conducted on U. S. soldiers. General George C. Marshall recruited from Hollywood Frank Capra, who had directed popular movies such as *Mr. Smith Goes to Washington*, to make a series of documentary films, titled *Why We Fight*, that explained the reasons and principles behind the U.S. role in the war. Capra produced seven fifty-minute films, such as *Prelude to War* and *The Battle of Britain*, that became part of the Army's training program for recruits. A team of social scientists from Yale conducted surveys of trainees before and after they watched the films, and compared the results to those of control groups that had never seen the movies. The scholars concluded that, although viewing the films did help soldiers to learn facts and in some cases change attitudes, they were not effective at strengthening the overall motivation or morale of the viewers. In short, these social scientists argued, mass communication effects were not powerful but instead were quite limited.

[19]Elmer Davis, "Report to the President," *Journalism Monographs* 7 (August 1968).

Expansion in Corporate PR

Despite the growing belief among scholars of public opinion that people were not easily persuaded by mass communication, the post-World War II era was one of unprecedented expansion in public relations. As before the war, public relations was important in every sector: corporate, government, and non-profit. In 1950 there were 19,000 "public relations specialists," according to the U.S. Department of Labor. A decade later there were 31,000. The field grew in size, scope, and professionalism after World War II, but in fundamental ways public relations counseling remained the same.

The postwar growth in public relations occurred for several reasons. Industrial relations were particularly important. Several waves of strikes after the war cost industry in lost production and in consumer dissatisfaction. Additionally, one survey indicated that in 1948 nearly half the American public demanded government regulation of big business, often arguing that prices were too high. Many business managers, including public relations counselors, believed that people felt this way only because they did not understand the contributions big business had made to the American standard of living. Therefore, they insisted that corporate advertising and public relations should do more than just promote products: they should also promote capitalism. Among business priorities after the war, one survey revealed, were "indicating the company's contribution to the general welfare, building confidence in the company's product, and promoting a belief in the free enterprise system."[20] This opened the door for increased public relations budgets, invigorating the field.

Over the years, corporations gradually de-emphasized the idea of selling "free enterprise," but they continued to use public relations activities to manage government regulation of business. One of the best-known examples involved a bitter fight between truckers in Pennsylvania and the Eastern Railroads. During the early 1950s the Pennsylvania Motor Truck Association lobbied the state legislature to increase truck weight limitations so that trucks could carry heavier loads on the state's highways. The Eastern Railroads Presidents Conference worried about the truckers' growing power; and, fearing that larger loads would take away business from the railroads, they hired Carl Byoir and Associates to implement a campaign opposing the truckers.

Byoir's campaign for the railroads had an important unintended effect: the legal controversy it created resulted in a Supreme Court opinion that gave First Amendment protection to public relations activities. Byoir ran an advertising campaign, commissioned free-lance writers to prepare magazine articles, sought radio airtime on the controversy, and recruited support from other organizations by suggesting that heavier loads were dangerous and would ruin the state's roads. When the truckers obtained a copy of Byoir's file on the railroad campaign, they charged the Railroad Presidents and Byoir with violating the antitrust laws by engaging in a conspiracy to eliminate competition. In particular they questioned Byoir's use of the "third party technique," when seemingly independent citizen's groups were formed by the agency specifically to support the client's position. Litigation on the case continued all the way to the U.S. Supreme Court, which ruled in 1961 that attempts to influence the passage or enforcement of laws did not violate the Sherman Act, even when the petitioner's motive was to seek legislation that would damage a competitor.[21]

Public relations also maintained its important role in product publicity. New York counsel Benjamin Sonnenberg, for example, promoted several large department store chains such as Bergdorf-Goodman and Federated Department Stores, which operated Bloomingdale's, Filene's of Boston, and other prominent shops. In addition to holding fashion shows and pitching feature stories to the press, Sonnenberg put live models pretending to be mannequins in store windows to capture public attention. To celebrate Bergdorf-Goodman's fiftieth anniversary, in 1951, Sonnenberg planned a dinner and dance at the famed Plaza Hotel in New York City. As many as 800 people attended, paying $50 each.

Another area of growth occurred due to the acceleration of the trend of establishing in-house public relations departments. In the decade following the war such corporations as Ford, Allis-Chalmers, the Pennsylvania Railroad, Socony-Vacuum, Gulf Oil, Chrysler, and Northwestern Mutual Life Insurance created their own public relations departments. In later years non-profit and government organizations, ranging from hospitals and voluntary organizations to public utilities, also increasingly established internal counsel.

In-house public relations did not grow at the expense of outside counsel. In 1960 *Printers' Ink* reported that there were 704 public relations agencies in New York City alone. These ranged from giants like Hill and Knowlton and Byoir "to the one-man operation whose apartment is his office."[22] Along with H&K, which both public relations executives and newspaper editors ranked as the best firm, other top agencies included Ivy Lee and T. J. Ross, Selvage and Lee (later Manning, Selvage and Lee), Dudley-Anderson-Yutzy, and Ruder and Finn.

Perhaps the most important development of the postwar era was the creation of the modern PR agency. During the first part of the twentieth century, public relations firms were identified with the individuals or partners who founded them. When George Parker left Parker & Lee, for example, the agency simply dissolved. The modern agency was more than a consultancy built around an individual. Carl Byoir and Associates and Hill and Knowlton had large staffs — each with more than 200 employees — with many executives who shared the responsibility of counseling clients, and both continued to operate for many years after the principals retired. An agency did not have to be large to be modern. Earl Newsom's firm, for example, had five partners — Newsom, Fred

[20] "Industry's Public Relations Job," *Business Record* 2 (March 1945), 75.

[21] *Eastern Railroad Presidents Conference v. Noerr Motor Freight, Inc.*, 365 U.S. 127 (1961).

[22] "Public Relations: A Communication System Ripens," *Printers' Ink* 273 (25 November 1960), 66.

Palmer, Arthur B. Tourtellot, William A. Lydgate, and Richard Aszling — and at its peak only twenty-three employees. But it represented such prestigious clients as Campbell's Soup, CBS Television, Eli Lilly, Ford, General Motors, International Paper, Merrill Lynch, the New York Stock Exchange, and Trans-World Airlines, and continued to do so long after Newsom retired.

International Public Relations

Still more growth lay overseas. After World War II many American businesses began to invest in other nations — direct foreign investment tripled in the decade immediately following the war — and to market their products to a war-torn world. Hill and Knowlton, which had become the leading U.S. agency, recognized that American business was moving overseas, and it was the first public relations firm to establish successful offices in foreign countries. The agency fashioned a network of associated public relations firms in Europe by affiliating with leading practitioners in England, France, the Netherlands, and Belgium, beginning in 1954. H&K paid each affiliate a $500 retainer. In return, the affiliates promised to work with Hill and Knowlton exclusively, and to handle any public relations activities H&K clients might require in Europe on a per-job basis. The agency also opened an international office in Geneva, headed by Loet Velmans, a Dutch citizen who had trained in H&K's New York office, and a subsidiary in Australia.

The American practice of public relations counseling did not transfer easily to other nations. One German industrialist, for example, could not see a need for public relations activities at all. He explained to Hill and Knowlton representatives that prices were fixed by the German cartels, so product promotion was not necessary; that industries had significant influence over legislation affecting them; and that German public opinion already favored industry. U.S. public relations counselors thus first had to sell public relations in general and then sell their own services in particular. For some years H&K found it easier to obtain U.S. clients who were working in other nations (multinational corporations like California Texas Oil and American Cyanamid) than to find foreign employers.

One agency, Barnet & Reef, specialized in international public relations during the 1960s. By the end of 1958, the year it was founded, its international client list included Dow Chemical and American Machine and Foundry. Within a few years it added such powerhouse clients as Goodyear, Philip Morris, United Fruit, and John Deere. At its peak Barnet & Reef associates worked in forty-eight nations, although its New York headquarters had only fifteen employees.

The Professionalization of Public Relations

The postwar era also saw a drive to improve the professionalism of public relations. In 1948 two organizations (the National Association of Accredited Publicity Directors and the American Council on Public Relations) combined to form a national professional organization, the Public Relations Society of America (PRSA). The PRSA developed a system of accreditation, which involved a practitioner's taking an examination to demonstrate expertise in public relations and pledging to uphold the Society's Code of Standards, which was adopted in 1954. Herbert Muschel created a special public relations wire service, the *PR NewsWire*, that same year. New journals, including *PR News* (1944), *Public Relations Journal* (1945), and *PR Reporter* (1958), also testified to the growing interest in improving the practice and reputation of public relations.

Professionalization also included a push for better public relations education, which developed rapidly after the war. Immediately after World War II, only about two dozen U.S. universities offered instruction on public relations. In a trend that can be traced back to Bernays' reliance on his uncle's theories about psychology, public relations educators increasingly drew from other fields of study (including organizational and consumer behavior, rhetoric, and electoral behavior) to develop a better understanding of the most effective ways to communicate with and persuade their diverse audiences. Educators and practitioners alike displayed an increasing reliance on computers, using them to target audiences and to analyze survey results that could help them influence opinions and behaviors. By the 1990s more than 300 colleges and universities offered courses in public relations, including many that offered graduate degrees.

Educators also recommended greater attention to interpersonal communication than Lee, Bernays, and other pioneer counselors had considered. One study of political decision-making suggested that persuasion was actually a two-step process. *The People's Choice*, published in 1948, analyzed the behavior of voters in Erie County, Ohio. The investigators found that some individuals were opinion leaders who paid close attention to political messages and who shared what they had learned with others. It seemed that ideas flowed from radio or print to the opinion leaders and from them to less active members of the population.

Public relations practitioners quickly adopted the notion of targeting opinion leaders for their messages, with the assumption that certain individuals would use their personal influence to sway others' opinions. Paul Lazarsfeld, who led *The People's Choice* research team, suggested that the study's results "have a meaning for the changing of minds in commercial advertising campaigns as well as in a political campaign."[23] For this reason public relations practitioners began to send materials, such as brochures and newsletters, directly to opinion leaders such as clergy or teachers, instead of trying to place articles in any newspaper or magazine that would print them. They also planned grass roots campaigns by providing information and materials to the leaders of local organizations, such as farm or women's groups, that could be used at small group meetings.

[23] Paul F. Lazarsfeld, "Who Influences Whom—It's the Same for Politics and Advertising," *Printers' Ink* 21 (8 June 1945), 32.

Presidential PR

Television changed the nature of presidential relations with the press and public. National commercial television had begun during the presidency of Harry Truman, but it was during the presidency of Dwight Eisenhower (left) that it became a national force. Through his press secretary, James Hagerty, he experimented with televised "fireside chats" and then with edited television news conferences. TV's need for compelling visuals and drama made the president's image and public speaking ability increasingly important. One might say that image over substance became the norm. Political public relations responded by providing opportunities for coverage that gave television reporters ample time to prepare for evening network newscasts. Unlike other presidential administrations that tried to control the flow of important information from the White House, the Richard Nixon administration (1969-1974) attempted to set the news agenda. Because Nixon (right) had an intense distrust of the news media, he created the White House Office of Communications to manage media relations and shield him from the press.

The American Medical Association's campaign to halt President Truman's plan for compulsory medical insurance in the late 1940s and early 1950s was an example of a campaign that utilized the "two-step flow" approach. The association retained California's Whitaker and Baxter, which spent over $4.5 million in three and a half years. The public relations agents prodded doctors to support voluntary group insurance plans and then promoted that position with the slogan "The Voluntary Way Is the American Way." It paid for billboards and posters of the famous painting "The Doctor," by Sir Luke Fildes, which showed a "bearded, frock-coated physician" turning "a compassionate glance on his small patient," a sick child, and the words "Keep Politics Out of This Picture."[24] Whitaker and Baxter mobilized doctors by providing speeches, resolutions, and press releases to the many state and county medical societies across the country. The materials could be modified to fit the local situation and then used to help publicize the doctors' fight against what they called "socialized medicine" at the local level. They distributed over 54 million pieces of literature in 1949 alone.

Not all practitioners, however, adopted the new approach. Hollywood publicists, for example, continued to utilize some of the tactics of the old railroad press agents. Rogers and Cowan, based in Los Angeles, went to any length to publicize the actors they represented — Joan Crawford, Frank Sinatra, Marlene Dietrich, Jane Wyman, Dean Martin, and Bette Davis, to name a few. The agency told a series of extravagant lies to get Rita Hayworth on the cover of *Look* magazine in a photo that made her famous. The only purpose of such campaigns was to obtain positive press coverage for clients.

GROWTH IN POLITICAL PR

Public relations also continued to grow in importance in the political arena. The 1952 Democratic and Republican presidential nominating conventions were the first to be televised coast-to-coast, and elected officials began to rely more heavily on television to reach their constituents. President Dwight D. Eisenhower's press secretary, James Hagerty, and his staff had constant access to the chief executive, meaning that they could provide counsel much like Hill or Newsom did for their corporate accounts. The Eisenhower administration experimented with televised "fireside chats," and then with specially edited television news conferences. Presidents Kennedy and Johnson then began the practice of allowing live broadcast of their news conferences.

Some scholars argue that the increasingly active role of public relations in political policymaking has been a detriment to the democratic process. The increasing importance of television and of "image" rather than substance has made PR a more dominant force in politics. Yet PR is not part of classical democratic theory, which posited the press as an intelligence service for the people. The complexity of both government and society means that reporters can no longer keep up, and they must depend on public relations practitioners to help.

Because of these factors, the White House public relations apparatus continued to expand until 1969, when President Richard M. Nixon created the White House Office of Communication. This office functioned in addition to the White House Press Office headed by the press secretary, Ronald Ziegler. The Office of Communication's four staff members, directed by a former journalist, Herbert Klein, coordinated the flow of information from the entire Executive Branch. Klein reported to H.R. Haldeman, the White House Chief of Staff, who had been an advertising executive at J.

[24] "The Doctors Gird for Battle," *Newsweek* 33 (20 June 1949), 50.

Reagan, "The Great Communicator"
The media's role in influencing public opinion has required modern American presidents to devote considerable attention to public relations. One of the most effective was Ronald Reagan. Even though journalists generally were hostile toward him, he managed to appeal directly to the public through such activities as well-planned news conferences.

Walter Thompson.

Nixon used the Office as a political tool to influence — not just inform — the public, and when the administration's lies to the public and to Congress were exposed in the Watergate scandal, the entire White House public relations operation was discredited. But the Office survived. Presidents Ford and Carter attempted to rebuild a good relationship with journalists and the public by being open about all their decisions and activities. By the Reagan era, White House staff engaged in public relations activities numbered in the hundreds.

Public Relations Today

By 1990 the number of public relations specialists had risen to more than 160,000. Far more significant was their increasing diversity. At the turn of the century there were apparently no full-time, paid public relations counselors who were women. In 1968 about one-quarter of PR specialists were female, and in 1993 nearly 60% were women.

Women's entry into the field was not easy, but the outstanding work of a few pioneers paved the way for others after World War II. The career of Jane Stewart provides an example. After graduating from Ohio Wesleyen in 1939, Stewart found a job as secretary to the president of Hill and Knowlton. Recognizing her skills, including leadership and a talent for writing, John Mapes recruited her when he left H&K to form a survey research company, Group Attitudes Development Corporation. A few years later, Hill and Knowlton bought Group Attitudes, making it a subsidiary of H&K, where it had its own clients in addition to doing work for H&K clients when needed. Stewart was entirely responsible for running the subsidiary when she was named president in 1961, and she did the job with great success. A few other women became executives during the 1960s, and in 1970 Marion Pinsdorf became the first woman vice-president on H&K's general account staff.

Minority participation in public relations remained smaller, but it too grew. About 11% of public relations practitioners in 1991 were minorities. D. Parke Gibson, an African American who opened a New York City agency during the 1960s, is one person who found it difficult to move into the mainstream of public relations practice. African Americans constituted a multi-million dollar market and therefore could not be ignored. Practitioners were therefore able to find work targeting other people of the same minority group. But many minority practitioners could find work only in minority-owned organizations, and, as Gibson discovered, minority-owned agencies had difficulty obtaining accounts other than those targeting minority audiences exclusively.

Because minorities were marginalized by society, they used public relations techniques to forward the cause of civil rights during the 1950s and 1960s. The Southern Christian Leadership Conference, headed by Martin Luther King, Jr., did not retain external counsel, but it did practice public relations. PR figured in many of the SCLC's activities, including alliance building, political advocacy, consumer boycotts, and grassroots communication. The SCLC conducted citizenship and political education campaigns designed to recruit volunteers, increase voter registration, and train citizens about nonviolent methods to solve social problems. Its public relations activities contributed to the eradication of both segregation and African-American disenfranchisement.

Mass communication research after World War II continued to undermine the idea that people are uniformly or directly affected by media messages, but it also indicated that effects do exist. Scholars argued that variables such as education, media use, and individual needs for information contribute to how much any individual pays attention to or is affected by messages. Public relations practitioners responded by developing methods of targeting audiences through messages tailored to meet individual needs and through media such as direct mail and the Internet.

One final significant trend in public relations counseling was the development of the mega-agency. A series of mergers of public relations firms with advertising and lobbying firms created a small number of huge, full-service agencies. In 1977, for example, Carl Byoir and Associates was sold to advertising giant Foote, Cone and Belding. Hill and Knowlton joined the J.W.T. Group, which included the advertising agency J. Walter Thompson, in 1980. Over the next several years H&K purchased ten public relations and lobbying firms, including its long-time rival, Byoir. In

Jane Stewart
Working as a secretary to the president of Hill and Knowlton, Jane Stewart left to join a survey research company, Group Attitudes Development Corporation. After Hill and Knowlton bought Group Attitudes, making it a subsidiary of H&K, she was named president in 1961.

1987 a British firm, the W.P.P. Group, executed a hostile takeover of J.W.T. Even smaller agencies like Newsom's merged with larger ones — Adams & Rinehart in 1983, which in turn merged with Ogilvy Public Relations.

Public relations changed dramatically during the twentieth century — the number of practitioners expanded geometrically, persuasion theory became increasingly sophisticated, and the practice of public relations modified in response — but at least one thing has remained constant throughout the history of PR counseling. In 1971 pioneer Bernays claimed that "this profession makes it possible for minority ideas to be more readily accepted by the majority"; but he also admitted that "regrettably, public relations, like other professions, can be abused and used for anti-social purposes."[25] The discrepancy between the ideal model of two-way communication for social good and the reality of public relations practice had not altered since Bernays first wrote about it fifty years earlier. Although there exist plenty of examples of public relations activities that have benefited the democratic process, PR techniques and counseling have also made negative contributions.

[25]Edward L. Bernays, "Emergence of the Public Relations Counsel: Principles and Recollections," *Business History Review* 45 (Autumn 1971): 297, 299.

RECOMMENDED READINGS

BOOKS

Allen, Craig. *Eisenhower and the Mass Media: Peace, Prosperity, and Prime-Time TV.* Chapel Hill, N.C., 1993. Eisenhower used the new medium of television as a regular part of his administration's public relations practices.

Bloom, Melvyn H. *Public Relations and Presidential Campaigns: A Crisis in Democracy.* New York, 1973. Political campaigns have changed dramatically since the founding of the United States, and public relations has not been an entirely positive force for democracy.

Cutlip, Scott M. *The Unseen Power: Public Relations, A History.* Hillsdale, N.J., 1994. A review of the history of public relations agencies concludes that PR has been a dominant, if unrecognized, force in twentieth-century U.S. history.

Ewen, Stuart. *PR! A Social History of Spin.* New York, 1996. The meanings of public, public opinion, and persuasion and the ways these ideas were applied to visual and verbal propaganda changed dramatically during the twentieth century.

Hiebert, Ray Eldon. *Courtier to the Crowd: The Story of Ivy Lee and the Development of Public Relations.* Ames, Iowa, 1966. Lee's career is best seen as a part of the democratic crisis that resulted when the mass — mass culture, mass production, mass communication — replaced pluralism. Lee developed techniques that allowed groups to express themselves, thus maintaining pluralism.

Honey, Maureen. *Creating Rosie the Riveter: Class, Gender, and Propaganda during World War II.* Amherst, Mass., 1984. The U.S. government's strategy to recruit women for war work was carefully constructed so that women's participation did not threaten traditional gender roles.

Juergens, George. *News from the White House: The Presidential-Press Relationship in the Progressive Era.* Chicago, 1981. The flow of power from Congress to the White House during the Progressive era created both the modern Presidency and the modern Washington press corps. Presidents and reporters needed each other, but also at times antagonized each other.

Maltese, John Anthony. *Spin Control: The White House Office of Communications and the Management of Presidential News.* Chapel Hill, N.C., 1992. When Nixon created the Office of Communications, he lifted presidential public relations to a new — although not better — level, creating a precedent with which presidents since have had to contend.

Miller, Karen. *The Voice of Business.* Chapel Hill, N.C., 1999. Examines the founding and operation of Hill and Knowlton.

Olasky, Marvin. *Corporate Public Relations: A New Historical Perspective.* Hillsdale, N.J., 1987. Business and public relations executives did not use PR to stop government intervention in business. Instead, they "worked diligently to kill free enterprise" by promoting an alliance between government and business.

Raucher, Alan R. *Public Relations and Business, 1900-1929.* Baltimore, 1968. The rise of corporate public relations was related to both the internal and the external problems of corporations, but the policy of adopting public relations techniques was initiated primarily as a political device.

Tedlow, Richard S. *Keeping the Corporate Image: Public Relations and Business, 1900-1950.* Greenwich, Conn., 1979. Public relations was a product of "a general movement to increase efficiency" and the need to respond to "journalistic criticism which was reaching a wider audience than ever before." Business leaders wanted to control the news that corporations could not help generating.

ARTICLES

Bernays, Edward L. "Emergence of the Public Relations Counsel: Principles and Recollections." *Business History Review* 45 (Autumn 1971): 296-316. Bernays describes key clients and campaigns in his career as counsel on public relations.

Cutlip, Scott M. "Public Relations in Government." *Public Relations Review* 2 (Summer 1976): 5-28. Government public relations "is a weapon of power," but the history of public information operations shows that journalists need assistance to cover the government adequately.

Endres, Fred F. "Public Relations in the Jackson White House." *Public Relations Review* 2 (Fall 1976): 5-12. Amos Kendall, who managed President Jackson's campaigns and press relations, should be considered the first public relations counselor.

Ferré, John P. "Protestant Press Relations in the United States, 1900-1930." *Church History* 62 (December 1993): 514-27. Many churches conducted public relations activities, and clergy considered publicity an effective way to increase attendance and contributions.

Henry, Susan. "Anonymous in Her Own Name: Public Relations Pioneer Doris E. Fleischman." *Journalism History* 23 (1997): 51-62. Fleischman remained behind the scenes, but she played a significant role in the development of the Bernays agency and public relations generally.

Lucarelli, Susan. "The Newspaper Industry's Campaign Against Spacegrabbers, 1917-1921." *Journalism Quarterly* 70 (1993): 883-92. Account of the newspaper industry's campaign after World War I against press agents who were accused of trying to get free space. The hostility between the two factions that continues today.

Miller, Karen S. "Smoking Up a Storm: Public Relations and Advertising in the Construction of the Cigarette Problem, 1953-1954." *Journalism Monographs* 136 (December 1992). The tobacco industry used public relations and advertising programs to defuse the first major cigarettes-and-health scare, by arguing that scientists lacked proof that cigarettes caused cancer or other diseases.

Miller, Karen S. "Woman, Man, Lady, Horse: Jane Stewart, Public Relations Executive." *Public Relations Review* 23 (1997): 249-69. Stewart was one of the first women to take on the counseling role at a major agency.

Murphree, Vanessa. "Public Relations, 1900-1950: Tool for Profit or for Social Reform?" Chap. 16 in Wm. David Sloan, *Perspectives on Mass Communication History*. Hillsdale, N.J., 1991. Analyzes the approaches that historians have taken to explaining public relations.

Olasky, Marvin. "Retrospective: Bernays' Doctrine of Public Opinion." *Public Relations Review* 10 (Fall 1984): 3-12. Bernays "stuck to his belief that the job of the public relations counsel was to produce socially useful propaganda."

Ponder, Stephen. "Presidential Publicity and Executive Power: Woodrow Wilson and the Centralizing of Government Information." *American Journalism* 11 (1994): 257-69. Many government agencies had press bureaus in the early twentieth century, and Wilson took steps to consolidate the flow of information from the executive branch.

Raucher, Alan R. "Public Relations in Business: A Business of Public Relations." *Public Relations Review* 16 (Fall 1990): 19-26. Public relations "emerged and grew as an institutional response to the distinctive features of a democratic America."

23

The Media in Transition

1945 - 1974

The phenomenon of television swept through America in the decades after World War II, asserting itself as the premier mass medium, modifying most other media, and changing the way people lived their lives. It introduced a new kind of journalism best defined by the title of an early television magazine program, *See It Now*.

The other media reacted and tried to meet the new competitor. Newspapers, the media with the longest tradition, attempted to hold on to their practices more than the other media did, but even they ultimately found that they had to change also. The story of the mass media in America following World War II is, then, in many ways the story of television.

The Television Phenomenon

The first public demonstration of television took place on September 7, 1927, from the laboratory of Philo Farnsworth in San Francisco. The experiment, which consisted of the transmission of a photograph, might have been demonstrated months earlier, but investors wanted to wait until a photo could be used, thinking it more impressive than the triangles and dollar signs that had been used in earlier private demonstrations.

Farnsworth's television system had gone unnoticed by the corporate giant RCA until the 1930s, when Farnsworth and RCA became fierce competitors. RCA had tried to purchase Farnsworth's patents, but he did not want to sell, since he had royalty payments in mind. RCA, however, did not want to pay royalties, insisting instead on an outright purchase of the patent rights.

Despite the setbacks and corporate battles that engaged his attention, today hundreds of patents are filed under the name of Farnsworth, "the father of television." He was the last of the independent inventors, a scientist rather than an entrepreneur.

The development of television moved slowly throughout the 1930s as the Federal Communications Commission proceeded cautiously in its determination of technical and regulatory standards. Not only was there fierce competition between television's development engineers, but several television proposals were placed before the FCC to consider, including one from CBS for color television. The FCC did not act on television until 1941, and then World War II interrupted progress on its development. It was not until after the war that television was widely introduced. In 1946 there were six television stations in the United States. By 1970 there were 900.

What is the distinctive nature of television? It combines spoken sound and natural sound, writing, and pictures. It does this all at once in a continually changing effusion of stimuli that can be transmitted instantaneously over a wide area. One does not simply see and hear television — one experiences television. At every given moment of every day millions are experiencing television. Thus, it is an incredibly rich medium for broadcasters. Television is chronological in nature. It operates on a schedule. One "sees it now" or never; or at least not until "it" is rerun. It is heavily dependent on sophisticated electronic technology.

At first people were transfixed by the miracle of television. They would look with wonder at the lines and numerals of the test pattern on a tiny seven-inch set. Stores put sets in their windows, and crowds gathered outside to watch. A home with a television attracted the neighbors, much as a literate person with a newspaper and a good reading voice attracted illiterate listeners in the early days of newspapers. Soon the illiterate in those days learned to read. Soon, in the days of television, every home had a set (more than 95% by 1970). By the early 1950s urban apartment roofs had sprouted television antennas and looked as if they had contracted a metallic fungus. Rickety sharecropper cabins in the rural South seemed to be supported by a TV antenna pole on one side and a pre-war used car on the other.

Early television content was influenced by radio and the movie industry. Radio was an electronic medium under the supervision of the Federal Communications Commission. It was primarily an entertainment industry with news and cultural events as ancillary content. It was financed by advertising revenue, with sponsoring businesses often producing their own content to be distributed by

The Visual Entertainer
Even before commercial television went on the air, its primary appeal was conceived to be entertainment rather than news and information. This 1944 ad told consumers that with television the most popular radio programs "could all become real visual experiences...experiences for you to watch as well as hear."

networks. Radio developed a full array of content: news, drama, comedy, music, lectures — using sound alone. Early television developed from this heritage.

From Hollywood motion pictures, television inherited all the techniques needed to add visual stimuli to the sound. At first, TV programming was live. A drama had to be performed on a set in front of a camera, with commercials performed live at the appropriate moment. If something went wrong, everyone watching knew it. For example, John Cameron Swayze was a radio journalist who became the pitch man on Timex watch commercials. After putting a watch through a terrible ordeal, he would hold it up to the camera and exult, "It takes a licking and keeps on ticking!" But once a Timex was lashed to an outboard motor propeller and thrashed about in a barrel of water. When the propeller emerged from the water, the Timex had disappeared, leaving Swayze speechless.

Early TV programming (such as Milton Berle's *Texaco Star Theater*, the first popular comedy) was not recorded. Lucille Ball's *I Love Lucy* show was one of the first to be filmed at the same time it was broadcast, and it still is in reruns.

Television's popularity spurred technological change. Early developments that modified the content of television included the film chain and the use of 16mm film. The film chain is a device that points a television camera at a movie projector and at slide projectors, putting images from either on the TV screen. No longer was live programming the only possibility. The 16mm format rapidly replaced 35mm, which was the motion picture industry standard. The smaller format was popular as an educational audio/visual tool. It was less bulky, less expensive, and easier to handle. Very soon most stations were doing their own 16mm processing and editing. By the mid-1960s, videotape was replacing film.

In the 1950s cities were linked, eventually coast to coast, by coaxial cable and later by microwave transmission, allowing instantaneous network broadcasting. In small towns individual receivers were linked by coaxial cable to a tall community antenna tower that could bring in signals from a city at some distance. This was the beginning of cable television. By 1970, 80% of local stations had a network affiliation and 2,800 community antenna systems (the largest with 50,000 subscribers) were serving 6,000,000 households in 5,300 communities.

Miniaturization of electronics and development of sophisticated rockets had allowed earth satellites to orbit the earth and bounce back television signals over large areas. The first trans-Atlantic live satellite transmission occurred in 1962 between Andover, Maine, and locations in Cornwall, England, and Britanny, France. RCA (the Radio Corporation of America) launched the first satellite specifically designed for television in 1975.

Two of the radio networks, CBS and NBC, and a manufacturer of television sets, Dumont, organized the first television networks in the 1940s. Soon Dumont went out of business, and ABC joined the list. The FCC at first authorized twelve VHF channels, later adding two dozen UHF channels. The VHF channels had wider range and better quality, and the network stations dominated them. The networks of stations provided a superb national advertising medium. Universities and other public entities established "educational" stations that were required to have no advertising. Governmental and public subsidies sustained them, and in the late 1960s PBS was established as a network of public stations.

Following the experience of radio, success of a television program or series was based on the number of sets tuned in. A successful program or a popular national issue, event, or personality on one network led the other networks to duplicate or match what their competitors were doing. The measure of success was not of the quality or importance of what was communicated; the measure was of how well the communication appealed to the current popular appetite.

The dominance of the three commercial networks and the great popularity of television allowed the medium to set a national agenda of what the public experienced. Sports blossomed, particularly the national professional sports of baseball, football, and later basketball. People talked about "America's team" instead of their own high school team. The television commercial emerged

FILMS RADIO VIDEO MUSIC STAGE

VARIETY

VOL. 186 No. 4 NEW YORK, WEDNESDAY, APRIL 2, 1952 PRICE 25 CENTS

'CUT OUT RADIO-TV CONFUSION'

Wear & Tear Sisters Find Legit Gold In Coast Valley Fruit-Grove Circuit

B'CASTERS CHART INDUSTRY FUTURE

TV May Become Greatest Ballyhoo For Films, Theatre Exec Tells D.C.

Danny Kaye's Vidpic Accent in NBC Dicker

ASCAP to Divvy Out $3,000,000 For Quarterly Record

TV Webs Still Optimistic Despite 'Soft' Market, Feel Corner's Turned

Benny to Stick On Sunday Radio For Next Season

New Radio Co-op To 'Sell' World War 2½

News of Television

With the advent of commercial television, *Variety* added it to the topics that the weekly entertainment publication covered. The 1952 page-one story "B'casters Chart Industry Future" examined the proposed lifting of a freeze on television channel allocations and the consequent millions of dollars in profits that the channels would make for those receiving one.

as a creative kind of communication in which dialogue, music and sound, and imagery were distilled into an intense instantaneous experience. One of the results was to change the nature of political campaigning from long messages such as speeches, to short commercials or news clips. The mass communication philosopher Marshall McLuhan defined what television was achieving with the term "global village."

Early Television News

Television news had its beginnings at the local level based on radio news practices. Announcers read items gleaned from the wire services, from local newspapers, or from original reporting. They brought news sources into their studios and interviewed them. They pointed their cameras at still news photographs. Soon, however, TV reporters were taking advantage of 16mm motion picture film and following the lead of the new network news programs.

CBS premiered *Douglas Edwards and the News* in 1948, and NBC followed with John Cameron Swayze's *Camel Caravan* the next year. They relied on newsreel companies such as Fox, Hearst, and MGM for film footage. Beginning in the mid-1950s, NBC started to upgrade its newsgathering operation and obtained good evening news ratings with the successful combination of Chet Huntley, reporting from New York, and David Brinkley, headquartered in Washington, D.C. Their popular closing, "Good Night, Chet...Good Night, David...and Good Night for NBC News," became the source of parody on entertainment shows, on a par with Walter Cronkite's "and that's the way it is..." in the late 1960s and 1970s.

The evening network news programs were limited until the 1960s to a fifteen-minute time slot, evidence of their secondary role to entertainment in television. NBC was also addressing the issues of the day on a weekly basis as early as 1947 with *Meet the Press* (which survives to this day). CBS followed suit with *Face the Nation* in 1954, and ABC initiated *Issues and Answers* six years later. Panels of journalists interviewed officials and other important news sources. The programs usually were relegated to unpopular viewing hours.

The lines between news, public affairs, and entertainment became less distinct in the 1950s with the introduction of talk and interview shows such as *Today*, which won acclaim under host Dave Garraway, and *Tonight* with Steve Allen. Along with the popular *Jack Paar Show*, these were entertainment-oriented, programmed in the early morning or late weeknights. They became serious-minded only with a visit from a political dignitary or with the intrusion of a major news event.

Edward R. Murrow was the most distinguished early television journalist. His background was radio. He had broadcast for CBS from London and even from a British bomber over Berlin in the early days of World War II. The print journalists, such as Cronkite, whom he recruited for CBS during the war were the nucleus of CBS news for its first decades. Murrow pioneered the television documentary looking at the darker side of American life in such offerings as *Harvest of Shame*, reporting the abysmal conditions of migrant workers. His *See It Now* offerings of "Christmas in Korea" (1953) and "Annie Lee Moss Before the McCarthy Committee" (1954) are classics in early in-depth television reporting. On a lighter note his *Person to Person* celebrity interviews were primarily entertainment.

Television's Impact on Other Media

As television increasingly captured the attention of the public, it had a profound effect on radio and the print media.

Television pre-empted drama and variety programming from radio. Radio networks began to specialize in news and sports, providing segments of local stations' programming. Local stations

Quiz Show Scandals

Cerebral Celebrity Becomes a Living Symbol of Shame

On November 28, 1956, Charles Van Doren grinned into a television camera and became a celebrity.

His popularity was not just because he came from a family of famous writers. Not just because he taught at Columbia University. Not just because of his boyish good looks, which a producer called "sexy yet wholesome."

Van Doren, who appeared that night on the quiz show *Twenty-One*, became an instant celebrity because of his mind, of all things. Audiences revered him and other contestants because of their intellectual, not (necessarily) their physical characteristics. One person gratefully called Van Doren the "antidote to Elvis."

However, in a matter of months he would become the living symbol of shame in the so-called "quiz show scandals."

In the mid-1950s, more than two dozen quiz shows ruled network television. The sponsor of the first one saw its sales go up 200% in two months. Such high stakes moved producers to manipulate contestants. They supplied them with questions and answers in advance and even prescribed their on-air dress and mannerisms.

When complaints started trickling out, no one wanted to believe them. But eventually, the cat got out of the bag.

A grand jury investigation, congressional hearings, and national publicity finally forced the shows, along with contestants like Van Doren, to their knees. He was convicted of lying to the grand jury but spent no time in jail. Fired from Columbia, he moved to Chicago, raised a family, and worked for *Encyclopedia Britannica* before retiring to Connecticut.

The scandal finished advertiser control over television programming. It also marked the end of America's innocence. Out of the era was born a phrase of a popular show today: "Trust no one."

Paul Adams
California State University, Fresno

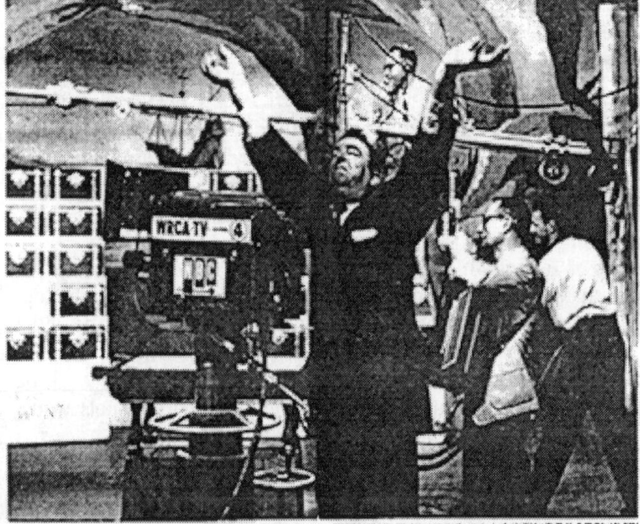

'TV QUIZ BUSINESS IS ITSELF QUIZZED ABOUT FIX CHARGES

The first of the big-money giveaway quiz shows was *The $64,000 Question*. Its popularity was phenomenal. Virtually overnight it caught the imagination of millions of viewers and spawned a host of similar quiz shows like *The $64,000 Challenge*, *Tic Tac Dough*, and *Twenty-One*. Contestants could be elevated instantly to wealth and fame. Charles Van Doren, the big winner on *The $64,000 Question*, became a national celebrity — including a full feature in *Life* magazine (top left) in early 1957.

The quiz shows' wildly successful ride came to a crashing end in 1958. Questions had been raised by the middle of 1957 (as indicated by the *Look* magazine feature at the top right) when a disgruntled contestant claimed that the programs were rigged. A subsequent congressional investigation found that program sponsors, who had acquired nearly total control over the quiz shows, had decided to feed answers to Van Doren and certain other contestants to assure that the most popular or most colorful ones would win. *Life's* feature in September 1958 (bottom) indicated the changed attitude about the quiz shows and contestants. Van Doren still declared that he knew nothing of the fixing. "I was completely fooled," he avowed. "I thought [the disgruntled contestant] was sweating as hard as I was [trying to answer questions]."

emphasized music programs presided over by disc jockeys, and in metropolitan areas stations targeted niche audiences by age group or cultural preferences.

Most of the bulging, high-circulation weekly national magazines disappeared. Television pre-empted the national advertising that had made *Collier's, Saturday Evening Post, Look,* and *Life* extremely profitable. *Life* appeared in a new, expensive, skinny monthly reincarnation. The news weeklies, *Time*, *Newsweek*, and *U.S. News*, slimmed down and became pricy in order to survive. Magazine publishers sought out consumer niches that the networks could not serve, and the number of titles increased as mass circulations declined.

Newspapers found television was taking some of their advertising revenue and making substantial inroads into the time their subscribers previously had spent reading. And although they realized television was a major competitor, newspaper editors were soon reporting copiously on television. That was what their readers wanted.

While editors soon came to realize that they could never enthrall the public the way television could, they also realized that their print medium could often inform readers in ways television and radio could not. The newspaper was a manufactured product. Readers could pick it up when they wanted to and turn to the content on their own schedule, rather than on the schedule of the broadcast station. The entire newspaper was produced locally; so its content could be tailored to the interests of the locality. At the same time it could carry items of interest to only a few of its readers without boring those who were not interested. Words in print were permanent and not fleeting. They could be studied at leisure and saved for the future. The newspaper could publish coupons in its advertisements, and it could classify advertising in the want-ad section, allowing a potential customer to seek out the product or service desired. Television primarily entertained. Newspapers primarily informed. Thus an environment existed in which the broadcast and print media co-existed.

A Community Newspaper, 1940s

In the period between 1945 and 1974, newspaper technology was revolutionized as publishers embraced computers and new ways of getting ink on paper. In 1945, for example, a small city newspaper's technology included only one electronic device, the Associated Press teletype machine.

The newsroom of the *Evening Mirror* (circulation 6,000) in Hillsboro, Texas, right after World War II was typical of American newspapers. It was equipped with the AP teletypewriter that punched out state, national, foreign, sports, and feature stories at forty-five to sixty words a minute. It also had a double desk for the news editor (who edited all the copy, wrote headlines, and laid out the pages) and a reporter. Two other desks equipped with battered typewriters were occupied by the society editor (who also took classified ads and sold back issues at a counter near the

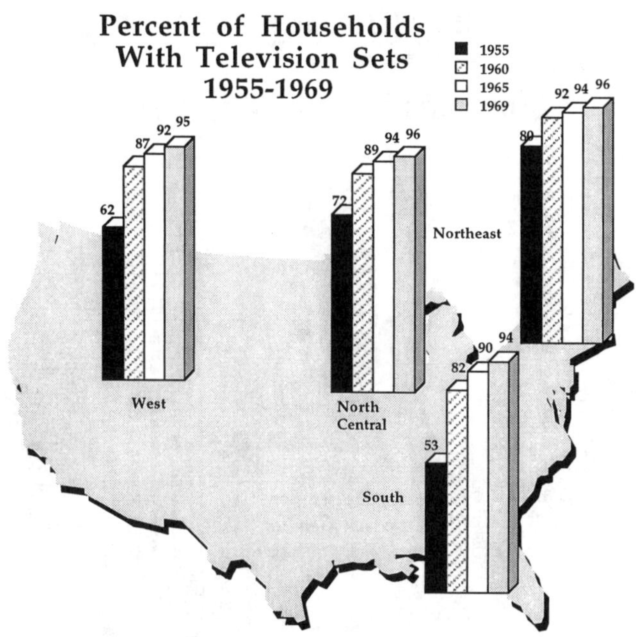

door) and a reporter who also wrote sports.

A closet darkroom and a Speed Graphic camera, which used 4" x 5" film, completed the news staff's equipment. The two advertising salespeople, who shared the room next door with the bookkeeper and circulation manager, also used the camera from time to time, but most illustrations for their ads came from a mat (short for "matrix") service — line drawings and photographs that had been engraved in metal and then, through the process of stereotyping, impressed into papier-mâché, with the impression mailed to the newspaper.

The composing room, which also housed the press, was at the rear of the building. It was the busy nerve center. There printers who were paid much more than reporters sat tapping on the keyboards of three clattering eight-foot-high Linotype machines that shot two to four lines of metal type a minute into trays. Other printers slid galleys of type into metal frames, along with zinc engravings of pictures, and locked the hundreds of individual pieces of metal tightly into page forms. With the stereotyping process, printers made mats of entire pages. The mats then were used as molds to make semi-cylindrical metal plates to put on rotary presses. Bigger papers also could afford a new device the AP called Wirephoto, an amazing machine that would transmit and receive photographs using telephone lines. The production process had been universal on small papers and large for the first half of the twentieth century. Every word typed in the newsroom had to be edited with pencil, scissors, and pastepot, re-keyboarded, and set in metal type in the composing room.

The rationale for newspaper content was as firmly established as the production method. The First Amendment to the Constitution had for more than 150 years indicated to publishers and editors that news was defined as what they and they alone decided to print. Most publishers (even if they were not owners) tried to present themselves as pillars of the community — capable of deciding

MASON CITY GLOBE-GAZETTE

North Iowa Edition

Sea-to-Sea Landslide--

HST Suggests Parley With Eisenhower

GOP Seems Assured of Delicate Control in Congress

Republican Over Moody in Michigan Election

New Chief Reaffirms Korea Trip

Union Bosses Take Licking in Election

State-by-State

Begin Transfer of 150 Convicts From Ohio Prison

Beardsley Edges Foe; Big Vote for General

Other GOP Are Elected

McCarthy Wins

BULLETIN

Election Comment

The Weather

The Newspaper of the Early '50s

The typical newspaper front page after World War II was reserved for news of major importance. This one from the *Mason City* (Iowa) *Globe-Gazette*, published on November 6, 1952, carried the story of President Harry Truman's proposal to confer with Dwight Eisenhower, who had just won the presidential election. In the face of new ideas and new competition, newspapers in the era just ahead were to change their concepts of both content and design.

on the basis of their knowledge of newspaper work and of their community what their readers wanted to read and how it should be presented.

Of reporters they asked for "objectivity" in the sense that news should be presented impersonally with the newspaper reacting to events, reporting attributable information in a straightforward style. Opinions, judgments, criticism, and advice emanating from the newspaper office itself would appear on the editorial page as editorials, columns, or cartoons.

The front page was reserved for news of major importance, spiced with a humorous short item frequently, and on rare occasions with a longer "human interest" feature. More features and straight news filled the inside news pages. There was a society page that included women's news centering around club, home, food, clothing, and cosmetics. For men there was the sports page, and the comics page ostensibly was aimed at children. Reporters and editors always were white, and almost always male, except for the society page staff and an occasional feature writer.

Newspapermen considered it a good system. The public voted daily with their nickels (or 45¢ weekly for subscriptions) as to whether the paper was doing its job. Most larger cities had competing newspapers (although increasingly only one published in the morning and one in the evening).

Although chain ownership of newspapers was continuing to grow, the newspaper still was viewed as a local institution. On the editorial page below the name of the newspaper there usually appeared opposite the title of publisher or president the name of a local family of long-standing. Such was as true in small cities as in New York City (where the name was Sulzberger or Reid), or in Dallas and Houston (Dealey and Hobby), or Los Angeles and Oakland (Chandler and Knowland).

New Technology and Changing Newspapers

Revolutionary change in newspaper technology most significantly began with paper tape, an inch wide. It came in rolls about a foot in diameter and was installed so that it ran through a small black box called a "perforator." An operator could tap on a keyboard, and the attached perforator would punch holes across the tape in combinations of one to six holes. These combinations represented every letter, figure, punctuation mark, and spacing combination that a Linotype machine could produce.

Small newspaper chains developed and used the system, and the wire services rapidly adopted it. When a wire service editor decided a story punched into the tape should go to a thousand newspapers across the country, he would run the tape through a black box called a "reader" that put the story on the teletypewriter circuits. In the thousand newspaper offices the tape was reproduced by perforators at the same time the story was printed on the teletypewriter. If the local editor chose to use the article, he sent the tape to the composing room along with the printed version that was marked with headline and editing information. One Linotype operator could keep tapes running through the black boxes (labeled Teletypesetter) hooked to several Linotypes, greatly increasing his productivity.

By the mid-1950s the system was almost universal in non-unionized newspapers. Papers bought their own perforator keyboards and used low-salaried clerical workers to produce tapes instead of depending on expensive Linotype operators.

The system was called Teletypesetter, and it had a noteworthy impact beyond productivity on the way newspapers were produced. Teletypesetter made it easier and much less expensive to use wire service material than previously, and it created a difference between the low cost of using wire service material (precomposed) and more expensive local material (although the latter could be produced by Teletypesetter less expensively than before). By paying the wire service a modestly increased tariff for Teletypesetter, the publisher dramatically reduced his labor costs.

Teletypesetter created trends toward newspaper uniformity in three ways. First, it was easier and less expensive for an editor to print a wire service story written by a skilled national writer than to assign a local story to a reporter and go through all the steps of

The Newspaper Technology Revolution

In the late 1940s newspapers still were using the hand-operated Linotype machine, which had been invented in the late 1800s, for setting type. Despite the boasts of the Linotype company (left) for its new "Blue Streak" machine, the manual process was slow – and it was about to be revolutionized through the Teletypesetter system (middle). With it, newspapers would enter a new technological age. The Teletypesetter system, invented in the 1950s, sped the process of setting newspaper type and reduced labor costs by connecting a tape-perforating machine to Linotype machines. Unplanned by its inventor, however, was the standardization it helped to bring to newspaper writing, content, and design. Along with the Teletypesetter system, the other great innovations in the printing industry in the decade after World War II were photocomposition and offset printing (right). By eliminating the use of metal type, they speeded up the printing process, reduced costs, and changed much of the newspaper printing process from a heavy industry into quiet office work.

producing it.

Second, the technology of Teletypesetter locked up punctuation, capitalization, abbreviation, and usage style. The Associated Press, United Press, and International News Service agreed on a basic style in the 1950s, and their jointly prepared stylebook set the standards for style in mainstream newspapers.[1]

Third, the Teletypesetter system also locked newspapers into a narrow range of column widths, making one American newspaper look like and read like all others. The tendency was alleviated greatly when computerized editing and typesetting became almost universal in the 1970s.

The other great technological innovation of the first twenty years after World War II was the adaptation of photocomposition and offset printing to newspaper production. Since Gutenburg's time, most printing had been done from raised surfaces on metal or wooden type. Photocomposition produces type by photographic processes. The type then is "pasted up" on the newspaper page. Newspaper offset printing is a form of lithography, using a photographic process to produce the plate and making it easier to reproduce pictures.

Computers in the Newsroom

Computers entered newspaper offices as a means of streamlining the way the right side of a column of type is evened up (justification). Justification always has been done by varying the amount of space between words from one line to the next and, if a particularly long word came at the end of the line, by hyphenating the word. Both Linotype operators and Teletypesetter operators were required to slow down at the end of each line and make sure they did not crowd the type together. In the 1960s computer salesmen convinced publishers that a hyphenation dictionary and the width table for any font of type could be stored in a computer, allowing it to determine where and how each line of type ended. After the introduction of these first-generation newspaper computers, Teletypesetter operators' fingers could fly over the keys at an unvarying speed as they produced "idiot tape" with no line endings. The idiot tape was fed into the computer, and it produced a second tape containing the perforator codes to justify the lines.

The next step was to combine this kind of computer with a photocomposition machine. The computer rode herd on the machinery, making sure it did all the typing and typesetting functions at a steady maximum speed as Teletypesetter tape was fed into it.

For a long time computer operators had been using teletypewriter keyboards to give instructions to their machines, and the machines would respond with material fed out through printers.

[1]International News Service and United Press eventually merged into United Press International.

Once computer people began to use cathode ray tubes (video screens) to look into computer memories, they realized that they had a new and useful communications tool — a text-editing system. They combined the data storage and retrieval capabilities of computers with what is now known as word processing and created a "front end system." Reporters could write on their keyboards and rewrite from the words on the cathode ray tubes. Copy editors could edit the stories on their terminals and write headlines, with the computer checking to see if the heads were too long or too short. Great savings were accomplished because there was no need for re-keyboarding at any time.

What a difference in production the video display terminals made. In classified advertising, for example, a clerk would take information by phone and type the want-ad into a VDT along with data about publication and the advertiser. The computer would automatically make a credit check and do the necessary bookkeeping while the ad copy went into storage. At deadline time, all of the previous day's ads that were not to be run again were purged. Previously, all these chores had to be done separately by hand.

The entire atmosphere of newspaper plants changed. Composing rooms shrank as they lost their clatter, heat, and inky grime. They became light, carpeted, and populated by printers in white shirts who with knives and rulers pasted up pages at sloping tables. In newsrooms the banging of typewriters and scurrying of copy boys were gone. When the newspaper went to press, its contents existed almost identically in two forms — the pasteups in the composing room and the stories in the computer memories.

Heavy and repeated capital investments by newspapers in the years since World War II gave them greater flexibility, content resources, and productivity. Yet increased competition from other media made publishers more concerned about the future of newspapers than they had been in 1945.

McCarthy and Objectivity

Senator Joseph McCarthy of Wisconsin gained notoriety, much of it through televised hearings his committee conducted, in the early 1950s by making largely unsubstantiated charges about Communist subversion in the U.S. government and other institutions including the media. The Soviet Union and China had powerful Communist governments with professed policies of international domination. United Nations forces, predominantly American and commanded by an American, were opposing North Korean and Chinese invasion of South Korea. The charges of McCarthy and others struck a responsive chord of fear in the American public.

"McCarthyism" played a major part in bringing about a change in the way journalists perceived their role in society. The change was caused in great part by the issues and the social changes on which journalists found themselves reporting. The case of Associated Press war correspondent Edward Kennedy illustrates the relation of reporters to government at the end of World War II. Kennedy and other correspondents, although they had witnessed the signing of an armistice at Allied Headquarters, had agreed not to report the end of the war in Europe (V-E Day) until next morning. When at midnight he heard Radio Berlin telling the news to the defeated Germans, Kennedy decided to break the embargo and let Americans in on the facts. The Associated Press fired him to stay in the good graces of the military. By contrast, in the latter stages of the Vietnam War, a wire-service reporter, Seymour Hersh, frustrated not only with military and governmental information policies, but also with wire service policies, quit his job and, despite the refusal of major news media to pay attention to his story, got it published and won a Pulitzer Prize for international reporting.[2]

A change in reporting and publishing the news had taken place between the two events that had nothing to do with "marketing" the newspaper. At the beginning of the period "objectivity" was a reporter's highest ideal. As time and events moved on, for many journalists getting the "real" story — the story beyond the official statements and surface events — was the ideal. *A Free and Responsible Press*, which the media criticized when it was released, contained ideas that newspaper reportage reflected more and more: "a truthful, comprehensive and intelligent account of the day's events in a context which gives them meaning" and the accurate portrayal of all social groups.[3]

The old concept of objectivity required reporters to lay aside most of their own wisdom when they sat down to write a story. They told what they had seen, what witnesses or spokesmen had said, and what written sources could provide for background. That was reporting and that was what Sen. Joseph McCarthy capitalized on as he alleged the existence of substantial numbers of Communists in the State Department, elsewhere in government, and finally in many private institutions such as newspapers that took exception to his tactics. Reporters dutifully reported his statements and speeches, which seemed to be paced so that rebuttals and denials never caught up with the on-going story.

At its 1953 meeting, the Associated Press Managing Editors Association raked coverage of McCarthy over the coals in one of its most rancorous debates. McCarthy was the subject, but "objectivity" was the issue. The *Washington Post's* J.R. Wiggins warned that "if we circulate day after day...month after month the infamous allegations that there's treason in the White House, in the Chiefs of Staff, in the Secretary of State and in all the other departments of government, we need not be surprised if an hour comes when the American people have confidence in no one." Robert P. Early of the *Indianapolis Star* said he was "surprised that McCarthy's name came up at all. I don't think we should snipe at the way McCarthy handles his news conferences. After all, he is a United States Senator."[4]

[2]Thirty-six newspapers ran Hersh's series of stories through a syndication service, the Dispatch News Service, created solely for the series. The first article was published in, among other newspapers, the *St. Louis Post-Dispatch*, 13 November 1969.

[3]Commission on Freedom on the Press, *A Free and Responsible Press* (Chicago, 1947), 21.

[4]Victor Hackler, ed., *The APME Red Book 1953* (New York, 1953), 57, 58.

The Media and McCarthyism
Senator Joseph R. McCarthy demonstrated how an uncritical mass media could be manipulated for ideological purposes. Ironically, a CBS *See It Now* television program and live television coverage of the Army/McCarthy hearings signalled his decline in popularity.

Later, new reporters who came on the scene in the 1960s and 1970s studied a textbook, *Interpretative Reporting*, written by a crusty Northwestern University professor named Curtis MacDougall, or other texts that also questioned "pure objectivity." The debate over "objectivity" and the new kind of "interpretive" reporting has continued.

Edward R. Murrow was among the first to point out the weakness of McCarthy's allegations and his use of loose innuendo to damage the reputations of public officials and private citizens. In *A Report on Senator Joseph R. McCarthy*, Murrow and his associate, Fred Friendly, used film of McCarthy's speeches and interviews to demonstrate contradictions and point out that his accusations extended to highly respected publications and military heroes.

However, it was the nationally televised Army-McCarthy Senate hearings that demonstrated the power of television to present an event to the public unmediated by a journalist. The hearings pitted Army Secretary Robert Stevens, a mild-appearing executive, and his attorney, an elderly New Englander named Joseph Welch, against the heavy-jowled McCarthy and his two aides, a hulking David Schine and a glowering attorney, Roy Cohn. When McCarthy tried to link one of Welch's aides to an alleged Communist front, Welch put his finger on the danger of character assassination that McCarthy represented before a television audience of millions of Americans. McCarthy steadily lost credibility thereafter and was censured by the Senate.

The Army-McCarthy hearings, like the Kefauver organized crime hearings that preceded them and the Watergate hearings that came two decades later, allowed television cameras and microphones to bring the national public face to face with important issues and key players.

The Media and Civil Rights

In 1954 the Supreme Court issued its landmark decision on school desegregation, and the beginning of a story called Civil Rights went up like a Fourth of July skyrocket. For the first time African Americans and other minorities seemed to have articulate spokesmen and effective strategies for combating discrimination from the national level down to county courthouses. The activism began with the black lawyers who fought the *Brown v. Board of Education* case through to the 1954 decision and its implementation. It included Dr. Martin Luther King; college students and others who conducted sit-ins, freedom rides, and voter registration projects; a rejuvenated black press including new national magazines; and a new crop of ambitious black political leaders.

There was strong opposition in southern states, and both sides in the conflict used all the tools of persuasion they could command. News people were challenged. Whom should they believe? Whom should they quote? What should they cover? Were events staged solely for media coverage? What was the real picture? No ultimate authority provided answers. More than ever before, media professionals made up their own minds at the scene of the news. In the South some newspapers simultaneously labeled black people as too backward for desegregation and condemned them for using cunning and unfair methods. The great majority of newspapers deplored the threat to law and order and supported the existing pattern of segregation. A few warned their neighbors that changes were inevitable and argued for fair play for African Americans. Nine newspaper men and women received the Pulitzer Prize for their editorial stands on civil rights.[5]

[5]Typical was Hazel Brannon Smith's "Arrest of Bombing Victim is Grave Disservice," Lexington (Miss.) *Advertiser*, 16 May 1963, one of the editorials for which Mrs. Smith was awarded the Pulitzer Prize. Similar writings by other editors are included in W. David Sloan and Laird Anderson, *Pulitzer Prize Editorials*, 2nd ed. (Ames, Iowa, 1994).

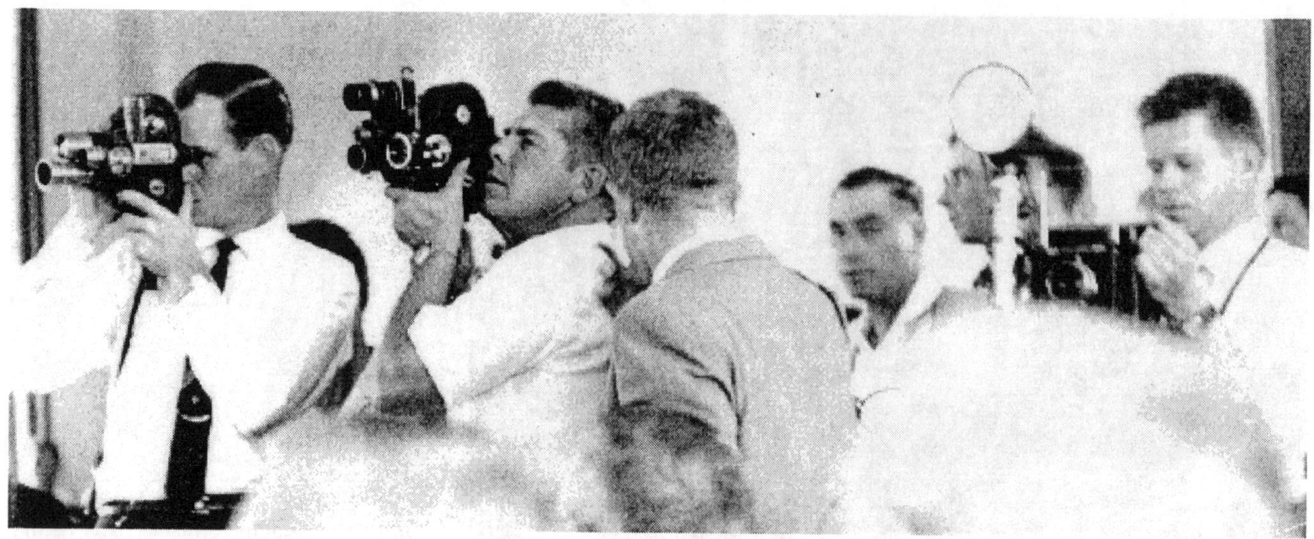

National Television and the Emmett Till Trial
Members of the news media from around the nation converged on the 1955 trial of two men charged in the murder of Emmett Till, a black teenager. The trial was one of the first that national television cameramen covered. Till's murder and the acquittal of the accused men provided much of the impetus for the media's coverage of the early Civil Rights movement. (Photo by Harry Marsh)

The power of local television news was demonstrated in 1955 by coverage of the funeral in Chicago of a black teenager, Emmett Till. Till's shot and mutilated body had been discovered in the Tallahatchie River in Mississippi. Two white men had taken him from his uncle's plantation cabin at night. The boy allegedly had whistled at the wife of one of the abductors. The boy's mother asked for an open-casket service. Televised pictures of the mutilated body brought thousands of mourners to the church. The story reached most of the northern industrialized centers that had large populations of blacks who had migrated from the South.

The trial of the two men, which ended in their acquittal, attracted more than 100 reporters from across the nation. Film was shot in the courtroom during recesses. Interviews were conducted outside on the courthouse lawn. Interviewees sat in folding chairs in front of microphones. Movie cameras on tripods were pointed at them, and reporters behind the cameras shouted questions at them.

The Till trial was the first of the major Civil Rights stories that took television reporters all across the South — to the Montgomery bus boycott, the Little Rock school desegregation crisis, the Birmingham Sunday School bombing, the sit-ins, the freedom rides, and eventually to Dr. Martin Luther King's "I Have a Dream" address on the steps of the Lincoln Memorial. Two decades later PBS broadcast the *Eyes on the Prize* documentaries that documented not only the Civil Rights movement, but the new kind of television news. Television went to crises and reported not only the official views, but the views and the pictures of ordinary people directly involved. Reporters developed a skeptical attitude toward officials that was to be a hallmark of journalism for the rest of the century.

For the national press, civil rights was a story about the South that became a story about the national condition. The *New York Times'* Atlanta bureau, headed by Claude Sitton, the wire service bureaus, and a few dozen southern newspapers provided bases of operations for correspondents from many metropolitan papers who roamed the South. They and their broadcast colleagues developed into a corps of expert reporters who eventually replaced the aging World War II correspondents on all the big stories. There existed for them no clear line of what was in the national interest — as had existed for the World War II press corps. The new generation sifted through pronouncements from the highest levels right down to quotes from illiterates at the scene of the action in attempting to determine what was of real significance.

A spin-off from the civil rights story resulted in a Supreme Court decision that strongly affected media coverage into the following decades. In *New York Times v. Sullivan* (a case involving an advertisement by a civil rights group placed in the *Times*) the court established the doctrine that public officials (later expanded to public figures) must prove actual malice before successfully suing for libel.[6] The definition of "public official" and "public figure" was argued strenuously in many cases, and courts demanded that reporters and editors reveal their motivations — as evidenced by notes and thoughts — regarding stories in litigation in order to determine whether malice existed. Although *Times v. Sullivan* and subsequent decisions complicated the lives of both news sources and news people, their general effect was to provide the media with a much fuller opportunity to report and comment on public matters.

Television and the Space Race

In 1957 the "beep-beep" radio signal emanating from Sputnik I, the first artificial satellite launched successfully from Earth, gave

[6] *New York Times Co. v. Sullivan,* 376 U.S. 254 (1964).

the American educational, scientific, military, and political institutions as well as the general public a rude wakeup call. The Soviet Union, considered well behind the Western Europeans and Americans scientifically, was leading what became known as the Space Race. Soon television viewers were seeing American attempts to launch a satellite fail, then eventually succeed. They saw a Russian dog emerge from a satellite that had been brought back home, and they got to know a monkey named Ham who performed as directed in an American satellite. Yuri Gagarin became a world hero as the first human to leave the earth's atmosphere and orbit in a Russian space capsule.

When the United States began to launch two-man Gemini spacecraft, television cameras accompanied them. Throngs in New York's Grand Central Station watched live pictures of Earth on giant screens. On July 20, 1969, a television camera mounted on the lunar lander Eagle transmitted live pictures of Neil Armstrong putting a human foot on the moon for the first time.

The Space Race was made for television. Public interest was combined with a government agency (NASA) eager to build public support. Journalists and experts explained with ingenious audio-visual models and graphics everything that was happening. The countdown to launch, the live pictures from space, and the moments of danger during re-entry stretched and sharpened the capabilities of television to go anywhere and show everything. The program was so successful that the exploration of space soon seemed commonplace. A manned space exploit was just another item of national news.

DIGEST

Farm subsidy lid voted

Story: PAGE 28

The Telegraph-Herald

Viet battle toll lowest in 3½ years

'Red Chinese key to future of Indochina'

New base

U.S. general is missing

Who's liable for rock fest damage?

Will speed up Viet pullout

Clarke-Loras Singers place high at festival

Woe is me!

The Press and Vietnam

Most newspapers supported United States involvement in the Vietnam war in its early stages. By the late 1960s, however, opposition had grown strong. Some critics claimed that the media opposition led to biased coverage and the ultimate military defeat. Whatever a newspaper's stance on involvement, however, the war was one of the biggest stories in the post-World War II era. The attention it occupied in the press can be gleaned from this front page of the *Dubuque* (Iowa) *Telegraph-Herald* in 1970.

The Media and Vietnam

When the next great issue, the Vietnam War, increasingly began to dominate front pages, two kinds of reporters — war correspondents and veterans of the civil rights story — packed off to Southeast Asia. Their backgrounds would influence their reporting.

Vietnam in Southeast Asia was a prosperous agrarian nation of villages and peasants that for centuries had endured the domination of China, France, and Japan. When the Japanese were defeated at the end of World War II, France attempted to renew its colonial rule and was defeated by Vietnamese forces. Two governments existed, a Communist regime in Hanoi and a pro-Western dictatorship in Saigon (now Ho Chi Minh City). The United States became unilaterally involved in the resulting war between the two regimes because it feared a Communist victory would lead to a "domino effect" in that region with numerous developing nations coming under Soviet and Chinese Communist domination. American participation escalated from non-combatant advisers on the scene to hundreds of thousands of troops (many of them draftees) carrying the brunt of the fighting with the support of Air Force and Navy units operating from distant bases.

An incident described by David Halberstam illustrated the difference between the traditional and the new reporting of the Vietnam war. After graduation from Harvard in the 1950s, Halberstam went to work on a small Mississippi daily. He wrote little for the paper about the civil rights story that swirled all about, but wrote a lot on it for the *Reporter* and other magazines. From this background where his own ideals required him to question not only the local social and political establishment but also his own editor, he moved through the *Nashville Tennessean* to the *New York Times*. In Saigon he began to cover the war with the same type of skepticism toward the U.S. military and the South Vietnamese government.

He became convinced that the American military had underestimated the strength and "historical dynamism" of the enemy and that the American policy of "small war, use technology to get in cheap, hope for the best" was proven wrong. He and others reported those problems, and "that made us different from war reporters in the past." Halberstam recalled a two-day tour of the Mekong Delta in 1963 (he was twenty-eight years old) with one of his journalistic heroes — Richard Tregaskis, World War II correspondent and author of *Guadalcanal Diary*. He introduced Tregaskis to several of his valued, non-government sources and discussed the war at length. As they returned to Saigon, Tregaskis quietly told him, "If I were doing what you are doing I would be ashamed of myself."[7] The stony silence that followed was symptomatic of the changes underway in reporting. Halberstam won a Pulitzer Prize for his Vietnam coverage, although he was one of a number of reporters whom the military and the government accused of not knowing whose "team" they were on.

The media's reporting contributed to the disaffection of the American public toward the war in Vietnam and toward the leaders in Washington, D.C. The respected columnist Walter Lippmann opposed the war very early and carried on a dove-hawk debate with Joseph Alsop on alternate days in the same spot on the editorial page of the *New York Herald Tribune*. Harrison Salisbury of the *New York Times* was criticized severely for going to North Vietnam and reporting major U.S. bombing damage to nonmilitary targets. But after the Pentagon Papers were published and the My Lai massacre became public, American disillusionment with the war was irreversible.

CBS questioned government policy as early as 1965 in *Vietnam: The Hawks and the Doves* and later in a series titled *Vietnam Perspective*. NBC presented a full year of *Vietnam Weekly Review*, and ABC addressed the Vietnam question in more than 100 half-hour documentaries. In 1966 when CBS declined to carry Senate committee hearings on involvement in Southeast Asia, Fred Friendly resigned as president of CBS News.

The news media covered the Vietnam story on three fronts: with the combatants in Vietnam, with the officials usually in Washington, D.C., and with the public that was deeply divided between those who vehemently opposed the war and those who resented what they viewed as disloyalty on the part of the opponents.

Television reporting from the scene was dramatically different from what Americans were accustomed to. World War II newsreels had shown American troops welcomed into European cities liberated from Nazi domination, American amphibious forces ousting Japanese from Pacific islands they had invaded, and United Nations forces fighting alongside South Koreans defending themselves from a North Korean and Chinese invasion. From Vietnam in 1965 Americans saw the burning of a Vietnamese village, Cam Ne, by U.S. Marines with Morley Safer of CBS providing the narration. They saw a Buddhist holy man burn himself to death in Saigon in protest of the violence. They saw a South Vietnamese policeman take out his pistol and summarily execute a bound prisoner in the middle of a street, with Jack Perkins of NBC describing the scene. They saw reports of the South Vietnamese president's assassination by his own Army, and they saw civilians including a naked six-year-old girl fleeing from American bombs. These were pictures of conflict inconsistent with what the American public felt it could support.

[7]Frances Ring, ed., "Excerpts from Conference Panels," *The Journalist* (University of Southern California School of Journalism, May 1983), 34.

1968 Convention Coverage
Protest over the Vietnam war had become widespread by 1968 as the national political conventions were set to begin. The national television networks were well prepared to cover the conventions, as this cover story in the August 8 issue of *TV Guide* demonstrated, but their biggest story became the violent demonstrations outside the Democratic convention hall in Chicago. Coverage of the rioting showed to the nation a Democratic party that appeared incapable of governing.

The news from U.S. cities and campuses was also disturbing. Thousands of young people, many politicized and energized by the Civil Rights movement, demonstrated peacefully against America's involvement in the war. Some became violent, burning buildings and seizing university administrative offices. Pro-war Hawks and anti-war Doves of all ages debated the war.

The domestic climax came at the 1968 Democratic National Convention in Chicago, when thousands of anti-war demonstrators took up residence in Grant Park. The demonstrations and eventual violence detracted from the convention (where reporter Dan Rather was physically assaulted on the floor) and culminated in "a police riot," in the words of the Walker Report, an official inquiry into the events. Former CBS News chief William Small described the final hours of the convention: "It reached its climax, not in the nomination of Hubert Humphrey but in the confrontation between anti-war demonstrators and jumpy police.... The consequent loss of control and restraint by police offered a violent scene that was carried around the world."[8] Reporters, clearly identified by press credentials, were "hit, maced or arrested" by the police without provocation, according to the report.

Turmoil and dissent over Vietnam drove the incumbent president, Lyndon Johnson, from office. His initial attempts to deal with the issue in a temperate, even low-key, manner on radio and television were in stark contrast to his personal attempts to manage the news and stifle dissent later. His press aides not only hounded broadcast company executives at work but also placed personal calls to the homes of network reporters. Johnson, overwhelmingly popular in 1964, chose not to seek re-election in 1968.

The "Pentagon Papers" drove another stake into America's war effort and another wedge between the media and the government. The papers were documents taken from Defense Department files by Daniel Ellsberg and given first to congressmen and then to the press. They indicated that the government had not been frank with the American people about its intentions in Vietnam. When the *New York Times* began publishing the papers, the government got a court order halting publication. The *Washington Post* and other newspapers picked up the publication, bringing further court orders. Eventually the *Times* and the *Post* won in the courts on the issue of prior restraint of publication.

Whereas the Pentagon Papers indicated deception at home, My Lai demonstrated dehumanization abroad. Using a modest foundation grant, his own money, and his knowledge of the military, reporter Seymour Hersh began from a brief Defense Department announcement about the scheduled court martial of Lieutenant William Calley and discovered the details of the massacre of hundreds of Vietnamese civilians by American soldiers in the village of My Lai. He uncovered the story by traveling across the country interviewing returned veterans who had been at the village. Hersh offered the story to leading publications and, after being rejected, placed the story in a few score newspapers through a small news service headquartered in Washington, D.C. Soon all the media were seeking every detail they could get about the incident. Pictures of the victims being shot and of their bodies eventually were published.

Richard Nixon, elected president in 1968 on a platform of ending the war, was dogged by Vietnam as the conflict dragged into the 1970s. CBS broadcast *The Selling of the Pentagon*, with Roger Mudd detailing government efforts to promote U.S. intervention and equally widespread efforts to deceive reporters regarding events in Vietnam. A Congressional committee investigated the matter, and an attempt to hold CBS President Dr. Frank Stanton in contempt of Congress failed in the House of Representatives by a 226-181 vote. Two military officers, Lieut. Col. Anthony Herbert and Gen. William C. Westmoreland, sued the network over postwar telecasts. Westmoreland, who commanded U.S. forces in Vietnam for a time, received an out-of-court settlement.

[8]William Small, *To Kill A Messenger: Television News and the Real World* (New York, 1970), 204.

"All the News That's Fit to Print"

The New York Times

LATE CITY EDITION

Tricia Nixon Takes Vows In Garden at White House

CITY TO DISCLOSE BUDGETARY TRIMS FOR DEPARTMENTS

Vietnam Archive: Pentagon Study Traces 3 Decades of Growing U. S. Involvement

U.S. URGES INDIANS AND PAKISTANIS TO USE RESTRAINT

NIXON CRITICIZED AS MAYORS MEET

Vast Review of War Took a Year

The Washington Post

Court Rules for Newspapers, 6-3

Vote at 18 Ratified Into Law

Decision Allows Printing of Stories On Vietnam Study

War File Articles Resumed

The Pentagon Papers

After the *New York Times*, on June 13, 1971, began printing the "Pentagon Papers," the federal government obtained an injunction to prevent further publication. In the meantime, other newspapers started publishing the classified documents. On July 1 the *Washington Post* exulted that the Supreme Court had voted to lift the injunction. The episode convinced many journalists that the government was their enemy, and the military viewed publication of the papers as another instance of reckless behavior by the press.

Politics and Presidents

Politicians, including presidents, recognized the power of television that might drive them from office, but they also recognized it as a tool to put them in office and keep them there. President Franklin Roosevelt had used radio to promote his New Deal reforms to combat the Great Depression and mobilize the nation after the 1941 attack on Pearl Harbor led the United States into World War II. He used radio as his direct link to the citizenry.

Television enhanced this direct link between office holder or candidate and the voting public. It changed the nature of politics and particularly presidential politics. Local political bosses found their ability to deliver the vote to a candidate more difficult when voters were given the opportunity to see and hear all the candidates frequently and make their own choices. State political conventions at which delegates to national conventions were chosen gave way to presidential primaries. Soon, by the time the national convention took place, the candidate it would choose already had been determined. The convention became a pep rally for the party faithful in which the candidate was showcased to the nation.

President Harry Truman was the first to use television, broadcasting from the White House and inviting cameras into some cabinet meetings. He was the first to be televised tossing out the baseball at the start of a major league season.[9] But he did not exploit the medium as some of his successors did. Dwight Eisenhower's smile was made for television, but his speaking style was not. He hired actor Robert Montgomery to be his television adviser. His inauguration was the first to be televised, and segments of his press conferences were released for television; but it was Richard Nixon, his 1952 running mate, who first exploited the medium to enhance his political fortunes.

When Nixon was accused of having set up a personal, political slush fund, he responded with an address televised by CBS and NBC. He disclosed details of his finances and provided a careful examination of his family history and work ethic. He noted that his wife had no furs but wore a "good Republican cloth coat" and concluded with a plea of support for Eisenhower and a staunch promise to retain a gift, a little dog named Checkers, from a Texas supporter to his daughter. The Checkers speech resulted in an outpouring of public support and Nixon's retention on the ticket.

However, it was Nixon's opponent in the 1960 campaign who emerged as the master of television. By 1960 mobile equipment allowed television journalists to follow the candidates about. John F. Kennedy showed his willingness to chance embarrassment by allowing cameraman Robert Drew to accompany him behind the campaign scenes, and in the first of four television/radio debates, he excelled on television although Nixon did better on radio.

Historians and critics have questioned the relevance of the debates to key issues of the day, but there is no question that they elevated the interest level of the electorate. In assessing their impact, Kurt and Gladys Lang maintained in *Politics and Television* (1968) that Kennedy's performance strengthened his support among uncertain Democrats.

Kennedy introduced the live television news conference and was a master at the ad lib response to reporters as well as at defusing tough questions with a one-word answer. He had a cultured delivery and youthful appearance that worked to his advantage. Perhaps his most effective use of the medium to inform the public and enlist its support was his open facedown of the Soviet Union over the installation of missiles in Cuba in 1962. He vowed to get rid of them and mobilized the military, all the while keeping the nation informed and working through diplomatic channels with Soviet leader Nikita Khrushchev. Perhaps the image of a resolute leader supported by Congress and the public played a role in the peaceful resolution of the crisis. Certainly television had a central role in international relations. A criticism, described by historian Eric Barnouw, was that the public was "left with the misleading picture of a good guy/bad guy crisis.... It was oversimplification — a defect not uncommon in television messages."[10]

[9]Raymond L. Carroll, "The 1948 Truman Campaign: The Threshold of the Modern Era," *Journal of Broadcasting* 24 (Spring, 1980): 175.

[10]Eric Barnouw, *Tube of Plenty: The Evolution of American Television* (New York, 1975), 319.

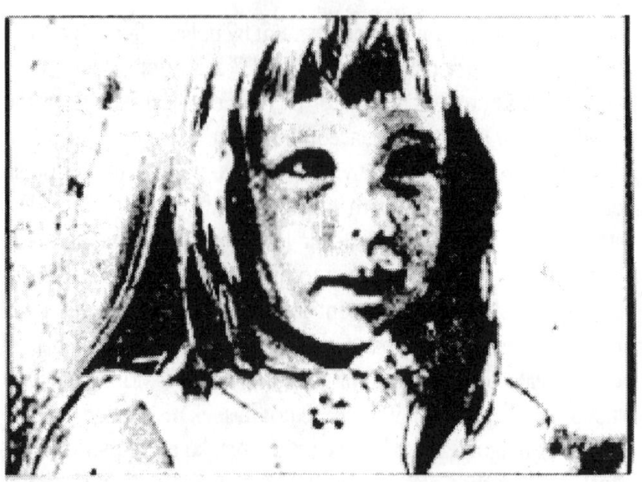

Six. Five. Four.

LYNDON JOHNSON (OVER): These are the stakes.

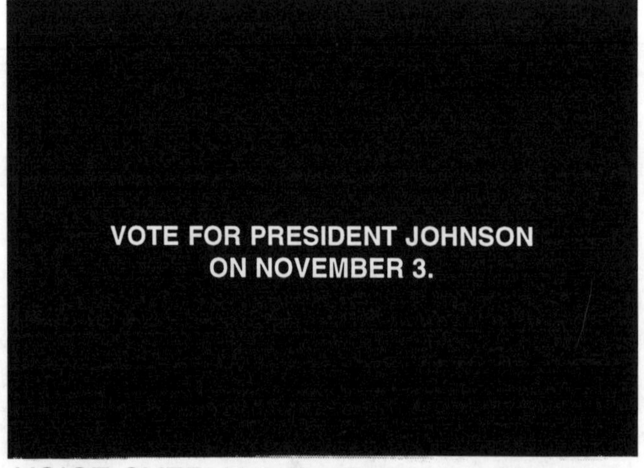

VOICE OVER: Vote for President Johnson on November third. The stakes are too high for you to stay home.

Political Advertising
Politicians began extensive use of TV commercials in the 1960s. The most infamous was this one. It implied that presidential candidate Barry Goldwater would start a nuclear war if elected.

When Kennedy was assassinated in November 1963, television was just barely mature enough to cover the story live from Dallas. The televising of Lee Harvey Oswald's murder and the Kennedy funeral could not have been broadcast live only a dozen years earlier, because the technology to do so was not available. Also, coincidentally, CBS and NBC had expanded their evening news programs to one-half hour less than three months before the assassination. Expansion at ABC occurred later. The assassination and funeral were media events of the first order. The networks suspended regular programming for nearly three and a half days. The tragedy was an example of the McLuhan global village concept, an event in which the world shared an experience via television. Taped footage of later assassination attempts on major figures such as Pope John Paul, Presidents Ford and Reagan, and Alabama Governor George Wallace were all on-the-air within minutes after they occurred.

Kennedy shared a quality with Roosevelt and (at times) Truman that is vital to good television communication. He spoke to the person sitting on the other side of the television screen without pomposity. His successor, Lyndon Johnson, though he wanted to project the image of a great commoner, never achieved informality, nor did Nixon. The Vietnam War put both Johnson and Nixon on the defensive at their press conferences, and both were reduced to making speeches at military installations and a few safe campuses, because of public hostility.

The Nixon administration was hostile to both public and commercial broadcasters, with Vice President Spiro Agnew delivering addresses in which he first described network journalists as "a tiny and closed fraternity of privileged men, elected by no one," and later attacked them as liberals who were "nattering nabobs of negativity." The trial of Lt. William Calley Jr. for his part in the massacre of civilians at My Lai in Vietnam and the death of four students at Kent State University at the hands of National Guardsmen during an anti-war demonstration exacerbated this hostility. The president called on a "silent majority" of citizens to make their views known in support of the government. His television adviser, Clay Whitehead, warned the Indianapolis chapter of the Society of Professional Journalists that broadcasters would suffer the wrath of their local communities at license renewal time, if they did not adhere to a standard of balanced reporting.

Suspicion
From the beginning of Richard Nixon's presidency in January 1969, many journalists believed that he hated the media. Some claimed that he used a wide rage of tactics to intimidate them, posing a danger to the very institution of the press itself. The feature story in this 1973 issue of *Newsweek*, as the Watergate investigation was heating up, declared that "journalists and politicians have many things in common, but these days their most notable shared characteristic seems to be suspicion."

THE MEDIA AND WATERGATE

Ultimately for Nixon, it was the media that brought the climax to his presidency. The courts and the newspapers first brought to the public eye the incident — known as "Watergate" — that finally resulted in the only resignation of a U.S. president. When television joined the hunt, there was no escaping for Nixon.

The story began with a botched burglary attempt in the summer of 1972 at Democratic campaign offices in a Washington building named Watergate. Carl Bernstein and Bob Woodward, two city desk reporters for the *Washington Post*, doggedly pursued the Watergate story from the day five burglars were caught in the act until the Judiciary Committee of the House of Representatives conducted impeachment proceedings.

They traced the chain of responsibility for the burglary and the funds to pay for it through the president's re-election campaign organization, past the gates of the White House, and into the Oval Office itself. They used the techniques of scrutinizing every record they could find and pounding the pavements and telephoning day and night to discover sources and elicit information. They had the resources of the biggest newspaper in the nation's capital behind them, and they and their editors avoided being discredited by having two reliable sources for every fact they published. Their tenacity resulted in Nixon and his closest aides having to admit again and again that they had been less than candid with the public. The Watergate cover-up became a bigger story than the Watergate burglary.

The Woodward-Bernstein coverage led other newspapers and the wire services to increase their attention to Watergate. The

Nixon quitting!

Full coverage below and on Pages 2, 4, 6, 7, 8 and 9

Chicago Daily News

1st lottery winning numbers

Man, it's a real ball, this lottery drawing

President goes on TV at 8 p.m.

Formal action due Friday

Ford: the man they call Jerry and admire for work devotion

Surge of Nixon emotion here

Dollar gets stronger

The Outcome of Watergate

When the 1972 burglary of the Democratic Party headquarters at the Watergate office building was discovered, hardly anyone paid much attention. *Washington Post* reporters Bob Woodward and Carl Bernstein, however, began tracking down evidence as crime investigators would. What they found finally convinced public officials and other journalists to investigate. President Richard Nixon eventually was implicated and, unable to escape the scandal, resigned from office in 1974, the only American president ever to do so.

New York Times put reporter Seymour Hersh on the story in an effort to match the *Post's* coverage. What the public read in the papers was supplemented by what it saw and heard daily on television, as cabinet members, campaign officials, and the president's advisers faced sharp questioning from reporters, Congress, and the courts.

Two nationally televised sets of Congressional hearings turned Watergate into a national scandal. The first was before a Congressional Committee chaired by Sen. Sam Ervin of North Carolina. The networks carried it live day after day, as the burglars admitted their crimes and officials from the White House and the Committee to Re-Elect the President testified under oath. Ultimately the existence of audio tapes that recorded all Oval Office conversations came to light, and the tapes demonstrated that the president's denials of knowledge and complicity in the break-in were false.

The second round of hearings was before the House Judiciary Committee chaired by Rep. Peter Rodino. It was here that members of Congress examined the evidence and related it to the law of the land. They bared their own consciences, debated what to do, and then voted to recommend impeachment before the national public.

President Nixon was forced to defend himself repeatedly in public addresses, and the few press conferences he held became increasingly sharp. When it became apparent to him in August 1974 that he would face impeachment, he resigned. By that time, the courts had heard testimony from the burglars, and a series of trials was underway that sent them along with presidential advisers at the highest level to prison.

Woodward and Bernstein won the Pulitzer Prize for reporting. Perhaps a more significant measure of the impact of their story on the public was the eagerness of the two leading motion picture actors — Robert Redford and Dustin Hoffman — to perform the Woodward-Bernstein roles in a film based on the reporters' book on how they covered Watergate, *All The President's Men*.

It provided a model for investigative reporting, an increasingly popular term in newsrooms. Investigative reporting is characterized by the use of conventional reporting techniques, but with reporters zeroing in on a specific subject and pursuing it relentlessly. It is one manifestation of the goal of getting to the truth behind the facts. Because the reporter stands aloof from the story, investigative reporting contrasts with another manifestation of the truth-behind-the-facts goal, the New Journalism of the 1960s and '70s.

In New Journalism, newspaper writers immersed themselves in stories, giving subjective reports. They even delved into what they thought their sources were thinking. Tom Wolfe, author of *The Kandy-Colored Tangerine Flake Steamlined Baby*, and Gay Talese, author of *The Kingdom and the Power*, became the best-known of the New Journalists. However, fiction writers such as Truman Capote, in his nonfiction novel *In Cold Blood*, and Norman Mailer, in *Armies of the Night*, did the same kind of reporting.

CONTROL AND CRITICISM

In the United States the government has more control over radio and television than it does over newspapers, magazines, and books. When the Bill of Rights to the Constitution was enacted in the eighteenth century, the press was excluded from any government control. This concept represented libertarian thinking: let all kinds of information compete in an open marketplace, and the truth will rise to the surface. But the idea of social responsibility for human enterprises was stronger in this century when radio and later television were introduced. The Commission on Freedom of the Press, for example, emphasized the responsibility of the media to provide a meaningful and complete presentation of

Sunlight and Blacklisting
During its first decade, commercial television experienced dramatic changes and faced dramatic situations. One of the early technological problems was the weak screen image in lighted rooms. House Jameson, the salesman in this ad for a "daylight television" set, starred on one of the most popular programs, *The Aldrich Family.* His co-star, Jean Muir, was one of those blacklisted for suspected Communist activity.

the news in its report, *A Free and Responsible Press.*

Orderly allocation of broadcast frequencies was the responsibility of the Federal Communications Commission under the law, and the FCC had established regulations seeking to assure that broadcasting would be carried out in the public interest. One effect of this system was to make broadcasters much more sensitive than print journalists were to public and official criticism.

Regulations regarding political campaigns influenced news and public affairs television programming. For example, Congress had to enact legislation to allow candidates Kennedy and Nixon to debate one-on-one in 1960 because the Equal Time regulations contained in the FCC's Fairness Doctrine required broadcasters to give every candidate for an office the same access to the airways and there were a dozen or so minor party candidates for president.

Outside the political arena the Fairness Doctrine resulted in the 1969 *Red Lion* decision by the Supreme Court in which an author took exception to criticism leveled at him by a television evangelist. The court ruled that the station, owned by Red Lion Broadcasting, would have to allow the author time to respond.

In this era the three major networks dominated the airways. Their technical ability to gather and edit information into effective communications was recognized. Thus, when a documentary like *Selling of the Pentagon* in 1971 set off a debate over foreign policy and defense department self-promotion, CBS came under criticism for the way it had edited and presented its material. A Defense Department official and an Army officer claimed their comments were used out of context and distorted their intent. A complaint was filed with the FCC, and a U.S. House of Representatives subcommittee launched an investigation, subpoenaing all material used in preparing the telecast. After the network refused to provide unbroadcast videotape and film (called "outtakes"), the effort to cite CBS President Frank Stanton was brought before the entire House and failed as indicated earlier.

The FCC could refuse to renew a station's license, as it had done in Jackson, Mississippi. (In that case, station WLBT-TV had lost its license when African Americans demonstrated that its programming had failed to address the concerns of the black community.) Congress could act, as in the *Selling of the Pentagon* incident. The Supreme Court could rule, as in the *Red Lion* case. In addition, advertisers could exert strong pressure by threatening to withdraw commercials. In the early 1950s when fear of Communist domination was at its height, government agencies and some businesses were demanding that employees sign loyalty oaths. Blacklisting, the practice of barring employment to someone alleged to have Communist sympathies or ties, developed in broadcasting as well as in the motion picture industry. Single-sponsor programming developed a strong link between talent and product. A byproduct of the blacklist phenomenon was a 1950 document, *Red Channels: The Communist Influence in Radio and Television*, which listed more than 100 persons in broadcasting alleged to have such sympathies. The most prominent cases involved Jean Muir, an actress for NBC's *The Aldrich Family*, and John Henry Faulk of CBS, both of whom lost their jobs in radio. Faulk's distinction lies in his successful legal battle over more than a decade to clear his name. His 1954 autobiography, *Fear on Trial*, became the subject of a television docudrama.

The networks were also responsive to the reports of government commissions. In the 1960s black contributions to society were brought to the forefront and represented in documentaries such as *Black History: Lost Stolen or Strayed?* narrated by Bill Cosby. They were offered in response to the Kerner Commission's examination of television's role in fostering prejudice by not reporting racial issues and failing to address black Americans.

Conservatives, liberals, and others established organizations such as Accuracy in Media (AIM) to examine and comment on media performance, particularly television. At the same time, broadcast news coverage faced its share of critics. In *News from Nowhere* (1973), Edward Epstein studied the decision-making process for network news coverage and put into perspective the idiosyncrasies of what gets covered and why. He described the logistics of putting together a network news program and the priorities, including time and visual content, that frequently dictate whether a story is told. *TV Guide* columnist Edith Efron confronted the issue of liberal news bias during the 1968 election in her book *The News Twisters* (1972). Some academics criticized her methodology and the extent to which it could be replicated. Nonetheless, the book received a great deal of attention; and Efron, along with an associate, Clytia Chambers, went on to document a public relations campaign by CBS News against publication of *The News Twisters*, ostensibly because of her indictment of CBS's performance in the 1968 election and its decidedly liberal bias. Another popular publication addressed methods of political campaigning and reporting. In *The Boys on the Bus* (1972), Tim Crouse accused the press corps of "pack journalism" on the political trail.

New Competition for Newspapers

The numbers of daily newspapers remained stable around the 1,750 level until 1980 when they slumped to 1,700. Television became a dominant medium, and the big magazines disappeared. Soon, newspapers turned to what had been the big magazines' staple: displays of photography and graphic art and lengthy nonfiction prose. With radio, television, billboards, and other media from which to choose, advertisers hesitated to buy space in more than one newspaper in a city with competing dailies. The newspaper falling behind in circulation and advertising lineage therefore usually continued to lose ground as time passed, rather than regaining first place.

One time-tested way to combat rising production and distribution costs was to increase newsstand and subscription prices. But an increase also tended to hasten busy media consumers' decision to forsake their second (often an afternoon) paper in favor of television or of more time spent elsewhere. Another way to combat high overhead was to abandon subscribers outside the newspaper's trade area. The *Fort Worth Star-Telegram*, for example, which had carrier delivery routes 350 miles from its Central Texas presses in the 1940s, had retreated to its local county and surrounding environs by the late 1960s.

NUMBER OF WEEKLY NEWSPAPERS IN THE UNITED STATES, 1935–1960

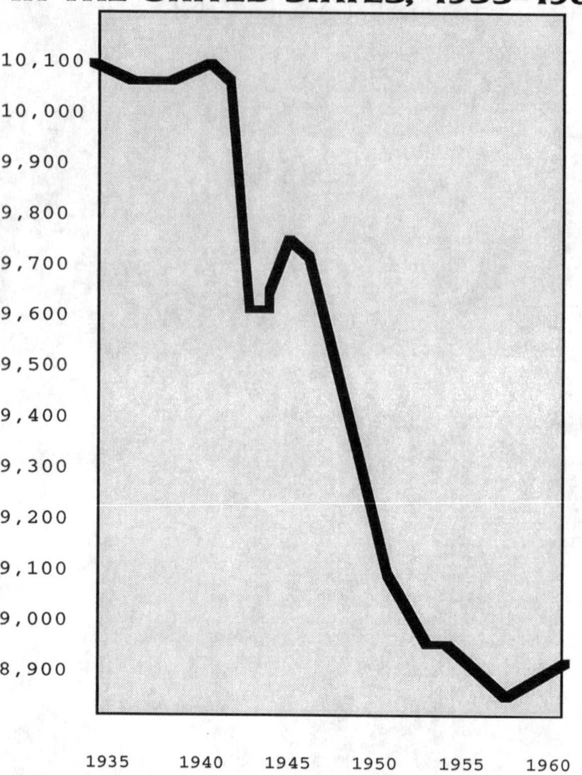

Three other kinds of competition appeared largely because of the new print technology. First, suburban newspapers succeeded. Some were chains surrounding a city and sometimes owned by a big downtown paper. Others, like *Newsday* of Long Island, New York, rivaled the metropolitan papers in size, coverage, and profitability.

City and regional magazines sprang up. Some prospered. Some soon withered away.

Most ubiquitous of the new print competitors were the shoppers, distributed free to every address in the market area. By trimming the news staff to a person who processed publicity releases and by aggressive advertising sales, these "throwaways," as traditional editors called them, operated with minimal editorial costs. The established papers countered with "TMC" (total market coverage) schemes in which they distributed streamlined editions to all non-subscribers.

In cities and towns too small to support a television station but big enough to have a substantial base of advertisers, daily and weekly newspapers thrived. The computerized newsroom-composing room let these "community" newspapers do things they had never done before. At last they were freed from expensive engraving of photographs; and the offset printing press, more efficient for small press runs than for giant runs, gave them the opportunity for as good or better printing quality than the big city paper had. Community papers banded together in joint printing ventures. A weekly or small daily publisher would put the paste-ups of the current edition on the truck seat beside him and drive to a central printing plant (sometimes a larger morning paper that got extra revenue by using its idle press time to roll out a half dozen smaller papers). A few hours later, after calling on possible advertisers or playing a round of golf, the publisher would head home with his bundles of papers ready for distribution. Sometimes they would be mailed directly from the printing site.

The trend toward chain — or "group," the term publishers preferred — ownership of newspapers accelerated. In part, this trend can be explained by the fact that chain management was more attuned than individual publishers to the competitive imperatives. Another part of the explanation can be found in two quirks in tax laws. Media groups embraced the law that allowed them to avoid paying capital gains taxes by investing their profits in additional "properties." At the same time, many newspaper families were finding it difficult to deal with inheritance laws that required them to seek large amounts of credit to pay the taxes required when the newspaper passed from one generation to the next.

Corporate practices began to replace traditional community journalism practices. They included aggressive as opposed to paternalistic management practices and credibility for the newspaper as opposed to credibility for the local editor-publisher. Many a city afflicted with generations of inept or even venal local newspaper ownership found that the management sent in by a major group produced a newspaper that served both advertisers and readers far better. Others, where a community-minded publisher sold his paper to a chain, discovered that a bright young publisher (perhaps an Ivy League MBA) might be around just long enough to get some local wisdom, only to be transferred to a bigger job and replaced by another bright young man or woman. Numerous communities found the local paper was being run by mediocre management sent in by owners, such as the Australian newspaper tycoon Rupert Murdock and London's Lord Thomson, who lived half a continent away or on the other side of the world.

Advertising and news departments began to use social science research soon after World War II, most notably when Rudolph Flesch's formula for the "fog index" of complicated writing came to the attention of editors. An Austrian-born readability expert, Flesch found that many advertisements were not only poorly written but also were difficult to read. Consequently, he promoted the use of simple words and short sentences. Soon information on readership and on the income and spending habits of the public was a routine part of newspaper planning.

In the face of the competition, the executives of newspaper groups turned, not surprisingly, to the kind of social science research other major corporations had used to increase the sales and acceptability of their products. In speeches before media groups, Robert Marbut, president of Harte-Hanks newspapers, could be heard during the early 1970s quoting the demographic statistics researcher Daniel Yankelovich had uncovered, to the effect that more and more young people were reading newspapers less and less, that they were more interested in information about their own lives than about the world, and that newspapers must reach them or suffer. The newspaper had to be "marketed."[11]

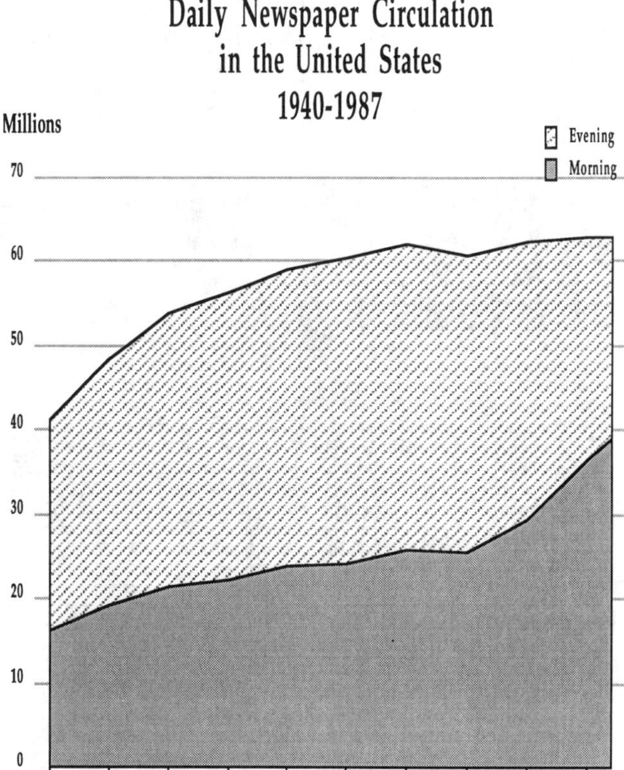

The traditional society and women's pages vanished to be replaced by "lifestyle" sections. Old-line newspaper people shook their heads when "people" pictures (as opposed to "news" pictures) and fluffy features began to appear on front pages every day. Vigor and style replaced much of the stuffiness of newspapers, but traditionalists questioned whether an analysis of the world's best-fitting jogging shoe matched in news value an analysis of the world's political health.

The Tribune's Struggle

In cities where newspaper competition continued to exist, it became cut-throat. Such competition existed for the *New York Herald Tribune.* A look at its effort to survive and why it failed illuminates the concerns with which newspapers struggled during these decades.

[11]"Marketing" of the newspaper was urged by Marbut in numerous speeches and in articles in professional publications. The remarks cited here are from an address delivered at the Southwest Journalism Symposium, San Antonio, Tex., 14-16 October 1978.

NEW YORK
Herald Tribune

Impact of Viet War Cost on 'Great Society': Defense Budget Up, Home Spending Is Cut

Johnson Sees Top Advisers On U.S. Outlay

MINISTER'S MURDER: SELMA WHITES FREE

City Bond Plan On Borrowing Wins in Court

Smoking Up a Burning Issue

Milwaukee's Boycott Priest —Archbishop Praises 'Cuts'

In The News This Morning

The Trib
In its struggle for survival, the *New York Herald Tribune* brought in James Bellows as editor. One of the best designed newspapers even before his arrival, it continued to win awards afterwards. The imaginative changes he made, however, were unsuccessful in the face of competition from the *New York Times* and the tabloid *Daily News*.

In the late 1950s John Hay Whitney, a wealthy member of an old East Coast family, purchased the *Herald Tribune* from the Reid family. He hoped to reverse the 120-year-old newspaper's decline in advertising and circulation, to make it the voice of the moderate wing of the Republican party, and to return it to a prominent position among the city's seven daily newspapers.[12]

He hired as editor the typographically innovative John Denson to provide a showcase for the *Trib's* stable of brilliant writers and reporters, including Walter Lippmann, Joseph Alsop, Marguerite Higgins, Robert Donovan, Art Buchwald, Walter Kerr, Judith Crist, Tom Wolfe, and Jimmy Breslin. The *Tribune's* stately vertical makeup had won many awards for typographical excellence. That look changed radically. Denson used large, terse one-line headlines spread across the page on a liberal background of white space, with stories and pictures packaged by bold borders. Promotional boxes at the top or bottom of page one touted inside content. A two-column summary of all the day's news always ran on the left side of page one to help readers crowding subways, buses, and commuter trains get the news without struggling to turn pages.

An advertising agency was employed to create a new image for the *Trib*. Soon billboards and carcards were asking New Yorkers: "Who Says a Good Newspaper Has to be Dull?" Not long after, the *Tribune's* logo appeared beneath the slogan to confirm to the public which newspaper was livelier than the fat, gray *New York Times* and more serious than the flashy tabloids, the *Daily News* and the *Mirror*.

Although circulation began to rise, the newspaper still was losing money. In 1962 Denson was replaced by James Bellows not long before all seven Manhattan dailies were shut down for 114 days by a labor-management dispute. Bellows and his top editors used the hiatus to design an entirely new *Sunday Herald Tribune* and a new Sunday magazine supplement, *New York*. Their goal was total design, and when publication resumed they came close to achieving it. A rule framed the front page of each section of the newspaper. Photographs, drawings, headlines, and type were integrated to provide the reader with logical and attractive packages of information.

New York magazine was pure lifestyle. The February 9, 1964, issue capitalized on Valentine's Day with a "Love in New York" theme. Tom Wolfe described a languorous weekend of apartment living in "A Sunday Kind of Love." In another article, Jimmy Breslin captured a raucous City Hall wedding in "When the Last of the Roths Got Married." The back of the magazine had columns in which the critics gauged the impact of romance on the cultural scene in art, dance, and the rest.

The good news about the *Trib*, however, was just a silver lining to dark clouds. Its competitors, the comprehensive *Times*, with the largest news staff of any U.S. paper, and the sensational *News*, with more than twice the circulation of any other, remained fat with advertising. When the strike ended, the four morning papers doubled their newsstand prices to a dime. Almost at once the tabloid *Mirror* went out of business, despite its half-million circulation. The *Tribune* lost circulation as many readers who had been willing to spend a dime to buy it and one of the other papers now chose to dump the *Trib* and spend the same dime on just one paper.

In 1964 moderate Republicans (including Whitney and the *Tribune*) failed to stop the nomination of conservative Barry Goldwater for the presidency; and for the first and only time in its history, the *Tribune* supported a Democratic presidential candidate, Lyndon Johnson. The goal of Republican leadership had not been reached. It was time to retrench. The last *Trib* was published in March 1966. An attempt to merge it with two afternoon papers failed.[13]

The *Herald Tribune*'s experience was different in some ways

[12] *Time*, 8 September 1958, 49.

[13] The story of the demise of the *WJT* is detailed in Joseph Sage, *Three to Zero: The Story of the Birth and Death of the World Journal Tribune* (New York, 1967).

The End
When competition brought the merger in 1966 of the *New York Herald Tribune*, the *World-Telegram*, and the *Journal-American*, it marked the end of the famous newspapers founded in the 1800s by James Gordon Bennett, Horace Greeley, Joseph Pulitzer, and William Randolph Hearst. The combined *World Journal Tribune* published for less than a year before it, too, died.

from that of most newspapers of the post-1945 era: its competition was with other newspapers, not other media, and it did not have the new technology available to enhance productivity. But the things it did to make itself more appealing to its readership — new design, new kinds of content, new marketing methods — were prophetic for the 1970s.

Professionalism and Self-Awareness

Forces in addition to media competition and new technology contributed to changes in news content of newspapers. Professionalization of news staffs through education, introspective examination by the media, scrutiny by social scientists, the impact of powerful institutions (government and business particularly), and national and world events contributed to changes in coverage and writing.

College educated reporters and editors came to dominate news rooms. A mid-1950s study showed that fewer than 20% of the staff members of Texas papers had been to college. An early 1970s study found the figure was approaching 90%.[14] College journalism programs burgeoned during the 1960s and '70s. Journalism courses dealt with historical, ethical, and theoretical perspectives of the media, as well as with the practical skills needed to work for the media. Upon graduation students took their college perspectives to their jobs. They looked upon fellow students and their professors as professional partners, and they established informal nationwide networks of alumni and colleagues who shared their views.

The mass communications scholars delved into critical and scientific examination of the media. The Graduate School of Journalism at Columbia University established the *Columbia Journalism Review* in the early 1960s, the prototype and one of the few survivors of several dozen academic and professional journals dedicated to critiquing media performance. Thousands of research reports on the media went onto library shelves as masters and doctoral theses, journal articles, and books. One of the most popular and useful was Philip Meyer's *Precision Journalism*, a book that explained the techniques and limits of social science research and showed how reporters could use it as a source of newsworthy information.

Education contributed to an attitude of self-examination by the media. So did immediate past events. The press had been compelled to deal with two world wars and the Great Depression during the first half of the century. Editors came to believe that they no longer could be satisfied to say, as a nineteenth-century editor had, that the role of the newspaper was to "print the news and raise hell."[15]

One journalist, Henry Luce, founder and publisher of *Time*, *Life*, and other news-oriented magazines, funded the Commission on Freedom of the Press in the late 1940s. Headed by Robert M. Hutchins, president of the University of Chicago, the Commission included in its inquiry all of the major instruments of the press at that time — radio and motion pictures as well as newspapers, magazines, and books. It addressed itself to "the responsibilities of owners and managers of the press to their consciences and the common good for the formation of public opinion." Despite the great technical achievements of the press, the Commission found that, in general, the press was failing to meet the needs of society. It was disturbed by the concentration of ownership of the press and questioned if the "struggle for power and profit [had] been carried to such a point in this field that the public interest...[had] suffered." The Commission also concluded that the press devoted too little time and space to information and discussion about public affairs and too much to "scoops and sensations." The press was too prone to accommodate itself to the whims and pressures of

[14] Alan Scott and Raymond West, "Personnel Turnover on Small Texas Dailies," *Journalism Quarterly* 32 (1955): 183-9; and Harry Marsh, "Correlates of Professionalism and News Performance Among Texas Newsmen" (Ph.D. diss., University of Texas, 1974), 51.

[15] This description of how journalism should be approached was popularized in the 1890s by Wilbur Storey of the Chicago *Times*, a brash, bold, sensational paper. Storey's attitude toward newspapering is chronicled in Justin E. Walsh, *To Print the News and Raise Hell* (Chapel Hill, N.C., 1968).

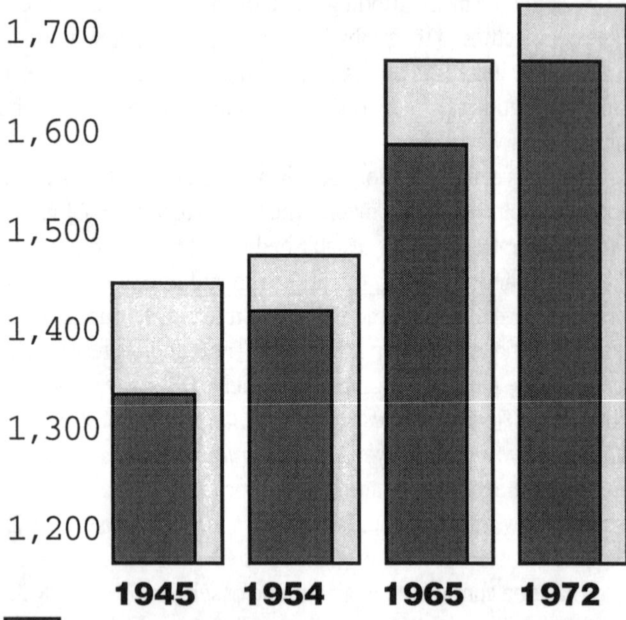

the audience on the one hand and to the preferences of owners on the other, the Commission believed.[16] Its report, *A Free and Responsible Press*, led in establishing responsibility to society, alongside freedom to publish, as a tenet of American journalism.

Codes of ethics, largely unenforceable under the First Amendment, gained renewed popularity. Joining the 1923 Canons of Journalism of the American Society of Newspaper Editors, were codes by the Society of Professional Journalists-Sigma Delta Chi, the National Conference of Editorial Writers, and others.

A Media Watershed

The Vietnam issue had ousted one president, and the Watergate controversy ousted his successor. The mass media had focused attention on both, and in the process they had changed also. As the third quarter of the twentieth century came to a close they seemed to have unprecedented power. Television stations and newspapers were being bought and sold at highly inflated prices. Journalism schools were experiencing record enrollments. It was a watershed for the media with new challenges ahead.

[16]The above quotations are from the Commission on Freedom of the Press, *A Free and Responsible Press*, 50-1 and 54.

RECOMMENDED READINGS

BOOKS

Allen, Craig. *Eisenhower and the Mass Media: Peace, Prosperity, and Prime-Time TV*. Chapel Hill, N.C., 1993. Eisenhower should be considered the first television president because he and his staff masterfully managed the new medium.

Arlen, Michael. *Living Room War*. New York, 1966. Essays from *The New Yorker* representing some of the best writing about television coverage from Vietnam.

Aronson, James. *The Press and the Cold War*. Indianapolis, 1970. The press between 1945 and 1970 helped lead the United States into a dangerous political reactionarianism.

Avery, Robert K., and Robert Pepper. *The Politics of Interconnection: A History of Public Television at the National Level*. Washington, 1979. Account of the internal politics of public television from 1968 to 1976.

Barnouw, Eric. *The Image Empire*. New York, 1970. The third part of the widely acclaimed trilogy on the history of broadcasting focuses on television.

Baughman, James L. *Television's Guardians: The FCC and the Politics of Programming, 1958-1967*. Knoxville, Tenn., 1985. The FCC was unsuccessful at regulating television because it could not get cooperation from either the legislative, executive, or judicial branch of the federal government.

—. *The Republic of Mass Culture: Journalism, Filmmaking, and Broadcasting in America since 1941*. Baltimore, 1992. By becoming the primary mass medium in the 1960s, television altered the lives of Americans and forced newspapers, film, radio, and magazines to adapt to a rapidly changing media marketplace.

Bayley, Edwin R. *Joe McCarthy and the Press*. Madison, Wis., 1981. A detailed summary of the anti-Communist senator's battles with — and many victories over — the press.

Bluem, A. William. *Documentary in American Television*. New York, 1965. A detailed, if dated, look at television documentaries containing a listing of films.

Braestrup, Peter. *Big Story: How the American Press and Television Reported and Interpreted the Crisis of Tet 1968 in Vietnam and Washington*. Boulder, Colo., 1977. In the Tet military offensive during the Vietnam war, logistical and structural problems in press operations and the press' negative reaction to President Lyndon Johnson's tactics resulted in distorted news and interpretations and outright falsification.

Bray, Howard. *The Pillars of the Post: The Making of a News Empire in Washington*. New York, 1980. Favorable history of the *Washington Post* from Eugene Meyer's purchase of the paper in 1933 to Donald Graham's becoming chairman of the board in 1979, including financing in the early years, Vietnam, racism on the paper's staff, and Watergate.

Brown, Lee. *The Reluctant Reformation: On Criticizing the Press in America*. New York, 1974. Outlines the major themes, patterns, and concerns of media criticism.

Felsenthal, Carol. *Power, Privilege and the Post: the Katharine Graham Story*. New York, 1993. Describes the life of the *Washington Post* publisher and how she built a profitable media empire through her will and determination.

Friendly, Fred W. *Due to Circumstances Beyond Our Control*. New York, 1967. Murrow's associate gives his personal account of the early days at CBS News.

Garay, Ronald. *Gordon McClendon: The Maverick of Radio*. New York, 1992. Fast-paced biography of a radio broadcaster known for his innovations in programming and management in the 1950s and 1960s.

Halberstam, David. *The Powers That Be*. New York, 1979. Examines the rise to power by the *Washington Post*, *Los Angeles Times*, CBS, and Time Inc. The huge media dominated American public thought and often shaped politics and society, acquiring status and large profits for themselves.

Hammond, Charles Montgomery, Jr. *The Image Decade: Television Docu-*

mentary, 1965-1975. New York, 1981. This study considers the period since Murrow and Friendly did their work and updates Bluem's study.

Hammond, William M. *Pubic Affairs: The Military and the Media, 1968-1973*. Washington, D. C.: Center of Military History, United States Army, 1996. Relations between the military and press deteriorated during the Vietnam War.

James, Doug. *Walter Cronkite: His Life and Times*. Brentwood, Tenn., 1991. Traces the 41-year career of the veteran CBS newscaster.

Kendrick, Alexander. *Prime Time: The Life of Edward R. Murrow*. Boston, 1969. Murrow was an outstanding broadcast journalist. He would have made the news even better had it not been for pressure from advertisers and CBS management.

Kluger, Richard. *The Paper*. New York, 1986. Details the rise of the *New York Tribune* and the *New York Herald*, their merger, and their decline as a newspaper subsidized by two influential families. Covers the same newspaper environment as Talese's *The Kingdom and the Power*.

Lashner, Marilyn A. *The Chilling Effect in TV News: Intimidation by the Nixon White House*. New York, 1984. The Nixon administration used a wide range of tactics to intimidate television journalism, diminishing its freedom and willingness to report.

Lindstrom, Carl E. *The Fading American Newspaper*. Garden City, N.Y., 1960. Newspapers in the 1950s failed to compete effectively with television and became primarily business enterprises.

Mickelson, Sig. *The Decade That Shaped Television News: CBS in the 1950s*. Westport, Conn.: 1998. An insider's account of the rise of television journalism in its first full decade.

Rader, Benjamin G. *In Its Own Image: How Television Has Transformed Sports*. New York, 1984. Television has had a major impact on the nature of sports since the late 1940s.

Rucker, Bryce. *The First Freedom*. Carbondale, Ill., 1968. Examines the danger that economic motives presented to the press, concluding that overwhelming economic concentration transformed the news media in the 1960s into gigantic interconnected conglomerates that approached every aspect of the news process as a business.

Sims, John Cameron. *The Grass Roots Press: America's Community Newspapers*. Ames, Iowa, 1969. Examines the state of weekly, community, and suburban newspapers, their operating conditions, their journalistic idealism, and their vigor in crusading.

Small, William. *To Kill A Messenger*. New York, 1970. One of the best accounts of broadcast news treatment of events of the 1960s.

Smith, Anthony. *Goodbye Gutenburg: The Newspaper Revolution of the 1980s*. New York, 1980. A summary of the revolution in newspaper economics brought about by changing demographics and improved printing methods.

Sperber, Ann M. *Murrow: His Life and Times*. New York, 1986. This biography emphasizes Murrow's professional career, from the development of radio news in the 1930s to the documentaries of the 1960s.

Talese, Gay. *The Kingdom and the Power: The Story of the Men Who Influence the Institution That Influences the World — The New York Times*. New York, 1969. Provides an inside view of *New York Times* reporters, editors, executives, and publishers, focusing on the struggle among them to determine the nature of the paper and the direction it would take.

Udell, Jon G. *Economic Trends in the Daily Newspaper Business, 1946 to 1970*. Madison, Wis., 1970. A recitation of economic trends buffeting newspapers in the postwar years, particularly rising costs and trends in advertising and readership.

Waldron, Ann. *Hodding Carter: The Reconstruction of a Racist*. Chapel Hill, N.C., 1993. Account of the editor of the *Delta Democrat-Times* in Greenville, Miss., whose progressive racial views made him a leader among moderate editors in the South after World War II.

Watson, Mary Ann. *The Expanding Vista: American Television in the Kennedy Years*. New York, 1990. Television was instrumental to the civil rights movement, expanding democracy, and other major facets of American society.

Wyatt, C. R. *Paper Soldiers: The American Press and the Vietnam War*. Chicago: University of Chicago Press, 1995. The media did not exercise a profound impact on the war.

ARTICLES

Ashdown, Paul G. "WTVJ's Miami Crime War: A Television Crusade." *Florida Historical Quarterly* 28 (1980): 427-37. Miami television station's 1966 campaign against Dade County crime was possibly "television's first and most significant editorial crusade."

Barrett, Edward. "Folksy TV News." *Columbia Journalism Review* (November-December, 1973): 16-20. Summary analysis of the happy news phenomenon examining the role of consultants.

Bliss, Robert M. "Development of Fair Comment as a Defense to Libel." *Journalism Quarterly* 44 (1967): 627-37. Analyzes the *New York Times v. Sullivan* case, tracing the historical development of the doctrine of fair comment in libel cases.

Cook, David A., ed. "The Economic and Political Structure of American Television." *Quarterly Review of Film Studies* 8, 3 (1983): 1-55. This special issue of *QRFS* contains two historical articles: David A. Cook, "The Birth of the Network: How Westinghouse, GE, AT&T, and RCA Invented the Concept of Advertiser-Supported Broadcasting," pp. 3-8, providing an economic explanation of the motives of the founders of the NBC radio network; and Gary Edgerton and Cathy Pratt, "The Influence of the Paramount Decision on Network Television in America," pp. 9-24, a discussion of the 1948 antitrust decision against Paramount.

Cranston, Pat. "Political Convention Broadcasts: Their History and Influence." *Journalism Quarterly* (1960): 186-94. Overview of political convention coverage with attention to trends.

Garay, Ron. "Television and the 1951 Senate Crime Committee Hearings." *Journal of Broadcasting* 22 (1978): 469-90. The 1951 Kefauver Committee hearings on organized crime "captured the attention of millions, transformed obscure politicians into national figures, and promoted television during the industry's formative years."

Hensher, Alan. "No News Today: How Los Angeles Lost a Daily." *Journalism Quarterly* 47 (1970): 684-8. The death of the *Los Angeles Daily News* in 1954 resulted not so much from television or suburban press competition but from debilitating labor union demands and lack of the immense capital required in a metropolis.

Hofstetter, Richard C. "News Bias in the 1972 Campaign: A Cross-Media Comparison." *Journalism Monographs* 58 (November 1978). Network television, the wire services, and two newspapers gave biased coverage of the 1972 presidential campaign because of the nature of the media and their structure, rather than because of partisan bias.

Larson, Carl M. "The Struggle of Paddock Publications Versus Field Enterprises, Inc." *Journalism Quarterly* 48 (1971): 700-6. The success of a group of suburban Chicago papers resulted from market research, good management, and new information systems.

Logue, Cal M. "Ralph McGill: Convictions of a Southern Editor." *Journalism Quarterly* 45 (1968): 647-52. McGill, editor of the *Atlanta Constitution*, was a crusader for equal rights, justice, education, economic opportunity, and freedom for black Americans.

Long, Stewart L. "A Fourth Television Network and Diversity: Some Historical Evidence." *Journalism Quarterly* 56 (1979): 341-5. The demise of the DuMont network in the 1950s decreased the diversity of programming.

Lorenz, Lawrence. "Truman and the Broadcasters." *Journal of Broadcasting* 113 (1968-69): 17-22. Review of radio's role in the beginning with attention to the rise of television in politics.

McIntyre, Jerilyn S. "The Hutchins Commission's Search for a Moral Framework." *Journalism History* (1979): 54-7 and 63. Examines the questions confronted by the Hutchins commission on freedom of the press and ethics and how "the implementation of moral principles is shaped by practical restrictions."

Nixon, Raymond B., and Jean Ward. "Trends in Newspaper Ownership and Inter-

Media Competition." *Journalism Quarterly* 38 (1961): 3-14. The newspaper industry after World War II attained the highest degree of stability in its history, and fears of a monopoly on the expression of ideas caused by the decline in newspaper competition were unfounded.

O'Brien, Michael. "Robert Fleming, Senator McCarthy and the Myth of the Marine Hero." *Journalism Quarterly* 50 (1973): 48-53. Praises the work of a *Milwaukee Journal* reporter in debunking the myth that McCarthy was a war hero.

O'Kelly, Charlotte G. "Black Newspapers and the Black Protest Movement, 1946-1972." *Phylon* 41 (1980): 313-24. Examines four large black newspapers and finds that they favored integration and non-violence.

Peterson, Wilbur. "Loss in Country Weekly Newspapers Heavy in 1950s." *Journalism Quarterly* 38 (1961): 15-24. The blame for the decline in the number of weekly newspapers was poor economies in small towns, increasing newspaper production costs, and the failure of papers to increase their advertising and subscription prices to keep pace with cost increases.

Sharp, Harry. "Live from Washington: The Telecasting of President Kennedy's News Conferences." *Journal of Broadcasting* 113 (1968-69): 23-32. Provides reporters' views on advantages/disadvantages of live telecasting of presidential press conferences.

Sloan, Wm. David. "The Contemporary Press, 1945-Present: Profiteering Business or Professional Journalism?" 104-22, in *Perspectives on Mass Communication History* (Hillsdale, N.J., 1991). Analyzes the approaches that historians have taken.

Smith, F. Leslie. "CBS Reports: The Selling of the Pentagon." In *Mass News*, eds. David Leroy and Christopher Sterling, 200-12. Englewood Cliffs, N.J., 1973. Concise overview of the controversy with an appendix of sources and film availability.

Sterling, Christopher H. "Trends in Daily Newspaper and Broadcast Ownership, 1922-70." *Journalism Quarterly* 52 (1975): 247-56, 320. While the number of newspapers decreased, the expansion of broadcasting meant an increase in the total number of outlets and voices. However, the trend is toward increasing concentration.

Wiebe, Gerhart D. "An Historical Setting for Television Journalism." *Journal of Broadcasting* 1 (1956): 33-8. Television seems to be a means by which officials can present their ideas to the public, who have clamored to participate in making political decisions but who prefer only to be spectators.

Wyatt, Clarence R. "'At the Cannon's Mouth': The American Press and the Vietnam War." *Journalism History* 13 (Autumn-Winter 1986): 104-13. An analysis of six newspapers' coverage of the Vietnam conflict shows that the press was not overly adversarial.

Yaeger, Murray R. "The Evolution of See It Now." *Journal of Broadcasting* 1 (1956): 337-44. Narrative of the development and history of the "See It Now" television program: where the idea came from, its radio background, changes, etc.

24

The Contemporary Media

1974 - Present

In the years immediately after Vietnam and Watergate, the power of the media seemed unprecedented. Stories having their genesis in the news media had toppled two administrations. Media properties were being sold at record prices. Enrollments at schools of journalism and mass communication broke records every year.

Money follows power; and in the next two decades, media chains and entrepreneurs such as Rupert Murdoch purchased newspapers and broadcast stations large and small at prices often exceeding their expected profits.

Television journalists and newspaper reporters comprised a new national media elite. TV personalities such as Barbara Walters and Walter Cronkite achieved celebrity status, as did newspaper reporters such as Bob Woodward and Carl Bernstein. Here were individuals who had seen their stories measurably influence national public opinion and, in some instances, change American policy. Journalists in newsrooms throughout the land emulated them.

Despite the triumphs, all was not bright on the media horizon. For some journalists, the quest for prestige superseded the quest for quality performance. Even as newspapers gained national recognition for their coverage of political and international events, they faced a growing economic threat from television. As television gained prominence as a news medium, it bore the brunt of wide-ranging criticism from the public and from within the media's own ranks. As the news media's visibility in public affairs grew, their credibility shrank. Even as they were buoyed by professional, economic, and technological success, the media faced major difficulties in the last quarter of the twentieth century.

With more attention and an infusion of new dollars, television news made significant improvements in personnel. Some network news departments grew to a size comparable to those on the nation's leading newspapers. Reporters at both the national and local levels became more specialized, and coverage was enhanced. One station, WCCO-TV in Minneapolis, set up its own Washington, D.C., bureau, the first local station to do so.

The great bulk of radio and television journalists at the local level remained general assignment reporters, but in major cities specialization in such areas as consumer affairs and medical and science reporting became commonplace. Some local feature reporters began syndicating their work nationally. They included automotive specialists, food experts, pharmacists, and others. In meteorology, a province once populated by "weather girls" on television, bona fide atmospheric scientists with graduate training and membership in the American Meteorological Association became the norm in most major population centers and in some smaller communities, particularly those vulnerable to more radical and severe changing weather patterns.

Some broadcast reporters, particularly at the network level, were recruited from the ranks of the nation's major newspapers, and specialization continued. Bill Lawrence had joined ABC in the early 1960s after serving as White House correspondent for the *New York Times* for more than twenty years. Ray Brady, a former *Wall Street Journal* staffer, became business correspondent at CBS News, and Dan Cordtz joined ABC as economics editor. Investigative reporter and columnist Jack Anderson teamed up with ABC's *Good Morning America,* and Carl Bernstein of Watergate fame and the *Washington Post* did a stint at ABC. The Watergate story also elevated two lawyers, Fred Graham and Carl Stern, to specialized positions in television news.

There were also advances in the status of women and minorities. In 1974, ABC named Ann Compton chief White House correspondent, a television "first." Lesley Stahl covered the Watergate Committee hearings for CBS, moved to the White House beat, and then joined the staff of *60 Minutes*. Catherine Mackin's appointment as NBC floor reporter made news at the political conventions even though another female, Pauline Frederick, had worked for the network as early as 1948 as a United Nations specialist. Nancy Dickerson also covered the capital for NBC. At ABC Marlene Sanders anchored an early news broadcast, produced documentaries for the innovative *Close-Up* series, and in 1976 became the first female news vice president at ABC. Barbara Walters got a mil-

Marlene Sanders
Marlene Sanders was part of a growing trend of more women in journalism at the national level. She anchored an early ABC news broadcast and in 1976 became the network's first female news vice president.

lion-dollar contract from ABC in 1976, setting off a public debate over the relative worth of a broadcast interviewer/reporter. Connie Chung joined NBC News from the CBS affiliate station KNXT-TV in Los Angeles, and Jane Pauley followed in Barbara Walters' shoes on NBC's *Today* after Walters' defection to ABC. Diane Sawyer won high praise as co-anchor of the *CBS Morning News*, joined the staff of *60 Minutes*, and then switched to ABC. In an unprecedented move, NBC reporter Judy Woodruff left commercial broadcasting to join PBS's news team in the early 1980s before joining CNN. Charlayne Hunter-Gault, one of the two black students integrating the University of Georgia in the early 1960s, served as key reporter and sometimes host for the *Newshour*.

While fewer in number, minority journalists made significant strides in the 1970s and '80s. William Raspberry and Thomas Sowell, among others, worked as syndicated columnists. *Black Journal* and *Tony Brown's Journal* started on public television. Two black males achieved "celebrity" status at the commercial network level as hosts of nationally televised series. Ed Bradley, a former Philadelphia school teacher, emerged at CBS News as a weekend anchorman, documentary narrator, and then host of *60 Minutes.* Sportscaster Bryant Gumbel excelled as host of NBC's *Today* morning program before joining CBS in 1997. ABC experimented briefly with anchor desks for its evening newscast centered in three locales. Chicago, one of the three cities chosen for the experiment, featured minority journalist Max Robinson at the helm. But the three-anchor approach was shelved after the death of Frank Reynolds, one of the anchors. CNN's Bernard Shaw won laurels for his reporting on the Gulf War against Iraq as a first-hand observer in 1991.

Numerous other minority journalists achieved prominent positions at the local level, and some turned down lucrative offers with national media to stay in their communities. The minority reporters who achieved high-level positions almost universally shunned the notion that they be given assignments on the basis of a tie-in with their race, as was the practice in both print and broadcast journalism in many locales.

Revolutions in Technology

One of the most visible changes in mass communication was the advance in technology. It had a pervasive influence in both broadcast and print media.

Mobile equipment came into wide use in commercial broadcasting. The editorial uses of modern technology were supplementing important changes being made in news personnel. The history of the development of television news has been like a game of editorial and technological leapfrog in which equipment bolstered news coverage in order to further support advances in technology.[1] This progression took a dramatic leap forward in 1974 with the introduction of highly mobile electronic news gathering (ENG) equipment, allowing for live transmission from the field using microwave technology. CBS affiliate KMOX-TV (now KMOV), St. Louis, was the first all-ENG station. ENG reporters learned a special need for sensitivity to situations and an awareness of potential legal and ethical problems that live coverage of events presents. Because of the pitfalls associated with live ENG reporting, it often was limited even at the network level, where more of the budget traditionally went to specialized staff.

Newspapers also made technological advances in newsgathering. In addition to the traditional notebook, pencil, and camera, the newspaper journalist began carrying an audio cassette recorder and a portable computer terminal. Many reporters used data bases and computerized financial programs to track the activities of business, government, and other public institutions. Technology enhanced accuracy and efficiency in gathering the news, writing stories, and getting them to the public. In contrast, the high-technology used by television news demanded a team including reporter and camera operator and equipment that was relatively cumbersome and obtrusive.

Along with changing newsgathering, technology affected newspaper production. Display advertisements up to four columns wide were being produced routinely on single pieces of photo-

[1] Av Westin, *Newswatch* (New York, 1982).

The Cable Landscape
Along with the home use of computers, the most visible change brought about by new communication technology was the proliferation of television offerings. Cable television had been available in the 1950s, but it was the 1980s that saw the introduction of the huge variety of programming that some people had originally envisioned. As the opportunities multiplied, however, a small number of large corporations dominated the programming landscape. MSNBC, for example, was started as a business venture co-owned by Microsoft and the NBC television network. Its activities in the 1990s included, in addition to this giant television screen in New York City's Times Square, a 24-hour-a-day television news channel, a digital satellite network seen on DirectTV and Primestar, and a web news service.

graphic paper. They used graphic design VDTs (video display terminals) that allowed blocks of type, borders, line drawings, logos, and even screened photographs to be sized and coordinated on the screen before being produced photographically. In some plants (beginning with the Rockland-Westchester papers of New York state) all the type and pictures were laid out on a page-sized VDT and then transmitted directly to a plate maker, a process called pagination.

In another technological development, newspaper pages were scanned and committed to computer memory and then transmitted via satellite to one or more printing plants hundreds of miles distant for simultaneous publication of the same newspaper in more than one city. The *Wall Street Journal* pioneered multiple-site publication using Teletypesetter technology. Dow Jones, the parent company, correctly predicted that the growing interest in financial, investment, and business information would make the *Journal* a national financial newspaper if it could be distributed on the day of publication. Gannett's *USA Today*, a national newspaper, utilized the same technology. In five years it became the nation's biggest newspaper in circulation totals and set the pace in use of color and graphics.

Amazingly, on smaller newspapers a new revolution in production was taking place by the end of the 1980s. The waist-high photocomposition machines that in the 1960s had made the Linotypes obsolete were themselves gathering dust in storerooms, displaced by laserprinters the size of a desktop copying machine. The new technology was appropriately named desktop publishing and combined the laserprinters, which used xerography rather than photochemicals, with generic personal computers and software capable of producing text and graphics. More than half of American newspapers were using this technology in 1987.

New technology also affected methods of delivering newspapers to readers. The newly developed interactive videotex systems used combinations of data bases stored in large computers. Through ingenious linkages of satellite, microwave, and telephone lines, the data bases were made available to the subscriber's home computer. By asking for categories of information (business, sports, classifieds, news, new products, etc.), the subscriber could get a broad choice from current information. If subscribers knew what they wanted, one or two key words typed into their computer could bring up the specific information.

Viewdata, based in Miami and founded by Knight-Ridder, a newspaper chain, began offering its service in the early 1980s at a monthly subscription of $12 (about one-third higher than that of a metropolitan newspaper) plus the cost of the user's computer and 90¢ an hour for phone line charges. The service was, however, unsuccessful and in 1987 was discontinued. Michael Bloomberg, however, succeeded on a grand scale with Bloomberg Financial Markets in the field of information services.

A variety of newspapers attempted more modest efforts to take advantage of the large bodies of information they acquired. The *Albuquerque Tribune* each day published a password to allow users of personal computers with modems to gain access to expanded information contained in its computers. The *Kansas City Star* launched an extensive "Startouch" program whereby readers could use their touch-tone telephones to get additional information through audio reports, to express their opinions, and even to order merchandise. Such services indicated an awareness on the part of publishers that no longer were they strictly in the business of putting ink on paper.

The Satellite Age

Multi-channel cable television (a potential of 100 or more program choices) made possible the all-news format, specialized content for various age groups and interests, and new opportunities for local programming and advertising.

Ted Turner, the operator of "superstation" WTBS-TV in Atlanta, based his marketing on transmission of the station signal by satellite and acceptance by cable systems nationwide. When he

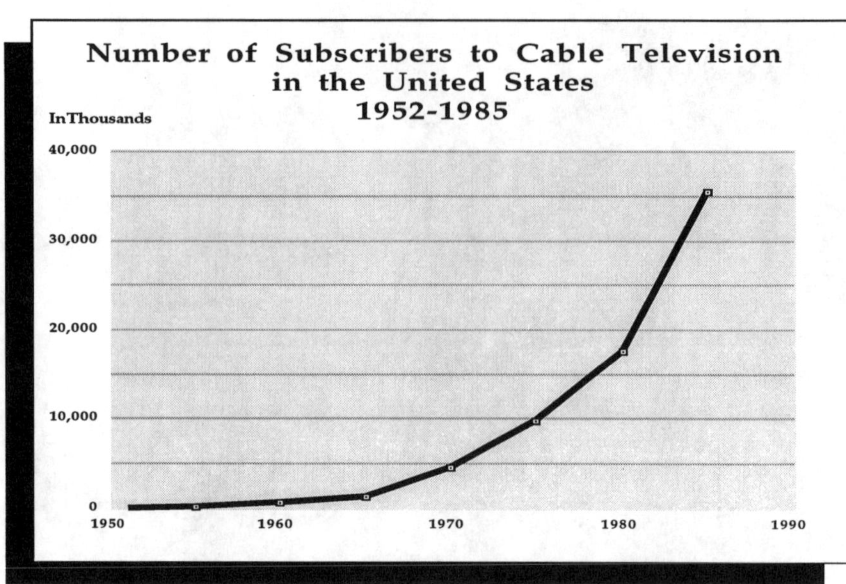

The Cable Technology Revolution
Among the many technological advances in television in the 1970s and 1980s, one of the most important was cable. Freeing broadcasting from a limited airwave spectrum, it allowed a multiplication of stations and programming operations. Its rapidly growing popularity is evident from this chart.

launched Cable News Network (CNN), the nation's first 24-hour television news service, he predicted news channels eventually would fulfill all the needs of newspaper readers. He hired Reese Schonfeld, founder of the Independent Television News Association, as president of the network and recruited former CBS News correspondent Daniel Schorr to serve as chief Washington correspondent.

CNN soon demonstrated the advantages of round-the-clock news broadcasting. In 1983 national attention was focused on Atlanta when the accused murderer of twenty-eight black youths, Wayne Williams, went on trial. Photographers were barred from the courtroom, but reporters in an elaborate press room viewed closed-circuit television cameras that focused only on the judge and jury. CNN, by virtue of its Atlanta base of operations, was able to provide hourly updates and won praise for the coverage. But the next year, CNN came under fire for coverage of two criminal trials, opening up the issue of invasion of privacy and free press/fair trial debates.

Both controversies revolved around the use of cameras in the courtroom that forty-nine states allowed, with varying restrictions, in the early 1980s. The first case involved a Massachusetts rape trial in which four men were charged. Although CNN did not show the face of the victim in its extensive coverage, her name was mentioned in court while the network was on the air. As a consequence, other news organizations felt justified in providing her name and CNN was regarded as "smut peddling" and infringing on the victim's right of privacy. In a second sensational trial in California, a 115-count indictment charged the proprietor of a nursery school and six teachers with sexual abuse of over 100 children. CNN requested permission to provide live coverage of pretrial hearings and temper its reporting while studying use of a time-delay system, to avoid the problem of exposing identity encountered in the Massachusetts case.

Cable offerings soon proliferated. A non-profit public service network, C-SPAN expanded to twenty-four hours a day in 1982. The National Broadcasting Company started CNBC, a 24-hour cable business news channel, to compete with CNN. Specialized cable networks — such as the Health Network — offered viewers a steady diet of nutrition-related features. Warner Cable's Qube experiment in Columbus, Ohio, offered interactive capability (two-way television) to cable subscribers. The U.S. Chamber of Commerce gave birth to the American Business Network (BIZNET) in 1982.

The Christian Broadcasting Network (CBN) began specialized news coverage in the 1980s with an emphasis on topics of interest to evangelical Christian viewers. In addition, evangelical groups received broadcast coverage of their efforts to effect change in broadcast programming. When broadcasters came under fire by religious groups in 1982, Moral Majority leader Jerry Falwell could claim administration support since he had campaigned vigorously for Ronald Reagan's candidacy and for Reagan's stand on controversial issues such as abortion and aid to private schools. Both Reagan and his deregulation-minded FCC chairman, Mark Fowler, spoke to the National Religious Broadcasters' 1982 convention. The leader of another group, the Reverend Donald Wildmon, founder of the National Federation for Decency, threatened broadcasters with a boycott if the content of popular television programming were not improved. Reagan sided with the religious supporters although he steered clear of the boycott issue.

The addition of cable television to the media complex presented challenges to the newspaper industry. Far from starting a mad rush to the new technology, however, publishers exhibited considerable skepticism along with their interest. Multi-channel television seemed to offer two competitive advantages to newspapers. Just as the introduction of radio and television had increased competition for the potential subscriber's time, additional television channels increased the competition for the television audience's time. In particular, the competition was expected to lessen the dependence of the public and of advertisers on the three major networks and their affiliated stations.

REVOLUTIONS IN TV PROGRAMMING

To their credit the TV networks went beyond technology in their efforts to improve news and public affairs programming. They produced more specialized programs and did some experimentation. Public broadcasting offered the weekly business-oriented series *Wall Street Week* beginning in 1970 and then added a *Nightly Business Report*. William F. Buckley introduced a steady diet of political views on *Firing Line,* and three weekly PBS talk shows — *Agronsky and Company, Washington Week in Review,* and the *McLaughlin Group* — all focused on Capitol Hill. In the 1970s the networks began to employ politicians to provide insight and commentary on special stories. ABC hired two famous presidential "losers," Barry Goldwater (1964) and George McGovern (1972), to provide perspective at the 1976 political conventions.

Noncommercial television presented a weekly interview program, *The Dick Cavett Show,* which also aired briefly over ABC. Cavett had guests from politics as well as from the arts and entertainment fields. In a talk show initially syndicated from the Midwest, Phil Donahue invited audience participation in questioning guests on controversial issues. He achieved a unique distinction among television talk-show hosts in 1984, when the FCC agreed that his show qualified as a bona fide news program, thus freeing him to invite political candidates without having to air the views of opponents. He concluded twenty-nine years on the air in 1996.

The early ABC experiment of *World News Tonight* with anchor desks in three important locales, including London, was an important attempt to provide international perspective. In the mid-1970s, *NBC Nightly News* introduced a mini-documentary series, three or four minutes in length, titled "Segment Three." This extended-format coverage allowed the network to go into more detail on the more significant, ongoing stories. ABC News followed suit with a "Special Assignment" series with related stories on a particular issue running in sequence for as many as three or four evenings in a row. The series was a forerunner of *Nightline*.

Despite such advances, many people, including some prominent broadcasters, still considered broadcast news a headline service. Progress was acknowledged when PBS extended its *MacNeil-Lehrer* report to one full hour in the early 1980s; but, plugged as "no nonsense news," the program became the *NewsHour with Jim Lehrer* and was an exception to the standard news format. Even with technical imperfections and lack of manpower by comparison to the commercial networks, the *MacNeil-Lehrer News Hour* provided flexibility and perspective in covering stories in more depth. It also forced the commercial networks to take notice and got the attention of critics, bringing welcome relief for cutbacks in documentaries that had occurred in the 1970s.

FROM DOCUMENTARIES TO DOCUDRAMAS

The 1960s had been a growth era for television documentaries. *CBS Reports* and ABC News *Close-Up* led the field with important treatment of political and social issues. NBC also aired more than thirty-five documentaries a year that decade. Since that time, documentary production had dwindled to the point that by 1983 the networks were providing fewer than half that number.[2] The decline resulted from the buildup of news departments, the re-alignment of internal resources in favor of successful magazine shows such as *60 Minutes*, and the poor ratings documentaries attracted.

It was especially difficult for public broadcasters to justify high expenditures to attract viewership without a sensational interest-grabbing component. Two PBS documentary efforts were *World* and *Frontline*. *World* included some provocative stories with veteran broadcaster Daniel Schorr serving as narrator. One topic examined was the international press. Another was America's dominance of communications technology and flow of information, preliminary to the controversial UNESCO debates along the same lines. A 1980 docudrama, "Death of a Princess," investigated the execution of a Saudi princess for adultery and set off a dispute between Saudi Arabia and Great Britain. It also resulted in a law suit and alienated the American oil industry but, in so doing, achieved the fifth highest viewer rating in PBS history. Another PBS series aired its first episode in 1983. In it, *Frontline* alleged that National Football League games had been rigged and that the owner of one team, the Los Angeles Rams, who reportedly drowned in 1979, actually had been "more or less murdered." The veracity of the report was questioned as well as the policy of paying some key sources appearing in the program.

In spite of the flaws of some of these efforts, television can be credited with taking itself more seriously, for the most part, in the 1970s and early 1980s, risking public criticism, both in news and entertainment programming, and showing a greater willingness to tackle tough issues. Of course, the public can also be credited for showing a greater appetite for these new directions. Network documentary dramas, while taking liberties with historical events, dealt with some of broadcasting's controversies and principal figures such as John Henry Faulk, Edward R. Murrow, and Joseph McCarthy. NBC's portrayal of McCarthy in the 1977 presentation of "Tail Gunner Joe" was attacked for sensationalism; and McCarthy's former colleague Roy Cohn claimed that dramatic license, caused by commercial pressures, destroyed the true McCarthy story.

In 1974 *ABC Theatre* broadcast a re-creation of "The Trial of Ethel and Julius Rosenberg." The Rosenbergs were executed for espionage and conspiracy to deliver atomic secrets to the Soviet Union. Ten years later, public television aired another docudrama in two parts, presenting the story of Whittaker Chambers and Alger Hiss — the basis for much of the anti-communist hysteria of the 1950s. Other documentary dramas dealt with President Kennedy's Cuban missile crisis performance in "The Missiles of October" and with another international crisis in "Pueblo," the story

[2]Bill Carter, "Whatever Happened to TV Documentaries?" *Washington Journalism Review* (June, 1983): 43-6.

of a Navy intelligence ship that the North Koreans captured in 1968. Political overtones were felt again in 1977, when a thinly veiled mini-series on Watergate was presented on network television featuring Jason Robards as President Richard Monckton, who bore a transparent similarity to Richard Nixon. ABC also presented "Friendly Fire," the true story of Gene and Peg Mullen of La Porte, Iowa, whose son had been killed in Vietnam. The show was an example of popular television making news with attention to an unpleasant reality.

Gradually the networks began to integrate actuality footage into these docudramas to add realism. In 1982, footage from an Air Florida jet crash outside Washington's National Airport was used a short time after the actual event in a drama about the disaster. The tape was available because news crews from local television stations were coincidentally on hand and witnessed the chaos as the plane crashed on a bridge jammed with commuters on their way home. Another made-for-television docudrama, "Special Bulletin," simulated how a television network might handle a nuclear incident involving terrorism; and an international sensation was created in 1983 when ABC broadcast "The Day After," the fictionalized account of events surrounding the start of a nuclear exchange between the United States and the Soviet Union set in Kansas City, Missouri, and Lawrence, Kansas. Since the showing of the film coincided with deployment of Pershing II missiles in West Germany, some critics ascribed the motivation to the network's being either pro- or anti-nuclear freeze, while others viewed it as a comment on America's lack of preparedness. After the program aired, a public debate ensued among scientists over whether the extent of damage depicted in the film was exaggerated or moderate when compared to the potential from a real attack.

Surprisingly little public dissent was heard when public television aired a bona fide documentary, *Vietnam: A Television History*, at about the same time in 1983. In thirteen hour-long segments the series presented what was generally considered to be a dispassionate, evenhanded chronicle of the conflict employing interviews with participants and documentary footage gathered from more than fifty film archives around the world. Lawrence Lichty, a television historian, directed research for the project that took six years and more than $4,000,000 to complete. Ken Burns became television's key documentarian, with thirteen historical efforts, during the 1980s and '90s. His works included *The Civil War* (1990), *Empire of the Air: The Men Who Made Radio* (1992), *Lewis and Clark* (1997), and *Frank Lloyd Wright* (1998).

INFO-TAINMENT

Obviously, though, more news is not better news; and at times it became hard to discriminate between news and entertainment. Television discovered an industry news equivalent of *Variety* or *People* magazine in the 1980s. A syndicated series, *Entertainment Tonight*, concentrated on information about television and the movies. Used as a lead-in to local newscasts in many cities, the series attracted a large viewership. This program was followed by others with descriptive titles such as *A Current Affair*, *Inside Edition*, and *Hard Copy*, raising once again the term "tabloid television." Syndicated talk shows also proved to be popular with viewers.

While good for the television industry and profitable for local stations, these "Info-tainment" programs, in the view of many critics, contributed to stunting the medium's growth as a serious news source. The success of *60 Minutes*, ABC's *Nightline*, and *20/20*; the expansion of *MacNeil-Lehrer*; and the presentation of informational programming — although not fulfilling the expectations of the early years — helped counter this trend toward purely entertainment-oriented news.

60 MINUTES

Even as *60 Minutes* served up much criticism of its subjects, the show itself was not without its own critics. Until the success achieved by *60 Minutes*, however, few national news programs attracted enough of a following to make a difference. Historically, news and public affairs shows have done poorly in attracting audiences. Edward R. Murrow was apt to point out that he was enabled to do *See It Now* by virtue of the ratings success of his celebrity interview series, *Person to Person*. Although the formats of Murrow's two shows differed, together they exemplified the best of what *60 Minutes* put forth. It was not without a struggle, however, that *60 Minutes* achieved popular acceptance.

Over the years *60 Minutes*, which went on the air in 1968, sustained its share of criticism. Media critic David Shaw concluded that leading network news and public affairs shows such as *60 Minutes* were guilty of ignoring important stories in favor of "subjects with an immediate emotional impact — sex, crime, consumer rip-offs...." Pointing to the use of confrontational interview techniques, Shaw accused one of television's best known investigative reporters, Mike Wallace, of playing a character in the "prime-time-news-as-soap-opera saga that *60 Minutes* often is."[3] The show also was accused of "checkbook journalism." It compensated Sirhan Sirhan, G. Gordon Liddy, and H. R. Haldeman for personal interviews. CBS paid former Nixon aide Haldeman $100,000 for a two-part interview. *60 Minutes* aired a talk with Nixon himself in 1984, in spite of the network's staunch refusal to purchase an interview with Nixon that British expatriate broadcaster David Frost had conducted eight years earlier. A special network of more than 150 stations broadcast four ninety-minute segments of these extended talks. Later, CBS admitted paying $10,000 to an unnamed informant who claimed to have information regarding the mysterious disappearance of labor leader Jimmy Hoffa.

One of *60 Minutes*' most intensely contested segments, which aired in 1975, revolved around the depiction of Syrian Jews.[4] The

[3]David Shaw, "The Trouble with TV Muckraking," *TV Guide*, 10 October 1981, 7. Also see "Magazines prime earners in prime time," *Broadcasting and Cable*, 9 May 1994, 40.

[4]Robert Chandler, Vice President and Director, Public Affairs Broadcasts, CBS News, letter to the author, 20 April 1978. See also "Steadfast at *60 Minutes*," *Quill* (March, 1976): 19-

Barbara Walters – Journalist, Celebrity
By the 1970s, television journalists and newspaper reporters comprised a new national media elite. Barbara Walters, for example, got a million-dollar contract from ABC in 1976 It set off a debate – among both journalists and the general public – over the worth of a broadcast interviewer/reporter.

American Jewish Congress accused the show of inaccuracy and distortion in a complaint to the National News Council.

Two decades later, *60 Minutes* made headlines when CBS management permitted broadcast of a tape of an assisted-suicide by Dr. Jack Kevorkian. The broadcast was widely criticized.[5] An earlier controversy erupted when *60 Minutes* suspended its popular commentator, forty-year-broadcast veteran Andy Rooney, for alleged racially derogatory off-air comments that an alternative publication attributed to him. The program's ratings declined briefly until Rooney was reinstated, using the occasion to deny ever having made the remarks. In one program, responding to public criticism of repeated television screening of the Los Angeles police beating of Rodney King, Rooney broke with fellow TV journalists and presented an extended analysis of the portions of the beating videotape that the networks edited out.

The popularity of *60 Minutes* encouraged experiments such as *48 Hours* and *60 Minutes II* at CBS. NBC tried *Weekend*, *First Tuesday*, and *Chronolog* before settling with *Dateline NBC*, hosted by Jane Pauley and Stone Phillips. At ABC, *20/20* with Hugh Downs and Barbara Walters became a success; and the interest in news stirred by *20/20* may have been responsible for helping *Nightline*, as well as *Prime Time Live* and an expanded *20/20* with Diane Sawyer and Sam Donaldson.

Dangers to Newspapers

As television became the dominant medium, newspapers found that their own status and fortunes were more fragile than journalists previously had imagined. The stresses on newspapers fell under the broad heading of increased competition.

The stakes in the press business were high. The value of media properties increased. Newspapers had operating profit margins that were attractive to investing companies, and the sale prices of newspapers soared dramatically.

As corporations bought up newspapers, local ownership decreased, a trend that concerned critics. Chain ownership of newspapers increased substantially. Whereas in 1960 a total of 114 chains had owned 563 dailies (32% of all dailies), by 1977 chains owned 1,061 dailies (60% of the total).

A related trend was the elimination of competing newspapers in the same city. Whereas 117 cities had had competing dailies in 1945, only thirty-four had them in 1990. In cities such as St. Louis, Dallas, and Little Rock, newspapers that had coexisted profitably for most of the century were locked in a struggle for survival. Eventually, each of those three cities had only one newspaper. Overall, the numbers of daily newspapers remained stable around the 1,750 level until 1980 when they slumped to 1,700, but the decrease did not mean competition from other media had declined.

Alert to the economic dangers that television posed, publishers attempted to restrict some of the competitors. They closed ranks, for example, in an effort to prevent regional telephone companies from adding information services to their traditional communication services.

Despite such efforts, newspapers faced increasing economic difficulties. All newspapers had to face dramatic increases in the costs of their basic raw materials: paper and ink. Beginning in the 1970s the cost of energy to run presses and to power delivery trucks more than doubled. Increases in labor costs also were substantial. Publishers needed the increased productivity brought about by new technology in offsetting the increased costs.

When chains and other owners found that their efforts to compete — whether with other newspapers or other types of media — were unsuccessful, they frequently sold out. This happened to the *Oakland Tribune*, long owned by the politically powerful Knowland family of California. Gannett Corporation purchased the paper but, when it failed to be profitable, decided to close it. A Gannett executive, however, Robert Maynard, joined with Oakland business leaders in the early 1980s and, going against the tide of chain ownership, bought it from Gannett. In 1990, with the paper again threatening to close, the Gannett Foundation (now known as the Freedom Forum) bailed it out with a multi-million dollar grant. Maynard was one of few blacks to become publisher-

20; and John J. O'Conner, "How Fair is the Fairness Doctrine?" *New York Times*, 15 June 1975, 27.

[5]See Frazier Moore, "TV Gets Downright Ghastly," *Newsday*, 2 January, 1999, C3.

ORIOLES FLY HIGH

USA TODAY

BEST FRIENDS?

NEWSLINE

Plot thickens in mystery flight

Making her mark

Productive summit ends on high note

Yuppies trim their spending

NBC calls on advertisers to resist threats

COVER STORY

Barbara Bush defines role, steals show

Green colors daydreams

USA SNAPSHOTS

THURSDAY Real Life

Best buddies:

The Birmingham News

Final debate: Critical Dole jabs at Clinton

Social Security benefits go up 2.9 % in 1997

State to ground drivers who lag in child support

Lonely livestock

Fewer animals, goods for judging at State Fair

Board looks ready to vote on Wright

Sessions outraises Bedford 2-1 in 3rd quarter funding

TODAY

USA Today
When *USA Today* was founded in 1982, journalists saw it as a visual competitor with television. With its short stories, modular format, and lavish use of illustrations and color – demonstrated by its front page (left) – it soon provided a new design formula. Many newspapers, as typified by this issue of the *Birmingham* (Ala.) *News* (right), began borrowing visual elements from it.

owner of a mainline newspaper; but, with his paper again facing financial problems, he sold it to a chain in 1992.

New Newspaper Approaches

Faced with competition from television, newspapers explored new techniques for making themselves more relevant to the audience. Publishers and editors looked at shrinking household penetration figures and unfavorable results of public opinion polls and began to question whether their traditional methods would provide the profits the new owners expected. For the most part newspapers maintained or enhanced their profitability into the 1980s, but stresses caused long-established metropolitan newspapers to disappear, and trends in circulation sent executives of newspaper groups to social science researchers seeking to find new ways to attract and keep readers.

First, newspapers had to face, in the 1970s, the "credibility" issue as a public reaction to the anti-establishment tone of the investigative reporters and New Journalists. Then, in the 1980s, after the arrival of *USA Today* in a rainbow of graphics, publishers, circulation managers, advertising directors, and editors created such slogans as "customer obsession" in an effort to make newspapers more appealing. In the 1990s, newspapers more and more were turning to "value added" efforts such as reader hotlines, telephone information services, shopping discount cards, and personal computer links.

Despite the problems that confronted newspapers, their advocates argued that the changes in newspapers and in the whole media situation actually worked to newspapers' advantage. The position of newspapers as the basic source of information and local advertising messages would be strengthened, reasoned newspaper executives. With dozens of television channels from which to choose, viewers more than before needed an up-to-date and detailed schedule of what was available on their sets, with concise descriptions of content. Newspapers provided the information in convenient formats updated daily. Editors expected reader-viewers to increase their dependence on newspapers for the service.

Newspapers, print journalists claimed, maintained superiority over other media in the quantity of important and interesting information they originated and made available to the public. Most of the news gathering still was done by newspaper reporters and made available to all the media by major and supplementary news services. In the broadcast media, news was still a mostly ancillary operation; and videotex services admitted that they were conveyors, rather than originators, of information.[6]

Newspapers continued to offer tangibility and availability. Even now, newspapers' defenders declare, the latest edition remains on the coffee table until the next day's issue supplants it. Professors tape comic strips and political cartoons to their office doors. Obtuse students can find relief from lectures in crossword puzzles. Clippings are mailed across the continent or pressed in family Bibles. No capital investment is required of the user. A coin gains access to a paper in a vending machine, and a paid subscription routinely brings one to the front door (or under the nearby rose bush). The newspaper remains the traditional source of daily information for the public.

Media-Government Relations

As the news media increasingly took on characteristics of big busi-

[6]Viewdata employed three "mini-reporters" during its first years of operation.

ness, they also developed as a profession. Activities oriented to professional journalism — such as college training, professional journals, and organizations of working journalists — flourished as they never had before. These factors and others contributed to an increasing recognition of journalism — in both its print and broadcast forms — as a well-defined field with its own training, practices, sets of ethics, and other features denoting an occupation as a profession.

One of the manifestations of professional self-awareness by journalists in the 1970s and '80s was the First Amendment Congress movement that sought public support and awareness through local and regional convocations on the need for an unfettered media. The Reporters Committee on Freedom of the Press reported on legal and procedural efforts to stifle the flow of public information, and the Investigative Reporters and Editors Association sought to spread the techniques of in-depth investigation of important issues by bringing successful practitioners together with other professionals and with students at conferences.

Perhaps the most marked change that the increased professionalization brought about was the media's relationship with government. Whereas the media prior to the Vietnam War generally were neutral toward or slightly supportive of government, the period after the war saw a swing toward a neutral-to-antagonistic attitude. Many critics claimed such an attitude indicated that the media had a liberal bias — a claim borne out by surveys that showed that the majority of journalists held liberal political and social views — but it appears also that the attitude represented journalists' institutionalized, professionalized view of themselves as the "watchdogs" of government and other institutions such as business and religion. Such attitudes had grown out of the Vietnam War and the Watergate political scandal. In these episodes, the media found themselves critical of the government power structure.

Many journalists accepted media opposition to established institutions as a professional standard. Some believed that support of the underdog was a function of the media and that the proper role of the press was to serve as a watchdog or adversary of established institutions. They sometimes viewed journalism in terms of the media fighting evil in American politics and society. Their heroes were journalists crusading to correct the ills and problems of their communities and the nation; and the opposition, they believed, was composed of authorities or groups that espoused repression and injustice, the wealthy class in American society, demagogues, or government. Some journalists and publications went so far as to declare that one of the government's paramount designs was to control information, silence the media, and deceive the public.[7]

[7]For examples of this view, see William Rivers, *The Adversaries: Politics and the Press* (Boston, 1970), and William E. Porter, *Assault on the Media: The Nixon Years* (Ann Arbor, Mich., 1976). The latter argued, for example, that President Richard Nixon viewed the press with hostility and waged a deliberate campaign to "intimidate, harass, regulate and damage" the news media.

Despite that outlook, there was considerable crossover of journalists into government employment.[8] When Richard Nixon resigned the presidency in 1974, broadcast reporters must have mused as his successor, Gerald Ford, appointed one of their own as White House press secretary. Ron Nessen, a one-time Vietnam War correspondent for NBC, became the first network broadcast veteran to become a chief press aide.

During his short presidency (1974-1976), Ford enjoyed generally congenial relations with the media. Journalists, however, seemed to delight in portraying him, a former football player at the University of Michigan, as clumsy. Every time Ford stumbled, it seemed that camera shots made network news and newspaper front pages. A similar media fascination with the superficial surfaced during the presidency of Ford's successor. One of the long-running stories about Jimmy Carter was of a "killer rabbit," as journalists dubbed it, that tried to bite the president during a fishing trip.

THE CARTER YEARS

The 1976 political campaign between Ford and Carter evolved against a backdrop of unprecedented circumstances tied to the first resignation of an American president and the result that the incumbent up for election had never before been on his party's presidential ticket. Ford's use of television was limited, of course, by his short term in office, although he did preside over the formal end of America's Vietnam involvement. Carter emerged initially as a Washington outsider intent on restoring integrity to national government. He derived advantage from a small, cohesive organization that provided continuity for his campaign and was the only primary candidate who in 1976 never changed media directors or broadcast advertising techniques. He did a credible job in the 1976 televised debates, and Ford's confusion over the geopolitics of Europe hurt his election prospects.

After winning the election, Carter experienced a brief grace period with the press, as has been the case with most American presidents. His media specialist, Gerald Rafshoon, encouraged his participation in televised town meetings, a radio call-in show, and gala dinners with news executives to enhance his press relations and image. But the image-making strategies wore thin as the economy worsened. The perceived theatricality associated with a televised "Fireside Chat" in which Carter dressed in a cardigan sweater and sat by a fireplace in the White House addressing the energy issue probably had the effect of undermining his substantive achievements such as his efforts in international peace negotiations. Coverage of his brother Billy Carter's drinking problem de-

[8]Edward R. Murrow once headed the United States Information Agency; and John F. Kennedy's press secretary, Pierre Salinger, eventually went to work for ABC in Europe. Bill Moyers also accomplished this feat in reverse, going from a former print journalist/publisher and press secretary for President Johnson to become an influential broadcast journalist with both PBS and CBS. John Chancellor served briefly as Director of the Voice of America under Lyndon Johnson; and another of broadcasting's elder statesmen, John Scali, achieved cabinet rank as ambassador to the United Nations, a post he held for two years before returning to ABC News as a senior correspondent.

Jimmy Carter's Media Difficulties
After winning election in 1976, President Jimmy Carter experienced a brief honeymoon with journalists. As the national economy worsened and the hostage crisis in Iran dragged on, media scrutiny became harsher. Carter's efforts to improve his public image with planned media appearances were not effective, and his popularity slowly diminished.

tracted from his image as a national leader in the tradition of F.D.R. In *The Other Side of the Story* (1978), Carter press aide Jody Powell insisted that unfair press attention to specious allegations of drug use by another close aide, Hamilton Jordan, also affected his boss' public stature and chance for reelection. Beyond these problems, the economy, fueled by excessive inflation, took its toll.

Media reporting on the important issues of the day was increasingly under study during Carter's term in office and throughout the 1970s and 1980s. The Media Institute, a Washington-based non-profit but corporate-sponsored research organization designed to improve business and economic reporting, gave the media a failing grade for their coverage of both the 1973-74 and 1978-79 oil crises — crises that included reports from gas lines at America's service stations. Carter was damaged also by negative coverage of a major news item that was due, more or less, to unanticipated circumstances abroad.

When about 500 Iranians seized the U.S. Embassy in Teheran in 1979, the action caught most Americans, including the news media, off guard. Taken in retaliation for cooperation of the United States with the Shah of Iran and because of the growing influence of Western culture and industrialization, it resulted in a demand that the Shah, seeking medical attention in New York, be returned to stand trial. Because of his failing health, return was impossible. The television networks were ill-equipped to handle this kind of international story although a decade earlier ABC had concentrated a great deal of energy, manpower, and money on exhaustive coverage of the 1972 Munich Olympics. The reporting of ABC's sports team during an Arab terrorist attack on Israeli athletes won high praise for the network, the traditional follower in news. It also brought attention to ABC sports chief Roone Arledge. He later was made head of the network's news operation, although his lack of journalism credentials became a cause of concern in some quarters. When the Iranian situation developed, Arledge requested special airtime for the story. The result was "The Iran Crisis: America Held Hostage," a series of twenty-minute updates that ran nearly four months until ABC formally established *Nightline* as a regular part of its program schedule with more than thirty segments devoted to Iran.

For the first three and a half days of the crisis, ABC News had a virtual monopoly on coverage because one of its reporters, Bob Dyk, was able to slip into the country the day after the takeover with a cameraman at his side. Iranian television allowed ABC to send reports via satellite using electronic newsgathering equipment. The competing networks were forced to rely on film shot by British and West German news organizations and shipped by air. This arrangement gave ABC an edge in covering the story even if the exclusive lasted only a few days.

Later, when the United States attempted to rescue the hostages, *Nightline* provided after-the-fact coverage, including biographical information on the eight American servicemen who lost their lives on the mission. When the American hostages were finally released and Ronald Reagan was inaugurated as president, both on January 20, 1981, *Nightline*, along with the other news media, provided detailed coverage. Follow-up stories — such as treatment of the hostages by the press once they returned to the United States — helped the show and an offspring, *Viewpoint*, gain high regard as a media monitor. The continued success of the series could be attributed also to ABC's willingness to extend coverage on special occasions, the performance of the series' master interviewer, Ted Koppel, and extensive use of satellite coverage of breaking events.

REAGAN: MASTER OF THE MEDIA

Sometimes referred to in press reports as "The Great Communicator," Ronald Reagan was regarded as the most effective television president since John F. Kennedy. He held the distinction of having been an actor and host of a television series, *General Electric Theatre*. His presidency helped usher in a new age of technology. Cable News Network provided live coverage of the major events surrounding his first inaugural — and some of the minor ones — and the inauguration was the first to be closed captioned for the hearing impaired for television.

A study of the 1980 election found, however, that the media, especially CBS, were predominantly negative in reporting about the candidates.[9] Even before the election, Reagan was involved in a television controversy when NBC News projected his win before voters in the West, Alaska, and Hawaii had gone to the polls. It was argued that Carter's early concession speech had the effect of turning away voters in those states. A later CBS News poll showed that nearly 10% of those who did not vote cited Carter's apparent loss in their decision.

Once in office, Reagan's television performances received rave reviews. After his first televised press conference, Tom Shales reported in the *Washington Post* that "whatever else he does during his administration, at least President Reagan won't be wasting his time learning how to look good on television.... It may not be possible to look any better on television than he already does."[10]

Reagan courted reporters in a manner not unlike John F. Kennedy. When a mini-press conference was held to address a drop in unemployment in 1983, Mrs. Reagan interrupted with a birthday cake for her husband halfway into the meeting. Television cameras from all three networks caught news correspondents in a chorus of "Happy Birthday to You," Reagan's 72nd, before returning to regular programming.

Reagan had trouble with press leaks during his early administration and suffered major setbacks with the televised Congressional grilling of some of his advisors, nominees, and appointees. Media coverage tended to be negative in several areas. An independent study of network economics reporting found an anti-administration bias at CBS. A follow-up study of CBS, NBC, and ABC reporting as the economy turned around in early 1983 discovered a sense of skepticism on the part of the news media. The study concluded that among the television networks ABC was providing the most comprehensive view of the economy while CBS was doing the least effective job.[11]

Reagan's major media problem during his presidency was an international guns-for-money deal that was dubbed the Iran-Contra scandal. The story was broken, not in the United States, but in the Middle East by an obscure magazine. What it reported and the rest of the world's press expanded on was the sale of arms by the United States through Israel to Iran, then under a U.S. embargo, and the use of millions of dollars from the sale to finance the Contra rebels fighting the Marxist government of Nicaragua, despite a federal law prohibiting the U.S. government from financing the Contras. Iran-Contra raised questions in the minds of many liberal critics as to whether American media were carrying out adequately their responsibility to inform the public of what official institutions were doing.

MEDIA ACCESS TO WAR

Reagan also became embroiled in the issue of press access to government information, particularly access to military operations in foreign countries — an issue largely forgotten in the United States since the Vietnam conflict.

In 1983, when American troops invaded tiny Grenada in the Caribbean, the military invited no reporters to go along, and those who appeared on the scene in the first days were not allowed to file stories. Journalists and news organizations expressed their dismay when the government restricted press coverage of military action on the island of Grenada. *NBC Nightly News* commentator John Chancellor was widely quoted for his condemnation of the action — an invitation to bureaucrats, he said, to "Do anything. No one is watching."

When journalists complained about the restrictions, public sentiment sided with the government. Journalists seemed almost as alarmed over the public's apparent unwillingness to support their demand for access as they had been over the original military restrictions. Although surveys found that opposition to the press was less pronounced than journalists might have thought,[12] Chancellor — dipping into his mailbag and recounting a dozen letters from viewers in response to his Grenada commentary — noted that most letter writers felt restrictions placed on the press were justified. He concluded with an advisory that military censorship outside the context of a declared war courts disaster in a democracy, as had been evidenced by Vietnam.[13]

In the wake of the Grenada invasion, a consortium of news organizations banded together to try to negotiate an understanding for future access to combat zones. PBS's *Inside Story* presented highlights of the dispute including the views of prominent reporters and public reaction against the journalists' position. Michael Burch, assistant secretary of defense for public affairs, pointed to the absurdity of a hypothetical military operation in which a television news program such as *60 Minutes* is allowed access to information from American forces, and then leaves to cover the story from the other side, getting the views of opposing troops. He also noted the additional space requirements for television equipment, the logistics of transporting technicians, and the other unique problems associated with operating television equipment in a combat zone.[14]

To attempt to accommodate both military and press interests, the military instituted a "pool system" that reduced the number of news people allowed direct contact with the fighting. The pool was used in Panama when the U.S. military intervened to capture

[9]See Michael Robinson, "Media, Rate Thyselves," *Washington Journalism Review* (December, 1983): 31-3. Surprisingly, this study showed a disproportionate amount of negative reporting by the press in stories about itself.

[10]Quoted in *Broadcasting*, 16 February 1981.

[11]See David Gergen, "How Television Weakens the Presidency," *Channels of Communication* 10 (March-April, 1984): 63-4; and Vernon Guidry, "How Television Covered the Recovery," *Washington Journalism Review* (July-August, 1983): 41-4.

[12]Carl Sessions Stepp, "In the Wake of Grenada," *Quill* (March, 1984): 12-5.

[13]Chet Huntley Memorial Lecture, New York University, reprinted in John Chancellor, "The Media and the Invasion of Grenada: Facts and Fallacies," *Television Quarterly* 20:4 (1984): 27-33.

[14]Lyle Denniston, "Planning for Future Grenadas," *The Quill* 72 (January, 1984): 10-16.

President Manuel Noriega. The system required an officer to be present whenever a reporter interviewed a serviceman. Most journalists condemned what they claimed was interference with independent reporting. Military officials responded that battlefield conditions and concern for the safety of civilian reporters necessitated the precautions.

Journalists voiced similar complaints during the Persian Gulf War in 1991. Media pool operations and video press briefings by General Norman Schwarzkopf were often cited as examples of military control of outgoing information; but coverage of the conflict won both big audiences and critical acclaim for newspapers and the television networks, especially CNN, which provided around-the-clock coverage. The pool setup resulted in much less cost for the news organizations, although CNN still spent $18 million on its war coverage and each of the other networks invested twice as much, over $40 million apiece.[15]

A number of reporters emerged from this coverage receiving wide praise: CNN's Bernard Shaw and Peter Arnett, for example; as well as Bob McKeown of CBS News, who was among the first to enter a liberated Kuwait City just ahead of coalition troops; and NBC's Arthur Kent, whom the national press colorfully dubbed "the Scud Stud," referring to his live broadcast performance in an area under attack by Scud missiles. Arnett and Kent were treated as media celebrities upon their return stateside, and their opinions were sought on a variety of political and domestic issues.[16] NBC fired Kent in 1992, however, for refusing to report from war-torn areas in Yugoslavia.

Dan Rather
Dan Rather won praise when he inherited the coveted CBS news anchor job of Walter Cronkite. In 1988, though, he became the focus of national attention when he refused to appear on-air in protest over a sporting event running over into the news slot. Republican presidential candidate George Bush referred to the episode during a confrontational live interview Rather conducted with him.

The Bush Presidency

Even before he became President, George Bush made broadcast performance an issue while appearing live on television in 1988. The then Vice President confronted Dan Rather on the *CBS Evening News*, claiming his appearance was being used as an excuse to cross examine his role in the Iran-Contra scandal. "It's not fair to judge my whole career by a rehash on Iran," Bush said. "How would you [Rather] like it if I judged your career by those seven minutes when you walked off the set in New York?"[17] Bush's reference was to an incident five months earlier when Rather refused to appear on the air as a protest over a sporting event running over into the news slot. For seven minutes, the network telecast went dead. Rather responded that Bush's campaign for the presidency was much more important than Rather's gaffe. Bush's handling of this interview, along with other campaign issues — such as the airing of a political advertisement in which his opponent, Michael Dukakis, was criticized for a Massachusetts prison furlough program that resulted in repeat offenses — provided television controversy.

During the Bush presidency, the role and propriety of journalists, particularly broadcasters, performing as commentators, which had been widely accepted in an earlier era, were being questioned. Broadcasters functioning as quasi-mediators and interpreters of events arose in a variety of international contexts, including the fall of the Berlin Wall.

The importance of television in modern world affairs seemed to have been epitomized by a joint appearance by Soviet premier Mikhail Gorbachev and Russian president Boris Yeltsin on ABC. Their appearance occurred in the wake of the disintegration of the Soviet Union and its Communist system. Admitting the failure of the system, Russian television began its newscast with: "Today, September 5, 1991, we all began living in a new country: The Soviet Union is no more."[18]

During the 1992 campaign, Vice President Dan Quayle made news when he was quoted as castigating fictional television host "Murphy Brown," played by Candace Bergen on CBS, for her decision to have an out-of-wedlock baby. The ensuing debate, in

[15] See Richard Zoglin, "Assessing the War Damage: ABC Establishes Air Supremacy," *Time*, 18 March 1991, 88-9; "CNN: Where Have All the Viewers Gone?" *Broadcasting*, 1 July 1991, 45-7.

[16] See Thomas J. Collin, "Will Success Spoil 'Bagdad Pete'?" *Washington Journalism Review* (May 1991): 18.

[17] CBS Evening News, 25 January 1988. Copies of the nine-minute exchange between Bush and Rather are available from C-SPAN, c/o Purdue University Video Archive.

[18] "Communism Failed, Soviets Agree in American TV Show," *St. Louis Post-Dispatch*, 6 September 1991, 1.

which the influence and values of Hollywood and television were often raised, became central to the campaign.

Congress was also a target of criticism. Members of the Senate Judiciary Committee were castigated, for example, for their handling of the televised confirmation hearings on the U.S. Supreme Court nomination of Judge Clarence Thomas, while the networks were praised for their decision to preempt profitable daytime programming to air the hearings. Focusing on charges of sexual harassment, the hearings had the unique distinction of outdrawing a major league championship baseball game on opening night.

The Media Under Scrutiny

Periodically throughout history the American news media have become the subject of intense criticism. Penny and yellow journalism in the nineteenth century attracted much denunciation. Likewise, in the twentieth century muckraking and conservative newspaper ownership during the New Deal bore many attacks. Rarely, however, was the criticism more widespread than in the last three decades. It came not just from special-interest groups and the elite segments of society. Suspicion about the media seemed at times pervasive. Generally, the criticism revolved around the issue of media bias.

Much of the criticism was aroused by journalists who appeared to think that their role was to be critical of almost everyone else. On the legal front, there was a slight reaction. Often journalists measured their own accomplishments in terms of their ability to expose some other person's or institution's weaknesses. The public and important institutions reacted against what seemed to be an arrogant mass media. Public opinion polls indicated low esteem for journalists and even a willingness to have government control certain press practices if abuses occurred. In the first Nixon term, Vice President Spiro Agnew had attacked the television networks and the big eastern papers as constituting an unrepresentative elite that had too much power. The criticism of the media continued to enlarge over the following years.

The expansive freedom that the media earlier had enjoyed began to be restricted. The courts, led by the Supreme Court under Chief Justice Warren Burger, limited the *N.Y. Times v. Sullivan* rule by narrowing the definition of public figure[19] and public official. The right to privacy was strengthened against media intrusion by court decisions and by legislative action to protect the rights of the accused following their arrest and during court actions. On the other hand, many official acts and records previously closed to the public became available through legislation calling for open records and open meetings.

Big business, long a target of critical press investigation, began to return fire. Both the skeptical investigative reporters and the more conventional writers in the lifestyles sections were interested in business matters. The influence of major corporations on political life, waste in public contracts, the contribution of manu-

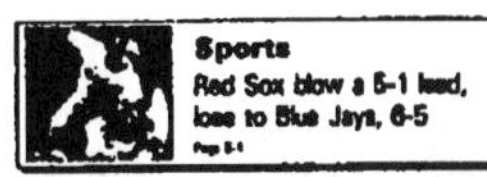

Sports
Red Sox blow a 5-1 lead, lose to Blue Jays, 6-5

Providence
Police union rejects contract, 243 to 33

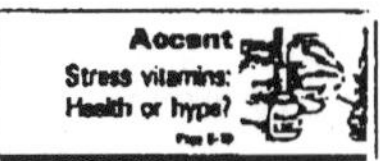

Accent
Stress vitamins: Health or hype?

The Providence Journal

City Edition

Bevilacqua panel quits for night; no word

Earlier suggestion of progress fades; hearing to resume this morning

5 hostages use news conference to beg Reagan not to try rescue

Hijack victims say they are 'well,' urge Israel to release 766 Shiite prisoners

Hostage and Victim

Fleet, partners hold RIHMFC to lease at Fleet Center

Rites of summer: 'Do what you want' on school's last day

Witnesses say killers of 13 sought out four Marines

Inside today's Journal

Television Criticism

As television became pervasive and demonstrated its capacity for immediacy in covering events, critics subjected it to increasing scrutiny. Among their charges was that TV journalists allowed themselves to be used irresponsibly because of their desire to get breaking news. Some of the most intense criticism of the 1980s occurred when television crews carried live a "news conference" that Islamic terrorists staged with American hostages in an attempt to influence negotiations with Israel. Most American daily newspapers carried, as the *Providence Journal* did, stories of the conference on page one.

facturing and of manufactured products to environmental pollution, the effects of conglomerates on the companies they acquired, prices as compared to costs — all these issues made headlines. In response, many elements of the business community began to monitor media performance in such areas as energy, pollution, and consumer information, becoming sharply critical of perceived anti-business biases. In public relations campaigns, they refuted media coverage and spoke out frankly and harshly on many occasions. They were joined by women's groups, ethnic groups, religious groups, and single-issue political groups across a wide spectrum in calling for careful reporting — and even careful

19 *Time, Inc.*, v. *Firestone*, 424 U.S. 448 (1976).

use of nouns, pronouns, and adjectives — when topics sensitive to them were in the news.

60 Minutes faced public humiliation in the late 1970s, when the subject of one of its investigative reports, Illinois Power, waged a public relations campaign circulating over one thousand copies of a videotape to community groups and stockholders pointing out *60 Minutes*' flaws in preparing a report of the company. The tape employed excerpts from the original *60 Minutes* broadcast, and some outtakes not included in the story as aired.[20]

Many journalists recognized the seriousness of the credibility problem they were facing and took steps to resolve it. They began publishing in the late 1960s and early '70s, often in league with college journalism departments, magazines that focused on press practices. Joining these journalism reviews as monitors of media performance were a dozen local and state press councils in which media consumers met with practitioners to air grievances and discuss current issues.

The National News Council, founded in 1974 and funded privately, accepted complaints from the public against the national news media — wire services, networks, major newspapers, and the like — studied them, and reported its findings. The Council was often called upon to render judgments on behalf of aggrieved parties who were willing to have a decision prepared by peers working on their behalf rather than taking their case to court. It ceased operation in 1984, never having gained adequate support from the news media.

Another effort to reconcile the media and the public, the institution of the ombudsman was imported from Europe by newspapers seeking new ways of being responsible.[21] Of the several dozen ombudsmen newspapers employed, most were readers' representatives, taking complaints from the public, looking into them, and reporting to executives and the staff of the newspaper and the complainant. Others independently critiqued their newspapers systematically and wrote reports, sometimes published in the paper and often highly critical of its performance.

Typifying the concern that journalists had for adherence to proper standards was the media reaction to the Janet Cooke affair in the early 1980s. That episode represented the ultimate in overreaching to achieve journalistic success. A young reporter for the *Washington Post*, Cooke wrote about an eight-year-old heroin addict named Jimmy, including direct quotes from the child and his mother and explicit descriptions of the two. Only after Cooke received a Pulitzer Prize for reporting was it discovered that there was no Jimmy and, indeed, that in applying for a job with the *Post*, Cooke had claimed an academic degree she did not have. The child that *Post* readers had been led to believe existed was, Cooke admitted, a composite created from what she had learned about addiction. The Pulitzer was withdrawn. Cooke and the *Post* parted company. An irony was that Bob Woodward was Cooke's editor.

Another paradox was that whereas the affair received great concern from journalists, public awareness of it was limited. The general public was more concerned about general media bias. On that issue, journalists' normal response was that they simply were not biased. Thus, journalists' reaction to the Cooke episode indicated that even though they were concerned about reporting accuracy, the nature of their professional concerns differed from those concerns that meant most to the public.

Television Under Attack

With television news occupying so much of the public's attention and other forms of television programming such as "The Day After" and "Roots," the historic mini-series on a black family's ancestry, having such a wide social impact, more serious attention to television was justified. Publications such as *Variety*, *Broadcasting and Cable*, and *Radio-Television Age* offered mostly specialized treatment for the trade; but as television's informational programming progressed, America's print media began to take the broadcast scene more seriously. Magazines such as *Saturday Review*, *The New Yorker*, and *TV Guide* contained some serious writing about broadcasting and for many years went beyond program listings for the general reader. Newspapers progressed more slowly in their coverage, no doubt hampered by their competitive position and traditional mindset toward entertainment programming and the "boob tube."

The *New York Times* covered broadcasting for more than twenty-five years with informed critiques by Jack Gould and, since 1972, John J. O'Connor. Les Brown was added as a broadcast correspondent and later became known for his authorship of two important books about television and editorship of *Channels of Communication* magazine. Over the years the *Times* received criticism for assignment of reporters with little or no radio or television experience to the broadcast beat.[22] In light of the fact that some medium-sized newspapers such as the *Louisville Courier-Journal* employed former television news directors for their broadcast beats, perhaps the criticism was justified. Most television columnists, however, by virtue of their limited numbers were required to go beyond broadcast news in their coverage, and an argument could be made that they needed to be generalists.

Some of the nation's other big newspapers, including the *Los Angeles Times*, employed a team of entertainment reporters, sometimes using smaller papers as training ground for broadcast critics. For awhile, the *New York Times* employed five television critics with a division of labor drawn between fiction and nonfiction programming, including Sally Bedell, a former *TV Guide* writer and author of *Up the Tube: Prime Time and the Silverman Years* (1981). In addition to the *New York Times* and the *Los Angeles Times*, metropolitan newspapers employed many of the nation's most respected television critics. One of the nation's pre-

[20]See Sandy Graham, "Illinois Power Pans *60 Minutes*," *Wall Street Journal*, 27 June 1980; or Tom Dorsey, "*60 Minutes* Can Skirt the Spotlight As Well As Wield It," *Louisville Courier Journal*, 9 June 1981, C1.

[21]An ombudsman is an official or agent who receives, investigates, and attempts to resolve complaints and problems between parties within an institution or organization.

[22]See "Television and the Times," *Broadcasting*, 7 March 1983, 86-9.

Walter Cronkite
The dean of network television news reporters and anchors, Walter Cronkite was one of many members of the CBS News team, including Eric Sevareid and Charles Kuralt, to criticize attempts to jazz-up newscasts in an effort to attract viewers. Cronkite is remembered also for his visit to Vietnam and subsequent stand against the American war effort. He also advocated the expansion of network evening news to one hour. He is shown here (third from left) in a 1981 White House photograph being toasted by President Ronald Reagan and other dignitaries upon his retirement from CBS.

mier broadcast critics made the transition to print from National Public Radio in 1972. Tom Shales joined critics Lawrence Laurant and John Carmody at the *Washington Post* and was made chief television critic seven years later. In *On the Air* (1982), a compilation of his columns, he presented perceptive, tongue-in-cheek commentary on the major events and personalities of television journalism of the 1970s and early '80s. In the essay "Jugular Journalism" he assessed the debate over a program produced and aired in 1980 over CBS-owned WBBM-TV in Chicago titled "Watching the Watchdog," which questioned the methods of ABC's investigative reporter Geraldo Rivera and CBS's own Mike Wallace. Shales also presented provocative profiles of television journalism's other key performers including Walter Cronkite, Dan Rather, Tom Brokaw, Ted Koppel, and Barbara Walters.

Most of the attention of critics focused on the issue of salaries. The question of excessive compensation for television figures was raised with the publication of Barbara Matusow's *The Evening Stars: The Rise of the Network Anchors* (1983). High-paid television journalists reacted passionately to such criticism from their newspaper counterparts. Matusow quoted CBS newsman Eric Sevareid as pointing out to publishers that "broadcast journalism is the only business in the country I can think of that has its chief competitor as its chief critic."[23] Veteran CBS producer Don Hewitt claimed professional jealousy was one motivation for the attention broadcasters' salaries received from print columnists. Another prominent broadcaster questioned the sanity of exorbitant salaries when Bill Leonard published *In the Storm of the Eye: A Lifetime at CBS* (1990), detailing Dan Rather's contract negotiations on the eve of Walter Cronkite's retirement. Cronkite aired his own views on the subject in his book *A Reporter's Life* (1996) and in a variety of speeches.

Despite such occasional attention to media practices, there were few instances in which broadcasters took a critical look at their own industry. Rarely did they examine their own network or their competition as harshly as they scrutinized outside individuals and organizations. Most reports examining the media came in special editions of ABC's *Viewpoint*, *Inside CBS News'* broadcasts from affiliate stations, CBS's *Eye on the Press*, and public television's *Inside Story*. *CBS Reports'* "Inside Public Television" focused on a competitor and came under fire from many members of the media when it aired in 1976. It dealt with growing commercialization, especially the use of auctions, at the tax-supported network. The reporter on the story, Charles Kuralt, questioned the sincerity of PBS executives in their pledge to stay out of the ratings war with commercial competitors. Later, National Public Radio's own *All Things Considered* reported on that network's mismanagement that contributed to the near financial collapse of NPR in 1983. Rare reports by in-house critics such as Jeff Greenfield, then of ABC, and Ron Powers at CBS provided some examination of broadcast programming, trends, policy, or political uses at their own networks.

Happy News

In 1974, Eric Sevareid, in his analysis section for the *CBS Evening News with Walter Cronkite*, questioned his broadcast brethren for jazzing up reality in their nightly newscasts: "In city after city, the news is delivered by newsmen turned actors, very bad actors. They grin, they laugh, they chuckle or moan the news....They kid each other or applaud each other. And any day now, one of them will sing the news while doing a buck-and-wing stark naked."[24] Sevareid's satire was consistent with other serious criticism concerning the emergence at the local level of "happy news" or "eyewitness" formats. In an effort to attain higher ratings many broadcasters followed the advice of consultants, placing more emphasis on shorter and more entertaining stories and appearance rather than substance in story selection.

[23] Quoted in Barbara Matusow, "Intrigue at NBC," *Washington Journalism Review* (July-August, 1983): 83.

[24] *The CBS Evening News with Walter Cronkite*, CBS News, 22 April 1974.

One of Sevareid's colleagues at CBS News, Charles Kuralt, well known for a decade of "On the Road" reports and host of *CBS Sunday Morning*, told the Radio-Television News Directors' Association that his lasting impression of local television news was of the anchorman's hair. In *The Newscasters: The News Business as Show Business* (1978), Ron Powers made a persuasive case that beginning in the late 1960s and early 1970s broadcast managers sacrificed good news judgment and turned some of their decision-making authority over to "news doctors," consultants who depended on marketing strategy to win an audience.

Philadelphia's KYW-TV and its former news chief, Al Primo, frequently were identified with the trend of letting reporters tell their own story in their own way, rather than relying on the old style news anchor approach. Broadcast historian Edward W. Barrett profiled the consultants and found an increased emphasis on show-business techniques.[25] In similar fashion to commercial television, San Francisco's public television station, KQED, responded to a newspaper strike by initiating *Newsroom*, a format in which reporters discussed stories on a set designed to encourage interaction and emphasize appearance.

A decade later, the show business elements of television news were spotlighted by a law suit brought by Christine Craft, a former anchorwoman for KMBC-TV, Kansas City, Missouri. She sued Metromedia, the station's owner, for $1.2 million charging sex discrimination, unequal pay, and fraud. *Craft vs. Metromedia* raised issues regarding television's journalistic integrity and, because Craft had been asked to improve her appearance in deference to viewers, the distinction between news and entertainment.

Inevitably the "show-business" trend resulted in what CBS's *60 Minutes* referred to as "tabloid news." A graduate journalism class at the University of California, Berkeley, taped all news programs for a week at top-rated KGO-TV in San Francisco during 1974.[26] *60 Minutes* reported that more than half of all stories fell into the tabloid category consisting of "fire, sex, tear-jerkers, accidents, and exorcism." This "eyewitness news" approach included more frequent exchanges between on-air personnel and a greater degree of specialized reporting. Within a decade, the formation of investigative units, or "I Teams," was challenged at some stations as being extensions of the "happy talk" format because of their orientation toward melodrama. Many would produce special, sensational reports aired during ratings periods, sometimes including the confrontation or "ambush" interview device.

In the O. J. Simpson case, which included elements of sex and murder — and which followed a trial of police brutality involving another black man, Rodney King — the nation was overwhelmed with more than 2,000 hours of live broadcast and cable coverage.

[25]Edward W. Barrett, "Folksy TV News," *Columbia Journalism Review* (November-December, 1973): 16-20. See also Gabriel Pressman, "Local Newscasts—A Continuing Identity Crisis," *Television Quarterly* (Summer, 1974); and "Local News in 31 Different Flavors," from *The Quill*, reprinted in Leonard L. Sellers and William L. Rivers, eds., *Mass Media Issues: Articles and Commentaries* (Englewood Cliffs, N.J., 1977), 76-85.

[26]*60 Minutes*, CBS Television Network, 10 March 1974. The study is reviewed in Edwin Diamond, *The Tin Kazoo: Television, Politics, and the News* (Cambridge, Mass, 1975), 65-6.

NEWSPAPERS UNDER TV ATTACK

While occasionally finding their own journalistic standards challenged, broadcast journalists seldom took their print counterparts to task for sloppy reporting or lack of professionalism. Only rarely did they make press performance a part of their job.

In 1974 Harry Reasoner castigated the *New York Times* for attention it paid to the motion picture *The Exorcist*, with five stories devoted to the film. "I'm afraid," he concluded, "the good old paper is possessed. Rites of exorcism in the city room and every bureau, performed by some tough minded city editor, are indicated.... If the union would permit the rites in the composing room, it might even reduce the typographical errors in the early edition."[27] In a more serious mood, Reasoner took *Time* and *Newsweek* to task in his ABC commentary for lack of objectivity in the handling of Watergate. He condemned *Newsweek* especially for reporting on indictments before they were given to Judge John Sirica and for "spoon-feeding conclusions in the style of pejorative pamphleteering."

In another exception to the rule, Hughes Rudd examined "The Business of Newspapers" in a television documentary, using an intense struggle for advertising dollars in Boston between the *Boston Globe* and *Boston Herald-American* as its base. The documentary included an analysis of newspaper chain ownership, which writers such as Ben Bagdikian also had criticized.

THE CLINTON PRESIDENCY

While the nation was experiencing tremendous economic prosperity and growth during Bill Clinton's presidency, the media became preoccupied with stories of sex and scandal. Bolstered by excessive coverage of the O. J. Simpson case in California, came charges of a dissolution of standards and of radical changes in news orientation. This "tabloidization," critics claimed, created a new norm for covering public affairs. Some observers argued that the media paid an inordinate amount of attention to the so-called Whitewater affair, which dated back to Clinton's term as governor of Arkansas. It involved financial dealings of his wife, Hillary, and close friends and placed them under close scrutiny. While some involved in the scandal did go to jail, the President himself was cleared. Investigations expanded from Whitewater to allegations of improper sexual conduct dating back to his years as governor and then targeted his more recent relations with a White House intern, Monica Lewinsky. When independent counsel Kenneth Starr released his office's voluminous report on its investigations, many newspapers reprinted it in its entirety, and some cable television networks gave the report continuous coverage. Clinton's testimony before a grand jury and Congressional hearings prior to his impeachment likewise received extensive newspaper and television coverage, and a variety of radio and television shows for

[27]*The ABC Evening News with Howard K. Smith and Harry Reasoner*, ABC News, 28 January 1974.

Clinton-Lewinsky Affair

The Tuscaloosa News $1.50

354 • 8 Sections SUNDAY, DECEMBER 20, 1998 Tuscaloosa/Northport and West Alabama

ARTICLE ONE	ARTICLE TWO	ARTICLE THREE	ARTICLE FOUR
APPROVED 228-206: First article of impeachment, alleging that Clinton perjured himself before a grand jury.	**REJECTED 229-205:** An article accusing Clinton of committing perjury in the Paula Jones lawsuit.	**APPROVED 221-212:** An article accusing Clinton of obstruction of justice in the Monica Lewinsky matter.	**REJECTED 285-148:** An article alleging Clinton abused the powers of his office by giving false answers to Congress.

HOUSE IMPEACHES CLINTON

■ House approves two of the four articles against Clinton ■ Livingston resigns, urges president to do the same ■ Five Republicans, five Democrats break party lines

Photo/The Associated Press

President Clinton addresses Democratic lawmakers who joined him outside the Oval Office of the White House Saturday after the House of Representatives voted to impeach the president.

By ALISON MITCHELL
N.Y. Times News Service

House Speaker nominee Rep. Bob Livingston, R-La., shown in this television image, speaks during the House session Saturday in Washington during debate on the four articles of impeachment against President Clinton.

Livingston will quit Congress, urges the president to resign

By KATHARINE Q. SEELYE
N.Y. Times News Service

WASHINGTON — Rep. Bob Livingston, who confessed to his colleagues Thursday night that he had had adulterous affairs, stunned the House chamber Saturday morning by saying in the impeachment debate on President Clinton that he would not serve as speaker and would quit Congress in six months. He urged the president to follow his example and quit, too.

But at the White House, where calls for Clinton's resignation are derided as a Republican strategy, the president sent a spokesman into the driveway to urge Livingston to reconsider his resignation.

Livingston stood in the well of the House he has served for two decades and called on Clinton to resign his

Please see QUIT Page 9A

Please see IMPEACH Page 6A

INSIDE

■ **SURPRISE:** 7A

■ **ANALYSIS:** 8A

■ **CHRONOLOGY:** Key events in the investigation that led to Clinton's impeachment. 10A

White House Sex Scandal Absorbs the News Media

What began as a second-hand report circulated by an obscure on-line journalist culminated in saturation coverage by major news organizations. Disclosure of President Bill Clinton's affair with a White House intern dominated the national news media in 1998 as no political scandal had before.

Matt Drudge broke the story on the Internet in January. He reported that *Newsweek* had delayed publication of a report that Clinton had a sexual relationship with Monica Lewinsky, a White House intern and staff member from 1995 to 1997. Within hours, mainstream news outlets enthusiastically pursued the story. Critics said all-news cable channels and Internet sites forced reporters to rely recklessly on rumors and anonymous sources for fresh angles.

Questioned by reporters in January, Clinton indignantly denied a sexual relationship with Lewinsky. After being called to testify before a federal grand jury in August, he gave a televised speech admitting he had lied but insisting that he broke no laws.

Independent Counsel Kenneth Starr disagreed, sending Congress a 445-page report alleging eleven impeachable acts, including perjury and obstruction of justice. The document included explicit descriptions of sexual acts committed in the White House. Editors and broadcasters were forced to reconsider their own standards for language and taste. Many newspapers and on-line sources published the entire report, warning readers of its content. Starr later released a videotape of Clinton's grand jury testimony. While most TV and radio news programs broadcast excerpts, cable news channels repeatedly showed the whole tape.

Some columnists and commentators called the coverage excessive. The public seemed to agree. Yet, while polls indicated that Americans thought the story was out of proportion to its importance, audience ratings for coverage remained high.

In early 1999 the U. S. Senate acquitted Clinton on two articles of impeachment that the House of Representatives passed against him, one alleging that he lied under oath and the second accusing him of obstructing justice.

Kenton Bird
Colorado State University

The Clinton-Lewinsky scandal and the resultant Senate impeachment trial provided one of the biggest media stories of the last half of the twentieth century. Television, magazines, and newspapers repeatedly showed photographs (top) of the president and the intern. The affair gave countless opportunities for editorial cartoonists (right). Newspapers around the country played the impeachment story with banner headlines.

Deering—*Arkansas Democrat-Gazette*

Nightline
Ted Koppel emerged as one of television news' master interviewers during the American hostage crisis in Iran. His authoritative and engaging live broadcasts on Nightline helped to establish ABC-TV as a leading news organization. (Photo courtesy ABC. Copyright 1990 Capital Cities/ABC, Inc.)

months devoted their daily programs to the scandals and investigations and to the House proceedings and Senate trial.

Criticism of media coverage came from a variety of quarters. Former television anchor Walter Cronkite took journalists to task for excessive use of unidentified sources and investigative leaks.[28] A number of other journalists echoed those charges. Other criticisms, however, clearly were tinged with ideology. Steve Brill, liberal publisher of *Brill's Content*, castigated journalists for what he claimed was a lack of fairness and balance, particularly targeting the use of anonymous sources and hearsay. He accused several publications and specific journalists, including NBC correspondent David Bloom and ABC's Jackie Judd, of being virtual extensions of Starr's investigation.[29] Starr himself sharply attacked Brill's charge as bordering on libel. Conservative critics, for their part, believed that the media's attention to Clinton's problems finally brought some ideological balance to the news media; but, they argued, had it been a Republican president involved in the scandals, media treatment would have been much harsher.

Because of the controversies surrounding the Clinton presidency, they dominated media coverage, and he made a number of efforts to direct attention elsewhere. One of the most notable was a visit to China in 1998. There, he was allowed to conduct a live, uncensored seventy-minute news conference broadcast across China and telecast back to the United States. Taking a generally conciliatory approach to China — whose record of human rights' abuses, critics pointed out, had been highlighted in 1989 with a crackdown on demonstrators in Tiananmen Square — Clinton predicted that democracy would eventually come to the world's most heavily populated country, aided by the fact that it was "moving into the world of cellular phones and the Internet."[30] At the same time that his broadcast in China received much play, some American journalists saw a paradox in the fact that the President had given a press conference in a foreign country while avoiding such give-and-take meetings with the American media after news of his relationship with Lewinsky broke.

Future Trends

By the latter part of the twentieth century, broadcast news and information programming — once a throwaway item at the major television networks — had become a mainstay and a major moneymaker. A public affairs series, *60 Minutes*, was consistently rated in the top ten most watched programs; while ABC News' *This Week* and NBC's *Meet the Press* with Tim Russert frequently made news with important interviews from the nation's capital. *Nightline* also provided insight and perspective on the critical issues of the day while attracting record numbers of viewers for late-night news programming. NBC also succeeded with its multipart series *Dateline NBC*, which forced both ABC and CBS to rethink their once-a-week airing of *20/20* and *60 Minutes*. PBS offered an hour's worth of news daily and scored a major ratings coup with a twelve-hour documentary series, "The Civil War," in 1990. The Cable News Network performed admirably on many occasions. It started "Special Assignment," which won praise for coverage of serious stories, such as the savings and loan scandal, investigations of former Panamanian dictator Manual Noriega, coverage of the release of Nelson Mandela after twenty-seven years in South African prisons, and a Washington, D.C., summit conference between President George Bush and Soviet President

[28] Joel Connelly, "Walter Cronkite Pontificates on Trends in TV News Today," *St. Louis Post-Dispatch*, 15 May 1998.
[29] *Brill's Content*, June 1998.

[30] "Clinton, Leaving China, Predicts Democracy Will Come," *St. Louis Post-Dispatch*, 4 July 1998.

Mikhail Gorbachev.

The anticipated development of additional networks such as Fox News provided evidence of further growth potential for broadcast news and public affairs programming, notwithstanding the effects of corporate takeovers such as Capital Cities' acquisition of ABC, General Electric's takeover of NBC in 1985, and major management changes at CBS. At the local level news was, beyond commercial time sales, the major source of employment at network-affiliate and independent television stations and the peg around which the station image was formed and promoted. Technological developments should enhance local prospects for covering national and international stories. Specialized news services such as those that Michael Bloomberg developed should improve financial and business reporting.

Broadcasting came into its own in the past few decades as a fairly reliable conveyer of news and information, but also as a major moneymaker. With continued support, perhaps expansion of news and increased emphasis on public affairs programs will enhance the public's belief in the medium and lead to an even more credible performance by broadcasters. Electronic journalism now presents unprecedented opportunities to cover events as they happen and to provide unique perspectives on important issues. A revolution in journalism is under way.

The future depends on the quality and direction broadcasters take in news programming efforts and support by management. The elimination of minimum guidelines for news coverage by the FCC may have the effect of limiting coverage in lean economic times, but expanded news and public affairs programming appears to have earned a permanent niche.

Even though confronted with major threats from television in the last twenty-five years, newspaper people nevertheless feel at home in what is labeled the Information Age. They find themselves challenged anew. They find it imperative to be willing to adapt to new technology, to be aware of the changing nature and continued innovation in all mass media, and to be sensitive to the continual changes in public tastes and needs.

The news media bear much of the nation's burden for providing an ever-rising level of understanding of an ever-more complicated society. Three centuries after the founding of America's first newspaper, they continue to have informing the public as their primary responsibility. How they can best do that is a point on which disagreement exists. Some journalists, as indicated by the *Washington Post's* publisher Katherine Graham, believe the method is for "hard-nosed editors and digging reporters"[31] to continue to employ professional practices vigorously.

Others believe the answer is to erase the professional detachment that the media have established between themselves and the rest of society, restoring some features of the communal relationship that existed between the two before the Vietnam War. While there are differences of opinion about the best means of approaching the media's role in the future, one thing is clear. With the American media having begun their fourth century and now entering the third millennium, they continue as indispensable parts of the American democracy and its day-to-day life.

[31]Address to national convention of the Society of Professional Journalists/Sigma Delta Chi, Chicago, 1969.

RECOMMENDED READINGS

BOOKS

Arnett, Peter. *Live From the Battlefield: From Vietnam to Baghdad — 35 Years in the World's War Zones*. New York, 1994. Memoirs of a veteran war correspondent.

Beniger, James R. *The Control Revolution*. Cambridge, Mass., 1986. Treats the media as part of the process leading to the Information Society, emphasizing technological and economic growth.

Bloomberg, Michael. *Bloomberg on Bloomberg*. New York, 1997. Business-information giant outlines the development of his service.

Brandt, J. Donald. *A History of Gannett, 1906-1993*. Arlington, Va., 1993. Insider's account of the growth of the media giant.

Brinkley, David. *A Memoir*. New York, 1995. The NBC anchor and commentator provides his personal account of television's development.

Brown, Les. *The New York Times Encyclopedia of Television*. New York, 1977. Comprehensive guide to television people, programs, and news organizations.

Craft, Christine. *Too Old, Too Ugly, and Not Deferential to Men*. New York, 1988. Anchorwoman provides personal account of her removal from airwaves and subsequent litigation.

Cronkite, Walter. *A Reporter's Life*. New York, 1996. Memoirs of the dean of television news.

Dawkins, Wayne. *Black Journalists: The NABJ Story*. Sicklerville, N.J., 1993. Anecdotal history of the early years of the National Association of Black Journalists.

Diamond, Edwin. *Behind the Times: Inside the New New York Times*. New York, 1994. Profiles changes at the *New York Times* in the 1960s, 1970s, and 1980s.

Donahue, Hugh Carter. *The Battle To Control Broadcast News: Who Owns the First Amendment?* Cambridge, Mass., 1989. Argues against special interest involvement in broadcast news.

Goldberg, Robert, and Gerald Jay Goldberg. *Anchors: Brokaw, Jennings, Rather and the Evening News*. New York, 1990. Uses 1989 stories as the basis for examination of broadcast news staff performance.

Hertsgaard, Mark. *On Bended Knee*. New York, 1988. Story of "coordinated" news activity in the Reagan White House.

Matusow, Barbara. *The Evening Stars: The Rise of the Network News Anchors*. Boston, 1983. This is primarily a criticism of the superficiality of television news, but it does provide some historical background. Selection of anchors is based too much on appeal rather than journalistic ability.

Murray, Michael, ed. *Encyclopedia of Television News*. Phoenix, 1999. Includes entries on major figures and issues.

O'Connor, John E., ed. *American History/American Television: Interpreting the Video Past*. New York, 1983. Collection of fifteen essays. "[I]n a very real sense, *television is American Culture*.... At least for the vast majority of Americans — people who may never attend a play or a concert, visit a museum, or read a book — TV is all there is."

Powers, Ron. *The Newscasters: The News Business as Show Business*. New York, 1977. To get higher ratings, TV executives from the 1960s to 1977 debased their local newscasts by using marketing principles to determine what viewers wanted to see, thus pushing news toward show business.

Read, Donald. *The Power of News: The History of Reuters*. New York, 1992. Detailed history of the rise of the worldwide news service, from the start of telegraphy in the 1840s to the present.

Robertson, Nan. *The Girls in the Balcony: Women, Men and The New York*

Times. New York, 1992. Sketches of women reporters at the *Times* through the years and an insider's account of gender discrimination.

Rozell, Mark J. *The Press and the Ford Presidency*. Ann Arbor, Mich., 1992. A survey of press coverage of the Ford presidency, concluding that the press was unduly harsh toward the president.

Salisbury, Harrison E. *Without Fear or Favor: The New York Times and Its Times*. New York, 1980. The *New York Times* became a powerful independent voice with its stands on such issues as civil rights, McCarthyism, and the Pentagon Papers.

Shawcross, William. *Murdoch*. New York, 1992. Biography of the publisher who built a worldwide media empire on a foundation of sensationalism.

Smoller, Frederic T. *The Six O'Clock Presidency: A Theory of Presidential Press Relations in the Age of Television*. Westport, Conn., 1990. CBS coverage of the presidency was "determined by the political, technical and commercial nature of the medium itself, producing a bias toward negative coverage."

Tifft, Susan E., and Alex S. Jones. *The Patriarch: The Rise and Fall of the Bingham Dynasty*. New York, 1991. Profiles the Bingham family of Louisville and the dissolution of its media empire.

Trotta, Liz. *Fighting for Air: In the Trenches with Television News*. New York, 1991. First woman correspondent in Vietnam and twenty-year network news veteran critiques changes in TV news.

Udelson, Joseph. *The Great Television Race: A History of the American Television Industry, 1925-1941*. Tuscaloosa, Ala., 1982. The history of television technology: survey of research, experiments, and telecasting prior to 1941, when commercial television was authorized.

ARTICLES

Allen, Craig. "Television, 1948-Present: Entertainment or Information?" in Wm. David Sloan, ed., *Perspectives on Mass Communication History*, 334-46. Hillsdale, N.J., 1991. Historiographical essay provides useful overview of explanations of television history.

Hahn, Dan. "The Effect of Television on Presidential Campaigns." *Communication Quarterly* (1970): 4-17. Argues that television has upgraded the public's awareness and knowledge.

Murray, Michael. "Network Insiders Look at CBS." *American Journalism* (1988): 248-57. Review essay examines half-dozen books about CBS.

Olmsted, Kathryn. "'An American Conspiracy': The Post-Watergate Press and the CIA." *Journalism History* 19 (1993): 51-8. Argues that the press was often deferential to the executive branch in the years after the Watergate scandal.

Pogrebin, Abigail. "Lack Attack." *Brill's Content* (February 1999): 93-9. Provides background on the recent success of NBC News and president Andrew Lack.

Schaefer, Richard J. "Reconsidering 'Harvest of Shame': The Limitations of a Broadcast Journalism Landmark." *Journalism History* 19 (1994): 121-32. The famous 1960 television documentary failed to affect public policy because its moralistic presentation lessened its impact.

Shmanske, Stephen. "News as a Public Good: Cooperative Ownership, Price Commitments, and the Success of the Associated Press." *Business History Review* 60 (Spring 1986): 55-80. In a free-market economy, the non-profit AP succeeded because of its cooperative ownership structure and because it was dealing with a commodity (news) that was a "public good."

Index

D

O

Q-R

XYZ